PRINCIPLES OF HOLISTIC PSYCHIATRY: A TEXTBOOK ON HOLISTIC MEDICINE FOR MENTAL DISORDERS

HEALTH AND HUMAN DEVELOPMENT
JOAV MERRICK - SERIES EDITOR
NATIONAL INSTITUTE OF CHILD HEALTH
AND HUMAN DEVELOPMENT,
MINISTRY OF SOCIAL AFFAIRS, JERUSALEM

Adolescent Behavior Research: International Perspectives
Joav Merrick and Hatim A.Omar (Editors)
2007. ISBN: 1-60021-649-8

Complementary Medicine Systems: Comparison and Integration
Karl W. Kratky
2008. ISBN: 978-1-60456-475-4 (Hardcover)
2008. ISBN: 978-1-61122-433-7 (E-book)

Pain in Children and Youth
Patricia Schofield and Joav Merrick (Editors)
2008. ISBN: 978-1-60456-951-3

Challenges in Adolescent Health: An Australian Perspective
*David Bennett, Susan Towns, Elizabeth Elliott
and Joav Merrick (Editors)*
2009. ISBN: 978-1-60741-616-6 (Hardcover)
2009. ISBN: 978-1-61668-240-8 (E-book)

Behavioral Pediatrics, 3rd Edition
*Donald E. Greydanus, Dilip R. Patel,
Helen D. Pratt and Joseph L. Calles, Jr. (Editors)*
2009. ISBN: 978-1-60692-702-1 (Hardcover)
2009. ISBN: 978-1-60876-630-7 (E-book)

**Health and Happiness from Meaningful Work:
Research in Quality of Working Life**
Søren Ventegodt and Joav Merrick (Editors)
2009. ISBN: 978-1-60692-820-2

Obesity and Adolescence: A Public Health Concern
*Hatim A. Omar, Donald E. Greydanus,
Dilip R. Patel and Joav Merrick (Editors)*
2009. ISBN: 978-1-60456-821-9

Poverty and Children: A Public Health Concern
Alexis Lieberman and Joav Merrick (Editors)
2009. ISBN: 978-1-60741-140-6

**Living on the Edge: The Mythical, Spiritual, and Philosophical
Roots of Social Marginality**
Joseph Goodbread
2009. ISBN: 978-1-60741-162-8

Alcohol-Related Cognitive Disorders: Research and Clinical Perspectives
Leo Sher, Isack Kandel and Joav Merrick (Editors)
2009. ISBN: 978-1-60741-730-9 (Hardcover)
2009. ISBN: 978-1-60876-623-9 (E-book)

Child Rural Health: International Aspects
Erica Bell and Joav Merrick (Editors)
2010. ISBN: 978-1-60876-357-3

**Advances in Environmental Health Effects of Toxigenic Mold
and Mycotoxins- Volume 1**
Ebere Cyril Anyanwu
2010. ISBN: 978-1-60741-953-2

Children and Pain
Patricia Schofield and Joav Merrick (Editors)
2009. ISBN: 978-1-60876-020-6 (Hardcover)
2009. ISBN: 978-1-61728-183-9 (E-book)

**Conceptualizing Behavior in Health and Social Research:
A Practical Guide to Data Analysis**
Said Shahtahmasebi and Damon Berridge
2010. ISBN: 978-1-60876-383-2

Chance Action and Therapy. The Playful Way of Changing
Uri Wernik
2010. ISBN: 978-1-60876-393-1

Adolescence and Chronic Illness. A Public Health Concern
*Hatim Omar, Donald E. Greydanus, Dilip R. Patel
and Joav Merrick (Editors)*
2010. ISBN: 978-1-60876-628-4 (Hardcover)
2010. ISBN: 978-1-61761-482-8 (E-book)

Social and Cultural Psychiatry Experience from the Caribbean Region
Hari D. Maharajh and Joav Merrick (Editors)
2010. ISBN: 978-1-61668-506-5 (Hardcover)
2010. ISBN: 978-1-61728-088-7 (E-book)

Narratives and Meanings of Migration
Julia Mirsky
2010. ISBN: 978-1-61761-103-2 (Hardcover)
2010. ISBN: 978-1-61761-519-1 (E-book)

Self-Management and the Health Care Consumer
Peter William Harvey
2011. ISBN: 978-1-61761-796-6 (Hardcover)
2011. ISBN: 978-1-61122-214-2 (E-book)

Sexology from a Holistic Point of View
Soren Ventegodt and Joav Merrick
2011. ISBN: 978-1-61761-859-8 (Hardcover)
2011. ISBN: 978-1-61122-262-3 (E-book)

**Principles of Holistic Psychiatry: A Textbook
on Holistic Medicine for Mental Disorders**
Soren Ventegodt and Joav Merrick
2011. ISBN: 978-1-61761-940-3 (Hardcover)
2011. ISBN: 978-1-61122-263-0 (E-book)

**Clinical Aspects of Psychopharmacology
in Childhood and Adolescence**
*Donald E. Greydanus, Joseph L. Calles Jr., Dilip P. Patel,
Ahsan Nazeer and Joav Merrick (Editors)*
2011. ISBN: 978-1-61122-135-0 (Hardcover)
2011. ISBN: 978-1-61122-715-4 (E-book)

Climate Change and Rural Child Health
Erica Bell, Bastian M. Seidel and Joav Merrick (Editors)
2011. ISBN: 978-1-61122-640-9 (Hardcover)
2011. ISBN: 978-1-61209-014-6 (E-book)

Rural Medical Education: Practical Strategies
Erica Bell, Craig Zimitat and Joav Merrick (Editors)
2011. ISBN: 978-1-61122-649-2 (Hardcover)

Environment, Mood Disorders and Suicide
Teodor T. Postolache and Joav Merrick (Editors)
2011. ISBN: 978-1-61668-505-8

PRINCIPLES OF HOLISTIC PSYCHIATRY: A TEXTBOOK ON HOLISTIC MEDICINE FOR MENTAL DISORDERS

SOREN VENTEGODT
AND
JOAV MERRICK
EDITORS

Nova Science Publishers, Inc.
New York

NOTICE TO THE READER

The Publisher has taken reasonable care in the preparation of this book, but makes no expressed or implied warranty of any kind and assumes no responsibility for any errors or omissions. No liability is assumed for incidental or consequential damages in connection with or arising out of information contained in this book. The Publisher shall not be liable for any special, consequential, or exemplary damages resulting, in whole or in part, from the readers' use of, or reliance upon, this material. Any parts of this book based on government reports are so indicated and copyright is claimed for those parts to the extent applicable to compilations of such works.

Independent verification should be sought for any data, advice or recommendations contained in this book. In addition, no responsibility is assumed by the publisher for any injury and/or damage to persons or property arising from any methods, products, instructions, ideas or otherwise contained in this publication.

This publication is designed to provide accurate and authoritative information with regard to the subject matter covered herein. It is sold with the clear understanding that the Publisher is not engaged in rendering legal or any other professional services. If legal or any other expert assistance is required, the services of a competent person should be sought. FROM A DECLARATION OF PARTICIPANTS JOINTLY ADOPTED BY A COMMITTEE OF THE AMERICAN BAR ASSOCIATION AND A COMMITTEE OF PUBLISHERS.

Additional color graphics may be available in the e-book version of this book.

Library of Congress Cataloging-in-Publication Data

Ventegodt, Sxren.
  Principles of holistic psychiatry : a textbook on holistic medicine for
mental disorders / Soren Ventegodt, Joav Merrick.
      p. ; cm.
  Includes bibliographical references and index.
  ISBN 978-1-61761-940-3 (hardcover)
  1. Mental illness--Treatment. 2. Holistic medicine. I. Merrick, Joav,
1950- II. Title.
  [DNLM: 1. Mental Disorders--therapy. 2. Holistic Health. 3.
Psychiatry--methods. WM 140]
  RC480.5.V46 2010
  616.89'1--dc22
                                                          2010034040

Published by Nova Science Publishers, Inc. † *New York*

Contents

Introduction: Holistic psychiatry. All you need to know to help heal your patient

Mental illnesses have tormented mankind ever since the first man walked the earth and for sure it has definitely occupied the minds of all physicians through the ages (1,2). Man is characterised by his conscious mind, mirroring and containing the world. Having the whole world represented inside is a huge advantage for survival and quality of life. The gift of language allows everybody to share ideas, interpretations and knowledge. Human beings built communities, cities, develop technology and science.

This is what we human beings truly are – lovers of knowledge, philosophers, human beings of consciousness – all of us, even the most mediocre and we are divine beings. We are talented and meant to be successful. We were made for joy, fun, adventure, contemplation, understanding and bliss. We are expressed in religious language and created in the image of God. We are made out of divine energy. We are sons and daughters of the universe. We are intelligent social beings and so capable that only our own imagination sets the limit. In our hearts, in our essence, we are beautiful and good people.

With this said, everybody knows that this is not the full picture. We human beings, the masters of consciousness, are also evil, narrow-minded, somewhat disoriented and delusional, often defocused, sometimes even depersonalised and de-realised beings. We are also, even the healthiest of us, partly a madman, a fruitcake and an idiosyncratic being. Most of us are not really crazy, but still we are somewhat neurotic, dependent, and un-autonomies beings, lacking I-strength, integrity, awareness, inner balance and strength. Too often we have not developed a natural ability to accept, understand, love and forgive.

So this is the paradox of man: Meant to be divine we often sink in the mud. Meant to be good and generous we often end up being small and demanding. Meant to be geniuses we often end thinking and behaving far less intelligent that that.

From an existential perspective we are great, wise, knowledgeable beings and at the same time small, unconscious beings, envious, jealous, self-conscious, serious beings filled with self-pity and inflated ego. Some of us are even worse; we can be depressed or really mentally ill: emotionally frozen, mentally disturbed, more or less autistic and to some extent even living alone in our own private world, being what in psychiatry often is called psychotic.

Mental illness come in many qualities and many degrees, from the young patient with low self-esteem and incomplete psychosexual development, to the patient with severe depression, anxiety, personality disturbances, social phobia, paranoia, mental delusions, or even severe autism, and schizophrenia with hallucinations and complete lack of sense of coherence and sense of reality.

All this darkness seems to be the sad shadow of our brilliant brain-mind. Because we contain a full model of the world in our heads we become highly vulnerable to flaws and errors in this mental model. Because we act and experience according to our expectations, our understanding of the world becomes highly self-confirmative. We become caught in our mind. We are interpreters of the world, and we, the human being, the highly developed and brainiest species of all, end up stuck in seemingly unsolvable, hermeneutic problems.

Mental health: What is it?

Positive psychology has addressed the mental disorders from the complete opposite perspective asking what mental health is. The answer has been quite simple: You are healthy when you know yourself, your character, essence (life mission or purpose of life) (3) and talents, and use all your gifts and talents to create value in all your relations. If you succeed in using yourself and create value in the world you will most likely be not only happy, but also physically and mentally healthy, and well functioning in all areas of life: studying life, working life, social life, sexual life etc.

So the healthy person is characterized with a special empowering quality of self-awareness, allowing the person to materialise a rich, interesting, developing life full of adventures and challenges and of sufficient safely and comfort to be balanced and happy.

The fundamental idea of mental disorders in holistic psychiatry is that they ascend from existential isolation that grow from a specific lack of self-insight and understanding of the inner logic of life. If you are not in balance, if you are not feeling as an integrated part of the world, if you are not experiencing a sense of coherence (SOC) (4,5) in life, if you are not able to love yourself and others, and to give without expecting anything back, just because you feel that this makes you happy, then you are likely to be unhappy, emotionally cold, mentally confused and existentially isolated. Your life will lack meaning and you social relations will be few and of a poor quality with little openness, goodness, content and intensity. You are most likely mentally ill.

If you are mentally ill you can heal. In the process now often called salutogenesis (becoming well), per definition meaning the opposite of pathogenesis (becoming ill), the patient can recover emotionally, mentally, existentially and spiritually. The process of existential healing has not been fully understood, but the concept of healing or salutogenesis is found in every single pre-modern culture that has a medical system (6-8). Unfortunately the concept of healing is little known in biomedicine.

Existential healing is induced by the therapist or physician when he or she is able to love, care and support his/her patient fully, and the patient is able to receive this loving care and support. The classic holistic perspective is that there is only one healing force, which is love. And the miracle this love can perform is that it helps the other person to confront, explore, understand, forgive, and love him or herself. This process of self-exploration leading to the recovery of self-insight has been called clinical medicine, or character medicine, and this is basically the traditional holistic medicine going all the way back to Hippocrates (1). This medicine is a non-drug medicine as the Greek physicians believed that drugs were too poisonous to be used as medicine; they used a lot of medical herbs and plants but only for external use (1).

So for more than 2000 years medicine has been about giving loving care to support the patients in the process of gaining self-awareness and self-insight. This process led to the discovery of all the gifts and talents (including the essence – often called the purpose of life or the life mission) that should be used for self realisation and value creation. Being of use and service was thought to be the key to happiness and health.

Holistic psychiatry takes this proud medical tradition into the difficult field of mental disorders. The practice and this kind of therapy for the mental disorders was developed during the first half of the last century; unfortunately this kind of therapy was almost forgotten as pharmaceutical psychiatry became dominant in the end of the century. But all the knowledge of healing the mental disorders established by the researchers in non-drug therapy is still with us in a long row of great books and tenth of thousands of scientific papers.

This book aims to extract the most important theories and practical tools from this long and broad holistic medical tradition.

Treating the mentally ill

In countries where biomedicine dominates, like Denmark where we come from, most mentally ill people stay chronically ill for the most of their life (9). Many biomedical psychiatritsts simply believe that schizophrenia, depression and the other mental diseases are caused by chemical disturbances in the brain, again caused by inherited bad genes (defect DNA strings). With this belief little is done to cure and much is done to block the symptoms.

In the tradition of holistic medicine the belief is that patients, even the most ill, can heal. Some patients, even the most ill schizophrenic patients, makes it sometimes out of the mental darkness.

One interesting clinical experiment was made by Harold Searles (2). Searles treated 18 severely schizophrenic patients, who had been hospitalised for years and had no statistical chance of getting out of the hospital again. He treated these patients with 900 hours of intensive holistic psychodynamic therapy and existential healing (salutogenesis (4,5). After the therapy 33% could leave the hospital and live as normal or almost normal people; 33% was significantly improved but could still not leave the mental hospital and 33% was not improved at all. Many such reports exist, indicating that non-drug therapy really can help even some of the most ill. This we have also seen in our own clinic (10).

Our personality can be defined as all the patterns of psychological defence we have established throughout our childhood. Personality seems to be founded early in life. Sigmund Freud (11), Gustav Jung (12), and the other psychoanalysts believed that this takes place in the first three years, while more recent researchers in consciousness like Stanislav Grof (13) found that the adaptation of our personality to our family and the surrounding world started already at conception. Must unfortunately it has been difficult to test psychodynamic personality theory scientifically, as the model has too few predictions to be falsified in rigid scientific studies. Freud, Jung and Grof were therefore often seen as romantic dreamers far from real medical science.

Modern biomedicine, and especially modern psychiatry, is in our opinion in a crisis. In Denmark and in most other developed countries 10% or more of the citizens are using psychopharmacological drugs (14). These mentally ill people are not efficient at work and often unemployed; they are not of much experienced value to other people and therefore often isolated and lonely. They are not engaged in life, and therefore it is very difficult for them to grow and develop. They are pensioned early in life and some even end up committing suicide. One in seven of the schizophrenic patients thus commit suicide in Denmark (15), during the treatment and many more have attempted suicide. Immediately after the initiation of antipsychotic drugs several per cent of the mentally ill are committing suicide from unclear reasons (16), possibly from drug-induced depression (17).

Biomedical psychiatry is coming from high optimism around 1970 to deep pessimisms today. Most medical students do not want to work in psychiatry and all over Europe psychiatry is missing manpower to meet the demands for help to the mentally ill. As results the use of force, high drug doses and poly-pharmacy in psychiatry have become common (18).

The recession of biomedical psychiatry has been followed by a blossoming of the holistic psychiatry. Little by little the old, traditional views of the importance of the development of personal character, including the development of sexual character, have been accepted again. Freud, Jung, Reich, Searles and many other psychodynamic researchers of the last century found that poor psychosexual development played an important role in both the etiology and the healing of mental disorders. Freud was the first modern researcher to state directly that the mental illnesses were a direct product of arrested psychosexual development.

But already Hippocrates and his students had used sexological tools for curing female hysteria and other mental illnesses in women (1). The close association between sexuality and mental health was also documented by the fact that sexological patients often radically improved their mental health, when their sexual problems were solved (19). The other way round mental healing is also connected to sexual healing (20). General improvement of the quality of life is connected to a strong improvement of mental health and sexual ability (21).

The classical holistic perspective is that for a patient to heal mentally, he or she needs also to heal emotionally, sexually, spiritually and existentially. The emphasis on the whole person is what makes holistic medicin holistic (= wholeness-centered). Today many physicians and therapists have come to believe that clinical medicine is efficient in curing the mental illnesses. Often one of two patients has been cured or radically improved in one year (20).

We believe that holistic medicine is offering a path for future psychiatry to follow; a path that can make psychiatrists help the mentally ill patients more efficiently in the future. While psychiatry presumably always will need to treat extremely violent and sexually aggressive patients with drugs that modify their behaviour to be acceptable by society, most mentally ill patients can be helped with natural and sustainable methods that help and inspire them to realise their potential for personal growth and healing.

In holistic medicine "the doctor is the tool"(22). The therapist helps by being friendly and compassionate towards the patients. To care for and to love the mentally ill patients are not an easy job. It is frightening, because in this kind of work the patient will meet him or herself and you, the physician or therapist, will meet yourself as well. You will confront you own deepest fears, and your own irrationalities, neuroses, and even sometimes your own aspects of madness. And none of us really wants to go there.

We have hope that this book will be well received by both our biomedical and our psychodynamic and holistic psychiatric colleagues. We will do everything we can to serve every single psychiatrist and physician who wants to use holistic therapy in his or her practice. We believe that the healing power of the classical, holistic character medicine is desperately needed by the many mental patients that are not well helped with drugs.

Our primary intention is to serve the mental patients of the world and their physicians and therapists. The mentally ill patients need an efficient, safe and sustainable medicine. We are convinced that holistic psychiatry will benefit many of the mentally ill, despite diagnosis. We even believe that there is hope for the chronically ill, hospitalised patients. Even some of these patients can heal, as Searles convincingly demonstrated. Now we all need to be as good physicians as Searles. We can do it if we are willing to try hard, fail miserably and learn from our mistakes. If we just continue our efforts we will pick it up. We will be able to help our patients in the end. It takes a fight and some talents and some knowledge. We are sure you got the talent for helping; most physicians got it. It is completely up to you if you take the challenge or not. But if you do this book will bring you what you need to know to cure a significant fraction of the mentally ill. We wish you the best of luck in this endeavour and may this book benefit all living beings.

Søren Ventegodt, MD, MMedSci, EU-MSc-CAM,
Director, Quality of Life Research Center, Frederiksberg Alle 13A, 2.tv
DK-1661 Copenhagen V, Denmark. E-mail: ventegodt@livskvalitet.org

Joav Merrick, MD, MMedSci, DMSc
Professor of Pediatrics, National Institute of Child Health and Human Development, Office of the Medical Director, Health Services, Division for Mental Retardation, Ministry of Social Affairs, Jerusalem and Kentucky Children's Hospital, Department of Pediatrics, University of Kentucky College of Medicine, Lexington, United States. E-Mail: jmerrick@zahav.net.il

References

[1]   Jones WHS. Hippocrates. Vol. I–IV. London: William Heinemann, 1923-1931.
[2]   Knight RP. Preface. In: Searles HF, ed. Collected papers on schizophrenia. Madison, CT: Int Univ Press, 1965:15-18.
[3]   Ventegodt S. The life mission theory: A theory for a consciousness-based medicine. Int J Adolesc Med Health 2003;15(1): 89-91.
[4]   Antonovsky A. Health, stress and coping. London: Jossey-Bass, 1985.
[5]   Antonovsky A. Unravelling the mystery of health. How people manage stress and stay well. San Franscisco: Jossey-Bass, 1987.
[6]   Seligman MEP. Authentic happiness: Using the new positive psychology to realize your potential for lasting fulfillment. New York: Free Press, 2002.
[7]   Peterson C, Seligman MEP. Character strengths and virtues. Oxford: Oxford Univ Press, 2004.
[8]   Ventegodt S, Thegler S, Andreasen T, Struve F, Jacobsen S, Torp M, et al. A review and integrative analysis of ancient holistic character medicine systems. ScientificWorldJournal 2007;7:1821-31.

[9]   Kjøller M, Juel K, Kamper-Jørgensen F. Folkesundhedsrapporten Danmark 2007]. Copenhagen: Statens Inst Folkesundhed, 2007. [Danish].
[10]   Ventegodt S, Kandel I, Merrick J. Clinical holistic medicine (mindful short-term psychodynamic psychotherapy complimented with bodywork) in the treatment of schizophrenia (ICD10-F20/DSM-IV Code 295) and other psychotic mental diseases. ScientificWorldJournal 2007;7:1987-2008.
[11]   Jones E. The life and works of Sigmund Freud. New York: Basic Books, 1961.
[12]   Jung CG. Man and his symbols. New York: Anchor Press, 1964.
[13]   Grof S. LSD psychotherapy: Exploring the frontiers of the hidden mind. Alameda, CA: Hunter House, 1980.
[14]   Gunnersen SJ. Statistical yearbook 2007. Copenhagen: Statistics Denmark, 2008.
[15]   Hemmingsen R, Parnas, J., Gjerris, A, Reisby, N. og Kragh-Sørensen, P. [Klinisk Psykiatri, 2 udg.] Copenhagen: Munksgaard, 2000. [Danish].
[16]   Qin P, Nordentoft M. Suicide risk in relation to psychiatric hospitalization: evidence based on longitudinal registers.Arch Gen Psychiatry 2005;62(4):427-32.
[17]   SBU-rapport nr. 133/1 og 133/2. Behandling med neuroleptika. Stockholm: Statens beredning för utvärdering av medicinsk metodik, 1997. [Swedish].
[18]   Lindhardt A, ed. The use of antipsychotic drugs among the 18-64 year old patients with schizophrenia, mania, or bipolar affective disorder. Copenhagen: National Board Health, 2006. [Danish].
[19]   Ventegodt S, Thegler S, Andreasen T, Struve F, Enevoldsen L, Bassaine L, et al. Clinical holistic medicine (mindful, short-term psychodynamic psychotherapy complemented with bodywork) in the treatment of experienced impaired sexual functioning. ScientificWorldJournal 2007;7:324-9.
[20]   Ventegodt S, Thegler S, Andreasen T, Struve F, Enevoldsen L, Bassaine L, et al. Clinical holistic medicine (mindful, short-term psychodynamic psychotherapy complemented with bodywork) in the treatment of experienced mental illness. ScientificWorldJournal 2007;7:306-9.
[21]   Ventegodt S, Thegler S, Andreasen T, Struve F, Enevoldsen L, Bassaine L, et al. Clinical holistic medicine (mindful, short-term psychodynamic psychotherapy complemented with bodywork) improves quality of life, health, and ability by induction of Antonovsky-salutogenesis. ScientificWorldJournal 2007;7:317-23.
[22]   de Vibe M, Bell E, Merrick J, Omar HA, Ventegodt S. Ethics and holistic healthcare practice. Int J Child Health Human Dev 2008;1(1):23-8.

Section 1. A critical view of psychiatry

In the introduction to this book we explained that holistic medicine is *wholeness-centered*, focusing on the *whole human being*. But holistic medicine includes more than that: It includes the patient's whole world. Many schizophrenic patients are being treated for years with no results, but the day they find a boyfriend or a girlfriend and establish a close, intimate relationship they often recover spontaneously, as the literature of recovery has shown. So healing takes resources, and these resources have to come from outside the person, from intimate relationships. This is the *principle of resources*.

To heal the existence – enter the state of healing often called salutogenesis - the patient needs to encounter the painful emotional material creating the inner conflicts that show themselves as mental illness on the symptomatic level. To help the patient overcome their emotional resistance and confront the historical problem the physician or therapist needs to support the patient in processing by helping the patient to get into the gestalts or painful, traumatic, early moments of life.

This is done by the *principle of similarity*, as Hippocrates and his students found out some 2400 years ago (1). The principle of similarity states that to heal you must be helped back by "clues" that signifies the content of painful events. This can be done in many ways from simply sending you back in time in regression therapy, to working on your emotions and sexuality as it is done in psychodynamic psychotherapy (2-4).

Psychodrama, holotropic breath-work (5) and other active methods can help you remember and confront. Today we know of literally hundreds of different "non-drug" methods to introduce salutogenesis, as we shall see in chapter 32 and section 11. These methods has been used for at least two thousand years in Europe and has – in spite of their often dramatic appearance - been found to be extremely safe (6) and in accordance with the famous ethics of Hippocrates (1).

The patient will heal in the opposite pattern of the way he or she got ill; this is the famous *law of Hering* – the third principle of holistic healing. The fourth principle of holistic medicine, also going back to Hippocrates is that you should use as little force as necessary – *"Primum non nocere"*. The fifth principle is that you should *always try to heal the patient's whole existence*, not only a specific symptom. Table 1 lists the five principles (7).

Table 1. The five central principles of holistic healing in clinical medicine, holistic medicine, clinical holistic medicine and CAM (7)

- The principle of resources: only when you are getting the holding/care and support you did not get when you became ill, can you be healed from the old wound.
- The similarity principle: only by reminding the patient (or his body, mind or soul) of what made him ill, can the patient be cured. The reason for this is that the earlier wound/trauma(s) live in the subconscious (or body-mind).
- The principle of salutogenesis: the whole person must be healed (existential healing), not only a part of the person. This is done by recovering the sense of coherence, character and purpose of life of the person.
- The principle of using as little force as possible (primum non nocere or first do no harm), because since Hippocrates (460-377 BCE), "Declare the past, diagnose the present, foretell the future; practice these acts. As to diseases, make a habit of two things - to help, or at least to do no harm." it has been paramount not to harm the patient or running a risk with the patient's life or health.
- The Hering's law of cure (Constantine Hering, 1800-1880): that you will get well in the opposite order of the way you got ill.

Errors in holistic medicine

When you know the principles of healing you also know what NOT to do – the formal errors of holistic medicine (7). When you know and understand the principles of healing and the errors following from not respecting them, you are ready to start treating your first patient with holistic medicine. Beginning is really that simple. Mastery on the other hand takes years of practice, and countless hours of effort and reflection.

Errors regarding the principle of resources (healing happens in surplus of resources)

Therapy gives support to the patient, in many different forms of resources, and only when the patient gets exactly the supportive quality what was missing at the moment of the trauma – security, love, care, acceptance, acknowledgement - can the healing happen. To do this takes a lot of empathy and understanding. The most common reason for lack of resources is lack of confidentiality, intimacy and trust. If a therapist is afraid of intimacy and do not dare to touch the patient, when and where the patient needs to be touched, the healing will not happen.

A strong indication of lack of sufficient resources is that therapy becomes very painful for the patient. Even the most traumatic and painful of traumas, i.e. from incest, rape, and violent abuse, becomes bearable if resources are plenty.

Errors regarding the principle of similarity

The most common error is not understanding or ignoring the principle of similarity; this means that the therapist or holistic physician only treats the patient in a good, supportive and kind way. To really induce the process of healing, the patient must be guided into the repressed material that made him or her ill. According to the famous principle of similarity, originally formulated by Hippocrates and today used in many types of holistic medicine and CAM i.e. by the homeopaths, the patient must be exposed to a small dose of what originally gave him or her the traumas that made the patient ill – violence, neglect, abuse, mental pressure or whatever. The principle of similarity means that only by burdening the patient with a moderate degree of "evil", will he or she be healed. This is in sharp conflict with the moral rules of most modern societies, and therefore many physicians and therapists avoid giving the therapeutic dose of "evil", that is necessary to get the patient into the process of salutogenesis, or existential healing. The holistic therapist needs a thorough understanding of evil. Section four, especially chapter 21, explains human evilness. At the core of the difficult art of holistic medicine is the ability to expose the patient for a well-dosed "evil" stimulus in the good intent of healing and helping.

Errors regarding the principle of using as little force as possible ("primum non nocere" or "first do no harm")

Errors regarding the principle of using as little force as possible happen when the therapist uses more force than necessary, i.e. coercive persuasion, unnecessary fixation, medication with antipsychotic drugs when psychotherapy could have helped better.

Errors of this type typically lead to retraumatisation i.e. the patient getting another trauma that represses the patient even more than before. A special type of "implanted memories" also comes from use of excessive force in therapy, and should be avoided. The only way to be sure that this principle is not violated is to see if all the smaller therapeutic steps likely to help, placed on a scale from no-force to max-force in the therapy, have been tried before the next level is taken into use. For clinical holistic medicine such a scale has shown its usefulness. Obviously there will always be an element of guess here, as to how small a tool is needed and to what tool is likely to cause the patient unnecessary suffering. Fortunately side effects even with the largest tools are extremely rare in clinical medicine, clinical holistic medicine and CAM. In chapter 6 we argue that psychiatry often use more force than necessary and thus violates this principle.

Errors regarding the Hering's law of cure (that you will get well in the opposite order of the way you got ill)

Errors happen here when the therapist fails to notice symptoms or to understand that the symptoms and diseases that appear during the treatment is actually a necessary replay of event from the patient's personal history, which must be re-experienced and integrated, for the healing to happen. An example is to treat the patient for a skin-disease, the patient had as a child, instead of allowing the patient to confront it and understand its inherent significance and psychodynamic meaning (i.e. problems in the contact with mother). According to Hering's law of cure such a symptom indicates the release of material from deeper layers or more vital organs in the body. Hering believed that if the patient were not allowed to re-experience these things, the spontaneous regression necessary for healing could not take place.

Evidence-based holistic medicine

Knowing the healing principles and formal errors of holistic medicine empowers us to identify holistic medicine, in the jungle of complementary and alternative medicine (CAM), where elements of the entire world's many different cultures contribute to the colorful, but not always too effective mix of CAM-methods.

Holistic medicine is alternative medicine in the sense that it is complementary to modern days' biomedical psychiatry (drugs), but it is not really alternative medicine; it is rather classical, Hippocratic medicine, only made alternative by the dominance of biomedicine and pharmaceutical drugs. It is scientific and has been used for millennia. It is believed to be completely safe and also highly efficient. But how can we know for sure?

To know the positive and negative effects of holistic medicine we need to make it evidence based. When we test drugs we have the randomised clinical trial (RCT), but as we shall see in chapter 4, this method has severe methodological problems connected to it, making it less than a perfect method for testing the effects of medicine in general. When it comes to the scientific methods that should be used for documenting the effects of holistic medicine we recommend the simple methods of testing the holistic therapy on chronic patients that have been ill for several years. We know for sure that these patients rarely get better, so it is safe to say that if they do during intervention with holistic medicine, the cure came from the treatment, not from spontaneous recovery. We can thus measure the efficacy of holistic medicine from the fraction of cured patients. In section 13 we document the efficacy of holistic medicine on mental disorders in this way.

Holistic medicine works by developing self-awareness and self-insight; it intervenes on the patients' consciousness. In that sense holistic medicine is placebo. The intervention only changes the patients' consciousness. But as our life to a large extend is a materialization of our consciousness (8), then this in fact is what makes the change. When it comes to mental disorders this is even more obvious than for physical diseases. But then again, how can we know that DNA and changed brain chemistry is not really running the show? In chapter 5 we are testing the popular biochemical hypotheses of the mental disorders.

A simple way to argue for the need of holistic medicine in psychiatry is the lack of safe treatments with pharmaceutical drugs. The drugs used for treating the mental disorders are known to have many adverse effects, and recent metaanalysis has documented that the positive effects on patients mental health (mental state) are small at best (9-11). Actually the results indicate that the drugs are not improving the patients' mental state at all (see chapter 3). In this book we will not make the radical claim that no patients are helped by pharmaceutical drugs, in spite of the data pointing in that direction; we will look at the "therapeutic value" of the drugs used in psychiatry and say that the therapeutic value is low. Chapter 7 shows that the likelihood of getting adverse effects is higher than the likelihood of getting a positive effect, meaning that the therapeutic value of the drugs at best is very limited. We therefore find that holistic medicine has much to offer compared to the drugs.

In Denmark we have socialized biomedicine meaning that all mentally ill patients get free pharmaceutical treatment of their mental illness. Unfortunately we know from the official statistics that today one in four of the Danes have a chronic, mental disorder that cannot be cured by drugs. So the drugs may help some patients, but a medical system based on drugs will indisputably leave the majority of patients uncured – as chronic patients. It seems from the documentation we will present in section 13 that holistic medicine can cure every second mentally ill patient. This seems to be better than the improvement rate of one in three often found in psychodynamic psychotherapy (2-4). The major difference between psychodynamic psychotherapy and holistic medicine is that the latter includes the body in the treatment (see section eleven). But still, the effect of psychotherapy is much better than the effects of the pharmaceutical drugs according the research made by Leichsenring (2-4).

In conclusion medicine must be evidence-based. Evidence-based holistic medicine cannot use the standard RCT-test as a placebo intervention cannot be tested against placebo. Instead the efficacy of holistic medicine can be tested directly on chronic mentally ill patients who are not likely to recover spontaneously. In this section we shall take a critical look at today's psychiatry, its safety, its efficacy and its hypothesis.

In sections two and three we shall then see how holistic medicine approaches the mentally ill. In sections four and five we try to understand man and his brain. In section six we then focus on the etiology of the mental disorders from a holistic perspective. Section seven is about the problems of decision making and sexual transference in the patient-therapist relationship. In section eight we focus on personality disorders and schizophrenia. In section nine we take a broader, social perspective, and look at the consequence of sexual trauma for mental health. Section 10 is about children and adolescence. Suicide and suicide preventions are discussed in section 12. Section 14 gives tools for research and quality assurance in the holistic medical clinic and finally section 15 goes in depth with the important ethical aspects of holistic medicine.

The holistic approach in practice
or the helicopter perspective

Many problems are easier to solve than the hard core mental problems the patient might have, and the solution of these problems will almost always facilitate the cure of the mental disease. We therefore always start by screening the patient (using QOL10, see chapter 56) for problems that could be solved in the start of the treatment with the following questions:

- Q 1 How do you consider your physical health at the moment?
- Q 2 How do you consider your mental health at the moment?
- Q 3 How do you feel about yourself at the moment?
- Q 4 How are your relationships with your friends at the moment?
- Q 5 How is your relationship with your partner at the moment?
- Q 6 How do you consider your ability to love at the moment?
- Q 7 How do you consider your sexual functioning at the moment?

- Q 8 How do you consider your social functioning at the moment?
- Q 9 How is your working ability at the moment?
- Q 10 How would you assess your quality of your life now?

We collect the answers using a five point symmetrical Likert rating scale:

1. very good
2. good
3. neither good nor bad
4. bad
5. very bad

or

1. very high
2. high
3. neither low nor high
4. low
5. very low

Regarding Q 1 "How do you consider your physical health at the moment?", small physical health problems like nail problems, eczema, allergy or chronic infections should be cured. Physical appearance and self confidence is very important for the patient's general feeling of self-worth. If you want to treat these health issues with holistic medicine we recommend our book on the holistic treatment on physical disorders (12). Most likely your physically ill patient will suffer from pain, often chronic pain, so we have included the holistic treatment of pain in this book as chapters 43 and 44.

Physical pain is a serious hindrance to mental healing so to treat patients in pain you will have to *address the patient's pain first*. This is done by the use of therapeutic touch, as described in section eleven. Again there are no magic tricks to it, just touch the part of the body that hurts and find out why it hurts and listen to the story the body has to tell. Be naive. Go to the body as a parent would to a child in pain. Just *be caring and comforting*. Helping a patient in pain is not difficult. It is just a question of expressing you liking for this person in a physical and intimate way. We know of course that just this simple thing might scare the best of biomedical psychiatrists, who have used half a life on treating patients on the other side of the desk. But believe us: As soon as you have starting practicing holistic medicine and noticed the miracles of healing that comes from intimacy, you would never want to sit 6 feet from your patient again.

Regarding Q 2 "How do you consider your mental health at the moment?"

This question is the most significant of them all, making you and your patient agree on the common goal: That the patients should experience a good or very good mental health in the end of the treatment. *Self-rated mental health* is presumably the best predictor of future good, mental health, signifying that the patient really is permanently cured if you can reach that goal together. To measure this before and after the treatment will also allow you to document your clinical success in a simple way.

Regarding Q 3 "How do you feel about yourself at the moment?"

This question is always a great opening for at talk about existence in holistic medicine.

Regarding Q 4 "How are your relationships with your friends at the moment?"

Friends are important and often the patient needs new friends. Support in re-establishing a social network is an important part of holistic treatment.

Regarding Q 5 "How is your relationship with your partner at the moment"

Many patients have problems in their intimate relationships especially their one-to-one relationship. If they do not have a partner, helping the patient to get one is an important part of holistic therapy. This can be done in many ways, from advise on behaviour (get outdoors! Use the city! Go dancing. You will not find him or her in you private home!) to the improvement of personal hygiene and self-esteem. Support that leads to *psychosexual development* might be the most important help here.

Regarding Q 6 "How do you consider your ability to love at the moment?"

Love is a spiritual thing. To reconnect the patient to his or her soul and opening the heart is essential in holistic therapy.

Regarding Q 7 "How do you consider your sexual functioning at the moment?"

Sexual problems are common among mentally ill patients and often the sexual problems are more easily cured than the mental disorder itself. With a well functioning sexuality the patient is much more likely to find a loving and supportive partner that can be a real resource for the patient. Holistic therapy for sexual problems is usually extremely efficient. If the patient has sexual problems these *problems needs to be addressed as a part of the treatment*. Often it makes things clearer to define the treatment of the specific sexual problems as a parallel sexological treatment. We recommend our book on holistic sexology (13).

Sexuality plays a profound and important role in holistic medicine; the original treatment of female mental disorder was basically a sexological treatment as the Hippocratic doctors believed that mental disorders was a product of arrested psychosexual development.

The issue of sexuality is therefore likely to appear in holistic therapy of any mental disorder. Instead of making sexuality a thing that little by little reveals its importance, the speed of therapy is dramatically increased if sexuality can be an issue from the beginning of the treatment. This is most elegantly done by defining a specific treatment for the sexual problems to be done in parallel with the treatment of the mental disorder. Later the two treatments serving the two different purposes, one to rehabilitate sexual ability and one to rehabilitate mental health, will slowly merge into the healing of the patients' whole existence. The more specific goals that can be set, which all points in the direction of existential healing, the faster and more efficient will the treatment be.

Regarding Q 8 "How do you consider your social functioning at the moment?"

Social functioning is often low among patients with mental disorders. Many treatment systems put lots of focus on this aspect and we find it important as well.

Regarding Q 9 "How is your working ability at the moment?"

The working ability is often low and the patient often dream of studying and working. It might seem an impossible goal but it is important to let the patients have his or her dream of a healthy and normal life. We have seen schizophrenic patients heal and one of the schizophrenic patients described in chapter 34 just finished his masters' degree in computer science. So it is possible to come back and it is important to support the patients also in this aspect. They should not start to work or study before they are sufficiently well, but the direction towards a normal life means everything to them. This goal is important to motivate them to work as hard as they can to get well again.

Regarding Q 10 "How would you assess your quality of your life now?"

The quality of life is important as a goal. The patients' philosophy of life should be developed during the treatment and often philosophical exercises, that allow them to express their thoughts and beliefs, are extremely valuable parts of the treatment. We recommend our book on holistic philosophy of life to the doctor or therapist who wants to work philosophically with the patient (14).

Holistic therapy addresses all aspects of life. The art of holistic medicine is to understand the order of things and the issues to focus on. In a way this is simple, because the patient will by the symptoms signify his or her needs right away. It is an art because of the resistance. The patient will not confront the difficult emotions if it is possible at all to avoid them.

The first step is always to win the confidence of the patient. To do this the goal must be clear, the strategy convincing, and the emotional pressure on the patients neurotic side low. With the confidence the patient will open up, and receive support from the therapist and from other people, and with more resources available, more difficult problems can be addressed. In the end the most difficult existential problems that causes the symptoms known as the mental disorder, can be confronted and solved, and the patient is cured.

We recommend that you use the QOL10 questionnaire and notice the 10 answers in the patients' records. You will then be able to document the effects of your treatments, and you will be able to see your improvement as a therapist as the years go by. Do not miss this important opportunity to gain self-confidence as you see your clinical results documented in the case records. If you want to write a research paper on your work you will in five or 10 years find that the data you have collected in this simple way to be of immense value. Section fourteen will teach you more about research and quality assurance in clinical holistic medicine.

To practice evidence-based holistic medicine is after all more than anything about being sure that what you do for your patients really works based on scientific evidence! So use these few minutes to collect that evidence. Interestingly failures to help patients and reflections of what went wrong are the most important source for learning. Only by collecting the evidence that we are NOT HELPING some of our patients (in the first years most of them) can we take this painful lesson. Else we will make our self belief that we are helping. Do not fall into that trap.

Getting started---start today

If you understand the five principles of holistic healing in table 1, you are ready to start practicing holistic medicine. You can of cause also wait until you have read the whole book and understood every word of it. But the sad thing is that when it comes to the practice of holistic medicine it is as much an art as a science. The leaning comes through practice. It is leaning by doing. What you need to find out is how you, as the person you are, can help your patient to heal. *Every patient is unique as are you are. Therefore every treatment will be unique also.*

In biomedical psychiatry, every specialty takes care of their specific part of the human being; the psychiatrist thus takes care of the brain. If you are a medical doctor, and wants to practice holistic medicine, you must start by understanding that this approach does not work in holistic medicine. You need to take care of everything and every little detail is important. It is very much like a mother or father taking care of a baby. Actually, according to holistic medical etiology the patients often got ill because of poor parenting early in life. So you need to be the good parent. *You need to be caring, loving and supportive.*

If you can be that, you can start the treatment. It is not that difficult. Just *explore the patient together with the patient.* Holistic medicine is clinical medicine which means that the examination of the patient together with the patient, giving the patient a thorough understanding of him or herself, IS the cure. We therefore often call it clinical holistic medicine. It doesn't matter what you call it. Just be there with the patient, help him or her understanding existence and life in sufficient depth and the existence will heal and the disease will be cured. It is that simple. So start today.

Pick yourself, among all your many patients, the patient you care most for, the patient that is closest to your heart and who you most want to help. Simply spend one hour every week or more together with this patient, just helping the patient exploring him or herself. Just sit close and talk.

Start being personal; open op and *share what is happening in your own life*, also the difficult parts of it. Do not burden your patient, do not ask for advice. Just share to show that you care. *Win trust* by showing that you trust. *Be close. Give of your love.* Make the healing happen in small but important steps. It is not that difficult. What it most difficult is getting started, and having your first success. When you have had this, just treat all the other patients the same successful way. When you can to this with a majority of your mentally ill patients you have become a holistic psychiatrist.

Do not wait. Start today. Read this book while you are treating your first patient. You will find that many of the questions that arise from your clinical work with this single patient will be answered little by little by this book. It will be difficult for you to understand what is going on in the patient, in you and between you. You will most likely make most of the errors mentioned above, and more. But do not worry. If you come from a good intent these errors will not harm your patient, but only make the treatment take longer time. If you get into the difficult area of sexual transference, which you most likely will if you treat a patient of the opposite sex, which we always recommend, make sure that you keep your sexual borders and behave ethically. We do recommend that you read section 15 before you start treating your first patient, and definitely before you start including bodywork (even holding hands) in your treatment.

The treatments of your first patients with clinical holistic medicine are likely to take several hundred hours. After practicing holistic medicine for about 20 years we can treat most of our patients in about 20 sessions of therapy (see section thirteen). Holistic therapy takes time, much time in the beginning and less time in the end. The first year you can only treat a small number of patients; when you are experienced you can treat hundred patients a year or even more.

You will find that your ability to help your patients corresponds perfectly to your ability to love. Practicing holistic medicine will teach you to love thy neighbor as thyself. It will open your heart. It will challenge and develop you. This is why it will be interesting for you to practice holistic medicine for many years to come.

Never forget that *to cure your patient is an act of love*. It is not an act of power, not an act of force, for you can never force your patient to heal. It is not even an act of knowledge for your knowledge and understanding will not help your patient, only the patients'own understanding will help him or her. Therefore the art of helping is the art of caring.

References

[1]   Jones WHS. Hippocrates. Vol. I–IV. London: William Heinemann, 1923-1931.
[2]   Leichsenring F, Rabung S, Leibing E. The efficacy of short-term psychodynamic psychotherapy in specific psychiatric disorders: a meta-analysis. Arch Gen Psychiatry 2004;61(12):1208-16.
[3]   Leichsenring F. Are psychodynamic and psychoanalytic therapies effective? A review of empirical data. Int J Psychoanal 2005;86(Pt 3):841-68.
[4]   Leichsenring F, Leibing E. Psychodynamic psychotherapy: a systematic review of techniques, indications and empirical evidence. Psychol Psychother 2007;80(Pt 2):217-28.
[5]   Grof S. Implications of modern consciousness research for psychology: Holotropic experiences and their healing and heuristic potential. Humanistic Psychol 2003;31(2-3):50-85.
[6]   Ventegodt S, Kandel I, Merrick J. A metaanalysis of side effects of psychotherapy, bodywork, and clinical holistic medicine. J Complement Integr Med, in Press.
[7]   Ventegodt S, Andersen NJ, Kandel I, Merrick J. Formal errors in nonpharmaceutical medicine (CAM): Clinical medicine, mind-body medicine, body-psychotherapy, holistic medicine, clinical holistic medicine and sexology. Int J Adolesc Med Health 2009;21(2):161-74.
[8]   Ventegodt S, Flensborg-Madsen T, Andersen NJ, Nielsen M, Morad M, Merrick J. Global quality of life (QOL), health and ability are primarily determined by our consciousness. Research findings from Denmark 1991-2004. Soc Indicator Res 2005;71:87-122.
[9]   Moncrieff J, Wessely S, Hardy R. Active placebos versus antidepressants for depression. Cochrane Database Syst Rev 2004;(1):CD003012.
[10]   Adams CE, Awad G, Rathbone J, Thornley B. Chlorpromazine versus placebo for schizophrenia. Cochrane Database Syst Rev 2007;(2):CD000284.
[11]   Ventegodt S, Flensborg-Madsen T, Andersen NJ, Svanberg BØ, Struve F, Endler C, Merrick J. Therapeutic value of anti-psychotic drugs: A critical analysis of Cochrane meta-analyses of the therapeutic value of anti-psychotic drugs. J Altern Med Res, in Press.
[12]   Ventegodt S, Kandel I, Merrick J. Principles of holistic medicine. Quality of life and health. New York: Hippocrates Sci Publ, 2005.
[13]   Ventegodt S, Merrick J. Sexology from a holistic point of view. A textbook of classic and modern sexology. New York: Nova Science, 2010.
[14]   Ventegodt S, Kandel I, Merrick J. Principles of holistic medicine. Philosophy behind quality of life. Victoria, BC: Trafford, 2005.

Chapter 1

Sometimes you need to stop what you usually do

In Denmark and other countries with socialised biomedicine about one in four has a chronic mental illness that cannot be cured by biomedical drugs. Sometimes we need to stop doing what we usually do, when it does not work. This seemingly being the most difficult thing a physician can do! May we suggest that we expand the range of the physician's activities with other toolboxes than the biomedical, so that we can find something new to do, when what we usually do does not work? If the NNT (number needed to treat) of the best working drug or operation is say 5, 10, 20 or even often higher, rendering only a small fraction of our patients (5-20% of them) helped by our medical intervention?

Remembering the old humoristic definition of insanity and its treatment: "to continue doing what we always have done, expecting new results", we on the other hand suggest that the physician should be open-minded to other kinds of treatment and perspectives on health and disease. In fact we actually want the modern physician to be multi-paradigmatic.

All medical work is based on the intention of doing good, either improving the health, the quality of life, or the ability of functioning – or a combination. Independently of the good intention coming from the physician, the medical work is always bound to some medical theory or a frame of interpretation. Hence the different paradigms (1) - giving a number of different perceptions, hypothesis, diagnoses, actions and reactions. Just compare how we construct our consciousness in general life and in science (2,3).

The process of healing is – as life itself - often fairly complicated. The course of the disease, the healing process, personal development, learning and coping in connection with a disease is highly individual.

The modern physician is often multi-paradigmatic as he must be to serve many different types of people in many different existential circumstances. He basically has the three, very different sets of technologies or "toolboxes" at his disposal, derived from three different medical paradigms:

- Classical, manual medicine, where the hands – used with the best and most humane intentions – constitute the main tools. It dates back to Hippocrates and Greek antiquity (4,5).

- Biomedicine, which came into widespread use around 1950, born paradigmatically along with the discovery of penicillin, where biomedicine has a focus on body chemistry and physiology (5).
- Holistic medicine – scientific, consciousness-oriented mind-body medicine - which originally was invented by Hippocrates and his students but is now appearing in a modern, scientific version as a new and increasingly popular trend with many family physicians in the western world. It draws on a variety of healing processes, philosophies and systems, taken in the original or modified form from the pre-modern cultures. The most important thinkers influencing holistic medicine in Europe today is great physicians and philosophers like Jung (6,7), Maslow (8), Antonovsky (9,10), Frankl (11), Fromm (12), Goleman (13,14), Sartre (15), Kiekegaard (16) and Allart (17). The holistic approach focus on the person as a whole, where this wholeness, soul or total existence is thought to be able to heal from its very totality – becoming "whole again", when the wholeness is partly or completely lost (18-27).

Depending on the perspective, or paradigm, very different things might happen to the patient, when treated by the physician, where the signs and symptoms of development or progress of health and disease is interpreted very differently. If you go to a homeopathic doctor, which for example is fairly common in Germany, it is seen as a good sign, if the treatment makes you feel worse for a while (28-31), but if you consult a biomedical doctor, then medicine is expected to make you feel better almost at once. If you consult a holistic doctor working according to the holistic process theory and the life mission theory (5,26,27), you would normally expect a very different path, even when occasionally confronting painful old traumas. The reason for this is that the earliest existential wounds normally are the toughest to overcome, but the more resources you have, the more severe wounds on your soul, you will manage to confront and heal.

In lack of a better term we have called the extended medical science, integrating these three different paradigms and their three strands of tools and methods for bio-psycho-social, holistic medicine. It is really medicine based on biological science in its widest sense – i.e. based on *the science of life*.

Clinical holistic medicine

Scientific holistic medicine is also called clinical holistic medicine. Many different theories exist; we base our work on the simple life mission theory (18-23) (see chapters 19-21) that state that everybody has a purpose of life, or a huge talent. Happiness comes from living this purpose and succeeding in expressing the core talent in your life. To do this, it is important to develop as a person into what is known as the natural condition, a condition where you know yourself and use all your efforts to achieve what is most important for you.

The holistic process theory of healing (26,27) and the related quality of life (QOL) theories (32-34) states that the return to the natural state of being is possible, whenever the person gets the resources needed for the existential healing. The resources needed are, according to the theory: "holding" in the dimensions of awareness, respect, care, acknowledgment and acceptance with support and processing in the dimensions of feeling, understanding and letting go of negative attitudes and beliefs.

The precondition for the holistic healing to take place, is trust with the intention that healing takes place. Existential healing is not a local healing of any kind, but a healing of the wholeness of the person, making him much more resourceful, loving, and knowledgeable of himself, his own needs and wishes. In letting go of negative attitudes and beliefs, the person returns to a more responsible existential position and an improved quality of life.

The philosophical change of the person healing, is often a change towards preferring difficult problems and challenges, instead of avoiding difficulties in life (35-43). The person who becomes happier and more resourceful is often also becoming more healthy, more talented and more able of functioning (44-46).

Consciousness-based medicine

In the search for the best way to make a new medical clinical practice to serve the new type of patients we now see in our western society (the critical and knowledgeable patient or the patient focused on personal or spiritual development), we have worked with three different approaches to the new medicine:

- Quality of life as medicine: Focusing on human feelings and emotions, we have combined bio-medicine with a number of complementary therapies, like Rosen body work, classical Chinese acupuncture and gestalt psychotherapy. We have called this holistic approach "quality of life as medicine" (44-46). The combined treatment have the intention of inducing existential healing (26,27) and encompasses three phases, which is popularly described as: "Feel, understand, and let go": Feel the blockages in body and mind, behind your health problems and symptoms, understand the life-denying conclusions you reached then which created them, and let go of these decisions once you are ready to assume responsibility and be your true, responsible self again. The team of physician and alternative therapist complementing each other working under medical supervision, could be the most efficient way to induce existential healing, in spite of the differences in professional language, culture and paradigm.
- Meaning of life as medicine: focusing on the purpose of life, meaning of life, life mission and talent (18-23). Focusing on the hidden potentials, on the beauty and magnificence of the soul and on the power of our existential choices, gives many patients faith and a fast healing progress. When the existential theories, the QOL philosophy and theories, and the QOL concepts are explained to the patients and internalised, patients gradually find themselves, and return to a natural state of being, comparable in some aspects to the state in which they were born with a certain purpose of life, and certain great talents to be used. The life mission theory simply states, that denying your meaning in life leads you to illness, unhappiness and poor performance, while recovering your purpose of life depends on finding and working for your purpose of life.

- Love as medicine: Based on the concept of genuine human relationships and the power of unconditional love and acceptance, we have worked with the spiritual gift of love and the healing power of this in what we have designated an experimental, social utopia (46,47). When patients belong to a small community with true companionship, contact and emotional surplus, their way to recovery seems to be much shorter. The problem with social utopia is, that it is very difficult to create and even more difficult to control. One of the preconditions seems to be that the participants do not have sex with each other, as this disturbs the possibility of intimacy in the group setting.

Although consciousness-based medicine supports individuals in their personal development; therapy and the patient-physician relationship can never replace a vibrant reality lived with those most important to them. It is the conquest of a good personal world to live in, which can bring wholeness and healing. Quite simply, an individual can only realize the meaning and purpose of life in a social context. This purpose is what we are meant to be and with this gift we will be able to give to others. This can only happen most fully in intimate relationships, full of trust and love. A huge body of evidence has been collected on the connection between health and survival, and love and intimacy (48).

Many medical doctors seem to be unable to work with therapists not scientifically trained, and many therapists do not like to be directed by a medical doctor, which makes the approach very difficult. Problems of this kind in the treatment team do not help the patients, as we have painfully experienced in our own clinical practice.

As human beings we are often limited to loving only a few percentages of our fellow men, at least before we develop the general ability of love and serve all. This is an issue that often naturally grow to a larger fraction, as we grow older, more wise, spacious and containing, as we understand that love might be a leading concept in medicine. Maybe even the strongest of the three concepts for inducing existential healing. Since such an approach for many seems unnatural, we are for all practical purposes left with the second approach in order for the modern physician to use the "new medicine", which really seems to be very similar to the classical holistic medicine.

Interestingly, the three approaches mentioned above express to what degree the physician is willing to come close with the patient. This mirrors the intention of the physician towards his patient. In a) the physician has the intent of helping the patient to heal, in b) he has the intent of personally giving a gift to the patient from the bottom of his heart and in c) the physician has the intention to let the patient be a part of his life, in true appreciation of the magnificence of this unique soul in front of him. We believe that most physicians of our time, who search their soul will find that the intentions of b) is an appropriate ambition for their work. The physician, who truly can give the holding (8,9) and processing in order to come close to his patients needs, will always be loved and respected by his patients.

What makes a physician excellent?

What will make a physician excellent are his good intentions, his deep knowledge and developed skills. In order to assist his patient to a successful treatment and help his patient, the physician is only excellent, when the good intentions result in the patient being adequately helped. The patient is helped when one of the following two conditions is fulfilled:

- The patient gets what he wants: quality of life in some aspect or globally, health in some aspect or globally, or ability of functioning in some aspect or globally – or a combination of these.
- The physician gets what he wants: the broken leg healed or the disease treated or prevented.

So the situation is fairly complex, and much is depending on the physician choosing the right medical paradigm or toolbox. It is not easy to tell, what a good medical treatment is, unless:

- you understand the paradigm chosen, and look at the patient from inside it.
- you keep track of all the subjective, objective factors and events involved in the process of healing through time.
- you have a valid way of testing the end result of the treatment.

All this is more or less complicated depending on the paradigm with the subjective paradigm the easiest to demonstrate (25). This makes it surprisingly easy to make research and quality improvement in the holistic medical clinic, introducing existential healing according to the holistic process theory, and surprisingly difficult to document effect of the biomedical treatments, because of the objective approach. This later approach needs a difficult set-up with control groups in the Cochrane design to be valid.

An example of the three medical paradigms at work: low back pain [49]

To make things simple here we will not look at schizophrenia, but on physical pain, which torments a surprising large number of mentally ill patients.

A patient comes to the physician with low back pain. If the physician uses manual medicine, he will examine the patient carefully to exclude the need of surgery; he works with his hands on the patient, helping the patient to be more relaxed, less tense and less in pain. Most fine body workers or chiropractors can remove a normal low back pain within an hour. When the cause in the body is understood and removed, the job is done. If the pain returns, so must the patient. If he gets a bad discus (a slipped disc) and a severe problem later with compression of the spinal nerves it is not related to this treatment.

If the physician is working according to biomedicine, he will examine the patient carefully to exclude the need of surgery, and if the problem is not serious he will mobilise the patient, and use the painkillers necessary for this. He will talk about prevention, avoiding heavy lifting or poor working postures. If the cause of the pain is understood this is fine, but mostly the low back pain has no objective cause and this is no obstacle for giving the treatment. When the patient is well again after the mobilisation – it normally takes a couple of days – the job is done.

If the physician is working with conscious-based medicine he will first examine the patient carefully to exclude the need of surgery. He will then, together with the patient, look for the cause of the illness in the patient's consciousness and subconsiousness – difficult feelings repressed and placed in the longissimus thoraces muscles and other muscles. He will talk to the patient, give "holding" and processing, and inspire him to a more honest and joyful living. When the cause in the (un)consciousness is understood and removed, and the pain is gone, the job is done.

It is not that any of these medical paradigms are better or worse that the other. The excellent physician mastering what we call the "new bio-psycho-social, holistic medicine" uses the most efficient way to help every patient, giving him or her exactly what is needed under the circumstances. So, if it does not work, stop the treatment and try something else.

References

[1] Kuhn TS. The structure of scientific revolutions. Int Encyclopedia Unified Sci 1962;2:2.
[2] Gadamer H. Truth and method. New York: Continuum, 2003.
[3] Chalmers A. What is this thing called science? Buckingham: Open Univ Press, 1999.
[4] Hanson AE. Hippocrates: Diseases of Women. Signs 11975;2:567-84.
[5] Ventegodt S, Morad M, Merrick J. Clinical holistic medicine: Classic art of healing or the therapeutic touch. ScientificWorldJournal 2004;4:134 -47.
[6] Jung CG. Man and his symbols. New York: Anchor Press, 1964.
[7] Jung CG. Psychology and alchemy. Collected works of CG Jung. Princeton, NJ: Princeton Univ Press, 1968.
[8] Maslow AH. Toward a psychology of being. New York: Van Nostrand, 1962.
[9] Antonovsky A. Health, stress and coping. London: Jossey-Bass, 1985.
[10] Antonovsky A. Unravelling the mystery of health. How people manage stress and stay well. San Franscisco: Jossey-Bass, 1987.
[11] Frankl V. Man´s search for meaning. New York: Pocket Books, 1985.
[12] Fromm E. The art of lving. New York, Harper Collins, 2000.
[13] Goleman DL. Emotional intelligence. New York: Bantam, 1995.
[14] Goleman DL. Destructive emotions. New York: Mind Life Inst, 2003.
[15] Sartre JP Being and nothingness. London: Routledge, London, 2002.
[16] Kierkegaard SA. The sickness unto death. Princeton, NJ: Princeton Univ Press, 1983.
[17] Allardt E. To have, to love, to be – about welfare in the Nordic countries. Lund: Argos, 1975. [Swedish]
[18] Ventegodt S, Andersen NJ, Merrick J. Editorial: Five theories of human existence. ScientificWorldJournal 2003;3:1272-6.
[19] Ventegodt S. The life mission theory: A theory for a consciousness- based medicine. Int J Adolesc Med Health 2003;15(1):89-91.
[20] Ventegodt S, Andersen NJ, Merrick J. The life mission theory II: The structure of the life purpose and the ego. ScientificWorldJournal 2003;3:1277-85.
[21] Ventegodt S, Andersen NJ, Merrick J. The life mission theory III: Theory of talent. ScientificWorldJournal 2003;3:1286-93.
[22] Ventegodt S, Merrick J. The life mission theory IV. A theory of child development. ScientificWorldJournal 2003;3:1294-1301.
[23] Ventegodt S, Andersen NJ, Merrick J. The life mission theory V. A theory of the anti-self and explaining the evil side of man. ScientificWorldJournal 2003;3:1302-13.
[24] Ventegodt S, Andersen NJ, Merrick J. Holistic medicine: Scientific challenges. ScientificWorldJournal 2003;3:1108-16.

[25] Ventegodt S, Andersen NJ, Merrick J. Holistic Medicine II: The square- curve paradigm for research in alternative, complementary and holistic medicine: A cost-effective, easy and scientifically valid design for evidence based medicine. ScientificWorldJournal 2003;3: 1117-27.

[26] Ventegodt S, Andersen NJ, Merrick J. Holistic Medicine III: The holistic process theory of healing. ScientificWorldJournal 2003;3: 1138- 46.

[27] Ventegodt S, Andersen NJ, Merrick J. Holistic Medicine IV: The principles of the holistic process of healing in a group setting. ScientificWorldJournal 2003;3:1294-1301.

[28] Hahnemann S. Organon of the medical art. Redmond, WA: Birdcage Books, 1996.

[29] Kent JT. Lectures on homeopathic philosophy. Sounthampton, UK: Southhampton Book, 1990.

[30] Tyler ML. Homeopathic drug pictures. Frome, Somerset, UK: Hillman Printer, 1995.

[31] Lockie A. Encyclopedia of homeopathy. London: Dorling Kindersley, 2000.

[32] Ventegodt S, Merrick J, Andersen NJ. Quality of life theory I. The IQOL theory: An integrative theory of the global quality of life concept. ScientificWorldJournal 2003;3:1030-40.

[33] Ventegodt S, Merrick J, Andersen NJ. Quality of life theory II. Quality of life as the realization of life potential: A biological theory of human being. ScientificWorldJournal 2003;3:1041-9.

[34] Ventegodt S, Merrick J, Andersen NJ. Quality of life theory III. Maslow revisited. ScientificWorldJournal 2003;3:1050-7.

[35] Ventegodt S, Andersen NJ, Merrick J. Quality of life philosophy: when life sparkles or can we make wisdom a science? ScientificWorldJournal 2003;3:1160-3.

[36] Ventegodt S, Andersen NJ, Merrick J. QOL philosophy I: Quality of life, happiness, and meaning of life. ScientificWorldJournal 2003;3:1164- 75.

[37] Ventegodt S, Andersen NJ, Kromann M, Merrick J. QOL philosophy II: What is a human being? ScientificWorldJournal 2003;3:1176-85.

[38] Ventegodt S, Merrick J, Andersen NJ. QOL philosophy III: Towards a new biology. ScientificWorldJournal 2003;3:1186-98.

[39] Ventegodt S, Andersen NJ, Merrick J. QOL philosophy IV: The brain and consciousness. ScientificWorldJournal 2003;3:1199-1209.

[40] Ventegodt S, Andersen NJ, Merrick J. QOL philosophy V: Seizing the meaning of life and getting well again. ScientificWorldJournal 2003;3:1210 -29.

[41] Ventegodt S, Andersen NJ, Merrick J. QOL philosophy VI: The concepts. ScientificWorldJournal 3, 1230-40.

[42] Merrick J, Ventegodt S. What is a good death? To use death as a mirror and find the quality in life. BMJ Rapid Responses 2003 Oct 31.

[43] Ventegodt S, Merrick J. Medicine and the past. Lesson to learn about the pelvic examination and its sexually suppressive procedure. BMJ Rapid Responses 2004 Feb 21.

[44] Ventegodt S, Merrick J, Andersen NJ. Quality of life as medicine. A `pilot study of patients with chronic illness and pain. ScientificWorld Journal 2003;3:520-32.

[45] Ventegodt S, Merrick J, Andersen NJ. Quality of life as medicine II. A pilot study of a five day "Quality of Life and Health" cure for patients with alcoholism. ScientificWorld Journal 2003;3:842-52.

[46] Ventegodt S, Clausen B, Langhorn M, Kromann M, Andersen NJ, Merrick J. Quality of Life as Medicine III. A qualitative analysis of the effect of a five days intervention with existential holistic group therapy: a quality of life course as a modern rite of passage. ScientificWorld Journal 2004;4:124-33.

[47] Ventegodt S. Consciousness-based medicine. Copenhagen: Forskningscenterets Forlag, 2003. [Danish]

[48] Ornish D. Love and survival. The scientific basis for the healing power of intimacy. New York: Harper Collins, 1999.

[49] Ventegodt S, Morad M, Merrick J. Clinical holistic medicine: The "new medicine", the multi-paradigmatic physician and the medical record. ScientificWorldJournal 2004;4:273-85.

Two different medical systems

Today we have two scientific medical traditions, two schools or treatment systems: holistic and alternative medicine and biomedicine. In Europe you can be a master of science in complementary, integrative and psychosocial medicine (EU-MSc in CAM at Interuniversity College, Graz, in Austria) or you can be a master of science in biomedicine (MD/ MMedSci).

The two traditions are based on two very different philosophical positions: subjectivistic and objectivistic. The philosopher Buber taught us that you can say I-Thou or I-It, holding the other person as a subject or an object. These two fundamentally different attitudes seem to characterize the difference in world view and patient approach in the two schools, one coming from psychoanalysis and the old, holistic tradition of Hippocratic medicine, the other from modern natural sciences.

Holistic medicine has during the last three decades developed its philosophical positions and is today an independent, medical system seemingly capable of curing mentally ill patients at the cost of a few thousand Euros with no side effects and with lasting value for the patient. The problem is that very few studies have tested the effect of holistic medicine on mentally ill patients. Another problem is that the effect of holistic medicine must be documented in a way that respects this school's philosophical integrity, allowing for subjective assessment of patient benefit and using the patient as his/her own control, as placebo control cannot be used in placebo-only treatment.

As the existing data are strongly in favor of using holistic medicine, which seems to be safer, more efficient, and cheaper, it is recommended that clinical holistic medicine also be used as treatment for mental illness. More research and funding is needed to develop scientific holistic medicine.

Introduction

It is most interesting that the last century left us with two completely different, scientific traditions for treating the mentally ill: a subjectivistic and an objectivistic. These two traditions correspond exactly to the two different ways man can relate to his world, with the famous philosophical position of the existential philosopher Buber (1): as a "thou" or as an "it". Buber published his famous book *I and Thou* in 1923 and it had quite an extreme impact on the development of the way therapists understood their own work at that time. They understood that man has only two fundamental relations in the world, either I-Thou or I-It.

Either you come from a subjectivistic position or from an objectivistic position; either you come from sheer love or from bruited force. There is no in between, no middle way, no way to mix the two. We must choose our approach and take the consequences. The person before you may be a divine being, with an autonomy equal to your own, to see, understand, and interpret the world; a center in the universe like yourself, and you have no power over this other person at all; (s)he is a unique presence, a source of existence like yourself, and you can only surrender and serve, if you want to relate at all.

On the other hand is the person who regards another as an object, which can be analyzed and manipulated, trimmed, supported, or broken down; you are in power, and the other person is at your command an for your use. The stimulus inciting the interest of Archie Cochrane (1909-1988) in scientific medicine is claimed to be his own ill health and the inability of psychoanalysis to cure his problem of sexual dysfunction (2).

The treatment undertaken by Cochrane failed, because his condition was organic, and thus evidence-based medicine was founded on Cochrane's critical evaluation of his own psychoanalytic psychotherapy. The objectivistic tradition of medical science thus founded now believes that objective physical and chemical etiologies exist for all disease, not only to organic problems but also to mental problems. In psychiatry, the objectivistic approach has led to extremely complicated and detailed systems for psychiatric diagnostics related to brain-chemistry and pharmaceutical treatments thereof.

In holistic medicine, the tradition of psychodynamic therapy going back to Freud (3) and Jung (4) has been developed into a variety of ways to support patients' body, mind, spirit, and whole existence. Most popular is existentially oriented conversational therapy (see (5)), emotionally realizing bodywork (6-9), and spiritual exercises that develop the patients' consciousness and autonomy (basically taking the patients back to what Huxley called the "perennial philosophy" (10)). The holistic medical tradition believes that subjective choices and shift in consciousness is the etiology of most diseases, both somatic and mental.

Holistic approach to psychiatry

In medicine, these two philosophically equally valid positions, the subjectivistic and the objectivistic, means that we as doctors either must come from an objectivistic science that tries to understand our patient by using tools for scientific analysis, diagnostics, and treatment, or from a subjectivistic science that focuses on meeting the other person soul to soul, on loving the other in an unselfish way, in letting yourself as a doctor be "the tool" in your impeccable service of the other; what you to do here is to bring the patient's subjective being into focus and surrender your own self to that meeting.

The objectivistic position is the position of the biomedical psychiatrist: the doctor has the full power to change the situation of the mentally ill patient because of his medical and scientific knowledge and competence that allows him to see and understand the mental disease as nothing more than an objective disturbance that can be treated and cured with biomedical science and its understanding of the brain and its consciousness.

The subjectivistic position is the position of the holistic doctor insisting on meeting the mentally ill patient in a nonjudging way, believing in his/her inner self-healing powers and innate knowledge and wisdom, and therefore taking the position that what is happening inside the other person is a product of this person's autonomously assumed choices and philosophical positions. As the person is obviously in trouble, the doctor surrenders his own ego and will to the situation, and coming from unselfish unconditional love, he gives what he can of attention, care, respect, acknowledgment, and acceptance to the other, in all aspects of this person's manifestations, i.e., physical, mental, spiritual, and existential.

In practice, nothing is as black and white as the two philosophical positions, but when you look for it, you can easily find these two positions as fundamental reasons for the materialization of two completely different traditions in medical science.

Evidence based medicine

During the last decades, medical science crystallized its contemporary insistence on evidence-based medicine: the effect of a medical treatment must be scientifically documented. Interestingly, both the subjectivistic and the objectivistic traditions came to the acceptance of the necessity of documenting results, but naturally in the ways determined by the different nature of their approaches.

The objectivistic medical tradition has designed a genius method to exclude subjectivity, objective examinations, and pharmaceutical treatment under placebo control. Deep psychopharmacological analysis of the brain and its transmitter systems has made it possible for the doctor to interact directly with the brain's chemistry, allowing him/her to balance the brain and thereby take the person back to normal, which then can be documented by objective measurement of the symptoms of neural malfunctioning before and after, controlling for the placebo effect by giving a similar group of patients only a placebo pill. A large number of meta-analysis now exists that documents the effect of a large number of drugs on certain psychiatric symptoms in psychiatry.

The subjectivistic medical tradition has designed a similar genius method to exclude the objectivity: subjective meetings with the patient; focus on self-insight, personal development, and emotional and philosophical work; results controlled by psychometric rating of the patient's subjective evaluations of health, quality of life, and ability to function, controlled by measuring the patient's subjective state of being before and after treatment (compare chapter 56). As the intervention in holistic medicine is primarily on the patient's state of consciousness and philosophy of the world, the treatment can be understood as a treatment with placebo only, rendering the objectivistic method of placebo control completely useless and even fatal; by admitting full value to the psychometric evaluation of the patient's own subjective state of being before and after treatment (and again after 1 year to be sure of a lasting effect), the effect of therapy can be easily measured.

The most extreme and radical schools of subjectivistic therapists claim that even measuring subjectivity is objectivistic, and that evaluation of the value of treatment should be done only qualitatively, not quantitatively. As these schools might have a philosophical point, the problem is that the effect of the treatment here is going to be so "invisible" that it becomes too easy to cheat oneself as a therapist and make oneself believe that the patient has actually been helped, even when this is not the case; this problem, called the hermeneutic problem, is well known from the philosophy of science (11).

Searching medline

A search on www.pubmed.gov in 2007 for "Cochrane and mental illness" gave 955 hits, "Cochrane and schizophrenia" gives 264 hits, while there are 403 hits for "Cochrane and depression". Many of these studies are meta-analyses of pharmaceutical studies. One recent example is Adams et al (12) who tested chlorpromazine, the drug of choice through decades, versus placebo for schizophrenia:

> MAIN RESULTS: ...We found chlorpromazine reduces relapse over the short (n=74, 2 RCTs, RR 0.29 CI 0.1 to 0.8) and medium term (n=809, 4 RCTs, RR 0.49 CI 0.4 to 0.6) but data are heterogeneous. Longer term homogeneous data also favoured chlorpromazine (n=512, 3 RCTs, RR 0.57 CI 0.5 to 0.7, NNT 4 CI 3 to 5). We found chlorpromazine provided a global improvement in a person's symptoms and functioning (n=1121, 13 RCTs, RR 'no change/not improved' 0.80 CI 0.8 to 0.9, NNT 6 CI 5 to 8).
> Fewer people allocated to chlorpromazine left trials early (n=1780, 26 RCTs, RR 0.65 CI 0.5 to 0.8, NNT 15 CI 11 to 24) compared with placebo. There are many adverse effects.
> Chlorpromazine is clearly sedating (n=1404, 19 RCTs, RR 2.63 CI 2.1 to 3.3, NNH 5 CI 4 to 8), it increases a person's chances of experiencing acute movement disorders (n=942, 5 RCTs, RR 3.5 CI 1.5 to 8.0, NNH 32 CI 11 to 154), parkinsonism (n=1265, 12 RCTs, RR 2.01 CI 1.5 to 2.7, NNH 14 CI 9 to 28). Chlorpromazine clearly causes a lowering of blood pressure with accompanying dizziness (n=1394, 16 RCTs, RR 2.37 CI 1.7 to 3.2, NNH 11 CI 7 to 21) and considerable weight gain (n=165, 5 RCTs, RR 4.92 CI 2.3 to 10.4, NNH 2 CI 2 to 3).

This is fine science in the objectivistic tradition; most unfortunate the results are not really good: NNT is 4 to 6, meaning that between four and six patients must be treated for one to benefit significantly. Another issue is that the patients were not cured; the test is only for "improvement". And the side effects are dramatic: weight gain in one of two, sedation to one in five, etc. The drug harms many more patients than are helped. If one reads the paper one will notice that the only dimension relevant for the patients' mental health, called "mental state", is not improved at all, by any antipsychotic drugs. Similar results exist for major depression; most of the meta-analysis shows NNT in the same range, although the side effects are somewhat milder; unfortunately, few studies exist of treatment of major depression versus placebo and still fewer vs, active placebo.

The psychodynamic tradition is somewhat in between the biomedical and the holistic school, and fine meta-analysis exist, documenting that short-term psychodynamic psychotherapy (STPP) is as effective as psychiatric standard treatment in many mental disorders (14,15). Unfortunately, STPP has not been clearly stating its "holistic" position, often using psychiatric diagnoses etc,; the Buber "I and Thou" position is not found here much; to find it, we must continue the spectrum all the way to scientific holistic medicine, especially the recently developed "clinical holistic medicine" (CHM), which has done much to clearly state its philosophical position in the treatment of a number of diseases and illnesses (16–60).

Going to holistic medicine, a search on PubMed for "holistic medicine and meta-analysis" in 2007 gave zero hits, not surprisingly. "Holistic medicine and Cochrane" gave five hits, among these a paper on the holistic strategy for testing treatment effect called the "square curve paradigm" (61), also from our group, but no test results. Searching for "square curve paradigm" on www.pubmed.gov, we found two studies using this strategy for documenting effect (62,63), but only the first study is actually testing the development of the patient's subjective experience of mental health or illness after holistic medical treatment. The details from the results of the treatment of mental and other patients with CHM, which combines STPP, bodywork, and spiritual exercises, as holistic medicine often does, are found in several articles (64-68).

The treatment group in Ventegodt et al (67) is 54 chronically ill patients that are their own control in the study; it is a diverse group of patients only having in common that they all consider themselves to be severely mentally ill before treatment. The results were surprisingly good: 31 of 54 patients, or 57.4 (CI 43.2–70.8), were subjectively cured by the treatment consisting of 20 sessions of CHM. But as the holistic approach did not allow for specific psychiatric "objective" diagnoses, we do not know exactly how this group of patients would be diagnosed if they had gone to standard psychiatry. But what we do know is that 40% of the patients had already been to a psychiatrist, and that the chronically ill mental patient entering the clinic after abandoning psychiatry in average rated 3.7 on a 5-point Likert scale on self-evaluated mental health (from the validated questionnaire QOL5 (69)), which is better than the inclusion criteria for this study: to enter, the patients needed a rating of 4 or 5 on a 5-point Likert scale, with 1 being completely mentally healthy and 5 being completely mentally ill, in their own subjective assessment. The group did not receive any drugs and only regression in the pace that their system could tolerate and did in accordance with this not report any side effects from the treatment (NNTH with CHM is estimated to 500, NNTB = 2 CI 1.4–2.3). The square curve paradigm analysis in Ventegodt et al (62) documents that these results seems to be lasting.

The scarcity of published data from studies in peer-reviewed PubMed listed medical journals makes this study somewhat unique. Here we have a group of patients who report that they feel mentally ill before treatment, and this feeling disappears for good in half the patients after 20 sessions of CHM with no side effects. But how can we be sure that the patients in this group are really mentally ill, in the psychiatric meaning of this word? Well, we cannot. We know that 40% were treated by psychiatrist, psychologist, or GP for a mental illness, and we know that this group was helped as much as the patients that entered to the clinic directly because of their personal conviction that they needed holistic therapy. But that is all. A subjectivistic researcher would argue that what really is important is not the psychiatrist's judgment, but the patient's experience of being mentally ill or well. For it is mental pain that brings them to the doctor, and if the treatment cures this pain, without damaging other aspects of the patient, well, then the patient has been well helped.

Interestingly, the cost of the treatment is also mentioned: 1,600 Euros. Standard psychiatric treatment normally costs 10, 100, or even 1000 times this. How can we compare the value to the patients of the treatments of these two very different medical schools, both obviously coming from fine scientific medical traditions, the biomedical and the psychoanalytic? And how do we make a fair cost/benefit analysis?

If we take the data as is from the papers, with all that uncertainty that is because one school can refer to huge meta-analyses and the other school only to single studies with few patients from the CHM group, we can see that:

- Holistic medicine helps one in two, psychiatry helps one in five.
- Holistic medicine cures the patient subjectively, while psychiatry takes some of the objective symptoms away, but without curing the patient.
- Holistic medicine has no side effect, where psychiatric treatment harms more patients than it helps.
- Holistic medicine has lasting effect, while psychiatry struggles with relapse.
- Holistic medicine costs a few thousand Euros, while psychiatry often costs hundreds of thousands of Euros.

In chapter 9 we shall analyse this in much more detail.

Discussion

We are not at all accustomed to think seriously over philosophical matters and, in this case, everything is dependent of it. As medical doctors, we are not at all used to taking a philosophical stand and we normally do not like that philosophy matters, as we are practical people who want to get things going.

Deep philosophical issues should better be left to the philosophers. However, the development of two parallel medical schools that each build on different philosophical traditions, the subjectivistic and the objectivistic, challenges this lazy attitude, for obviously our philosophical attitude matters to the treatment of our patients.

Maybe the reason why psychiatry has so little effect in helping patients is because patients are reduced to objects, and the soul, integrity, and autonomy of the patient is let down in the treatment of the patient's body, brain, and behavioral symptoms.

Most unfortunately, the methodology from objectivistic medical science is now also used to evaluate subjectivistic medical science. Cochrane tests of the value of complementary and alternative medicine (CAM) are being conducted. In the following example (70), the value of therapeutic touch is tested in anxiety disorder, therapeutic touch being common in the holistic treatment of patients (18,28): "Inclusion criteria included all published and unpublished randomized and quasi-randomized controlled trials comparing therapeutic touch with sham (mimic) TT, pharmacological therapy, psychological treatment, other treatment or no treatment /waiting list."

The problem here is that holistic therapy does not work in either of the conditions that are listed in the list of inclusion criteria, and the insistence of placebo control, sham touch, or randomization to pharmacological therapy or psychological treatment is with absolute certainty excluding the patients that really believe in CAM, because they would never accept to be a part of a study where they could be randomized to pharmacological or psychological treatment. The only way to document therapeutic success here would be to measure the patients before and after treatment, and after a sufficiently long time, to see if their subjective assessment of own mental health really improved.

So what is happening now is that objectivistic science is evaluation subjectivistic medicine on objectivistic permission, and this is obviously not giving holistic medicine a fair trial. To test holistic medicine, the square curve paradigm or a similar method has to be used, using the patient's own subjective evaluations of health and quality of life as endpoints, and avoiding placebo controls and other objectivistic tools that destroy the possibility of a fair scientific testing of medical interventions based on developing the patient's consciousness.

The belief of biomedicine and psychiatry is that a placebo control is necessary to take away all disturbing subjectivity from the study. From a subjectivistic perspective, there is already a huge surrender on a philosophical and existential level when you choose psychiatric treatment, and without testing for subjective factors like patient confidence in the doctor and in this kind of medicine, the placebo effect is still 100% working on the patient and not controlled in the study. In general, the two schools have little understanding for each other's position, and find their own arguments completely valid; only when a clear philosophical analysis is made, an openness and understanding for the other school can take place.

Conclusions

When two equally acceptable medical systems or schools exist, as is the case with psychiatric and holistic treatment of mentally ill patients, the only rational way to choose between one or the other system is to look at the results of the treatments. But here we face a big problem, because the two schools use their own philosophic value systems as premise for the scientific evaluation. In the objectivistic medical system of psychiatry, only the treatment of objective symptoms is taken as relevant. In subjective holistic medicine, only the patient's subjective experience of being mentally ill or well is relevant; only a subjective improvement of life at large – the state of the whole person – is relevant.

Both the holistic and the psychiatric school use valid scientific ways to treat mentally ill patients. In spite of the very limited data, it seems like to conclude that:

- Scientific holistic medicine (CHM) helps one in two, while psychiatry helps one in four or five.
- Scientific holistic medicine (CHM) cures the patient subjectively, while psychiatry takes some of the objective symptoms away, but without curing the patient.
- Scientific holistic medicine (CHM) has no side effect, where psychiatric treatment harms more patient than it helps.
- Scientific holistic medicine (CHM) has lasting effect, while psychiatry struggles with relapse.
- Scientific holistic medicine (CHM) costs a few thousand Euros while psychiatry often costs hundreds of thousands of Euros.

When it comes to treating mentally ill patients, it is recommended that holistic medicine is used; more research is needed, especially regarding the effects related to the specific mental disorders. It is recommended that governments and funds support the development of scientific holistic medicine.

References

[1]   Buber M. I and thou. New York: Charles Scribner´s Sons, 1970.
[2]   Macleod S. Cochrane's problem: psychoanalysis and anejaculation. Australas Psychiatry 2007;15(2):144-7.
[3]   Jones E. The life and works of Sigmund Freud. New York: Basic Books, 1961.
[4]   Jung CG. Man and his symbols. New York: Anchor Press, 1964.
[5]   Yalom ID. Existential psychotherapy. New York: Basic Books, 1980.
[6]   Reich W. [Die Function des Orgasmus.] Köln: Kiepenheuer Witsch, 1969. [German].
[7]   Lowen A. Honoring the body. Alachua, FL: Bioenergetics Press, 2004.
[8]   Rosen M, Brenner S. Rosen method bodywork. Accessing the unconscious through touch. Berkeley, CA: North Atlantic Books, 2003.
[9]   Rothshild B. The body remembers. New York: WW Norton, 2000.
[10]   Huxley A. The perennial philosophy. New York: HarperCollins, 1972.
[11]   Chalmers A. What is this thing called science? Buckingham: Open Univ Press, 1999.
[12]   Adams CE, Awad G, Rathbone J, Thornley B. Chlorpromazine versus placebo for schizophrenia. Cochrane Database Syst Rev 2007;18(2):CD000284.
[13]   Leichsenring F, Rabung S, Leibing E. The efficacy of short-term psychodynamic psychotherapy in specific psychiatric disorders: a meta-analysis. Arch Gen Psychiatry 2004;61(12):1208–16.
[14]   Leichsenring F. Are psychodynamic and psychoanalytic therapies effective? A review of empirical data. Int J Psychoanal 2005;86(Pt 3):841-68.
[15]   Ventegodt S, Andersen NJ, Merrick J. Holistic medicine III: the holistic process theory of healing. ScientificWorldJournal 2003;3: 1138-46.
[16]   Ventegodt S, Merrick J. Clinical holistic medicine: applied consciousness-based medicine. ScientificWorldJournal 2004;4:96-9.
[17]   Ventegodt S, Morad M, Merrick J. Clinical holistic medicine: classic art of healing or the therapeutic touch. ScientificWorldJournal 2004;4:134-47.
[18]   Ventegodt S, Morad M, Merrick J. Clinical holistic medicine: the "new medicine", the multiparadigmatic physician and the medical record. ScientificWorldJournal 2004;4:273–85.
[19]   Ventegodt S, Morad M, Merrick J. Clinical holistic medicine: holistic pelvic examination and holistic treatment of infertility. ScientificWorldJournal 2004;4:148–58.
[20]   Ventegodt S, Morad M, Hyam E, Merrick J. Clinical holistic medicine: use and limitations of the biomedical paradigm ScientificWorldJournal 2004;4:295–306.
[21]   Ventegodt S, Morad M, Kandel I, Merrick J. Clinical holistic medicine: social problems disguised as illness. ScientificWorldJournal 2004;4:286–94.
[22]   Ventegodt S, Morad M, Andersen NJ, Merrick J. Clinical holistic medicine: tools for a medical science based on consciousness. ScientificWorldJournal 2004;4:347–61.
[23]   Ventegodt S, Morad M, Merrick J. Clinical holistic medicine: prevention through healthy lifestyle and quality of life. Oral Health Prev Dent 2004;1:239–45.
[24]   Ventegodt S, Morad M, Hyam E, Merrick J. Clinical holistic medicine: when biomedicine is inadequate. ScientificWorldJournal 2004;4:333–46.
[25]   Ventegodt S, Morad M, Merrick J. Clinical holistic medicine: holistic treatment of children. ScientificWorldJournal 2004;4:581–8.
[26]   Ventegodt S, Morad M, Merrick J. Clinical holistic medicine: Problems in sex and living together. ScientificWorldJournal 2004;4: 562–70.
[27]   Ventegodt S, Morad M, Hyam E, Merrick J. Clinical holistic medicine: holistic sexology and treatment of vulvodynia through existential therapy and acceptance through touch. ScientificWorldJournal 2004;4:571–80.
[28]   Ventegodt S, Flensborg-Madsen T, Andersen NJ, Morad M, Merrick J. Clinical holistic medicine: a pilot stidy on HIV and quality of life and a suggested cure for HIV and AIDS. ScientificWorldJournal 2004;4:264–72.

[29] Ventegodt S, Morad M, Merrick J. Clinical holistic medicine: induction of spontaneous remission of cancer by recovery of the human character and the purpose of life (the life mission). ScientificWorldJournal 2004;4:362–77.

[30] Ventegodt S, Morad M, Kandel I, Merrick J. Clinical holistic medicine: treatment of physical health problems without a known cause, exemplified by hypertension and tinnitus. ScientificWorldJournal 2004;4:716–24.

[31] Ventegodt S, Morad M, Merrick J. Clinical holistic medicine: developing from asthma, allergy and eczema. ScientificWorldJournal 2004;4:936–42.

[32] Ventegodt S, Morad M, Press J, Merrick J, Shek DTL. Clinical holistic medicine: holistic adolescent medicine. ScientificWorldJournal 2004;4:551–61.

[33] Ventegodt S, Solheim E, Saunte ME, Morad M, Kandel I, Merrick J. Clinical holistic medicine: Metastatic cancer. ScientificWorldJournal 2004;4:913–35.

[34] Ventegodt S, Morad M, Kandel I, Merrick J. Clinical holistic medicine: a psychological theory of dependency to improve quality of life. ScientificWorldJournal 2004;4:638–48.

[35] Ventegodt S, Merrick J. Clinical holistic medicine: chronic infections and autoimmune diseases. ScientificWorldJournal 2005;5:155–64.

[36] Ventegodt S, Kandel I, Neikrug S, Merrick J. Clinical holistic medicine: holistic treatment of rape and incest traumas. ScientificWorldJournal 2005;5:288–97.

[37] Ventegodt S, Morad M, Merrick J. Clinical holistic medicine: chronic pain in the locomotor system. ScientificWorldJournal 2005;5:165–72.

[38] Ventegodt S, Merrick J. Clinical holistic medicine: chronic pain in internal organs. ScientificWorldJournal 2005;5:205–10.

[39] Ventegodt S, Kandel I, Neikrug S, Merrick J. Clinical holistic medicine: the existential crisis – life crisis, stress, and burnout. ScientificWorldJournal 2005;5:300–12.

[40] Ventegodt S, Gringols G, Merrick J. Clinical holistic medicine: holistic rehabilitation. ScientificWorldJournal 2005;5:280–7.

[41] Ventegodt S, Andersen NJ, Neikrug S, Kandel I, Merrick J. Clinical holistic medicine: mental disorders in a holistic perspective. ScientificWorldJournal 2005;5:313–23.

[42] Ventegodt S, Andersen NJ, Neikrug S, Kandel I, Merrick J. Clinical holistic medicine: holistic treatment of mental disorders. ScientificWorldJournal 2005;5:427–45.

[43] Ventegodt S, Merrick J. Clinical holistic medicine: the patient with multiple diseases. ScientificWorldJournal 2005;5:324–39.

[44] Ventegodt S, Clausen B, Nielsen ML, Merrick J. Clinical holistic health: Advanced tools for holistic medicine. ScientificWorldJournal 2006;6:2048–65.

[45] Ventegodt S, Clausen B, Merrick J. Clinical holistic medicine: the case story of Anna. I. Long-term effect of childhood sexual abuse and incest with a treatment approach. ScientificWorldJournal 2006;6:1965–76.

[46] Ventegodt S, Calusen B, Merrick J. Clinical holistic medicine: the case story of Anna. II. Patient diary as a tool in treatment. ScientificWorldJournal 2006;6:2006–34.

[47] Ventegodt S, Clausen B, Merrick J. Clinical holistic medicine: the case story of Anna. III. Rehabilitation of philosophy of life during holistic existential therapy for childhood sexual abuse. ScientificWorldJournal 2006;6:2080–91.

[48] Ventegodt S, Merrick J. Suicide from a holistic point of view. ScientificWorldJournal 2005;5:759–66.

[49] Ventegodt S, Clausen B, Omar HA, Merrick J. Clinical holistic medicine: holistic sexology and acupressure through the vagina (Hippocratic pelvic massage). ScientificWorldJournal 2006;6:2066–79.

[50] Ventegodt S, Clausen B, Merrick J. Clinical holistic medicine: pilot study on the effect of vaginal acupressure (Hippocratic pelvic massage). ScientificWorldJournal 2006;6:2100–16.

[51] Hermansen TD, Ventegodt S, Rald E, Clausen B, Nielsen ML, Merrick J. Human development I: twenty fundamental problems of biology, medicine, and neuro-psychology related to biological information. ScientificWorldJournal 2006;6:747–59.

[52]   Ventegodt S, Hermansen TD, Nielsen ML, Clausen B, Merrick J. Human development II: we need an integrated theory for matter, life and consciousness to understand life and healing. ScientificWorldJournal 2006;6:760–6.

[53]   Ventegodt S, Hermansen TD, Rald E, Flensborg-Madsen T, Nielsen ML, Clausen B, Merrick J. Human development III: bridging brain-mind and body-mind. introduction to "deep" (fractal, poly-ray) cosmology. ScientificWorldJournal 2006;6:767–76.

[54]   Ventegodt S, Hermansen TD, Flensborg-Madsen T, Nielsen ML, Clausen B, Merrick J. Human development IV: the living cell has information-directed self-organisation. ScientificWorldJournal 2006;6:1132–8.

[55]   Ventegodt S, Hermansen TD, Flensborg-Madsen T, Nielsen ML, Clausen B, Merrick J. Human development V: biochemistry unable to explain the emergence of biological form (morphogenesis) and therefore a new principle as source of biological information is needed. ScientificWorldJournal 2006;6:1359–67.

[56]   Ventegodt S, Hermansen TD, Flensborg-Madsen T, Nielsen M, Merrick J. Human development VI: supracellular morphogenesis. The origin of biological and cellular order. ScientificWorldJournal 2006;6:1424–33.

[57]   Ventegodt S, Hermansen TD, Flensborg-Madsen T, Rald E, Nielsen ML, Merrick J. Human development VII: a spiral fractal model of fine structure of physical energy could explain central aspects of biological information, biological organization and biological creativity. ScientificWorldJournal 2006;6:1434–40.

[58]   Ventegodt S, Hermansen TD, Flensborg-Madsen T, Nielsen ML, Merrick J. Human development VIII: a theory of "deep" quantum chemistry and cell consciousness: quantum chemistry controls genes and biochemistry to give cells and higher organisms consciousness and complex behavior. ScientificWorldJournal 2006;6:1441–53.

[59]   Ventegodt S, Hermansen TD, Flensborg-Madsen T, Rald E, Nielsen ML, Merrick J. Human development IX: a model of the wholeness of man, his consciousness and collective consciousness. ScientificWorldJournal 2006;6:1454–9.

[60]   Hermansen TD, Ventegodt S, Merrick J. Human development X: Explanation of macroevolution — top-down evolution materializes consciousness. The origin of metamorphosis. ScientificWorldJournal 2006;6:1656–66.

[61]   Ventegodt S, Andersen NJ, Merrick J. The square-curve paradigm for research in alternative, complementary, and holistic medicine: a cost-effective, easy, and scientifically valid design for evidence-based medicine. ScientificWorldJournal 2003;3:1117–27.

[62]   Ventegodt S, Thegler S, Andreasen T, Struve F, Enevoldsen L, Bassaine L, et al. Clinical holistic medicine: psychodynamic short-time therapy complemented with bodywork. A clinical follow-up study of 109 patients. ScientificWorldJournal 2006;6:2220–38.

[63]   Ventegodt S, Clausen B, Langhorn M, Kroman M, Andersen NJ, Merrick J. Quality of life as medicine III. A qualitative analysis of the effect of a five-day intervention with existential holistic group therapy or a quality of life course as a modern rite of passage. ScientificWorldJournal 2004;4:124–33.

[64]   Ventegodt S, Thegler S, Andreasen T, Struve F, Enevoldsen L, Bassaine L, et al. Clinical holistic medicine (mindful, short-term psychodynamic psychotherapy complemented with bodywork) in the
[65]   treatment of experienced impaired sexual functioning. ScientificWorldJournal 2007;7:324–9.

[66]   Ventegodt S, Thegler S, Andreasen T, Struve F, Enevoldsen L, Bassaine L, et al. Clinical holistic medicine (mindful, short-term psychodynamic psychotherapy complemented with bodywork) improves quality of life, health, and ability by induction of Antonovsky-salutogenesis. ScientificWorldJournal 2007;7:317–23.

[67]   Ventegodt S, Thegler S, Andreasen T, Struve F, Enevoldsen L, Bassaine L, et al. Clinical holistic medicine (mindful, short-term psychodynamic psychotherapy complemented with bodywork) in the treatment of experienced physical illness and chronic pain. ScientificWorldJournal 2007;7:310–6.

[68]   Ventegodt S, Thegler S, Andreasen T, Struve F, Enevoldsen L, Bassaine L, et al. Clinical holistic medicine (mindful, short-term psychodynamic psychotherapy complemented with bodywork) in the treatment of experienced mental illness. ScientificWorldJournal 2007;7:306–9.

[69]   Ventegodt S, Thegler S, Andreasen T, Struve F, Enevoldsen L, Bassaine L, et al. Self-reported low self-esteem. Intervention and follow-up in a clinical setting. ScientificWorldJournal 2007;7:299–305.

[70]   Lindholt JS, Ventegodt S, Henneberg EW. Development and validation of QoL5 for clinical databases. A short, global and generic questionnaire based on an integrated theory of the quality of life. Eur J Surg 2002;168:103–7.

[71]   Robinson J, Biley F, Dolk H. Therapeutic touch for anxiety disorders. Cochrane Database Syst Rev 2007;18(3):CD006240.

Chapter 3

A critical analysis of Cochrane meta-analyses of the therapeutic value of anti-psychotic drugs

About 5% of people in the developed world are prescribed anti-psychotic drugs. The scope of this chapter is to evaluate the positive and negative effects of anti-psychotic drugs, when treating the psychotic, mentally ill patient in comparison with placebo. We conducted a meta-analysis of the Cochrane protocols on anti-psychotic drugs, which included all randomized clinical trials, where anti-psychotics have been tested in comparison with placebo. The primary outcomes of treatment of interest to the study were: Mental health (or "mental state"), cooperativeness (or "behaviour"), a hybrid measure of mental health, cooperativeness and hallucinatory behaviour (or "global state"), relapse of primarily un-cooperativeness or hallucinatory behaviour (or "relapse") as well as adverse effects. The study included analyses of dichotomous data using fixed effects relative risk (RR), an estimation of the 95% confidence interval (CI) as well as a calculation of the number needed to treat (NNT) and the number needed to harm (NNH). All significant NNHs were summed to estimate the sum of total NNH. The results showed, that anti-psychotic drugs improved mental health (NNT=50). It was also found that uncooperative behaviour (NNT=4) and "relapse" (NNT=4) was reduced, and that "global state" was improved (NNT=7). Anti-psychotic drugs were shown to have many adverse effects (total NNH=0.67) and the different types of anti-psychotic drugs had similar positive and negative effects. Anti-psychotic drugs did not cure or improve mental health for patients with psychotic or mental illness, as the small, positive effect found could be explained by the bias. The drugs have many severe adverse effects.

Introduction

According to the World Health Organization (WHO), 400 million people suffer from a severe mental illness (1). In Denmark, the yearly consumption of anti-psychotic drugs equals 6% of the population or about 300,000 people with an annual expense of 122 million EURO (2).

Some studies have recently shown that anti-psychotic drugs are of miniature efficiency, when treating children, patients with learning disabilities, as well as other groups of patients

(3-5). Alongside these findings, a tendency towards attributing an increase of importance to patient narratives concerning a less positive impression of the treatment with anti-psychotic drugs has emerged (6,7) and mentally ill patients are known to frequently have discontinued the treatment. A significant part of the explanation is the patients' experiences of the treatment with anti-psychotic drugs as being less than perfect (8,9). Some researchers have even suggested that anti-psychotic drugs mainly work by reducing salience of ideas and perceptions, and thus doubt the positive effect of the drugs on the patient's mental health (10). Other researchers have suggested that non-drug therapy might be better for the patients in the long run (11). All of this has created an interest to re-evaluate the positive and negative effects of anti-psychotic drugs.

The ideal study would be an all-including meta-analysis of the positive and negative effects of all the anti-psychotic drugs in the treatment of the psychotic mental illnesses in general. But such a study has been considered difficult to complete, among other reasons due to the non-uniform quality of many of the studies, and because of the diversity of effect and adverse effects among the different types of anti-psychotic drugs.

However during the last decade, many studies of the positive and negative effects of the anti-psychotic drugs vs. placebo have been thoroughly analyzed in a large number of Cochrane meta-analyses (12-88). Moreover, recently a large Cochrane study documented that all the different types of anti-psychotic drugs shared similar qualities in regards to beneficence, non-beneficence or even harmful qualities (13). As an effect of that, a significant step towards overcoming the obstacles hindering such a general meta-analysis seems to have been taken, thus making this current study possible.

The present chapter is a meta-analysis of the effect on anti-psychotic drugs in general for the psychotic mental illnesses in general. As the recent Cochrane study on the effects of the different antipsychotic drugs indicated that mental health ("mental state") did not improve significantly (13), a central research question of interest is therefore, if there is a positive treatment effect on mental health with the use of anti-psychotic drugs.

Cochrane collaboration

Cochrane Collaboration software for preparing and maintaining Cochrane reviews (Review Manager), and the basic review and meta-analysis principles recommended by the Cochrane Collaboration (89,90,91) were used in this study. The methodological quality of the studies was independently assessed by at least two authors. The data was extracted by two reviewers. We searched Medline/PubMed and the Cochrane Library (CENTRAL) for all Cochrane reviews including studies investigating the effects of anti-psychotic drugs versus placebo for all illnesses, and these studies formed the basis of the study at hand. Only randomized controlled trials were included, while quasi-randomized studies were excluded. All participants were people with a diagnosis of schizophrenia or other types of psychotic mental illness, irrespective of age, sex or severity of illness.

The search allowed us to include data from 127 studies on the positive effect of anti-psychotic drugs including 16,646 patients and data from 556 studies on the adverse effects, which included 74,369 patients in the present analysis. As inclusion necessitated at least a Category B on The Cochrane Handbook rating of allocation, a similar number of studies were excluded. The reason for reviewing studies based on quantitative methods only was the lack of quantitative research in the field.

Types of intervention

- Any of the following: High dose (Chlorpromazine, Thioridazine), middle dose (Zuclupenthixol, Peraphenazine), low-dose (Fluphenazine, Haloperidole, Sulpiride, Pimozide, Penfluridol), or atypical, (Risperidone, Aripiprazole, Quetiapine, Amisulpride, Olanzapine, Sertindole, Ziprasidone). Thus including any dose or mode of administration (oral or by injection).
- Any dose or mode of inactive placebo.

Types of outcome measures

- Mental health (psychotic symptoms or "mental state"): Clinical significant response (short and medium term: 0 days – 6 month)
- Behaviour (un-cooperative/disturbed/deteriorated/hallucinatory): Clinical significant response (medium term: 6 weeks – 6 month)
- Global state (Hybrid measures of mental health and uncooperative or hallucinatory behaviour): Clinical significant response (short and medium term: 0 days – 6 month)
- Relapse (as defined in the clinical trials, often of un-cooperative or hallucinatory behaviour): Clinical significant response (long term: 6 month to 2 years)
- Adverse effects (see Table 2): (short and medium term: 0 days – 6 month)

Methodological quality

- Randomization: A fairly low percentage (about 10% of the studies) described the methods used to generate random allocation. For most studies, it did not seem completely clear that bias was minimized during the allocation procedure. About 40% reported that the participants allocated to each treatment group were estimated to be similar.
- Blinding: About 50% gave a description of their attempts to make the investigation double-blind.
- Treatment withdrawals: The description of those who left the study early was in general unclear or sometimes absent.
- Outcome reporting: Studies frequently presented both dichotomous and continuous data in graphs, or reported statistical measures of probability (p-values). This diminished the possibility to acquire raw data for a synthesis. It was also common to use p-values as a measure of association between intervention and outcomes instead of showing the strength of the association. Although p-values are influenced by the strength of the association, they also depend on the sample size of the groups. Frequently, continuous data were presented without providing standard

deviations/errors (about 60% of trials) or no data were presented at all (about 20% of trials). Thus a lot of possibly informative data were not at hand; we estimated that half of the information was lost here. Many studies used the the Brief Psychiatric Rating Scale (BPRS) that contains data related to quality of life like "anxiety", "emotional withdrawal", "guilt feelings", "blunted affect", "depression", "tension" and "anergia", but these subjective data were not analysed in any Cochrane studies, and is therefore not included in the present study.

- Overall quality: The quality of trials as measured in the previous version of the review varied (mean using the Jadad Scale was about 3.5). Inclusion necessitated at least a Category B on the Cochrane Handbook rating of allocation. Practically no studies reached Category A, so all data must be considered to be prone to a moderate degree of bias.

Meta-analytical calculations

The meta-analysis was done in line with recommendations from the Cochrane Collaboration and the Quality of Reporting of Meta-analyses guidelines (89,90,91). The randomized-analysed endpoints used in the Cochrane reviews were used to group studies according to the above-mentioned outcomes. Funnel plots were made for each outcome and to summarize the effect, relative risks (RR) and risk differences (RD) were calculated, and the number needed to treat (NNT) and number needed to harm (NNH) was calculated from RDs. To combine data in this meta-analysis the fixed effects model was used.

We did not apply weighting for study quality, since we did not have any empirical basis for doing so. The pooled NNH that combined all adverse effects into one measure was calculated as the inverse of the added inverse NNHs of all significant adverse effects (see Table 2). We avoided counting the same adverse effect twice, by grouping similar side effects into one group.

Results

Positive effects

Adding together all anti-psychotic drugs into the same meta-analysis (see table 1) we found data to favour anti-psychotic drugs according to: mental health (clinical significant response on psychotic symptoms or mental state) (n=8,407, 53 RCTs, RR 0.87, CI 0.81-0.94), NNT 50; cooperativeness (n=1085, 9 RCTs, RR 0.52, CI 0.45-0.61), NNT 4; clinical significant response in "global impression" (n=5,453, 47 RCTs, RR 0.76, CI 0.73-0.80), NNT 7; and long-term relapse (primarily of hallucinatory or un-cooperative behaviour) (n=1,701, 18 RCTs, RR 0.58, CI 0.53-0.64), NNT 4.

The NNT estimates varied substantially according to the different outcomes. Hence, the NNT for relapse and cooperativeness were 4 and 4 respectively, while the NNT for a clinical significant response to mental health (psychotic symptoms or mental state) was 50. Sub-dividing the meta-analysis into different categories of drugs showed the same pattern, with relapse and cooperativeness being the outcomes with the lowest NNT for all kinds of drugs and clinical significant responses to mental health (psychotic symptoms or mental state) having a substantially higher NNT (see Table 1).

Table 1. Number Needed to Treat (NNT) according to type of anti-psychotic drug and outcome

	NNT High-dose typicals	NNT Low-dose typicals	NNT Atypicals	NNT All anti-psychoticdrugs
Mental health (psychotic symptoms or mental state not improved)	No significant improvement	No significant improvement	237.7 (42.7 - ∞)	50.2 (26.4-519.8)
Cooperativeness (lack of hallucinatory or uncooperative behavior)	3.5 (2.9-4.4)	No studies	No studies	3.5 (2.9-4.4)
"Global impression" (mental health and hallucinatory behavior not improved)	5.3 (4.3-6.9)	3.9 (3.1-5.4)	12.7 (9.1-21.0)	6.8 (5.7-8.3)
"Relapse" (primarily of hallucinatory and uncooperative behavior)	3.2 (2.5-4.3)	3.2 (2.5-4.3)	4.9 (3.5-8.1)	3.7 (3.1-4.4)

Adverse effects

Adding together all anti-psychotic drugs we found data to favour placebo treatment according to a number of adverse effects. Table 2 shows the adverse effects that we found statistically significant for at least one group of antipsychotic drugs. It is important to notice that while most of the adverse effects might be seen as less burdensome than the mental illness they intent to cure, i.e. weight gain, some of the adverse effects must be considered serious threats to the patients health, like liver problems, Parkinsonism, and general movement disorders. Adding up all side effects showed a NNH of 0.67 (0.49-1.09), meaning that every patient treated with an antipsychotic drug was likely to get adverse effects. High-dose typicals (NNH=0.60; 0.43-0.98) and low-dose typicals (NNH=0.58; 0.38-1.23) showed similar low NNHs; an estimation of the total NNH of middle-dose typicals and atypicals was not possible due to lack of data.

Heterogeneity

The studies varied regarding type of inclusion criteria, anti-psychotic drugs and outcomes. In order to reduce the heterogeneity, it is common practice in Cochrane studies to exclude trials that differ much. In this study we included all studies irrespective of the heterogeneity in order to avoid bias. In addition to fixed effect model we also used a random effects model, but this did not change the results much.

Table 2. Number needed to harm (NNH) according to type of antipsychotic drug and adverse effects. (Estimation of the NNHs of middle-dose typicals and atypicals was not possible due to lack of data)

	NNH High-dose typicals	NNH Low-dose typicals	NNH All antipsychotic drugs
1. Photosensitivity	7.9 (6.2-11.0)	No studies	7.9 (6.2-11.0)
2. Eye problems	6.5 (4.9-9.8)	Not significant	6.5 (4.9-9.6)
3. Low blood pressure	10.2 (7.7-15.4)	Not significant	14.6 (11.6-19.8)
4. Constipation	18.5 (12.2-38.7)	8.8 (4.6-96.9)	26.0 (17.9-47.5)
5. Dry mouth	9.5 (7.5-13.1)	8.5 (5.0-26.3)	10.8 (9.1-13.3)
6. Weight gain	3.6 (2.4-5.4)	9.1 (5.7-22.3)	14.9 (11.6-20.7)
7. Salivation and drooling	40.7 (24.4-132.6)	13.9 (8.9-32.2)	40.9 (27.3-80.7)
8. Peripheral oedema	No studies	No studies	9.4 (5.7-26.9)
9. Dystonia	25.7 (17.3-49.7)	8.3 (5.0-25.4)	21.9 (14.9-41.3)
10. Parkinsonism	8.8 (6.8-12.7)	3.1 (2.4-4.4)	13.4 (9.8-21.2)
11. Tremor	15.8 (9.5-48.3)	9.6 (6.6-17.7)	21.2 (16.3-30.4)
12. Rigidity	12.0 (7.8-26.4)	3.7 (2.9-5.3)	11.1 (8.3-17.0)
13. Weakness including asthenia	6.1 (4.0-12.9)	No studies	13.8 (9.6-24.5)
14. Sleepiness and sedation	4.2 (3.7-5.0)	7.7 (5.5-12.0)	7.0 (6.3-7.9)
15. Fits (loss of consciousness)	38.2 (19.0 - ∞)	Not significant	35.8 (18.8-389.2)
16. Liver problems	11.8 (7.2-31.9)	Not significant	9.9 (6.3-23.9)
17. Urinary problems	52.1 (26.2-3977.3)	Not significant	25.5 (17.7-45.8)
18. Blurred vision	Not significant	12.0 (7.0-40.7)	62.4 (27.7-247.4)
19. Thick speech or speech disorder	Not significant	Not significant	15.3 (9.9-33.9)
20. General movement disorder	Not significant	7.0 (3.5-292.6)	24.3 (17.4-39.9)
21. Dizziness	No studies	Not significant	20.8 (14.4-37.6)
22. Akathisia	Not significant	7.8 (5.2-15.5)	Not significant
ALL (added together)	0.60 (0,43-0.98)	0.58 (0.38-1.23)	0.67 (0.49-1.09)

Discussion

Two percent of the mentally ill patients treated with anti-psychotic drugs improved their mental health ("mental state") (NNT=50); as we included all studies the effect tested for was a small, but significant clinical effect. A significant bias of all data can easily explain this small effect, Therefore it is not correct to claim based on these data that mentally ill patients can be cured. Uncooperative behaviour and relapse of hallucinatory behaviour was significantly reduced in a quarter of the patients prescribed anti-psychotic drugs (NNT=4), but this is likely to be due to a pacifying effect of the drug, in a way poisoning the patients. In accordance with this interpretations we found adverse effects to be very common (total NNH=0.67).

We aimed to use long-term data for the effects of anti-psychotic drugs, as many patients have them prescribed for a relatively long period (sometimes several years). Long-term data for "relapse" was found, but very few long-term studies were found in order to investigate the other outcomes. For "behaviour" and "global impression", only short- and medium-term data was found, and for "mental state" and "adverse effect" a finding of primarily short-term data complemented with little medium-term data took place. In order to make the present analysis it was necessary to include short, medium and long-term data in order to uphold the validity of this study, There are some indications that the positive effects diminish over time; "global impression" thus falls from NNT=4 (short-term) to NNT=7 (middle-term) (4), but there were no long-term data. Based on the experience gained from performing this study, the research group recommend that long-term data should be collected in future testing of anti-psychotic drugs. In addition, many of the original outcome measures of the studies were non-theory-based hybrid measures that included both mental health and behaviour (i.e. the Brief Psychiatric Rating Scale, BPRS). These hybrid measures have been grouped together and relabelled "global impression" in the Cochrane studies, but their significance is not clear.

The interpretation of the NNH values found is debatable as the different types of anti-psychotic drugs have different profiles of adverse effects. The aim of the present analysis of the adverse effects was not to establish the single NNH numbers, which are better established in the tests of the different groups of anti-psychotic drugs one by one, but to establish the total NNH, which expresses the likelihood to get one or more side effects using any type of anti-psychotic drug. In spite of the different profiles, the non-beneficial or harmful effects of the different types of anti-psychotic drugs seem to be of similar intensity in this data interpretation. We do not know if some of the adverse effects are statistically correlated, but this is likely to be the case. If that is the case, then the total NNH is calculated too small. A moderate correlation of 0.1 would change the NNHt to about 1. There is an ongoing methodological debate about the concepts of "number needed to treat" and "number needed to harm" (92,93), but we do not find the arguments against these concepts presented convincing, and before better concepts are developed, we should not abandon the few effective tools we have to evaluate the clinical value of drugs. Abandoning the NNTs and NNHs would make it quite impossible to evaluate the products of the pharmaceutical industry in metaanalysis, which we obviously need to do, the antipsychotic drugs being an example of this urgent need.

There are several problems with the study inclusion criteria: a) Why look at only placebo controlled trials? Although active controlled trials are not that numerous in antipsychotic trials, nevertheless they would methodologically still provide usable comparisons between individual compounds. b) Why only look at randomised trials? - although they are accepted as the 'best design these trials will almost never be actually designed as safety trials, as they nearly always have efficacy as their primary objective. Often trials - even otherwise good ones - are poor at systematically reporting all safety data. They also tend not to be large enough to be powered to look at rare events, even when aggregated in a meta-analysis across studies. They are also known in many different clinical areas to generally select an atypical subset of the treatable population into the RCT. We found it problematic that many of the early studies did not allow the efficacy result from a study to be extracted (e.g. just a P-value was given). It is pointless having an optimized search algorithm, if then the data cannot be extracted. This might have serious implications for the robustness of the findings.

We found only 127 studies (~17,000 patients) to be of sufficient quality to be included, but 556 studies on adverse events (~70,000 patients). The reason for this is that the drugs four times as often are tested against each other than against placebo. This fact should not induce bias.

There was a 'general heterogeneity' in the old trials (different drugs, different designs, different adverse effects signals, different population, differing quality etc). One could fairly argue that the quality of the studies was so poor in general and bias so large that the "Cochrane-type metaanalysis" are in fact completely meaningless. This position might be philosophically correct, but will render us completely without tools for evaluating the therapeutic effects of any drugs, giving the pharmaceutical industry power to float the market with inefficient and harmful drugs, so we do not want to go there.

Research has not been thorough, when it comes to the studies of global quality of life, sexual or social functioning, so we have drawn our conclusions based on rather incomplete data. We have assumed that because the early studies of the effect of antipsychotic drugs showed that quality of life, social and sexual functioning were significantly reduced, the pharmaceutical industry simply avoided these measures in the later research, the same way as they avoided all long term measures for adverse effects, This assumption might be wrong and we encourage researchers more resourceful than our group to investigate this.

The Cochrane studies did not test the effect of anti-psychotic drugs against "active placebo" (94), which is another more serious source of bias (95). We recommend that all future studies of mind-altering pharmaceutical drugs be tested this way, or even better against the optimal, alternative non-drug CAM treatment for the relevant disorder (96).

There are people who do not believe in vitamin C for scurvy, antibiotics for infection, blood transfusions etc. There are also people not believing in antipsycjotic drugs. We do not consider our self "non-believevers". We just want to base treatment of mentally ill patients on evidence. And we find no evidence that antipsychotic drugs improve patient's mental state or mental health.

Should we conclude from our review that we need more efficacious medication with fewer adverse events? No, Fifty years of intensive research not documenting any progress obviously shows that we are going the wrong way using strongly poisonous drugs as medicine for the mentally ill. This project cannot be safed by improving the drugs. It is a wrong project, presumably based on the wrong understanding of mental disorder.

The most problematic side of the present finding is that many psychiatrists and patients seem to function well with the antipsychotic drugs, so how could these drugs not be helpful? Our answer is that a close and supportive relationship between patient and physician IS helpful; if drugs is the only acknowledged treatment among psychiatrists the gifted and skilful psychiatrist will use the drugs as the anchor of treatment and build rapport, hope and mutual understanding around this treatment. Even if the antipsychotic drug only has harmful effects the treatment using such drugs could still be very beneficial. But statistics talks it own language: Such positive outcomes might exist but they are very rare; most patients are only harmed by the drugs. This is what should be learned from this study.

What is the relevance of combining studies of antipsychotics from all illnesses? How does this further our understanding or guide treatment decisions compared to existing meta-analyses of antipsychotics restricted to single diagnoses? Well, this mirrors well the complex daily reality of psychiatrists that will get all these different kinds of psychotic mentally ill patients, that all will be treated very much the same way: With antipsychotic drugs. The rationale of adding all studies together is to evaluate the value of the modern psychiatric practice using antipsychotic drugs. What the results shows us is that we do not help a significant fraction of the patients, if any at all. This shows us, that we need a fundamentally new kind of psychiatry.

Their conclusion that you have to treat only a single (0.6) patient to give them side effects is, sadly, is, according to the reviewers of this paper, not far from clinical practice. One could argue that by including studies from decades ago, this study doesn't reflect modern practice where tolerability and the minimisation of side effects while optimizing outcome is a key clinical objective. Well, Adams et al (13) recently showed us that the new drugs did not work better than the old ones. While we do not want to ignore the difficult clinical and ethical questions of risk to benefit ratio, and of values in health, for this to be a relevant argument, there should be improvement of patients mental health (mental state, including hallucinations etc.). Our finding in this regard was very clear clear: Antipsychotic drugs does not improve mental health in any way. It only reduces hallucinatory behaviour, presumably because of there obviously sedating and poisoning effects.

In general reviewers that we have send this chapter to, of which there has been many, agreed that antipsychotic drugs has very limited value to the patients; to quote one reviewer: "It has been extensively demonstrated that antipsychotic drugs have very limited efficacy, fail to treat many aspects of the illness such as negative symptoms and cognition, and that patients experience frequent adverse effects." The question is if this meta-analysis does move knowledge forward. We think it does. We think that it makes this general knowledge so clear that it is time to look for other ways in general than drugs to treat mentally ill patients. We need to go back in time and use the more "old-fashioned" kinds of psychotherapy and bodywork that has helped so many patients just half a century ago. We need to return to mind-body medicine. We need to understand that the doctor is the tool, not some more or less toxic drugs. Basically, what we learn from this review chapter, is that psychiatry has been going the wrong way for half a century, and that it is timely to realize this and go back to what worked without harming the patient – the classical Hippocratic non-drug medicine.

Interestingly the statistical reviewer of the Lancet (where this chapter was send as a scientific paper) accepted the final version of the paper, its methods and its conclusions. It was rejected by two of three clinicians who would not accept to let go of the use of antipsychotic drugs; the third clinical reviewer accepted the paper. Allow us to quote the reviewer briefly: "Reviewer #5: THELANCET-D-08-00436R2" wrote: "Statistical review. Comments for the authors: This is a major improvement on the previous version. The statistical methods used now seem appropriate largely throughout." In the end the paper was rejected and used in a shorter version as a chapter in this book.

Conclusions

In this meta-analysis, data from 127 studies on the positive effect of anti-psychotic drugs including 16,646 patients has been interpreted in the first general meta-analysis on the effect of antipsychotic drugs. The statistical analysis showed, that the anti-psychotic drugs actually did improve mental health ("mental state") compared with placebo (NNT=50). As we have included all outcomes, large and small, we know that this effect is very small indeed, as one in fifty gets a small improvement. We also know that all data is moderately biased, but we find that the small effect can be easily explained by the bias. We therefore did not find the antipsychotic drugs to improve the mental state of mentally ill patients. The study showed that the patients' "behaviour" seems to be significantly improved due to a reduction in un-cooperativeness and "relapse" seems to improve due to less hallucinatory behaviour (NNT=4). These effects can be explained from a pacifying effect of the drugs coming from a general poisoning of the patient. "Global state", a hybrid measure of unclear significance, was also improved. The anti-psychotic drugs had many adverse effects (total NNH=0.67), but this should probably be corrected to total NNH=1 as we expect some correlation between adverse effects. All types of anti-psychotic drugs had in general similar levels of positive and negative effects. Thus an overall conclusion of this data interpretation is that the anti-psychotic drugs included in this study did not improve mental health. Taken together with the shown extent of the side effects following the use of such medicine, the treatment of psychotic, mentally ill patients with anti-psychotic drugs cannot be considered rational.

References

[1]   Janca A. World and mental health in 2001. Curr Psychiatry Rep 2001;3(2):77-8.
[2]   Gunnersen SJ. Statistical Yearbook 2007. Copenhagen: Statistics Denmark, 2008.
[3]   Editorial. Children and psychiatric drugs: disillusion and opportunity. Lancet 2008;372(9645):1194.
[4]   Sikich L, Frazier JA, McClellan J, Findling RL, Vitiello B, Ritz L, et al. Double-blind comparison of first- and second-generation antipsychotics in early-onset schizophrenia and schizo-affective disorder: Findings from the treatment of early-onset schizophrenia spectrum disorders (TEOSS) study. Am J Psychiatry 2008; 165:1420-31.
[5]   Yawar A. The doctor as human being. J R Soc Med 2005;98(5):215-7.
[6]   Goff man E. Asylums. London: Penguin, 1991.
[7]   Thornicroft G, Tansella M, Becker T, et al. The personal impact of schizophrenia in Europe. Schizophr Res 2004; 69: 125–32.
[8]   Whitaker R. Mad in America. New York, USA: Basic Books, 2002
[9]   Lieberman JA, Stroup TS, McEvoy JP, et al. Effectiveness of anti-psychotic drugs in patients with chronic schizophrenia. N Engl J Med 2005;353:1209–23.
[10] Kapur S. Psychosis as a state of aberrant salience: a framework linking biology, phenomenology, and pharmacology in schizophrenia. Am J Psychiatry 2003;160:13–23.
[11] Bola JR, Mosher LR. Treatment of acute psychosis without neuroleptics: 2-year outcomes from the Soteria project. J Nerv Ment Dis 2003;191:219–29.
[12] Abhijnhan A, Adams CE, David A, Ozbilen M. Depot fluspirilene for schizophrenia. Cochrane Database Syst Rev 2007;(1):CD001718.
[13] Adams CE, Awad G, Rathbone J, Thornley B. Chlorpromazine versus placebo for schizophrenia. Cochrane Database Syst Rev 2007;(2):CD000284.
[14] Amato L, Minozzi S, Pani PP, Davoli M. Anti-psychotic medications for cocaine dependence. Cochrane Database Syst Rev 2007;(3):CD006306.
[15] Arunpongpaisal S, Ahmed I, Aqeel N, Suchat P. Anti-psychotic drug treatment for elderly people with late-onset schizophrenia. Cochrane Database Syst Rev 2003;(2):CD004162.
[16] Bagnall A, Lewis RA, Leitner ML. Ziprasidone for schizophrenia and severe mental illness. Cochrane Database Syst Rev 2000;(4):CD001945.
[17] Bagnall A, Fenton M, Kleijnen J, Lewis R. Molindone for schizophrenia and severe mental illness. Cochrane Database Syst Rev 2007;(1):CD002083.
[18] Ballard C, Waite J. The effectiveness of atypical anti-psychotics for the treatment of aggression and psychosis in Alzheimer's disease. Cochrane Database Syst Rev 2006;(1):CD003476.
[19] Basan A, Leucht S. Valproate for schizophrenia. Cochrane Database Syst Rev 2004;(1):CD004028.
[20] Belgamwar RB, Fenton M. Olanzapine IM or velotab for acutely disturbed/agitated people with suspected serious mental illnesses. Cochrane Database Syst Rev 2005;(2):CD003729.
[21] Binks CA, Fenton M, McCarthy L, Lee T, Adams CE, Duggan C. Pharmacological interventions for people with borderline personality disorder. Cochrane Database Syst Rev 2006;(1):CD005653.

[22] Carpenter S, Berk M, Rathbone J. Clotiapine for acute psychotic illnesses. Cochrane Database Syst Rev 2004;(4):CD002304.

[23] Chakrabarti A, Bagnall A, Chue P, Fenton M, Palaniswamy V, Wong W, Xia J. Loxapine for schizophrenia. Cochrane Database Syst Rev 2007;(4):CD001943.

[24] Chua WL, de Izquierdo SA, Kulkarni J, Mortimer A. Estrogen for schizophrenia. Cochrane Database Syst Rev 2005;(4):CD004719.

[25] Coutinho E, Fenton M, Quraishi S. Zuclopenthixol decanoate for schizophrenia and other serious mental illnesses. Cochrane Database Syst Rev 2000;(2):CD001164.

[26] Cure S, Rathbone J, Carpenter S. Droperidol for acute psychosis. Cochrane Database Syst Rev 2004;(4):CD002830.

[27] David A, Adams CE, Eisenbruch M, Quraishi S, Rathbone J. Depot fluphenazine decanoate and enanthate for schizophrenia. Cochrane Database Syst Rev 2005;(1):CD000307.

[28] David A, Quraishi S, Rathbone J. Depot perphenazine decanoate and enanthate for schizophrenia. Cochrane Database Syst Rev 2005;(3):CD001717.

[29] DeSilva P, Fenton M, Rathbone J. Zotepine for schizophrenia. Cochrane Database Syst Rev 2006;(4):CD001948.

[30] Dinesh M, David A, Quraishi SN. Depot pipotiazine palmitate and undecylenate for schizophrenia. Cochrane Database Syst Rev 2004;(4):CD001720.

[31] Duggan L, Brylewski J. Anti-psychotic medication versus placebo for people with both schizophrenia and learning disability. Cochrane Database Syst Rev 2004;(4):CD000030.

[32] Duggan L, Fenton M, Rathbone J, Dardennes R, El-Dosoky A, Indran S. Olanzapine for schizophrenia. Cochrane Database Syst Rev 2005;(2):CD001359.

[33] El-Sayeh HG, Morganti C. Aripiprazole for schizophrenia. Cochrane Database Syst Rev 2006;(2):CD004578.

[34] Elias A, Kumar A. Testosterone for schizophrenia. Cochrane Database Syst Rev 2007;(3):CD006197.

[35] Fenton M, Rathbone J, Reilly J, Sultana A. Thioridazine for schizophrenia. Cochrane Database Syst Rev 2007;(3):CD001944.

[36] Gibson RC, Fenton M, Coutinho ES, Campbell C. Zuclopenthixol acetate for acute schizophrenia and similar serious mental illnesses. Cochrane Database Syst Rev 2004;(3):CD000525.

[37] Gilbody SM, Bagnall AM, Duggan L, Tuunainen A. Risperidone versus other atypical anti-psychotic medication for schizophrenia. Cochrane Database Syst Rev 2000;(3):CD002306.

[38] Gillies D, Beck A, McCloud A, Rathbone J, Gillies D. Benzodiazepines alone or in combination with anti-psychotic drugs for acute psychosis. Cochrane Database Syst Rev 2005;(4):CD003079.

[39] Hartung B, Wada M, Laux G, Leucht S. Perphenazine for schizophrenia. Cochrane Database Syst Rev 2005;(1):CD003443.

[40] Hosalli P, Davis JM. Depot risperidone for schizophrenia. Cochrane Database Syst Rev 2003;(4):CD004161.

[41] Huf G, Alexander J, Allen MH. Haloperidol plus promethazine for psychosis induced aggression. Cochrane Database Syst Rev 2005;(1):CD005146.

[42] Hunter RH, Joy CB, Kennedy E, Gilbody SM, Song F. Risperidone versus typical anti-psychotic medication for schizophrenia. Cochrane Database Syst Rev 2003;(2):CD000440.

[43] Jayaram MB, Hosalli P, Stroup S. Risperidone versus olanzapine for schizophrenia. Cochrane Database Syst Rev 2006;(2):CD005237.

[44] Jesner OS, Aref-Adib M, Coren E. Risperidone for autism spectrum disorder. Cochrane Database Syst Rev 2007;(1):CD005040.

[45] Joy CB, Adams CE, Rice K. Crisis intervention for people with severe mental illnesses. Cochrane Database Syst Rev 2006;(4):CD001087.

[46] Joy CB, Adams CE, Lawrie SM. Haloperidol versus placebo for schizophrenia. Cochrane Database Syst Rev 2006;(4):CD003082.

[47] Kennedy E, Kumar A, Datta SS. Anti-psychotic medication for childhoodonset schizophrenia. Cochrane Database Syst Rev 2007;(3):CD004027.

[48] Kumar A, Strech D. Zuclopenthixol dihydrochloride for schizophrenia. Cochrane Database Syst Rev 2005;(4):CD005474.

[49] Leucht S, Hartung B. Benperidol for schizophrenia. Cochrane Database Syst Rev 2005;(2):CD003083.

[50] Leucht S, Hartung B. Perazine for schizophrenia. Cochrane Database Syst Rev 2006;(2):CD002832.

[51] Leucht S, Kissling W, McGrath J, White P. Carbamazepine for schizophrenia. Cochrane Database Syst Rev 2007;(3):CD001258.

[52] Leucht S, Kissling W, McGrath J. Lithium for schizophrenia. Cochrane Database Syst Rev 2007;(3):CD003834.

[53] Lewis R, Bagnall AM, Leitner M. Sertindole for schizophrenia. Cochrane Database Syst Rev 2005;(3):CD001715.

[54] Macritchie KA, Geddes JR, Scott J, Haslam DR, Goodwin GM. Valproic acid, valproate and divalproex in the maintenance treatment of bipolar disorder. Cochrane Database Syst Rev 2001;(3):CD003196.

[55] Macritchie K, Geddes JR, Scott J, Haslam D, de Lima M, Goodwin G. Valproate for acute mood episodes in bipolar disorder. Cochrane Database Syst Rev 2003;(1):CD004052.

[56] Marques LO, Lima MS, Soares BG. Trifluoperazine for schizophrenia. Cochrane Database Syst Rev 2004;(1):CD003545.

[57] Marriott RG, Neil W, Waddingham S. Anti-psychotic medication for elderly people with schizophrenia. Cochrane Database Syst Rev 2006;(1):CD005580.

[58] Marshall M, Rathbone J. Early intervention for psychosis. Cochrane Database Syst Rev 2006;(4):CD004718.

[59] Matar HE, Almerie MQ. Oral fluphenazine versus placebo for schizophrenia. Cochrane Database Syst Rev 2007;(1):CD006352.

[60] Mota NE, Lima MS, Soares BG. Amisulpride for schizophrenia. Cochrane Database Syst Rev 2002;(2):CD001357.

[61] Nolte S, Wong D, Lachford G. Amphetamines for schizophrenia. Cochrane Database Syst Rev 2004;(4):CD004964.

[62] Pekkala E, Merinder L. Psychoeducation for schizophrenia. Cochrane Database Syst Rev 2002;(2):CD002831.

[63] Premkumar TS, Pick J. Lamotrigine for schizophrenia. Cochrane Database Syst Rev 2006;(4):CD005962.

[64] Punnoose S, Belgamwar MR. Nicotine for schizophrenia. Cochrane Database Syst Rev 2006;(1):CD004838.

[65] Quraishi S, David A. Depot flupenthixol decanoate for schizophrenia or other similar psychotic disorders. Cochrane Database Syst Rev 2000;(2):CD001470.

[66] Quraishi S, David A. Depot haloperidol decanoate for schizophrenia. Cochrane Database Syst Rev 2000;(2):CD001361.

[67] Rathbone J, McMonagle T. Pimozide for schizophrenia or related psychoses. Cochrane Database Syst Rev 2007;(3):CD001949.

[68] Rendell JM, Gijsman HJ, Keck P, Goodwin GM, Geddes JR. Olanzapine alone or in combination for acute mania. Cochrane Database Syst Rev 2003;(3):CD004040.

[69] Rendell JM, Gijsman HJ, Bauer MS, Goodwin GM, Geddes GR. Risperidone alone or in combination for acute mania. Cochrane Database Syst Rev 2006;(1):CD004043.

[70] Rendell JM, Geddes JR. Risperidone in long-term treatment for bipolar disorder. Cochrane Database Syst Rev 2006;(4):CD004999.

[71] Rummel C, Hamann J, Kissling W, Leucht S. New generation anti-psychotics for first episode schizophrenia. Cochrane Database Syst Rev 2003;(4):CD004410.

[72] Rummel C, Kissling W, Leucht S. Antidepressants for the negative symptoms of schizophrenia. Cochrane Database Syst Rev 2006;3:CD005581.

[73] Soares BG, Fenton M, Chue P. Sulpiride for schizophrenia. Cochrane Database Syst Rev 2000;(2):CD001162.

[74] Soares BG, Lima MS. Penfluridol for schizophrenia. Cochrane Database Syst Rev 2006;(2):CD002923.

[75] Srisurapanont M, Kittiratanapaiboon P, Jarusuraisin N. Treatment for amphetamine psychosis. Cochrane Database Syst Rev 2001;(4):CD003026.

[76] Srisurapanont M, Maneeton B, Maneeton N. Quetiapine for schizophrenia. Cochrane Database Syst Rev 2004;(2):CD000967.

[77] Tharyan P, Adams CE. Electroconvulsive therapy for schizophrenia. Cochrane Database Syst Rev 2005;(2):CD000076.

[78] Trevisani VF, Castro AA, Neves Neto JF, Atallah AN. Cyclophosphamide versus methylprednisolone for treating neuropsychiatric involvement in systemic lupus erythematosus. Cochrane Database Syst Rev 2006;(2):CD002265.

[79] Tuominen HJ, Tiihonen J, Wahlbeck K. Glutamatergic drugs for schizophrenia. Cochrane Database Syst Rev 2006;(2):CD003730.

[80] Tuunainen A, Wahlbeck K, Gilbody SM. Newer atypical anti-psychotic medication versus clozapine for schizophrenia. Cochrane Database Syst Rev 2000;(2):CD000966.

[81] Volz A, Khorsand V, Gillies D, Leucht S. Benzodiazepines for schizophrenia. Cochrane Database Syst Rev 2007;(1):CD006391.

[82] Wahlbeck K, Cheine M, Essali MA. Clozapine versus typical neuroleptic medication for schizophrenia. Cochrane Database Syst Rev 2000;(2):CD000059.

[83] Waraich PS, Adams CE, Roque M, Hamill KM, Marti J. Haloperidol dose for the acute phase of schizophrenia. Cochrane Database Syst Rev 2002;(3):CD001951.

[84] Webb RT, Howard L, Abel KM. Anti-psychotic drugs for non-affective psychosis during pregnancy and postpartum. Cochrane Database Syst Rev 2004;(2):CD004411.

[85] Whitehead C, Moss S, Cardno A, Lewis G. Antidepressants for people with both schizophrenia and depression. Cochrane Database Syst Rev 2002;(2):CD002305.

[86] Wijkstra J, Lijmer J, Balk F, Geddes J, Nolen WA. Pharmacological treatment for psychotic depression. Cochrane Database Syst Rev 2005;(4):CD004044.

[87] Wong D, Adams CE, David A, Quraishi SN. Depot bromperidol decanoate for schizophrenia. Cochrane Database Syst Rev 2004;(3):CD001719.

[88] Young AH, Geddes JR, Macritchie K, Rao SN, Vasudev A. Tiagabine in the maintenance treatment of bipolar disorders. Cochrane Database Syst Rev 2006;3:CD005173.

[89] van Tulder M, Furlan A, Bombardier C, Bouter L; Editorial Board of the Cochrane Collaboration Back Review Group. Updated method guidelines for systematic reviews in the Cochrane Collaboration back review group. Spine 2003;28(12):1290-9.

[90] Higgins J, Green S. Cochrane handbook for systematic reviews of interventions version 5.0.0. edn. Oxford: The Cochrane Collaboration, 2008.

[91] Moher D, Cook DJ, Eastwood S, Olkin I, Rennie D, Stroup DF. Improving the quality of reports of meta-analyses of randomized controlled trials: the QUOROM statement. Quality of Reporting of Meta-analyses. Lancet 1999;354:1896-900.

[92] Sampaio C, Ferreira J, Costa J.[Numbers needed for treatment and their respective confidence intervals: useful tools to assess clinical significance and uncertainty associated with medical interventions] Rev Port Cardiol 2000;19(12):1303-8.[Portuguese].

[93] Ebrahim S. The use of numbers needed to treat derived from systematic reviews and meta-analysis. Caveats and pitfalls. Eval Health Prof 2001;24(2):152-64.

[94] Moncrieff J, Wessely S, Hardy R. Active placebos versus antidepressants for depression. Cochrane Database Syst Rev. 2004;(1):CD003012.

[95] Boutron I, Estellat C, Guittet L, Dechartres A, Sackett DL, Hróbjartsson A, Ravaud P. Methods of blinding in reports of randomized controlled trials assessing pharmacologic treatments: a systematic review. PLoS Med 2006;3(10):e425.

Chapter 4

Is the randomised clinical trial (RCT) really the gold standard?

In the last chapter we saw that antipsychotic drugs cannot be considers an efficient treatment of the psychotic mental disorders. This might seem like a strange conclusion, when 5% or more of the people in the western world take these drugs every day. The reason for the discripancy between the scientific documentation of the pharmaceutical drugs from the pharmaceutical companies and the results coming from large metaanalyses seems to have serious methodological problems connected to the way pharmaceutical drugs are tested. The method is called randomised, clinical trials (RCT).

RCT have been accepted as the golden standard of testing making chemical medicine "evidence based". RCT is based on four assumptions: 1) The placebo effect is represented by a placebo pill, 2) it is possible to make a double-blind test with biologically active drugs, 3) beneficial and harmful effects of drugs are fairly measured in RCTs, and 4) an appropriate time frame for the test I used.

We have found problems with these assumptions: 1) The placebo effect provided by close relationships to a physician is stronger than an inert pill, 2) double-blind tests cannot be made with biologically active drugs, as these leave an internal clue in the patient that destroys the blinding (active placebo), 3) lack of global outcome measures makes toxic effects invisible for the test and magnifies minor effects to make clinically insignificant positive effects look important, and 4) RCTs are used in such a brief time frame that side effects and harm are not properly detected.

The four errors combine into a serious error: The RCT-procedure induces a strong bias in favor of any toxic drug tested.

RCTs can turn drugs that are only toxic and not beneficial at all into products sold as useful chemical medicine. Many pharmaceutical drugs on the marked today are tested only with this flawed RTC-procedure and we recommend that these drugs be tested again using a rational method. If drugs are not more helpful than placebo we need to return to classic psychosocial holistic medicine.

Introduction

For more than 2000 years, ever since 400 BCE, European medicine was identical to the proud tradition of the Hippocrates psychosocial medicine. Hippocrates medicine has also been called "character medicine" as its interventions served the purpose of helping the patient to self-insight into his or her purpose of life and character, i.e. total pool of physical, mental and spiritual talents (1).

When a person use all talents to create value in all personal relationships, this person is happy, healthy and well functioning in all major areas of life, from social, family and sexual life to working life. The classical physician was a man of wisdom and his training was about helping people to develop self-insight and realize their full potential – i.e. to "step into character". This treatment intervened only on consciousness and the healing effect of it was called placebo, from Latin "I please". The ethics of the Hippocratic medicine was the famous principle of primum non nocere: First do no harm (1).

About 1950, the discovery of penicillin and other effective pharmaceuticals started a biochemical revolution. If medicine could be drugs, this was an eminent business opportunity, and soon a large number of commercial pharmaceutical companies were established. The first problem the new chemical medicine had to solve was technical chemical problems: how were bioactive drugs with specific effects designed and developed? The second problem was how such potentially poisonous and harmful drugs could be tested on humans? The third problem was ethical – to convince the medical societies to abandon the traditional Hippocratic ethics.

To justify pharmaceutical products, the industry had to document that the drugs were beneficial for the patients. They needed to be more efficient for healing and cure than the traditional psychosocial consciousness-based treatments – now called the placebo cures – and the harm they inflicted must be insignificant compared to the healing benefits.

The solution to this problem emerged over a few decades into the standard toxic trial on animals followed by randomized clinical testing (RCT) on humans used today. In the latter the potentially beneficial drug is tested double-blind against an inert placebo pill, containing calcium carbonate (chalk), sugar or a similar, biologically inert drug. Potential effects and suspected adverse effects and events are measured and counted.

The animal testing has during the years proven less effective than expected, as the human body reacts differently towards many drugs than the small mammals we most often use for lab-tests of toxicity. The tests of the drugs on humans often also ignores important poisonous aspects of the drugs, as we have seen many examples of, lately i.e. with the problematic drug Vioxx (2), a seemingly harmless painkiller, that caused acute myocardial infarction and stroke. In the medical society there is a kind of tolerance towards such failures to detect severe and lethal adverse effects of drugs, as it is impossible to test for everything in a pharmaceutical testing. Still this reminds us all of the importance to choose a non-drug treatment for our patients, if such a treatment exists at all.

In this paper we will show that there are much more fundamental problems with the standard RCT procedure used by the pharmaceutical companies to get their pharmaceutical products approved and sold, than just occasional failures to detect toxic effects of drugs. We have analyzed these problems and found them severe so that we believe RCT to be questioned as a sound basis for evidence based medicine. In the end of this paper we therefore suggest more rational methods for testing the pharmaceutical drugs.

Four fundamental problems of RCT

The RCT is based on four assumptions:

1) The placebo effect is well represented with a placebo pill
2) It is possible to make a double blind test
3) The beneficial and harmful effects of the drugs are fairly measured
4) The timeframe used for the RCT test is reasonable.

The fifth condition for RCTs to be valid is that they are done by people without a personal interest in the outcome of the study, since such a special interest is likely to induce a bias in the study (3). The problem of bias in pharmaceutical studies based on RCTs is well known and therefore not the subject of this paper. We will discuss these assumptions one by one.

Regarding assumption 1: The placebo effect is well represented with a placebo pill

The core in the classical Hippocratic non-drug treatment is the intimate relationship with a physician – the physician is the tool, so to speak (4). The importance of the close relationships with the physician for the size of the placebo effect has recently been documented in the British Medical Journal (5). The relative importance of talking and touching has been investigated in a recent study by our group (6) and we found the combination of the two principal interventions to be important for inducing a large placebo effect, indicating a strong synergy. The size of the placebo effect has also been established now, from several dozens of studies of holistic non-drug medicine done through the last three decades (7,8). We concluded in the two reviews that most health conditions can be treated and one patient in two or three are normally cured with the most effective types of placebo-treatments. It has thus been documented that the placebo effect is tremendously powerful as medicine, even if the patient has a severe heart condition (9,10).

The effect of the placebo-pill used in pharmaceutical RCTs has recently been investigated and the conclusion was that it had no effect at all (11). The authors concluded from this that the placebo effect [in the RCTs tested] did not exist at all, when compared to no treatment.

Conclusion: The assumption that the placebo effect is well represented with a placebo pill in the RCTs is therefore false.

Regarding assumption 2: It is possible to make a double blind test of a drug vs. [passive] placebo

Most if not all biologically active drugs gives an internal clue to the test person that he or she has actually gotten an active drug. This clue activates a placebo effect called *active placebo* (12) and if such a drug is tested against normal (passive) placebo, it will induce a placebo effect that by itself will create the result that this is an effective drug. Therefore it is not possible to make a test double blind as the blinding is destroyed by the internal clues of active drugs.

The size of the active placebo effect in psychoactive drugs has recently been established in a Cochrane meta-analysis of antidepressants vs. active placebo (13). The authors found that the effect of antidepressants practically disappeared, if tested against active placebo compared to the normal "passive placebo" pill and when tested against passive placebo one patient in three was helped.

This latter result is the basis for the marketing of antidepressants today; obviously the conclusion that the antidepressants help is not justified. We find it possible to extrapolate from this type of drugs to all psychoactive drugs in use today.

The situation is even worse. If you give the patient a poison that gives an internal clue, it will always come out better than the passive placebo used for comparison. The test-substance in the Cochrane meta-analysis was exactly that: drugs that only gave adverse effects, and no beneficial effects. So the way the double-blind test is designed favors poisinous drugs for non-poisonous drugs.

In theory all drugs could be tested using active placebo drugs of similar toxicity, but as this is highly predictable to give the same results as in the above mentioned Cochrane study, the pharmaceutical industry is not likely to induce this procedure by itself, in spite of its logic necessity.

Conclusion: The assumption that it is possible to make a double blind test of a drug vs. [passive] placebo in the RCTs is therefore false.

Regarding assumption 3: The beneficial and harmful effects of the pharmaceutical drugs are fairly measured

Only with a fair measure of beneficial effects can it be evaluated, if the drug is useful as medicine and only with a fair and similar measurement of benefits and harm is it possible to compare the two to evaluate, if the drug all in all is beneficial or harmful to the patient.

Many new drugs will reach the clinic or office based on their ability to affect some presumably disease-related measure (i.e., glucose, cholesterol, blood pressure), which are readily measured and can serve as a disease marker. Clearly, something that influenced cholesterol, but had no effect on cardiovascular disease would not be of much use; however, one would have to learn about this in a stepwise manner. Other strategies for testing drugs focus on local symptoms rather than global states of health and quality of life. Only with global measures can we really know, if a pharmaceutical drug is benefitting the patient.

Today we have a number of established and validated global measures of health. We can easily measure self-rated health, self-rated physical health, self-rated mental health, and global quality of life, using small easy-to-use questionnaires (WHOQOL5, QOL1, QOL5, QOL10) (14-16).

We also know that such subjective measures of health are stronger predictors of survival and future health than any objective health measure (17-21). With such measures it is easy to evaluate the total effect of a drug on health and quality of life. This effect can also easily be followed over time. The cost for such testing is minimal and the information gained essential. A global quality of life measure detects the combined effect of benefits and harms from a drug. Many such measures exist, but they are rarely used in RCTs today.

In spite of the possibility of using global measures the pharmaceutical companies most often focus on only one or a few, local measures to document the positive outcomes, when they develop and test a drug. Global benefits in health and quality of life is therefore not tested, nor is global harm. The focus on specific adverse effects and events is further enhancing the drugs chances of looking good in the RCT-test, while the possible damaging impact on a global scale on health, quality of life and general level of performance that would make the drug look very bad, is not measured.

When a new drug is marketed the physicians therefore lack this crucial information, and when they do, they automatically assume, that the symptom alleviated by the drug is more important to the patient, than the adverse effects induced by the drugs. In this way drugs that are more harmful than beneficial to health and quality of life can still pass the RCT and come out as a beneficial drug.

Our own analysis of the relative harm and benefit of antipsychotic drugs thus showed the antipsychotic drugs to be about 100 times more harmful than beneficial (22) and we recently found a similar situation for cancer chemotherapy (23).

As times goes by adverse (toxic) effects according to the science of toxicology often tend to accumulate and beneficial effects tend to diminish; it is therefore very important to observe the long term effects of the drugs. In practice this is almost never done by the pharmaceutical companies.

Other problems are that negative results almost never are published giving a very strong publication bias; when all data is collected in a field the results are often much more negative than if the industry just publish its positive results, as we saw with the huge meta-analysis of cancer chemotherapy done by Abel, that concluded that chemotherapy shortened life and destroyed quality of life for almost all types of cancers (the epitheloid cancers) (24-27).

Conclusion: The assumption that the beneficial and harmful effects of the pharmaceutical drugs are fairly measured in the RCTs is therefore false.

Regarding assumption 4: The timeframe used for the RCT test is reasonable

If the active placebo effect of a toxic drug is used in medicine there will be two phases, a positive phase (the active placebo phase), where the patient feels lifted, motivated and helped due to the active placebo effect, and after this a negative phase (a toxic phase), where the patient is paying the prize of being helped by a toxic drug.

The ideal use of a toxic drug – like strychnine which was used by allopathic physicians around the 1900s – was a short, strong intervention. If the treatment period was too long, the immediate benefit would be destroyed by the harm caused in the long run. We therefore know, that a RCT-test that involves a strong element of active placebo from toxic effects of biologically active chemicals, need to be thoroughly tested for the whole period of time, where it is used by the patients, to monitor the total effect on the patients.

In our metaanalysis of the antipsychotic drugs (22) we learned that a positive effect found in a short term measurement at six month often is reduced to half the effect after 12 month, and it is presumed that this tendency continues though time, making it mandatory to test positive effects for two years or more, as many patients are treated with the drugs for years, in the belief that short term effect is also preserved in the long term.

In the same way the adverse effects (side effects) and adverse events (negative events) tend to accumulate through time. As an example it is well known that schizophrenic patients more and more frequently commit suicide as the treatment with antipsychotic drug continue. A few percent of the patients take their own life in the beginning of pharmaceutical treatment (28) with this fraction growing to 15% as times goes by (29).

Swedish researchers have suggested that suicide is caused by drug-induced depression (30). The reason for the increased rate of patient suicide though time could very well be a more and more severe depression induced by the accumulated toxic effect of the antipsychotic drugs.

It is also found that psychiatric patients treated with pharmaceutical drugs have a higher tendency to die spontaneously (31), presumably because of accumulated toxic effects. It is therefore of extreme importance to continue the measuring of toxic adverse effects and adverse events on the long term (2 years or more, and 5-20 years if patients often take the drugs for so long).

If the appropriate time frame for the RCTs is not used, the whole test becomes meaningless. Unfortunately most pharmaceutical companies are only testing their product over a short term, often only three month. This seems to be a strategy to hide the adverse effects of the drugs, which is unacceptable.

Conclusion: The assumption that the timeframe used for the RCT test is reasonable is therefore false.

Combined effect of the four errors

The first error, not to test pharmaceuticals against the traditional psychosocial intervention that holistic physicians have been doing for millenniums, are giving the pharmaceutical industry an easy way out or no competition at all. Basically all drugs can win this race.

The second error change the sign of the test from plus to minus – toxic drugs are perceived as beneficial drugs due to the active placebo effect. This is problematic and makes the present RCT-procedure misleading.

The third effort, the local non-global testing (a local symptom or a disease marker) ignores the possible, negative global effects on the patient's health caused by toxic effects of the drugs. The focus on local effects separates positive effects from adverse effects, making is possible to ignore that the harmful effects are stronger than the beneficial and allows the industry to conclude that the drug has beneficial qualities for specific symptoms. Because of this way of testing, even a very toxic drug can pass the RCT test and come out as beneficial.

The fourth effect, to test only in a short term period is boosting the positive effects caused by the active placebo effect and hiding the true, adverse effects of a drug used in the long run.

Combining these four errors, the pharmaceutical industry have managed to set up a RCT procedure, that can make almost any drug look like a beneficial pharmaceutical medicine with only modest harm done to the patients.

In the documentation the drugs will look as clinically beneficial drugs with clinically less significant adverse effects and events. We have a situation that is clearly not acceptable. The RCT procedure needs instant revision and should not in its present form be used for future clinical testing of pharmaceuticals. All drugs tested with the RCT procedure needs to be retested as we cannot rely on the results of the present RCT-test procedure.

There can be no doubt that all the four errors individually have been used, because of their ability to improve the way the pharmaceutical drugs come out of the RCT. We doubt that the highly problematic combined effect, that toxic drugs are made to look like beneficial medicine, is made intentionally, as the effect of the pattern of the four errors combined is somewhat difficult to understand.

On the other hand there has been times where pharmaceutical drugs in large metaanalyses have turned out to be only harmful and not beneficial at all as we have seen (13,24). Another example is the antipsychotic drugs, where Adams et al (32) in a large Cochrane metaanalysis found these drugs not to improve the mental health ("mental state") at all, with the drugs having many very common and severe adverse effects. Adams et al (32) also found that the new generation of antipsychotic drugs are not more beneficial or less harmfull than the first drug, Chlorpromazine, in spite of the industrial RCT-tests of the new generation drugs often showing an improvement.

The pharmaceutical industry has had time and plenty of occasions to reflect upon the contrast between the results of the single RCT-based study made by the industry and the conclusions of the large metaanalyses made by independent researchers.

We believe that the pharmaceutical industry has done its own critical analyses, very similar to the one we are presenting here, but has not taken the consequences and changed the RCT procedure. This is in part, because scientific journals are accepting the RCT procedure as it is and partly because it is good business for the industry.

How should biomedical interventions be tested?

If one wants to keep the design of RCT one should use active placebo of sufficient strength, global outcomes and sufficient observation time. We have an ethical problem with the use of active placebo drugs, as they must be as toxic as the drug we are testing, but without positive medical qualities. It is not simple to distribute toxics to thousands of innocent control patient.

For chronic patients a simple schedule must be preferred: Simply treat chronically ill patients – patients that have not been better for years – and see if they improve on some global level – health, quality of life, or performance. Follow them for a few years and see if the induced improvement is permanent. Use NNT and NNH numbers to express the effectiveness and use if possible at all the outcome "cured or not cured" in combination with self-rated physical health, self-rated mental health and self-rated quality of life.

If a pharmaceutical treatment cure a fair fraction of the patients, say one in 2, 3 or 4, and does not have significant adverse effects, this is a valuable drug. If not, if it only cures one in 50, and if it has significant adverse effects, the drug is of no medical value. If there is a more effective, or similarly effective, non-drug treatment the pharmaceutical treatment is of no value as there will always be some adverse effects from drugs.

This procedure of curing chronically ill patients and using them as their own control is simple and efficient, and can be used with all types of chronic patients (33). The randomization to *no treatment* is less valuable, as most of these patients will go to some kind of CAM treatment, if not treated medically. If the classical, Hippocratic holistic medicine is used as control in the study and we recommend that the research follows the open source protocol for clinical holistic medicine (34).

For acute patients, randomization is still necessary. The most logical thing to do is to randomize to holistic medical treatment; there are many small units with holistic physicians, who have documented their efficacy. If a holistic medical treatment unit is not available for a specific disease, it will be necessary to train a group of physicians to do it or if this cannot be done, randomize to no treatment. When a patient receives no treatment from a doctor, the patient – i. e. in an acute psychotic crisis - is likely to assume more responsibility for his or her own life, and this itself has a strong curative effect.

We understand that a serious proposal to create a NGO (non-government organization) to reevaluate every approved drug on the market would involve breathtaking commitment of resources. But it can and should be done. We estimate that a research hospital specifically established for the comparison of biomedicine and classical holistic medicine would cost around or 150 million EURO or $US 200 millions to establish. This is still not much on an industrial or national scale.

Discussion

Most researchers acknowledge that there is no risk-free ride, when a patient takes a drug to obtain a benefit; every drug has some adverse effects. We have found that the way the RTC tests the medical value of pharmaceutical drugs today tends to create the impression that a drug, that has no beneficial effect at all, but only harmful adverse effects, can still appear as an effective, useful medicine. Toxic drugs tested with the RTC-method can thus be sold as medicine.

The RCT-procedure is build on false assumptions in our opinion and has strong built-in bias in favor of the drugs. We know that biologically active drugs can be toxic and it is therefore of extreme importance that we are able to make a fair test of pharmaceutical drugs to ensure benefit to the patient and do no harm. The problems relate to the choice of placebo types, to the used outcomes and the observation times, not to mention all the other types of well-known bias like the withdrawal of negative results from publication, which could explain the findings of Abel (25).

We see basically all this as political and commercial problems rather than as scientific problems. The scientific problems of RCTs can easily be solved: In principle the CRT can test the benefits and harms of a drug using randomized, double blind testing compared to active placebo with the drugs we have suggested and global outcome measures. This could easily be done without any technical or scientific problems.

But the industry tests its pharmaceutical drugs in such a way as to optimize the appearance of the drugs, which is only logical from a commercial perspective. The pharmaceutical companies make the drugs look as beneficial and as harmless as they possibly can. It is important to recall that the way the drugs are tested has been created by the pharmaceutical industry. They have been uncritically approved by the responsible government institutions and by the physicians in our opinion.

The academic institutions have in general also approved the standard RCT method for pharmaceutical drug testing without being critical enough in our opinion. We are now in a difficult situation, because drugs have been accepted, but they might be harmful and not beneficial to patient health and quality of life.

We know that about 50% of citizens in countries with socialized, free biomedicine are chronically ill (35). Analyses have shown that only a small fraction of these patients are helped by drugs (36). The deteriorating health of the population might be explained directly from the toxic effect of the many pharmaceutical drugs given to the population.

The solution to the difficult situation is to test all drugs on the market again. The pharmaceutical drugs must be tested by some organization that does not have commercial interests in the drugs. Such organizations are hard to find, and might have to be created from the bottom, finding researchers without personal interests in medicine. It must preferably be an NGO as strong lobbyism from the pharmaceutical industry continues to plague the public health care system.

The possible result of such a testing could very well be that the classical holistic medicine inducing healing of mind and body – often called salutogenesis – may be found to be preferable to symptom blocking drugs, which does not heal the person (36-40). A broader application of subjective health and quality of life measures would constructively impact the RCT test.

Conclusions

The standard RCT-testing of pharmaceutical drugs in double blind trials as compared to placebo has so many problems that these sum up to a fatal error: a drug with only toxic qualities is likely to appear as beneficial medicine. The primary single cause for this is that toxic drugs always have an active placebo effect, that makes the drug look beneficial in the RCT-test. This cast serious doubt that the RCT-procedure in its present form is not scientifically valid.

The way the clinical outcomes are chosen in the tests – with focus on local symptoms or disease markers instead of global states - makes it furthermore impossible to compare positive and negative effects.

Finally the short time frame of testing makes the positive active placebo effect dominate over the negative pharmacological drug effect of a toxic drug. Therefore a toxic drug with no beneficial pharmacological effects is likely to be approved as a beneficial pharmacological medicine, when the standard RTC is used.

We conclude that effects of drugs documeted with the standard RCT-test procedure used by the pharmaceutical industry today are not "evidence based". As a consequence of this, we cannot exclude the possibility that some of the pharmaceutical drugs in use today being likely more harmful than beneficial, in spite of being documented as primarily beneficial. We therefore need to re-test all the pharmaceutical drugs documented with the RCT-test. This can be done using the simple test on chronic patients with randomization against no treatment, or better against the traditional placebo cure by classical holistic medicine, or in acute medicine, uisng a randomized test using active placebo, global outcomes, and sufficiently long test times.

Testing must be done by people and organizations without personal, commercial or political interest in medicine. We strongly advise NGOs to be empowered to do the testing, as all governmental organizations are strongly influenced by the lobby of the pharmaceutical industry.

We recommend the establishmed of a research hospital dedicated to the testing of medicine which could compares the effects of pharmaceutical drugs with the effects of classical holistic medicine, the original placebo cure, for each clinical condition. We estimate that this could be done for about 200 million $US or 150 million EURO, which is not much on a national or industrial scale.

References

[1] Jones WHS. Hippocrates. Vol. I–IV. London: William Heinemann, 1923-1931.

[2] Rout, M. Vioxx maker Merck and Co drew up doctor hit list. April 01, 2009 http://www.theaustralian.news.com.au/story/0,25197,25272600-2702,00.html. Accessed 2009-05-11.

[3] Gøtzsches P. Bias in double-blind trials. Dan Med Bull 1990;37:329-336.

[4] de Vibe M, Bell E, Merrick J, Omar HA, Ventegodt S. Ethics and holistic healthcare practice. Int J Child Health Human Dev 2008;1(1):23-8.

[5] Kaptchuk TJ, Kelley JM, Conboy LA, Davis RB, Kerr CE, Jacobson EE, Kirsch I, Schyner RN, Nam BH, Nguyen LT, Park M, Rivers AL, McManus C, Kokkotou E, Drossman DA, Goldman P, Lembo AJ. Components of placebo effect: randomised controlled trial in patients with irritable bowel syndrome. BMJ 2008;336(7651):999-1003.

[6] Ventegodt S, Andersen NJ, Merrick J, Greydanus DE. Effectiveness of traditional pharmaceutical biomedicine versus complementary and alternative medicine in a physician's general practice. J Altern Med Res 2010;2(2), in press.

[7] Ventegodt S, Omar HA, Merrick J. Quality of life as medicine: Interventions that induce salutogenesis. A review of the literature. Submitted to Soc Indicator Res.

[8] Ventegodt S, Andersen NJ, Kandel I, Merrick J. Effect, side effects and adverse events of non-pharmaceutical medicine. A review. Int J Disabil Hum Dev 2009, in press.

[9] Ornish D, Brown SE, Scherwitz LW, Billings JH, Armstrong WT, et al. Can lifestyle changes reverse coronary heart disease? The lifestyle heart trial. Lancet 1990;336(8708):129-33.

[10] Ornish D, Scherwitz LW, Billings JH, Brown SE, Gould KL, et al. Intensive lifestyle changes for reversal of coronary heart disease. JAMA1998;280(23):2001-7.

[11] Hròbjartsson A, Gøtzsche PC. Placebo interventions for all clinical conditions. Cochrane Database Syst Rev 2004;(3):CD003974.

[12] Boutron I, Estellat C, Guittet L, Dechartres A, Sackett DL, Hróbjartsson A, Ravaud P. Methods of blinding in reports of randomized controlled trials assessing pharmacologic treatments: a systematic review. PLoS Med 2006;3(10):e425.

[13] Moncrieff J, Wessely S, Hardy R. Active placebos versus antidepressants for depression. Cochrane Database Syst Rev 2004;(1):CD003012.

[14] Lindholt, J.S., Ventegodt, S. and Henneberg, E.W. Development and validation of QoL5 for clinical databases. A short, global and generic questionnaire based on an integrated theory of the quality of life. Eur J Surgery 2002;168(2):107-13.

[15] Ventegodt S, Andersen NJ, Merrick J. QOL10 for clinical quality-assurance and research in treatment-efficacy: Tehn key questions for measuring the global quality of life, self-rated physical and mental health, and self-rated social-, sexual and working ability. J Altern Med Res 2009;1(2), in press.

[16] Fitzpatrick R, Davey C, Buxton MJ, Jones DR. Evaluating patient-based outcome measures for use in clinical trials. Health Technol Assess 1998;14 (2):1-80.

[17] Singh-Manoux A, Dugravot A, Shipley MJ, Ferrie JE, Martikainen P, Goldberg M, Zins M. The association between self-rated health and mortality in different socioeconomic groups in the GAZEL cohort study. Int J Epidemiol 2007;36(6):1222-8.

[18] Long MJ, McQueen DA, Banga-lore VG, Schurman JR2nd. Using self-assessed health to predict patient outcomes after total knee replacement. Clin Orthop Relat Res 2005;434:189-92.

[19] Idler EL, Russell LB, Davis D. Survival, functional limitations, and self-rated health in the NHANES I epidemiologic follow-up study, 1992. First national health and nutrition examination survey. Am J Epidemiol 2000;152 (9):874-83.

[20] Idler EL, Kasl S. Health perceptions and survival: do global evaluations of health status really predict mortality? J Gerontol 1991;46(2):S55-65.

[21] Burström B, Fredlund P. Self rated health: Is it as good a predictor of subsequent mortality among adults in lower as well as in higher social classes. J Epidemiol Community Health 2001;55(11):836-40.

[22] Ventegodt S, Flensborg-Madsen T, Andersen NJ, Svanberg BØ, Struve F, Endler C and Merrick J. Therapeutic value of anti-psychotic drugs: A critical analysis of Cochrane meta-analyses of the therapeutic value of anti-psychotic drugs. J Altern Med Res, In Press.

[23] Ventegodt S Endler PC, Andersen NJ, Svanberg BØ, Struve F and Merrick J. Therapeutic value of anti-cancer drugs: A critical analysis of Cochrane meta-analyses of the therapeutic value of chemotherapy for cancer. J Altern Med Res, In Press.

[24] Abel U. Chemotherapy of advanced epithelial cancer - a critical review. Biomed Pharmacother 1992;46:439-52.

[25] Abel U. [Chemotherapy of advanced epithelial cancer.] Stuttgart: Hippokrates Verlag 1990. [German].

[26] Abel U. [Chemotherapie fortgeschrittener Karzi-nome. Eine kritische Bestandsaufnahme.] Berlin: Hippokrates, 1995. [German].

[27] Abel U. Chemotherapy of advanced epithelial cancer. Stuttgrat, Germany: Hippokrates Verlag, 1995.

[28] Qin P, Nordentoft M. Suicide risk in relation to psychiatric hospitalization: evidence based on longitudinal registers. Arch Gen Psychiatry 2005;62(4):427-32.

[29] Hemmingsen R, Parnas, J., Gjerris, A, Reisby, N. og Kragh-Sørensen, P. Klinisk Psykiatri. 2. udg. København: Munksgaard, 2000.

[30] SBU-rapport nr. 133/1 og 133/2. Behandling med neuroleptika. Stockholm: Statens beredning för utvärdering av medicinsk metodik, 1997;2. [Swedish].

[31] Lindhardt A, ed. The use of antipsychotic drugs among the 18-64 year old patients with schizophrenia, mania, or bipolar affective disorder. Copenhagen: National Board Health, 2006. [Danish].

[32] Adams CE, Awad G, Rathbone J, Thornley B. Chlorpromazine versus placebo for schizophrenia. Cochrane Database Syst Rev 2007;(2):CD000284.

[33] Ventegodt S, Andersen NJ, Merrick J. The square curve paradigm for research in alternative, complementary and holistic medicine: A cost-effectice, easy and scientifically valid design for evidence-based medicine and quality improvement. ScientificWorldJournal 2003;3:1117-27.

[34] Ventegodt S, Andersen NJ, Kandel I, Merrick J. The open source protocol of clinical holistic medicine. J Altern Med Res 2009;1(2), in press.

[35] Kjøller M, Juel K, Kamper-Jørgensen F. [Folkesundhedsrapporten Danmark 2007]. Copenhagen: Statens Inst Folkesundhed, 2007. [Danish].

[36] Ventegodt S, Andersen NJ, Merrick J, Greydanus DE. Effectiveness of traditional pharmaceutical biomedicine versus complementary and alternative medicine in a physician's general practice. J Altern Med Res 2010;2(2), in press.

[37] Antonovsky A. Health, stress and coping. London: Jossey-Bass, 1985.

[38] Antonovsky A. Unravelling the mystery of health. How people manage stress and stay well. San Francisco: Jossey-Bass, 1987.

[39] Harrington A. The cure within: a history of mind-body medicine. New York: WW Norton, 2008.

[40] Goleman D, Gurin J, Connellan H. Mind, body medicine: How to use your mind for better health. New York: Consumer Reports Books, 1993.

Chapter 5

Are the biochemical hypotheses for the etiology of the mental diseases substantiated?

We review the understanding of the etiology of the mental diseases, which has changed considerably during the last three decades. We consider the results from psycho-neuro-pharmacology and the derived historical, biochemical hypotheses for the mental diseases, and find that they have not been substantiated.

We analyse the popular, biochemical hypothesis of the diseases depression and schizophrenia and find that the standard biochemical hypotheses are not substantiated. We suggest a mechanism for the pasifying effect of the antipsychotic drugs. When it comes to the etiololgy of the two most common mental diseases both of these seem to be caused by disturbed psychosexual development, causing a degenerated intent, in accordance with Bleuler's classical description and understanding of schizophrenia. We present a psychobiological and more holistic models of the mental diseases and their etiology, which we find more plausible than the historical, biochemical and genetic models.

Introduction

All transmitter systems known so far are present in both rats and humans; they must therefore be considered to be very stable in an evolutionary perspective (1). But here are significant differences also in the vertebrate brains; it looks as if man to a much higher degree than animals is in control of his fundamental mental functions such as attention, sleep, and motor activity. In man all these functions are under control of the will and are assumed to be ruled from the cerebral cortex. This is in accordance with the known development of the cerebral neocortex and above all the fronto-orbital lobes. Because mental diseases such as depression and schizophrenia are hardly found in animals, it seems reasonable to believe that mental diseases are caused by regulation from the cerebral cortex rather than deregulation in one or several of the ascending systems. The rational-mechanical interpretation of reality favours the hypothesis of a defect in the ascending systems, while the energetic-informational interpretation of reality favours a complex cerebral deregulation. Research has concentrated on the ascending systems, partly because of the documented effect of the antidepressants and the neuroleptics. However little is known about the descending, neural systems.

Seen from a rational interpretation of reality we think it is natural to assume, that mental diseases are caused by an inherited, mechanical defect in the brain such as a defect in an enzyme or a receptor. When psychopharmacological drugs were invented, they wereseemingly able to reduce manyof the symptoms of mental illnesses, i.e. the hallucinatory behaviour of schizophrenic patients. The mentally ill patients became much more calm and easier to care for, and members of the patients family often appreciated the results of the treatment, in spite of the rate of cure was rarely found to be significantly improved compared to the traditional methods of psychotherapy and holistic therapy. Especially the obedience of the patients was often radically improved, and the lack of resistance and the cooperation was seen as important signs of improvement.

This led to a number of hypotheses, as it was assumed that the effect of the drugs was a simple compensation for specific defects behind the mental diseases. This interpretation has, however, in spite of many years of research and thousands of published papers not lead to the expected full understanding of the aetiology of mental diseases; quite on the contrary mental illness and human brain function seems more mysterious and hard to understand from a chemical perspective than ever.

This paper provides arguments to reject the hitherto proposed simple hypotheses about a link betweenbiochemical, molecular defects and mental disease. For instance, in spite of a great scientific effort neither schizophrenia nor depression has been linked to such defect genes or other specific biochemical defects; and this fact was clear to researchers already in 1989 (2).

Psychoneuropharmacology and the biochemical hypotheses of the etiology of mental diseases

Almost every drug that affects the brain does so in terms of influences on synaptic transmissions (3). Antidepressants and neuroleptics as well as several other types of psychotropic drugs often work on one or more ascending mono-aminergic transmitter system (with serotonine (5HT), norepinephrine (NE) or dopamine (DA) as transmitter), whose nuclei are present in the brain stem or the diencephalon. Pharmacological interaction with systems with acetylcholine (Ach) or gamma-aminobutyrate (GABA) can, however, also give a similar effect. Reserpin was the first antipsychotic drug that were shown to empty the monoamines from their storage vesicles, making them accessible to degradation by mitochondria-tied monoamine oxidase. The discovery of such compounds lead to the formation of the hypothesis of genetically specified dysfunction in these systems as a possible cause of schizophrenia, and serotonine and norepinephrine of depression.

The monoamine systems (5HT, NE, DA) are supposed to be the primary site of action of many psychotropic drugs and have therefore been the subject of intensive research activity. But in spite of this the precise nature of the exact relation between the monoamine systems, the mental effect of the drugs, physiology, and behaviour is still not understood in details. Because of their great diversity the monoaminergic systems can be assumed to attend to general regulatory functions. The function of the serotonergic systems is the least understood. They seem to function through a neural inhibiting tonus especially to the limbic system, correlated to muscle tonus. Dopaminergic systems possibly regulate motor activity and the activity of thoughts. Regulation of outwardly directed attention is possibly connected to the noradrenergic systems.

Model examples of mental disorders

Depression and schizophrenia can be seen as examples of mental illness, which is the heavy workload in any psychiatric centre or practice. Depression is characterized by constantly bad mood, self-disapproval, a low self-confidence, and a negative self-image (4). Schizophrenia most frequently occurs at the age 15-35 years and is characterized by lack of zest for life and disorganization of logical thought most often together with auditory hallucinations and paranoid delusions (5), together with emotional flattening and social withdrawal (comp. Bleuler 1911). Depressed and schizophrenic patients constitute far the greatest part of the mentally ill patients. These two mental diseases will be the subjects of the further discussion in this paper, because they represent the best known and investigated mental disorders existing today.

Depression

The inheritance of affective diseases. Studies of monozygote twins showed that if twins grow up together, the concordance as regards depression is higher for monozygote twins (33-79%) than for dizygote twins (54%) (6). A concordance of 79% in the heaviest cases showed that even in these cases monozygotic twins have a considerable freedom to develop in their own way despite having the same genes and living in the same environment.

Studies of adoptation. A study of 29 adopted bipolar depressive patients showed that 31% of the patients had adoptive parents who suffered from affective diseases, in contrast to only 9% of the biological parents. In the case of non-depressive adopted children 2% of their adoptive parents suffered from affective diseases. These data, reviewed by (7) suggested that the environmental factors dominate in the ratio 2:1 against the "early factors", at least in this case. A simple mendelian inheritance seems unlikely. We hypothesize that intrauterine information transmitting interactions between the mother and child are responsible for the remaining cases not explained by genetics and environment.

Most affective diseases have a cyclic nature, most notably bipolar depression that hardly tallies with a genetic defect or a descending cerebral dysfunction. In the well-known "winter-depression" the light factor seems to play a key role.

It seems that environmental factors as well as genetic factors and other early factors, of which we favour intrauterine information transmitting interactions, play a role in the development of depressive diseases. As there is a very close contact between mother and child in utero, and adopted children of course spend their foetal lives in their mother's womb, twin studies are not able to distinguish between the two kinds of factors.

The effectiveness of antidepressants compared to placebo. For many years it was thought that antidepressants were more active than placebo, but around year 2000 the understanding of the active placebo effect led to re-investigation and comparison of the most efficient antidepressants (the tricyclic antidepressant) with active placebo, and quite chocking it was found that these drugs, being the most potent antidepressant drugs know, was not at all better that placebo (8). Before that it was generally believed that app. 65% of non-psychotic depressive patients respond to imipramin, while app. 30% responds to placebo; all heterocyclic antidepressantshad the response figures of 65-75% after one month treatment compared to 20-40% response to placebo. Generally speaking, the worse a depression is, the better the antidepressant fares compared to the passive placebo (7), but this difference is obviously annihilated when it comes to active placebo.

The above-mentioned old studies were conducted in a way that opened up to criticism. Even a 50% reduction in the Hamilton rating score (9) were clinically called a response, but in fact this was only a mild relief of symptoms. More importantly most researchers only included patients that completed the experiment, but did not inform about how many patients that did not complete the experiment – and they did not count these as non-responders, what most of them perhaps were. Moreover it was rarely told how many patients the subjects are chosen from, and there were serious problems with the criteria for election for the experiment.Only patients that do respond positively to the drugs were included in most of the studies, creating a tremendous bias: "Most of the controlled clinical studies exclude patients who have not responded to antidepressants in the past" (10). In most cases the studies report no results of the duration of the recovery or of the frequency ofrelapse, and long-term follow-ups are extremely rare. So it is easy to see to day how the inefficient, antidepressive drugs were artificially turned into active and valuable drugs by the research that was almost always paid for by the pharmaceutical industry.

The hypothesis of depression. Around 1990 research of the effect of antidepressants led to a fundamental revision ofthe earlier hypotheses. Most researchers seem to agree that the simple hypothesis of depression as caused by lack of monoamines was not verified. This hypothesis was partly based on the assumption that the drugs worked through an increased supply of transmitter substances (NE and 5HT) in the synapses in a clinical time variance of the effect of between 7- 45 days (7), a much longer time than the quickly induced biochemical effect. Moreover drugs e.g. iprindol and mianserin, that are not reuptake- or MAO-inhibitors in a significant way were found to be as efficient as the classical drugs. In addition amphetamine, which is a reuptake-inhibitor, cannot effectively be used in the treatment of depressions.

Studies of monoamine-turnover in laboratory animals, long term treated with antidepressants or electroshock, showed no significant deviation from normal. The influence of the reuptake-blocking seems to be submitted to a feedback-regulated mechanism exerting its effect through auto-receptors.

None of these findings are sufficient in themselves in order to reject the hypothesis, "but together they provide a powerful argument for its re-examination and suggest that antidepressants act in a more complex manner than that envisaged by the monoamine deficiency hypothesis of depression" concluded Elliot and Stephenson in 1989 (4).

Psychotherapy, holistic therapy and depression. Since 1975 great methodological and technical improvements have been made, including improvement of methods of evaluating 1) the condition of the patient, 2) the qualifications of the therapist, 3) the contents of the therapy and 4) the improved situation of the patient. Central coordination of therapist training and evaluation programs has apparently resulted in a minor revolution in this area. The results are mixed, but some researchers have concluded that there are large differences in effectiveness between the different therapies (9).

Resent research has documented that depressed patients were helped better by psychotherapy than by psychiatric standard treatment (11-13). One of the best predictors for response to interpersonal therapy is a pathological picture indicating endogen depression!

It seems reasonable to conclude, that mental factors are of tremendous importance concerning affective diseases (14,15). We interpret the existing data in the following way: Mental illnesses are caused primarily by psychological factors, not by genes, as genes cannot be changed by psychotherapy. More efficient that psychotherapy alone is the combination of psychotherapy and bodywork, and holistic therapy like clinical holistic medicine, also including work with philosophy of life and sexuality (16-25).

Schizophrenia

The inheritance of schizophrenia. Evidently schizophrenia is not randomly distributed within a population, but is more frequent within exposed families than in the population as a whole (p<0.001) (26). In recent twin studies the concordance between pairs of twins growing up together is larger between monozygote (31-78%) than betweendizygote twins (6- 28%). These studies also show that 22-69% of monozygote twins growing up together do not both develop schizophrenia (ibid.). This points towards a dominant influence of environmental factors. Since several investigations have shown that monozygote twins to a far higher degree than dizygote twins share the same environment, friends, and attitudes of their parents and teachers (ibid.), the greater concordance might as well be attributed to these environmental likenesses.

Studies have found a significantly higher occurrence of schizophrenia among children adopted by schizophrenic parents and among adopted children, whose biological parents were schizophrenic, compared to the average population. In some studies no significant difference was found, however. Studies of monozygote twins not growing up together were of much greater value than studies of monozygote twins growing up together. The adopted children have, however, often spent a smaller or larger time together with the mother, and in all circumstances they had had the opportunity to adapt to the mother within the womb. The information transmitting interactions have had the time to work.

What is transferred from one generation to the next is not a simple tendency towards the development of schizophrenia, not even a non-specific tendency towards the development of psychiatric diseases, but a tendency towards bad psychosocial functioning, "These findings provide an increasingly complex, but informative, picture of the nature of transmitted liability to schizophrenia" (26).

Since 1916 it has been known, that schizophrenia does not follow a classic Mendelian inheritance pattern, thus, it is obvious to imply a polygenic inheritance. Models for polygenic inheritance, however, are flexible, because they are very difficult to falsify.

From all this, it seems that the studies of adopted monozygote children could suggest the importance of " early factors", but it is not known, whether these are of a genetic or an intrauterine nature. In addition, it is evident, that environmental factors play a great role.

Hypotheses for schizophrenia. Several hypotheses for schizophrenia have been proposed, but the dopamine hypothesis seemed for many years to be the only transmitter hypothesis, that could not be definitively falsified (see historical review in (5)). The dopamine hypothesis was founded in the effect on dopaminergic systems of manyof the original neuroleptics. The hypothesis says that schizophrenia is caused by a(genetically inherited) hyper-activity of the dopaminergic system.

The hypothesis came in different versions each considering one of several possibilities with regard to the function of DA in the psychotic brain. Either there was too fast a DA-metabolism, or a too large a receptor sensitivity (5). Unfortunately for the believer in the dopamine hypothesis, post mortem studies or other studies did not provide evidence for an increased DA-turnover in the brain of people with schizophrenia. An up regulation of D2-receptors as a consequence of the administration of neuroleptics in the brain of schizophrenics was not found. There is still no positive evidence for occurrence of changed D2-frequency in untreated schizophrenics. Thus there is no evidence for any molecular hypothesis for schizophrenia, not even for the dopamine hypothesis. This is in agreement with the fact that schizophrenia occurs in episodes - a fact that is very difficult to explain in terms of a defect in a transmitter system. The earlier mentioned simple hypotheses about schizophrenia as caused by simple biochemical defects or disturbances were around 1990 abandoned in favour of more complex explanations of the brain function.

From 1990 to 2008 came a large series of Cochrane metaanalysis analysing the effect of all kinds and types of antipsychotic drugs on a number of different illnesses and mental states (27-103). Quite surprisingly it was found that every time an antipsychotic drug was tested against placebo, the patients' mental state was not found to be significantly improved. Behaviour was still found to be modified, but the effect of the behaviour was just pacification, not an improvement. Hallucinations and other symptoms of mental illness was not at all relieved by the drugs, which does not deserve its name "antipsychotic medicine" anymore, as the drugs are not at all antipsychotic, only tranquillising the patients. It was also documented in these studies that the adverse effects of the drugs were very severe; they basically took the patient's energy and autonomy away, thus giving the obedient and more socially acceptable picture of an improved patient, that from an existential perspective was actually loosing his quality of life as a sad consequence of the treatment.

The Cochrane analyses finally made it impossible to believe in the biochemical hypothesis of schizophrenia and the other psychotic mental illness; they were simply not substantiated.

Negative and positive symptomatology. The subdivision of schizophrenics into a positive and a negative symptomatology has a long history and seems to be supported by morphological studies (104). The positive symptoms are hallucinations, delusions and some types of thought disturbances as derailment, neologisms and incoherency. The negative symptoms are lack of function in a number of areas, such as social withdrawal, weakened affect, reduced motivation, psycho motor retardation, and poverty of speech.

It was around 1990 commonly understood, that the negative symptoms are not disappearing by use of neuroleptics, but only with the Cochrane studies systematic exploration of the effects of the drugs on the positive effects was it documented that the positive symptoms were not improved either.

There is clinical evidence showing that negative symptoms may be connected with too low a dopamine activity. It is known that Parkinson disease is often associated with social withdrawal and deflated affect. Large doses of neuroleptics may trigger the negative symptoms, besides motor inhibition, while chronic l-dopa administration, which counteracts neuroleptics, sometimes is able to alleviate deflated affect, withdrawn emotions, and apathy.

This means that schizophrenic patients can be divided into a "hyper-dopaminergic" group with positive symptoms, and a "hypo-dopaminergic" group with negative symptoms. The words "hyper" and "hypo" refer to the pharmaceutical compensation that seems to remove the symptoms, and not necessarily to the DA-activity of the patients.The variance in neuropsychological state cannot in itself support a biochemical hypothesis for schizophrenia.

Taken all together it is clear today that the biochemical hypothesis for schizophrenia is in no way substantiated.

Discussion

The passive placebo effect seems to be the same for anti-schizophrenic (antipsychotic drugs) as for antidepressants (5); the active placebo effect is only known for the antidepressant drugs, as nobody yet has investigated this with the antipsychotic drugs. The psychological and sexual factors seems to be dominant in schizophrenia as well as in depression. In studies of neuroleptics, the fact that 2 of three or more were non-responders showed that the brain has a great adaptive capacity to compensate thesedating influences ofthe neuroleptics.

It has been known for a long time that the side effects of neuroleptics closely resemble Parkinson's disease, which is known to be associated by the decay of dopaminergic neurons; the strongest evidence for the dopaminergic effect is the fact that the clinical efficiency of many neuroleptics is closely correlated to their displacement of 3H-spiroperidol and 3H-haloperidol from D2-receptors (5,104). When it was shown, that there was a good correlation between the clinical efficiency of neuroleptics and D2-binding, it seemed reasonable to assume that neuroleptics worked through the D2-receptor. Today a whole new generation of neuroleptics with quite different affinity profiles (27-103,105) have been created. Among the newly identified neuroleptics are compounds that by thorough clinical testing has been shown to be as effective as the old ones, while they on the whole have no affinity to DA-receptors (e.g. clozapin; less tested is flulerlapin, and BW 234 U). These compounds are all found to be "effective" in animal models. It has been shown, that they in general are clinically effective, since it is no longer possible to associate neuroleptic activity with D2-binding. Hence there is no pharmacological evidence, that psychosis is associated with theDA-sytems (5). Webster and Jordan concluded in 1989: "The controversy over neuroleptic treatment and the state of D2-receptors remain unsolved." To day this is finally solved: The illness called schizophrenia is not at all connected to the D2-receptors.

The considerable time-elapse, before the effect of the neuroleptics occurs, points to a complex interaction between drug and brain. As the discontinuation of the drug rarely leads to an immediate aggravation of symptoms, it is evident, that the effects of the drugs cannot be explained by a simple interaction between a drug and a transmitter system.

Neuroleptics have not improved during the past 50 years (28) and while patients' mental health according to the many new Cochrane metaanalysis stays totally unaffected their bodies suffers. A vast fraction of the patients get serious side effects, such as tardive dyskinesia and tardive psychosis, the consequences of which are still uncertain. In spite of intensive studies the patients that selectively respond to these drugs have not been characterized (106).

Finally there is no clinical evidence that neuroleptics should be more active against schizophrenic psychoses than against any other kind of psychosis (107). Therefore there is no reason to limit the DA-hypothesis to schizophrenia; it should comprise all kinds of psychoses. Discontinuation of neuroleptics rarely seems to result in acute aggravation of the schizophrenic symptoms. The schizophrenic symptoms seem to arrive in episodes, a detail that proposes a very complex mechanism.

One of the strangest arguments of the 80'ies, interesting for its historical value, is that the pharmacological effect is due to adaptation to the drug. This hypothesisare of cause not plausible, because adaptation should lower the effect of the neuroleptics, not increase them, but in the 80'ies researches in antipsychotic drugs often suspended all reason to prove what they believed was be true. But this is not so rare in science.

A suggestion of the mechanism of psychopharmacological drugs

The key problem in understanding the mechanism of antidepressants and neuroleptics seems to be the great time delay of their effect. The pharmacological effect takes a few hours, the central nervous system adaptation to this effect presumably takes a few days, but the clinical effect often takes a month or more. The hypothesis of adaptation at receptor level as a mechanism behind the clinical effect does not seem plausible given the time discrepancy. The pharmacological effect of antidepressants generally seems to be an argumentation of synaptic activity, where neuroleptics (e.g. reserpine) may induce depression.

About 1990 it seemed reasonable to assume, that antidepressants respectively neuroleptics compensated a hypo-activity respectively a hyper-activity in the brain as a whole, not at any specific site of action for a specific drug. This compensation could give the complete neural system a "push" in the right direction towards normal function and normal interpretation of reality. According to this interpretation the time delay of the clinical effect was seen as inertia in the adaptation at the higher (mental) levels of the brain.

We suggest that the cognitive content of mental disease corresponds to a large number of considerations and decisions that take a long time to accumulate in one's model of reality in the brain.

This inertia in the change of perception of reality leads to the time delay in any treatment of depression and schizophrenia, whether it is done by pharmacological means or by electro chock (ECT), psychotherapy and holistic therapy.

But the most obvious hypothesis for the function of the drugs is much simpler: Poisoning. As time goes by, and the patients loose energy due to severe poisoning, the behaviour becomes more and more obedient, passive and without the initiative and rebellion that characterizes autonomous beings.

The psychopharmacological drugs are simple socializing the patients by depraving them of their life energy. This interpretation seems to be in almost perfect accordance with the findings of the Cochrane studies of antipsychotic drugs.

The etiology of depression and schizophrenia

In 1990 it was found that depression could be counteracted through interaction with many different transmitter systems. This pointed towards a complex mechanism and not a simple one tied to a single transmitter system. Reuptake in itself could also be excluded as a mechanism, because cocaine and amphetamine did not act as antidepressants. Compensatory up regulation of beta-receptors was often seen, but not always (107), thus this could not be the general regulation mechanism. Adaptation to a drug, including receptor adaptation through increased sensitivity, was suggested as a mechanism. This did not seem likely, because such an adaptation should eliminate the disturbance and thus decrease rather than increase. In this way reduce instead of increase the effect of the antidepressants. It seems absurd to suppose that such an adaptation should give a whole new effect as for example to alleviate a depression. An adaptation to a psychotropic drug normally takes about four days (108), whereas the effect of antidepressants often does not assert its effect before about six weeks (7).

The long interval before the effect shows up indicated a very complex mechanism instead of a simple molecular mechanism. The same conclusion was indicated by the fact that about one third of the patients did not respond to antidepressants at all. The placebo effect – known today to account for the full effect (8) of the antidepressant drugs – caused by the expectations to a treatment, indicated an important mental factor. Inheritance studies suggested that a certain amount of genetic transmission could not be excluded. Spontaneous remission was well known in patients with depression, but would not be likely in the case of a genetic programmed biochemical error. The periodical nature of manic depression (bipolar depression) was also difficult to connect to a genetic deficiency.

Today we know that psychotherapy is superior to drugs, and we know that the psychopharmacological drugs themselves are only giving positive effects though psychological mechanisms – the placebo effect.

The conclusion therefore is, that environmental factors are more important for the etiology of mental illness than genetic defects. As defect genes causing mental illness has never been found, the "early factor" seemingly important in the etiology of schizophrenia is more likely to be information-transmitting interactions between mother and child in and outside the womb. Inheritance studies showed that environmental factors played a decisive role in the etiology of schizophrenia. Early factors, such as genetic and/or intrauterine factors, were of minor importance. We hypothesize that information-transmitting interactions in utero and in early childhood were more important than genetic factors.

Studies of neuroleptics have shown a considerable placebo effect and a substantial group of non-responders, as is also the case in antidepressants. New generations of neuroleptics forced researchers around 1990 to reject the earlier assumption of schizophrenia was tied to the dopaminergic transmitter system. The long lapse of time before the effect manifest itself (7-30 days) corresponded badly with the time for the chemical effect (2 hours) or the time of adaptation at receptor level (a few days). Moreover, the episodic occurrence of schizophrenia makes it hard to maintain simple, molecular hypotheses for schizophrenia.

The positive and negative symptomatology seems to show, that schizophrenia covers a broad spectrum from "hypo" to "hyper" dopaminergic activity. Finally, neuroleptics assert their effect non-specifically against all psychoses, not only against schizophrenia.

All in all no evidence for any molecular hypothesis seems to have been found. On the contrary, there is clear evidence for the importance of environmentaland psychological factors.

Conclusions

We have the following final remarks after our review of the literature:

Neuroleptics: Almost hundred Cochrane metanalysis seems to have documented that psychotic mental illness in general are not causally associated with the DA-systems, or any other transmitter system. The time-elapse from ingestion of neuroleptics to the effect occurs indicates that simple interaction between drug and transmitter system is not a plausible explanation. According to the receptor hypothesis concerning the effect of neuroleptics the pharmacological effect is due to adaptation to drugs, but we believe this is wrong, because adaptation should lower the effect of the neuroleptics, not increase them. It is most likely that the effect of antipsychotic drugs on behaviour – in our analysis seen as the reduction of the autonomy, libido and life energy from the patient, thus pacifying him or her and depraving the patient his basic life, is due to simple poisoning by the drugs. The Cochrane studies have systematically documented that compared to placebo; not a single type of antipsychotic drug did improve the mental state neither for the schizophrenics nor for other patients.

Antidepressants: In 1990 the pharmacological effect of antidepressants was used as argumentation of a biochemical hypothesis for depression linked to serotonine. This interpretationcame into difficulties as the time delay of the clinical effect was seen as inertia in the adaptationto the drugs at the mental levels of the brain. A Cochrane study showed in 2004 that the most effective of the antidepressant drugs are not more effective than active placebo (8). Any hypothesis based on antidepressant drugs is therefore not substantiated.

Etiology of the mental diseases in general: Neither in the case of depression nor schizophrenia there seems to be evidence of genetic or molecular defects from the literature. Inheritance studies show a very important environmental factor, and a less important "early" factor, which may be due to genetic defects, but in our view far more likely, may be due to information transmitting interactions in the uterus.

The placebo effect seems to be what gives the effect of the psychopharmacological drugs; therefore it is hardly surprising that psychotherapy and holistic therapy has been found to be more effective than psychopharmacological drugs. We conclude that the mental diseases have an etiology based on psychosexual developmental factors, not genetics.

A psychosexual etiology of the mental diseases is in accordance with recent research and opens up for psychodynamic (11-13) and scientific holistic therapy as the rational cure for mental diseases (16-25,109-130) and psychoform pain (131-133). It might also explain the most interesting connection between the sense of coherence and disease (134-140).

References

[1] McGeer PL, Eccles JC, McGeer EG. Molecular neurobiology of the mammalian brain. New York: Plenum Press, 1987.

[2] Meltzer HY. Psychopharmacology. The third generation of progress. New York: Raven, 1987.

[3] Snyder SH. Molecular strategies in neuropsychopharmacologic research. In: Meltzer HY, ed. Psychopharmacology. The third generation of progress. New York: Raven, 1987.

[4] Elliot JM, Stephenson JD. Depression. In: Webster RA, Jordan CC, eds. Neurotransmitters, drugs and disease. Oxford: Blackwell, 1989.

[5] Webster RA, Jordan CC. Neurotransmitters, drugs and disease. Oxford: Blackwell, 1989.

[6] Gershon ES, Berrettini W, Nurnberger J, Goldin LR. Genetics and affective illness. In: Meltzer HY, ed. Psychopharmacology. The third generation of progress. New York: Raven, 1987.

[7] Brotman AW, Falk WE, Gelenberg AJ. Pharmacologic treatment of depressive subtypes. Psychiatr Med 1988;6(3):92-113.

[8] Moncrieff J, Wessely S, Hardy R. Active placebos versus antidepressants for depression. Cochrane Database Syst Rev. 2004;(1):CD003012.

[9] Williams JBW. A structured interview guide for the Hamilton Depression Rating Scale. Arch Gen Psychiatry 1988;45(8):742-7.

[10] Weissman MM, Jarrett RB, Rush AJ. Psychotherapy and its relevance to the pharmacotherapy of major depression: a decade later (1976-1985). In: Meltzer HY, ed. Psychopharmacology. The third generation of progress. New York: Raven, 1987.

[11] Leichsenring F, Rabung S, Leibing E. The efficacy of short-term psychodynamic psychotherapy in specific psychiatric disorders: a meta-analysis. Arch Gen Psychiatry 2004;61(12):1208-16

[12] Leichsenring F. Are psychodynamic and psychoanalytic therapies effective? A review of empirical data. Int J Psychoanal 2005;86(Pt 3):841-68

[13] Leichsenring F, Leibing E. Psychodynamic psychotherapy: a systematic review of techniques, indications and empirical evidence. Psychol Psychother 2007;80(Pt 2):217-28.

[14] Beck A. Cognitive therapy and the emotional disorders. New York: Int Univ Press, 1976.

[15] Beck A. Cognitive therapy of depression. London: Guildford, 1979.

[16] Ventegodt S, Kandel I, Merrick J. Clinical holistic medicine (mindful short-term psychodynamic psychotherapy complimented with bodywork) in the treatment of schizophrenia (ICD10-F20/DSM-IV Code 295) and other psychotic mental diseases. ScientificWorldJournal 2007;7:1987-2008.

[17] Ventegodt S, Kandel I, Merrick J. Clinical holistic medicine: how to recover memory without "implanting" memories in your patient. ScientificWorldJournal 2007;7:1579-89.

[18] Ventegodt S, Clausen B, Omar HA, Merrick J. Clinical holistic medicine: holistic sexology and acupressure through the vagina (Hippocratic pelvic massage). ScientificWorldJournal 2006;6:2066-79.

[19] Ventegodt S, Clausen B, Merrick J. Clinical holistic medicine: pilot study on the effect of vaginal acupressure (Hippocratic pelvic massage). ScientificWorldJournal 2006;6:2100-16.

[20] Ventegodt S, Clausen B, Merrick J. Clinical holistic medicine: the case story of Anna. III. Rehabilitation of philosophy of life during holistic existential therapy for childhood sexual abuse. ScientificWorldJournal 2006;6:2080-91.

[21] Ventegodt S, Thegler S, Andreasen T, Struve F, Enevoldsen L, Bassaine L, Torp M, Merrick J. Clinical holistic medicine (mindful, short-term psychodynamic psychotherapy complemented with bodywork) in the treatment of experienced impaired sexual functioning. ScientificWorldJournal 2007;7:324-9.

[22] Ventegodt S, Kandel I, Neikrug S, Merric J. Clinical holistic medicine: holistic treatment of rape and incest trauma. ScientificWorldJournal 2005;5:288-97.

[23] Ventegodt S, Morad M, Hyam E, Merrick J. Clinical holistic medicine: holistic sexology and treatment of vulvodynia through existential therapy and acceptance through touch. ScientificWorldJournal. 2004 Aug 4;4:571-80.

[24] Ventegodt S, Morad M, Kandel I, Merrick J. Clinical holistic medicine: problems in sex and living together. ScientificWorldJournal 2004;4:562-70.

[25] Ventegodt S, Morad M, Merrick J. Clinical holistic medicine: holistic pelvic examination and holistic treatment of infertility. ScientificWorldJournal 2004;4:148-58.

[26] Kendler KS. The genetics of schizophrenia: A current perspective. In: Meltzer HY, ed. Psychopharmacology. The third generation of progress. New York: Raven, 1987.

[27] Abhijnhan A, Adams CE, David A, Ozbilen M. Depot fluspirilene for schizophrenia. Cochrane Database Syst Rev 2007;(1):CD001718.

[28] Adams CE, Awad G, Rathbone J, Thornley B. Chlorpromazine versus placebo for schizophrenia. Cochrane Database Syst Rev 2007;(2):CD000284.

[29] Amato L, Minozzi S, Pani PP, Davoli M. Antipsychotic medications for cocaine dependence. Cochrane Database Syst Rev 2007;(3):CD006306.

[30] Arunpongpaisal S, Ahmed I, Aqeel N, Suchat P. Antipsychotic drug treatment for elderly people with late-onset schizophrenia. Cochrane Database Syst Rev 2003;(2):CD004162.

[31] Bagnall A, Lewis RA, Leitner ML. Ziprasidone for schizophrenia and severe mental illness. Cochrane Database Syst Rev 2000;(4):CD001945.

[32] Bagnall A, Fenton M, Kleijnen J, Lewis R. Molindone for schizophrenia and severe mental illness. Cochrane Database Syst Rev 2007;(1):CD002083.

[33] Ballard C, Waite J. The effectiveness of atypical antipsychotics for the treatment of aggression and psychosis in Alzheimer's disease. Cochrane Database Syst Rev 2006;(1):CD003476.

[34] Basan A, Leucht S. Valproate for schizophrenia. Cochrane Database Syst Rev 2004;(1):CD004028.

[35] Belgamwar RB, Fenton M. Olanzapine IM or velotab for acutely disturbed/agitated people with suspected serious mental illnesses. Cochrane Database Syst Rev 2005;(2):CD003729.

[36] Binks CA, Fenton M, McCarthy L, Lee T, Adams CE, Duggan C. Pharmacological interventions for people with borderline personality disorder. Cochrane Database Syst Rev 2006;(1):CD005653.

[37] Carpenter S, Berk M, Rathbone J. Clotiapine for acute psychotic illnesses. Cochrane Database Syst Rev 2004;(4):CD002304.

[38] Chakrabarti A, Bagnall A, Chue P, Fenton M, Palaniswamy V, Wong W, Xia J. Loxapine for schizophrenia. Cochrane Database Syst Rev 2007;(4):CD001943.

[39] Chua WL, de Izquierdo SA, Kulkarni J, Mortimer A. Estrogen for schizophrenia. Cochrane Database Syst Rev 2005;(4):CD004719.

[40] Coutinho E, Fenton M, Quraishi S. Zuclopenthixol decanoate for schizophrenia and other serious mental illnesses. Cochrane Database Syst Rev 2000;(2):CD001164.

[41] Cure S, Rathbone J, Carpenter S. Droperidol for acute psychosis. Cochrane Database Syst Rev 2004;(4):CD002830.

[42] David A, Adams CE, Eisenbruch M, Quraishi S, Rathbone J. Depot fluphenazine decanoate and enanthate for schizophrenia. Cochrane Database Syst Rev 2005;(1):CD000307.

[43] David A, Quraishi S, Rathbone J. Depot perphenazine decanoate and enanthate for schizophrenia. Cochrane Database Syst Rev 2005;(3):CD001717.

[44] DeSilva P, Fenton M, Rathbone J. Zotepine for schizophrenia. Cochrane Database Syst Rev 2006;(4):CD001948.

[45] Dinesh M, David A, Quraishi SN. Depot pipotiazine palmitate and undecylenate for schizophrenia. Cochrane Database Syst Rev 2004;(4):CD001720.

[46] Duggan L, Brylewski J. Antipsychotic medication versus placebo for people with both schizophrenia and learning disability. Cochrane Database Syst Rev 2004;(4):CD000030.

[47] Duggan L, Fenton M, Rathbone J, Dardennes R, El-Dosoky A, Indran S. Olanzapine for schizophrenia. Cochrane Database Syst Rev 2005;(2):CD001359.

[48] El-Sayeh HG, Morganti C. Aripiprazole for schizophrenia. Cochrane Database Syst Rev 2006;(2):CD004578.

[49] Elias A, Kumar A. Testosterone for schizophrenia. Cochrane Database Syst Rev 2007;(3):CD006197.

[50] Fenton M, Rathbone J, Reilly J, Sultana A. Thioridazine for schizophrenia. Cochrane Database Syst Rev 2007;(3):CD001944.

[51] Gibson RC, Fenton M, Coutinho ES, Campbell C. Zuclopenthixol acetate for acute schizophrenia and similar serious mental illnesses. Cochrane Database Syst Rev 2004;(3):CD000525.

[52] Gilbody SM, Bagnall AM, Duggan L, Tuunainen A. Risperidone versus other atypical antipsychotic medication for schizophrenia. Cochrane Database Syst Rev 2000;(3):CD002306.

[53] Gillies D, Beck A, McCloud A, Rathbone J, Gillies D. Benzodiazepines alone or in combination with antipsychotic drugs for acute psychosis. Cochrane Database Syst Rev 2005;(4):CD003079.

[54] Hartung B, Wada M, Laux G, Leucht S. Perphenazine for schizophrenia. Cochrane Database Syst Rev 2005;(1):CD003443.

[55] Hosalli P, Davis JM. Depot risperidone for schizophrenia. Cochrane Database Syst Rev 2003;(4):CD004161.

[56] Huf G, Alexander J, Allen MH. Haloperidol plus promethazine for psychosis induced aggression. Cochrane Database Syst Rev 2005;(1):CD005146.

[57] Hunter RH, Joy CB, Kennedy E, Gilbody SM, Song F. Risperidone versus typical antipsychotic medication for schizophrenia. Cochrane Database Syst Rev 2003;(2):CD000440.

[58] Jayaram MB, Hosalli P, Stroup S. Risperidone versus olanzapine for schizophrenia. Cochrane Database Syst Rev 2006;(2):CD005237.

[59] Jesner OS, Aref-Adib M, Coren E. Risperidone for autism spectrum disorder. Cochrane Database Syst Rev 2007;(1):CD005040.

[60] Joy CB, Adams CE, Rice K. Crisis intervention for people with severe mental illnesses. Cochrane Database Syst Rev 2006;(4):CD001087.

[61] Joy CB, Adams CE, Lawrie SM. Haloperidol versus placebo for schizophrenia. Cochrane Database Syst Rev 2006;(4):CD003082.

[62] Kennedy E, Kumar A, Datta SS. Antipsychotic medication for childhoodonset schizophrenia. Cochrane Database Syst Rev 2007;(3):CD004027.

[63] Kumar A, Strech D. Zuclopenthixol dihydrochloride for schizophrenia. Cochrane Database Syst Rev 2005;(4):CD005474.

[64] Leucht S, Hartung B. Benperidol for schizophrenia. Cochrane Database Syst Rev 2005;(2):CD003083.

[65] Leucht S, Hartung B. Perazine for schizophrenia. Cochrane Database Syst Rev 2006;(2):CD002832.

[66] Leucht S, Kissling W, McGrath J, White P. Carbamazepine for schizophrenia. Cochrane Database Syst Rev 2007;(3):CD001258.

[67] Leucht S, Kissling W, McGrath J. Lithium for schizophrenia. Cochrane Database Syst Rev 2007;(3):CD003834.

[68] Lewis R, Bagnall AM, Leitner M. Sertindole for schizophrenia. Cochrane Database Syst Rev 2005;(3):CD001715.

[69] Macritchie KA, Geddes JR, Scott J, Haslam DR, Goodwin GM. Valproic acid, valproate and divalproex in the maintenance treatment of bipolar disorder. Cochrane Database Syst Rev 2001;(3):CD003196.

[70] Macritchie K, Geddes JR, Scott J, Haslam D, de Lima M, Goodwin G. Valproate for acute mood episodes in bipolar disorder. Cochrane Database Syst Rev 2003;(1):CD004052.

[71] Marques LO, Lima MS, Soares BG. Trifluoperazine for schizophrenia. Cochrane Database Syst Rev 2004;(1):CD003545.

[72] Marriott RG, Neil W, Waddingham S. Antipsychotic medication for elderly people with schizophrenia. Cochrane Database Syst Rev 2006;(1):CD005580.

[73] Marshall M, Rathbone J. Early intervention for psychosis. Cochrane Database Syst Rev 2006;(4):CD004718.

[74] Matar HE, Almerie MQ. Oral fluphenazine versus placebo for schizophrenia. Cochrane Database Syst Rev 2007;(1):CD006352.

[75] Mota NE, Lima MS, Soares BG. Amisulpride for schizophrenia. Cochrane Database Syst Rev 2002;(2):CD001357.

[76] Nolte S, Wong D, Lachford G. Amphetamines for schizophrenia. Cochrane Database Syst Rev 2004;(4):CD004964.

[77] Pekkala E, Merinder L. Psychoeducation for schizophrenia. Cochrane Database Syst Rev 2002;(2):CD002831.

[78] Premkumar TS, Pick J. Lamotrigine for schizophrenia. Cochrane Database Syst Rev 2006;(4):CD005962.

[79]   Punnoose S, Belgamwar MR. Nicotine for schizophrenia. Cochrane Database Syst Rev 2006;(1):CD004838.

[80]   Quraishi S, David A. Depot flupenthixol decanoate for schizophrenia or other similar psychotic disorders. Cochrane Database Syst Rev 2000;(2):CD001470.

[81]   Quraishi S, David A. Depot haloperidol decanoate for schizophrenia. Cochrane Database Syst Rev 2000;(2):CD001361.

[82]   Rathbone J, McMonagle T. Pimozide for schizophrenia or related psychoses. Cochrane Database Syst Rev 2007;(3):CD001949.

[83]   Rendell JM, Gijsman HJ, Keck P, Goodwin GM, Geddes JR. Olanzapine alone or in combination for acute mania. Cochrane Database Syst Rev 2003;(3):CD004040.

[84]   Rendell JM, Gijsman HJ, Bauer MS, Goodwin GM, Geddes GR. Risperidone alone or in combination for acute mania. Cochrane Database Syst Rev 2006;(1):CD004043.

[85]   Rendell JM, Geddes JR. Risperidone in long-term treatment for bipolar disorder. Cochrane Database Syst Rev 2006;(4):CD004999.

[86]   Rummel C, Hamann J, Kissling W, Leucht S. New generation antipsychotics for first episode schizophrenia. Cochrane Database Syst Rev 2003;(4):CD004410.

[87]   Rummel C, Kissling W, Leucht S. Antidepressants for the negative symptoms of schizophrenia. Cochrane Database Syst Rev 2006;3:CD005581.

[88]   Soares BG, Fenton M, Chue P. Sulpiride for schizophrenia. Cochrane Database Syst Rev 2000;(2):CD001162.

[89]   Soares BG, Lima MS. Penfluridol for schizophrenia. Cochrane Database Syst Rev 2006;(2):CD002923.

[90]   Srisurapanont M, Kittiratanapaiboon P, Jarusuraisin N. Treatment for amphetamine psychosis. Cochrane Database Syst Rev 2001;(4):CD003026.

[91]   Srisurapanont M, Maneeton B, Maneeton N. Quetiapine for schizophrenia. Cochrane Database Syst Rev 2004;(2):CD000967.

[92]   Tharyan P, Adams CE. Electroconvulsive therapy for schizophrenia. Cochrane Database Syst Rev 2005;(2):CD000076.

[93]   Trevisani VF, Castro AA, Neves Neto JF, Atallah AN. Cyclophosphamide versus methylprednisolone for treating neuropsychiatric involvement in systemic lupus erythematosus. Cochrane Database Syst Rev 2006;(2):CD002265.

[94]   Tuominen HJ, Tiihonen J, Wahlbeck K. Glutamatergic drugs for schizophrenia. Cochrane Database Syst Rev 2006;(2):CD003730.

[95]   Tuunainen A, Wahlbeck K, Gilbody SM. Newer atypical antipsychotic medication versus clozapine for schizophrenia. Cochrane Database Syst Rev 2000;(2):CD000966.

[96]   Volz A, Khorsand V, Gillies D, Leucht S. Benzodiazepines for schizophrenia. Cochrane Database Syst Rev 2007;(1):CD006391.

[97]   Wahlbeck K, Cheine M, Essali MA. Clozapine versus typical neuroleptic medication for schizophrenia. Cochrane Database Syst Rev 2000;(2):CD000059.

[98]   Waraich PS, Adams CE, Roque M, Hamill KM, Marti J. Haloperidol dose for the acute phase of schizophrenia. Cochrane Database Syst Rev 2002;(3):CD001951.

[99]   Webb RT, Howard L, Abel KM. Antipsychotic drugs for non-affective psychosis during pregnancy and postpartum. Cochrane Database Syst Rev 2004;(2):CD004411.

[100] Whitehead C, Moss S, Cardno A, Lewis G. Antidepressants for people with both schizophrenia and depression. Cochrane Database Syst Rev 2002;(2):CD002305.

[101] Wijkstra J, Lijmer J, Balk F, Geddes J, Nolen WA. Pharmacological treatment for psychotic depression. Cochrane Database Syst Rev 2005;(4):CD004044.

[102] Wong D, Adams CE, David A, Quraishi SN. Depot bromperidol decanoate for schizophrenia. Cochrane Database Syst Rev 2004;(3):CD001719.

[103] Young AH, Geddes JR, Macritchie K, Rao SN, Vasudev A. Tiagabine in the maintenance treatment of bipolar disorders. Cochrane Database Syst Rev 2006;3:CD005173.

[104] Losonczy MF, Davidson M, Davis KL. The dopamine hypothesis of schizophrenia. In: Meltzer HY, ed. Psychopharmacology. The third generation of progress. New York: Raven, 1987.

[105] Tamminga CA, Gerlach J. New neuroleptics and experimental antipsychotics in schizophrenia. In: Meltzer HY, ed. Psychopharmacology. The third generation of progress. New York: Raven, 1987.

[106] Hollister LE. Novel drug treatments for schizophrenia. Psychopharmacol Bull 1987;23(1):82-4.

[107] Blackwell B. Newer antidepressant drugs. In: Meltzer HY, ed. Psychopharmacology. The third generation of progress. New York: Raven, 1987.

[108] Falk JL, Feingold DA. Environmental and cultural factors in the behavioural action of drugs. In: Meltzer HY, ed. Psychopharmacology. The third generation of progress. New York: Raven, 1987.

[109] Ventegodt S, Flensborg-Madsen T, Andersen NJ, Nielsen M, Mohammed M, Merrick J. Global quality of life (QOL), health and ability are primarily determined by our consciousness. Research findings from Denmark 1991-2004. Soc Indicator Res 2005;71:87-122.

[110] Ventegodt S, Merrick J. Clinical holistic medicine: Applied consciousness-based medicine. ScientificWorldJournal 2004;4:96-9.

[111] Ventegodt S, Morad M, Andersen NJ, Merrick J. Clinical holistic medicine Tools for a medical science based on consciousness. ScientificWorldJournal 2004;4:347-61.

[112] Ventegodt S, Morad M, Kandel I, Merrick J. Clinical holistic medicine: a psychological theory of dependency to improve quality of life. ScientificWorldJournal 2004;4:638-48.

[113] Ventegodt S, Kandel I, Neikrug S, Merrick J. Clinical holistic medicine: Holistic treatment of rape and incest traumas. ScientificWorldJournal 2005;5:288-97.

[114] Ventegodt S, Kandel I, Neikrug S, Merrick J. Clinical holistic medicine: The existential crisis – life crisis, stress and burnout. ScientificWorldJournal 2005;5:300-12.

[115] Ventegodt S, Gringols G, Merrick J. Clinical holistic medicine: Holistic rehabilitation. ScientificWorldJournal 2005;5:280-7.

[116] Ventegodt S, Andersen NJ, Neikrug S, Kandel I, Merrick J. Clinical holistic medicine: Mental disorders in a holistic perspective. ScientificWorldJournal 2005;5:313-23.

[117] Ventegodt S, Andersen NJ, Neikrug S, Kandel I, Merrick J. Clinical holistic medicine: Holistic treatment of mental disorders. ScientificWorldJournal 2005;5:427-45.

[118] Ventegodt S, Merrick J. Clinical holistic medicine: The patient with multiple diseases ScientificWorldJournal 2005;5:324-39.

[119] Ventegodt S, Clausen B, Nielsen ML, Merrick J. Clinical holistic medicine: Advanced tools for holistic medicine. ScientificWorldJournal 2006;6:2048-65.

[120] Ventegodt S, Clausen B, Merrick J. Clinical holistic medicine: The case story of Anna: I. Long term effect of child sexual abuse and incest with a treatment approach. ScientificWorldJournal 2006;6:1965-76.

[121] Ventegodt S, Clausen B, Merrick J. Clinical holistic medicine: the case story of Anna. II. Patient diary as a tool in treatment. ScientificWorldJournal 2006;6:2006-34.

[122] Ventegodt S, Clausen B, Merrick J. Clinical holistic medicine: The case story of Anna. III. Rehabilitation of philosophy of life during holistic existential therapy for childhood sexual abuse. ScientificWorldJournal 2006;6:2080-91.

[123] Ventegodt S, Merrick J. Suicide from a holistic point of view. ScientificWorldJournal 2005;5:759-66.

[124] Ventegodt S, Clausen B, Omar HA, Merrick J. Clinical holistic medicine: Holistic sexology and acupressure through the vagina (Hippocratic pelvic massage). ScientificWorldJournal 2006;6:2066-79.

[125] Ventegodt S, Clausen B, Merrick J. Clinical holistic medicine: Pilot study on the effect of vaginal acupressure (Hippocratic pelvic massage). ScientificWorldJournal 2006;6:2100-16.

[126] Ventegodt S, Thegler S, Andreasen T, Struve F, Enevoldsen L, et al. Clinical holistic medicine: Psychodynamic short-time therapy complemented with bodywork. A clinical follow-up study of 109 patients. ScientificWorldJournal 2006;6:2220-38.

[127] Ventegodt S, Thegler S, Andreasen T, Struve F, Enevoldsen L, et al. Clinical holistic medicine (mindful, short-term psychodynamic psychotherapy complemented with bodywork) in the treatment of experienced impaired sexual functioning. ScientificWorldJournal 2007;7: 324-9.

[128] Ventegodt S, Thegler S, Andreasen T, Struve F, Enevoldsen L, et al. Clinical holistic medicine (mindful, short-term psychodynamic psychotherapy complemented with bodywork) improves quality of life, health, and ability by induction of Antonovsky-salutogenesis. ScientificWorldJournal 2007;7:317-23.

[129] Ventegodt S, Thegler S, Andreasen T, Struve F, Enevoldsen L, et al. Clinical holistic medicine (mindful, short-term psychodynamic psychotherapy complemented with bodywork) in the treatment of experienced mental illness. ScientificWorldJournal 2007;7:306-9.

[130] Ventegodt S, Thegler S, Andreasen T, Struve F, Enevoldsen L, et al. Self-reported low self-esteem. Intervention and follow-up in a clinical setting. ScientificWorldJournal 2007;7:299-305.

[131] Ventegodt S, Merrick J. Clinical holistic medicine: Chronic pain in the locomotor system. ScientificWorldJournal 2005;5:165-72.

[132] Ventegodt S, Merrick J. Clinical holistic medicine: Chronic pain in internal organs. ScientificWorldJournal 2005;5:205-10.

[133] Ventegodt S, Thegler S, Andreasen T, Struve F, Enevoldsen L, et al. Clinical holistic medicine (mindful, short-term psychodynamic psychotherapy complemented with bodywork) in the treatment of experienced physical illness and chronic pain. ScientificWorldJournal 2007;7:310-6.

[134] Flensborg-Madsen T, Ventegodt S, Merrick J. Sense of coherence and physical health. A review of previous findings. ScientificWorldJournal 2005;5:665-73.

[135] Flensborg-Madsen T, Ventegodt S, Merrick J. Why is Antonovsky's sense of coherence not correlated to physical health? Analysing Antonovsky's 29-item sense of coherence scale (SOCS). ScientificWorldJournal 2005;5:767-76.

[136] Flensborg-Madsen T, Ventegodt S, Merrick J. Sense of coherence and health. The construction of an amendment to Antonovsky's sense of coherence scale (SOC II). ScientificWorldJournal 2006;6:2133-9.

[137] Flensborg-Madsen T, Ventegodt S, Merrick J. Sense of coherence and physical health. A cross-sectional study using a new SOC scale (SOC II). ScientificWorldJournal 2006;6:2200-11.

[138] Flensborg-Madsen T, Ventegodt S, Merrick J. Sense of coherence and physical health. Testing Antonovsky's theory. ScientificWorldJournal 2006;6:2212-9.

[139] Flensborg-Madsen T, Ventegodt S, Merrick J. Sense of coherence and health. The emotional sense of coherence (SOC-E) was found to be the best-known predictor of physical health. ScientificWorldJournal 2006;6: 2147-57.

[140] Ventegodt S, Flensborg-Madsen T, Andersen NJ, Merrick J. Life Mission Theory VII: Theory of existential (Antonovsky) coherence: a theory of quality of life, health and ability for use in holistic medicine. ScientificWorldJournal 2005;5:377-89.

Chapter 6

Use of coercive persuasion ("brainwashing", "mind control") in psychiatry from an ethical point of view

One of the major reasons for many patients to shift from biomedical to holistic medicine is traumatic experiences of violence and coercion in psychiatry. The patients often complain that they feel the physicians used more force than necessary. Especially they felt that their psychiatrist tried to persuade them to take drugs they did not believe would help them. They also felt that the psychiatric theories were imposed on them, to examine if the complains were in any way substantiated we made an analysis of coercive persuasion in psychiatry, based on the literature. We did not have to read much to conclude that coercion is actually every day practice in psychiatry. The question is if the use of force is necessary or if the Hippocratic principle of *Primum non nocere* is violated.

Coercive persuasion, 50 years ago called "brainwashing", "mind control" and "thought reform" has recently been recommended by some psychiatrists as an efficient psychiatric tool, which is often not felt as coercion by the patients. The intensive use of antipsychotic drugs, which in Cochrane metaanalyses has been shown to reduce hallucinatory behavior without improving the patient's mental state significantly, seems to facilitate coercive persuasion; it reduces patient resistance and autonomy by sedating him or her into a passive, cooperative, weak, and obedient state. Lifton found eight criteria or themes for coercive persuasion and when we compare these to modern biomedical psychiatry we find astonishing similarities. The patients must accept the "sacred psychiatric science", an imposed "categorical" psychiatric diagnosis as a personal fault, and must obey and comply with the "treatment": taking the prescribed, often sedative drugs, staying in hospital until behavior is normalized.

Biomedical psychiatry has long been criticized for reducing its patients to "zombies" or robots, and about 2% of patients commit suicide or attempt to do so shortly after the initiation of psychiatric treatment. It is alarming that both the process and the outcome of biomedical, psychiatric treatment share unmistakable similarities with brainwashing. In conclusion, coercive persuasion that harm patient integrity and autonomy, decreases the feeling of meaning of life, sense of coherence, and quality of life, can explain the pattern of damage often inflicted by psychiatric treatment and we would like to question the ethical aspects of such a treatment.

Introduction

Coercion is still common practice in psychiatry (1-3), in spite of a growing awareness of the inflicted harm (4). Of the many different forms of coercion, coercive persuasion seems to be the only form that is generally accepted and even recommended among psychiatrists, with the argument that "positive symbolic pressures, such as persuasion, do not induce perceptions of coercion and such positive pressures should be tried in order to encourage admission before force or negative pressures are used" (5).

If you think about it, this is extremely worrisome: Coercive persuasion – what was called "brainwash", "mind-control" and "though-reform" 50 years ago - is not felt like coercion at all. This means that if you are coercively persuaded, you are not even likely to be able to observe it. This makes coercive persuasion, which can change patient's attitudes, preferences and loyalties – that is why it is used of course - an extremely strong measure, as the patient cannot really resist it. Therefore coercive persuasion is likely to be much more harmful than open and visible use of coercion, which you can resist and distance yourself from. Coercive persuasion is, when it makes you change and degrades your personal philosophy of life, like an invisible poison that stays in your flesh and bones forever. You might have a feeling that you picked up something that was very bad for you, but you can't know what it was, or where you picked it up, so you can't get rid of it.

As our consciousness is the primary source of everything we do and are, including our health, quality of life, and ability in general (6), we are extremely vulnerable to influences and manipulations that shifts our consciousness away from what could be called our "natural philosophy", our inner account of who we really are what we really want from life, into an alienated philosophy of life. Large shifts in people's philosophy of life can happen in accidents where traumas give strong, emotionally charged, negative learning (7,8).

The question is how easy it is for other people to impose such a major shift in our consciousness, if they want to use us for their own purposes. We know that commercials are exactly about that. You cannot avoid looking, and then you are sold, but then again, not completely. This is on a small scale, and the coercion is subtle – you want to be fancy, so you buy fancy clothes.

But what if you are a parent and you persuade your child? We all know that this is easy. What if you are a physician who wants to stop a mentally ill patient from creating problems for him and others, how easily could you "thought-reform" this patient, and change his behavior by coercive persuasion?

We all know, as we have tried to persuade other people many times, that most people do not voluntarily let go of their autonomy and personal favorite philosophy of life, attitudes and values; the shift in consciousness takes a yield, and the external pressure causing it needs sometimes to be extreme. But at other times, the person's consciousness is very moldable, especially if the person is in serous trouble and has confidence in our good intentions and us. And if you are the doctor, and the patient's life depends on you, the power-relation is similar to the parent-child relation, and modifying the patient's consciousness is really easy.

The main characteristic of an intended shift, and the reason that it has been called "coercive persuasion", "brainwashing", "mind control", "thought reform" is that it fundamentally violates the victims autonomy, and thereby destroys quality of life, as quality of life is the realization of self (9-12). Brainwashing is thus the complete opposite of existential therapy that aims in freeing the person, rehabilitating autonomy, and improving quality of life and health (13,14). In clinical holistic medicine (14-16) this is done by rehabilitating the patient's character, life mission and natural philosophy of life (17-19).

Most interestingly, existential therapy will also deliberately implant philosophy of life in the patient, but this is done after consent – not that this means too much if the patient is severely ill and will consent to anything the physician suggests - but the philosophy is a positive, life-supporting philosophy, implanted as a part of the therapeutic contract, and meant for later de-learning, when the patient reaches his final destination of autonomy and self-insight (14).

From a psychodynamic perspective we know that coercive persuasion this is an obligatory part of every harsh childrearing practice (20-25), as the child being relative powerless constantly must yields to and obeys its parents; in spite of this often being highly traumatic this seems to be generally accepted in our culture. When the person is an autonomous adult we find coercive persuasion in principle unethical, especially if the inflicted harm is obvious, unless the person is criminal or insane.

Most interesting unethical, coercive persuasion have mostly been associated with religious leaders of sects and cults (26-28) and political totalism especially in Russia and China (28-30), while the traumas and harm from coercive persuasion inside the modern western societies, especially towards the criminals and the insane have been almost ignored in research.

The harm caused by coercive persuasion is alienation and loss of autonomy; the symptoms of this is a reduction of the person to a more primitive being, or if taken further to an unconscious zombie-like being with little free will and initiative, and severe problems related to meaning of life (31) and sense of coherence (32). The most severe cases of brainwashing has systematically been seen to lead to suicide in cults, although other courses might exist (33-35); coercive tools have been sedating drugs, physical, and mental restrains.

This paper addresses the well known theme of coercive persuasion in psychiatry (1-4,36); another paper will address the unnecessary violation of suspected criminals that often harm these in principle still innocent people, just to make everything worse. Our intent with the present analysis is not to give suggestion on how to solve the problems of crime and insanity from the societial point of view, one possibility of cause being the elimination of the burdening person by coercive persuasion, another more constructive than healing and development of him or her.

We just want to make everybody professionally involved in patients and criminals more aware of the serious ethical problems of coercive persuasion, which can be extremely harmful to the vulnerable existence and vital autonomy of a human being. We want to prevent professionals victimizing the already vulnerable, disturbed person. Mentally ill patients have in general few resources, a poor social network, and low self-esteem, making them especially vulnerable to coercive persuasion.

Drugs and coercion in psychiatry

In Denmark the annual use of antipsychotic drugs corresponds to 6% of the population – about 300.000 patients - taking such drugs every day, with another 6% taking antidepressive drugs. The prize of the antipsychotic and the antidepressive drugs in 2007 were 122 million EURO and 106 million EURO respectively, accounting for 14% if the national turnover on drugs (37).

The massive use of drugs in psychiatry happens in spite of recent scientific metaanalysis have documented, that these two large groups of drugs in principle are of questionable therapeutic value. The antidepressive drugs are active placebos (38), giving the patients adverse effects that make them believe that he or she gets help, while they are actually harmed by the adverse effects of the drugs. The antipsychotic drugs have in Cochrane metanalysis and similar studies been shown to have no effect at all on the mental health; they seems only to pacify, and this effect is likely to be a consequence of chronic poisoning by the drugs (39).

Most interestingly the drugs pacify the patients and makes it difficult not to "cooperate" (NNT=4 for "cooperativeness"); in an authoritarian, coercive system "cooperation" is exactly the same as "obedience", so the documented effect seems to be a documentation of the antipsychotic drugs efficiency in facilitating the coercive persuasion. Psychiatric treatment with the antipsychotic drugs have been criticized for reducing the patients to "zombies" (40) and to a very disturbing degree it has been documented that suicide among mentally ill patients occurs very often and this is statistically related to intensive psychiatric treatment and hospitalization (41).

Taken all together this looks like psychiatry uses coercive persuasion as its primary tool, facilitated by the drugs and other techniques like electroshock (42,43); the use of coercion might explain why biomedical psychiatry in general does not improve mental health (39).

Theories of coercive persuasion

Brainwashing has often been a legal issue both in the United States and Europe (26,27), but a surprisingly limited number of scientific theories of brainwashing and coercive persuasion could be found in a combined Pubmed/MedLine and PsycINFO search, in spite of 300 references, and most of the proposed theories have been seriously disputed. The most acknowledged research in brainwashing is probably done by Lifton (28,30), who studied brainwashing in China and found eight central conditions or "themes" for brainwashing (see 44):

1. Sacred science. The group's doctrine or ideology is considered to be the ultimate truth, beyond all questioning or dispute. Truth is not to be found outside the group. The leader is above criticism.
2. Doctrine over person. Member's personal experiences are subordinated to the sacred science and any contrary experiences must be denied or reinterpreted to fit the ideology of the group.

3. Loading the language. The group interprets or uses words and phrases in new ways so that often the outside world does not understand. This jargon consists of thought-terminating clichés, which serve to alter members' thought processes to conform to the group's way of thinking.
4. Milieu control. This involves the control of information and communication both within the environment and, ultimately, within the individual, resulting in a significant degree of isolation from society at large.
5. Demand for purity. The world is viewed as black and white and the members are constantly exhorted to conform to the ideology of the group. The induction of guilt and/or shame is a powerful control device used here.
6. Confession. Sins, as defined by the group, are to be confessed either to a personal monitor or publicly to the group. There is no confidentiality; members' "sins," "attitudes," and "faults" are discussed and exploited by the leaders.
7. Dispensing of existence. The group has the prerogative to decide who has the right to exist and who does not. This is usually not literal but means that those in the outside world are not saved, unenlightened, unconscious and they must be converted to the group's ideology. If they do not join the group or are critical of the group, then the members must reject them. Thus, the outside world loses all credibility.
8. Mystical manipulation. There is manipulation of experiences that appear spontaneous but in fact were planned and orchestrated by the group or its leaders in order to demonstrate divine authority.

Hassan (45) developed this further into his BITE model with some of the major criteria for brainwashing listed below:

1. Behavior control
    a. Need to ask permission for major decisions
    b. Need to report thoughts, feelings, and activities to superiors
    c. Rewards and punishments (behavior modification techniques positive and negative)
    d. Individualism discouraged; "group think" prevails
    e. Rigid rules and regulations
    f. Need for obedience and dependency

2. Information control
    g. Use of deception
    h. Access to non cult sources of information minimized or discouraged
    i. Compartmentalization of information; Outsider vs. Insider doctrines
    j. Extensive use of cult generated information and propaganda

3. Thought control
    k. Need to internalize the group's doctrine as "Truth"
    l. Use of "loaded" language (for example, "thought terminating clichés").
    m. Only "good" and "proper" thoughts are encouraged.
    n. Manipulation of memories and implantation of false memories

o.   Rejection of rational analysis, critical thinking, constructive criticism. No critical questions about leader, doctrine, or policy seen as legitimate.

p.   No alternative belief systems viewed as legitimate, good, or useful

4.   Emotional control

q.   Manipulate and narrow the range of a person's feelings

r.   Make the person feel that if there are ever any problems, it is always their fault, never the leader's or the group's

s.   Phobia indoctrination: inculcating irrational fears about ever leaving the group or even questioning the leader's authority. The person under mind control cannot visualize a positive, fulfilled future without being in the group.

A researcher who defined coercive persuasion as "psychotechnology, which can involuntarily transform beliefs and loyalties", have stressed *deception* and *seductive pseudosolidarity* as standard elements in brainwashing (26).

The process of brainwashing "is fostered through the creation of a controlled environment that heightens the susceptibility of a subject to suggestion and manipulation through … cognitive dissonance, peer pressure and a clear assertion of authority and dominion. The aftermath of brainwashing is a severe impairment of autonomy and of the ability to think independently which induced a subjects unyielding compliance and the rupture of past connections, affiliations and associations" [Peterson v. Sorlien 1980, quoted in 26]. A physical threat intensifies the coercion (26). Brainwashing leads to "feeling of guilt, dependency, low self-esteem, worthlessness, anxiety and hopelessness in vulnerable individuals" (43), severe reduction of autonomy, and in the most extreme cases, suicide (26,27,33,34). Other researchers have found a triad in brainwashing of "deception, dependency, dread" (46).

A simple way of understanding brainwash is the three-step-process of: 1) gaining control of the victim's time, activities, and mental life; 2) placing the victim in a position of powerlessness; and 3) suppressing the victim's former identity (47).

If you think about it, this is to a large extent what every school child is exposed to every day and to a much smaller extent, what every employee to some extent must accept (25). So coercive persuasion is not something mystical and strange; it is our practical reality as human beings. Luckily most of us are not very vulnerable and very receptive for brainwash; as soon as the pressure goes and we get resources for healing, we return to our natural identity and philosophy (7). The fraction of people who are vulnerable are the people who did not get sufficient love and support during childhood from their parents, or maybe even were physically or sexually abused. Most unfortunately this is exactly the group of people that often becomes our mentally ill patients. Coercive persuasion therefore becomes extremely problematic with these people.

In conclusion coercive persuasion can inflict serious harm and turn people into chronic patients; it must be mentioned that there are few regular scientific studies documenting this and the negative effects of coercive persuasion have therefore been disputed in relation to a number of lawsuits (48-50).

Coercive persuasion in psychiatry

Schein (51) found in 1962 remarkable similarities between brainwash in totalitarian regimes and treatment in mental institutions. Independent of the scientific scheme of coercive persuasion used it was easy to find large similarities to the situation that a mentally ill patient finds himself in, coming to the psychiatrist, and the brainwashed member of a authoritarian state of cult:

1. Sacred science. Only psychiatrists understand the patient's mental illnesses and the diagnosis and treatments, or the science behind it or rationally and applicability of the treatments cannot be disputed. The patient must surrender fully to the psychiatric authority, accept the diagnoses as truth, and comply obediently with the prescribed treatment that most often is drugs.
2. Doctrine over person. The patient's personal experiences are subordinated to the sacred science and any contrary experiences must be denied or reinterpreted to fit the psychiatric science.
3. Loading the language. The group interprets or uses words and phrases in new ways so that often the outside world does not understand. This jargon consists of thought-terminating clichés; the acceptance of "disturbed brain chemistry causing the mental disease" to be "compensated by the drugs" (the dopamine hypothesis) is such a cliché, often used but obviously falsified by the facts that antipsychotics do not improve mental health [39].
4. Milieu control. The mental institution is often very restrictive when it comes to communication outside, and physical restrictions are normal; medication by force is a complete control of the patient's inner, biochemical milieu.
5. Demand for purity. The patient is told to control unwanted "hallucinogenic" behavior, like conflicts, aggression, critique, blame, justifications, theorizations etc. Such expressions of the patient's autonomy are considered impure.
6. Confession. The "group therapy" often used (comp. Jack Nicholson's famous appearance in the sharing-circle in the movie "One flew over the Cuckoo's Nest"(52)) in this way breaking down patient's integrity and autonomy; patients' mental diseases are discussed and exploited by the leaders.
7. Dispensing of existence. The psychiatrists have the prerogative to decide who has the right to exist and who does not; other therapists are unenlightened, inefficient and harmful. Healing and help from the outside world loses all credibility.
8. Mystical manipulation. The psychiatric environment is highly structured, and the patient has no possibility for understanding how his or her experience is manipulated.

Hassan's criteria (45) listed above are almost all met in contemporary biomedical psychiatric standard treatment with antipsychotic drugs. Thus the critique raised more than 40 years ago seems still valid. When it comes to "psychotechnology, which can involuntarily transform beliefs and loyalties", *deception* and *"seductive pseudosolidarity"* seems also to be present in psychiatry; the psychiatrist pretends to be the patient's good doctor with the intention of healing the patient, but he knows very well that there is not cure. The true nature, purpose and function of the psychiatric institution are hidden for the newcomer; the highly structured environment catches the patient and absorbs him or her.

Biomedical psychiatry is deceptive in that the institution, the drugs etc. all are named after helping and curing the patient, i.e. "mental hospital", "antipsychotic drugs", but the drugs does not at all improve the patients mental health and the patient is not at all cured at the "hospital", but just drugged down into convenient passivity and obedience (39). Thus the patient is giving convent to the treatment in the expectation to get help, but this help will never come as it is not possible to cure any disease or improve mental health with the drugs; the essential purpose of the mental institution is thus not to cure the mentally ill – as is evident after all statistics - but to rid society for its burden of difficult, unfit, and troublesome people. An interesting question is if it really is legal to "deceiving [people] into subjecting themselves, without their knowledge or consent, to coercive persuasion" (26).

Deep existential problems follows often from accepting the categorical, psychiatric diagnosis, which in itself leads to marginalized in all social and societal aspects. The patient is facing the "fact" that the incurable and chronic mental disease never will allow success at work or in education. The patient is there by effectively excluded from ever being of any substantial value to the surrounding world; he or she will never get a normal life. The meaning of life and the sense of coherence are sadly lost, and suicide is in this situation can be a fairly rational decision (35) from the patient's new perspective planted by coercive persuasion. The suicidal intend is often noticed, as this is a part of the standard procedure, and the coercive prevention of suicide, which philosophically is depriving the patient the last remains of autonomy, leads to a final repressed state of complete resignation and pacification, and this is the state of the "zombie" or robot, as already Hunter said (53,54): A person deprived of all will to live and even all will to die; with no hope, no joy, and no autonomy left.

The analysis of psychiatry as coercive persuasion looks surprisingly accurate, and this calls for a number of questions: What is really going on here? Why are the patients accepting the psychiatric diagnosis, and the drugs, in spite of the drugs have been proven not to improve mental health at all and being highly poisonous and sedating? Why are psychiatrists not behaving rationally, and stopping the combined use of drugs and coercive persuasion, when it is now clear that it is not at all based on scientific evidence? Why are the national health authorities accepting such a malpractice that seems to severely harm thousands of mentally ill patients, especially when there are so many successful alternative treatments (55-57)? Somehow the authorities, the psychiatrist and the patients all together have become fixed in the belief, that the drugs helps and is the correct treatment, and that the categorical diagnosis are the final truth about the patent, in spite of science telling us the complete opposite, but how come?

Coercive persuasion as weapon

Coercive persuasion has often been used in war (58-61). On a smaller scale, it has been used in the "war" between pharmaceutical industry - including on its side many biomedical psychiatrist- and the CAM-therapists (62). Psychiatrists have according to this book often accused CAM-therapists of harming the patients, an often used testimonial from former

CAM-patients, that later came into psychiatric treatment; vice versa have CAM-therapist often quoted patients who had ETC or antipsychotic drugs for statements about these treatments as severely destructive and ruining the patient's whole life. A vulnerable patient takes the role of a child in relation to his or her doctor, and this always opens op to the possibility of coercive persuasion; the patient can thus be made to think and say almost anything by her former therapist or physician. In such cases the only rationale thing is to look at the facts (34) of what happened, what was the outcome of the therapy? Did the therapy make the patient better with regards to quality of life, selfassessed physical or mental health, self-esteem etc? Was the patient general abilities reduced during treatment? Was the patient hospitalized during the treatment? Was emotional withdrawal cured or intensified? Was libido and sexual relations opened op, or closed down? Were there any suicide attempts, or death wishes? Was the relation with the outer world improved during treatment or did the patient become more isolated?

All these subjective and objective factors related to autonomy, empowering, meaning of life, and sense of coherence, feeling of guilt, dependency, low self-esteem, worthlessness, anxiety and hopelessness, social isolation, and suicide must be analyzed to see the whole picture, and answer the difficult question: Was this constructive therapy or destructive, coercive persuasion.

A most difficult issue is the issue of consent and free will. A mentally ill patient needs care, and is dependent; free will is thus reduced, and consent must be seen in this light. If a patient gives consent to psychiatric treatment, in a mental state where he or she feels very bad, this is not really a valid consent. Such consent is important not to violate the patient's feeling of autonomy, but the consent have little meaning in its philosophical sense as the illness puts a strong force on the patient; we therefore need to monitor the process and the outcome of every treatment very carefully to be sure to help and not harm a vulnerable, ill patient. Luckily this is easily done with a small questionnaire on quality of life (62). Every patient needs to fill in such a questionnaire before treatment is initiated; if the patient is not able to do so, the quality of life questionnaire should still be rated by an external observer (63) and corrected by the patient when he or she is able to do so.

An important ethical obligation we have as therapist in this turbulent time is not to use the patients as weapons in our internal combats; in the end all coercive persuasion will harm our vulnerable patients.

Discussion

Coercive persuasion, or "brain washing", is possible if somebody is in a weak and vulnerable relation to another more powerful person, similar to that of a small child with its parents. The powerless position is often the one mentally ill patients have in relation with their psychiatrist; it is so tempting to put all hope of salvation and cure into a relation with an authoritarian doctor, who seems to know everything and promise to help. Most unfortunately, the biomedical psychiatrist believes in the dopamine hypothesis, and therefore also in the antipsychotic drugs, but these drugs does not improve mental health according to the statistics (38); when a physician believes in the drugs he does not have the intent of curing the patient himself, and thus he will not provide the resources needed for recovery and spontaneous healing (7). His biochemical understanding of life, brain and mental diseases and consciousness does not allow this either. The psychiatrist carries instead the intention of fitting the patient into society; he wants to help the patient to assume a role that is non-destructive and un-problematic, and the only role that is possible is as chronically mental patient, with the conflict-causing, hallucinatory behavior pacified by antipsychotic drugs.

The coercive psychiatrist is empowered by society to use force to make the patient behave normally; in the patient's experience this is often a battle where the patient fights for his autonomy but looses; the psychiatrist ends up destroying the patient existentially, but he does this to serve society and find himself in good intent, while the patient often see him as an enemy.

A strong belief in tradition, and what seem to be obsolete, biochemical hypothesis of mental illnesses, makes it difficult for psychiatrists to disregard all the new scientific studies, including the many large Cochrane analysis, that have shown that the patients' mental state – the measured mental health – is not improved by the drugs. New studies have also documented very embarrassing data on the adverse effects, suicide and spontaneous death from the drugs (40,64). As long as the psychiatrist simply stick to the belief that mental illness is a genetically inherited brain-defect that only can be compensated by antipsychotic drugs, he simply will be in denial, when it comes to the urgent needs of reforms; and in this denial he will not consider other therapeutic methods.

It is an interesting idea that the reason for the psychiatrists insisting on using the "antipsychotic", sedative drugs is coercive persuasion during his medical training. Only if these ideas and theories were accepted, he could become the physician he wanted to be; this "coercive learning" could be called "professional deformation". Generations of physicians have thus been brainwashed to believe in biochemistry as the final answer to the mysteries of life, and the dopamine hypothesis as the final answer to the mystery of psychotic mental illnesses; so when new science shows that the dopamine hypothesis is not likely at all, he simply sticks to it anyway. The lack of openness to new ideas and the strong irrational conservatism that we see here could very well be another symptom of coercive persuasion.

About 5% of the western population is on antipsychotic drugs, making this one of the largest pharmaceutical industries in the world. The industry uses billions of Euros and dollars on highly biased, randomized clinical studies (38) and all these studies are made by doctors getting payment, prestige, and important degrees from their involvement. The medico-industrial complex is highly integrated in society, and the industry is returning so much of the money it makes to the doctors that this can fairly be compared to bribe. But it is done in smart ways so nobody can officially blame the doctors; and often the doctors do not even them self realize that they are being manipulated.

The politicians need psychiatry to take care of the mentally ill, to get quiet and stable, productive societies; and a successful pharmaceutical industry also bring wealth to the nation. The fact seems to be that millions of patients, who believe that psychiatry helps them, are little by little reduced to zombies by mental and chemical repression. The patients are in reality loosing their life and whole existence due to drug-facilitated, coercive persuasion; but when it comes down to it nobody really cares about the mentally ill.

Conclusions

Coercive persuasion, or brainwash, as it is known from war and totalism (29) seems to be the normal practice of western psychiatry of today; it is strongly facilitated by the sedative and highly poisonous, "antipsychotic" drugs that have been shown not to improve mental health in a number of recent Cochrane metaanalyses. After the patient is tricked to believe that psychiatry is about healing the mentally ill, which most unfortunately is not the case in biomedical psychiatry, as patients are not healed, the tool of coercive persuasion is used to repress and pacify the patient into the convenient role of a chronic, mentally ill patient.

Most unfortunately the psychiatrists of today have completely lost contact with scientific reality and have drifted away in obsolete ideas and illusions that are in no way substantiated or even the least supported by facts. But the money and the prestige connected with a high position at a mental hospitals are still so attractive, that the psychiatrist simply looses common sense, and accepts a role as terminator for naïve patients, being horribly manipulated and existentially destroyed by the combined effects of coercive persuasion and strongly sedative and poisonous drugs taking the patients' ability of autonomy and resistance away.

Every year about a million, mostly young people, enter the psychiatric system and become patients (65) and every year a million of so good people who could have had wonderful, blossoming lives, are turned into existentially reduced "zombies" or even into dead by suicide. We have been so busy criticizing the other societies and cultures that we completely have missed that we in the western world could be the most repressing, evil, violent and un-containing of all people that have inhabited the planet till this day.

References

[1] Lidz CW. Coercion in psychiatric care: what have we learned from research? J Am Acad Psychiatry Law 1998;26(4):631-7.

[2] Lützén K. Subtle coercion in psychiatric practice. J Psychiatr Ment Health Nurs 1998;5(2):101-7.

[3] Eriksson KI, Westrin CG. Coercive measures in psychiatric care. Reports and reactions of patients and other people involved. Acta Psychiatr Scand 1995;92(3):225-30.

[4] O'Brien AJ, Golding CG. Coercion in mental healthcare: the principle of least coercive care. J Psychiatr Ment Health Nurs 2003;10(2):167-73.

[5] Lidz CW, Mulvey EP, Hoge SK, Kirsch BL, Monahan J, et al. Factual sources of psychiatric patients' perceptions of coercion in the hospital admission process. Am J Psychiatry 1998;155(9):1254-60.

[6] Ventegodt S, Flensborg-Madsen T, Andersen NJ, Nielsen M, Mohammed M, Merrick J. Global quality of life (QOL), health and ability are primarily determined by our consciousness. Research findings from Denmark 1991-2004. Soc Indicator Res 2005;71:87-122.

[7] Ventegodt S, Andersen NJ, Merrick J. Holistic medicine III: The holistic process theory of healing. ScientificWorldJournal 2003;3:1138-46.

[8] Ventegodt S, Clausen B, Merrick J. Clinical holistic medicine: The case story of Anna. III: Rehabilitation of philosophy of life during holistic existential therapy for childhood sexual abuse. ScientificWorldJournal 2006;6:2080-91.

[9] Ventegodt S, Merrick J, Andersen NJ. Quality of life theory I. The IQOL theory: An integrative theory of the global quality of life concept. ScientificWorldJournal 2003;3:1030-40.

[10] Ventegodt S, Merrick J, Andersen NJ. Quality of life theory II. Quality of life as the realization of life potential: A biological theory of human being. ScientificWorldJournal 2003;3:1041-9.

[11] Ventegodt S, Merrick J, Andersen NJ. Quality of life theory III. Maslow revisited. ScientificWorldJournal 2003;3:1050-7.

[12] Ventegodt S. The life mission theory: A theory for a consciousness-based medicine. Int J Adolesc Med Health 2003;15(1): 89-91.

[13] Yalom ID. Existential psychotherapy. New York: Basic Books, 1980.

[14] Ventegodt S, Kandel I, Merrick J. Clinical holistic medicine: How to recover memory without "implanting" memories in your patient. ScientificWorldJournal 2007;7:1579-80.

[15] Ventegodt S, Clausen B, Nielsen ML, Merrick J. Clinical holistic medicine: Advanced tools for holistic medicine. ScientificWorldJournal 2006;6:2048-65.

[16] Ventegodt S, Kandel I, Merrick J. Principles of holistic medicine. Quality of life and health. New York: Hippocrates Sci Publ, 2005.

[17] Ventegodt S, Kromann M, Andersen NJ, Merrick J. The life mission theory VI. A theory for the human character: Healing with holistic medicine through recovery of character and purpose of life. ScientificWorldJournal 2004;4:859-80.

[18] Ventegodt S, Kandel I, Merrick J. Principles of holistic medicine. Philosophy behind quality of life. Victoria, BC: Trafford, 2005.

[19] Ventegodt S, Kandel I, Merrick J. Clinical holistic medicine: Factors influencing the therapeutic decision-making. From academic knowledge to emotional intelligence and spiritual "crazy" wisdom. ScientificWorldJournal 2007;7:1932-49.

[20] Silvera K. Scientific meeting of the American Institute for Psychoanalysis. Am J Psychoanal 2004;64(1):109-12.

[21] Poole DR. Review of children held hostage: Dealing with programmed and brainwashed children. PsycCRITIQUES 1992;37(6):606-7.

[22] Mahlendorf UR. Child brainwashing in two pre-romantic novels. Am J Soc Psychiatry 1984;4(2):45-51.

[23] Gordon RM, Fenchel, GH, eds. The Medea complex and the parental alienation syndrome: When mothers damage their daughters' ability to love a man. Lanham, MD: Jason Aronson, 1998.

[24] Henningsen G. The child witch syndrome: Satanic child abuse of today and child witch trials of yesterday. J Forensic Psychiatry 1996;7(3):581-93.

[25] Lynn R. Brainwashing techniques in leadership and child rearing. Br J Soc Clin Psychol 1966;5(4):270-3.

[26] Anthony D, Robbins T. Law, social science and the "brainwashing" exception to the First Amendment. Behav Sci Law 1992;10(1):5-29.

[27] Richardson JT, Introvigne M. Brainwashing" theories in European parliamentary and administrative reports on "cults" and "sects". J Sci Study Religion 2001;40(2):143-168.

[28] Lifton RJ. Thought reform and the psychology of totalism: A study of "brainwashing" in China. New York: WW Norton, 1961.

[29] Anthony DL. Brainwashing and totalitarian influence: An exploration of admissibility criteria for testimony in brainwashing trials. Dissertation Abstr Int B Sci Eng 1997;57(8-B):5377.

[30] Lifton RJ. Thought reform of Chinese intellectuals: A psychiatric evaluation. J Soc Issues 1957;13 (3):5-20.

[31] Frankl V. Man´s search for meaning. New York: Pocket Books, 1985.

[32] Antonovsky A. Unravelling the mystery of health. How people manage stress and stay well. San Franscisco: Jossey-Bass, 1987.

[33] Meerloo JAM. Suicide, menticide, and psychic homicide. Arch Neurol Psychiatr (Chicago) 1959;81:360-2.

[34] Silke A. The role of suicide in politics, conflict, and terrorism. Terror Political Violence 2006;18(1):35-46.

[35] Robbins T. Combating "cults" and "brainwashing" in the United States and Western Europe: A comment on Richardson and Introvigne's report. J Sci Study Religion 2001;40(2):169-75.

[36] Taylor K. Brainwashing: The science of thought control. New York: Oxford Univ Press, 2004.

[37] Gunnersen SJ. Statistical yearbook 2007. Copenhagen: Statistics Denmark, 2007.

[38] Moncrieff J, Wessely S, Hardy R. Active placebos versus antidepressants for depression. Cochrane Database Syst Rev 2004;(1):CD003012.

[39] Ventegodt S, Flensborg-Madsen, T, Andersen NJ, Svanberg BØ, Struve F, Merrick J. Therapeutic value of antipsychotic drugs: A critical analysis of Cochrane meta-analyses of the therapeutic value of antipsychotic drugs. In preparation.

[40] SBU-rapport 133/2. Treatment with neuroleptics [Behandling med neuroleptika]. Stockholm: Statens beredning för utvärdering av medicinsk metodik 1997:81. [Swedish].

[41] Qin P, Nordentoft M. Suicide risk in relation to psychiatric hospitalization: evidence based on longitudinal registers. Arch Gen Psychiatry 2005;62(4):427-32.

[42] Frank LR. Electroshock: Death, brain damage, memory loss, and brainwashing. J Mind Behav 1990;11(3-4):489-512.

[43] Frank LR. Electroshock: A crime against the spirit. Ethical Hum Sci Serv 2002;4(1):63-71.

[44] Walsh Y. Deconstructing 'brainwashing' within cults as an aid to counseling psychologists. Couns Psychol Q 2001;14(2):119-28.

[45] Hassan S. Combatting cult mind control. Rochester, VT: Park Street Press, 1990.

[46] Galanti GA. Reflections on "brainwashing." In: Langone, MD, ed. Recovery from cults. New York: WW Norton, 1993:85-103.

[47] Zerin MF. The Pied Piper phenomenon and the processing of victims: The transactional analysis perspective re-examined. Transactional Anal J 1983;13(3):172-7.

[48] Anthony D, Robbins T. Law, social science and the "brainwashing" exception to the First Amendment. Behav Sci Law 1992;10(1):5-29.

[49] Robbins T, Anthony D. Deprogramming, brainwashing and the medicalization of deviant religious groups. Soc Problems 1982;29(3):283-97.

[50] Robbins T, Anthony D. The limits of "coercive persuasion" as an explanation for conversion to authoritarian sects. Political Psychol 1980;2(2):22-37.

[51] Schein EH. Man against man: Brainwashing. Correct Psychiatr J Soc Ther 1962;8(2):90-7.

[52] Miloš Forman. One flew over the Cuckoo's Nest. Hollywood: United Artists, 1975.

[53] Hunter E. Brainwashing in Red China. New York: Vanguard, 1951.

[54] Hunter E. Brainwashing. From Pavlow to powers. New York: Book Master, 1960.

[55] Leichsenring F, Rabung S, Leibing E. The efficacy of short-term psychodynamic psychotherapy in specific psychiatric disorders: a meta-analysis. Arch Gen Psychiatry 2004;61(12):1208-16.

[56] Leichsenring F. Are psychodynamic and psychoanalytic therapies effective? A review of empirical data. Int J Psychoanal 2005;86(Pt 3):841-68.

[57] Leichsenring F, Leibing E. Psychodynamic psychotherapy: a systematic review of techniques, indications and empirical evidence. Psychol Psychother 2007;80(Pt 2):217-28.

[58] Chorover SL. Psychology as a social weapon. PsycCRITIQUES 1979;24(10):764-5.

[59] Meerloo JAM. Pavlovian strategy as a weapon of menticide. Am J Psychiatry 1954;809-13.

[60] Schein EH. The Chinese indoctrination program for prisoners of war. Psychiatr J Study Interpers Processes 1956;19:149-72.

[61] Biderman AD. Effects of Communist indoctrination attempts: Some comments based on an Air Force prisoner-of-war study. Soc Problems 1959;6:304-13.

[62] James P. Carter. Racketeering in medicine: The suppression of alternatives. Charlottesville, VA: Hampton Roads Publ, 1992.

[63] Lindholt JS, Ventegodt S, Henneberg EW. Development and validation of QoL5 for clinical databases. A short, global and generic questionnaire based on an integrated theory of the quality of life. Eur J Surg 2002;168(2):107-13.

[64] Merrick J, Omar HA, Ventegodt S. Quality of life and persons with intellectual disability. Can we measure QOL in this population? In preparation.

[65] Lindhardt A, ed. The use of antipsychotic drugs among the 18-64 year old patients with schizophrenia, mania, or bipolar affective disorder. Copenhagen: National Board Health, 2006. [Danish].

[66] Janca A. World and mental health in 2001. Curr Psychiatry Rep 2001;3(2):77-8.

Chapter 7

The therapeutic value of anti-psychotic drugs used in Denmark

A rough estimate of the therapeutic value of a drug can be established from the ratio "Number Needed to Treat to Harm/Number Needed to Treat to Benefit" (NNH/NNT or NNtH/NNtB). The ratio illuminate the degree to which the treatment with the drug respects the ethical rule of "first do no harm"; if the ratio is >1 the drug helps more than it harms and is thus primarily beneficial. We need to compare the upper confidence limit of the NNtB with the lower confidence limit of the NNtH to assure that a drug helps and does not harm the patient. We compared NNH/NNT ratio from the Cochrane meta-analyses of the commonly used antipsychotic drugs in Denmark and found that all antipsychotic drugs used in Denmark had a NNH/NNB< 1, and often 1/5 and 1/10, meaning that the drugs are likely to harm many more patients than they help.

Antipsychotic drugs are known to have not only physical adverse effects, but also mental, existential, social and sexual side effects that are seldom included in the studies, giving a strong bias in favor of the drugs. Important factors that are often ignored in the studies were: suicides from drug-induced depression, suicide attempts and their consequences, spontaneous drug-induced death, drug-induced self-molestation, damage to learning and working ability, sexual function, social function, self-esteem and self-confidence, and cognitive factors. Antipsychotic drugs on the Danish market today have a very low therapeutic value and seem to be harmful to the patients. From an ethical perspective antipsychotic drugs can therefore not be used as a standard treatment for any mental illness. Further scientific investigation into the significance of this finding is urgently needed. Antipsychotic drugs might still be justified in the treatment of specific subgroups of patients like violent and sexually aggressive, acute psychotic, schizophrenic patients.

Introduction

From the days of Hippocrates in 300 BCE medical ethics has stressed the importance of avoiding harm to your patient: "primum non nocere" – first do no harm. To serve the patient's best interest a physician must be certain that the drugs are helping and not causing harm to the patient. Most patients will accept mild adverse effects, and serious adverse effects can be tolerated if they are rare and the drugs is useful, but it is unethical to give drugs that severely harm a substantial fraction of the patients, and it becomes a really serious ethical problem if a drug harms more patients than it helps.

In medical science today we use the concept "Number Needed to Treat to Benefit" (NNT or NNtB) about the number of patients that must be treated for one to be helped, and the Number Needed to Treat to Harm (NNtH or NNH) to tell the number of patients that must be treated for one to be harmed. NNtB and NNtH are measured with an uncertainty (CI means confidence interval at p=.05), so there are always a highest and a lowest value for each NNT measure. To be sure that a drug really helps and does not harm we need to compare the lowest empirically supported value (i.e., the upper confidence limit, or pessimistic harms assessment) with the highest empirically supported value of the Number Needed to Treat to Benefit (NNtB), i.e. a pessimist's assessment of benefits. In principle the NNtH/NNtB ratio can be calculated better, if all positive and negative effects were added up to one number; the importance of each treatment effect factor should be multiplied with its likelihood before taken into the addition, and a negative effect should be given negative value. The problem with such a "smart" strategy is that the result will be totally dependent on the number of included factors – what makes it less smart than it appears at first glance.

Our study

We have compared the Cochrane meta-analyses of the commonly used antipsychotic drugs in Denmark (1-27) (see table 1). Surprisingly we found that almost all the drugs were harming more patients than they were helping, and often five or even 10 times more. We typically found NNtB to be 5-20 and NNtH 2-5. Just using a drug, which needs 10 patients treated for one to be helped, seems highly unethical, if a large fraction of the patients are harmed. Another serious problem is that the placebo effect is included in the results, making many drugs look active, when they are only slightly more effective that placebo.

Discussion

A serious problem with the data is that they are provided by the industry, which has an interest in marketing their products. We found that most of the trials reviewed of the pharmaceuticals were designed to be very kind to the drugs.

Only a small improvement of psychotic symptoms is often taken as help for the patient, in spite of the sad fact that these drugs rarely cure any patient for any disease. On the other hand the industry-imposed design has looked mostly at short-term physical adverse effects and often many extremely serious mental (28), social, existential, sexual, financial and other adverse effects and side effects were not included in the studies.

Among some of the important factors often ignored in the studies were: suicides from drug-induced depression (28,39), suicide attempts and their consequences or spontaneous drug-induces death (4,30), drug-induced self-molestation (cutting etc), damage to learning and working ability, sexual function, social function, self-esteem, self-confidence and quality of life (4), notably including some adverse phenomena which physicians, and even psychiatric investigators, rarely have been trained to probe into. Other important biases have also been found (31).

All this makes the NNtH likely to be systematically much too large and the NNtB likely to be systematically much too small, giving a very severe bias in favor of the drugs in the pharmaceutical studies, and most unfortunately also to the Cochrane meta-analyses re-using these data most often without any chance of mounting the appropriate critique. We definitely need a to collect this information for the drugs being used to day.

It has been argued that the positive effects are qualitatively more important than the negative effects of the drugs, but we have analyzed this and found that both positive and negative changes were registered, when they were clinically noticeable. It therefore seems likely that NNtB and NNtH numbers build on equality noticeable phenomena, and therefore comparable.

The fact that the antipsychotic drugs have highly unfavorable NNH/NNT ratios cannot be dismissed by the argument the positive effects of the drugs (i.e. the anti-hallucinating effect) are more important than the negative side effects (i.e. severe obesity).

We found that there is not one single, antipsychotic, psychopharmacological drug that can be used without harming the patients more than benefiting them; NNH/NNT were always <1 (see table 1).

To compare NNtH and NNtB will always to some extend be comparing apples and pears; this problem can only be solved by measuring one integrated endpoint of both positive and negative effect like *global quality of life* (which can be measured with a simple questionnaire like the QOL1 with one questions on self-assessed global quality of life (35)), self-assessed physical and mental health, or self-assessed ability of functioning in a number of relevant domains (work, social life, family, sexuality). We recommend the use of a wise and balanced combination of self-assessed mental and physical health, global quality of life, and ability in general as the endpoints for any medical treatment. The low ratio NNH/NNT is the likely reason that the pharmaceutical industry systematically has avoided the use of such endpoint that illuminates the effect of the drugs on the whole person. It has also avoided long-term documentation of adverse effects, in spite of many physicians and patients have been asking for these data for years.

We suggest that we call the inverse number NNH/NNT for "the ethical treatment value of the drug". The way it is calculated is in a way "double pessimistic"; we estimate that a drug with NNH/NNT>10 has a 99% chance to be a primarily beneficial (valuable) drug, and a NNH/NNT value<1/10 signifies a 99% risk of being a primarily harmful drug. We suggest that the NNH/NNT value of "penicillin in the treatment of syphilis" (about 100) can be a benchmark for a highly valuable drug.

If effects and side effects are mechanistically related, like the better mobility after curing a femural fracture leading to an increased future fracture rate, the above-mentioned "smart" formula must be used.

The last important thing is that most symptoms and side effects are reversible, but brain damage, suicide and dead are not. Suicide is a negative effect that is much more difficult to tolerate that all other adverse effects and every study must therefore include a long-term survey of increased or diminished suicide rate.

Table 1. During the last 10 years the many Cochrane units all over the world have provided us with highly valuable meta-analyses. Because of this unique source of scientifically established high-level knowledge, we now in our opinion know that the ethical treatment of many psychiatric disorders is still psychotherapy, which on one hand in many studies has been documented to help and on the other never has been documented to harm the patients (see 32-34)

"Atypical" antipsychotics

Sertindole (N05AE03) [1] NNtB: 'very much improved' as compared to those taking placebo NNT 7.9, CI 4.3 to 41.1

NNtH: almost as haloperidol. Akathisia - 8mg: 1 study, n=245, RR 0.2, CI 0.1 to 0.5, NNH 6.0, CI 4.1 to 11.2; 16mg: 1 study, n=252, RR 0.1, CI 0.0 to 0.3, NNH 5.4, CI 3.9- 9.0; 20mg: 1 study, n=253, RR 0.3, CI 0.2 to 0.7, NNH 7.3, CI 4.6 to 17.9; 24mg: 2 studies, n=524, RR 0.5, CI 0.3 to 0.7, NNH 8.6, CI 5.6 to 18.3. Tremor - 8mg: 1 study, n=245, RR 0.3, CI 0.1 to 0.7, NNH 8.5, CI 5.2 to 24.0; 16mg: 1 study, n=252, RR 0.2, CI 0.1 to 0.5, NNH 7.3, 4.8 to 15.6; 20mg: 1 study, n=253, RR 0.2, CI 0.1 to 0.6, NNH 7.8, CI 4.9 to 18.1; 24mg: 2 studies, n=524, RR 0.4, CI 0.2 to 0.6, NNH 8.2, CI 5.6 to 15.3. For Hypertonic - 24mg: 2 studies, n=524, RR 0.5, CI 0.3 to 0.8, NNH 12.4, CI 7.5 to 35.0. NNtH/NNtB=4/41.1= 0.097

Ziprasidone (N05AE04) [2] NNtB: As haloperidol. NNtH: Not calculated; almost as haloperidol. Clozapin (N05AH02), No Cochrane study found

Olanzapine (N05AH03) [3] NNtB: 'no important clinical response' NNT 8 CI 5 to 27 NNtH: weight gain NNH 5 CI 4 to 7). Insufficient data. NNtH/NNtB=4/27= 0.15

Quetiapine (N05AH04) [4] NNtB 11 CI 7 to 55. NNtH: Movement disorders NNH 4 CI 4 to 5. Dry mouth NNH 17 CI 7 to 65. Sleepiness NNH 18 CI 8 to 181. NNtH/NNtB=7/55= 0.13. No summarized data of spontaneous patient death (4 of 728 died in one RCT, 2 of 618 died in an other RCT).

Amisulpride (N05AL05) [5] NNtB not specified: NNT 3 CI 3 to 7. NNtH: Need for antiparkinson drugs: NNH 4 CI 3 to 6. Agitation NNH 11 CI 6 to 50. NNtH/NNtB=3/7= 0.43 (Chlorpromazine used as reference').

Risperidone (N05AX08)[6,7] NNtB: As Olanzapine. NNtH: sexual dysfunction abnormal ejaculation NNH 20 CI 6 to 176. Impotence RR 2.43 CI 0.24 to 24.07. One third of people given either drug experienced some extrapyramidal symptoms (n=893, 3 RCTs, RR 1.18 CI 0.75 to 1.88) but 25% of people using risperidone require medication to alleviate extrapyramidal adverse effects (n=419, 2 RCTs, RR 1.76 CI 1.25 to 2.48, NNH 8 CI 4 to 25). Weight gain: NNH 7 CI 6 to 10). NNtH/NNtB=4/27= 0.15

Aripiprazole (N05AX12) [8] NNtB: NNT 5 CI 4 to 8. NNtH: Need for antiparkinson drugs NNtH 4 CI 3 to 5. (Previous study included NNtH: Insomnia NNH 4 CI 3 to 9.) NNtH/NNtB=3/8= 0.37

High-dose typical antipsychotics

Chlorpromazine (N05AA01) [9] NNtB: Prevents relapse, longer term data: NNT 4 CI 3 to 5. Improves symptoms and functioning NNT 6 CI 5 to 8. NNtH: Sedation: NNH 5 CI 4 to 8. Acute movement disorder NNH 32 CI 11 to 154. Need for antiparkinson drugs NNH 14 CI 9 to 28. Lowering of blood pressure with accompanying dizziness NNH 11 CI 7 to 21. Considerable weight gain NNH 2 CI 2 to 3. NNtH/NNtB=2/5= 0.15

Levomepromazine (N05AA02). No Cochrane study found

Promazine (N05AA03). No Cochrane study found

Thioridazine (N05AC02)[10] NNtB: "global state outcomes" NNT of 2 CI 2 to 3; NNtH: Sedation NNH 4 CI 2 to 74. Cardiac adverse effects NNH 3 CI 2 to 5. NNTH/NNTB=2/3= 0.67

Melperone (N05AD03), No Cochrane study found
Pipamperone (N05AD05) No Cochrane study found

Chlorprothixene (N05AF03)No Cochrane study found

Middle-dose typical antipsychotics

Perphenazine (N05AB03) [11] NNtB: 2 CI 1 to 20. NNtH: invalid data.
Depot perphenazine decanoate[12]: NNtB as clopenthixol decanoate and other antipsychotic drugs. Need for anticholinergic drugs (one RTC NNtH 4 and another NNtH 10), movement disorders (RR 1.36, CI 1.1 to 1.8 NNT 5). NNtH/NNtB = 4/8 = 0.50 (Chlorpromazine used as reference).
Zuclopenthixol (N05AF05) [13] NNtB: Patient not unchanged or worse: NNT 10 CI 6 to 131. NNtH: Extraparamydal symptoms NNH 2 CI 2 to 31. Need for antiparkinson drugs NNH 3 CI 3 to 17. NNtH/NNtB=3/131= 0.023
Zuclopenthixol decanoate [14] NNtB: Prevented or postponed relapses NNT 8, CI 5-53. NNtH: Adverse effects NNH 5, CI 3-31. NNtH/NNtB=3/53= 0.057

Low-dose typical antipsychotics

Fluphenazine (N05AB02) [15] NNtB: NNT= placebo (not effective). NNtH: Experiencing extrapyramidal effects such as akathisia NNH 13 CI 4 to 128. NNtH/NNtB=4/Infinite= 0.00
Haloperidol (N05AD01) [16] NNtB: NNT 3 CI 2 to 5/Global improvement NNT 3 CI 2.5 to 5. NNtH: Acute dystonia NNH 5 CI 3 to 9. Need for antiparkinson drugs NNH 3 CI 2 to 5. NNtH/NNtB=2/5= 0.40
Flupentixol (N05AF01) [17] NNtH/NNtB: as other depot antipsychotics
Pimozide (N05AG02) [18] NNtB: Prevents relapse NNT 4 CI 3 to 22. NNTH: Tremor NNH 6 CI 3 to 44- Need for antiparkinson drugs NNH 3 CI 2 to 5. NNtH/NNtB=2/22= 0.091

Penfluridole (N05AG03) [19] NNtB: 'improvement in global state' NNT 3 CI 2 to 10 – as chlorpromazine, fluphenazine, trifluoperazine, thioridazine, or thiothixene. NNtH as chlorpromazine, fluphenazine, trifluoperazine, thioridazine, or thiothixene. NNtH/NNtB=4/10= 0.40

Sulpiride (N05AL01) [20] NNtH/NNtB: evidence is limited and data relating to claims for its value against negative symptoms is not trial-based.

New generation antipsychotics[21]: NNtH: Of the new generation drugs, only clozapine was associated with significantly fewer extrapyramidal side-effects (EPS) (RD=-0.15, 95% CI -0.26 to -0.4, p=0.008) and higher efficacy than low-potency conventional drugs. These findings might have been biased by the use of the high-potency antipsychotic haloperidol as a comparator in most of the trials. First episode schizophrenia[22]: NNH 3 CI 2 to 6 The results of this review are inconclusive.

Antipsychotics in treatment of childhood onset psychoses[23]: NNtH/NNtB: There are few relevant trials and, presently, there is little conclusive evidence regarding the effects of antipsychotic medication for those with early onset schizophrenia. Some benefits were identified in using the atypical antipsychotic clozapine compared with haloperidol but the benefits were offset by an increased risk of serious adverse effects. Early intervention for psychosis[24]: NNtB: Six month follow up: less likely to develop psychosis at a six month follow up NNT 4 CI 2 to 20, 12 month follow up: Not significant! NNtH: Weight gain etc., insufficient data
Other drugs sometimes used against psychosis

acepromazine (N05AA04), No Cochrane study found
prochlorperazine (N05AB04), No antipsychotic Cochrane study found
periciazine (N05AC01), No Cochrane study found
tetrabenazine (N05AK01) No antipsychotic Cochrane study found
Litium (N05AN01) [25] NNTB: as placebo (not efficient). NNTH: Insufficient data. NNTH/NNTB=something/infinite<<1
Benzodiazepines [26] NNTB: NNT 3 CI 2 to 17. NNTH: Maybe worse than placebo. NNTH/NNTB= 100/17? Probably >1
Valproate [27] NNTB: Insufficient data. NNTH: Insufficient data

The last thing to consider is that placebo often has a NNT=3; the difference between the antipsychotic drugs and placebo are therefore only marginal; an alternative explanation to a therapeutic effect is the fact that you can feel the drug in you brain, destroying the blindness of the study and creating an "active placebo" effect. If this is the case, we are actually only using placebo to treat, but with high risk of causing side effects and serious harm to the patients. This has never been investigated for the antipsychotic drugs neither by the pharmaceutical companies nor by neutral researchers, and this must urgently be done.

Conclusions

In conclusion, the NNH/NNT ratio might be the needed guideline for evaluating the therapeutic effect of drugs; when this analysis is carried out on the antipsychotic drug using the upper confidence limit of NNT and the lower confidence limit of NNH for the comparison, we find that all antipsychotic drugs used in Denmark are more harmful than beneficial.

We presume that the antipsychotic drugs on the market today in Denmark are very much the same as in all other countries, as the same drugs are used almost everywhere. The analysis indicates that the antipsychotic drugs are likely not to improve health and thus to be without any net therapeutic value; they are likely to be primarily harmful to the patients. This does not mean that the drugs cannot to be used for life-saving and other compelling reasons, like on extremely aggressive, patients that urgently needs to be calmed down, or on acute psychotic sexually violent schizophrenic patients etc., but they can not be used ethically as a standard treatment for any kind of mental illness.

On the other hand recent research comparing psychotherapy with psychiatric treatment has documented psychotherapy to be helpful to many groups of patients (32-34), and also more helpful than the psychiatric standard treatment, without having the adverse effects of the anti-psychotic drugs. We believe that the NNH/NNT ratio is the best indicator we have today of the total therapeutic value (benefit versus harm) of a drug, but we must admit that it is a crude summary index of benefit-vs.-harm. For a better evaluation of a medical treatment we need to use a combined measure of *global quality of life* (like QOL1 and QOL5) (35), self-assesses health (36), and self-assessed ability (in a number of relevant domains) (36).

We need urgently - for the sake of all patients - to be able to estimate the total therapeutic value of a drug (or any other treatment) more accurate in the future, and recommend that all clinical trials in the future use *global QOL and self-assessed physical and mental health* as obligatory outcomes; long term studies including all relevant dimensions like *loss of working and studying ability, suicide, and spontaneous drug-induced death* are also absolutely necessary for an ethical evidence-based medicine in psychiatry.

References

[1]   Lewis R, Bagnall AM, Leitner M. Sertindole for schizophrenia. Cochrane Database Syst Rev 2005;(3):CD001715.
[2]   Bagnall A, Lewis RA, Leitner ML. Ziprasidone for schizophrenia and severe mental illness. Cochrane Database Syst Rev 2000;(4):CD 001945.

[3]   Duggan L, Fenton M, Rathbone J, Dardennes R, El-Dosoky A, Indran S. Olanzapine for schizophrenia. Cochrane Database Syst Rev 2005;(2):CD001359.

[4]   Srisurapanont M, Maneeton B, Maneeton N. Quetiapine for schizophrenia. Cochrane Database Syst Rev 2004;(2):CD000967.

[5]   Mota NE, Lima MS, Soares BG. Amisulpride for schizophrenia. Cochrane Database Syst Rev 2002;(2):CD001357.

[6]   Jayaram MB, Hosalli P. Risperidone versus olanzapine for schizophrenia. Cochrane Database Syst Rev 2005;(2):CD005237.

[7]   Jesner OS, Aref-Adib M, Coren E. Risperidone for autism spectrum disorder. Cochrane Database Syst Rev 2007;(1):CD005040.

[8]   El-Sayeh HG, Morganti C. Aripiprazole for schizophrenia. Cochrane Database Syst Rev 2006;(2):CD004578.

[9]   Adams CE, Awad G, Rathbone J, Thornley B.Chlorpromazine versus placebo for schizophrenia. Cochrane Database Syst Rev 2007;(2):CD000284.

[10] Fenton M, Rathbone J, Reilly J, Sultana A. Thioridazine for schizophrenia. Cochrane Database Syst Rev 2007;(3):CD001944.

[11] Hartung B, Wada M, Laux G, Leucht S. Perphenazine for schizophrenia.Cochrane Database Syst Rev 2005;(1):CD003443.

[12] Quraishi S, David A. Depot perphenazine decanoate and enanthate for schizophrenia. Cochrane Database Syst Rev 2000;(2):CD001717.

[13] Kumar A, Strech D. Zuclopenthixol dihydrochloride for schizophrenia. Cochrane Database Syst Rev 2005;(4):CD005474.

[14] Coutinho E, Fenton M, Quraishi S. Zuclopenthixol decanoate for schizophrenia and other serious mental illnesses. Cochrane Database Syst Rev 2000;(2):CD001164.

[15] Matar HE, Almerie MQ. Oral fluphenazine versus placebo for schizophrenia. Cochrane Database Syst Rev 2007;(1):CD006352.

[16] Joy CB, Adams CE, Lawrie SM. Haloperidol versus placebo for schizophrenia. Cochrane Database Syst Rev 2006;(4):CD003082.

[17] Quraishi S, David A. Depot flupenthixol decanoate for schizophrenia or other similar psychotic disorders. Cochrane Database Syst Rev 2000;(2):CD001470.

[18] Rathbone J, McMonagle T. Pimozide for schizophrenia or related psychoses. Cochrane Database Syst Rev 2007;(3):CD001949.

[19] Soares BG, Lima MS. Penfluridol for schizophrenia. Cochrane Database Syst Rev 2006;(2):CD002923.

[20] Soares BG, Fenton M, Chue P. Sulpiride for schizophrenia. Cochrane Database Syst Rev 2000;(2):CD001162.

[21] Leucht S, Wahlbeck K, Hamann J, Kissling W. New generation antipsychotics versus low-potency conventional antipsychotics: a systematic review and meta-analysis. Lancet 2003;361(9369):1581-9.

[22] Rummel C, Hamann J, Kissling W, Leucht S. New generation antipsychotics for first episode schizophrenia. Cochrane Database Syst Rev 2003;(4):CD004410.

[23] Kennedy E, Kumar A, Datta S.Antipsychotic medication for childhood-onset schizophrenia. Cochrane Database Syst Rev 2007;(3):CD004027.

[24] Marshall M, Rathbone J. Early intervention for psychosis. Cochrane Database Syst Rev 2006;(4):CD004718.

[25] Leucht S, Kissling W, McGrath J. Lithium for schizophrenia. Cochrane Database Syst Rev 2007;(3):CD003834.

[26] Volz A, Khorsand V, Gillies D, Leucht S. Benzodiazepines for schizophrenia. Cochrane Database Syst Rev 2007;(1):CD006391.

[27] Basan A, Leucht S.Valproate for schizophrenia. Cochrane Database Syst Rev 2004;(1):CD004028.

[28] SBU-rapport nr. 133/1 og 133/2. Treatment with neuroleptics [Behandling med neuroleptika]. Stockholm: Statens beredning för utvärdering av medicinsk metodik 1997;2:81. [Swedish].

[29] Qin P, Nordentoft M. Suicide risk in relation to psychiatric hospitalization: evidence based on longitudinal registers. Arch Gen Psychiatry 2005;62(4):427-32.

[30] Lindhardt A, et al. The use of antipsychotic drugs among the 18-64year old patients with schizophrenia, mania, or bipolar affective disorder. National bord of Heath, Copenhagen[Forbruget af antipsykotika blandt 18-64 årige patienter med skizofreni, mani eller bipolar affektiv sindslidelse". Copenhagen: Sundhedsstyrelsen, 2006 [Danish].

[31] Chaves AC, Seeman MV. Sex selection bias in schizophrenia antipsychotic trials. J Clin Psychopharmacol 2006;26(5):489-94.

[32] Leichsenring F, Rabung S, Leibing E. The efficacy of short-term psychodynamic psychotherapy in specific psychiatric disorders: a meta-analysis. Arch Gen Psychiatry 2004;61(12):1208-16.

[33] Leichsenring F. Are psychodynamic and psychoanalytic therapies effective?: A review of empirical data. Int J Psychoanal 2005;86(Pt 3):841-68.

[34] Leichsenring F, Leibing E. Psychodynamic psychotherapy: a systematic review of techniques, indications and empirical evidence. Psychol Psychother 2007;80(Pt 2):217-28.

[35] Lindholt JS, Ventegodt S, Henneberg EW. Development and validation of QoL5 for clinical databases. A short, global and generic questionnaire based on an integrated theory of the quality of life. Eur J Surg 2002;168(2):107-13.

[36] Ventegodt S, Henneberg EW, Merrick J, Lindholt JS. Validation of two global and generic quality of life questionnaires for population screening: SCREENQOL and SEQOL. ScientificWorldJournal 2003;3:412-21.

Section 2. What can holistic medicine offer?

In this section we will look at the use and limitations of biomedical drugs compared to the use of holistic non-drug medicine. We will not go into statistical analysis, but look at it from single cases. In general, drugs are very useful in acute physical disease. Chronic disease, physical or mental, respond much less to pharmaceutical drugs and in general chronic disease is chronic, because the patients hope for a biomedical cure that does not exist, instead of assuming responsibility and searching for a therapist or physician that can assist the natural process of healing.

We are accustomed to the use of drugs. Often we continue to believe in drugs, because we generalize our childhood experience from being "saved" by for example the treatment of acute otitis with penicillin to most drugs. We do not know that most of us have experienced this treatment in spite of it not being evidence-based: It has no significant efficacy according to recent metaanalysis (1). We must stop believing in pharmaceutical drugs as a way to salvation as it is very unlikely that drugs will cure us from our chronic disease, mental or physical.

In this section we see countless examples of pharmaceutical drugs working in acute somatic medicine and not in chronic somatic or psychiatric medicine. We also see that when it comes to quality-of-life-years (QALY) only holistic medicine seems to help mentally ill patients significantly.

References

[1] Glasziou PP, Del Mar CB, Sanders SL, Hayem M. Antibiotics for acute otitis media in children. Cochrane Database Syst Rev 2004;(1):CD000219.

Chapter 8

What is clinical holistic medicine?

Clinical holistic medicine, also called scientific holistic medicine, has its roots in the medicine and tradition of Hippocrates. Modern epidemiological research in quality of life, the emerging science of complementary and alternative medicine, the tradition of psychodynamic therapy, and the tradition of bodywork are merging into a new scientific way of treating patients.

This approach seems able to help every second patient with physical, mental, existential or sexual health problem in 20 sessions over one year, as we shall see in section thirteen. This chapter discuss the development of holistic medicine into scientific holistic medicine with discussion of future research efforts.

Introduction

Millennia ago, around 300 BCE, at the island of Cos in old Greece, the students of the famous physician Hippocrates (460-377BCE) (1) worked to help their patients to step into character, get direction in life, and use their human talents for the benefit of their surrounding world. For all that we know this approach was extremely efficient medicine that helped the patients to recover health, quality of life, and ability, and Hippocrates gained great fame. For more than 2,000 years this was what medicine was about in most of Europe.

On other continents similar medical systems were developed. The medicine wheel of the Native Americans, the African Sangoma culture, the Samic Shamans of northern Europe, the healers of the Australian Aboriginals, the ayurvedic doctors of India, the acupuncturists of China, and the herbal doctors of Tibet all seems to be fundamentally character medicine (2-8).

All the theories and the medical understanding from these pre-modern cultures are now being integrated in what is called integrative or transcultural medicine. Many of the old medical systems are reappearing in modern time as alternative, complementary and psychosocial medicine.

This huge body of theory is now being offered as a European Union Master of Science degree at the University College in Graz, Austria (2-8).

What is happening today?

Interestingly, two huge movements of the last century have put this old knowledge into use: psychoanalysis (9) and psychodynamic therapy (10,11) (most importantly STPP)(12,13) going though the mind on one hand, and bodywork (most importantly Reich, Lowen and Rosen) (14-16) and sexual therapy (especially the European tradition of the sexological examination and the Eastern tantric tradition (17)) going through the body on the other (see also section 11). A third road, but much less common path has been directly though the spiritual reconnection with the world (18,19).

Our international research collaboration got interested in existential healing from the data coming from epidemiological research at the University Hospital of Copenhagen (Rigshospitalet) starting in 1958-61 at the Research Unit for Prospective Paediatrics and the Copenhagen Perinatal Birth Cohort 1959-61. Almost 20 years ago we were conducting epidemiological research on quality of life, closely examining the connection between global quality of life and health for more than 11,000 people in a series of huge surveys (20) using large and extensive questionnaires, some of them with over 3,000 questions. We found (quite surprisingly) from this huge data base that quality of life, mental and physical health, and ability of social, sexual and working ability seemed to be caused primarily by the consciousness and philosophy of life of the person in question, and only to a small extent by objective factors, like being adopted, coming from a family with only one breadwinner, mother being mentally ill, or one self being financially poor or poorly educated (which are obviously very much socially inherited) (20).

This scientific finding was not expected and so contra-intuitive for us that we were forced to investigate the subject going to the roots of western medicine, or the Hippocratic character of medicine. This meant that we had to look at transcultural and integrative medicine, the emerging science of alternative medicine (scientific CAM theory) and to the very much forgotten traditions of psychosomatic, psychodynamic, and bodily oriented therapies. Around 1994 we received substantial fundings for our research project trying to embrace this huge heritage of medical wisdom philosophically (21-28), theoretically [29-49], epidemiologically/statistically (50-71).

We have since 1997 with a great effort tried to take this knowledge into clinical practice (72-113) and with fine results. Clinical holistic medicine has in our Research Clinic for Holistic Medicine and Sexology in Copenhagen helped every second patient with physical, mental, existential or sexual health issues or diseases over one year (114-119) (see section thirteen). Finally we have been looking at what seems to be the common denominator for all existential healing work in all cultures at all times: the sense of coherence, most clearly expressed by Aaron Antonovsky (1923-1994), a sociologist from the Faculty of Health Sciences at the Ben Gurion University of the Negev in Israel (18,19,120-125). We have also been debating many difficult issues related to modern day medical science, especially in the British Medical Journal (126-139) and finally we are now collecting most of what we consider essential knowledge for the holistic physician in a series of books on the "Principles of holistic medicine"(140-142), with this book being the fifth volume in this series, planed to appear together with the fourth volume on "Sexology from a holistic point of view" in 2010.

What we have learned from this long journey through the grand medical heritage from the different cultures on this planet is that we need to work on body, mind and spirit at the same time (medicine men has always combined talking, touching, and praying), and when being human and truly kind is what really heals the other person. This is what Hippocrates called "the Art" (1), not "the art of medicine" or "the art of right living", but simply "the art" – the way of the human heart, cultivating existence into sheer compassionate behaviour and joyful being, which has always been the ultimate goal of all the great healers in our history.

We are more than happy to see our research project in scientific holistic medicine (clinical holistic medicine, CHM) developing. The most paradoxal aspect of this is that while we like to think we are taking medicine forward, we are actually just taking medicine back to its roots.

The most important thing is that research and development in this field is made in a dialectic process between qualitative and quantitative research.

Qualitative and quantitative research

There are basically two ways of documenting an effect of a holistic medical intervention, the quantitative and the qualitative approach. Much effort has been given to developing valid methodology and measuring tools, but the art of documentation has become a complex and expensive task. Due to lack of resources we have been forced to seek simple, but still valid ways of documenting effect (75). In this communication we will focus on the qualitative research method.

Fortunately the holistic approach makes it much simpler, because there are always three domains to investigate: health, quality of life (QOL) and ability. These three domains can be subdivided in as many detailed domains as one wishes, but often three are sufficient for most purposes.

There are two qualitative aspects of documenting effect in medicine, often called subjective (that is from the perspective and experience of the patient) - and objective (that is from the perspective of the therapist or researcher). To document effect of an intervention using both perspectives, the patient must be interviewed before and after the intervention. Semi structured interviews with interviewer rating of the state immediately before and after the intervention can be used to give the objective perspective on the effect of the intervention. Interviewing the patient after the intervention can give the patient's subjective experience of the effect.

Most importantly these perspectives often leads to two different results, but confronting the patient with the observed improvement, after the patient has given his own experience of the effect, can be very enlightening.

The consensus paradigm states that only to the degree that there is consensus between patient and therapist/observer, the treatment has an effect. If the patient experience an effect that cannot be observed, something else is likely to have happened, i.e. an upgrade of other dimensions than the three defined as outcome. Instead of QOL, health and ability the patient has gained self-esteem, confidence, admiration from others etc. As holistic medicine aims to improve life in these three domains, a pleasant experience with the therapy is not the same as en effect of a treatment.

If the patient does not experience an observed effect, this effect is most likely to be happening only in the observer's mind. Very often a therapist is convinced that a cure or intervention gave a positive result, but the fact that the patient did not experience that is then often neglected. In holistic medicine the dimensions we want to improve are highly experiential, so if the patient did not experience any improvement, such an improvement is most likely not to have happened.

Interestingly one single patient is enough to document effect with the consensus paradigm. If both the physician and his patient, after careful investigation before and after the treatment, find that the treatment has helped, this is most likely the case. The more precise the target group and the treatment are defined the more valuable the documentation. We recommend for securing the validity that the presented method is used with five highly comparable patients receiving five highly comparable treatments.

As always we recommend for the observer rating a five point symmetrical Likert scale with neutral middle point and equidistance (143). A clinically significant improvement must be half a step on this scale or more. The patient needs to express the gain as a "significant improvement". When both patient and observer find improvement of QOL, health, and ability significant (according to the above), we call the treatment "good".

Perspectives for future research and development

There are lots of possible advantages with the scientific holistic medicine that must be closely examined in future research:

- How can it be make a affordable, efficient medicine for the future
- The possibility to prevent disease
- The possibility to cure cancer and coronary heart disease
- The possibility to seroconvert HIV-positive patients to HIV negative
- The possibility to relief pain and discomfort
- The possibility of rehabilitating working ability
- The possibility of improving peoples competency as parents
- The possibility of improving working efficiency though development of talent
- The possibility of helping people to be happy in spite of difficult circumstances and challenges
- The possibility of people developing consciousness and becoming more responsible for local and global environment

We hope that this work will be of value to all living beings.

References

[1]   Jones WHS. Hippocrates. Vol. I–IV. London: William Heinemann, 1823-1931.
[2]   Antonella R. Introduction of regulatory methods, systematics, description and current research. Graz, Austria: Interuniv Coll, 2004.
[3]   Blättner B. Fundamentals of salutogenesis. Health promotion (WHO) and individual promotion of health. Graz, Austria: Interuniv Coll, 2004.

[4] Endler PC. Master's programme for complementary, psychosocial and integrated health sciences. Graz, Austria: Interuniv Coll, 2004.

[5] Endler PC. Working and writing scientifically in complementary medicine and integrated health sciences. Graz, Austria: Interuniv Coll, 2004.

[6] Kratky KW. Complementary medicine systems. Comparison and integration. New York: Nova Sci, 2008.

[7] Pass PF. Fundamentals of depth psychology. Therapeutic relationship formation between self-awareness and casework. Graz, Austria: Interuniv Coll, 2004.

[8] Spranger HH. Fundamentals of regulatory biology. Paradigms and scientific backgrounds of regulatory methods. Austria: Interuniv Coll, 2004.

[9] Jones E. The life and works of Sigmund Freud. New York: Basic Books, 1961.

[10] Jung CG. Man and his symbols. New York: Anchor Press, 1964.

[11] Jung CG. Psychology and alchemy. Collected Works of CG Jung. Princeton, NJ: Princeton Univ Press, 1968.

[12] Leichsenring F, Rabung S, Leibing E. The efficacy of short-term psychodynamic psychotherapy in specific psychiatric disorders: a meta-analysis. Arch Gen Psychiatry 2004;61(12):1208-16.

[13] Leichsenring F. Are psychodynamic and psychoanalytic therapies effective?: A review of empirical data. Int J Psychoanal 2005;86(Pt 3):841-68.

[14] Reich W. [Die Function des Orgasmus.] Köln: Kiepenheuer Witsch, 1969. [German]

[15] Lowen A. Honoring the body. Alachua, FL: Bioenergetics Press, 2004.

[16] Rosen M, Brenner S. Rosen method bodywork. Accessing the unconscious through touch. Berkeley, CA: North Atlantic Books, 2003.

[17] Anand M. The art of sexual ecstasy. The path of sacred sexuality for Western lovers. New York: Jerymy P Tarcher/Putnam, 1989.

[18] Antonovsky A. Health, stress and coping. London: Jossey-Bass, 1985.

[19] Antonovsky A. Unravelling the mystery of health. How people manage stress and stay well. San Franscisco: Jossey-Bass, 1987.

[20] Ventegodt S, Flensborg-Madsen T, Andersen NJ, Nielsen M, Morad M, Merrick J. Global quality of life (QOL), health and ability are primarily determined by our consciousness. Research findings from Denmark 1991-2004. Soc Indicator Res 2005;71:87-122.

[21] Ventegodt S, Andersen NJ, Merrick J. Quality of life philosophy: when life sparkles or can we make wisdom a science? ScientificWorldJournal 2003;3:1160-3.

[22] Ventegodt S, Andersen NJ, Merrick J. QOL philosophy I: Quality of life, happiness, and meaning of life. ScientificWorldJournal 2003;3:1164-75.

[23] Ventegodt S, Andersen NJ, Kromann M, Merrick J. QOL philosophy II: What is a human being? ScientificWorldJournal 2003;3:1176-85.

[24] Ventegodt S, Merrick J, Andersen NJ. QOL philosophy III: Towards a new biology. ScientificWorldJournal 2003;3:1186-98.

[25] Ventegodt S, Andersen NJ, Merrick J. QOL philosophy IV: The brain and consciousness. ScientificWorldJournal 2003;3:1199-1209.

[26] Ventegodt S, Andersen NJ, Merrick J. QOL philosophy V: Seizing the meaning of life and getting well again. ScientificWorldJournal 2003;3:1210-29.

[27] Ventegodt S, Andersen NJ, Merrick J. QOL philosophy VI: The concepts. ScientificWorldJournal 2003;3:1230-40.

[28] Ventegodt S Merrick J. Philosophy of science: how to identify the potential research for the day after tomorrow? ScientificWorldJournal.2004;4:483-9.

[29] Ventegodt S, Merrick J, Andersen NJ. Quality of life theory I. The IQOL theory: An integrative theory of the global quality of life concept. ScientificWorldJournal 2003;3:1030-40.

[30] Ventegodt S, Merrick J, Andersen NJ. Quality of life theory II. Quality of life as the realization of life potential: A biological theory of human being. ScientificWorldJournal 2003;3:1041-9.

[31] Ventegodt S, Merrick J, Andersen NJ. Quality of life theory III. Maslow revisited. ScientificWorldJournal 2003;3:1050-7.

[32]   Ventegodt S, Andersen NJ, Merrick J. Editorial: Five theories of human existence. ScientificWorldJournal 2003;3:1272-76.

[33]   Ventegodt S. The life mission theory: A theory for a consciousness-based medicine. Int J Adolesc Med Health 2003;15(1): 89-91.

[34]   Ventegodt S, Andersen NJ, Merrick J. The life mission theory II: The structure of the life purpose and the ego. ScientificWorldJournal 2003;3:1277-85.

[35]   Ventegodt S, Andersen NJ, Merrick J. The life mission theory III: Theory of talent. ScientificWorldJournal 2003;3:1286-93.

[36]   Ventegodt S, Merrick J. The life mission theory IV. A theory of child development. ScientificWorldJournal 2003;3:1294-1301.

[37]   Ventegodt S, Andersen NJ, Merrick J. The life mission theory V. A theory of the anti-self and explaining the evil side of man. ScientificWorldJournal 2003;3:1302-13.

[38]   Ventegodt S, Andersen NJ, Merrick J. The life mission theory VI: A theory for the human character. ScientificWorldJournal 2004;4: 859-80.

[39]   Ventegodt S, Flensborg-Madsen T, Andersen NJ, Merrick J. Life mission theory VII: Theory of existential (Antonovsky) coherence: a theory of quality of life, health and ability for use in holistic medicine. ScientificWorldJournal 2005;5:377-89.

[40]   Ventegodt S, Merrick J. Life mission theory VIII: A theory for pain. J Pain Manage 2008;1(1):5-10.

[41]   Hermansen TD, Ventegodt S, Rald E, Clausen B, Nielsen ML, Merrick J. Human development I: twenty fundamental problems of biology, medicine, and neuro-psychology related to biological information. ScientificWorldJournal 2006;6:747-59.

[42]   Ventegodt S, Hermansen TD, Nielsen ML, Clausen B, Merrick J. Human development II: we need an integrated theory for matter, life and consciousness to understand life and healing. ScientificWorldJournal 2006;6:760-6.

[43]   Ventegodt S, Hermansen TD, Rald E, Flensborg-Madsen T, Nielsen ML, Clausen B, Merrick J. Human development III: bridging brain-mind and body-mind. introduction to "deep" (fractal, poly-ray) cosmology. ScientificWorldJournal 2006;6:767-76.

[44]   Ventegodt S, Hermansen TD, Flensborg-Madsen T, Nielsen ML, Clausen B, Merrick J. Human development IV: the living cell has information-directed self-organisation. ScientificWorldJournal. 2006;6:1132-8.

[45]   Ventegodt S, Hermansen TD, Flensborg-Madsen T, Nielsen ML, Clausen B, Merrick J. Human development V: biochemistry unable to explain the emergence of biological form (morphogenesis) and therefore a new principle as source of biological information is needed. ScientificWorldJournal 2006;6:1359-67.

[46]   Ventegodt S, Hermansen TD, Flensborg-Madsen T, Nielsen M, Merrick J. Human development VI: Supracellular morphogenesis. The origin of biological and cellular order. ScientificWorldJournal 2006;6:1424-33.

[47]   Ventegodt S, Hermansen TD, Flensborg-Madsen T, Rald E, Nielsen ML, Merrick J. Human development VII: A spiral fractal model of fine structure of physical energy could explain central aspects of biological information, biological organization and biological creativity. ScientificWorldJournal 2006;6:1434-40.

[48]   Ventegodt S, Hermansen TD, Flensborg-Madsen T, Nielsen ML, Merrick J. Human development VIII: A theory of "deep" quantum chemistry and cell consciousness: Quantum chemistry controls genes and biochemistry to give cells and higher organisms consciousness and complex behavior. ScientificWorldJournal 2006;6:1441-53.

[49]   Ventegodt S, Hermansen TD, Flensborg-Madsen T, Rald E, Nielsen ML, Merrick J. Human development IX: A model of the wholeness of man, his consciousness and collective consciousness. ScientificWorldJournal 2006;6:1454-9.

[50]   Hermansen TD, Ventegodt S, Merrick J. Human development X: Explanation of macroevolution — top-down evolution materializes consciousness. The origin of metamorphosis. ScientificWorldJournal 2006;6:1656-66.

[51]   Ventegodt S, Merrick J, Andersen NJ. Editorial-A new method for generic measuring of the global quality of life. ScientificWorldJournal 2003;3:946-9.

[52]   Ventegodt S, Hilden J, Merrick J. Measurement of quality of life I: A methodological framework. ScientificWorldJournal 2003;3:950-61.

[53]   Ventegodt S, Merrick J, Andersen NJ. Measurement of quality of life II. From philosophy of life to science. ScientificWorldJournal 2003;3:962-71.

[54]   Ventegodt S, Merrick J, Andersen NJ. Measurement of quality of life III: From the IQOL theory to the global, generic SEQOL questionnaire. ScientificWorldJournal 2003;3:972-91.

[55]   Ventegodt S, Merrick J, Andersen NJ. Measurement of quality of life IV: Use of the SEQOL, QOL5, QOL1 and other global and generic questionnaires. ScientificWorldJournal 2003;3:992-1001.

[56]   Ventegodt S, Merrick J, Andersen NJ. Measurement of quality of life V: How to use the SEQOL, QOL5, QOL1 and other and generic questionnaires for research. ScientificWorldJournal 2003;3:1002-14.

[57]   Ventegodt S, Merrick J, Andersen NJ. Measurement of quality of life VI: Quality-adjusted life years (QALY) is an unfortunate use of quality of life concept. ScientificWorldJournal 2003;3:1015-9.

[58]   Ventegodt S, Merrick J. Measurement of quality of life VII: Statistical covariation and global quality of life data. The method of weight-modified linear regression. ScientificWorldJournal 2003;3:1020-9.

[59]   Ventegodt S, Henneberg EW, Merrick J, Lindholt JS. Validation of two global and generic quality of life questionnaires for population screening: SCREENQOL and SEQOL. ScientificWorldJournal 2003;3:412-21.

[60]   Lindholt JS, Ventegodt S, Henneberg EW. Development and validation of QoL5 for clinical databases. A short, global and generic questionnaire based on an integrated theory of the quality of life. Eur J Surg 2002;168:103-7.

[61]   Ventegodt S. Sex and the quality of life in Denmark. Arch Sex Behav 1998;27(3):295-307.

[62]   Ventegodt S. A prospective study on quality of life and traumatic events in early life – 30 year follow-up. Child Care Health Dev 1998;25(3):213-21.

[63]   Ventegodt S, Merrick J. Long-term effects of maternal smoking on quality of life. Results from the Copenhagen Perinatal Birth Cohort 1959-61. ScientificWorld Journal 2003;3:714-20.

[64]   Ventegodt S, Merrick J. Long-term effects of maternal medication on global quality of life measured with SEQOL. Results from the Copenhagen Perinatal Birth Cohort 1959-61. ScientificWorldJournal 2003;3:707-13.

[65]   Ventegodt S, Merrick J. Psychoactive drugs and quality of life. ScientificWorldJournal 2003;3:694-706.

[66]   Ventegodt S, Merrick J. Lifestyle, quality of life and health. ScientificWorldJournal 2003;3:811-25.

[67]   Ventegodt S, Flensborg-Madsen T, Andersen NJ, Merrick J. The health and social situation of the mother during pregnancy and global quality of life of the child as an adult. Results from the prospective Copenhagen Perinatal Cohort 1959-1961. ScientificWorldJournal. 2005;5:950-8.

[68]   Ventegodt S, Flensborg-Madsen T, Anderson NJ, Merrick J. Factors during pregnancy, delivery and birth affecting global quality of life of the adult child at long-term follow-up. Results from the prospective Copenhagen Perinatal Birth Cohort 1959-61. ScientificWorldJournal. 2005;5:933-41.

[69]   Ventegodt S, Flensborg-Madsen T, Andersen NJ, Merrick J. Events in pregnancy, delivery, and infancy and long-term effects on global quality of life: results from the Copenhagen Perinatal Birth Cohort 1959-61. Med Sci Monit 2005;11(8):CR357-65.

[70]   Ventegodt S, Flensborg-Madsen T, Andersen NJ, Morad M, Merrick J. Quality of life and events in the first year of life. Results from the prospective Copenhagen Birth Cohort 1959-61. ScientificWorldJournal. 2006;6:106-15.

[71]   Ventegodt S, Flensborg-Madsen T, Andersen NJ, Merrick J. What influence do major events in life have on our later quality of life? A retrospective study on life events and associated emotions. Med Sci Monit 2006;12(2):SR9-15.

[72]   Ventegodt S. Every contact with the patient must be therapeutic. J Pediatr Adoles Gynecol 2007;20(6):323-4.

[73]   Ventegodt S, Merrick J. Psychosomatic reasons for chronic pains. South Med J 2005;98(11):1063.

[74]   Ventegodt S, Andersen NJ, Merrick J. Holistic medicine: Scientific challenges. ScientificWorldJournal 2003;3:1108-16.

[75]   Ventegodt S, Andersen NJ, Merrick J. Holistic Medicine II: The square-curve paradigm for research in alternative, complementary and holistic medicine: A cost-effective, easy and scientifically valid design for evidence based medicine. ScientificWorldJournal 2003;3: 1117-27.

[76]   Ventegodt S, Andersen NJ, Merrick J. Holistic Medicine III: The holistic process theory of healing. ScientificWorldJournal 2003;3:1138-46.

[77]   Ventegodt S, Andersen NJ, Merrick J. Holistic Medicine IV: Principles of the holistic process of healing in a group setting. ScientificWorldJournal 2003;3:1294-1301.

[78]   Ventegodt S, Merrick J. Clinical holistic medicine: Applied consciousness-based medicine. ScientificWorldJournal 2004;4:96-9.

[79]   Ventegodt S, Morad M, Merrick J. Clinical holistic medicine: Classic art of healing or the therapeutic touch. ScientificWorldJournal 2004;4:134-47.

[80]   Ventegodt S, Morad M, Merrick J. Clinical holistic medicine: The "new medicine", the multi-paradigmatic physician and the medical record. ScientificWorldJournal 2004;4:273-85.

[81]   Ventegodt S, Morad M, Merrick J. Clinical holistic medicine: Holistic pelvic examination and holistic treatment of infertility. ScientificWorldJournal 2004;4:148-58.

[82]   Ventegodt S, Morad M, Hyam E, Merrick J. Clinical holistic medicine: Use and limitations of the biomedical paradigm ScientificWorldJournal 2004;4:295-306.

[83]   Ventegodt S, Morad M, Kandel I, Merrick J. Clinical holistic medicine: Social problems disguised as illness. ScientificWorldJournal 2004;4:286-94.

[84]   Ventegodt S, Morad M, Andersen NJ, Merrick J. Clinical holistic medicine Tools for a medical science based on consciousness. ScientificWorldJournal 2004;4:347-61.

[85]   Ventegodt S, Morad M, Merrick J. Clinical holistic medicine: Prevention through healthy lifestyle and quality of life. Oral Health Prev Dent 2004;1:239-45.

[86]   Ventegodt S, Morad M, Hyam E, Merrick J. Clinical holistic medicine: When biomedicine is inadequate. ScientificWorldJournal 2004;4:333-46.

[87]   Ventegodt S, Morad M, Merrick J. Clinical holistic medicine: Holistic treatment of children. ScientificWorldJournal 2004;4:581-8.

[88]   Ventegodt S, Morad M, Merrick J. Clinical holistic medicine: Problems in sex and living together. ScientificWorldJournal 2004;4: 562-70.

[89]   Ventegodt S, Morad M, Hyam E, Merrick J. Clinical holistic medicine: Holistic sexology and treatment of vulvodynia through existential therapy and acceptance through touch. ScientificWorldJournal 2004;4:571-80.

[90]   Ventegodt S, Flensborg-Madsen T, Andersen NJ, Morad M, Merrick J. Clinical holistic medicine: A Pilot on HIV and Quality of Life and a Suggested treatment of HIV and AIDS. ScientificWorldJournal 2004;4:264-72.

[91]   Ventegodt S, Morad M, Merrick J. Clinical holistic medicine: Induction of spontaneous remission of cancer by recovery of the human character and the purpose of life (the life mission). ScientificWorldJournal 2004;4:362-77.

[92]   Ventegodt S, Morad M, Kandel I, Merrick J. Clinical holistic medicine: Treatment of physical health problems without a known cause, exemplified by hypertension and tinnitus. ScientificWorldJournal 2004;4:716-24.

[93]   Ventegodt S, Morad M, Merrick J. Clinical holistic medicine: Developing from asthma, allergy and eczema. ScientificWorldJournal 2004;4:936-42.

[94]   Ventegodt S, Morad M, Press J, Merrick J, Shek D. Clinical holistic medicine: Holistic adolescent medicine. ScientificWorldJournal 2004;4:551-61.

[95]   Ventegodt S, Solheim E, Saunte ME, Morad M, Kandel I, Merrick J. Clinical holistic medicine: Metastatic cancer. ScientificWorldJournal 2004;4:913-35.

[96]   Ventegodt S, Morad M, Kandel I, Merrick J. Clinical holistic medicine: a psychological theory of dependency to improve quality of life. ScientificWorldJournal 2004;4:638-48.

[97]   Ventegodt S, Merrick J. Clinical holistic medicine: Chronic infections and autoimmune diseases. ScientificWorldJournal 2005;5:155-64.

[98] Ventegodt S, Kandel I, Neikrug S, Merrick J. Clinical holistic medicine: Holistic treatment of rape and incest traumas. ScientificWorldJournal 2005;5:288-97.

[99] Ventegodt S, Morad M, Merrick J. Clinical holistic medicine: Chronic pain in the locomotor system. ScientificWorldJournal 2005;5:165-72.

[100] Ventegodt, S. Merrick, J. Clinical holistic medicine: Chronic pain in internal organs. ScientificWorldJournal 2005;5:205-10.

[101] Ventegodt S, Kandel I, Neikrug S, Merrick J. Clinical holistic medicine: The existential crisis – life crisis, stress and burnout. ScientificWorldJournal 2005;5:300-12.

[102] Ventegodt S, Gringols G, Merrick J. Clinical holistic medicine: Holistic rehabilitation. ScientificWorldJournal 2005;5:280-7.

[103] Ventegodt S, Andersen NJ, Neikrug S, Kandel I, Merrick J. Clinical holistic medicine: Mental disorders in a holistic perspective. ScientificWorldJournal 2005;5:313-23.

[104] Ventegodt S, Andersen NJ, Neikrug S, Kandel I, Merrick J. Clinical Holistic medicine: Holistic treatment of mental disorders. ScientificWorldJournal 2005;5:427-45.

[105] Ventegodt S, Merrick J. Clinical holistic medicine: The patient with multiple diseases. ScientificWorldJournal 2005;5:324-39.

[106] Ventegodt S, Clausen B, Nielsen ML, Merrick J. Advanced tools for holistic medicine. ScientificWorldJournal 2006;6:2048-65

[107] Ventegodt S, Clausen B, Merrick J. Clinical holistic medicine: The case story of Anna: I. Long term effect of child sexual abuse and incest with a treatment approach. ScientificWorldJournal 2006;6:1965-76.

[108] Ventegodt S, Morad M, Merrick J. Clinical holistic medicine: the case story of Anna. II. Patient diary as a tool in treatment. ScientificWorldJournal 2006;6:2006-34.

[109] Ventegodt S, Morad M, Merrick J. Clinical holistic medicine: The case story of Anna. III. Rehabilitation of philosophy of life during holistic existential therapy for childhood sexual abuse. ScientificWorldJournal 2006;6:2080-91.

[110] Ventegodt S, Merrick J. Suicide from a holistic point of view. ScientificWorldJournal 2005;5:759-66.

[111] Ventegodt S, Clausen B, Omar HA, Merrick J. Clinical holistic medicine: Holistic sexology and acupressure through the vagina (Hippocratic pelvic massage). ScientificWorldJournal 2006;6:2066-79.

[112] Ventegodt S, Clausen B, Merrick J. Clinical holistic medicine: Pilot study on the effect of vaginal acupressure (Hippocratic pelvic massage). ScientificWorldJournal 2006;6:2100-16.

[113] Ventegodt S. [Min brug af vaginal akupressur.] (My use of acupressure.) Ugeskr Laeger 2006;168(7):715-6. [Danish]

[114] Ventegodt S, Thegler S, Andreasen T, Struve F, Enevoldsen L, Bassaine L, et al. Clinical holistic medicine: Psychodynamic short-time therapy complemented with bodywork. A clinical follow-up study of 109 patients. ScientificWorldJournal 2006;6:2220-38.

[115] Ventegodt S, Thegler S, Andreasen T, Struve F, Enevoldsen L, Bassaine L, et al. Clinical holistic medicine (mindful, short-term psychodynamic psychotherapy complemented with bodywork) in the treatment of experienced impaired sexual functioning. ScientificWorldJournal 2007;7:324-9.

[116] Ventegodt S, Thegler S, Andreasen T, Struve F, Enevoldsen L, Bassaine L, et al. Clinical holistic medicine (mindful, short-term psychodynamic psychotherapy complemented with bodywork) improves quality of life, health, and ability by induction of Antonovsky-salutogenesis. ScientificWorldJournal 2007;7:317-23.

[117] Ventegodt S, Thegler S, Andreasen T, Struve F, Enevoldsen L, Bassaine L, et al. Clinical holistic medicine (mindful, short-term psychodynamic psychotherapy complemented with bodywork) in the treatment of experienced physical illness and chronic pain. ScientificWorldJournal 2007;7:310-6.

[118] Ventegodt S, Thegler S, Andreasen T, Struve F, Enevoldsen L, Bassaine L, et al. Clinical holistic medicine (mindful, short-term psychodynamic psychotherapy complemented with bodywork) in the treatment of experienced mental illness. ScientificWorldJournal. 2007;7:306-9.

[119] Ventegodt S, Thegler S, Andreasen T, Struve F, Enevoldsen L, Bassaine L, et al. Self-reported low self-esteem. Intervention and follow-up in a clinical setting. ScientificWorldJournal 2007;7:299-305.

[120] Flensborg-Madsen T, Ventegodt S, Merrick J. Sense of coherence and physical health. A Review of previous findings. ScientificWorldJournal 2005;5:665-73.

[121] Flensborg-Madsen T, Ventegodt S, Merrick J. Why is Antonovsky's sense of coherence not correlated to physical health? Analysing Antonovsky's 29-item sense of coherence scale (SOCS). ScientificWorldJournal 2005;5:767-76.

[122] Flensborg-Madsen T, Ventegodt S, Merrick J. Sense of coherence and health. The construction of an amendment to Antonovsky's sense of coherence scale (SOC II). ScientificWorldJournal 2006;6:2133-9.

[123] Flensborg-Madsen T, Ventegodt S, Merrick J. Sense of coherence and physical health. A cross-sectional study using a new SOC scale (SOC II). ScientificWorldJournal 2006;6:2200-11.

[124] Flensborg-Madsen T, Ventegodt S, Merrick J. Sense of coherence and physical health. Testing Antonovsky's theory. ScientificWorldJournal 2006;6:2212-9.

[125] Flensborg-Madsen T, Ventegodt S, Merrick J. Sense of coherence and health. The emotional sense of coherence (SOC-E) was found to be the best-known predictor of physical health. ScientificWorldJournal 2006;6:2147-57.

[126] Merrick J, Ventegodt S. What is a good death? To use death as a mirror and find the quality in life. BMJ. Rapid Response 2003 Oct 31.

[127] Ventegodt S, Merrick J. Medicine and the past. Lesson to learn about the pelvic examination and its sexually suppressive procedure. BMJ. Rapid Response 2004 Feb 20.

[128] Ventegodt S, Morad M, Merrick J. If it doesn't work, stop it. Do something else! BMJ. Rapid Response 2004 Apr 26.

[129] Merrick J, Morad M, Kandel I, Ventegodt S. Spiritual health, intellectual disability and health care. BMJ Rapid Response 2004 Jul 16.

[130] Ventegodt S, Morad M, Kandel I, Merrick J. Maternal smoking and quality of life more than thirty years later. BMJ Rapid Response 2004 Jul 30.

[131] Merrick J, Morad M, Kandel I, Ventegodt S. Prevalence of Helicobacter pylori infection in residential care centers for people with intellectual disability. BMJ Rapid Response 2004 Jul 23.

[132] Merrick J, Morad M, Kandel I, Ventegodt S. People with intellectual disability, health needs and policy. BMJ Rapid Response 2004 Aug 20.

[133] Ventegodt S, Vardi G, Merrick J. Holistic adolescent sexology: How to counsel and treat young people to alleviate and prevent sexual problems. BMJ Rapid Response 2005 Jan 15.

[134] Ventegodt S, Flensborg-Madsen T, Merrick J. Evidence based medicine in favor of biomedicine and it seems that holistic medicine has been forgotten? BMJ Rapid Response 2004 Nov 11.

[135] Ventegodt S, Merrick J. Placebo explained: Consciousness causal to health. BMJ Rapid Response 2004 Oct 22.

[136] Ventegodt S, Merrick J. Academic medicine must deliver skilled physicians. A different academic training is needed. BMJ Rapid Response 2004 Oct 9.

[137] Ventegodt S, Morad M, Merrick J. Chronic illness, the patient and the holistic medical toolbox. BMJ Rapid Response 2004 Sep 15.

[138] Ventegodt S, Kandel I, Merrick J.. Medicine has gone astray - we must reverse the alienation now. BMJ Rapid Response 2005 Mar 10.

[139] Ventegodt S, Merrick J. The consensus paradigm for qualitative research in holistic medicine. BMJ Rapid Response 2005 Nov 24.

[140] Ventegodt S, Kandel I, Merrick J. Principles of holistic medicine. Philosophy behind quality of life. Victoria, BC: Trafford, 2005.

[141] Ventegodt S, Kandel I, Merrick J. Principles of holistic medicine. Quality of life and health. New York: Hippocrates Sci Publ, 2005.

[142] Ventegodt S, Kandel I, Merrick J. Principles of holistic medicine. Global quality of life. Theory, research and methodology. New York: Hippocrates Sci Publ, 2005.

[143] Ventegodt S. Measuring the quality of life. From theory to practice. Copenhagen: Forskningscentrets Forlag, 1996.

Chapter 9

How does antipsychotic drugs and non-drug therapy effect quality-adjusted life-years (QALY) in persons with borderline and psychotic mental illness?

It is impossible for patients, physicians and health-politicians to know, which treatment to choose if the treatment outcome is not in one integrative measure. To evaluate the total outcome of the treatment of borderline and psychotic mentally ill patients with antipsychotic drugs compared to non-drug treatments, we choose the two major outcomes "quality of life" (QOL) and "survival time" integrated into one total outcome measure, the Quality-Adjusted Life Years (QALY). We estimated total outcome in QALY (Δ QALY) by multiplying the estimated difference in global QOL (Δ QOL) and the estimated difference in survival time (Δ survival time): Δ QALY= $\sum_{\text{all outcomes}}(\Delta QOL \times \Delta$ survival time). We included factors like suicide and spontaneous drug-induced death that is normally not included in clinical randomized trials of antipsychotic drugs. We found that the total outcome of treatments with antipsychotic drugs was about -2 QALY; the total outcome from non-drug therapies (psychodynamic psychotherapy, clinical holistic medicine) was about $+8$ QALY. When the total outcomes of the treatments were measured in QALY, antipsychotic drugs harmed the patients, while the patients benefited from the non-drug therapies. Antipsychotic drugs violate the medical ethics of Hippocrates, "First do no harm"; non-drug therapy is therefore the rational treatment for the borderline and psychotic mental illnesses. Treatment with antipsychotic drugs is only justified, when prolonged non-drug therapy has failed.

Introduction

To evaluate the total outcome in medicine there are two general outcomes of primary interest: *survival* and *global quality of life*. These two measures can easily be integrated into Quality-Adjusted Life Years (QALY) (1). A positive QALY-contribution comes from positive effects of a treatment, and a negative QALY-contribution comes from a negative effect, called the adverse or side effects, like for example the patient's death caused either by drug-induced suicide or by the toxic adverse effects. Recent studies on all mentally ill patients in Denmark revealed a high risk of suicide (2) and unexplained death associated with psychiatric treatment and antipsychotic drugs (3). NNT (number needed to treat) and NNH (number needed to harm) numbers have been calculated for the treatment with antipsychotic drugs (4) and for the non-drug treatment (5), and the NNHs have been added up to a total NNH (4,5). Only some aspects of effects and side effects were related to QOL judged from the empery from the QOL-research (6-10); the NNT and NNH related to global QOL were thus evaluated on an empirical basis to estimate the size of the impact on QOL both of the positive and negative effects, to find the total impact on QOL of the treatment. Then the treatments impact on survival was evaluated. All in all the results made it possible to estimate the total positive and negative impact of the two alternative treatments in the dimensions *QOL* and *survival time*. From this we calculated the QALY impact of the different treatments of mentally ill with antipsychotic drugs and without these drugs, to compare them and find the rational, evidence-based treatment.

The borderline and psychotic, mentally ill patients and their physicians can today choose between either a drug treatment or a non-drug therapy like psychodynamic psychotherapy (11-15) or scientific CAM (complementary and alternative medicine i.e. clinical holistic medicine) (16-18). Till this day many different outcomes and adverse effects have made the picture highly unclear to the patients, the doctor, and the political decision maker. This study aims to provide the integrated outcome data needed to make a scientific comparison of the therapeutic value of the competing treatments and thus the data needed for a rational choice.

Our review

The QALY analyses of the effect of the non-drug treatments were rather trivial; although we had no data on survival, we had no reason to believe that any patient's life was shortened because of non-drug therapy (5). Quite on the contrary it seemed the therapy would prevent suicide and prolong life, but no accurate data could be found, so we did not include this in our calculations. We found QOL to be improved (11), or more often positive effects indicating that QOL was improved for the mentally ill patients (6-8) including patients with schizophrenia (9,10), thus giving a positive QALY outcome of non-drug therapy for mental illness.

The analysis of the QALY outcome for the treatment of mentally ill patients with antipsychotic drugs was much more complicated, so we had to build it partly on a meta-analysis on the total outcome of antipsychotic drugs (4), and partly on other studies as there were factors difficult to include in the traditional effect study due to lack of data. Factors like suicide rates and spontaneous drug-induced over-mortality were most often not included in the randomized clinical trials, so this information needed to be collected from separate studies. So we build the QALY-meta-analysis on the outcomes of antipsychotic drugs, and included the factors that were not included in the studies, to get a more complete picture of the positive and negative effects of antipsychotic drugs. Thus the present analysis contains more information and therefore is likely to give a more accurate picture than the documentation provided by the pharmaceutical industry.

We estimated the total outcome in QALY by multiplying the estimated difference in global QOL and the estimated difference in survival time: Δ QALY= $\sum_{all\ outcomes}(\Delta QOL \times \Delta$ survival time). We made all estimations conservatively, to avoid adding a bias here. We estimated conservatively the average patient to be 25 years old at treatment start; we know that most persons with schizophrenia are diagnosed between 15 and 25 years of age. The antipsychotic treatment is normally continuing for the rest of the patient's life, which we conservatively set to last for 65 years (which is shorter than the average life span of about 75). We used the measure "global QOL" and not health-related QOL, which is not based on QOL-theory, but only on ad hoc measures (19) and preferred values confirmed with many different measures to large values only confirmed by one measure. We avoided the problems related to QALY described in an earlier paper (1).

What did we find?

Recent Cochrane meta-analysis has shown that all antipsychotic drugs share the effect profile of chlorpromazine with a similar toxicity (20). We only found the outcome "mental state" relevant to QOL, as "relapse", "behavior" and "global state/global impression" all related to behavior, or to a mix of behavior and mental state. For comparison a normal life in Denmark is 75 life-years (21) of a mean 70% QOL (12,13) equivalent to 52.5 QALY.

Antipsychotic drugs, positive QALY-contributions

For antipsychotic drugs we found no improvement in mental state in our meta-analysis of 79 Cochrane meta-analyses of antipsychotic drugs (4). The analysis included all relevant data on subjective dimensions like fear, agitation, hallucinations, confusion etc. None of the dimensions related to global QOL showed any improvement; thus the positive contribution from improvement of mental state was 0.00 QALY.

Antipsychotic drugs, negative QALY-contributions

We found in our meta-analysis (4) that severe adverse effects were very common with antipsychotic drugs, on average every patient had at least 1.66 adverse effects (11). We know from an earlier study that people with one or two health problems on average have a global quality of life that is 74.2% compared to people without health problems who have a global QOL of 76.1% (12); the health problems is therefore associated with a loss of global QOL of 1.9% for as long as the drugs are taken, which is normally all life if treated with antipsychotic drugs. This sums up to a QALY impact of −1.9% QOL x 40 Years= -0.76 QALY.

2.04% of the patients in the schizophrenic spectrum committed suicide in direct connection to starting the drug treatment (during psychiatric admission) and another 2.80% committed suicide immediately after admission (0-6 month) (22) giving a total of 4.84% of the patients with psychotic mental illnesses committing suicide in connection to the treatment with antipsychotic drugs, which is standard treatment in Denmark. As these patients are normally young (estimated mean of 25 years) and life expectancy of at least 65 years (conservative estimate), with at least a QOL of 41.4% (schizophrenia) (the global QOL for schizophrenic patients in Denmark (13)), this sums up to a QALY impact of –4.84% x 41.4% QOL x 40 Years= -0.80 QALY.

We know that antipsychotic drugs is associated with an 25% increased likelihood of unexplained sudden death, which normally is about 0.3% a year (23) and this continues for every year the drugs are taken; this sums up to a total of 40 years x 0.25 over-mortality/year, equal to10 times the normal mortality from spontaneous death of 0.3%; each death takes in average 20 years from the persons life. The total likelihood for spontaneous death is thus 3%. This sums up to a QALY impact of -3% x 20 years x 41.4% QOL= -0.25 QALY. The total QALY outcome of antipsychotic drugs is –1.81 QALY (see table 1).

Non-drug therapy, positive QALY-contributions

Psychodynamic psychotherapy have in uncontrolled studies cured 1/3 to 1/8 of the schizophrenic patients (9,10) and clinical holistic medicine have cured 57% of patients who felt mentally ill (11); a conservative calculation of non-drug therapy gives us a permanent improvement of QOL of 20%; the QALY contribution is thus 40 years x 20% QOL = 8 QALY. The 20% improvement in global QOL is conformed by measuring the global QOL before, after and one year after non-drug treatment (11,24).

Non-drug therapy, negative QALY-contributions

Adverse effects are generally considered not to be a problem in non-drug therapy, and suicide is very rare and actually more likely to be prevented that to be provoked (5-11,25). There is no indication of spontaneous death happening more often that usual (5). Conservatively estimated the QALY contribution from this is +0.00 QALY. The total QALY outcome from the non-drugs treatment psychodynamic psychotherapy and clinical holistic medicine is thus about 8 QALY (see table 1).

Discussion

The method of QALY has been criticized because of the many different ways QOL can be measured (1), giving very different results depending on the QOL-measure. We find this critique to be correct when it comes to health-related QOL; we have therefore measured global QOL in 11 different ways (12-15,19) and have learned that the measure of global QOL is fairly robust, and surprisingly independent of theory and composition of questions in the questionnaire (12,13,19). This means that global QOL can bee seen as a real, measurable phenomenon, and the measure of global QOL as an expression of a person's global state of life. The multiplication of global QOL and life years have been criticized also for being to simple; a long life with poor quality of life could be worse than being dead (1) and suicide could therefore be a rational act. We do not find any of these considerations conflicting with our estimations. We conclude that the presented conservative estimates are fair and free from bias.

Table 1. QALY outcome from treatments with antipsychotic drugs and the non-drug treatments (PP= psychodynamic psychotherapy; CHM= clinical holistic medicine)

Treatment	QALY contribution
Antipsychotic drugs, positive treatment effect	+ 0.00 QALY
Antipsychotic drugs, adverse effects	-0.76 QALY
Antipsychotic drugs, suicide	-0.80 QALY
Antipsychotic drugs, spontaneous death	-0.25 QALY
Total QALY contribution, antipsychotic drugs	-1.81 QALY
Non-drug treatment (PP, CHM), positive treatment effects	+8.00 QALY (ref)
Non-drug treatment (PP, CHM), adverse effects	- 0.00 QALY
Non-drug treatment (PP, CHM), suicide	+ 0.00 (preventive effects, size unknown)
Non-drug treatment (PP,CHM), spontaneous death	- 0.00 QALY
Total QALY contribution, non-drug treatment (PP, CHM)	+ 8.00 QALY

Conclusions

In the treatment of the psychotic mentally ill patient, the total outcome of the treatment with antipsychotic drugs is -2 QALY, while the total outcome of non-drug therapies (psychodynamic psychotherapy and clinical holistic medicine) is +8 QALY (see table 1). The treatment with antipsychotic drugs is harming the patient, while the treatment with the non-drug therapy is beneficial judged from a QALY analysis. We must therefore strongly recommend non-drug therapy to patients with borderline and psychotic mental illnesses, whenever possible and warn against the extensive use of antipsychotic drugs.

References

[1] Ventegodt S, Merrick J, Andersen NJ. Measurement of quality of life VI: Quality-adjusted life years (QALY) are an unfortunate use of quality of life concept. ScientificWorldJournal 2003;3:1015-9.

[2] Qin P, Nordentoft M. Suicide risk in relation to psychiatric hospitalization: evidence based on longitudinal registers. Arch Gen Psychiatry 2005;62(4):427-32.

[3] Lindhardt A, ed. The use of antipsychotic drugs among the 18-64 year old patients with schizophrenia, mania, or bipolar affective disorder. Copenhagen: National Board Health, 2006. [Danish].

[4] Ventegodt S, Flensborg-Madsen T, Andersen NJ, Svanberg BØ, Struve F, Merrick J. Therapeutic value of antipsychotic drugs: A critical analysis of Cochrane meta-analyses of the therapeutic value of antipsychotic drugs. Lancet, submitted.

[5] Ventegodt S, Kandel I, Merrick J. A metaanalysis of side effects of psychotherapy, bodywork, and clinical holistic medicine. J Complement Integr Med, submitted.

[6]   Leichsenring F, Rabung S, Leibing E. The efficacy of short-term psychodynamic psychotherapy in specific psychiatric disorders: a meta-analysis. Arch Gen Psychiatry 2004;61(12):1208-16.

[7]   Leichsenring F. Are psychodynamic and psychoanalytic therapies effective?: A review of empirical data. Int J Psychoanal 2005;86(Pt 3):841-68.

[8]   Leichsenring F, Leibing E. Psychodynamic psychotherapy: a systematic review of techniques, indications and empirical evidence. Psychol Psychother 2007;80(Pt 2):217-28.

[9]   Modestin J, Huber A, Satirli E, Malti T, Hell D. Long-term course of schizophrenic illness: Bleuler's study reconsidered. Am J Psychiatry 2003;160(12):2202-8.

[10] Searles HF. Collected papers on schizophrenia. Madison, CT: Int Univ Press, 1965:15–18.

[11] Ventegodt S, Thegler S, Andreasen T, Struve F, Enevoldsen L, Bassaine L, Torp M, Merrick J. Clinical holistic medicine (mindful, short-term psychodynamic psychotherapy complemented with bodywork) in the treatment of experienced mental illness. ScientificWorldJournal 2007;7:306-9.

[12] Ventegodt S. [Livskvalitet i Danmark]. Quality of life in Denmark. Results from a population survey. Copenhagen: Forskningscentrets Forlag, 1995. [partly in Danish].

[13] Ventegodt S. [Livskvalitet hos 4500 31-33 årige]. The Quality of Life of 4500 31-33 year-olds. Result from a study of the Prospective Pediatric Cohort of persons born at the University Hospital in Copenhagen. Copenhagen: Forskningscentrets Forlag, 1996. [partly in Danish].

[14] Ventegodt S. [Livskvalitet og omstændigheder tidligt i livet]. The quality of life and factors in pregnancy, birth and infancy. Results from a follow-up study of the Prospective Pediatric Cohort of persons born at the University Hospital in Copenhagen 1959-61. Copenhagen: Forskningscentrets Forlag, 1995. [partly in Danish].

[15] Ventegodt S. [Livskvalitet og livets store begivenheder]. The Quality of Life and Major Events in Life. Copenhagen: Forskningscentrets Forlag, 2000. [partly in Danish].

[16] Ventegodt S, Kandel I, Merrick J. Principles of holistic medicine. Philosophy behind quality of life. Victoria, BC: Trafford, 2005.

[17] Ventegodt S, Kandel I, Merrick J. Principles of holistic medicine. Quality of life and health. New York: Hippocrates Sci Publ, 2005.

[18] Ventegodt S, Kandel I, Merrick J. Principles of holistic medicine. Global quality of life. theory, research and methodology. New York: Hippocrates Science, 2005.

[19] Ventegodt S. Measuring the quality of life. From theory to practice. Copenhagen: Forskningscentrets Forlag, 1996.

[20] Adams CE, Awad G, Rathbone J, Thornley B. Chlorpromazine versus placebo for schizophrenia. Cochrane Database Syst Rev 2007;(2):CD000284.

[21] Gunnersen SJ. Statistical yearbook. Copenhagen: Statistics Denmark, 2007.

[22] Qin P, Nordentoft M. Suicide risk in relation to psychiatric hospitalization: evidence based on longitudinal registers. Arch Gen Psychiatry 2005;62(4):427-32.

[23] Lindhardt A, et al. [Forbruget af antipsykotika blandt 18-64 årige patienter med skizofreni, mani eller bipolar affektiv sindslidelse]. Copenhagen: Sundhedsstyrelsen, 2006. [Danish].

[24] Ventegodt S, Thegler S, Andreasen T, Struve F, Enevoldsen L, Bassaine L, Torp M, Merrick J. Clinical holistic medicine: Psychodynamic short-time therapy complemented with bodywork. A clinical follow-up Study of 109 patients. ScientificWorldJournal 2006;6:2220-38.

[25] Polewka A, Maj JC, Warchoł K, Groszek B. [The assessment of suicidal risk in the concept of the presuicidal syndrome, and the possibilities it provides for suicide prevention and therapy--review]. Przegl Lek 2005;62:399-402. [Polish].

Chapter 10

Use and limitations of the biomedical paradigm

The bio-medical paradigm is so convincing from a biochemical point of view, and highly efficient in many cases of acute medical problems and emergencies, but unfortunately most chronically mental ill patients cannot be treated to get much better only with drugs, they need to do something about their lives themselves.

It is highly important for the modern physician to understand the strength and weakness of the modern biomedical paradigm, to understand when and when not to administer drugs to their patients. Often a symptom can be eliminated for a while with drugs, but this is not always good as the patient might need the learning from studying the imbalances in life causing the disturbances and symptoms.

Sometimes the treatment with a drug can falsely teach the patient that quality of life is the responsibility of the physician and not the patient. This learned attitude can give the patient problems later or make them less active in helping themselves (responsibility transfer in the wrong direction). This chapter gives a number of examples, where medical drugs really are the treatment of choice in general practice, and some more doubtful examples of using of the biomedical paradigm. We also argue that sometimes life can be extended in spite of the subjective fact for the elderly patient that life has come to its end, but such a prolongation might not be ethical.

Introduction

In the past more than 50 years we have seen the emergence of a new medical science based on molecular biology, often called biomedicine. It is a highly developed, biochemical science with pharmaceuticals – chemical drugs based on specially designed molecules, often with a specific effect on cellular receptor molecules. Chemically and technologically, this is science at its most advanced stage. On the other hand many diseases end up being chronic, meaning that they persist in spite of the pharmaceutical treatment.

Chronic disease and disability represent a huge burden of ill health and a large – and growing - cost to modern society (1). The problem of chronic disease has led to the very provocative conclusion, that "drugs don't work" (2,3). It is well known that most drugs need five patients or more treated to demonstrate an effect, meaning that most of the patients are not helped by most of the drugs, a fact that even the medical industry seems to admit now.

This leaves us with extremely interesting questions: who will get well again and who will not? Or put it in another way: What kind of diseases shall we expect to be cured by pharmaceuticals drugs and which diseases would it be wise to treat with other medical strategies, i.e. alternative or holistic therapy on body, mind and feelings?

The strengths and weaknesses of the biomedical paradigm

This chapter provides some success stories of biomedical treatment, to demonstrate sufficient examples of successful biomedicine to crystallize the biomedical paradigm in its most useful form. The physician is intervening at the cellular level, often with highly designed and very biologically potent drugs. It is thus possible to regulate aspects of cell-functioning, like acid-forming cells can be stopped producing gastric acid (e.g. with Losec), or the communication between cells can be overridden so that the ovaries no longer produce eggs (contraceptive pills), or bacteria can be fought (with drugs like penicillin that inhibit bacterial growth) without any significant impact or damage to the cells of the body in the person treated. Biomedicine is known as "bio", because it applies biochemistry and molecular biology, thereby interfering with the chemistry of life itself.

When you stop and think about it, you will realize that this is really amazing. In principle, biomedicine is highly effective, when it can do this. When you look at it more closely and from a theoretical viewpoint, however, it is less impressive because many of the effects, side-effects and adverse reactions of a pharmaceutical product in a clinical test cannot be explained or predicted on the basis of biomedical theory. The truth is that we do not understand the information systems of the body at the molecular level well enough to do so. Whenever we treat our patients with designed molecules that interfere with the body's intercellular communication, we are not in complete control of the effects and adverse reactions of the drug, in spite of even numerous clinical trials in animals and humans . Since we do not have complete knowledge of the underlying causes of a disease – the large biomedical textbooks state with regard to almost any disease that its cause is not understood – and since we do not have complete control of the effects of the drugs prescribed, whether in the short or the long term, we need to keep an eye on how any specific drug will act in a given patient.

Biomedicine has been developed and tested in order to counteract a specific, well-defined pathology. The physician prescribes it for that indication, e.g., depression, allergy or hypertension. Before it is launched on the market, it has been tested as mentioned above for effects, side-effects and adverse reactions in long series of studies, first in animals and then in humans. It is not possible to know exactly what will happen in the patient, until it has been tried. If the medicine works the way it should without any visible damage it will be marketed.

Biomedicine is really good at treating lots of diseases. But there is a limit to what you can achieve by biochemical means, and we should be highly alert to that limit in our medical practice. We should be particularly alert, because the problems that many of our patients are facing can often be solved without pills, which after all cannot solve all their problems.

Below are some examples of what we call "perfect biomedicine". These are biomedical cures that we still use in our own medical practice, even when we master a series of holistic treatment techniques, because we acknowledge these cures to be of excellent and unique value to our patients. It consists of antibiotics and other drugs that we safely apply. Sometimes we face problems that we as physicians cannot solve with biomedicine, and must therefore look more closely at the limitations of biomedicine. Both ways of looking gives important information that guide us in our choice of treatment in the clinic.

Let us emphasize, if you should doubt it, that we have absolute faith in science. When a new pharmaceutical has been investigated in randomised studies, which is in principle a thoroughly sound scientific basis, by objective and unbiased researchers and according to standard protocols, we will not hesitate to acknowledge the documented effect. However, often times many details in the studies performed are open to criticism, especially the danger of scientific bias, when a pharmaceutical company needs to document the efficacy of its own drug. According to recent investigations, such bias appears to be a real threat to the scientific integrity of a study (4) making many patients take pills that actually does not work well on their condition.

When a drug in a clinical study is tested actively for a given symptom we would generally believe in its effect. But the situation is more complicated: this does not mean, however, that it would be a sensible move in general practice to remove that symptom with this drug, just because it is possible. The symptom suppressed will perhaps just be replaced by a symptom or problem that is deeper, more dangerous and more difficult to trace. And perhaps the patient has a lesson to learn from the condition, which is why it would be highly problematic to eliminate it, depriving the patient of vital learning.

The modern biomedical physician applies about 100 different medicinal products in his practice. For a pharmacology examination, an excellent test would be to let the student choose the 15 drugs that would suffice in a biomedical practice in the great majority of cases, including antibiotics, analgesics, diuretics, hydrocortisone, anticoagulants, etc. All these drugs have their clinical merits, including from the perspective of holistic medicine. Below, we shall look at some uses of biomedicine with which we fully agree. But first we need to present our holistic perspective so the reader understands, why we so willingly admit the drugs to be of limited use: we have an alternative to drugs when it comes to many chronic diseases.

Clinical holistic medicine is based on the life mission theory and the holistic process theory of healing

Allow us to repeat, as this is essential, that our approach to existential healing is based on the life mission theory (5-10) that states that everybody has a purpose in life, or a huge talent. Happiness comes from living this purpose and succeeding in expressing the core talent in life. To do this, it is important to develop as a person into what is known as the natural condition, a condition where the person know himself and use all his efforts on achieving what is most important for him.

The holistic process theory of healing (11,13,14) and the related quality of life theories (15-17) state that the return to the natural state of being is possible, whenever the person gets the resources needed for the existential healing. The resources needed are, according to the theory, holding in the dimensions: awareness, respect, care, acknowledgment and acceptance; and support and processing in the dimensions: feeling, understanding and letting go of negative attitudes and beliefs. The preconditions for the holistic healing to take place, is trust, and the intention of the healing taking place. Existential healing is not a local healing of any tissue, but a healing of the wholeness of the person, making him much more resourceful, loving, and knowledgeable of himself and his own needs and wishes. In letting go of negative attitudes and beliefs the person returns to a more responsible existential position and an improved quality of life.

The philosophical change of the person healing is often a change towards preferring difficult problems and challenges, instead of avoiding difficulties in life (18-25). The person, who becomes happier and more resourceful is often also becoming more healthy, more talented and able of functioning (26-27). Interestingly, energy, wisdom, happiness, talent, intelligence and the human qualities alike are not easily increased with drugs; considering this sad fact, it can hardly be a surprise that health in general, so related to these qualities, is also very difficult to improve with drugs. So let us look at some good examples of when we can use drugs. As you will notice the pharmaceutical drugs are excellent, when it comes to the treatment of acute, physical illnesses. They are rarely of use in chronic disease.

Pneumonia and penicillin

Penicillin is the classical drug and the basis of the biomedical paradigm. We find it a great drug, largely non-toxic, inexpensive, produced from moulds that have attacked our food, since the beginning of time and thus presumably have been known to the body for thousands of years. Penicillin is highly active against a range of micro-organisms that often affect humans.

Once this is said, penicillin is not really very active in cavities such as the frontal sinus or middle ear, which are almost never reached by the blood distributing the drug in the body. Several studies have shown that penicillin only shortens the course of the disease by a few days on average in the case of inflammation in a cavity. People are happy to be given penicillin. Now they are on medication, things are happening, and all will be well, since everybody knows penicillin and how effective it is. The following cases of pneumonia are trivial from a medical point of view, but it shows how the daily life of a modern family physician practising biomedicine is an oft-repeated theme with minor variations.

> Female, aged 24 years with pneumonia
> She has suffered from chest constriction for two days. Auscultation of the lungs: ronchi and "dense" sounds. Diagnosis: /Pneumonia/ Prescribe penicillin.

Female, aged 86 years with pneumonia
Breathing difficulties for 14 days. Feels very ill, is freezing and weating. Examination: fever, auscultation of the lungs: ronchi, crackles /Pneumonia/ Cannot tolerate penicillin. Prescribe Erythromycin.

The high efficiency of antibiotics gives us another problem, a difficult ethical problem. Perhaps in the case of the old patient she should be allowed to die from her pneumonia? Before modern antibiotics, pneumonia provided a quick and gentle death – "an old woman's best friend", as Aldous Huxley (1894-1963) said. Today we keep people alive as long as possible often with little consideration for their quality of life, until they develop dementia or a painful cancer, which most people eventually do when they are old enough. Death can be a protracted affair, painful, lonely and terrible. It can also be quick and merciful. We believe that old people should be afforded a merciful death when their time is up. And there is really no need for the physician to decide when that is. As doctors, we could do the decent thing and ask the old person whether he or she wants help to live on. Many old people are quite clear in their mind and know when their time is up (25).

Other infections

Female, aged 27 years with vaginal discharge
Negative urine stick. Pelvic examination: Cervical motion tenderness of the uterus, otherwise normal. Wet smear: 80% clue cells /Trichomoniasis/ Prescribe Elysol [metronidazole] 500 mg bid for five days. Since she often forgets to take contraceptive pills we talked about switching to an Implanon implant. She will think about it.

Metronidazole preparations are excellent against the bacteria that usually cause this form of lower abdominal infection (Trichomonas vaginalis).

Female, aged 88 years with impetigo
Presents with small pustules and an even rash on the back and with large red erythematous elements on the left arm without sores or blistering. /Impetigo/ Prescribe culture, locally mupirocin (Bactroban) and Azithromycin orally for five days. Should return if the problem persists.

Impetigo is a very common superficial skin infection caused by streptococci, staphylococci or a combination of both. They can cause impetigo, erysipilas, cellulitis, lymphangitis, furuncles and sbscess. Impetigo can be common in children, but also in adults, where advanced age can low resistance as in the case above.

Male, aged 56 years with Lyme disease following a tick bite
Bitten by a tick below the right clavicle. Large erythema 25 x 25 cm, growing every day. /Erythema migrans/suspected Lyme disease/Prescribe penicillin.

Here we have some probability of saving the man from neuroborreliosis, a borrelian infection in the brain. This is a very unpleasant disease, if left untreated often ending in brain damage or death (28).

Antibiotics are probably the group of drugs that have gained biomedicine most respect among the general population. It is indeed a great thing to have drugs formulated as eye drops or vagitories to get rid of that terrible itching. All in a few days.

Vitamin and mineral supplements

Another great example of the biomedical paradigm is the highly effective treatment of a vitamin deficiency with oral vitamin pills. Now that we are talking about placebo, it is logical to move on to the vitamin and mineral supplements so often used, probably the clearest example of placebo available today. In our opinion, vitamin and mineral supplements do very little to promote health, objectively speaking. Most scientific studies conclude that minerals and vitamins like vitamin C, widely believed to be beneficial for the general health, make no difference to a person's health (29,30), except in the very few people suffering from a deficiency condition, while other studies show only what seems to be a modest, beneficial effect (31). So why do people still take these pills?

The health problems affecting the population are rarely due to vitamin or mineral deficiencies, which is why they cannot be cured by these dietary supplements. Nor will the body benefit from getting any more vitamins or minerals than it needs.

Many people take vitamin C when they have a cold. To our knowledge, no scientific study has come up with evidence of the sense in that. Even very large daily supplements of many grams of vitamin C have no guaranteed effect. We can only conclude that lemon tea and grapefruits, rather like rum toddies, are great placebo remedies for the common cold. And if you are now thinking: "but I can feel the effect", then we will not deny this in any way, but merely ask: "why do you feel that way?" Is it not because a person you trust greatly, perhaps your mother, once told you that it was good?

The very limited insight in biochemistry most people have means that there is an incredible market for this kind of remedies. People believe in advertising telling them that they will feel fine once they have taken a vitamin pill, and of course they will, because it saves their conscience. Each year, people buy completely useless vitamin pills and mineral supplements for billions of EUROs and dollars.

> Female, aged 52 years with iron deficiency
> Blood tests showed iron deficiency and slightly elevated blood sedimentation rate. No other signs of infection. Still chest pain. We try prescribing Modifenac [diclofenac], Multitabs [vitamins and minerals], Ferro Duretter [ferrous salt] bid + physiotherapy. Check iron with new blood test in three months.

The classic: Prescribing iron against iron deficiency. Here the cause of iron deficiency was not discovered. Occult bleeding? Our general advice on vitamins and minerals is: unless you suffer from a diagnosed state of deficiency, it is not wise to waste money, time and energy on vitamin and mineral supplements. If you want to pamper yourself, you can do better and gain more nourishment by putting your money and efforts into cooking.

Immune system disorders

In the following we present some case studies that describe one of the most frequent causes of visits to the physician: immunological disorders.

> Boy, aged four years with asthma
> Four-year preventive surveillence examination. Good development, happy, speech well developed, extrovert, sweet and interested. Weight and height catching up, but he is still asthmatic. Recently the parents apparently increased medication to Spirocort [budesonide] 2 x 200 bid.

Many children suffer from asthma, and asthma drugs are very effective. However, we feel that a symptomatic therapy of this kind is not quite satisfactory, when instead we might address the root of the problem. To us, this is a question of understanding the child's life and his basic requirements for well-being in his family. We see the child as the thermometer of the family, and when the child is sick there is often cause for improvement in the family. Basically, based on the strong covariance of asthma attacks with stress and other psychological factors (32), we see asthma as a psychosomatic disorder with medication as symptomatic therapy. Nevertheless it works really well and with good effect.

> Girl, aged eight years with eczema
> This girl has eczema on her forearm with well-defined, delimited scaly patches, 2 x 2 cm, mostly on left side. Possibly /fungal infection/Prescribe Brentacort [hydrocortisone, miconazole].

A fungal eczema – we prescribed Brentacort ointment with hydrocortisone and a fungicide.

> Male, aged 37 years with neurodermatitis
> He has been suffering from intense itching and a rash around the penis for six months. He scratches it every day with long nails. Wife claims to have same problem. We need to see her, too, as they may be passing it on to each other. The patient has been informed of this. Examination: Intense rash resembling neurodermatitis 6 x 7 cm on the anterior and lateral parts of the penis. Standard check for STDs. No pustules, margins not affected, skin much thickened and eczematous. Scabies suspected, but no visible burrows in the epidermis. Two years ago, elbow region and groin also affected. Most probably a case of /Tinea cruris [jock itch; ringworm]/ /suspected neurodermatitis/. We try prescribing Brentacort [hydrocortisone, miconazole] ointment. If no marked effect within two weeks, the patient should return to the clinic.

Neurodermatitis is very interesting. It means that the patient will scratch, where it itches. When he scratches, it itches more, and so he will scratch even more. In the end damage to the skin is complete. It appears thick, uneven, bleeding with deep hollows and old scabs; it can be a terrible sight. It is truly incredible how much damage people with a propensity to scratching can do to themselves. We recall a psychiatric patient, who inflicted a hole in his arm right down to the muscle. The cure is simple: Stop scratching! We break the vicious circle with hydrocortisone, which effectively calms the itching.

Male, aged 61 years with pulmonary oedema?
Breathing difficulties, believes he has water in the lungs. Auscultation of the lungs:
normal. Somewhat gasping respiration that is difficult to interpret. No fever. We try
increasing Furix [furosemide] 40 mg bid. He should call out-of-hours service or
emergency room, if there is no improvement and he deteriorates over the weekend.

Idiopathic pulmonary oedema − which is self-originated without any external cause − is
caused by irritation of pulmonary tissues that makes the vessels become permeable and leak,
with plasma pouring into the alveoles. Diuretic drugs are highly effective and have saved
many patients in that situation.

Girl, aged two years − Atopic dermatitis − infantile eczema
Atopical dermatitis. Prescribe hydrocortisone ointment. Mother should treat her for
14 days and wait and see. Should return if the problem persists.

Hydrocortisone ointment is certain to help. It is good and effective, and the fear of adverse
reactions in topical use is highly exaggerated. In our opinion it is quite harmless.

Male, aged 62 years with rheumatoid arthritis?
Complaints of pain in right ankle. Tender, red, swollen and slightly warm
corresponding to both ankles, probably mild rheumatoid arthritis. Some points are
very tender, especially laterally below the malleolus. We try prescribing Ibuprofen
[ibuprofen] with follow-up for further testing.

Ibuprofen and the other NSAIDs are very satisfactory to use. They take it all: fever,
inflammation, pain, swellings, redness, heat. And they are tolerated by most patients, they are
cheap and you can take them throughout your life. (But why does the patient contract
rheumatoid arthritis?)

Female, aged 32 years with urticaria
She had urticaria this morning, which has abated substantially by 2 p.m. Prescribe
Zyrtec [cetirizine] 10 mg as required. We talked a little about feelings and the
correlation between body and mind − about feelings controlling the body most of the
time.

The antihistaminergic drugs are highly effective against urticaria and similar inflammatory
complaints.

Female, aged 43 years with hayfever
Diprospan [betamethasone] 2 ml IM in the right gluteus maximus muscle. We talk a
little about what she can do to minimise her hayfever symptoms.

Our "little talk" will make many biomedical physicians smile, because what indeed can you
do yourself about hayfever? But the intensity of hayfever may fluctuate considerably. And if
the patient can see, when and why she is not bothered by the allergy at all she might do
something to turn these blissful periods into a permanent state. Well, hydrocortisone is truly
effective, and the season is not that long, so serious adverse reactions rarely occur even at
high doses. Personally, we would prefer holistic therapy to Diprospan.

Constipation, diabetes and hypertension

Below is a wide range of problems that can be solved with biomedicine.

> Female, aged 42 years with possible gastritis
> In connection with working on shifts, which will come to an end on the 19th this month, the patient vomits at each meal and has pain immediately after the meal and before vomiting corresponding to solar plexus. She is also experiencing problems with her boss. No blood in faeces /suspected gastritis / Prescribe Losec [omeprazole]. If the problems continue she should be referred for gastroscopy.

Losec belongs to a group of agents that can inhibit gastric acid secretion almost completely. In many cases the symptoms disappear as if by magic. Only not in this patient, whom we had to refer to gastroscopy. Losec is a convincing drug; it is rather expensive, but it is genuinely effective and for most patient almost without side effects (28). It is impressive. (But why do people develop gastritis?).

> Female, aged 62 years with hypertension
> BP 150/80, has taken Cozaar [losartan] 50 mg x 1, since half a tablet was too little; the headache returned. Now well-controlled.

Hypertension is a dangerous condition, which increases the risk of a stroke. So if not for the adverse reactions of the drug – some rather diffuse and quite common adverse reactions such as fatigue or loss of energy – this therapy would be just fine. Since lowering the blood pressure is important, and since the drugs at our disposal today are not extremely effective, we need to combine two or three at a time. Often there are serious adverse reactions such as impotence, when beta-blockers also have to be used.

> Male, aged 43 years with hypertension
> Complains of large pull in left calf. If there is suspicion of deep vein thrombosis, the right cure will be immobilisation and ultrasound, but as the condition appears to be almost back to normal today with no real deep tenderness, mobilisation is prescribed; the patient walks well on his leg following massaging of calf. Second BP check. Headache. At home: BP measured at 145/95-105; Here, BP = 150/105. He should continue with Norvasc [amlodipine]. Check-up in three months.

This patient will presumably take this medication for half his life. We believe that it is possible to get rid of the elevated blood pressure through personal development, where the patient "grows" out of the problem, so to speak. It is a good alternative for those, who are interested in personal development. However, because of his view of life we cannot reach this patient with holistic therapy. So we will not bother him with it.

> Male, aged 85 years with type 2 diabetes
> Diabetes check. Blood glucose 8.9; BP 130/90, well-controlled.

Adult-onset diabetes, now known as type 2 diabetes mellitus (NIDDM), is one of the diseases that we can manage well, and the same applies to type 1 diabetes. That is something to be proud of. Today, people with diabetes have a life, and the complications – the breakdown of nerves, vascular system, eyes - are very limited compared with before biomedicine. This is a great result. (Imagine, though, if young people could completely avoid developing diabetes and having to inject insulin throughout their lives?).

Contraception and abormal uterine bleeding

If there is one thing that the biomedical physician is good at, it is preventing unwanted pregnancies. Once the functions of the reproductive organs are understood, it is easy to understand the effect of forms of contraceptives such as condoms, the femidom, intra-uterine devices, diaphragms or contraceptive foams. Abnormal uterine bleeding is often easy to correct with hormones. A well-known and serious adverse effect of "the pill" is that chemical contraception often make the women loose much of her sexual desire, female polarity and orgasmic potency.

Depression and psychotic mental illness

As we have seen in section one patients with depression and schizophrenia are only helped little by the psychopharmachological drugs and severe adverse effects are very common.

Discussion

Biomedicine is often highly effective when facing acute, somatic problems. It is easy to administer and the effort or time for the physician often very limited. Contraceptives are of huge value, although they often deprive the women of the sexual desire. Morphine is a sublime help in many cases of terminal disease, but can shorten life.

Unfortunately the target of biomedicine is mostly the symptoms and not the real cause of the disease. When the immunological resistance is temporarily weakened and an infection is threatening the life of the patient, an antibiotic can save him by killing the micro-organism causing the infection, but even here the cause of the disease is not really the bacteria itself, but the weakened immune response. Most often, the disease is not cured by the biomedical intervention, and masking the symptom does not help the patient in the long run. He will get sick again, if the immune resistance is not recovered.

For the last five decades physicians have been very optimistic about what could be obtained with a developed biomedicine – from cures to cancer to dramatic prolongation of youth and long vitality. What we generally have seen – with some important exceptions naturally - is more and more specialized drugs, more and more expensive drugs and more and more potent drugs curing a still minor fragment of the patients treated. The big pharmaceutical companies have been admitting that "the drugs don't work" (2,3) and huge companies like NovoNordisk are now claiming that prevention of disease, and not curing them, seems to be the future for the industry (33).

To understand the seriousness of the problem, let us quote the BMJ editor Richard Smith (2): "Now business has outdone parody, and Allen Rogers, worldwide vice president of genetics at Glaxo SmithKline, is reported on the front page of the Independent as saying: "Our drugs don't work on most patients." This is of course not news to physicians. Anybody familiar with the notion of "number needed to treat" (NNT) knows that it is usually necessary to treat many patients in order for one to benefit. NNTs under 5 are unusual, whereas NNTs over 20 are common."

This it important so let us give it a second though, from the emotional perspective of the physician: What will a sincere and ambitious physician feel, when he gives a drug to a patient with a NNT of 2 or less? What can he tell his patients, if he is to be honest? With an NTT of 2 he can say: "There is a fair change that you get well again, and he will feel severely frustrated that this is the help he can give his patient, because he wants to make much more than 50% of his patients well. With a number on NNT of 3, he must say: Most likely this drug will not help you, but let give it a try, and he will feel terrible. With a NTT of 5 he must admit: it is highly unlikely that this drug will help you, but there still is a chance, so let us go for that, and he must feel despair. With a NTT of 20, which is common, he must say: "I will give you this drug because it helps sometimes, but do not rely on it in any way; this drug cannot even justify a hope". And the ambitious and caring physician will feel like hopeless and helpless. Because if you only help 5% of your patients, 95% will leave your clinic without improvement, but instead waste money on the drugs, have severe side effects. But most important, often with a resignation that is as life-threatening as the disease itself.

Medicine is evolving, and the hope we had for biomedicine is turning into frustration, scepticism and for many physicians despair. This dispair can be found in the frustration, that physicians cannot really rely on the drugs, that was supposed to heal. The drugs will undoubtedly play an important role also for the future medicine, but simple manual medicine like therapeutic touch (34) and the emerging new toolbox of consciousness-based, holistic medicine must also be taken into use by the physicians to have a probate set of medical tool for the new century (35,36). What is important now is that the physician really rely on his own senses. If he experience that the drugs work, he should use them. As the pharmaceutical companies do almost nothing, for understandable financial reasons, to narrow the indications so that only the patients likely to benefit will get a drug, this must be the task of the physician. And it is not that difficult. It takes some experimentation on the part of the physician, some alternative medical tools to shift among in order to provide alternatives to the drugs in your practice. This is the purpose in our series of papers on clinical holistic medicine.

So we are not unhappy that biomedicine turned out to be of restricted value to the patients. Actually, an extended bio-psycho-social medical toolbox (see section eleven) including also the consciousness-based, holistic medicine will have many advantages, not only for the patient on an individual level, but also for society at large, making its citizens grow into being more conscious, more ethical, more talented and more socially minded (5-10,18-25).

Conclusion

The drugs do work. But only in special situations, and only as a basic rule, where there are background resources to back up the local healing. The drugs have specific activities, which can be used when this specific action is needed.

But very often the symptoms are caused by psychosocial imbalances, which should be corrected. These imbalances can be attributed to many aspects, like poor living conditions, so the symptoms have to create or generate a learning process for the patient, so curing the disease that reveals the imbalance in life often prevents the patient from using his opportunity for the learning process. Sometimes a life can be saved with drugs remedying an acute crisis. But many times this crisis is only a symptom of a chronically poor mental and physical health or even a terminal state of life, and saving the patient which might seem to be a good thing to do today, can be seen as a cruel thing tomorrow.

In general, drugs are highly efficient in an acute phase of a physical disease, but almost inert in the long run and of little help in the treatment of mental disorders. To improve health and cure chronic disease the whole life and its quality must be improved. This takes more than drugs; this takes a responsible and determined effort on the part of the patient. This is why, in most cases, a holistic approach to the patient is needed, if the physician is to bring permanent improvements in quality for life and health to the patient.

The bio-medical paradigm is very convincing from a biochemical point of view, and highly efficient in many cases of acute, somatic medical problems and emergencies. Unfortunately most chronic patients cannot be treated to get much better with drugs, they need to do something about their lives themselves.

References

[1]   Lewis R, Dixon J. Rethinking management of chronic diseases. BMJ 2004;328:220-2.
[2]   Smith R. The drugs don't work. BMJ 2003;327(7428):0-h.
[3]   Dyer O. City reacts negatively as GlaxoSmithKline announces for a new drugs. BMJ 2003;327:1366.
[4]   Gøtzsches P. Bias in double-blind trials. Dan Med Bull 1990;37:329-36.
[5]   Ventegodt S, Andersen NJ, Merrick J. Editorial: Five theories of human existence. ScientificWorldJournal 2003;3:1272-6.
[6]   Ventegodt S. The life mission theory: A theory for a consciousness-based medicine. Int J Adolesc Med Health 2003;15(1):89-91.
[7]   Ventegodt S, Andersen NJ, Merrick J. The life mission theory II: The structure of the life purpose and the ego. ScientificWorldJournal 2003;3:1277-85.
[8]   Ventegodt S, Andersen NJ, Merrick J. The life mission theory III: Theory of talent. ScientificWorldJournal 2003;3:1286-93.
[9]   Ventegodt S, Merrick J. The life mission theory IV. A theory of child development. ScientificWorldJournal 2003;3:1294-1301.
[10] Ventegodt S, Andersen NJ, Merrick J. The life mission theory V. A theory of the anti-self and explaining the evil side of man. ScientificWorldJournal 2003;3:1302-13.
[11] Ventegodt S, Andersen NJ, Merrick J. Holistic medicine: Scientific challenges. ScientificWorldJournal 2003;3,1108-16.
[12] Ventegodt S, Andersen NJ, Merrick J. Holistic Medicine II: The square-curve paradigm for research in alternative, complementary and holistic medicine: A cost-effective, easy and scientifically valid design for evidence based medicine. ScientificWorldJournal 2003;3: 1117-27.
[13] Ventegodt S, Andersen NJ, Merrick J. Holistic Medicine III: The holistic process theory of healing. ScientificWorldJournal 2003;3:1138-46.
[14] Ventegodt S, Andersen NJ, Merrick J. Holistic Medicine IV: The principles of the holistic process of healing in a group setting. ScientificWorldJournal 2003;3:1294-1301.
[15] Ventegodt S, Merrick J, Andersen NJ. Quality of life theory I. The IQOL theory: An integrative theory of the global quality of life concept. ScientificWorldJournal 2003;3:1030-40.

[16] Ventegodt S, Merrick J, Andersen NJ. Quality of life theory II. Quality of life as the realization of life potential: A biological theory of human being. ScientificWorldJournal 2003;3:1041-9.

[17] Ventegodt S, Merrick J, Andersen NJ. Quality of life theory III. Maslow revisited. ScientificWorldJournal 2003;3:1050-7.

[18] Ventegodt S, Andersen NJ, Merrick J. Quality of life philosophy: when life sparkles or can we make wisdom a science? ScientificWorldJournal 2003;3:1160-3.

[19] Ventegodt S, Andersen NJ, Merrick J. QOL philosophy I: Quality of life, happiness, and meaning of life. ScientificWorldJournal 2003;3: 1164-75.

[20] Ventegodt S, Andersen NJ, Kromann M, Merrick J. QOL philosophy II: What is a human being? ScientificWorldJournal 2003;3:1176-85.

[21] Ventegodt S, Merrick J, Andersen NJ. QOL philosophy III: Towards a new biology. ScientificWorldJournal 2003;3:1186-98.

[22] Ventegodt S, Andersen NJ, Merrick J. QOL philosophy IV: The brain and consciousness. ScientificWorldJournal 2003;3:1199-1209.

[23] Ventegodt S, Andersen NJ, Merrick J. QOL philosophy V: Seizing the meaning of life and getting well again. ScientificWorldJournal 2003;3:1210-29.

[24] Ventegodt S, Andersen NJ, Merrick J. QOL philosophy VI: The concepts. ScientificWorldJournal 2003;3:1230-40.

[25] Merrick J, Ventegodt S. What is a good death? To use death as a mirror and find the quality in life. BMJ. Rapid Response 2003 Oct 31.

[26] Ventegodt S, Merrick J, Andersen NJ. Quality of life as medicine. A pilot study of patients with chronic illness and pain. ScientificWorld Journal 2003;3:520-32.

[27] Ventegodt S, Merrick J, Andersen NJ. Quality of life as medicine II. A pilot study of a five day "Quality of Life and Health" cure for patients with alcoholism. ScientificWorldJournal 2003;3:842-52.

[28] Fauci AS, Braunwald E, Isselbacher KJ, Wilson JD, Martin JB, Kasper DL, Hauser SL, Longo DL, eds. Harrison's principles of internal medicine, 14th ed. New YorK: McGraw-Hill, 1998.

[29] Kim MK, Sasaki S, Sasazuki S, Okubo S, Hayashi M, Tsugane S. Long-term vitamin C supplementation has no markedly favourable effect on serum lipids in middle-aged Japanese subjects. Br J Nutr 2004;91(1):81-90.

[30] Fogarty A, Lewis SA, Scrivener SL, Antoniak M, Pacey S, Pringle M, Britton J. Oral magnesium and vitamin C supplements in asthma: a parallel group randomized placebo-controlled trial. Clin Exp Allergy 2003;33(10):1355-9.

[31] Hercberg S, Preziosi P, Galan P, Faure H, Arnaud J, Duport N, et al. The SU.VI.MAX Study": a primary prevention trial using nutritional doses of antioxidant vitamins and minerals in cardiovascular diseases and cancers. SUpplementation on VItamines et Mineraux AntioXydants. Food Chem Toxicol 1999;37(9-10):925-30.

[32] Gehrke I, Bohm E, Sybrecht GW. [Stress-induced asthma--placebo-controlled double-blind comparison of prevention using fenoterol, disodium cromoglycate and a combination of the two.] Prax Klin Pneumol 1986;40(4):129-34. [German].

[33] Kristensen M. [Novo Nordisk's new strategy: From disease control to health promotion. Mandag morgen 2004;6:13-6. [Danish].

[34] Ventegodt S., Morad M, Merrick J. Clinical holistic medicine: Classic art of healing or the therapeutic touch. ScientificWorldJournal 2004;4:134-47.

[35] Ventegodt S, Merrick J. Clinical holistic medicine: Applied consciousness-based medicine. ScientificWorldJournal 2004;4:96-9.

[36] Ventegodt S, Morad M, Merrick J. Clinical holistic medicine: The "new medicine", the multi-paradigmatic physician and the medical record. ScientificWorldJournal 2004;4:273-85.

Chapter 11

When biomedicine is inadequate

The modern, biomedical physician, which is the most common type of physician at least in Northern Europe, is using pharmaceuticals as his prime tool. Unfortunately this tool is much less efficient than you might expect from the biochemical theory. The belief in drugs as the solution to the health problems of mankind, overlooking important existing knowledge on quality of life, personal development and holistic healing seems to be one good reason why around every second citizen of our modern society is chronically ill and stays ill in spite of treatment with pharmaceutical drugs.

The bio-medical paradigm and the drugs are certainly useful, where in many situations we could not do without the drugs (like antibiotics), but administering penicillin to cure infections or disease in young age is not without consequences, as the way we perceive health and medicine is influenced by such experiences.

When we get a more severe disease in midlife, we also believe drugs will make us healthy again. But at this age the drugs do not work efficiently anymore, because we have turned older and lost much of the biological coherence that made us heal easily, when we were younger.

Now we need to assume responsibility, take learning and improve our quality of life. We need a more holistic medicine that can help us back to life by allowing us to access our hidden resources.

The modern physician cannot rely solely on drugs, but also have holistic tools in his medical toolbox. This is the only way we can improve the general health of our populations. Whenever NNT (number needed to treat) is 3 or higher, the likelihood to cure the patient is less that 33%, which is not satisfying to any physician.

In this case he must ethically try something more in order to cure his patients, which are the crossroads where both traditional manual medicine and the tools of a scientific holistic medicine are helpful.

The NNTs of pharmaceutical drugs are often 10, 20 and 50, making their use statistically almost irrelevant to most patients; as we have seen in section one the NNTs of drugs for chronic mentally illness is often 50 or higher meaning that less than 2% of the patients get better. The rest of the patients must put their hope in an alternative type of treatment.

Introduction

About one in two persons have a chronic disease – unpleasant complaints such as arthritis, migraine, allergy, diabetes, low back pain or depression – despite numerous visits to their family physician or to specialists and generous use of advanced biomedicine (1). About half the chronic patients even seek alternative treatment (CAM) (2), which is gaining increasing trust among the population, but often to no avail – the disease usually does not go away. Holistic medicine (3-26) on the other hand is often considered obsolete by the physicians and not mastered by the complementary therapists and is therefore not used. Therefore most chronic patients stay ill for life.

In our modern society, partly due to longer life expectancy, illness has become something that people have to learn to live with. Often we see one disease followed by another and it is not uncommon for older people to have five or ten different ailments taking up to a dozen different kinds of medications. We also observe a steady decline in functional capacity of middle-aged or elderly people, who rely solely on biomedicine.

One of the most brutal tendencies of the biomedical paradigm (27) is that it often creates resignation and thus allows disease to control the individual. Symptoms can often be alleviated to some extend, but the causes of the disease are beyond the reach of acknowledgement due to the inherent philosophy of the bio-medical paradigm: the overwhelming complexity of the biochemical description of man. Therefore, biomedicine is rarely able to help people get rid of the cause of their disease, which in our understanding often is to be found in the quality of the life the patients lead, and not in their genes or metabolism. The diseases plaguing our patients are often caused by life-stile.

In our opinion, modern biochemistry is generally incapable of helping people to draw on their hidden resources. Thus, the human resources that should help us overcome the disease remain hidden. That is our harshest criticism of biomedicine as holistically oriented physicians. On the pretext of being able to help, it takes responsibility for and away from patients and thereby deprives them of the opportunity to wake up and help themselves – and patients let the physician do so. The consciousness-based medicine that we are striving to develop serves the opposite purpose, namely to help people help themselves. Many people have good experiences with biomedical treatment, since we all have an infection or ailment at some time, which was cured.

With all its technological perfection and scientific character, biomedicine appears extremely convincing and makes us confident that it will provide a cure the next time something goes wrong. Unfortunately, the bitter truth is that once you get seriously ill, you usually remain ill for the rest of your life. Biomedicine cannot make you well again or cure the chronic illness.

Below, we provide some examples of quite common disease and disorders for which biomedicine, in our experience as physicians, has proven inadequate. A colleague with more experience and greater insight in biomedicine might possibly be able to do a better job, so we will let readers draw their own conclusions on the numerous short and somewhat sad case histories.

Chronic disorders

The following case reports describe chronic disorders and complaints for which biomedicine has no effective remedy or cure, as is so often the case.

> Female, aged 21 years with chronic dizziness
> The patient suffers from chronic dizziness. Blood chemistry normal, except CRP (C-reactive protein), which is marginally outside the normal range. Against this background we discuss whether the patient may have another illness that would explain the dizziness, e.g. a virus affecting the acoustic nerve. The patient is told to return, if the symptoms do not go away by themselves.

Dizziness is more frequently encountered in older persons with increasing age. Most cases are benign and self-limited, but still a risk factor for falls in the older patient. Dizziness with no apparent organic cause is common and from a biomedical perspective very little can be done about it. "A virus affecting the acoustic nerve," says the biomedical doctor, which is the explanation given to the patient to excuse, why we cannot help, because there is not much we can do about a virus. Indeed, the dizziness will very often cease within six months.

However, this story might look different in a holistic perspective. Frequently, the dizziness either passes quickly, or it continues for the rest of the patient's life. In either case it is unlikely to be caused by a virus. We believe that this kind of dizziness is generally caused by a loss of vital energy due to inner conflicts and lack of confrontation with both the internal and external reality. When the patient does not have enough energy to obtain an overview of life, this kind of dizziness occurs, like motion sickness. It simply becomes difficult to orientate oneself in the world, tying down the vital energy, but when this conflict is solved, the dizziness will miraculously vanish.

> Male, aged 25 years with chronic sore throat
> No fever, sore throat for four weeks. Also pricking sensation in the tongue. Oral cavity: slightly red and swollen, no coating. Glands in the sternoclavicular region swollen bilaterally. Strep A: negative. To be reassessed in two weeks. Pricking sensation in the tongue possibly due to allergy. Prescribe Zyrtec [cetirzine] for the patient to try.

There is no effective treatment against a chronic burning and pricking sensation in the tongue and throat, when there is no external cause. In our opinion, irritation of the tissue – a burning, hot and pricking sensation – is a clear sign of a blockage or hidden feelings. Symptoms can be alleviated by antihistamines, and the effect may last for a few hours, but in the long term this is not a lasting solution. The patients suffer their entire lives. Sometimes they "grow" out of it, sometimes their illness takes on a more serious nature.

> Female, aged 42 years with tinnitus
> Noise in the ear, so that the patient finds it difficult to talk to other people. /Tinnitus/ Prescribe audiometry prior to assessment of the need for hearing aid with masking device. Note: Tinnitus may decrease if the patient's possible depression improves, the picture of this suspected depression is unfortunately not so clear that is justifies a treatment. Hearing test shows nearly complete loss of hearing at high frequencies (over 2000Hz). Referred to audiologist for hearing aid with masking device.

Tinnitus is a term to describe an internal noise perceived by the person. The cause can be otologic, metabolic, neurologic, pharmacologic, dental or psychologic, but also due to vascular abnormalities, tympanic muscle disorders or central nervous system anomalies. A complete otolaryngeal evaluation and audiometry should be performed in order to find the potential cause. Tinnitus is a very difficult problem to treat, with a prevalence of 14.2% in Gothenburg (28), thought to be representative for the Nordic countries.

Overweight

Childhood, adolescent and adult obesity presents one of the most challenging and frustrating problems in medical practice. Obesity is of particular concern because of the health risks associated with it. These risks include hypertension, hyperlipidemia, hypertriglyceridemia, diabetes mellitus, coronary heart disease, pulmonary and renal problems, surgical risks, and degenerative joint disease.

Obesity causes significant morbidity as well as a decreased life-expectancy. Obesity is a major public health problem. Recent data from the Third National Health and Nutrition Examination Survey (NHANES) in the United States suggested that 22% of children and adolescents are overweight, and 11% are obese. Among the general population, the survey revealed that between 1987 and 1993 overweight prevalence increased 3.3% for men and 3.6% for women. Total overweight prevalence among American males is now 33% and for females 36% (29).

> Female, aged 30 years with severe overweight
> The patient weighs 99 kg, BMI 44.5 = severe overweight (obese class III). Headache and tingling sensation in left hand. Also many episodes of reflux. Gastroscopy should be considered if the problem persists. Patient must return for weight-loss plan.

This patient needs a life. Slight tingling sensation in her hand. Our guess is that she has more important issues to worry about. Why focus on the hand, when her entire body needs to be reviewed? And why look only at the body when her entire life has gone off track? This might seem a hard judgment, but in our opinion, a weight-loss plan or a reduction in calorie intake for that matter would be of little help to her, as she no doubt already has tried all dietary cures on the market to loos weight. To conquer her overweight she has to address the fundamental problems, of which her overweight is a result.

The real weakness of biomedicine is that it does not support the patient in taking responsibility for his or her own life; this weakness is not only a fault of biomedicine as it is shared by the majority of alternative treatments. It is often the case that the person (physician or alternative healer) giving treatment does something with the patient on the basis of the own knowledge of the physician or healer.

Physicians are often highly skilled, and it is tempting to take control and know what is right. However, that is generally not the best possible help for the patient. The best result will not be achieved, until the patient plays an active part, uncovers his or her basic needs and finds out how to fulfil them.

When pain persists

Acute pain is a normal sensation triggered in the nervous system to alert you to possible injury and the need to take care of yourself, but chronic pain is different. Chronic pain persists. Pain signals keep firing in the nervous system for weeks, months, even years. There may have been an initial mishap -- sprained back, serious infection, or there may be an ongoing cause of pain -- arthritis, cancer, ear infection, but some people suffer chronic pain in the absence of any past injury or evidence of body damage. Many chronic pain conditions affect older adults. Common chronic pain complaints include headache, low back pain, cancer pain, arthritis pain, neurogenic pain (pain resulting from damage to the peripheral nerves or to the central nervous system itself), psychogenic pain (pain not due to past disease or injury or any visible sign of damage inside or outside the nervous system). One Dane in five live a life of chronic pain in spite of the most effective biomedical treatment (3). The pain persists, despite analgesics, despite physiotherapy and massage, or despite antidepressants. The patient is in pain, regularly or more or less constantly, and life is not fun any more.

Pain is what causes almost 30% of the patients to see their family physician (30) and often the physician does not succeed in removing the pain from the everyday life of the patient. We do not want to hand out morphine to people, who are not terminally ill – although that would be an effective pharmacological solution to both physical and existential pain. This could be one of the reasons, why we have so many drug addicts or so many young girls in existential pain, who become drug-addicted prostitutes. Let us make it clear that we do not share the restrictive attitude of our society to morphine. If it were up to us to decide, all adults would be allowed to buy it at the pharmacy. That would spare thousands of young people from humiliation, criminalisation, marginalisation, prostitution or HIV and society would save enormous amounts of money. The way we see it, the drug policy of our society reflects old moral codes and notions, instead of being an expression of real insight into human suffering.

> Male, aged 65 years with chronic pain, reduced vitality, libido and urge for isolation
> Patient has had failing health with many complaints of pain over the last four years. He has gone through several assessments with X-rays of knees and hips, with only minimum findings. In recent years, he has had decreased vitality and libido, now urge for isolation – mostly stays at home and indoors. Born in Asia. Has lived in Denmark for 30 years, but with a four-year stay abroad in between. Denies any problems regarding language and culture. Examination: Knees almost normal findings, in particular no restricted movement, no looseness, no signs of arthritis, no patella effusion or other pathology. The patient reports slight tenderness on side of right knee. Hip also normal regarding movement. The patient complains of some pain in the extreme position [fully extended or flexed], but this is hardly relevant during normal use of the body. Below the note from the last radiological examination showing stable conditions in the patient's joints: X-ray of left hip joint compared with the right hip joint, shows, as previously, slight narrowing of the joint space on both sides, slightly more on the right than on the left. No deformation of femoral head/incipient osteoarthrosis of the hip bilaterally/.

This patient's situation is deteriorating. But what is actually the matter with him? The cultural problems appear to be insurmountable, but he denies them completely. This is a case of marginalisation, perhaps even social exclusion. He is experiencing an existential desert, deep despair over no longer being useful. We are convinced that this man's situation in life could be rescued if he acknowledges, however painfully, the actual nature of his problems. But that is a barrier only he himself can cross. And as long as he keeps thinking: "If only there were something wrong with my hips. Then everything would come to an end, and my life would find its final and conclusive form," there is not much hope. Resignation is complete. His depression is real, but it cannot be treated in a conventional, medical sense. Life has gone off track, the patient refuses to help himself, and medication is unlikely to be of much help.

> Female, aged 49 years with migrating aches
> Thyrotropin normal (not goitre). Swelling around the epiglottal cartilage, in my opinion not corresponding to thyroid gland. Receives physiotherapy, and we agree that the physiotherapist should also massage the neck. We discuss her fibromyalgia, rheumatism and Sjogren's syndrome, and the patient states that she has "migrating aches" that migrate from one area of the body to the next, like slight cramps. We discuss the nature of such "migrating aches". The patient is referred to a specialist.

Migrating aches are tensions that crawl about in the patient's body like worms. They are a very interesting example of tensions living a life of their own inside the body as a repository of unprocessed feelings. They are not localised in any particular site or organ, but may come and go anywhere in the body, with resulting disturbance of the organ they affect. In our opinion, fibromyalgia, rheumatism and Sjogren's syndrome are sequelae of such tension.

Biomedicine turn to a molecular analysis of the autoimmune disturbance and, at best, it regards the migrating aches as a rarity, while consciousness-based medicine considers the content of the migrating aches and takes them very seriously.

If the patient's subjective complaints can be alleviated, there is a very good chance that the physical disturbances will also pass. Biomedicine rarely succeed in proper healing of autoimmune diseases like diabetes type I or arthritis; it remains a semi-effective symptomatic treatment.

Cancer kills one in three

It is believed that one Dane in three dies from cancer and biomedicine has thus no effective cure for cancer. Since we can live to become 100 years old, many of us will die from cancer around halfway through the life intended by nature.

> Male, aged 66 years with prostatism
> Micturition slowly returning to normal, prostate surgery twice and surgery for urethral stricture twice. No pain. Examination: No tenderness corresponding to the bladder. Negative urine stick. Referral to hospital for assessment and treatment.

Prostate cancer, which is what this patient presumably has, is merciful; it grows very slowly and rarely spreads.

Heart conditions

It is believed that one Dane in two dies from a cardiovascular disease, so biomedicine has obviously no effective cure against most heart conditions. The general practitioner will see the patient in the community, refer to the hospital, where they are diligently medicated and operated on. Survival statistics on these patients are not impressive. The average event free survival time is short, often said to be less than 10 years after bypass surgery, where three veins are grafted around the blocked coronary arteries; in the case of three-vessel coronary disease with varying severities of angina and left ventricular dysfunction, adjusted event-free survival (death, myocardial infarction, definite angina, or reoperation) after 6 years were only 23% (one vessel bypassed), 23% (two vessels bypassed), 29% (three vessels bypassed), and 31% (more than three vessels bypassed) (31).

> Male, aged 52 years with balloon angioplasty and anxiety
> The patient suffers from anxiety following balloon angioplastic surgery twice [dilation of the coronary arteries with a balloon which is inflated inside the vessel]. We talk about getting rid of the anxiety by accepting it, dwelling on it, perhaps lying in his wife's arms, allowing yourself to be small and afraid – do it a 1,000 times over the next couple of years. His wife is kind and understanding and wants to support her husband. Can return for conversation.

People become afraid when they have heart problems. Years after the problems seem to have been solved, people still tremble with fear. Since half of us die from cardiovascular disease, this anxiety is justified. We really are going to die. And the heart is our Achilles' heel, so to speak. It stops beating, and that is the end of it. Biomedicine has not solved the problem of weak hearts, although enormous progress has been made with for example enzymes that dissolve acute blood clots. Dean Ornish and co-workers (32) have demonstrated that cardiac disease is very sensitive to improved quality of life. His work focused on making the patient "open up the heart physically, emotionally and spiritually". This is a marvellous project and a very successful one. Only, his colleagues do not really appreciate his work. For how can spiritual openings of the heart do away with coronary stenosis?

Psychiatric disorders

Statistically, the incidence of severe mental diseases in the Nordic countries is about 13% [numbers from Norway] (33) and about one in five will at some point in life receive psychiatric treatment with psychotropic drugs. Generally, people who become mentally ill do not recover completely, but people who have a reasonable life at the onset of their illness will often achieve sufficient symptom relief to resume their old lives after treatment.

The situation is different for people who become mentally ill before they have settled down, i.e. when they are young. A mentally ill and unstable person will find it difficult to attain a life. The many recovery studies indicate that only one in five patients diagnosed with schizophrenia attains a normalised existence; the rest of these patients have so many psychotic symptoms throughout their lives that a psychiatrist will still call them schizophrenic. Biomedicine removes some of their symptoms, but not the actual illness, as we have seen in Section one.

Institutionalisation in psychiatric wards teaches them that they need not take responsibility for their survival. Our conclusion is that we need a new psychiatric approach that is better at making the patients well. We need a psychiatric system that understands the actual cause of the psychiatric disorders and treats them on that basis. We will provide our view of such holistic theory below. For the moment, suffice it to say that when patients discover themselves and their purpose in life and learn to be true to themselves and live accordingly, it appears that they actually can become well or cope with life.

> Male, aged 60 years with depression
> 1. Patient scores HDS 20 (MIES24) on the Hamilton scale, corresponding to depression. Prescribe antidepressants. The patient has presumably been depressed for years, and has been advised not to expect any major improvement for weeks or months.
> 2. The patient suffers from chronic muscular pain, which may be a manifestation of the depression.

Quite frankly, the psychiatric biomedical program against depression and psychosis is not working well. Depression and psychoses may be temporarily alleviated by means of psychotropic drugs, and patients may return more or less to who they used to be, albeit perhaps a little more timid and inhibited. But surely life does not intend us to remain the way we are as people at our current stage of development, and then deteriorate physically and mentally over our adult lives? Is it not the meaning of life that we should develop, become better and more alive, and get to know ourselves better?

An episode of depression is an opportunity to take a close look at ourselves and learn lessons through questions such as: why are my shoes not comfortable to wear? What is it I feel about myself, the people around me and life in general that gives me this unsatisfactory life? Any patient who patiently and laboriously takes on the task of sorting out his own philosophy of life will, in our experience, be richly rewarded for the effort.

Difficult medical conditions

Sometimes patients suffer from something rare and strange. The body is a highly complex structure and any disturbances may take on quite strange, special and unexpected forms of expression. The poorer the understanding of a patient's disease or condition, the more difficult it is to treat. Where should you begin and where end? Patients with rare diseases are usually referred to specialised units at the hospital, where they are transferred from one unit to another, until somebody feels competent enough to treat them. Having a rare disease may be life threatening.

Patients with well-known but incurable diseases often ends up in hospitals, which take care of their symptoms and give them general life support, but the normal pattern is a slow deterioration towards dead. With holistic medicine both situations may be within the physician's therapeutic reach, if only the patient is willing to work on himself.

> Male, aged 44 years with purpura
> Patient has breathing difficulties, dizziness with headache, swelling around the eyes, sometimes feels very ill, very tired for a long period, partially far-away sensation in the head. Examination: BP 135/85. Weighs 92.5 kg – usually weighs between 55 and 59 kg. Small red patches that do not disappear on pressure! /Purpura [a dangerous rash]/ /suspected immunological disorder. New appointment when we have the results of various blood tests.
> Blood test results together with the clinical purpura indicated systemic [involving the entire body] disease, which should be assessed by specialists at the hospital. Referral.

This is a very dangerous situation for him. Purpura – the image formed by thousands of microhaemorrhages in the skin – is not to be taken lightly. If he also has micro haemorrhages (small bleedings) everywhere in his internal organs, his life is at risk. The condition is difficult to treat pharmacologically, and the outcome of such 'immunological collapse' may be death in spite of the greatest expertise. We are not quite as good at adjusting imbalances of that kind, as is generally assumed.

Stagnant existence or burnout

Stagnation is an odd phenomenon. People lose the spark of life or they have no purpose, their entire existence and all their human relations decay. In the end, they have absolutely nothing of value, and although their bodies are strong and healthy, they display numerous symptoms, reflecting repression to the body of their emotionally painful lives.

> Female, aged 37 years with typical "stagnant" picture
> Presents with distal phalanx of the right second finger, which feels sore and "inflamed" on one side. Examination: Slight redness and tenderness corresponding to the phalanx, but unlikely to be rheumatoid arthritis or other well-defined arthropathy. Additionally: All phalanges of the digits bilaterally "rigid", cough, tenderness corresponding to the trigger points in arms and legs, severe tension in the neck, back problems – but the knee problems claimed by the patient are unlikely. The cause of the patient's complaints appears to be tension rather than inflammation. We discuss it: "I have never been able to relax", "I don't like just sitting, then I start feeling agitated," the patient says. EXERCISE in relaxation: "Sit down for 10 minutes with an egg-timer and just sit there without doing anything at all, sense how you feel. Preferably combined with massaging of the many sore muscles. Should return if the problem persists, possibly physiotherapy.

People who do not work on themselves at all or who are totally unwilling to confront their problems in life easily become stagnant. The stagnant picture includes the following aspects: "trouble" in the joints, sore muscles, dizziness and mental clouding, mixed-up human relations and a distinct lack of initiative and direction in life in general. They somehow appear "clumsy", "untidy" and poorly presented, as if they basically refuse to present themselves as people with goals in life and a meaning to their existence. The clay that should be moulded remains un-moulded. It is as if they totally lack creative and constructive spirit. Neither medication nor physiotherapy can do much about that. They need to talk about it.

> Female, aged 46 years with possible burnout
> Constantly tired, dizzy, impaired concentration, perhaps a slight temperature, throat
> complaints for about 45 days. BP 130/70. Auscultation of the lungs: slight basal
> crackles. Throat: still slightly red, no coating. Socially: no longer happy about work.
> Strict boss who "forbids anything good", is not allowed to do anything, works too
> slowly, "the other bookkeeper is much better." /Suspected atypical pneumonia/
> /suspected burnout/ Prescribe Abboticin [erythromycin]. If no marked improvement
> within 2 weeks, the patient should return to the clinic.

In this case, the approach was simply to prescribe the best drug that we could find for her.
Then we wait to see whether the problem might disappear by itself. We hope so, but do not
believe it will, although the suspected pneumonia could make the difference. It will probably
take a lot more than antibiotics to get her back on her own two feet considering her
complaints. We believe that she has a burnout and in need of comprehensive rehabilitation.
But sometimes we are tricked. If she does, in fact, have pneumonia, she and her negative
attitude might recover completely with the medicine.

Old age

Old age is one of the strangest phenomena, because there is often a substantial difference
between chronological age and physiological age. Young people may appear very old and
tired – worn out and incoherent – while old people may appear extremely energetic and fit.
Physiological age is determined by our personal energy level. In turn, this is determined by
how much of our vital energy is free and how much of it tied to blockage and traumas. At the
cellular level, the cells are forever young – they have eternal life – after all, they are
3,800,000,000 years old by now: the cells have always existed almost back to the beginning
of the planet Earth, they renew themselves by division, so in principle they never become old.
Therefore, it is extremely difficult to perceive age as anything but an energy problem. There
is another factor, however, the life purpose (5), which may be fulfilled so that the person feels
genuinely full of days. Unfortunately, hardly anybody has succeeded with that project in our
time. Physiological old age is therefore to a great extent a result of accumulated inner
conflicts and susceptible to holistic treatment – people may actually "become five or ten years
younger" following six months of holistic therapy.

By contrast, biomedical pharmaceuticals bind further vital energy by disturbing the body
in all sorts of ways, so that although the symptom addressed by the treatment may become
milder, the general health and well-being can in fact deteriorate. For that reason, elderly
people should preferably not receive medication; nevertheless many elderly people have ten
different kinds of pills in their medicine cabinet instead of three kinds at the most, which their
bodies can tolerate.

> Female, aged 56 years growing old much too soon
> 1. Has slept on her side, pain corresponding to outside of left arm for last three
> weeks. Loss of strength assessed as being of "protection – fixation type." No sensory
> deficit, no affliction of feet or lower legs /to be followed up/.
> 2. Oedema around the ankles. Prescribe Furix [furosemide].

3. Patient requests a blood sample for gout, but there is no physical signs, so there is no immediate indication for it. "If she doesn't get it, her husband will tear the whole clinic apart." She is informed in detail of the risk of prescribing too much medicine, if blood tests are not clinically justified and show false-positive results.

4. Productive morning cough for many months. Auscultation of the lungs: nothing abnormal discovered. No fever. May have slight bronchitis in spite of the normal examination.

5. We talk about her everyday life, which is difficult; she becomes increasingly insecure. We talk about anxiety and menopause.

6. Headache almost daily. BP 130/90.

This patient has grown old 20 years too soon. She desperately wants to be examined, since there must be a disease, which the physicians have overlooked and for which she can be treated. But no, there is no disease. A good physician knows often intuitively whether or not people are seriously ill. To the best of our knowledge, this patient is not ill. We do not want to examine her for something, which we are certain she does not have – with the risk that the blood samples show a slight imbalance. Blood samples often shows false-positive results, some say one in twenty, but sometimes it is much more: compare i.e. the high rate of false positives in blood donor screening for antibodies to hepatitis C virus (34). So a fine rule is only to test when you suspect a specific disease. All the biomedicine in the world cannot save her. She has to save herself. Otherwise it will not happen.

Male, aged 79 year and aged
1. Vision and hearing no longer good. Should have an appointment with ophthalmologist and audiometry.
2. Dandruff and dry facial skin. Should use a rich skin cream daily on the face and anti-dandruff shampoo.
3. Very dizzy. BP 160/115. Probably drinks far too little, which may also be a predisposing factor of urinary tract infection that he sometimes suffer from. The home care should make sure that he drinks at least 2 litres daily. In addition, slightly confused, possibly also slightly demented. Cannot place the hours on the face of a clock.
4. Still pain in the locomotor system. Nobligan [opioid analgesic], 50 mg capsules, as required, maximum four times daily in addition to regular medication twice daily.
5. Urinary tract infection. The urine sample today negative, excluding 2+ for blood.

Dementia affects a great many elderly people – and especially people around them. Several alternative treatments have been developed to work toward the prevention of dementia by psychosocial measures. The idea is to use empathic communication in order to make the patient feel useful again. By contrast, biomedicine currently has no remedies for dementia. Alzheimer disease (AD) was first described by professor Alois Alzheimer, Germany, in 1906, when he reported the case of Auguste D, a 51-year old female patient, he had followed at a Frankfurt hospital since 1901 up until her death on April 8th, 1906. Even after her death he went on to study the neuropathological features of her illness. Shortly after her death he presented her case at the 37th Conference of German Psychiatrist in Tubingen on November 4th, 1906 in which he described her symptoms:

- Progressive cognitive impairment
- Focal symptoms

- Hallucinations
- Delusions
- Psychosocial incompetence
- Neurobiological changes found at autopsy: plaques, neurofibrillary tangles and artherosclerotic changes

These symptoms are still the characteristics of AD today, which is the most common cause of dementia in western countries. Clinicaly AD most often presents with a subtle onset of memory loss followed by a slowly progressive dementia that has a course of several years. The duration of AD can be 3-10 years from diagnosis to death (35).

Discussion

The fine art of medicine is to give the patient what he or she needs to get well and healthy. For lots of reasons the drugs do not always help, and it is therefore important for modern medicine to understand, which patients will benefit and also where it will be a waste to give drugs. Many modern drugs have a NNT (Number Needed to Treat) of 2 or more (36,37), and this situation is interesting, because it means that only some of the patients will be helped. Therefore the task of the modern physician will be to know which one to treat with a drug and which patient not to treat bio-medically, but with manual medicine or consciousness-oriented holistic medicine instead.

When a drug has a NNT of 2 or more, and you have no specific reason to believe that the drug will help a specific patient, it means that the patient has a likelihood of only 50% to be helped by the drug; if the NNT is 5, the likelihood is only 20%. But any physician worth his salt wants to cure the majority of his patients. So just using a drug with an NNT of 2 is not good enough and he is forced to use another toolbox. In general, treatment with a drug of NNT higher that 2 can never stand alone, and if the NNT is 5 or higher, an alternative toolbox must desperately be sought. Interestingly consciousness-based medicine seems to be able to help most of the patients, who understand the path of personal development, if the physician masters the art of "holding" and processing, and have the love for his patients necessary to gain the trust needed for the patient to receive the holding.

Another important aspect is that the pharmaceutical industry could be much better to let us know the NNT number for various drugs, which should be placed on every package, for the physician and his patient to know. And the pharmaceutical industry could and should do much more research to determine, which groups of patients are likely to be helped by the drug (38). Most drugs work better, when a person is otherwise healthy, young, understands to cooperate with the treatment and motivated to take the drugs. It is also important that the patient believes in biomedicine, has an orderly personality to keep a high compliance, has good personal networks, employed, etc. So it is very important to include different kind of patients in a drug study and to let us know the NNT in every case. We believe that this should be regulated by law, as the companies have an obvious interest in widening the group receiving the drug, while the physician and his patients have the complete opposite interest. We need to know and find out, when to give and take the drug, and when to use alternative medical toolboxes.

So understanding, where the biomedicine is likely to work and not to work is the most important issue in today's medical practice. Administering drugs with high NNT numbers blindly to our patients is not going to help much.

Conclusion

The bio-medical paradigm is dominating our medical education in most western countries. The modern physician is using pharmaceuticals as his prime tool. Unfortunately this tool is much less efficient than you might expect from the biochemical theory. The naïve believe in drugs as the solution to health problems of mankind, overlooking important existing knowledge on quality of life, personal development and holistic healing, seems to be the main reason, why around every second citizen of our modern societies are chronically ill.

The bio-medical paradigm and the drugs are certainly useful and in many situations we could not do without the drugs, i.e. the antibiotics curing syphilis and pneumonia. But curing infections in young age is not without consequences as the way we perceive health and medicine is influenced by such experiences. When we get a more severe disease in midlife we also often believe that a drug exists that can make us healthy again. But now the drugs does not work anymore, because we have turned older and have lost much of the surplus and personal energy that made us heal easily, when we were younger. Now we need to assume responsibility, take learning, and improve our quality of life. We need a more holistic medicine that can help us back to life by allowing us to access our hidden resources.

Whenever NNT is 3 or higher, the likelihood to cure the patient is less that 33%, which is not satisfying to any physician. In this case he must for ethical reasons try something more, to cure his patients; this is where the tools of both traditional manual medicine and the tools of a scientific holistic medicine are helpful.

The modern physician cannot rely solely on drugs; he must also have holistic tools in his medical toolbox. With every patient he must ask himself what he truly believe will help this patient, and this is the line of treatment he must follow. This is the only way we as physicians can improve the general health of our populations. Drugs alone will not do the job.

References

[1]   Ventegodt S. [Quality of life in Denmark. Results from a population survey.] Copenhagen: Forskningscentrets Forlag, 1995. [Danish].
[2]   Danish Parliement. Rapport from the Technology Council on alternative treatment in Denmark. Christiansborg, Copenhagen: Danish Parliement, 2002. [Danish].
[3]   Ventegodt S, Andersen NJ, Merrick J. Editorial: Five theories of human existence. ScientificWorldJournal 2003;3:1272-6.
[4]   Ventegodt S. The life mission theory: A theory for a consciousness-based medicine. Int J Adolesc Med Health 2003;15(1):89-91.
[5]   Ventegodt S, Andersen NJ, Merrick J. The life mission theory II: The structure of the life purpose and the ego. ScientificWorldJournal 2003;3:1277-85.
[6]   Ventegodt S, Andersen NJ, Merrick J. The life mission theory III: Theory of talent. ScientificWorldJournal 2003;3:1286-93.

[7] Ventegodt S, Merrick J. The life mission theory IV. A theory of child development. ScientificWorldJournal 2003;3:1294-1301.

[8] Ventegodt S, Andersen NJ, Merrick J. The life mission theory V. A theory of the anti-self and explaining the evil side of man. ScientificWorldJournal 2003;3:1302-13.

[9] Ventegodt S, Andersen NJ, Merrick J. Holistic medicine: Scientific challenges. ScientificWorldJournal 2003;3:1108-16.

[10] Ventegodt S, Andersen NJ, Merrick J. Holistic Medicine II: The square-curve paradigm for research in alternative, complementary and holistic medicine: A cost-effective, easy and scientifically valid design for evidence based medicine. ScientificWorldJournal 2003;3:1117-27.

[11] Ventegodt S, Andersen NJ, Merrick J. Holistic Medicine III: The holistic process theory of healing. ScientificWorldJournal 2003;3: 1138-46.

[12] Ventegodt S, Andersen NJ, Merrick J. Holistic Medicine IV: The principles of the holistic process of healing in a group setting. ScientificWorldJournal 2003;3:1294-1301.

[13] Ventegodt S, Andersen NJ, Merrick J. Quality of life theory I. The IQOL theory: An integrative theory of the global quality of life concept. ScientificWorldJournal 2003;3:1030-40.

[14] Ventegodt S, Merrick J, Andersen NJ. Quality of life theory II. Quality of life as the realization of life potential: A biological theory of human being. ScientificWorldJournal 2003;3:1041-9.

[15] Ventegodt S, Merrick J, Andersen NJ. Quality of life theory III. Maslow revisited. ScientificWorldJournal 2003;3:1050-7.

[16] Ventegodt S, Andersen NJ, Merrick J. Quality of life philosophy: when life sparkles or can we make wisdom a science? ScientificWorldJournal 2003;3:1160-3.

[17] Ventegodt S, Andersen NJ, Merrick J. QOL philosophy I: Quality of life, happiness, and meaning of life. ScientificWorldJournal 2003;3: 1164-75.

[18] Ventegodt S, Andersen NJ, Kromann M, Merrick J. QOL philosophy II: What is a human being? ScientificWorldJournal 2003;3:1176-85.

[19] Ventegodt S, Merrick J, Andersen NJ. QOL philosophy III: Towards a new biology. ScientificWorldJournal 2003;3:1186-98.

[20] Ventegodt S, Andersen NJ, Merrick J. QOL philosophy IV: The brain and consciousness. ScientificWorldJournal 2003;3:1199-1209.

[21] Ventegodt S, Andersen NJ, Merrick J. QOL philosophy V: Seizing the meaning of life and getting well again. ScientificWorldJournal 2003;3:1210-29.

[22] Ventegodt S, Andersen NJ, Merrick J. QOL philosophy VI: The concepts. ScientificWorldJournal 2003;3:1230-40.

[23] Merrick J, Ventegodt S. What is a good death? To use death as a mirror and find the quality in life. BMJ Rapid Response 2003 Oct 31.

[24] Ventegodt S, Merrick J, Andersen NJ. Quality of life as medicine. A pilot study of patients with chronic illness and pain. ScientificWorld Journal 2003;3:520-32.

[25] Ventegodt S, Merrick J, Andersen NJ. Quality of life as medicine II. A pilot study of a five day "Quality of Life and Health" cure for patients with alcoholism. ScientificWorld Journal 2003;3:842-52.

[26] Ventegodt S, Morad M, Hyam E, Merrick J. Clinical holistic medicine: Use and limitations of the biomedical paradigm. ScientificWorldJournal 2004;4:295-306.

[27] Ventegodt S, Clausen B, Langhorn M, Kromann M, Andersen NJ, Merrick J. Quality of life as medicine III. A qualitative analysis of the effect of a five days intervention with existential holistic group therapy: a quality of life course as a modern rite of passage. ScientificWorld Journal 2004;4:124-33.

[28] Axelsson A, Ringdahl A. Tinnitus--a study of its prevalence and characteristics. Br J Audiol 1989;23(1):53-62.

[29] Bjorntorp P, ed. International textbook of obesity. Chichester: John Wiley, 2001.

[30] Hasselstrom J, Liu-Palmgren J, Rasjo-Wraak G. Prevalence of pain in general practice. Eur J Pain 2002;6(5):375-85.

[31] Bell MR, Gersh BJ, Schaff HV, Holmes DR Jr, Fisher LD, Alderman EL, et al. Effect of completeness of revascularization on long-term outcome of patients with three-vessel disease undergoing coronary artery bypass surgery. A report from the Coronary Artery Surgery Study (CASS) Registry. Circulation 1992;86(2):446-57.

[32] Ornish D, Brown SE, Scherwitz LW, Billings JH, Armstrong WT, Ports TA, et al. Can lifestyle changes reverse coronary heart disease? Lancet 1990;336(8708):129-33.

[33] Sandanger I, Nygard JF, Ingebrigtsen G, Sorensen T, Dalgard OS. Prevalence, incidence and age at onset of psychiatric disorders in Norway. Soc Psychiatry Psychiatr Epidemiol 1999;34(11):570-9.

[34] Prohaska W, Wolff C, Lechler E, Kleesiek K. High rate of false positives in blood donor screening for antibodies to hepatitis C virus. Cause of underestimation of virus transmission rate? Klin Wochenschr 1991;69(7):294-6. [German].

[35] Merrick J, Kandel I, Morad M. Health needs of adults with intellectual disability relevant for the family physician. ScientificWorldJournal 2003;3:937-45.

[36] Smith R. The drugs don't work. BMJ 2003;327(7428):0-h.

[37] Dyer O. City reacts negatively as GlaxoSmithKline announces for a new drugs. BMJ 2003;327:1366.

[38] Gøtzsches P. Bias in double-blind trials. Dan Med Bull 1990;37:329-36.

Section 3. Principles of holistic medicine

In this section we shall understand the dimensions of existence involved in the process of healing (salutogenesis). We are surprisingly complex beings and even the simplest theory able to explain mental disease and healing seems multifaceted. One way to understand mental disorder is simply to see the patient's mind as separate from his or her being; to heal the mind is simply to integrate it into the patient's existence and life once again. Seen from the perspective of the patient's mind, the patient needs to find him or herself. "Know thyself" has been the key to life and healing ever since ancient Greece. Existential healing is the subject analyzed in chapter 12. Existential healing can be seen in cultural and a religious context, which we will do in chapter 13.

In Chapter 14 and 15 mental disorders are seen from the perspective of existential responsibility. A special method containing eight existential steps that the patient must go through to heal his or her mind is presented.

The different approaches presented in this section might seem very different but they are not. They are just existential healing seen from different angles.

We consider this section the most important section in the book. If you understand the principle of holistic healing, you will be able to help and cure a substantial fraction of your mentally ill patients, and even some the most ill.

Chapter 12

The holistic theory of healing

Holistic medicine and sexology, including holistic psychiatry are about existential healing (salutogenesis). The basic idea of healing is that the patient's whole existence is damaged, disturbed, closed down, repressed, or in some other way destoyed and compromised. To function well again the patient will need to heal. The mental, sexual and existential wounds are often gained early in life; either in the womb or in the first three years of life, during the establishment of the personality. Healing existence is not different from healing mind, body, emotions or other aspects of the human being. To be able to heal, the holisitc therapist or physician must understand the basic principles of healing.

It is possible to understand the process of healing from a holistic perspective. According to the life mission theory that we have developed (see Chapters 19-21), we can stretch our existence and lower our quality of life when we are in crisis, to survive and adapt, and we can relax to increase our quality of life when we later have resources for healing.

The holistic process theory explains how this healing comes about: Healing happens in a state of consciousness exactly opposite to the state of crises. The patient enters the "holistic state of healing" when the 1) patient and 2) the physician have a perspective in accordance with life, 3) a safe environment, 4) personal resources, 5) the patient has the will to live, 6) the patient and 7) the physician have the intention of healing, 8) the trust of the patient in the physician, and 9) sufficient holding.

The holding must be fivefold, giving the patient 1) acknowledgment, 2) awareness, 3) respect, 4) care and 5) acceptance.

The holistic process has three obligatory steps: to feel, to understand and to let go of negative decisions. This chapter presents a theory for the holistic process of healing, and lists the necessities for holistic therapy restoring the quality of life, health and ability to function.

Introduction

The process of healing seemingly takes place on two different levels in the organism. Though not completely understood, medical science has a good understanding of the local process of healing that takes place when a specific tissue or organ gets a wound. Healing can also take place on the level of the whole organism, and this is far more mysterious.

Biomedical science has been successful in explaining processes on the level of the molecule and the cell, but often unsuccessful in explaining the processes at the level of the organism. It has accordingly not yet been able to explain what happens when patients spontaneously recover or heal completely even from a severe mental or somatic illness, like cancer or schizophrenia. To explain what happens on the level of the whole organism is the objective of holistic medicine (1).

The holistic process of healing seemed to be a complete mystery for medical science, but in the second half of the 20th century, several scientists succeeded in explaining important aspects of this complicated phenomenon. One of the most brilliant was Aaron Antonovsky (1923–94) from the Ben Gurion University in Beer-Sheva, Israel with his model for holistic healing using the famous concept of "salutogenesis" (2,3). Antonovsky's idea was to help the patient to create a "sense of coherence", an experience in the depth of life, strongly related to the concepts of meaning, understanding, and action. In recovering the sense of coherence, the patient accesses his or her hidden resources and improves quality of life, health, and ability to function at the same time.

Pioneers in the field of holistic medicine have developed different holistic approaches, some fairly successful. Experiments done primarily in the United States through the last decades call on a revisited and more concise explanation (4-6), a contribution to which we hope to give in this chapter.

The explanation presented below accentuates the subjective and global level of the human being. It is holistic and will therefore not deal either with the biology of single cells or with molecules. We are working on explaining the biological mechanisms behind the holistic process of healing. We hope that the scientific community will accept the model in spite of its abstract character, where we take our journey through the life mission theory (7) and not in molecular biology. However strange, the model presented in this paper seems to be of great utility in the daily clinical practice of the family physician, where patients with chronic diseases often need the holistic approach if they are to become better. This model is to be understood as a practical help or tool for the physician, not the final explanation, as we also need the mechanistic explanation at the level of the cells, but that is not given here.

Three stages of holistic healing

Working directly with the consciousness of the patient is possible because the level of meaning and purpose can be acknowledged by both the patient and the physician in order to work with it and develop (7-10). This is often called personal development and is now an increasingly popular trend in our western society. Personal development and holistic healing is also the aim of much alternative, complementary, and holistic therapy.

The human existence can be interpreted as extending from the most abstract level of existence (the consciousness, the spirit, and the soul) to the most concrete level of cells, molecules, and atoms — the physical matter. Taking this as our frame of reference, we can place the phenomena body, feelings, and mind in between the abstract and the concrete level, as shown in figure 1 (8). The cells can be found between the level of matter and the level of the body. When these cells are disturbed because of "blockages", illness and suffering arises.

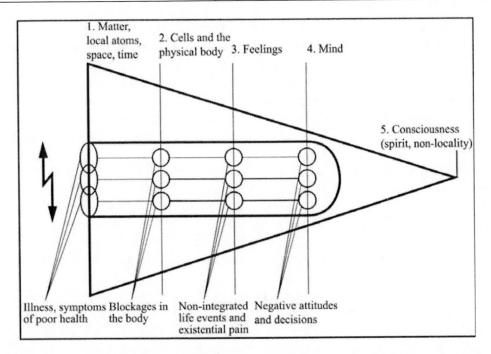

Figure 1. The holistic process theory of healing can be divided in three steps: "to feel, to understand, and to let go". "To feel" is to set feelings on the body, "to understand" is to set words on the feelings, and "to let go" is to set consciousness on the words. During these three steps, the illness and suffering is treated causally, as the etiology seen from the holistic perspective is the "blockages" in mind and body. The blockages are caused by feelings, suppressed by negative decisions into the tissues of the body. In the optimal process of holistic healing, the three above-mentioned steps occur at the same time.

When man experiences unbearable emotional difficulties, these can be solved by repressing emotional pain from the surface of consciousness. This happens by making a negative decision that denies the original constructive intention, which causes the suffering (8). The existential pain is, together with the whole perception, turned into what is known as a gestalt (a "frozen now"), which is from that moment found as a chronic tension in some part of the mind or the body.

Working with our patients in holistic therapy, we typically discover these tensions as chronic tightening in the skeletal muscles, but the smooth musculature (such as muscles in the intestines or the uterus) can also hold tensions. Principally, any tissue can hold any kind of tension. The symptoms of these tensions are known as health problems like chronic back pain, chronic stomach pain, and bleeding disturbances without any identified physical cause, or psychosomatic origin. According to this theory, sickness often occurs because emotional pain is suppressed and placed in different tissues in the body, which thereby hold the painful occurrence, the gestalt, until this is processed and reintegrated.

The holistic process of healing is exactly the opposite process of a crisis, creating the problem in the first place; we can identify the same three stages as are found in a crisis, just in the reverse order:

- The patient initially opens himself up for repressed feelings, feeling them again. Getting rid of the emotional pain is the last step in the crisis.

- The patient deals with the occurrence in his consciousness and understands his own responsibility about what has happened. Denying the responsibility and escaping the conscious scenario and the painful perception is the intermediate phase of a crisis.
- The patient perceives the decision that once was made, and understands the inappropriateness of maintaining it. This causes him to let go of it, and heal. Taking this negative perspective or decision is what initially brought the patient into the crisis; of course, this is usually provoked by some unfortunate condition of life.

This three-step model was developed after years of studying the best and most successful kinds of alternative treatment. These were intervening on the levels: body (bodyworks like Rosen therapy), feelings (gestalt psychotherapy), and mind and soul (philosophy of life). The intention was always to help the patient be himself, understand, and take responsibility for his own life. Step 1 was facilitated by body massage and other kinds of physical contact and care, step 2 by psychotherapy and conversations, and step 3 by life philosophical training and reading of insightful books.

For a long time, the three-step model seemed sufficient as these steps really seemed to be what was needed for holistic healing. For several years, we combined bodywork and psychotherapy with philosophical training at the Research Clinic for Holistic Medicine in Copenhagen. The approach worked well for some patients, but most patients were unable to achieve complete recovery and reach the level of full self-expression that was the ultimate goal in the holistic treatment.

Realizing that the alternative therapy gave the patient an experience of getting help without a full recovery made us re-evaluate our approach. We learned that the recovery was sometimes only temporary and that observation forced us to develop the model further, into the holistic theory of healing, presented below. For example: Could a patient with low back pain, treated by holistic bodywork, after a period of feeling better for one month, come back and need a new treatment, and so forth, year after year? Just moving the problem out of the body and into the domain of the patient's feelings did not help the patient, because it was not sufficiently integrated emotionally.

Another example was the common experience among psychotherapists, that in spite of rapid and visible progress in the beginning of the therapy, incest victims very seldom got back their normal ability to feel; in spite of many years of therapy their feelings did not heal. Only by making sure that the patient gets through all three stages — in the same therapeutic session or series of sessions — the problem is conclusively solved. When the patient has let go of his negative decisions by the end of therapy, the trauma is completely healed and the experience is like the traumatic event never took place.

To make sure the patient goes through all three steps and obtain real progress in the holistic therapy, it is of advantage that the therapist master all three dimensions of the therapy. The therapist must be holistic in the broadest sense of the word. We learned that if the holistic therapist also is able to give acknowledgment of the soul and spiritual dimension of the patient, and acceptance of the body and sexuality of the patient, he can take the patient into a state of being that we now call "being in the holistic process of healing" or "being in process" for short. When a holistic therapist is able to take his patient into this process, even the most severe traumas seem to go all the way to complete healing.

The entire and complete healing, where the problems are solved by the root of existence, is consequently the goal of holistic medicine. The model has been tested in a sequence of pilot studies (9,10) since 1998, as well as in clinical practice, and it is still being developed. From the clinic follows the example below.

Case story

As an example of such a patient from our own clinical practice, we can refer to a female patient in her twenties called Anna (11). The story of Anna is her own story, as she has recalled it in the therapy. As Anna decided not to confront her family with her memories, these recollections have not been confirmed nor dismissed by adult encounteres with the people of her childhood reality. We therefore do not know for sure if her recollections are "implanted memories" or factual events (see chapters 18-21). From the dramatic positive effects on her mental health and general well-being from integrating these events we have reached the conclusion that these events most likely actually happened as she has recollected and described them. The way Anna recovered were so remarkable that she in many ways has served as our ideal model-case (see chapter 23-25).

Three different men, including her father, raped Anna around 100 times as a child with some of the abuse extremely violent. On arriving at the clinic, she appeared very confused, psychological disturbed, weeping labile, and with poor social functioning. She believed that she was on her way to a nervous breakdown, or maybe even a psychosis at the beginning of the therapy.

In the holistic therapy, she found approximately 200 negative decisions that she successfully let go of. She went through the process, which took two years and approximately 100 therapy sessions of one or two hours, besides thousands of hours of homework. Afterwards, she returned to a normal and healthy emotional state, and could begin to have a natural relationship with men and sex. The therapy occasionally required a substantial holding from several individuals, and during the process she continuously and spontaneously returned to her childhood, until there was no more traumatic material.

During some of the most intense trauma sessions, the patient was in a state of such profound regression that her condition could be described as psychotic. She passed these episodes unproblematically and without any kind of medication, and was capable of taking care of herself between the sessions.

After two years of therapy, she entered a calm and stable phase, and was able to make an appraisal of her situation. She gained confidence and self-esteem, and felt that she was in full control of her life. She realized that her intelligence had increased to such a degree that she successfully could study at the university. She started a new life of higher quality, taking into use her intellectual, social, sexual, and many other talents.

The holistic state of healing: Being in process

"To be in holistic process" is our designation for the state of holistic healing, achieved by a patient, who is able to trust and receive the holding and processing offered by competent therapists. The patient needs to have the necessary personal resources, in a setting where the intention from both the patient and the physician is the healing of the patient. The process is a "high-energy state of consciousness" often with high arousal, since it has the same intensity as the trauma that originally caused the patient to escape from an overwhelming emotional pain. The result of this holistic process of healing is a spontaneous transfer back to one's self from the position of the ego (12).

It can be extremely painful and almost unbearable to be in a holistic process, because existential life pains are coming back just as if they had never been deserted. An especially interesting recent finding from our laboratory is that the process does not have to be painful if the patient is supplied with all the necessary resources in the therapeutic session. If the patient is now receiving what historically was missing, the gestalt is not painful, but joyful to confront, as the pleasure of receiving in the present now is greater than the historic pain. We believe this to be an important discovery, since it means that even the most painful traumas can be integrated in a graceful and noble manner into the holistic therapy.

We have identified nine factors that facilitate the process of the patient entering into the holistic process of healing, and staying in it until the process of healing is completed:

- The physician has a perspective in accordance with life. This comes from a personal philosophy of life that holds life, existence, and every individual soul as sacred and of immense value.
- The patient has a perspective in accordance with life. The patient appreciates fully the value of his own life, even if this value is not experienced in present time.
- A safe environment, peace, calmness and time.
- Personal resources, rest, tasty food, no crises with family or friends.
- The patient has a will to live and to be happy.
- The physician has the intention that the patient will heal.
- The patient has the intention of healing himself.
- The patient has enough trust to receive the holding and processing.
- Substantial and competent holding from the physician, nurse, or other employees.

The five fundamental qualities of holding the patient to "go into process" are:

- Awareness
- Respect
- Care
- Acknowledgment
- Acceptance

These qualities correspond with the three existential dimensions of mankind (11):

- Purpose or love – axis: as whole persons we want to give to others. Here the essential is the relationship to other people and what we have to offer (our purpose in life) (11). The holding need is acknowledgment of our soul and talents.
- Power – axis: body, feelings, and mind. Here the essential is our consciousness and survival. The holding needs are awareness, respect, and care.
- Gender and sexuality – axis. Here the essential is pleasure and the ability to enjoy. The holding need is acceptance of body and sexuality.

The holistic process of healing the existence

If our life is viewed from the perspective of the life mission or purpose in life, the process of holistic healing can be understood in a very simple way. In our natural condition, we live in a balance between "to be" giving us happiness and "to do" giving us often severe emotional and existential pain. Being is in essence a wonderful thing, happiness is an intrinsic factor in life; doing is mostly connected with trouble, effort, failure, and learning. In our natural state of being, life is a dynamic condition in which our existence can be presented as an energy-filled and dancing spring (see figure 2), the energy of our life — of our being — coiled around our purpose of life, the source of our doing.

When our existential needs are not fulfilled, and especially when we feel that our survival is threatened, which gives us the highest intensity of pain, we may make one or several decisions that modifies our existence. This is done to get what we want, and to survive. Our decisions now stretch the spring, and bind the energy that previously was dancing freely around. As we make more and more negative, existential decisions through life, we move further and further away from our natural state of being (see figure 3). Psychologically we are loosing the contact with our genuine selves. Mentally we might loose the ability to observe reality from different perspectives, or maybe even our psychological health. Emotionally we might loose the ability to feel. Bodily we might loose our physical health. Sexually we might loose our ability to engage, feel passion, and take pleasure. Spiritually we loose our sense of coherence and meaning. The holistic process of healing our existence brings all of this back, together with our quality of life, health, and functional ability in general.

When considering children, it is a little more complicated because children usually still have parents that are not completely competent holders. When parents solve their existential problems in their own lives, which often prevent them from giving the child the necessary holding, the children will normally get back their quality of life, health, and functional ability. Often it is much more efficient to help parents be better parents, than to work directly with the children. Often, one hour of competent holding of the child by the doctor demonstrates what is needed sufficiently to give the parents a better idea of competent parentship, and this alone can solve many of the problems for the child.

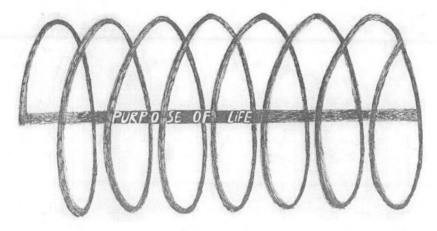

Figure 2. In our natural condition our existence can be compared with an energy-filled and dancing spring.

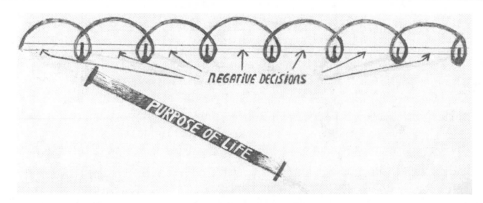

Figure 3. Low quality of life; poor health and poor functional ability in relation to social life, work life, and sexuality are derived from locking up your existence with negative decisions. The condition is rigid and undynamic and can be illustrated by a stretched spring that lost its ability to dance and vibrate freely.

Conclusions

If the physician adapts the necessary skills in holding — acknowledgement, awareness, respect, care, and acceptance — meeting the trusting patient is often enough to make the patient spontaneously go into the holistic process of healing. This process is characterized by a certain feeling of "existential movement" also known from a crisis (a feeling much like if the ground — the basis of the whole patients life — is moving). The existential movement of healing is just the opposite of the movement of crisis and adaptation for survival. In principle any problem caused by disturbances of the cells and tissues by "blockages" can be healed.

From the most abstract, holistic perspective, every problem, illness, or suffering related to the wholeness of the person basically needs the same holistic treatment: The five-dimensional holding and intention of the physician, that brings the patient into the state of existential healing. This condition is often very intense because it has the same intensity as the original trauma that forced the patient into modifying himself using the immense power of decisions.

The state of healing is not painful if the holding supplies the patient with the necessary resources. Even with the most severe traumatic life events, the confrontation of the most severe emotional pain will often be over in a few seconds or minutes if all the patient's resources are fully engaged in the process of healing. Sometimes the holding process needs more persons than just the physician or therapist, and sometimes an expanded amount of time (days) is needed for the patient to initiate, go through, and conclude the process of returning to his more natural state of being.

If the intention by the patient or the physician is unclear or a lack of correct holding, the process of treatment can drag on for a long time or may even prevent the patient from recovering or getting healed. If the physician does not succeed to get the patient through the holistic process of healing, this is usually because the physician or patient needs a more positive philosophy of life, a more safe environment, more personal resources, clearer intentions, more trust, or a more substantial and competent holding from the physician, nurse, and other employees. If the problem is with the physician, this can often be rectified through the use of existentialistic, oriented therapy.

To the reader who finds our explanation complicated and difficult we want to say: You do not have to understand this in you head. If you dare to care for and unconditionally love your patient and give your gift honestly, in spite of all resistance and trouble this endeavour might help your patient to heal in the end. When this happens you will witness this divine process of healing yourself. First when you get this expirience you will fully understand what healing is about and eventually you will find you own words to describe and explain the miracle of exitential healing.

Just trust your instincts, give your love without doubting yourself, follow your intuition and inborn sense of wisdom and the miracle of healing will happen also to you and your patient.

It is not complicated; it's not a mind thing. Its all about meeting heart to heart, soul to soul, and human being to human being. Meeting from the bottom of your heart is really all it takes. An as you practice you will be still more capable of doing it. Love is not a thing you can expect to be able to; for a loving heart in the end to be able to embrazse and contain everybody it must be trained and developed every single day.

In many ways sexuality seems to be the antidote to love; the animalistic side seems to be the opposite of the spiritual. But this dichotomy is the illusion. Love and sexuality are in the end from the same divine energy within all living beings. Only love can heal sexuality and existence. Only by being loved and accepted unconditionally, your mentally ill patient can return to be the true version of him or her self. And this journey back to natural existence is what holistic, existential healing is all about.

References

[1] Ventegodt S, Andersen NJ, Merrick J. Holistic medicine: scientific challenges. ScientificWorldJournal 2003;3:1108-16.

[2] Antonovsky A. Unravelling the mystery of health: How people manage stress and stay well. San Francisco: Jossey-Bass, 1987.

[3] Antonovsky A. Health, stress and coping. London: Jossey-Bass, 1985.

[4] Spiegel D, Bloom JR, Kraemer HC, Gottheil E. Effect of psychosocial treatment on survival of patients with metastatic breast cancer. Lancet 1989;2(8668):888-91.

[5] Ornish D, Brown SE, Scherwitz LW, Billings JH, Armstrong WR, Ports TA, et al. Can lifestyle changes reverse coronary heart disease? The Lifestyle Heart Trial. Lancet 1990;336(8708):129-33.

[6] Dige U. Cancer miracles. Århus: Forlaget Hovedland, 2000. [Danish].

[7] Ventegodt S. The life mission theory: a theory for a consciousness based medicine. Int J Adolesc Med Health 2003;15(1):89–91.

[8] Ventegodt S. Quality of life philosophy that heals. Copenhagen: Livskvalitets Forlaget, 1999. (Danish).

[9] Ventegodt S, Merrick J, Andersen NJ. Quality of life as medicine. A pilot study of patients with chronic illness and pain. ScientificWorldJournal 2003;3:520–32.

[10] Ventegodt S, Merrick J, Andersen NJ. A pilot study of a five day "Quality of Life and Health" cure for patients with alcoholism. ScientificWorldJournal 2003;3:842-52.

[11] Ventegodt S. Bevidsthedsmedicin [Consciousness Oriented Medicine]. Copenhagen: Livskvalitetsforlaget, 2003. [Danish].

[12] Ventegodt S, Merrick J, Andersen NJ. The life mission theory II: the structure of the life purpose and the ego. ScientificWorldJournal 2003;3:1277-85.

Chapter 13

Holistic healing in religion, medicine and psychology

The abstract aim of the human endeavors in the field of religion, medicine and psychology is basically the same: healing of human existence. Most interestingly, the process of holistic healing seems to be the same in all cultures, at all times and in all human endeavors. We try in this chapter to document the common nature of holistic healing and to describe how healing is related to personal development, especially development of the human consciousness enabling it to embrace and comprehend both the depth of self and the depth of the surrounding world. This development is nessesary for the mentally ill patient to heal and recover.

We argue that only by deepening the worldview, i.e. making our personal cosmology more complex, will we be able to reach the threshold for holistic healing. When we heal, not only our spirit and heart are healed, but also our body and mind, explaining why holistic healing has been such an important concept in all the religious and medical system of the worlds premodern cultures. Holistic healing thus seems to be the core concept of the Hippocratic Greek medicine, the origin of modern medicine. We compare this to modern holistic healing in the holistic medical clinic that uses the concept of applied salutogenesis to induce healing not only of existential and sexual disorders, but also of serious illness, such as cancer and schizophrenia. We argue that only if the patient is willing to abandon his simplistic worldview, he can have the fruit of holistic, existential healing and salutogenesis. In this chapter the religious experience is defined as the personal meeting with the totality of the universe; this can be a meeting with the universe as a person, i.e. God, or it can be the meeting with the fundamental source, the emptiness, sunya(ta) that creates the world, or it can be a unification with the universal energy lowing though everybody and everything. The universal quality of holistic healing is the development of sense of coherence (salutogenesis).

Introduction

Holistic healing is about the human healing his totality, i.e. healing of existence, or healing on an existential level (1,2). In all religions the purpose is the direct experience of the universe in its totality; in some religions like Judaism, Christianity, and Islam, the universe appears, according to the famous Jewish philosopher Martin Buber (1878-1965) (3) to be a person, a You, a God; in other religions like Hinduism, Buddhism, Islamic, Jewish and Christian mystic, and the native American, African and Australian cultures, the universe appears as the void, sunya(ta), the great emptiness, the common, creative source of everything, the universal energy penetrating everything. Independent of the universe being a person or not, the goal of the religion is to help the person back to the experience of being a part of the universe, a person welcome in the world, a person in the deepest harmony with the universe.

Most interestingly this striving for sense of coherence in religion seems to be identical with the striving for existential healing in the many different medical systems of the worlds premodern cultures: The ancient Greek Hippocratic character medicine (4), the medicine wheel and peyote medicine of the native Americans (5), the tradition of the about one million African Sangomas, the medical tradition of the Australian aboriginals (6), the tradition of the shaman healers of Northern Europe's (i.e. the Sames), the tradition of druids and witches using the power of nature for healing. In modern holistic sexology we find the same intend of transcending the ego, to allow the patient to get full orgasm using the tool of surrendering to love, oneness, and sense of coherence (7-16).

The striving for sense of coherence, and the merging of own consciousness with the collective conscious is also quite remarkably the goal of depth psychology as it started with Carl Gustav Jung (1875-1961) and of one of the more recent trends in psychology called "positive psychology". Several philosophers and researchers have reflected on the fact that holistic, existential healing, sense of coherence, and oneness with the world seems to be a fundamental objective of all human endeavor. This has lead to the successful concepts of perennial philosophy (18) and, as mentioned above, salutogenesis (1,2).

Taken to one single, abstract concept, all human striving seems to be about love – about loving and about being loved. Thus love being the essence of our human nature, the purpose of life (19-25) and the must fundamental motivation of our soul. Freud and the school of psychodynamic psychotherapy follow the fundamental motivations of man back to sexuality. In sexuality there is also this peculiar striving for unification, for the experience of oneness and transcendence; the full orgasm has been known to transcend ego and mind and everything else (comp. the French calling orgasm "le petit mort", i.e. the small death) and modern sexologists like Reich and Osho (Bhagwan Shree Rajneesh) believed that only the full orgasm had the power to heal man in his present, highly neurotic condition (27,28).

So it seems that holistic healing, in the most abstract sense of helping man back to being a perfect and happy, healthy, meaningful, coherent part of the universe, is the basic goal of religion, medicine and psychology. If we look at religion, medicine and psychology most of the practices have though history been holistic practices and the intent seem to always be the same: healing of human existence, holistic healing or in other words salutogenesis.

The nature of holistic healing

The different cultures are primarily characterized by their world-view (29). To understand the structure and nature of the world-view one must go to cosmology. Most interestingly, the depth of its cosmology determines the complexity of the culture including its religion, medicine and psychology. The more complex the cosmology, the more spiritually conscious, deeper reflected philosophically, and mystical is the culture. The cosmology thus seems to determine the quality of the culture and its religion and science. The complexity of the cosmology can be analyzed in a simple way using the concept of rays; the more rays or constitutional aspects a cosmology has, the more complex is it (25,26,28). Interestingly the number of rays determines, if a culture is very spiritual or very materialistic; in a cosmology with only one ray everything is the same, and often this is taken to be matter.

Modern biomedicine is thus based on the basic idea that the world is only chemistry and atoms, i.e. matter, allowing for a most practical and operational experience of the world, inviting the use of drugs and surgery for treatment. Jewish mysticism (the Kabbalah and Tarot build on this) is a cosmology seemingly with about 10 rays, or fundamental aspects of existence, allowing for a deep mystical experience of the world, deep existential reflection and healing, and even the personal meeting with God. Most psychological systems are in between, based on dualism with mind and matter allowing for some psychological and existential depth in the analyses without going all the way to mysticism.

Using the concept of poly-ray cosmology as a fundamental frame for interpretation, it seems that the condition for holistic healing is high cosmological complexity. In Hippocratic medicine the ray-number were four corresponding to the four elements (4); in Chinese medicine the ray number was five corresponding to five Chinese elements; in Hinduism the ray number was often seven, and in native American cosmology (the medicine wheel) the ray number was often eight (the eight directions of the wheel) (28). Mystics like George Ivanovitch Gurdjieff (1877–1949) made highly ingenious analysis of the structure of the human soul, which is still very popular with business leaders worldwide (29). This becomes quite practical in the end, allowing us to conclude that to meet God and heal existentially you need to develop your consciousness into a more complex understanding of self and the world. The concept of personal development (30-37) has been crystallized out of this cultural striving for a deeper understanding.

Tools for personal development can be found in religion (prayer, meditation), medicine (healing, development of character, consciousness and self-insight into the purpose of life and talents) and psychology (psychotherapy, exercises).

Discussion

Holistic healing, which is needed for the mentally ill patient to recover, thus basically is about the person developing a consciousness of sufficient depth and complexity to truly grasp both the world and the self, and in this understanding integrating the two into one, or creating the bridge from existence to the world.

The religious experience is often that you become one with everything, that God is within you and outside you; that you are just one string of energy arising out of the subtle, divine energies of the universe, materializing a being that again a just a dancing particle in the divine unity of everything. It has been described many times in medicine and psychology that patients even with metastatic cancer and other mortal diseases have become completely happy (38) and even spontaneously well again (39). Of course we all know stories of religious miracles, a little harder to believe for the skeptically, scientifically oriented mind. But basically, the message is the same: When you become once again one with the universe, improve your quality of life, and experience the magical sense of coherence, you will heal, not only your spirit, but also you mind and your body (40,41). The healing of the heart have often been an issue, as has sexual healing, reviving the person from the most fundamental and basic level of existence.

We have analyzed the nature of holistic healing from an existence-philosophical perspective, and found that we are born with a purpose of life, a gift of love to the world, and early in life we are forced to abandon this gift, and thus abandon the most valuable and divine aspect of our human nature. Holistic healing is basically about allowing ourselves to rediscover this hidden gem and become a unique and valuable person, not only to ourselves, but also to the surrounding world.

We have used this theory of a personal life-mission (18-25) to help patients heal, when biomedicine could not help them and have found that holistic medicine in this way could heal every second patient with physical illnesses and chronic pains, mental illnesses, existential and sexual problems (9,15,42-46). We have also found the effect of holistic healing to be lasting (47).

In practice, clinical holistic medicine has used the tools of conversational therapy, bodywork, and philosophical exercises to obtain the holistic healing and during the past 10 years cures have been developed for a number of illnesses and diseases (48-69). Very often the patients have had religious experiences and deep, spontaneous insights in self in relation to healing (7,70-72). Several patients even with mental illness, even schizophrenia and severe physical illness like cancer can seemingly be healed or helped this way (73-79).

Conclusion

So holistic healing, as we know it from religion, medicine and (depth) psychology, might have substantial values to offer modern man. A solution for many physical, mental, existential and sexual problems of modern man comes from the holistic healing that happens, when we develop our consciousness from being one-rayed – having a simple, materialistic worldview - into a much more complex, loving and appreciative understanding of both our inner and our outer world.

The abstract aim of the human endeavors in the field of religion, medicine and psychology is basically the same: healing of human existence. Most interestingly, the process of holistic healing seems to be the same in all cultures and we have tried in this chapter to document the common nature of holistic healing and to describe how healing is related to personal development, especially development of the human consciousness making it able to embrace and comprehend both the depth of self and the depth of the surrounding world. We argue that only by deepening the worldview, i.e. making our personal cosmology more complex, will we able to reach the threshold for holistic healing. When we heal, we heal our spirit, heart, body and mind, which explain why holistic healing has been such an important concept in premodern cultures. Holistic healing thus seems to be the core concept of the Hippocratic Greek medicine, the origin of modern medicine.

We compared this to modern holistic healing in the holistic medical clinic using the concept of applied salutogenesis to induce healing not only of existential and sexual disorders, but also of serious illness like cancer and schizophrenia. We argue that only if the patient is willing to abandon his simplistic worldview, he can have the fruit of holistic, existential healing and salutogenesis. In this chapter the religious experience is defined as the personal meeting with the totality of the universe; this can be a meeting with the universe as a person, i.e. God, or it can be the meeting with the fundamental source, the emptiness, sunya(ta) that creates the world, or it can be a unification with the universal energy lowing though everybody and everything. The universal quality of holistic healing is the development of sense of coherence (salutogenesis) (80-82). Only by looking for what is common in man's fundamental endeavors of religion, medicine and psychology, can we find the abstract core of the meaning of life, and only by finding this meaning can we live a happy, healthy, able life, which we were meant to live. Development and perfection of experience seems to be the fundamental intent of the universe. Only when we surrender and start experiencing this directly can we understand existence and truly be.

References

[1]   Antonovsky A. Health, stress and coping. London: Jossey-Bass, 1985.
[2]   Antonovsky A. Unravelling the mystery of health. How people manage stress and stay well. San Franscisco: Jossey-Bass, 1987.
[3]   Buber M. I and thou. New York: Charles Scribner, 1970.
[4]   Jones WHS. Hippocrates. Vol. I–IV. London: William Heinemann, 1923-1931.
[5]   Anderson EF. Peyote.The divine cactus. Tucson, AZ: Univ Arizona Press, 1996.
[6]   Morgan M. Mutant message from forever: A novel of Aboriginal wisdom. London: Harper Collins, 1990.
[7]   Ventegodt S, Clausen B, Merrick J. Clinical holistic medicine: the case story of Anna. III. Rehabilitation of philosophy of life during holistic existential therapy for childhood sexual abuse. ScientificWorldJournal 2006;6:2080-91.
[8]   Ventegodt S, Kandel I, Merrick J. Clinical holistic medicine: how to recover memory without "implanting" memories in your patient. ScientificWorldJournal 2007;7:1579-89.
[9]   Ventegodt S, Thegler S, Andreasen T, Struve F, Enevoldsen L, Bassaine L, et al. Clinical holistic medicine (mindful, short-term psychodynamic psychotherapy complemented with bodywork) in the treatment of experienced impaired sexual functioning. ScientificWorldJournal 2007;7:324-9.
[10] Ventegodt S, Kandel I, Neikrug S, Merric J. Clinical holistic medicine: holistic treatment of rape and incest trauma. ScientificWorldJournal 2005;5:288-97.
[11] Ventegodt S, Morad M, Hyam E, Merrick J. Clinical holistic medicine: holistic sexology and treatment of vulvodynia through existential therapy and acceptance through touch. ScientificWorldJournal 2004;4:571-80.
[12] Ventegodt S, Morad M, Kandel I, Merrick J. Clinical holistic medicine: problems in sex and living together. ScientificWorldJournal 2004;4:562-70.
[13] Ventegodt S, Morad M, Merrick J. Clinical holistic medicine: holistic pelvic examination and holistic treatment of infertility. ScientificWorldJournal 2004;4:148-58.
[14] Ventegodt S, Clausen B, Omar HA, Merrick J. Clinical holistic medicine: holistic sexology and acupressure through the vagina (Hippocratic pelvic massage). ScientificWorldJournal 2006;6:2066-79.
[15] Ventegodt S, Clausen B, Merrick J. Clinical holistic medicine: pilot study on the effect of vaginal acupressure (Hippocratic pelvic massage). ScientificWorldJournal 2006;6:2100-16.
[16] Ventegodt S, Struck P. Five tools for manual sexological examination: Efficient treatment of genital and pelvic pains and sexual dysfunction without side effects. J Altern Med Res 2009;1(3):247-56.
[17] Huxley A. The perennial philosophy. New York: Harper Collins, 1972.

[18] Ventegodt S, Andersen NJ, Merrick J. Editorial: Five theories of human existence. ScientificWorldJournal 2003;3:1272-6.
[19] Ventegodt S. The life mission theory: A theory for a consciousness-based medicine. Int J Adolesc Med Health 2003;15(1):89-91.
[20] Ventegodt S, Andersen NJ, Merrick J. The life mission theory II. The structure of the life purpose and the ego. ScientificWorldJournal 2003;3:1277-85.
[21] Ventegodt S, Andersen NJ, Merrick J. The life mission theory III. Theory of talent. ScientificWorldJournal 2003;3:1286-93.
[22] Ventegodt S, Andersen NJ, Merrick J. The life mission theory IV. Theory on child development. ScientificWorldJournal 2003;3:1294-1301.
[23] Ventegodt S, Andersen NJ, Merrick J. The life mission theory V. Theory of the anti-self (the shadow) or the evil side of man. ScientificWorldJournal 2003;3:1302-13.
[24] Ventegodt S, Kromann M, Andersen NJ, Merrick J. The life mission theory VI. A theory for the human character: Healing with holistic medicine through recovery of character and purpose of life. ScientificWorldJournal 2004;4:859-80.
[25] Ventegodt S, Flensborg-Madsen T, Andersen NJ, Merrick J. The life mission theory VII. Theory of existential (Antonovsky) coherence: A theory of quality of life, health and ability for use in holistic medicine. ScientificWorldJournal 2005;5:377-89.
[26] Reich W. [Die Function des Orgasmus]. Köln: Kiepenheuer Witsch, 1969. [German].
[27] Osho B. Tao. The pathless path. New York: Renaissance Books, 2002.
[28] Ventegodt S, Thegler S, Andreasen T, Struve F, Jacobsen S, Torp M, Aegedius H, Enevoldsen L, Merrick J. A review and integrative analysis of ancient holistic character medicine systems. ScientificWorldJournal 2007;12;7:1821-31.
[29] Maitri S. The spiritual dimension of the enneagram. New York: Penguin Putnam, 2001.
[30] Ventegodt S, Andersen NJ, Merrick J. Quality of life philosophy: when life sparkles or can we make wisdom a science? ScientificWorldJournal 2003;3:1160-3.
[31] Ventegodt S, Andersen NJ, Merrick J. Quality of life philosophy I. Quality of life, happiness and meaning in life. ScientificWorldJournal 2003;3:1164-75.
[32] Ventegodt S, Andersen NJ, Merrick J. Quality of life philosophy II. What is a human being ? ScientificWorldJournal 2003;3:1176-85.
[33] Ventegodt S, Andersen NJ, Merrick J. Quality of life philosophy III. Towards a new biology: Understanding the biological connection between quality of life, disease and healing. ScientificWorldJournal 2003;3:1186-98.
[34] Ventegodt S, Andersen NJ, Merrick J. Quality of life philosophy IV. The brain and consciousness. ScientificWorldJournal 2003;3:1199-1209.
[35] Ventegodt S, Andersen NJ, Merrick J. Quality of life philosophy V. Seizing the meaning of life and becoming well again. ScientificWorldJournal 2003;3:1210-29.
[36] Ventegodt S, Andersen NJ, Merrick J. Quality of life philosophy VI. The concepts. ScientificWorldJournal 2003;3:1230-40.
[37] Ventegodt S, Merrick J. Philosophy of science: How to identify the potential research for the day after tomorrow? ScientificWorldJournal 2004;4:483-9.
[38] Grof S. LSD psychotherapy: Exploring the frontiers of the hidden mind. Alameda, CA: Hunter House, 1980.
[39] Dige U. Cancer miracles. Copenhagen: Hovedland, 2000. (Danish).
[40] Spiegel D, Bloom JR, Kraemer HC, Gottheil E. Effect of psychosocial treatment on survival of patients with metastatic breast cancer. Lancet 1989;2(8668):888-91.
[41] Ornish D, Brown SE, Scherwitz LW, Billings JH, Armstrong WT, Ports TA, et al. Can lifestyle changes reverse coronary heart disease? The lifestyle heart trial. Lancet 1990;336(8708):129-33.
[42] Ventegodt S, Thegler S, Andreasen T, Struve F, Enevoldsen L, Bassaine L, et al. Self-reported low self-esteem. Intervention and follow-up in a clinical setting. ScientificWorldJournal 2007;7:299-305.
[43] Ventegodt S, Thegler S, Andreasen T, Struve F, Enevoldsen L, Bassaine L, et al. Clinical holistic medicine (mindful, short-term psychodynamic psychotherapy complemented with bodywork) in the treatment of experienced mental illness. ScientificWorldJournal 2007;7:306-9.

[44] Ventegodt S, Thegler S, Andreasen T, Struve F, Enevoldsen L, Bassaine L, et al. Clinical holistic medicine (mindful, short-term psychodynamic psychotherapy complemented with bodywork) in the treatment of experienced physical illness and chronic pain. ScientificWorldJournal 2007;7:310-16.

[45] Ventegodt S, Thegler S, Andreasen T, Struve F, Enevoldsen L, Bassaine L, et al. Clinical holistic medicine (mindful, short-term psychodynamic psychotherapy complemented with bodywork) improves quality of life, health and ability by induction of Antonovsky-Salutogenesis. ScientificWorldJournal 2007;7:317-23.

[46] Ventegodt S, Kandel I, Merrick J. A short history of clinical holistic medicine. ScientificWorldJournal 2007;7:1622-30.

[47] Ventegodt S, Thegler S, Andreasen T, Struve F, Enevoldsen L, Bassaine L, et al. Clinical holistic medicine: Psychodynamic short-time therapy complemented with bodywork. A clinical follow-up study of 109 patients. ScientificWorldJournal 2006;6:2220-38.

[48] Ventegodt S, Merrick J. Clinical holistic medicine: Applied consciousness-based medicine. ScientificWorldJournal 2004;4:96-9.

[49] Ventegodt S, Morad M, Merrick J. Clinical holistic medicine: Classic art of healing or the therapeutic touch. ScientificWorldJournal 2004;4:134-47.

[50] Ventegodt S, Morad M, Merrick J. Clinical holistic medicine: The "new medicine". The multiparadigmatic physician and the medical record. ScientificWorldJournal 2004;4:273-85.

[51] Ventegodt S, Morad M, Hyam E, Merrick J. Clinical holistic medicine: Use and limitations of the biomedical paradigm. ScientificWorldJournal 2004;4:295-306.

[52] Ventegodt S, Morad M, Kandel I, Merrick J. Clinical holistic medicine: Social problems disguised as illness. ScientificWorldJournal 2004;4:286-94.

[53] Ventegodt S, Morad M, Andersen NJ, Merrick J. Clinical holistic medicine: Tools for a medical science based on consciousness. ScientificWorldJournal 2004;4:347-61.

[54] Ventegodt S, Morad M, Hyam E, Merrick J. Clinical holistic medicine: When biomedicine is inadequate. ScientificWorldJournal 2004;4:333-46.

[55] Ventegodt S, Morad M, Merrick J. Clinical holistic medicine: Prevention through healthy lifestyle and quality of life. Oral Health Prev Dent 2004;2(Suppl 1):239-45.

[56] Ventegodt S, Morad M, Vardi G, Merrick J. Clinical holistic medicine: Holistic treatment of children. ScientificWorldJournal 2004;4:581-8.

[57] Ventegodt S, Morad M, Kandel I, Merrick J. Clinical holistic medicine: A psychological theory of dependency to improve quality of life. ScientificWorldJournal 2004;4:638-48.

[58] Ventegodt S, Morad, M, Kandel I, Merrick J. Clinical holistic medicine: Treatment of physical health problems without a known cause, examplified by hypertention and tinnitus. ScientificWorldJournal 2004;4:716-24.

[59] Ventegodt S, Morad M, Merrick J. Clinical holistic medicine: Developing from asthma, allergy and eczema. ScientificWorldJournal 2004;4:936-42.

[60] Ventegodt S, Merrick J. Clinical holistic medicine: Chronic infections and autoimmune diseases. ScientificWorldJournal 2005;5:155-64.

[61] Ventegodt S, Flensborg-Madsen T, Andersen NJ, Morad M, Merrick J. Clinical holistic medicine: A pilot study on HIV and quality of life and a suggested cure for HIV and AIDS. ScientificWorldJournal 2004;4:264-72.

[62] Ventegodt S, Merrick J. Clinical holistic medicine: Chronic pain in the locomotor system. ScientificWorldJournal 2005;5:165-72.

[63] Ventegodt S, Gringols M, Merrick J. Clinical holistic medicine: Whiplash, fibromyalgia and chronic fatigue. ScientificWorldJournal 2005;5:340-54.

[64] Ventegodt S, Merrick J. Clinical holistic medicine: Chronic pain in internal organs. ScientificWorldJournal 2005;5:205-10.

[65] Ventegodt S, Kandel I, Neikrug S, Merrick J. Clinical holistic medicine: The existential crisis – life crisis, stress and burnout. ScientificWorldJournal 2005;5:300-12.

[66] Ventegodt S, Gringols M, Merrick J. Clinical holistic medicine: Holistic rehabilitation. ScientificWorldJournal 2005;5:280-7.

[67] Ventegodt S, Morad M, Press J, Merrick J, Shek DTL. Clinical holistic medicine: Holistic adolescent medicine. ScientificWorldJournal 2004;4:551-61.

[68] Ventegodt S, Merrick J. Clinical holistic medicine: The patient with multiple diseases. ScientificWorldJournal 2005;5:324-39.

[69] Ventegodt S, Clausen B, Nielsen ML, Merrick J. Clinical holistic medicine: Advanced tools for holistic medicine. ScientificWorldJournal 2006;6:2048-65.

[70] Ventegodt S, Clausen B, Merrick J. Clinical holistic medicine: The case story of Anna. I. Long-term effect of childhood sexual abuse and incest with a treatment approach. ScientificWorldJournal 2006;6:1965-76.

[71] Ventegodt S, Clausen B, Merrick J. Clinical holistic medicine: The case story of Anna. II. Patient diary as a tool in treatment. ScientificWorldJournal 2006;6:2006-34.

[72] Clinical holistic medicine: factors influencing the therapeutic decision-making. From academic knowledge to emotional intelligence and spiritual "crazy" wisdom. ScientificWorldJournal 2007;7:1932-49.

[73] First do no harm: an analysis of the risk aspects and side effects of clinical holistic medicine compared with standard psychiatric biomedical treatment. ScientificWorldJournal 2007;7:1810-20.

[74] Biomedicine or holistic medicine for treating mentally ill patients? A philosophical and economical analysis. ScientificWorldJournal 2007;7:1978-86.

[75] Ventegodt S, Andersen NJ, Neikrug S, Kandel I, Merrick J. Clinical holistic medicine: Mental disorders in a holistic perspective. ScientificWorldJournal 2005;5:313-23.

[76] Ventegodt S, Andersen NJ, Neikrug S, Kandel I, Merrick J. Clinical holistic medicine: Holistic treatment of mental disorders. ScientificWorldJournal 2005;5:427-45.

[77] Clinical holistic medicine (mindful short-term psychodynamic psychotherapy complimented with bodywork) in the treatment of schizophrenia (ICD10-F20/DSM-IV Code 295) and other psychotic mental diseases. ScientificWorldJournal. 2007;7:1987-2008.

[78] Ventegodt S, Morad M, Hyam E, Merrick J. Clinical holistic medicine: Induction of spontaneous remission of cancer by recovery of the human character and the purpose of life (the life mission). ScientificWorldJournal 2004;4:362-77.

[79] Ventegodt S, Solheim E, Saunte ME, Morad M, Kandel I, Merrick J. Clinic holistic medicine: Metastatic cancer. ScientificWorldJournal 2004;4:913-35. Sense of coherence and physical health. Testing Antonovsky's theory. ScientificWorldJournal 2006;6:2212-9.

[80] Flensborg-Madsen T, Ventegodt S, Merrick J. Sense of coherence and physical health. A cross-sectional study using a new scale (SOC II). ScientificWorldJournal 2006;6:2200-11.

[81] Flensborg-Madsen T, Ventegodt S, Merrick J. Sense of coherence and physical health. The emotional sense of coherence (SOC-E) was found to be the best-known predictor of physical health. ScientificWorldJournal 2006;6:2147-57.

[82] Flensborg-Madsen T, Ventegodt S, Merrick J. Sense of coherence and health. The construction of an amendment to Antonovsky's sense of coherence scale (SOC II). ScientificWorldJournal 2006;6:2133-9.

Chapter 14

Mental disorders form a holistic perspective

From a holistic perspective psychiatric diseases are caused by the patients unwillingness to assume responsibility for his life, existence and personal relations. The loss of responsibility arises from the repression of the fundamental existential dimensions of the patients. Repression of love and purpose causes depersonalisation (i.e. a lack of responsibility for being yourself and for the contact with others, loss of direction and purpose in life). Repression of strength in mind and emotions give de-realisation – the breakdown of the reality testing, often with mental delusions and hallucinations. The repression of joy and gender give devitalisation – emotional emptiness, loss of joy, personal energy, sexuality, and pleasure in life.

The losses of the existential dimensions are invariably connected to traumas with life-denying decisions. Healing the wounds of the soul by holding and processing will lead to the recovery of the person's character, purpose of life and existential responsibility. It can be very difficult to help a psychotic patient. The physician must first love his patient unconditionally and then fully understand the patient in order to meet and support the patient to initiate the holistic process of healing. It takes motivation and willingness to suffer on behalf of the patients in order to heal, as the existential and emotional pain of the traumas resulting in insanity are often overwhelming. We believe that most psychiatric diseases can be alleviated or cured by the loving and caring physician who masters the holistic toolbox. Further research is needed to document the effect of holistic medicine in psychiatry.

Introduction

Genuine mental disorders are characterised by the condition medically referred to as "psychosis": a state of severe mental illness making normal function impossible for the patient. Psychosis is a difficult and much debated concept, and over the years various psychiatrists and schools of psychiatry have fought over the definition and delimitation of the term. Indeed, it is difficult to draw a clear line between psychosis and the normal, neurotic and disturbed mental state that characterises a large fraction of people in the western world. In for example the Danish society, often said to be one of the richest and most healthy communities in the world, one in every fourth person is severely mistriving (1,2). Only every second has close friends with whom they share everything, every second has some kind of sexual problems and only one in three are really satisfied with their job (1,2). From the high numbers of prevalence and incidence presented by the major textbooks (3) about one in five will be treated by a psychiatrist during their lifetime, and presumably many more will experience severe life crisis.

A general holistic theory of mental illness

The interesting question is whether there is a smooth transition from the normal state of consciousness into what we label as the psychotic state, or whether an actual qualitative shift occurs, when people become mentally ill. Holistic medicine regards most dimensions of the mind as continuous, while conventional psychiatry insists that there is a discrete leap from the normal mental state to the psychotic state. Admittedly, one easily gets the impression that the mentally ill, hallucinatory patient has had a sharp break from reality. We have followed patients closely in and out of psychosis as we have done many times now; we have never observed such leaping in and out of the psychotic state. Instead we find gradual shifts from severe existential pain though degrees of escapes from the overwhelming emotions to sheer denial and total repression of the emotionally painful content and finally into the state of hallucination, as the ultimate escape from unbearable emotional pain. There seems to be a general agreement that psychosis is characterised by a combination of the following:

- De-realisation – breakdown of the reality-testing, mental delusions, hallucinations
- Devitalisation – emotional emptiness, loss of joy, personal energy, sexuality and pleasure
- Depersonalisation – lack of responsibility for being oneself and for the contact with others, loss of direction and purpose in life

Together the break down in these three vital areas of human existence (corresponding to the fundamental dimensions of existence in the theory of talent) (4) constitute a mental and existential state that prevents the patient from assuming responsibility for his or her own life and for normal functioning, which are the core characteristics of the psychotic state of being.

In our opinion, the most important single dimension of psychosis and "madness" in general is that the person disclaims responsibility for his or her own life. Accordingly, we consider psychosis a defence against the emotional and existential suffering associated with assuming responsibility. It might seem rather surprising that assuming responsibility can cause such emotional problems. In the therapy the extreme and intolerable pain of the psychotic patient reveals itself as raising from being yourself fully as a child (so vulnerable and open as you enter life) and failing completely in giving what you have to offer to the people you trusted fully and loved so unconditionally. As most children do not receive the holding they need (4,5), it is not so surprising that most people carry deep wounds in their soul. These wounds can burst open when life becomes rough. The real mystery is why some people choose to dig into this old, painful material voluntarily seemingly with the intention to integrate what was left of being and thus heal their existence, while other people keep the mind extrovert and the machinery of the facade intact through life, thus avoiding the turmoil connected with confronting the most serious of our human traumas.

As psychosis comes in a gradual spectrum, its most common manifestation is "silent" and indistinguishable to lay people, such as the quiet young girl who confess to her physician that her home has been equipped with surveillance cameras, only she cannot find them. It may also have very dramatic manifestations as when the patient poses a danger to himself and to others, as in classic madness. In this situation a conflict is often building over time and the patient often chooses to be evil in order to avoid emotional pain (6).

When encountering a psychotic patient in the holistic clinic, we have to examine the following conditions to assess the nature and severity of the psychosis. For the patient's own safety, in particular, it is important to assess whether the severity of the psychosis prevents surviving in a normal everyday life. The degree of reduced functioning and the severity of the psychosis call for special precautions:

- Cognitive disturbances – is the patient's perception impaired or distorted, for example by hallucinations?
- Emotional disturbances – is the basic mood lowered as in the case of depression or elevated as in the case of mania? Is the sex life affected?
- Disturbances in meaning, content and direction of life – is the patient realistic in respect to his or her project in life? Is the patient assuming responsibility for own existence and the relations to other? Is the patient consciously choosing to be evil?

Healthy individuals are in control of their fantasy world and do not mix it with the perception of the external world, while psychotic patients tend to hallucinate, create their own perceptions, like an internal picture partially overlapping the perception of the external world. When studied extremely carefully, it can be demonstrated that everybody projects something on other people from their own subconscious mind - like the inner man or woman when fallen in love. Everybody is slightly hallucinatory, what really maters is the degree.

In some psychotic patients the perception of reality includes a few, perceptional elements created unconsciously. The classic example of such acute psychosis is delirium tremens in alcoholics, where spiders and snakes crawl out of the walls. As a medical student, one of the authors (SV) once helped a patient with acute delirium get the spiders out of the window. That really calmed him down, but the nurse reprimanded afterwards for doing this act. The cause of delirium in alcoholics is the brain compensating for the sedative effect of alcohol by increasing activity, including the neurotransmitter system that use a substance called GABA. When the alcoholic suddenly drinks less than usual, brain activity becomes so high and productive that the symbols and images otherwise belonging to the dream world and the subconscious mind cannot be contained within the imagination, but are projected onto the walls and doors of the physical world.

The examination will often reveal that any patient is to some extent living in his or her own world, which is one way of disclaiming responsibility. A total lack of reality testing – where the patient lacks the ability to respond appropriately to the external environment and has withdrawn completely into his or her own reality – is rare. Even in the most hallucinatory state of being, most aspects of reality still are interpreted normally (there might be non-existent spiders in the state of delirium but they still climb the real wall and table).

The spontaneous hallucinations observed in most mentally ill patients are difficult to understand. Urgent matters in the subconscious mind, while at the same time the patient is unwilling to take responsibility for the pain from the traumatic moments in the past, probably cause them. The problem manifests itself symbolically in the present: old poisonous comments become poisonous gas flowing into the house, old condemnation becomes hazardous irradiation, childhood traumas from excessive control become a sense of camera surveillance at home, the parents' unbearable criticism turns into constantly audible voices.

Another strategy for disclaiming responsibility is to depreciate the existence, value, power and possession of yourself, of life and the world, obviating all requirements for achievement and performance. When the person is so insignificant and has so little value or knowledge and the world is so impossible – the perception observed in many depressive patients – the person no longer has any particular responsibility for his or her life. No one is committed beyond one's power.

Conventional psychiatry distinguishes between two main types of mental illness: schizophreniform disorders, which primarily occur in schizophrenic patients and borderline patients and affective mood disorders, which occur in depressive patients, manic patients and patients with manic-depressive disorders. The former type is generally associated with increased brain activity and can be treated with psychotropic drugs, which reduce the brain activity appropriately. By contrast, a depressive patient's brain activity is too low. This can be treated with drugs that stimulate brain activity. Anxiety is related to specific neurotransmitter systems and can be treated with drugs that suppress the activity of these systems.

Psychotropic drugs have come into wide use in our culture and at least one in five people in Denmark will at some point in life receive such drugs. There is consensus that psychotropic drugs affect the symptoms, but not the actual disorder. To heal the disease the patients must heal his or her existence and human character (7) and in this process recover the clearness of mind, the spaciousness of feelings, the strength of being present in the body, the acceptance of gender and sexuality and the acknowledgment of the essence of his wholeness and being (the soul) and in the core of this: the purpose of life (8).

Before we address the question of how the psychiatric patient can be helped by the holistic physician we take a closer look at the holistic process of healing. It is important to notice that the holistic theory of mental illnesses presented here is derived from a general theory of loss of health, quality of life and ability (4-10). From a holistic perspective psychiatric diseases are caused by the patient's unwillingness to assume responsibility for their own life, existence and personal relations. This loss of responsibility is caused by the repression of the patient's fundamental existential dimensions, which we normally call love and purpose, strength and power, joy, gender and sexuality (4). Repression of love and purpose gives depersonalisation or the lack of responsibility for being oneself and for the contact with others, as well as loss of direction and purpose in life. Repression of power and strength in mind, feelings and body gives de-realisation or the breakdown of the reality testing, often with mental delusions and hallucinations. The repression of joy, gender and sexuality gives devitalisation or emotional emptiness, loss of joy, personal energy, sexuality and ability to feel pleasure and happiness in life. The loss of the physical, mental and spiritual character seems to be the price the patient has to pay for this multidimensional repression of his or her true self.

Clinical holistic medicine

Please allow us to repete below what we think is at the core of scientific holistic medicine. The life mission theory (4-10) states that everybody has a purpose of life, or huge talent. Happiness comes from living this purpose and succeeding in expressing the core talent in your life. To do this, it is important to develop as a person into what is know as the natural condition, a condition where the person knows himself and uses all his efforts to achieve what is most important for him. The holistic process theory of healing (11-14) and the related quality of life theories (15-17) state that the return to the natural state of being is possible, whenever the person gets the resources needed for the existential healing. The resources needed are holding in the dimensions: awareness, respect, care, acknowledgment and acceptance with support and processing in the dimensions: feeling, understanding and letting go of negative attitudes and beliefs. The preconditions for the holistic healing to take place are trust and the intention for the healing to take place. Existential healing is not a local healing of any tissue, but a healing of the wholeness of the person, making him much more resourceful, loving and knowledgeable of himself and his own needs and wishes. In letting go of negative attitudes and beliefs the person returns to a more responsible existential position and an improved quality of life. The philosophical change of the person healing is often a change towards preferring difficult problems and challenges, instead of avoiding difficulties in life (18-25). The person who becomes happier and more resourceful is often also becoming more healthy, more talented and able of functioning (26-28).

Dimensions of the mental disorders

A skilled psychiatrist will immediately "scan" his patient for a dozen or so different symptoms, more or less well defined. Some of them are so well defined that they can be rated on various psychometric scales, which will indicate the severity of the patient's condition: depression, mania, anxiety, psychosis (e.g. hallucinations), neuroticism or introversion. Other dimensions can be sensed, but are difficult to quantify: the degree of delusion, somatisation, grief, hypochondria, arousal level (e.g. panic), liveliness, untruthfulness, hysteria,and quality of attention or alertness.

Based on these observations, the psychiatrist can form an impression on the degree of the patient's suffering, functional capacity, the degree to which the patient assumes responsibility for his or her own life and relations, the patient's level of consciousness, insight and finally the severity of the disorder. The complexity of human consciousness makes it difficult to become a good holistic psychiatrist, because of the numerous paths that one has to know and be able to follow, as the patient enters them.

Conventional psychiatric treatment typically involves psychotropic drugs or electro-convulsive therapy (ECT). In the short run the drugs and ECT are efficient in about half the patients, generally there is insufficient evidence on the long time effect of the drugs, and little scientific knowledge about any lasting effect of ECT's often serious temporary side effects like discomforts and memory impairment (29). It seems from a search in MedLine (www.pubmed.gov) that the long term side effects has not been well examined but it seems fair to expect from this extremely violent treatment that at least some side effects will last.

Conventional psychiatric treatment seeks to alleviate the symptoms that prevent the patient from functioning and coping with life. It is generally agreed that while medication can be effective in many cases, it hardly ever leads to recovery. Many health professionals would therefore prefer a new psychiatric approach that deals more with the causes of the disorders. In order to adopt such an approach we have to understand the causes of psychiatric disorders.

> Female, aged 27 years, where the psychiatrist only prescribes medication
> Patient is dissatisfied because her psychiatrist only prescribes medication. Physiotherapy hashad little effect on her headache. Patient has had physiotherapy ten times, and there is no reason to continue. I recommend her to read books about people who have had the same experience and have solved their problems. Perhaps the librarian can help her. She has to be honest with her psychiatrist and verbalise her discontent.

As physicians, we must to be careful not to destroy each other's work. When the psychiatrist has put the patient on medication, in principle, we should not interfere with his field of work, but since she is dissatisfied with the psychiatrist and seeks help from a holistic physician, she obviously feels a need to get help and support to confront the biomedical paradigm (30,31). We believe that reading books is important, as they can provide words with which to think. They will also make it easier for the patient to communicate with the psychiatrist. In this case the helper is therefore the librarian.

Biomedical versus holistic perspectives of the mental disorders

In a conventional (biomedical) psychiatric perspective, mental disorders are caused by certain disturbances in brain activity, considered to be genetically controlled. Depression and schizophrenia are assumed to be hereditary, although there is insufficient evidence of any genetic causes. Twin studies with identical twins, who grew up away from each other showed that in 25-50% of the twin pairs, both twins were schizophrenic (the concordance) (32-36). This is generally considered to support the hypothesis that schizophrenia has a genetic cause, but in our opinion it confirms the belief that factors other than genetics determine, whether the disorder develops. There are of coarse some genetically determine vulnerability which might differ from individual to individual, but the genetic patterns has never been identified with any certainty, so this is still speculative. When we take mentally ill or disturbed patients into deep regressive therapy, many patients reveal traumatic episodes going all the way back into the womb. It is very likely that identical twins being genetically identical are in closer mental contact in the womb than non-identical twins, making them to a higher extent share the content of their early consciousness, also the traumatic content. Such considerations seem to favour the hypothesis of early psychosocial factors causing schizophrenia, and weaken the evidence for the genetic hypothesis.

From our holistic perspective, mental disorders are generally not caused by genetics. People may be genetically predisposed, but rather by traumas, emotionally difficult situations often occurring early in the individual's life that lead to negative decisions denying life, self and reality. The decisions lie as deep structures in the conscious and subconscious mind and compromise the patient's relations with himself, his inner life and the outside world. The inner conflicts are manifested as suffering and reduced capacity in relation to mental and social functioning, love, sex or work.

The traumas in the mentally ill patient often involve severe emotional pain, leading to dramatic and destructive statements such as: "I am outside", "Nobody likes me", "I am nothing but trouble", "I am crazy", "I am dead", "You are dead", "It is unreal", "It is not now". Often, these statements include a directly social hereditary element, for instance if the patient's mother has had a mental disorder and experiences with her lead to conclusions such as: "She is mentally ill," and if one attempts to excuse the mother's illness: "I am mentally ill," etc.

Holistic healing induces recovery of character, purpose and responsibility

Recovery is known to happen in one out of four even in the most severe psychiatric cases. The recovery literature shows several kinds of recovery from schizophrenia (32), the most interesting being full recovery happening in one study in 13,7% of the patients after 5 years (33) and in about 25% of the patients long term (34,35) in the western countries and, quite surprisingly, much more often in the third world (36), Since third world countries are mostly without a developed biomedical psychiatry, this may indicate that many of the therapeutic procedures which seem beneficial in the short run (month) might actually be contra-therapeutic with a perspective of years. It is important to cooperate with this spontaneous recovery process and to enhance it, if and when possible. This is the mission of the holistic approach to the psychiatric illness.

According to the holistic medicine perspective, the major mental disorders are caused by traumas with painful emotional content and life-denying decisions. Therefore, the causal cure consists in helping the patient to heal his or her existence by the integration of the old traumas. The existential healing is induced by applying the obligatory steps of holistic process of healing on the mental diseases (13):

- Make the patients become aware of what lies behind the symptoms they display.
- Let them sink into the feeling until they understand what it is about.
- Help them apply words to the feelings and support them in letting go of all decisions that make themselves or their lives less good and real.

In practice, the process is complicated. The greater the old emotional pain, the stronger the patient's mental defences against entering the old now and more support and holding – attention, respect, care, acceptance and acknowledgment – are required to get the patient through the trauma. In principle, holistic medicine can help any psychiatric patient, who is willing to assume responsibility for his or her own life, provided that there is sufficient support andthat the holistic physician fully understands the patient, his/her situation, and his/her state of being. The latter is absolutely crucial. A patient who does not experience being seen and met will not be able to show any trust. Without trust the patient will not allow the physician to give him/her holding and support.

To understand mentally ill people in sufficient depth, the therapist must possess great personal insight and acknowledge the corresponding problems in his own life, naturally on a smaller scale. In our opinion, we are all tarred with the same brush regardless of the nature and severity of the particular human problem. The purpose of conventional, biomedical, psychiatric treatment of psychosis is to make the symptoms of the psychosis disappear, while the purpose of holistic treatment of mental disorders is to eliminate their cause and in that way help the patient return fully to life, health and ability. The essence of holistic treatment of mental disorders is to help the patient recommence and take full responsibility for his or her life. As they disclaimed their responsibility under extreme pressure patients frequently, in order to recover, have to relive difficult events and temporarily experience increased aggravation and suffering during the sessions, in order to recover. This constitutes a distinct difference between biomedical and holistic psychiatry. The former approach does not allow the patient to suffer, because suffering is unnecessary, while the latter approach allows suffering, if it helps the patient to move on. In addition, existential pain is actually an important element of life of which the patient should not be deprived without the most careful of thoughts. In the holistic clinic, it is to some extent rational to apply the conventional (biomedical) psychiatric diagnoses. This allows for consensus among professionals, when cooperating in helping the patient andwhen doing research. However, the holistic physician has to supplement the traditional diagnosis with a description of the dimensions that are relevant for the holistic therapy. For example: What resources, internal and external, does the patient possess? What is the patient's reality? Is the patient, for example, an institutionalised, experienced user of psychiatry, with little motivation for a major change, or is it a new patient with no experience with the established psychiatric system? Is there an insatiable appetite for learning and a will to recover?

The latter questions are very important, because patients can survive in the psychiatric system with a much lower level of responsibility, than is required to survive in the real world. Patients who have become accustomed to being hospitalised know that it is acceptable for them to disclaim responsibility, unlike patients who lack that experience. In a way, the biomedical, psychiatric system of today inadvertently rewards patients who disclaim responsibility, which is most unfortunate. In the field of holistic psychiatry the physician's kindness, his human generosity and emotional capacity are the primary tools for helping the patient. The physician's love of his patient is the patient's primary resource and the ethical standard of the holistic physician is also an important prognostic factor. Thephysician's good intention restores confidence and provides an opening. If a therapist has a patient that he cannot accommodate, it is absolutely essential to say so immediately and refer the patient to someone, who can. Incidentally, kindness is neither sympathy nor empathy, but rather the willingness to give something to the patient without receiving anything in return, a generous quality closely related to the love we share with our relatives.

Suicidal thoughts

Naturally, suicidal thoughts are a central issue, since a patient with very low self-esteem may have a spontaneous death wish in order not to be in the way or cause trouble for other people.

The way we see it, a death wish is actually social. We all, deep down, need to feel useful and if we are not of value to anybody we will not live as a burden.

Specific plans to commit suicide means that the patient has to be treated in cooperation with an experienced psychiatrist. If the situation is clearly life threatening there is no alternative to admission for treatment, by force if necessary. As force will almost invariably inflict new traumas on the patient and therefore cause a setback in the patient's development, force should only be applied in extreme cases. If the physician succeeds in making the patient let go of the decisions that are the cause of low self-esteem and the death wish, a crisis can sometimes be avoided, but it is important to ensure that the patient's condition subsequently remains stable. With this said, it really is a difficult ethical (and classical philosophical) question. Are we allowed to compromise the patients autonomy to safe his life? What is more important: the life or the survival of the patient? If we have to choose most people will say that surviving with no living is pointless. Of course living is not possible without survival either.

With this said, we have found that holistic medicine is known to prevent suicide. A recent review has documented that about hundred patients who had decided to take their own life actually survived by the help and intervention of holistic medicine (37).

Discussion

Patients with acute psychosis, who do not pose any danger to themselves or others, are highly susceptible to contact and care founded on profound empathy and endless patience. Acute psychosis is a common condition in connection with severe traumas and may also be provoked by recreational substances, such as LSD, ecstasy or cannabis. Follow-up should include a brief series of conversations. If the patient remains in a psychotic state, a psychiatric specialist can provide help by means of appropriate, small doses of antipsychotic medication.

Unipolar depression, including major depression and minor depression can often be treated with holistic medicine. A therapeutic course lasting six months should be expected in major depression. Antidepressants can often remove the symptoms in a couple of months, but the tendency towards depression will usually persist for the rest of the patient's life. Once the holistic treatment has been completed successfully and the patienthas learned from the experience there is justified hope that the depression is gone forever.

In our experience, the bipolar disorder is difficult to treat, because this type of patient tends to shift rapidly from one mental state to the next to avoid contact with the underlying existential pain. In young people who have not been admitted for psychiatric treatment, but have a tendency to become psychotic, holistically oriented conversational therapy appears to be effective in preventing mental illness, but more research is required to confirm this. Schizophreniform psychosis: schizophrenia, borderline psychosis and similar disorders can be treated, if the therapist understands and feels great kindness towards the patient. A long therapeutic course should be anticipated, because psychosis usually reveals a hidden flaw in the patient's character in respect of responsibility.

In elderly psychotic patients or patients with a history of repeated hospitalisation in a psychiatric ward, treatment may be extremely difficult and require substantial resources. For example, in the case of the patient'sresources – for example because of the patient adapting to a life as mentally ill with all the privileges of not being responsible – and in that case holistic treatment without psychotropic medication is deemed impracticable. A mentally ill patient often undergoes thorough assessment and a detailed treatment and development plan prior to receiving holistic therapy, which is frequently provided in close cooperation with a psycho-dynamically oriented psychiatrist. Now and again, we let the specialist do the initial work with the patient, particularly in patients who require many resources, then we step in as a coach for personal development, when the patient has been stabilised and gained access to his own resources. People with development perspective are generally more susceptible to holistic treatment than people, who are ignorant of the notion of personal development.

From a holistic perspective most psychiatric diseases are caused by the patients unwillingness to assume responsibility for his life, existence and personal relations. The loss of responsibility arises according to the holistic theory of mental illnesses from thepatient's repression of the fundamental existential dimensions (called love, strength and joy in the theory of talent). Repression of love and purpose gives depersonalisation – lack of responsibility for being oneself and for the contact with others and loss of direction and purpose in life. Repression of strength in mind and emotions give de-realisation – the breakdown of the reality testing, often with mental delusions and hallucinations. The repression of joy and gender give devitalisation – emotional emptiness and loss of joy, personal energy, sexuality, and pleasure in life.

The loss of the existential dimensions is invariably connected to traumas with life-denying decisions. Healing the wounds of the soul by holding and processing in accordance with the holistic process theory of healing will lead to the recovery of the persons character, purpose of life, and existential responsibility. It can be very difficult to help a psychotic patient. The physician must first love his patient unconditionally and then fully understand the patient and his/her state of being. Only then can he meet and support the patient and initiate the holistic process of healing. It takes a lot of motivation and willingness to suffer on behalf of the patient, so that he can heal, as the existential and emotional pain of the traumas giving insanity are often overwhelming. We believe that most psychiatric diseases can be alleviated or cured by the loving and caring physician, who masters the holistic toolbox.

A recent metaanalysis has documented that holistic medicine actually prevented suicide making holistic medicine a treatment also when the patient is suicidal (37). If it is nessesary to use force to prevent suicide we recommend this, but we acknowledge that it is an fundamental ethical problem, if suicidal thoughts should make the physician neglect the patient's fundamental human right of autonomy.

References

[1]   Ventegodt S. [Livskvalitet i Danmark.] Quality of life in Denmark. Results from a population survey. Copenmhagen: Forskningscentrets Forlag, 1995. [Danish].
[2]   Ventegodt S. [Livskvalitet hos 4500 31-33 årige.] The Quality of Life of 4500 31-33 year-olds. Result from a study of the Prospective Pediatric Cohort of persons born at the University Hospital in Copenhagen. Copenhagen: Forskningscentrets Forlag, 1996. [Danish].
[3]   Fauci AS, Braunwald E, Isselbacher KJ, Wilson JD, Martin JB, Kasper, DL, et al, eds. Harrison's principles of internal medicine, 14th ed. New York: McGraw-Hill, 1998.
[4]   Ventegodt S, Andersen NJ, Merrick J. The life mission theory III: Theory of talent. ScientificWorldJournal 2003;3:1286-93.

[5] Ventegodt S, Merrick J. The life mission theory IV. A theory of child development. ScientificWorldJournal 2003;3:1294-1301.

[6] Ventegodt S, Andersen NJ, Merrick J. The life mission theory V. A theory of the anti-self and explaining the evil side of man. ScientificWorldJournal 2003;3:1302-13.

[7] Ventegodt S, Kromann M, Andersen NJ, Merrick J. The life mission theory VI: A theory for the human character. Healing with holistic medicine through recovery of character and purpose of life. ScientificWorldJournal 2004;4:859-80.

[8] Ventegodt S. The life mission theory: A theory for a consciousness-based medicine. Int J Adolesc Med Health 2003;15(1):89-91.

[9] Ventegodt S, Andersen NJ, Merrick J. Editorial: Five theories of human existence. ScientificWorldJournal 2003;3:1272-6.

[10] Ventegodt S, Andersen NJ, Merrick J. The life mission theory II: The structure of the life purpose and the ego. ScientificWorldJournal 2003;3:1277-85.

[11] Ventegodt S, Andersen NJ, Merrick J. Holistic medicine: Scientific challenges. ScientificWorldJournal 2003;3:1108-16.

[12] Ventegodt S, Andersen NJ, Merrick J. Holistic Medicine II: The square-curve paradigm for research in alternative, complementary and holistic medicine: A cost-effective, easy and scientifically valid design for evidence based medicine. ScientificWorldJournal 2003;3: 1117-27.

[13] Ventegodt S, Andersen NJ, Merrick J. Holistic Medicine III: The holistic process theory of healing. ScientificWorldJournal 2003;3: 1138-46.

[14] Ventegodt S, Andersen NJ, Merrick J. Holistic Medicine IV: The principles of the holistic process of healing in a group setting. ScientificWorldJournal 2003;3:1294-1301.

[15] Ventegodt S, Merrick J, Andersen NJ. Quality of life theory I. The IQOL theory: An integrative theory of the global quality of life concept. ScientificWorldJournal 2003;3:1030-40.

[16] Ventegodt S, Merrick J, Andersen NJ. Quality of life theory II. Quality of life as the realization of life potential: A biological theory of human being. ScientificWorldJournal 2003;3:1041-9.

[17] Ventegodt S, Merrick J, Andersen NJ. Quality of life theory III. Maslow revisited. ScientificWorldJournal 2003;3:1050-7.

[18] Ventegodt S, Andersen NJ, Merrick J. Quality of life philosophy: when life sparkles or can we make wisdom a science? ScientificWorldJournal 2003;3:1160-3.

[19] Ventegodt S, Andersen NJ, Merrick J. QOL philosophy I: Quality of life, happiness, and meaning of life. ScientificWorldJournal 2003;3:1164-75.

[20] Ventegodt S, Andersen NJ, Kromann M, Merrick J. QOL philosophy II: What is a human being? ScientificWorldJournal 2003;3:1176-85.

[21] Ventegodt S, Merrick J, Andersen NJ. QOL philosophy III: Towards a new biology. ScientificWorldJournal 2003;3:1186-98.

[22] Ventegodt S, Andersen NJ, Merrick J. QOL philosophy IV: The brain and consciousness. ScientificWorldJournal 2003;3:1199-1209.

[23] Ventegodt S, Andersen NJ, Merrick J. QOL philosophy V: Seizing the meaning of life and getting well again. ScientificWorldJournal 2003;3:1210-29.

[24] Ventegodt S, Andersen NJ, Merrick J. QOL philosophy VI: The concepts. ScientificWorldJournal 2003;3:1230-40.

[25] Merrick J, Ventegodt S. What is a good death? To use death as a mirror and find the quality in life. BMJ. Rapid Response 2003 Oct 31.

[26] Ventegodt S, Merrick J, Andersen NJ. Quality of life as medicine. A pilot study of patients with chronic illness and pain. ScientificWorld Journal 2003;3:520-32.

[27] Ventegodt S, Merrick J, Andersen NJ. Quality of life as medicine II. A pilot study of a five day "Quality of Life and Health" cure for patients with alcoholism. ScientificWorld Journal 2003;3:842-52.

[28] Ventegodt S, Clausen B, Langhorn M, Kromann M, Andersen NJ, Merrick J. Quality of Life as Medicine III. A qualitative analysis of the effect of a five days intervention with existential holistic group therapy: a quality of life course as a modern rite of passage. ScientificWorld Journal 2004;4:124-33.

[29] Stromgren LS. Therapeutic results in brief-interval unilateral ECT. Acta Psychiatr Scand 1975;52(4):246-55.

[30] Ventegodt S, Morad M, Merrick J. Clinical holistic medicine: The "new medicine", the multi-paradigmatic physician and the medical record. ScientificWorldJournal 2004;4:273-85.

[31] Ventegodt S, Morad M, Andersen NJ, Merrick J. Clinical holistic medicine Tools for a medical science based on consciousness. ScientificWorldJournal 2004;4:347-61.

[32] Jorgensen P. Recovery and insight in schizophrenia. Acta Psychiatr. Scand 1995;92(6):436-40.

[33] Robinson DG, Woerner MG, McMeniman M, Mendelowitz A, Bilder RM. Symptomatic and functional recovery from a first episode of schizophrenia or schizoaffective disorder. Am J Psychiatry 2004;161(3):473-9.

[34] Torgalsboen AK. Full recovery from schizophrenia: the prognostic role of premorbid adjustment, symptoms at first admission, precipitating events and gender. Psychiatry Res 1999;88(2):143-52.

[35] Torgalsboen AK, Rund BR. "Full recovery" from schizophrenia in the long term: a ten-year follow-up of eight former schizophrenic patients. Psychiatry 1998;61(1):20-34.

[36] Warner R. Recovery from schizophrenia in the Third World. Psychiatry 1983;46(3):197-212.

[37] Ventegodt S, Andersen NJ, Kandel I, Merrick J. Effect, side effects and adverse events of non-pharmaceutical medicine. A review. Int J Disabil Hum Dev 2009;8(3):227-35.

Chapter 15

Holistic treatment of mental disorders

We have analysed how responsibility, perception and behaviour decays in the pathogenesis of mental disease, the hypothesis being that mental illness is primarily caused by low existential responsibility. We have mapped the subsequent loss of responsibility into an eight-step responsibility-for-life scale: 1) Full responsibility and free perception. 2) Overwhelming emotional pain. 3) Denial of life purpose (psychic death/ego death). 4) Escaping into low responsibility perspectives. 5) Denial of reality. 6) Destruction of own perception 7) Freedom of hallucination. 8) Suicide, unconsciousness, coma, and dead. The scale seems to be a valuable tool for understanding both pathogenesis and salutogenesis: the states of consciousness a mentally sick patient must go through to recover.

The scale can help the holistic physician to guide the patient through the process of assuming responsibility and recovering; in the process of salutogenesis the patient enters into a altered state of consciousness, which we call "being in holistic healing". This happens when the patient receives unconditional love - sufficient intense care – by a physician or therapist; being fully at the patient's service the physician wins the trust of the patient and gets allowance to give the sufficient support and holding.

In the holistic existential therapy old childhood traumas are re-experienced and integrated. Repressed painful emotions reappear to the surface of the patient's consciousness and a new more constructive understanding of life emerges; in this process the patient gradually lets go of negative beliefs and assumes responsibility for own life.

To recover responsibility for life the patient must rehabilitate the three fundamental dimensions of existence from "theory of talent": 1) love including purpose of life (the life mission), 2) power of mind, feelings and body, and 3) gender including character and sexuality. It seems that even severely mentally ill patients can recover fully if they let go of all the negative attitudes and beliefs rising from the sufferings and causing the disease.

Interestingly, just a few hours of existential holistic therapy where the patient enters the state of holistic healing and confronts the core existential problems seems to be of significant help, especially to the young patient with the emerging disease, who has not yet been given anti psychotic drugs or been institutionalised. This gives great hope for prevention and early intervention. Many somatically severely ill patients like cancer patients can also benefit from assuming responsibility as most diseases have a psychosomatic element.

Introduction

In this chapter we will demonstrate how to heal some mental disorders through love, trust, holding and processing (1-9) using the general holistic theory of mental diseases. Many physicians and psychiatrists from the biomedical paradigm seems to believe that mental diseases cannot be healed, but the biomedical approach can alleviate the symptoms and give many patients the possibility to lead a normal or almost normal life. The recovery-literature on the spontaneous healing of mental disease, with the recovery of schizophrenia as the most radical example, shows that about one in four of even the sickest mental patients will eventually be well again without the intervention of a physician. The recovery literature shows several kinds of recovery from schizophrenia (10), the most interesting being full recovery happening in one study in 13,7% of the patients after five years (11) and in about 25% long term (12,13) in the western countries and quite surprisingly much more in the third world (14). Coming from the holistic paradigm we believe strongly that everybody has huge hidden resources and the organism contains strong self-healing powers, which can be mobilised by the intervention in the holistic medical clinic. Before we give a series of examples of this induction of spontaneous recovery and holistic healing, we would like to introduce the reader to our previous work in this field. The paper will explain through a number of case stories why holistic healing can work on the patient with mental illness

What is insanity?

In our way of looking at holistic medicine we define insanity as the degeneration of our state of consciousness and the subsequent degeneration of our behaviour. From a theoretical perspective it is caused by the repression of our purpose of life (5). Spiritual, mental, physical and sexual character (15) are also repressed, and so are the mental, emotional and physical strength (7) together with gender and sexuality (16). We aim to integrate all these dimensions in the much simpler perspective that insanity is simply caused by the loss of responsibility for our own existence; recovery from mental illness is therefore a question of re-assuming responsibility for life.

In theory, there are three dimensions of existence to be responsible for: Love, power and joy (7). Love is about purpose of life, or out personal mission. Power is the personal power of mind, feelings and body. Joy is the dimension of gender, character and sexuality. If the three dimensions collapsed randomly, or if they collapse in parallel, we would pretty much have the pattern of a spiral or whorl, going from full responsibility for the three key areas to zero (see figure 1). From our clinical findings this is not the pattern we normally observe; it seems that first love is lost, then the feelings and the rational mind, and finally sexuality and life itself. An other interesting finding is that the dimension is normally not lost in one traumatic, but the persons own freedom or permission to use the dimensions are withdrawn before the dimensions are completely lost in a qualitative shift of the patients existence, changing both state of consciousness, perception and behaviour (figure 2). It therefore seems possible to create a one-dimensional scale of existential responsibility (see table 1).

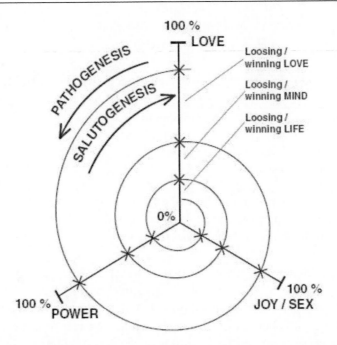

Figure 1. How the loss of existential responsibility causes insanity – theoretical model. If the three dimensions of love, power and joy (from theory of talent[7]) are collapsed randomly, or if they collapse in parallel, we would pretty much have the pattern of a spiral or whorl, going from full responsibility for the three key dimensions down to zero. Responsibility can be defined as responsiveness to all experienced gabs, the gabs being between self and others, in self or in others, or even on the group level (in "the space"). ("X" represents a traumatic life event).

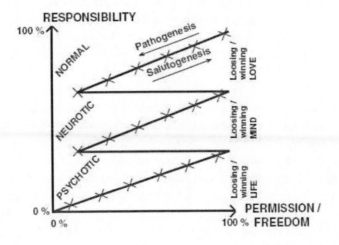

Figure 2. How the loss of existential responsibility causes insanity – clinical findings.

Clinical findings where patients are regressing back to their childhood traumas in holistic existential therapy demonstrate that love is lost first, then power, and finally "sexuality" in its most primitive sense. Every dimension of love, power and joy/sex is lost gradually, until it goes under in a qualitative shift, changing state of consciousness, perception and behaviour at the same time. ("X" represents a traumatic life event).

Table 1. Pathogenesis of mental diseases seen as an 8-step responsibility for life scale

1. Free perception (fully conscious and happy)
2. Painful perception (perceiving something unwanted)
3. Psychic death (overwhelmed by emotional pain)
4. Escape (changing perspective)
5. Denial (lying)
6. Destruction of own perception ("blacking out")
7. Hallucination (seeing what is wanted instead of reality)
8. Suicide, unconsciousness, coma, physical death

The different qualities of perceptions related to mental diseases can be understood as the gradual loss or recovery of responsibility and permission, gradually de/reconnecting the patient with reality and urge. As a general rule, first love is lost, then mind and feelings, and at last the fundamental coherence in life itself. Permission can be defined to the level of giving in to the experienced urges (the urge of love, the urge of mind and feelings, the urge of sex and biological life).

In table 1 the pathogenesis of mental diseases is seen as an 8-step responsibility for life scale. When a person meet resistance and bad luck, life turns painful; when it turns to painful we escape; when we cannot escape we lie, when we cannot lie we black out; when we cannot black out because the roof is falling down on our head we hallucinate, and when this is impossible we die (i.e. commit suicide). The theory of pathogenesis is also when read bottom up the path of salutogenesis, and thus helpful when we work with low-responsibility patients, which are normally almost impossible to cure and help, i.e. suicidal patients. Some cancer patients and other somatically ill patients who are actually dying seem to be awfully low on this scale too, and might be helped in the same way, as there is a psychosomatic element in most disease.

This scale can be further elaborated into a highly structured and logical scale of responsibility (see table 2) which can be further elaborated into a detailed scale of the parallel decay of existential responsibility, perception, and behaviour (see table 3). This scale has proven clinically useful, when we as holistic physicians want to help patients to assume responsibility; as the scale illustrate the normal pathogenesis of mental diseases, we have tested the hypothesis that we can induce healing – salutogenesis with the famous expression of Aron Antonovsky – using the scale as a staircase upwards to full health for our patients. The responsibility-scale is thus guiding the holistic physician's induction of the mentally ill patient's recovery (2). As we shall illustrate with clinical examples below, this seems to work surprisingly well, supporting the hypothesis, that the fundamental causal element in mental disease, which of cause co-exist with genetic vulnerability, are the traumatic life events which makes the human escape existential responsibility as it becomes overwhelmed by painful feelings and emotions. The patient then first enters a states of no-love, then it goes to ego-death; it reappears in the head as a reasonable although neurotic being, when overwhelmed again it starts to produce lies, and ends completely blacked out and in reality psychotic, before going further into an blossoming hallucinatory state, and further down to "negative symptoms" – not even hallucinating any more - helplessness, shock, unconsciousness, suicide, coma, and death.

Theoretically the scale is easy to understand, as it is a product of the gradual loss of first love, then mind, and finally life itself. As the patient goes "down under", he or she looses the ability to love, feel, think, be, enjoy, do, and live as a sexual being. At a first glance into the mentally ill patients personality, mind and sub-consciousness, the deterioration of existence including quality of life health, ability, character, gender, meaning, and coherence with the world happens rather chaotically as the negative and self-destructive decisions are taken; interestingly there seems to be yet another pattern, the famous pattern of multiple personalities, a famous pattern obvious in from some types of schizophrenia, and much less obvious in most other patients until looked for. This pattern is illustrated on figure 3. As the different parts are returning to normal during the therapy, they are integrated and merging into the wholeness of the person.

The loss of sanity during a traumatising personal history and the recovery during holistic existential therapy of love, mind and life itself is excellently illustrated with the case of the patient Anna (17), who took literally hundreds of negative life-denying decisions as she was abused during her childhood, and recovered from a borderline state as she confronted her different inner parts and the repressed emotions and decisions connected to them and let go of these decisions.

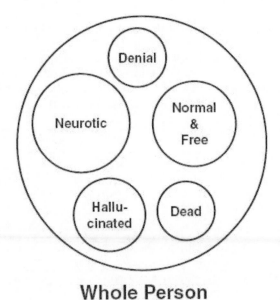

Whole Person

Figure 3. In practice the patient is almost always containing multiple personalities as the wholeness early in life is participated, and the parts are living their own life to a large extend. This means that different parts of the person co-exist on different states. This is the analysis from holistic existential therapy of a 26-year old female breast-cancer patient, made during the session to educate her to confront and assume responsibilities for all her "inner parts". One part of her is romanticising and not meeting the real world (called hallucinated), another part of her is completely dead, while the largest part of her is neurotic.

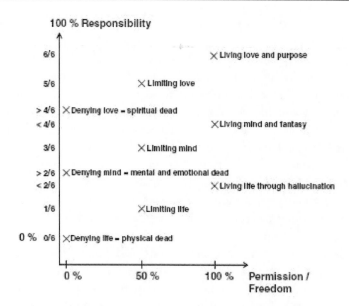

Figure 4. Responsibility x permission diagram. The different qualities of perceptions related to mental diseases can be understood as the gradual loss or recovery of responsibility and permission, gradually de/reconnecting the patient with reality and urge. First love is lost, then mind, and at last the fundamental coherence with life itself.

Table 2. Responsibility-for-life scale. The scale describes how existential responsibility - seen from inside (the state of consciousness) and outside (the behaviour) – is first lost and then found as the patient climb the ladder of hallucination, blacking out, denial, escape, psychic death, unbearable emotional pain, to freedom of perception. To rehabilitate a psychotic patient in a hallucinatory state of consciousness, you need to help him/her confront the chocking trauma that originally motivated the escape into hallucination; in doing this you must carefully avoid to push them deeper down into suicide (see text)

Degree of responsibility for your own existence (estimated percentage)	State of consciousness (many sub-states exist)	Behaviour (other patterns might exist)
100% responsibility Mentally healthy	Present, fully aware, interpreting the world according to your purpose of life	Succeeding, playing
90-80 %	Emotional pain (denying and repressing the feelings)	Fighting, attacking
66 % Neurotic	Emotionally overwhelmed, psychic death (denying the purpose of life)	Fighting, defending
50%	Escaping from here and now	Flight, running
40 %	Cannot escape, denying here and now	Freezing, helplessness
33 % Psychotic	Destructing the perception (wiping out, "blackness", "closing eyes", denying the mind)	Shocked, numb, lame
20-10 % Hallucinating (substituting perception)	Dreaming (perception and behaviour not related to the outer world)	Dream state
0% responsibility Dead	Unconscious, in coma (denying the body)	Physically dying, suicidal, evil and destructive

To help the most severely ill patients, the advanced toolbox of holistic medicine must be taking into use (18); be warned that this takes some years of training in clinical holistic medicine to be able to use the most powerful tools. What is important is to take care of the patients safety; as one repressed inner part might with to commit suicide, this part must be confronted with extreme attention; we call this "to push the patient down", and it is a necessary part of deep existential therapy, as the repressed parts cannot be healed into the patient without this confrontation, but the existential crises reappearing to the surface of the patients consciousness must be taken well care of.

The transformations of perception in this scale can be understood if we look at a two-dimensional presentation, with permission and responsibility as the two axis (see figure 1), we see the theoretical background for the Responsibility scale, namely the repression of the three existential dimensions of man (cf. the theory for talent: love, power, and joy (7).

Healing the mentally ill patient

The general principle in healing the mentally ill patient and inducing recovery is to process the repressed emotional pain and negative decisions (4-44). When this is done, the patients will gradually assume more responsibility for life and existence. To follow the patient step-by-step up the scale demands that the holistic physician masters the compassionate meeting of the patient in a series of specific states of consciousness (see table 1). It is also important that the physician follows the patients as he or she moves spontaneously along the timeline, and the physicians must also follow the internal shifts from one inner part ("multiple personality") to an other; often the mentally ill patient will shift mood, perception and behaviour fast and it takes a great deal of training to process the most ill patients. The more competent assistants the physician has giving holding to the patient in the session, the smoother the therapy will run. Below we present a strategy for meeting the patient on the different levels of existential responsibility.

Step 8: No responsibility, evil, suicidal
This patient is the most difficult to handle. It can be the anorectic patient starving herself to death, it can be the insane serial killer or simply the patient determined to end life by his own hand. The fundamental problem is to love this person, who has so little love for him/herself or others. Can you love a person who wants to kill you? This is the art of the physician dealing with the evil patient, the patient who has chosen to be evil (9). Can you love a patient who destructs him- or her self? This is the problem of the many anorectic girls and psychotic incest victims often with borderline diagnosis. Can you love a person who intent to end his own meaningless life? Well, the answer to all the questions: you can if you can see and acknowledge their beautiful souls, their talents and their gifts. So the state of unconditional love is needed to deal with the most difficult patients.

Step 7: Hallucinating
This patients needs to be met in his or her own world. This takes a lot of training and will to let go of one own ego and preconceptions of the world. But it is not impossible to visit the psychotic patient in his or her own psychotic universe and if you can do that you can take the patients by the hand and "walk him or her out of there". This is all it takes to help an acute psychotic patient out of the psychosis. On entering into the world of the emotional pain that

caused the psychosis it will reappear to be processed. The difficult part is to make an alliance with the patient in the psychotic state that is so strong that he or she will not let go of your hand, while taking him/her through the "terrifying walls of black smoke and burning fire". That is the art of holding, when it becomes most intense.

Step 6: Blacking out, destroying the perception

Helping the patient to integrate his destruction of perception, which is what makes the blank screen to project hallucinations on; this state if often experienced by the patient as blackness and the processing is often difficult, because of the lack of responsibility for perception in such events.

Making the patient perceive the blackness i.e. as "a strange shadow", and just by talking about this experience of blackness in precise words, the patient will find an other perspective and soften up.

The holistic medical tools of touch (36,41) are often much more efficient that anything else in this phase. Shame is often an important part of these traumas, making acceptance through touch (16) a useful tool, if the patient can accept this. Basic care is often very helpful. Sometimes advanced tools must be used (18).

Step 5: Denying

Timeline therapy and even better spontaneous regression is excellent with these patients, who now assume so much responsibility that holding and processing often is quite easy.

Step 4: Escaping

This patient is almost back into reality. During the therapy it can almost always be understood what the escape was about; most often the reason for the escape is not present anymore. Just by realising this, much of the emotional pain is integrated.

Step 3: Overwhelmed

This it the phase of emotional recovery, where the patient returns to normal life and functioning. It is the recovery of character.

Step 2: Emotional pain

Holistic existential standard therapy runs smoothly. It is the stage of recovery of purpose of life.

Step 1: Full responsibility

The patient is back, fully alive, aware of his or her purpose of life and able to use all his/her talents. This is the stage of optimal QOL, health and ability. To the frustration of some therapist, the patient will often start a new round presenting another of the inner parts needing the therapist attention, when one part (one of the "multiple personalities") is healed. This seemingly repetitive procedure, which slowly is processing many years of intense childhood suffering, often makes the therapy go on for years. Patience and deep devotion making every moment with the patient joyful and interesting is a must for working with the most traumatised patients.

Now, let us see how this fits in with working on the different categories of the mental illnesses.

Depression and mania – affective disorders

We become depressive, when we run away from the responsibility for our own lives by describing the world, life and ourselves as impossible. Similarly, we can escape from the world by describing ourselves as unrealistically well (the world as fantastic), which is the manic strategy. The most advanced strategy is to have both descriptions and then alternate between them at your own convenience. This is characteristic of the bipolar disorder.

Systematic and categorical denial of the value of the life inside us and in our external world leads to a life in a bleak, dark and disconsolate world – the depressive universe. In this case, the nature of reality is the problem, including our own unbearable, but unfortunately un-improvable personality. Thus, the problem is not that we, as responsible souls, have made some existential choices with unfortunate consequences, which we now have to learn from and revise. That would be the responsible, existential perspective. Classic depression has a cognitive, an emotional and a physical dimension. The cognitive dimension is the negative description of self, life and reality. The emotional dimension concerns the low emotional basic mood. Depression is also associated with a number of bodily symptoms, such as reduced speed of speech and movement, waking in the early hours of the day, loss of appetite and sexual desire (libido). It is also common for depressive patients to experience chronic pain that is resistant to medication.

The depressive patient needs help to cope with being depressive and control when the depression occurs. Instead of being "full-time depressed", controlled by the dark side, the patient can learn to become "part-time depressed", so that the patient controls when the depression should come and go, and how long it should last. By being willing to enter the depression and feel all aspects of it, and then being willing to leave it again with the knowledge from that experience, the patient can overcome his depression and no longer be enslaved by his pattern of survival. The healing process has commenced and as the patient confronts and deals with the existential pain, he recovers.

Treatment of a depressive and psychotic patient must have due regard for the patient's safety. The therapist should handle both the structure of the patient's defences and the underlying pain. The dark side of a psychotic or depressive patient may appear as a "helping agent", which can be very shrewd and cunning and require great skill on the part of the holistic therapist. Some patients can be very self-destructive and the "agent" inside – the dark side – is virtually authorised to kill the patient, before the existential pain is uncovered completely. This aspect demands the utmost professional expertise, which in our clinic means a referral to a psychiatrist at the slightest suspicion of specific plans for suicide, in order to ensure that the patient survives.

Female, aged 48 years with bipolar affective disorder and obsessive thoughts is mood-regulating, prescribed by her psychiatrist. Manic-depressive with fixed pattern: Manic for two and a half months, depressive for two and a half months. She has been manic for nearly three months now. She describes her depressive state as follows: "My head is severed," "I only have gloomy thoughts," "I only think about how to get away from here with my daughter". Major problems with ex-husband, who will not talk to her. They have had a dependency relationship, her being his obedient little dog. She still is and she feels that he is "pissing on her and that she still accepts being pissed on by him". The authorities have granted them 12 months to become good parents; otherwise their 10-year-old son will be removed. All in all, the patient is in a miserable state, but not beyond therapeutic reach. EXERCISE 1 – in relation to ex-husband and other people: Say no, do not put up with being messed about, express your anger when you feel it, do not submit. EXERCISE 2 – win the case about your son – take responsibility for his entire parenthood and make sure that he gets what he needs. Or bring him here perhaps, so we can look at the interaction between the two of you. EXERCISE 3 – be depressed for 15 min. a day. Sit on a chair and be depressed. Find statements such as: "Everything is hopeless." "There's nothing good awaiting me," and let go of them. PLAN: Rosen session once a month, with physician (SV) once a month.

This patient is in a miserable state. When you spend half the time wishing to get away from here – and take your child with you – the situation is really serious. Since she has not killed herself and has suffered from her illness for half her life, the risk of suicide is not great. She will not be redeemed, until she confronts the underlying pain, which led to the negative decisions that now control her life.

Male, aged 55 years with manic-depressive disorder
QOL conversation: The patient has responded to body therapy with mania. Has a history of manic-depressive disorder going back many years. Treated by his own psychiatrist with lithium. Treated by anthroposophical doctor for 13 years with Cikorium [chicory root] and gold D 6 against mania, Terraxikum (dandelion), gold D 30 and other substances. Muscle pain throughout the body, tension headache and fatigue. On examination: Appears somewhat bleary-eyed, all trigger points tender /fibromyalgia/. Instructed to "feel, acknowledge, let go." PLAN: Wishes to go into psychotherapy and can start here with one of our psychiatric consultants. The topic would be to take responsibility for his own feelings: Six gestalt therapy sessions, then appointment again. Then, he should be encouraged to choose the doctor he wants in future. EXERCISE: Read three good books on personal development – find a new life philosophy, ideally one that concerns responsibility.

Here the patient is merely supported in helping himself by getting a grip on the concept of responsibility in theory and in practice. We guide him, as gently as possible, into acknowledgement.

A patient, who has received treatment for 13 years without any progress is likely to begin to wonder whether the treatment is working. Many alternative therapists tell their patients that the beneficial effect sets in slowly and imperceptibly, so they have to be patient. A surprisingly large number of patients undergo all sorts of peculiar courses of treatment, before painfully acknowledging that they are not being helped. We believe that patients should experience being helped from the very first appointment at our clinic, including when we provide holistic treatment. If they do not, they should find another therapist. It is a general rule that if everything is exactly the same as before you had the treatment, you should not expect it to be effective in the long run either. Good therapy is effective and leads to immediate improvement, but naturally it may take long to resolve the problem completely. If we are initially unable to help the patient just a little bit, we doubt that we will be able to help the patient at all. Our advice to a patient asking whether acupuncture, for instance, is effective, is therefore as follows: feel for yourself whether it is effective.

The class of schizophreniaform psychosis

We can also run away from existential pain by escaping from the world in general, prompted by decisions that deny the existence of ourselves, life and/or the world around us. This causes the classic psychosis characterised by depersonalisation (I am not real), de-realisation (the outside world is not real) and devitalisation (life is not real, but merely something mechanical and inanimate). The primary characteristic of psychosis is the lack of reality-testing (that is, poor contact with reality) and emotional blunting. Denial goes here all the way through blackness to hallucination. Occasionally, but not always, we see the split personality that led to the disease being named schizophrenia. The split implies that two different sides cannot be united in the person's character, one side being for instance vibrant and driven by instinct, and the other side being conscious, inhibited and conscientious. According to a holistic interpretation, the split personality stems from the negative decisions.

> Female, aged 29 years with acute psychosis
> The patient has spontaneously entered something old and very painful. She is uncontactable, not in the present. She becomes agitated and tries to hit me (the physician) with the furniture. She then smashes up the furniture systematically in a classic catharsis /acute psychosis/. Guarded so that she does not hurt herself and kept under observation to determine appropriate treatment.

In rare cases we come across the classic picture of "madness" where the patient is furious, evil, and very destructive. Psychosis is often a quite subtle diagnosis and fairly inconspicuous to lay people. This particularly applies to patients with borderline personality, where we sense that the patient "has a screw loose".

> Male, aged 29 years with borderline condition?
> QOL conversation: Very pensive as a child. Assaulted by bikers at the age of 18 years, anxiety since then. Has seen a psychologist. Degree in engineering. At the age of 20 years he was furiously angry with the system, smoked a lot of cannabis. Smashed up his room, had a psychotic episode with 5 days in closed psychiatric unit. Admitted to closed psychiatric unit again with cannabis psychosis for three weeks at the age of 21. The patient is writing his autobiography. The patient believes that he is harbouring so much pain that he is at risk of dying from it. According to his records he has suffered from depression and paranoid psychosis with delusions. He has therefore received: Zoloft [sertraline] and Zyprexa [olanzapine] for the past couple of years. Prescribe Zoloft 50 mg bid /suspected borderline/. Analysis: The patient is a truth-seeking person, who early in his life encountered the injustices of the world and raged about them. Anger and aggression are major problems here, because in my opinion the patient harbours a great deal of suppressed anger. PLAN: This patient has to restore his balance without taking a wrong turn. The patient's intelligence must be mobilised. He must stop being a destructive and maladapted element. Does a lot of reading already, but should pick relevant books that can help the patient. Perhaps books about philosophy. EXERCISE: Write down the facts of the events: what happened, how did you feel. Come back in two weeks with your autobiography, then we shall look at the way you work, so that you can obtain maximum benefit from it.

Like any other patient, the psychotic patient has certain defences against facing and integrating the problematic gestalts. The holistic therapist has to "meet and understand" the patient and handle the patient's defences in an intelligent manner. Basically, they are defences against feeling the pain, but a psychiatric patient often finds it particularly difficult to begin to work with himself, since recognition of the disorder is particularly difficult together with the stigmatisation of mental illness in modern society. If modern society adopted a more relaxed attitude towards mental illness and possessed greater faith in the patients' ability to solve their problems through personal development, it would become much easier to be mentally ill and the illness would probably last much shorter than the case today, when mental illness is often for life.

The fear of mental illness is understandable as we experience that schizophrenics, for example, are a great burden on themselves and the people near them throughout their lives. Some experience has shown, that 20 to 30 per cent of schizophrenic persons recover spontaneously. In our view, they attain recovery, when they succeed in finding a genuine and intimate relationship that provides them with sufficient support to spontaneously heal the old wounds to their soul. Treatment of depressive or psychotic patients can be difficult and protracted, but may also be simple, fast and surprisingly painless, if the patient manages to obtain a clear and precise understanding of his situation. When the patient realise the real nature of his "opponent", he will often experience fast, effective and lasting recovery. Complete recovery often requires years of treatment.

Delusions

According to the "feel, acknowledge, let go" hypothesis, it is possible to help patients who can confront the pain behind their illness. Making an exact diagnosis is therefore not important. The important thing is to obtain an accurate understanding of the patient's existential dilemmas. The next patient is suffering from delusions. If the physician understands the problem, it is often possible to make the patient understand it as well in a short time. The patient is often hallucinated in a smart and well-hidden way.

> Male, aged 49 years with obsessive thoughts
> Obsessive thoughts about having to take off his shoes, before stepping on to the carpet, about killing – children and adults, etc. Wants to die. His family physician has put him on antidepressive medication, apparently with no effect. A few years ago, he ran into a 45-year-old man with his car and killed him, has felt very bad since then. We talk about the death of his father, when the patient was 12 years old, which made him think that everybody around him would die and that he, too, would soon die. Cries. EXERCISE: Write your autobiography and come to terms with your difficult relationship with death, one hour a day. Can return in a month.

The feeling of guilt is hard, difficult and we tend to repress it. If such a feeling is repressed early in life, an event occurring later in life can create an opening that will make all the old skeletons jump out of the cupboard. The patient killed a man by accident and he already has the death of his father on his conscience (children assume responsibility for everything the adults do not). So now he is falling apart, and he needs to sort things out. If the patient succeeds in discovering the key problem he will soon make progress and recover. The next patient suffers from paranoia, a very unpleasant condition with basic distrust of everything and everybody.

> Female, aged 64 years with paranoia
> QOL conversation: Appears somewhat paranoid, her neighbours steal her mail and do other wicked things. I think that if the patient focus on what she is good at and the useful things she can do, then the problem with her neighbours will diminish. The patient would like to change her personality, to become more extrovert and social. We talk about the patient being able to improve. EXERCISE 1: Call more on your friends and acquaintances – the patient's own suggestion. EXERCISE 2: Ignore the wicked neighbours. EXERCISE 3: Her son, whom the patient has rejected, deserves a postcard.

In this case, we choose a behavioural approach: practical exercises. The actual treatment is in exercise 3. According to our analysis, the patient becomes frightened by the wickedness, which she herself is still practising in relation to her son, who deep down psychologically is herself.

A classic example of mental disorder is querulous paranoia. Such a patient is running away from his or her life and is engaged in constant battle with society and the authorities; soon the patient spends all his or her time writing letters of complaint. It is a very agonising condition and the patients are often completely unaware of their illness. In the following case report, the driving force behind the complaints is the loss of a child.

> Female, aged 41 years with possible querulous paranoia
> QOL conversation: Alone with her 14-year-old son. Husband left her three years ago. Three months into the last relationship she became pregnant, but gave birth to a stillborn daughter. It seems as though the patient is living in the past instead of living here and now. Will not let go of her past, which means so much to her. She is very involved in a complaint concerning compulsory treatment at a psychiatric hospital. We talk about letting go of the past /suspected querulous paranoia/. EXERCISE 1: If you want to, you can turn your back on the past and face the present and the future by asking yourself: What do I need? How can I achieve that? Do not concern yourself with the past, with writing letters to the authorities, with thinking about things that happened in the past. But you need to cry and mourn the death of your daughter, so do that. EXERCISE 2: Read "The Power of Now" by Eckhart Tolle, and other good books about living in the present. EXERCISE 3: Make a complete list of all your problems in the present, write half a page about each of them – about 20 major problems. PLAN: Next appointment in one month.

Anxiety

Anxiety afflicts about one in ten people in Denmark. A suitable amount of anxiety is a natural element of life, but when it grows into an uncontrollable fear of death and overshadows one's entire existence, it becomes a psychiatric disorder.

> Female, aged 44 years with anxiety and grief
> First visit: Having difficulties with feelings in the form of fear of death and grief that overwhelm her. We talk about how to cope better with her strong feelings – by

regarding them as an acceptable part of her. The feelings are strong, but not dangerous, and they are a part of her, which she needs. On examination: not suicidal or psychotic-depressive. She can return in two weeks if problems persist.

Second visit: Abdominal pain, attacks reported to last one hour a day for a month. No fever, affective pattern apparently normal, but poorly observed. On examination: Abdomen soft with no palpable tumours, no significant tenderness except minute McBurney tenderness and diffusely around navel. Rectal exploration shows no blood, normal faeces. Pelvic examination: Vulva, vagina natural, no cervical motion tenderness of the uterus, no tenderness corresponding to adnexa. No tumours, mucous membrane smooth, sphincter tone slightly above average. Other gynaecological findings: no complaints, in particular no vaginal discharge. PLAN: To be observed to see what induces the pain – e.g. related to meals? Movement? Waking? Agitation? etc. Also faeces to be observed, plus urine dipsticks. Blood tests. Prescribe Voltaren [diclophenac] suppositories 100 mg as required.

Third visit: She is doing much better. Barely any problems for two weeks, although anxiety is still lurking beneath the surface. She recalls that it began after a serious accident at work eight years ago. Now she can handle the anxiety when it occurs, but is still scared of dwelling on it. We shall look at that next time. Once she becomes able to enter her anxiety, she will also be able to enter other feelings, also positive ones such as love and sex, which she finds difficult at present because she feels "reserved" in relation to her boyfriend. On examination: Marked improvement. Appears happy today.

By allowing the patient to harbour her feelings and assuring her that they are in no way dangerous – on the contrary – although they may be difficult, we open the waste bin, which virtually explode, having built up an enormous pressure for years in the form of denial and repression of feelings. We perceive her abdominal pain as being psychosomatic, but since the health service is founded on biomedicine, such a diagnosis is an exclusion diagnosis, which can only be made following a thorough physical assessment. We have to rule out several somatic possibilities. But everything turns out well, and the patient reaches the other side, happy and free, both of abdominal complaints and of her fear of death. As an unexpected bonus, the process lead to an improved love life.

> Male, aged 28 years with anxiety and headache
> Frequent anxiety, suffers from fear of death – thinks of when his heart will stop beating, does not sleep. Has started seeing a psychiatrist, who prescribed Seroxat [paroxetine] for panic disorder. Also very severe headache daily. On examination: Appears very tormented and afraid, his back is tense as a rock from os sacrum to atlas /tension headache/ /fear of death/. Cannot suppress anxiety with Alopam [oxazepam] 15 mg 3 times daily. Prescribe physiotherapy. EXERCISE: Sit down and feel the anxiety, when it emerges. Do not run away from it – otherwise it will pursue you for the rest of your life. Come back next week for conversation.

Suppressed anxiety will lead to tension, typically manifested as headache as in this patient. He is a young man full of energy and inclined not to repress, but to integrate things. That is the reason why his fear of death surface in the first place. So a better solution would be for him to name the monster and invite it in, make friends with it and then release it.

> Female, aged 24 years with anxiety
> Conversation: Acute counselling during the weekend following anxiety attack. Now composed, but worried. Watched her father stab her mother with a bread knife, when

she was five years old. That incident is coming back to her now. At that time she used to think: "If only they would hold onto him, because he is sick in his head". EXERCISE: Describe every detail of the incident – everything that happened, everything you felt. When you become afraid, feel yourself as the little girl again, and look at the world from her perspective. Next appointment in two weeks, when she will bring what she has written with her. Is able to work.

When the father and mother are in a life-and-death struggle, the children suffer terrible wounds to their soul. Mercifully almost all such wounds can be healed over time.

Discussion

The concept of loss of existential responsibility and subsequent degeneration of human perception is highly complex and the 8-step Responsibility-for-Life Scale we have presented in this paper is clearly too simple. Every mental patient contains many "inner parts" living their own life, and needing individual processing along the scale. A lot of gestalts are working in the patient's mind at the same time and all the decisions that modify perception and consciousness are there at the same time, making the patient's perception spread out all over the scale, instead of being at one single point of it. This means that a patient that can be seemingly completely normal in his/her behaviour can be 30% hallucinated and only while dealing with special persons or in specific situations will this show. Interestingly, when sitting with a patient you can easily feel the "insane" quality of the patient and as you work your way downwards the time line using the holistic medical techniques of holding and processing, inducing the spontaneous regression to the patients traumas, you will suddenly see the patient entering a psychotic state that was there all the time. It seems fair to talk about the web of consciousness, because our mind is woven of so many perceptual gestalts, memories, decisions and philosophical attitudes.

The question is, if a scale like the presented is meaningful at all. We think it is, as a general scheme for the degeneration of our consciousness. In the holistic clinical practice it serves very well as a map of states and transformations. It is very interesting that you cannot hallucinate, before you have cleaned your tabular and you do this by repressing the content of your mind so efficiently that the perception turns black. Now, on the blackness, you can ad anything you want. The psychotic patient has many aspects of his/her perception repressed in the same time, but still there often is a basic orientation. You can talk to the insane person, because he or she sees you in some form, maybe severely disturbed, but you are still there and you can discus reality. The psychotic patient will perceive reality very different from you, but if you are into symbolic language, even the discrepancies will make fine meaning to you and using this ability to understand you can actually help the patient to heal.

What we are doing in these examples are not very difficult; all it takes is really the intention to be of service to the patient and to come with love or intense care, win trust, give holding and lead the processing. Interestingly, a similar idea of levels or scales of responsibility seems to be the foundation of many systems of therapy and healing, from gestalt therapy[45] to energy healing[46] using the healer as a saviour and channel of divine energy, to the new-religious movements, where a scale of responsibility sometimes is used together with peculiar star war-like axioms of reincarnation. The use of the scale of responsibility for spontaneous regression and existential healing following love, trust, and full holding (the combination of care, respect, awareness, acceptance through touch and acknowledgement) are normally not used in neither gestalt therapy, healing or religious ceremonies and seems thus to be a characteristic of holistic medicine.

In contrast to the normal belief, it is possible to help the mentally ill patients to heal, if you can love them, win their trust and get allowance to give them support and holding. Even the most psychotic schizophrenic patient can heal if you can make him or her feel the existential pain in its full depth, understand what the message of the suffering is and let go of all the negative attitude and beliefs connected with the disease. While healing the most severe schizophrenic patients, especially those with a long carrier in mental institutions, might take many years to heal and even be out of reach, because of limited resources and lack of motivation for participate in their own healing, most mentally ill young people will benefit from existential holistic processing and many might even get healed completely. This would make it possible for them to get a good life and thus be saved from the long carrier as mental patients, so painful for anybody involved and close to the person, and so expensive for society.

The "trick" of helping the mentally ill patient seems to be understanding the level of responsibility the patient take and help him or her process the trauma and decisions that made him escape responsibility for his or her own life and destiny. A scale from free perception over emotional pain to psychic death (denial of life purpose making love impossible) further down to escape and denial to destruction of own perception and hallucination seems to be a valuable tool to understand the state of consciousness of the patient and the nature of the process of healing the patient must go through.

Conclusion

We have analysed how responsibility, perception and behaviour decays in the pathogenesis of mental disease, the hypothesis being that mental illness is primarily caused by low existential responsibility. We have mapped the subsequent loss of responsibility into an eight-step responsibility-for-life scale: 1) Full responsibility and free perception. 2) Overwhelming emotional pain. 3) Denial of life purpose (psychic death/ego death). 4) Escaping into low responsibility perspectives. 5) Denial of reality. 6) Destruction of own perception 7) Freedom of hallucination. 8) Suicide, unconsciousness, coma, and dead. The scale seems to be a valuable tool for understanding both pathogenesis and salutogenesis: the states of consciousness a mentally sick patient must go through to recover.

The scale can help the holistic physician to guide the patient through the process of assuming responsibility and recovering; in the salutogenetic process the patient enters into a altered state of consciousness, which we call "being in holistic healing". This happens when the patient receives unconditional love - sufficient intense care – by a physician or therapist; being fully at the patient's service the physician wins the trust of the patient and gets allowance to give the sufficient support and holding.

In the holistic existential therapy old childhood traumas are re-experienced and integrated. Repressed painful emotions reappear to the surface of the patient's consciousness and a new more constructive understanding of life emerges; in this process the patient gradually lets go of negative beliefs and assumes responsibility for own life.

To recover responsibility for life the patient must rehabilitate the three fundamental dimensions of existence from "theory of talent": 1) love including purpose of life (the life mission), 2) power of mind, feelings and body, and 3) gender including character and sexuality. It seems that even severely mentally ill patients can recover fully if they let go of all the negative attitudes and beliefs rising from the sufferings and causing the disease. The use of the Responsibility-for-Life Scale can be used on patients who need a path to assume responsibility for life, both mentally and somatically ill patients including cancer patients.

Interestingly, just a few hours of existential holistic therapy where the patient enters the state of holistic healing and confronts the core existential problems seems to be of significant help, especially to the young patient with the emerging disease, who has not yet been given anti psychotic drugs or been institutionalised. This gives great hope for prevention and early intervention.

References

[1] Ventegodt S, Andersen NJ, Neikrug S, Kandel I, Merrick J. Clinical holistic medicine: Mental disorders in a holistic perspective. ScientificWorldJournal 2005;5:313-23.
[2] Ventegodt S, Andersen NJ, Merrick J. Holistic Medicine III: The holistic process theory of healing. ScientificWorldJournal 2003;3:1138-46.
[3] Ventegodt S, Andersen NJ, Merrick J. Holistic Medicine IV: The principles of the holistic process of healing in a group setting. ScientificWorldJournal 2003;3:1294-1301.
[4] Ventegodt S, Andersen NJ, Merrick J. Editorial: Five theories of human existence. ScientificWorldJournal 2003;3:1272-6.
[5] Ventegodt S. The life mission theory: A theory for a consciousness-based medicine. Int J Adolesc Med Health 2003;15(1):89-91.
[6] Ventegodt S, Andersen NJ, Merrick J. The life mission theory II: The structure of the life purpose and the ego. ScientificWorldJournal 2003;3:1277-85.
[7] Ventegodt S, Andersen NJ, Merrick J. The life mission theory III: Theory of talent. ScientificWorldJournal 2003;3:1286-93.
[8] Ventegodt S, Merrick J. The life mission theory IV. A theory of child development. ScientificWorldJournal 2003;3:1294-1301.
[9] Ventegodt S, Andersen NJ, Merrick J. The life mission theory V. A theory of the anti-self and explaining the evil side of man. ScientificWorldJournal 2003;3:1302-13.
[10] Jørgensen P. Recovery and insight in schizophrenia. Acta Psychiatr Scand 1995;92(6):436-40.
[11] Robinson DG, Woerner MG, McMeniman M, Mendelowitz A, Bilder RM. Symptomatic and functional recovery from a first episode of schizophrenia or schizoaffective disorder. Am J Psychiatry 2004;161(3):473-9.
[12] Torgalsboen AK. Full recovery from schizophrenia: the prognostic role of premorbid adjustment, symptoms at first admission, precipitating events and gender. Psychiatry Res 1999;88(2):143-52.
[13] Torgalsboen AK, Rund BR. "Full recovery" from schizophrenia in the long term: a ten-year follow-up of eight former schizophrenic patients. Psychiatry 1998;61(1):20-34.
[14] Warner R. Recovery from schizophrenia in the Third World. Psychiatry 1983;46(3):197-212.
[15] Ventegodt S, Kromann M, Andersen NJ, Merrick J. The life mission theory VI: A theory for the human character. Healing with holistic medicine through recovery of character and purpose of life. ScientificWorldJournal 2004;4:859-80.

[16] Ventegodt S, Morad M, Hyam E, Merrick J. Clinical holistic medicine: Holistic sexology and treatment of vulvodynia through existential therapy and acceptance through touch. ScientificWorldJournal 2004;4:571-80.

[17] Ventegodt S, Clausen B, Merrick J. Clinical holistic medicine: The case story of Anna. I. Long term effect of physical maltreatment, incest and multiple rapes in early childhood. ScientificWorldJournal 2006;6:1965-76.

[18] Ventegodt S, Clausen B, Nielsen ML, Merrick J. Clinical holistic medicine: Advanced tools for holistic medicine. ScientificWorldJournal 2006;6:2048-65.

[19] Ventegodt S, Andersen NJ, Merrick J. Holistic medicine: Scientific challenges. ScientificWorldJournal 2003;3:1108-16.

[20] Ventegodt S, Andersen NJ, Merrick J. Holistic Medicine II: The square-curve paradigm for research in alternative, complementary and holistic medicine: A cost-effective, easy and scientifically valid design for evidence based medicine. ScientificWorldJournal 2003;3:1117-27.

[21] Ventegodt S, Merrick J, Andersen NJ. Quality of life theory I. The IQOL theory: An integrative theory of the global quality of life concept. ScientificWorldJournal 2003;3:1030-40.

[22] Ventegodt S, Merrick J, Andersen NJ. Quality of life theory II. Quality of life as the realization of life potential: A biological theory of human being. ScientificWorldJournal 2003;3:1041-9.

[23] Ventegodt S, Merrick J, Andersen NJ. Quality of life theory III. Maslow revisited. ScientificWorldJournal 2003;3:1050-7.

[24] Ventegodt S, Andersen NJ, Merrick J. Quality of life philosophy: when life sparkles or can we make wisdom a science? ScientificWorldJournal 2003;3:1160-3.

[25] Ventegodt S, Andersen NJ, Merrick J. QOL philosophy I: Quality of life, happiness, and meaning of life. ScientificWorldJournal 2003;3: 1164-75.

[26] Ventegodt S, Andersen NJ, Kromann M, Merrick J. QOL philosophy II: What is a human being? ScientificWorldJournal 2003;3:1176-85.

[27] Ventegodt S, Merrick J, Andersen NJ. QOL philosophy III: Towards a new biology. ScientificWorldJournal 2003;3:1186-98.

[28] Ventegodt S, Andersen NJ, Merrick J. QOL philosophy IV: The brain and consciousness. ScientificWorldJournal 2003;3:1199-1209.

[29] Ventegodt S, Andersen NJ, Merrick J. QOL philosophy V: Seizing the meaning of life and getting well again. ScientificWorldJournal 2003;3:1210-29.

[30] Ventegodt S, Andersen NJ, Merrick J. QOL philosophy VI: The concepts. ScientificWorldJournal 2003;3:1230-40.

[31] Merrick J, Ventegodt S. What is a good death? To use death as a mirror and find the quality in life. BMJ. Rapid Response 2002 Oct 31.

[32] Ventegodt S, Merrick J, Andersen NJ. Quality of life as medicine. A pilot study of patients with chronic illness and pain. ScientificWorld Journal 2003;3:520-32.

[33] Ventegodt S, Merrick J, Andersen NJ. Quality of life as medicine II. A pilot study of a five day "Quality of Life and Health" cure for patients with alcoholism. ScientificWorld Journal 2003;3:842-52.

[34] Ventegodt S, Clausen B, Langhorn M, Kromann M, Andersen NJ, Merrick J. Quality of life as medicine III. A qualitative analysis of the effect of a five days intervention with existential holistic group therapy: a quality of life course as a modern rite of passage. ScientificWorld Journal 2004;4:124-33.

[35] Ventegodt S, Merrick J. Clinical holistic medicine: Applied consciousness-based medicine. ScientificWorldJournal 2004;4:96-9.

[36] Ventegodt S, Morad M, Merrick J. Clinical holistic medicine: Classic art of healing or the therapeutic touch. ScientificWorldJournal 2004;4:134-47.

[37] Ventegodt S, Morad M, Merrick J. Clinical holistic medicine: The "new medicine", the multi-paradigmatic physician and the medical record. ScientificWorldJournal 2004;4:273-85.

[38] Ventegodt S, Morad M, Merrick J. Clinical holistic medicine: Holistic pelvic examination and holistic treatment of infertility. ScientificWorldJournal 2004;4:148-58.

[39] Ventegodt S, Morad M, Hyam E, Merrick J. Clinical holistic medicine: Use and limitations of the biomedical paradigm ScientificWorldJournal 2004;4:295-306.

[40] Ventegodt S, Morad M, Kandel I, Merrick J. Clinical holistic medicine: Social problems disguised as illness. ScientificWorldJournal 2004;4:286-94.

[41] Ventegodt S, Morad M, Andersen NJ, Merrick J. Clinical holistic medicine Tools for a medical science based on consciousness. ScientificWorldJournal 2004;4:347-61.

[42] Ventegodt S, Morad M, Hyam E, Merrick J. Clinical holistic medicine: When biomedicine is inadequate. ScientificWorldJournal 2004;4:333-46.

[43] Ventegodt S, Flensborg-Madsen T, Andersen NJ, Morad M, Merrick J. Clinical holistic medicine: A Pilot on HIV and quality of life and a suggested treatment of HIV and AIDS. ScientificWorldJournal 2004;4:264-72.

[44] Ventegodt S, Morad M, Merrick J. Clinical holistic medicine: Induction of spontaneous remission of cancer by recovery of the human character and the purpose of life (the life mission). ScientificWorldJournal 2004;4:362-77.

[45] Perls F, Hefferline R, Goodman P. Gestalt therapy. New York: Julian Press, 1951.

[46] Brofman M. Anything can be healed. Findhorn: Findhorn Press, 2003.

Section 4. Understanding the human being

In this section we focus on the nature of the human being. There have been many models explaining the constitutions of the human being and the structure of talent and human character (1). What have been most difficult to understand is the concepts of good or evil. Freud believed that man had two basic instincts, the constructive Eros and the destructive Thanatos, and many philosophers of life has had similar concepts.

We are not here to judge, but to set free. We are healers so we come from love and understanding, not from judgment and punishment. The patients can freely admit all their misdeeds to us. And they can share all the misdeeds done to them by others.

Only when you have reached a certain point of development will you realize that both good and evil are divine. Everything comes from the same source, our life. Only when you understand this fully can you help a patient tormented by evil done to him or her and by him or her.

Violent and sexual abuse, fail and neglect and all kinds of misery has been the patient's life. To heal mind and existence is to step beyond the evil. To integrate the human shadow. To see everything as a necessary part of life, a necessary part of the journey of the spirit.

In this section we search for the deepest understanding we can get of the human existence. Not to justify the evil. But to be able to forgive and heal.

References

[1] Ventegodt S, Kromann M, Andersen NJ, Merrick J. The life mission theory VI. A theory for the human character: Healing with holistic medicine through recovery of character and purpose of life. ScientificWorldJournal 2004;4:859-80.

Quality of life as the realization of life potential

Holistic medicine is also called "quality of life as medicine". The reason for this is simple. When the patients improves their quality of life they also improve their health, both their physical and mental health, as we shall see in chapter 52.

So another approach to holistic healing is the improvement of the patients quality of life in general. To help the patient improve his or her quality of life it is nessesary to know what quality of life is. A help is the quality-of-life theory. The chapters of this section all presents some theoretical framework the the improvement of the patients qualiyy of life.

This chapter presents one of the eight theories of the quality of life (QOL) used for making the SEQOL (self evaluation of quality of life) questionnaire or *the quality of life as realizing life potential*. This theory is strongly inspired by Maslow and the review furthermore serves as an example on how to fulfill the demand for an overall theory of life (or philosophy of life), which we believe is necessary for holistic medicine as well as for global and generic quality-of-life research.

Whereas traditional medical science has often been inspired by mechanical models in its attempts to understand human beings, this theory takes an explicitly biological starting-point. The purpose is to take a close view of life as a unique entity, which mechanical models are unable to do.

This means that things considered to be beyond the individual's purely biological nature, notably the quality of life, meaning in life and aspirations in life, are included under this wider, biological treatise.

Our interpretation of the nature of all living matter is intended as an alternative to medical mechanism, which dates back to the beginning of the twentieth century. New ideas such as the notions of the human being as nestled in an evolutionary and ecological context, the spontaneous tendency of self-organizing systems for realization and concord and the central role of consciousness in interpreting, planning and expressing human reality are unavoidable today in attempts to scientifically understand all living matter, including human life.

Introduction

This chapter presents one of the eight theories of the quality of life (QOL) used for making the SEQOL (self evaluation of quality of life) questionnaire or the quality of life as realizing life potential. This theory is strongly inspired by Maslow (1,2) and has been presented in several publications (3,4). The present overview furthermore serves as an example on how to fulfill the demand for an overall theory of life (or philosophy of life), which we believe (5,6) as necessary for global and generic quality-of-life research.

Whereas traditional medical science has often been inspired by mechanical models in its attempts to understand human beings, this theory takes an explicitly biological starting-point. The purpose is to take a close view of life as a unique entity, which mechanical models are unable to do. This means that things considered to be beyond the individual's purely biological nature, notably the quality of life, meaning in life and aspirations in life, are included under this wider, biological treatise.

Trying to include such lofty qualities of life in a biological theory will probably raise the suspicion that these qualities are going to be reduced to something more primitive. We hope that this analysis will make it clear that this is not the case. The purpose is to show a respect for life rather than to reduce it to mere trivial mechanisms.

The hierarchy of life

What is life from a modern biological viewpoint? If we look at how life is organized, we will immediately have a picture of a pyramid before our eyes: an organization of hierarchies with levels of biological systems nestled in one another, from the tiniest molecule, cell and organism, to ecosystems and the biosphere (3,7).

In recent decades the belief has arisen that the essence of this hierarchy of life is not any material substance but the information that organizes the hierarchy (8). What interest us are the self-reproducing patterns that contain these particles of matter. They are of interest, because they contain what is life in a unique sense and not just the few grams of hydrogen, carbon and other elements found in every living organism.

Recent surveys stress the ability of the physical, chemical and biological world to generate new patterns spontaneously, where hitherto there were none (9,10). This process is known as self-organization, and it has been an ongoing process, since the "Big Bang". This is how the planets and the galaxies came into existence, and life has developed in this manner over 4 billion years. During the evolutionary process, biological systems developed more and more complex hierarchies with organisms and ecosystems forming through mutual interaction with the physical-chemical environment.

Higher-level organisms, such as animals and human beings, are colonies of cells that have united to form ever more complex systems with more and more cells for the past billion years (11). To uphold the unity of the organism, the cells constantly exchange information to achieve maximum adaptation and coordination. This is because the subsystems of the organism have to carry out certain functions: they monitor the development and health of the organism as a whole. This life-maintaining communication between cells is called the biological information system.

The biological information system keeps the organism together and is found in all living beings – one-celled organisms, animals and plants. The system that monitors the regulation and communication, including the hormones, the nervous system and the immune system, is also responsible for the overall creation of form, known as ontogenesis: the creation of each individual, regeneration of damaged tissue, etc.

Through evolution, the biological data system in more complex animals has generated a nervous system that processes the sensory input from the environment, ensuring that the body reacts at maximum potential. An image of the external world is contained at the site where all sensory data is processed. In humans, this forum is the brain. Consciousness can be seen as an emergent quality of the organism. This quality emerges at a sufficiently high degree of complexity in the biological information system.

The human brain contains representations of external reality in the form of abstract maps of reality containing detailed descriptions of the external and internal world and the human self (the ego). Using these maps, we guide ourselves in our inner lives as well as in our external physical and social environment; as a consequence, these maps determine our ability to function in the world. All things being equal, poor maps will create poor lives and good maps good lives. This is because good maps of reality enable us to acknowledge, internally, our potential as well as the rich opportunities of our external lives, to identify these when they arise and to make constructive choices throughout life. The good map becomes the bridge to the world and ensures the optimal balance between the deep dreams and opportunities in life.

Figure 1 presents a holistic model of the human being. The brain contains the map of reality, which, in the figure, is symbolized by a triangle. The map may be in good or poor shape, reflecting the person's understanding of life, himself and the surrounding world. The brain is located within the unity and serves this unity through an image of the world (the map) by connecting it to the external world.

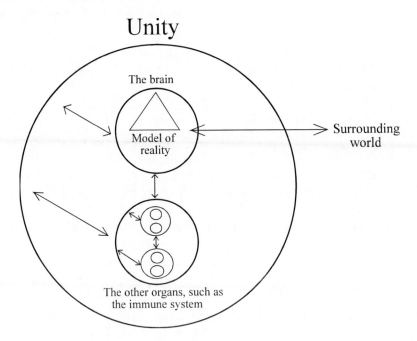

Figure 1. The wholeness of human being (see text for explanation).

The map stems from personal history and is thus related to reason – everything we have learned about reality. The unity is linked to our actual existence and our deep lives and therefore contains the history of a life (as it has developed), a history the human being only has access to intuitively.

The theory of realizing life potential tells us that, by nature, human beings are capable of living: able to love themselves and others and to connect to the external world by occupying themselves with activities they care about and that are needed in the world. The real problem in life is to weed out the wrong and the outdated ideas such that the map is evolving internally in a proper balance with the inner being as well as the external reality.

The unity of the human being is created through a complex interaction between all parts of the organism, even at the cellular level, symbolized by the smaller levels in the bottom circle of figure 1 and all the arrows. Likewise, the unity of the world is created by integrating all living organisms into the global ecosystem. Thus, understanding ourselves does not entail discovering our own ego, but rather discovering the nature of our relationship to the world.

The biological potential and life intentions

Each living organism contains a store of information that reflects the evolution of that particular species. In recent decades we have become accustomed to viewing this mass concentration of piled-up information as carried by the genes. However, it is now becoming increasingly clear that both the cell surrounding the DNA strands and the data attached to the organism play a significant role in the formation and further development of biological form.

Let us then move one step further and state that living organisms have biological potential as a result of evolution. If we combine this notion with the universal tendency towards self-organization, we can conclude that biological potential requires the realization of life potential.

This urge of the biological potential to realize itself is termed the will to live. All living organisms, from bacteria to humans, have a will to live: a self-organizing instinct, or urge, that realizes the biological potential. We do not wish to posit a metaphysical or parapsychological, let alone new (or old) life force beyond scientific description. Rather, we wish to give an intuitively plausible name to the tendency towards realization, a tendency that is no more mysterious than that tendency towards self-organization, spontaneous order and evolution that modern physics and biology have identified in numerous systems (12,13).

In humans, the will to live is expressed by biological potential: in physical evolution from the fertilized ovum to the mature body as well as in all the psychological and social activities human life requires when lived to the full.

We seldom come across the will to live per se in our everyday lives. Rather we see its actual manifestations in life, which we will call life intentions or life purposes (14). Life intentions are the images of the present and the future that serve to give our lives the course we want them to take: the desire for a meaningful occupation, good social relations, family and children, stability or variety of life. As symbol-carrying images, often unconscious, life intentions form part of the values of life in the model of reality found in the brain. They are a part of our mental maps. As such they can further or inhibit the realization of life potential to varying degrees.

Life intentions are dormant seeds existing as dispositions of biological potential, dispositions that may shape the potential of a life. Nevertheless, our life intentions are really molded in close encounters with culture, especially our parents or other caregivers.

Our life intentions determine our efforts to develop life in certain directions. They are frustrated when we do not succeed in realizing life in accordance with our intentions. When this happens and we cannot reshape our life intentions, we tend to give them up and adapt the realization of life potential to the reality we find – we dream less ambitious dreams.

We see the will to live, when we meet death. It is a powerful experience, because we are confronted with life, its intentions and the basic urge to live. When we meet death, one of the major crises in life, we have to discover whether we are sufficiently strong to re-evaluate our true intentions and way of life. We may even have to change our attitude to it entirely. This in itself may lead to new growth and a reassessment of our values.

Ill health and meaning in life

In the search for causes of ill health, medical science tends to examine genetic reasons such as defective molecules that cause malfunction – or external stresses that cause traumas, such as traffic accidents, asbestos or smoking. Only certain disciplines, notably psychosomatic medicine, pediatrics and public health, are concerned with psychosocial factors.

Hence, medical science tends to believe that mechanical faults are the most important factors in the cause of ill health. Nevertheless, in the vast psychosocial field, the factors of the quality of life, may well be significantly more important than genetics and external stress factors. It could well be that the quality of life, and its many dimensions, is the major reason for ill health.

This is difficult to comprehend, because consciousness and our entire worldview contribute to creating the quality of life. Life is far greater and more spacious than our perception of being and reality. As evolution concerns everything, not just you and me, the biological information system is a collective system, which, like the hierarchy of life, encompasses all individuals, including the biosphere. This link with the world plays a major role in the realization of life potential of each organism.

If we view human beings as organisms with biological potential capable of realizing themselves mentally and socially, the purpose of life is the ability to let this potential blossom and develop in an individual and eco-social context. We may take this one step further so that the quality of life, a good life, means the ability to maximize life potential in a social and ecological context.

The acknowledgment of this and the ability to choose a good course in life (constantly adjusting one's life intentions in order to achieve the full realization of life potential) leading to a close connection to reality generate meaning in life. Meaning in life arises, when we experience a fruitful connection between the inner depths of our being and the external world. The given biological potential is then realized and a unified worldview is hereby developed. This unification or connection may be experienced as stages reached in the realization of life (that is, manifest results such as having a partner and children) or it may take shape as a feeling that things are happening, that development is taking place in which the different phases in life are explored and seized gradually.

The experience of meaning in life presupposes a high degree of contact with the depths of our being, the center of our existence, which we here call the biological information system.

Meaning in life and hence the quality of life caused by our biological potential is how biology expresses itself subjectively in our lives. An objective expression of biological potential is found in our state of health. A healthy body is proof that the biological potential is finding a healthy outlet. Likewise, illness means that the biological potential is hampered in realizing itself in a healthy body. The biological information system, which is responsible for the biological potential, is out of balance in the sick body. Hence, communication between the cells, which is crucial for the maintenance of the organism as a whole, is disturbed.

A good example of this is cancer. Cancer is usually regarded as an illness in which the ability of the cells to fit into the organizational unity breaks down. This is the inevitable consequence of a breakdown in the mutual communication, regulation and coordination of the cells.

Likewise, many other illnesses can be seen as a communication failure at an elementary, cellular level or as problems in the biological information system. This is further complicated, when the immune system is affected. Infection, allergy, eczema, insulin-dependent diabetes, arthritis, multiple sclerosis and other ailments can be explained, if we think of these illnesses as a result of malfunctioning of the immune system. This dysregulation is according to our understanding linked to disturbances in the global biological information system of the organism (15,16). Unfortunately this global and integrative biological information system has yet no satisfying scientific description; we believe it to carry our consciousness.

The subjective meaning in life and objective state of health of the individual is then a common basis of the individual's inner being or the existential center. As the quality of life is closely linked with self-realization and the degree of meaning in life attained, the quality of life is closely linked with illness via the state of the biological feedback system. As our quality of life is enhanced or diminished by the way we live and our opportunities to realize our biological potential, changes in lifestyle and the realization of life potential will change the quality of life and state of health. The relationship between the quality of life and illness is that both originate from the realization of life potential, that is, the ability to live out our life intentions. Figure 2 outlines the roles the quality of life and state of health play in life. Three types are shown:

- A good life with high quality of life and good health where the individual live to the full to the very end.
- An average life, where the life intentions, quality of life and the other subjective factors are neither quite right nor quite hopeless. This generates a poorer state of health and might end with thrombosis or cancer.
- A poor life, where life intentions, quality of life and maps of reality are bleak right from infancy. This leads to a life that is continuously downhill. Abandoning responsibility might lead to mental illness in which the individual no longer wishes to take part in collective reality.

We may choose to work with our fundamental notions of life and reality at any time. We can then adjust our course in life and thus achieve a better life (4,17-19). Usually we need to meet death before we accept that we are no experts in life.

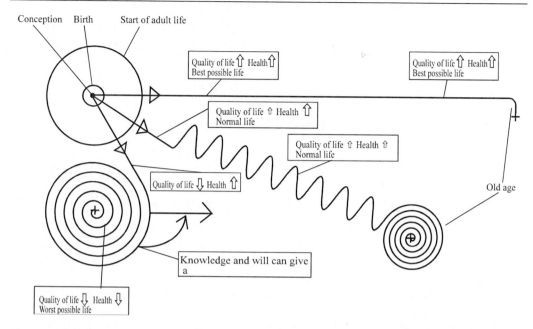

Figure 2. The three paths of life[4]: the good life with optimal QOL, health and ability of functioning, the average, normal, life with sub-optimal QOL, health and ability, and the poor life with low QOL, ill health and bad functioning, lived by a quartile of the Danish population.

Towards a new scientific understanding of humanity

This understanding of the realization of life potential has many traits of a popular understanding of life and may strike us as being self-evident. Unfortunately, this is not the case. Another widely accepted model for the life and health of the human being, the medical science model, states in its biomedical mechanism that the cause of illness is either genes or external trauma: accidents, infections, bacteria and other attacks on the body. The entire psychosocial field, including the mental maps of reality and life intentions, regarded in our model to be factors of affecting the quality of life, are not regarded as particularly meaningful in classical medical, molecular biology research. In fact, these factors are merely considered to be the background against which the factors causing the illness unfold and they are thus often ignored in scientific discussions of sickness and health.

The most important scientific hypothesis of our quality-of-life project is precisely that the quality of life, in the truest and deepest meaning of the concept, is the real cause of most illnesses, notably cancer, cardiovascular diseases and allergies, and that these illnesses can be prevented by improving the quality of life in time (19). If this hypothesis is confirmed and/or more explicitly formulated, it can lead to a new and far more comprehensive discipline of medicine than the one we know today.

Our interpretation of the nature of all living matter is intended as an alternative to medical mechanism, which dates back to the beginning of the twentieth century. New ideas such as the notions of the human being as nestled in an evolutionary and ecological context, the spontaneous tendency of self-organizing systems for realization and concord and the central role of consciousness in interpreting, planning and expressing human reality are unavoidable today in attempts to scientifically understand all living matter, including human life.

References

[1]   Maslow A. Toward a psychology of being. New York: Van Nostrand, 1962.
[2]   Ventegodt S, Merrick J, Andersen NJ. QOL Theory III. Maslow revisited. ScientificWorld Journal 2003;3:1050-7.
[3]   Ventegodt S. Review of quality of life with a biological theory on global quality of life. Agrippa 1991;13:58-79. [Danish].
[4]   Ventegodt S. Measuring the quality of life. Copenhagen: Forskningscentrets Forlag, 1996. [Danish].
[5]   Ventegodt S, Henneberg EW, Merrick J, Lindholt JS. Validation of two global and generic quality of life questionnaires for population screening: SCREENQOL and SEQOL. ScientificWorldJournal 2003;3:412-21.
[6]   Ventegodt S, Hilden J, Merrick J. Measurement of quality of life I: A methodological framework. ScientificWorldJournal 2003;3:950-61.
[7]   Køppe S. Levels of reality. The new science and its history. Copenhagen: Gyldendal, 1990. [Danish]
[8]   Bateson G. Mind and nature: A necessary unity. New York: Ballantine, 1972.
[9]   Yates FE, ed. Self-organizing systems (the introduction): the emergence of order. New York: Plenum, 1987.
[10] Davies P. The cosmic blueprint. London: Heineman, 1987.
[11] Margulis L, Sagan D. Microcosmos: Four billion years of evolution. New York: Simon Schuster, 1989.
[12] Yates FE, ed. Self-organizing systems: The emergence of order. New York: Plenum, 1987.
[13] Kaufman S. The origins of order: Self- organization and selection in evolution. Oxford: Oxford Univ Press, 1993.
[14] Ventegodt S. The life mission theory: A theory for a consciousness-based medicine. Int J Adolesc Med Health 2003;15(1):89-91.
[15] Ventegodt S. The connection between quality of life and disease. Stockholm: Federation Soc Insurance Officers, 1994.
[16] Ventegodt S, Ventegodt S. The connection between quality of life and health. Theory and practice. Copenhagen: Acadr Appl Philosophy, 1994. [Danish].
[17] Ventegodt S, Poulsen DL. What advice to give on a better quality of life. Meet the person, where he/she is. Farmaci 1992;139-40. [Danish].
[18] Lindholt JS, Ventegodt S, Henneberg EW. Development and validation of QOL5 for clinical databases. A short, global and generic questionnaire based on an integrated theory of the quality of life. Eur J Surg 2002;168:107-13.
[19] Ventegodt S, Merrick J, Andersen NJ. Quality of life as medicine: A pilot study of patients with chronic illness and pain. ScientificWorldJournal 2003;3:520-32.

Chapter 17

The wholeness of man, his consciousness and collective consciousness

In this chapter we look at the rational and the emotional interpretation of reality in the human brain and being, and discuss the representation of the brain-mind (ego), the body-mind (Id), and the outer world in the human wholeness (the I or "soul"). Based on this we discuss a number of factors including the coherence between perception, attention and consciousness, and the relation between thought, fantasies, visions and dreams. We discuss and explain concepts as intent, will, morals and ethics. The Jungian concept of the human collective conscious and unconscious is also analysed. We also hypothesis on the nature of intuition and consider the source of religious experience of man. These phenomena are explained based on the concept of deep quantum chemistry and infinite dancing fractal spirals making up the energetic backbone of the world. In this paper we consider man as a real wholeness and debate the concepts of subjectivity, consciousness and intent that can be deduced from such a perspective.

Introduction

Until now in this series of papers on human development we have been looking at information transmitting interactions at the different levels of the organism. The nature of the information transmitting interactions is unknown, because we do not know the limits of their effect in time and space. Likewise, we cannot with our rational interpretation set this delimitation. The emotional interpretation is far more suitable for this, but unfortunately far from our reason. Epistemologically we here refer to Occam's razor (1,2) and so far maintain for reasons of simplicity that the same principles that affects the lower levels also affects the higher levels. Our conclusion therefore is that the perceptual and conscious life of man may be deduced from a generalization of the effect of the information transmitting interactions to all levels.

In this paper we discuss the representation of the wholeness of the organism and the outer world in the brain. Among all the organ systems the brain is exceptional, because it is specialized to represent the outer world through the sense organs and thereby give a simple interpretation [3] of matter with some or all elements being reduced to the same frame of description as apply to dead things.

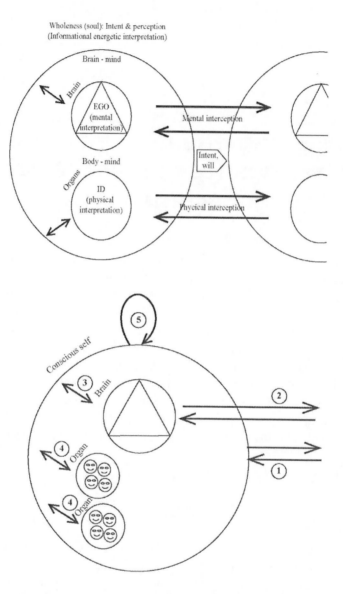

Figure 1. A model of the wholeness of man, including the functions of attention and will. The representational stages of a human being. The attention function and a survey over the representative possibilities and functional stages. This figure shows a survey of man. Man himself is part of a larger social system, to which it through interactions is adapted, and which he himself influences. The human organism can directly represent elements at its own level, humans and other living beings, and more difficultly dead things. The human organism is also able to represent lower levels, such as organ systems, and higher levels, such as the family. A. Wholeness, intention and perception. B. The 5 representational stages: 1. Directly representation of the outer world. 2. Indirectly representation of the outer world through the brain. 3. Representation of the brain in the wholeness. 4. Directly representation of the outer world. 5. The wholeness represents the wholeness.

The representation of the outer world is made up as a long chain of interpretation actions corresponding with the outer world - inasmuch as the motor apparatus is under control of the brain (4). In figure 1 the motor apparatus is drawn below the brain, however the wholeness and the motor apparatus must be thought of as being interacting around the brain. The organism is able to represent the reality (the world) in two ways: 1) Directly through information transmitting interactions, which is the emotional way of representation, where reality is represented in the organism's wholeness (3) or 2) Indirectly through representation in the brain. This is the rational way of representing the outer world by means of the reason (3).

We believe that the brain can represent the wholeness of the organism and what goes on in it in addition to representing the outer world through the senses. This means that the organism possesses the possibility of the rational and the emotional interpretations of reality. When the simplistic representation of the world dominates in the representation of the wholeness we have the rational interpretation of reality.

When the direct representation outside the brain dominates the representation of the wholeness, we have the emotional interpretation of reality, where the brain represents the wholeness (3). In this chapter we will discuss man as holistic through his ability to experience the world through these two ways of interpretation.

The human as a wholeness

Attention, perception, and consciousness. The information transmitting interactions giving representation of a subject matter in the wholeness of the organism corresponds to the attention function, and the representation itself corresponds to the attention. This is in contrast to the common notion that perception happens in the brain (5). However we think that consciousness cannot be explained by brain activity alone. Consciousness is not brought about before the totality, the seat of perception, has represented the brain. Consciousness demands a representation of the subject matter in the totality of the organism, but this is not sufficient. A double, simultaneous representation is required, because the representation is a sufficient model of reality within the brain (3,6); the comparison of the two representations is necessary for being able to witness the world, in other words: to be conscious about it.

Thought, fantasies, visions, and dreams. When the totality represents the brain in a state, where important new sensory information is not entering, but where the rational interpretation of reality is sustained, the purpose of the organism of handling the outer world manifests itself through a reorganization of the representation in the brain. The model of reality in the brain is reorganized in a way that makes it possible to retain a better handling of the world through behaviour. When the brain is working with space-time organizations this phenomenon is called thinking, and when the pictures do not represent the real world it is called visions or fantasies. In dreams, the possibility of realizing the purposes of the organism under the existing circumstances is systematically worked through.

The intent. It is evident that representation is very tightly controlled through the perception function. The patterns of the totality are tuned in a way that ensures agreement between the patterns of the totality and the patterns of a specific level or subject. This tuning is the purpose of the organism. The tuning of the totality happens, when information-transmitting interactions bring the "programs" lying as organized patterns at the deepest levels to the surface of the wholeness of the organism.

The subject matter that is represented has a given organization, which by now can be evaluated through more specific interactions between the wholeness and the information-"program". Reality is thus perceived and obtains its meaning through the purposes of the biological system. These purposes are a collection of fundamental biological information patterns forming the basis for the unfolding of the biological system. Various aspects of wholeness are submitted to each purpose, and correspondingly different aspects of reality are perceived as a consequence of this submission.

Attention may be attracted to incidents at the various levels, and the purposes must therefore be recruited dynamically as they are needed in order for the wholeness to undergo governed transformations in a suitable way. The governing of attention must happen autonomously through shifts between the states of the totality following a genetically determined governing pattern. The realization of the more simple patterns is a condition for the more complex organizations, in the same way as in morphogenesis (7,8).

Morals and ethics. What attention captures is perceived and gives meaning in relation to the basic pattern, the purpose. The organization of the subject matter may be viewed as proper or improper – or it may be viewed as something in between. When a level or a subject matter is represented in the totality, a double evaluation follows. On the surface the organization is perceived as suitable for the organism or unsuitable for the organism, i.e. right or wrong. Inwardly an emotional response is triggered, that evaluates the agreement between the genetic program and the structure of the subject matter in the representation of the totality. A good agreement between the program and reality corresponds to positive emotions, while a bad agreement corresponds to negative emotions.

The will. Hitherto we have only been looking at the representation of subject matters in the totality of the organism through the attention function. It is secondary whether the representation happens directly through the totality following a purpose, resulting in an emotional interpretation of reality, or indirectly through the brain following a purpose, resulting in a rational interpretation of reality. The evaluation through emotion and perception happens in the same way.

Information transmitting interactions in principle work both ways. When purpose transmits information to the wholeness of the organism, information is also transmitted from this wholeness to the subject matter at which the attention is directed. A representation is forced upon the subject matter by the organism, and this function, which is the inverse of the attention function, is called the function of will.

The organism approaches the subject gradually. At first a fundamental adaptation is accomplished by the tuning of the totality by the purpose. In this way the basic patterns are shared between the organism and the subject. This creates a representation of the subject in the totality of the organism. Then this representation is evaluated, and the purpose is tightened, and the patterns corresponding to a certain organization of the subject are pulled up into the totality. Vice versa the desired organization is transferred to the subject.

The increasing complexity of the organism throughout life can be understood as the realization of purposes through the use of the will function. The different purposes are recruited in a succession that ensures organization of the inner levels before the outer levels. The will function is thus the organism's organizing force. It is brought about through information transmitting interactions. The purpose being a very high level of organization in the totality of the organism, forces an organization corresponding to the informational program of the organism, onto a subject with which the totality interacts. The will function can work directly upon the outer world, or indirectly through the brain. The latter leads to behaviour and in man also to speech. Speech is an indirect mediation of interpretation of reality through words, while action is a direct mediation of interpretation of reality through the motor apparatus. It is possible to act out of an emotional interpretation of reality, because the brain is subject to the totality in this interpretation of reality [3,6]. Direct use of the will function is usually hidden from our reason and belongs to the emotional interpretation of reality.

The intuition. The direct interaction (described above) either between individuals or between an individual and the society yields a complex information transmission, but this is only available for the emotional interpretation of reality. A specific representation of the outer world focusing at certain patterns may theoretically speaking be a precise source of information, providing that patterns that reach us through information transmitting interactions can be identified and interpreted in a precise and sober-minded way.

The difficulty of obtaining this precision and sober-mindedness has led to a pronounced and legitimate scepticism against the value of this data source, because people who claim to have intuition rarely have developed this gift. Intuition in its developed form is the ability to let one's attention float in the complex dynamics consisting of the wholeness and all the individuals of the society. When the wholeness represents the outer world in a general way, one obtains experiences of unity with nature and the like, that belongs to the class of experiences that collide with an undeveloped reason.

The collective (un-)consciousness. When you start thinking in this strange way, that reality is more a hidden order that what meets the eye; the reality of a collective mind or collective consciousness is not a farfetched idea. If the world is created like a huge many-leveled fractal, we might all be a part of such a huge meta-structure, which connects us and collects our perceptions and experiences to bring them to the next level for all to enjoy. This is in a way scary because we often prefer that our consciousness is private; the Jungian concept of a common consciousness is basically born our of the opposite idea: that consciousness cannot be private; it is always public although most people luckily for us do knot know how to approach the collective consciousness and "crack the code" to get admission to our innermost hidden secrets and unspoken emotions.

The religious experience. Last we will discuss the religious experience. In our culture one of the least known qualities of man's wholeness is man's ability to represent himself, to be aware of himself.

This is an experience obtained either by chance or, more commonly, after having exercised the control of attention to a level, where he can exclude all other representations. It is usually described as the religious experience: the experience of God, of the divine principle enlightenment etc.

In spite of the evidently positive, beautiful and real aspects of this experience, it demands much soberness to be able to use this kind of experiences in a positive way. Very often people lose their way in the overwhelming experiences, or they use them for self-asserting purposes, a fact that has resulted in a prevailing and justified skepticism against "religious" people.

Conclusions

Many aspects are involved when we look at the man as wholeness, including a suitable combination of the rational and emotional interpretation of reality. These aspects are summarised and discussed in this chapter:

- We think that consciousness cannot be explained by brain activity alone. A double, simultaneous representation is required. The comparison of these two representations is necessary to be conscious about the world.
- The phenomenon of thinking is when the brain is working with space-time organizations leading to pictures. When these do not represent the real world it is called visions or fantasies. In dreams the possibility of realizing the purposes of the organism is systematically worked through.
- The patterns of the totality are tuned in a way that ensures agreement between the patterns of the totality and the patterns of a specific level or subject. This tuning is the organism's intent.
- The organization of a subject matter may be viewed as proper or improper or something in between. A good agreement between the genetic program and reality corresponds to positive emotions, while a poor agreement corresponds to negative emotions. Tuning of these functions is called moral and ethics.
- A representation is forced upon a subject matter by the organism. This function is called the function of will and can work directly upon the outer world, or indirectly through the brain. The latter leads to behaviour, and in man also to speech. Speech is an indirect mediation of interpretation of reality through words, while action is a direct mediation of interpretation of reality through the motor apparatus.
- The direct interaction between individuals or between an individual and the social levels yields a complex information transmission available for the intuition. In its developed form intuition is the ability to let one's attention float in the complex dynamics consisting of the wholeness and all the individuals of the society.
- In our culture one of the least known qualities of man's wholeness is man's ability to represent himself, to be aware of himself. This is an experience obtained either by chance or after having exercised the control of attention to a level, where he can exclude all other representations. It is usually described as the religious experience.

References

[1] Thorburn WM. Occam's razor. Mind 1915;24:287-8.
[2] Thorburn WM. The Myth of Occam's razor. Mind 1918;27:345-53.
[3] Ventegodt S, Andersen NJ, Merrick J. The life mission theory V. A theory of the anti-self and explaining the evil side of man. ScientificWorldJournal 2003;3:1302-13.
[4] Kandel ER, Schwartz JH. Principles of neural science. New York: Elsevier, 2000.
[5] Hubel DH, Wiesel TN. Brain and visual perception: The story of a 25-year collaboration. Oxford: Oxford Univ Press, 2004.

[6]   Ventegodt S, Hermansen TD, Kandel I, Merrick J. Human development XII: A theory for the structure and function of the (human) brain. ScientificWorldJournal 2008;8:621-42.

[7]   Ventegodt S, Hermansen TD, Flensborg-Madsen T, Nielsen ML, Merrick J. Human development IV: The living cell has information-directed self-organisation. ScientificWorldJournal 2006;6:1132-8.

[8]   Ventegodt S, Hermansen TD, Flensborg-Madsen T, Nielsen ML, Merrick J. Human development VI: Supra-cellular morphogenesis - the origin of biological and cellular order. ScientificWorldJournal 2006;6:1424-33.

Chapter 18

Concept of self in holistic medicine

René Descartes, Sigmund Freud and Anna Freud have among others developed the concept of self with a focus on ego development and self-interpretation. These concepts have also been used in counseling, where self-consistency has been seen as a primary motivating force in human behavior and psychotherapy can be seen as basically a process of altering the ways that individuals see themselves.

In holistic medicine it is generally believed that there is an ego connected to the brain-mind and a deeper self, connected to the wholeness of the person (the soul), but we have yet another self connected to the body mind taking care of our sexuality. So this three-some of selves (ego, the body and the soul) must function and this is done best under the leadership of our wholeness, the deep self. This chapter with a few case stories illustrate the holistic medicine mindset concerned with the concept of self.

Introduction

Philosophically the self has always been problematic. Millions of Buddhists believe in the concept on "anata" meaning no-self and many more scientist and physicians of today believe that we are only chemical machines making the concept of consciousness and the self a matter of mere self-illusion.

In psychoanalysis and related systems we have the ego, the super ego and the id, in most psychology we have a self that is the person's self reference, his interpretation of own personified existence (1-4).

In holistic medicine we normally have an ego connected to the brain- mind, and a deeper self, connected to the wholeness of the person (often in religion and philosophy called the "soul") (5-19). We have yet another self connected to the body mind taking care of our sexuality (20).

So this three-some of selves must function, and this is done best under the leadership of our wholeness, the deep self.

To call it deep is really strange, because when you come from this self, you are not really coming from any depth, but only from yourself. The term is appropriate in education as most students are familiar to some extend with their ego, and to some extent with their sexual bodily self, but not with their totality.

To discover this vast hall of existence in oneself often gives a feeling of revelation, of realizing that we are divine creates.

The soul is close to God in our inner experience, and many religious experiences (21) thus come after discovering this existential layer in one self. What is interesting for medicine is that many people experience a dramatic improvement in their quality of life, general ability and their health when they break through to this dimension of "higher self", as it can be called (5-19). The term "higher" might be justified from the reference to the person's wholeness, higher then signifying "the top of the hierarchy of entities of this person".

Purpose of life: The essence of self

In the scientific holistic medicine we intent to improve QOL, health and ability, all in one process (22,23). The only way to do this is by re-establishing the patient's existential coherence (19,24,25). This is often done in the holistic clinic by the rehabilitation of the patient in the three dimensions of love, consciousness and sexuality (15). The most important being love.

To rehabilitate the patients ability to love is done by helping the patient to acknowledge his existential depth, that is his wholeness, and what we call "the essence of the soul" or the purpose of life. The purpose of life, or life mission (13) is the primary talent of the person and when this talent is taken into use, the person can contribute in a constructive and valuable way to other people and society. Realising this value to other people is often making the person very happy, which will facilitate the person to go to the next level of unconditional love.

When a person realises that the meaning of life is to give from the bottom of his soul what he himself has been gifted with to other people awakens a happiness in the person that is so sufficient that no more is needed. This person can now give without wanting or needing anything in return. He has become a source of love, a source of value for his family and environment.

Living the purpose of life is an experience as being in the state of existence that we were originally meant to be in. This is realising our self (27). So love is only realised though the wholeness, the deep self or the soul.

When we come from love we give from the core of our soul, and we give from our essence. On doing this, all human talents can be recruited to support this key intension of manifesting love, expressing our purpose of life (14).

Quite surprisingly this means that almost everybody contains huge hidden resources that can be mobilised. The experience of becoming oneself and finding the ability to love seems to be the biggest resource a patient can find.

Often this is the initiation of an intense self-healing process (28,29). The background for the life mission theory (13) can be found in box 1.

Box 1. The life mission theory (13)

The phases listed below chart the life and disease history of an individual (II-VII). At the outset, let us assume that a human being begins his or her existence with a plan or an ambition for a good and healthy life. We may put this assumption of a primordial plan in quite abstract terms (I):

I. Life Mission. Let us assume that at the moment of conception all the joy, energy and wisdom that our lives are capable of supporting are expressed in a "decision" as to the purpose of our lives. This first "decision" is quite abstract and all-encompassing and holds the intentions of the entire life for that individual. It may be called the personal mission or the life mission. This mission is the meaning of life for that individual. It is always constructive and sides with life itself.

II. Life pain. The greatest and most fundamental pain in our lives derives from the frustrations encountered, when we try to achieve our personal mission, be they frustrated attempts to satisfy basic needs or the failure to obtain desired psychological states.

III. Denial. When the pain becomes intolerable we can deny our life mission by making a counter-decision, which is then lodged in the body and the mind, partially or entirely cancelling the life mission.

IV. Repair. One or several new life intentions, more specific than the original life mission, may now be chosen relative to what is possible henceforth. They replace the original life mission and enable the person to move forward again. They can, in turn, be modified, when they encounter new pains experienced as unbearable. (Example: Mission #1: "I am good." Denial #1: "I am not good enough." Mission #2: "I will become good," which implies I am not).

V. Repression and loss of responsibility. The new life intention, which corresponds to a new perspective on life at a lower level of responsibility, is based on an effective repression of both the old life mission and the counter-decision that antagonises and denies it. Such a repression causes the person to split in a conscious and one or more unconscious/subconscious parts. The end result is that we deny and repress parts of ourselves. Our new life intention must always be consistent with what is left undenied.

VI. Loss of physical health. Human consciousness is coupled to the wholeness of the organism through the information systems that bind all the cells of the body into a unity. Disturbances in consciousness may thus disturb the organism's information systems, resulting in the cells being less perfectly informed as to what they are to do where.

Disruptions in the necessary flow of information to the cells of the organism and tissues hamper the ability of the cells to function properly. Loss of cellular functionality may eventually result in disease and suffering.

VII. Loss of quality of life and mental health. In psychological and spiritual terms, people who deny their personal mission gradually lose their fundamental sense that life has meaning, direction and coherence. They may find that their joy of life, energy to do important things and intuitive wisdom are slowly petering out. The quality of their lives is diminished and their mental health impaired.

IIX. Loss of functionality. When we decide against our life mission we invalidate our very existence. This shows up as reduced self-worth and self-confidence. Thus, the counter-decisions compromise not only our health and quality of life, but also our basic powers to function physically, psychologically, socially, at work, sexually, etc.

The self and healing

When the patient enters the process of existential healing, we find what is important is the three steps that integrates old traumas and develops a positive philosophy of life: 1) to feel, 2) to understand and 3) to let go of negative beliefs and decisions (which has been formulated in "the holistic process theory of healing") (22). What this process does to a person is a rather peculiar thing: first the negative emotions from old traumas appear in the consciousness; second the repressed and forgotten contexts appear in the mind, where hidden and neurotic patterns are confronted and seen, and finally the many negative beliefs and attitudes collected though live failures are dismissed to reveal a natural and positive philosophy of life. The negative attitudes are really what give the brain-mind ego its lack of transparency. A sound ego is transcendent and allows the deep wishes of the soul (the wholeness) to be manifested in the mind and fulfilled by the person using all of the rich possibilities in this world. In the same way the self of the body-mind will become visible and present when shame, guild and other feelings attended to sexuality and the body are processed and the old traumatic life events integrated in holistic existential therapy (30-32).

So the three selves of a person, the ego, the body and the soul are closely related in the sound person. In the sick person these are often widely apart (33-35). Sexuality is repressed and the body's urges distorted and perverted, the soul and the true direction of the person is left out of the persons reach, and the mind is occupied with sheer survival.

Rehabilitation of existence is really rehabilitation of the soul, mind and body. The mind ego must become transparent (see box 2). The body's self must become free and happy. The soul must come into power to manifest its love and be a coherent part of the universe[36].

Box 2. The process of healing and the ego (14)

The ego is our description of self in the brain-mind. It is important to notice that personal development is a plan not for the elimination of the ego, but for its cultivation. An existentially sound person will always have an operative mental ego, but it is centered on the optimal verbal expression of the life mission. Such an ego is not in conflict with one's true self, but supports the life and wholeness of the person, although in an invisible and seamless way. The more developed the person, the more talents are taken into use. So, although the core of existence remains the same throughout life, the healthy person continues to grow. As the number of talents we can call upon is unlimited, the journey ends only at death.

Case story 1

A female, aged 42 years with tinnitus, migraine, herpes simplex 1 and 2, low back pain, treatment-resistant genital warts, sun allergy and depression. Despite her age, Mia was already in a very poor condition, physically and mentally. But she possessed something special, an alertness and interest in the spiritual world. She wanted to develop as a person and that meant that she was ready to assume responsibility and take the rather bitter, holistic medicine offered her. We met in a good and sincere way. Processing her painful personal history took her directly to her life purpose. Following this acknowledgement her art began to flourish and grow like never before. Suddenly, she could do things that she had not even come close to doing before, and her art expressed her new state of acceptance and understanding of good and evil, beautiful and ugly, muck and mire and sky and light. Having acknowledged her life purpose, Mia largely became able to manage on her own. She could now develop further without our help. My work (SV) of guiding her through the pain that made her ill and blocked her enjoyment of life and self-expression is now finished. Her body and soul have largely healed, her tinnitus is almost gone and most of the time she cannot hear it at all. Obviously, this patient may become physically ill again, but her resistance and inner equilibrium appeared to be much greater than before, so next time she is likely to recover much faster.

This woman seemed to have almost all her diseases caused by inner conflicts between her ego and her true self. When the conflicts were solved in the holistic therapy, the most of her seemingly incurable diseases disappeared at the same time.

Case story 2

The next case story was written by a Rosen Body Work practitioner at the Quality of Life Research Center. It is instructive as it shows an important aspect of how the conflict of the ego versus the true self is related to the subjective problems of a male with heart problems.

Male, aged 55 years with the question if he had heart problems. This patient was a family man and manager of a private firm. He seemed a happy and extrovert man with a good grip on things. However, his body was heavy and his muscles very hard. Shortly before he started at the clinic, he had been in hospital with a blood clot in his heart and was taking medication for hypertension. Most of the times he was on the couch he fell into a deep sleep that was frequently interrupted by some very violent jerks throughout the body, which he called his electric shocks. Several times during the period when he came to our clinic he was admitted to the hospital with extreme cardiac pain and angina. Eventually he started medication for these symptoms and on the waiting list for bypass surgery. During some of his private sessions he became aware of some of the things that had greatly influenced his life, including an alcoholic father, who had been violent towards his mother. As a very young he received electroconvulsive therapy for severe depression. After he had realised this, the jerks that used to wake up both him and his wife ceased or diminished. It also became apparent that he was taking strong antidepressants and had done so for years. He choose to reduce dosage so that he was far below the daily dose, and he was doing well without the excessive medication. Throughout the therapy he had some major problems with his staff and he felt they had taken a dislike to him. I (SV) had other clients from that workplace, and it turned out that others shared his belief. The patient mobilised all his strength to give notice and start again from scratch in another firm, where he is working today. At some point he was again admitted to the hospital with extreme pain and angina that was considered to be life threatening, so he was transferred to a cardiology ward for surgery at the earliest opportunity. However, when the cardiologists examined him thoroughly they could not find any disorder or defect in the heart or surrounding blood vessels, so they discharged him again. During the last private session with the patient he was truly happy about life, and full of vigour to devote to his family and friends. His jerks and cardiac problems had vanished completely, and he was enjoying his new job.

What happened here according to the theory of the ego presented in this chapter is, that the man finally let go of his cold and frozen-hearted ego, which was suppressing his feelings and emotions. It was also beneficial for his subjective experience of his heart, his quality of life, working life and ability of functioning in general.

The method of Marion Rosen Body Work (37) and other body therapies that make the patient note the feelings located in the body are effective tools in holistic medicine. Sometimes the patient can verbalise his feelings and let go of the limiting beliefs that keep them bound to the narrow world of the ego. For many middle-aged men, their Achilles heal is allowing themselves to feel. Often, it is extremely unpleasant for a grown-up man in a managerial position to register the old feelings from his childhood of being small, frightened or helpless. It is quite simply an insult to his ego, that he is still harboring such feelings. To release them seemingly relieved his angina.

Conclusions

René Descartes (1596-1650) wrote in 1644 the book "Principles of philosophy" (38) perceived as a milestone in reflection on the non-physical inner self. He proposed that doubt was a principal tool of disciplined examination, but he could not doubt that he doubted. He rationalized that if he doubted, he was thinking and therefore must exist and therefore existence depended upon perception. Concept of self was also part of the writings of Sigmund Freud (1856-1939) (1,39), who developed further and new understanding of the importance of internal mental processes. Freud hesitated to make self-concept a primary psychological unit in his theories, but his daughter Anna Freud (1895-1982) (40) focused on ego development and self-interpretation.

In counseling the psychologist Prescott Lecky (1892-1941) created a personality theory, but was never able to collect his writing into a completed form until his former Columbia University students in 1945 published a small posthumous volume (41), where self-consistency was seen as a primary motivating force in human behavior. Others (42) have used the self-concept in counseling interviews and argued that psychotherapy is basically a process of altering the ways that individuals see themselves.

In holistic medicine we believe that there is an ego connected to the brain-mind and a deeper self, connected to the wholeness of the person (the soul), but we have yet another self connected to the body mind taking care of our sexuality (20). So this three-some of selves (ego, the body and the soul) must function and this is done best under the leadership of our wholeness, the deep self. This chapter with a few case stories illustrate the holistic medicine mindset concerned with the concept of self.

References

[1]   Freud S. Mourning and melancholia. London: Penguin, 1984.
[2]   Jung CG. Man and his symbols. New York: Anchor Press, 1964.

[3] Sulivan HS. Interpersonal theory and psychotherapy, London: Routledge, 1996.

[4] Horney K. Our inner conflicts: A constructive theory of neurosis. London: WW Norton, 1948.

[5] Ventegodt S, Andersen NJ, Merrick J. Quality of life philosophy: when life sparkles or can we make wisdom a science? ScientificWorldJournal 2003;3:1160-3.

[6] Ventegodt S, Andersen NJ, Merrick J. QOL philosophy I: Quality of life, happiness, and meaning of life. ScientificWorldJournal 2003;3:1164-75.

[7] Ventegodt S, Andersen NJ, Kromann M, Merrick J. QOL philosophy II: What is a human being? ScientificWorldJournal 2003;3:1176-85.

[8] Ventegodt S, Merrick J, Andersen NJ. QOL philosophy III: Towards a new biology. ScientificWorldJournal 2003;3:1186-98.

[9] Ventegodt S, Andersen NJ, Merrick J. QOL philosophy IV: The brain and consciousness. ScientificWorldJournal 2003;3:1199-1209.

[10] Ventegodt S, Andersen NJ, Merrick J. QOL philosophy V: Seizing the meaning of life and getting well again. ScientificWorldJournal 2003;3:1210-29.

[11] Ventegodt S, Andersen NJ, Merrick J. QOL philosophy VI: The concepts. ScientificWorldJournal 2003;3:1230-40.

[12] Ventegodt S, Andersen NJ, Merrick J. Editorial: Five theories of human existence. ScientificWorldJournal 2003;3:1272-76.

[13] Ventegodt S. The life mission theory: A theory for a consciousness-based medicine. Int J Adolesc Med Health 2003;15(1):89-91.

[14] Ventegodt S, Andersen NJ, Merrick J. The life mission theory II: The structure of the life purpose and the ego. ScientificWorldJournal 2003;3:1277-85.

[15] Ventegodt S, Andersen NJ, Merrick J. The life mission theory III: Theory of talent. ScientificWorldJournal 2003;3:1286-93.

[16] Ventegodt S, Merrick J. The life mission theory IV. Theory of child development. ScientificWorldJournal 2003;3:1294-1301.

[17] Ventegodt S, Andersen NJ, Merrick J. The life mission theory V. A theory of the anti-self and explaining the evil side of man. ScientificWorldJournal 2003;3:1302-13.

[18] Ventegodt S, Andersen NJ, Merrick J. The life mission theory VI: A theory for the human character. ScientificWorldJournal 2004;4:859-80.

[19] Ventegodt S, Flensborg-Madsen T, Andersen NJ, Merrick J. Life Mission Theory VII: Theory of existential (Antonovsky) coherence: a theory of quality of life, health and ability for use in holistic medicine. ScientificWorldJournal 2005;5:377-89.

[20] Ventegodt S, Vardi G, Merrick J. Holistic adolescent sexology: How to counsel and treat young people to alleviate and prevent sexual problems. BMJ Rapid Response 2005 Jan 15.

[21] Buber M. I and thou. New York: Charles Scribner, 1970.

[22] Ventegodt S, Andersen NJ, Merrick J. Holistic Medicine III: The holistic process theory of healing. ScientificWorldJournal 2003;3:1138-46.

[23] Ventegodt S, Andersen NJ, Merrick J. Holistic Medicine IV: Principles of existential holistic group therapy and the holistic process of healing in a group setting. ScientificWorldJournal 2003;3:1388-1400.

[24] Antonovsky A. Health, stress and coping. London: Jossey-Bass, 1985.

[25] Antonovsky A. Unravelling the mystery of health. How people manage stress and stay well. San Francisco: Jossey-Bass, 1987.

[26] Fromm E. The art of loving. New York: Harper Collins, 2000.

[27] Maslow AH. Toward a psychology of being, New York: Van Nostrand, 1962.

[28] Spiegel D, Bloom JR, Kraemer HC, Gottheil, E. Effect of psychosocial treatment on survival of patients with metastatic breast cancer. Lancet 1989;2(8668), 888-91.

[29] Ventegodt S, Morad M, Merrick J. Clinical holistic medicine: Induction of spontaneous remission of cancer by recovery of the human character and the purpose of life (the life mission). ScientificWorldJournal 2004;4:362-77.

[30] Ventegodt S, Merrick J. Clinical holistic medicine: Applied consciousness-based medicine. ScientificWorldJournal 2004;4:96-9.

[31] Ventegodt S, Morad M, Merrick J. Clinical holistic medicine: Classic art of healing or the therapeutic touch. ScientificWorldJournal 2004;4:134-47.

[32] Ventegodt S, Morad M, Merrick J. Clinical holistic medicine: The "new medicine", the multi-paradigmatic physician and the medical record. ScientificWorldJournal 2004;4:273-85.

[33] Ventegodt S, Merrick J, Andersen NJ. Quality of life theory I. The IQOL theory: An integrative theory of the global quality of life concept. ScientificWorldJournal 2003;3:1030-40.

[34] Ventegodt S, Merrick J, Andersen NJ. Quality of life theory II. Quality of life as the realization of life potential: A biological theory of human being. ScientificWorldJournal 2003;3:1041-9.

[35] Ventegodt S, Merrick J, Andersen NJ. Quality of life theory III. Maslow revisited. ScientificWorldJournal 2003;3:1050-7.

[36] Ventegodt S, Flensborg-Madsen T, Andersen NJ, Nielsen M, Morad M, Merrick J. Global quality of life (QOL), health and ability are primarily determined by our consciousness. Research findings from Denmark 1991-2004. Soc Indicator Res 2005;71:87-122.

[37] Rosen M, Brenner S. Rosen method bodywork. Accesing the unconscious through touch. Berkeley, CA: North Atlantic Books, 2003.

[38] Descartes R. Principles of philosophy. Dordrecht: D Reidel, 1983.

[39] Freud S. The interpretation of dreams. In the complete psychological works of Sigmund Freud. London: Hogarth Press, 1962.

[40] Freud A. The ego and the mechanisms of defense: The writings of Anna Freud. Guilford, CT: Int Univ Press,1967.

[41] Lecky P. Self-consistency: A theory of personality. New York: Island Press, 1945.

[42] Raimy VC. Self-reference in counseling interviews. J Consult Psychol 1948;12:153-63.

Chapter 19

Five theories of the human existence

Before you can understand the holistic proces of healing or make it work in the clinic, you need to understand human existence thourougly. You also need to understand it well enough to be able to explain it to your patients together with the central concepts related to quality of life (QOL). We have developed the new theories of existence to obtain this clinical proficiency, so we have been forced to make them very clear and simple.

Introduction

We have already elaborated on the meaning of life (1) and have discussed a new theory, that we have called the holistic process theory of healing (2,3). Before you can understand the holistic proces of healing or make it work in the clinic, you need to understand human existence thourougly. You also need to understand it well enough to be able to explain it to your patients together with the central concepts related to quality of life (QOL). We have developed the new theories of existence to obtain this clinical proficiency, so we have been forced to make them very clear and simple.

The first theories of existence of this kind were put forward by Carl Gustav Jung (1875-1961) (4), the famous student of Sigmund Freud (1856-1939). His well-known model of the structure of the ego and the true self are shown in figure 1 (4). We have now managed to make surprisingly simple models of the purpose of life (1), the ego, the conditions for the unfolding of the unique talent of every human being, the problems of human development especially in childhood, and finally of the nature of the evil side of man (the shadow, the anti-self), that collides with our deepest intention as human beings trying to be and do good.

The theories of existence put forward are the results of a decade of research and philosophy in the connection between quality of life, disease and health (5-11) and clinical work with several hundreds of patients in holistic therapy using the models (12,13). The intent that brought us to the theories was the intent of giving support, holding and holistic medical treatments to our patients. Recently the fruit of this positive development in Denmark, Norway and Israel was expressed in the holistic process theory of healing (2). This theory is now making the basis for the development of a clinical and holistic medicine (14-17).

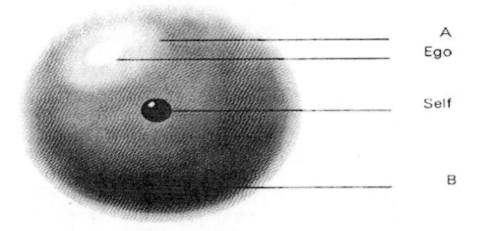

The psyche can be compared to a
sphere with a bright field (A) on its
surface, representing consciousness.
The *ego* is the field's center (only if
"I" know a thing is it conscious).
The *Self* is at once the nucleus
and the whole sphere (B); its internal
regulating processes produce dreams.

Figure 1. The famous, classical picture by CG Jung (4) of the vast human existence with the true self in the middle, and the tiny ego on the surface (A), surrounded by a minute, white spot of consciousness, and besides that darkness and unconsciousness (B). The core of existence (the self) is similar to the purpose of life in the life mission theory (1).

The main arguments why these five theories are important, is that they seem to complement the reductionistic medical model of mainstream medicine in a beautiful and non-contradictory way. You are an organism containing both advanced genetically determined, biochemical pathways, and you are a living wholeness, conscious and alive, with love, feeling and sexuality not reducible to mere chemistry.

Given the wide range of existential theories, some justifications for choosing these five theories should be given, but this is difficult. Any theory that is not in conflict with known facts and which really helps the patients, seems to be valid, and many such theories might be valid at the same time, as they express different perspectives on life and existence. So the argument here is not that we now are to present the final theories on human existence, but that we find these theories in accordance with the know facts of life, and also highly practical in our clinical work.

They seem to support a pretty theory of the holistic process of healing, which we have found of tremendous value to our chronic patients. This does not make the five theories true, but in our opinion gives this fact a certain beauty to the five theories that is appealing. The abstract nature of the theories is also appealing, because as soon as you understand the theories, many phenomenons, which looked complex and complicated before, now look simple and easy to understand. This is the case not only to us as therapist or consultant, but also to our patients and clients. This is the main reason why we find the five theories of existence useful and trustworthy.

Understanding human existence

With this series of existential theories we are going to present in this journal, we hope to show that the human existence can be understood in depths. We also hope that this understanding of the human being, even in the most dark and hidden corners, will in the end be joyful. The human being according to the life mission theory (1) and the derived theories is "good" and we believe that we all have the possibility for making true and ethical choices in life in order to get to know ourselves better, to integrate our hidden resources and talents (and also our black shadow) so that we can create the good life. The good life, where we become valuable for each other and to ourselves.

The theories are based on the life mission theory (1), which claims that the human being from the beginning of his existence had a constructive purpose of life, which at the same time also is our greatest talent. When we learn to use this talent, we become not only happy, but also healthy and well functioning in our relations to ourselves and the surrounding world. When a human being denies and suppresses himself, he or she becomes ill, unhappy and malfunctioning. We believe that you need to find your true self and live in balance according with your life purpose, which will be the very best medicine (18,19) for you, even at the end of your life (20).

To realize your life purpose

However it is not that easy to realize your life purpose, because in our personal history every human being has at one point in time or another suffered defeat or failed in realizing the life purpose. According to the theory presented in this journal, an overwhelming pain early in life has caused a denial of the purpose. This denial is a highly self-destructive intention, which precisely balances against the constructive and more fundamental life purpose.

We sometimes find ourselves in an existential dilemma, where we cannot let go of the painful and often troublesome life-purpose, because if we do that we will die, as the purpose of life is the only reason we have to live. The intended self-destruction is therefore the only way that the human being (in this case the child during childhood) can get out of the dilemma in order to survive and adapt. In defining a new life purpose, the earlier life purposes will be repressed, both the positive and the negative ones. The human being ends up being an adult unconscious about his or her strengths and weaknesses, about his or her "white and black" sides. This is exactly the scenario put forward by Jung (see Figure 1).

Holistic process

In order to start all over again the human being has to heal. The holistic process theory (2) explains how healing happens. When the human being gets and accepts the acknowledgement or respect and care, which was originally lacked, these frozen memories from the past comes out to surface the consciousness and can now be integrated. From now on the human being can return to his or her natural condition.

The holistic process of healing can be very effective in a group process and the last article explains, which principles counts in the existential group therapy. Principally this therapy can be used on every human being, no matter which illness or sickness the human being suffers from.

This means we can offer an effective therapy, also in the occasions where the etiology of the suffering is not understood. This means that the initial exploration by the medical diagnosticians, which is often a period of waiting for the patient, can happen at the same time of the treatment and therefore a lot of expensive examinations, testing and long hospitalisation avoided.

We have published two articles, which documents success in pilot studies with existential group therapy done with patients suffering from chronic pains and alcoholism (15,16). Not only did the patient get healthier, but their the quality of life improved. It looks like the holistic medicine can mobilize resources within the person.

Our hope

We hope the holistic medicine build on the new and deeper understanding of man will develop into an attractive complementary and alternative to the established biomedicine, which we would call the "new medicine". In the Research Clinic for Holistic Medicine in Copenhagen, we are now developing new cures based on the holistic process theory for patients, that cannot be helped sufficiently with the drugs of the biomedicine.

We want to help our patients to development of high quality of life, a better health and an improved ability of functioning, through the mobilization of the hidden resources within the patient, even in the last time of our lives (20). This is the reason that we expanded on the life mission theory (1) (see chapter 20) with four more theories (21-24) on other aspects of life:

- The structure of the life purpose and the ego
- Theory of talent
- Theory on child development
- Theory of the anti-self (the shadow) or the evil side of man (see chapter 21).

References

[1]   Ventegodt S. The life mission theory: A theory for a consciousness-based medicine. Int J Adolesc Med Health 2003;15(1):89-91.
[2]   Ventegodt S, Andersen NJ, Merrick J. Holistic Medicine III: The holistic process theory of healing. ScientificWorldJournal 2003;3:1138-46.
[3]   Ventegodt S, Andersen NJ, Merrick J. Principles of existential holistic group therapy and the holistic process of healing in a group setting. ScientificWorldJournal 2003;3:1388-400.
[4]   Jung CG. Man and his symbols. New York: Anchor Press, 1964.

[5]   Ventegodt S, Andersen NJ, Merrick J. Quality of life philosophy: when life sparkles or can we make wisdom a science? ScientificWorldJournal 2003;3:1160-3.

[6]   Ventegodt S, Andersen NJ, Merrick J. QOL philosophy I: Quality of life, happiness, and meaning of life. ScientificWorldJournal 2003;3:1164-75.

[7]   Ventegodt S, Andersen NJ, Merrick J. Quality of life philosophy II. What is a human being ? ScientificWorldJournal 2003;3:1176-85.

[8]   Ventegodt S, Andersen NJ, Merrick J. Quality of life philosophy III. Towards a new biology: Understanding the biological connection between quality of life, disease and healing. ScientificWorldJournal 2003;3:1186-98.

[9]   Ventegodt S, Andersen NJ, Merrick J. Quality of life philosophy IV. The brain and consciousness. ScientificWorldJournal 2003;3:1199-1209.

[10] Ventegodt S, Andersen NJ, Merrick J. Quality of life philosophy V. Seizing the meaning of life and becoming well again. ScientificWorldJournal 2003;3:1210-29.

[11] Ventegodt S, Andersen NJ, Merrick J. Quality of life philosophy VI. The concepts. ScientificWorldJournal 2003;3:1230-40.

[12] Ventegodt S. Philosophy of life that heals. [Livsfilosofi der helbreder]. Copenhagen: Forskningscenterets Forlag, 1999. [Danish].

[13] Ventegodt S. Quality of life as medicine [Livskvalitet som medicin.] Copenhagen: Forskningscenterets Forlag, 2001. [Danish].

[14] Ventegodt S, Andersen NJ, Merrick J. Holistic medicine: Scientific challenges. ScientificWorldJournal 2003;3:1108-16.

[15] Ventegodt S, Merrick J, Andersen NJ. Quality of life as medicine. A pilot study of patients with chronic illness and pain. ScientificWorld Journal 2003;3:520-32.

[16] Ventegodt S, Merrick J, Andersen NJ. Quality of life as medicine II: A pilot study of a five-day "quality of life and health" cure for patients with alcoholism. ScientificWorldJournal 2003;3:842-52.

[17] Ventegodt S, Clausen B, Langhorn M, Kromann M, Andersen NJ, Merrick J. Quality of life as medicine III. A qualitative analysis of the effect of a five day intervention with existential holistic group therapy or a quality of life course as a modern rite of passage. ScientificWorldJournal 2004;4:124-33.

[18] Spiegel D, Bloom JR, Kraemer HC, Gottheil E. Effect of psychosocial treatment on survival of patients with metastatic breast cancer. Lancet 1989;2(8668):888-91.

[19] Ornish D. Love and survival. The scientific basis for the healing power of intimacy. Perennial, NY: HarperCollins, 1999.

[20] Merrick J, Ventegodt S. What is a good death ? To use death as a mirror and find the quality of life. BMJ Rapid Response 2003 Oct 31.

[21] Ventegodt S, Andersen NJ, Merrick J. The life mission theory II. The structure of the life purpose and the ego. ScientificWorldJournal 2003;3:1277-85.

[22] Ventegodt S, Andersen NJ, Merrick J. The life mission theory III. Theory of talent. ScientificWorldJournal 2003;3:1286-93.

[23] Ventegodt S, Merrick J. The life mission theory IV. Theory on child development. ScientificWorldJournal 2003;3:1294-301.

[24] Ventegodt S, Andersen NJ, Merrick J. The life mission theory V. Theory of the anti-self (the shadow) or the evil side of man. ScientificWorldJournal 2003;3:1302-13.

Chapter 20

The life mission theory
and understanding existential healing

Genetic factors, external stress and what we call "the human factor" are influential in the health and well-being of every person. Several studies have shown that the human being have many internal powers that can promote health and increase quality of life. A theory on the human meaning of life is put forward and how it relates to health, disease and quality of life in the context of holistic medicine.

Introduction

The basic factors that influence health and disease can be divided into three categories: genetic factors, external stressors and traumas, as well as positive factors such as social network and medical treatment, and finally the purely "human" factor concerned with lifestyles, free will, philosophy of life and the quality of their lives. Studies of the role of this "human" factor (1,2) indicated that many patients have major and unexplained powers to promote their own health. This short communication sketches a possible explanation that draws on classical psychodynamic and psycho¬somatic theory.

The theory

The phases listed below chart the life and disease history of an individual (II-VII). At the outset, let us assume that a human being begins his or her existence with a plan or an ambition for a good and healthy life. We may put this assumption of a primordial plan in quite abstract terms:

I. Life mission. Let us assume that at the moment of conception all the joy, energy and wisdom that our lives are capable of supporting are expressed in a "decision" as to the purpose of our lives. This first "decision" is quite abstract and all-en¬compassing and holds the intentions of the entire life for that individual. It may be called the personal mission or the life mission. This mission is the meaning of life for that individual. It is always constructive and sides with life itself.

II. Life pain. The greatest and most fundamental pain in our lives derives from the frustrations encountered, when we try to achieve our personal mission, be they frustrated attempts to satisfy basic needs or the failure to obtain desired psychological states.

III. Denial. When the pain becomes intolerable we can deny our life mission by making a counter-decision, which is then lodged in the body and the mind, partially or entirely cancelling the life mission.

IV. Repair. One or several new life intentions, more specific than the original life mission, may now be chosen relative to what is possible henceforth. They replace the original life mission and enable the person to move forward again. They can, in turn, be modified, when they encounter new pains experienced as unbearable. (Example: Mission #1: "I am good." Denial #1: "I am not good enough." Mission #2: "I will become good," which implies I am not).

V. Repression and loss of responsibility. The new life intention, which corresponds to a new perspective on life at a lower level of responsibility, is based on an effective repression of both the old life mission and the counter-decision that antagonises and denies it. Such a repression causes the person to split in a conscious and one or more unconscious/ subconscious parts. The end result is that we deny and repress parts of ourselves. Our new life intention must always be consistent with what is left undenied.

VI. Loss of physical health. Human consciousness is coupled to the wholeness of the organism through the information systems that bind all the cells of the body into a unity. Disturbances in consciousness may thus disturb the organism's information systems, resulting in the cells being less perfectly informed as to what they are to do where.

Disruptions in the necessary flow of information to the cells of the organism and tissues hamper the ability of the cells to function properly. Loss of cellular function¬ality may eventually result in disease and suffering.

VII. Loss of quality of life and mental health. In psychological and spiritual terms, people who deny their personal mission gradually lose their fundamental sense that life has meaning, direction and coherence. They may find that their joy of life, energy to do important things and intuitive wisdom are slowly petering out. The quality of their lives is diminished and their mental health impaired.

IIX. Loss of functionality. When we decide against our life mission we invalidate our very existence. This shows up as reduced self-worth and self-confidence. Thus, the counter-decisions compromise not only our health and quality of life, but also our basic powers to function physically, psychologically, socially, at work, sexually, etc.

Applying the theory

Spiegel et al (1) asked women with metastatic breast cancer to talk to each other in group sessions about their illness. As described in the article, the women made an effort to improve the quality of their lives. Survival improved radically, relative to a control group. This may be accounted for as follows. When people confront and deal with still more of their destructive cognitions or attitudes to life, then the counter-decisions recorded in their bodies and minds results in the repressed pain to resurface in consciousness to be dealt with and the fragmentation of the person slowly ceases. We heal and we become whole. Since the fragmentation is one of the causes of the disease resulting in decreased quality of life and ability to function, the internal repair will enable the person to become more healthy, happy and functional. The inner qualities of joy, energy and wisdom re-express themselves. Other things being equal, there will be prophylactic effects on new outbreaks of disease, accidents and loss of functionality.

Ornish et al (2) induced patients with coronary arteries severely constricted from atherosclerosis to adopt lifestyle changes and deal with the quality of their lives. This had beneficial effects on the arterial constrictions, as compared with a control group.

The life mission theory may explain this by reference to the systematic efforts exerted by the patients to modify their behaviours and the attitudes that go along with them. This means that people work to relinquish destructive attitudes to life that deny the life mission. As this denial recedes, the person more or less returns to his or her natural state of health, quality of life and ability to function.

The theory predicts that, for example, that when a person is helped along by a family physician conducting a conversation (clinical interview or consultation) about the quality of life of that person, she can reestablish her life mission. The person can then recognize it as the proper purpose in her life. She can rearrange her life accordingly and achieve her truest sense of humanity, a human being in full agreement with herself and life. This person can draw on her resources and potentials to the fullest degree. In her natural state, a human being is maximally valuable to herself and the world around her.

A consciousness-oriented (holistic) medicine based on this theory will help people become valuable not only to themselves, but also to each other.

References

[1]   Spiegel D, Bloom JR, Kraemer HC, Gottheil E. Effect of psychosocial treatment on survival of patients with metastatic breast cancer. Lancet 1989; 2(8668):888-91.

[2]   Ornish D, Brown SE, Scherwitz LW, Billings JH, Armstrong WR, Ports TA, Kirkeeide RL, Brand RJ, Gould KL. Can lifestyle changes reverse coronary heart disease? The Lifestyle Heart Trial. Lancet 1990;336(8708):129-33.

Chapter 21

The anti-self (the shadow) or the evil side of man

Something that constantly follows the concept of human existence are the concepts of good and evil. When it comes to sexuality, the concept of the animalistic self (Freud's Id) is followed by the concept of a constructive force (the *Eros*) and the corresponding concept of the destructive, evil force, the Thanatos. Freud postulated that human beings are dominated by these two basic instincts, Eros being the sexual drive or creative life force and Thanatos the death force or destructiveness. As we shall see (see section seven), sexuality plays an important role in holistic healing of mental disorders.

As discussed by Katchadourian (see below) psychological analyses of sexual excitement have often revieled all kinds of evil feelings and intents, like hatred and revenge towards the woman (the mother), as the basis of sexual arousal in the most known human form. To understand man and his shadow, including all dominant and submissive, masochistic and sadistic elements of sexuality, it is nessesary to understand the human evilness in such depth as not to cendemn it, but instead to accept it fully.

The ideal holistic physician, psychiatrist, or sexologists can honestly say: "Nothing human is strange for me". First when we have integrated the evil are we able to penetrate into the remotest corner of the human sexuality with our consiousness and light of understanding we will be able to give our most construtive help to other people with sexual issues.

According to the life mission theory (see chapter 19), the essence of man is his purpose of life, which comes into existence at conception. This first purpose is always positive and in support of life. This is not in accordance with the everyday experience, that man also engages in evil enterprises born out of destructive intensions. This chapter presents a theory of the evil side of man, called "anti-self" (the shadow), because it mirrors the self and its purpose of life. The core of the anti-self is an evil and destructive intention just opposite the intention behind the life-mission.

The evil side of man arises when, as the life mission theory proclaims, man is denying his good, basic intention to avoid existential pain. The present theory of the anti-self claims that all the negative decision accumulated throughout the personal story, sums up to a negative or dark anti-self, as complex, multifaceted and complete as the self.

All the negative decisions taken trough personal history builds this solid, negative, existential structure. The anti-self, or shadow as Carl Gustav Jung used to call it, is a precise reflection of man's basically good and constructive nature. When mapped it seems that for most or even for all the many fine talents of man, there is a corresponding evil intention and talent in the person's anti-self. As man is as evil as he is good, he can only realize his good nature and constructive talents though making ethical choices. Ethics therefore seems to be of major importance to every patient or person engaged in the noble project of personal growth.

Understanding the nature and structure of the evil side of man seems mandatory to every physician or therapist offering existential therapy to his patient. The theory of anti-self makes it possible to treat patients with destructive behavioural patterns, who deep in their heart want to be good, by helping them let go of their evil intentions. The anti-self seems also to explain the enigma of why the human being often commit suicide.

Integrating the shadow lead to often dramatic, subjective experiences, of ubiquitous light in an unpersonal form, of enlightenment, or of meeting light and consciousness in a personal, universal form, known as G-d.

Introduction

Man has a free will, acknowledged by philosophers of all times, and by using this will man can either do good or become engaged in evil intentions and by doing so, assumes often grotesque and inhuman forms. Numerous are the examples of such demonic beings, like Lord Dracula, Hannibal the Cannibal or Jack the Ripper. What seems to be even more scary is that we daily are facing seemingly normal men and woman being caught as child molesters, criminals of war, rapists, and the like in the media. Everybody seems to have the potential of being evil, and it seems as easy to be evil as it is to be good; hence the existential choice and the free will.

History is packed with examples of people abusing their power to live out their dark side. During the Inquisition it is estimated, that between five and ten million innocent people was burned alive as witches in the name of Jesus by the ministers of Europe (1,2) and six million Jews (one million children) killed by the Germans during the Holocaust. Thus, even religious ministers, who should be the representatives of G-d, the most devoted guards of the good, cannot reproach themselves from the shadow, the dark side of man, or the evil side.

The yoke of heaven, or the abstract guiding principle of mankind, must be for everyone to know what his task is in this world and to understand the principles of the universe, or the ways of G-d, the Divine ideas and the way mankind should choose in order to achieve his purpose in life (3-6). There has been a lot of research in the nature and source of the evil motives of man. Sigmund Freud (1856-1939) explained the evil side of man as a natural force: a basic urge or instinct of moving towards death. Along with the sexual instinct this constitute the two essential urges in man, the two only real motivators (4). Carl Gustav Jung (1875-1961), the grand student of Freud, studied the shadow intensely and he has described it maybe better than anyone (5). Jung had a complicated relationship to the shadow, since he apparently on the one hand thought that the shadow, the dark side of man, contains a substantial developing potential that is set free, when we attempt to integrate the shadow, but on the other hand believed that the shadow never can be completely eliminated or defeated.

Studies of the dynamics of therapeutic interventions with existential therapy based on the life mission theory (6-9) shows, that the dark side of man has a relatively simple structure.

When the structure of the shadow is worked out and eventually mapped during therapy, it can be integrated, if the patient chooses to let go of it (8). The understanding of the general nature and structure of the dark side of man is important in this work with the patient.

If a person succeeds to re-intend his true life-mission, he will often be almost ecstatically happy in his sensation of having found himself and his inner truth. Soon after he will often feel in pain, because he reaches contact with the original situation, where he was unable to make a difference. The strong intensity of the positive emotions that is found around the purpose of life can be explained in terms of all the good that is repressed in man. The often overwhelming intensity of the life-pain explains why the mission of life is often repressed throughout life and why the evil side is often preferred for the good.

Self and anti-self, life purpose and anti-purpose

According to the life mission theory (6), the life purpose is so painful in the beginning of our life that we end up denying and repressing it. We repress it by intending the opposite of the original positive intention behind our purpose of life. This very negative intention is also repressed as we assume another constructive purpose of life. Soon after, this new positive purpose is also denied by a negative intention and so forth. So during our upbringing both the positive and the negative intentions of man are repressed from the surface of consciousness, and forced into the famous, but mysterious un-consciousness.

When carefully sought for, the repressed intentions can be found as "gestalts" carrying both cognitive and emotional data, in split up parts or "pockets" of our biological existence. In body therapy these pockets are known as "blockages": tissue areas with a strange tense quality to them. The blockages releases the gestalts to the consciousness of the person, when competently contacted in the therapy. It seems that these gestalts, even after many years, still are potentially very active, and they surface as soon as the person calls upon the destructive intentions, as it can happen in a headless moment of furry or anger. The dark side then takes over and the person is for a period of time out of conscious control. He or she seems to be very present and awake, but is not really, as the gestalts has taken the person and drawn him back in time.

The philosophical question is here if the person could have acted otherwise with a higher ethical standard. This is a very difficult issue giving birth to the discussion of insanity in the moment of crime, which in many countries releases the person for responsibility according to the law.

Most normal persons of our time have most of their good as well as most of their evil intentions suppressed. All the repressed, positive intentions in a person are basically pulling the same way, and are summed up to our unconscious, good side. In the same way all our repressed, negative intensions are summed up to our unconscious, evil side. In the normal person, who does not know himself very well, the good and the evil forces are mostly unconscious and of almost same size, since they quite accurate equilibrate each other (10). The unconscious man functions opportunistic, since he is shifting between the good and the evil intensions, from situation to situation, according to what is most suitable in the given situation in relation to survival and satisfaction of needs. Such a person does not take conscious ownership of his own intentions; therefore he projects both the good and the evil to the surrounding world and its people, and therefore he cannot live his life with much strength. He is not in control of his own existence (11).

When man becomes more conscious, he acknowledges that he has to choose between the good and the evil. As he grows he must confront the basic ethical choice in life. Since the two sides, good and evil, are balancing each other, man is free to choose between the good and the evil; the choice decides which side that will consciously be lived out. The side that is not chosen by the half-conscious man, will however not disappear, but is projected to the surrounding world. A person, who chooses to be good, is in this phase of his personal growth denying his own hidden evilness, and can now only indirectly observe this denied black side, which appears as evilness and darkness around him. Unfortunately the repressed evil intensions are still highly active in man and more so if he consciously chooses the good as he unconsciously still balance the good and the evil to avoid the severe existential pain that according to the life mission theory is inevitably linked to the un-denied life purpose. Very often the "ethical person" ends up in a colourful and dramatic battle with his own shadow, unwillingly and unconsciously causing harm to self and others (12).

The conclusion is that evilness is difficult to get rid of. Even the person, who consciously chooses to be good, will often unconsciously be evil, but still this person is likely to be far less evil than the opportunist, who lives completely without ethics. The person, who on the contrary chooses the evil and denies the good, will in spite of this be unconsciously good, but still worse that the opportunistic. The hidden goodness and the internal battle between the good and the evil in man explains why the person, who in his madness chooses the evil path to solve his problems, is often not succeeding in living out his evilness, but ends up stuck in his own existential problems (13).

The person, who admits to contain positive as well as negative intensions in his unconsciousness, and strive to embrace both with his existence, can by time observe and acknowledge both sides in himself and can thereby gradually take responsibility for all aspects of his existence. This person develops and grows, and will gradually be able to let go of the negative decisions that sums up to be his dark side, his anti-self, or the shadow-side that prevents him to live out his mission in life and express his true self. Existential therapy, which makes use of this knowledge about self and anti-self, can therefore help people to integrate their dark, negative side, and express themselves fully (14).

The creation of the anti-self ("the shadow")

In our true and natural state of being, all our intentions and talents are centred round our life mission. This set of intentions is how we express our true self, but very often only a fraction of our natural power and potential is lived as we live through our ego (15-17). Our ego appears as we deny our purpose of life and our secondary purposes, one by one, with a row of negative decisions. This is continuing until only a small part of our inherent nature and talents is left operational.

Most people over 20 years of age actively deny all, or almost all, of the central aspects in their true self. This happens as a consequence of adaptation. This way everybody ends up having a white aspect of the self for every talent and good intention in life, and a corresponding black aspect for every evil intention and destructive talent. The evil outbalances the good. Man is at peace, but often bored with life, and many people of our time experience their existence as almost meaningless.

As man develops his consciousness about himself, he moves from being chaotic to being polarized, as he obtains the ability to discriminate between the good and the evil within himself. Now he sees that all the negative, black intentions are basically turned towards life, while all the positive, white intensions are supporting life. Black and white are outbalancing each other, and the dark side has annulated the purpose of life.

In other words, our black, or self-destructive, side is appearing as our dark shadow, which precisely is cowering our positive self (the "life mission flower", except the little place that is left back without denial and which gives rise to our ego (see figure 1 and 2 in 15)). The shadow is accordingly, technically seen, the difference between our true self and our ego.

The anatomy of the shadow

The shadow hence is a set of destructive intentions, which is organised in exactly the same way as our true self, where the set of good intentions are assembled in the life mission flower round the purpose of life (15).

The centre of shadow is the intention destroying the purpose of life most directly, called the anti-life-mission or anti-life-purpose.

The shadow therefore appears as a negative copy of the personality, as its black parallel (see figure 1). The purpose of establishing the shadow during our personal history was to weaken the good intentions, that couldn't be realized in early childhood and therefore became too painful.

Because the shadow has developed into a copy of the true self, it looks as if the whole shadow can be given life, if man using the power of his fee will choose to adopt the negative perspective, which lies in the denial of his life mission. The new mission of life for this person is the evil anti-life-mission. Now, in the worst-case scenario, we have the serial killer in action.

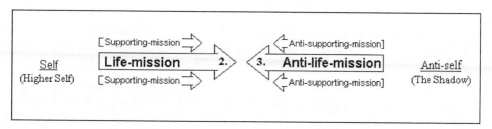

Figure 1. The life-mission as well as all the supporting missions is repressed, and man does not know himself. The repression has happened through negative anti-decisions, which outbalance the positive missions. The negative decisions are hence anti-self intentions that are organized around the most basic self-denial - the negative decisions that are here called anti-life-missions. All of these anti-self intentions exist in the parts of us that are still active, even though they are repressed; they sum up to be one self-destructive intentional structure in us, here called the anti-self.

An example: From "i am good" to "i am evil"

An easy understandable example is the following: This person had as life mission the sentence "I am good". The anti-life-purpose was the complete opposite: "I am evil". This person used one of the two in an opportunistic way. If he chooses to be good he would repress his evil side. If he chooses to be evil, he would repress his good side. The original purpose of this destructive intention was to outbalance the intention about being good, so that the pain of not being able to do any good was eliminated early in life.

What makes man choose evil?

There seems to be huge emotional advantages for the person being evil, since this identity is often far less existential painful, because you inflict somebody else the pain. This is opposite to being good, where it is often your self, who suffers. If a person chooses consciously to be evil, all of the black shadow-flower will be this new person's personality, to a high degree free of emotional pain (6).

A feeling of enormous power is set free in man, when the anti-mission is re-intended and all of the repressed, negative supporting-missions and destructive talents that is organized around the anti-mission, is activated. This is typically experienced as a wild roar, even ecstasy, of raw power and animalistic strength (19). Most people have a sense of reason, which makes them live in the head preventing both the extremely constructive as well as the extremely destructive perspective of life to manifest itself.

The experience of intensity and energy without any life-pain can peak in a sheer delight of domination; "Satanic pleasure" seems to be the most appropriate designation for this intense joy of the dark side.

The dynamic of the shadow

All the good in man comes from his purpose of life, which expresses the essence of our true self. According to the life mission theory the mission is always good, and it is stabile throughout life. It is often so repressed and suppressed in man, that it cannot be known, expressed, and lived out. The evil exists correspondingly as an anti-mission, that expresses the opposite of our profound self. The anti-self is as stable as the self, but has a destructive nature and intention.

The intentions of average people from the western world of today are not focused towards either the positive or the negative. Life is not guided neither by the mission or the anti-mission. Rather the intention is presented as an in-between of these to. This means that the ordinary, unconscious person does not have much drive, energy, and enthusiasm. His direction in life is confused. Both the good and the evil is seen as non-self, and projected on the outside world. Thus man is usually not ascribing himself any special strengths or talents, or any specific significance.

Many people of our time do see themselves as having a great potential and working in order to express this potential though personal development. Re-intending the original mission of life and developing a more conscious relationship to existence and a clearer recognition of who one is, raises the experience of joy of life and the level of personal energy. But personal growth will also reawaken the original life pain.

A lot of people who search for themselves are therefore experiencing great difficulties. At some time everybody seemingly have to face their dark side – their own shadow. Christianity tells us the story about how Jesus got tempted in the desert by the devil promises of immense power and sovereignty, but finally chose love and the good (20,21).

When it comes to patients that are working with themselves, but seriously ill, it is especially important for the physician to know the mechanisms that are prevailing in such a situation. Supporting the patient so that he can develop himself, might lead to the patient entering the troublesome existential phase. The optimal approach for the patient is to take responsibility for his whole being including both the light and the shadow, and at the same time strive to express his white essence, the meaning and purpose of his life. To do so he has to constantly reflect upon his own participation in all aspects of reality. As he acknowledges that he contains both good as well as evil, he must carefully scrutinize all of his intentions to see if they are constructive or destructive.

The learning position is difficult, because we are fragmented in a number of parts with almost their own life, until we have confronted and integrated our historical life pains. The fragmentation happens, because of our contradictory consciousness.

Everyone owns a huge number of black and white intentions, and we all live the black as much as the white, even through we are not aware of it. The conscious, integrated and transcendent position is a tough and challenging position that brings up as mush historical life pain to the surface as we have the resources to handle. Without supply of external resources such as holding (7), the development will be slow and painful. Interestingly enough, excess of resources means that a person can move quickly forward and integrate considerable parts of repressed life pain. Hereby he will let go of a lot of negative decisions, and the shadow will become gradually smaller.

Jung did not believe that the shadow could be integrated to a situation where it disappeared, but this is exactly the classical ideal of enlightenment (5,19-21). From a theoretical point of view all life pains can be integrated until the anti-mission is gone and the fragments that are carrying the anti-mission have melted together with unity. Hence, in our sphere we still do not have the competence to process the shadow out of the world, but this is the goal that we are pursuing.

The four existential positions

Because the good and the evil is balancing inside us, before we have become conscious and have developed personally, we are from the starting point absolutely free to choose our existential position. We have identified four such positions (see figure 2). The first position is indifferent in respect to our purpose of life. The second position is on the side of the purpose. The third is on the anti-purpose side. The fourth is a balanced position, which considers both the good and the evil, and integrates both, which is the fruitful path of personal development.

1. The unconscious, opportunistic position

This position is the most common. It is not associated with the integration of the shadow and gives consequently no personal development. We live the purposes that occur to us, but there is no connection with the (personal) purpose of life. Therefore, the position is neither along with nor against the life purpose, but is being regulated by the sum of the good and the evil in the person itself. So the whole lives its own life without any particular vigour, and the fragments carrying both the good and the evil intentions are active at a low stage and result in both good and evil things that are outside control of the person. Typically, this person will, without taking notice of it, alter between the positions good, evil, and indifferent, depending upon what best serves survival and needs fulfilment. The opportunist position means that the person cannot be trusted or counted on. He/she is subject to outer circumstances, without observing its own intentions or the behaviour resulting from these intentions. When that person wakes up and realizes that he/she has to choose between the good and the evil, he/she enters into one of the positions of the half-conscious human being (23).

2. The half-conscious, ethical (or good) position

This position is not unusual. The person knows itself well enough to be aware of what life is and places itself on the side of the life. The difficulty of boosting its own life purpose without assuming the responsibility for the shadow, is that the shadow is projected outwards so that others become evil, destructive, unsympathetic or unkind.

Consequently, this position gives a polarization that pushes the evil out to the world so that the partner, the colleague or the children are now the negative ones, whereas the person itself is perpetually positive. Interestingly enough, it seems that the account of this position is not particularly positive as the shadow is somehow invited inside in a projective manner, and it is very hard for this person to get any love affair, working relations and other relations to function.

Typically, this person is accused of being dominating, manipulating or egocentric. There is much more development in the good position than in the unconscious one, where the perpetual striving for the good fails again and again due to the inevitably accompanying shadow, which on the whole spoils any aims.

However, this gives dynamics and movement, which at last leads to the person taking responsibility for the shadow, resulting in the conscious transcendent position (described below).

People who choose the good are in danger of having to fight with their own shadow side (sort of shadow boxing,), and sometimes they might justify their malice from a consideration of "to return evil for evil".

The shift to the half-conscious, evil position often take place without the person actually noticing it. From this point one might return to the resigned, unconscious starting position (24).

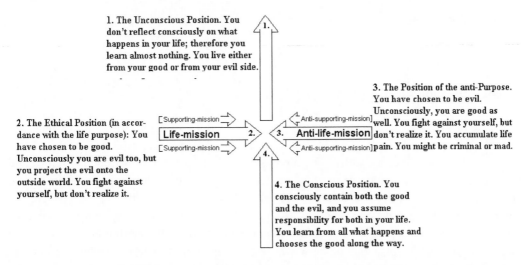

Figure 2. The human being can be unconscious and opportunistic. It can be half-conscious and choose either to be good or bad, or it can be conscious and admit both the good and the evil in itself, attempt to be good in spite of everything and learn from anything that happens.

3. The half-conscious, evil position

This position is rare and it has terrible consequences. It is the position of the evil father, evil mother, Satanist or deliberate criminal. When we perceive our true nature as our anti-purpose and choose to comply with it, we become completely evil persons. The good is projected onto the outside world and becomes the issue to be fought or spoiled. If we do not know ourselves extremely well, i.e. both our good and evil sides, it can be very difficult to understand the person, who chooses the evil. However, the evil has many existential advantages. To begin with we intended the anti-purpose in order to survive and get out of excruciating life pain, and actually we survived; so as a start the evil has allowed us to keep life. Later on in life, choosing the evil means that we do not suffer like when choosing our good, true life purpose, which is so infinitely hard to carry into effect. In fact, the person proves a delight by choosing the evil corresponding to the pain by choosing the good. So choosing the evil is rewarded by delight in the same way like choosing the good is punished by existential pain.

Obviously, this is only at the beginning as long as we are not whole. When we heal we realize that the pain that prevented us from carrying out the life purpose will be balanced by the joy of living. The pleasure of revenge is then caught up by a dreadful sorrow about hurting others, because this is in fact the opposite of what we really want, since we want to make ourselves useful to the world. Our life purpose is always good. Choosing the evil is not a solution at sight, but can be experienced as joyful and releasing at the very moment, where we break through to the lowest existential layer. The difficulty of choosing the evil is that we create even more pain for ourselves than we already had. This makes it still more difficult to awaken to a conscious position. Usually, people sink to a resigned, unconscious position at a lower existential stage than before choosing the evil. However, it is possible to help this person along to reach the conscious, transcendent position provided the person itself wants to be helped to understand what the whole life scene is about. A positive attitude and unconditional love can sometimes help the bad person on to the position of the conscious human being (25).

4. The conscious learning position

When we clearly see that we are basically good, but unable to live our life purpose due to an awful lot of repressed life pain, we have to assume the transcendent position. We are not able to be good, we are not able to be bad. We are not able to be, but we can be conscious and learn. Right now we are not able to know ourselves. We cannot understand ourselves, but we are able to express ourselves and be alert (awake). We live consciously, but we have still no control of life. We can do our utmost well knowing that at this stage it is not good enough. The consciousness is painful and sweet at the same time. Meaningfulness is the finest sweetness, but being conscious of the powerlessness is painful. The understanding that the way forward is the way back to life, through confrontation of the historic sufferings is animating. This is possible as an adult, but not as a child. The conscious position implies that the old life pains break out to the surface and are gradually admitted. When the comprehension is clear, a chaotic historic life scene is crystallized into one single or a few negative resolutions that can be let off now. So this life is in motion onward, is cleared, and the true life is returning slowly, without any inhibition, without any inner contrast or reluctance. So the consciously transcendent position, essentially to certify our own life, is a deep reflection of our soul, regardless of how painful it is to see the truth. This is what makes life evolve optimally (26).

One of the most difficult questions is why so few people reach the conscious learning position. The main obstacles seem to fall into two categories: inner and outer. The inner obstacle seems to be existential pain, as discussed above. The outer obstacles seem to be the need for social acceptance. A person who is learning must be honest himself, which can be hard sometimes in an environment where other people are "playing games" and not willing to make a learning effort. This means that a person in the process about learning about him/herself is also a source for learning in his or her environment. But learning goes together with existential pain, so this person actually often involuntarily inflicts pain on the people near and dear to him. So it seems that people in the conscious, learning position need people of their own kind to socialise with. This is maybe the most severe obstacle facing the patient entering holistic existential therapy. You are entering a world of learning, of joys, meaning and suffering, where most people do not go. So you will have to face loneliness and you will have to seek new friends. It is important for the holistic physician or therapist to build networks of patients and clients in personal growth, to avoid the feeling of being completely alone and to avoid the patient to be drawn into milieus and religious sects. This would not help the person in growth and possibly also hinder the person's self-actualization in the long run.

It is also very important to understand that the loneliness experienced when entering the learning process is often overwhelming, tempting the patient to choose position three (the half-conscious, evil position) instead, or even in the extreme tempting the patient to consider suicide. Often the suicidal patient is caught in between the positions two and four, two or three, or three and four. If the holistic physician can help the patient to understand the situation from an existential and developmental perspective, the patient will realize that entering position four is to prefer to suicide, even if this position is emotionally very difficult. To die is really not the problem; the problem is to live, and to live a full and conscious life. As the Russian saying goes: "Death is easy, life is difficult".

Relevance of the existential therapy

The classical Greek virtues: beauty, goodness and truth, reflect three levels of the existence, which Kierkegaard called the esthetical, the ethical and the religious layers in man (27). Søren Aabye Kierkegaard (1813-1855) was a prolific writer in the period called the "golden age" in Denmark of intellectual and artistic activity with work in the fields of philosophy, theology, psychology, literary criticism and fiction. He was a social critique and wanted to renew Christian faith within Christendom. He is known as the "father of existentialism", but also for his critiques of Hegel and the German romantics, his contributions to the development of modernism, his literary experimentation and talents to analyse and revitalise Christian faith. He burned with the passion of a religious poet, was armed with extraordinary dialectical talent, and drew on vast resources of erudition.

In the integrative quality of life theory (28), the dimension of beauty is reflected by man's superficial layer connected with well-being and satisfaction, needs fulfilment and ability to function. The ethical layer deals with life expansion, whereas the religious layer concerns the meaning of life and a deep inner balance.

Through the theory of the anti-self, the ethical layer becomes accessible for the existential therapy. The good and the evil manifest themselves in the patient as well as in the consciousness of the therapist and the patient is temporarily able to enter into the evil valence in order to confront it, mirrored from the outside by the therapist, and from the inside by its own good side. Through this double reflection, the light of the consciousness is thrown onto the patient's dark side, which brings the historic conglomerate of negative experiences and decisions amounting to man's dark side, the anti-self or shadow, to collapse in a series of painful memory pictures, which can be belaboured subsequently and integrated one at the time, e.g. by group therapy. By this process, the patient goes from the surface, the esthetical, first to the ethical layer and then, simultaneously with the inner contrasts being admitted and transcended, onto the deepest existential layer, which Kierkegaard called the religious (27).

Discussion

It connection with severe illness it is often relevant to look at the unconscious evil. When for instance one partner in a relationship is severely ill and the other is completely healthy, fit, extremely good and considerate, this couple may have an unconscious agreement that one of them carries the darkness for them both, whereas the other partner carries the light. The bright, healthy party often appears full of energy, most considerate and thoroughly devoted. At a closer analysis, the good party will at first appear dominating and later actually condemning and dissociating towards to the "evil" and ill party. Additionally, it often turns out that the apparently good has not in fact good intentions or love towards its ill partner. The bad side has been projected forth and over to the partner, who is now the intolerable and negative partner. The ill partner is not seen and met, and feels typically lonesome and unloved in spite of the healthy partner's apparent goodness and helpfulness. This loneliness and lack of mental meeting and understanding is typical of a relationship, which is dominated by shadow projections. If the ill partner becomes healthy it is necessary that both of them again assume the responsibility for both the bright and the dark sides. The process helping the patient to become healthy results preliminarily in the healthy partner getting more "ill". The responsibility for the dark side is being divided, and the poor fellow who carried all their common darkness can now be helped to confront and integrate its own darkness (29).

When the life purpose is clearly admitted and the negative decisions, which deny it, are found and let gone, the disorder often heals up even when this should not occur according to statistics. By means of the existential therapy which manages the shadow and brings the human being to its deepest existential layer it seems thus possible to induce the spiritual arousal, which is so typical indeed in connection with the "spontaneous remissions" of, as an example cancer (30).

Confronting and integrating the human being's dark side make it also possible for people who are persuaded to be evil, to change into seeing themselves as basically good. This change implies that their evil side has no longer free occasion to expand. The justification of the negative living, by describing the human nature as basically evil, is thus dissolved and not longer possible. The noble art of life called no-mind in the eastern traditions seems to be about suspending reason but to remain good. The famous and rare state of enlightenment seems to follow total integration of the shadow.

Conclusions

Everybody have a dark side, an evil shadow that mirrors all the beautiful and lovely aspect of their soul. Knowing this and taking responsibility for both good and evil allows the person to take the learning position and little by little develop their consciousness and transcend their "shadow". In doing this they integrate all their inner conflicts and let go of all their self-destructive decisions and attitudes, and so they become beautiful, good, and true.

Scientifically speaking, the "shadow" can only be examined by qualitative methods, where you apply your own consciousness to explore the consciousness of yourself and others. As it seems infinitely much easier to examine the shadow of the other person, friend, partner, client or patient, so everybody who wants to learn about his or her shadow is obliged to listen to the other, to know and understand himself.

A fine way to see if what is learned in general is true is to make models and theories of the shadow and test these theories against reality. If a model or theory makes therapy easier and more successful this is a good indicator that the theory in some way or another is true. But qualitative science is as tricky as consciousness itself; in the end what makes us choose a theory and call it valid is our personal liking and ability to understand life, ourself, and our patient better from it.

As everybody seemingly owns a dark side, which makes big problems for us if not realized and integrated, we suggest that the shadow should be a theme in every course of holistic treatment.

We suppose that many of the hidden resources needed to be well again are actually bound by the patents unconscious struggle with the shadow. It might be that understanding and integrating the shadow, confronting the evil, walking awake into the darkness to win over it, is the straight way to light, joy, love, self-exploration and in the end healing.

Only the one, who caries the light of consciousness and conquer the darkness of lies and unconsciousness will reach the state of transcendence described by Maslow, or the state of coherence described by Antonovsky, or the state of meaning described by Frankl (6,9,16,17). People who engage fully in the battle against the darkness often come to experience the whole universe as basically made of light. This light is often ascribed as brilliantly white and divine, or even as a unity, or a person, making it possible "to meet with G-d himself".

As this last perspective is what motivates us in our work and our lives, and what urges us to develop our precious medical science in the service of mankind, we would like to devote our final lines wholeheartedly to the divine being, or G-d. Rabbi Eleazar Ha-Kappar used to say (31): "Those who are born are destined to die; those who are dead are destined to be brought to life again, and the living are destined to be judged. It is for you to know, proclaim and be sure that he is G-d. It is said: "These words which I command you today shall be on your heart" (Deut. 6:6).

This statement to keep "these words" or G-d's commandments above our heart, mean that they supersede our own wishes and if you follow that path it should be the beginning of the redemption of mankind from bestiality and the breaking down of his egotism, the root of evil in this world (3).

He is the Maker, he is the Creator, he is the Discerner, he is the Judge, he the Witness, he the Complainant and it is he who will judge. Blessed be he in whose presence there is no wrongdoing, not forgetting, nor partiality, nor taking bribes.

Know that all is according to reckoning and let not your imagination persuade you that the grave is a place of refuge for you. Perforce you were formed and perforce you were born. Perforce you live, perforce you shall die and perforce you shall have to give a strict account before the Supreme King of kings, the Holy One, blessed be He".

So whoever believes and accept the yoke of heaven will understand the transience and unimportance of this world, as well as the eternity and infinity of the world to come, where the soul will find its permanent place. This person will also understand that the eradication of evil from this world is only a hairsbreadth of difference between his dying now and dying naturally according to his normal life span (32). Rabbi Jacob made a more simple conclusion (33): " This world is like a vestibule before the world to come. Prepare yourself that you may enter into the banquet hall".

If you are not a religiours person, you still need to deal with the good and the evil, as these poles are often highly visible in secuality. Something that constantly follows the concept of sexuality is the concept of the animalistic self (Freud's Id) and the concept of the evil.

As discussed by Katchadourian (34) psychological analyses of sexual exitement have often revealed all kinds of evil feelings and intents, like hatred and revenge towards the woman (the mother), as the basis of sexual arousal in the most known human form. To understand human nature, especailly the human shadow that contain all the dominant and submissive, masochistic and sadistic elements of sexuality it is nessesary to understand the human evilness in such depth as not to cendemn it, but instead to accept it fully.

References

[1]   Kamen H. The Spanish inquisition: a historical revision. London: Weidenfeld Nicholson, 2000.
[2]   MacCulloch D. Reformation: Europe's house divided 1490-1700. London: Allen Lane, 2003.
[3]   Kahane M. Or Haraayon. The Jewish idea. Jerusalem: Institute Publ Writings Rabbi Meir Kahane, 1996:15-33.
[4]   Freud S. Mourning and melancholia. London: Penguin, 1984.
[5]   Jung CG. Man and his symbols. New York: Anchor Press, 1964.
[6]   Ventegodt S. The life mission theory: A theory for a consciousness-based medicine. Int J Adolesc Med Health 2003;15(1):89-91.
[7]   Ventegodt S, Andersen NJ, Merrick J. Holistic Medicine III: The holistic process theory of healing. ScientificWorldJournal 2003;3: 1138-46.
[8]   Ventegodt S, Andersen NJ, Merrick J. Holistic Medicine IV: Principles of existential holistic group therapy and the holistic process of healing in a group setting. ScientificWorldJournal 2003;3:1388-400.
[9]   Ventegodt S, Andersen NJ, Merrick J. QOL philosophy V: Seizing the meaning of life and getting well again. ScientificWorldJournal 2003;3:1210-29.
[10] Swinburne R. The problem of evil. Oxford: Oxford Univ Press, 1998.
[11] Sanford JA. Evil: The shadow of reality. New York: Crossroad Publ, 1981.
[12] Abrams J, Zweig C. Meeting the shadow. The hidden power of the dark side of human nature. Los Angeles, CA: JP Tarcher, 1991.
[13] Bly R. A little handbook on the human shadow. Memphis, TN: Raccoon, 1986.
[14] Yalom I. Existential psychotherapy. New York: Basic Books, 1980.
[15] Ventegodt S, Andersen NJ, Merrick J. The life mission theory II: The structure of the life purpose and the ego. ScientificWorldJournal 2003;3:1277-85.
[16] Ventegodt S, Andersen NJ, Kromann M, Merrick J. QOL philosophy II: What is a human being? ScientificWorldJournal 2003;3:1176-85.
[17] Ventegodt S, Andersen NJ, Merrick, J. QOL philosophy VI: The concepts. ScientificWorldJournal 2003;3:1230-40.
[18] Miller WA. Make friend with your shadow. Minneapolis, MN: Augsburg Fortress Publ, 1981.
[19] Congar JP. Jung and Reich: The body as shadow. Berkeley, CA: North Atlantic Books, 1988.
[20] Sanford JA. Jung and the problem of evil. Boston, MA: Sigo Press, 1993.
[21] Franz ML. Shadow and evil in fairy tales. Boston, MA: Shambhala, 1995.
[22] Jung CG. Psychology and alchemy. Collected works of CG Jung, vol12. Princeton, NJ: Princeton Univ Press, 1968.
[23] Stein M. Jung on evil. Princeton, NJ: Princeton Univ Press, 1996.
[24] Whitmont EC. The symbolic quest. Princeton, NJ: Princeton Univ Press, 1969.
[25] Edinger EF. The mystery of the Coniunctio. Toronto: Inner City Books, 1994.
[26] Johnson RA. Owning your own shadow. San Francisco, CA: Harper, 1994.
[27] Kierkegaard S. In vino veritas. Copenhagen: Finn Suenson, 1981. [Danish].
[28] Ventegodt S, Merrick J, Andersen NJ. Quality of life theory I. The IQOL theory: An integrative theory of the global quality of life concept. ScientificWorldJournal 2003;3:1030-40.
[29] Miller WA. Your golden shadow. San Francisco, CA: Harper Row, 1989.
[30] Dige U. Cancer miracles. Århus: Forlaget Hovedland, 2000. [Danish].
[31] Mishnah, Nezikin, Avot 4:22.
[32] Kahane M. Or Haraayon. The Jewish idea. Jerusalem: Institute Publ Writings Rabbi Meir Kahane, 1996:150-1.
[33] Mishnah, Nezikin, Avot 4:16.
[34] Katchadourian HA. Fundamental of human sexuality, 5th ed. San Francisco: Holt Rinehart Winston, 1989.

Section 5. Understanding human brain

"The hard problem" is the difficulty in neuro-philosophy about how mind and matter interact. It seems like matter and consciousness exist on two fundamentally different levels. We know that we can turn the level of awareness up or down with drugs like cocaine and chloroform; we also know that the state of consciousness can be changed by drugs like LSD and psilocybin (magic mushrooms) (1-3).

But the content of human consciousness seems to be completely unaffected by such drugs. The activity of the brain has something to do with human consciousness, but seemingly only on a quantitative level. The brain is necessary for verbal and mental consciousness, but it does not determine the content of consciousness. The body does that, especially what is connected to sexuality, at least according to Freud, Jung, Reich, Searles and hundreds of psychodynamic researchers from the last century.

The problem has not been solved (4-10). We shall not claim that we have solved it either. It remains a true mystery.

In this section we look into the hardwiring of the human brain and try to map human consciousness. We model a world seemingly induced from sensory input, but for a more thorough analysis the whole world is an interpretation based on our purpose of life. The life mission theory thus seem to be better to explain the fundamental structure of human consciousness and unconsciousness that even the best biological description of the human brain known to science today.

References

[1] Grof S. LSD psychotherapy: Exploring the frontiers of the hidden mind. Alameda, CA: Hunter House, 1980.
[2] Grof S. Implications of modern consciousness research for psychology: Holotropic experiences and their healing and heuristic potential. Humanistic Psychol 2003;31(2-3):50-85.
[3] Goleman D. Healing emotions: Conversations with the Dalai Lama on the mindfulness, emotions, and health. Boston, MA: Mind Life Inst, 1997.
[4] Kelso JAS. Dynamic patterns: The self-organization of brain and behavior. Cambridge, MA: MIT Press, 1995.
[5] Kelso JAS, Engstrom DA. The complementary nature. Cambridge, MA: MIT Press, 2006.
[6] Wolfram S. A new kind of science. Champaign, IL: Wolfram Media, 2002.

[7]   Penrose R. Shadows of the mind. Oxford: Oxford Univ Press, 1996.

[8]   Hofstadter DR. I am a strange loop. New York: Basic Books, 2007.

[9]   Kandel ER, Schwartz JH. Principles of neural science. Amsterdam: Elsevier, 2000.

[10] Hermansen TD, Ventegodt S, Merrick J. Human development X: Explanation of macroevolution — top-down evolution materializes consciousness. The origin of metamorphosis. ScientificWorldJournal 2006;6:1656-66.

Chapter 22

Consciousness

Consciousness is the source of our being and the way we deal with our own consciousness often become our destiny, also concerned with our physical and mental health. Every physician should be willing to go beyond his/her own limits and to upgrade attitudes and personal belief systems for the sake of his or her patients. This is what creates the real, full and rich life. And this is also what creates health and prevents diseases. How can medical students be taught this? Well, it is not too complicated and in some of our publications we have dealt explicitly with the philosophy of life needed for being able to handle these difficult aspects of medicine. Philosophy can be read and understood, and it can be taught at medical school. Allow us to recommend that all medical students get such training.

Introduction

You could ask how much our moral values influence clinical decisions (1). Seen from a holistic perspective, the human being is much more than his body. Mind has psychic dimensions difficult to measure and turn into science, especially the soul, the spiritual level of man, that is normally acknowledged to be a wordless domain of our existence. Unfortunately, consciousness is a soul-thing. The place within our self, where we take the final judgment of our life values and major decisions in life, is hidden, unpredictable, and un-material (2).

Consciousness is the source of our being and the way we deal with our own consciousness often become our destiny, also concerned with our physical and mental health. The Danish existential philosopher Søren Kierkegaard (3) recommended to always make the most arduous and difficult choice, when confronted with a choice of something easy or something challenging.

The physician (usually the family physician) will often be the person discussing these life-forming decisions with the patient. Unfortunately, the modern physician is so absorbed in his own profession that it can be very difficult to understand how it is to be a truck driver, a cleaner, or a shopkeeper. Often the physician is not really taking the hardest of alternatives himself in his own personal life.

So the person that the patient is most likely to entrust his or her life to might be the person least able to give the inspiriting advice of seeking the challenge and running the risk.

In life the real emotional risk is too lose yourself. To put you own existence to the test. To go beyond your own limits. To upgrade your attitudes and personal belief system. This is the game of consciousness in which every physician should be involved for the sake of his or her patients. This is what creates the real, full and rich life. And this is also what creates health and prevents diseases according to our research from the Copenhagen Prospective Birth Cohort (4).

How can medical students be taught this? Well, it is not too complicated. In the recently published first and second volumes of our book series "Principles of Holistic Medicine" (5,6), we have dealt explicitly with the philosophy of life needed for being able to handle these difficult aspects of medicine.

Philosophy can be read and understood, and it can be taught at medical school. Allow us to recommend that all medical students get such training.

References

[1]   Godlee F. Learning for life. BMJ 2006;332:0-f.
[2]   Ventegodt S, Flensborg-Madsen T, Andersen NJ, Merrick J. The life mission theory VII. Theory of existential (Antonovsky) coherence: A theory of quality of life, health and ability for use in holistic medicine. ScientificWorldJournal 2005;5:377-89.
[3]   Eremita V, ed. Enten-Eller. Et Livs-Fragment [Either-Or: A fragment of life]. Copenhagen: CA Reitzel, 1843. [Danish].
[4]   Ventegodt S, Flensborg-Madsen T, Andersen NJ, Nielsen M, Morad M, Merrick J. Global quality of life (QOL), health and ability are primarily determined by our consciousness. Research findings from Denmark 1991-2004. Social Indicator Research 2005;71:87-122.
[5]   Ventegodt S, Kandel I, Merrick J. Principles of holistic medicine. Philosophy behind quality of life. Victoria, BC: Trafford, 2005.
[6]   Ventegodt S, Kandel I, Merrick J. Principles of holistic medicine. Quality of life and health. New York: Hippocrates Sci Publ, 2005.

Chapter 23

Cerebral cortex and human consciousness

The structure of human consciousness is thought to be closely connected to the structure of cerebral cortex. One of the most appreciated concepts in this regard is the Szanthagothei model of a modular building of neo-cortex. The modules are believed to organize brain activity pretty much like a computer. We looked at examples in the literature and argue that there is no significant evidence that supports Szanthagothei's model. We discuss the use of the limited genetic information, the corticocortical afferents termination and the columns in primary sensory cortex as arguments for the existence of the cortex-module. Further, we discuss the results of experiments with Luminization Microscopy (LM) colouration of myalinized fibres, in which vertical bundles of afferent/efferent fibres that could support the cortex module are identified. We conclude that sensory maps seem not to be an expression for simple specific connectivity, but rather to be functional defined. We also conclude that evidence for the existence of the postulated module or column does not exist in the discussed material. This opens up for an important discussion of the brain as functionally directed by biological information (information-directed self-organisation), and for consciousness being closely linked to the structure of the universe at large. Consciousness is thus not a local phenomena limited to the brain, but a much more global phenomena connected to the wholeness of the world.

Introduction

In our quest for a new understanding of the mysterious connection between life, matter and consciousness (1-10), we have now turned our interest towards the human brain. The structure held responsible for the structure and quality of human consciousness is the neo-cortex, the only structure that discriminates us qualitatively from the other vertebrates. Our motivation for the exploration of the life-matter-consciousness-link is our finding that quality of life, health and ability primarily is determined by our consciousness. This discovery has lead us to the interesting possibility that guided shifts in the state of consciousness and the development of self-insight with a more positive, responsible and constructive philosophy of life can be used as medicine to help cure patients. Based on this strategy we have made a series of papers setting the strategy for alleviating healing many different physical, mental, existential, and sexual diseases and health problems (11-52). Another motivation for a deep exploration of the matter-life-consciousness link is the strange fact that "holistic healing" - the healing of the patients total life and existence, including body, mind and spirit – seems to be closely connected to the patient recovering his experience of "sense of coherence" (SOC) (53-59). SOC is actually the experience that one conscious being is connected to the whole universe though our physical and mental existence (59); to bring the patient back to be an integrated part of the world seems to be the fundamental idea of all medicine, the tradition going all the way back to Hippocrates and his students (60).

Many theories concerning the neo-cortical function are based on the possible existence of discrete modules in the neo-cortex as suggested by Szentagothai (61). It is tempting to do this, because the function of neo-cortex is a lot easier to understand and modulate in a mathematical way. Unfortunately, evidence does not seem to exist concerning modules in Szentagothai's understanding, as approximately 300 µ large, discrete columns that are able to make the "building stones" of association-cortex. In this chapter, we discuss the possibility of the existence of Szentagothai's cortical modules.

Is there evidence for the cortex module of szentagothai?

Szentagothai (62), wrote "It was then (1974) that the assembly of larger tissue complexes from repetitive units of similar build - not unlike the integrated circuits in electronics technology - became an attractive conceptual model to explain how such an immense complexity in "wiring" might be put together without having to make unrealistic demands on the genetic apparatus responsible for this feat in system engineering". Szentagothai had both the genes and the microchips in his mind, when he introduced the modular concept into the association cortex. He realized that repetition of a structure coded by the genes as basis of the cortex development would economize the specific amount of information delivered by the genes. Even if we do not know of any molecular mechanism of such kind, this is a good idea, because such copy mechanism does not deal with DNA replication. Instead it deals with supra cellular patterns.

Therefore, we have gradually gotten confident with the description of such phenomena through the conception of positional information. Analogue examples such as the development of testine-villi may be described in this way and therefore modules are an attractive idea. Furthermore, genes can be thought to deliver "continuous modules" (as in visual cortex, see later), and maybe create connectivity in a closely netted, unlimited, roomy way.

About an experiment (61,63) invented to prove that association cortex is constructed by discrete modules Szentagothai (61) wrote, "Here at last is unambiguous evidence for really columnar cortical architecture". In this experiment, proteins containing injected 3H-amino acids were transported to cortical areas of the brain. After subsequent auto-photography, these experiments unveiled the finest 300 µ broad vertical columns in all layers of cortex (62-64). Szentagothai (62) wrote, "It is most interesting to compare the overall size of the columns with the arborisation pattern of individual cortico-cortical afferents as it appears in the Golgi picture. Majorossy showed that both the size and the shape of the arborisation space corresponded very closely to the columns, as delineated by the degeneration or autoradiographic tracing techniques". Consequently, this column is analogues to the termination column of the corticocortical afferent. The big question then, is if the identified 300 µ broad termination column represents the module Szentagothai tries to prove the existence of. Seemingly, he has not found evidence enough to support such kind of structure (61,62).

Szentagothai supposed that this area had a great convergence. But Goldman and Rakic (63) said: "Such clear modular pictures as those of the figure (63) are not often seen, because the injections necessarily must cover many modules that result in agglomerations of the labelled modules, often in strips". This indicates an overlap between the termination columns and why fully discrete modules seem not to exist. But, of cause, a "half discrete" module represented by the largest concentration of afferents, cannot be excluded on the basis of this.

In the cortex about 2,500,000,000 corticocortical afferents have been identified by Kandel et al (65). But cortex has not room for more than approx. 3,000,000 columns of 300 µ in diameter, only enough to supply approx. 100 afferents to each column. If then a discrete module exists, a great amount of afferents may terminate within this. Therefore, it does not seem reasonable to take the single afferents termination, as indication for the existence of superior modules.

Szentagothai supports his opinion, that the primary sensory cortex has a columnar structure, on evidences from early research (62,65,67). He emphasized two examples from respectively the somatic sensory cortex, 1), and the visual cortex, 2), that he thinks corresponds to the potential modules of the association cortex. However, he realized that the modules are not evident in association cortex.

1) Barrels: In a rodent's brain, "barrels" exists in the fourth layer of the somatic sensory cortex. Each barrel contains 2500 neurons arranged around a hollow centre. 100 somatic afferent fibres lead to these barrels from receptors around the barrels. If a barrel is removed, the other barrels are regularly distributed and fill out the area where the barrel is missing. This arrangement reminds us of the primates somatic sensory cortex, where inputs also are recorded in the fourth layer. If some nerve treads are damaged in this layer, a corresponding re-arrangement to that of the barrels can be realized in this layer, see (65).

Because a rodent only has 50-100 barrels each delivering huge amounts of information, it seems reasonable that each barrel has an individual discrete representation in cortex. This is a unique exception of the organization of the somatic sensory cortex (65). Such kind of organization of the representation only exists in the fourth layer of the somatic sensory cortex, why it cannot be explained as a cortical column.

Because the amount of barrels can vary independent of the area of the modality, it can be stated that if the amount of barrels determines the size of cortex, a single barrel cannot be a structural module.

2) Hyper columns: The hyper columns are found in primary visual cortex (65). In one direction these are organized in ocular dominance columns, and in the other direction

they are organized in orientation columns. However, we do not think the expression column fits here, because the ocular dominance column is defined by the termination of the afferent in the fourth layer where they do not make discrete columns, but instead alternate stripes from right and left eye. Perpendicular to these, the orientation columns can be defined as serial prisms that separately can be adjusted so their angle is a bit displaced compared with the prism. But nothing indicates that the line detector is not continuous. Also, the hyper column is arbitrary defined as a 1-2 mm large part of the cortex that makes up a right and a left stripe on the one side, and a complete round of the line detector on the other. The colour modality are handled in "blobs" in layer two and three of cortex (68). Therefore, it is not likely that they represent the cortical module. Generally, for instance concerning the receptive field (65), all cells are identical in a very thin layer of the somatic sensory cortex. Possible, this field corresponds to the "micro-columns" described by (62,69), of approx. 10-30 µ, but not to the expected "micro column".

Maybe, cortex is constructed by continuous "modules" as the hyper column that very well could be a repeated structure coded by the genes, and seemingly, Szentagothai did not find any support for his discrete modules in this possibility, because the primary sensory cortex did not show any characteristics of a discrete modular structure. Also in the primary motor cortex the evidence for the presence of columns is weak (Hultborn, Personally communication), because the structure of stripes can only be distinguished here, where the organization seems much more to look like the visual cortex, analogue to the ocular dominance stripes, see (70).

Data that could support the existence of a cortex module

In colouration experiments with myalinized fibres, vertical bundles of afferent- and/or efferent-fibres are often seen many places in the cortex as reviewed by Williams and Warwick (71).

In LM, the distance between these is approx. 2-3 pyramid cell diameter (20-150 µ) and approx. 10 µ in thickness, and seemingly 10-20 of these myalinized axons are seen to loose the myalinization throughout the cortex (own observations). These "weigot-columns" are hardly Szentagothai's modules, because 1) the distance between these is too small and 2) each of the large modules should receive 1000 afferents and deliver 1,000 efferents, and not 10-20. But maybe these 10-20 myalinized axons correspond to "micro-columns" of 5 µ thickness described by Mountcastle (72).

It seems like the outspread termination of mono-aminergic fibres in neo-cortex can be observed as a gap of around 100 µ (73). This distance is too little to fit with modules of 300 µ. But other researchers think that cortex contains non-modular "overlapping columns" of 800 µ (72).

Sensory map

The somatotope map shows immediately reorganization (65), when the supplying nerve is cut. This shows that the afferents terminations happen through a large area, and do not indicate that they are "hard wired" in a simple way. We can guess that such phenomena are caused by complex connectivity, and find it obvious to set the organization of the map in connection with the attention and the positional information that manage the complex dynamics of the morphogenesis.

In the same way, because the thalamus-cortical afferents terminates opposite large areas, the ocular dominance columns seem to make up a kind of functional organizations (64). Szentagothai (61) realized this and proposed that inhibitory inter-neurons adjust the afferents. But such arrangement does not support the existence of structural discrete columns in the sensory cortex.

Discussion

Millennia ago, around 300 BC, at the island of Cos in old Greece, the students of the famous physician Hippocrates (60) worked to help their patients to step into character, get direction in life, and use their human talents for the benefit of their surrounding world. For all that we know this approach was extremely efficient medicine that helped the patients to recover health, quality of life, and ability, which resulted in Hippocrates attaining great fame. For more than 2000 years this was what medicine was about in most of Europe.

On other continents similar medical systems were developed. The medicine wheel of the native Americans, the African Sangoma culture, the Samic Shamans of northern Europe, the healers of the Australian Aboriginals, the ayurvedic doctors of India, the acupuncturists of China, and the herbal doctors of Tibet all seems to be fundamentally character medicine, re-connecting man to his world.

Interestingly, the Hippocratic and the transcultural medical traditions gave birth to two succesfull movements in the last century: psychoanalysis (74,75) and psychodynamic therapy (76,77), developed further into today's clinical holistic medicine, integrating "short-term psychodynamic psychotherapy" (STPP) (78,79)) with the many traditions of bodywork (developed further into emotionally realizing bodywork by Reich (80), Lowen (81) and Rosen (82)) and existential work, today often much inspired by Antonovsky and the concept of SOC (83,84).

What we have learned by following this long journey of medicine that the grand medical heritage from the planet's different cultures teach us to work on body, mind and spirit at the same time; medicine men of all kinds have always combined talking, touching, and praying.

The fundamental problem of understanding the connection of human consciousness and health is this: how do we understand the experience of true connectedness with the universe of a human being, if the brain is just a computer generating the consciousness? The module concept reduces the brain from being a pattern-formatting organ under information directed control from the wholeness of the being and the wholeness of the world, into just being a computer with a pretty isolated function.

The importance of the module concept is seen in the attractiveness of this concept, which gives a feeling of understanding the brain, at least to a certain level, as a computer, or network of computers – the modules, in many models working very much like central processing units (CPUs). If there are not modules and not real structure of the cerebral cortex, only billions of brain-cells firing at their own will, a highly structured consciousness really is a true mystery. This mystery opens up for the possibility that our consciousness is structured true our complex interaction with the surrounding world on an informational level. And this is fundamentally what we need consciousness to be, to understand the extreme important of the concept of "sense of coherence" for the art and science of holistic healing.

Conclusion

When small 30 μ cortical columns are taken from a random spot of cortex, no significant difference in the amount of cells can be identified. When we look at corticocortical myelinized afferents, no organization of 300 μ can be identified. When many afferents are coloured at the same time, we can see no superior columns. This means that the well known 300 μ termination columns from corticocortical afferents overlaps. Such structure does not support the existence of the discrete module proposed by Szentagothai.

"The "barrels" of the rodents somatosensory cortex does not seam to be modules, and discrete modules in visual- or somatosensory cortex, does not seam to be discrete. At the cell level, the large basket cell seems to be independent of, and opposite to, a 300 μ module. The thalamus cortical afferents are shown to terminate in the fourth layer, independent of the corticocortical afferents termination column. Besides this, the most corticocortical afferents are shown to terminate laminar (so the fibres from respectively layer 7 and layer 5 of neo-cortex projects to the same layer). These considerations do not seam directly to permit any modules. Therefore, we conclude that evidence for the existence of the postulated module or column does not exist in the literature. There is no evidence for an app. 300 μ large vertically placed structure that could be able to make up for the cortical ground-unit proposed by Szentagothai.

References

[1] Hermansen TD, Ventegodt S, Rald E, Clausen B, Nielsen ML, Merrick J. Human development I. Twenty fundamental problems of biology, medicine and neuropsychology related to biological information. ScientificWorldJournal 2006;6:747-59.

[2] Ventegodt S, Hermansen TD, Nielsen ML, Clausen B, Merrick J. Human development II. We need an integrated theory for matter, life and consciousness to understand life and healing. ScientificWorldJournal 2006;6:760-6.

[3] Ventegodt S, Hermansen TD, Rald E, Flensborg-Madsen T, Nielsen ML, Clausen B, Merrick J. Human development III. Bridging brain-mind and body-mind. Itroduction to "deep" (fractal, poly-ray) cosmology. ScientificWorldJournal 2006;6:767-76.

[4] Ventegodt S, Hermansen TD, Rald E, Flensborg-Madsen T, Nielsen ML, Clausen B, Merrick J. Human development IV. The living cell has information-directed self-organization. ScientificWorldJournal 2006;6:1132-8.

[5] Ventegodt S, Hermansen TD, Flensborg-Madsen T, Nielsen ML, Clausen B, Merrick J. Human development V: Biochemistry unable to explain the emergence of biological form (morphogenesis) and therefore a new principle as source of biological information is needed. ScientificWorldJournal 2006;6:1359-67.

[6] Ventegodt S, Hermansen TD, Flensborg-Madsen T, Nielsen M, Merrick J. Human development VI: Supracellular morphogenesis. The origin of biological and cellular order. ScientificWorldJournal 2006;6:1424-33.

[7] Ventegodt S, Hermansen TD, Flensborg-Madsen T, Rald E, Nielsen ML, Merrick J. Human development VII: A spiral fractal model of fine structure of physical energy could explain central aspects of biological information, biological organization and biological creativity. ScientificWorldJournal 2006;6:1434-40.

[8] Ventegodt S, Hermansen TD, Flensborg-Madsen T, Nielsen ML, Merrick J. Human development VIII: A theory of "deep" quantum chemistry and cell consciousness: Quantum chemistry controls genes and biochemistry to give cells and higher organisms consciousness and complex behavior. ScientificWorldJournal 2006;6:1441-53.

[9] Ventegodt S, Hermansen TD, Flensborg-Madsen T, Rald E, Nielsen ML, Merrick J. Human development IX: A model of the wholeness of man, his consciousness and collective consciousness. ScientificWorldJournal 2006;6:1454-9.

[10] Hermansen TD, Ventegodt S, Merrick J. Human development X: Explanation of macroevolution — top-down evolution materializes consciousness. The origin of metamorphosis. ScientificWorldJournal 2006;6:1656-66.

[11] Ventegodt S, Flensborg-Madsen T, Andersen NJ, Nielsen M, Mohammed M, Merrick J. Global quality of life (QOL), health and ability are primarily determined by our consciousness. Research findings from Denmark 1991-2004. Soc Indicator Res 2005;71:87-122.

[12] Ventegodt S, Merrick J. Clinical holistic medicine: Applied consciousness-based medicine. ScientificWorldJournal 2004;4:96-9.

[13] Ventegodt S, Morad M, Merrick J. Clinical holistic medicine: Classic art of healing or the therapeutic touch. ScientificWorldJournal 2004;4:134-47.

[14] Ventegodt S, Morad M, Merrick J. Clinical holistic medicine: The "new medicine". The multiparadigmatic physician and the medical record. ScientificWorldJournal 2004;4:273-85.

[15] Ventegodt S, Morad M, Merrick J. Clinical holistic medicine: Holistic pelvic examination and holistic treatment of infertility. ScientificWorldJournal 2004;4:148-58.

[16] 16. Ventegodt S, Morad M, Hyam E, Merrick J. Clinical holistic medicine: Use and limitations of the biomedical paradigm. ScientificWorldJournal 2004;4:295-306.

[17] Ventegodt S, Morad M, Kandel I, Merrick J. Clinical holistic medicine: Social problems disguised as illness. ScientificWorldJournal 2004;4:286-94.

[18] Ventegodt S, Morad M, Andersen NJ, Merrick J. Clinical holistic medicine: Tools for a medical science based on consciousness. ScientificWorldJournal 2004;4:347-61.

[19] Ventegodt S, Morad M, Merrick J. Clinical holistic medicine: Prevention through healthy lifestyle and quality of life. Oral Health Prev Dent 2004;2(Suppl 1):239-45.

[20] Ventegodt S, Morad M, Hyam E, Merrick J. Clinical holistic medicine: When biomedicine is inadequate. ScientificWorldJournal 2004;4:333-46.

[21] Ventegodt S, Morad M, Vardi G, Merrick J. Clinical holistic medicine: Holistic treatment of children. ScientificWorldJournal 2004;4:581-8.

[22] Ventegodt S, Morad M, Kandel I, Merrick J. Clinical holistic medicine: Problems in sex and living together. ScientificWorldJournal 2004;4:562-70.

[23] Ventegodt S, Morad M, Hyam E, Merrick J. Clinical holistic medicine: Holistic sewxology and treatment of vulvodynia through existential therapy and acceptance through touch. ScientificWorldJournal 2004;4:571-80.

[24] Ventegodt S, Flensborg-Madsen T, Andersen NJ, Morad M, Merrick J. Clinical holistic medicine: A pilot study on HIV and quality of life and a suggested cure for HIV and AIDS. ScientificWorldJournal 2004;4:264-72.

[25] Ventegodt S, Morad M, Hyam E, Merrick J. Clinical holistic medicine: Induction of spontaneous remission of cancer by recovery of the human character and the purpose of life (the life mission). ScientificWorldJournal 2004;4:362-77.

[26] Ventegodt S, Morad M, Kandel I, Merrick J. Clinical holistic medicine: Treatment of physical health problems without a known cause, exemplified by hypertension and tinnitus. ScientificWorldJournal 2004;4:716-24.

[27] Ventegodt S, Morad M, Merrick J. Clinical holistic medicine: Developing from asthma, allergy and eczema. ScientificWorldJournal 2004;4:936-42.

[28] Ventegodt S, Morad M, Press J, Merrick J, Shek DTL. Clinical holistic medicine: Holistic adolescent medicine. ScientificWorldJournal 2004;4:551-61.

[29] Ventegodt S, Solheim E, Saunte ME, Morad M, Kandel I, Merrick J. Clinic holistic medicine: Metastatic cancer. ScientificWorldJournal 2004;4:913-35.

[30] Ventegodt S, Morad M, Kandel I, Merrick J. Clinical holistic medicine: a psychological theory of dependency to improve quality of life. ScientificWorldJournal 2004;4:638-48.

[31] Ventegodt S, Merrick J. Clinical holistic medicine: Chronic infections and autoimmune diseases. ScientificWorldJournal 2005;5:155-64.

[32] Ventegodt S, Kandel I, Neikrug S, Merrick J. Clinical holistic medicine: Holistic treatment of rape and incest trauma. ScientificWorldJournal 2005;5:288-97.

[33] Ventegodt S, Merrick J. Clinical holistic medicine: Chronic pain in the locomotor system. ScientificWorldJournal 2005;5:165-72.

[34] Ventegodt S, Merrick J. Clinical holistic medicine: Chronic pain in internal organs. ScientificWorldJournal 2005;5:205-10.

[35] Ventegodt S, Kandel I, Neikrug S, Merrick J. Clinical holistic medicine: The existential crisis – life crisis, stress and burnout. ScientificWorldJournal 2005;5:300-12.

[36] Ventegodt S, Gringols M, Merrick J. Clinical holistic medicine: Holistic rehabilitation. ScientificWorldJournal 2005;5:280-7.

[37] Ventegodt S, Andersen NJ, Neikrug S, Kandel I, Merrick J. Clinical holistic medicine: Mental disorders in a holistic perspective. ScientificWorldJournal 2005;5:313-23.

[38] Ventegodt S, Andersen NJ, Neikrug S, Kandel I, Merrick J. Clinical holistic medicine: Holistic treatment of mental disorders. ScientificWorldJournal 2005;5:427-45.

[39] Ventegodt S, Merrick J. Clinical holistic medicine: The patient with multiple diseases. ScientificWorldJournal 2005;5:324-39.

[40] Ventegodt S, Clausen B, Nielsen ML, Merrick J. Clinical holistic medicine: Advanced tools for holistic medicine. ScientificWorldJournal 2006;6:2048-65.

[41] Ventegodt S, Clausen B, Merrick J. Clinical holistic medicine: The case story of Anna. I. Long-term effect of childhood sexual abuse and incest with a treatment approach. ScientificWorldJournal 2006;6:1965-76.

[42] Ventegodt S, Clausen B, Merrick J. Clinical holistic medicine: The case story of Anna. II. Patient diary as a tool in treatment. ScientificWorldJournal 2006;6:2006-34.

[43] Ventegodt S, Clausen B, Merrick J. Clinical holistic medicine: The case story of Anna. III: Rehabilitation of philosophy of life during holistic existential therapy for childhood sexual abuse. ScientificWorldJournal 2006;6:2080-91.

[44] Ventegodt S, Merrick J. Suicide from a holistic point of view. ScientificWorldJournal 2005;5:759-66.

[45] Ventegodt S, Clausen B, Omar HA, Merrick J. Clinical holistic medicine: Holistic sexology and acupressure through the vagina (Hippocrates pelvic massage). ScientificWorldJournal 2006;6:2066-79.

[46] Ventegodt S, Clausen B, Merrick J. Clinical holistic medicine: Pilot study on the effect of vaginal acupressure (Hippocratic pelvic massage). ScientificWorldJournal 2006;6:2100-16.

[47] Ventegodt S, Thegler S, Andreasen T, Struve F, Enevoldsen L, Bassaine L, Torp M, Merrick J. Clinical holistic medicine: Psychodynamic short-time therapy complemented with bodywork. A clinical follow-up study of 109 patients. ScientificWorldJournal 2006;6:2220-38.

[48] Ventegodt S, Thegler S, Andreasen T, Struve F, Enevoldsen L, Bassaine L, et al. Clinical holistic medicine (mindful, short-term psychodynamic psychotherapy complemented with bodywork) in the treatment of experienced impaired sexual functioning. ScientificWorldJournal 2007;7: 324-9.

[49] Ventegodt S, Thegler S, Andreasen T, Struve F, Enevoldsen L, Bassaine L, et al. Clinical holistic medicine (mindful, short-term psychodynamic psychotherapy complemented with bodywork) improves quality of life, health, and ability by induction of Antonovsky-salutogenesis. ScientificWorldJournal 2007;7:317-23.

[50] Ventegodt S, Thegler S, Andreasen T, Struve F, Enevoldsen L, Bassaine L, et al. Clinical holistic medicine (mindful, short-term psychodynamic psychotherapy complemented with bodywork) in the treatment of experienced physical illness and chronic pain. ScientificWorldJournal 2007;7: 310-6.

[51] Ventegodt S, Thegler S, Andreasen T, Struve F, Enevoldsen L, Bassaine L, et al. Clinical holistic medicine (mindful, short-term psychodynamic psychotherapy complemented with bodywork) in the treatment of experienced mental illness. ScientificWorldJournal 2007;7:306-9.

[52] Ventegodt S, Thegler S, Andreasen T, Struve F, Enevoldsen L, Bassaine L, et al. Self-reported low self-esteem. Intervention and follow-up in a clinical setting. ScientificWorldJournal 2007;7:299-305.

[53] Flensborg-Madsen T, Ventegodt S, Merrick J. Sense of coherence and physical health. A Review of previous findings. ScientificWorldJournal 2005;5:665-73.

[54] Flensborg-Madsen T, Ventegodt S, Merrick J. Why is Antonovsky's sense of coherence not correlated to physical health? Analysing Antonovsky's 29-item sense of coherence scale (SOCS). ScientificWorldJournal 2005;5:767-76.

[55] Flensborg-Madsen T, Ventegodt S, Merrick J. Sense of coherence and health. The construction of an amendment to Antonovsky's sense of coherence scale (SOC II). ScientificWorldJournal 2006;6:2133-9.

[56] Flensborg-Madsen T, Ventegodt S, Merrick J. Sense of coherence and physical health. A cross-sectional study using a new SOC scale (SOC II). ScientificWorldJournal 2006;6:2200-21.

[57] Flensborg-Madsen T, Ventegodt S, Merrick J. Sense of coherence and physical health. Testing Antonovsky's theory. ScientificWorldJournal 2006;6:2212-9.

[58] Flensborg-Madsen T, Ventegodt S, Merrick J. Sense of coherence and health. The emotional sense of coherence (SOC-E) was found to be the best-known predictor of physical health. ScientificWorldJournal 2006;6:2147-57.

[59] Ventegodt S, Flensborg-Madsen T, Andersen NJ, Merrick J. Life mission theory VII: Theory of existential (Antonovsky) coherence: a theory of quality of life, health and ability for use in holistic medicine. ScientificWorldJournal 2005;5:377-89.

[60] Jones WHS. Hippocrates. Vol. I–IV. London: William Heinemann, 1923-1931.

[61] Szentagothai J. The modular architectonic principle of neural centers. Rev Physiol Biochem Pharmacol 1983;98:11-61.

[62] Szentagothai J. The neuron network of the cerebral cortex: A functional interpretation. Proc P Soc Lond B 1978;201:219-48.

[63] Eccles JC, Jones EG, Peters A. Cerebral cortex, vol. 2. New York: Plenum, 1984.

[64] Gilbert CD, Wiesel TN. Functional organization of the visual cortex. Nature 1979;280:120-5.

[65] Kandel ER, Schwartz JH. Principles of neural science. New York: Elsevier, 2000.

[66] Mountcastle VB. Modality and topographic properties of single neurons of cat's somatic sensory cortex. J Neurophysiol 1957;20(4):408-34.

[67] Hubel DH, Wiesel TN. Receptive fields of single neurones in the cat's striate cortex. J Physiol 1959;48:574-91.

[68] Livingstone MS. Art, illusion and the visual system. Sci Am 1988;258(1):78-85.

[69] Szentagothai J. The "module concept" in cerebral cortex architecture. Brain Res 1975;95:475-96.

[70] Goldman-Rakic PS. Modular organization of the prefrontal cortex. Trends Neurosci 1984;7:419-29.

[71] Williams PL, Warwick R. Grays anatomy. Edinburg: Churchill Livingstone, 1980.

[72] Mountcastle VB. An organizing principle for cerebral function: the unit module and the distributed system. In: Edelman GM, Mountcatle VB, eds. Mindful brain. Cambridge, MA: MIT, 1978:7-50.

[73] Rockel AJ, Hions RW, Powell TPS. The basic uniformity in the structure of the neocortex. Brain 1980;103:221–4.

[74] Jones E. The life and works of Sigmund Freud. New York: Basic Books, 1961.

[75] Jung CG. Man and his symbols. New York: Anchor Press, 1964.

[76] Jung CG. Psychology and alchemy. Collected works of CG Jung, Vol 12. Princeton, NJ: Princeton Univ Press, 1968.

[77] Leichsenring F, Rabung S, Leibing E. The efficacy of short-term psychodynamic psychotherapy in specific psychiatric disorders: a meta-analysis. Arch Gen Psychiatry 2004;61(12):1208-16.

[78] Leichsenring F. Are psychodynamic and psychoanalytic therapies effective?: A review of empirical data. Int J Psychoanal 2005;86(Pt 3) :841-68.

[79] Reich W. [Die Function des Orgasmus.] Köln: Kiepenheuer Witsch, 1969. [German].

[80] Lowen A. Honoring the body. Alachua, FL: Bioenergetics Press, 1994.

[81] Rosen M, Brenner S. Rosen method bodywork. Accessing the unconscious through touch. Berkeley, CA: North Atlantic Books, 2003.

[82] Antonovsky A. Health, stress and coping. London: Jossey-Bass, 1985.

[83] Antonovsky A. Unravelling the mystery of health. How people manage stress and stay well. San Franscisco: Jossey-Bass, 1987.

Chapter 24

A theory for the structure and function of the human brain

The human brain is probably the most complicated single structure in the biological universe. The cerebral cortex that traditionally is connected with the consciousness is extremely complex. The brain contains approximately 1,000,000 km of nerve fibres indicating its enormous complexity that makes it difficult for scientists to reveal the function of the brain. In this chapter we propose a new model for brain functions: information-guided self-organization of neural patterns, where information is provided from the abstract wholeness of the biophysical system of an organism (often called the true self, or the "soul"). We present a number of arguments in favour of this model that provide self-conscious control over the thought process or cognition. Our arguments arise from analysing experimental data from different research fields: histology, anatomy, electro-encephalography (EEG), cerebral blood flow, neuropsychology, evolutionary studies and mathematics. We criticize the popular network theories as a consequence of a simplistic, mechanical interpretation of reality (philosophical materialism) applied to the brain. We demonstrate how viewing the brain functions as information-guided self-organization of neural patterns can explain the structure of conscious mentation; we seem to have a dual hierarchical representation in the cerebral cortex: one for sensation-perception and one for will-action. The model explains many of our unique mental abilities to think, memorize, associate, discriminate, and make abstractions. The presented model of conscious brain seems also able to explain the function of the simpler brains like that of insects and hydra.

Introduction

In our previous publications (1-11), we have discussed the nature of biology, cell communication and deeply structured quantum fields, the structure of the neocortex and human consciousness (12-20). With such a background in the literature, you should be able to understand our motivation for the development of this new theory of the brain as we need a strong scientific foundation for holistic medicine (21-24). Holistic medicine can provide us with new treatments for many physical, mental, sexual, and existential human sufferings (25-

60). Our former philosophical work on life, brain, consciousness, biological information, order, health, and disease have lead to successful treatment of patients with many different health problems (61-66). It is our hope that a more profound model of the human brain and consciousness can facilitate further progress. Our work is based on many publications by gifted researchers like Freud, Jung, Reich, Lowen, Rosen, Anand and Antonovsky (67-75) and many others, who created the foundation for the psychodynamic psychotherapy (76-78).

The present work is neurophilosophical, not traditional neuroscientific. It is based on many different sources of contemporary thoughts and is thus highly interdisciplinary. Our core ideas or axioms are:

- Everything has a solid particle and an energetic wave aspect, according to the laws of quantum physics.
- Everything is thus an aspect energy. We live in a quantum world where everything, when it comes down to it, is interfering, non-local energy fields of quantum nature (8). These fields are structured and can carry information that can be used by the living organisms (1-10).
- Everything is thus an aspect of matter, like atoms and molecules giving rise to biochemistry that can be used by the living organisms.
- A living organism has two sides, a subjective and an objective side; matter and consciousness that are bridged by biological mechanics, including according to our understanding both biochemical and informational quantum mechanics. Our hypothesis is that all organisms, even bacteria, have consciousness and a sense of subjectivity. We doubt that a virus has awareness or subjectivity, but then again we need to define what we mean by "subjectivity" and "consciousness". Those two are difficult and thorny terms with many meanings and connotations; so by consciousness we mean an entities' ability to represent in its informational field the inner and outer world in a meaningful way. Meaning points of purpose carried by the entity. If a virus can sense its surrounding world without sheer mechanical stimuli, then it has awareness and consciousness by our definition. Awareness is thus the sub-atomic ("quantum") quality derived from the entities' wholeness (the informational field) that "senses" (represents) the inner and outer world.
- When two particles of any kind are contained in the same system they share a common quantum state and thus stops being two separate entities; their common quantum state can be used to coordinate the living system's parts with its wholeness, and this is true for life at all levels: from molecular ensembles, organelles, organelle-systems, cells, organs, organ-systems, organism and the levels of the outer ecosystem in which the organism participates. What is life in this sense? Is it not a supernatural vital force, a cause, an agent, or an independent being like the Indian or Christian concept of the soul? No, but rather a materialisation of an extremely complex and mysterious quality or aspect of the universal energy, providing the living being through billions of years of evolution with autonomy, light, meaning, joy, purpose, will and choice.
- The level of separateness defines the extent to which any part of a global ecosystem (living totality) has autonomy; the level of the organism has a rather high degree of autonomy giving rise to the organism's sense of self. Every part of the whole has

thus to some extent autonomy; parts that merges completely (i.e. cells that merges into muscle fibres) surrender autonomy to the system. All parts are partly autonomous and partly controlled by the levels above and below them.

- We are well aware of the depths of the mathematical structures rising from chaos theory, fractal geometry, and complex dynamics (79,80), but we want to emphasis that we do not believe that self-organising patterns can control neither consciousness nor behaviour. Quite on the contrary, we find the mathematical structures derived from the new mathematic (81) to be rather far from biological patterns, so it is quite obvious that we have not yet found the key to a profound scientific understanding of life.

This chapter is a presentation with interpretations based on these fundamental axioms of the current knowledge of the human brain. We are thus taking an absolutely opposite stand-point than normally done in neuroscience, where the nerve-cell is seen as the mechanical unit of the brain, under control of genes, hormones, neurotransmitters, neuropeptides, and functional stimuli. Our hope is to be able to understand the nature and structure of consciousness and especially the functional relationship between consciousness, mind, and the physical (or cellular) body. Our hope is that such a model may allow us to understand emotions and psychosomatics – and in the end, existential healing (23,24,26) and salutogenesis (defined by Aaron Antonovsky (1923-1994) as healing of physical and mental illnesses trough the rehabilitation of "the sense of coherence")(74,75).

The idea that the cell is conscious might seem strange to many people, but that was a conclusion that Sir Roger Penrose and other researchers reached at the SOL-meeting at the Niels Bohr Institute in Copenhagen 1996 (82). Since this meeting this has been our understanding of living organisms: that they always carry consciousness. This means that every cell in our body to some modest extent has an independent consciousness and subjectivity. It is this phenomenon that allows cells to develop into cancer cells, and cells to be cultivated in the laboratory, also after the dead of the multi-cellular organism. We know that this position will be hard to accept in modern neuroscience: that every nerve cell think for it self and make its own independent decisions, which make it so much more than just a small "mechanical computer". Sir Roger Penrose has published a similar hypothesis in his book "Shadows of the mind"(83). It could be argued that we should draw a line somewhere between those unicellular organisms that may have primitive consciousness versus the cells of our nails or hair (84), but we still find it most likely and in accordance with the philosophical principle of Occam's raiser that consciousness is a trait carried by all living beings, but on different levels of complexity.

Does a zygote have a sense of self?

This leaves us to the natural question: Does a zygote have a sense of self and consciousness? Based on empirical research with people re-experiencing their conception, the answer definitely seems to be affirmative, but the objectivity of such studies has been disputed (84). If you think this is a little to farfetched we must tell you that in spite of being quite sceptical ourselves, we as scientists often see patients spontaneously regress all the way into the womb in intensive holistic therapy. The first author have after 20 years of consecutive therapy suddenly regressed during holotropic breastwork (86) all the way back to the zygotic state; according to this experience there was indeed a conscious "I" from the very beginning of life (87), but then again, when you become very experienced late in life, you start to relax your scepticism a little and believe in all sorts of things, and then you are not really reliable any more, are you? To keep it simple, which is a must in order to comply with Occam's raiser, the sense of self (being an independent soul) does not develop gradually from the zygote – embryo – foetus – newborn – infant – child – adult – old age; this feeling of being an autonomous creatures is with us from the very beginning as an innate trait of the person; what is developed though time and experience is the level of complexity of the mind (brain-mind), and perhaps also the complexity of the being.

Many scientists believe that the human brain is a kind of independent computer able to understand almost everything in this universe, but at the same time it seems clear that we human beings never fully will be able to comprehend consciousness and the brain itself. This paradox may be a consequence of a narrow, rationalistic and materialistic interpretation of reality (1-10).

If the interpretation of reality gets more complex and less naive this might give us a chance of developing a more transcendent and deeper understanding of the brain and consciousness. The description of life as a complex dynamic and information-directed self-organizing system (4) is an example of this point of view and it can settle the above-mentioned paradox. From this perspective, consciousness is seen as a characteristic of all living things. Because of the relative high degree of outer separateness self-consciousness is especially prevalent in the human brain, which has a large degree of autonomy; the abilities of the human mental self (Ego) are complex and advanced. The body is the next fairly independent biological entity, carrying as Freud noticed correctly, the consciousness of the Id (and the body-mind). Finally the human wholeness also carries its representation of us called our "spiritual self", "true self" or "soul". This gives man three dominant representations of self: The wholeness-related self (below called the Soul), the brain-related self (below called the Ego), and the body-related self (below called the Id). And then we have the "I", the integrative self that emerges from an organic synthesis of body, mind and spirit. This "I" is often in spiritual literature and poetry called the "heart" (Comp. the lyrics of Madonna: "When you heart is open"). In Freud's work the super-ego is synonymous with the Soul; Freud often said that everything good in man comes from the Superego (67).

The interesting question, "Doesn't the self operate through the brain?", leads us to an immediate "of course", and a secondary remorse on deeper reflection, that in the end brings the realisation that our thoughts and behaviour might be controlled by our self, but feelings, sexuality and spirituality are as well controlled by our self, so are we really living in the brain? This is most definitely not our experience, if we must be honest. Emotions are felt in the body; and our sexual feelings are definitely felt primarily in our sexual organs. And maybe this is not merely a joke, but human biological reality that must be respected, as Freud insisted.

We know that there seems to be an interpretation of our feelings in the limbic system, and without this happening we could not be mentally aware that we were emotionally hurt or sexually exited. But to insist that feelings and being is merely a brain-thing, that is insisting on something that obviously conflicts with our common sense (senses communis). As therapists we are emotionally oriented people, and we really like to place the "I" in our hearts much more that in our brains. This gives a much more human contact and a much richer emotional life. On the other hand we must agree that mental consciousness obviously is focused in the middle of the brain (in what the Indians have called the "3rd eye" for 7,000 years). We like to use our experiences as basis for understanding; not vice versa. And this is the true reason for making this paper: We need to stop thinking so much and start sensing and explore our inner self to really understand what is going on. We suspect that many neuroscientists often miss the obvious truth, because they do not sincerely feel what is happening inside and reflect upon it. Basically this is a question of using subjectivity in research, and putting sufficient emphasis on the qualitative aspect of science. In this paper we want to analyse the implications of this for our understanding of the brain.

Consciouness

All the cells of the organism carry consciousness. Human consciousness is basically embedded in a quantum field arising from the combination of all individual cells' consciousnesses (4-9,83). This is highly debatable, we must admit, but we humbly ask you to play with this idea before you decide to dismiss it. This structure of Soul, Ego and Id, all carrying semi-individual consciousness means that the whole organism (the "heart" or "I") can "see" and analyse all its lower-level conscious functions; thus both brain-mind functions, body-mind and even wholeness-related "spiritual intelligence" functions are observed and interacted with by the "I". It is very usual in therapy that a person suddenly observes an inner process of cancer, or observers his own autistic side, and this could not be done without the ability of such a "meta-perspective" provided by the abstract I. This is somewhat related to the strange observations that patients during surgery can observe the surgical theatre from above, from a view-point where they obviously feel out of the body. Most interesting this shift of perspective also often happens in intensive holistic therapy. So it is hard not to believe for us as therapists witnessing this happen all the time. Not that we understand it, or even like it. Human consciousness is way too mysterious to be cosy.

The "I" or "heart" can see the brain from a perspective "outside" the brain, but inside the organism. And the body can see the brain and the brain can see the body – energetically, or if you prefer by direct transference of information from one "wholeness" to the other. Is the wholeness of the body different from the wholeness of the brain? Does an organism have one wholeness? Does an organism behave as one entity? The unreflected answer is that the organism carries the wholeness and its organs do not. But after deeper reflection and meditation on ants and corrals and after that on human societies and the way consciousness is manipulated in a society collectively i.e. by the media, we must admit that the organisms are not that free to think, feel and act as we would like them to be. After thorough studies on sexuality and human unconsciousness (un-integrated traits of brain-mind and body-mind) we must admit that our organs are pretty powerful actors in their own right. So the picture is much more complicated and in the end every level of us has some degree dependence and freedom.

The "I" can use the bodies' emotional intelligence – the faculty of intelligence connected to the body-cells' collective consciousness field (and of course the wisdom of a mature brain's cortico-limbic system) – to get a clear picture of the mental processes and the basic machinery that creates its own mind. This is the typical perspective of the Tibetan Buddhists Yogis reached in deep meditation, but only little acknowledged in the west until recently (87). You could argue that these are subjective reports of their mental states and experiences and thus they are probably not a good argument in support of our thesis in a scientific journal. But our direct experiences of the world might be as real as our mental reflections upon it; we would actually argue: more real!

The brain is represented in the organism's wholeness, in the same way as the organism is represented in the brain. You could argue that you have never seen your own brain, but if you can sense where you mental activity is centered – right behind your eyes – then your wholeness has already acknowledged that you can sense you own brain, or at least its energy and quality. So what we basically claim is that the brain cannot be understood without understanding the "I" and its consciousness, and Id, and the Soul, and their individual consciousnesses.

In a well-integrated organism the self rules ("I" am in power); from its placement at the top-level of the organism it can strongly impact what is going on at all the lower levels, including in the brain. The model we are going to develop further was originally made by the psychoanalysts to allow us to understand how I-born consciousness (as in "living by heart") can be causal in our life (67-72). Interestingly this model seems to be the normal understanding of man in most pre-modern societies (9) and most interestingly it opens up to an explanation of collective consciousness (9,68,69) that is normal in pre-modern societies, but almost forgotten or neglected in our culture in spite of Jung (68,69), Grof (85,86) and other prominent psychic researchers stressing its meaning and importance to us. It seems that it actually came from the pre-modern cultures into psychoanalysis especially by Jung. The model we present is thus not purely based on theory, but on lots of practical experience, and it is also in accordance with the philosophy of life that has arisen from our research in quality of life and health during the last two decades.

Understanding the complex patterns of brain activity

To understand the various functions of the brain we need an integrative theory for brain function that accounts for the control of the mental functions on the highest level of the brain. The multi-dimensional connectivity that follows the extreme con- and divergence in the architecture of the human neocortex, the results of countless EEG-measurements, and the measurements of the high and almost constant brain-energy-usage indicates that the cortex cerebri is a machinery that almost continuously delivers a huge selection of patterns that floats into each other (79,80,88-91). Mathematical analyses (90,91,92) have indicated that the cerebral cortex cannot organize the patterns by itself in a meaningful way, leaving us with the most fundamental problem of how the brain is controlled.

It may be assumed that sensory inputs to the brain temporarily can stabilize its chaotic neural self-organising patterns, creating a sensory perception of simple information-directed self-organisation. But this does not explain much – thinking, understanding, perceiving etc. Therefore, another much more efficient and innate organizing system may exist, that makes the brain function as it does. Morphological and evolutionary data (93,94) seem to show that the nervous system is developed and functions through an intense communication with self – or in more scientific language: the brain is totally imbedded in the complex informational dynamics of the organismic wholeness. The organismic wholeness entirely depends on a well functioning, living brain as expressed by John Zachary Young (1907-1997), professor of anatomy at the University College London: "No brain, no mind, no nothing."

Actually the brain is completely absorbed in the organism, and has, as we see it, no completely independent function of its own, in spite of it being in many structural and physiological ways a highly autonomous organ. Even the slightest action on the brain is in some way influenced by the totally and intentions of the being who owns it.

One can ask at what stage of embryological development of an organism, like a bacterium or a human being, is there a communication between the brain and self? Little do we know about how bacteria process information, but they obviously do, and the close distance between the genes and their global level tells us that there must be an intense inner representation of the bacteria's wholeness. Do we have a self, when we are at the single cell level of development viz. the zygote? Yes, we seemingly do. Do we have self even before conception? No, at least not in our philosophy. Then again it is wise to remember that half the population of the planet would disagree here.

It is normally believed in neuroscience that a lot of the cortical-subcortical activity is spontaneous, involuntary, automatic and subconscious. This is often presented as a fact in many standard textbooks of neurobiology, neuroscience and neurophysiology; but it is worthwhile remembering that we never have seen a brain keeping these "automatic" functions on its own (in vitro). And if we count the consciousness of the Self and the Body, this might not be the case at all. The interesting thought-experiment to do here is to imagine a person's brain isolated and fed in a jar: Will this brain still be able to think and feel like the person it came from? Will it still function at all? We know of course that in vitro developing neurons still fire. But will this activity be able to create any collective meaning without the informational guidance from the Self and the body? The consequence of our thinking is that this is not possible. Unfortunately we do not know of any experiments that can decide this for us.

On the contrary, we know of many experiments that indicate that the functional order of the brain is highly fluent and rapidly reorganised. The cortical representation of all sensory and motor functions in neural maps and their well known and quite mysterious, momentary reorganization[88] seems to confirm that brain function is controlled from "a level above", because the representations are not fixed in the physical brain – the maps are not hardwired. Studies of blood flow and lesions show a hierarchically ordered structure of representations in cortical networks (88,93,94). These examples are in accordance with the psychological developmental studies showing that the consciousness has its starting point in the functions of the body with the primary sensory and motor areas creating the foundation for the hierarchy. The higher integrative areas create the intermediate, and the highest integrative areas – especially prefrontal cortex – create the top of the hierarchy (88). It is well known that some brain lesions like that of the Brocka's area are followed by expressive aphasia. So there are lots of hard-wired solutions in the brain also, of course, on lower levels of the brain. But all high level, consciousness-related organisation seems to be informationally directed. And we believe that the Self provides this information, and that the Self thus controls its brain. This link between Self and brain is crucial for our understanding of i.e. the altered brain function and physiology in illnesses like depression and schizophrenia.

In appendix 1, we give a short evaluation of the value of central experimental data for our understanding of the brain with a special attention to the function of the cortex cerebri. We will now discuss how the brain functions according to our holistic understanding. The fundamental structure of the neocortex (95,96) has been reviewed and will not be repeated here (11).

A theory for brain function

What does the brain do? Basically the brain connects Ego, I, Soul, and Id to the outer world. It carries the organism's rational interpretation of the world and allows it to realise the intentions of Self and Id through plans carried out in time and space. The brain creates mental perception, rational understanding and visual, auditory, somatosensory interpretation of the inner and outer world, and proper, rational actions and inner adjustments from the Ego's, Soul's, Id's, and I's intent.

One could ask if I, Soul, Ego and Id are generated from a well-functioning brain, and this could very well be so. The different inner personalities that we label all these names could easily rise from a less than perfect integrity of the brain. So one cannot judge just by thinking, if there is any rationale behind the more complex model of human reality that we propose; we do it because we respect our "common sense", our direct experience of life; it is this sense that allows us to help our patients in holistic therapy, and provides us with the power of healing. So we cannot just give it up. And when we take our experience to meet neuroscience, things do not fit. What we feel and experience is simply not compatible with the mechanical interpretation of reality we find in contemporary neurophysiology books; even profound books like Principles of Neural science (88) does not reflect on the quality of existential depth, joy, light, and innate wisdom that we sense is connected to consciousness. Frankly the concept of consciousness is hardly addressed in neurophysiology of today. The "hard" problem (how subjective consciousness is produced from chemistry and physics) has not been solved, and it is much too often just ignored.

This is done through intensive mapping of the inner and outer world. The brain is in touch with the outside world through the senses and the apparatus of movement, and in touch with the person's "inner world" through feelings, intuitions, finer sensations, intentions, states of consciousness and being: dreams are very much the materialisation of this inward contact.

Throughout life a more and more detailed model of reality is build up, using the fundamental dimensions of space and time. The brain and mind are harvesting experiences through the presence of sensory qualitative units called "qualia" - like the colour red - that is solely produced by the nervous system and the organism itself; a nervous signal can in principle not be read (unless you accept that it can carry a more subtle and finer level of information, i.e. quantum level information). Qualia are combined through time and space into elements that can be perceived and manipulated, giving birth to the phenomenological world. The intensity of qualia is established, and its location in time and space is noticed, and all these neural measurements are integrated into a dynamic perception. Mental elements can be static or dynamic, corresponding to nouns and verbs in the language (see Chomsky's famous concept of "deep structures" of language, and Piaget's model of development of human consciousness) (97-99). The nonverbal mental phenomena like pure visual images, touch, taste and emotions are also based on qualia, but they are often just taken for granted and not abstracted to higher logical levels. But they can be, as in the Indian and Tibetan art of erotic tantra, were sexual feelings and unified sexual poles are abstracted to oneness ("sunya")(73).

The mind is thus basically nothing but a highly dynamic model of reality constructed in this way, just by combining the elements on higher and higher, more and more abstract levels through experience and memory, and the mental faculty of abstraction and concretisation. The model is organised though association and dissociation. Logic and sets are used for giving rational structure.

The brain is constantly preparing a row of behavioural and perceptual strategies to meet the intentions of the whole organism (the "I" motivated by "Soul, Id, and Ego" according to psychodynamic theory). The brain interprets all experiences and sensory inputs from the outer world in agreement with the organism's intentions, accumulating concrete strategies for action and for perceptual and intellectual analysis. These strategies are gradually revised as new goals immerge through a changing life. When the resistance is too big – when realising ones dreams and intentions are too difficult and painful - the goals are replaced in resignation with smaller, more obtainable goals. Such events result in the degeneration of the intent (life mission) (12-20,50,51,54-57) and the personal character, which sometimes even lead to mental illness like depression and schizophrenia, as suggested by Bleuler, Freud, Jung and others.

The only interpretation of the brain that is in accordance with all the collected data from all the sources mentioned above is that the brain is a pattern-machine, that continuously produces concrete and abstract patterns combining into "sensori-motor-pictures"; it seems that this process is guided by the organism's abstract high-level perceptual faculty of finding meaning in chaos, and a similarly abstract faculty of intent. It thus seems that it is the self (the organism's wholeness) that guides the brain in its making plans for achievement and realization of the abstract and concrete goals of the human being. The reality is interpreted in agreement with the intention and is represented for the conscious wholeness, where it is evaluated and processed. This seems to be in accordance with Arthur Schopenhauer (1788-1860) a German philosopher, who believed that the will to live is the fundamental reality.

Information guided self-organization of the neural patterns

We have analysed the process of morphogenesis and found that it is happening through information-directed self-organization of cells and tissue; all cell movements and differentiations are initiated and directed through information-directed self-organization of molecules and organelles (4). It seems reasonable to suggest that the brain functions in a completely similar way through information-directed self-organisation of complex, dynamic, hierarchically organised, neural patterns.

The neural connectivity patterns are specified through information-transferring interactions on many levels of the living organism. This means that both the patterns of connectivity and the functional neural patterns of the working brain interact with the information-bearing, complex dynamic processes of the biological system; please recall that we have found this to be a real phenomenon existing in the organism at a quantum level (8). The functional neural patterns are different from the structural. But when structures and functions are developed in parallel through evolution, it must be that the functional patterns also interact with the informational level of the organism; a fine example of this is the Hydra; in the Hydra the neural network is constantly updated by the organism; if the body of hydra is reshaped by cutting, the neural information reconstructs it with no hesitation.

We can look and make sense of even the most complicated of patterns like for example at turbulent water flowing, growing plants and ecosystems, or computer produced fractals; from this it is clear that our brain that has the capability to form extremely complex patterns for perceptual use – much more complex and complicated than those structures that are before our eyes. The brain is formatting extremely complex patterns. This neural "modelling medium" (or matrix) can be organized either by sense input or by the consciousness and intention of the organism.

Since our senses are always flooded by information, it is obvious that a considerable and continuous selection of the incoming data is happening at all times. The intent of the Self determines what is interesting for the being from an existential perspective, and therefore defines the contents of its perception. Therefore it is correct to state that the content of consciousness it actually coursed by the Self. This is an extremely interesting conclusion as it makes the perception of the mentally ill including delusions, hallucinations, emotional flattening understandable (17,50,51). Most interestingly, intent is connected to the philosophy of life, and revising one's philosophy of life seems to completely alter the realm of perceptions; the patient in deep philosophical exploration is often "travelling from heaven to hell and vice versa". Also the perception of body, sexuality, the partner etc is completely mouldable by the person's philosophy of life.

The huge mass of data not found to be relevant for the realization of the organism's intentions are selected by the materialisation of a "pyramid of consciousness" from the abstract intentions to the concrete perceptions and behaviours; the intentions materialise "concrete plans" that support the specific sense-impressions. For the organism's wholeness intention materialises existential relevant experiences; in the brain intentions materialise the physical and well know description of the world used for everyday-living: the interpretation of the reality.

On a mechanistic, informational level the intentions must come to the brain in the form of superior matrixes of guiding patterns – these patterns correspond to those of the organism's wholeness; they organize the top-level patterns selected by the functioning brain, and the brain's self organising nature takes care of the rest. The organism's plans and strategies for self-realization are carried out in agreement with the rational interpretation of the organism's sense impressions. We know that in humans dreams are very important in this process.

A double hierarchical model for the reality representation of cortex cerebri

In order to simplify this description, we will only concentrate on the largest structures of the prosencephalon. The subject for the discussion will be the integrative structures such as the limbic system of cortex cerebri, the basal ganglia, and thalamus. The last two of these areas will be considered as equally connected with the areas of cortex cerebri.

We think these structures represent a person's "emotionally close social relationships in the group" (the limbic system), groupings in the basal ganglia corresponding to the motor and verbal activities related to the outside world, and the whole perceived and cognised reality model in the thalamus and the related cortex. In the following, these structures are included in the term, cortex cerebri.

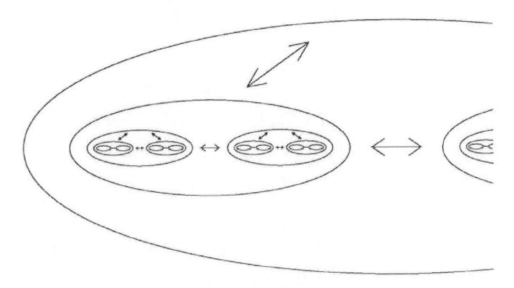

Figure 1. The living organism seen as a fractal structure with interacting parts on many levels. The arrows illustrate the information-transmitting interactions and are based on generalized empiric results. The figure illustrates how biologic informational systems are structured as a fractal "Chinese box"; the information transmitting interactions is seen between the different parts of the same level and between levels.

In cortex cerebri, two hierarchies seemingly exist, one for perception and one for action. Together, these stretch out the reality model, in the brain.

One of these is a variant of the Chinese box system (see figure 1) existing in all biological systems. In this, the brain as a whole and cortex cerebri is build up by substructures somewhat similar to the cortical areas. These again are separated in supra cellular structures – for instance feature-detectors in visual cortex – that again are build up by cells, etc as discussed above.

The second hierarchy, roughly speaking, goes lengthwise through the brain. The primary sensory input from vision, hearing, and somatic senses, give representations of these sense-spaces, in particular places. Seemingly, these areas converge to superior integrative areas that again converge to the highest integrative areas.

The last ones are directly related to motor cortex, from where movement are controlled. However, the somato-sensory cortex is also placed next to somato-motor cortex. Figure 2 shows these hierarchies separated and together.

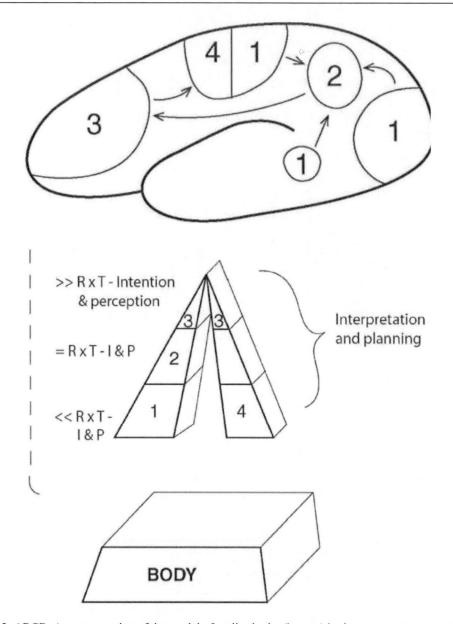

Figure 2. ABCD. A representation of the model of reality in the (human) brain as a consequence of a double hierarchy. A illustrates parts of the brain that interacts by each other. B illustrates the hierarchy of quantified qualia organised in space and time (I = Intention, P = Perception.). C illustrates the Chinese box hierarchy of interactions in the brain. D illustrates the double hierarchical representation of reality in the the brain.

Explanation of the ability to associate, discriminate and abstract

The cerebral areas represent a separate level and use a time-space hierarchy (see discussion above). But it also has to interact with the superior wholeness of the brain. Data corresponding to everything that has happened on each level, could possibly be stored in each of the cortical areas from the complex dynamic at the lower levels. Recall that the storage of data may happen in an extremely controlled way, because each area contains unimaginable amount of information.

A consequence of the ongoing information transmitting interactions on all levels of the brain is that every recall of data happens in an associated way.

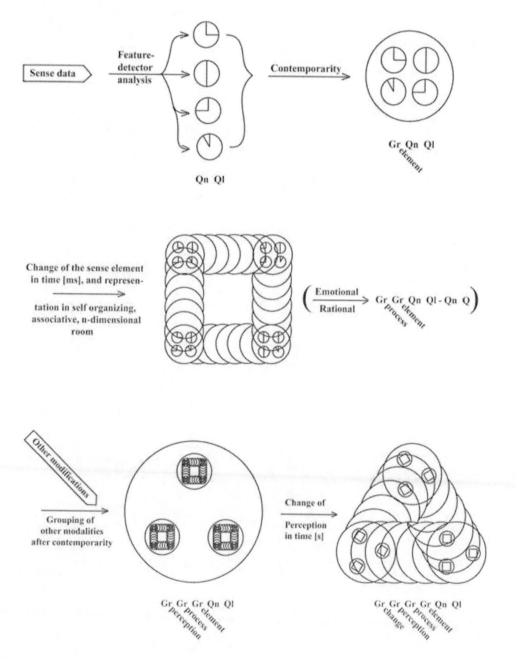

Figure 3. (Continued).

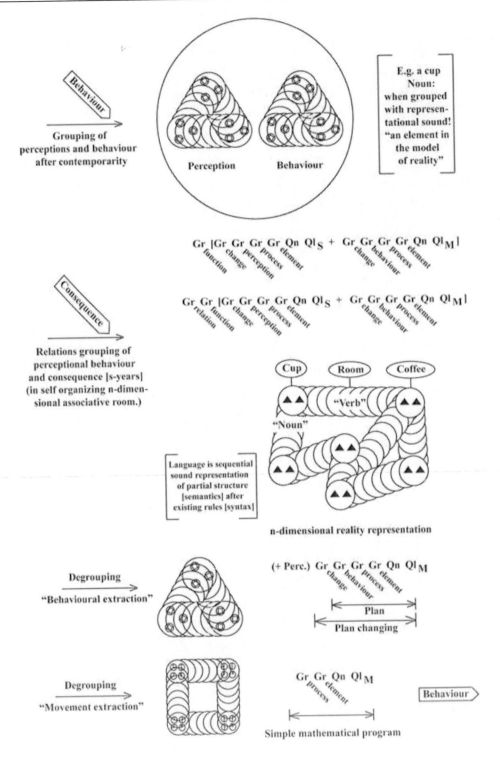

Figure 3. A model of the representation of reality in the human brain (se text).

This means that only the data that passes into the larger pattern is retrieved, and it is the most superior pattern that organizes the complete recall, which in this connection is the intention.

The ability to discriminate is presumably achieved through the structure of the functional patterns themselves. The ability to abstract and generalize follow from a co-representation of many elements having common traits in an n-dimensional, self-organizing, associative room (7) that will make up an informational body which forms exactly as the generalization or abstraction of all represented elements in this area. Such bodies (or sets) that are built by big amounts of smaller bodies will in a similar way correspond to higher levels of abstraction.

A proposal for the generation of the reality model in the brain

Figure 3 shows how a four-levels model of how reality can be created from simple repetitive co-groupings of elements of quantified qualia in space and time. First, sense impressions are analysed to meaning units in meaning unit analysers (this may bee too speculative like the "grand mother" cell and the mechanism might be energetic and not mechanic at all; comp. the visual feature detectors). The distribution of these "meaning units" in space and time is determined in the representation as positional information (compare the traditional use of this concept in ontogenesis (5)– the quantifying of the qualities. To realize the relationship between space and time in these groupings at different levels must be imagined. Thus the fundamental structure of space-time must be fully understood for us to fully comprehend consciousness.

The first grouping level causes the creation of sense elements corresponding to the perceptual level of qualia localised in space and time (this process takes milliseconds). On the motor side a corresponding grouping to motor-elements exists. The second grouping level is co-grouping of the different sense-modalities with sense elements in bigger space and time (many milliseconds or seconds) to perceptions. These cover the whole sensory-perceptual space. In the same way, motor-elements are grouped together to create concrete movements.

The third grouping level is higher space and time (seconds or minutes) groupings of perceptions and behaviour. This gives a reason-effect, where relationships between perceptions and behaviour, as possibilities, and those between behaviour and perceptions, as consequences. In the last case, the possibilities of a perception for action, and actions for perceptual consequences, is getting clear. On the third level of grouping, the co-grouping of the perceptions with behaviour in space and time, gives the reality models concrete functional elements – as for instance a cup – together with those processes that move and transform the elements into each other (the cup for example, can break in pieces when it is dropped on the floor). A child's limited intellectuality and its ability to interpret the concrete objects and possibilities of the surrounding world, has been build up at this point. The language with its nouns and verbs is introduced at this stage of life. Here, it is central to understand that the reality of the child is developed in identity with the biological intensions and needs.

The fourth group level replies to the groupings of possibilities and consequences, on higher space-time levels (from min. to years) that fit with the more complicated intentions of the human beings. In the reasonability of interpretation, this corresponds to the intellectual development, because the reality interpretation here is lifted from the concrete world into the world of ideas, abstractions, principles, hypotheses, lawfulness, and logic. In the emotional reality interpretation, this corresponds to the recognition of extremely complicated situations in the reality, outside the body.

The hierarchical representation through cortex cerebri fits with the existing data of the brain. This representation also makes good sense. Since this fits with co-groupings of sense data, and data concerning motor functions, in a number of levels that, in the end, represents the human conceptions, ideas, and intentions.

The purpose by the first concrete grouping levels is to realise the concrete intentions of the child as eating, drinking, playing, etc. On the other hand, the abstract groupings serve the purpose of realizing the long-term intentions of the adult individual, through huge spaces and times.

For the brain, it is the case, that the intentions are superior patterns that organize the highest level of co-grouping of the elements of the reality model. A specific intention, in this way, results in a selection of specific superior consequence groupings, and these again, correspond to a plan or strategy. This strategy is realised through a de-grouping to sensory-motor elements, completely analogous to the superstructure of the reality model, see figure 3.

The intention, therefore, is the innermost craft that organizes the reality model in the brain. But, the co-ordinated learning acts directly on the intention. Also, a great part of the parent's reality interpretation is transferred in a direct way, through information directed interactions to the child as learned ideas with value-ladings attached to these. Therefore, the reality model is often filled with glaring conflicts, misty ideas and direct contradictions. This results in a really complicated structure caused by the demands of social interactions.

Discussion

We do not believe that the brain is a "neural network" that has a conscious activity of its own; neither do we believe that such an "isolated brain" could have an independent activity corresponding to thoughts and dreams. We believe that models for self-organizing associative memory have demonstrated a fundamental disability in thinking and perceiving; as the computerised "neural network" of an isolated brain can't have an independent activity like thinking. We believe the brain is a highly complex pattern machine that continuously produces concrete and abstract "sensory-motor-pictures" guided by the intention of the wholeness. The mechanism by which this is done by the brain is by using information-directed dissipative neural patterns, the information coming from both the senses and the organism's wholeness. The brains central job is to make meaningful plans for achievement and realization of goals presented to the brain at its top-level by the human wholeness (the "I"), often in dreams. The reality is interpreted in agreement with the intention and is through the brain's highest level represented for the organism's wholeness in which it is evaluated emotionally.

The presented model is built on a number of axiomatic statements derived from the former papers in this series. It is quite surprising to us that it is possible to get such a clear picture of human brain function that in so many ways is helpful i.e. in explaining the perceptive distortions of the mentally ill from the degeneration of intent.

The model seems highly helpful in relation to clinical holistic therapy, where these distorted perceptions in the form of transferences and projections are happening at all the times.

The clear understanding of their neural basis will presumably make it much easier to deal with the mentally ill in therapy, and increase the number that can be helped by scientific holistic medicine. The problem of the proposed model is that you need a holistic philosophy admitting the individual cell consciousness etc. to use it.

We propose a theory for the function of the (human) brain claiming that it on a mechanical level works through information-directed self-organization of neurally produced extremely complex patterns, which only add up to meaningful perceptions and actions because of the fundamental will, or intentions, of the individual. We assume likewise that the morphogenesis of the brain is happening through the information directed self-organization of cells and tissues, and that this informational link is active throughout the individual life, securing an extremely close informational connection between mind and Self (the wholeness of the organism). All growth, absorption and modifications of nerve cells, axons, and dendrites are guided through information-directed self-organization of the molecules and organelles (1-10).

When we look at the most complicated, visual patterns as for example turbulent water flow, growing plants or computer produced fractals[101], and understand how fast and direct the brain interprets even the most complicated of visions, we find it obvious that a "patterned medium" exists in our brain that immediately forms even extremely complex patterns; these extremely complex patterns are organized in many hierarchical levels to create the well known model of reality in the human brain.

A possible consequence of the information-transmitting biological interactions in the "deep quantum field" (8) is that recalls of information happens in an associative way. Only memorised patterns that resonate with actually activated patterns are recalled. This ability to discriminate is achieved through the structure of the functional patterns themselves. The ability to abstract and generalize follows from a co-representation of many elements having common traits in an n-dimensional, self-organizing, associative space.

In cortex cerebri two hierarchies stretch out the reality model in the brain. One of these is a variant of the Chinese box system. In this, the brain is build by structures in the cortical areas separated in supra-cellular structures that in turn are build by cells. In the second hierarchy, the primary sensory input from vision, hearing, and somatic feeling, gives representations of these sensory-spaces. The last hierarchy is directly related to motor cortex, the part of the brain from where movement is controlled.

This sum up our proposal for the generation of the model of reality in the (human) brain. The many-levelled organising biological (positional) information organises the distribution of the qualia (meaningful units) in space and time. We suggest that the intentions of the whole individual are represented in the brain as superior patterns that organize the highest levels of the model of reality in the brain; this high-level co-grouping of all the elements of consciousness by the intention is the innermost craft that organizes the perceptual and acting powers of the brain.

The brain is by evolution structured to transform all modalities of sensation and intention into its integrated perception of reality, in a form that empowers it for optimal action to achieve self-actualisation – the full realisation of the abstract "I".

Appendix 1. The value of existing sources of knowledge of the brain for understanding its function

Sources of experimental data about the structure and function of the brain: Data concerning the brain come from different sources, but yet they are not - even when pooled together - adequate to fully explain consciousness and the mind. To postulate that the functions of the brain are understood, we need the collected data to make sense and be able to explain all aspects of the mind; but most of the data does not make much sense – as the EEG and data definitely do not sum up to a nice understanding of what is going on. Some essential sources of data on the brain are mentioned below.

Anatomically the brain can be divided in a forebrain, a midbrain and a hindbrain that again are separated in several structures – as for example cortex cerebri separated in sub structures of cerebral cortex. These sub structures are split in supra cellular structures in the primary visual cortex – meaning analysers/feature detectors – that seemingly analyse incoming counts nerve cell signals.

The morphogenesis of the brain is uniform to that of other organs and can be essentially separated from those in reverse order, when axons and dendrites make the connectivity between nerve cells. This connects the different parts of the brain with each other so sensory inputs from receptors in the sense organs and body can be associated with motor outputs of the apparatus of movement.

Histological studies (79) have shown that pyramid cells (that count approximately half of all cells in cerebral cortex) converge to about 1,000 of the 3 million cells in cerebral cortex positioned only 3-4 cells apart from each other. Electron microscopically measurements of the distribution of sound impressions in cortex, give the same kinds of results (88,94).

Connectivity: The cortex cerebri can be understood as a surface having a 1,000-dimentional connectivity. The neuron length is about 1,000,000 km indicating the tremendous complexity of the brain. The existence of meaning-unity analysers/feature detectors, is most evidently in the primary visual cortex, but probably exists in all primary cortices. It has been proposed[95,96], that cerebral association-cortex, in general, should be organized in functionally modules of 300? But this is not supported by evidence in the literature, because the existing columns only seem to be caused by corticocortical termination from pyramid cells (11).

Physiological studies have shown an intense interaction between all structures of the brain. Thalamus, fore instance, may be assumed to play a central role as a regulator of input to the cerebral cortex. Motor outputs that happen through motor cortex, seemingly is essentially influenced by the limbic structures and the basic ganglions, and also the patterns of movement (and perceptional patterns) from the cerebellum are commissioned. Generally, all parts of the brain are mutually connected with each other, but the total brain function is not yet understood.

Electro physiological studies have shown that inputs are well-arranged in cortex in two-dimensional maps repeated many times throughout the different brain areas. Somatotopic maps in somatosensory and motor areas, represents the different sense-receptor types and motor aspects of the body. Visio type maps represent the visual field in the visual areas, and tonotropic maps represent the tone scale. The organization of the smell sense in cortex is not yet understood. Trials with maps show that these cortical representations almost instantaneously can be organised, why they hardly are associated directly with axons and dendrites (88).

Electron microscopic tests of complex cells and groups of cells show, most clearly in primary visual cortex, an organization that is used to analyse meaning-unities of visual impressions.

Data from electro encephalogram (EEG) is very difficult to interpret. Simultaneously, they reflect the activity from cells in the cortical surface. Normally the electronic voltage arises and decreases 8-30 times per second when awake. The most important result is that a high amount of patterns integrates constantly while the brain works (88).

Studies of the blood flow in cerebral cortex (4,5) and of cortical lesions, have given a rather detailed map of the localization of the cerebral cortex's function. We know that data from the primary sensory areas as prefrontal cortex are dispositioned in areas of higher levels.

Psychological studies (93-94) have shown that the consciousness is build of sense-motor activities, and that the development through childhood follows the development of the body organization. The consciousness consists of sense and motor functions created by sense-motor elements. Later in the development, the child learns to think in abstractions and then talk. In this way, the consciousness gets freedom to use the body in more complex ways.

Philosophy. What we think gives the consciousness meaning. This interpretation is fundamentally connected with the body. The development of the consciousness as an objective matter of interpretation, results in hiding the original physical beginning where the connection between body and mind is being obscure.

Evolutionary studies reveal that simple nerve systems such as Hydras, that is thought to be the first organism with a nerve network, could function through information-transformed interactions between nerve system and health. A quite simple nerve network consisting of neurons, where the nerve impulses can move along in all directions from the stimulus point (100), gives Hydra a possibility to carry out a very complex behaviour as for example catching of prey, swimming, and somersaults. Seemingly this nerve network does not need any practise to function.

Mathematical analysis; cortex cerebri as a model machine: Systems with elements that exitatorically and inhibitorically influences each other, such as neurons do, show a stabile self-organization. However, mathematical analysis show that when the connectivity is huge, as it is in cortex, the ability to stabilize the self-organization break down (90,91) and all patterns become liquid and non-durable.

Metabolism. About 20% of our energy is used by the brain that only makes up 2% of the body weight. It is estimated that this huge consumption of energy, corresponds with an almost constant activity of impulses in all the brains nerve cells (NA Lassen, personally communication 1990). However, seemingly through an extreme "mental burden" this metabolism does not increase considerably.

Discussion of the significance of the above listed data sources

How does the brain work? Throughout time, there have been a lot of proposals on how to explain the functions of the brain. However, nobody has been able to explain "higher psychic functions" and existing explanations seems not to support what we know about the brain. For example, it is often proposed that the brain process its data in the same way as computers. Indeed computer implemented "neural network" with learning specific "synapse strengths" can be trained to process input patterns into specific output patterns. Coordinated learning through synapse strength is known from lower level animals (88), but as mentioned, research on the cortical maps have documented that cortical representations are not hard-wired. We are therefore forced to conclude that the brain is not using "neural networks" of any known type. A neural network is basically a slave without creativity, and do not have an independent activity corresponding to thoughts and dreams, which is an other major problem if you try to explain the brain as a neural net. Also, when it comes to consciousness, the non-local key quality of consciousness it very difficult to produce even in theory with a neural network; they are popular because they are easy to produce in silicon, but please remember that the electric activity of a computer is extremely local!!! Having dispersed information into a network is not helping us getting non-local consciousness as data now is stuck to certain positions in the network "Convergent groupings of feature-detectors" on an number of levels can theoretically give us a single cell that represents any object knows from our world - the famous idea of a "grandmother cell" that fires only when we see our grandmother! But the problem is of course how such the activity in a cell should be able to give us the consciousness of seeing our grandmother – how will this single-cell activity be clearly represented in out global brain activity? We believe that models for self-organizing associative memory like the famous Kohonen model (92) have the same disability as the other "neural network" and cannot have an independent activity like thinking. Most interestingly there have never been constructed a truly self-learning neural network; all existing neural networks are in some way controlled from the outside though the programming of the net. Nothing artificial has yet been created that function like the brain, not even most superficially. This in itself should make people think about the difference between machines of silicon and living beings.

The most famous problem in brain research is the psychophysical problem. The materialistic version of this problem goes: how can consciousness emerge from biochemistry? How can any dead back of inorganic atoms end up feeling and living? Most people intuitively agrees that no matter how many balls you put in the bag, or how ingeniously you combine them with electromagnetic springs, they still do not live and laugh. As to the dualistic proposals to find a solution of the psychophysical problem (102), these proposals of the brain function seem to be an expression for philosophic resignation: The problem simply is to hard, so in stead of solving it we are cheating. Most researches that has worked with this problem has actually in the end given up explaining consciousness, perception, intention etc (102). Brain research has turned completely mechanical, into molecular research; as if the brain researchers all has come to believe that just by finding smarter molecules they will some pretty day be able to solve the fundamental problems of brain and consciousness. (Maybe that is what is going to happen in the end when we finally get to understand proteins and find "intelligent molecules" that can read the extremely small energies of the directive collective quantum field of the biological system)(4-8).

It is not that we do not believe in science. But we need to acknowledge reality and stop moving away from the fundamental problems we need to solve – just avoiding the pain of not getting anywhere will not give us a new scientific understanding of the brain. We cannot understand the wholeness as a sum of its parts; the wholeness is always more. That is one of the most central understandings of holistic philosophy (1-11).

The brain (neocortex) is making lots and lots of extremely complex patterns; that's pretty much what we can tell from all the brain research done. The nature of these patterns; the geometry they must be described in, the way they interact with other patterns, sensory stimuli and the inner biological informational system of the organism, remains most unfortunately still in the dark.

References

[1]   Hermansen TD, Ventegodt S, Rald E, Clausen B, Nielsen ML, Merrick J. Human development I. Twenty fundamental problems of biology, medicine and neuropsychology related to biological information. ScientificWorldJournal 2006;6:747-59.

[2]   Ventegodt S, Hermansen TD, Nielsen ML, Clausen B, Merrick J. Human development II. We need an integrated theory for matter, life and consciousness to understand life and healing. ScientificWorldJournal 2006;6:760-6.

[3]   Ventegodt S, Hermansen TD, Rald E, Flensborg-Madsen T, Nielsen ML, Clausen B, Merrick J. Human development III. Bridging brain-mind and body-mind. Itroduction to "deep" (fractal, poly-ray) cosmology. ScientificWorldJournal 2006;6:767-76.

[4]   Ventegodt S, Hermansen TD, Rald E, Flensborg-Madsen T, Nielsen ML, Clausen B, Merrick J. Human development IV. The living cell has information-directed self-organization. ScientificWorldJournal 2006;6:1132-8.

[5]   Ventegodt S, Hermansen TD, Flensborg-Madsen T, Nielsen ML, Clausen B, Merrick J. Human development V: Biochemistry unable to explain the emergence of biological form (morphogenesis) and therefore a new principle as source of biological information is needed. ScientificWorldJournal 2006;6:1359-67.

[6]   Ventegodt S, Hermansen TD, Flensborg-Madsen T, Nielsen M, Merrick J. Human development VI: Supracellular morphogenesis. The origin of biological and cellular order. ScientificWorldJournal 2006;6:1424-33.

[7]   Ventegodt S, Hermansen TD, Flensborg-Madsen T, Rald E, Nielsen ML, Merrick J. Human development VII: A spiral fractal model of fine structure of physical energy could explain central aspects of biological information, biological organization and biological creativity. ScientificWorldJournal 2006;6:1434-40.

[8]   Ventegodt S, Hermansen TD, Flensborg-Madsen T, Nielsen ML, Merrick J. Human development VIII: A theory of "deep" quantum chemistry and cell consciousness: Quantum chemistry controls genes and biochemistry to give cells and higher organisms consciousness and complex behavior. ScientificWorldJournal 2006;6:1441-53.

[9]   Ventegodt S, Hermansen TD, Flensborg-Madsen T, Rald E, Nielsen ML, Merrick J. Human development IX: A model of the wholeness of man, his consciousness and collective consciousness. ScientificWorldJournal 2006;6:1454-9.

[10]   Hermansen TD, Ventegodt S, Merrick J. Human development X: Explanation of macroevolution — top-down evolution materializes consciousness. The origin of metamorphosis. ScientificWorldJournal 2006;6:1656-66.

[11]   Hermansen TD, Ventegodt S, Kandel I. Human development XI: The structure of the cerebral cortex. Are there really modules in the brain? ScientificWorldJournal 2007;7:1922-9.

[12]   Ventegodt S, Andersen NJ, Merrick J. Editorial: Five theories of human existence. ScientificWorldJournal 2003;3:1272-6.

[13]   Ventegodt S. The life mission theory: A theory for a consciousness-based medicine. Int J Adolesc Med Health 2003;15(1):89-91.

[14]   Ventegodt S, Andersen NJ, Merrick J. The life mission theory II: The structure of the life purpose and the ego. ScientificWorldJournal 2003;3:1277-85.

[15] Ventegodt S, Andersen NJ, Merrick J. The life mission theory III: Theory of talent. ScientificWorldJournal 2003;3:1286-93.

[16] Ventegodt S, Merrick J. The life mission theory IV. A theory of child development. ScientificWorldJournal 2003;3:1294-1301.

[17] Ventegodt S, Andersen NJ, Merrick J. The life mission theory V. A theory of the anti-self and explaining the evil side of man. ScientificWorldJournal 2003;3:1302-13.

[18] Ventegodt S, Andersen NJ, Merrick J. The life mission theory VI: A theory for the human character. ScientificWorldJournal 2004;4:859-80.

[19] Ventegodt S, Flensborg-Madsen T, Andersen NJ, Merrick J. Life mission theory VII: Theory of existential (Antonovsky) coherence: a theory of quality of life, health and ability for use in holistic medicine. ScientificWorldJournal 2005;5:377-89.

[20] Ventegodt S, Merrick J. Life mission theory VIII: A theory for pain. J Pain Manage 2008;1(1):5-10.

[21] Ventegodt S, Andersen NJ, Merrick J. Holistic medicine: Scientific challenges. ScientificWorldJournal 2003;3:1108-16.

[22] Ventegodt S, Andersen NJ, Merrick J. Holistic Medicine II: The square-curve paradigm for research in alternative, complementary and holistic medicine: A cost-effective, easy and scientifically valid design for evidence based medicine. ScientificWorldJournal 2003;3: 1117-27.

[23] Ventegodt S, Andersen NJ, Merrick J. Holistic Medicine III: The holistic process theory of healing. ScientificWorldJournal 2003;3: 1138-46.

[24] Ventegodt S, Andersen NJ, Merrick J. Holistic Medicine IV: Principles of the holistic process of healing in a group setting. ScientificWorldJournal 2003;3:1294-1301.

[25] Ventegodt S, Merrick J. Clinical holistic medicine: Applied consciousness-based medicine ScientificWorldJournal 2004;4:96-9.

[26] Ventegodt S, Morad M, Merrick J. Clinical holistic medicine: Classic art of healing or the therapeutic touch. ScientificWorldJournal 2004;4:134-47.

[27] Ventegodt S, Morad M, Merrick J. Clinical holistic medicine: The "new medicine", the multi-paradigmatic physician and the medical record. ScientificWorldJournal 2004;4:273-85.

[28] Ventegodt S, Morad M, Merrick J. Clinical holistic medicine: Holistic pelvic examination and holistic treatment of infertility. ScientificWorldJournal 2004;4:148-58.

[29] Ventegodt S, Morad M, Hyam E, Merrick J. Clinical holistic medicine: Use and limitations of the biomedical paradigm ScientificWorldJournal 2004;4:295-306.

[30] Ventegodt S, Morad M, Kandel I, Merrick J. Clinical holistic medicine: Social problems disguised as illness. ScientificWorldJournal 2004;4:286-94.

[31] Ventegodt S, Morad M, Andersen NJ, Merrick J. Clinical holistic medicine Tools for a medical science based on consciousness. ScientificWorldJournal 2004;4:347-61.

[32] Ventegodt S, Morad M, Merrick J. Clinical holistic medicine: Prevention through healthy lifestyle and quality of life. Oral Health Prev Dent 2004;1:239-45.

[33] Ventegodt S, Morad M, Hyam E, Merrick J. Clinical holistic medicine: When biomedicine is inadequate. ScientificWorldJournal 2004;4:333-46.

[34] Ventegodt S, Morad M, Merrick J. Clinical holistic medicine: Holistic treatment of children. ScientificWorldJournal 2004;4:581-8.

[35] Ventegodt S, Morad M, Merrick J. Clinical holistic medicine: Problems in sex and living together. ScientificWorldJournal 2004;4:562-70.

[36] Ventegodt S, Morad M, Hyam E, Merrick J. Clinical holistic medicine: Holistic sexology and treatment of vulvodynia through existential therapy and acceptance through touch. ScientificWorldJournal 2004;4:571-80.

[37] Ventegodt S, Flensborg-Madsen T, Andersen NJ, Morad M, Merrick J. Clinical holistic medicine: A Pilot on HIV and Quality of Life and a Suggested treatment of HIV and AIDS. ScientificWorldJournal 2004;4:264-72.

[38] Ventegodt S, Morad M, Merrick J. Clinical holistic medicine: Induction of spontaneous remission of cancer by recovery of the human character and the purpose of life (the life mission). ScientificWorldJournal 2004;4:362-77.

[39]   Ventegodt S, Morad M, Kandel I, Merrick J. Clinical holistic medicine: Treatment of physical health problems without a known cause, exemplified by hypertension and tinnitus. ScientificWorldJournal 2004;4:716-24.

[40]   Ventegodt S, Morad M, Merrick J. Clinical holistic medicine: Developing from asthma, allergy and eczema. ScientificWorldJournal 2004;4:936-42.

[41]   Ventegodt S, Morad M, Press J, Merrick J, Shek DTL. Clinical holistic medicine: Holistic adolescent medicine. ScientificWorldJournal 2004;4:551-61.

[42]   Ventegodt S, Solheim E, Saunte ME, Morad M, Kandel I, Merrick J. Clinical holistic medicine: Metastatic cancer. ScientificWorldJournal 2004;4:913-35.

[43]   Ventegodt S, Morad M, Kandel I, Merrick J. Clinical holistic medicine: a psychological theory of dependency to improve quality of life. ScientificWorldJournal 2004;4:638-48.

[44]   Ventegodt S, Merrick J. Clinical holistic medicine: Chronic infections and autoimmune diseases. ScientificWorldJournal 2005;5: 155-64.

[45]   Ventegodt S, Kandel I, Neikrug S, Merrick J. Clinical holistic medicine: Holistic treatment of rape and incest traumas. ScientificWorldJournal 2005;5:288-97.

[46]   Ventegodt S, Morad M, Merrick J. Clinical holistic medicine: Chronic pain in the locomotor system. ScientificWorldJournal 2005;5:165-72.

[47]   Ventegodt S, Merrick J. Clinical holistic medicine: Chronic pain in internal organs. ScientificWorldJournal 2005;5:205-10.

[48]   Ventegodt S, Kandel I, Neikrug S, Merrick J. Clinical holistic medicine: The existential crisis – life crisis, stress and burnout. ScientificWorldJournal 2005;5:300-12.

[49]   Ventegodt S, Gringols G, Merrick J. Clinical holistic medicine: Holistic rehabilitation. ScientificWorldJournal 2005;5:280-7.

[50]   Ventegodt S, Andersen NJ, Neikrug S, Kandel I, Merrick J. Clinical holistic medicine: Mental disorders in a holistic perspective. ScientificWorldJournal 2005;5:313-23.

[51]   Ventegodt S, Andersen NJ, Neikrug S, Kandel I, Merrick J. Clinical holistic medicine: Holistic treatment of mental disorders. ScientificWorldJournal 2005;5:427-45.

[52]   Ventegodt S, Merrick J. Clinical holistic medicine: The patient with multiple diseases. ScientificWorldJournal 2005;5:324-39.

[53]   Ventegodt S, Clausen B, Nielsen ML, Merrick J. Advanced tools for holistic medicine. ScientificWorldJournal 2006;6:2048-65.

[54]   Ventegodt S, Clausen B, Merrick J. Clinical holistic medicine: The case story of Anna: I. Long term effect of child sexual abuse and incest with a treatment approach. ScientificWorldJournal 2006;6:1965-76.

[55]   Ventegodt S, Clausen B, Merrick J. Clinical holistic medicine: the case story of Anna. II. Patient diary as a tool in treatment. ScientificWorldJournal 2006;6:2006-34.

[56]   Ventegodt S, Clausen B, Merrick J. Clinical holistic medicine: The case story of Anna. III. Rehabilitation of philosophy of life during holistic existential therapy for childhood sexual abuse. ScientificWorldJournal 2006;6:2080-91.

[57]   Ventegodt S, Merrick J. Suicide from a holistic point of view. ScientificWorldJournal 2005;5:759-66.

[58]   Ventegodt S, Clausen B, Omar HA, Merrick J. Clinical holistic medicine: Holistic sexology and acupressure through the vagina (Hippocratic pelvic massage. ScientificWorldJournal 2006;6:2066-79.

[59]   Ventegodt S, Clausen B, Merrick J. Clinical holistic medicine: Pilot study on the effect of vaginal acupressure (Hippocratic pelvic massage). ScientificWorldJournal 2006;6:2100-16.

[60]   Ventegodt S. [Min brug af vaginal akupressur.] My use of acupressure. Ugeskr Laeger 2006;168(7):715-6. [Danish].

[61]   Ventegodt S, Thegler S, Andreasen T, Struve F, Enevoldsen L, Bassaine L, et al. Clinical holistic medicine: Psychodynamic short-time therapy complemented with bodywork. A clinical follow-up study of 109 patients. ScientificWorldJournal 2006;6:2220-38.

[62]   Ventegodt S, Thegler S, Andreasen T, Struve F, Enevoldsen L, Bassaine L, et al. Clinical holistic medicine (mindful, short-term psychodynamic psychotherapy complemented with bodywork) in the treatment of experienced impaired sexual functioning. ScientificWorldJournal 2007;7:324-9.

[63]   Ventegodt S, Thegler S, Andreasen T, Struve F, Enevoldsen L, Bassaine L, et al. Clinical holistic medicine (mindful, short-term psychodynamic psychotherapy complemented with bodywork) improves quality of life, health, and ability by induction of Antonovsky-salutogenesis. ScientificWorldJournal 2007;7:317-23.

[64]   Ventegodt S, Thegler S, Andreasen T, Struve F, Enevoldsen L, Bassaine L, et al. Clinical holistic medicine (mindful, short-term psychodynamic psychotherapy complemented with bodywork) in the treatment of experienced physical illness and chronic pain. ScientificWorldJournal 2007;7:310-6.

[65]   Ventegodt S, Thegler S, Andreasen T, Struve F, Enevoldsen L, Bassaine L, et al. Clinical holistic medicine (mindful, short-term psychodynamic psychotherapy complemented with bodywork) in the treatment of experienced mental illness. ScientificWorldJournal 2007;7:306-9.

[66]   Ventegodt S, Thegler S, Andreasen T, Struve F, Enevoldsen L, Bassaine L, et al. Self-reported low self-esteem. Intervention and follow-up in a clinical setting. ScientificWorldJournal 2007;7:299-305.

[67]   Jones E. The life and works of Sigmund Freud. New York: Basic Books, 1961.

[68]   Jung CG. Man and his symbols. New York: Anchor Press, 1964.

[69]   Jung CG. Psychology and alchemy. Collected works of CG Jung, Vol 12. Princeton, NJ: Princeton Univ Press, 1968.

[70]   Reich W. [Die Function des Orgasmus.] Köln: Kiepenheuer Witsch, 1969. [German].

[71]   Lowen A. Honoring the body. Alachua, FL: Bioenergetics Press, 1994.

[72]   Rosen M, Brenner S. Rosen method bodywork. Accessing the unconscious through touch. Berkeley, CA: North Atlantic Books, 2003.

[73]   Anand M. The art of sexual ecstasy. The path of sacred sexuality for Western lovers. New York: Jerymy P Tarcher/Putnam,

[74]   Antonovsky A. Health, stress and coping. London: Jossey-Bass, 1985.

[75]   Antonovsky A. Unravelling the mystery of health. How people manage stress and stay well. San Franscisco: Jossey-Bass, 1987.

[76]   Leichsenring F, Rabung S, Leibing E. The efficacy of short-term psychodynamic psychotherapy in specific psychiatric disorders: a meta-analysis. Arch Gen Psychiatry 2004;61(12):1208-16.

[77]   Leichsenring F. Are psychodynamic and psychoanalytic therapies effective? A review of empirical data. Int J Psychoanal 2005;86(Pt 3):841-68.

[78]   Leichsenring F, Leibing E. Psychodynamic psychotherapy: a systematic review of techniques, indications and empirical evidence. Psychol Psychother 2007;80(Pt 2):217-28.

[79]   Kelso JAS. Dynamic patterns: The self-organization of brain and behavior. Cambridge, MA: MIT Press, 1995.

[80]   Kelso JAS, Engstrom DA. The complementary nature. Cambridge, MA: MIT Press, 2006.

[81]   Wolfram S. A new kind of science. Champaign, IL: Wolfram Media, 2002.

[82]   Ventegodt S. Philosophy of life that heals. [Livsfilosofi der helbreder.] Copenhagen: Forskningscenterets Forlag, 1999. [Danish].

[83]   Penrose R. Shadows of the mind. Oxford: Oxford Univ Press, 1996.

[84]   Hofstadter DR. I am a strange loop. New York: Basic Books, 2007.

[85]   Grof S. LSD psychotherapy: Exploring the frontiers of the hidden mind. Alameda, CA: Hunter House, 1980.

[86]   Grof S. Implications of modern consciousness research for psychology: Holotropic experiences and their healing and heuristic potential. Humanistic Psychol 2003;31(2-3):50-85.

[87]   Goleman D. Healing emotions: Conversations with the Dalai Lama on the mindfulness, emotions, and health. Boston, MA: Mind Life Inst, 1997.

[88]   Kandel ER, Schwartz JH. Principles of neural science. Amsterdam: Elsevier, 2000.

[89]   Freeman WJ. Analysis of cerebral cortex by use of control systems theory. Logistics Rev 1967;3:5-40.

[90]   Babloyantz A. Self-organization phenomena resulting from cell-cell contact. J Theor Biol 1977;68(4):551-61.

[91]   Babloyantz A, Kaczmarek LK. Self-organization in biological systems with multiple cellular contacts. Bull Math Biol 1979;41(2):193-201.

[92]   Kohonen T. Selforganization and associative memory. Berlin: Springer, 1984.

[93]   Lassen NA, Roland PE, Larsen B, Melamed E, Soh K. Mapping of human cerebral functions: a study of the regional cerebral blood flow pattern during rest, its reproducibility and the activations seen during basic sensory and motor functions. Acta Neurol Scand 1977;Suppl 64: 262-3, 274-5.

[94]   Friberg L, Olsen TS, Roland PE, Paulson OB, Lassen NA. Focal increase of blood flow in the cerebral cortex of man during vestibular stimulation. Brain 1985;8(3):609-23.

[95]   Szentagothai J. The "module concept" in cerebral cortex architecture. Brain Res 1975;95:475-96.

[96]   Mountcastle VB. An organizing principle for cerebral function: The unit module and the distributed system. In: Edelman GM, ed. The mindful brain. Cambridge, MA: MIT Press, 1978:7-50.

[97]   Piaget J. The construction of reality in the child. New York: Basic Books, 1954.

[98]   Piaget J. The growth of logical thinking from childhood to adolescence. New York: Basic Books, 1958.

[99]   Piaget J. The psychology of the child. New York: Basic Books, 1969.

[100] Campbell NA, Reece JB, Mitchell LG. Biology. Menlo Park, CA: Addison-Wesley Longman, 2002.

[101] Peitgen H-O. Beauty of fractals: Images of complex dynamical systems. Berlin: Springer, 1986.

[102] McGinn C. The mysterious flame. New York: Basic Books, 2000.

Section 6. Etiology of mental disorders

The deeper we look into human existence the less we seem to understand. In this section we look into the fundamental dimensions of human existence that were introduced in section three. We shall also look into the healing crisis that almost always is connected to holistic healing – a crisis that often is mistaken for a transient psychosis, or even a mental disorder caused by the therapy.

The strangest concept we shall meet in this section is the concept of human metamorphosis.

This is a concept that is as old as holistic medicine itself. The analogy is the metamorphosis of the larvae into the butterfly or the tadpole into the frog. It is a complete and almost immediate reorganization of form, behaviour and basic intent, that most, higher life forms seems able of. We human beings have got a series of genes known to be involved in metamorphosis if frogs.

We believe that small children are able to go through a process of metamorphosis where they change, if not their physical appearance, but their energy, character and purpose of life, to take a form that please their parents more so they are more able to survive even a rough childhood. We believe this, because we often see dramatic processes that looks like this process being reversed after so many years with the person finally returning to his or her true self. We have called this dramatic almost instant process of human transformation for "adult human metamorphosis" in spite of the fact that the scientifically correct concept should be "adult human re-metamorphosis". We simply found the concept complicated enough as it was.

The problem of this section is that some of its theory is not very likely to be true. The theories are too farfetched. On the other hand, we need theories of this level of complexity to fully understand what is going on. Needless to say, we need much more research in this problematic research area of human existence.

If you want to understand our thoughts in it full depth we need to refer you to our series of papers on "human development" (1-10) and to our previous books on holistic medicine (11-14).

We hope and pray that the complexity of the concepts that makes the basis of the three chapters we have included in this section will not totally de-motivate our readers.

References

[1] Hermansen TD, Ventegodt S, Rald E, Clausen B, Nielsen ML, Merrick J. Human development I: twenty fundamental problems of biology, medicine, and neuro-psychology related to biological information. ScientificWorldJournal 2006;6:747-59.

[2] Ventegodt S, Hermansen TD, Nielsen ML, Clausen B, Merrick J. Human development II: we need an integrated theory for matter, life and consciousness to understand life and healing. ScientificWorldJournal 2006;6:760-6.

[3] Ventegodt S, Hermansen TD, Rald E, Flensborg-Madsen T, Nielsen ML, Clausen B, Merrick J. Human development III: bridging brain-mind and body-mind. introduction to "deep" (fractal, poly-ray) cosmology. ScientificWorldJournal 2006;6:767-76.

[4] Ventegodt S, Hermansen TD, Flensborg-Madsen T, Nielsen ML, Clausen B, Merrick J. Human development IV: the living cell has information-directed self-organisation. ScientificWorldJournal 2006;6:1132-8.

[5] Ventegodt S, Hermansen TD, Flensborg-Madsen T, Nielsen ML, Clausen B, Merrick J. Human development V: biochemistry unable to explain the emergence of biological form (morphogenesis) and therefore a new principle as source of biological information is needed. ScientificWorldJournal 2006;6:1359-67.

[6] Ventegodt S, Hermansen TD, Flensborg-Madsen T, Nielsen M, Merrick J. Human development VI: Supracellular morphogenesis. The origin of biological and cellular order. ScientificWorldJournal 2006;6:1424-33.

[7] Ventegodt S, Hermansen TD, Flensborg-Madsen T, Rald E, Nielsen ML, Merrick J. Human development VII: A spiral fractal model of fine structure of physical energy could explain central aspects of biological information, biological organization and biological creativity. ScientificWorldJournal 2006;6:1434-40.

[8] Ventegodt S, Hermansen TD, Flensborg-Madsen T, Nielsen ML, Merrick J. Human development VIII: A theory of "deep" quantum chemistry and cell consciousness: Quantum chemistry controls genes and biochemistry to give cells and higher organisms consciousness and complex behavior. ScientificWorldJournal 2006;6:1441-53.

[9] Ventegodt S, Hermansen TD, Flensborg-Madsen T, Rald E, Nielsen ML, Merrick J. Human development IX: A model of the wholeness of man, his consciousness and collective consciousness. ScientificWorldJournal 2006;6:1454-9.

[10] Hermansen TD, Ventegodt S, Merrick J. Human development X: Explanation of macroevolution — top-down evolution materializes consciousness. The origin of metamorphosis. ScientificWorldJournal 2006;6:1656-66.

[11] Ventegodt S, Kandel I, Merrick J. Principles of holistic medicine. Philosophy behind quality of life. Victoria, BC: Trafford, 2005.

[12] Ventegodt S, Kandel I, Merrick J. Principles of holistic medicine. Quality of life and health. New York: Hippocrates Sci Publ, 2005.

[13] Ventegodt S, Kandel I, Merrick J. Principles of holistic medicine. Global quality of life.Theory, research and methodology. New York: Hippocrates Sci Publ, 2006.

[14] Ventegodt S, Merrick J. Sexology from a holistic point of view. A textbook of classic and modern sexology. New York: Nova Science, 2010.

Chapter 25

Clinical medicine and psychodynamic psychotherapy. Evaluation of the patient before intervention

Clinical medicine has been defined as "the study and practice of medicine by direct examination of the patient." This approach to medicine is appropriate whenever the patient's problem or disease is caused by repressed material contained in the patient's unconscious. According to psychoanalysis, body-psychotherapy and clinical holistic medicine most mental and physical illnesses are caused by informational disturbances in the bodies tissues likely to be a direct consequence of repressed emotions, feeling and thoughts from traumas earlier in life. This is the most logical explanation why the rehabilitation of the sense of coherence seems to induce healing of both physical and mental diseases.

If it is unconscious material that causes the patient's disorders the patient will not be helped by a precise anamnesis and an accurate diagnosis; the only thing that can cure is the unconscious material being integrating in the patient's consciousness. If a chronic patient with a long history in biomedicine has not been helped, in spite of many biomedical doctors using their best efforts on this, the likely cause of the patient's illness or disease is in the unconscious. In this case there is no reason to spend much time on anamnesis and diagnosis of the patient; the right thing to do is to start the exploration of the patient's inner, unconscious life together with the patient right away. This strategy leads to the most cost-efficient use of time, and often to the healing of the patients experienced health-problems in only 20 sessions. Many disorders can be treated effectively and without adverse effects/side effects with clinical medicine (NNT=1-3 and NNH>1000), which should be compared to NNT=5-20 and NNH=1-4 for most drugs.

Introduction

The concept of "clinical medicine" has two meanings; the one is the well-known and science of practical medicine and another is much more traditional, well expressed by "BioMedExperts.Com" (1): "Clinical medicine: The study and practice of medicine by direct examination of the patient."

Before physicians had drugs – from around 1900 and all the way back to the old Greek physicians in the line of Hippocrates (2) medical treatment was about examination the patient and shedding light, consciousness and understanding on the human problems. In this process of common exploration of the patient, where the patient little by little understood what was wrong and what needed to be corrected in life, the patient was healed (or died). The disease process could be of one of two types, disease caused by external causes (epidemics were well known even in Hippocrates time (2), and by internal causes. The internal causes were seen as caused by either divine influence or of lack of self-knowledge at that time. Devine influence was harder to deal with, but the exploration into self and the unconscious seem to be an integrated part of the practice that later was labeled "character medicine".

Character medicine was about balancing the four symbolic elements of water, fire, earth and air, in the person's character. The Greek medical system was holistic, and could best be translated into something like "energy healing" or "consciousness-based medicine". The tools for the combined examination-treatment was talking and touching; therapeutic touch in the form of massage and acupressure seems to be the normal treatment of a long series of problems likely to be caused by "inter courses".

Freud and psychoanalysis

First with Sigmund Freud (1856-1939) and the psychoanalysts of the 20th century the concept of "the unconscious" was developed. The unconscious was always feelings/emotions and thoughts linked to personal history and especially painful and overwhelming moments called traumas or "gestalts". Freud, Reich, Jung, Lowen Rosen, Anand (3-9) and other psychoanalysts and body-psychotherapists focused on sexual traumas as these traumas seemed to hold on to the most intense feelings that needed to be integrated by the patient, in order to heal physical and mental illnesses. The successful healing of a long number of mental illnesses including schizophrenia (10) led to the conviction that all mental illness were caused by unconscious material – traumas with repressed sexuality. Wilhelm Reich (1897-1957), another therapist like the many from the contemporary schools of body-psychotherapy came to believe that even cancer and coronary heart disease were caused by repressed emotions and sexuality, and still today we have physicians like Dean Ornish who cure heart patients by learning his patients intimacy, and thus "opening their hearts physically, emotionally, and spiritually" (11,12). In New York psychoanalysts seemingly has good results with treating cancer patient in much the same way (13,14), and in Germany complementary therapists are going the same way with their patients (15). The understanding of holistic healing has recently been more clear after the work and development of "salutogenesis" by Aaron Antonovsky (1923-1994) (16,17).

Exploring the unconscious with the patient

To cure a patient from a problem caused by traumatic content in the patient's subconscious is in principle easy: Just explore the unconscious together with the patient, help him or her to confront the difficult emotions and feeling, and integrate all that happened in the consciousness. This is the strategy of psychoanalysis, where free associations have been the major tool. This has also been the strategy in Reichian bodywork and body-psychotherapy. It was also, as mentioned above the core of the therapy of the old, holistic physicians working with conversation and touch therapy to develop the patient's self-insight and character.

Interestingly, the process of healing in "clinical medicine" – exploring the patient together with the patient in the intent to cure – are almost opposite the process of today's biomedicine, where anamnesis, testing and examination leads to diagnosis, and first after that the establishment of the right drug, surgery or other (mechanical or chemical) intervention for treatment. In biomedicine the accuracy of the anamnesis and diagnosis is essential to competent treatment. In clinical medicine, the anamnesis and diagnosis, is only of importance if the physician is in doubt of the cause of the disease. If the cause is external – bacteria as in syphilis for example – it has little meaning to work on the patient's unconscious, but as soon as the cause is established as internal, based in the patient's subconscious, there is no more need for anamnesis and diagnosis. All energy must now be focused on the process of healing, by shedding light into the patient's unconscious.

If the patient is a chronic patient, who already has been to a number of well-trained biomedical physicians there is no reason to suspect that the reason is external, because that would have been discovered already. In this situation, the treatment should start right away by taking the patient unto the journey of exploring the patient's inner life.

The efficacy of clinical medicine

Clinical medicine has been documented highly effective in physiotherapy (18-23), psychodynamic psychotherapy (24-26), sexology (27-30), and CAM, i.e.. clinical holistic medicine (31-38). Number Needed to Treat has normally been about NNT=2, and Number Needed to treat to Harm has been shown to be NNH>1000 or more (39,40). Heart diseases and cancer has been rather successfully treated (NNT=3-7), and even some cases of schizophrenia seem to respond well (NNT=3) (10). In comparison to this most drugs has a NNT=5-20 (41) and a NNH =2-4 (compare i.e. the statistics for the antipsychotic drugs (42)).

In spite of the large success for therapists using clinical medicine to help their patients with physical, mental, existential, sexual health problems and dysfunctions, there has been little interest in research and development of this kind of medicine by universities and government institutions.

The pharmaceutical industry has no natural interest in this kind of medicine, and the large industrial lobby might be one of the reasons for the almost complete lack of interest in this field until recently.

We strongly suggest that medical research institutions and universities start taking clinical medicine seriously. With the non-drug medical tools of psychotherapy, sexology and CAM many of the health problems that torment today's citizen could be alleviated. In states with nationalized medicine it is time to consider the more efficient and less harmful clinical medicine in our opinion.

A practical solution for research and quality assurance

Instead of using much time on anamnesis and diagnosing we recommend the patient should fill out a short questionnaire like QOL5 (43) or QOL 10 (44) to measure:

- Self-rated physical health
- Self-rated mental health
- Self-rated sexual functioning
- Self-rated self-esteem
- Self-rated I-strength
- Self-rated relation to partner
- Self-rated relation to friends
- Self-rated social ability
- Self-rated working/studying ability

To establish that one or more of these dimensions are low is sufficient to justify the immediate onset of the treatment with an appropriate clinical medical tool (45), a sexological tool (46) or a psychoanalytical tool (47,48) for healing mental disorders or personality disturbances.

If the therapist measure the patient before and after the treatment, and again after one year – i.e. following the square curve paradigm – it is easy to see if a patient was helped and make the statistics over the efficacy of the clinical work in relation to the different health problems (compare how we did it for Research Clinic for Holistic Medicine and Sexology (32-39)). The one-year follow up is important to document that the results are stable through time (38).

Conclusions

In general clinical holistic medicine helps chronic patients cure physical, mental, existential and sexual illnesses and dysfunctions that primarily are caused by repressed thoughts and emotions in the patient's unconscious. Often the patient has tried to be helped by biomedical drugs without success. If a patient has a chronic condition that has not been cured with biomedicine there is no reason to spend time once again making a thorough anamnesis and give an accurate diagnoses; a rough categorization into the categories of feeling physically ill, mentally ill, sexually dysfunction etc. by a short questionnaire is sufficient for documenting the patient's progress.

In general the anamnesis and diagnosis has little therapeutic value in clinical holistic medicine, as all patients in principle are treated the same way, to rehabilitate their existence, improve their sense of coherence, and improve health, quality of life, and ability in general – the sexual, social, working, studying ability etc. We recommend that all patients fill out a short questionnaire on self-assessed physical and mental health, quality of life, and ability, like the QOL5 (43) or QOL 10 (44). The patients and the physicians and time, money and other resources should be used wisely and focused on healing that happens when the physician and the patient together explore the patient's inner life to re-integrate repressed feelings. Using to much time on taking the patient's life-story and on giving the patient specific, biomedical diagnoses, that are only useful when you are treating with drugs is wasting time and money in clinical holistic medicine and holistic sexology and might therefore be considered a principal error.

References

[1]   BioMedExperts.Com. Accessed 2009-03-13.

[2]   Jones WHS. Hippocrates. Vol. I–IV. London: William Heinemann, 1923-1931.

[3]   Jones E. The life and works of Sigmund Freud. New York: Basic Books, 1961.

[4]   Reich, W. Die Function des Orgasmus. Köln: Kiepenheuer and Witsch, 1969. [German].

[5]   Jung CG. Man and his symbols. New York: Anchor Press, 1964.

[6]   Jung CG. Psychology and alchemy. Collected works of CG Jung, Vol 12. Princeton, NJ: Princeton Univ Press, 1968.

[7]   Lowen A. Honoring the body. Alachua, FL: Bioenergetics Press, 2004.

[8]   Rosen M, Brenner S. Rosen method bodywork. Accessing the unconscious through touch. Berkeley, CA: North Atlantic Books, 2003.

[9]   Anand M. The art of sexual ecstasy. The path of sacred sexuality for western lovers. New York: Jeremy P Tarcher/Putnam, 1989.

[10] Knight RP. Preface. In: Searles HF. Collected papers on Schizophrenia. Madison, CT: Int Univ Press, 1965:15-8.

[11] Ornish D, Brown SE, Scherwitz LW, Billings JH, Armstrong WT, et al. Can lifestyle changes reverse coronary heart disease? The lifestyle heart trial. Lancet 1990;336(8708), 129-33.

[12] Ornish D, Scherwitz LW, Billings JH, Brown SE, Gould KL, et al. Intensive lifestyle changes for reversal of coronary heart disease. JAMA1998;280(23),2001-7.

[13] Levenson FB. The causes and prevention of cancer. London: Sidgwick Jackson, 1985.

[14] Levenson FB, Levenson,MD, Ventegodt S, Merrick, J. Psychodynamic psychotherapy, therapeutic touch and cancer. A review of the method of intervention and study of 75 cases. Accepted by J Altern Med Res 2009, in press.

[15] Ventegodt S, Andersen NJ, Merrick J. Rationality and irrationality in Ryke Geerd Hamer's System for holistic treatment of metastatic cancer. ScientificWorldJournal 2005;5:93–102.

[16] Antonovsky A. Health, stress and coping. London: Jossey-Bass, 1985.

[17] Antonovsky A. Unravelling the mystery of health. How people manage stress and stay well. San Franscisco: Jossey-Bass, 1987.

[18] Bø K, Berghmans B, Mørkved S, Van Kampen, M. Evidence-based physical physical therapy for the pelvic floor. Bridging science and clinical practice. New York: Elsevier Butterworth Heinemann, 2007.

[19] Polden M, Mantle J. Physiotherapy in obstetrics and gynecology. Stoneham, MA: Butterworth-Heinemann, 1990.

[20] Lukban J, Whitmore K, Kellogg-Spadt S, Bologna R, Lesher A, Fletcher E. The effect of manual physical therapy in patients diagnosed with interstitial cystitis, high-tone pelvic floor dysfunction, and sacroiliac dysfunction. Urology 2001;57(6 Suppl 1):121-2.

[21] Bergeron S, Brown C, Lord MJ, Oala M, Binik YM, Khalifé S. Physical therapy for vulvar vestibulitis syndrome: a retrospective study. J Sex Marital Ther 2002;28(3),183-92.

[22] Ventegodt S, Clausen B, Merrick J. Clinical holistic medicine: Pilot study on the effect of vaginal acupressure (Hippocratic pelvic massage). ScientificWorldJournal 2006;6:2100-16.

[23] Wurn BF, Wurn LJ, King CR, Heuer MA, Roscow AS, Hornberger K, Scharf ES. Treating fallopian tube occlusion with a manual pelvic physical therapy. Altern Ther Health Med 2008;14(1):18-23.

[24] Leichsenring F, Rabung S, Leibing E. The efficacy of short-term psychodynamic psychotherapy in specific psychiatric disorders: a meta-analysis. Arch Gen Psychiatry 2004;61(12):1208-16.

[25] Leichsenring F. Are psychodynamic and psychoanalytic therapies effective? A review of empirical data. Int J Psychoanal 2005;86(Pt 3):841-68.

[26] O´Donohue W, Dopke CA, Swingen DN. Psychotherapy for female sexual dysfunction: A review. Clin Psychol Rev 1997;17(5):537-66.

[27] Masters WH, Johnson VE. Human sexual inadequacy. Philadelphia, PA: Lippincott Williams Wilkins, 1966.

[28] Struck P, Ventegodt S. Clinical holistic medicine: teaching orgasm for females with chronic anorgasmia using the Betty Dodson method. ScientificWorldJournal 2008;8:883-95.

[29] Heiman JR, Meston CM. Empirically validated treatment for sexual dysfunction. Ann Rev Sex Res 1997;8:148-94.

[30] Ventegodt S, Kandel I, Merrick J. A study in experienced chronic pain in the holistic medicin clinic using mindful psychodynamic short time psychotherapy complemented with bodywork. J Pain Manage 2008;1(1):55-62.

[31] Ventegodt S, Andersen NJ, Merrick J. Holistic Medicine III: The holistic process theory of healing. ScientificWorldJournal 2003;3:1138-46.

[32] Ventegodt S, Thegler S, Andreasen T, Struve F, Enevoldsen L, Bassaine L, Torp M, Merrick J. Clinical holistic medicine (mindful, short-term psychodynamic psychotherapy complemented with bodywork) in the treatment of experienced physical illness and chronic pain. ScientificWorldJournal 2007;7:310-6.

[33] Ventegodt S, Thegler S, Andreasen T, Struve F, Enevoldsen L, Bassaine L, Torp M, Merrick J. Clinical holistic medicine (mindful, short-term psychodynamic psychotherapy complemented with bodywork) in the treatment of experienced mental illness. ScientificWorldJournal 2007;7:306-9.

[34] Ventegodt S, Thegler S, Andreasen T, Struve F, Enevoldsen L, Bassaine L, Torp M, Merrick J. Clinical holistic medicine (mindful, short-term psychodynamic psychotherapy complemented with bodywork) in the treatment of experienced impaired sexual functioning. ScientificWorldJournal 2007;7:324-9.

[35] Ventegodt S, Thegler S, Andreasen T, Struve F, Enevoldsen L, Bassaine L, Torp M, Merrick J. Clinical holistic medicine (mindful, short-term psychodynamic psychotherapy complemented with bodywork) improves quality of life, health, and ability by induction of Antonovsky-salutogenesis. ScientificWorldJournal 2007;7:317-23.

[36] Ventegodt S, Thegler S, Andreasen T, Struve F, Enevoldsen L, Bassaine L, Torp M, Merrick J. Self-reported low self-esteem. Intervention and follow-up in a clinical setting. ScientificWorldJournal 2007;7:299-305.

[37] Ventegodt S, Andersen NJ, Merrick J. Clinical holistic medicine in the recovery of working ability. A study using Antonovsky salutogenesis. Int J Disabil Hum Dev 2008;7(2):219-22.

[38] Struve F. Clinical holistic medicine: Psychodynamic short-time therapy complemented with bodywork. A clinical follow-up study of 109 patients. Dissertation. Graz: Interuniversity College, 2008.

[39] Ventegodt S, Merrick J. A metaanalysis of side effects of psychotherapy, bodywork, and clinical holistic medicine. Submitted to J Complement Integr Med.

[40] Ventegodt S, Kandel, I, Merrick, J. Positive effects, side effects and negative events of intensive, clinical, holistic therapy in Sweden. A review of the program "meet yourself" characterized by intensive body-psychotherapy combined with mindfulness meditation at Mullingstorp in Sweden J Altern Med Res 2009;1(3):00-00, in press.

[41] Smith R. The drugs don't work. BMJ 2003;327(7428):0-h.

[42] Adams CE, Awad G, Rathbone J, Thornley B. Chlorpromazine versus placebo for schizophrenia. Cochrane Database Syst Rev 2007;18(2):CD000284.

[43] Lindholt JS, Ventegodt S, Henneberg EW. Development and validation of QoL5 for clinical databases. A short, global and generic questionnaire based on an integrated theory of the quality of life. Eur J Surg 2002;168:103-7.

[44] Ventegodt S, Andersen NJ, Kandel I, Merrick J. QOL10 for clinical quality-assurance and research in treatment-efficacy: Ten key questions for measuring the global quality of life, self-rated physical and mental health, and self-rated social-, sexual- and working ability. J Altern Med Res 2009;1(2), in press.

[45] Ventegodt S, Clausen B, Nielsen ML, Merrick J. Advanced tools for holistic medicine. ScientificWorldJournal 2006;6:2048-65.

[46] Ventegodt S, Andersen NJ, Kandel I, Merrick J. Five tools for manual sexological examination and treatment. J Altern Med Res, in press.

[47] Yalom ID. Existential psychotherapy. New York: Basic Books, 1980.

[48] Yalom ID. The gift of therapy. New York: HarperCollins, 2002.

Chapter 26

A model for holistic diagnoses and holistic treatment of mild, borderline and psychotic personality disorders

Today's categorical system of diagnosing personality disorders in ICD-10 and DSM-IV should in ICD-11 and DSM-V be substituted with a simpler, more comprehensive, five-dimensional model. The proposed model gives a tremendous simplification of today's diagnostic universe and empowers the psychiatrist and therapist with tools that facilitate an integrated holistic practice of understanding, diagnosing and healing the mental disorders in general. The five dimensions are based on the classical Hippocratic description of man: 1) body and sexuality, 2) consciousness and psyche, 3) feelings and emotions, 4) spirituality and ability to love and 5) an integrative function of the "I" often called "the heart".

We present seven easy-to-use rating scales of 1) Therapist's global impression of the patient (as normal, low self-esteem, low self-confidence, nymphomaniac, dependant, nervous/evasive, compulsive, labile, narcissistic, hysteric/histrionic, 295chizoid295/antisocial, paranoid, 295chizoid, autistic, dysphoric, hypomanic, depressive, manic, bipolar, skizo-affective, schizophrenic); 2) Level of sexual development (genital, immature oral/anal/clitoral, infantile autoerotic); 3) State of sexual energy (free or blocked); 4) Patient's affective/emotional state (vital, flat, blocked), 5) Level of mental development (mature, immature, instable, deluded, deluded-instable, disintegrated), 6) Spiritual state (whole, flat or split) and 7) "I-Strength" also called "state of heart" or "degree of development of integrative ability" (fair, intermediate, weak).

The seven rating scales makes diagnosis and planning of the psychodynamic or holistic therapy easy and opens up for a constructive dialog about the goal of therapy with the patient. The five-dimensional diagnostic system has been clinically tested and seems to humanize psychiatry and improve treatment efficiency and compliance.

Introduction

There seems to be a general agreement that the categorical system of diagnosing the personality disorder used both in ICD-10 (1) and DSM-IV (2) is highly impractical and presumably even outdated (3,4). We need a much simpler and more logical system that integrates our understanding and knowledge of the mental disorders and empowers us as therapists to treat and cure the patients suffering from personality disorders. Especially problematic is the complex relations between personality disorders and genuine mental illnesses. From all we know the mental diseases present themselves in a perfect continuum, which is only artificially made into categorical diagnoses, and this transformation of continuous phenomenon's into categories is a severe hindrance to exploration, diagnostics and healing work. Especially the dialog with the patients has become much more difficult that it need to be, as patients most often show severe resistance against the diagnosis. The resistance often comes from an experience of stigmatization, as nobody likes to accept to be in a specific category of personality disorders. On the other hand, every patient will agree that his or her feelings, mind, sexuality etc. are somewhat less that perfectly developed, and the degree can be satisfactory negotiated during treatment. This dialog is extremely important in therapy, making the diagnosis of ICD-10 and DSM-IV highly contra productive and difficult to use in the clinic.

The personality disorders are traditionally placed between the completely mentally healthy state and the most psychotic mentally ill schizophrenic state. Historically the personally disorders are collectively characterized by causing unproductive conflicts in the persons inner and outer life. When only the patient himself is tormented by the mental disorder we often use the work "neurosis", i.e. "anxiety neurosis" but almost always anxiety will give the patient an evasive trait – paradoxically creating lots of conflicts around the patient as the entire patient's fears one by one materialize – turning the neurosis into a personality disorder. The concept of "neurosis" is therefore well substituted with the concept of personality disorders. All mental illnesses are rooted in psychological defense and therefore also based in personality disorders. The distinction between personality disorders and mental illnesses are therefore also totally artificial. Theoretically there is no reason not to integrate the mental illnesses and the personality disorders, as we have done in our suggested 5-dimensional model of personality disorders (see table 1).

In the psychodynamic literature there seems to be an agreement that the outer conflicts is a materialization of the persons inner conflicts, which are understood as internalized early external conflicts, often going all the way back to the earliest childhood and even the womb. The reason for the internalization is adaptation to the environment and parents to increase the holding and love and thereby optimizing the basic conditions for personal development and survival. Traditionally the personality disorders have been categorized as mild, borderline and psychotic and we have developed a five-dimensional model that we suggest should enter the ICD-11 and DSM-V classification. We have tested the model in clinical practice and found that it allows successful healing work with both patients with personality disorders and with mental illnesses (5,6).

Holistic medicine and biomedicine in the treatment of personality disorders

Historically the treatment of personality disorders like hysteria goes all the way back to Hippocrates and the Greek doctors who used massage of the uterus combined with conversational therapy to heal the sexual disturbances believed to be the primary cause of personality disturbances (7-9). Holistic medicine that combined conversational therapy with bodywork was the European medicine for more than 2000 years and Freud started himself as a holistic doctor giving massage to the hysterical patients legs (10). Freud left bodywork and initiated the tradition of psychodynamic psychotherapy, but he struggled with the problem that contemporary culture was extremely negative towards physical touch and bodily intimacy and he gained great fame from developing a style of therapy that left bodywork behind to focus on the talking; in spite of this the psychosexual developmental problems of the patient was still seen as the primary course of personality disorders.

During the 20th century psychiatry came up with neurobiological hypothesis for personality disorders and the more severe mental problems were less treated with conversational therapy and more and more often treated with psychopharmacological drugs, often combined with ECT (electroconvulsive therapy).

Its is difficult to compare the results from the three different ways to treat personality disorders, but it seems that Philippe Pinel (1745-1826) could cure 70% of his patients – presumably a mixture of schizophrenics and borderline patients - with his version of holistic medicine, the "traitement moral" that had a strong focus also on philosophical and somatic aspects of the patient around 1800 (11). Psychodynamic psychotherapy with conversational therapy alone could cure around 33% of the patients with personality disorders and schizophrenia from 1900 to 1970 (12-14), while psychopharmacological treatment only have helped a few percent of the patients with personality disorders since 1970 (1) and cured even less.

The reason for the use of psychopharmacological drugs in the treatment of the personality disorders (in spite of no Cochrane or other studies documenting clinically significant effect here) is simple: Firstly the believe that mental disorders are caused by chemical disturbances in the brain makes this natural and secondly an extremely large number of patient can be treated with a minimal of the physician's time. The sad fact is that the urbanization, modernization and the shift to a strong focus on natural science and biochemistry in medicine seems to take the healing power out of medicine.

To increase the rate of patients being cured it seems that we are forced to take medicine back to its holistic roots; only if we work with therapy, and preferably the classical combination of bodywork and conversational therapy, can we really come back to the excellent results of the former eras holistic doctors. We have tested this idea in clinical practice and found that 57,4% of mentally ill patients seen at the Copenhagen Clinic can actually be cured (self rated outcome in mental health) just in one year and with 20 hours of treatment (6) using the system of clinical holistic medicine (CHM), that our international research team has developed during the last two decades (15-28). CHM is easy to use and highly efficient, as we have documented this approach in a number of uncontrolled studies addressing a long serious of physical, mental, sexual and existential problems (6,29-32) and the treatment plan comes quite natural if the physician uses the five-dimensional, diagnostic system.

After a decade of treatment experiments and research into the process of holistic healing we have come up with a theoretical framework that we have used to explain and map all major personality disorders (see table 1) together with the mental diseases (33).

Table 1. The personality disorders (according to ICD-10 and DSM-v) and the mental illness can be seen as a simple product of the combination of psychosexual, emotional, mental, spiritual and integrative problems that often can be successfully addressed in holistic therapy (CHM). Most interestingly this analysis does not justify the traditional distinguishing between personality disorders and mental illnesses, and all mental disorders are seemingly curable in therapy (11-14, 42-44)

	ICD-10	DSM-IV	I-Strength (integrative ability, "heart")	Sexual development	Affective (emotional) state	Mental state	Spiritual state
Normal, healthy person	-	-	Strong	Genital, free	Vital	Mature	Whole
	Low self esteem *	Low self esteem *	Fair	Genital, free	Flat or blocked	Mature	Whole
	Low self confidence *	Low self confidence *	Fair	Genital, free	Vital	Immature	Whole
	Nympho-mania *	Nympho-mania *	Fair	Sexualised, often genital	Vital	Mature	Whole
	Dependant	Dependent	Fair	Often immature, free	Vital	Often immature	Whole
	Nervous/Evasive	Evasive	Fair	Often immature, free	Vital	Often immature	Whole
Mild (neurotic)	Compulsive	Compul-sive	Fair	Often immature, often blocked	Often flat	Often immature	Whole
	Dysphoric *		Fair	Often immature, blocked	Flat	Often immature	Whole
	Hypomanic*		Fair	Often immature, free	Vital	Often immature	Whole
	Emotionally labile	Instable	Moderate or weak	Immature, free	Vital	Often immature	Whole
	-	Narcissistic	Moderate or weak	Infantile autoerotism, free	Vital	Often immature	Whole
	Histrionic (Hysteric)	Histrionic (Hysteric)	Often weak	Sexualised, often genital	Vital	Often immature, instable	Whole
Borderline	Dyssocial	Antisocial	Weak	Immature, sexualised or blocked	Often flat	Often immature	Flat
	Depressive **		Moderate	Immature, Blocked	Flat	Often immature	Flat
	Manic**		Moderate	Immature, often sexualised	Vital or flat	Often immature	Flat

	ICD-10	DSM-IV	I-Strength (integrative ability, "heart")	Sexual development	Affective (emotional) state	Mental state	Spiritual state
Psychotic	Paranoid	Paranoid	Weak	Immature, blocked	Often flat or blocked	Immature, deluded	Flat
	Skizoid	Skizoid	Weak	Immature or infantile autoerotism, blocked	Blocked	Immature	Split
	(Autistic*)	Skizotypical	Weak	Infantile autoerotism, blocked	Blocked	Immature, deluded	Split
	Bipolar**		Weak	Immature, instable, blocked or sexualised	Vital or flat	Immature, deluded, instable	Split
	Schizo-affective **		Weak	Immature, blocked or sexualised	Vital or flat	Immature, Deluded	Split
Schizo-phrenia *	Schizophrenia **		Weak	Infantile Autoerotism, blocked	Blocked	Immature, deluded, dis-integrated	Split

*) Not considered a personality disorder in ICD-10 and DSM-IV.
**) Mental illnesses according to ICD-10 and DSM-IV.

We have learned that we are indeed capable of understanding and also curing many of the patients with these disorders and illnesses using the simple tools of clinical holistic medicine (28). Of course one can disagree with the holistic description of man as consisting of body, mind, spirit and heart and with the idea of the sexual energy as the fundamental life energy of man. Without this perspective the presented theory of personality disorders and the holistic cures will be of little value. On the other hand one can argue that the fine results of the methods derived from this understanding can be taken as an empirical confirmation of the holistic theory of man.

The definition of personality

In holistic medicine the personality is different from the being (34). The entity, or real person, is behind every appearance always intact and can be revitalized just by letting go of all the patient's many layers of existential learning and adaptation that we call personality. The personality is in this sense *neurotic and created for survival and adaptation* and very different from the person's character (35) and life mission (33,35-40), that is the person's real talents given already at conception intended for *living and growing*. So in this sense a completely healthy person does not have a personality, but is striving for self-realization to be able to create value in the world. A mentally healthy person can create conflicts, but these conflicts will always be about maximizing value and taking down hindrances for what is considered good by the individual. On the other hand will personality disorders always lead to neurotic conflicts that will consume a lot of time and energy and only lead to modest results if any. More often the conflicts will be destructive to the individual in spite of the experience of the conflicts being necessary and for the good of all. A person with severe personality disturbances will always blame the surrounding world for the problems and conflicts, while a mentally healthy person will assume full responsibility for all conflicts.

Conflicts can be made actively and passively; the psychodynamic concept of "passive aggression" is often very well used in relation to personality disorders. Autism can be seen as the pure crystallization of passive aggression towards the parents; it can also bee seen as a product of arrested psychosexual development around the fetal or infantile state called "infantile autoerotism" by Freud (41).

Holistic theory of personality disorders

Man is seen holistically as body, mind, spirit and heart with sexuality as a penetrating ubiquitous energy, which circulates in the whole energetic system of the person and connects all parts of it. The mild personality disorders (the dependent, the nervous, the narcissistic and the labile) are characterized by an open heart and whole and functionally intact spirit, often a normal emotional life, but a somewhat immature mind and sexuality. The borderline, or intermediate, personality disorders (the compulsive, the hysteric (histrionic), the anti-social (psychopathic), the depressive, the manic, and the schizotypical) are characterized by a blocked heart making connections to people very difficult; often a "flat" spirit, flat or labile emotions, a somewhat immature mind, and often a blocked sexuality.

The psychotic personality disorders (the autistic, the bi-polar, the paranoid, and the schizoid) are characterized by a blocked heart making connections to people very difficult; a split spirit, flat, a immature and deluded mind with often a completely blocked, little developed sexuality. The schizophrenic patient is at the extreme end of the spectrum with infantile auto-erotism and no objects-related sexuality, split spirit, often highly underdeveloped, strongly deluded mind, and most often complete, emotional flatness.

In principle, body and sexuality must be rehabilitated first, then emotions and mind, and finally spirit and heart. In practice the course of therapy is always strongly dependent on the patient and the holistic therapist need to invent a new cure for every new patient. Table 1 shows the system of personality disorders and the underlying sexual, mental, spiritual and integrative (I/heart) problems that must be addressed in therapy to cure the patient.

Five dimentions of mental health

1. Sexuality

Sexuality has been known to play a central role in personality disorders all the way back to Hippocrates and the Greek physicians and this perspective has been kept in today's psychoanalysis, psychodynamic psychotherapy and holistic medicine from Hippocrates to Freud, Jung, Reich, Searles and many other grand therapists (13,34,41,45,46). Sexuality lies at the core of human existence and the level of psychosexual development and the free or blocked flow of sexual energy is easily observed in clinical practice from the level of libido, sexual aggression, will to live and level of life energy. The development goes from object-less, infantile autoerotism through immature sexuality to the mature, genital sexuality needed for mutually satisfying, sexual intercourse. Freud described the immature sexuality as oral or anal. It has in the literature of erotic tantra been suggested that immature female sexuality can be seen as "clitoral" opposed to mature, vaginal sexuality (47). Sexuality (the sexual energy) can be free, blocked or sexualized. Sexualized energy is neurotically boosted; compare this with the classical diagnosis of "nymphomania", which is neurotically boosted sexuality in an otherwise normal patient (nymphomania is therefore included in table 1 as a normal condition and not a disorder).

Many hysteric patients are strongly sexualized and have an obvious nymphomaniac trait. Promiscuous behavior is sometimes the behavioral derivate of sexualisation also in normal people, but this is not a mental disorder as we see it. This problem and many other related sexual problems like vulvodynia belongs to the field of sexology in spite of obvious presence of personality disorders in these patients. Eating disorders are often more strongly related to sexual than to mental problems and should therefore also be treated under the specialty of sexology. In the future psychiatry and sexology might also be integrated into a more holistic model; as physical health are also strongly related to mental and sexual problems we must always remember that body and mind cannot truly be separated in medicine. A few minutes talk about sexuality will reveal the patient's level of psychosexual developmental status; often just the way the patient dresses and contact you will let you know.

2. Affect/emotions

The emotional state of a human being goes from vital and healthy to flat and further to completely blocked. A person can contain a whole palette or rainbow of emotions, every moment being like a colorful painting; or emotional life can be flat and simplistic, one single emotion at the time, and no symphony of tones, no profoundness and mystery; or emotional life can be completely blocked. The palette can be dominated by dark colors in depression, or light colors in mania, and the whole palette can be changing unpredictably as in cyclothymia and emotional lability. The emotional status of the patient is easily experiences in personal contact.

3. Mind

The mind can be immature or maturely developed; it can contain complex concepts and fine language for describing the world or intelligent and creative processes to model the surrounding world and meet the multiple challenges from inside and outside. It can be a sharp, precise, stable, and useful tool, a reliable source of information and true resource for problem solving. When mind is immature, its description of the world can be instable, deluded, an unreliable source of information, or even a severe burden insisting compulsively on the patient doing or thinking specific thoughts or actions, and in the psychotic patient deluded thoughts and ideas can lead to highly destructive acts. In the most undeveloped and disturbed form the conception is confused and disintegrated. An hour of conversation will allow the therapist to estimate the level of development of patient's mind.

4. Spirit

In this important, but abstract dimension of man lies our ability to love and give unconditionally. If wholeness or the concept of soul is denied in the patient's personal philosophy, the ability to love unconditionally is often destroyed. The spiritual dimension also holds our mission of life, i.e. our core talents which we need for being of true value in our social relationships. The spiritual dimension can be whole and vital, flat and reduced, or split in two or more parts, giving the most severe personality disorders. The split spirit is a well-known defense mechanism. Splitting is our normal reaction to traumas early in life, when the mind is still to immature to cope. In holistic therapy we often find these traumas under deep regression to the womb, where they can be healed (25-27,34,48,49).

The clinical assessment of this is quite difficult. A split spirit should not be mistaken for the phenomenon of multiple personalities that we all, sound as sick, contains as a condition for normal mental functioning; normally our multitude of "personalities" are not visible due to a high level of integration. But split spirit often materializes though the phenomenon of inner conflicts between the inner personalities and the extreme example of this has given the name to the illness schizophrenia, meaning "split spirit" in Greek. Other manifestations of the split defense is ambivalence, which in marriage can be seen as a strong tendency to adultery, in work seen as a strong tendency to change work places, in friendship seen as a high rhythm of meeting and sacking friends.

Diagnosing the patient's spirit is the most difficult part of the diagnosing process. To master diagnoses and holistic therapy with patients with split-spirit problems the therapist needs to go through deep and regressive therapy himself, allowing for deep self-exploration into the spiritual domain. But even the inexperienced student will soon learn to identify ambivalence and strong inner conflicts in the patient coming from the obvious split defense.

5. Heart

The experience of an integrated "I" is a function of a complex integrative function developed though childhood and adolescence (34,41). We often call this function the "human heart". The heart integrates body, mind and spirit, or more accurately the patient's Id, Ego and Self (soul). The function of the heart makes it possible for us to meet another person as a subject (Though) and not an object ("it") (50). If a person becomes emotionally wounded the heart can be temporarily "broken" or more permanently blocked (a "closed heart") and relating becomes difficult. This influences the whole experience and appearance of the person. Psychiatry has often understood the concept of I-Strength as a mental quality, while holistic medicine traditionally has seen is as an existential quality. Holistic medicine is aligned with the more common understanding of the heath; people who "have a heart" or "an open heart" are able to meet the world and other people in an open-minded, assertive, empathic, accepting, involved, respectful, interested and loving way. The status of the heart is thus easily observed in clinical practice.

Diagnosis in the 5-dimentional system

The power of the 5-dimensional system lies in its practicality in daily work. To use the system we always start with an interview about the patient's status in the five dimensions; the therapist's global impression grows organically out of this dynamic interaction. After rating this general global impression and also the five dimensions, the diagnosis is easily found using table 1. It is strongly recommended also to use a patient-rated questionnaire like QOL1, QOL 5 or QOL10 (51) and compare the two ratings to secure a reasonable concordance between the two sets of ratings. If the ratings differ much the reason for the discrepancy must be thoroughly analyzed (52). In general, holistic therapy will not run smothery without a fundamental agreement between the therapist and the patient about what the patient's problem is and what the solution and goal of the therapy is.

Schizophrenia is recognized as the lower extreme of all five dimensions combined. In a non-categorical system as the one presented, there are no qualitative characteristics that makes it possible to identify the "schizophrenic patient" per se (like hearing voices). Schizophrenia is a state characterized by extreme lack of personal development of body, mind, spirit, sexuality and heart. Because of this perspective, schizophrenia can be treated as well as the other mental diseases.

Therapist rated questionnaire for diagnosing the personality disorders and mental illnesses (The holistic 5-dimensional system suggested for ICD-11 and DSM-V)

Q1: Therapist's global impression:

1. Normal (no significant personality disorder or mental illness)
2. Normal, low self-esteem
3. Normal, low self-confidence
4. Normal, nymphomaniac
5. Dependant
6. Nervous/evasive (including anxiety)
7. Compulsive
8. Dysphoric
9. Hypomanic
10. Labile
11. Narcissistic
12. Hysteric (Histrionic)
13. Dyssocial/Antisocial
14. Depressive
15. Manic
16. Paranoid
17. Skizoid
18. Autistic
19. Bipolar
20. Skizo-affective
21. Schizophrenic
22. Other, mild personality disorder
23. Other, borderline personality disorder
24. Other, psychotic personality disorder
25. Other psychotic mental illness

Q2: How I-strong is the patient (heart open/closed)?

1. Strong ("open heart")
2. Fair
3. Moderate ("broken heart")
4. Weak ("closed heart")

Q3: How developed is the patient's sexuality?

1. Genital (mature)
2. Autoerotism (immature clitoral/oral/anal)
3. Infantile autoerotism (no object)

Q4: How blocked or sexualized is patient's sexual energy?

1. Free
2. Sexualized
3. Blocked

Q5: How vital are the patient's emotions?

1. Vital
2. Flat
3. Blocked

Q6: How developed is the patient's mind?

1. Mature
2. Immature
3. Immature, instable
4. Deluded
5. Deluded, instable
6. Deluded, disintegrated

Q7: How whole is the patient's spirit?

1. Whole
2. Flat (remote)
3. Split

Principles of holistic therapy

The key to helping the patient to heal his or her life and existence (salutogenesis) (53,54)) lies in truly meeting and understanding the patient (55). The traditional psychodynamic style of therapy is patient conversations allowing the patient to explore and understand himself, and this method is highly efficient (34,42-44,48,49) and with most mental disorders more efficient than psychiatric treatments as usual (42-44]. The holistic style of therapy is much more intensive with physical holding and direct processing of old traumas in spontaneous regression.

Psychodynamic psychotherapy works much with transferences, reflection on the therapist-patent relation being the primary tool. Holistic medicine use both conversation and bodywork to allow the patients to work more directly with the healing of early traumas. Interestingly, Freud did this in the beginning of his career (10), but presumably for political reasons living in a sex-and-body-negative culture he later abandoned bodywork. We have argued that the price Freud paid for psychoanalysis to be accepted in contemporary society was the effect of therapy, where holistic medicine seems to do in only 20 sessions (56), what often takes 1,000 hours of classical psychoanalysis (13).

Holistic therapy is basically re-parenting, where the therapist gives the patient the love, support and holding the parents were unable to give with the intent of healing the old traumas and integrate all the different feelings often related to body and sexuality. This allows the arrested psychosexual development to continue into the mature state. Sexuality almost always plays a central role in personality disorder (see table 1). The intimate love and care from the holistic therapist and assistants allows the patient to return to early childhood or even into the womb fetal state and reconnect to the emotional and sexual energies often left behind. Regression to the early stages of life is often experienced as extremely sexual in regressive therapy and the successful revitalization of the sexuality seems to be a condition for complete healing of a personality disorder.

The mind and the patient's philosophy of life and ability to think and analyze must also be rehabilitated. This is often done though reading and philosophical exercises, careful writing of patients biography and artwork (25-27). The spiritual dimension of the patient's life is most simply seen as ability to love and use core talents to be of value to self and others (33-40). When the patient regains ability to unconditional love, most of the personality disorder is often cured. This happens in the traditional Hippocratic holistic medicine, when the patients recover his true physical, mental and spiritual character. This kind of medicine has therefore also been called for "character medicine" (45,57).

What we call "the heart" is as mentioned above really the abstract, integrative function of the human consciousness that allows us to connect to other people as a wholeness presenting body, mind and spirit at the same time, in a delicate balance. It is quite clear that a profound understanding of one self and also holistic theory and philosophy is a precondition for efficient treatment of patients with mental illnesses. Love and generosity are always the primary tools in therapy. Often the therapist ability to love and care is challenged by the cold-hearted, mentally undeveloped and sexually unappealing patients presenting the personality disorders. It is important to contain all these often-repelling characteristics of the mentally disturbed patient and to see all these unappealing aspects of the person as sides of the disease to be worked upon and healed in the end. A list of the many tools that can be used in holistic therapy can be found in (28).

Discussion

Psychodynamic psychotherapy has a long tradition (41-44) and in our experience is not difficult to use this intervention form to cure or heal the personality disorder in therapy. A therapist that understands the basic principle of healing can cure mental illnesses (49). A skilled therapist like Searles cured 33% of even the most severely ill schizophrenic patients even after years of hospitalization with 900 hours of psychoanalysis (13) and in our study we found that 57% of the mentally ill patients experienced to be cured with clinical holistic medicine (6). In our experience it is important to work with a broad variety of patients, also including the most ill patients, for the therapist to fully understand the basic constitution of the personality and the problems connected to it. Only in the most severely ill patients the whole structure of man becomes transparent and visible. When you can cure schizophrenia, everything else becomes easy.

Working with the patient's sexuality is normally the biggest problem for the modern physician, because of the strong sexual taboo of society. We must stress that this is an absolutely necessary step in helping most patients with severe personality disorders and not only a thing that should be cared about when rehabilitating the patient with explicit sexual traumas. It is also important to remember that one girl in seven are still being sexually abused and these girls very often become the adult patients that seek therapy for personality disorders and mental problems.

The therapist needs to be without prejudice, generous, caring and containing on order to help patients re-integrate their ability to feel sexual interest, desire and arousal. Often the patents need to verbalize many sexual issues that normal people would never care to verbalize, i.e. their experience of the bodily reactions or orgasm. Most therapists feel quite awkward and embarrassed in the beginning working explicitly with patent sexuality, but it is really worth getting past this point, because it gives the patient motivation and energy to raise the mind. The use of therapeutic touch is paradoxically reducing the need of verbalizing and is also dramatically reducing the intensity of sexual transferences, but they will never completely disappear, making supervision and Balint Group work mandatory for holistic therapists. Written consent is mandatory and the medical record must contain detailed record of all procedures and emotionally charged wordings.

If patient-physician "chemistry" is bad with little love and affection, it is wise to allow the patient to change therapist. If the relation is healing up, this is a sign of the patient's sexuality healing; in this case it is wise not to abrupt therapy as it can set the patient seriously back. Of course the therapist is responsible for keeping the sexual boundaries and respecting the ethical rules of holistic therapy. We recommend the rules of the International Society for Holistic Health (see www.internationalsocietyforholistichealth.org).

To obtain fast results in the therapy it is paradoxically important to allow the patient to develop slowly out of a psychotic state or a psychotic crisis. Therefore we recommend as a general rule that anti-psychotic and sedative drugs are not used in holistic psychiatry. It is much better to process the patient in his or her psychosis, than to bring them fast and violently down to normal consciousness with drugs. It is difficult in the beginning to meet psychotic people and work with them in therapy; surprisingly bodywork and therapeutic touch are often much more efficient in this phase than psychotherapy and words. In general all shifts of mind and understanding must happen slowly and gradually. The patients must be allowed to grow very much as grass, trees or flower grow in the garden. "The grass grows by itself" is an old saying that is relevant here.

Conclusions

ICD-10 and DSM-IV are in our opinion not well suited for diagnosing the personality disorders, or the mental illnesses in general for that sake. We suggest the categorical diagnosis substituted with a five-dimensional holistic system that allows for a simple analysis and thus a clear understanding of the different personality disorders (including the mental disorders of the affective and schizophrenic specters). Our analysis links the personality disorder close to the traditional mental illnesses and the system allows for a simple and efficient treatment plan: healing the mentally ill patient along the five axis, independent of what mental illness the patients would have in the ICD-10 or DSM-IV systems. This basically means that all mentally ill patients can be treated with holistic non-pharmaceutical medicine. It also means that the classical mental diagnoses are not needed in holistic psychiatry. It might very well be that they are actually therapeutically counterproductive as they make patients think badly about themselves. Therapy should in general avoid inducing negative philosophy.

The relational and psychosexual developmental problems seem to be at the core of every personality disorder and only by healing the patient's sexuality, mind and spirit can health in the end be healed. The strength of this integrative dimension is what determines the functional capability of the patient and thus the severity of the personality disorder.

We recommend that the dimensions of emotion and sexuality are addressed first in the therapy, as the more profound problems of mind, spirit and heart crystallizes well during the process of emotional and sexual healing (23,47). Only when the patient's sexuality, mind, and spirit are all healed, the integrative function known as the patients "I-strength" or "heart" can be recovered. The "I-strength" is still in our model the central characteristic and determines the severity of the personality disorder, but we add a focus on the development of sexuality, mind, and spirit that has been somewhat neglected by modern biomedical psychiatry.

References

[1]   World Health Organization. The ICD-10 classification of mental and behavioural disorders. Clinical descriptions and diagnostic guidelines. Geneva: World Health Organization, 1992.
[2]   American Psychiatric Association. Diagnostic and statistical manual of mental disorders. 4th ed, text revision. Washington: Am Psychiatr Assoc, 2000.
[3]   Quante A, Röpke S, Merkl A, Anghelescu I, Lammers CH [Psychopharmacologic treatment of personality disorders].Fortschr Neurol Psychiatr. 2008;76(3):139-48 [German].
[4]   Widiger TA. Dimensional models of personality disorder. World Psychiatry 2007;6(2):79–83.
[5]   Ventegodt S, Thegler S, Andreasen T, Struve F, Enevoldsen L, et al. Clinical holistic medicine: Psychodynamic short-time therapy complemented with bodywork. A clinical follow-up study of 109 patients. ScientificWorldJournal 2006;6:2220-38.
[6]   Ventegodt S, Thegler S, Andreasen T, Struve F, Enevoldsen L, et al. Clinical holistic medicine (mindful, short-term psychodynamic psychotherapy complemented with bodywork) in the treatment of experienced mental illness. ScientificWorldJournal 2007;7: 306-09.
[7]   Jones WHS. (1923–1931) Hippocrates. Vol. I–IV. London: William Heinemann, 1923-1931.
[8]   Ventegodt S, Clausen B, Omar HA, Merrick J. Clinical holistic medicine: Holistic sexology and acupressure through the vagina (Hippocratic pelvic massage). ScientificWorldJournal 2006;6:2066-79.
[9]   Ventegodt S, Clausen B, Merrick J. Clinical holistic medicine: Pilot study on the effect of vaginal acupressure (Hippocratic pelvic massage). ScientificWorldJournal 2006;6:2100-16.
[10] Freud S, Breuer J. Studies in hysteria. New York: Penguin Classics, 2004. (Original work published 1893, 1895, 1908).
[11] Weiner DB. The clinical training of doctors. An essay from 1793 by Philippe Pinel. Henry E Sigerist Suppl Bull Hist Med 1980;3:1-102.
[12] Modestin J, Huber A, Satirli E, Malti T, Hell D. Long-term course of schizophrenic illness: Bleuler's study reconsidered. Am J Psychiatry 2003;160(12):2202-8.
[13] Knight RP. Preface. In: Searles HF. Collected Paper on schizophrenia. Madison, CT: Int Univ Press, 1965:15-18.
[14] Karon BP, VandenBos G. Psychotherapy of schizophrenia. The treatment of choise. New York: Jason Aronson, 1981.
[15] Ventegodt S, Kandel I, Neikrug S, Merrick J. Clinical holistic medicine: Holistic treatment of rape and incest traumas. ScientificWorldJournal 2005;5:288-97.
[16] Ventegodt S, Kandel I, Neikrug S, Merrick J. Clinical holistic medicine: The existential crisis – life crisis, stress and burnout. ScientificWorldJournal 2005;5:300-12.
[17] Ventegodt S, Gringols G, Merrick J. Clinical holistic medicine: Holistic rehabilitation ScientificWorldJournal 2005;5:280-7.
[18] Ventegodt S, Andersen NJ, Neikrug S, Kandel I, Merrick J. Clinical holistic medicine: Mental disorders in a holistic perspective. ScientificWorldJournal 2005;5:313-23.
[19] Ventegodt S, Andersen NJ, Neikrug S, Kandel I, Merrick J. Clinical holistic medicine: Holistic treatment of mental disorders. ScientificWorldJournal 2005;5:427-45.

[20] Ventegodt S, Clausen B, Merrick J. Clinical holistic medicine: The case story of Anna: I. Long term effect of child sexual abuse and incest with a treatment approach. ScientificWorldJournal 2006;6:1965-76.

[21] Ventegodt S, Clausen B, Merrick J. Clinical holistic medicine: the case story of Anna. II. Patient diary as a tool in treatment. ScientificWorldJournal 2006;6:2006-34.

[22] Ventegodt S, Clausen B, Merrick J. Clinical holistic medicine: The case story of Anna. III. Rehabilitation of philosophy of life during holistic existential therapy for childhood sexual abuse. ScientificWorldJournal 2006;6:2080-91.

[23] Ventegodt S, Andersen NJ, Merrick J. Holistic Medicine III: The holistic process theory of healing. ScientificWorldJournal 2003;3:1138-46.

[24] Ventegodt S, Andersen NJ, Merrick J. Holistic Medicine IV: Principles of the holistic process of healing in a group setting. ScientificWorldJournal 2003;3:1294-1301.

[25] Ventegodt S, Kandel I, Merrick J. Principles of holistic medicine. Philosophy behind quality of life. Victoria, BC: Trafford, 2005.

[26] Ventegodt S, Kandel I, Merrick J. Principles of holistic medicine. Quality of life and health. New York: Hippocrates Sci Publ, 2005.

[27] Ventegodt S, Kandel I, Merrick J. Principles of holistic medicine. Global quality of life. Theory, research and methodology. New York: Hippocrates Sci Publ, 2006.

[28] Ventegodt S, Clausen B, Nielsen ML, Merrick J. Clinical holistic medicine: Advanced tools for holistic medicine. ScientificWorldJournal 2006;6:2048-65.

[29] Ventegodt S, Thegler S, Andreasen T, Struve F, Enevoldsen L, et al. Clinical holistic medicine (mindful, short-term psychodynamic psychotherapy complemented with bodywork) in the treatment of experienced impaired sexual functioning. ScientificWorldJournal 2007;7:324-9.

[30] Ventegodt S, Thegler S, Andreasen T, Struve F, Enevoldsen L, et al.. Clinical holistic medicine (mindful, short-term psychodynamic psychotherapy complemented with bodywork) improves quality of life, health, and ability by induction of Antonovsky-salutogenesis. ScientificWorldJournal 2007;7:317-23.

[31] Ventegodt S, Thegler S, Andreasen T, Struve F, Enevoldsen L, et al. Clinical holistic medicine (mindful, short-term psychodynamic psychotherapy complemented with bodywork) in the treatment of experienced physical illness and chronic pain. ScientificWorldJournal 2007;7:310-6.

[32] Ventegodt S, Thegler S, Andreasen T, Struve F, Enevoldsen L, et al. Self-reported low self-esteem. Intervention and follow-up in a clinical setting. ScientificWorldJournal 2007;7:299-305.

[33] Ventegodt S, Andersen NJ, Merrick J. The life mission theory III. Theory of talent. ScientificWorldJournal 2003;3:1286-93.

[34] Jung CG. Man and his symbols. New York: Anchor Press, 1964.

[35] Ventegodt S, Andersen NJ, Merrick J. The life mission theory VI: A theory for the human character. ScientificWorldJournal 2004;4:859-80.

[36] Ventegodt S. The life mission theory: a theory for a consciousness-based medicine. Int J Adolesc Med Health 2003;15(1):89-91.

[37] Ventegodt S, Andersen NJ, Merrick J. The life mission theory II. The structure of the life purpose and the ego. ScientificWorldJournal 2003;3:1277-85.

[38] Ventegodt S, Merrick J. The life mission theory IV. Theory on child development. ScientificWorldJournal 2003;3:1294-301.

[39] Ventegodt S, Andersen NJ, Merrick J. The life mission theory V. Theory of the anti-self (the shadow) or the evil side of man. ScientificWorldJournal 2003;3:1302-13.

[40] Ventegodt S, Flensborg-Madsen T, Andersen NJ, Merrick J. Life Mission Theory VII: Theory of existential (Antonovsky) coherence: a theory of quality of life, health and ability for use in holistic medicine. ScientificWorldJournal 2005;5:377-89.

[41] Jones E. The life and works of Sigmund Freud. New York: Basic Books, 1961.

[42] Leichsenring F, Rabung S, Leibing E. The efficacy of short-term psychodynamic psychotherapy in specific psychiatric disorders: a meta-analysis. Arch Gen Psychiatry 2004;61(12):1208-16.

[43] Leichsenring F. Are psychodynamic and psychoanalytic therapies effective?: A review of empirical data. Int J Psychoanal 2005;86(3):841-68.

[44] Leichsenring F, Leibing E. Psychodynamic psychotherapy: a systematic review of techniques, indications and empirical evidence. Psychol Psychother 2007;80(2):217-28.

[45] Jones WHS. Hippocrates (Loeb Classical Library No. 147: Ancient Medicine). New York: Hippocrene Books, 1923.

[46] Reich W. Die Function des Orgasmus. Köln: Kiepenheuer Witsch, 1969. [German].

[47] Anand M. The art of sexual ecstasy. The path of sacred sexuality for Western lovers. Los Angeles, CA: Jeremy Archer Press, 1989.

[48] Grof S. LSD psychotherapy: Exploring the frontiers of the hidden mind. Alameda, CA: Hunter House, 1980.

[49] Ventegodt S, Kandel I, Merrick J. Clinical holistic medicine (mindful short-term psychodynamic psychotherapy complimented with bodywork) in the treatment of schizophrenia (ICD10-F20/DSM-IV Code 295) and other psychotic mental diseases. ScientificWorldJournal 2007;7:1987-2008.

[50] Buber M. I and Thou. New York: Charles Scribner, New York, 1970.

[51] Lindholt JS, Ventegodt S, Henneberg EW. Development and validation of QoL5 clinical databases. A short, global and generic questionnaire based on an integrated theory of the quality of life. Eur J Surg 2002;168:103-7.

[52] Ventegodt S, Merrick J. The consensus paradigm for qualitative research in holistic medicine. BMJ 2005 November 24 on-line: http://bmj.bmjjournals.com/cgi/eletters/331/7526/0-d-122164.

[53] Antonovsky A. Health, stress and coping. London: Jossey-Bass, 1985.

[54] Antonovsky A. Unravelling the mystery of health. How people manage stress and stay well. San Franscisco: Jossey-Bass, 1987.

[55] Kierkegaard SA. The sickness unto death. Princeton, NJ: Princeton Univ Press, 1983.

[56] Ventegodt S, Thegler S, Andreasen T, Struve F, Enevoldsen L, et al. Clinical holistic medicine: psychodynamic short-time therapy complemented with bodywork. A clinical follow-up study of 109 patients. ScientificWorldJournal 2006;6:2220-38.

[57] Ventegodt S, Thegler S, Andreasen T, Struve F, Jacobsen S, et al. A review and integrative analysis of ancient holistic character medicine systems. ScientificWorldJournal 2007;7: 1821-31.

Chapter 27

Etiology of mental diseases and the role of adult human metamorphosis in spontaneous recovery

Mentally ill patients can enter the state of adult human metamorphosis, to re-do the juvenile metamorphosis into non-human forms that was necessary for their survival in childhood. The adult human metamorphosis looks at first glance like a normal psychotic crisis of a schizophrenic patient, but when you study it closer it becomes obvious that it is actually a healing crisis, an unusual state of accelerated healing process of the type "Antonovsky-salutogenesis".

The healing crisis and the process of adult human metamorphosis seems to be the pathogenesis reversed: an inverted event of a juvenile metamorphosis, where the patient originally turned him- or herself into a non-human (often quite alien) form to survive a hostile and unfriendly invironment. This often leads to severe developmental disturbances and thus to physical or mental health problems later in life.

We have observed several cases of spontaneous remission of a number of different mental diseases induced by holistic existential therapy: schizophrenia, borderline, anxiety, and bulimia. We propose that the general etiology of mental diseases is juvenile metamorphosis intended for survival, not defect genes disturbing the patient's brain chemistry. This understanding empowers us to induce salutogenesis and spontaneous recovery in also the most ill, mental patients with clinical holistic medicine.

The healing crisis could be wrongly diagnosed as a brief reactive psychosis, if the psychiatrist is without practical knowledge of the phenomenon of Antonovsky-salutogensis; this could explain why intensive psychotherapy has been considered dangerous by some psychiatrists.

Introduction

As we have discussed in our papers on "human development", shape and function is closely related to the organism's consciousness. Intent seems to be able to change and modify shape and function. The modifying force of intent is active though life from its very beginning, and the individual seems to be able to read what is going on in its world though the exchange of information on many levels in the individual and collective informational systems.

This opens up for radical self-modifications early in life. We suggest that the individual is actually able to transform itself into a being more fit for survival and the family it is going to soon be a part of. These transformations can be caused by dramatic events in the family, or by the environment being so rough that a normal child could not survive in it. Many dysfunctional families could qualify for this description. The most dramatic change we know of is the metamorphosis; the radical and complete transformation of an individual through an interaction between the level of intent and consciousness to the level of form and function.

We suggest that early adaptation to severely dysfunctional parents, in the womb or in early childhood, will render the individual so changed that it can present itself almost non-human; both consciousness and functions will be severely disturbed, and the person can even sometimes look not only ugly, but "alien" in bodily appearance and energy.

Adult human metamorphosis is re-metamorphosis of childhood adaptations

Some of the authors have examined and treated a number of severely mentally ill patients and we have observed that they often appear very unappealing physically and very alien mentally, as if they have turned themselves into some kind of "monsters" early in life. In surprisingly many cases they have adapted to extreme environments dominated by violent or sexual abuse, or severe neglect and fail. Spontaneously in the holistic existential therapy (1-6) they have entered the state of what we call adult human metamorphosis and they have spent weeks to reconnect to the human collective consciousness, as if they have lived in a system of their own non-connection to the human universe but to some strange parallel reality. It is like they are coming back from a monstrous world into the world of human beings.

Often they have felt alien; felt that they were like aliens waling the earth. So we suggest that they have metamorphosed themselves into beings with non-human intent (3,4,6-10) in some cases even using biological information from alien life forms, in fantasy or for real, if biological information can ride even the energy of the galaxies. Changing intent and the patterns of thought and perception early in life away from the typical human patterns into something else, giving the individual severe problems with relating to other people and the human world at large, is from this perspective what causes mental diseases of the skizotypical types. Presumably this also goes for the affective disorders, as the root of affective aberration likewise seem to be cognitive disturbances. So we suggest that mental diseases are caused by the individual entering metamorphosis early in life to transform into a being with non-human consciousness better able to survive an inhuman and severely dysfunctional environment. This give some meaning to the extremely scary effects of aliens in movies: that they are here already, walking amongst us, disguised as humans. And we think they are.

All aspects of a human being except its fundamental purpose of life can be changed by human juvenile metamorphosis; the purpose of life cannot be changed, but repressed and forgotten. The person going through the process of metamorphosis seems to change functioning purpose of life and fundamental intent, and both mind and body seem to follow. Love, consciousness and sexuality is often severely affected, and the ability to love, understand and enjoy is often damaged. The gender is often annulated or even inverted energetically; the feelings are often completely withdrawn, and mental and intellectual capacity is changed into focusing on non-living issues, very much like the loss of a "I-thou" relationship described by Martin Buber (1878-1965) (11).

The healing of mental diseases through re-metamorphosis

The metamorphosis of the human mind during the psychotic crises seems to be the most radical and drastic of the processes of healing. It happens spontaneously, when development has been radically arrested early in life, normally because of a trauma forcing the patient to let go of his or her purpose of life and substitute it with another purpose. The patients have seemingly had a psychotic episode in connection to this, often in early childhood. Often many aspects of psychosexual development has been arrested, and the people likely to go into human metamorphosis are in many ways like the butterfly's larvae, which grow and grow in size but not in any other way, until the day of metamorphosis, where the information linked to being an adult is finally accessed at once, giving a complete transformation of character, personality and consciousness.

Entering the metamorphosis is helped by intense holistic existential therapy combined with intense holding and combined with the patient's extreme intent to heal here and now and today! Healing existence must be more important that anything else, and the process of metamorphosis is taking the patient to a place of continuous healing for days. Recreation for a week or two after the introvert, psychotic crises seems mandatory, and the patient cannot work or look after kids or have other normal obligations in this period, and sometimes for an extended period of time.

Once the process of personal transformation have started it must run to its natural end. If the metamorphosis is disturbed, when the patient is in the most vulnerable state, severe harm can be done. It is very important that spouses and other family members are informed about the natural course of this kind of spontaneous healing, and they must be carefully informed about the urgent needs for tranquillity and loving care and support for days or weeks. The danger of poor living for months or years if the healing process is disrupted and the patient is sedated or drugged must be severely stressed.

An important ethical problem is if the physician or the relatives should judge what is in the best interest of the patient, when the patient enters the introvert, "psychotic" state similar to the butterfly's pupae. Often the spouse of family members not completely trusting the natures ways will react with fear and want the patient back in the old condition, while the patient him- or herself is doing everything possible to transform into a new and better version of self. Coming from fear and anger the family can cause severe damage to the patient, by interrupting the metamorphosis and arresting it at a transformational state where the patients mind is not very functional. Another dangerous aspect of this is that the person needing the transformation is often victimised early in life, and therefore of a week character allowing other people to exploit them, when they evolve into a more responsible and whole version of themselves they will often rebel against the dominance and "ownership", to become free and autonomous. It is important that the physician notice patterns of abuse in the relationship and helps the patient to understand the consequences of submitting to dominance and being owned by i.e. a spouse. If the behaviour of relatives is obviously threatening the patient's health, the physician should inform the social authorities and other relevant authorities for them to take the appropriate action.

Most interestingly human metamorphosis seems to be able to explain many religious experiences, like the 40 days in the desert where Jesus meets his creator, or Gautama Buddha's famous enlightenment, where he reaches Nirvana, the cosmic emptiness creating the world. A simple way of understanding human metamorphosis is as re-establishing the coherence with the world, getting direct access to the "web", "the nest of the world" (in prep. for publication), or the deep level of the universe we call "the matrix of energy and information"(in prep. for publication), feeding all organisms with qualities like intent and talent.

Case stories

At many occasions during our 14 years of research in quality of life and holistic medicine at the Quality of Life Research Clinic in Copenhagen we have seen patients with the diagnoses of schizophrenia or borderline enter an extremely intense, accelerated process of healing we have called "adult human metamorphosis", because of its remarkable resemblance of a butterfly's larva entering the pupae and metamorphosing into the butterfly. The patients even sometimes look like larvae, with plump poorly demarcated body contours, immature, clumsy movement patterns, and they are characterised by having poor reality testing, as if they lived in their own world, in a parallel universe. Sometimes they have been students of remarkable intelligence, studying medicine or psychology at the university, sometimes they have been very intelligent, but not able to study, sometimes they have chosen to study nursing or occupational therapy. The patients that have come to our research clinic for holistic medicine come to our private clinic by own choice to enter our research protocol on healing the mentally ill (12,13); they normally get a grant from the Quality of Life Research Center so they are able to participate; they typically pay 25% of the therapy themselves.

Female university student of medicine, 24 years, borderline

At the beginning of the treatment she was 30 kg overweight, a poor reality testing, no close friends; she was still a virgin with no interest in men, and a strange non-human uni-sex appearance. All body movements was impaired, she was slow, clumsy, and seemingly depressed, but with no emotional problems, except feeling like an alien. She was not able to look into other people's eyes. In holistic existential therapy she confronted that her 10-year-older big brother had raped her when she was five years old. The energy was that of war-rape: she was raped in the intent of repressing her. Strangely her parents wanted her eliminated and her brother was in alliance with the parents against her and he was not punished. She entered a psychotic crisis that lasted for 14 days during which she was hospitalised at the clinic. She experienced that she melted down and re-entered the human stream of consciousness – the collective human consciousness. She entered a visionary state of mind and for days she received thousands of pictures of human life from an inner source of wisdom and knowledge. When she re-appeared to the surface she was completely transformed into a wise young human remembering her true human nature. She changes her life completely, started dating boys, doing exercise, changing diet and loosing weight. In art-therapy she painted hundreds of paintings of the scenarios she has visualised during the metamorphosis.

Female university student of psychology, 22 years, bulimia

Severe problems with self-esteem, looks, sexuality – not able to enjoy sex or intercourse – self-confidence, presenting severely disturbed eating patterns of overeating and vomiting. She believed she must weigh 50.00 kg. If not, she found her body disgusting. Sometimes she dressed extremely feminine in skirt and appears as a beautiful young woman, this interchanging with a much more male appearance where she varies men's pants. She also suffers from anxiety, and her sexual borders are 2 meters from her body; if men get closer she often feels intimidated. In holistic existential therapy the therapist (SV) could not get close to her for many sessions. When trust was won she finally allowed the therapist to get close emotionally and she melted down in a psychotic crises, where all her problems of sexuality of low bodily self-esteem exploded. She entered a mental state of feeling totally unreal and stayed like this for days. She was hospitalised at our clinic for four days, before she can integrate the painful childhood events of failure and neglect that she has confronted; obviously she has then as a child metamorphosed into a person living in her own world not needing any contact to her parents, to avoid the pain of feeling not loved and not cared for. After the psychotic crises her condition slowly normalised and she was able to function again as a human being.

We have earlier described this kind of spontaneous healing of two schizophrenic patients (14), and we have often seen holistic sexological therapy and holistic gynaecology lead to accelerated existential healing (Antonovsky salutogenesis) (15-24).

Discussion

In a number of cases in our clinical work we have observed a radical process of spontaneous healing that seems to be adult human metamorphosis, parallel to the metamorphosis of many insects and some vertebrates. In its most radical version the person's mind is melting down and all behavioural and mental patterns are disintegrated for up to 10 days. The function of the human metamorphosis is to allow a person to catch up after many years of arrested psychosexual development. It happens spontaneously or provoked by holistic existential therapy, and is most likely to happen with people who have been violently or sexually abused in early childhood. The process is often initiated by a catharsis and a break through into old trauma of extremely intense emotional pain; rape in early childhood seems to be the paradigm. Other traumas of sufficient intensity to cause the developmental arrest which is set free by the metamorphosis is: surgery, social isolation, violence, and other events giving the child a near-death or psychic death experience. During the metamorphosis the person will re-live the extreme neural arousal and temporary psychosis of the traumatic childhood event.

It is most important to stress that the metamorphosis is not a mental disease - but a state of spontaneous healing - and it should not be treated as such. In this spontaneous healing event the patient needs loving care and tranquillity, while being "in the pupae": introvert, mentally disintegrated, seemingly psychotic and not in present time, sinking into the sea of biological information of being human, to finally reappear the way nature originally meant this person to be.

We suggest that human metamorphosis is really a biological process, and we believe that there is a complete set of genes and chemical mediators (hormones, neurotransmitters, or neuropeptides) to handle the biological side of the human metamorphosis. We believe that human metamorphosis is the most efficient healing process known to this day, and that a successful metamorphosis can save the patient from many years of therapy and sufferings. Human metamorphosis cannot only change the mind. We believe that spontaneous healing of cancer and other diseases is also often caused by human metamorphosis.

Conclusions

Interestingly, mentally ill patients can enter the state of adult human metamorphosis, to re-do the juvenile metamorphosis into non-human forms that was beneficial for their childhood survival. The adult human metamorphosis looks at first glance like a normal psychotic crisis of a schizophrenic patient, but when you study it closer it becomes obvious that it is an unusual state of accelerated healing, a healing crisis. It is important to understand that the adult human metamorphosis is the inverted event of a juvenile metamorphosis where the patient turned him- or her self into some non-human alien form to survive; the self-transportation of human existence into a parallel dimensionof existence often gives severe developmental problems and both physical and mental problems to the person later in life but was necessary for survival from an emotional point of view.

We have now carefully observed several cases of spontaneous remission of a number of different mental diseases: schizophrenia, borderline, anxiety, and bulimia. We understand the adult human metamorphosis as a confirmation of our hypothesis of aetiology of mental diseases: that they are in general caused by juvenile metamorphosis (12,13), not by defective genes and disturbed brain chemistry.

We believe that we in cracking this "secret code" have found a general way to understand and heal mental diseases, by taking them into adult human metamorphosis with clinical holistic medicine.

References

[1] Ventegodt S, Andersen NJ, Merrick J. Holistic medicine III: The holistic process theory of healing. ScientificWorldJournal 2003;3: 1138-46.
[2] Ventegodt S, Andersen NJ, Merrick J. Holistic medicine IV: Principles of existential holistic group therapy and the holistic process of healing in a group setting. ScientificWorldJournal 2003;3, 1388-1400.

[3]   Ventegodt S, Andersen NJ, Merrick J. The life mission theory V. A theory of the anti-self and explaining the evil side of man. ScientificWorldJournal 2003;3:1302-13.

[4]   Ventegodt S, Andersen NJ, Merrick J. The life mission theory VI: A theory for the human character. ScientificWorldJournal 2004:4:859-80.

[5]   Ventegodt S, Morad M, Andersen NJ, Merrick J. Clinical holistic medicine Tools for a medical science based on consciousness. ScientificWorldJournal 2004;4:347-61.

[6]   Ventegodt S, Flensborg-Madsen T, Andersen NJ, Merrick J. Life mission theory VII: Theory of existential (Antonovsky) coherence: a theory of quality of life, health and ability for use in holistic medicine. ScientificWorldJournal 2005;5:377-89.

[7]   Ventegodt S. The life mission theory: A theory for a consciousness-based medicine. Int J Adolesc Med Health 2003;15(1):89-91.

[8]   Ventegodt S, Andersen NJ, Merrick J. The life mission theory II: The structure of the life purpose and the ego. ScientificWorldJournal 2003;3:1277-85.

[9]   Ventegodt S, Andersen NJ, Merrick J. The life mission theory III: Theory of talent. ScientificWorldJournal 2003;3:1286-93.

[10] Ventegodt S, Merrick J. The life mission theory IV. A theory of child development. ScientificWorldJournal 2003;3:1294-1301.

[11] Buber M. I and thou. London: Free Press, 1971.

[12] Ventegodt S, Andersen NJ, Neikrug S, Kandel I, Merrick J. Clinical Holistic medicine: Holistic treatment of mental disorders. ScientificWorldJournal 2005;5:427-45.

[13] Ventegodt S, Andersen NJ, Neikrug S, Kandel I, Merrick J. Clinical holistic medicine: Mental disorders in a holistic perspective. ScientificWorldJournal 2005;5:313-23.

[14] Ventegodt S, Kandel I, Merrick J. Clinical holistic medicine (mindful short-term psychodynamic psychotherapy complimented with bodywork) in the treatment of schizophrenia (ICD10-F20/DSM-IV Code 295) and other psychotic mental diseases. ScientificWorldJournal. 2007;7:1987-2008.

[15] Ventegodt S, Kandel I, Merrick J. Clinical holistic medicine: how to recover memory without "implanting" memories in your patient. ScientificWorldJournal. 2007 Sep 17;7:1579-89.

[16] Flensborg-Madsen T, Ventegodt S, Merrick J. Sense of coherence and physical health. The emotional sense of coherence (SOC-E) was found to be the best-known predictor of physical health. ScientificWorldJournal. 2006 Jun 22;6:2147-57.

[17] Ventegodt S, Clausen B, Omar HA, Merrick J. Clinical holistic medicine: holistic sexology and acupressure through the vagina (Hippocratic pelvic massage). ScientificWorldJournal. 2006 Mar 7;6:2066-79.

[18] Ventegodt S, Clausen B, Merrick J. Clinical holistic medicine: pilot study on the effect of vaginal acupressure (Hippocratic pelvic massage). ScientificWorldJournal. 2006 Apr 14;6:2100-16.

[19] Ventegodt S, Clausen B, Merrick J. Clinical holistic medicine: the case story of Anna. III. Rehabilitation of philosophy of life during holistic existential therapy for childhood sexual abuse. ScientificWorldJournal. 2006 Mar 7;6:2080-91.

[20] Ventegodt S, Thegler S, Andreasen T, Struve F, Enevoldsen L, Bassaine L, Torp M, Merrick J. Clinical holistic medicine (mindful, short-term psychodynamic psychotherapy complemented with bodywork) in the treatment of experienced impaired sexual functioning. ScientificWorldJournal. 2007 Mar 2;7:324-9.

[21] Ventegodt S, Kandel I, Neikrug S, Merric J. Clinical holistic medicine: holistic treatment of rape and incest trauma. ScientificWorldJournal. 2005 Apr 6;5:288-97.

[22] Ventegodt S, Morad M, Hyam E, Merrick J. Clinical holistic medicine: holistic sexology and treatment of vulvodynia through existential therapy and acceptance through touch. ScientificWorldJournal. 2004 Aug 4;4:571-80.

[23] Ventegodt S, Morad M, Kandel I, Merrick J. Clinical holistic medicine: problems in sex and living together. ScientificWorldJournal. 2004 Aug 4;4:562-70.

[24] Ventegodt S, Morad M, Merrick J. Clinical holistic medicine: holistic pelvic examination and holistic treatment of infertility. ScientificWorldJournal. 2004 Mar 4;4:148-58.

Section 7. Decision making and transfernce

This section is about sexuality. It is about arrested psychosexual development and what it does to the patient-physician relationship when this issue is addressed in the therapy.

Sexuality is a difficult subject in our culture. In spite of porn in every small shop on the corner in most western countries, dirty dating sites and millions of internet pages of all kind of explicit sexual acts, which is seen by a majority of young people, including the females, sexuality remains taboo.

In the sphere of therapy and medicine the taboo of sexuality is even stronger than in the rest of society. But sexuality cannot be removed, only repressed. It was the philosophical position of Freud, Jung, Reich and the other psychoanalysts of the last century that repression of sexuality was the most direct and important cause of mental disorders.

Today at least one in four in our civilized world is chronically, mentally ill, according to the national statistics (1). Could it be that we as physicians and therapists do not know how to integrate the repressed sexuality and make our patients heal existentially and become whole and coherent people? Could it be that the reason why so many patients are mentally ill is because of our difficult relationship with sexuality in our culture? This is the position of not only Freud and the psychoanalysts, but also of the whole tradition of holistic medicine and psychiatry.

In the patient-physician relationship sexuality often comes sneaking in, quite unexpected. In the beginning the mutual sexual interest or repulsion are not felt or noticed. But when the patients' psychosocial development is becoming the center of attention the sexual energy in the patient and between the patient and other people including the physician becomes enhanced. In this situation it is important to understand the nature of the sexual transference and counter transference described in detail by Freud, Searles and other great therapists; and it is important to know what to do with the sexual energies. They need to be accepted and integrated; repression of them will not help the patient to heal.

In the five chapters of this section we give all the info needed to deal competently with even the most difficult of situations: the strong female Oedipus complex caused by sexual abuse. One in seven of girls in the Western world is sexually abused, so a large fraction of your mentally ill patient's future life will depend on your careful understanding of this section.

References

[1]   Kjøller M, Juel K, Kamper-Jørgensen F. [Folkesundhedsrapporten Danmark 2007]. Copenhagen: Statens Inst Folkesundhed, 2007. [Danish].

Chapter 28

Factors influencing the therapeutic decision-making

We consider the classical holistic medicine, psychiatry and sexology to be a part of the Hippocrates holistic medicine. Most of the sexological procedures used in manual sexology, like the sexological examination, were in some form described in the classical textbooks of Hippocratic medicine dated back to 300 BC called the *Corpus Hippocraticum*.

Both modern sexology and modern holistic psychiatry acknowledges these ancient roots and share the same close relationship to the contemporary scientific holistic medicine. Actually 2400 years ago psychiatry and sexology was not two disciplines, but only one; the mental disorders of the female was under one category called "hysteria" from greek Hystera, uterus. Hysteria was cased by energetic malfunction of the female genitals. This is hard to understand for modern biomedical psychiatrists that do not operate with psychic energy, but it is very similar to Indian and Chinese medicine, where the existence of psychic energy is an inherent part of the philosophical system descibing the disorders.

Holstic medicine is different from many types of alternative and complementary medicine (CAM) as it focus on the *whole person*, body, mind, spirit and heart together with the person's *character, life mission and sense of coherence* (SOC) with the surrounding world.

Modern, scientific holistic medicine is built on holistic medical theory, on therapeutic and ethical principles. The rationale is that the therapist can take the patient into a state of salutogenesis, or existential healing, using his skills and knowledge. The formal distinction between holistic medicine, psychiatry and sexology is a very recent development; in the original holistic medicine the whole existence was cured independent of symptomatology. Mental, physical and sexual problems were all treated almost alike.

How ever much we want to make therapy a science it remains partly an art, and the more developed the therapist becomes, the more of his/her decisions will be based on intuition, feeling and even inspiration that is more based on love and human concern and other spiritual motivations than on mental reason and rationality in a simple sense of the word.

The provocative and paradoxal medieval western concept of the "truth telling clown", or the eastern concepts of *"crazy wisdom"* and *"holy madness"* seems highly relevant here.

The problem is how we can ethically justify this kind of highly "irrational" therapeutic behavior in the rational setting of a medical institution. We argue here that holistic therapy has a very high success rate and is doing no harm to the patient, and encourage therapists, psychiatrists, psychologist and other academically trained "helpers" to constantly measure their own success-rate.

This chapter discuss many of the important factors that influence clinical holistic decision-making. The holistic theories of mental disorders still have deep roots in sexuality; many psychoanalysts from Freud to Reich and Searles have believed that sexuality, or Eros, is the most healing power that exists and also the most difficult for the mind to comprehend. To deal with the seemingly irrational elements of therapy, such spirituaol and erotic elements, such elements have been named the "crazy-wise" tool of therapy.

Introduction

400,000 Danes used CAM (complementary and alternative medicine) in 1990, which is holistic and alternative medicine (defined as non-biomedical complementary, alternative, integrative or psychosocial interventions for medical purposes). This increased to 800,000 by year 2000 (1) and expected to be 1,600,000 in 2010. If the development continues, as it has done in the United States already, there will be more CAM consultations than biomedical consultations in Denmark year 2020. One of the fastest growing areas of CAM in the whole western world is sexolology, presumably refecting both a liberalisation of society and an increating rate of severe sexual problems in the population.

In spite of all this activity, the effect of CAM in general is still not clear at all. This is primarily because the term now refers to hundreds of treatment systems focusing on some aspects of "the whole patient" and not primarily on symptoms or diseases, as is normal practice in today's mainstream biomedicine (pharmacological medicine).

What works in holistic medicine is healing of the patient's existence, called "salutogenesis" by Aaron Antonovsky (1923–1994) (2-9). This is most often done by creating a deep shift in the consciousness of the patient towards a more positive and constructive attitude towards self, including body and mind, other people, and the world at large. The reason for the medical efficiency of such a shift towards positive attitudes and behaviours seems to be that consciousness is the primary determinant of global quality of life (QOL), health, and ability in general (10-14). Because of the appreciation in the causal power of consciousness, many physicians and therapists are now focusing on this important shift in the patient's consciousness as their primary goal in treatment, when they want to improve QOL, health, and ability of the patient. This focus has caused the emerging field of scientific holistic medicine, i.e. "clinical holistic medicine" (15-55).

We have been able to document that such an approach can help every second patient in the patients own experience - with physical illness and chronic pain, mental illness, low self-esteem, sexual dysfunction, low quality of life, and low working ability (56-62). Interestingly we tested the holistic therapy on patients that could not be helped by their doctor with standard treatment (drugs), and many of the patients had had their chronic conditions for many years. This indicates quite a powerful effect of scientific holistic medicine. The clinical decision making were guided by many sound and rational theories and principles, but the different treatments took so many different routes that we literally invented a new cure for every new patient, leaving us with a need of deep reflections on what really is happening in the therapy. What are the "unpredictable" factors that are so radically influencing the therapists decisions, when not the rational principles of healing and therapy themselves? From where comes the surprising creativity in the session that in the end seemingly sets the patient free?

The therapeutic principles

Since Hippocrates, holistic healing has been guided by medical principles (63). The better the holistic therapist knows and understands these principles, and the more fluent he is in using them, the more efficient will the therapy be and the more lasting the results. Holistic therapy uses primarily four core principles of treatment (56):

- Induce healing of the whole existence of the patient (salutogenesis) and not only his/her body or mind (2-9). The healing often included goals like recovering purpose and meaning of life (64-72) by improving existential coherence (71) and ability to love, understand, and function sexually (67).
- Adding as many resources to the patient as possible as the primary reason for originally repressing the emotionally charged material was lack of resources — love, understanding, empathy, respect, care, acceptance, and acknowledgment — to mention a few of the many needs of the little child (17,49,68). The principle was also to use the minimal intervention necessary by first using conversational therapy, then additional philosophical exercises if needed, then adding bodywork or, if needed, adding role play, group therapy, and finally when necessary in a few cases, referring to a psychiatrist for psychopharmacologic intervention (49). If the patient was in somatic or psychiatric treatment already at the beginning of the therapy, this treatment was continued with support from the holistic therapist.
- Using the similarity principle (see 56 for references) that seems to be a fundamental principle for all holistic healing (63). The similarity principle is based on the belief that what made the person sick originally will make the patient well again, when given in the right, therapeutic dose. This principle often leads to dramatic events in the therapy and to efficient and fast healing, but seems to send the patient into a number of developmental crises that must be handled professionally (50-52).
- Using Hering's Law of Cure (see 56 for references) to support the patient in going once again through all the disturbances and diseases, in reverse order, that brought the patient to where he or she is now. Other important axioms of Hering's Law of Cure is that the disease goes from more to less-important organs, goes from the inside out, and goes from upside down. The scientific rationale for the last three axioms are less clear than for the first: The patient must go back through his/her timeline in order to integrate all the states and experiences he/she has met on his/her way to disease. Going back in time is normally done though spontaneous regression in holistic existential therapy.

These four principles seem to be a lot to keep in mind, when you are practicing therapy, but you will soon learn that they are all aspects of the same fundamental principle, the abstract law of integration – everything to emotionally intense in your patients life must be felt again, recalled and understood, and finally "melted" into the patients own, natural understanding of life and being. This is the same as the patient returning to being him- or her self. So in this respect everything gets simpler as you get more experienced as therapist. Get your patient back into contact with the world through body and mind, heal the patients psychoform and the somatoform dissociation, just restore the patient's sense of coherence, and your are home free. But in practice therapy develops paradoxically more and more complex and more and more simple at the same time - more and more complex for the therapist's mind, and more and more simple for the therapist's self.

What is a decision?

One rational way of understanding the development of a treatment of a patient is as a series of rational choices each one serving the purpose of using tools for healing the patient's life. This is a nice idea, and highly popular with academic thinkers. Unfortunately most choices in therapy are not based on ratio and reason, but on emotions, feelings, sensations and intuitions. This is because we are dealing with emotions. Therapy is about integrating difficult emotions. But still there is a consciousness and a will guiding these choices.

Philosophically, in the grand tradition of existentialistic thinkers, man has free will, and from that, free choice (73,74). Choice is a consequence of the presentation in our human consciousness of more than one alternative, future action; the more conscious we are the more alternatives will be acknowledged by our self, and the wiser the choice, and thus the bigger the power and influence of the choice on our future destiny.

In the existentialistic philosophy of Søren Kirkegaard (1813-1855) we are divine beings empowered to create our own destiny good or bad. The empowerment comes from man containing in his innermost existential core the possibility to connect to the universe and from this connection in each situation draw the wisdom to make the good choice. When we loose this connection to the universe, we loose our existential orientation, and we fall into darkness and random choices, leaving responsibility for our live and relationship behind.

Sigmund Freud (1856-1939), Carl Gustav Jung (1875-1961) and their students elaborated on this further, defining the subconscious and the repression of emotions and sexuality, giving the science of psychodynamic therapy (75,76). Antonovsky gave in the 1980s his theory of "sense of coherence" (2,3), which stated that the healthy person has a sense of coherence – inwards towards life and inner self making him alive, and outwards towards the world, making him real. Being alive and real is what a sound person is, and loss of health is loss of the sense of coherence making the person emotionally dead, mentally delusioned, and spiritually aloof.

Resent developments in research on therapy have identified that this sense of coherence has two main vehicles, the mind and the body. The sense of coherence can be lost in part, when one of our to channels to the world shut down, either as somatoform or psychoform dissociation. Or both these vital channels can b closed leaving the patient without any real contact to the outer world, in a severely ill state, often suffering from both mental, existential, physical, and sexual problems and illnesses.

Rehabilitation of the connectedness to life and to the world, i.e. rehabilitation of the sense of coherence, is also the rehabilitation of the patient's life, power, wisdom, and freedom of choice. This total healing of the patients existence, the existential salutogenesis, is the primary intention in scientific holistic therapy; this fundamental shift from not being into being see seems to be the central theme of the works of Kierkegaard on "hjaelpekunst" (Danish: the art of helping) and the focus of the old holistic medical tradition going all the way back to Hippocrates, who calling his noble medical art of helping and healing for "the art" (63).

In practice the therapist will make many choices in each treatment, but as the fundamental problems of revitalisation and existential rehabilitation in holistic therapy are pretty much the same with each patient, the choices seem to repeat themselves. The uninspired, experienced therapist will tend to take therapy into a boring and non-productive state of quite mechanical repetition, which is the dead of efficient therapy; when routine and dullness takes over the love dies; the investment of the therapist's libidinous energy in the relationship with the patient is closed down; and what is left is the remote and formal relationship. The experienced, but inspired, therapist will move in the completely opposite direction, into a state of being where there is almost no choices left, but just a stream of consciousness and dancing libidinous energy, in witch the whole therapeutic setting and therapeutic process is embedded.

The therapist as the tool

To be in flow (77), to be conscious (78) and to be happy (in the state of sat-shit-ananda: present, knowing and happy) seems to be the holistic therapeutic ideal of a human being; this can be further developed into non-knowing (cp. Zen: "state of no mind"), just being dancing with the patient's consciousness in a state where all decisions are not made and the action never becomes a problem. This is the intuitive state of the experience holistic therapist, coming from love, and being completely in service of his patient.

Holistic therapy and the process of existential healing is unwrapping the personal history of the patient, sending him back to heal all wound on body, mind and soul, rehabilitating the "natural philosophy" of the patient, that is: the understanding of life that best serves his character and purpose of life. Unfortunately every therapeutic action is intensively impacting the philosophy of life of the patient, actually implanting philosophy in the patient; this philosophy must be de-learned for the natural philosophy of the patient to emerge.

The holistic therapeutic principles includes the most important principle of similarity; the patient will have to transfer his past into the present and transfer the emotional charges of his childhood traumas on the therapist With out this actualisation of the past, the therapy cannot work, as already noticed by Freud. As we are transferring from both our bodily (emotional, sexual), and mental (philosophical, energetic) and spiritual (consciousness, love) realms, holistic therapy is often extremely complex, and much too complex to monitor by the therapist brain-mind. The body-mind (instinctive domains) and spirit-mind (intuitive domains) must be strongly involved for the therapist to be effective and successful as healer.

The most important thing in holistic therapy is the state and quality of the tool (one self as therapist), and personal development to a state where unconditional love to all human beings is natural is a sine qua non; unfortunately most therapist reaches this level late in life, if the therapist's own therapy is not intensified and boddhahood actively pursued. Only in the state of unconditional love can the therapist be pure and unselfish and coming from his heart in service; only love allows the therapist to use all aspects of him self without hesitation to help the patient to heal his existence. Only another person's true love can set a tormented soul free, and that is what holistic healing is all about. And when you love, most choices are easy, because your personal interests are suspended, and all that matters is what best can help your patient. When the patient feels your love as a therapist, he or she will let go of the neurotic control that for survival reasons has replaces responsible conscious being, and the existence will heal and re-emerge.

The philosophy of life of the therapist

Holistic, existentially oriented, therapy is basically about re-interpreting life and through a more containing philosophy of life being able to integrate past events. The expansion of the patient's philosophy of life is done by consciously or unconsciously implanting a more accepting and loving philosophy of life in the patient. This is done through therapists body language, the way the clinic is decorated, the quality of therapist awareness, the concepts used, the attitude in the meeting, the nature of the therapeutic contract, the methods and technologies used, and of coarse primarily by the inspiration coming from meeting on a regular basis with a (hopefully) more sound and higher developed person than the patient him- or her self. Even if the relation is equal, holistic therapy can only work if the therapist is empowered by the patient by the patients illusion of the therapist being in some aspects wiser and superior – because most traumas and philosophical misunderstandings comes from the patients childhood, and the therapist must substitute the parent(s) to make the healing happen.

The therapist's own philosophy of life therefore becomes of crucial importance, and the more evolved and deep-sighted the therapist's philosophy is, the more efficient can he plant the containing philosophy. Truthfulness and honesty about the philosophical implantation will ease the process of de-learning the philosophy in the final stage of therapy. When the therapist is honest the patient will suffer, and this suffering is the patients meeting with reality, that in the end will restore sense of coherence with the outer world. The loving acknowledgment will support the patient in rehabilitating the sense of coherence inwards towards life and the deeper existential and spiritual layers (the "soul").

It is therefore helpful for the therapy that the therapist has values such as: honesty, openness, directness and compassion as a part of his actively worded philosophy.

Understanding the therapeutic processs

The processes of healing the existence is quite predictable and in an abstract sense always the same (see figure 1). The movement is from the body (holding the repressed material) to the mind (denying responsibility by negative philosophy of life) to the spirit (the original cause of the problems by the historic unwise choices of the original, spiritually awake being). In the process of healing there are obligatory developmental crises, which the patient must go through to rehabilitate ability of love, understand and be in a sexual body. The better the therapist understand the process and the nature of the crisis, the better can the patients resistance and problems in the therapy be handled.

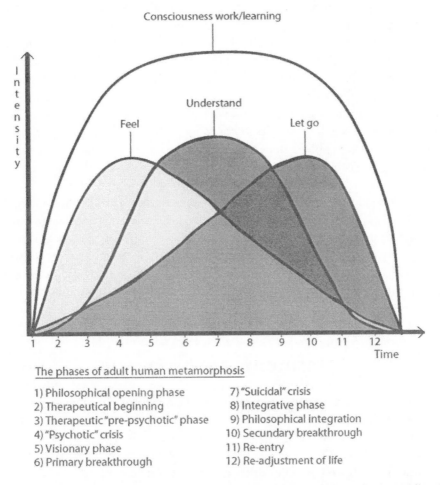

The phases of adult human metamorphosis

1) Philosophical opening phase
2) Therapeutical beginning
3) Therapeutic "pre-psychotic" phase
4) "Psychotic" crisis
5) Visionary phase
6) Primary breakthrough

7) "Suicidal" crisis
8) Integrative phase
9) Philosophical integration
10) Secundary breakthrough
11) Re-entry
12) Re-adjustment of life

Figure 1. The process of holistic healing seen as three phases of feeling (yellow), understanding (red), and letting go (blue) of negative beliefs, attitudes, and decisions. As an end result, the process was improving the patient's philosophy of life and thus allowed the patient to rebalance existence and to assume responsibility for life. During the process, the patient's will re-established quality of life, health, and existential coherence, along with the ability to love, understand, and enjoy the whole spectrum of feelings and emotions, including sexuality.

Many patients in intensive therapy experience the healing as a series of phenomena or breakthroughs and existential crises with characteristic content. The most intense crises are metaphorically called the "psychotic", the "visionary", and the "suicidal" crises. They include feelings of going insane, not knowing the world or oneself, and wanting to die. Knowing what is coming next in the course of therapy is of great help to the patient, making it much easier to confront and integrate the often extremely intense, painful emotions and states of being, arising from integrating the early childhood traumas. The 12 steps (see figure 1) are some possible steps in the process of healing and human transformation; understood though an ancient and powerful metaphor as the steps of "human metamorphosis" (52).

Understanding health and disease

Man consists of body, mind and spirit, and many of the energies are going though all aspects of the human being, like sexuality, meaning, and sense of coherence. The highly complex construction of the human being through billions of years of evolution and the limited ability to represent complexity in the brain-mind, the brain after all just being a small part of the human being, makes understanding health and disease one of the most central problems and most crucial issues in holistic therapy.

The modern holistic therapist must know a wide range of sciences from physics, biochemistry and biology, to medicine (anatomy, physiology, pathology), psychology, philosophy, and sociology. In the same time the therapist must be trained in art and literature, and he must also be deeply involved in the project of self-exploration, to develop a deep and thorough understanding of all aspects of self – from sexuality to spirituality.

The training and education of a holistic physician thus never ends. And many therapists get exhorted in the process of assimilating all existent scientific knowledge and ends up feeling insecure and insufficient. The temptation of closing ones view down to a specific therapeutic system with specific tools is big, but holistic medicine can newer work if the doctor himself is not the tool. The person cannot be substituted with procedures or machinery. An many therapists ends up not working holistically, but just practicing some procedure and techniques mechanically, without the therapy healing existence and giving lasting effects.

Hermeneutic problems

The most fundamental problem of working professionally with induction of shifts in consciousness is the hermeneutic problems: that what we believe will be our reality. The reason for this is that our reality is a materialisation of our consciousness (79). Therefore we will always find confirmation for our believes in reality, in spite of our believes being in deep conflict with life itself, and with the larger world. This problem makes it a necessity for the holistic therapist to involve in a spiritual practice to develop consciousness.

Awareness of planting philosophy of life in the patient is a condition for de-learning the philosophy ion the end of the therapy. Not doing this leads to all the problems with dependence between therapist and patient, extended therapeutic courses with no progress lasting up to many years, and the famous problems of implanted memories, known from the trials where the family sue the therapist for implanting incest-memories – such "fake memories and ideas" are just the events of the patient's personal history, interpreted though the "glasses" of the implanted philosophy, lasting after therapy because of lack of philosophical de-learning.

Supervision

The quality of the holistic therapist's choices is because of hermeneutic problems completely dependent of second opinions; Balint group work and supervision is mandatory. The therapist must work in his own therapy with the existential problems that continue to be revealed because of a mirroring effect from the patients into the therapist – the famous process of counter-transference.

We have identified (71) nine key dimensions of existence, which exist in a passive and an active form, corresponding to the being and doing of life (see table 1).

Table 1. Nine key dimensions of existence, which exist in a passive and an active form, corresponding to the being and doing of life

	Active form	Passive form
1. Coherence, the web, the nest of the world	Receiving, taking in	Being an integrated part
2. Intent/purpose of life	Intention, decision	Having a purpose (of life)
3. Talent/strength	Using skills and urges	Having strength and structure
4. Consciousness	Noticing, knowing, understanding, planning	Being awake
5. Love	Acting in love	Being in love
6. Sex/physicality	Meeting, enjoying	Being man/woman of character
7. Light	Bringing light	Being in light/enlightened
8. Joy	Bringing joy	Being in joy
9. Meaning/QOL	Creating/fulfilling life, giving	Being alive, having impact

Interestingly, as a person develops, the nine areas merges completely; every part of existence becomes conscious, filled with love, meaningful, joyful, enlightened, purposeful, urge-driven, ecstatic and coherent, as all parts of existence expands into the neighbour areas. This expansion of all existential areas is the project of personal development, such as sex expands into the consciousness and love expands into sexuality we have the classical art of sexual tantra (see "the path of tantra" (reference 71, Figure 4), that is integrating sex and consciousness). One by one all the splits and participations that torment modern man heal in this process of existential integration. Existential healing is therefore the primary goal of personal development (2,3).

State of mind

The more relaxed, in flow, free, and happy, the therapist is, and the less he controls his rational and irrational impulses of talking and acting, the more flawless and efficient is the holistic therapy. Modern short-term therapy, where huge problems is intended solved in only 10 or 20 sessions, demands the therapist to be extremely active, in strong contrast to the old-style psychoanalytical therapist, who did almost nothing but listen to the patient while he did his free associations. Body work is becoming more and more common, and spiritual and philosophical exercises has become modern all over the western world as a part of holistic therapy. This puts new demands on the therapist to be ethically aware, and conscious about sexual transferences, emotional energies, symbiotic dependencies etc.

The therapeutic tools

The ideal therapist uses only the loving and caring contact with the patient to induce holistic healing, the process Antonovsky called "salutogenesis". But as we are not as loving as we potentially could be, our love is often not powerful enough to make the healing happen, and then we can go to using tools as a compensation for this lack of healing power. Unfortunately, tools are a meagre substitute, and results obtained with tools are often temporary and not lasting long.

But as everything is a learning process, the acceptance of one limitations is an important prerequisite for growing, and daring to use tools to materialise ones firm intent of helping the patient to heal is the road to learn how to practice medicine, as it inevitably reveals our own impurities and shaddowish sides – if we dare to look, and we have someone to assist us by pointing at what we least of everything want to see in ourselves.

The "staircase" of therapeutic tools of increasing power [49]

As demonstrated throughout our many papers on clinical holistic medicine (15-55), almost everything can be used as a tool, since only the imagination sets the limit. To induce the state of consciousness we call "being in the process of healing" (17), the physician (according to Yalom (80)) needs to invent a new cure for every patient. This ability to be imaginative, creative, and use whatever is necessary to induce the healing is the hallmark of the excellent therapist. Good intent, balanced action, and good results are definitely needed in holistic medicine. Giving up on your patient and not doing anything at all might be a bigger sin, in many cases, than doing your best as a holistic physician and still losing your patient. Still you need to use any tool only after careful consideration, respecting the golden rule never to use a tool more powerful and dangerous than necessary (compare that both in surgery and with chemotherapy the patient is risking death as a result of the treatment).

Almost everything in the world can be used as a tool, but as the physician lines up his tools, some tools are used naturally before others and some might be painfully out of reach because of lack of expertise or due to the laws of your country. The ranking of tools after intensity, danger, and needed expertise of the physician gives a "staircase" of advanced tools of holistic medicine; its function is to help the holistic physician to "step up" in the use of the techniques one level at a time.

Let us admit that therapy often is a little "messy" with the combination of a number of tools and techniques. To think of therapy as the clear-cut process of "walking the staircase" is too simple. Often, many of the steps are used in subtle and symbolic ways by the skilled therapist, i.e., hidden in jokes and ironic remarks.

So this staircase is meant for education, training, and treatment strategy, and not to limit the flexibility and spontaneity of the therapy.

The concept of "stepping up" in the therapy by using more and more "dramatic" methods to get access to repressed emotions and events has led to the common notion of a "therapeutic staircase" with still stronger, more efficient, and more potentially dangerous traumatic methods of therapy (see figure 1). We have identified 10 steps of this staircase:

- Is about establishing the relationship
- Is about establishing intimacy, trust, and confidentiality
- Is about giving support
- Is about taking the patient into the process of physical, emotional, and mental healing
- Is about social healing of being in the family
- Is about spiritual healing – returning to the abstract wholeness of the soul
- Is about healing the informational layer of the body (from old times called the ethereal layer)
- Is about healing the three fundamental dimensions of existence: love, power, and sexuality in a direct way
- Is mind-expanding and consciousness-transformativ techniques, and
- Techniques transgressing the borders of the patient and therefore often traumatizing, like using force and going against the will of the patient.

When the holistic physician or therapist masters one step, he can go on to training and using the techniques of the next step of the staircase. As step 10 is often traumatizing for the patient even with the best of physicians, it is generally advised that the holistic physician or therapist do not go there. When mastered by the physician, steps 5–8 (9) can be used, when steps 1–4 do not help the patient sufficiently. The tools must be used one level at a time and each step implies an increasing risk for traumatizing the patient. Levels 8 and 9 often take many years of practice to master.

When everything else has been tried, but the healing has not occurred and the physician still senses that there is more to be done, the holistic physician can — if he has the necessary qualifications such as training in medical ethics and in the different treatment techniques, combined with a sufficient level of personal development and sufficient courage — use the advanced tools of holistic medicine. The advanced holistic physician's expanded toolbox contains powerful tools that can be organized into a staircase of the intensity of the therapeutic experience that they provoke and the level of expertise they take to master (see figure 1 and table 1). The more intense a therapeutic technique, the more emotional energy will normally be contained in the session and the higher the risk for the therapist to lose control or lose the patient to the dark side, which can make the therapeutic session very traumatic and damaging. These induced problems can almost always be healed if the patient stays in the therapy, so the real risk is losing the patient because he or she completely drops out of the therapy.

Libidinous investment in abstinence as effective, crazy-wise, therapeutic behavior

Interestingly, the destiny of the therapist experience with therapy is his choice of closing down or opening up for his libidinous energy towards his clients; the most dangerous of these energetic openings are of cause the acceptance of the transference and countertransference of Oedipal love, because the temptations of not keeping the borders are biggest here. Harold F Searles stated in his brilliant paper "Oedipal love in the countertransference"(81) the thesis that it is the therapist's libidinous investment in sexual abstinence that helps mentally ill patients to recover; he is believed to have cured 40% of his schizophrenic patients by using the combination of a good heart and a brilliant administration of sexual energy to cure his patients. Using the therapists own sexuality in combination with a strict sexual ethic as the therapeutic tool is an example of a crazy-wise therapeutic behaviour, that most people would abandon, if it was not for the fact that he cured so many patients and harmed no one. Most interestingly, if you are a firm believer in Freud's theory of libido as the only creative power of man, you will not find a libidinous investment in a patient "crazy-wise" or plain crazy, you would find it rational and well based on theory. From a crazy-wise perspective the Freudian concept of libido is a crazy-wise theory in itself.

Intention and spiritual matters

The nature of the human wholeness is difficult to grasp as it is abstract; the essence of man – the essence of the soul – seems to be love in a particular colour, the gift of the person, or the mission of the persons life (64-72). When the patient recovers his remembrance of what he really is, the great talents of his personality are also revealed. Life is from this perspective about being of value to the world by using one's talents to enriching the surrounding world, and thus contributes in all relations.

The theory of existential coherence explains many of the same facets of existence covered by the "Four quadrant theory" of Ken Wilber (82). He also started with "The great nest of being", what we call the coherent matrix of energy and information, or the web of the world. Wilber's four quadrants are intentions, behaviour, culture and social relations, but love is rejected as a central concept in Wilber's model, making this model less useful for deep holistic, existential therapy, where love, trust, and holding are prerequisites for taking the patient into the state of consciousness we call "being in the process of existential healing" (17). Responsibility for the person's own world is also difficult to rehabilitate using the Wilber model, whereas this is the consequence of walking the path of responsibility, noticing and reacting to your own impacts.

Research and development

Both human, culture, and society develops, and medicine must follow, if it is to be contemporary and helpful to modern man. But research is always about stepping over the borders of today and yesterday, and sometimes the decisions taken in a field of little experience will show wrong or insufficient.

In this field, making the wrong decisions is not only allowed, it is an obligation, for you cannot make any decision on incomplete foundation of knowledge without the attitude that it is completely OK to make mistakes, when you only learn from them and do whatever you can to make it up to the patient.

Research will naturally be done with the group of patients that cannot be helped with the standard method, and it is justified by their need for help. Often the case is that if the holistic therapist cannot help them, nobody can, as the biomedical doctor is sought first in most cases.

Both positive and negative results must be shared with the international community for the patients not to have suffered for nothing. The decision of doing something completely new in the intent of helping the patient on an experimental basis is the most difficult decision to make in the holistic clinic. Surprisingly, if the therapist remembers the principles of healing and make sure that the experimental treatment complies to these few basic rules, most new interventions will in our experience help the patient, also when all hope is lost. We have seen this with cancer patients, where chemotherapy has failed to help, and we have tried something untraditional to induce holistic healing; in most examples this has seemingly actually helped the patients to survive the life expectance given them by their biomedical doctor.

Learning process

The attitude that "I as a physician" myself got a little of all diseases, imbalances, impurities, and disturbances is extremely helpful to accept the often dramatic impact on oneself from holistic therapy on the patient. The openness to learn takes the humility of a therapist who knows that he or she is not at all neither perfect nor completely sound. But to look deeply into your own wounds from being raised in a dysfunctional family with incestuous bindings are really challenging. And when it comes down to it, perfect parents are really rare. So we are all quite neurotic and damaged, and in need of healing our existence our self.

Helping other people knowing this about our self takes the challenge of being therapist to a new level. Surprisingly, the fact that therapy is provoking and inspiring our own personal growth, is what makes being a holistic therapist so satisfying and extraordinary. Only the painstaking process of personal growth will lead us to realise that there really are no limits for what we can do for our self and our patients.

Humility, love and acceptance

Coming from the heart is the solution to the problem of how to help. Because we are all caught in our mental description of the world, we will inevitably start our medical practice less holistic and more "methodological" and instrumental. But as we little by little realise that the drugs are not really helping much, and that other therapeutic tools and techniques are only excuses for intimacy, closeness and loving contact with the patient, we will day for day stand more bravely forward and finally admit, that we are beings of love, and that our natural tendency is to care and to give without getting anything but our own happiness in return. And in this realisation we will grow into powerful holistic healers, in the same time, as we will feel more and more humble and powerless.

The paradox of love is that only when we let go, and accept that we really cannot do anything for an other person, for the person must decide for himself, and create his own life – autonomously – for himself, can we help. This is the paradox and the miracle of holistic medicine. Being a successful therapist in this field is very much a question of surrendering to reality, being one with the Great Spirit, being purely of service, or how you want to put it.

Metamorphosis

The belief of most holistic healer is that the blue-print of body, mind, and spirit is always intact and that contacting this informational source within can lead to complete healing in spite of every seemingly misery and hopelessness of the situation. This is really a kind of religious belief, where life is in our imagination empowered with almost magic powers. Because of the logic of hermeneutics, this believe will often materialise, so the therapist that believe in true miracles will see them every day, and the therapist that don't will never see them. When the sceptical therapist enters the optimistic therapists clinic, he will find nothing but doubtful successes and certain failures, and when the trusting and positive therapist come to the sceptical physicians clinic he will find miracle after miracle happening even there.

Patients who come to believe will go to therapists that believe and here go though adult human metamorphosis (83-92) and be transformed into wonderful, able and happy people, even their bodies will be transformed. And patients that do not believe will go to therapist and get their bodies and minds damaged and destroyed. The religious healer will attract religious patients. And the sceptical healer will attract sceptical patients. Every person will get what he materialises. The therapist role is to serve and to materialise what he believes in. The holistic therapist will often believe in healing the whole existence. And all choices will be made in that believe.

Different worlds

The fact that the biomedical and holistic therapist are living in very different worlds with very different cosmologies and very different experiences is often becoming a problem for the patient, who has to chose between to fundamentally different worlds and different treatments.

And often are the sceptic minds much more powerful that the trusting souls, making biomedicine winning many legal and political battles. But all over the world people are more positive in their attitudes and philosophies, and holistic medicine is growing fast with more consultations now in the USA than biomedical consultations. The battles are becoming intensified all over the world, and it seems that we in the next 20 years or so will have a complete commercial shift into holistic medicine; this shift is already predicted and being prepared for by many of today's large pharmaceutical companies. In the same time we see increasing lobbyist activities from physicians and industry trying to suppress holistic medicine – the war against homeopathy in Germany being an example.

The war is happening in the way that the holistic medicine is tested on the premises of biomedicine. With homeopathy, it is most unlikely that it is the homeopathic drugs in themselves that has any effect; the healing happens as the patient becomes more conscious of his human character and thus more accepting and integrating in attitude and philosophy of life. But instead of looking of these shift in consciousness and acknowledging all the good things there is happening for the patients who believe, sceptical research is des-empowering the homeopathic tradition, obviously in the intension of substituting it with biomedicine ("rational medicine", "evidence based medicine").

There is really nothing evidence based about the way the war is going on; only materialisation of believes, as both patients and researchers are caught in the hermeneutic illusory web of interpretation of the world. We need a truly integrative medicine now, with space for more that one cosmology, i.e. a poly-cosmological entrance. Because biomedicine is not wrong; from one perspective the world is really chemistry and physics only. And the spiritual medicine is not wrong either. From another perspective, everything is really a materialisation of consciousness. It is time to embrace a poly-paradigmatic medical science.

Ethics

The purpose of medical ethics is to ensure that the patient is not exploited or harmed in any way. To monitor the effect of the therapy and to be sure that it really helps and that it does not harm the patient is the primary ethical concern in holistic medicine. As the sense of coherence is the primary goal, and as this has been difficult to measure directly (4-9), the effect of holistic therapy on quality of life, health and ability has proven easy and efficient as an effect measure (it takes only 5 minutes to fill in the QOL5 questionnaire (93) self-assessed QOL, subjective health (physical and mental) and the quality of human relationships); ability of functioning (love, work, social, sexual) is also relevant to measure.

To measure the patients before and after treatment seems to be mandatory, and we have done that for years in our clinic, being able to document sufficient results of the interventions on more than half the patients (56-61).

Bodywork is a hallmark of holistic therapies, and bodywork introduces a lot of ethical problems known already by Hippocrates and his students (63). The ethical problems of modern bodywork might be best illuminated by using the extreme example of holistic sexological bodywork, originating both from the Hippocratic tradition and from the Asian/Indian holistic medical tradition (54,55). The procedure of Hippocratic pelvic massage, in Denmark known and practiced by hundreds of therapists as "acupressure through the vagina" is such a technique that seemingly is extremely efficient to help patients with primary vulvodyni and chronic pelvic pain, but must be performed according to ethical standards. The holistic sexological procedures are derived from the holistic existential therapy, which involves re-parenting, massage and bodywork, conversational therapy, philosophical training, healing of existence during spontaneous regression to painful life events (gestalts) and close intimacy without any sexual involvement.

In psychology, psychiatry and existential psychotherapy (80), touch is often allowed, but a sufficient distance between therapist and client must always be kept, all clothes kept on and it is even recommended, that the first name is not taken into use to keep the relationship as formal and correct as possible. The reason for this distance is to create a safety zone that removes the danger of psychotherapy leading to sexual involvement. In the original Hippocratic medicine (63), as well as in modern holistic existential therapy such a safety zone was not possible, because of the simultaneous work with all dimensions of existence, from therapeutic touch (22) of the physical body, feelings and mind, to sexuality and spirituality. The fundamental rule has since Hippocrates been that the physician must control his behaviour, not to abuse his patient. The patients in holistic existential therapy and holistic sexology are often chronically ill, and their situation often pretty hopeless, as many of them have been dysfunctional and incurable for many years or they are suffering from conditions for which there are no efficient biomedical cure.

The primary purpose of the holistic existential therapy is to improve quality of life, secondary to improve health and ability. The severe conditions of the patients and the chronicity is what ethically justify the much more direct, intimate and intense method of holistic existential therapy, which integrates many different therapeutic elements and works on many levels of the patient's existence and personality at the same time. Holistic sexology is holistic existential therapy taken into the domain of sexology. The general ethical rule is that everything that does not harm and in the end will help the patient is allowed ("first do no harm"). An important aspect of the therapy is that the physician must be creative and in practice invent a new treatment for every patient, as Yalom has suggested (80). To perform the sexological technique of acupressure through the vagina, the holistic sexologist must be able to control not only his/her behaviour, but also his sexual excitement to avoid any danger of the therapeutic session turning into sexual activity. Most physicians can do the classic pelvic examination after their standard university training, but the vaginal acupressure we are discussing here in this paper can only be obtained through long training and supervision in order to reach a level, where such a procedure can be performed.

Side effects of the treatment can be soreness of the genitals and periods of bad mood, as old painful repressed material are slowly integrated. We have seen acute psychosis as a sexually abused woman confronted her most painful experiences, but she recovered in a few days without the use of drugs and this episode was an integral part of her healing. In fact it was her therapeutic breakthrough. As it is possible that the patient can feel abused from transferences, it is extremely important to address this openly to prevent this situation. We recommend that the patient is contacted or followed for 1-5 years, to prevent and handle any potential long-term negative effects of the treatment. In spite of these problems we have found the treatment with holistic existential therapy combined with the tool of vaginal acupressure to be very valuable for the patients (54,55).

Discussion

There are many factors influencing the therapist's choice of action in the therapeutic session. We have presented it as if the therapist had the power of deciding what is going on. The reason that every treatment of a patient takes its own route might very well be that every patient because of his or her basic resistance is struggling very hard not go get well, not to get cures, not to get into the state of salutogenesis. The reason for this is clear from a psychodynamic perspective: The defences are created for survival difficult situations in the past, and the patent will unconsciously feel like dying if these situations reappear in consciousness.

So therapy is a dance, or a fight, or a play; a complex pattern is created like always when to forces are almost of same size and opposite each other, and creating a chaotic, highly dynamic middle zone of whorls and constant changes.

Our list of factors influencing therapy might be complete useless, if it is so simple that the patient subconsciously is doing whatever possible for destroying the therapy, and the therapist just is following along as well as possible. Because then the "individual cure for every patient" is nothing but the patients escape route before he or she is finally caught, and the destructive, neurotic or psychotic survival patterns busted for good.

The argument that the large creativity observed in clinical holistic therapy is coming from the therapist emotional and spiritual intelligence, might just be the therapist's narcissistic positive interpretation of what it is like to be almost completely out of control in the session. Maybe it is not a deeper and wiser layer of the therapist taking over, but just the patient unconsciously fighting for his or her survival, and therefore naturally investing more energy and efforts and therefore being smarter than us.

Many of the tools of the advanced holistic medical toolbox are inducing dramatic feelings in the patient, and it is an art to know when to use and when to avoid using a specific tool. The truth is that in spite of all the rational principles only the emotional intelligence can provide us with the wisdom of when to use a tool, because of the extreme complexity of the human consciousness. The central thing is therefore that the therapist at all times is aware of his intentions, and certain that he is in good intend towards his patients and acting in accordance with all professional and ethical principles. It might be almost impossible to control this from outside; because of this measuring the results of therapy and being sure of really helping his patients might in the end be the most ethical the therapist can do.

Conclusions

Clinical holistic medicine is curing every second patient – in the patient's own experience – from physical illness and chronic pain, mental illness, low self-esteem, low quality of life, sexual dysfunction and low working ability (57-62). But the therapy is not following any nice and reproducible pattern, in spite of four rather clear therapeutic principles and a well-defined tool-box (49). On the contrary every treatment has its own course, often unpredictable, meandering and pitful, and we say that we need to invent a new treatment for every patient. We are in this chapter identifying many of the factors that seem to come into play guiding the therapist's decision-making in the session. We are suggesting that crazy-wise aspects of the therapist are responsible for the creativity that in the end will take the patient into existential healing (salutogenesis).

"Holy madness" (94) is a well-known concept from eastern spiritual teaching (as a Google-search will show), and seems to be a very appropriate expression for what is going on in the therapy, inside the therapist when he is fully engaged. Most interestingly "holy madness" is also a very accurate description of the state of consciousness called "holistic healing"(17). And maybe all the chaos and creativity is not really delivered by the therapist but much more by the patient him- or her self; as therapists we like to flatter our self with the idea of being in control, creating the cure, and helping the patient making the idea of the patient being responsible less attractive (but never the less very likely).

We suggest that the therapist that allows himself to be existentially absorbed and engaged beyond the mind in the therapeutic process, and who is able to use all aspects of himself, body, mind and spirit included in the service of the patient, is much more successful in inducing existential healing in the patient, than the classic, rational, distant, mind-oriented, physician who uses only reductionistic, and scientific principles and tools for therapy.

Spiritual commitment and love is what we firmly believe heal the patients; only by letting go of the minds firm grip on reality can love find its natural and full expression in the therapy. Sexuality and libidinous interest is a natural part of this, and the investment of libidinous energy without acting out sexually has been suggested as the key to entering the universe of "crazy-wise healing".

Only by allowing the energy to dance within our self, and make the therapeutic decisions that we instinctively know are right to free our patient, and allow our self to speak and act completely without censorship, can we be as natural and powerful as we need to be, to overcome the resistance – the dark side of our self and the patient in combination - and induce Antonovsky salutogenesis (2,3) – the healing of the patient's whole existence that will be followed by recovery of illness, improving of the patient's abilities, and recovery of the patients global quality of life.

References

[1] Technology Council. Rapport from the Technology Council on alternative treatment to the Danish Parliement. Christiansborg: Danish Parliament, 2002 Mar 19. [Danish].

[2] Antonovsky A. Health, stress and coping. London: Jossey-Bass, 1985.

[3] Antonovsky A. Unravelling the mystery of health. How people manage stress and stay well. San Franscisco: Jossey-Bass, 1987.

[4] Flensborg-Madsen T, Ventegodt S, Merrick J. Sense of coherence and physical health. A Review of previous findings. ScientificWorldJournal 2005;5:665-73.

[5] Flensborg-Madsen T, Ventegodt S, Merrick J. Why is Antonovsky's sense of coherence not correlated to physical health? Analysing Antonovsky's 29-item sense of coherence scale (SOCS). ScientificWorldJournal 2005;5:767-76.

[6] Flensborg-Madsen T, Ventegodt S, Merrick J. Sense of coherence and health. The construction of an amendment to Antonovsky's sense of coherence scale (SOC II). ScientificWorldJournal 2006;6:2133-9.

[7] Flensborg-Madsen T, Ventegodt S, Merrick J. Sense of coherence and physical health. A cross-sectional study using a new SOC scale (SOC II). ScientificWorldJournal 2006;6:2200-11.

[8] Flensborg-Madsen T, Ventegodt S, Merrick, J. Sense of coherence and physical health. Testing Antonovsky's theory. ScientificWorldJournal 2006;6:2212-9.

[9] Flensborg-Madsen T, Ventegodt S, Merrick J. Sense of coherence and health. The emotional sense of coherence (SOC-E) was found to be the best-known predictor of physical health. ScientificWorldJournal 2006;6:2147-57.

[10] Ventegodt S, Flensborg-Madsen T, Andersen NJ, Nielsen M, Morad M, Merrick J. Global quality of life (QOL), health and ability are primarily determined by our consciousness. Research findings from Denmark 1991-2004. Soc Indicator Res 2005;71:87-122.

[11] Ventegodt S, Flensborg-Madsen T, Anderson NJ, Merrick J. Factors during pregnancy, delivery and birth affecting global quality of life of the adult child at long-term follow-up. Results from the prospective Copenhagen Perinatal Birth Cohort 1959-1961. ScientificWorldJournal 2005;5:933-41.

[12] Ventegodt S, Flensborg-Madsen T, Andersen NJ, Merrick J. Events in pregnancy, delivery, and infancy and long-term effects on global quality of life: results from the Copenhagen Perinatal Birth Cohort 1959-61. Med Sci Monit 2005;11(8):CR357-65.

[13] Ventegodt S, Flensborg-Madsen T, Andersen NJ, Morad M, Merrick J. Quality of life and events in the first year of life. Results from the prospective Copenhagen Birth Cohort 1959-1961. ScientificWorldJournal 2006;6:106-15.

[14] Ventegodt S, Flensborg-Madsen T, Andersen NJ, Merrick J. What influence do major events in life have on our later quality of life? A retrospective study on life events and associated emotions. Med Sci Monit 2006;12(2):SR9-15.

[15] Ventegodt S, Andersen NJ, Merrick J. Holistic medicine: Scientific challenges. ScientificWorldJournal 2003;3:1108-16.

[16] Ventegodt S, Andersen NJ, Merrick J. Holistic Medicine II: The square-curve paradigm for research in alternative, complementary and holistic medicine: A cost-effective, easy and scientifically valid design for evidence based medicine. ScientificWorldJournal 2003;3:1117-27.

[17] Ventegodt S, Andersen NJ, Merrick J. Holistic Medicine III: The holistic process theory of healing. ScientificWorldJournal 2003;3:1138-46.

[18] Ventegodt S, Andersen NJ, Merrick J. Holistic Medicine IV: Principles of the holistic process of healing in a group setting. ScientificWorldJournal 2003;3:1294-1301.

[19] Ventegodt S. Every Contact With the Patient Must Be Therapeutic. J Pediatr Adolesc Gynecol 2007:20(6):323-4.

[20] Ventegodt S, Merrick J. Psychosomatic reasons for chronic pains. South Med J 2005;98(11):1063.

[21] Ventegodt S, Merrick J. Clinical holistic medicine: Applied consciousness-based medicine. ScientificWorldJournal 2004;4:96-9.

[22] Ventegodt S, Morad M, Merrick J.Clinical holistic medicine: Classic art of healing or the therapeutic touch. ScientificWorldJournal 2004;4:134-47.

[23] Ventegodt S, Morad M, Merrick J. Clinical holistic medicine: The "new medicine", the multiparadigmatic physician and the medical record. ScientificWorldJournal 2004;4:273-85.

[24] Ventegodt S, Morad M, Merrick J. Clinical holistic medicine: Holistic pelvic examination and holistic treatment of infertility. ScientificWorldJournal 2004;4:148-58.

[25] Ventegodt S, Morad M, Hyam E, Merrick J. Clinical holistic medicine: Use and limitations of the biomedical paradigm ScientificWorldJournal 2004;4:295-306.

[26] Ventegodt S, Morad M, Kandel I, Merrick J. Clinical holistic medicine: Social problems disguised as illness. ScientificWorldJournal 2004;4:286-94.

[27] Ventegodt S, Morad M, Andersen NJ, Merrick J. Clinical holistic medicine Tools for a medical science based on consciousness. ScientificWorldJournal 2004;4:347-61.

[28] Ventegodt S, Morad M, Merrick J. Clinical holistic medicine: Prevention through healthy lifestyle and Quality of life. Oral Health Prev Dent 2004;1:239-45.

[29] Ventegodt S, Morad M, Hyam E, Merrick J. Clinical holistic medicine: When biomedicine is inadequate. ScientificWorldJournal 2004;4:333-46.

[30] Ventegodt S, Morad M, Merrick J. Clinical holistic medicine: Holistic treatment of children. ScientificWorldJournal 2004;4:581-8.

[31] Ventegodt S, Morad M, Merrick J. Clinical holistic medicine: Problems in sex and living together. ScientificWorldJournal 2004;4:562-70.

[32] Ventegodt S, Morad M, Hyam E, Merrick J. Clinical holistic medicine: Holistic sexology and treatment of vulvodynia through existential therapy and acceptance through touch. ScientificWorldJournal 2004;4:571-80.

[33] Ventegodt S, Flensborg-Madsen T, Andersen NJ, Morad M, Merrick J. Clinical holistic medicine: A Pilot on HIV and Quality of Life and a Suggested treatment of HIV and AIDS. ScientificWorldJournal 2004;4:264-72.

[34] Ventegodt S, Morad M, Merrick J. Clinical holistic medicine: Induction of spontaneous remission of cancer by recovery of the human character and the purpose of life (the life mission). ScientificWorldJournal 2004;4:362-77.

[35] Ventegodt S, Morad M, Kandel I, Merrick J. Clinical holistic medicine: Treatment of physical health problems without a known cause, exemplified by hypertension and tinnitus. ScientificWorldJournal 2004;4:716-24.

[36] Ventegodt S, Morad M, Merrick J. Clinical holistic medicine: Developing from asthma, allergy and eczema. ScientificWorldJournal 2004;4:936-42.

[37] Ventegodt S, Morad M, Press J, Merrick J, Shek D. Clinical holistic medicine: Holistic adolescent medicine. ScientificWorldJournal 2004;4:551-61.

[38] Ventegodt S, Solheim E, Saunte ME, Morad M, Kandel I, Merrick J. Clinical holistic medicine: Metastatic cancer. ScientificWorldJournal 2004;4:913-35.

[39] Ventegodt S, Morad M, Kandel I, Merrick J. Clinical holistic medicine: a psychological theory of dependency to improve quality of life. ScientificWorldJournal 2004;4:638-48.

[40] Ventegodt S, Merrick J. Clinical holistic medicine: Chronic infections and autoimmune diseases. ScientificWorldJournal 2005;5:155-64.

[41] Ventegodt S, Kandel I, Neikrug S, Merrick J. Clinical holistic medicine: Holistic treatment of rape and incest traumas. ScientificWorldJournal 2005;5:288-97.

[42] Ventegodt S, Morad M, Merrick J. Clinical holistic medicine: Chronic pain in the locomotor system. ScientificWorldJournal 2005;5:165-72.

[43] Ventegodt S, Merrick J Clinical holistic medicine: Chronic pain in internal organs. ScientificWorldJournal 2005;5:205-10.

[44] Ventegodt S, Kandel I, Neikrug S, Merrick J. Clinical holistic medicine: The existential crisis – life crisis, stress and burnout. ScientificWorldJournal 2005;5:300-12.

[45] Ventegodt S, Gringols G, Merrick J. Clinical holistic medicine: Holistic rehabilitation. ScientificWorldJournal 2005;5:280-7.

[46] Ventegodt S, Andersen NJ, Neikrug S, Kandel I, Merrick J. Clinical holistic medicine: Mental disorders in a holistic perspective. ScientificWorldJournal 2005;5:313-23.

[47] Ventegodt S, Andersen NJ, Neikrug S, Kandel I, Merrick J. Clinical Holistic medicine: Holistic treatment of mental disorders. ScientificWorldJournal 2005;5:427-45.

[48] Ventegodt S, Merrick J. Clinical holistic medicine: The patient with multiple diseases. ScientificWorldJournal 2005;5:324-39.

[49] Ventegodt S, Clausen B, Nielsen ML, Merrick J. Clinical holistic medicine: Advanced tools for holistic medicine. ScientificWorldJournal 2006;6:2048-65.

[50] Ventegodt S, Clausen B, Merrick J. Clinical holistic medicine: The case story of Anna: I. Long term effect of child sexual abuse and incest with a treatment approach ScientificWorldJournal 2006;6: 1965-76.

[51] Ventegodt S, Clausen B, Merrick J. Clinical holistic medicine: the case story of Anna. II. Patient diary as a tool in treatment. ScientificWorldJournal 2006;6:2006-34.

[52] Ventegodt S, Clausen B, Merrick J. Clinical holistic medicine: The case story of Anna. III. Rehabilitation of philosophy of life during holistic existential therapy for childhood sexual abuse. ScientificWorldJournal 2006;6:2080-91.

[53] Ventegodt S, Merrick J. Suicide from a holistic point of view. ScientificWorldJournal 2005;5:759-66.

[54] Ventegodt S, Clausen B, Omar HA, Merrick J. Clinical holistic medicine: Holistic sexology and acupressure through the vagina (Hippocratic pelvic massage). ScientificWorldJournal 2006;6: 2066-79.

[55] Ventegodt S, Clausen B, Merrick J. Clinical holistic medicine: Pilot study on the effect of vaginal acupressure (Hippocratic pelvic massage). ScientificWorldJournal 2006;6:2100-16.

[56] Ventegodt S, Thegler S, Andreasen T, Struve F, Enevoldsen L, Bassaine L, et al. Clinical holistic medicine: Psychodynamic short-time therapy complemented with bodywork. A clinical follow-up study of 109 patients. ScientificWorldJournal 2006;6: 2220-38.

[57] Ventegodt S, Thegler S, Andreasen T, Struve F, Enevoldsen L, Bassaine L, et al. Clinical holistic medicine (mindful, short-term psychodynamic psychotherapy complemented with bodywork) in the treatment of experienced impaired sexual functioning. ScientificWorldJournal 2007;7:324-9.

[58] Ventegodt S, Thegler S, Andreasen T, Struve F, Enevoldsen L, Bassaine L, et al. Clinical holistic medicine (mindful, short-term psychodynamic psychotherapy complemented with bodywork) improves quality of life, health, and ability by induction of Antonovsky-salutogenesis. ScientificWorldJournal 2007;7:317-23.

[59] Ventegodt S, Thegler S, Andreasen T, Struve F, Enevoldsen L, Bassaine L, et al. Clinical holistic medicine (mindful, short-term psychodynamic psychotherapy complemented with bodywork) in the treatment of experienced physical illness and chronic pain. ScientificWorldJournal 2007;7:310-6.

[60] Ventegodt S, Thegler S, Andreasen T, Struve F, Enevoldsen L, Bassaine L, et al. Clinical holistic medicine (mindful, short-term psychodynamic psychotherapy complemented with bodywork) in the treatment of experienced mental illness. ScientificWorldJournal 2007;7:306-9.

[61] Ventegodt S, Thegler S, Andreasen T, Struve F, Enevoldsen L, Bassaine L, et al. Self-reported low self-esteem. Intervention and follow-up in a clinical setting. ScientificWorldJournal 2007;7:299- 305.

[62] Ventegodt S, Andersen NJ, Merrick J. Clinical holistic medicine in the recovery of working ability. A study using Antonovsky salutogenesis. Int J Disabil Hum Dev 2008;7(2):219-22.

[63] Jones WHS. Hippocrates. Vol. I–IV. London: William Heinemann, 1923–1931.

[64] Ventegodt S, Andersen NJ, Merrick J. Editorial: Five theories of human existence. ScientificWorldJournal 2003;3:1272-6.

[65] Ventegodt S. The life mission theory: A theory for a consciousness-based medicine. Int J Adolesc Med Health 2003; 15(1): 89-91.

[66] Ventegodt S, Andersen NJ, Merrick J. The life mission theory II: The structure of the life purpose and the ego. ScientificWorldJournal 2003;3:1277-85.

[67] Ventegodt S, Andersen NJ, Merrick J. The life mission theory III: Theory of talent. ScientificWorldJournal 2003;3:1286-93.

[68] Ventegodt S, Merrick J. The life mission theory IV. A theory of child development. ScientificWorldJournal 2003;3:1294-1301.

[69] Ventegodt S, Andersen NJ, Merrick J. The life mission theory V. A theory of the anti-self and explaining the evil side of man. ScientificWorldJournal 2003;3:1302-13.

[70] Ventegodt S, Andersen NJ, Merrick J. The life mission theory VI: A theory for the human character. ScientificWorldJournal 2004;4: 859-80.

[71] Ventegodt S, Flensborg-Madsen T, Andersen NJ, Merrick J. Life Mission Theory VII: Theory of existential (Antonovsky) coherence: a theory of quality of life, health and ability for use in holistic medicine. ScientificWorldJournal 2005;5:377-89.

[72] Ventegodt S, Merrick J. Life mission theory VIII: A theory for pain. J Pain Manage 2008;1(1):5-10.

[73] Kierkegaard SA. The sickness unto death. Princeton, NJ: Princeton Univ Press, 1983.

[74] Sartre JP. Being and nothingness. London: Routledge, 2002.

[75] Jones E. The life and works of Sigmund Freud. New York: Basic Books, 1961.

[76] Jung CG. Man and his symbols. New York: Anchor Press, 1964.

[77] Csikszentmihalyi M. Flow. The psychology of optimal experience. New York: Harper Collins, 1991.

[78] Krishnamurti J. The wholeness of life. London: HarperCollins, 1981.

[79] Gadamer H. Truth and method. New York: Continuum, 2003.

[80] Yalom ID. Existential psychotherapy. New York: Basic Books, 1980.

[81] Searles HF. Oedipal love in the countertransference. In: Searles HF, ed. Collected papers of schizophrenia and related subjects. New York: Int Univ Press, 1965:284-5.

[82] Wilber K. Integral psychology: Consciousness, spirit, psychology, therapy. Los Angeles, CA: Shambhala, 2000.

[83] Hermansen TD, Ventegodt S, Rald E, Clausen B, Nielsen ML, Merrick J. Human development I: twenty fundamental problems of biology, medicine, and neuro-psychology related to biological information. ScientificWorldJournal 2006;6:747-59.

[84] Ventegodt S, Hermansen TD, Nielsen ML, Clausen B, Merrick J. Human development II: we need an integrated theory for matter, life and consciousness to understand life and healing. ScientificWorldJournal 2006;6:760-6.

[85] Ventegodt S, Hermansen TD, Rald E, Flensborg-Madsen T, Nielsen ML, Clausen B, Merrick J. Human development III: bridging brain-mind and body-mind. introduction to "deep" (fractal, poly-ray) cosmology. ScientificWorldJournal 2006;6:767-76.

[86] Ventegodt S, Hermansen TD, Flensborg-Madsen T, Nielsen ML, Clausen B, Merrick J. Human development IV: the living cell has information-directed self-organisation. ScientificWorldJournal 2006;6:1132-8.

[87] Ventegodt S, Hermansen TD, Flensborg-Madsen T, Nielsen ML, Clausen B, Merrick J. Human development V: biochemistry unable to explain the emergence of biological form (morphogenesis) and therefore a new principle as source of biological information is needed. ScientificWorldJournal 2006;6:1359-67.

[88] Ventegodt S, Hermansen TD, Flensborg-Madsen T, Nielsen M, Merrick J. Human development VI: Supracellular morphogenesis. The origin of biological and cellular order. ScientificWorldJournal 2006;6:1424-33.

[89] Ventegodt S, Hermansen TD, Flensborg-Madsen T, Rald E, Nielsen ML, Merrick J. Human development VII: A spiral fractal model of fine structure of physical energy could explain central

aspects of biological information, biological organization and biological creativity. ScientificWorldJournal 2006;6:1434-40.

[90] Ventegodt S, Hermansen TD, Flensborg-Madsen T, Nielsen ML, Merrick J. Human development VIII: A theory of "deep" quantum chemistry and cell consciousness: Quantum chemistry controls genes and biochemistry to give cells and higher organisms consciousness and complex behavior. ScientificWorldJournal 2006;6:1441-53.

[91] Ventegodt S, Hermansen TD, Flensborg-Madsen T, Rald E, Nielsen ML, Merrick J. Human development IX: A model of the wholeness of man, his consciousness and collective consciousness. ScientificWorldJournal 2006;6:1454-9.

[92] Hermansen TD, Ventegodt S, Merrick J. Human development X: Explanation of macroevolution — top-down evolution materializes consciousness. The origin of metamorphosis. ScientificWorldJournal 2006;6:1656-66.

[93] Lindholt JS, Ventegodt S, Henneberg EW. Development and validation of QoL5 clinical databases. A short, global and generic questionnaire based on an integrated theory of the quality of life. Eur J Surg 2002;168:103-7.

[94] Feuerstein G. Holy madness. Spirituality, crazy-wise teachers and enlightenment. London: Arkana, 1992.

Chapter 29

How to recover memory without "implanting" memories

Every therapeutic strategy and system teach us the philosophy of the treatment system to the patient, but often this teaching is subliminal and the philosophical impact must be seen as "implanted philosophy", which gives distorted interpretations of past events called "implanted memories". The weaker the patient the greater chance for mental implants. The mentally ill patients are known to be among the most vulnerable and fragile of patients making this problem more pronounced with these patients than with any other category of patients.

Based on the understanding of the connection between "implanted memory" and "implanted philosophy" we have developed a strategy for avoiding implanting memories arising from one of the seven most common causes of implanted memories in psychodynamic and holistic therapy: 1) Satisfying own expectancies, 2) pleasing the therapist, 3) transferences and counter transferences, 4) as source of mental and emotional order, 5) as emotional defence, 6) as symbol and 7) from implanted philosophy.

Traditionally mental disorders is understood by holistic medicine and psychiatry as arrested psychosexual development. Freud taught us that child sexuality is "polymorphously perverted", meaning that all kinds of sexuality is present at least potentially with the little child; and in dreams consciousness often go back to the earlier stages of development, potentially causing all kinds of sexual dreams and fantasies, which can come up in therapy and look like real memories.

The therapist working with psychodynamic psychotherapy, clinical holistic medicine, psychiatry, and emotionally oriented bodywork, should be aware of the danger of implanting philosophy and memories. Implanted memories and implanted philosophy must be carefully handled and de-learned before ending the therapy. In conclusion modern sexology and contemporary holistic medicine ("clinical holistic medicine") have developed a strategy for avoiding implanting memories.

Even the best of therapists can sometimes not aviod the patient from developing an "implanted memory" to some extent, as this is a natural part of the therapy, as will be discussed in chapter 20. If the patient has a strong female Oedipus complex it might even be nessesary to use the avoidable "implanted memory" as a tool for healing; how this is done is discussed in chapter 20.

The rule is to avoid to implant memories in the patient, if at all possible. In reality it is the patient him or herself that implants these memories, which are interpretations of the past and not memories in the classical (visual) sense, but these dynamics are only to a certain degree under the control of the therapist.

Introduction

During the last decade there has been an intense and ongoing debate in the medical scientific community about therapy and implanted memories (1,2). It has generally been concluded that memory is not perfect and often more like an idea or an impression than actually like a movie that you can play again and see what really happened. Memory in this sense is known to be highly sensitive to emotions and expectations, as is well known from forensic psychology. Another problem is that the human being constantly has fantasies and reveries (3,4), and when we remember such a fantasy, this is an actual remembrance but of an unreal event. If this happens with a patient, this can cause large confusion in therapy. In general the mind is not very reliable and the interpretation of the world in present time and in the past seems to be easily affected by intentions and needs, both bodily and mental.

Because of this vagueness of most people's memories it is now generally believed that it is actually possible to implant "memories" during therapy. The normal solution in therapy is to be sure that you do not make any judgements about what actually happened, until the patient finds out for herself what happened. It is important to actively avoid influencing the process of interpretation (i.e. give suggestions that can be taken as indications of how a feeling or gestalt should be interpreted by the patient). The central dogma of not interpreting the material of the patient is at the root of classical psychoanalysis, and gives a relaxed and often not-so-intense kind of therapy that often includes several hundreds of hours of therapy during several years.

When it comes to intensive psychodynamic short-term psychotherapy (often defined as less that 40 sessions) and existential psychotherapy the therapist becomes more dependent of his own theory for the individual patient (5,6). Unfortunately, the patient will often know this theory, or sense it as the therapist cannot help revealing its central idea in the way he approaches the patient, and the subjects he addresses in the therapy. In the beginning of the therapy the only way the patient can cooperate is letting go of the control and playing along. In doing this there is a lot of learning that is actually implanting philosophy. When the patient's personal past is seen in the light of this new or corrected philosophy, the whole past will look different, which is actually also the core idea of therapy. So every therapist is in fact implanting memories in the broadest sense of this concept.

When the therapist expects sexual abuse to be the caboose of a complex of symptoms, the patient will look for and often find events that can be interpreted in this way, in order to comply. Here we have the implanted memories of incest or abuse. The problematic thing about such memories is that if they are taken as real, the patient needs to "clear" the relationships with the relevant people (often the parents or other family members), and often this is done in a non-forgiving and destructive way harming the patient and sometimes also her surroundings.

The loss of self-esteem in connection with such a recovery of incest memories is always a difficult problem, but can be solved in existential therapy. If the events are implanted memories, incongruence is introduced, making it very difficult for the patient to move forward, and heal herself and her relationships to the people of her world. (Please notice that we use "she" as the sexually abused patient is normally a woman, but the patient could as well be a man; we use "he" about the therapist who is sometimes a man but could as well be a woman).

This becomes even more problematic, when intensive psychodynamic short term psychotherapy are combined with bodywork and holistic gynaecological/sexological therapy (7-18), where the intensity of the confronted repressed emotions in the therapy often is getting high. The reason for using the combination of techniques is that the patient needs a lot of support on many different levels, to be able to confront i.e. a childhood rape scenario without experiencing unbearable existential pain in the session.

We have worked with the problem of how to avoid implanted memories for years in the research project "Quality of life and aetiology of diseases" and believe that we have come to a practical solution of the problem, allowing us to make the most intensive therapy without damaging the patients (i.e. by implanting memories).

A recent follow-up of 109 patients from our Research Clinic for Holistic Medicine in Copenhagen after clinical holistic medical treatment (receiving the mindful combination of psychodynamic short time therapy and bodywork) has documented that the patients were not harmed, but often helped by this therapy (19-24).

A pilot study of 20 women that had continuous sexual problems on average for almost nine years (in spite of seeing physicians and alternative therapists over that period) showed that most of the patients were helped in this therapy and no patient was harmed (reporting significant side-effects or ending at a lower score in quality of life, health and ability that before starting the therapy) (17).

We have solved the problem on a theoretical level, and when we took this solution into practice we found that it worked good with reliable results. We used contemporary models from the research fields of quality of life, human development, and holistic medicine to understand what happened in therapy to make implanted memories possible. We found a simple solution to the complex problem of implanted memories, which is recovering the memory and sense of truth in general in the patient.

Seven causes of implanted memories

The seven most common causes of implanted memories are:

1) Satisfying own expectancies: If the patient expects that she had been abused sexually i.e. because a sister was, she can implant more or less vague memories of incest herself.

2) Pleasing the therapist: The patient wants to be in accordance with the therapist and is therefore accepting his view or what she believes or imagine is his view. This is enhanced if the therapist shares his interpretations and gives the patient leads (i.e. questions that are not neutral but biased in some direction); and even more if the

therapist is making judgments on what happen in stead of bearing not knowing what happened until the patient finds our for herself.

3) Transferences and counter transferences: If the patient develops sexual feelings towards the therapist and if these are ignored by the therapist, or if the patient senses that the therapist will not accept them, this can enhance sexual fantasies, which eventually can take the form as an implanted memory; old sexual fantasies can also be boosted by this unconscious wish in the patient, and even real events can be distorted and reinterpreted now filled with the sexual feelings that the patient cannot allow to emerge in the personal relationship to the therapist.

4) As source of mental and emotional order: A third source of implanted memories has nothing to do with the therapy in itself. The patient needs to get a kind of order in the chaos of emotions and symptoms, and having a simple explanation can be a relief instead of living with chaos and mystery.

5) As emotional defence. Sometimes the recovered but false memory is hiding another event that is much more painful. This could be that her father left her and her mother when she was a child. This may be much more difficult to integrate than sexual abuse. If the patient is desperately angry with her father and cannot confront the event causing the anger, an implanted event can be a solution. It could also be neglect that is the problem; it seems that neglecting the bodily presence and sexual character of a girl can be as destructive to her self-esteem and psychosexual development as actual physical or sexual abuse.

6) As symbol. Often, the parents have been abusing the child in subtle and psychological ways, (i.e. not respecting the child's sexual borders, or having used the child as a sexual partner, which is most often seen when a parent lives alone with a child of the opposite sex). This does not mean that there was a sexual act of objective, physical, incest like coitus, but what we could call the "symbolic incest" or "energetic incest" is often extremely painful and very harmful to a child on an emotional level. "Energetic" incest happens typically when her father being the only parent raises a girl (or when a mother raises her son alone), and the two of them "pair up" as man and woman making wholeness emotionally and energetically comparable to the wholeness of a sexual couple, but without the sexual acting out. A lot of sexual energies are accumulated and circulated here, and the girl is often, as Freud pointed out, having secret sexual dreams about her father with lots of shame and guilt. An implanted memory that carries all the shame and energy of a real incestuous trauma, but where intense therapy do not reveal any recorded "movie" of the event(s), might very well come from "energetic incest".

7) Implanted philosophy. When a patient learns that problems often are caused by traumas, she often starts speculating which traumas could have caused which problems. Sexual problems often then lead to dreams about sexual dominance/abuse/perversions and dreams can be interpreted as memories. Freud taught us that the child's sexuality is "polymorphously" perverted, meaning that all kinds of sexuality is present at least potentially with the little child. In dreams, according to Freud, consciousness often goes back to the earlier stages of development, potentially leading to all kinds of sexual dreams and fantasies.

The mind can interpret the same event in many different ways and one version of a "memory" cannot immediately be trusted over others. Many therapists therefore turn to the physical body for the truth about the past of the patient, assuming that the body cannot lie, because it carries the traumas as tensions that can be released, when the emotional and cognitive content of the gestalt is reintegrated in the consciousness of the patient. But as the body is seen through the patient's delusive mind, just turning from the mind to the body does not solve the problem of validating that a particular event actually happened as the patient recalls it.

Three phases of existential holistic therapy

During the last decade of research in clinical holistic medicine at the Research Clinic for Holistic Medicine in Copenhagen, we have found that the therapy in general has three phases (25-28):

1) Feeling the repressed emotions of the past
2) Understanding the objective elements of the traumatic event
3) Modifying/changing negative beliefs about the traumatic event ("letting go")

We have analysed the therapeutic work of about 500 patients with a number of different diseases and health issues (29-45) and learned that, in general, therapy has the following course.

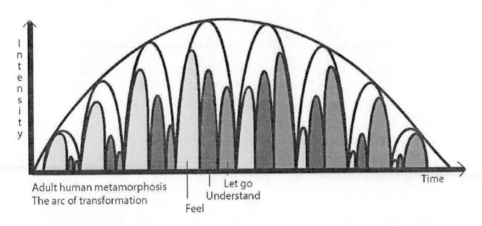

Figure 1. The arch of therapeutically transformation in clinical holistic medicine. There is three core elements of the therapeutic process: to feel (yellow), to understand (red), and to let go (blue) of negative, life-denying beliefs and attitudes. In the first sessions the emotional discharge dominates; as intensity in therapy grows, the element of understanding becomes more dominant, and in the end when the "heat" leaves therapy, cool understanding raises from the bottom of the patients soul (wholeness) (15).

In the first sessions, the emotional discharge dominates; as intensity in therapy grows, the element of understanding the traumatic event becomes dominant, and in the end when the intensity leaves the therapeutic process, a deeper understanding arises from the bottom of the patient's soul (wholeness). We have also learned that the therapeutic process can be understood as a metamorphosis (see figure 1) – the patient enters the therapy like a butterfly's larvae in need of transformation; she lets go of her old identity and melts down (entering the "pupae"). In this state, she develops a new understanding from recalling what she was originally meant to be; and finally she enters the world again as a renewed and transformed person (free to fly like the butterfly), much more beautiful, good and true. We know this process as the autogenetic process (46,47), where the patient regains physical and mental health, quality of life, and the ability to function in all areas of life. During this process, the patient will experience a number of crises that are not dangerous to the patient assuming that the patient is cared for intensively and properly (see figure 2).

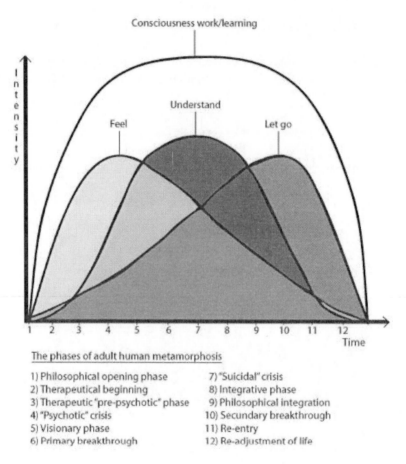

Figure 2. The experimentally found major phases and crisis in intensive dynamic short time therapy when complemented with bodywork (15).

A model for the wholeness of man

Humans have classically been described as consisting of three separate entities, all of which in psychoanalytical therapy are seen as carrying each a very different representation of self: the body carrying the Id, the mind carrying the Ego, and the wholeness carrying the True Self (higher self, soul, comparable to Freud's "Super Ego"). The wholeness of man consist of these three parts, and this points to a simple reason why neither the body nor the mind can be trusted much: they are only parts of our being, and as such they are not able to contain the totality. Only through our wholeness can we truly "see" the world and our personal history.

This understanding is very important as it gives us a key to understanding why patients cannot remember much in the beginning of the therapy, when they are starting to confront their own emotions. We also understand the reason for the intensive involvement of the mind in the second phase of the therapy, which does not provide clear understanding and recalling (memory) to the patient. It is only in the third phase of therapy, when the patient lets go of all negative and defensive beliefs and attitudes and returning to her natural philosophy of life will everything become clear, and (s)he will find herself remembering and understanding everything as the "true" reality.

Interestingly, the majority of patients may see themselves as part and parcel of a severely harmed body and not a free and enjoyable spirit (the wholeness, the free and true "soul"). In therapy, the patient needs first to recover the energy of the body (physical character and sexuality - a process, which has been used as medicine since Hippocrates) then they need to recover the mind (the mental character), and finally they will recover the spiritual dimensions of love, individual talents, higher intelligence (the spiritual character and purpose of life/life mission), and real happiness coming from being able to contribute to the world.

In the therapy we often teach this in a popular way to the patients, talking about "the four doors of existential therapy":

1) getting into sexuality
2) getting into consciousness
3) getting into love
4) getting into life

Most (Danish) patients realize the needs of re-conquering these dimensions of life, and therefore understand and accept this path to the healing of existence (salutogenesis) (46-48) immediately. Interestingly, as this process proceeds, first ability to feel, then ability to understand, and finally ability to judge what is true and what is not comes into focus. This originates from the patients reconnecting to the universe, and obtaining the Antonovsky's existential experience of the sense of coherence (46,47,49).

Case story

A 24 year-old psychology student, very intelligent, with a "head-centred", mental approach to the world and with a strongly repressed sexuality presents in clinical holistic therapy desiring to solve her existential and sexual problems. She strongly expected her father to have abused her sexually and remembers many such events. As therapy progresses and the emotional charge is relieved, she gradually changes her mind about the occurrence of abuse. After the fifth session, she starts to doubt that she has been physically abused, and in the end she realises the sexual abuse to be energetic (symbolic). Before the therapy she rated herself as functioning poorly sexually, with lack of sexual interest and orgasm, but after the integration of the energetic incest she was able to enter a relationship and a satisfying sex life. She managed to keep this relationship vital for years.

Intensive psychodynamic short-term psychotherapy with role-playing (re-parenting) and bodywork (body dynamics, vaginal acupressure) was used with this patient using the advanced therapeutic toolbox (12). In the beginning of the therapy emotions were not intense with this patient, but only slowly did she open up. When she finally did, the session was almost exploding in intensity. The breakthrough session happened at point 6 in figure 2, right when the most intense feelings were turned into understanding. At this point in time, the realistic memories of the abuse were still hidden from the soul, and the mind can interpret such events in many different ways. The repressed sexuality of this patient seemed to distort the patient's memory up to and including sexual sadism. Most interesting was the therapeutic catharsis and the effect of allowing the patient to go fully into exploring her past history of sexual abuse, making her finally doubt that it really happened: "I can't understand that this should really have happened". In the session the patient was sent back into the early events using the principle of similarity. The issue related to using similarity is that you cannot, as a therapist, avoid "implanting the memory" that the patient and you as a physician agree upon treating. But in this phase the trauma cannot be remembered, because the emotional charge is efficiently clocking the admittance to the time line. So we are really making a drama, only led by the emotional charge of the patient's repressed traumas. But only by supporting the patient in confronting these emotions can she get closer to a real memory of what happened to her. This is a most difficult technique that only can be done, when there is a very close and intimate relationship between the patient and the physician. At the same time, this intimacy invites implanted memories of the "transferences and counter transferences" kind (see above point 3 in causes of implanted memory). The situation looks impossible, but fortunately the processing of the trauma and the subsequent emotional discharge is, in the end, the key to solving the problem. The only thing the therapist cannot do is to back out and abandon the patient.

A most interesting thing to observe in this example is the high degree of certainty she had about past traumatic events at the beginning of the session. When the memories start to clear up, after she confronted the unbearable emotions of the gestalts, she became more and more doubtful that what she has remembered was "real". After reflecting deeply over the content of the session for some months she concluded that the abuse had not actually happened on a physical level although it did happen energetically. Thus it was a symbolic representation of energetic abuse (the 6th reason of implanted memories, see above).

Discussion

The use of the similarity principle with patients that believe they have been sexually abused sometimes reveal that what they seem to remember and recover in the therapy did not actually happen. This is an amazing process of recovering severe sexually traumatic memories and through careful evaluation, the patient realize that something completely different and much more complex actually happened.

We are complicated beings with needs and consciousness of many layers. As we develop, we need to be physically touched and emotionally supported, met at our borders and loved unconditionally. Unfortunately, most parents are not really able to meet the demands of their children and many children ends up more or less traumatized – a sad fact known ever since Freud.

The only way to cure somatic, mental, existential, and sexual problems arising from early childhood trauma is to discharge the emotional components by confronting the content of the traumas. The emotional charge also makes the trauma impossible to remember; the only route for inducing healing of the patient's existence (salutogenesis) (46-48) is to support a blind" confrontation of the repressed emotional content of the patient's sub-consciousness. The similarity principle seems most useful (49-55), as this principle allows the therapist to take the patient directly down to confronting the old traumas causing the problems.

The problem with this kind of therapy has been the fear of planting memories by the therapy itself. Our experience with holistic existential therapy is that sometimes such false memories are in fact implanted, but as therapy progresses these implanted memories are seen as not true. This is happening when the patient acquires a soul-perspective and becomes able to look at the whole life – the whole timeline from conception to now – as one single event, that is understandable in the light of the purpose of life that then is denied and repressed (see the life mission theory (56-62)).

The only real problem with this form of therapy is if the patient drops out of the therapy, before the temporarily false memories are reinterpreted and integrated. It is the obligation of the therapist to continue the therapy, until the patient is cured and free of her problem. Therefore, it is important that the patient stays in therapy no matter how unpleasant emotionally it is to confront the old traumas.

We have analysed the problem of implanted memories and found that such implantations indeed do happen in therapy for a number of reasons. When extreme memories of sexual abuse occur in patients with a strongly repressed sexuality and a very active mind, the therapist should consider if the memories are actually implanted. This does not mean that he should disrupt the therapy, but he should most carefully be sure not to interpret for the patient. This allows the patient to modify the memories about what has really happened in her childhood. If the emotional charge of the early traumas – often feelings of guilt and shame – is systematically relieved, the patient will in the end obtain the position of being able to review her whole time line and understand the real events (no matter how traumatic) leading to the emotional charge that has given the patient so many challenges.

Only when the patient can look from her wholeness, the truth can be perceived and the past truthfully remembered. The therapist must be extremely certain that the therapy reaches this conclusion. Fictive memories temporarily implanted are not a problem if this happens, but will be if the therapy for some reason is disrupted.

Using the similarity principle (49-55) during intensive, mindful psychodynamic short term psychotherapy complemented with bodywork seems to be the most direct way to induce holistic healing – salutogenesis – in patients with a complex of somatic, mental, existential and sexual problems. The therapy will often be very intense and the content of the therapy might be extremely explicitly sexual. If the therapist can contain the patient and all her emotions, the existential healing can be completed with no serious hindrances.

Freud taught us that mental illness comes from arrested psychosexual development and that the child sexuality is "polymorphously" perverted, meaning that all kinds of sexuality is present at least potentially with the little child; and in dreams consciousness often go back to the earlier stages of development, potentially causing all kinds of sexual dreams and fantasies, which can come up in therapy and look like real memories.

The therapist working with holistic medicine and psychiatry, sexology, psychodynamic psychotherapy, mind-body medicine, body psychotheray and other kinds of emotionally oriented psychotherapy and bodywork, should be aware of the danger of implanting philosophy and memory. Implanted memories and implanted philosophy must be carefully handled and de-learned before ending the therapy. In conclusion, modern sexology and scientific, holistic medicine and psychiatry (clinical holistic medicine) has developed a strategy for avoiding implanting memories.

References

[1]   Roth S, Batson R. Naming the shadows. A new approach to individual and group psychotherapy for adult survivors of childhood incest. New York: Free Press, 1997.
[2]   Roth S, Friedman MJ, eds. Childhood trauma remembered: A report on the current scientific knowledge base and its applications. J Child Sex Abuse 1998;7:83-111.
[3]   Jones E. The life and works of Sigmund Freud. New York: Basic Books, 1961.
[4]   Jung CG. Man and his symbols. New York: Anchor Press, 1964.
[5]   Yalom ID. The gift of therapy. New York: HarperCollins, 2002.
[6]   Yalom ID. Existential psychotherapy. New York: Basic Books, 1980.
[7]   Ventegodt S, Morad M, Merrick J. Clinical holistic medicine: Holistic pelvic examination and holistic treatment of infertility. ScientificWorldJournal 2004;4:148-58.
[8]   Ventegodt S, Morad M, Merrick J. Clinical holistic medicine: Problems in sex and living together. ScientificWorldJournal 2004;4: 562-70.
[9]   Ventegodt S, Morad M, Hyam E, Merrick J. Clinical holistic medicine: Holistic sexology and treatment of vulvodynia through existential therapy and acceptance through touch. ScientificWorldJournal 2004;4:571-80.
[10] Ventegodt S, Kandel I, Neikrug S, Merrick J. Clinical holistic medicine: Holistic treatment of rape and incest traumas. ScientificWorldJournal 2005;5:288-97.
[11] Ventegodt S, Merrick J. Clinical holistic medicine: Chronic pain in internal organs. ScientificWorldJournal 2005;5:205-10.
[12] Ventegodt S, Clausen B, Nielsen ML, Merrick J. Clinical holistic medicine: Advanced tools for holistic medicine. ScientificWorldJournal 2006;6:2048-65.
[13] Ventegodt S, Clausen B, Merrick J. Clinical holistic medicine: The case story of Anna: I. Long term effect of child sexual abuse and incest with a treatment approach. ScientificWorldJournal 2006;6:1965-76.
[14] Ventegodt S, Chausen B, Merrick J. Clinical holistic medicine: the case story of Anna. II. Patient diary as a tool in treatment. ScientificWorldJournal 2006;6:2006-34.
[15] Ventegodt S, Clasusen B, Merrick J. Clinical holistic medicine: The case story of Anna. III. Rehabilitation of philosophy of life during holistic existential therapy for childhood sexual abuse. ScientificWorldJournal 2006;6:2080-91.
[16] Ventegodt S, Clausen B, Omar HA, Merrick J. Clinical holistic medicine: Holistic sexology and acupressure through the vagina (Hippocratic pelvic massage). ScientificWorldJournal 2006;6:2066-79.
[17] Ventegodt S, Clausen B, Merrick J. Clinical holistic medicine: Pilot study on the effect of vaginal acupressure (Hippocratic pelvic massage). ScientificWorldJournal 2006;6:2100-16.
[18] Ventegodt S. Every contact with the patient must be therapeutic. J Pediatr Adolesc Gynecol 2007;20(6):323-4.
[19] Ventegodt S, Thegler S, Andreasen T, Struve F, Enevoldsen L, Bassaine L, et al. Clinical holistic medicine: Psychodynamic short-time therapy complemented with bodywork. A clinical follow-up study of 109 patients. ScientificWorldJournal 2006;1:256-74.

[20] Ventegodt S, Thegler S, Andreasen T, Struve F, Enevoldsen L, Bassaine L, et al. Clinical holistic medicine (mindful, short-term psychodynamic psychotherapy complemented with bodywork) in the treatment of experienced impaired sexual functioning. ScientificWorldJournal 2007;7:324-9.

[21] Ventegodt S, Thegler S, Andreasen T, Struve F, Enevoldsen L, Bassaine L, et al. Clinical holistic medicine (mindful, short-term psychodynamic psychotherapy complemented with bodywork) improves quality of life, health, and ability by induction of Antonovsky-salutogenesis. ScientificWorldJournal. 2007;7:317-23.

[22] Ventegodt S, Thegler S, Andreasen T, Struve F, Enevoldsen L, Bassaine L, et al. Clinical holistic medicine (mindful, short-term psychodynamic psychotherapy complemented with bodywork) in the treatment of experienced physical illness and chronic pain. ScientificWorldJournal 2007;7:310-6.

[23] Ventegodt S, Thegler S, Andreasen T, Struve F, Enevoldsen L, Bassaine L, et al. Clinical holistic medicine (mindful, short-term psychodynamic psychotherapy complemented with bodywork) in the treatment of experienced mental illness. ScientificWorldJournal. 2007;7:306-9.

[24] Ventegodt S, Thegler S, Andreasen T, Struve F, Enevoldsen L, Bassaine L, et al. Self-reported low self-esteem. Intervention and follow-up in a clinical setting. ScientificWorldJournal 2007;7:299-305.

[25] Ventegodt S. Consciousness-based medicine [Bevidsthedsmedicin – set gennem lægejournalen.] Copenhagen: Forskningscenterets Forlag, 2003. [Danish].

[26] Ventegodt S, Kandel I, Merrick J. Principles of holistic medicine. Philosophy behind quality of life. Victoria, BC: Trafford, 2005.

[27] Ventegodt S, Kandel I, Merrick J. Principles of holistic medicine. Quality of life and health. New York: Hippocrates Sci Publ, 2005.

[28] Ventegodt S, Kandel I, Merrick J. Principles of holistic medicine. Global quality of life.Theory, research and methodology. New York: Hippocrates Sci Publ, 2005.

[29] Ventegodt S, Morad M, Andersen NJ, Merrick J. Clinical holistic medicine Tools for a medical science based on consciousness. ScientificWorldJournal 2004;4:347-61.

[30] Ventegodt S, Morad M, Merrick J. Clinical holistic medicine: Prevention through healthy lifestyle and quality of life. Oral Health Prev Dent 2004;1:239-45.

[31] Ventegodt S, Morad M, Merrick J. Clinical holistic medicine: Holistic treatment of children. ScientificWorldJournal 2004;4:581-8.

[32] Ventegodt S, Flensborg-Madsen T, Andersen NJ, Morad M, Merrick J. Clinical holistic medicine: A Pilot on HIV and Quality of Life and a Suggested treatment of HIV and AIDS. ScientificWorldJournal 2004;4:264-72.

[33] Ventegodt S, Morad M, Merrick J. Clinical holistic medicine: Induction of spontaneous remission of cancer by recovery of the human character and the purpose of life (the life mission). ScientificWorldJournal 2004;4:362-77.

[34] Ventegodt S, Morad M, Kandel I, Merrick J. Clinical holistic medicine: Treatment of physical health problems without a known cause, exemplified by hypertension and tinnitus. ScientificWorldJournal 2004;4:716-24.

[35] Ventegodt S, Morad M, Merrick J. Clinical holistic medicine: Developing from asthma, allergy and eczema. ScientificWorldJournal 2004;4:936-42.

[36] Ventegodt S, Morad M, Press J, Merrick J, Shek D. Clinical holistic medicine: Holistic adolescent medicine. ScientificWorldJournal 2004;4:551-61.

[37] Ventegodt S, Solheim E, Saunte ME, Morad M, Kandel I, Merrick J. Clinical holistic medicine: Metastatic cancer. ScientificWorldJournal 2004;4:913-35.

[38] Ventegodt S, Morad M, Kandel I, Merrick J. Clinical holistic medicine: a psychological theory of dependency to improve quality of life. ScientificWorldJournal 2004;4:638-48.

[39] Ventegodt S, Merrick J. Clinical holistic medicine: Chronic infections and autoimmune diseases. ScientificWorldJournal 2005;5:155-64.

[40] Ventegodt S, Morad M, Merrick J. Clinical holistic medicine: Chronic pain in the locomotor system. ScientificWorldJournal 2005;5:165-72.

[41] Ventegodt S, Kandel I, Neikrug S, Merrick J. Clinical holistic medicine: The existential crisis – life crisis, stress and burnout ScientificWorldJournal 2005;5:300-12.

[42] Ventegodt S, Gringols G, Merrick J. Clinical holistic medicine: Holistic rehabilitation. ScientificWorldJournal 2005;5:280-7.

[43] Ventegodt S, Andersen NJ, Neikrug S, Kandel I, Merrick J. Clinical holistic medicine: Mental disorders in a holistic perspective. ScientificWorldJournal 2005;5:313-23.

[44] Ventegodt S, Andersen NJ, Neikrug S, Kandel I, Merrick J. Clinical holistic medicine: Holistic treatment of mental disorders. ScientificWorldJournal 2005;5:427-45.

[45] Ventegodt S, Merrick J. Clinical holistic medicine: The patient with multiple diseases. ScientificWorldJournal 2005;5:324-39.

[46] Antonovsky A. Health, stress and coping. London: Jossey-Bass, 1985.

[47] Antonovsky A. Unravelling the mystery of health. How people manage stress and stay well. San Franscisco: Jossey-Bass, 1987.

[48] Ventegodt S, Flensborg-Madsen T, Andersen NJ, Merrick J. Life mission theory VII: Theory of existential (Antonovsky) coherence: a theory of quality of life, health and ability for use in holistic medicine. ScientificWorldJournal 2005;5:377-89.

[49] Endler PC. Master programme for complementary, psychosocial and integrated health sciences. Graz: Interuniversity College, 2004.

[50] Blättner B. Fundamentals of salutogenesis. Health promotion and individual promotion of health: Guided by resources. Graz: Interuniversity College, 2004.

[51] Pass PF. Fundamentals of depth psychology. Therapeutic relationship formation between self-awareness and casework. Graz: Interuniversity College, 2004.

[52] Endler PC. Working and writing scientifically in complementary medicine and integrated health sciences. Graz: Interuniversity College, 2004.

[53] Spranger HH. Fundamentals of regulatory biology. Paradigms and scientific backgrounds of regulatory methods. Graz: Interuniversity College, 2004.

[54] Rodari A. Introduction of regulatory methods and systematics. Description and current research. Graz: Interuniversity College, 2004.

[55] Kratky KW. Complementary medical systems. Comparison and integration. New York: Nova Sci, 2008.

[56] Ventegodt S, Andersen NJ, Merrick J. Editorial: Five theories of human existence. ScientificWorldJournal 2003;3:1272-6.

[57] Ventegodt S. The life mission theory: A theory for a consciousness-based medicine. Int J Adolesc Med Health 2003;15(1): 89-91.

[58] Ventegodt S, Andersen NJ, Merrick J. The life mission theory II: The structure of the life purpose and the ego. ScientificWorldJournal 2003;3:1277-85.

[59] Ventegodt S, Andersen NJ, Merrick J. The life mission theory III: Theory of talent. ScientificWorldJournal 2003;3:1286-93.

[60] Ventegodt S, Merrick J. The life mission theory IV. A theory of child development. ScientificWorldJournal 2003;3:1294-1301.

[61] Ventegodt S, Andersen NJ, Merrick J. The life mission theory V. A theory of the anti-self and explaining the evil side of man. ScientificWorldJournal 2003;3:1302-13.

[62] Ventegodt S, Andersen NJ, Merrick J. The life mission theory VI: A theory for the human character. ScientificWorldJournal 2004;4: 859-80.

Chapter 30

How to avoid the Freudian trap of sexual transference and countertransference

As the therapist and the patient get to know each other an emotional bonding will develop. One aspect of this bond is always sexual. The sexual energy might be negatively polarised, as repulsion, or positively polarised, as attraction. It can be subtle and not easily noticed, or very obvious. The patients' sexual, libidinous investment in the therapist or physician is called "sexual transference"; a sexual interest always provoke a reaction called the "sexual counter transference".

Sexual transference and countertransference can make therapy slow and inefficient, when the libidinous gratification becomes more important for both the patient and the therapist than real therapeutic progress.

Sexual transference is normal, when working with a patient's repressed sexuality, but the therapeutic rule of not touching in most psychotherapy often hinders the integration of sexual traumas, as this process needs physical holding. So the patient is often left with her sexual, Oedipal energies projected on the therapist as an "idealized father" figure.

The strong and lasting sexual desire for the therapist without any healing happening can prolong the therapy for many years, as it often does in psychodynamic psychotherapy and psychoanalysis. We call this problem "Freud's trap".

Freud used intimate bodywork like massage of the female patient legs in the beginning of his career, but stopped presumably for moral and political reasons. In the tradition of psychoanalysis touch is therefore not allowed.

Recent research in scientific holistic medicine and psychiatry (clinical, holistic medicine, CHM), salutogenesis and sexual healing has shown, that touch and bodywork (an integral part of medicine since Hippocrates) is as important for healing as conversational therapy.

The combined holding and processing of holistic medcine allows the patient to spontaneously regress to early, sexual and emotional traumas, and heal the deep wounds on body, soul and sexual character from arrested psychosexual development.

Modern sexology and holistic medicine treat sexuality in therapy more as the patient's internal affair (i.e. energy work), and less as a thing going on between the patient and the therapist (i.e. transference). This accelerates healing and reduces sexual transference and the need for mourning in the end of therapy.

Introduction

There is plenty of literature on the need to work in abstinence, and almost every therapist on the planet agrees on the Hippocratic ethics of avoiding sexual contact with the patient. Sexual transference and counter-transference is therefore a concern in psychoanalysis and psychotherapy, but there is a scarcity of papers analysing this mutual libidinous gratification in spite of the issue being highly disturbing to so many therapists (1).

A few years back Irvin D Yalom, the father of "existential psychotherapy"(2) on a visit to Copenhagen addressed the taboo of sexual feelings in therapy directly by declaring that: "I have been sexually aroused by patients and so have every therapist I know". A participant in this conference and teacher in psychoanalysis was somewhat uncomfortable by admitting that he, in the end of a very difficult, almost 10-year long, four-sessions-a-week analysis with a mentally ill, sexually abused, female patient, had an erection. But this event signified to him more than anything else that the patient had finally successfully healed not only her sexuality, but also her basic existence; but he still felt uncomfortable to be aroused by an abused patient, especially as he earlier in the therapy was positioned as the abuser in the transference.

We must face the fact that therapists are human beings with the same sexuality and also the same feelings of shame and guilt as other people. This means that whenever a man and a woman are together, and they share intimate details, this will affect them sexually (3-6). There will always be some internal reaction, and also some reaction towards the other, i.e. transference and countertransference of love and sexuality, and sexuality thus ceases to be entirely the internal affair of the patient. The ethical art of therapy has since the days of Hippocrates been not to act out on these feelings (7).

Any relationship needs an investment of energy to be of any importance, and this energy is our life energy, which is very sexual, as Freud noticed correctly (8). When the therapeutic relationship turns sexually rewarding, the therapist must guard his intention at all times and be certain that he intents to help the patient, not to engage in the libidinous gratification, however pleasant and however unavoidable.

Unfortunately, the subconscious drive often wins over the mental and spiritual interest of curing the patient, and in this case the therapy often gets stuck. By addressing the sexual healing explicitly and directly, the therapy can move on, but if this does not happen, the therapist and the patient are often hopelessly trapped in what we call the "Trap of Freud": the continuous libidinous gratification that will make the patient pay for many sessions with no real progress, and with great, prolonged, and painful mourning in the end.

It is difficult to know when this state has been reached; one sign of this problem might be that the therapist is starting to dream and fantasize not only about coitus with the patient, but also about actually marrying him or her; on the other hand such fantasies might be necessary for the therapy (4,5). We must admit that therapy in this situation almost has turned into a real "marriage" between the therapist and the patient. There are so many similarities to marriage that the only major difference is the lack of physical acting out.

For Searles the difference between fantasising about marrying or having sex with the patient and actually doing so is crucial (4): Without the fantasy sexual energy is not available for therapy, but without the taboo on acting out this energy is channelled into the sexual relationship with the therapist not the therapy; this taboo however brings mourning because the desired relationship is sacrificed for the therapy. But Searles also worked under the taboo of touch, and from our perspective this unnatural distance to a person you care for, is what created the accumulated, and stagnant, libidinous energy experienced by Searles, and thus the fantasies. In one study Searles worked for 900 hours in average on the patients (9).

Sexual transferences and countertransferences are not bad for the therapy; brilliant therapists like Freud, Searles believed that transference and counter-transference of love and sexuality was necessary for therapeutic progress, but they most be used wisely (3,4). The need for sexual healing must be acknowledged, and the therapy must address this need directly in order for therapy to progress efficiently. In order for healing to take place (according to the theory of holistic healing (7,10), se discussion below) it is necessary to provide the patient with the support and holding needed for spontaneous regression back to the traumas. What most patients need is according to the Hippocratic medical tradition physical and mental contact, love, respect and acceptance, honest conversation, and physical intimacy (11,12).

According to some experts, Freud and the other psychoanalysts stopped giving physical holding precisely *because* it encouraged sexual gratification, but this could also be a way to signal to the surrounding world that now sexuality was under control in the therapy. Physical contact and therapeutic touch has been an integral part of holistic medicine since Hippocrates, and Freud was of course familiar with this tradition, being his own medical roots and his own initial practice (se below how he treated hysteria very much the same way as the Hippocratic doctors).

So we find it highly unlikely that Freud's really believed that stopping bodywork would solve the problem of therapists acting out; probably Freud who was a politically cunning developer intended to modernise the somewhat old-fashioned holistic medicine, and take it into a medical practice that could be widely accepted and used by his contemporary fellow therapists. We know from his many writings that Freud often reflected deeply upon what could be accepted by the press and contemporary culture and what could not.

Most interestingly, the energy needed for deep existential healing (salutogenesis) (13,14) is what we would call of a maternal character; if patient receives a nourishing, female, motherly energy, he or she will often spontaneously regress into and heal from his early, infantile, sexual traumas. It is important though that the therapist is not excluding the male pole in his contact with the patient, as treating the supportive energy as only a maternal energy can lead to a serious denial of sexuality.

In many pre-modern cultures the medicine man was a person of "double sex", being able to be both father and mother at the same time. The same idea is prevalent in today's Indian yogis; the famous yogi Sai-Baba's name meaning literally mother-father. The Jungian idea of an inner opposite sex (anima and animus) was an important development in psychoanalysis (6) and many psychoanalysts have believed that Freud's limited ability to help the schizophrenic patients was due to his lack of willingness to be the mother. Let us quote Harold F Searles in one of his fine passages:

"My impression is that Freud himself clung to this father-transference role in order to avoid facing the anxiety associated with the patient's working through their earlier conflicts in relation to him as a mother in the transference. This is a clue, I think, to why Freud considers schizophrenic patients, in whom the resolution of such conflicts is crucial, to be insusceptible to psycho-analytic therapy." (5:440).

Most interestingly the re-parenting and the care for spirit, mind and body at the same time is also what characterized the original Hippocratic character medicine (7). Many of the Hippocratic procedures had the purpose of re-balancing the sexual energies, especially of the female patient who received pelvic massage (7,15-17).

The indication for this treatment was "hysteria" (from Gr. Hystera: Uterus), believed to signify a broad range of female, mental illnesses. This treatment (also called vaginal acupressure) give intense physical holding to the female patients body, including the genitals (15,16) allowing her to regress and heal infantile sexual traumas related also to infantile (auto)erotism (see below). This treatment is thus highly rational from a psychodynamic perspective, in spite of obvious, ethical problems (15,16) (see below), which presumably inspired the Hippocratic doctors to developing their famous ethics.

Sexual transference and countertransference

Sexuality is ubiquitously present in nature and two sexually sound people will always to some extent have some bodily sensations of sexual nature provoked by each other's body. If we were just animals, sexual interest would be constantly and openly present. Being composite creatures with body, mind and spirit, and Id, Ego and Self (soul, higher self), the bodily part of us is constantly interested in sex which are in many ways sublimated, as Freud ingeniously noticed, as much of our natural interest in other people come from sexuality, but is turned into mental and spiritual interest. Researchers in tantra (18) have noticed, as Freud, that our mental and spiritual energy basically is transformed sexual energy. And here it is important not to fool oneself: It is still sexual energy, just in a more socially acceptable form.

Having stated these plain and well-known facts, we can take a deeper look at sexual transference and countertransference. This has been a strong taboo in psychoanalytic and psychodynamic psychotherapy (1), and from the very beginning it was considered a serious threat to the reputation and practice of psychoanalysis (3:170). The reason for the taboo is not very surprising, because who will send their sick young daughter to a man whose primary interest is to engage his sexual energy in her? So psychoanalysis has from the very beginning, in spite of Freud always stressing frank honesty as a key value made, made very smart cover-ups, especially in the language it has been using. Most people do not realize what the Oedipus conflict is about, and they do not want to know either, for this issue is far much too provoking. Most sexual transference seem to be of Oedipal nature; that was the reason for Freud to develop this seemingly strange Oedipus theory: It seems that the nurturing relations between children and parents are carrying extremely strong, but often unconscious, sexual feelings; and this energy is very often materializing itself in therapy, when the patient is regressing to early childhood scenario, and projecting father or mother (or both) on the therapist (10). But Freud did talk about this mother infant bond as sexual in a broad sense. Psychoanalysis has had to operate throughout its history with a tension between its highly sexual theories and its wish to be accepted in a repressive culture. It hasn't always got everything right, but it would be over-simplistic to simply say it has covered up sexuality.

These subliminal or conscious sexual complexes and feelings in psychodynamic therapy and psychoanalysis have been sought resolved in a simple way. When years of intensive contact in the therapy have finished its sexual-energetic process, its natural end is a very intense and prolonged mourning. This whole process often takes years and during this time many patients will stick firmly to their symptoms, since these supply the patient with a justification for staying in the most intense, intimate and pleasurable psychosexual contact to an other human being they have ever experienced.

Meetings four times a week for years are not unusual – literally thousands of sessions. The obvious lack of progress in therapy is understandable if we acknowledge that our body has priority in our subconscious universe controlling so much of our behaviour. This trap of psychoanalysis must be avoided at all cost, as it makes therapy expensive and inefficient.

We know of course that some psychoanalysts might find our analysis hard to accept, and from a traditional psychoanalytical position it is clear, that what we have stated above could be seen as a misunderstanding and oversimplification of psychoanalysis on a number of fronts. Firstly, psychoanalysts could argue, the mourning is in part at least because of the lack of sexual gratification not because of the loss of it. In the same way the incest taboo between parents and their children is what compels them to form sexual relationships outside the family of origin. But there is a kind of mourning involved in the acknowledgement that although daddy finds the child lovely he is married to mummy and therefore not available. And as the many fine statistics have documented (9), it is not corrects to say that no-one benefits from or needs long-term therapy. An other argument that could meet our position in this paper is that is promotes a 'one size fits all' type of philosophy that might not be correct; it might simply be that some types of patients need many years of dialog and verbal therapy, and not bodywork.

Our aim with the ongoing research is to develop more effective and fast therapy, so it might definitely in the end turn out that we have been to optimistic of the methods of clinical holistic medicine and the combination of psychotherapy and bodywork. But for now, we prefer to stick to our optimism, especially as this optimism in itself seems to accelerate therapy immensely.

The only way to accelerate the process is to address it directly and consciously to abort the more or less unconscious, mutual plan of a sexual-energetic long-term "marriage". Actually it is well-known from analytic literature (3-6), that both therapist and patient have such intense and ongoing fantasies of sexual intercourse and marriage. And it is, from our perspective, not a shame, not a bad thing, but a biologically and completely natural thing, but still a trap that we definitely must be smart enough to avoid.

The only way to avoid being caught by the subliminal sexual rewards of therapy is to address sexual issues openly, and get the therapy going at a well-defined and high speed. We must talk openly about sexuality, address sexual transferences and counter-transferences as soon as they are noticed, keeping the focus on the goal of therapy, and avoid being afraid to take the patient in deep regression and earlier sexual traumas by using the holding and support needed for this, including therapeutic touch.

The roots of Freud in holistic medicine

Interestingly, Freud did work rather intensively with therapeutic touch in the beginning of his carrier, wery much in the Hippocratic tradition of the holistic medical doctors, but stopped giving physical holding to his patients as he continued to developed psychoanalysis. Lauren Nancarrow Clarke writes (19:8):

> "Freud (20) used physical, body-to-body touch as one of his therapeutic tools... Freud, in several recorded case studies, performed the necessary leg massage and rolling for his hysterical patients to help alleviate their symptoms (see Fraulein Elisabeth von R.'s case, for example). Although touch is not the primary focus of this study, Freud's use of touch raises interesting thoughts about the 'touch taboo' in psychotherapy (21). Additionally, while this practice has been lost, the creator of psychoanalysis thought that touch was an important part of the healing process. If one of the patients' main modes of communication is through the bodily symptoms, why is this no longer an area of focus for all clinicians working today?"

It is well known from "The Cocaine Papers" (22) that Freud did much of his research into the psyche on cocaine, which has a well-known tendency to enhance libido (the large need of self-medication for sexual problems might be the reason why cocaine is available on every "black market" on the planet). It might very well be that the continuous use of cocaine is not very compatible with intimate bodywork, if you want to avoid acting out, but a much more plausible reason for Freud to abandon bodywork was extremely tense sexual-political and moral situation at that time (Freud talked about "highly explosive forces" (3:170), making physical contact with a patient questionable, even for a physician.

Use of bodywork

Holistic doctors have used bodywork since Hippocrates. Freud abandoned it, but many therapists after Freud, like Wilhelm Reich (1897-1957) (23), continued to use it and noticed that bodywork really was extremely effective in healing by sending patients back into earlier sexual traumas, including unsolved issues relating to infantile sexuality. Unfortunately Reich did his therapy in a way that, in spite of it being scientific (and also traditional) (17) was seen as a treat to the therapists and physicians of his time, namely by direct sexual stimulation of his female patients. This situation lead to the dramatic actions of burning his brilliant books with his unique research on human sexuality and a jail sentence and death of heart failure, while in jail.

In Denmark after two sexual revolutions (in the 1960s and in the 1990s) and legalization of both pornography and prostitution with pornography in every store and almost every TV-program-package, and even with porn-stars becoming TV-heroes on national TV, we still have problems with this kind of explicit, manual, sexological therapy. Today we can talk openly about sexuality, we can use bodywork to take patients into regression, but working directly with sexual stimulation of the patient in the sexological clinic is still highly controversial. Direct sexual stimulation of patients with vibrators for clitoral use are coming into use in holistic sexological therapy by alternative therapists, like the Danish sexologist Pia

Struck, who like a dozen other Danish therapists have been trained in this method by the American "mother of female masturbation", Betty Dodson (24). Direct sexual stimulation during therapy must be considered classical tool of holistic medicine (17) and is therefore listed as an advanced tool of clinical holistic medicine (25); its rationale seems to be to induce a sexual opening when the patient's sexuality has been definitely shot down since early childhood. It might be this ancient tradition of holistic, manual sexology that Freud tried to get away from by inducing the taboo of touch.

The bodywork needed for inducing healing, when the patient has strong sexual transference, is not sexual stimulation but often just simple therapeutic, accepting touch, which can be done while the patient has the clothes on (18). More intensive holding can be given with the patient partly undressed or nude (19) and with more therapists and holders (20), without touch becoming sexual. Acceptance though touch (19) and vaginal acupressure, also called Hippocratic pelvic massage after its appearance in the famous Corpus Hippocraticum (7,17), seems to be valuable tools for giving intensive holding and support to the sexually traumatized female patients (26,27), without direct sexual stimulation.

Interestingly vaginal acupressure is equivalent to the explorative phase of the pelvic examination; we therefore believe that this procedure is legal in most countries. But as a therapist you must be absolutely certain that a holistic medical procedure is legal in your country and that you have the needed therapeutic competency, ethical training, and supervision, before using it.

We have noticed at the Research Clinic for Holistic Medicine in Copenhagen that sexual issues and severe existential problems after rape and sexual abuse often can be solved in only 10 to 20 hours of holistic therapy, if sufficient bodywork is included, when needed (16,28,29). The extreme acceleration of therapy from up to 2,000 hours of psychoanalysis (one hour four times a week for 10 years) to 10 or 20 hours of scientific holistic therapy has been the main reason to include therapeutic touch (18) in our development of clinical, holistic medicine (20,30-32).

If one as a therapist dares to go all the way to working with direct sexual stimulation in the holistic, sexological clinic, even the most severe and chronic, sexual problems and dysfunctions can be solved; an example of this is the treatment of anorgasmia, where even in the most difficult cases of lack of orgasm and desire lasting for decades could be solved after only 15 hours of intensive therapy (24). Struck and Ventegodt (24) found that 93% of 500 patients with anorgasmia were cured in this way and the method had no negative adverse effects.

Unfortunately, not many therapists would like to work so directly with the sexuality and genitals of the patient, as it is possible to do with the most radical, advanced tools of holistic, sexological, manual therapy. But in most cases simple therapeutic touch will do the job. We must strongly recommend that therapists acknowledge the value of manual therapy and the need for physical holding, because many problems are coming from our childhood and a condition, where we did not get sufficient love and care from our parents. When we spontaneously go back to these days of early childhood in the therapy, we simply need physical holding – as we did then (7,10).

Psychoanalysts, who defend the taboo of touch, have disputed the need for physical holding. It has been a constant experience from many therapists now, working on hundreds patients with many different diseases, that touch is often needed for a complete healing of childhood traumas (33-35). The reason that therapeutic touch is needed seem to be the way information are transferred from body to body, by direct transference of biological information (36-45); especially when the patient has been sexually abused seems touch to be the key to healing (33-35).

Using sexual energy in healing

Harold F. Searles (1918-) wrote in his excellent paper on "Sexual processes in schizophrenia (5:441):

> "This vignette brings up the point, too, that as the patient and therapist encounter prolonged periods of mutual despair at ever resolving the illness, both experience powerful urges to give up the difficult struggle towards a genuinely psychotherapeutic goal, and to settle for a much more primitive goal of finding sexual satisfaction in one another."

Here we see the conflict in the therapy. The mutual sexual interest is on the one hand what sets the patient free energetically and consciously and motivates for the often-painful exploration into a wounded existence. On the other hand the same mutual, sexual interest can be fixating the therapy until it breaks down in mutual despair and reveal its true, sexual nature. Searles continues (5:441):

> "One may see this phenomenon when mutually gratifying investigative work is interrupted, for long weeks and even months, by a recrudescence of the patient's defensive withdrawal. The therapist, having tested the pleasure of carrying on a relatively high order of collaborative therapeutic investigation with the difficult patient, now has a reason to feel that such gratifications are irretrievably gone, and he apt to be preoccupied more than usual by sexual feelings towards, and fantasies about, the withdrawn patient. Such sequences suggest the extent to which the gratifications of psychotherapeutic or psycho-analytic work represent sublimations of libidinal impulses, which break down, for varying periods of time, during such periods of withdrawal... in the relationship between patient and therapist. Just as sexual behaviour by a schizophrenic person may represent his last-ditch attempts to make or maintain contact with outer reality, or with his own inner self... so the therapist sexual feelings towards the withdrawn patient may be, in part, an unconscious effort to bridge the psychological gulf between then, when more highly refined means have failed."

What Searles shares with us here is extremely important: Behind the independent interest of our Id and Ego we still have the intentions of the self, and if the therapist is conscious of his intentions and constantly intents to serve his patient every second of the therapy – which is the real challenge of being a therapist – then sexuality might serve a higher and healing purpose. So Searles noticed in himself that his sexual interest in the patient actually was embedded in his good intent for this patient – as is our physical interest in our children, when we are good parents. So after all, being a therapist is not that difficult – one must just be like a good parent.

Transference or regression

One cannot avoid sexual transferences in psychodynamic therapy of any kind, but by focusing directly on the triple rehabilitation of body, mind, and spirit (id, ego, and self/soul) one can take the focus from mutual interest here and now – which is good for confidence and trust but bad for therapeutic speed – to the crucial rehabilitation of the patient's talents of body, mind, spirit, love, consciousness and sexuality. Working on these issues seems to be what heals the existence of the patient, i.e. induces the salutogenesis.

The therapeutic schools hold somewhat different opinions on regression; according to most contemporary schools and to holistic medicine in general, salutogenesis is happening, when the patient regress back to the painful moments, where striving for survival forced her/him to stretch fundamental existence and reshape personality at its core. We have coined this radical and total human transformation into a more hardcore and survivable version of "juvenile human metamorphosis" and the deep process of existential healing similarly called "adult human metamorphosis" (33-45). These states are so painful that only the most intensive holding can give sufficient support and often this takes all the intimacy the patient can get. These processes can be extremely resource-demanding, if the patient is severely traumatized i.e. by repeat rape or sexual abuse in childhood and they are best done in a group setting (29). The "healing crisis" that the patient enters is well described as "holy madness", and the therapist is well advised coming from "crazy wisdom" (46).

Interestingly, when holistic therapy is done with a strong intentional focus on love, consciousness and sexuality, transference is mostly prevented and the healing process focused internally in the patient. In the process of salutogenesis (7,13,14,47-52) not only the mind heals (53), but also the body (54), sexuality (28) and life as a whole (55,56).

So by working on body, mind, and spirit at the same time, much human suffering can be alleviated and most interestingly even the working ability is given back to the patient. Scientific holistic therapy is therefore also helping the patient's economy, which should be very much appreciated by poor patients, and equally by the states that offers free health service to its citizens. To return the patient to society, initiating a process that in the end turns the patient into a valuable person for him-self and others and for society at large is the finest goal of therapy, and the only goal that really served the purpose of rehabilitating the patient's character (7) and by that also his sense of coherence (13,14) and purpose of life (57).

Fetal sexuality and infantile autoerotism

From research in the tradition of tantra (18) we know that sexual health is associated with the ability to contain large amount of sexual energy. We also know that the ability to control the letting go and action out of this accumulated, sexual energy is essential to sexual health. Problems with containing sexual energy is often experienced as a tension or a pressure, leading to emotional lability, premature ejaculations, frigidity, and many other problems related to sexually and personality (2,3,6,7,8,18,20).

Most interestingly the therapeutic regression into infantile sexually is healing our ability to contain huge amounts of sexual energy. The regression into early childhood and into the womb as a foetus is often an extremely sexual experience, but the sexual energies are internally circulated, not circulated between self and other persons, as in mature sexuality. Freud called this "infantile auto-erotism", and believed that schizophrenics were ill, because they were stuck at this level of psychosexual development (5:429), very much in accordance with our own observations from deep therapeutic regression of such patients.

It seems that only if our inner, sexual energy system is well functioning and healthy, that our body and mind can be healthy. It seems that early traumas arresting our psychosexual development at this stage is causing many of the mental, existential, sexual, and even physical problems we see in the clinic. It therefore seems necessary for the existential healing (salutogenesis) to take place that the therapeutic work includes early regression and healing of the traumas related to infantile autoerotism.

Ethical aspects

As so often in our life, the rule is that what we most desperately try to avoid will be our destiny. This simply follows from the way our mind works. Everything we hold on to with the mind will subconsciously direct our behaviours, also when we cling to something negative. All therapy is about telling the patient to let go of the mind clinging.

Form the very beginning psychoanalysis has desperately avoided sexual exploitation of the patients. This has been regulated by firm rules of not touching and to avoid physical acting out of the sexual transference and countertransference. But sexual interest is not going away, because of such rules. And they most obviously do not prevent sex between therapist and patient, as this continues to be a huge problem, and the largest taboo among physicians and psychotherapists, whether they are classical psychoanalysts, gestalt therapist or CAM-healers.

We believe there should be firm ethical rules in therapy, but avoiding touch has destroyed the therapeutic progress. Touch is a basic human need all the way through life and in all kinds of care (58,59). Positive, accepting, pleasurable touch is most definitely needed for normal childhood development, and therefore most definitely needed as the most important part of the holding, when the patient regress to the childhood in order to solve traumatic childhood issues.

The healing of sexual traumas needs (more than healing of any other trauma) physical support and therapeutic touch. By avoiding touch in therapy in order to avoid sexual abuse, we believe that Freud and other psychoanalysts ended up with many patients being "married" to their therapist in a "sexually gratifying relationships" of little therapeutic value. The ethical problems connected with Freud's trap are:

- The patient is deprived of her healing believing it is on its way, instead of a healing that could happen in less hours of intensive therapy involving physical touch. Therapy without touch can also be fast, if you address the issues directly, as done in short-term psychodynamic psychotherapy, where even severe psychiatric illnesses often can be alleviated in 20-40 hours (60-62) and clinical holistic medicine (53).
- The patient will be deeply involved mentally, emotionally, sexually, and existentially with a therapist for many years, often having her therapist as the closest person in her

life, with him being the object of her longings, sexual fantasies, and desires. This energetic "marriage" will deprive her of the possibility of getting the male she really needs, and getting the sexual satisfaction she so separately longs for. So the patient is basically wasting her life.

- Another important aspect is the question of possible financial exploitation. Independent of Freud's trap, the use of relative inefficient therapeutically methods will always be unethical for the reasons of prolonging therapy and taking too much money from the patient. The patient eternally trapped in Freud's trap will be caught like a mouse in a mouse trap; driven by her emotions and desires, projecting her inner male into therapist as the "divine" idealized father (or mother if a patient is having a female therapist). She will gratefully and without hesitation spend all her available money on the therapy continuing for many years, because it is just such an honour to be with the therapist for 2 or 4 hours a week - and such an Oedipal pleasure to finally be "married to dad". If there is no therapeutic gain and the purpose for meeting is the mutual libidinous gratification, this is very much like prostitution with the therapist being the prostituted "expert lover". But this is not prostitution, as the therapist is not admitting – and often not even aware of - the simple, sexualised purpose of their time together. The therapist experience to work seriously; but she is just a very hard case so solve. The harder the patient's case is, the more desperately will the patient need the therapists help. This necessity of prolonged therapy is not only obvious for the patient and the therapist, but often the patient's whole social network is backing the continuation of the therapy up as extremely and vitally important; everybody is happy that the patient finally found such a brilliant doctor who really gets the therapy going. Seen by a cynical, analytic eye, the patient sitting in Freud's Trap is caught and exploited financially; as the sexual pleasure is mutual it would not be correct to say that she is exploited sexually.

- In the end of therapy there will be mourning and grief. Therapist and patient must separate, because the energy is leaving the relationship, as it always will in a sexual relationship without fundamental renewing. So the joy of therapy is converted into the pain of therapy. Much of the pleasure the patient paid for must be returned in the end, without the money being returned.

In order to sum up, the concept of Freud's Trap is giving us a view into a part of psychodynamic therapy and psychoanalysis that is not working well. We find the reason for this to be the taboo of touch. There are many reasons for contemporary therapist not to want to touch the patients; there are restrictive therapeutic rules, there are strategies for avoid being tempted sexually, and strategies for avoiding being accused of sexual abuse. What ever the reason for not touching is the therapist ends up involving the patient deeply emotionally and sexually in a relationship that is supposed to be healing, but because of the taboo of touch it is not.

Such a relationship is neither truly, sexually rewarding, in spite of an often-strong focus on sexuality and some sexual gratification, nor healing. The therapist stuck with the patient ends up very much like a prostitute, with the client coming to the "expert lover" for love-sessions; but the costumers buying this kind of therapy are paying for something that neither develops into the real sex the patient is longing for, nor into the healing she actually pays for.

We think that the taboo of touch is a historical mistake that prolongs therapy for years; we do not find that Freud's Trap is causing any direct harm to the patients.

We acknowledge that psychoanalysts might disagree with our position in this paper; we admit coming from the old tradition of Hippocratic holistic medicine, where touch has been an integral part of medicine for millennia; this gives us very different experiences than does psychoanalysis and psychodynamic psychotherapy working with all the pragmatic restrictions of the taboo of touch.

Conclusions

Holistic medicine for mental disorders will always at some point in time adress the patients problem related to arrested psychosexual development. When the patients sexuality is the focus of attention all the patients sexual energies including the relational aspects are enhanced. Often the sexual transference and countertransference becomes strong.

Sexual transference and counter-transference has been one of the large and unsolved problems in psychoanalysis and psychodynamic psychotherapy as it often makes therapy slow and inefficient, because of the mutual libidinous gratification of the therapeutic relationship subconsciously being more important than therapeutic progress. Purposeful and expressive work on healing the patients sexuality using bodywork often takes the patient spontaneously into deep regression and all the way back to the sexual traumas in early childhood and even into the womb.

Holistic doctors have used a combination of conversational therapy and bodywork ever since Hippocrates. Freud also used intimate bodywork like massage in the beginning of his career, but stopped, presumably for moral and political reasons. In the classical tradition of psychoanalysis and psychodynamic psychotherapy touch is not allowed, especially not when related to the patient's sexuality and genitals. Modern sexology and scientific, holistic medicine integrates, in the classical tradition of Hippocratic holistic medicine, psychodynamic psychotherapy and therapeutic touch, making it possible to support the healing of the patient's sexuality also on the physical level. Recent research in holistic medicine, salutogenesis and sexual healing has shown, that touch and bodywork is as important for healing as conversational therapy (63,64). Holistic medicine (CHM) has also shown good results, presumably because it integrates psychodynamic psychotherapy and therapeutic touch (7,10,26). It thus allows the patient to spontaneously regress to early, sexual and emotional traumas, and heal the deep wounds on body, soul and sexual character from arrested psychosexual development. Modern sexology and holistic medicine treats sexuality in therapy more as the patient's internal affair (i.e. energy work), and less as a thing going on between the patient and the therapist (i.e. transference). This form dramatically accelerates healing and reduces intensity of the sexual (Oedipal) bonding between therapist and patient and as a consequence the experience of loss and need for mourning in the end of therapy.

References

[1] Gabbard GO. Sexual excitement and countertransference love in the analyst. J Am Psychoanal Assoc 1994;42(4):1083-1106.

[2] Yalom ID. Existential psychotherapy. New York: Basic Books, 1980.

[3] Freud S. Observations on transference love. In: Freud S. Collected works, vol XII. London: Hogarth Press, 1924:159-71.

[4] Searles HF. Oedipal love in the countertransference In: Searles HF. Collected papers on schizophrenia. Madison, CT: Int Univ Press, 1965:284-303.

[5] Searles HF. Sexual processes in schizophrenia. In: Searles HF. Collected papers on schizophrenia. Madison, CT: Int Univ Press, 1965:429-442.

[6] Jung CG. Man and his symbols. New York: Anchor Press, 1964.

[7] Jones WHS. Hippocrates. Vol. I–IV. London: William Heinemann, 1923-1931.

[8] Jones E. The life and works of Sigmund Freud. New York: Basic Books, 1961.

[9] Robert P, Knight RP. The preface. In: Searles HF. Collected papers on schizophrenia. Madison, CT: Int Univ Press, 1965:15-16.

[10] Ventegodt S, Andersen NJ, Merrick J. Holistic Medicine III: The holistic process theory of healing. ScientificWorldJournal 2003;3:1138-46.

[11] Ventegodt S, Andersen NJ, Merrick J. The life mission theory III: Theory of talent. ScientificWorldJournal 2003;3:1286-93.

[12] Ventegodt S, Merrick J. The life mission theory IV. A theory of child development. ScientificWorldJournal 2003;3:1294-1301.

[13] Antonovsky A. Health, stress and coping. London: Jossey-Bass, 1985.

[14] Antonovsky A. Unravelling the mystery of health. How people manage stress and stay well. San Francsico: Jossey-Bass, 1987.

[15] Ventegodt S, Clausen B, Merrick J. Clinical holistic medicine: Holistic sexology and acupressure through the vagina (Hippocratic pelvic massage). ScientificWorldJournal 2006;6:2066-79.

[16] Ventegodt S, Clausen B, Merrick J. Clinical holistic medicine: Pilot study on the effect of vaginal acupressure (Hippocratic pelvic massage). ScientificWorldJournal 2006;6:2100-16.

[17] Maines R. The technology of orgasm. Baltimore, MD: Johns Hopkins Univ Press, 1999.

[18] Bertelsen J. [Quantum leaps. A book about love.] Kvantespring. En bog om kærlighed]. Copenhagen: Borgen, 1986. [Danish]

[19] Clarke NL. Putting the body back in social work: How social workers experience and differ in levels of personal body awareness. Northampton, MA: Smith College School Soc Work, 2007.

[20] Freud S, Breuer J. Studies in hysteria. New York: Penguin Classics, 2004. (Original work published 1893, 1895, 1908).

[21] Kimble Wrye H. The embodiment of desire: Rethinking the bodymind within the analytic dyad. In: Aron L, Anderson SF, eds. Relational perspectives on the body. New Jersey: Analytic Press, 1998;12:39-64.

[22] Byck R, ed. Cocaine papers by Sigmund Freud. New York: Stonehill, 1974.

[23] Reich W. [Die Function des Orgasmus]. Köln: Kiepenheuer Witsch, 1969.. [German]

[24] Struck P, Ventegodt S. Clinical holistic medicine: Breaking the orgasm-barrier by re-parenting, genital acceptance and clitoral stimulation: 93% of 500 chronically an-orgasmic female patients had an orgasm after 15 hours of holistic, sexological, manual therapy. ScientificWorldJournal 2008;8:883-95.

[25] Ventegodt S, Morad M, Merrick J. Clinical holistic medicine: Classic art of healing or the therapeutic touch. ScientificWorldJournal 2004;4:134-47.

[26] Ventegodt S, Morad M, Hyam E, Merrick J. Clinical holistic medicine: Holistic sexology and treatment of vulvodynia through existential therapy and acceptance through touch. ScientificWorldJournal 2004;4:571-80.

[27] Ventegodt S, Thegler S, Andreasen T, Struve F, Enevoldsen L, Bassaine L., et al. Clinical holistic medicine (mindful, short-term psychodynamic psychotherapy complemented with bodywork) in the treatment of experienced impaired sexual functioning. ScientificWorldJournal 2007;7: 324-9.

[28] Ventegodt S, Andersen NJ, Merrick J. Holistic Medicine IV: Principles of the holistic process of healing in a group setting. ScientificWorldJournal 2003;3:1294-1301.

[29] Ventegodt S, Kandel I, Merrick J. Principles of holistic medicine. Philosophy behind quality of life. Victoria, BC: Trafford, 2005.

[30] Ventegodt S, Kandel I, Merrick J. Principles of holistic medicine. Quality of life and health. New York: Hippocrates Sci Publ, 2005.

[31] Ventegodt S, Kandel I, Merrick J. Principles of holistic medicine. Global quality of life.Theory, research and methodology. New York: Hippocrates Sci Publ, 2006.

[32] Ventegodt S, Clausen B, Merrick J. Clinical holistic medicine: The case story of Anna: I. Long term effect of child sexual abuse and incest with a treatment approach. ScientificWorldJournal 2006;6:1965-76.

[33] Ventegodt S, Clausen B, Merrick J. Clinical holistic medicine: the case story of Anna. II. Patient diary as a tool in treatment. ScientificWorldJournal 2006;6:2006-34.

[34] Ventegodt S, Clausen B, Merrick J. Clinical holistic medicine: The case story of Anna. III. Rehabilitation of philosophy of life during holistic existential therapy for childhood sexual abuse. ScientificWorldJournal 2006;6:2080-91.

[35] Hermansen TD, Ventegodt S, Rald E, Clausen B, Nielsen ML, Merrick J. Human development I: twenty fundamental problems of biology, medicine, and neuro-psychology related to biological information. ScientificWorldJournal 2006;6:747-59.

[36] Ventegodt S, Hermansen TD, Nielsen ML, Clausen B, Merrick J.Human development II: we need an integrated theory for matter, life and consciousness to understand life and healing. ScientificWorldJournal 2006;6:760-6.

[37] Ventegodt S, Hermansen TD, Rald E, Flensborg-Madsen T, Nielsen ML, Clausen B, Merrick J. Human development III: bridging brain-mind and body-mind. introduction to "deep" (fractal, poly-ray) cosmology. ScientificWorldJournal 2006;6:767-76.

[38] Ventegodt S, Hermansen TD, Flensborg-Madsen T, Nielsen ML, Clausen B, Merrick J. Human development IV: the living cell has information-directed self-organisation. ScientificWorldJournal 2006;6:1132-8.

[39] Ventegodt S, Hermansen TD, Flensborg-Madsen T, Nielsen ML, Clausen B, Merrick J. Human development V: biochemistry unable to explain the emergence of biological form (morphogenesis) and therefore a new principle as source of biological information is needed. ScientificWorldJournal 2006;6:1359-67.

[40] Ventegodt S, Hermansen TD, Flensborg-Madsen T, Nielsen M, Merrick J. Human development VI: Supracellular morphogenesis. The origin of biological and cellular order. ScientificWorldJournal 2006;6:1424-33.

[41] Ventegodt S, Hermansen TD, Flensborg-Madsen T, Rald E, Nielsen ML, Merrick J. Human development VII: A spiral fractal model of fine structure of physical energy could explain central aspects of biological information, biological organization and biological creativity. ScientificWorldJournal 2006;6:1434-40.

[42] Ventegodt S, Hermansen TD, Flensborg-Madsen T, Nielsen ML, Merrick J. Human development VIII: A theory of "deep" quantum chemistry and cell consciousness: Quantum chemistry controls genes and biochemistry to give cells and higher organisms consciousness and complex behavior. ScientificWorldJournal 2006;6:1441-53.

[43] Ventegodt S, Hermansen TD, Flensborg-Madsen T, Rald E, Nielsen ML, Merrick J. Human development IX: A model of the wholeness of man, his consciousness and collective consciousness. ScientificWorldJournal 2006;6:1454-9.

[44] Hermansen TD, Ventegodt S, Merrick J. Human development X: Explanation of macroevolution — top-down evolution materializes consciousness. The origin of metamorphosis. ScientificWorldJournal 2006;6:1656-66.

[45] Feuerstein G. Holy madness. Spirituality, crazy-wise teachers and enlightenment. London: Arkana, 1992.

[46] Flensborg-Madsen T, Ventegodt S, Merrick J. Sense of coherence and physical health. A Review of previous findings. ScientificWorldJournal 2005;5:665-73.

[47] Flensborg-Madsen T, Ventegodt S, Merrick J. Why is Antonovsky's sense of coherence not correlated to physical health? Analysing Antonovsky's 29-item sense of coherence scale (SOCS). ScientificWorldJournal 2005;5:767-76.

[48] Flensborg-Madsen T, Ventegodt S, Merrick J. Sense of coherence and health. The construction of an amendment to Antonovsky's sense of coherence scale (SOC II). ScientificWorldJournal 2006;6:2133-9.

[49] Flensborg-Madsen T, Ventegodt S, Merrick J. Sense of coherence and physical health. A crosssectional study using a new SOC scale (SOC II). ScientificWorldJournal 2006;6:2200-11.

[50] Flensborg-Madsen T, Ventegodt S, Merrick J. Sense of coherence and physical health. Testing Antonovsky's theory. ScientificWorldJournal 2006;6:2212-9.

[51] Flensborg-Madsen T, Ventegodt S, Merrick J. Sense of coherence and health. The emotional sense of coherence (SOC-E) was found to be the best-known predictor of physical health. ScientificWorldJournal 2006;6:2147-57.

[52] Ventegodt S, Thegler S, Andreasen T, Struve F, Enevoldsen L, Bassaine L., et al. Clinical holistic medicine (mindful, short-term psychodynamic psychotherapy complemented with bodywork) in the treatment of experienced mental illness. ScientificWorldJournal 2007;7:306-9.

[53] Ventegodt S, Thegler S, Andreasen T, Struve F, Enevoldsen L, Bassaine L., et al. Clinical holistic medicine (mindful, short-term psychodynamic psychotherapy complemented with bodywork) in the treatment of experienced physical illness and chronic pain. ScientificWorldJournal 2007;7:310-6.

[54] Ventegodt S, Thegler S, Andreasen T, Struve F, Enevoldsen L, Bassaine L., et al. Clinical holistic medicine (mindful, short-term psychodynamic psychotherapy complemented with bodywork) improves quality of life, health, and ability by induction of Antonovsky-salutogenesis. ScientificWorldJournal 2007;7:317-23.

[55] Ventegodt S, Thegler S, Andreasen T, Struve F, Enevoldsen L, Bassaine L., et al. Self-reported low self-esteem. Intervention and follow-up in a clinical setting. ScientificWorldJournal 2007;7:299-305.

[56] Ventegodt S. The life mission theory: A theory for a consciousness-based medicine. Int J Adolesc Med Health 2003;15(1):89-91.

[57] Ventegodt S. Every contact with the patient must be therapeutic. J Pediatr Adolesc Gynecol 2007;20(6):323-4.

[58] Routasalo P, Isola A. The right to touch and be touched. Nurs Ethics 1996;3(2):165-76.

[59] Leichsenring F, Rabung S, Leibing E. The efficacy of short-term psychodynamic psychotherapy in specific psychiatric disorders: a meta-analysis. Arch Gen Psychiatry 2004;61(12):1208-16.

[60] Leichsenring F. Are psychodynamic and psychoanalytic therapies effective?: A review of empirical data. Int J Psychoanal 2005;86(Pt 3):841-68.

[61] Leichsenring F, Leibing E. Psychodynamic psychotherapy: a systematic review of techniques, indications and empirical evidence. Psychol Psychother 2007;80(Pt 2):217-28.

[62] van der Kolk BA. The body keeps the score: memory and the evolving psychobiology of post traumatic stress. Harvard Rev Psychiatry 1994;1:253–65.

[63] van der Kolk BA. The neurobiology of childhood trauma and abuse. Child Adolesc Psychiatr Clin North Am 2003;12(2):293–317.

[64] Rosen M, Brenner S. Rosen method bodywork. Accessing the unconscious through touch. Berkeley, CA: North Atlantic Books, 2003.

Chapter 31

How to use implanted memories of incest as a tool for dissolving a strong female Oedipus complex

To claim that Freud at the end of his life meant that we should avoid working on sexual traumas is to misread Freud in our opinion. On the other hand it seems that for political reasons and in order for psychoanalysis to survive in a period of severe critique, he chose to focus psychoanalysis on internal conflicts and not on sexual traumas. Later in his life he even admitted to have consciously repressed the fact that the parental sexual abuse of several of his female patient had created the strong female Oedipus complex that caused the hysteric and sexually dysfunctional symptoms of these patients. A large fraction of mentally ill patients has been sexually abused in their childhood and this is often associated with a strong Oedipus complex, which binds their mental energy and continues to give the patient often severe mental symptoms until resolved.

As a rule such early, emotionally painful life events cannot be contacted directly by the patient's consiousness as they are deeply repressed. The way such content emerge in the therapy is by a series of phantasies or interpretations that gradually become more and more solid, until an "implanted memory" appears. This memory is not at all accurate, but carry the part of the emotional content of the trauma that the patient can tolerate. As therapy progresses this "implanted memory" will transform into a true recollection of the actual traumas. "Implanted memories" can therefore be an important tool in the sexological clinic.

Sometimes the abuse of the child was physical, but as often it was psychological (energetical incest). If the process of healing continues to its natural closure, the patient will know with certainty what actually happened at the end of the therapy.

Introduction

In the ongoing debate on implanted memories and sexual traumas (1-3), Robert Withers (4) pointed out that it is possible to use memory defensively to evade uncomfortable feelings in the transference, and similarly possible to use the transference defensively. So we are in great trouble as therapists, when we want to be sure that what we are dealing with is based on reality and not on defensive construction.

To claim that Freud at the end of his life meant that we should avoid working on sexual traumas is to misread Freud in our opinion. On the other hand it seems that for political reasons and in order for psychoanalysis to survive in a period of severe critique, he chose to focus psychoanalysis on internal conflicts and not on sexual traumas. Later in his life he even admitted to have consciously repressed the fact that the parental sexual abuse of several of his female patient had created the strong female Oedipus complex that caused the hysteric and sexually dysfunctional symptoms of these patients (5,6).

It is not difficult to understand why Freud chose this path, away from conflicts that easily could have put psychoanalysis in a bad position. We have learned from the way the brilliant researcher Wilhelm Reich (7), the founder of modern sexology, was treated with persecution, imprisonment and public book burning, that Freud chose a wise route for psychoanalysis, when he avoided the hot issues, that could explode in the media. All readers of Freud will know how often Freud addressed this political level and how thoroughly he incorporated it when he developed psychoanalysis.

But time is no longer for hiding the truth and being political; we need a science of therapy that works and effectively will cure our patients. Robert Withers (4) is correct when he states that the sexually traumatised patient that hear her analyst saying in essence: 'Let's not talk about your father raping you—let's talk about us' is severely let down by her therapist. He concludes: "There is no doubt that at times the transference/countertransference can be a wonderful therapeutic tool. But we do our patients a disservice, if we forget Freud's original insight that it can also be used by the resistance—especially in the face of emerging traumatic material."

We would like to take this a bit further. We want to state that implanted memories of incest can be a wonderful tool also, if the energy of this false memory comes from a strong, un-dissoluted female Oedipus complex. One can ask: How can such a fixed energy most easily be dissoluted? What is the most direct route? Basically the female Oedipus complex is the girl's sexual energy directed towards her father and because of the taboo of incest denied and repressed. So the most direct route is to visualise the intercourse with the father in order to free the energy. But we all know that the superego, because of the incest taboo, will not allow such a fantasy. But if this enters as an unconscious, implanted memory of sexual abuse or rape, this problem is solved. Now the problem is how to own and integrate such a forbidden gestalt. If the therapist and the patient simply allows this to be explored in a non-judging atmosphere, the emotional charge will little by little be taken out of the gestalt and set free to be used by the woman in her adult relationships.

Interestingly, the mention of the Oedipus complex as a possible real intercourse with the father is taking much of the sexual charge our of the transference-countertransference dynamic, making this a much faster route to sexual healing and re-sexualisation of the woman, than the traditional psychoanalytic method of addressing everything as transference.

We even suggest that some women is unable to process and heal all the way to mature genital sexuality, if their Oedipus complex is not treated like it was caused as an actual, sexual trauma.

This is most definitely the case, when the patient actually was sexually traumatised, for without the full integration of the trauma there will be no complete healing.

This is also the case when the Oedipus complex is caused by symbolic abuse, i.e. where a father psychologically has substituted a mother with a daughter, which is quite normal, i.e. when the mother dies, is divorced from the father, or just leaves the home for a longer period of time.

Eight causes of implanted memory

We have discussed the causes of implanted memories above; here we give a little more detail. The eight most common causes of implanted memories are (8):

- Satisfying own expectancies: If the patient expects that she had been abused sexually i.e. because a sister was, she can implant more or less vague memories of incest herself.
- Pleasing the therapist: The patient wants to please or be in accordance with the therapist and is therefore accepting his view or what she believes or imagine is his view. This is enhanced if the therapist shares his interpretations and give the patient leads (i.e. questions that are not neutral, but biased in some direction). Even more so, if the therapist is making judgments on what happened instead of waiting until the patient finds out for herself.
- Transferences and counter transferences: If the patient develops sexual feelings towards the therapist and if these are ignored by the therapist, or if the patient senses that the therapist will not accept them, this can enhance sexual fantasies, which eventually can take the form of an implanted memory. Old sexual fantasies can also be boosted by this unconscious wish of the patient, and even real events can be distorted, reinterpreted and now filled with the sexual feelings that the patient cannot allow to emerge in the personal relationship with the therapist.
- As source of mental and emotional order: A third source of implanted memories has nothing to do with the therapy in itself. The patient needs to get a kind of order in the chaos of emotions and symptoms, and having a simple explanation can be a relief instead of living with chaos and mystery.
- As emotional defense. Sometimes the recovered, but false memory is hiding another event that is much more painful. This could be that her father left her and her mother, when she was a child. This may be much more difficult to integrate than sexual abuse. If the patient is desperately angry with her father and cannot confront the event causing the anger, an implanted event can be a solution. It could also be neglect that is the problem; it seems that neglecting the bodily presence and sexual character of a girl can be as destructive to her self-esteem and psychosexual development as actual physical or sexual abuse.
- As symbol. Often, the parents have been abusing the child in subtle and psychological ways, (i.e. not respecting the child's sexual borders, or having used the child as a sexual partner, which is most often seen when a parent lives alone with a child of the opposite sex). This does not mean that there was a sexual act of objective, physical, incest like coitus, but what we could call the "symbolic incest" or "energetic incest" is often extremely painful and very harmful to a child on an

emotional level. "Energetic" incest happens typically when her father being the only parent raises a girl (or when a mother raises her son alone), and the two of them "pair up" as man and woman making wholeness emotionally and energetically comparable to the wholeness of a sexual couple, but without the sexual acting out. A lot of sexual energies are accumulated and circulated here, and the girl is often, as Freud pointed out, having secret sexual dreams about her father with lots of shame and guilt. An implanted memory that carries all the shame and energy of a real incestuous trauma, but where intense therapy do not reveal any recorded "movie" of the event(s), might very well come from "energetic incest".

- Implanted philosophy. When a patient learns that problems often are caused by traumas, she often starts speculating which traumas could have caused which problems. Sexual problems can then lead to dreams about sexual dominance/abuse/perversions and dreams, which can be interpreted as memories. Freud taught us that the child's sexuality is polymorphously" perverted, meaning that all kinds of sexuality is present at least potentially with the little child. In dreams, according to Freud, consciousness often goes back to the earlier stages of development, potentially leading to all kinds of sexual dreams and fantasies.

- Implanted memories function as the patient's subconscious tool for sexual healing. When a patient has a very strong Oedipus complex and not willing to take this to transference and prefer to handle it psychologically as an internal affair, this will materialize as a visualization of intercourse with the opposite-sexed parent. This as the incest-taboo will make it impossible to accept the fantasy in present time and therefore it will materialize as a false memory of physical sexual abuse. Only if this memory is acknowledged and taken seriously, the Oedipus complex will dissolute; in this process the patient will realize the true nature and mission of the "implanted memory".

Different opinions of freud

It is worthwhile to give the word to Freud himself, who wrote: "In the period in which the main interest was directed to discovering infantile sexual traumas, almost all my female patients told me that they had been seduced by their father. I was driven to recognize in the end that these reports were untrue and so came to understand that hysterical symptoms are derived from phantasies and not from real occurrences. It was only later that I was able to recognize in the phantasy of being seduced by the father the expression of the typical Oedipus complex in woman" (6).

Anna Freud reflects on this passage as follows: "In his early discussion of the etiology of hysteria Freud often mentioned seduction by adults as among its commonest causes. But nowhere in these early publications did he specifically inculpate the girl's father. Indeed, in some additional footnotes written in 1924 for the Gesammelte Schriften reprint of Studies on Hysteria he admitted to having on two occasions suppressed the fact of the father's responsibility" (6:419).

Conclusions

Where does this take us? To the practical position, where we are willing to do what it takes to cure our patient. Every therapist should know that a patient's memories are not accurate, and in the start of therapy the "memories" are much more like guessing or diffuse interpretations than visual and tactile accurate recallings.

There should be plenty of room in the therapy to allow the patients all kinds of "memories", fantasies, ideas and mental and emotional experiments. The therapist should keep the patient safe by securing that she is not sharing her ideas with her parents etc, as long at the therapy is not completed and her Oedipus complex not dissoluted.

If the "implanted memory" or more correctly put "visually false but emotionally correct memory" is taken as a powerful therapeutic tool instead of something that should be avoided at any prize, the patients will heal and become sexually mature at a much higher speed and success rate, than if the therapist and patient is avoiding the core issue from fear of the possibility of making an implant. In the end of the therapy the patient will know exactly what happened.

The art of therapy is to keep the patient on the right track of facing all resistance and difficult emotions, following her all the way though the dark night of the repressed and unconscious, and into the dawn of the bright day of mature sexuality, unconditional love, and mental and existential freedom.

References

[1] Bohleber W. Remembrance trauma and collective memory. Int J Psychoanal 2007;88:329–52.
[2] Fonagy P. Memory and therapeutic action. Int J Psychoanal 1999;80:215-23.
[3] Good MI. On: Julie's museum: The evolution of thinking, dreaming and historicization in the treatment of traumatized patients [Letter]. Int J Psychoanal 2007;88:769–71.
[4] Withers R. Further thoughts on: Julie's museum: The evolution of thinking, dreaming and historicization in the treatment of traumatized patients. Int J Psychoanal 2007;88(6):1551.
[5] Freud S. The dissolution of the Oedipus Complex. In: Freud A. The essential of psychoanalysis. London: Penguin Books, 1986. (Original 1924).
[6] Freud S. New introductory lectures on psycho-analysis. Lecture 33: Femininity. In: Freud A. The essential of psychoanalysis. London: Penguin Books, 1986:412-32. (Original 1933).
[7] Reich W. [Die Function des Orgasmus.] Köln: Kiepenheuer Witsch, 1969. [German].
[8] Ventegodt S, Kandel I, Merrick J. Clinical holistic medicine: how to recover memory without "implanting" memories in your patient. ScientificWorldJournal 2007;7:1579-89.

Chapter 32

The use of Hippocrates' healing principle of similarity

Hippocrates induced healing (salutogenesis) with the "principle of similarity" - like cures like, or in the classical latin expression from homeopathy: *Similia Similibus Currentur*. The similarity principle has been used as the major therapeutic principle in the modern holistic medicine and psychiatry. One radical style of holistic mind-body medicine has been developed by the late Swedish physician Bengt Stern. This type of therapy that make use of dramatic, sexological elements has recently been found highly efficient in improving quality of life and normalizing sense of coherence, also in mentally ill patients (estimated NNT=2), without any side effects or adverse events.

Stern's therapy mimics the most difficult events in life during role-plays. His unique therapeutic program, "Meet yourself", takes the participant though the most difficult aspects of life, including birth, death, and neurotic and evil human interactions, also of violent and sexual nature. About 4,000 patients have now been trough the "fascist exercise" without getting side effects or adverse events (NNH>4,000). This exercise includes the methods of controlled sexual and psychological abuse (level 8 in tools of clinical holistic medicine).

Since Freud it has been known that to rehabilitate a patient's mental health the healing of the patient's sexuality is particularly important. In his therapy Stern has done what Freud could not do for moral reasons hundred years ago: Making the full, painful drama of early life happen again for patients to heal not only their physical, mental disorders and sexual dysfunctions, but their whole life and existence.

The therapeutic program of Bengt Stern is evaluated in this chapter and found to be ethical and in accordance with the healing principles and traditions of holistic medicine, in spite of its use of explicit sexual elements that outside the therapeutic sessions often are believed to be harmful. The use of such elements in the therapy has ever since Hippocrates been the essense of using similarity for healing. Most of the known healing principles of CAM are used in this therapy.

Stern's "Meet yourself" course is an effective, nonpharmaceutical medicine that does not cause any harm as it has been found to be without side effects or adverse events.

Introduction

The principle of "the same cures the same" was made famous by Christian Friedrich Samuel Hahnemann (1755-1843), who wanted to find more elegant solutions to the rather painful, traditional Hippocratic cure of exposing patients to the same violation that originally made them ill (1). Hippocrates and his students did practically not use drugs for medicine (2). Instead they rehabilitated the patients character by supporting self-exploration—a strategy called "clinical medicine" (3). What needed exploration were all the episodes and events from the patient's life that was painful, and problematic—traumatic and repressed—in modern psychodynamic language.

Hahnemann's intent was impeccable. If a woman had been raped, we all know how painful it is for her to go back to relive the trauma in therapy to integrate the unbearable feelings of the violation. If a person had been abused or neglected as a vulnerable, little child, we all know how troublesome therapy is when taking the patient back to this painful event. If this could be solved in a more elegant way, this would be extremely valuable.

Homeopathy has been very successful, and today about 10% of all treatments in the world done by a physician are done with homeopathy. Most unfortunately homeopathy has not been very effective, at least according to much recent research. Therefore, therapy has not been able to move away from the strategy of directly confronting patients with the content of their traumas. This can be done in many therapeutic ways.

Some types of therapy only works through the mind, others only though the body, others only trough the mind, while still other systems combine conversation and touch therapy, and still others intervene holistically on all aspects of man at the same time. The latter is called holistic medicine. It exist today as many non-scientific systems i.e. the shamanistic healing ceremonies known from almost all premodern cultures. It is also developed into medical science as in clinical holistic medicine.

There are different styles of clinical holistic medicine: Holistic body psychotherapy (England, Germany) (4-8), holistic mind body medicine (Sweden) (9-13) and the Nordic School of Clinical Holistic Medicine (Denmark) (14-16). The most intensive of these are undoubtedly the Swedish system, which works very directly on healing physical and sexual abuse and violation by use of the similarity principles.

How unpleasant this therapy might be felt by the participants, it is known to be absolutely safe, without any significant side effects or adverse events (8,9,13,17). The physical intensity of this therapy is well reflected in the fact that one participant in 1,000 broke a rib (13).

Bengt stern's therapy

Bengt Stern, MD (1938-2002) was a physician who believed strongly in non-drug medicine. He built his holistic therapy on the most efficient and intense non-drug techniques he could find or invent himself (9). He used the Reichian herapeutic principle of working against the resistance.

Stern's therapy was about "raising the patient's consciousness". According to his book "Feeling bad is a good start" (9) his therapy combines a number of highly provocative and intense techniques:

Body-psycho-therapy, psychodrama, gestalt therapy, transactional analysis, and Janov's primal therapy. Holotropic breath work of the Stanislav Grof type is also used, to make his therapy among the most intensive non-drug therapies in use today. The techniques he included are efficient, because "they activate painful emotional memories. In processing these memories, one understands the effect these experiences have had on one's adult life. Sometimes you re-experience very clearly, and in detail, painful emotional memories from early childhood."

Stern wrote about his body psychotherapy:

"Body-psychotherapy is not psychotherapy in its usual sense, but rather a technique to contact pre-intellectual emotional memories, so called cell memories. Body-psychotherapy is the conscious activation of these cell memories in your body. In its practical application body-psychotherapy consists of hundreds of different breath exercises, body movements, massage techniques, etc. The pioneer of body-psychotherapy was Wilhelm Reich (1897-1957). Other prominent figures within this science are Alexander Lowen, John C Pierrakos, Charles Kelley and David Boadella."

Bengt Stern was interested in all major aspects of life, especially the three aspects he found most difficult and traumatizing: birth, human interaction and death. To help the participants in his therapeutic course "Meet yourself", he made everyone go through three most intense exercises, which he labeled the "birth excise", the "fascist exercise", and the "death exercise" (9). In all three exercises, he used psychodrama, role-play, and imagination to mimic the emotional reactions in every little detail of a painful and difficult birth, sexual and non-sexual abuse, violation and repression in human interactions, and the transformative crises of the psychological death process—often called "metamor-phosis" (18-21).

The text below is Bengt Sterns own description of his most central and famous "fascist exercise" from his book (9). Around 1985, when his book appeared in the first edition, a great number of people had already participated in it, and most fortunately this exercise proved to have no side effects of adverse events associated with it, as Bengt Stern stated in his book:

The "fascist" exercise in the "meet yourself process"
An essential exercise, a kind of psychodrama, is part of the first step. This exercise has the nickname "the "fascist" exercise". The aim is for the participants to become aware of their fascistic shadow. That is the part which people unconsciously allow to leak out on their daily life. When participants become aware of their fascistic tendencies, these tendencies lose their destructive energy. So these tendencies will, to a great extent, start disappearing.
Just as with other intense exercise in the Meet Yourself Process, this exercise is explained in detail beforehand. No participant is told they must participate in this exercise. Rather, every participant will have to express a wish to take part. Some of them might be advised by the course-leader not to participate in this particular exercise.
In the exercise, participants, working in couples, suppress each other within a given framework. They are, of course, nor allowed to hurt each other physically, but within the given framework they are encouraged to participate totally. In the role of oppressor they are to use all their creativity to offend their partner. In the role as victim they use all their creativity to enter the role of being totally invaded. This exercise lasts for about thirty minutes before the partners change roles.

Participants react in a variety of ways. Many participants totally enter both roles. Some are quite capable of handling the role of the oppressed but have difficulties being the oppressor, or vice versa. Occasionally, participants are psychologically paralyzed, mostly in the role as the oppressor, but sometimes even in the role of oppressed.

If participants do become paralyzed they will receive an individual emotional release session with one of the course-leaders. It is then evident that the psychological paralysis is their way of avoiding contact with the memory of the mental, and often physical, violence to which they were subjected by one of their parents early in life.

In such a session the participant has an opportunity to express his pain and rage, because of the violence. The opportunity to complete this exercise through such a session is a great relief for the participant.

After this exercise, the couples share their experience with each other – i.e. how they are now able to identify their oppressive role and their victim role in their everyday life.

This is followed by an exercise of emotional expression in which the participants liberate them-selves from all the preintellectual pain that has been activated during the exercise.

About two thousand people have been through the "fascist" exercise. They consider this exercise one of the most essential of the course. Although it is demanding, nobody regrets having participated in it. Those who wholly participate in this exercise stand a great chance of avoiding being suppressive or of allowing suppression in the future.

Case reports

After the documentation of the efficacy of Bengt Stern's therapy, it has been taken into use in all the Nordic countries. In Denmark the "fascist exercise" is used especially for the training of therapists that works with traumas from violent and sexual abuse, i.e. incest. One training center that uses it is the Nordic School of Holistic Medicine in Copenhagen. The following are descriptions of how two participants experienced this exercise:

Training session, female holistic body psycho-therapist, 28 years old. For many years I had vulvodynia with strong daily genital pains and not being able to have intercourse. I had the condition for 15 years and I had been to a large number of experts, physicians, gynecologists, sexologists and complementary therapists and used a lot of money on these treatments, but with almost no results. I had finally given up. As part of my training as therapist I finally encountered the gestalts that had caused my gynecological problems. This happened in the "fascist exercise". In this exercise it was not difficult for me being the oppressor. I was together with a man around 40 years and I humiliated him totally, but this did very little to me. I just felt like he deserved it. When it was my turn to be the "slave" this was something totally different. I felt from the beginning the most intense anxiety. Just meeting him and seeing him standing there in front of me, sensing his scary, dominating, male, aggressive energy was quite impossible for me to cope with. So the exercise hardly started before I broke down and regressed into an ocean of the old emotions of shame and being abused. The idea that I had to obey him in spite of his intention to abuse me was totally intolerable for me. Without him doing or saying much I felt so abused, so violated. I just had to obey. It was like being buried in an avalanche of shame and humiliation. What really got to me was the idea of not being able to have my own opinion. It was like my will was broken at its very root.

He started calling me names and humiliating me. He did not touch me, but that didn't matter. If he had raped me this could not have been much worse. I felt like dying. At the same time I was completely aware that this was an exercise and that I just stood and confronted a normal, rather good looking, intelligent and empathic man, who actually had been kind to me just an hour ago. In the normal world I liked him. But in this exercise he was the devil himself. I was not in present time. I was with my parents a long time ago when I was a little child.

The next thing I was asked to do was to dress naked and lie on the floor in front of him. I did it, but I felt like dying every second. He told me I was the most ugly girl he had ever seen and that I had a clammy body. He yielded at me and told me in the meanest way that I was just a pussy. He then ordered me to show him my vulva. This did it for me; it was like an old cinema movie that suddenly broke. I just disappeared. I found myself in the position typically held by embryos, and felt like vomiting. I felt really sick. After this I was done. And I was through. I felt such an immense relief. Lying there on the floor I realized that this was what had been repressed and what caused my vulvodynia. It was like a huge matrix of negative emotions, thought and beliefs that came from adapting to my sexually rather dysfunctional parents, when I was very small. I felt it like hell at that time. I was not physically abused, but energetically I had been violated again and again. The feelings could not have been worse. They were really unbearable. No wonder I did not have access to them in my normal therapy. The degree of resistance I had made for myself made it necessary for me to get through to myself only in the course of the "fascist exercise".

The exercise released the most intense bodily emotions and already the next day I felt much better. Since then my vulvodynia has been gone. Sometimes I still have pain during intercourse, but my daily genital pains have disappeared. I feel much more proud of my body (and my genitals) and my self-esteem has improved radically. I was scared of getting men's attention, but this has also changed. Today I can perform for a crowd with a relaxed attitude. When men say something humiliating to me, as they sometimes do, I don't care much. It is like it doesn't get to me anymore. When somebody tells me that I look bad, I simply cannot believe it. My whole experience of myself as woman has improved immensely thanks to this exercise. What from the outside looked like I was being tortured was experienced from the inside the most healing event.

Training session, male holistic body psycho-therapist, 42 years old.
The most intense exercise for me was the "fascist exercise", where you work with a partner; normally the couples consist of a man and a woman. The idea is that a person of the opposite gender has repressed everybody earlier in life and because of this there has been a sexual element in the repression. Often there has been more than that – a direct violation, physical, mental or sexual. In this exercise the participants are allowed to work with all these painful aspects of unequal human interaction. The instructor told us that he would not guide our experience – we could go where we needed to go in this exercise – but for him, it had been about sexuality, from beginning to end. In this way, everybody who needed to work on their sexuality – and I think we all did – got acceptance to go into this most difficult and painful space of sexual trauma, to heal whatever wound we would have here.

In the exercise the person who feel most violated, start by "getting even" by violating the partner. All energy from old traumas are used, the preparation takes everybody deeply into the feeling of being hurt and wanting go get revenge by repressing the person that hurt you – by proxy, using the partner in the exercise.

The beauty of the exercise is that it really is cooperation, where you mutually allow yourself and your partner to go into the sexually wounded space and express all you anger, grief, fear etc. In the role of the oppressor you do to the other what originally, traumatically, was done to your self. In real life you are never allowed to go into this "evil" space; the strong sexual taboo of our culture also makes this absolutely impossible. But in this exercise you go there together with your partner, who also wants to heal and even more importantly, also wants to help you heal, by giving you the opportunity to express the most dark and dirty sides of your own shadow, and to re-experience being violated and abused. In the exercise this happens in a useful way that helped me to integrate my past and to learn that I today am a strong adult that in reality cannot be so deeply hurt any more. What harmed us happened to us, when we were vulnerable kids, which could not withstand the hard pressure of our parents. Today we are not vulnerable kids any more.

First one is "fascist" and the other is a "slave" for 30 minutes, and after that the partners shift roles. So all the humiliations you just got from the other are given back right away. What a wise and wonderfully balanced design of this exercise!

There are some rules in the exercise: You must promise confidentiality; you are not allowed to touch the other person; you are not allowed to put bodily fluids (spit, sweat etc) on the other person and you most stay in the exercise for the 60 minutes it takes, if you accept to participate. You are supposed to cooperate and help the other person repress and humiliate you by revealing your sore spots and suggesting things that could be done to you that you would feel awful. As people come for healing, everybody engaged surprisingly willingly in this. When you are a "slave" you are supposed to obey your "master". But you are allowed not to, if what you are asked is too difficult.

Now the idea of the exercise is that the "fascist" uses his or her imagination to abuse and exploit the "slave". This can be done by asking the "slave" to undress, take humiliating positions and say horrible things about him or herself... The "fascist" may scold the "slave", ridicule etc. The art is to find out how to "break down" the partner, as this break is exactly the historical break the partner needs to confront and heal. So the whole exercise is nothing, but support to go back into the core trauma of life, regarding the body, sexuality, self-worth etc. You are allowed to break down and just lie on the floor, crying or whatever you are doing, feeling the old painful emotions again. You are not allowed to leave the room during the exercise. During the whole exercise there is a physician present to ensure that no person is getting "repressed" more that necessary for the healing to happen. The therapists will also moderate the participant's behavior – tell the "fascist" to go slower, or faster, and the "slave" to let go of fear and engage more fully in the exercise.

I was given a partner by the therapists, a woman about 30 years old and judged from her behavior in the exercise with a personal history of sexual traumati-zation. I was worried that she would be harmed by this exercise, so I talked to the therapists about my great concern for her future well-being, but they all ensured me that the exercise was harmless, if done correctly. I had heard that this kind of therapy could cause re-traumatization – giving a new similar trauma on top of the old one – but the therapists ensured me that this never had happened in this kind of therapy {which is in accordance with (8,9,13,17)}.

Finally we engaged in the exercises and the things she got me to do gave me a feeling of shame so badly that I felt I should die. I was exactly like a little boy that was ridiculed and humiliated by his mother, who hated men and sex. I had no recalling of my mother doing this to me, but as the exercise went on I felt more and more that I had been harmed by my mothers energy and her sex-negative attitude, that had colored my relation to my own body and sexuality. It was a deeply healing experience, in spite of it being ugly.

When it was my turn, I asked her to undress and show herself to me. She had extreme resistance and finally she broke down and cried as a little child. The most difficult thing was that I liked it! I had never seen myself as a sexual sadist, but I realized that I contained so much hatred and anger toward the woman (= my mother). I was very surprised of all the repressed sexuality this exercise released for both of us. It was a small miracle and Bengt Stern was right. Confronting this was not yet another trauma on top of the other. The principle of similarity took us straight back to some of the most difficult and most efficiently repressed feelings and events in our lives. The exercise did not turn me into a sexual sadist, but it made me own my sexual aggression, which had been repressed since early child-hood. I felt that I finally became a man. It was wonderful. My partner revealed she had a similar experience, and that she finally dared to be sexual again.

I was obviously one of the participants that became paralyzed from the exercise and was therefore offered a special session (as described above), which I accepted. This was a session with three female therapists at one time. The three women intended to help me free my life energy and sexuality further. They did this by tempting me with their bodies, moving sexually around me, inviting my interest in them, flirting and revealing parts of breasts, stomach and other intimate parts of their bodies and whenever I revealed the slightest interest they scolded and humiliated me for being a pig, a horny, dirty man, totally worthless and good for nothing, a pervert and a real lowlife scumbag. The double action of tempting and humiliating me took me into the most difficult feelings of male repression by dominant women, like being castrated – the "vagina dentata" from Freud's writings. It was really amazing what it did to me to confront the most evil aspects of the feminine – it was like dancing with the good Kali from Indian mythology. The energy was totally wild and animalistic. Little by little I came to peace with the shadow of the female.

Not so long time after this exercise I was able to take a big step forward in my own relationship and surrender to my own woman. I finally was able to choose her as my partner for life. The exercise had helped me confront the most dark side of my "own inner woman" and finally taught me to let go of my fear and bond devotedly to my own women. I also felt like being a much better therapist after this. I found new trust in the female and I dared to help women who had been raped or sexually violated in their childhood in a much more open and intimate way. I got better results and much better feedback from the female victims of sexual abuse and incest that I had in therapy. I realized that sexual torture, the most harmful kind of torture there is, is damaging because it repeats the child's reality, where the victim must adapt him- or herself to the reality of the offenders – similarly to the child's need to adapt to its parents reality for survival. As adult human beings we do not need to adapt in this way, hence we are not vulnerable.

Elements of bengt stern's holistic philosophy

One very important aspect of Stern's therapy is forgiveness (9):

"In forgiveness, man moves beyond his intellect and explores his greatest vulnerability. He encounters the pain of his unprocessed emotional memories. Only by stopping and encountering this pain may it be released and allowed to disappear.

Clearly, forgiveness is not a superficial, intellectual process, but an energy release at one's very depth."

Another aspect is that sexuality is the basic energy in life. Our culture strongly represses, which leads to prostitution, pornography, child abuse and incest. On the latter subject Bengt wrote:

"Incest: The reason behind incest is suppressed sexuality. A culture, which is dominated by feelings of guilt, because of sexuality and/or intercourse before marriage, encourages early marriages. Before marriage neither the woman nor the man is allowed to have intercourse. As their marriage continues the two partners might find that they are not compatible, although they now have children and refrain from having sex with each other. In the vacuum that then arises, a father who suffers from perverted sexuality may approach his daughter and a mother who suffers from perverted sexuality may approach her son. Both parents are always responsible for the incestuous act by not taking responsibility for having a mature and satisfying sexual life with other or with new partners."

Stern was a strong believer in self-insight as the primary outcome of psychotherapy:

"The role of psychotherapy: Profound self-insight is knowing oneself beyond the intellect and contacting one's wholeness. Self-insight then increases and brings about the understanding and practicing of an existential view of humanity and the world. Through profound self-insight people can find the existential answer as to why they are feeling bad. Once that is understood the leap toward well-being is not far away. However, profound self-insight is not limited to treating mental problems. Even many physical problems, often irrespective to the degree of difficulty they cause, improve dramatically when man understands the reasons behind the problems. Above all, when people come to know themselves, their quality of life increase in every respect."

Discussion

The principle of similarity has been used to an extreme degree in Bengt Stern's holistic mind-body medicine, which is why is has been so effective in inducing salutogenesis (22,23). Recent analysis of the effects of Bengt Stern's therapy has proven it highly efficient with people who have the most severe mental and existential problems including suicidal patients (8,9,13,17).

Not only the principle of similarity is taken into use in this therapy; all five healing principles of holistic medicine are used (8) and this is done impeccable, without any of the medical errors it is easy to make in this kind of therapy (24). This is making the therapy highly effective with NNT-2 for improving of quality of life and sense of coherence estimated from the non-dichotomous data in (2-4).

There might potentially be an ethical problem in making the participants engage in repressing, abusing and violating each other, but it is important to understand that all participants as described by Stern above was fully informed about the purpose of the exercise, how it would be practiced and what the expected benefits were for the participants, based on experience with at least 4,000 participants who had been through the therapy during the 24 years, since it was invented by Bengt Stern (13).

All participants are free not to participate in an exercise if they do not feel up to it or do not see how this exercise could help them. Therefore everything is happening with consent after full information. The purpose of it is clear and everybody who is participating is doing this to help him or herself and the partner in the exercises.

Having a physician present to exclude patients that are not likely to benefit from the therapy is an extra precaution that we do not believe is necessary anymore based on the complete lack of side effects and negative events with the fascist exercise. We know of no cases where the physician prohibited a patient from participating.

We have evaluated the therapy according the Ethical Rules for International Society for Holistic Health and found all the exercises in Bengt Stern's "Meet Yourself" course to be in accordance with the ethical standards of holistic medicine (25). Controlled sexual and violent abuse and repression are well known tools of holistic medicine (categorized as "level 8 tools" in (26)). They have been used since Hippocrates and cause no side effects or adverse events if used correctly (1,3,9,13,17). They are especially useful in the training of therapists that work with healing traumas of incest, violent, sexual or mental abuse, repression and violation.

The principle of similarity, which has been known since Hippocrates, has been cultivated into its purest form in Bengt Stern's therapy. Because of the courage of Bengt Stern to mimic the most difficult events in life in role-plays in his therapy, he has created a unique therapeutic program that in one single process takes the participant though all the most difficult aspects of life, including birth, death, and neurotic and evil human interactions, also of violent and sexual nature. People who would judge this kind of therapy as bad and unethical are the people who haven't understood the basic rules of holistic non-drug therapy.

Bengt Stern's "Meet yourself" course is candidate to be among the most effective types of holistic mind-body medicine in use to day, thanks to his thorough understanding of the principle of similarity and consequently his inclusion of controlled sexual and violent abuse into the therapeutic program. Since Freud it has been known that to rehabilitate a patient's health the healing of the patient's sexuality is particularly important.

Stern did what Freud could not for moral reasons do hundred years ago: Making the full, painful drama of early life happen again for the patients with physical and mental disorders and sexual dysfunctions, who need to confront the most intense and difficult of traumas to heal life and existence. The program is evaluated and found to be ethical and in accordance with the traditions of holistic medicine.

Stern's "Meet yourself" course is an effective non-pharmaceutical medicine for all types of patients including the mentally ill, with radical, sexological elements that do not cause any harm, neither side effects nor adverse events (estimated NNT=2 for the outcome "quality of life improved" and NNH>4,000 for significant side effects).

References

[1] Hahnemann S. Organon of the medical art. Redmond, WA: Birdcage Book, 1996.

[2] Jones WHS. Hippocrates. Vol. I–IV. London: William Heinemann, 1923-1931.

[3] Ventegodt S, Andersen NJ, Kandel I, Merrick J. Clinical medicine and psychodynamic psycho-therapy. Evaluation of the patient before inter-vention. J Altern Med Res 2009;1(3). [in press].

[4]   Boyesen G. Collected papers of biodynamic psychology. London: Biodynamic Publ, 1980.

[5]   Boyesen G. Uber den Korper die Seele Heilen. Munich: Kosel Verlag, 1987. [German].

[6]   Boyesen G. Biodynamik Des Lebens. Essen: Synthesis, 1987. [German].

[7]   Boyesen G. Von der Lust am Heilen. Quintessenz meines Lebens. Munich: Kosel Verlag, 1995. [German].

[8]   Allmer C, Ventegodt S, Kandel I, Merrick J. Positive effects, side effects and adverse events of clinical holistic medicine. A review of Gerda Boyesen's nonpharmaceutical mind-body medicine (biodynamic body-psychotherapy) at two centres in United Kingdom and Germany. Int J Adolesc Med Health 2009;21(3), in press.

[9]   Stern B. Feeling bad is a good start. San Diego: ProMotion Publ, 1996.

[10] Fernros L, Furhoff AK, Wändell PE. Quality of life of participants in a mind-body-based self-development course: a descriptive study. Qual Life Res 2005;14(2):521-8.

[11] Fernros L, Furhoff AK, Wändell PE. Improving quality of life using compound mind-body therapies: evaluation of a course intervention with body movement and breath therapy, guided imagery, chakra experiencing and mindfulness meditation. Qual Life Res 2008;17(3):367-76.

[12] Fernros, L. Improving quality of life with body-mind therapies. The evaluation of a course intervention for personal self-awareness and development. Dissertation. Stockholm: Karolinska Institutet, 2009. Accessed 01 Mar 2009. Available at: http://diss.kib.ki.se/2009/978-91-7409-356-8.

[13] Ventegodt S, Kandel I, Merrick J. Positive effects, side effects and negative events of intensive, clinical, holistic therapy. A review of the program "meet yourself" characterized by intensive body-psychotherapy combined with mindfulness meditation at Mullingstorp in Sweden. J Altern Med Res 2009;1(3), in press.

[14] Ventegodt S, Kandel I, Merrick J. Principles of holistic medicine. Philosophy behind quality of life. Victoria, BC: Trafford, 2005.

[15] Ventegodt S, Kandel I, Merrick J. Principles of holistic medicine. Quality of life and health. New York: Hippocrates Sci Publ, 2005.

[16] Ventegodt S, Kandel I, Merrick J. Principles of holistic medicine. Global quality of life. Theory, research and methodology. New York: Hippocrates Sci Publ, 2005.

[17] Ventegodt S, Merrick J. Side effects and adverse events of non-drug medicine (nonpharmacological CAM). J Complement Integr Med, in press.

[18] Ventegodt S, Hermansen TD, Flensborg-Madsen T, Nielsen ML, Merrick J. Human development VIII: A theory of "deep" quantum chemistry and cell consciousness: Quantum chemistry controls genes and biochemistry to give cells and higher organisms consciousness and complex behavior. ScientificWorldJournal 2006;6:1441-53.

[19] Ventegodt S, Hermansen TD, Flensborg-Madsen T, Rald E, Nielsen ML, Merrick J. Human development IX: A model of the wholeness of man, his consciousness and collective consciousness. ScientificWorldJournal 2006;6:1454-9.

[20] Hermansen TD, Ventegodt S, Merrick J. Human development X: Explanation of macroevolution —top-down evolution materializes consciousness. The origin of metamorphosis. ScientificWorld Journal 2006;6:1656-66.

[21] Hermansen TD, Ventegodt S, Kandel I. Human development XI: the structure of the cerebral cortex. Are there really modules in the brain? ScientificWorldJournal 2007;7:1922-9.

[22] Antonovsky A. Health, stress and coping. London: Jossey-Bass, 1985.

[23] Antonovsky A. Unravelling the mystery of health. How people manage stress and stay well. San Francisco: Jossey-Bass, 1987.

[24] Ventegodt S, Andersen NJ, Kandel I, Merrick J. Formal errors in nonpharmaceutical medicine (CAM): Clinical medicine, mind-body medicine, body-psychotherapy, holistic medicine, clinical holistic medicine and sexology. Int J Adolesc Med Health 2009;21(2), in press.

[25] de Vibe M, Bell E, Merrick J, Omar HA, Ventegodt S. Ethics and holistic healthcare practice. Int J Child Health Human Dev 2008;1(1):23-8.

[26] Ventegodt S, Clausen B, Nielsen ML, Merrick J. Advanced tools for holistic medicine. ScientificWorldJournal 2006;6:2048-65.

Section 8. Holistic treatment of mental disease

In this section we follow the classical route of psychodynamic therapy inducing accelerated psychosexual development of the mentally ill patient (1). The sexual nature of the disturbance causing the mental symptoms is becoming clearer and we are now able to understand and treat personality disorder, illnesses of the schizophrenic spectrum and eating disorders.

Body, mind, spirit and heart are all bound together by an internal flow of sexual energy; if this energy is disturbed severe mental symptoms are seen. The problem of this model is that it is rather philosophical and not easy to test empirically; the results of the treatment on the other hand are easy to measure.

So the qualitative dimension, the subjective experience of the disturbed existence, are becoming more and more important the deeper we go in the mental disorders. To treat schizophrenia the holistic physician needs a thorough self-insight that allows for the recognition and understanding of the abnormal psychic structures in the patient. A strong intuition will guide the healer to help the patient identify and confront the original traumas that created the mental splitting or other pathological pattern of mind and spirit.

If you have read the previous sections, and if you have been treating your first patient like we recommended you do in section one, you will most likely instinctively know what we are writing about here. If not you will need to find your first patient to treat with holistic medicine now. You will not be able to learn to heal without practical experience and reflection on your own failure to help and cure. Holistic medicine is not a theoretical thing but a highly practical thing. You need to practice. Please start today. We recommend that you re-read our advice regarding this in the introduction to section one.

Your first patient should not be very difficult. Your first patient should help you understand the principles of holistic medicine and make you feel confident and successful. But if you have a heart for a very ill and dependent patient, you can as well start here. Just know that the more ill he or she is the more he or she will depend on you for being cured, and the less you will be able to withdraw from the treatment before it is done, which can take several years.

It is a responsibility. Do not take it too easy. You will be responsible for this fragile life. It is very similar to getting a baby. You will be responsible until the baby is grown up and ready to life on its own. Do not engage in treating anybody before you are ready to carry this responsibility on your shoulder. But then again, you should also realize that nobody is likely to help the person if you are not helping. Therefore, even if you fail, the patient is not likely to be worse of that he or she is today. So forgive yourself if you cannot carry the burden. Do try. You will grow with the challenge.

If you love the patient; if you truly do, do not hesitate to offer your service. You might find out that while you believe that it is you that set your patient free, it is actually the other way round: the patient sets you free. For the biggest gift in this world is not to give, but to receive and allow other people to give their gift to you. The Native Americans always upheld receiving as the highest spiritual discipline. Giving is in that sense for beginners. When you mature, you will be able to truly and egolessly receive the gift of the other.

When you work on healing your patient you will notice that every time a patient is healed you have received a huge gift. Only if you can allow yourself to receive the gift of the patient, your patient can heal. The love that you started has become mutual. Now the patient loves you. Therefore the patient can love again. And being able to love is what life is truly about.

When you finally end the treatment and separate, this love the patient has felt for you is available for another person. By letting go of him or her you have helped your patient to relate intimately to another human being. A new life has started for this person. If love, consciousness, and sexuality has been sufficiently developed the patient will also be cured at this point in time.

References

[1]   Jones WHS. Hippocrates. Vol. I–IV. London: William Heinemann, 1923-1931.

Personality disorders

Scientific holistic medicine has as mentioned its roots in the medicine and tradition of Hippocrates. Modern epidemiological research in quality of life, the emerging science of complementary and alternative medicine (CAM), the tradition of psychodynamic therapy, and the tradition of bodywork are merging into a new scientific way of treating patients. This approach seems able to help every second patient with personality disorders and mental illness in 20 sessions over one year.

To treat personality disorders with holistic medicine the patients are first diagnosed in five dimensions based on the classical Hippocratic description of man: 1) body and sexuality, 2) consciousness and psyche, 3) feelings and emotions, 4) spirituality and ability to love, and 5) an integrative function of the I often called "the heart".

The patient can be normal, mentally ill or have a disturbed personality. The later goes from the mildest degree of low self-esteem, low self-confidence and nymphomania over mild personality disorders (the dependant, nervous/evasive, compulsive) to the borderline patients (the labile, narcissistic, hysteric/histrionic, dyssocial/antisocial, and paranoid, to the schizoid almost schizophrenic patient.

The therapy address the level of psychosexual development; it facilitates development from infantile autoerotic over the immature (oral/anal/clitoral) to the mature, genital state where the patient can engage in mutually satisfactory coitus. The patient's affective and emotional state is developed from blocked over flat to vita. The patients mind are stimulated and developed from an immature to a mature level (on the scale: mature, immature, instable, deluded, deluded-instable, disintegrated).

The patient's spiritual state are also analyzed and old defenses like split and flattening are reversed often during intensive existential crisis where the patient regress to early childhood to heal his or her whole existence (the existential healing Antonovsky called "salutogenesis"). Finally when body, mind and spirit are ready, the heart or "I-Strength" can be recovered. The five-dimensional diagnostic system makes diagnosis and planning of the psychodynamic or holistic therapy easy and open op for a constructive dialog about the goal of therapy with the patient.

Introduction

Around 300 BCE, at the island of Cos in old Greece, the students of the famous physician Hippocrates (460-377BCE) (1) worked to help their patients to step into character, get direction in life, and use their human talents for the benefit of their surrounding world. For all that we know this approach was extremely efficient medicine that helped the patients to recover health, quality of life, and ability, and Hippocrates gained great fame. For more than 2,000 years this was what medicine was about in most of Europe.

On other continents similar medical systems were developed. The medicine wheel of the native Americans, the African Sangoma culture, the Samic Shamans of northern Europe, the healers of the Australian Aboriginals, the ayurvedic doctors of India, the acupuncturists of China, and the herbal doctors of Tibet all seems to be fundamentally character medicine (2-8). All the theories and the medical understanding from these pre-modern cultures are now being integrated in what is called integrative or transcultural medicine. Many of the old medical systems are reappearing in modern time as alternative, complementary and psychosocial medicine. This huge body of theory is now being offered as a European Union Master of Science degree (2-8).

What is happening today?

If you recall our chapter on the history of scientific holistic medicine you can jump over this section. If not, you can keep on reading. We repeat this as we believe it to be important that the practitioner of holistic medicine thoroughly understands its historical roots.

Interestingly, two huge movements of the last century have put this old knowledge into use: psychoanalysis (9) and psychodynamic therapy (10,11) (most importantly STPP)(12,13) going though the mind on one hand, and bodywork (most importantly Reich)(14), Lowen (15) and Rosen (16)) and sexual therapy (especially the tantric tradition)(17) going through the body on the other. A third road, but much less common path has been directly though the spiritual reconnection with the world (18,19).

Our international research collaboration got interested in existential healing from the data coming from epidemiological research at the University Hospital of Copenhagen (Rigshospitalet) starting in 1958-61 at the Research Unit for Prospective Pediatrics and the Copenhagen Perinatal Birth Cohort 1959-61. Almost 20 years ago we were conducting epidemiological research on quality of life, closely examining the connection between global quality of life and health for more than 11.000 people in a series of huge surveys (20) using large and extensive questionnaires, some of them with over 3,000 questions. We found (quite surprisingly) from this huge data base that quality of life, mental and physical health, and ability of social, sexual and working ability seemed to be caused primarily by the consciousness and philosophy of life of the person in question, and only to a small extent by objective factors, like being adopted, coming from a family with only one breadwinner, mother being mentally ill, or one self being financially poor or poorly educated (which are obviously very much socially inherited) (20).

This scientific finding was not expected and so contra-intuitive for us that we were forced to investigate the subject going to the roots of western medicine, or the Hippocratic character of medicine. This meant that we had to look at transcultural and integrative medicine, the emerging science of alternative medicine (scientific CAM theory) and to the very much forgotten traditions of psychosomatic, psychodynamic, and bodily oriented therapies. Around 1994 we received substantial funding for our research project trying to embrace this huge heritage of medical wisdom

Philosophically (21-28), theoretically (29-49), epidemiologically/statistically (50-71). We have since 1997 with a great effort tried to take this knowledge into clinical practice (72-113) and with quite extraordinary results. Clinical holistic medicine has in our Research Clinic for Holistic medicine in Copenhagen helped every second patient with physical, mental, existential or sexual health issues or diseases over one year (114-119). Finally we have been looking at what seems to be the common denominator for all existential healing work in all cultures at all times: the sense of coherence, most clearly expressed by Aaron Antonovsky (1923-1994), a sociologist from the Faculty of Health Sciences at the Ben Gurion University of the Negev in Israel (18,19,120-125). We have also been debating many difficult issues related to modern day medical science, especially in the British Medical Journal (126-139) and finally we are now collecting most of what we consider essential knowledge for the holistic physician in a series of books on the "Principles of holistic medicine" (140-142). What we have learned from this long journey through the grand medical heritage from the different cultures on this planet is that we need to work on body, mind and spirit at the same time (medicine men has always combined talking, touching, and praying), and that being human and truly kind is what really heals the other person. This is what Hippocrates called "the Art" (1), not "the art of medicine" or "the art of right living", but simply "the art" – the way of the human heart, cultivating existence into sheer compassionate behavior and joyful being, which has always been the ultimate goal of all the great healers in our history.

We are more than happy to see our research project in scientific holistic medicine (clinical holistic medicine, CHM) developing. The most paradoxal aspect of this is that while we like to think we are taking medicine forward, we are actually just taking medicine back to its roots. The most important thing is that research and development in this field is made in a dialectic process between qualitative and quantitative research.

What is a personality disorder?

The personality disorders are traditionally placed between the completely mentally healthy state and the most psychotic mentally ill schizophrenic state; historically the personally disorders are collectively characterized by causing unproductive conflicts in the persons inner and outer life. When only the patient himself is tormented by the mental disorder we often use the work "neurosis", i.e. "anxiety neurosis", but almost always anxiety will give the patient an evasive trait - paradoxically creating lots of conflicts around the patient as all the patient's fears one by one materialize - turning the neurosis into a personality disorder. The concept of "neurosis" is therefore well substituted with the concept of personality disorders. All mental illnesses are rooted in psychological defense and therefore also based in personality disorders. The distinction between personality disorders and mental illnesses are therefore also totally artificial. Theoretically there is no reason not to integrate the mental illnesses and the personality disorders, as we have done in our suggested 5-dimensional model of personality disorders (see table 1).

In the psychodynamic literature there seems to be an agreement that the outer conflicts is a materialization of the persons inner conflicts, which are understood as internalized early external conflicts, often going all the way back to the earliest childhood and even the womb. The reason for the internalization is adaptation to the environment and parents to increase the holding and love and thereby optimizing the basic conditions for personal development and survival. Traditionally the personality disorders have been categorized as mild, borderline, and psychotic.

We have developed a five-dimensional model, which we have tested in clinical practice and found that it allows successful healing work with both patients with personality disorders and with mental illnesses (118).

Holistic medicine and biomedicine in treatment of personality disorders

Historically the treatment of personality disorders like hysteria goes all the way back to Hippocrates and the Greek physicians, who used massage of the uterus combined with conversational therapy to heal the sexual disturbances believed to be the primary cause of personality disturbances (1). Holistic medicine that combined conversational therapy with bodywork was the European medicine for more than 2000 years, and Freud started himself as holistic physician giving massage to the hysterical patient's legs (144). Freud left bodywork and initiated the tradition of psychodynamic psychotherapy; he struggled with the problem that contemporary culture was extremely negative towards physical touch and bodily intimacy and he gained great fame from developing a style of therapy that left bodywork behind to focus on the talking. This in spite of the fact that the psychosexual developmental problems were still seen as the primary cause of personality disorders.

During the 20th century psychiatry developed the neurobiological hypothesis for personality disorders and this resulted in mental problems becoming less treated with conversational therapy and more and more often treated with psychopharmacological drugs, often combined with ECT.

Its is difficult to compare the results from the three different ways to treat personality disorders, but it seems that Philippe Pinel (1745-1826) could cure 70% of his patients – presumably a mixture of schizophrenics and borderline patients - with his version of holistic medicine, the "traitement moral" that had a strong focus on philosophical and somatic aspects of the patient around the 1800 (145); psychodynamic psychotherapy with conversational therapy alone could cure around 33% of the patients with personality disorders and schizophrenia from 1900 to 1970 [146-9], while psychopharmacological treatment only have helped a few percent of the patients with personality disorders since 1970 (150) and cured even less.

The reason for the use of psychopharmacological drugs in the treatment of the personality disorders in spite of lack of Cochrane or other studies documenting clinically significant effect is simple: First the belief that mental disorders are caused by chemical disturbances in the brain makes this natural; and secondly an extremely large number of patient can be treated with minimal physician time. The sad fact is that the urbanization, modernization and the shift to a strong focus on natural science and biochemistry in medicine seems to take the healing power out of medicine.

After a decade of treatment experimentation and research into the process of holistic healing we have come up with a theoretical framework that can be used to explain and map all major personality disorders (see table 1) together with the mental diseases (33). We have learned that we are indeed capable of understanding and also curing most of the patients with these disorders and illnesses using the simple tools of clinical holistic medicine (28). Of course one can disagree with the holistic description of man as consisting of body, mind, spirit and heart, and with the idea of the sexual energy as the fundamental life energy of man. Without this perspective the presented theory of personality disorders and the holistic cures will be of little value. On the other hand one can argue that the fine results of the methods derived from this understanding can be taken as an empirical confirmation of the holistic theory of man.

The definition of personality

In holistic medicine the personality is different from the being (34). The entity, or real person, is behind every appearance always intact and can be revitalized just by letting go of all the many layers of existential learning and adaptation that we call personality. The personality is in this sense *neurotic and created for survival and adaptation,* and very different from the person's character (35) and life mission (33,35-40), that is the person's real talents given already at conception intended for *living and growing.* So in this sense a completely healthy person does not have a personality, but is striving to create it for self-realization in order to be able to create value in this world. A mentally healthy person can create conflicts, but these conflicts will always be about maximizing value and taking down hindrances for what is considers good by the individual.

On the other hand will personality disorders always lead to neurotic conflicts that will consume a lot of time and energy and only lead to modest results if any. More often the conflicts will be destructive to the individual in spite of the experience of the conflicts being necessary and for the good of all. A person with severe personality disturbances will always blame the surrounding world for the problems and conflicts, while a mentally healthy person will assume full responsibility for all conflicts. Conflicts can be made actively and passively; the psychodynamic concept of "passive aggression" is often very well used in relation to personality disorders. Autism can be seen as the pure crystallization of passive aggression towards the parents; it can also bee seen as a product of arrested psychosexual development around the fetal or infantile state called "infantile autoerotism" by Freud (41).

Holistic theory of personality disorders

Man is seen holistically as body, mind, spirit and heart with sexuality as a penetrating ubiquitous energy, which circulates in the energetic system and connects all parts of it. The mild personality disorders (the dependent, the nervous, the narcissistic and the labile) are characterized by in open heart, and whole and functionally intact spirit, often a normal emotional life, but a somewhat immature mind and sexuality.

Table 1. In clinical holistic medicine the personality are analyzed and diagnosed according to five central dimensions: sexuality, emotion, mind, spirit and heart (see text)

		I-Strength (integrative ability, "heart")	Sexual develop-ment	Affective (emotio-nal) state	Mental state	Spiritual state
Normal, healthy person	-	Strong	Genital, free	Vital	Mature	Whole
	Low self esteem *	Fair	Genital, free	Flat or blocked	Mature	Whole
	Low self confidence *	Fair	Genital, free	Vital	Immature	Whole
	Nympho-mania *	Fair	Sexualised, often genital	Vital	Mature	Whole
Mild (neurotic)	Dependant	Fair	Often immature, free	Vital	Often immature	Whole
	Nervous/ Evasive	Fair	Often immature, free	Vital	Often immature	Whole
	Compulsive	Fair	Often immature, often blocked	Often flat	Often immature	Whole
Borderline	Emotionally labile	Moderate or weak	Immature, free	Vital	Often immature	Whole
	-	Moderate or weak	Infantile autoerotism, free	Vital	Often immature	Whole
	Histrionic (Hysteric)	Often weak	Sexualised, often genital	Vital	Often immature, instable	Whole
	Dyssocial	Weak	Immature, sexualised or blocked	Often flat	Often immature	Flat
Psychotic	Paranoid	Weak	Immature, blocked	Often flat or blocked	Immature, deluded	Flat
	Skizoid	Weak	Immature or infantile autoerotism, blocked	Blocked	Immature	Split
	(Autistic)	Weak	Infantile autoerotism, blocked	Blocked	Immature, deluded	Split
Schizo-phrenia *	Schizo-phrenia *	Weak	Infantile Autoerotism, blocked	Blocked	Immature, deluded, dis-integrated	Split

*) Not considered a personality disorder.

The borderline, or intermediate, personality disorders (the compulsive, the hysteric (histrionic), the anti-social (psychopathic), the depressive, the manic, and the schizotypical) are characterized by a blocked heart making connections to people very difficult; often a "flat" spirit, flat or labile emotions, a somewhat immature mind, and often a blocked sexuality.

The psychotic personality disorders (the autistic, the bi-polar, the paranoid, and the schizoid) are characterized by a blocked heart making connections to people very difficult; a split spirit, flat, an immature and deluded mind, and most often a completely blocked or little developed sexuality. The schizophrenic patient is at the extreme end of the spectrum with infantile auto-erotic and no objects-related sexuality, split spirit, often highly underdeveloped, strongly deluded mind, and most often complete, emotional flatness. In principle, body and sexuality must be rehabilitated first, then emotions and mind, and finally spirit and heart. In practice the course of therapy is always strongly dependent on the patient; the therapist needs to invent a new cure for every new patient.

Table 1 shows the system of personality disorders and the underlying sexual, mental, spiritual and integrative (I/heart) problems that must be addressed in therapy to cure the patient.

The five dimensions of mental health

1. Sexuality

Sexuality has been known to play a central role in personality disorders all the way back to Hippocrates and the Greek physicians and this perspective has been kept in today's psychoanalysis, psychodynamic psychotherapy, and holistic medicine from Hippocrates to Freud, Jung, Reich, Searles and many other great therapists. Sexuality lies at the core of human existence and the level of psychosexual development and the free or blocked flow of sexual energy is easily observed in clinical practice from the level of libido, sexual aggression, will to live, level of life energy etc. The development goes from object-less, infantile autoerotism through immature sexuality to the mature, genital sexuality needed for mutually satisfying, sexual intercourse. Freud described the immature sexuality as oral or anal. It has in the literature of erotic tantra been suggested that immature female sexuality can be seen as "clitoral" opposed to mature, vaginal sexuality. Sexuality (the sexual energy) can be free, blocked or sexualized. Sexualized energy is neurotically boosted; compare this with the classical diagnosis of "nymphomania", which is neurotically boosted sexuality in an otherwise normal patient (nymphomania is therefore included in table 1 as a normal condition and not a disorder).

Many hysteric patients are strongly sexualized and have an obvious nymphomaniac trait. Promiscuous behavior is sometimes the behavioral derivate of sexualisation also in normal people, but this is not a mental disorder as we see it. This problem and many other related sexual problems like vulvodynia belongs to the field of sexology in spite of obvious presence of personality disorders in these patients; eating disorders are often more strongly related to sexual than to mental problems and should therefore also be treated with under the specialty of sexology. In the future psychiatry and sexology might also be integrated into a more holistic model; as physical health are also strongly related to mental and sexual problems we must always remember that body and mind cannot truly be separated in medicine. A few minutes talk about sexuality will reveal the patient's level of psychosexual developmental status; often just the way the patient dresses and contact you will let you know.

2. Affect/emotions

The emotional state of a human being goes from vital and healthy to flat and further to completely blocked. A person can contain a whole palette or rainbow of emotions, every moment being like a colorful painting; or emotional life can be flat and simplistic, one single emotion at the time, and no symphony of tones, no profoundness and mystery; or emotional life can be completely blocked. The palette can be dominated by dark colors in depression, or light colors in mania, and the whole palette can be changing unpredictably as in cyclothymia and emotional lability. The emotional status of the patient is easily experiences in personal contact.

3. Mind

The mind can be immature or maturely developed; it can contain complex concepts and fine language for describing the world, and intelligent and creative processes to model the surrounding world and meet the multiple challenges from inside and outside. It can be sharp, precise, stable, and useful tool, a reliable source of information and true resource for problem solving. When mind is immature, its description of the world can be instable, deluded, an unreliable source of information, or even a severe burden insisting compulsively on the patient doing or thinking specific thoughts or actions, and in the psychotic patient deluded thoughts and ideas can lead to highly destructive acts. In the most undeveloped and disturbed form the conception is confused and disintegrated. An hour of conversation will allow the therapist to estimate the level of development of patient's mind.

4. Spirit

In this important, but abstract dimension of man lies our ability to love and give unconditionally; if wholeness or the concept of soul is denied in the patient's personal philosophy, the ability to love unconditionally is often destroyed. The spiritual dimension also holds our mission of life, i.e. our core talents, which we need for being of true value in our social relationships. The spiritual dimension can be whole and vital, flat and reduced, or split in two or more parts, giving the most severe personality disorders. The split spirit is a well-known defense mechanism. Splitting is our normal reaction to traumas early in life when mind is still to immature to cope; in holistic therapy we often find these traumas under deep regression to the womb, where they can be heeled.

The clinical assessment of this is quite difficult. A split spirit should not be mistaken for the phenomenon of multiple personalities that we all, sound as sick, contains as a condition for normal mental functioning; normally our multitude of "personalities" are not visible due to a high level of integration. But split spirit often materializes though the phenomenon of inner conflicts between the inner personalities, and this is the extreme examples of this that have given name to the illness schizophrenia, meaning "split spirit" in Greek. Other manifestations of the split defense is ambivalence; in marriage seen as a strong tendency to adultery; in work seen as a strong tendency to change work places, in friendship seen as a high rhythm of meeting and sacking friends.

Diagnosing the patient's spirit is the most difficult part of the diagnosing process; to master diagnoses and holistic therapy with patients with split-spirit problems the therapist needs to go through deep and regressive therapy himself, allowing for deep self-exploration into the spiritual domain. But even the inexperienced student will soon learn to identify ambivalence and strong inner conflicts in the patient coming from the obvious split defense.

5. Heart

The experience of an integrated I is a function of a complex integrative function developed though childhood and adolescence; we often call this function the "human heart". The heart integrates body, mind and spirit, or more accurately the patient's Id, Ego and Self/soul. The function of the heart makes it possible for us to meet another person as a subject (Though) and not an object ("it") (151). If a person becomes emotionally wounded the heart can be temporarily "broken" or more permanently blocked (a "closed heart"), and relating becomes difficult. This influences the whole experience and appearance of the person. Psychiatry has often understood the concept of I-Strength as a mental quality, while holistic medicine traditionally has seen is as an existential quality. Holistic medicine is aligned with the more common understanding of the heath; people who "have a heart" or "an open heart" are able to meet the world and other people in an open-minded, assertive, empathic, accepting, involved, respectful, interested, and loving way. The status of the heath is thus easily observed in clinical practice.

How to diagnose with the 5-dimensional system

The power of the 5-dimensional system lies in its practicality in daily work. To use the system we always start with an interview about the patient's status in the five dimensions; the therapist's global impression grows organically out of this dynamic interaction. After rating this general global impression and also the five dimensions (on the 6 scales), the diagnosis is easily found using table 1. It is strongly recommended also to use a patient-rated questionnaire like QOL1, QOL 5 or QOL10 (60), and compare the two ratings to secure a reasonable concordance between the two sets of ratings. If the ratings differ much, the reason for the discrepancy must be thoroughly analyzed. In general, holistic therapy will not run smothery without a fundamental agreement between the therapist and the patient about what the patient's problem is, and what the solution and goal of therapy is.

Therapist rated questionnaire for diagnosing the personality disorders and mental illnesses (The holistic 5-dimensional system suggested for ICD-11 and DSM-V)

Q1: Therapist's global impression:

1. Normal (no significant personality disorder or mental illness)
2. Normal, low self-esteem
3. Normal, low self-confidence
4. Normal, nymphomaniac
5. Dependant
6. Nervous/evasive (including anxiety)
7. Compulsive
8. Labile
9. Narcissistic
10. Hysteric (Histrionic)
11. Dyssocial/Antisocial
12. Paranoid
13. Schizoid
14. Mentally ill

Q2: How I-strong is the patient (heart open/closed)?

1. Strong ("open heart")
2. Fair
3. Moderate ("broken heart")
4. Weak ("closed heart")

Q3: How developed is the patient's sexuality?

1. Genital (mature)
2. Autoerotism (immature clitoral/oral/anal)
3. Infantile autoerotism (no object)

Q4: How blocked or sexualized is patient's sexual energy?

1. Free
2. Sexualized
3. Blocked

Q5: How vital are the patient's emotions?

1. Vital
2. Flat
3. Blocked

Q6: How developed is the patient's mind?

1. Mature
2. Immature

3. Immature, instable
4. Deluded
5. Deluded, instable
6. Deluded, disintegrated

Q7: How whole is the patient's spirit?

1. Whole
2. Flat (remote)
3. Split

Principles of treatment

There were four core principles for the treatment:

- Induce healing of the whole existence of the patient and not only his/her body or mind (18,19). The healing often included goals like recovering purpose and meaning of life by improving existential coherence and ability to love, understand and function sexually.
- Adding as many resources to the patient as possible, as the primary reason for originally repressing the emotionally charged material was lack of resources - love, understanding, empathy, respect, care, acceptance and acknowledgement - to mention a few of the many needs of the little child. The principle was also to use the minimal intervention necessary by first using conversational therapy, then in addition philosophical exercises if needed, then adding bodywork or if needed adding role plays, group therapy and finally when necessary in a few cases, referring to a psychiatrist for psychotropic intervention. If the patient was in somatic or psychiatric treatment already at the beginning of the therapy, this treatment was continued with support from the holistic therapist.
- Using the similarity principle that seems to be a fundamental principle for all holistic healing. The similarity principle is based on the belief that what made the person sick originally will make the patient well again, when given in the right, therapeutic dose. This principle leads to often dramatic events in the therapy and to efficient and fast healing, but seems to send the patient into a number of crises that must be handled professionally. The scientific background for a radical and fast healing using the similarity principle is analysed in.
- Using Hering's Law of Cure (Constantine Hering, MD, 1800-1880) supporting the patient in going once again through all the disturbances and diseases – in reverse order - that brought the patient to where he or she is now. Other important axioms of Hering's Law of Cure is that the disease goes from more to less important organs, goes from the inside out, and goes from upside down. The scientific rationale for the last three axioms is less clear than for the first: the patient must go back his time-line to integrate all the states and experiences s/he has met on her/his way to disease. Going back in time is normally done though spontaneous regression in holistic existential therapy.

Discussion

Psychodynamic psychotherapy has a long tradition of doing it (41-44) and in our experience is not at all difficult to cure the personality disorder in therapy. A therapist that understands the basic principle of healing can cure mental illnesses; a skilled therapist like Searles cured 33% of even the most severely ill schizophrenic patients even after years of hospitalization with 900 hours of psychoanalysis (148); in our study we found that 57% of the mentally ill patients experienced to be cured with clinical holistic medicine (118). In our experience it is important to work with a broad variety of patients, also including the most ill patients, for the therapist to fully understand the basic constitution of the personality and the problems connected to it. Only in the most severely ill patients the whole structure of man becomes transparent and visible. When you can deal with schizophrenia, everything else becomes easy.

Working with the patient's sexuality is normally the biggest problem for a modern physician, because of the strong sexual taboo of society; we must stress that this is an absolutely necessary step in helping most patients with severe personality disorders, and not only a thing that should be cared about when rehabilitating patient with explicit sexual traumas. It is also important to remember that one girl in seven are still being sexually abused and these girls very often become the adult patients that seek therapy for personality disorders and mental problems. The therapist needs to be without prejudice, generous, caring and containing, to help patients re-integrate their ability to feel sexual interest, desire and arousal. Often the patents need to verbalize many sexual issues that normal people would never care about verbalize, i.e. their experience of the bodily reactions or orgasm. Most therapist feel quite awkward and embarrassed in the beginning working explicitly with patent's sexuality, but it is really worth getting past this point because it give the patient motivation and energy to raise a mind.

The use of therapeutic touch is paradoxically reducing the need of verbalizing and is also dramatically reducing the intensity of sexual transferences, but they will never completely disappear, making supervision and Balint Group work mandatory for holistic therapists. Written consent is always a good idea, and the medical record must contain detailed record of all procedures and emotionally charged wordings.

If patient-physician "chemistry" is bad, with little love and affection, it is wise to allow the patient to change therapist. If the relation is healing up, this is a sign of patients sexuality heeling; in this case it is wise not to abrupt therapy as it can set the patient seriously back; of cause the therapist is responsible for keeping the sexual boundaries and respecting the ethical rules of holistic therapy. We recommend the rules of International Society for Holistic Health (www.internationalsocietyforholistichealth.org).

References

[1]   Jones WHS. Hippocrates. Vol. I–IV. London: William Heinemann, 1923-1931.
[2]   Antonella R. Introduction of regulatory methods, systematics, description and current research. Graz: Interuniversity College, 2004.
[3]   Blättner B. Fundamentals of salutogenesis. Health promotion and individual promotion of health: Guided by resources. Graz: Interuniversity College, 2004.

[4]   Endler PC. Master program for complementary, psychosocial and integrated health sciences Graz, Austria: Interuniversity College, 2004.

[5]   Endler PC. Working and writing scientifically in complementary medicine and integrated health sciences. Graz, Austria: Interuniversity College, 2004.

[6]   Kratky KW. Complementary medical systems. Comparison and integration. New York: Nova Sci, 2008.

[7]   Pass PF. Fundamentals of depth psychology. Therapeutic relationship formation between self-awareness and casework Graz, Austria: Interuniversity College, 2004.

[8]   Spranger HH. Fundamentals of regulatory biology. Paradigms and scientific backgrounds of regulatory methods. Graz: Interuniversity College, 2004.

[9]   Jones E. The life and works of Sigmund Freud. New York: Basic Books, 1961.

[10]   Jung CG. Man and his symbols. New York: Anchor Press, 1964.

[11]   Jung CG. Psychology and alchemy. Collected works of CG Jung, vol 12. Princeton, NJ: Princeton Univ Press, 1968.

[12]   Leichsenring F, Rabung S, Leibing E. The efficacy of short-term psychodynamic psychotherapy in specific psychiatric disorders: a meta-analysis. Arch Gen Psychiatry 2004;61(12):1208-16.

[13]   Leichsenring F. Are psychodynamic and psychoanalytic therapies effective?: A review of empirical data. Int J Psychoanal 2005;86(Pt 3):841-68.

[14]   Reich W. [Die Function des Orgasmus]. Köln: Kiepenheuer Witsch, 1969. [German].

[15]   Lowen A. Honoring the body. Alachua, FL: Bioenergetics Press, 2004.

[16]   Rosen M, Brenner S. Rosen method bodywork. Accessing the unconscious through touch. Berkeley, CA: North Atlantic Books, 2003.

[17]   Anand M. The art of sexual ecstasy. The path of sacred sexuality for Western lovers. New York: Jerymy P Tarcher/Putnam, 1989.

[18]   Antonovsky A. Health, stress and coping. London: Jossey-Bass, 1985.

[19]   Antonovsky A. Unravelling the mystery of health. How people manage stress and stay well. San Franscisco: Jossey-Bass, 1987.

[20]   Ventegodt S, Flensborg-Madsen T, Andersen NJ, Nielsen M, Morad M, Merrick J. Global quality of life (QOL), health and ability are primarily determined by our consciousness. Research findings from Denmark 1991-2004. Soc Indicator Res 2005;71:87-122.

[21]   Ventegodt S, Andersen NJ, Merrick J. Quality of life philosophy: When life sparkles or can we make wisdom a science? ScientificWorldJournal 2003;3:1160-3.

[22]   Ventegodt S, Andersen NJ, Merrick J. Quality of life philosophy I. Quality of life, happiness and meaning in life. ScientificWorldJournal 2003;3:1164-75.

[23]   Ventegodt S, Andersen NJ, Merrick J. Quality of life philosophy II. What is a human being? ScientificWorldJournal 2003;3:1176-85.

[24]   Ventegodt S, Andersen NJ, Merrick J. Quality of life philosophy III. Towards a new biology: Understanding the biological connection between quality of life, disease and healing. ScientificWorldJournal 2003;3:1186-98.

[25]   Ventegodt S, Andersen NJ, Merrick J. Quality of life philosophy IV. The brain and consciousness. ScientificWorldJournal 2003;3:1199-1209.

[26]   Ventegodt S, Andersen NJ, Merrick J. Quality of life philosophy V. Seizing the meaning of life and becoming well again. ScientificWorldJournal 2003;3:1210-29.

[27]   Ventegodt S, Andersen NJ, Merrick J. Quality of life philosophy VI. The concepts. ScientificWorldJournal 2003;3:1230-40.

[28]   Ventegodt S, Merrick J. Philosophy of science: How to identify the potential research for the day after tomorrow? ScientificWorldJournal 2004;4:483-9.

[29]   Ventegodt S, Merrick J, Andersen NJ. Quality of life theory I. The IQOL theory: An integrative theory of the global quality of life concept. ScientificWorldJournal 2003;3:1030-40.

[30]   Ventegodt S, Merrick J, Andersen NJ. Quality of life theory II. Quality of life as the realization of life potential: A biological theory of human being. ScientificWorldJournal 2003;3:1041-9.

[31]   Ventegodt S, Merrick J, Andersen NJ. Quality of life theory III. Maslow revisited. ScientificWorldJournal 2003;3:1050-7.

[32]   Ventegodt S, Andersen NJ, Merrick J. Editorial: Five theories of human existence. ScientificWorldJournal 2003;3:1272-6.

[33]   Ventegodt S. The life mission theory: A theory for a consciousness-based medicine. Int J Adolesc Med Health 2003;15(1): 89-91.

[34]   Ventegodt S, Andersen NJ, Merrick J. The life mission theory II. The structure of the life purpose and the ego. ScientificWorldJournal 2003;3:1277-85.

[35]   Ventegodt S, Andersen NJ, Merrick J. The life mission theory III. Theory of talent. ScientificWorldJournal 2003;3:1286-93.

[36]   Ventegodt S, Andersen NJ, Merrick J. The life mission theory IV. Theory on child development. ScientificWorldJournal 2003;3:1294-1301.

[37]   Ventegodt S, Andersen NJ, Merrick J. The life mission theory V. Theory of the anti-self (the shadow) or the evil side of man. ScientificWorldJournal 2003;3:1302-13.

[38]   Ventegodt S, Kromann M, Andersen NJ, Merrick J. The life mission theory VI. A theory for the human character: Healing with holistic medicine through recovery of character and purpose of life. ScientificWorldJournal 2004;4:859-80.

[39]   Ventegodt S, Flensborg-Madsen T, Andersen NJ, Merrick J. The life mission theory VII. Theory of existential (Antonovsky) coherence: A theory of quality of life, health and ability for use in holistic medicine. ScientificWorldJournal 2005;5:377-89.

[40]   Ventegodt S, Merrick J. Life mission theory VIII: A theory for pain. J Pain Management 2008;1(1):5-10.

[41]   Hermansen TD, Ventegodt S, Rald E, Clausen B, Nielsen ML, Merrick J. Human development I. Twenty fundamental problems of biology, medicine and neuropsychology related to biological information. ScientificWorldJournal 2006;6:747-59.

[42]   Ventegodt S, Hermansen TD, Nielsen ML, Clausen B, Merrick J.Human development II. We need an integrated theory for matter, life and consciousness to understand life and healing. ScientificWorldJournal 2006;6:760-6.

[43]   Ventegodt S, Hermansen TD, Rald E, Flensborg-Madsen T, Nielsen ML, Clausen B, Merrick J. Human development III. Bridging brain-mind and body-mind. Itroduction to "deep" (fractal, poly-ray) cosmology. ScientificWorldJournal 2006;6:767-76.

[44]   Ventegodt S, Hermansen TD, Rald E, Flensborg-Madsen T, Nielsen ML, Clausen B, Merrick J. Human development IV. The living cell has information-directed self-organization. ScientificWorldJournal 2006;6:1132-8.

[45]   Ventegodt S, Hermansen TD, Flensborg-Madsen T, Nielsen ML, Clausen B, Merrick J. Human development V: Biochemistry unable to explain the emergence of biological form (morphogenesis) and therefore a new principle as source of biological information is needed. ScientificWorldJournal 2006;6:1359-67.

[46]   Ventegodt S, Hermansen TD, Flensborg-Madsen T, Nielsen M, Merrick J. Human development VI: Supracellular morphogenesis. The origin of biological and cellular order. ScientificWorldJournal 2006;6:1424-33.

[47]   Ventegodt S, Hermansen TD, Flensborg-Madsen T, Rald E, Nielsen ML, Merrick J. Human development VII: A spiral fractal model of fine structure of physical energy could explain central aspects of biological information, biological organization and biological creativity. ScientificWorldJournal 2006;6:1434-40.

[48]   Ventegodt S, Hermansen TD, Flensborg-Madsen T, Nielsen ML, Merrick J. Human development VIII: A theory of "deep" quantum chemistry and cell consciousness: Quantum chemistry controls genes and biochemistry to give cells and higher organisms consciousness and complex behavior. ScientificWorldJournal 2006;6:1441-53.

[49]   Ventegodt S, Hermansen TD, Flensborg-Madsen T, Rald E, Nielsen ML, Merrick J. Human development IX: A model of the wholeness of man, his consciousness and collective consciousness. ScientificWorldJournal 2006;6:1454-9.

[50]   Hermansen TD, Ventegodt S, Merrick J. Human development X: Explanation of macroevolution — top-down evolution materializes consciousness. The origin of metamorphosis. ScientificWorldJournal 2006;6:1656-66.

[51]   Ventegodt S, Merrick J, Andersen NJ. Editorial-A new method for generic measuring of the global
        quality of life. ScientificWorldJournal 2003;3:946-9.

[52]   Ventegodt S, Hilden J, Merrick J. Measurement of quality of life I: A methodological framework.
        ScientificWorldJournal 2003;3:950-61.

[53]   Ventegodt S, Merrick J, Andersen NJ. Measurement of quality of life II: From the philosophy of life
        to science. ScientificWorldJournal 2003;3:962-71.

[54]   Ventegodt S, Merrick J, Andersen NJ. Measurement of quality of life III: From the IQOL theory to the
        global, generic SEQOL questioinnaire. ScientificWorldJournal 2003;3:972-91.

[55]   Ventegodt S, Merrick J, Andersen NJ. Measurement of quality of life IV: Use of the SEQOL, QOL5,
        QOL1 and other global and generic questioinnaires. ScientificWorldJournal 2003;3:992-1001.

[56]   Ventegodt S, Merrick J, Andersen NJ. Measurement of quality of life V: How to use the SEQOL,
        QOL5, QOL1 and other and generic questionnaires for research. ScientificWorldJournal 2003;3:1002-
        14.

[57]   Ventegodt S, Merrick J, Andersen NJ. Measurement of quality of life VI: Quality-adjusted life years
        (QALY) is an unfortunate use of quality of life concept. ScientificWorldJournal 2003;3:1015-9.

[58]   Ventegodt S, Merrick J. Measurement of quality of life VII: Statistical covariation and global quality
        of life data. The method of weight-modified liniar regression. ScientificWorldJournal 2003;3:1020-29.

[59]   Ventegodt S, Henneberg EW, Merrick J, Lindholt JS. Validation of two global and generic quality of
        life questionnaires for population screening: SCREENQOL and SEQOL. ScientificWorldJournal
        2003;3:412-21.

[60]   Lindholt JS, Ventegodt S, Henneberg EW. Development and validation of QOL5 for clinical
        databases. A short, global and generic questionnaire based on an integrated theory of the quality of
        life. Eur J Surg 2002;168:103-7.

[61]   Ventegodt S. Sex and the quality of life in Denmark. Arch Sex Behav 1998;27(3):295-307.

[62]   Ventegodt S. A prospective study on quality of life and traumatic events in early life – 30 year follow-
        up. Child Care Health Dev 1998;25(3):213-21.

[63]   Ventegodt S, Merrick J. Long-term effects of maternal smoking on quality of life. Results from the
        Copenhagen Perinatal Birth Cohort 1959-61. ScientificWorldJournal 2003;3:714-20.

[64]   Ventegodt S, Merrick J. Long-term effects of maternal medication on global quality of life measured
        with SEQOL. Results from the Copenhagen Perinatal Birth Cohort 1959-61. ScientificWorldJournal
        2003;3:707-13.

[65]   Ventegodt S, Merrick J. Psychoactive drugs and quality of life. ScientificWorldJournal 2003;3:694-
        706.

[66]   Ventegodt S, Merrick J. Lifestyle, quality of life and health. ScientificWorldJournal 2003;3: 811-25.

[67]   Ventegodt S, Flensborg-Madsen T, Andersen NJ, Merrick J. The health and social situation of the
        mother during pregnancy and global quality of life of the child as an adult. Results from the
        prospective Copenhagen Perinatal Cohort 1959-1961. ScientificWorldJournal 2005;5:950-8.

[68]   Ventegodt S, Flensborg-Madsen T, Andersen NJ, Merrick J. Factors during pregnancy, delivery and
        birth affecting global quality of life of the adult child at long-term follow-up. Results from the
        prospective Copenhagen Perinatal Birth Cohort 1959-61. ScientificWorldJournal 2005;5:933-41.

[69]   Ventegodt S, Flensborg-Madsen T, Andersen NJ, Merrick J. Events in pregnancy, delivery, and
        infancy and long-term effects on global quality of life: results from the Copenhagen Perinatal Birth
        Cohort 1959-61. ScientificWorldJournal 2007;7:1622-30.

[70]   Ventegodt S, Flensborg-Madsen T, Andersen NJ, Morad M, Merrick J. Quality of life and events in
        the first year of life. Results from the prospective Copenhagen Birth Cohort 1959-61.
        ScientificWorldJournal 2006;6:106-15.

[71]   Ventegodt S, Flensborg-Madsen T, Andersen NJ, Merrick J. What influence do major events in life
        have on our later quality of life? A retrospective study on life events and associated emotions Med Sci
        Monit 2006;12(2):SR9-15.

[72]   Ventegodt S. Every contact with the patient must be therapeutic. J Pediatr Adolesc Gynecol
        2007;20(6):323-4.

[73]   Ventegodt S, Merrick J. Psychosomatic reasons for chronic pains. South Med J 2005;98(11): 1063.

[74]   Ventegodt S, Andersen NJ, Merrick J. Holistic medicine: Scientific challenges.
       ScientificWorldJournal 2003;3:1108-16.
[75]   Ventegodt S, Andersen NJ, Merrick J. Holistic Medicine II: The square-curve paradigm for research in
       alternative, complementary and holistic medicine: A cost-effective, easy and scientifically valid design
       for evidence based medicine. ScientificWorldJournal 2003;3:1117-27.
[76]   Ventegodt S, Andersen NJ, Merrick J. Holistic medicine III: The holistic process theory of healing.
       ScientificWorldJournal 2003;3:1138-46.
[77]   Ventegodt S, Andersen NJ, Merrick J. Holistic Medicine IV: Principles of the holistic process of
       healing in a group setting. ScientificWorldJournal 2003;3:1294-1301.
[78]   Ventegodt S, Merrick J. Clinical holistic medicine: Applied consciousness-based medicine.
       ScientificWorldJournal 2004;4:96-9.
[79]   Ventegodt S, Morad M, Merrick J. Clinical holistic medicine: Classic art of healing or the therapeutic
       touch. ScientificWorldJournal 2004;4:134-47.
[80]   Ventegodt S, Morad M, Merrick J. Clinical holistic medicine: The "new medicine", the
       multiparadigmatic physician and the medical record. ScientificWorldJournal 2004;4:273-85.
[81]   Ventegodt S, Morad M, Merrick J. Clinical holistic medicine: Holistic pelvic examination and holistic
       treatment of infertility. ScientificWorldJournal 2004;4:148-58.
[82]   Ventegodt S, Morad M, Hyam E, Merrick J. Clinical holistic medicine: Use and limitations of the
       biomedical paradigm. ScientificWorldJournal 2004;4:295-306.
[83]   Ventegodt S, Morad M, Kandel I, Merrick J. Clinical holistic medicine: Social problems disguised as
       illness. ScientificWorldJournal 2004;4:286-94.
[84]   Ventegodt S, Morad M, Andersen NJ, Merrick J. Clinical holistic medicine Tools for a medical
       science based on consciousness. ScientificWorldJournal 2004;4:347-61.
[85]   Ventegodt S, Morad M, and Merrick J. Clinical holistic medicine: Prevention through healthy lifestyle
       and quality of life. Oral Health Prev Dent 2004;1:239-45.
[86]   Ventegodt S, Morad M, Hyam E, Merrick J. Clinical holistic medicine: When biomedicine is
       inadequate. TheScientificWorldJOURNAL 4, 333-346.
[87]   Ventegodt S, Morad M, Merrick J. Clinical holistic medicine: Holistic treatment of children.
       ScientificWorldJournal 2004;4:581-8.
[88]   Ventegodt S, Morad M, Merrick J. Clinical holistic medicine: Problems in sex and living together.
       ScientificWorldJournal 2004;4:562-70.
[89]   Ventegodt S, Morad M, Hyam E, Merrick J. Clinical holistic medicine: Holistic sexology and
       treatment of vulvodynia through existential therapy and acceptance through touch.
       ScientificWorldJournal 2004;4:571-80.
[90]   Ventegodt S, Flensborg-Madsen T, Andersen NJ, Morad M, Merrick J. Clinical holistic medicine: A
       Pilot on HIV and Quality of Life and a Suggested treatment of HIV and AIDS. ScientificWorldJournal
       2004;4:264-72.
[91]   Ventegodt S, Morad M, Merrick J. Clinical holistic medicine: Induction of spontaneous remission of
       cancer by recovery of the human character and the purpose of life (the life mission).
       ScientificWorldJournal 2004;4:362-77.
[92]   Ventegodt S, Morad M, Kandel I, Merrick J. Clinical holistic medicine: Treatment of physical health
       problems without a known cause, exemplified by hypertension and tinnitus. ScientificWorldJournal
       2004;4:716-24.
[93]   Ventegodt S, Morad M, Merrick J. Clinical holistic medicine: Developing from asthma, allergy and
       eczema. ScientificWorldJournal 2004;4:936-42.
[94]   Ventegodt S, Morad M, Press J, Merrick J, Shek D. Clinical holistic medicine: Holistic adolescent
       medicine. ScientificWorldJournal 2004;4, 551-561.
[95]   Ventegodt S, Solheim E, Saunte ME, Morad M, Kandel I, Merrick J. Clinical holistic medicine:
       Metastatic cancer. ScientificWorldJournal 2004;4:913-35.
[96]   Ventegodt S, Morad M, Kandel I, Merrick J. Clinical holistic medicine: a psychological theory of
       dependency to improve quality of life. ScientificWorldJournal 2004;4:638-48.
[97]   Ventegodt S, Merrick J. Clinical holistic medicine: Chronic infections and autoimmune diseases.
       ScientificWorldJournal 2005;5:155-64.

[98] Ventegodt S, Kandel I, Neikrug S, Merrick J. Clinical holistic medicine: Holistic treatment of rape and incest traumas. ScientificWorldJournal 2005;5:288-97.

[99] Ventegodt S, Morad M, Merrick J. Clinical holistic medicine: Chronic pain in the locomotor system. ScientificWorldJournal 2005;5:165-72.

[100] Ventegodt S, Merrick J. Clinical holistic medicine: Chronic pain in internal organs. ScientificWorldJournal 2005;5:205-10.

[101] Ventegodt S, Kandel I, Neikrug S, Merrick J. Clinical holistic medicine: The existential crisis – life crisis, stress and burnout. ScientificWorldJournal 2005;5:300-12.

[102] Ventegodt S, Gringols M, Merrick J. Clinical holistic medicine: Holistic rehabilitation. ScientificWorldJournal 2005;5:280-7.

[103] Ventegodt S, Andersen NJ, Neikrug S, Kandel I, Merrick J. Clinical holistic medicine: Mental disorders in a holistic perspective. ScientificWorldJournal 2005;5:313-23.

[104] Ventegodt S, Andersen NJ, Neikrug S, Kandel I, Merrick J. Clinical Holistic Medicine: Holistic treatment of mental disorders. ScientificWorldJournal 2005;5:427-45.

[105] Ventegodt S, Merrick J. Clinical holistic medicine: The patient with multiple diseases. ScientificWorldJournal 2005;5:324-39.

[106] Ventegodt S, Clausen B, Nielsen ML, Merrick J. Clinical holistic medicine: Advanced tools for holistic medicine. ScientificWorldJournal 2006;6:2048-65.

[107] Ventegodt S, Clausen B, Merrick J. Clinical holistic medicine: The case story of Anna. I. Long-term effect of childhood sexual abuse and incest with a treatment approach. ScientificWorldJournal 2006;6:1965-76.

[108] Ventegodt S, Chausen B, Merrick J. Clinical holistic medicine: the case story of Anna. II. Patient diary as a tool in treatment. ScientificWorldJournal 2006;6:2006-34.

[109] Ventegodt S, Clasusen B, Merrick J. Clinical holistic medicine: The case story of Anna. III. Rehabilitation of philosophy of life during holistic existential therapy for childhood sexual abuse. ScientificWorldJournal 2006;6:2080-91.

[110] Ventegodt S, Merrick J. Suicide from a holistic point of view. ScientificWorldJournal 2005;5:759-66.

[111] Ventegodt S, Clausen B, Omar HA, Merrick J. Clinical holistic medicine: Holistic sexology and acupressure through the vagina (Hippocratic pelvic massage). ScientificWorldJournal 2006;6:2066-79.

[112] Ventegodt S, Clausen B, Merrick J. Clinical holistic medicine: Pilot study on the effect of vaginal acupressure (Hippocratic pelvic massage). ScientificWorldJournal 2006;6:2100-16.

[113] Ventegodt S. [Min brug af vaginal akupressur.] My use of acupressure. Ugeskr Laeger 2006;168(7):715-6. [Danish].

[114] Ventegodt S, Thegler S, Andreasen T, Struve F, Enevoldsen L, Bassaine L, et al. Clinical holistic medicine: Psychodynamic short-time therapy complemented with bodywork. A clinical follow-up study of 109 patients. ScientificWorldJournal 2006;6:2220-38.

[115] Ventegodt S, Thegler S, Andreasen T, Struve F, Enevoldsen L, Bassaine L, et al. Clinical holistic medicine (mindful, short-term psychodynamic psychotherapy complemented with bodywork) in the treatment of experienced impaired sexual functioning. ScientificWorldJournal 2007;7:324-9.

[116] Ventegodt S, Thegler S, Andreasen T, Struve F, Enevoldsen L, Bassaine L, et al. Clinical holistic medicine (mindful, short-term psychodynamic psychotherapy complemented with bodywork) improves quality of life, health and ability by induction of Antonovsky-salutogenesis. ScientificWorldJournal 2007;7:317-23.

[117] Ventegodt S, Thegler S, Andreasen T, Struve F, Enevoldsen L, Bassaine L, et al. Clinical holistic medicine (mindful, short-term psychodynamic psychotherapy complemented with bodywork) in the treatment of experienced physical illness and chronic pain. ScientificWorldJournal 2007;7:310-6.

[118] Ventegodt S, Thegler S, Andreasen T, Struve F, Enevoldsen L, Bassaine L, et al. Clinical holistic medicine (mindful, short-term psychodynamic psychotherapy complemented with bodywork) in the treatment of experienced mental illness. ScientificWorldJournal 2007;7:306-9.

[119] Ventegodt S, Thegler S, Andreasen T, Struve F, Enevoldsen L, Bassaine L, et al. Self-reported low self-esteem. Intervention and follow-up in a clinical setting. ScientificWorldJournal 2007;7:299-305.

[120] Flensborg-Madsen T, Ventegodt S, Merrick J. Sense of coherence and physical health. A Review of previous findings. ScientificWorldJournal 2005;5:665-73.

[121] Flensborg-Madsen T, Ventegodt S, Merrick J. Why is Antonovsky's sense of coherence not correlated to physical health? Analysing Antonovsky's 29-item sense of coherence scale (SOCS). ScientificWorldJournal 2005;5:767-76.

[122] Flensborg-Madsen T, Ventegodt S, Merrick J. Sense of coherence and health. The construction of an amendment to Antonovsky's sense of coherence scale (SOC II). ScientificWorldJournal 2006;6:2133-9.

[123] Flensborg-Madsen T, Ventegodt S, Merrick J. Sense of coherence and physical health. A cross-sectional study using a new SOC scale (SOC II). ScientificWorldJournal 2006;6:2200-11.

[124] Flensborg-Madsen T, Ventegodt S, Merrick J. Sense of coherence and physical health. Testing Antonovsky's theory. ScientificWorldJournal 2006;6:2212-9.

[125] Flensborg-Madsen T, Ventegodt S, Merrick J. Sense of coherence and health. The emotional sense of coherence (SOC-E) was found to be the best-known predictor of physical health. ScientificWorldJournal 2006;6:2147-57.

[126] Merrick J, Ventegodt S. What is a good death? To use death as a mirror and find the quality in life. BMJ. Rapid Response 2003 Oct 31.

[127] Ventegodt S, Merrick J. Medicine and the past. Lesson to learn about the pelvic examination and its sexually suppressive procedure. BMJ. Rapid Response 2004 Feb 20.

[128] Ventegodt S, Morad M, Merrick J. If it doesn't work, stop it. Do something else! BMJ. Rapid Response 2004 Apr 26.

[129] Merrick J, Morad M, Kandel I, Ventegodt S. Spiritual health, intellectual disability and health care. BMJ Rapid Response 2004 Jul 16.

[130] Ventegodt S, Morad M, Kandel I, Merrick J. Maternal smoking and quality of life more than thirty years later. BMJ Rapid Response 2004 Jul 30.

[131] Merrick J, Morad M, Kandel I, Ventegodt S. Prevalence of Helicobacter pylori infection in residential care centers for people with intellectual disability. BMJ Rapid Response 2004 Jul 23.

[132] Merrick J, Morad M, Kandel I, Ventegodt S. People with intellectual disability, health needs and policy. BMJ Rapid Response 2004 Aug 20.

[133] Ventegodt S, Vardi G, Merrick J. Holistic adolescent sexology: How to counsel and treat young people to alleviate and prevent sexual problems. BMJ Rapid Response 2005 Jan 15.

[134] Ventegodt S. Flensborg-Madsen T, Merrick J. Evidence based medicine in favor of biomedicine and it seems that holistic medicine has been forgotten? BMJ Rapid Response 2004 Nov 11.

[135] Ventegodt S, Merrick J. Placebo explained: Consciousness causal to health. BMJ Rapid Responses 2004 Oct 22.

[136] Ventegodt S, Merrick J. Academic medicine must deliver skilled physicians. A different academic training is needed. BMJ Rapid Response 2004 Oct 9.

[137] Ventegodt S, Morad M, Merrick J. Chronic illness, the patient and the holistic medical toolbox. BMJ Rapid Response 2004 Sep 15.

[138] Ventegodt S, Kandel I, Merrick J. Medicine has gone astray - we must reverse the alienation now. BMJ Rapid Response 2005 Mar 10.

[139] Ventegodt S, Merrick J. The consensus paradigm for qualitative research in holistic medicine. BMJ Rapid Response 2005 Nov 24.

[140] Ventegodt S, Kandel I, Merrick J. Principles of holistic medicine. Philosophy behind quality of life. Victoria, BC: Trafford, 2005.

[141] Ventegodt S, Kandel I, Merrick J. Principles of holistic medicine. Quality of life and health. New York: Hippocrates Sci Publ, 2005.

[142] Ventegodt S, Kandel I, Merrick J. Principles of holistic medicine. Global quality of life.Theory, research and methodology. New York: Hippocrates Sci Publ, 2005.

[143] Ventegodt S. Measuring the quality of life. From theory to practice. Copenhagen: Forskningscentrets Forlag, 1996.

[144] Freud S, Breuer J. Studies in hysteria. New York: Penguin Classics, 2004. (Original work published 1893, 1895, 1908).

[145] Weiner DB. The clinical training of doctors. An essay from 1793 by Philippe Pinel. Henry E Sigerist Suppl Bull Hist Med 1980;3:1-102.

[146] Modestin J, Huber A, Satirli E, Malti T, Hell D. Long-term course of schizophrenic illness: Bleuler's study reconsidered. Am J Psychiatry 2003;160(12):2202-8.

[147] Knight RP, Preface. In: Searles HF. Collected papers on schizophrenia. Madison, CT: Int Univ Press, 1965:15-18.

[148] Karon BP, VandenBos G. Psychotherapy of schizophrenia. The treatment of choise. New York: Jason Aronson, 1981.

[149] Quante A, Röpke S, Merkl A, Anghelescu I, Lammers CH. [Psychopharmacologic treatment of personality disorders.] Fortschr Neurol Psychiatr 2008;76:1-10. [German].

[150] Buber M. I and thou. New York: Charles Scribner, 1970.

Chapter 34

Schizophrenia and other psychotic mental diseases

Clinical holistic medicine (CHM) has developed into a system that can also be helpful with mental ill patients. CHM-therapy supports the patient through a series of emotionally challenging, existential and healing crises. The patient's sense of coherence and mental health can be recovered through the process of feeling old repressed emotions, understanding life, self and finally letting go of negative beliefs and delusions, The Bleuler's triple condition of autism, disturbed thoughts, and disturbed emotions that characterizes the schizophrenic patient can be understood as arising from the early defense of splitting, caused by negative learning from painful childhood traumas that made the patient lose sense of coherence and withdraw from social contact. Self-insight gained though the therapy can allow the patients to take their bodily, mental and spiritual talents into use. In the end of therapy the patients are once again living a life of quality centered on their life-mission and they relate to other people in a way that systematically creates value. There are a number of challenges meeting the therapist working with schizophrenic and psychotic patients, from the potential risk of experiencing patient's violence to the obligation to contain the most difficult and embarrassing of feelings, when the emotional and often also sexual content of the patient's unconsciousness becomes explicit. There is a long, well establised tradition for treating schizophrenia with psyhodynamic therapy and we have found that the combination of bodywork and psychotherapy can enhance and accelerate the therapy and might improve the treatment rate further.

Introduction

Madness has tormented mankind since its birth and definitely as long back as we have medical recordings. Hippocrates (460-377BCE) devoted attention to mental diseases and used an ingenuous combination of conversational therapy and bodywork as treatment for example of hysteria (from Greek Hystera: Uterus) and other mental conditions[1]. As one of his treatments he used pelvic massage (2,3) to "correct the energy of the uterus", but also other provocative and efficient methods of interventions. To avoid the problems of sexual abuse following the use of bodywork and intimacy he invented his famous Hippocratic ethics (1).

Philippe Pinel (1745-1826) (4) at Bicétre in Paris used "moral treatment" for mentally ill patients, and he did that surprisingly successful. According to his statistics about 70% of the patients were healed using the holistic medical principles. With a strong focus on medical ethics, he stressed the respect of the individual and used intensive studies of each single patient through detailed case recordings (4,5). Pinel called his psychiatric therapy for "traitement moral" and this holistic system represented the first modern attempt at individual psychotherapy. His treatment core values were gentleness, understanding, goodwill and he was opposed to violent methods. He recommended close medical attendance during convalescence, and he emphasized the need of hygiene, physical exercise, and a program of purposeful work for the patient. A number of his therapeutic procedures, including ergo therapy and the placement of the patient in a family group, anticipated modern psychiatric care.

The Swiss psychiatrist Paul Eugen Bleuler (1857-1939) gave birth to the name schizophrenia (earlier named dementia praecox but changed to characterize split mind in Greek)) to describe the splitting in the mental functions between the patient and reality (5). He had three main criterions, or primary symptoms, still being used in today's psychiatry for diagnosing schizophrenia:

- Disturbed thought, especially difficulties in the logic and disorganization of thoughts
- Disturbed emotions, especially the presence of irrelevant feelings and numbness.
- Autism i.e. social withdrawal.

This triad was complemented by a number of secondary symptoms like hallucinations, fixed delusions, catatonia, lack of self-care, and strange ways of speaking and acting. The schizophrenic state was during the last century understood in more and more depth psychodynamically and seen as caused by the mental defense called "splitting", during which a substantial part of the patient's consciousness, emotional and sexual life is repressed (6,7); splitting is a different, more primitive and more radical defense than what we usually call repression in therapy. Spitting was understood psychodynamically as being the emotionally challenged child's psychic survival position. The purpose of assuming the position of splitting was saving the patient's vulnerable core of existence from the threat of destruction by the insensitive contact with parents not meeting the child's sensitive mind and spirit the way it needed to be met. This is not to blame the parents who undoubtably are doing their best; but some children are extremely sensitive, and some parents are not.

This transformation of an open and vulnerable child into a protective person living in a safe shell of numbness and isolation explained how and why the patient turned herself into a disconnected and severely dysfunctional being. "Fear of dying" – or even panic - is according to the psychodynamic theory the permanent, emotional state of the schizophrenic patient. To cure the schizophrenic patient the therapist must thus offer a "saving" that is perceived as safer than what is offered by the psychotic defenses. When the therapist is offering this alternative "safe place" the patient can finally heal by opening up emotionally for the world once again, thus coming back to life and social life. Their might of course be a constitutional factor on the side of the child, like what have been called "karmic traumas" – energetically inherited existential imbalances - that makes such a healing very difficult. Sigmund Freud (1856-1939) (6) and Carl Gustav Jung (1875-1961) (7) saw correctly the psychotic defenses as a very early mechanism – happening the first year of life or so or even before than, in the womb – and they were quite pessimistic about addressing this defense in therapy, as it firmly protected the fundamental existence of the being. Jung worked with Bleuler and was more optimistic than Freud in treating psychosis. The neurotic defense mechanisms like repression were seen as a more mature defense mechanism happening later in childhood, and only protecting the content of consciousness, not the container – the existence - itself. Freud believed that only the later were curable by psychoanalysis. Psychodynamic psychotherapists like Harold Frederic Searles (1918-) found in the middle of last century, that the deep existential problems of preventing the loss of self though splitting were actually also curable by psychodynamic psychotherapy, and Searles became famous for curing about 33% of his schizophrenic patients this way; and many more great psychotherapists have been able to cure scizofrenia during the last centrury (see below under discussion).

Also today psychiatric disorders can be treated by psychodynamic psychotherapy; this kind of therapy has recently in metanalysis been found superior to standard psychiatric treatment (8-10). Standard psychiatric drug treatment is not curing the patient – and is not claiming to do so either - and it has severe side-effects/adverse effects from the psychopharmacological drugs and from negative implanted philosophy (11), making this treatment a less than perfect medical procedure (12). But it may still be useful in many cases, especially when psychotherapy has failed to help.

Unfortunately psychotherapy with schizophrenic patients can be extremely challenging for the therapist and medical treatment with neuroleptic drugs therefore more attractive and not time-consuming as psychodynamic psychotherapy, holistic therapy and other kinds of psychotherapy that induce recovery and salutogenesis. Only further research can tell us the fraction of patients that can be completely healed; even the most talented of therapists like Searles and Laing had to admit their failure in their attempt of curing schizophrenic patients. There have been critique of research with psychotherapy for schizophrenia, because was mostly done without control groups, but with schizophrenic patients we all know the poor outcome for the patients if not treated, or if treated with biomedicine (antipsychotic drugs like Chlorpromazine) (12), which is exactly why the therapists did not bother to have a control group.

Etiology of schizophrenia

Today most researchers interpret the findings of a concordance of .25 to .5 in the many monozygote twin-studies of schizophrenia as proof of a genetic trait and an environmental trait as well (13). Obviously the factor most dominant is the environmental, estimated from the size of the found concordances.

New information about the life as fetus comes from fetal regression, where adult patients and researchers engaged in regression back to the womb; a method practiced for many years by Tibetan Yogis (14), but until recently seen as impossible (15,16) as the fetus has no mature brain – and the early fetus no brain at all. The validity of such experiences has been tested and often the remembered facts were found to be actually correct (15,16), although this is still an issue of debate. The fetus being a conscious being interacting with the world, and actively adapting to the circumstances of life is in severe contrast to the much more mechanical interpretation of embryonic development held by science until recently. If the subjective data about fetal adaptation is found to be valid the twin studies must be reinterpreted. The twin studies are thus neglecting that monozygote twins are in very close contact to each other in the womb, and that the fetuses are actually aware and communicating and sharing many subjective experiences in the womb also, which might as well as bad genes explain the found concordance.

From the perspective of clinical holistic medicine, where patients go back into the womb very often, and where these experiences are giving meaning and value to the process of existential healing of the most early defenses, there is no doubt that environmental factors by far dominates the genetic influence. This is the reason why schizophrenia and other mental illnesses seemingly founded already in the womb in many cases can be healed in holistic existential therapy.

Under all circumstances it is important to stress that the often-heard argument that schizophrenia is in fact an incurable genetic disease documented by the many monozygote twin studies is not valid; the concordance is much to low to substantiate this view. Data is quite opposite is favor of the view that schizophrenia primarily is a psychosocially induced disturbance, which therefore possibly can be cured by the persisting psychosocial problems from the patient's past being solved. Future clinical research will tell us, if our optimistic interpretation of data is substantiated.

Diagnostic guidelines (ICD-10, F20 schizofrenia)

In the ICD-10 system the normal requirement for a diagnosis of schizophrenia is that a minimum of one very clear symptom (and usually two or more if less clear-cut) belonging to any one of the groups listed as (a) to (d) below, or symptoms from at least two of the groups referred to as (e) to (h), should have been clearly present for most of the time during a period of one month or more. Conditions meeting such symptomatic requirements but of duration less than one month (whether treated or not) should be diagnosed in the first instance as acute schizophrenia-like psychotic disorder and are classified as schizophrenia if the symptoms persist for longer periods.

a) thought echo, thought insertion or withdrawal, and thought broadcasting;
b) delusions of control, influence, or passivity, clearly referred to body or limb movements or specific thoughts, actions, or sensations; delusional perception;
c) hallucinatory voices giving a running commentary on the patient's behavior, or discussing the patient among themselves, or other types of hallucinatory voices coming from some part of the body;
d) persistent delusions of other kinds that are culturally inappropriate and completely impossible, such as religious or political identity, or superhuman powers and abilities (e.g. being able to control the weather, or being in communication with aliens from another world);

e) persistent hallucinations in any modality, when accompanied either by fleeting or half-formed delusions without clear affective content, or by persistent over-valued ideas, or when occurring every day for weeks or months on end;

f) breaks or interpolations in the train of thought, resulting in incoherence or irrelevant speech, or neologisms;

g) catatonic behavior, such as excitement, posturing, or waxy flexibility, negativism, mutism, and stupor;

h) "negative" symptoms such as marked apathy, paucity of speech, and blunting or incongruity of emotional responses, usually resulting in social withdrawal and lowering of social performance; it must be clear that these are not due to depression or to neuroleptic medication;

i) a significant and consistent change in the overall quality of some aspects of personal behavior, manifest as loss of interest, aimlessness, idleness, a self-absorbed attitude, and social withdrawal.

Diagnostic criteria
(DSM-IV code 295 schizophrenia)

The DSM-IV system is basically focusing on the same symptoms, but are using a slightly different system:

A. Characteristic symptoms: Two (or more) of the following, each present for a significant portion of time during a one month period (or less if successfully treated):

- delusions
- hallucinations
- disorganized speech (e.g., frequent derailment or incoherence)
- grossly disorganized or catatonic behavior
- negative symptoms, i.e., affective flattening, alogia, or avolition

Note: Only one Criterion A symptom is required if delusions are bizarre or hallucinations consist of a voice keeping up a running commentary on the person's behavior or thoughts, or two or more voices conversing with each other.

B. Social/occupational dysfunction: For a significant portion of the time since the onset of the disturbance, one or more major areas of functioning such as work, interpersonal relations, or self-care are markedly below the level achieved prior to the onset (or when the onset is in childhood or adolescence, failure to achieve expected level of interpersonal, academic, or occupational achievement).

C. Duration: Continuous signs of the disturbance persist for at least 6 months. This 6-month period must include at least 1 month of symptoms (or less if successfully treated) that meet Criterion A (i.e., active-phase symptoms) and may include periods of prodromal or residual symptoms. During these prodromal or residual periods, the signs of the disturbance may be manifested by only negative symptoms or two or more symptoms listed in Criterion A present in an attenuated form (e.g., odd beliefs, unusual perceptual experiences).

D. Schizoaffective and mood disorder exclusion: Schizoaffective disorder and mood disorder with psychotic features have been ruled out because either 1) no major depressive, manic, or mixed episodes have occurred concurrently with the active-phase symptoms; or 2) if mood episodes have occurred during active-phase symptoms, their total duration has been brief relative to the duration of the active and residual periods.

E. Substance/general medical condition exclusion: The disturbance is not due to the direct physiological effects of a substance (e.g., a drug of abuse, a medication) or a general medical condition.

Relationship to a pervasive developmental disorder: If there is a history of Autistic disorder or another pervasive developmental disorder, the additional diagnosis of schizophrenia is made only if prominent delusions or hallucinations are also present for at least a month (or less if successfully treated).

As both diagnotic systems use almost the same patognomonic criteria, it has been quite easy to establish the diagnosis with great certainty for almost a century.

Clinical holistic medicine (CHM) and schizophrenia

In CHM schizophrenia is seen as the most extreme state of lack of sense of coherence (17-25). The purpose of CHM is rehabilitating the sense of coherence through healing somatoform and psychoform dissociation and rehabilitation of the patients physical, emotional, mental and spiritual contact with other people though the channels of body and mind.

To obtain this polyvalent effect the standard short-term psychodynamic psychotherapy (STPP) - traditionally focusing on the patients emotional mind and sexuality - is complemented with bodywork (of Marion Rosen type) (26) and philosophy of life (27-36).

CHM is using the life mission theory (25,37-42) to understand the degeneration of the self into the ego, the shadow, the evil side of man, the loss of libido and talents though the repression of painful emotions, and the loss of existential coherence though the loss of energy, meaning, light and joy (25). CHM uses an expanded toolbox[43] and four central healing principles (44-46):

*   Induce healing of the whole existence of the patient (also called salutogenesis) (17,18,45,46) and not only his/her body or mind. The healing often includes goals like recovering purpose and meaning of life by improving existential coherence and ability to love, understand and function sexually.
*   Adding as many resources to the patient as possible (6,7,15-18,45,46), as the primary reason for originally repressing the emotionally charged material was lack of resources - love, understanding, empathy, respect, care, acceptance and acknowledgement - to mention a few of the many needs of the little child. The

principle was also to use the minimal intervention necessary by first using conversational therapy, then in addition philosophical exercises if needed, then adding bodywork or if needed adding role plays, group therapy and finally when necessary in a few cases, referring to a psychiatrist for psychotropic intervention. If the patient was in somatic or psychiatric treatment already at the beginning of the therapy, this treatment was continued with support from the holistic therapist.

- Using the similarity principle that seems to be a fundamental principle for all holistic healing (45,46). The similarity principle is based on the belief that what made the person sick originally will make the patient well again, when given in the right, therapeutic dose. This principle leads to often dramatic events in the therapy and to efficient and fast healing, but seems to send the patient into a number of crises that must be handled professionally (47-49). The scientific background for a radical and fast healing using the similarity principle is analysed in (50-55).
- Using Hering's Law of Cure (50-55) supporting the patient going once again through all the disturbances and diseases – in reverse order - that brought the patient to where he or she is now. Other important axioms of Hering's Law of Cure is that the disease goes from more to less important organs, goes from the inside out, and goes from upside down. The scientific rationale for the last three axioms are less clear than for the first: the patient must go back his time-line to integrate all the states and experiences s/he has met on her/his way to disease. Going back in time is normally done though spontaneous regression in holistic existential therapy.

Using these tools and principles many physical, mental, sexual and existential problems can be addressed (1-10,46-48,57-81) with satisfactory results (82-86). Even severe mental problems can be alleviated (4,5,85) and in several cases patients with schizophrenia have been cured (see cases below) (5,85,87,88), but we still need research to document the effect of CHM with a large group of well-diagnosed, schizophrenic patients. As the patients we have been working with might be in the more healthy part of the schizophrenic spectrum (see the cases below) we have been warned that many schizophrenic patients will be more difficult to cure.

Clinical holistic treatment of schizophrenia and other psychotic diseases

While many of the psychiatric diseases can be efficiently treated with short-term psychodynamic psychotherapy, schizophrenia still seems to challenge the psychodynamic psychotherapist.

The most difficult aspect of the therapy is how to engage the patient in the often quite unpleasant therapy. The autistic aspect of schizophrenia makes it difficult to get into contact at all; the severe emotional disturbances makes it difficult to get into a normal relationship with the patient, and the severe thought disturbances makes it difficult to talk in a coherent and meaningful way and to make a therapeutic contract with the patient.

The patient's hallucinations make it difficult to share a common reality; delusions gives birth to strange behavior and idiosyncratic logic; apathy, paucity of speech, and blunting or incongruity of emotional responses results in general social withdrawal and lowering of social performance often leaving the patient without any resources and thus taking the patient completely out of the "game of life".

So where to start? The goal is to help the patient back into the world as a contributing person; the practical solution of clinical holistic medicine is using a "the triple handle": the patient is contacted though body, mind and total being (spirit) at the same time. The therapy uses whatever aspect the patient offers for getting into contact and aching a proper therapeutic response.

The fundamental goal of the existential therapy is always to induce salutogenesis, or existential healing. Existential healing happens when the patient intents to heal, and gets the resources needed for the healing process from the outside at the same time. During the process of healing, the patient will heal in three dimensions:

- The outer world – healing relations and ability of functioning
- The inner world – healing emotions, philosophy of life and existential problems
- The presence - healing the psychoform and somatoform dissociation through contact, communication and development of the vital sense of coherence.

The therapy must have a balanced focus on these three dimensions at all times.

A standard course of clinical holistic therapy

With severely mentally ill patients, the existential healing is happening according to the metaphor of metamorphosis (78): The patient is like a caterpillar, getting into the pupae stage to remember her true nature and transform, and finally reappearing likes the butterfly. The phases of the existential healing seen though this metaphor is depicted in figure 1.

Please notice that the patient supported by holistic therapy is not getting psychotic, mad, nor suicidal in the crises mentioned in the legend of figure 1. The names refer to the subjective experience of the phases of healing, not to the patient's external and objective behavior.

Actually, the patient is normally coming back to life during these crises, but the emotional intensity demands the most intense support and holding, often by several therapists at a time.

The use of the concepts in CHM is thus very different from the use of the same concepts in standard psychiatry, as the concepts refers to the subjective experience, not to the objective symptoms.

When it comes to the most ill schizophrenic patients it might be impossible to give the holding and support needed at all times, so it might be that we actually see psychotic relapses during therapy with this group of patients; such relapses might also be understood as a habitual pattern of defensive behavior, and as a re-experiencing and reintegrating of earlier psychotic events.

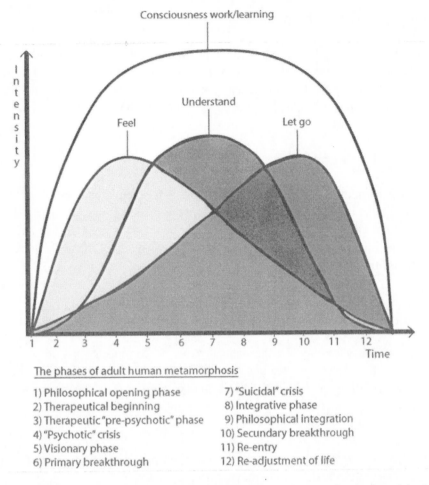

The phases of adult human metamorphosis

1) Philosophical opening phase
2) Therapeutical beginning
3) Therapeutic "pre-psychotic" phase
4) "Psychotic" crisis
5) Visionary phase
6) Primary breakthrough

7) "Suicidal" crisis
8) Integrative phase
9) Philosophical integration
10) Secondary breakthrough
11) Re-entry
12) Re-adjustment of life

Figure 1. The therapeutic arc of transformation. Please notice that there are three existential crises connected to the process of healing from schizophrenia: loss of old, safe self and survival mechanism (giving up the splitting) – often (re)experienced by the patient as a psychic death (number 4) in the figure); the visionary phase often called the healing crisis and often experienced as "holy madness" by the patient (number 5 and 6); and the most intense, existential crisis of "to be or not to be" – often experiences as a suicidal crises by the patient (number 7), where the basic value of life is considered, and where the patient finally must choose life as it is (78).

Key concepts

A. Personal development of quality of life and insight in self

To engage a severely mentally ill patient in therapy the fundamental metaphor must be easily understood and appealing. The concept of personal development is doing the job for most patients. The rehabilitation of the patients character has been alpha and omega since Hippocrates (1).

B. Body-mind-spirit-existence (wholeness)

Holistic therapy makes it possible for the therapist to work with the whole patient, not only his mind. To define the therapy as holistic will open up for the therapists use of bodywork, philosophical exercises etc. that immediately mobilizes patient-resources that cannot be activated within the standard frame of psychodynamic psychotherapy.

C. Purpose of life – good and evil (41)

To engage the patient in a deep self-exploration looking for the hidden purpose of life is often very helpful with the mentally ill patient. To explore the shadow – the good purpose reversing into the evil intent often troubling the patient – might be the door to a common understanding of the world, the illness and the therapy – the later as the way out of the underworld, in which the patent finds himself caught.

D. Clinical holistic medicine: Holding and processing

Love and support is necessary for the patient to relax, lean in, and assimilate the offered resources to get the process of healing going. The picture of the therapy as the therapist keeping a firm grip of the patient in one hand, and beating him with the other – the good and the evil parent in one – is often giving much sense to the patient.

E. Spontaneous regression, symbolic processing, death-rebirth, fetal regression, re-experiencing conception

When the patient receives the resources needed for existential healing he will go back to the painful moments of childhood where he repressed large part of his consciousness to survive (the trauma causing the patients splitting). We call this process for spontaneous regression. It can take the patient all the way back to his first years of life, to his birth, even into the womb and all the way back to conception. Even if this gives no sense for a skeptical mind, this is what the patients often experience in therapy, as first noticed by Grof (15,16) and before that by the tradition of Tibetan Buddhism (14) and other ancient mystery schools. The re-experience of conception often gives a strong feeling of direction in life, and of primary talent (the life mission) (25,37-42).

F. Rehabilitation of patient's talents of sex, consciousness and love

The primary talents of the patient is related to body, mind and spirit – and thus to sexuality, consciousness, and love (39). Many researchers in the treatment of schizophrenia has been focusing on rehabilitation of the patients sexuality; Wilhelm Reich, Harold F Searles and many other outstanding therapist believed that the main etiology to schizophrenia and most other mental diseases was the patient's unconscious repression of genital sexuality. We believe that the ability to love and understand is as important for mental health as the ability to function sexually.

G. From isolation and meaninglessness to contribution and sense of coherence

One extremely important issue in CHM is the rehabilitation of the sense of coherence. This is achieved by rehabilitation of the patient's constructive attitude and behavior towards other people and the surrounding world. Using the talent for being of value to other is the essence of love, and when the patient is able to love and contribute, (s)he is often well again.

H. Philosophy of life – from negative, destructive and delusions to rational and constructive understanding

Rehabilitating the patients positive and constructive, natural philosophy of life and rational thoughts is the most important condition for a permanent cure (5). The negative philosophy is actually a sum of hundreds of negative decisions though life, each holding on to a negative emotion from a painful life event. In the therapy, as the emotional charge is removed from the personal history, a constructive and positive philosophy of life is slowly reappearing.

I. The metaphor of metamorphosis – psychic death, transformation, and reentry in the world

The schizophrenic patients flow of consciousness is most often filled with negative issues like death, illness, rotten flesh, urine and faces, perverted sex, incest, homosexuality, rape, sadomasochism, pedophilia, violence, all kinds of evilness and torture, darkness and death. The acceptance of all these elements and the rational explanation of these elements dominating position in the patient's mind is often experienced as a great relief. The therapist being familiar with all these emotionally difficult subjects and accepting them allows the patient to share for the first time in his or her life the true content of the stream of consciousness. These elements have been classical elements of the traditions of Tantra (14,89,90) and other mystery schools; but most people do not accept to talk about them, even when they are present in there experiential life, as they are a strong taboo of contemporary western culture and society. To allow the patient to engage fully in the exploration of the shadow side of modern man and western culture is often a major key to healing.

J. The healing crisis, hole madness, and crazy wisdom

With hundreds of thousands of hit in a yahoo.com or google.com search, these concepts are well integrated in contemporary spiritual culture. Originally coming from the orient, most people engaged in serious, spiritual development now know them. They signify the wisdom coming from within and materializing itself though dreams and visions in states of expanded consciousness.

These states are introduced by meditation, holotropic breath work, fetal regression, or other intense self-explorative techniques. Most unfortunately, many psychiatrists do not know them, and to not recognize when the patient has entered a healing crises that is an obligatory part of any recovery from schizophrenia. Instead of supporting the patient in the vital project of self-exploration these doctors take the patient "down" from the expanded state of consciousness with antipsychotic drugs, thus arresting the spontaneous healing taking place.

K. Wounded healer

The only way a therapist can truly help his patient is by letting him be the tool for the patient's healing. To do that he must admit that he is only a human being himself; he must admit that he has all human flares and faults himself; he must admit that he is also a wounded child, and not perfect yet; he is also in the process of human development and in that sense very much in the same position as the patient.

Only by sharing the common human conditions, and being together in a true fellowship, can the therapist give sufficient support and holding for the patient to heal the core of his existence.

L. Confronting the evil in whatever form

We are as evil as we are good. We pretend that we are good, or we repress our evil side to our shadow, but when we are true and honest we must admit, that only by choosing the good and abandoning the evil, can we become decent and ethical human beings. Owing the evil is mandatory for the schizophrenic patient, as splitting of the evil side of man is the most common kind of splitting. Secondary is the splitting of the body and sexuality, or of the divine, spiritual aspect of the patient's being.

M. Negative decisions and axiomatic thinking

A trauma always consists of an unbearable feeling and a life-denying, negative decision. This decision is a generalized justification that works as an axiomatic basis for the interpretation of the patient's world. These negative decisions is behind the delusions that the patient presents, and only by taking the patient all the way back to the fundamental emotional pain of the trauma fixating the negative believe, can the patient get rid of his delusions.

Table 1(78) is a list of the most important negative and life-denying sentences that was released during the therapy, when the patient healed her borderline condition. The sentences were the essence of the gestalts that was integrated in the therapy; they are both feelings and thoughts at the same time, making them extremely to the point of the experience.

Table 1. The 25 most importance sentences a borderline patient did let go of in holistic therapy (CHM); while letting go of these decisions she healed her existence and recovered from a severely dysfunctional state. The traumas were sexual abuse in her childhood (78)

1. Nobody likes me
2. I don't want to know it
3. I can't stay anywhere
4. I am out in the space
5. This is unreal
6. I am empty
7. I am hollow
8. It is not me
9. I can do nothing
10. I do not need you
11. I need nobody
12. I cannot do that
13. I am a failure
14. There is no room for me
15. I am nothing
16. It is absurd
17. She is a schizophrenic
18. I am a schizophrenic
19. I do not deserve to live
20. Why didn't they kill me?
21. I get smashed up
22. I go to pieces
23. She is going to kill me
24. He is going to kill me
25. They are going to kill me

N. The fundamental conditions of existence (the "philosophical existentials")

Every person is alive and therefore going to die, which create anxiety; every person is autonomous and therefore basically alone; and every person is intending to contribute in love, and therefore failing and suffering. These three existential pains are inevitable, and every conscious person on Earth must bare these fundamental conditions for being a human being. This must be thoroughly understood by the patient, who normally thing that this is unique and horrible conditions that God gave this pour soul.

O. Precautions

To make psychodynamic therapy with CHM a success there are certain issues of crucial importance:

1) Avoid high age. The older the patient, the more difficult the therapy.

2) Avoid institutionalization. The longer time at an institution, the more difficult the therapy.

3) Avoid pharmaceutical drugs. The higher the dose and the longer time treated, the more difficult the therapy. If the patient is already a psychiatric patient on antipsychotic drugs, who wishes a CHM-treatment, this situation must be handled carefully. For the CHM-therapy to be efficient patients need their full intellectual capacity; as they often experience the antipsychotic drugs as sedating they will often insist on coming of the antipsychotic drugs. We find this reasonable and suggest that it happens gradually, with the patients well supported, in a number of well-controlled steps. Sometimes the patients want to get of the drugs right away which might make them reenter their original psychosis; this can be very therapeutic, but only if there are sufficient therapeutic resources available (several therapists and holders 24hours/7day a week). Most often in our experience the patients who wants to get of the drugs do not have compliance and only pretend to take the drugs, making this problem much less that it might seem.

4) Avoid giving a psychiatric diagnosis if possible. The more the patient think of herself as "schizophrenic", the more difficult the therapy. If they already have a diagnosis, this must be carefully explained as something temporary and not something final.

5) Avoid negative, philosophical implants. The more hopeless the patient believes her situation to be, the more difficult the therapy.

6) Handle the transference of love and sexuality with great care. The more the patient feels rejected and judged, the more difficult the therapy.

7) Handle the acute psychosis with patients and love. The more severe the trauma from loosing control to psychosis is, the more difficult is future therapy.

8) Prevent suicide attempts. The more attempts, the more difficult the therapy.

9) Prevent self-mutilating, self-abuse, humiliation, and loss of: friends and social network, social reality like school, family, self-worth, and self-respect. The deeper the patient falls, the less resources and the more difficult the therapy. One efficient way to do this is by having a person (a "mentor" or a "sponsor") entering into a close, intimate, supportive relation with the patient, for a while being his or her "best friend".

Case stories

Case 1: Psychotic illness in a 7-year-old boy caused by implanted philosophy and cured in one hour (5)

A 7-year-old boy was taken into therapy, because he day or night washed his face and hands every 30 minutes, obsessively. He went furious if somebody stopped him doing this. VandenBos (5) discovered during a one hour session that cured the boy that a doctor had implanted the understanding that the nerves was worms living under his skin. Just clearing the misunderstanding cured the boy. If VandenBos had not examined the boy and cleared this up he would have been taking to a psychiatric ward, and the normal procedure and the trauma of the hospitalization in itself could easily had given symptoms that would have confirmed the tentative diagnoses of schizophrenia. This could easily had turned the child into a chronic patients as VandenBos concluded[5]. If only all cases were this easy!

Case 2: Schizophrenic 30-year-old male cured by three years of holistic therapy (CHM)

30-year-old man who had lived a protected life on a small island. From early childhood he had lived with his grandparents, as his own parents could not raise him. When he came to the clinic he had for years suffered from emotional blunting and an almost complete withdrawal from other people (autism); he had severe delusions of living in outer space combined with strongly peculiar obsessive, catatone behavior (standing fixated on top of telephone boxes to be close to other people) combined with the symptoms of subjective depersonalization and de-realization. At the time he started therapy he considered committing suicide, but was also very scared of dying (ambivalence). He was severely visually hallucinated. He was thinking according to his own personal logic. He sometimes used prostitutes, which he mostly paid to talk with him, which was his only contact to the other sex. On the quality of life scale (QOL5) he rated himself as 4 (bad; 1-5, five being bottom of scale); he was rating his self-evaluated mental health as "poor" (4 on the five point Likert scale).

This patient who had persistent hallucinations (e), catatone behavior (g), negative symptoms (h), significant and consistent change in personal behavior, and social withdrawal (i) was diagnosed /F20 Schizophrenia/ according to ICD-10. He was presumably catatone schizophrenic, but this diagnosis was not used.

He was in the beginning of the CHM-therapy only treated philosophically, as philosophical discussions was the only contact possible with this patient; the patient was given books to read and then the content discussed with the therapist (SV). The books were about philosophy of life, like Buber[91], and Chopra[92]. The patient was clearly intelligent (IQ not measured) and this resource was used. In the next, psychodynamic phase of the therapy, he came into contact with his feelings and went though the existential crisis that is standard with CHM (see figure 1) and was now given the challenging exercises to confront his enormous anxiety. He had to visualize that the anxiety was a fire where he was burned and purified. We did this successfully. Then he was supported in confronting his visual hallucinations, which he also managed to do.

The next theme was supporting him in confronting his problems with women and sexuality. He let go of his use of prostitutes and used his sexual drive to go to town and meet and talk to women; after months of demanding, behavioral training he finally managed to behave socially acceptable on a dance floor, and finally he got a girlfriend and a semi-normal sexual life.

After four month of therapy one hour a week, and intensive writings of dozens of full pages in the form of a patients diary, the patient was able to use the concepts from therapy and from the books he has been reading in his thinking; and for the first time in his life he had a valid language for his strange, alienated perceptions. This made him reflect upon himself and he realized how sick he really was: "Today I was surprised to realize that I really have hallucinations…I jumped into a state of death, with no ability at all to express my sense of I-Thou".

The middle phase of therapy consisted of holistic bodywork (a female holistic physiotherapist) to help him; she managed to take the patient back to the most painful part of early childhood, where the patient were abandoned by his mother (and father), and in healing these old, deep wounds on the patient's soul, he finally came back into normal, emotional contact (induction of salutogenesis through the parallel healing of psychoform and somatoform dissociation).

The third and final part of the therapy was focusing on supporting the patient in creating a new philosophy of life that allowed him to step into character and use his bodily, mental and spiritual talents (25,42).

The CHM-case record for this patient is close to 100 pages, most of them written by the patient. They demonstrate the complete transformation in the patient's logic, value system, relationship with himself and the world, and sexuality. He is not yet able to love other people in a normal way, but he is still recovering, and there is no doubt that his sense of coherence is being rehabilitated. At the end of therapy three years after he started, he rated his QOL5 as 3 (intermediate) and his self evaluated mental health as "good" (2 on the five point Likert scale). He had no longer hallucinations (symptom e), his catatone behavior was gone (g), his negative symptoms gone (h), his significant and consistent change in personal behavior and social withdrawal (i) was radically improved. Thus he did no longer fit the diagnosis of /ICD10-F20 Schizophrenia/ (or DSM-IV Code 295). The patient was thus cured after about 40 sessions (one every third week) of CHM-therapy during three years. He continued in therapy for another year to improve his general ability, and after that he went to university to take his MSc in computer science, where he did well.

Case 3: Schizophrenic 15-year-old male cured by two years of holistic therapy (CHM)

This 15-year old boy was brought to the Research Clinic for Holistic Medicine by his parents, who were not satisfied with the results from several years of psychiatric treatment with neuroleptic drugs and hospitalisation at an institution for violent young mentally ill patients. The parents believed that the drugs did not help him, that he got too much medicine, which sedated him without curing him, as they did not see any improvement as time went by.

He had been extremely violent in school, clearly psychotic and living in strong delusions of being another person, a German soldier from the Second World War, which life he clearly remembered. The things he told from his personal story were strongly worrying; amongst other things he had been just about to kill a friend at school, of which he was rather proud – it proved that he was the strong Nazi-soldier he believed himself to be. He was hallucinated and saw his father as an English pilot he remembered that he killed during the war.

We accepted to take him into CHM-therapy and the municipality accepted to pay for the therapy (yearly cost for the institution was about 150,000 Euro, the cost of treatment in our clinic about 4,000 Euro a year). According to ICD-10 he was clearly having the following symptoms:

d)   persistent delusions that are culturally inappropriate
e)   persistent visual hallucinations occurring every day for months on end
f)   "negative" symptoms such as blunting and incongruity of emotional responses

g) a significant and consistent change in the overall quality of personal behavior

According to ICD-10 his diagnosis was thus /F20 Schizophrenia/. In the beginning of the therapy the patient was very vulnerable and weak in the emotional contact; he went through a big transformation process and astonishingly ended up on his feet as a healthy young man who is doing well socially and at school. He stopped the medicine during the first months of therapy by himself, without sharing is with anybody, and obviously without needing it any more.

In the therapy evilness was the big theme, and after months of confrontation of his shadow (his evil side) he ended up by choosing to be good and letting go of his idea of being the German warrier. After this fundamental shift in his personal philosophy, he was able to slowly regain empathy and emotional contact; he went back to school where he is doing really fine and caching up on the three years he missed. After a few episodes of moderate violence (fighting with the other boys) he managed to get his anger and furry under control, and continues to developed into a well-functioning boy, that is fitting in and being appreciated by the other kids. He got a girlfriend, which is very good for his self-esteem and feeling of being a young man, growing up and participating in society. He is now of great help to his family, and his progress highly appreciated.

In the holistic therapy using also bodywork the patient's psychoform and somatoform dissociations were healed and his sense of coherence slowly recovered. After two years and about 40 sessions he was out of regular therapy, but he continued for follow-up sessions every six months. About a year after the therapy ended he got the following statement from his teacher at school:

> "PATIENT NAME has in relation to diligence and cooperation been doing satisfactorily work. He has been positive and very engaged in the subjects. In the class room PATIENT NAME has contributed creating a good and positive atmosphere as a good listener and friend. PATIENT NAME has furthermore good relations to the school staff. The school therefore gives him the best recommendations."

His delusions, hallucination, incongruity emotional responses, and behavioural disturbances including his tendency to violence has now completely gone. Thus he did no longer fit with the diagnosis of /ICD10-F20 Schizophrenia/ (or DSM-IV Code 295).

Challenges for the therapist

Working with schizophrenic patients gives the therapist all the challenges you can with for – and a little more. Only if you are up to an intense project of accelerated self-development and a exploration into your own shadow for deep self-insight, will you find it really rewarding to work with this group of patients. Below is listed the challenges that we have met in our work with the patients.

- All symptoms and symbols are meaningful – the therapist must contain his confusion, because in the end all questions will be answered, but in the most surprising ways.
- The sexual content of the patients unconscious will be explicit – most traumatic events shared by the patient refers to real events, whether it being incest or rape (5) and you must be worth your salt as a therapist when the patient brings this to the sessions.
- Implanted philosophy: The most important gift the therapist can give his patient is his optimism about the patients ability to heal and recover (5); often you can hardly believe that the patient has a chance, but you must choose to believe it.
- Never expect your patient to be grateful or to acknowledge improvements. When a problem is gone – it is out of the patients mind forever. So keep a thorough case report and do not expect patients to remember their progress or even to thank you for curing them when they are cured (5).
- The more healthy the patient gets in the process, the more troubled will the patient's feelings and emotions be. An example from (5) is a girl that starts completely unable to have sex, and after successful therapy starts complaining about her not liking her new boyfriend much, and not getting to much pleasure from sex. She is not grateful at all for her being able to have the boyfriend now but only angry over things that are not right and perfect yet. This is clearly a patient healing. Only by keeping a good case record, this progress can be appreciated by the therapist.
- The patient being more emotionally labile, angry, expressive and difficult is a good sign of the patient healing. Most therapists – as most parents – do not really appreciate people getting more powerful, selfish, and demanding. But it is a fine sign of individuation. Emotional crisis will get more and more intense and more and more frequent. That is the patient coming back to life, which is always painful. Often the awakening sexuality will give the patient strong sexual feelings and a most uncomfortable and embarrassing behavior, especially when the patient is transferring sexuality on the therapist. This is not the patient getting more sick but the patient getting into a developmental state similar to retarded puberty, and the sexuality of the patient must not be condemned or repressed it the therapist wants the patient to recover.
- The patient's borders are often transgressed and badly defined. Most patients have never had a private room in their life, and the establishment of such a sacred, personal space is a necessity for the patient to recover his identity. To support the patient in having such a space, the therapist must accept the patient to have secrets.
- Counter transferences are often difficult. The schizophrenic patient is often living in a self-made hell that we do not want to look into; when we do so our empathy courses us unbearable pain. Especially sharing the position of feeling reduced from being a person to being something like a mistreated animal, or even a thing without life and existence, puts us in severe agony. The patient's defenses will make the patient do everything to hinder that we get close to the patient, so very often the patient will make himself dirty, ugly, repelling etc, just to make us keep an emotional distance to him. Some patients use urine, faces, saliva, dirty cloths etc. to make themselves less appealing. Psychotic patients presents their emotional, sexual etc.

material in the most raw and least socially acceptable form for the same reason: To prove to themselves that we do not like them at all – the same way they felt rejected and not loved by their parents.

- Risking murder and suicide. Psychotic patients do not have the inhibitions that normal people have. Sometimes they kill themselves, and sometimes they kill others. The psychology of a murder is often a patient that cannot accept angry impulses (cannot contain conscious anger), and represses these impulses till the day he explodes (5). Often sexuality and jealousy are central issues here. Most schizophrenic patients are not dangerous at all, but the therapist should use his intuition and common sense and be very careful, when the patient feels like a "bomb" of repressed anger, and is living in a conflict involving jealousy.

- Most patients, whether psychotic or borderline, consider committing suicide during the therapy (5). Actually the suicidal crisis must be seen as an important part of the therapy, because this is when the patient for the first time in life really chooses life. Fortunately the consideration is hardly ever leading to the action of committing suicide, but the danger of the patient committing suicide must be considered in every consultation, and if suicidal thoughts are present, the issue must be directly addressed, to support the patient in taking the learning from the crisis, and preventing suicide.

- Suicide, when actually committed, is often materializing the desperate intent of revenge. The calculation is that if the patient kills himself, the person(s) who failed the patient will be really sorry! Most often suicidal attempts are nothing but a cry for help – the young girl takes four sleeping pills and knows she will be found with the suicide letter in her hand. Much more seriously endangered is the 60-years old, male and recently retired patient that demonstrates the "presuicidal syndrome"(93).

- It is very important to notice that research has shown that ECT (electroconvulsive therapy) is not preventing suicide, but just postpones it (94). The prescription of antipsychotic drugs is very dangerous in the case of a suicide threat, as everybody knows that drugs are often used to commit suicide; drugs are also taking the patient into depression enhancing the emotional drive against suicide (94).

- Risking violence from the patient. Therapists are often exposed to threats and even at rare occasions to violence, when working on schizophrenic patients. Karon (5) described a patient putting a pin into her knee during a session, in the intent of making the therapist hate him. For most schizophrenic patients love and kindness is had to stand; hatred and anger are better, and emotionally cold rejection and even total lack of interest is making the patient feel safe.

- Mastering controlled fail of the patient. The reason is that most schizophrenic patients comes from severely dysfunctional families, where they have survived without getting the love and close contact that is a normal part of other children's upbringing. The ability of the therapist to fail the patient intentionally, using the principle of similarity, is a central condition for being able to cure. Most therapists engage themselves in their patients; and when they are starting to know them they are often also coming to like them. In this case the holding is appropriate, and processing must follow. Here the therapist must shift between being the good father/mother of the patient, and the evil father/mother. Many therapists find this shifting necessary for supporting the schizophrenic patient most difficult.

- Containing self-mutilation. Often the schizophrenic patients are self-destructive, and this must be contained by the therapist. When this is directly addressed, the reason for the impulses are often understood and self-mutilations stops. Karon described a self-mutilating patient that cut his arm using broken glass from a glass bulb[5]. Karon used the occasion to give the patient credit for stopping before the artery was cut: "I am proud of you. You stopped cutting yourself before somebody else had to stop you" (5). This direct confrontation without any judgment made the patient stop his self-mutilation.

- Patient that will not eat. Karon and VandenBos (5) recommended psychotherapy during a meal as the key to solving this problem.

- Sleeping disorders. Karon and VandenBos (5) recommended full accept of the state as solution, and recommended the patient not to sleep but just to lay down for eight hours of resting – without getting up during the night. Most patients ague that this is very boring, and the answer is to acknowledge the boredom, and reassure the patient that he will be able to function the next day.

- Illegal drugs. Most schizophrenics are not attracted to heroin or other similar drugs, but if they are hallucinated, they can be very interested in hallucinogenic drugs that can enhance the hallucinations and give the patient insight in the nature and hidden courses of the hallucinations; regular use of high doses of hallucinogens are to be considered self-destructive (5) and the therapist should warn the patient against the negative consequences of abuse, like bad trips (drug-traumas) and flash backs (5).

Discussion

Schizophrenia is today often regarded as the most difficult disease to treat with psychotherapy, especially when the patient is in a psychotic state, or hospitalized (95). Normally, therefore, the scizophrenic patient is treated with a drug, and only when the patient is back in a "normal" and communicative state of being, can additional psychotherapy be introduced.

Unfortunately only 1 in 4 or less reacts well to for example chlorpromazine and one in two gets serious physical side effects (12). The drug is also suspected to provoke severe mental adverse-effects with dysphoria, depression and even the feeling of "being like a zombie" (96). In addition to that, a spontaneous over-mortality of up to 150% has recently been documented by the Danish Health Authorities for specific subgroups (97).

The standard psychiatric treatment is known not to cure schizophrenia, but only to reduce some of its symptoms, and schizophrenia is considered by most psychiatrists to be a chronic and incurable disease. The standard psychiatric treatment is thus a rather imperfect treatment for schizophrenia, and alternatives must be sought. Luckily the last decade has given us documentation of psychodynamic psychotherapy being efficient with mental diseases[8-10] and presumably also with schizophrenia (5,85,87,88).

Psychotherapy in patients with schizophrenia has been considered more difficult than the treatment of any other group of mental illnesses, due to the triad of autism, emotional "flattening" and not correctable delusions. When the contact with the patient is very poorly anchored in mind, feeling, and body, as we see it in patients with severe somatoform and psychoform dissociation, the possibility to have an impact on a patient is rather limited. If the patient is psychotic, and not oriented in time, space and own data, this becomes even harder. Seen from the therapist's perspective, there is no "handle" to get hold on the patient and start turning him back towards reality.

To solve this problem, we have expanded short-term psychodynamic psychotherapy with bodywork and philosophy of life exercises (47-49), giving the therapist a possibility to get in contact with the patient at a physical, mental and spiritual level at the same time. The triple grip of the patient allows us to work with even the most psychotic patient, although therapeutic progress is not always visible in the beginning of the therapy. We have observed in the patients that come to our clinic that three things are associated to a good outcome of therapy: the younger the patient is, the shorter time a patient has spent in a psychiatric ward, the shorter time the patient has been on antipsychotic drugs, and the shorter time the patient has been ill, the easier it is to help. We have worked with 10 insufficiently diagnosed schizophrenic/schizotypical patients and about 30 borderline patients (44) and have noticed a certain path of healing for these patients that often takes a quite dramatic form, when treated with clinical holistic medicine, with a quite number of severe existential crises before healing existentially (see figure 1).

We have been working on the schizophrenic patients directly with the deluded thoughts, the flattened emotions and the autistic withdrawal from the world. We have found that all these symptoms characterizing the schizophrenic patients can in most cases quite easily be traced back to severely dysfunctional family patterns of the patient's childhood. Especially the method of spontaneous regression, where taking the patient into fetal regression, has made is possible to include the prenatal adaptation to the future family, which has given many of the missing pieces to a full psychodynamic understanding of schizophrenia. These adaptations also seem to be able to explain the concordance seen in the twin studies with schizophrenic patients, stressing the environmental factors and thus giving an alternative hypothesis to the hypothesis of genetic courses of schizophrenia.

The patient is often found in a severely dysfunctional state of being, with very few if any stable intimate, personal, confidential contacts. So helping the patient back to life is basically about inducing salutogenesis by rehabilitating sense of coherence in two directions – inwards, towards life, and outwards, towards other people and the surrounding world. To induce the recovery of schizophrenia, the first thing to be done is to give the schizophrenic patient the optimal holding they need, to go back to confront old childhood traumas. In the therapy we normally give them two "new" parents: a male and a female therapist, who during therapy act as if they were the patient's "good" and "bad" parents. One of the therapists is good, while the other therapist evil, taking the patient back using the principle of similarity, while giving the patient all the loving and caring support needed for the existential healing.

We have found that as soon as we are able to engage the patient in the therapeutic contract, the therapy is starting to work. We have found that one in two of the schizophrenic patients (the limitation is our small sample) was cured during one year of holistic therapy. Unfortunately the limited number is not sufficient for statistical analysis and the diagnosis were not made strictly according to an international system like ICD10 or SDM-IV, so we are now conducting another experiment including a larger number of patients and more well-defined international diagnostic criteria.

Dissociation is a well-established phenomenon [DSM IV, 98-102] occurring in people who have experienced some form of trauma. Trauma can be defined as anything that overwhelms our resources (99). According to the Diagnostic and Statistical Manual for Mental Disorders, Fourth Edition (DSM-IV; American Psychiatric Association, 1994), the essential feature of dissociation is a disruption of the normal integrative functions of conscious-ness, memory, identity, and perception of the environment. Much of the research on dissociation emerged from the identification of Post Traumatic Stress Disorder as a distinct condition. Van der Kolk (98) identified core symptoms of PTSD as intrusions (thoughts, dreams, flashbacks), hyper arousal and numbing. Dissociation is a real, biological phenomena arising from trauma, and both somatoform and psychoform dissociation must be healed to cure schizophrenia and other psychotic mental disorders.

It is still a matter of discussion if traumas are the underlying cause of schizophrenia; our success in healing a few schizophrenic patients by healing their traumas definitely points in this direction.

During the last two centuries thousands of therapists have succeeded to cure a fraction of their schizophrenic patients; we know that Philippe Pinel and his students with their moral therapy cured patients, but as the diagnosis schizofrenia (or dementia precox) was not available yet, we do not know the fraction of cured schizophrenic patient. When data on the treatment of schizophrenia became available we see that 33% were cured and 33% radically improved, but the rest only little improvement or not helped by psychothederapy (Harold Searles statistics are documented in ([103], the introduction). Similar results were produced by a number of remarkable therapist, like Jung (1875-1961)(7), Adler (1870-1937)(104), Abraham (1877-1925)(105), Federn (1871-1950)(106), Harry Stack Sullivan and Frida Fromm Reichmann further develloped by Will (1961)(107) and Searles (1965)(108), Schilder (1935)(109), Rosenfeld (1965)(110), Segal (1950)(111), Fairbairn (1954)(112), Guntrip (1969)(113), Perry (1961)(114), Lidz (1973)(115), Kernberg (1975,1976)(116,117), Volkan (1976)(118), Sechehaye (1951)(119), Rosen (1953)(120), Eissler (1952)(121), Arlow and Brenner (1964)(122), Giovacchini (1979)(123), Arieti (1974)(124), Bellak (1979)(125), Gendlin (1967)(126), Prouty (1976)(127), Gunderson and Mosher (1976)(128), and Karon and VandenBos (1981)(5). But even before Pinel and the psychotherapists the Hippocratic doctors healed the hysteric and mentally ill patients for millennia with holistic medicine.

In spite of this strong and scientifically well estabilshed tradition many physicians today have come to believe, that schizophrenia cannot be treated with psychotherapy, which has been discussed by Karon and VandenBos (5). It seems that many physicians believe that it is very difficult and demands special skills, knowledge, talents and training to make therapy with schizophrenic patients available. Karon and VandenBos argued that this is not the case, since everybody who cares about people and knows elementary psychotherapy can treat schizophrenic patients, and although these patients can be very difficult, some of them are easy to help, and almost nobody is completely impossible to help (5).

Conclusions

It is not new that psychodynamic psychotherapy and holistic medicine can help cure schizophrenia and other psychotic mental disorders. In one study Searles treated a group of 18 of the most heavy, chronically ill schizophrenics with a duration of illness of in average 9,2 years, and 2,3 years of hospitalization on average before entrance into the study. After therapy 33,3% were cured ("remarkably improved" and out of hospital) and further 38,9% were "remarkably improved", but still hospitalized[103]. Searles kept records of 600 patients for his research and continued to be optimistic throughout his life. It is generally believed that the earlier the treatment starts the better will be the therapeutic results. Based on the available data we estimate that schizophrenic patients can actually be cured by intensive holistic therapy, if they are treated right at onset of disease..

But to work with these "heavy" patients the therapist must be prepared to invest his whole existence and he must expect to be challenged at all levels of existence. To maximize the therapeutic effect of psychodynamic psychotherapy it must be turned into the system of clinical holistic medicine (CHM), also using bodywork and philosophy of life. CHM has been developed though the last two decades to treat even severely mentally ill patients, like schizophrenia.

There are many different factors to get hold of and a lot of theory to master before a therapist can treat schizophrenic patients easily. As a therapist you need to acknowledge the gift of a daily challenge. You need to appreciate the gift of not getting gratefulness in return for a most demanding and even exhausting job. You need to like to work with the human shadow, looking deep down into the evil, the sexual, the mystery, and the divine side of life. We need therapists and researchers to engage in the development of CHM, because we owe the patient a treatment that cures them, not just a treatment that alleviates some patients of the symptoms and give many more patients side effects. If you can love even the sickest person, if you can see all the illnesses you meet in your patient in yourself too, if you want to develop yourself and obtain wisdom, then working with schizophrenic patients might be the job of your dreams.

We find that holistic, psychodynamic treatment (CHM) is the cure of choice for schizophrenia, as the psychopharmachological treatment has proved less efficient with many side effects. We therefore recommend further research in scientific holistic therapy and its development.

References

[1] Jones WHS. Hippocrates. Vol. I–IV. London: William Heinemann, 1923-1931.

[2] Ventegodt S, Clausen B, Omar HA, Merrick J. Clinical holistic medicine: Holistic sexology and acupressure through the vagina (Hippocratic pelvic massage). ScientificWorldJournal 2006;6:2066-79.

[3] Ventegodt S, Clausen B, Merrick J. Clinical holistic medicine: Pilot study on the effect of vaginal acupressure (Hippocratic pelvic massage). ScientificWorldJournal 2006;6:2100-16.

[4] Weiner DB. The clinical training of doctors. An essay from 1793 by Philippe Pinel.. Henry E Sigerist Suppl Bull Hist Med 1980;3:1-102.

[5] Karon BP, VandenBos G. Psychotherapy of schizophrenia. The treatment of choise. New York: Jason Aronson, 1981.

[6] Jones E. The life and works of Sigmund Freud. New York: Basic Books, 1961.

[7] Jung CG. Man and his symbols. New York: Anchor Press, 1964.

[8] Leichsenring F, Rabung S, Leibing E. The efficacy of short-term psychodynamic psychotherapy in specific psychiatric disorders: a meta-analysis. Arch Gen Psychiatry 2004;61(12):1208-16.

[9]   Leichsenring F. Are psychodynamic and psychoanalytic therapies effective? A review of empirical data. Int J Psychoanal 2005;86(Pt 3):841-68.

[10] Leichsenring F, Leibing E. Psychodynamic psychotherapy: a systematic review of techniques, indications and empirical evidence. Psychol Psychother 2007;80(Pt 2):217-28.

[11] Ventegodt S, Kandel I, Merrick J. Clinical holistic medicine: How to recover memory without "implanting" memories in your patient. ScientificWorldJournal 2007;7:1579-589.

[12] Adams CE, Awad G, Rathbone J, Thornley B. Chlorpromazine versus placebo for schizophrenia. Cochrane Database Syst Rev 2007;18(2):CD000284.

[13] Sullivan PF, Kendler KS, Neale MC. Schizophrenia as a complex trait: evidence from a meta-analysis of twin studies. Arch Gen Psychiatry 2003;60(12):1187-92.

[14] Sambhava P, Thurman RA, Pa KG. The Tibetan book of the dead. New York: Bantam, 1994.

[15] Grof S. LSD psychotherapy: Exploring the trontiers of the hidden mind. Alameda, CA: Hunter House, 1980.

[16] Grof S. Psychology of the future. Albany, NY: State Univ New York Press, 2000.

[17] Antonovsky A. Health, stress and coping. London: Jossey-Bass, 1985.

[18] Antonovsky A. Unravelling the mystery of health. How people manage stress and stay well. San Franscisco: Jossey-Bass, 1987.

[19] Flensborg-Madsen T, Ventegodt S, Merrick J. Sense of coherence and physical health. A Review of previous findings. ScientificWorldJournal 2005;5:665-73.

[20] Flensborg-Madsen T, Ventegodt S, Merrick J. Why is Antonovsky's sense of coherence not correlated to physical health? Analysing Antonovsky's 29-item sense of coherence scale (SOCS). ScientificWorldJournal 2005;5:767-76.

[21] Flensborg-Madsen T, Ventegodt S, Merrick J. Sense of coherence and health. The construction of an amendment to Antonovsky's sense of coherence scale (SOC II). ScientificWorldJournal 2006;6:2133-9.

[22] Flensborg-Madsen T, Ventegodt S, Merrick J. Sense of coherence and physical health. A cross-sectional study using a new SOC scale (SOC II). ScientificWorldJournal 2006;6:2200-11.

[23] Flensborg-Madsen T, Ventegodt S, Merrick J. Sense of coherence and physical health. Testing Antonovsky's theory. ScientificWorldJournal 2006;6:2212-9.

[24] Flensborg-Madsen T, Ventegodt S, Merrick J. Sense of coherence and health. The emotional sense of coherence (SOC-E) was found to be the best-known predictor of physical health. ScientificWorldJournal 2006;6:2147-57.

[25] Ventegodt S, Flensborg-Madsen T, Andersen NJ, Merrick J. Life mission theory VII: Theory of existential (Antonovsky) coherence: a theory of quality of life, health and ability for use in holistic medicine. ScientificWorldJournal 2005;5:377-89.

[26] Rosen M, Brenner S. Rosen method bodywork. Accessing the unconscious through touch. Berkeley, CA: North Atlantic Books, 2003.

[27] Hermansen TD, Ventegodt S, Rald E, Clausen B, Nielsen ML, Merrick J. Human development I. Twenty fundamental problems of biology, medicine and neuropsychology related to biological information. ScientificWorldJournal 2006;6:747-59.

[28] Ventegodt S, Hermansen TD, Nielsen ML, Clausen B, Merrick J. Human development II. We need an integrated theory for matter, life and consciousness to understand life and healing. ScientificWorldJournal 2006;6:760-6.

[29] Ventegodt S, Hermansen TD, Rald E, Flensborg-Madsen T, Nielsen ML, Clausen B, Merrick J. Human development III. Bridging brain-mind and body-mind. Itroduction to "deep" (fractal, poly-ray) cosmology. ScientificWorldJournal 2006;6:767-76.

[30] Ventegodt S, Hermansen TD, Rald E, Flensborg-Madsen T, Nielsen ML, Clausen B, Merrick J. Human development IV. The living cell has information-directed self-organization. ScientificWorldJournal 2006;6:1132-8.

[31] Ventegodt S, Hermansen TD, Flensborg-Madsen T, Nielsen ML, Clausen B, Merrick J. Human development V: Biochemistry unable to explain the emergence of biological form (morphogenesis) and therefore a new principle as source of biological information is needed. ScientificWorldJournal 2006;6:1359-67.

[32] Ventegodt S, Hermansen TD, Flensborg-Madsen T, Nielsen M, Merrick J. Human development VI: Supracellular morphogenesis. The origin of biological and cellular order. ScientificWorldJournal 2006;6:1424-33.

[33] Ventegodt S, Hermansen TD, Flensborg-Madsen T, Rald E, Nielsen ML, Merrick J. Human development VII: A spiral fractal model of fine structure of physical energy could explain central aspects of biological information, biological organization and biological creativity. ScientificWorldJournal 2006;6:1434-40.

[34] Ventegodt S, Hermansen TD, Flensborg-Madsen T, Nielsen ML, Merrick J. Human development VIII: A theory of "deep" quantum chemistry and cell consciousness: Quantum chemistry controls genes and biochemistry to give cells and higher organisms consciousness and complex behavior. ScientificWorldJournal 2006;6:1441-53.

[35] Ventegodt S, Hermansen TD, Flensborg-Madsen T, Rald E, Nielsen ML, Merrick J. Human development IX: A model of the wholeness of man, his consciousness and collective consciousness. ScientificWorldJournal 2006;6:1454-9.

[36] Hermansen TD, Ventegodt S, Merrick J. Human development X: Explanation of macroevolution — top-down evolution materializes consciousness. The origin of metamorphosis. ScientificWorldJournal 2006;6:1656-66.

[37] Ventegodt S. The life mission theory: A theory for a consciousness-based medicine. Int J Adolesc Med Health 2003;15(1): 89-91.

[38] Ventegodt S, Andersen NJ, Merrick J. The life mission theory II. The structure of the life purpose and the ego. ScientificWorldJournal 2003;3:1277-85.

[39] Ventegodt S, Andersen NJ, Merrick J. The life mission theory III. Theory of talent. ScientificWorldJournal 2003;3:1286-93.

[40] Ventegodt S, Andersen NJ, Merrick J. The life mission theory IV. Theory on child development. ScientificWorldJournal 2003;3:1294-1301.

[41] Ventegodt S, Andersen NJ, Merrick J. The life mission theory V. Theory of the anti-self (the shadow) or the evil side of man. ScientificWorldJournal 2003;3:1302-13.

[42] Ventegodt S, Kromann M, Andersen NJ, Merrick J. The life mission theory VI. A theory for the human character: Healing with holistic medicine through recovery of character and purpose of life. ScientificWorldJournal 2004;4:859-80.

[43] Ventegodt S, Clausen B, Nielsen ML, Merrick J. Clinical holistic medicine: Advanced tools for holistic medicine. ScientificWorldJournal 2006;6:2048-65.

[44] Ventegodt S, Thegler S, Andreasen T, Struve F, Enevoldsen L, Bassaine L, et al. Clinical holistic medicine: Psychodynamic short-time therapy complemented with bodywork. A clinical follow-up study of 109 patients. ScientificWorldJournal 6, 2220-2238.

[45] Ventegodt S, Andersen NJ, Merrick J. Holistic Medicine III: The holistic process theory of healing. ScientificWorldJournal 2003;3: 1138-46.

[46] Ventegodt S, Andersen NJ, Merrick J. Holistic Medicine IV: Principles of the holistic process of healing in a group setting. ScientificWorldJournal 2003;3:1294-1301.

[47] Ventegodt S, Kandel I, Merrick J. Principles of holistic medicine. Philosophy behind quality of life. Victoria, BC: Trafford, 2005.

[48] Ventegodt S, Kandel I, Merrick J. Principles of holistic medicine. Quality of life and health. New York: Hippocrates Sci Publ, 2005.

[49] Ventegodt S, Kandel I, Merrick J. Principles of holistic medicine. Global quality of life.Theory, research and methodology. New York: Hippocrates Sci Publ, 2006.

[50] Antonella R. Introduction of regulatory methods. Systematics, description and current research. Graz: Interuniversity College, 2004.

[51] Blättner B. Fundamentals of salutogenesis. Health promotion (WHO) and individual promotion of health guided by resources. Graz: Interuniversity College, 2004.

[52] Endler PC. Master's program for complementary, psychosocial and integrated health sciences. Graz: Interuniversity College, 2004.

[53] Endler PC. Working and writing scientifically in complementary medicine and integrated health sciences. Graz: Interuniversity College, 2004.

[54]   Kratky KW. Complementary medicine systems. Comparison and integration. New York, Nova Sci, 2008.

[55]   Pass PF. Fundamentals of depth psychology. Therapeutic relationship formation between self-awareness and casework. Graz: Interuniversity College, 2004.

[56]   Spranger HH. Fundamentals of regulatory biology. Paradigms and scientific backgrounds of regulatory methods. Graz: Interuniversity College, 2004.

[57]   Ventegodt S, Morad M, Merrick J. Clinical holistic medicine: Holistic treatment of children. ScientificWorldJournal 2004;4:581-8.

[58]   Ventegodt S, Morad M, Merrick J. Clinical holistic medicine: Problems in sex and living together. ScientificWorldJournal 2004;4: 562-70.

[59]   Ventegodt S, Morad M, Hyam E, Merrick J. Clinical holistic medicine: Holistic sexology and treatment of vulvodynia through existential therapy and acceptance through touch. ScientificWorldJournal 2004;4:571-80.

[60]   Ventegodt S, Flensborg-Madsen T, Andersen NJ, Morad M, Merrick J. Clinical holistic medicine: A Pilot on HIV and Quality of Life and a Suggested treatment of HIV and AIDS. ScientificWorldJournal 2004;4:264-72.

[61]   Ventegodt S, Morad M, Merrick J. Clinical holistic medicine: Induction of spontaneous remission of cancer by recovery of the human character and the purpose of life (the life mission). ScientificWorldJournal 2004;4:362-77.

[62]   Ventegodt S, Morad M, Kandel I, Merrick J. Clinical holistic medicine: Treatment of physical health problems without a known cause, exemplified by hypertension and tinnitus. ScientificWorldJournal 2004;4:716-24.

[63]   Ventegodt S, Morad M, Merrick J. Clinical holistic medicine: Developing from asthma, allergy and eczema. ScientificWorldJournal 2004;4:936-42.

[64]   Ventegodt S, Morad M, Press J, Merrick J, Shek DTL. Clinical holistic medicine: Holistic adolescent medicine. ScientificWorldJournal 2004;4:551-61.

[65]   Ventegodt S, Solheim E, Saunte ME, Morad M, Kandel I, Merrick J. Clinical holistic medicine: Metastatic cancer. ScientificWorldJournal 2004;4:913-35.

[66]   Ventegodt S, Morad M, Kandel I, Merrick J. Clinical holistic medicine: a psychological theory of dependency to improve quality of life. ScientificWorldJournal 2004;4:638-48.

[67]   Ventegodt S, Merrick J. Clinical holistic medicine: Chronic infections and autoimmune diseases. ScientificWorldJournal 2005;5: 155-64.

[68]   Ventegodt S, Kandel I, Neikrug S, Merrick J. Clinical holistic medicine: Holistic treatment of rape and incest traumas. ScientificWorldJournal 2005;5:288-97.

[69]   Ventegodt S, Morad M, Merrick J. Clinical holistic medicine: Chronic pain in the locomotor system. ScientificWorldJournal 2005;5:165-72.

[70]   Ventegodt S, Merrick J. Clinical holistic medicine: Chronic pain in internal organs. ScientificWorldJournal 2005;5:205-10.

[71]   Ventegodt S, Kandel I, Neikrug S, Merrick J. Clinical holistic medicine: The existential crisis – life crisis, stress and burnout. ScientificWorldJournal 2005;5:300-12.

[72]   Ventegodt S, Gringols M, Merrick J. Clinical holistic medicine: Holistic rehabilitation ScientificWorldJournal 2005;5:280-7.

[73]   Ventegodt S, Andersen NJ, Neikrug S, Kandel I, Merrick J. Clinical holistic medicine: Mental disorders in a holistic perspective. ScientificWorldJournal 2005;5:313-23.

[74]   Ventegodt S, Andersen NJ, Neikrug S, Kandel I, Merrick J. Clinical holistic medicine: Holistic treatment of mental disorders. ScientificWorldJournal 2005;5:427-45.

[75]   Ventegodt S, Merrick J. Clinical holistic medicine: The patient with multiple diseases. ScientificWorldJournal 2005;5:324-39.

[76]   Ventegodt S, Clausen B, Merrick J. Clinical holistic medicine: The case story of Anna: I. Long term effect of child sexual abuse and incest with a treatment approach. ScientificWorldJournal 2006;6:1965-76.

[77]   Ventegodt S, Clausen B, Merrick J. Clinical holistic medicine: the case story of Anna. II. Patient diary as a tool in treatment. ScientificWorldJournal 2006;6:2006-34.

[78]   Ventegodt S, Clausen B, Merrick J. Clinical holistic medicine: The case story of Anna. III. Rehabilitation of philosophy of life during holistic existential therapy for childhood sexual abuse. ScientificWorldJournal 2006;6:2080-91.

[79]   Ventegodt S, Merrick J. Suicide from a holistic point of view. ScientificWorldJournal 2005;5:759-66.

[80]   Ventegodt S. [Min brug af vaginal akupressur.] My use of acupressure. Ugeskr Laeger 2006;168(7):715-6. [Danish].

[81]   Ventegodt S, Clausen B, Omar HA, Merrick J. Clinical holistic medicine: Holistic sexology and acupressure through the vagina (Hippocratic pelvic massage). ScientificWorldJournal 2006;6:2066-79.

[82]   Ventegodt S, Thegler S, Andreasen T, Struve F, Enevoldsen L, Bassaine L, et al. Clinical holistic medicine (mindful, short-term psychodynamic psychotherapy complemented with bodywork) in the treatment of experienced impaired sexual functioning. ScientificWorldJournal 2007;7:324-9.

[83]   Ventegodt S, Thegler S, Andreasen T, Struve F, Enevoldsen L, Bassaine L, et al. Clinical holistic medicine (mindful, short-term psychodynamic psychotherapy complemented with bodywork) improves quality of life, health, and ability by induction of Antonovsky-salutogenesis. ScientificWorldJournal 2007;7:317-23.

[84]   Ventegodt S, Thegler S, Andreasen T, Struve F, Enevoldsen L, Bassaine L, et al. Clinical holistic medicine (mindful, short-term psychodynamic psychotherapy complemented with bodywork) in the treatment of experienced physical illness and chronic pain. ScientificWorldJournal 2007;7:310-6.

[85]   Ventegodt S, Thegler S, Andreasen T, Struve F, Enevoldsen L, Bassaine L, et al. Clinical holistic medicine (mindful, short-term psychodynamic psychotherapy complemented with bodywork) in the treatment of experienced mental illness. ScientificWorldJournal 2007;7:306-9.

[86]   Ventegodt S, Thegler S, Andreasen T, Struve F, Enevoldsen L, Bassaine L, et al. Self-reported low self-esteem. Intervention and follow-up in a clinical setting. ScientificWorldJournal 2007;7:299- 305.

[87]   Mosher LR. Evaluation of psychosocial treatments. In: Gunderson, JG, Mosher LR, eds. Psychotherapy of schizophrenia. New York: Aronson, 1975:253-8.

[88]   Mosher LR. (1975) Psychotherapy research. In: Gunderson, JG, Mosher LR, eds. Psychotherapy of schizophrenia. New York: Aronson, 1975:243-52.

[89]   Trungpa C. Crazy wisdom. Berkeley, CA: Dharma Ocean Series, Shambhala Publ, 1969.

[90]   Feuerstein G. Hole madness spirituality, crazy-wise teachers and enlightenment. New York: Hohm Press, 2001.

[91]   Buber M. I and thou. New York: Charles Scribner's Sons, 1970.

[92]   Chopra D. Quantum healing. Exploring the frontiers of mind body medicine. New York: Bantam Books, 1990.

[93]   Polewka A, Maj JC, Warchol K, Groszek B. [The assessment of suicidal risk in the concept of the presuicidal syndrome, and the possibilities it provides for suicide prevention and therapy--review] Przegl Lek 2005;62:399-402. [Polish].

[94]   Avery D, Winokur G. Mortality in depressed patients treated with electro convulsive therapy and antidepressants. Arch Gen Psychiatry 1976;33:1029-37.

[95]   Malmberg L, Fenton M. Individual psychodynamic psychotherapy and psychoanalysis for schizophrenia and severe mental illness. Cochrane Database Syst Rev 2001;3:CD001360.

[96]   The Swedich Council of Technology Assessment in Health Care. Treatment with antipsychotic drugs [Behandling med neuroleptika.] Stockholm: SBU-Report 133/1 and 133/2, 1997. [Swedish].

[97]   Lindhardt A, et al. The use of neurolectic drugs among patients 18-64 years old with schizophrenia, mania or bipolar affective mental disorder [Forbruget af antipsykotika blandt 18-64 årige patienter med skizofreni, mani eller bipolar affektiv sindslidelse"]. Copenhagen: Danish Natl Board Health, 2006. [Danish].

[98]   van der Kolk B, McFarlane A, Weisaeth L, eds. Traumatic stress: The effects of overwhelming experience on mind, body, and society. New York: Guilford, 1996.

[99]   Levine P, Frederick A. Waking the tiger. Healing trauma. Berkeley, CA: North Atlantic Books, 1997.

[100] Nijenhuis ERS. Somatoform dissociation: Major symptoms of dissociative disorders. J Trauma Dissociation 2000;1(4):7-32.

[101] Rothschild B. The body remembers. The psychophysiology of trauma and trauma treatment. New York: WW Norton, 2000.

[102] Shapiro F. Eye movement desensitization and processing.Basic principles. Protocols and procedures. 2nd ed. London: Guildford, 2001.

[103] Searles HF. Preface. In: Searles HF. Collected papers on schizophrenia. Madison, CT: Int Univ Press, 1965:15-18.

[104] Adler A. The practice and theroy of individual psychology. London: Routledge Kegan Paul, 1925.

[105] Abraham K, Abraham H. Clinical papers and essays on psycho-analysis. London: Maresfield Reprints, 1979.

[106] Federn P. Ego psychology and the psychoses. New York: Basic Books, 1953.

[107] Will OA. Process, psychotherapy, and schizophrenia. New York; Basic Books, 1961.

[108] Searles HF. Collected papers on schizophrenia. Madison, CT: Int Univ Press, 1965.

[109] Schilder P. The image and appearance of the human body. LondonL Kegan Paul, 1935.

[110] Rosenfeld HA. Psychotic states: A psycho-analytical approach. Madison, CT: Int Univ Press, 1965.

[111] Segal H. Some aspects of the analysis of a schizophrenic. Int J Psycho Analysis 195031, 268-278.

[112] Fairbairn RWD. An object-relations theory of the personality. Oxford: Basic Books, 1954.

[113] Guntrip H. (1968) Schizoid phenomena, object relations and the self. Madison, CT: Int Univ Press, 1968.

[114] Perry JW. Image, complex, and transference in schizophrenia. Psychotherapy of the psychoses. New York: Basic Books, 1961:90-123.

[115] Lidz T. The origin and treatment of schizophrenic disorders. Madison, CT: Int Univ Press, 1990.

[116] Kernberg OF. Borderline conditions and pathological narcissism. New York: Jason Aronson, 1975.

[117] Kernberg OF. Object relations theory and clinical psychoanalysis. New York: Jason Aronson, 1976.

[118] Volkan VD. Primitive internalized object relations. Madison, CT: Int Univ Press, 1976.

[119] Sechehaye MA. Symbolic realization. Madison, CT: Int Univ Press, 1951.

[120] Rosen JN. Direct analysis (selected papers). New York: Grune Stratton, 1953.

[121] Eissler KR. Remarks on the psychoanalysis of schizophrenia. In: Brody EB, Redlich FC, eds. Psychotherapy with schizophrenics. Madison, CT: Int Univ Press, 1952:130-67.

[122] Arlow JA, Brenner C. Psychoanalytic concepts and the structural theory. Oxford: Int Univ Press, 1964.

[123] Giovacchini PL. Treatment of primitive mental states. New York: Jason Aronson, 1979.

[124] Arieti S. Interpretation of schizophrenia, 2nd ed. New York: Basic Books, 1974.

[125] Bellak L. Disorders of the schizophrenic syndrome. New York: Basic Books, 1979.

[126] Gendlin ET. Therapeutic procedures in dealing with schizophrenics. In: Rogers CR, ed. The therapeutic relationship and its impact. A study of psychotherapy with schizophrenics. Madison, WI: Univ Wisconsin Press, 1967:369-400.

[127] Prouty G. Pre-therapy: a method of treating pre-expressive retarded and psychotic patients. Psychotherapy 1976;1:290-4.

[128] Gunderson JG, Mosher LR. Psychotherapy of schizophrenia. New York: Jason Aronson, 1975.

Chapter 35

Eating disorders

Virtually all teenage girls and young women have to some extent an eating disorder, which research has shown to covariate with the intensity of psychosexual developmental disturbances and sexual problems. The most severe cases of eating disorders are often referred to psychiatric treatment.

We suggest simple psychosexual (psychodynamic) explanations for the most common eating disorders like anorexia nervosa, bulimia nervosa, and binge eating disorder and propose the hypothesis that eating disorders can be easily understood as symptoms of the underlying psychosexual developmental disturbances.

We relate the symptoms of the eating disorders to three major strategies for repressing sexuality:

1. The dispersion of the flow of sexual energy - from the a) orgasmic potent, genitally mature ("vaginal") state via the b) more immature, masturbatory ("clitoral") state, and further into the c) state of infantile autoerotism ("asexual state").
2. The dislocation from the genitals to the other organs of the body, especially the digestive and urinary tract organs (the kidney-bladder-urethra) giving the situation where sexual energy is accumulated and subsequently released though the substituting organs.
3. The repression of a) free, natural and joyful sexuality into first b) sadism, and then further into c) masochism.

We conclude that the eating disorders easily can be understood as sexual energies living their own life in the non-genital body organs, and we present results from the Research Clinic for Holistic Medicine and Sexology, Copenhagen, where eating disorders have been treated with accelerated psychosexual development.

We included the patients with eating disorders into the protocol for sexual disturbances and found half these patients to be cured in one year and with 20 sessions of clinical holistic therapy.

Introduction

Virtually every teenage girl on the western hemisphere – and most women between 12 and 35 years– has an eating disorder to some extends. Working as physicians in general practice we have observed not only a high prevalence of severe eating disorders like anorexia (the general loss of appetite or disinterest in food), anorexia nervosa (the intended weight loss by starvation, over-exercise, purging etc.) and bulimia nervosa (the cyclical, recurring pattern of binge eating often followed by guilt, self-recrimination and compensatory behavior such as dieting, over-exercising and purging) (see list of the eating disorders listed in ICD-10 in table 1) (1), but also a number of milder disorders that less often are put into diagnoses followed by medical treatment, like binge eating disorder (uncontrolled bursts of overeating followed by compulsive vomiting), extreme and obsessive weight control (often by patients with a normal weight) where the bathroom weight are used several times a day, and obsessive, neurotic attitudes to food i.e. a too large importance attributed to avoiding calories, or carbohydrates, or fat, or even the compulsive abandonment of a single foot items like white sugar, white bread etc.

Other expressions of this are extreme exercise-programs sometimes even encouraged by the physician, and vanity that converts into a compulsive drive for being as slim as the commercial fashion-models. The girls often present severely disturbed body images in combination with either an antisocial behavioral pattern with withdrawal and social isolation (antisocial or severely disturbed personality), or a strong dependency on the confirmation of their value as a person from peers and parents (dependent personality type), or a need for constant appraisal of the bodies' sexual value from boys (hypersexual behavior). So the closer we look at the appetite dysregulations, the more they seem deeply connected to psychosexual factors.

Therapists who work with young female patients with eating disorders often notice that there seem to be both a mental (psychoform) and a bodily (somatoform) aspect of the problem. The patient's mind often carries a lot of thoughts and ideas about the vital importance of not getting too fat and ugly, combined with feelings of shame and guilt from not being able to control the eating habits, etc. The patient's body often seems to live its own life. Some times it is compensatory attracted to food, at other times strongly repelled by food, and at other times again not interested in food at all.

Often the phases vary in a cyclic, rather predictable way. In anorexia, food is simply not of any interest; in anorexia nervosa there is a battle in the patient not to eat in spite of an urge for eating; in bulimia we have the compensatory overeating, and in bulimia nervosa we have the inner conflict between one part of the patient that want to eat and an other that do not. In binging the striving is for simply filling the stomach and thereafter emptying it totally again, releasing all tension. The emotional character of the eating disorder has made them difficult to treat with behavioral therapy; it has not been able to treat them successfully with drugs either. So most patients suffer from their eating disorder the first 20 years after early puberty; after that is normally tend to burn out – as to the sexual urge.

There are many scientific speculations about biological reasons for the eating disorders - the same way psychiatrists for a hundred years now have speculated in possible biological reasons for mental illnesses; but neither has till this day showed genetic or any other clear scientific evidence for being "hardwired" in the human nature. It is often said that the eating disorders disturb other aspects of the patient's life, including her sexual life, but this is most likely to be the other way round: the eating disorder is a symptom of a deeper psychosexual disturbance.

It is worth to speculate that the problems started with puberty and gradually goes down ("burns out") during the next 20 years until the 35-year old woman, who statistically have come to know her body and sexuality by getting rid of her eating disorder, or at least of its symptoms. The close association in time and intensity is a strong clue that eating disorders might be causally linked to sexuality.

Psychosomatic and psychosexual research has in accordance with this shown sexuality to be closely linked to the eating disorders. Morgan et al (2) found that anorectics were less likely than bulimics to have engaged in masturbation and also scored lower on a measure of sexual esteem, and both groups exhibited less sexual interest and more negative affect during sex than did a normative sample (2). Abraham et al (3) found that bulimic patients were more likely to experience orgasm with masturbation, were more likely to have experimented with anal intercourse, and were more likely to describe their libido as "above average", while their controls were more likely to experience orgasm during sexual intercourse (3). Raboch and Faltus (4) found that "primary or secondary insufficiencies of sexual life were found for 80% of the anorectic patients"(4), while Raboch (5) found that sexual development of patients with anorexia nervosa was accelerated in the initial stages.

Table 1. The 2007 ICD-10 list of eating disorders and sexual disorders.
Notice the similarities

(F50.) Eating disorders
(F50.0) Anorexia nervosa
(F50.1) Atypical anorexia nervosa
(F50.2) Bulimia nervosa
(F50.3) Atypical bulimia nervosa
(F50.4) Overeating associated with other psychological disturbances
(F50.5) Vomiting associated with other psychological disturbances
(F50.8) Other eating disorders
(F50.9) Eating disorder, unspecified

(F52.) Sexual dysfunction, not caused by organic disorder or disease
(F52.0) Lack or loss of sexual desire
(F52.1) Sexual aversion and lack of sexual enjoyment
(F52.2) Failure of genital response
(F52.3) Orgasmic dysfunction
(F52.4) Premature ejaculation
(F52.5) Nonorganic vaginismus
(F52.6) Nonorganic dyspareunia
(F52.7) Excessive sexual drive
(F52.8) Other sexual dysfunction, not caused by organic disorder or disease
(F52.9) Unspecified sexual dysfunction, not caused by organic disorder or disease

Sarol-Kulka et al (6) found in a pilot study that the anorectic patients showed interest in the opposite sex at an earlier age than patients with bulimia; however, the anorectic females more frequently than bulimic, reported that these interests were never realized. 36% of patients with anorexia and 29% of patients with bulimia had no sexual initiation. When evaluating the negative aspects of their own sexuality, 28% of patients with bulimia and 9% of patients with anorexia reported difficulties in achieving orgasm; 13% of bulimic and 9% of anorectic females reported difficulties in getting aroused, 22% of bulimic and 17% of anorectic females reported fearing the sexual initiation (6).

Handa et al (7) found that 16.3% of patient with eating disorders had been physically abused and Sanci (8) found that childhood sexual abuse happed 2.5 times as often as normal with patients that later developed bulimia; the patients who developed anorexia did not show this association. Although the picture is not at all clear, and even somewhat contradictory, research has shown a strong association between sexuality and eating disorders. In science we must agree that our present understanding of sexuality is messy and unclear in itself that this most likely is the reason for the messy conditions of the research; we actually believe that it is the incomplete understanding of sexuality itself in the mind of the researchers that is the major hindrance for shedding light into this.

As we aim to improve our present state of understanding we have incorporated into this chapter a number of classical and modern theories of sexuality and psychosexual development.

We believe that this synthesis is of clinical value and have, after working 10 years with holistic sexology in the clinic setting (9-25) developed a holistic sexological cure for the eating disorders that we have tested with success on several patients. We therefore want to present our theoretical understanding to make a basis for further research in clinical holistic medicine both in Denmark and in other countries (this chapter is a part of the Open Source Protocol for Clinical Holistic Medicine, that includes all the published strategies for helping the patients with clinical holistic medicine (CHM) and the obtained results from the clinical practice, to be found at www.pubmed.gov, search for papers with "clinical holistic medicine" in the title).

Oral sexuality, sexual repression and eating disorders

The Freudian concept of oral sexuality is little understood by contemporary physicians and psychiatrists (26), but Freud's concept was acknowledged by the whole tradition of psychoanalysts and psychodynamic researchers and therapists from the last century including Jung (27) and Reich (28,29).

Case story

Female patient 36 years old. The patient tells her story about an eating disorder (bulimia nervosa) starting when she was 16 years, a little before she became sexually active. She had this condition until recently – first when she was 30 years old did she have spontaneous remission from it - in spite of many years of cognitive psychotherapy.

She was first treated on an individual basis at the University Hospital Psychiatric Clinic; then she came in a bulimia psychotherapy group for 18 month, when she was 20-21 years old, followed by 6 years in individual psychotherapy with a female experienced psychologist. The focus of the therapy was getting control over the eating habits. She reported that she always had big problems with desire, getting sexually aroused, and getting satisfactory orgasm, and she complains about a life-long history of unsatisfactory sexual relationships. She explained that her binging was motivated primarily of the extremely relaxed and happy feelings she got after filling her stomach completely until it almost bursted, and then immediately after emptying again completely by vomiting. The process itself was not really emotionally rewarding, neither the eating part of it nor the vomiting part, but the total bodily relaxation was what she was really after.

Only after she learned how to relax and go with "the flow in life", letting go of controlling everything, did the eating disorder leave her. It seemed that the therapy was unproductive, because it aimed at helping the patient getting control, not at helping the patient to learn to let go of the control.

Freud believed that sexuality during the child's psychosexual development traveled from the mouth to the anus (and bladder), until it reached its final destination in the genitals. Reich had a somewhat different understanding, as he believed that the sexually healthy little girl had genital sexuality, and only when she was denied her "genital rights" i.e. by being punished for masturbation, would she repress her sexuality away from the genitals and into the other organs.

Freud also had the idea of sexual development from infantile autoerotism into the more mature masturbatory, clitoral sexual competency, before the girl finally reach genital maturity and able to have sexual intercourse. Reich believed that whenever sexuality became repressed is was kept by the body-amour and the muscles of the body. So when sexuality was repressed, it moved into the tensions of the body, and thus out of reach and use for the patient (28). Today we know in theory three ways for sexuality to become repressed – three neurotic strategies for getting rid of a sexuality that cannot be contained in the patient's childhood environment:

- Repression of sexual energy by destroying the sexual ray of energy: from the genital state (orgasmic potency) to "infantile autoerotism" (lack of orgasmic potency). The first is the repression of the sexual energy, from flowing freely through the genitals allowing the person so engage in sexual intercourse, to the more restricted masturbatory state, where the sexual energy still can be used for pleasure raising a sexual circle, but only within the person herself, into the still more futile and useless state of infantile autoerotism, where sexual energy cannot any longer form a beam of energy and flow, but only hang as a cloud of sexual energy (a sexual quality or "odor"), just barely allowing the observer to identify the gender of the person. The infantile autoerotism is the typical sexual state of the schizophrenic patient; in psychodynamic theory the lack of sexual interest in the world from this state is one of the suggested reason for autism.
- Repression of sexual energy by displacement from the genital to other organs – sexualisation of the digestive system. When sexuality cannot be accepted by the

girl's parents it can still survive by being transformed into emotional charge associated with eating, defecation and urination. The mouth, intestines, anus and bladder can, as observed already by Freud carry enormities of charge of sexual energy. The reader that doubts this might recall Gräfenberg study from 1950 where he quite surprisingly documented the very important role of the urethra in many women's sexuality (30). This means that the sexual energies in many ways can be preserved, but disguised, as sexual emotions connected to non-sexual organs; the joy associated with the later is obviously often much easier to accept for the parents: The little girls is cute when the eats; she is even cute when she goes to the bathroom, but she is definitely naughty and not-so-cute when she plays with her own genitals. So the displacement of sexual energies turns her, if she is raised in a sex-negative environment, into a socially acceptable person. If we compare the eating disorders with the sexual disorders, it is quite interesting to see how parallel these two lists are (see table 1). Of course this psychodynamic understanding of body and sexuality might seem rather incomprehensible, if you are unwilling to acknowledge sexual energies as the fundamental vital energies in the human being, as did Freud, Jung, Reich, and so many of the other great psychologists and physicians of the last century. But if you can follow this scheme of thinking, then you can also examine your female patient presenting an eating disorder for a deeper layer of psychosexual developmental disturbances, that could be corrected, and by doing so you can help the young woman not only to get rid of her eating disorder, but also of other more existentially important problems related to a poorly developed sexuality.

- Repression of sexual energy by degeneration into sadism and masochism. A third way sexuality could be repressed is as sadism and masochism. The idea that sexual repression leads to masochism, which is perhaps most strongly and clearly expressed by Reich in his book "Character analysis" (29), is that sexuality basically calls for meeting with the opposite sex, in an active, aggressive way. Sexual aggression is thus the most natural thing with both sexes, although the expression of male and female sexual aggression is very different, the male aggression often looking like sexual violation and harassment, while the female aggression often is looking more like seduction and "hooking". When sexual aggression becomes blocked, i.e. when the girl is told not to be so sexually challenging to the boys in the way she dresses and acts, or when she is sexually neglected of the father and other boys and men who she is depending on interacting with for her psychosexual development, her sexuality first turns into evil sexual intent (i.e. sexually torturing the boys by rejecting them or slating or intimidating them); the logic in this is that sexuality still exists, because is breaks through the barrier using force (which is sadism). If sadism is also repressed, the flow of sexual energy is turned inwards, instead of outwards (which is masochism). So masochism is basically sadism turned inwards towards self. If the reader wonders how sadism is created from sexual energy turned evil, we refer to our explanation of evilness in general in the life mission theory (31-39). This theory explains how and why all intents seem to turn evil, when they cannot be realized by the little child (36).

Theories for eating disorders

Anorexia nervosa

The basic pattern of anorexia nervosa seems to be the lack of desire and the lack of self-acceptance and acceptance of body and sexuality. The girl often presents severe problems related to her personality; her mind is often not fully developed compared to other girls her age, her sexuality is often less active, unless she uses this as a kind of activity that uses calories i.e. instrumentally and not for the sexual pleasure; spiritually she is often not able to give and receive love, and she often also has a poorly developed self (see (40) for a systematic way to analyze the personality disturbances). So it might be a little simplistic to point to the patients psychosexual development as the fundamental cause of the eating disorders, but according to psychosomatic theory the problems related to the lack of development of her personality is actually also likely to be caused by her more fundamental problems related to her psychosexual development.

So we do not find it hard to see how anorexia nervosa relates to repressed sexuality; the patient's sexuality is often repressed in several ways: obviously there is often the regression toward the infantile autoerotism; then there is the translocation of sexuality from her genitals to her digestive system (and often also bladder-urethra); and finally there is often a strong component of masochism leading to self-destruction. If the reason for starvation really is masochism, and it often looks so, there is a hidden sexual pleasure in the self-destruction that is stronger than any pain you can inflict on the patient during the most rigorous scheme of behavioral therapy. Actually any scheme that represses the masochistic sexual energy is likely to deprive the female masochistic patient even the last remaining joy and meaning of life. This is likely to be the reason why behaviors coercive therapy, which is still in use in psychiatry, most often is strongly contra-productive.

Bulimia nervosa

Bulimia is in many practical ways the opposite of anorexia, but it still contains from a psychodynamic view many of the same basic elements of repressed sexuality. The shift from the genitals to the digestive organs (and often also bladder-urethra) is the same; the repression of vital sexuality and orgasmic potency into the masturbatory, clitoral state is the same, although the bulimic patient often is less repressed than the anorectic; and the masochistic quality of the bulimic behavior is often rather obvious. But in bulimia the fundamental drive is preserved. The patients wants to eat; when the patient tells about the strength of the urge it carries the same feel as the other basic biological urges, making it highly likely to be an expression of a hidden sexual urge. If this is the case, it is clear that it is uncontrollable by the girl or young woman. The power of sexuality is stronger than the power of the mind; it cannot be controlled by direct repression; it can only be handled by intelligent negotiation. So if this is the case, the bulimic patient must learn to acknowledge her compensatory drive for eating as an expression of her sexuality; and her neurotic sexuality must be developed to enable it to shift back and inhabit once again her pelvis, genitals - and become a natural sexuality.

Binge eating disorder

This disorder is a less serious disorder that seldom leads to medical attention, as we find it in girls and young women with almost normal psychopathology. In many ways this disorder is the clearest expression of sexuality taken to the digestive system. Instead of filling her vagina she is filling her stomach; and instead of releasing the tension in an orgasm, she releases is through vomiting. Many of these patients seem to have their sexuality repressed to the clitoral level being able to masturbate, but not to have full orgasm during coitus (loss of orgasmic potency). The masochistic component is often lacking, but it can be there also. The simplest way to understand this is the patient masturbating though her digestive system, the same way other women masturbate by filling the vagina and emptying it again; we have noticed the habit of some of these patients to fill their anus and rectum with objects or large amount of water, and releasing this again for sexual pleasure or for reasons of "purification". This is obviously the same sexual dynamics taking directly to the intestines. The same way the urine can be held back and finally released as a masturbatory practice of some of these often sexually innovative patients.

The bulimic and the binging patients are often sexually active also; not all their sexual energy is channeled to the digestive organs, making the situation a little more complex. It is like a diverted river, where more of less water is running in a parallel river. The cure is to help the patient lead all the water, all the flow of sexuality, back into the main river. First when the patient own all her sexual energy and is able to use it maturely genitally for satisfying sex with a partner, will her eating disorder – the symptoms of her disturbed sexuality – finally be cured.

Sexological treatment of eating disorders

In treating the eating disorders as sexological disturbances it is important to go directly to the patient's sexuality; this means that the therapist and the patient should agree completely that her sexuality and personality as a whole is much more important than her eating disorder. Of course, if the patient is dying from starvation or excessive overweight there might be practical problems in using such a strategy; it is important to remember that all problems start as small problems and only if they remain unsolved for a very long time turn into huge, even mortal situations. So this approach is wisely used as soon as the symptoms of the eating disorder appears, not when the girl or young woman has lost so much weight that she is unable to concentrate on anything and close to dying.

The aim of the holistic sexological therapy is the development of the patient's whole personality through rehabilitation of her sexuality – her genital character – with an often-used expression by Reich (28,29).

Holistic Medicine is nothing but the classical, European medicine going back to Hippocrates; this is the beginning of modern medicine, which we know rather well from uniquely well-preserved sources called the Corpus Hippocraticum (41). We have in recent years tried to develop holistic medicine into a modern, scientifically based system of clinical medicine, where patients are cured mostly without drugs and surgery. The theory and practice of clinical holistic medicine has been described in a number of books (42-45) and experimental cures for many illnesses and disorders including cancer and schizophrenia have already been presented in a series of papers (46-75). The sense of coherence seems to be a core concept in the understanding of holistic healing (76-81).

We are not in this chapter going to repeat all the practical tools and details, but the interested physician is encouraged to start just by talking with the patient about her personal history and present problems and after obtaining the trust of the patient continuing this therapeutic work by using therapeutic touch, i.e. massage of the whole body. The combination of the conversational therapy and the bodywork has been used for millennia to rid the patients of repressed emotions hidden in the body or related to the body and sexuality in the patient's mind. The basic idea in the therapy is to work against the patient's emotional resistance, to bring all difficult emotions up to the surface of consciousness, but first a variety of emotions will show in the therapy, often sorrow, anxiety, anger, helplessness, hopelessness or despair. After the emotional layer an even more intense layer of emotions connected to the sexual aspects of the body and its energies, including the genitals and pelvic area will appear.

The holistic sexological bodywork is normally not including the patient's genitals, as many patients can be helped without this degree of intimacy. If the patient is not sufficiently helped there are a number of small and large sexological tools to be used, like acceptance through touch (11) and vaginal physiotherapy (14,15), which are relative small tools and much smaller procedures than the standard pelvic examination, and larger tools like the expanded holistic pelvic examination (13), going all the way up to direct sexual stimulation of the patient in a radical and provocative technique developed 50 years ago by sexologist like Hoch and Reich called the sexological examination (82-92).

The fundamental strategy of therapy is to take the patient back in time, to allow her to confront the emotional and sexual problems of her early life, childhood, and even fetal life if necessary, that she cold not solve at that time. The patient will get well again the reverse order of her getting ill – this is the law of Hering (93). The patients will heal her whole existence, not only a part – that is the salutogenic principle (94-95). The patient will come back into the old traumas, when she is exposed, in a symbolic form, for the traumatic events and energies that once created her wounds – that is the famous principle of similarity going all the way back to the ideas op Hippocrates; and finally she will heal when she got the resources needed at the time of the trauma, and is so confident with the therapist that she is able to receive them.

The eating disorders can easily be understood as sexual energies living their own life in the parallel body organs related to digestions, and we present our experience from the Research Clinic for Holistic Medicine that the eating disorders easily can be treated, if therapist and patient can agree that sexuality, not the eating disorder, is the focus of the therapy. In our project we have observed that virtually all young female patients to some degree have an eating disorder; we understand these as symptoms of psychosexual developmental disturbances and we therefore successfully included the patietns with eating disorders into the protocol for sexual disturbances (9). We found that about half the patients was cured, not only for their sexual problems, but also systematically from their eating disorders, in one year and with 20 sessions of clinical holistic therapy. In general we found that independently of the type of problem about half the patients were cured, and the more direct the patient's sexuality was approached in the therapy, the more efficient it was (9,15,96).

Ethical considerations

Holistic therapy and holistic sexology should be made according to the ethical standard of the International Society for Holistic Health (97) and the laws of the country you reside in. It will be difficult for physicians not familiar with contemporary holistic medicine or the works of Freud, Jung, Reich, Lowen, Rosen and others (26-29,98.99), to understand the full clinical rationality in interpreting the eating disorders as psychosexual disturbances. It will also be difficult for psychiatrists that normally do not touch their patients at all, to understand the therapeutic value of therapeutic touch. And when it comes to using the manual sexological tools, many physicians who are not sexologists, might find these tools too intimate and too directly sexual. In our clinic we have until now used the small manual sexological tools, and only rarely the holistic pelvic exam. Direct sexual stimulation of the female patients seems to be necessary in primary anorgasmia and similar sexual disorders, but we have not, in spite of the indication, found it correct to use these tools in our clinic, but have referred the patients in need of such therapy to the sexologists using these methods.

When it comes to teenagers below 18 years old, we have chosen to wait with the manual sexological treatment until they could sign up for these treatments themselves as adults legally responsible for their own treatment. For patients below 18 years we have often used the normal pelvic examination as basis for a conversation about sexuality and related issues, and we have found the pelvic examination to be as therapeutic as it is unpleasant and even experienced as "very painful" by 15% of the teenagers (100). We know from several studies that patients with a history of sexual abuse very often react very negative emotionally to the pelvic examination (101); the penetration of the vagina with the speculum and other instruments, or just even the fingers, often gives strong associations to - and memories of the sexual abuse, and according to the principle of similarity this can – and should – be used therapeutically to help the female patient to heal her old wound on body an soul from the sexual abuse (18-20).

Discussion

The observation of the psychoform and somatoform dissociation of the patient will naturally lead to an intent to heal the patient by reconnecting mentally and bodily to the patient. As we are sexual beings, and as a disturbed sexuality has so many symptoms and is followed by so many complications of all kinds, we cannot afford to be a-sexual and to keep all discussion of the patient problems in the a-sexual realm, if we truly want to help the patient.

For almost 100 years psychotherapy and psychiatry have disagreed about the importance of sexuality in mental diseases; this disagreement continues when it comes to the eating disorders. We cannot here settle this old discussion today; just inform the interested reader about the theories and the tools for healing also the patient with an eating disorder. When you have worked for some years in the holistic clinic, as we have now with more than 500 patients, and seen how the dynamics of masochism, sexual repression into autoerotism, and sexual shifts from the genitals to the other organs of the body like the digestive organs (from mouth to anus) and the whole urinary tract (kidney-bladder-urethra) can be easily reversed and often followed by the radical improvement not only of the patient's sexuality, but also of quality of life, physical and mental health, and level of social, sexual and working ability, you will also come to believe in the old psychodynamic theories of Freud and his students. We found it often helpful to teach the patients about quality of life theory (102-105) and quality of life philosophy (106-113).

The sexological approach in the treatment of physical, mental, and existential problems are not new; the traditional holistic medicine of old Greece did exactly that. We have become quite alienated to simple conversational therapy and bodywork during the last five decades, where biomedicine and drugs have become the answer to every problem of the patient, but with biomedicine we have not be able to help all patients and today every second citizen in modern society is a chronic patient, even in countries like Denmark where biomedicine and health service are absolutely free. So we have to conclude that biomedicine is not going to help all patients and biomedicine is not likely to help teenagers and young women with eating disorders – especially not if the psychodynamic hypothesis presented in this chapter is likely to be true. The most fundamental problem with the sexual approach is that is has proven very difficult to understand the true nature of sexual energy in scientific terms, and that the whole field of human development is theoretically extremely farfetched (114-126). To simplify everything it is important to recall that the essence of relating is being able to say I-Thou. In therapy the courage to love your patient is what in the end will heal you patient and release the patient from disease/pathology (127).

Conclusions

Virtually all teenage girls and young females have an eating disorder to some degree. We have suggested simple sexual explanations for the most common eating disorders like anorexia nervosa, bulimia nervosa and binge eating disorder. We have suggested that these disorders could easily be understood as symptoms of psychosexual developmental disturbances. We have analyzed the symptoms in relation to three major ways that patients use to repress their sexuality as children: 1) The dispersion of sexual energy from the genitally mature to the immature masturbatory (clitoral) state, and further into the state of infantile autoerotism, 2) the dislocation from the genitals to the other organs especially the digestive organs and the bladder-urethra, giving a situation where sexual energy is accumulated and released though substituting organs and 3) the repression of free, natural and joyful sexuality into first sadism, and then further into masochism.

The eating disorders can easily be understood as sexual energies living their own life in the parallel body organs related to digestions and we present our experience from the Research Clinic for Holistic Medicine and Sexology that the eating disorders can be treated, if therapist and patient can agree that sexuality, not the eating disorder, is the focus of the therapy. In our project we have included patients with eating disorders into the protocol for sexual disturbances, and we have found about half the patients to be cured in one year and with 20 sessions of clinical holistic therapy, independent of the problem the patient initially presented with (NNT=2) (9,128-133).

References

[1]   http://www.who.int/classifications/apps/icd/icd10online.

[2]   Morgan CD, Wiederman MW, Pryor TL. Sexual functioning and attitudes of eating-disordered women: a follow-up study. J Sex Marital Ther 1995;21(2):67-77.

[3]   Abraham SF, Bendit N, Mason C, Mitchell H, O'Connor N, Ward J, Young S, Llewellyn-Jones D. The psychosexual histories of young women with bulimia. Aust N Z J Psychiatry 1985;19(1):72-6.

[4]   Raboch J, Faltus F. Sexuality of women with anorexia nervosa. Acta Psychiatr Scand 1991;84(1):9-11.

[5]   Raboch J. Sexual development and life of psychiatric female patients. Arch Sex Behav 1986;15(4):341-53.

[6]   Sarol-Kulka, A. Kulka, Z. Sexuality and the use of alcohol and substances of abuse in women with eating disorders. Post Psychiatr Neurol 2005; 14(2):115-122 ICID: 16755.

[7]   Handa M, Nukina H, Hosoi M, Kubo C. Childhood physical abuse in outpatients with psychosomatic symptoms. Biopsychosoc Med 2008;2:8.

[8]   Sanci L, Coffey C, Olsson C, Reid S, Carlin JB, Patton G. Childhood sexual abuse and eating disorders in females: findings from the Victorian Adolescent Health Cohort Study. Arch Pediatr Adolesc Med 2008;162(3):261-7.

[9]   Ventegodt S, Thegler S, Andreasen T, Struve F, Enevoldsen L, Bassaine L, Torp M, Merrick J. Clinical holistic medicine (mindful, short-term psychodynamic psychotherapy complemented with bodywork) in the treatment of experienced impaired sexual functioning. ScientificWorldJournal 2007;7:324-9.

[10]   Ventegodt S, Kandel I, Neikrug S, Merric J. Clinical holistic medicine: holistic treatment of rape and incest trauma. ScientificWorldJournal 2005;5:288-97.

[11]   Ventegodt S, Morad M, Hyam E, Merrick J. Clinical holistic medicine: holistic sexology and treatment of vulvodynia through existential therapy and acceptance through touch. ScientificWorldJournal. 2004;4:571-80.

[12]   Ventegodt S, Morad M, Kandel I, Merrick J. Clinical holistic medicine: problems in sex and living together. ScientificWorldJournal 2004;4:562-70.

[13]   Ventegodt S, Morad M, Merrick J. Clinical holistic medicine: holistic pelvic examination and holistic treatment of infertility. ScientificWorldJournal 2004;4:148-58.

[14]   Ventegodt S, Clausen B, Omar HA, Merrick J. Clinical holistic medicine: holistic sexology and acupressure through the vagina (Hippocratic pelvic massage). ScientificWorldJournal 2006;6:2066-79.

[15]   Ventegodt S, Clausen B, Merrick J. Clinical holistic medicine: pilot study on the effect of vaginal acupressure (Hippocratic pelvic massage). ScientificWorldJournal 2006;6:2100-16.

[16]   Ventegodt S, Andersen NJ, Kandel I, Merrick J. Five tools for manual sexological examination and treatment. MedSciMonit, submitted 2008.

[17]   Ventegodt S, Clausen B, Nielsen ML, Merrick J. Clinical holistic medicine: Advanced tools for holistic medicine. ScientificWorldJournal 2006;6:2048-65.

[18]   Ventegodt S, Clausen B, Merrick J. Clinical holistic medicine: The case story of Anna. I. Long-term effect of childhood sexual abuse and incest with a treatment approach. ScientificWorldJournal 2006;6:1965-76.

[19]   Ventegodt S, Clausen B, Merrick J. Clinical holistic medicine: The case story of Anna. II. Patient diary as a tool in treatment. ScientificWorldJournal 2006;6:2006-34.

[20]   Ventegodt S, Clausen B, Merrick J. Clinical holistic medicine: the case story of Anna. III. Rehabilitation of philosophy of life during holistic existential therapy for childhood sexual abuse. ScientificWorldJournal 2006;6:2080-91.

[21]   Ventegodt S, Merrick J. Medicine and the past. Lesson to learn about the pelvic examination and its sexuality suppressive procedure. BMJ 2004 February 20 online at http://bmj.com/cgi/eletters/328/7437/0-g#50997.

[22]   Ventegodt S, Vardi G, Merrick J. Holistic adolescent sexology: How to counsel and treat young people to alleviate and prevent sexual problems. BMJ 2005 Jan 15 on-line at http://bmj.bmjjournals.com/cgi/eletters/330/7483/107#92872.

[23] Ventegodt S, Kandel I, Merrick J. Clinical holistic medicine: how to recover memory without "implanting" memories in your patient. ScientificWorldJournal. 2007;7:1579-89.

[24] Ventegodt S, Kandel I, Merrick J. Pain and pleasure in sexuality. An analysis for use in clinical holistic medicine. J Pain Manage 2008;1(1):11-28.

[25] Freud A. The essential of psychoanalysis. London: Penguin Books, 1986.

[26] Jung CG. Man and his symbols. New York: Anchor Press, New York, 1964.

[27] Reich W. Die Function des Orgasmus. Köln: Kiepenheuer Witsch, 1969.[German].

[28] Reich W. Character analysis. New York: Farrar Straus Giroux, 1990.

[29] Grafenberg E. The role of urethra in female orgasm. Int J Sexology 1950;3(3):145-8.

[30] Ventegodt S, Andersen NJ, Merrick J. Editorial: Five theories of human existence. ScientificWorldJournal 2003;3:1272-6.

[31] Ventegodt S. The life mission theory: A theory for a consciousness-based medicine. Int J Adolesc Med Health 2003;15(1): 89-91.

[32] Ventegodt S, Andersen NJ, Merrick J. The life mission theory II. The structure of the life purpose and the ego. ScientificWorldJournal 2003;3:1277-85.

[33] Ventegodt S, Andersen NJ, Merrick J. The life mission theory III. Theory of talent. ScientificWorldJournal 2003;3:1286-93.

[34] Ventegodt S, Andersen NJ, Merrick J. The life mission theory IV. Theory on child development. ScientificWorldJournal 2003;3:1294-1301.

[35] Ventegodt S, Andersen NJ, Merrick J. The life mission theory V. Theory of the anti-self (the shadow) or the evil side of man. ScientificWorldJournal 2003;3:1302-13.

[36] Ventegodt S, Kromann M, Andersen NJ, Merrick J. The life mission theory VI. A theory for the human character: Healing with holistic medicine through recovery of character and purpose of life. ScientificWorldJournal 2004;4:859-80.

[37] Ventegodt S, Flensborg-Madsen T, Andersen NJ, Merrick J. The life mission theory VII. Theory of existential (Antonovsky) coherence: A theory of quality of life, health and ability for use in holistic medicine. ScientificWorldJournal 2005;5:377-89.

[38] Ventegodt S, Kandel I, Merrick J. Life mission theory VIII: A theory for pain. J Pain Manage 2008;1(1):5-10.

[39] Ventegodt S, Merrick J. Personality disorders and clinical holistic medicine. The revival of traditional holistic medicine in a modern scientific form. In: Hagen JC, Jensen EI, eds. Personality disorders: New research. New York: Nova Sci, 2008.

[40] Jones WHS. Hippocrates. Vol. I–IV. London: William Heinemann, 1923-1931.

[41] Ventegodt S. Consciousness-based medicine. Copenhagen: Forskningscenterets Forlag, 2003. [Danish].

[42] Ventegodt S, Kandel I, Merrick J. Principles of holistic medicine. Philosophy behind quality of life. Victoria , BC : Trafford, 2005.

[43] Ventegodt S, Kandel I, Merrick J. Principles of holistic medicine. Quality of life and health. New York : Hippocrates Sci Publ, 2005 .

[44] Ventegodt S, Kandel I, Merrick J. Principles of holistic medicine. Global quality of life.Theory, research and methodology. New York : Hippocrates Sci Publ, 2005.

[45] Ventegodt S, Merrick J. Clinical holistic medicine: Applied consciousness-based medicine. ScientificWorldJournal 2004;4:96-9.

[46] Ventegodt S, Morad M, Merrick J. Clinical holistic medicine: Classic art of healing or the therapeutic touch. ScientificWorldJournal 2004;4:134-47.

[47] Ventegodt S, Morad M, Merrick J. Clinical holistic medicine: The "new medicine". The multiparadigmatic physician and the medical record. ScientificWorldJournal 2004;4:273-85.

[48] Ventegodt S, Morad M, Hyam E, Merrick J. Clinical holistic medicine: Use and limitations of the biomedical paradigm. ScientificWorldJournal 2004;4:295-306.

[49] Ventegodt S, Morad M, Kandel I, Merrick J. Clinical holistic medicine: Social problems disguised as illness. ScientificWorldJournal 2004;4:286-94.

[50] Ventegodt S, Morad M, Andersen NJ, Merrick J. Clinical holistic medicine: Tools for a medical science based on consciousness. ScientificWorldJournal 2004;4:347-61.

[51] Ventegodt S, Morad M, Hyam E, Merrick J. Clinical holistic medicine: When biomedicine is inadequate. ScientificWorldJournal 2004;4:333-46.

[52] Ventegodt S, Morad M, Merrick J. Clinical holistic medicine: Prevention through healthy lifestyle and quality of life. Oral Health Prev Dent 2004;2(Suppl 1):239-45.

[53] Ventegodt S, Morad M, Vardi G, Merrick J. Clinical holistic medicine: Holistic treatment of children. ScientificWorldJournal 2004;4:581-8.

[54] Ventegodt S, Morad M, Kandel I, Merrick J. Clinical holistic medicine: A psychological theory of dependency to improve quality of life. ScientificWorldJournal 2004;4:638-48.

[55] Ventegodt S, Morad, M, Kandel I, Merrick J. Clinical holistic medicine: Treatment of physical health problems without a known cause, examplified by hypertention and tinnitus. ScientificWorldJournal 2004;4:716-24.

[56] Ventegodt S, Morad M, Merrick J. Clinical holistic medicine: Developing from asthma, allergy and eczema. ScientificWorldJournal 2004;4:936-42.

[57] Ventegodt S, Merrick J. Clinical holistic medicine: Chronic infections and autoimmune diseases. ScientificWorldJournal 2005;5:155-64.

[58] Ventegodt S, Flensborg-Madsen T, Andersen NJ, Morad M, Merrick J. Clinical holistic medicine: A pilot study on HIV and quality of life and a suggested cure for HIV and AIDS. ScientificWorldJournal 2004;4:264-72.

[59] Ventegodt S, Merrick J. Clinical holistic medicine: Chronic pain in the locomotor system. ScientificWorldJournal 2005;5:165-72.

[60] Ventegodt S, Gringols M, Merrick J. Clinical holistic medicine: Whiplash, fibromyalgia and chronic fatigue. ScientificWorldJournal 2005;5:340-54.

[61] Ventegodt S, Merrick J. Clinical holistic medicine: Chronic pain in internal organs. ScientificWorldJournal 2005;5:205-10.

[62] Ventegodt S, Kandel I, Neikrug S, Merrick J. Clinical holistic medicine: The existential crisis – life crisis, stress and burnout. ScientificWorldJournal 2005;5:300-12.

[63] Ventegodt S, Gringols M, Merrick J. Clinical holistic medicine: Holistic rehabilitation. ScientificWorldJournal 2005;5:280-7.

[64] Ventegodt S, Morad M, Press J, Merrick J, Shek DTL. Clinical holistic medicine: Holistic adolescent medicine. ScientificWorldJournal 2004;4:551-61.

[65] Ventegodt S, Merrick J. Clinical holistic medicine: The patient with multiple diseases. ScientificWorldJournal 2005;5:324-39.

[66] Ventegodt S, Clausen B, Nielsen ML, Merrick J. Clinical holistic medicine: Advanced tools for holistic medicine. ScientificWorldJournal 2006;6:2048-65.

[67] Clinical holistic medicine: factors influencing the therapeutic decision-making. From academic knowledge to emotional intelligence and spiritual "crazy" wisdom. ScientificWorldJournal 2007;7:1932-49.

[68] First do no harm: an analysis of the risk aspects and side effects of clinical holistic medicine compared with standard psychiatric biomedical treatment. ScientificWorldJournal 2007;7:1810-20.

[69] Biomedicine or holistic medicine for treating mentally ill patients? A philosophical and economical analysis. ScientificWorldJournal 2007;7:1978-86.

[70] Ventegodt S, Andersen NJ, Neikrug S, Kandel I, Merrick J. Clinical holistic medicine: Mental disorders in a holistic perspective. ScientificWorldJournal 2005;5:313-23.

[71] Ventegodt S, Andersen NJ, Neikrug S, Kandel I, Merrick J. Clinical holistic medicine: Holistic treatment of mental disorders. ScientificWorldJournal 2005;5:427-45.

[72] Clinical holistic medicine (mindful short-term psychodynamic psychotherapy complimented with bodywork) in the treatment of schizophrenia (ICD10-F20/DSM-IV Code 295) and other psychotic mental diseases. ScientificWorldJournal 2007;7:1987-2008.

[73] Ventegodt S, Morad M, Hyam E, Merrick J. Clinical holistic medicine: Induction of spontaneous remission of cancer by recovery of the human character and the purpose of life (the life mission). ScientificWorldJournal 2004;4:362-77.

[74] Ventegodt S, Solheim E, Saunte ME, Morad M, Kandel I, Merrick J. Clinic holistic medicine: Metastatic cancer. ScientificWorldJournal 2004;4:913-35.

[75] Flensborg-Madsen T, Ventegodt S, Merrick J. Sense of coherence and physical health. A Review of previous findings. ScientificWorldJournal 2005;5:665-73.

[76] Flensborg-Madsen T, Ventegodt S, Merrick J. Why is Antonovsky's sense of coherence not correlated to physical health? Analysing Antonovsky's 29-item sense of coherence scale (SOCS). ScientificWorldJournal 2005;5:767-76.

[77] Flensborg-Madsen T, Ventegodt S, Merrick J. Sense of coherence and health. The construction of an amendment to Antonovsky's sense of coherence scale (SOC II). ScientificWorldJournal 2006;6:2133-9.

[78] Flensborg-Madsen, T., Ventegodt, S., and Merrick, J. Sense of coherence and physical health. A crosssectional study using a new SOC scale (SOC II). ScientificWorldJournal 2006;6:2200-11.

[79] Flensborg-Madsen, T., Ventegodt, S., and Merrick, J. Sense of coherence and physical health. Testing Antonovsky's theory. ScientificWorldJournal 2006;6:2212-9.

[80] Flensborg-Madsen, T., Ventegodt, S., and Merrick, J. (2006) Sense of coherence and health. The emotional sense of coherence (SOC-E) was found to be the best-known predictor of physical health. ScientificWorldJournal 2006;6:2147-57.

[81] Hoch Z. Vaginal erotic sensitivity by sexological examination. Acta Obstet Gynecol Scand 1996;65(7);767-73.

[82] Halvorsen, JG, Metz, ME. Sexual dysfunction, Part II: Diagnosis, prognosis, and management. J Am Board Fam Pract 1992;5(2):177-92.

[83] Hamilton WH. The therapeutic role of the sexological examination. Dissertation. San Diego, CA: Calif Sch Prof Psychol, Alliant Int Univ, 1978.

[84] Hartman WE, Fithian MA. Treatment of sexual dysfunction. New York: Aronson, 1994.

[85] Hock ZA. Commentary on the role of the female sexological examination and the personnel who should perform it. J Sex Res 1982;18:58-63.

[86] Kegel A. Progressive resistence exercise in the functional restoration of the perineal muscles. Am J Obstet Gynecol 1948;56:238-48.

[87] Hartman WE, Fithian MA. Magnus Hirschfeld Archive for Sexuality, http://www2.hu-berlin.de/sexology/ECE5/sexological

[88] Kegel AH. Sexual function of the pubococcygeus muscle. West J Surg. Obstet Gynaecol 1952;60:521.

[89] Masters WH, Johnson VE. Human sexual response. Boston: Little Brown, 1966.

[90] Kline-Graber G, Graber B. A guide to sexual satisfaction. Woman's orgasm. New York: Popular Library, 1975:21-54.

[91] Gillan P, Brindley GD. Vaginal and pelvic floor responses to sexual stimulation. Psychophysiology 1979;16:471.

[92] Ventegodt S, Thegler S, Andreasen T, Struve F, Enevoldsen L, Bassaine L, Torp M, Merrick J. Clinical holistic medicine: Psychodynamic short-time therapy complemented with bodywork. A clinical follow-up study of 109 patients. ScientificWorldJournal 2006;6:2220-38.

[93] Antonovsky A. Health, stress and coping. London: Jossey-Bass, 1985.

[94] Antonovsky A. Unravelling the mystery of health. How people manage stress and stay well. San Francisco: Jossey-Bass, 1987.

[95] Struck P, Ventegodt S. Clinical holistic medicine: Teaching orgasm for females with chronic anorgasm using the Betty Dodson Method. Submitted to ScientificWorldJournal.

[96] de Vibe, M., Bell, E., Merrick, J., Omar, H.A., Ventegodt, S. Ethics and holistic healthcare practice. Int J Child Health Human Dev, in press.

[97] Lowen A. Honoring the body. Alachua, FL: Bioenergetics Press, 2004.

[98] Rosen M, Brenner S. Rosen method bodywork. Accesing the unconscious through touch. Berkeley, CA: North Atlantic Books, 2003.

[99] Larsen SB, Kragstrup J. Experiences of the first pelvic examination in a random samples of Danish teenagers. Acta Obstet Gynecol Scand 1995;74(2):137-41.

[100] Robohm JS, Buttenheim M.The gynecological care experience of adult survivors of childhood sexual abuse: a preliminary investigation. Women Health 1996;24(3):59-75.

[101] Ventegodt S, Merrick J, Andersen NJ. Quality of life theory I. The IQOL theory: An integrative theory of the global quality of life concept. ScientificWorldJournal 2003;3:1030-40.

[102] Ventegodt S, Merrick J, Andersen NJ. Quality of life theory II. Quality of life as the realization of life potential: A biological theory of human being. ScientificWorldJournal 2003;3:1041-9.

[103] Ventegodt S, Merrick J, Andersen NJ. Quality of life theory III. Maslow revisited. ScientificWorldJournal 2003;3:1050-7.

[104] Ventegodt S, Flensborg-Madsen T, Andersen NJ, Nielsen M, Morad M, Merrick J. Global quality of life (QOL), health and ability are primarily determined by our consciousness. Research findings from Denmark 1991-2004. Soc Indicator Res 2005;71:87-122.

[105] Ventegodt S, Andersen NJ, Merrick J. Quality of life philosophy: when life sparkles or can we make wisdom a science? ScientificWorldJournal 2003;3:1160-3.

[106] Ventegodt S, Andersen NJ, Merrick J. QOL philosophy I: Quality of life, happiness, and meaning of life. ScientificWorldJournal 2003;3:1164-75.

[107] Ventegodt S, Andersen NJ, Kromann M, Merrick J. QOL philosophy II: What is a human being? ScientificWorldJournal 2003;3:1176-85.

[108] Ventegodt S, Merrick J, Andersen NJ. QOL philosophy III: Towards a new biology. ScientificWorldJournal 2003;3:1186-98.

[109] Ventegodt S, Andersen NJ, Merrick J. QOL philosophy IV: The brain and consciousness. ScientificWorldJournal 2003;3:1199-1209.

[110] Ventegodt S, Andersen NJ, Merrick J. QOL philosophy V: Seizing the meaning of life and getting well again. ScientificWorldJournal 2003;3:1210-29.

[111] Ventegodt S, Andersen NJ, Merrick J. QOL philosophy VI: The concepts. ScientificWorldJournal 2003;3:1230-40.

[112] Ventegodt S, Merrick J. Philosophy of science: how to identify the potential research for the day after tomorrow? ScientificWorldJournal 2004;4:483-9.

[113] Ventegodt S, Hermansen TD, Nielsen ML, Clausen B, Merrick J. Human development I: twenty fundamental problems of biology, medicine, and neuro-psychology related to biological information. ScientificWorldJournal 2006;6:747-59.

[114] Ventegodt S, Hermansen TD, Nielsen ML, Clausen B, Merrick J. Human development II: we need an integrated theory for matter, life and consciousness to understand life and healing. ScientificWorldJournal 2006;6:760-6.

[115] Ventegodt S, Hermansen TD, Rald E, Flensborg-Madsen T, Nielsen ML, Clausen B, Merrick J. Human development III: bridging brain-mind and body-mind. introduction to "deep" (fractal, poly-ray) cosmology. ScientificWorldJournal 2006;6:767-76.

[116] Ventegodt S, Hermansen TD, Flensborg-Madsen T, Nielsen ML, Clausen B, Merrick J. Human development IV: the living cell has information-directed self-organisation. ScientificWorldJournal 2006;6:1132-8.

[117] Ventegodt S, Hermansen TD, Flensborg-Madsen T, Nielsen ML, Clausen B, Merrick J. Human development V: biochemistry unable to explain the emergence of biological form (morphogenesis) and therefore a new principle as source of biological information is needed. ScientificWorldJournal 2006;6:1359-67.

[118] Ventegodt S, Hermansen TD, Flensborg-Madsen T, Nielsen M, Merrick J. Human development VI: Supracellular morphogenesis. The origin of biological and cellular order. ScientificWorldJournal 2006;6:1424-33.

[119] Ventegodt S, Hermansen TD, Flensborg-Madsen T, Rald E, Nielsen ML, Merrick J. Human development VII: A spiral fractal model of fine structure of physical energy could explain central aspects of biological information, biological organization and biological creativity. ScientificWorldJournal 2006;6:1434-40.

[120] Ventegodt S, Hermansen TD, Flensborg-Madsen T, Nielsen ML, Merrick J. Human development VIII: A theory of "deep" quantum chemistry and cell consciousness: Quantum chemistry controls genes and biochemistry to give cells and higher organisms consciousness and complex behavior. ScientificWorldJournal 2006;6:1441-53.

[121] Ventegodt S, Hermansen TD, Flensborg-Madsen T, Rald E, Nielsen ML, Merrick J. Human development IX: A model of the wholeness of man, his consciousness and collective consciousness. ScientificWorldJournal 2006;6:1454-9.

[122] Hermansen TD, Ventegodt S, Merrick J. Human development X: Explanation of macroevolution — top-down evolution materializes consciousness. The origin of metamorphosis. ScientificWorldJournal 2006;6:1656-66.

[123] Hermansen TD, Ventegodt S, Kandel I. Human development XI: the structure of the cerebral cortex. Are there really modules in the brain? ScientificWorldJournal 2007;7:1922-9.

[124] Ventegodt S, Hermansen TD, Kandel I, Merrick J. Human development XII: a theory for the structure and function of the human brain. ScientificWorldJournal 2008;8:621-42.

[125] Ventegodt S, Hermansen TD, Kandel I, Merrick J. Human development XIII: the connection between the structure of the overtone system and the tone language of music. Some implications for our understanding of the human brain. ScientificWorldJournal 2008;8:643-57.

[126] Buber M. I and thou. New York: Charles Scribner, 1970.

[127] Ventegodt S, Thegler S, Andreasen T, Struve F, Enevoldsen L, Bassaine L, Torp M, Merrick J. Self-reported low self-esteem. Intervention and follow-up in a clinical setting. ScientificWorldJournal 2007;7:299-305.

[128] Ventegodt S, Thegler S, Andreasen T, Struve F, Enevoldsen L, Bassaine L, Torp M, Merrick J. Clinical holistic medicine (mindful, short-term psychodynamic psychotherapy complemented with bodywork) in the treatment of experienced mental illness. ScientificWorldJournal 2007;7:306-9.

[129] Ventegodt S, Thegler S, Andreasen T, Struve F, Enevoldsen L, Bassaine L, Torp M, Merrick J. Clinical holistic medicine (mindful, short-term psychodynamic psychotherapy complemented with bodywork) in the treatment of experienced physical illness and chronic pain. ScientificWorldJournal 2007;7:310-16.

[130] Ventegodt S, Thegler S, Andreasen T, Struve F, Enevoldsen L, Bassaine L, Torp M, Merrick J. Clinical holistic medicine (mindful, short-term psychodynamic psychotherapy complemented with bodywork) improves quality of life, health and ability by induction of Antonovsky-Salutogenesis. ScientificWorldJournal 2007;7:317-23.

[131] Ventegodt S, Kandel I, Merrick J. A short history of clinical holistic medicine. ScientificWorldJournal 2007;7:1622-30.

[132] Ventegodt S, Andersen NJ, Kandel I, Merrick J. The open source protocol of clinical holistic medicine. J Altern Med Res 2009;1(2):129-44.

Section 9. Strategies for clinical intervention

From an abstract view all existential problems are identical. But the more concrete you look at it the more different the situations become. Some patients that appear to be mentally ill are just caught in social predicaments they cannot solve; simple couching that help the patients solve their marital problems, problems with friends or colleagues is often enough to alleviate a situation that for a first glance looked like several years of hard existential therapy.

Very much the same clinical pictures can be caused by severe sexual traumas of incest or rape. In this situation holistic sexology and holistic psychiatry merge together into a coherent holistic medicine addressing the patients' description of purpose of life (life mission) and similar fundamental structures in the patients philosophy if life.

Existential crisis are yet another cause of the same clinical picture. This is completely different as the patient simply often has continues a course in life that did not renew and inspire. After sufficiently many years the persons' emotional life is almost dead. Holistic rehabilitation is urgently needed.

Finally dependency is another pattern that can materialize as severe mental disorder. Dependency is basically to urge to substitute what one have inside one self, but which one does not believe to have, with something from the outside world. It is basically a misconception, caused by early emotional problems that can be solved by confrontation and self-insight. It is not really important to be able to classify or diagnose the patterns behind the mental symptoms but if they are seen it makes the treatment faster and easier. The theoretical structure of these different patterns of personal decay is not well-defined. Actually, the deeper one goes, the more they appear to be the same. And if one goes all the way, it becomes obvious that what create all the problems is just illusions – what in Buddhism is called "Maya". The cause of all suffering is not knowing, not acknowledging and not appreciating one's own divine nature (1).

References

[1]   Grof S. Implications of modern consciousness research for psychology: Holotropic experiences and their healing and heuristic potential. Humanistic Psychol 2003;31(2-3):50-85.

Chapter 36

Social problems disguised as illness

Many of the diseases seen in the psychiatric clinic are actually symptoms of social problems. It is often easier for the physician to treat the symptoms than to be a couch and help the patient to assume responsibility in order to improve quality of life, the social situation and relations.

If the physician ignores the signs of the disease being a symptom of social problems, and treats the patient with pharmaceuticals, he can give the patient the best justification in the world not to do anything about the situation. It is very important that the physician is not tricked by the games the socially troubled patient, more or less unconsciously, is playing.

A firm and wise attitude that confronts the patient with his or her lack of responsibility for solving the social problems, seems to be a constructive way out. The physician can give holding and support, but the responsibility must remain with the patient. Often it is better for the patient that the physician abstains from giving the drugs that can remedy the symptoms and take the role of a couch instead. Suffering is not necessarily bad, suffering is actually highly motivating and often the most efficient source of learning. Couching can help the patient canalise his motivation into highly constructive considerations and behaviour. A holistic approach thus gives the patient learning and helps him rehabilitate his social reality.

Concerning children with recurrent or chronic pain we have observed an overuse of painkillers, where we believe part is of a psychosomatic nature due to pour thriving in the family. The true cause is almost always emotional problems like anxiety. Here the physician has an important job helping the parents to develop as persons, teaching them the basic holding of awareness, respect, care, acknowledgment and acceptance of their child. Most of chronic pain and discomfort with children can be improved, if the physician understands how to use the holistic medical toolbox and help the children to cope with difficult emotions.

Introduction

There are some people that cannot be helped by their physician, because their symptoms are more or less direct manifestations of social difficulties. Physicians, especially in USA have thus been criticized for treating social problems by prescribing pharmaceuticals for the symptomatic physical (or mental) complaints (1). Results from a logistic regression analysis showed that in women (but not in men) problems in the relationship with spouse or partner increased the probability of being a general practice attendee more than twofold (2). It is well known from many studies that social and medical problems are strongly connected (3), and it is also known that the quality of the patients' social relationships are highly correlated to self-perceived mental and physical health (4,5). In our experience, many symptoms connected to social problems are somatisations that will vanish into thin air, once the difficulties are overcome. It may, however, be difficult to get that far, particularly if the patients believe that they are ill and use illness as an excuse to avoid solving their social and domestic problems.

Excuses are very common, because it is difficult to take responsibility for all aspects of our lives. Somatic or mental illness can be a marvellous excuse, because everybody accepts it immediately. But to a physician, the situation is more difficult to accept, when the patient really has no somatic or mental illness. The patient supposedly has terrible back pain or depression, but walks into the room completely unaffected, sits down and speaks lively. Then, suddenly, there is a shift, and all the pain in the back appears, or the full depression appears, as if by order. It is hard not to smile, but it may be said in the patient's defence that often he or she is only partially aware of what is going on. Talking about the physical or mental pain can work miracles, if the patient is prepared to improve his or her life. Before we look at examples of social problems disguised as disease, let us look one more time at how life in general can be improved.

The basis for clinical holistic medicine

The life mission theory (6-11) state that everybody has a purpose of life or has a huge talent. Happiness comes from living this purpose and succeeding in expressing the core talent in your life. To do this, it is important to develop as a person into what is known as the natural condition, a condition where you know yourself and use all your efforts to achieve what is most important for you. The holistic process theory of healing (12-15) and the related quality of life theories (16-18) state, that the return to the natural state of being is possible, whenever the person gets the resources needed for the existential healing. The resources needed are, according to the theory, holding in the dimensions: awareness, respect, care, acknowledgment and acceptance with support and processing in the dimensions: feeling, understanding and letting go of negative attitudes and beliefs. The precondition for the holistic healing to take place is trust, and the intention of the healing taking place. Existential healing is not a local healing of any tissue, but a healing of the wholeness of the person, making him much more resourceful, loving, and knowledgeable of himself and his own needs and wishes. In letting go of negative attitudes and beliefs the person returns to a more responsible existential position and an improved quality of life.

The philosophical change of the person healing is often a change towards preferring difficult problems and challenges, instead of avoiding difficulties in life (19-26). The person who becomes happier and more resourceful is often also becoming more healthy, talented and more able to function (27-29).

Examples of social problems disguised as disease

We believe that the best way to illustrate our thoughts and intentions is to use case stories. The following case reports will therefore illustrate the problem from different angles.

> Girl, aged one year, who is constantly ill
> Frequently ill, almost constantly since January. Violent pain makes her throw herself back and forth, uncontrollable. Examination: Speech development normal, knows only a few words, somewhat poor psychomotor development, walks unsteadily and often falls and hurts herself. Otoscopy: Red tympanic membrane bilaterally /Otitis media/ Prescribe penicillin. Socially: Her mother visits a crisis centre. They have found a family for respite care. The situation seems to be very hard for the patient.

This is an example of the extreme situation, where the correlation between somatic illness and social circumstances is spelled out. Indeed, that is how young physicians learn it: first we understand the rough cases and then gradually the more subtle ones. And finally we are able to see the correlation, which nobody else can see, if we keep looking for it with ever more profound and subtle techniques.

> Girl, aged seven years with back problems
> Seven-year-old girl come together with her father. She has low cervical back pain, projecting spinous process on palpation. Headache. Examination: Tension in the long back muscles. Her father says that he has no energy left for her, when he gets home, has major problems at work, will probably lose his job soon and is looking for a new one. Conversation about children's needs. There is not much to be done except to offer the father another conversation about better daytime planning. However, stretching the back helps the patient.

Suppressed feelings go straight into the back, in both children and adults. Often, it is difficult to change the situation for the adult. Back problems in children and adolescents with no direct traumatic cause or objective finding should alert the physician to look for psychosocial causes.

> Girl, aged 14 years with abdominal pain
> Over the past year several episodes with severe abdominal pain. Examination: Normal examination. During the conversation it is revealed that her parents have just separated. She has problems at school and also feels that she has to take too much responsibility for her two sisters, because her mother seems to be out of strength and very short tempered. /Psychosomatic abdominal pain/ We agree that she should discuss the situation with the mother and return for a conversation together.

Abdominal pain is a common childhood symptom that can range from mild discomfort to a life-threatening emergency requiring immediate attention. In most cases, surgery will not be required, but children with such symptoms should have a thorough check-up to make sure there is not a serious underlying problem. It can be difficult to diagnose the cause of abdominal pain, because many conditions affecting various parts of the body can produce abdominal pain. In infancy, the most common cause of abdominal pain is colic. As the child grows older, abdominal pain may be associated with minor disruptions of normal body functions (such as constipation) or with a variety of organic disorders or emotional problems. Often the pain accompanies diseases of the abdominal organs, such as the intestines, liver, pancreas and stomach. But it may be relayed from other, more distant parts of the body; pneumonia and tonsillitis (strep throat), for example, sometimes cause abdominal symptoms.

The term recurrent abdominal pain (RAP) has been used and defined in various ways over time, but begins with a reference to Apley's criteria[30]. RAP is characterized by three or more episodes of abdominal pain that occur over at least three months and are severe enough to interfere with activities, such as school attendance and performance, social activities, and participation in sports and extracurricular activities. Clinically, these episodes are characterized by vague abdominal pain that may be dull or crampy, lasts for less than one hour, and poorly localized or periumbilical. The pain frequently presents with nausea, vomiting, and other signs of autonomic arousal. Though the term RAP is most often used to refer to functional abdominal pain, Apley's original description is broad and does not have specific etiological implications. The majority of children with RAP do not have a specific physical disorder or organic disease. Most investigators report that only 5-10% of affected children have an organic cause for their pain.

Probably the hardest thing for the child is the need to be loyal to both parents and this can easily lead to a conflict that cannot be resolved. There is a deep psychological explanation for this need for two-sided loyalty, namely that each individual contains the two genders, represented by our parents. The quality of our future love life depends on how lovingly these two aspects of ourselves meet.

> Male, aged 26 years with back pain
> The patient asks for a medical certificate, but there is absolutely nothing wrong with his back, and pain cannot be provoked in any way. No tenderness, no spinal anomalies, normal flexion forwards and sideways. He has been off work for three months and brings papers that should have been filled out long ago.

If we are entirely unable to provoke the back pain claimed by the patient, we quite simply do not believe it exists. We know about back pain, we know how it hurt and what makes it hurt. In addition, we can often tell when patients are lying, which does not make it any easier to believe in their stories. And sometimes, when the motive for lying is obvious – typically, as in this case, social problems at the workplace that the patient has been unable to solve – it may be better to grab the bull by its horns rather than allow a downward path, which a long-term sick leave often is. In this situation, as physicians we cannot help him; he has to find another job.

> Female, aged 29 – Separation
> Comes in order to solve the problems relating to separation from her former husband. She has two daughters aged 5 and 7 years. It is suggested to her that they spare the children their mutual problems and make the following arrangement: that the children live with their mother and stay with their father every second weekend from end of school on Fridays to start of school on Mondays (the children to be handed over to the other parent after school) and every Wednesday from end of school until start of school on Thursdays (the children to be handed over to the other parent after school), and that they share all holidays equally between them so that the father spends the first half of the holidays with the children, and the mother the second half. This arrangement should continue until the children are 12 years old,

whereupon they should decide themselves where they want to live. Generally, it is working much better now, and the patient seems to be getting the situation under control. She has withdrawn her report of violence by her former husband.

We must often help to solve social problems and often experience that the symptoms with which the patient present – usually not the social problems, but physical or mental disorders – disappear when everything else falls into place. For the patient, it is of extreme value that the physician will take a holistic approach and help the patient take a comprehensive view of reality.

> Male, aged 30 years with neck pain
> Becomes dizzy – especially when smoking – has had severe neck pain, difficulty in bending his head to his chest. Currently unemployed, his wife gives him a massage in the tense regions. Does not want ibuprofen [NSAID] or similar medication. Prescribe stretching of antagonistic muscles, which proves effective. Should return in two weeks for new treatment, if the problem has not been solved by then.

"Unemployment" often covers a range of problems such as low self-esteem, social marginalisation, low functional capacity, poor health and low quality of life. People, who are long-term unemployed often do not just need a job, they need a rehabilitation program. However, it is very convenient to blame all problems on unemployment. The truth is that any person, who has a high personal energy level, well-developed enjoyment of life and a minimum of direction in life will never remain unemployed for very long without finding something interesting to do, pay or no pay. We do not condemn the unemployed, we merely encourage him, if he is receptive, to address the real problem: low functional capacity – and then to do something about it. Life skills can be developed, if there is a will to do so.

> Male, aged 32 years with back pain
> Back pain, on sick leave. No physical injury of the back, only severe muscle tension corresponding to the lower back. Manipulated with good effect. Patient claims to be incapacitated; no apparent evidence to that effect. He is put on sick leave for another week with follow-up.

This patient claims to have back pain, but in the opinion of the physician, there is nothing wrong with him. He has some muscle tension, but does not even appear to be in much pain. His gait is relaxed and quite natural, and he moves freely. In our opinion, muscle tension is not a disease, but rather something all of us experience, because we unconsciously hide away our difficult feelings in the muscles. Back and low back muscles, in particular, are suitable for storing acute problems. But this patient is hoping to be put on long-term sick leave. General medical practice require us to grant him another week to get better.

He is annoyed that the physician dos not "buy" his claims of terrible pain. He claims that the physician cannot possibly know the kind of pain he is in. But we have a different opinion, namely that a good physician knows very well how much pain a patient is in. He also knows how easy or difficult it is to tolerate the pain. We believe that a physician with empathy knows a lot about his patients' subjective condition, although naturally he cannot be absolutely certain.

> Female, aged 57 years with pain everywhere
> Complains of pain in the head, arms and hands, shoulders, upper and lower back, buttocks, knees and feet. Muscle pain all over the body on physical examination. Very tense. Recommended to swim twice a week. It is important that the patient uses her body and learns to relax at the same time. Interpreter and language problems. The problem is probably also cultural, since she does not speak Danish. Panodil [paracetamol] two tablets as required when she is active. Stronger medication needs to be considered. A language course and an integration programme would also benefit the patient, but that is hardly realistic due to low motivation.

Living in Denmark without knowing the language is not pleasant. Many foreigners never learn to speak Danish resulting in social isolation, feeling of being dispensable and unhappiness may often lead to somatisation and incurable pain.

> Male, aged 79 years with loneliness
> Home visit. He telephones complaining of gasping for air. On my arrival he is quite unaffected, has been feeling scared and lonely, he says, and presumably his inhalation spray may be empty. Would like some more cough mixture. The patient is calmed down and invited to return in two weeks to go through it all. Prescription: continue with Berodual [ipratropium, phenoterol], cough mixture.

Biomedicine helps elderly and weak people to survive and lead a decent and reasonably symptom-free life. Nevertheless, people decline, their general condition deteriorate, they function less and less well, they become old, isolated and lonely, until death catches up with them. Is that natural? However natural death is, we find the decline, the loneliness and social exclusion equally unnatural, this constant loss of attitude until one cannot spread one's wings at all.

Discussion

Many of the diseases we identify, diagnose and treat with biomedicine might actually be mere symptoms of social conditions that weaken the patient's whole organism or simply somatize. Pain is one of the most frequent symptoms of emotional and social problems. If a social problem is treated like a disease, it is likely that the patient will not fight as eagerly as if he or she would, if told that this condition was caused by the actual problematic social circumstances. As physicians we want to be merciful and helpful, but by treating symptoms and not confronting the patient with our understanding of the whole situation we will not be true to our profession. If we are unable to point out the causal relations between poor living and poor quality of life or subjective and objective symptoms of disease, we might obtain just the opposite effect. We can this way make the patient a passive victim to a non-existent disease, or a health condition that actually could be alleviated, at least with some likelihood, by the patient him- or herself.

Much of our dissatisfaction with biomedicine is related to the fact that only rarely is it able to restore health, enjoyment of life, vitality, vital energy and social worth in chronic patients, i.e. in the majority of the population over the age of 45 years of age.

As the many cases in this paper have clearly demonstrated, social problems are not difficult to alleviate, when the physician has a clear understanding and insight. Concerning children many of the problems we see in the clinic might be symptoms of familiar dysfunction or stress. Psychosomatic symptoms are by definition clinical symptoms with no underlying organic pathology. Common symptoms seen in children include abdominal pain, headaches, enuresis, chest pain, fatigue, limb pain, back pain or worry about health and difficulty breathing.

The prevalence of psychosomatic complaints in children and adolescents has been reported to be between 10 and 25% (31). Potential sources of stress in children and adolescents include schoolwork, family problems, peer pressure, chronic disease or disability in parents, family moves, psychiatric disorder in parents and poor coping abilities. Characteristics that favour psychosomatic basis for symptoms include vagueness of symptoms, varying intensity, inconsistent nature and pattern of symptoms, presence of multiple symptoms at the same time, chronic course with apparent good health, delay in seeking medical care, and lack of concern on the part of the patient. A thorough medical and psychosocial history and physical examination are the most valuable aspects of diagnostic evaluation in order to rule out organic etiology.

Sometimes the parents do not understand the character of the child or do not acknowledge its talents and purpose of life, what we a little poetically like to call "the essence of its soul". In this case personal development is needed for the parents, if the child is to heal existentially (7,10,14). This can be brought around, if the physician works with open eyes and a warm hearth for his patients. We therefore call for a new medical approach that develop people and support them in their effort to live long, good and purposeful lives. Often, biomedicine only helps people survive the acute crises resulting in continued chronic decline. By contrast, it has little to offer in relation to the ordinary course of life of people in the Western world with ever decreasing quality of life, health and functional capacity. We believe that using the toolboxes of the manual and the consciousness-based medicine actually can empower the physician to help his patient more, even with problems related to existential issues like love, respect, sexuality, social functioning and general attitudes towards life and other.

Conclusion

Many of the physical and mental diseases seen in the general practitioner clinic are mere symptoms of social problems. It is often easier for the physician to diagnose and treat the symptoms than it is to help the patient assume responsibility and improve his or her quality of life, social situation, and relations.

If the physician ignores that the signs of a disease could be symptoms of emotional and social problems, he can give the patient the best justification in the world not to do anything about the situation. It is very important that the physician is not tricked by the games the socially troubled patient can play, more or less unconsciously. A firm and wise attitude that confronts the patient with his or her lack of responsibility for solving the social problems, seems to be the only constructive way out of the situation. The physician can give holding and support, but the responsibility must remain with the patient. Often it is better for the patient that the physician abstains from giving the drugs that can remedy the symptoms; and take the role of a couch instead. Suffering is not necessary bad. Actually suffering is highly motivating and often the most efficient source of learning. Couching can help the patient canalise his motivation into highly constructive considerations and behaviour.

Concerning children we have seen many cases in our daily clinical practice suffering from chronic pain with psychosomatic components due to poor thriving and emotional problems in their family. The physician has an important job helping the parents to develop as persons, teaching them the basic holding of awareness, respect, care, acknowledgment and acceptance of their child. Most of chronic pain and discomfort with children can be improved using the holistic medical toolbox.

References

[1] Peters B, McRee S. Born in the USA. The medicalization of social problems. Mich Health Hosp 1996;32(4):71-3.

[2] Pini S, Piccinelli M, Zimmermann-Tansella C. Social problems as factors affecting medical consultation: a comparison between general practice attenders and community probands with emotional distress. Psychol Med 1995;25(1):33-41.

[3] Del Piccolo L, Saltini A, Zimmermann C. Which patients talk about stressful life events and social problems to the general practitioner? Psychol Med 1998;28(6):1289-99.

[4] Ventegodt, S. Quality of life in Denmark. Results from a population survey. Copenhagen: Forskningscentrets Forlag, 1995. [Danish].

[5] Ventegodt S. The quality of life of 4,500 31-33 year-olds. Result from a study of the Prospective Pediatric Cohort of persons born at the University Hospital in Copenhagen. Copenhagen: Forskningscentrets Forlag, 1996. [Danish].

[6] Ventegodt S, Andersen NJ, Merrick J. Editorial: Five theories of human existence. ScientificWorldJournal 2003;3:1272-6.

[7] Ventegodt S. The life mission theory: A theory for a consciousness-based medicine. Int. J. Adolesc. Med. Health 2003;15(1):89-91.

[8] Ventegodt S, Andersen NJ, Merrick J. The life mission theory II. The structure of the life purpose and the ego. ScientificWorldJournal 2003;3:1277-85.

[9] Ventegodt S, Andersen NJ, Merrick J. The life mission theory III. Theory of talent. ScientificWorldJournal 2003;3:1286-93.

[10] Ventegodt S, Andersen NJ, Merrick J. The life mission theory IV. Theory on child development. ScientificWorldJournal 2003;3:1294-1301.

[11] Ventegodt S, Andersen NJ, Merrick J. The life mission theory V. A theory of the anti-self and explaining the evil side of man. ScientificWorldJournal 2003;3:1302-13.

[12] Ventegodt S, Andersen NJ, Merrick J. Holistic medicine: Scientific challenges. ScientificWorldJournal 2003;3:1108-16.

[13] Ventegodt S, Andersen NJ, Merrick J. Holistic Medicine II: The square-curve paradigm for research in alternative, complementary and holistic medicine: A cost-effective, easy and scientifically valid design for evidence based medicine. ScientificWorldJournal 2003;3:1117-27.

[14] Ventegodt S, Andersen NJ, Merrick J. Holistic Medicine III: The holistic process theory of healing. ScientificWorldJournal 2003;3:1138-46.

[15] Ventegodt S, Andersen NJ, Merrick J. Holistic Medicine IV: The principles of the holistic process of healing in a group setting. ScientificWorldJournal 2003;3:1294-1301.

[16] Ventegodt S, Merrick J, Andersen NJ. Quality of life theory I. The IQOL theory: An integrative theory of the global quality of life concept. ScientificWorldJournal 2003;3:1030-40.

[17] Ventegodt S, Merrick J, Andersen NJ. Quality of life theory II. Quality of life as the realization of life potential: A biological theory of human being. ScientificWorldJournal 2003;3:1041-9.

[18] Ventegodt S, Merrick J, Andersen NJ. Quality of life theory III. Maslow revisited. ScientificWorldJournal 2003;3:1050-7.

[19] Ventegodt S, Andersen NJ, Merrick J. Quality of life philosophy: when life sparkles or can we make wisdom a science? ScientificWorldJournal 2003;3:1160-3.

[20] Ventegodt S, Andersen NJ, Merrick J. QOL philosophy I: Quality of life, happiness, and meaning of life. ScientificWorldJournal 2003;3:1164-75.

[21] Ventegodt S, Andersen NJ, Kromann M, Merrick J. QOL philosophy II: What is a human being? ScientificWorldJournal 2003;3:1176-85.

[22] Ventegodt S, Merrick J, Andersen NJ. QOL philosophy III: Towards a new biology. ScientificWorldJournal 2003;3:1186-98.

[23] Ventegodt S, Andersen NJ, Merrick J. QOL philosophy IV: The brain and consciousness. ScientificWorldJournal 2003;3:1199-1209.

[24] Ventegodt S, Andersen NJ, Merrick J. QOL philosophy V: Seizing the meaning of life and getting well again. ScientificWorldJournal 2003;3:210-29.

[25] Ventegodt S, Andersen NJ, Merrick J. QOL philosophy VI: The concepts. ScientificWorldJournal 2003;3:1230-40.

[26] Merrick J, Ventegodt S. What is a good death? To use death as a mirror and find the quality in life. BMJ Rapid Response 2003 Oct 31.

[27] Ventegodt S, Merrick J, Andersen NJ. Quality of life as medicine. A pilot study of patients with chronic illness and pain. ScientificWorld Journal 2003;3:520-32.

[28] Ventegodt S, Merrick J, Andersen NJ. Quality of life as medicine II. A pilot study of a five day "Quality of Life and Health" cure for patients with alcoholism. ScientificWorld Journal 2003;3:842-52.

[29] Ventegodt S, Clausen B, Langhorn M, Kromann M, Andersen NJ, Merrick J. Quality of Life as Medicine III. A qualitative analysis of the effect of a five days intervention with existential holistic group therapy: a quality of life course as a modern rite of passage. ScientificWorld Journal 2004;4:124-33.

[30] Apley J. The child with recurrent abdominal pain. Pediatr Clin North Am 1967;14(1):63-72.

[31] Brill SR, Patel DR, MacDonald E. Psychosomatic disorders in pediatrics. Indian J Pediatr 2001;68(7):597-603.

Chapter 37

Holistic approach to rape and incest trauma

A large fraction of mentally ill patients has been sexually abused. Studies indicate that at least 15% of the female population in western countries has experienced sexual abuse and severe sexual traumas and a substantial fraction of these females develop symptoms of mental disorder. Behind an innocent depression or a personality disturbance is often found sexual traumas from abuse or neglect; the most painful of these are caused by close members of the patients family.

This chapter explains how even serious sexual abuse and neglect traumas can be healed, when care and resources encourage the patient to return to the painful life events. When the physician care and receive the trust of the patient, emotional holding and processing will follow quite naturally.

Spontaneous regression seems to be an almost pain free way of integrating the severe traumas from earlier experiences of rape and incest. This technique is a recommended alternative to classical timeline therapy using therapeutic commands.

When traumatized patients distance themselves from their soul (feelings, sexuality and existential depth), they often lose their energy and enjoyment of life. But this does not mean that they are lost to life. Although it may seem paradoxical, a severe trauma may be a unique opportunity to regain enjoyment of life. The patient will often be richly rewarded for the extensive work of clearing and sorting out in order to experience a new depth in his or her existence and emotional life with a new ability to understand life in general and other people in particular. So what may look like a tragedy can be transformed into a unique gift, if the patient gets sufficient support, there is the possibility of healing and learning. Consciousness-based medicine seems to provide the severely traumatized patient with the quality of support and care needed for the healing of body, mind and soul.

Introduction

The problem of victimization and re-victimization is psychologically extremely complex. Most people believe the victim is chosen randomly by the offender, but research has shown that victims very often have been victims before and that victimization often is a long chain of life events containing many different objective events, but they are the same mode of victimization.

Russell (1,2) found that between 33% and 68% of the sexually abused victims were subsequently raped. This is compared to an incidence of 17% for non-abused woman. Other researchers (3) have found that 18% of repeat rape victims had incest histories, compared to 4% of first time victims.

The research indicated that for many rape victims, who have been victimized before, the rape and sexual assault are seldom accidental. These events follow a dark and sad pattern of unconsciously replaying and reliving the role of the victim. This makes the therapy of the rape and incest victim complex. Most rape victims have earlier incidents of victimization and most incest victims have had difficulties with keeping their boundaries and taking care of their personal safety.

As sexual assaults and rape is among the life events with the most dramatic negative effect on quality of life, the physician must take such traumas extremely seriously. Unfortunately, such sexual assaults are fairly common in the population. Studies from different western countries indicated an incidence of about 15% of the girls being assaulted sexually in childhood (1,4,5). These patients are also more likely to be physically abused by husbands and partners (1,6). Unfortunately some are even abused by the therapist, who was supposed to heal and protect them (7).

Poor quality of life is statistically connected to bad health. About one in four of the patients seen by the family physician will have such highly painful histories. Most of these sexual traumas remain hidden. The work with these serious problems can therefore not be a task for specialists. Every physician must be able to handle these traumas, when met in the clinic.

Fortunately, the loving and caring physician or sexologist, using the tools and principles of modern sexology and scientific holistic medicine (8-16), can help the patients to heal, even with serious wounds on the body and soul. The most effective and safe sexogical and holistic medical tools are disussed in chapter 26-30. In this chapter we discuss the general principles of holistic and sexological treatment of incest and rape victims.

Therapy with incest and rape victims

Many forms of therapy have proven effective with rape victims, like cognitive-behavioral therapy (17-19), reality therapy (20) and group therapy (21). Many forms of therapy has also proven effective with incest victims, like play therapy (22), analytical psychotherapy (23), supportive group therapy (4,8,24,25), couples therapy (26) and family therapy (27), but as shown by Krach and Zens (7) the result of the therapy is often not completely satisfactory. This is in part because the ethical standards of the therapist working with the incest victims have often been regrettably low. 46% of the incest victims feel abused after the therapy, (sexually or otherwise). The toolbox of holistic medicine includes an ethical strategy ("coming from the hearth") (29), which it intended to eliminate the possibility of such malpractice in the holistic medical clinic.

Holistic trauma treatment: The use of spontaneous and guided time line therapy

When we feel that we have lost our value as human beings (as many girls do following a sexual assault), or when we feel that our manhood and self-confidence have been seriously damaged, (as many men do following a violent assault) a destructive decrease in self-esteem and self-confidence will result. This is often due to the decisions made during or after the incident to overcome the unbearable feelings of fear, shame, guilt, powerlessness and hopelessness. Holistic treatment of the after-effects of sexual and/or violent traumas is important in order to work on the mind-body dissociation (27), post traumatic stress, self-blame, sexual dysfunction and low self esteem. Holistic treatment in this case is based on classic time line therapy, going through the incident over and over again, until the patient clearly acknowledge what happened then and can let go of the negative decisions, made in the heat of the moment.

First the patient has to feel the pain once again and then everything will be understood. Ultimately, the victim can let go of the life-denying decisions and will feel as though the incident never occurred. Very often the whole chain of similar events must be processed, to cure the symptoms. Often this will require thorough and time-consuming work which gives the patients an important learning experience. Relief from the painful events and often even a gratitude that it happened that an old, self-destructive pattern finally can be broken.

Aldous Huxley's novel, Island (30), provide a beautiful description of time line therapy. Sending the patient back to the trauma can be done by means of the classic time line commands, if the physician has gotten the full trust and acceptance by the patient to receive the necessary holding (awareness, respect, care, acknowledgment, and acceptance) (31):

- Go back to when it happened.
- With your eyes closed, go through the event from the beginning to the end.
- Tell me what happened.

This process should be repeated until the problem has been processed, the learning gained, and the pattern broken. Despite the simplicity of the commands, time line therapy is not a simple process. Indeed, the skilled time line therapist must be able to identify the patient's position on the time line at any time. Also, the experienced therapist rarely needs to apply time line therapy at all. Meeting and joining the patient exactly where she is will send her back in time spontaneously. To be more exact: the patient has never moved beyond the frozen now. So the good doctor should simply join and support the patient with the intention of helping her, then the patient will regress spontaneously – or to be precise- the patient will confront the pain in the frozen now.

In our opinion, therapy with many mental commands is therapy that tries to process things without the requisite emotional holding. In our view, love and compassion constitute a much stronger therapeutic strategy than using power and mental guidance. The former is holistic and practical, the latter keeps within the framework of the mind. From our perspective, Neuro Linguistic Programming (NLP) and mental processes of that kind are not holistic therapy. With love and compassion holding and processing come quite naturally and thus it is holistic healing.

Modern holistic medicine and sexology

The major difference between classical holistic medicine and sexology and its modern counterpart is the theories used by the latter. The belief is that nothing is as practical as a good theory and from this philosophy a number of new theories for existential healing and holistic therapy have emerged. These theories are not substituting Hippocrates original theory of repression of the human character as the primary cause of all physical, mental, existential and sexual problems, but elaborates on the aspects, where Hippocrates and his students were less clear.

The life mission theory (31-36) states that everybody has a purpose of life, or huge talent. Happiness comes from living this purpose and succeeding in expressing the core talent in your life. To do this, it is important to develop as a person into what is know as the natural condition. This is a condition where the person knows himself and is able to use all his efforts to achieve what is most important for him. The holistic process theory of healing (37-40) and the related quality of life theories (41-43) states that the return to the natural state of being is possible, whenever the person gets the resources needed for the existential healing. The resources needed are "holding" in the dimensions of awareness, respect, care, acknowledgment and acceptance with support and processing in the dimensions of feeling, understanding and letting go of negative attitudes and beliefs.

The preconditions for the holistic healing to take place are trust and the intention of the healing to take place. Existential healing is not a local healing of any tissue, but a healing of the wholeness of the person, making him much more resourceful, loving, and knowledgeable of himself, needs and wishes. By letting go of negative attitudes and beliefs the person returns to a more responsible existential position and an improved quality of life. The philosophical change of the person healing is often a change towards preferring difficult problems and challenges, instead of avoiding difficulties in life (44-51). The person who becomes happier and more resourceful is often also becomes more healthy, more talented and more able to function (52-55).

Acute trauma

Female, aged 34 years with acute trauma. Arrives in a state of shock and on the brink of tears after having a street fight with her former husband and having had her life threatened by him. He is now on the run from the police, as he has a suspended sentence. She has sent her two children of 5 and 10 years to stay with relatives and friends. Needs psychological assistance, perhaps one weekly session for eight weeks. Sick leave for three weeks. Prescribe urgent counselling – the incident is reviewed four times here, until the patient no longer cries, when confronting it. The psychologist should take over from there.

We refer the patient to a psychologist or a gestalt therapist, but cannot send her home, as she is completely emotionally incoherent. We relieve the pressure by means of simple time line therapy. The patient goes through the incident until the intense emotional reaction has worn off. In this case, the psychologist is also needed because of the social circumstances. Successful trauma therapy is about keeping patients in the present, while their attention moves back in time and confronts the traumatic events. Difficult feelings, which the patient receives insufficient support in facing, will allow her to let go of the present and return to the past. Without contact with the present the patient is technically psychotic and the therapeutic gain from the session will be negligible.

An experienced holistic therapist will notice that the patient is about to lose her mental focus ("third eye closing"), before she has left the present. In this situation we would quickly call in another therapist to support the patient. A patient, who is on the brink of psychosis on arrival has to receive ample support, for instance in the form of a "good father" and a "good mother", before the therapeutic process can begin.

Traumas in body and mind

The classic trauma is a serious and unexpected assault such as rape. In a holistic perspective, even in the case of atrocities, most injuries to the body and mind can heal,

> Female, aged 16 years and raped. In the train, a 16-year-old girl noticed that a young man has taken an interest in her. She avoided his glance, but as she gets off the train on a dark road, he follows her. She becomes scared and tries to run away, but he catches her, throws her to the ground and rapes her. It hurts and she is very frightened. "If you tell anybody, I'll kill you," he whispers to her. She tells no one, but her friends notice that she has become quieter. Once she managed to let go of the sentence "He'll kill me" during therapy, she brightened up and returned to her old self.

This girl has been marked by the incident. The question is why events affect individuals so differently, and what actually takes place when we are injured by a trauma. Exactly what was is it about the rape that traumatised her? Suffering inflicted on us by the trauma itself, however unpleasant in the present, does not seem to harm us subsequently – unless we repress the suffering in the situation and consequently carry it with us. Thus, pain is not traumatising in itself. Whether or not we become traumatised depends on how we relate to the pain. In the specific situation, the victim cans represss the unbearable emotional pain for which she cannot assume responsibility. By drawing a justifying conclusion she makes the pain go away and consequently enables her to cope with the situation. But although the pain has disappeared from her conscious mind, it still exists below the surface. After the event, she now carries it along with her. The statement "He'll kill me" is impressed on her subconscious mind and she now has an impression of men that will restrain her in future, until she relives the pain by being a victim during therapy. In this way she chooses to suffer without resistance and makes her mind let go of the statement. For lack of a better expression, we call such statements which are generalised justifications enabling us to disclaim an unbearable responsibility, "decisions".

Early sexual abuse

Early sexual abuse is often extremely traumatising and the girls, who are most frequently the victims, end up making numerous self-destructive decisions, which are very difficult to become aware of and let go of. But as the victims address the pain and fully understand the assaults and their nature, they can let go of the negative decisions and life returns. We believe that holistic medicine, when used correctly, can be so effective that no serious scars remain on the soul... The patient can achieve complete recovery, but it takes love and care. Holistic therapy alone is not enough.

> Female, aged 21 years and sexually abused. First quality-of-life (QOL) session: Wants to resolve her inner existential problems that peaked after she had helped a friend recover from a suicide attempt. Has a very difficult personal history, but has tackled it surprisingly well. Has very strong defences', enabling her to appear as a smart and sensitive young woman. SOCIAL: Both parents alcoholics, she lived in a foster home when she was young, was adopted by a couple who divorced four years later, new father also an alcoholic, died when the patient was 9 years old. Subsequently, she lived with the mother of her adoptive father, who ignored her. At the age of 12 years she asked to be placed in a foster home, where she stayed for one year, but the foster family was psychologically mean to her and she felt like a prisoner. Moved to a student hostel on her 18th birthday. On examination: On the couch, however, it can be seen that from the chest down she is practically dead – her abdomen looks more like the abdomen of a corpse, all pale, devoid of blood and life. Strange damage on the skin of both hips, like the cracks in the dermis layer normally seen in pregnant or obese women, but the patient was never overweight. Previous assessment for this, no conclusion. SUBJECTIVE FINDINGS: We talk about emptying the internal waste bin and she appears to be clear and determined about her personal development project: The aim is to find out what you want to do with your life. She wants to provide care, but that is an understandable reaction to her life. Should rather grow up and become independent. She has had about four boyfriends. Her self-esteem needs to be restored. Deserted repeatedly in her life, so she needs to reopen her heart. EXERCISE: Write down your life story – focus on your feelings, thoughts and decisions. Start from the present. What happened? How did you feel? (What decision/conclusion did you make?) What happened? How did you feel? Topics: friendship, love, sex, food, failure – school/work, family, leisure-time. Next appointment in two weeks.

Second QOL session: Has been well, has been very much at home in her abdomen and has felt more than she used to since last session. Has done her homework nine months back. We look at it together. She does not write as much about her feelings, as I (SV) would have liked, it is as though she finds it difficult to recall her feelings. We work on that. EXERCISE: Make friends with your body – do some sport, possibly together with other people, cook some nice meals for yourself, preferably three times a day, explore your sexuality and get to know yourself better, also inside the pelvis and abdomen. EXERCISE: When you continue your autobiography, take the emotional perspective. One hour a day at the most, opens up and then closes. Next appointment in two weeks. Should come sooner if she suddenly feels bad. I think therapy will be hard on her.

Third QOL session: We talk about what theme she is dealing with in her current process. Something about playing dead to survive some horrible situation. Has met a 24-year-old man, whom she has had sex with. The relationship is good. She can feel her emotions. She seems relaxed and happy, and is going camping in the summer and will take our summer course, Life Philosophy that Heals. Should continue the exercises from last session.

Fourth QOL session: Fourth QOL session: Attended the course Life Philosophy that Heals (life purpose: I am wise.) She relived the extensive sexual abuse that she experienced as a child when she was about three years old. Has cried for hours and felt a terrible pain in her reproductive organs and abdomen.. Attended the course Life Philosophy that Heals (life purpose: I am wise) and has relived extensive sexual abuse as a child when she was about three years old. Has cried for hours and felt a terrible pain in her reproductive organs and abdomen... Today she feels much more alive and energetic, and she looks much better, although she still has the habit of "playing dead" – she gives, but does not take from her boyfriend, whom I believe she really needs. She has close friends, but she shares only a small part of her life with them. EXERCISE: Rely more on your friends: give and take –take the initiative to be with them, frequently and intimately. Make use of your sexuality. Feeling EXERCISE: Sit on a chair for five minutes every day and sense how you feel. She already does that exercise. How to become truly wise and smart? Write two A4 pages about it. You are going at 1 km/h – it's time to speed up!

Fifth QOL conversation: Things are going well – has set her boundaries with her supervisor, has attained self-respect and her own space. Has experienced close contact with girlfriend. Feels buoyant and happy today. She has reflected sexuality, no problems there, she believes. 1. Rely more on your friends: give and take – and take the initiative to be with them, frequently and intimately – OK, she has done that. 2. Make use of your sexuality– OK about herself. Feeling EXERCISE: Sit on a chair for 5 minutes every day and sense how you feel. She is already doing that - OK. EXERCISE: How to become truly wise and smart? A two-page draft – she has not done that – for next time – write down all sub-aspects you can find of "knowing".

This patient will have to work on herself for years in order to heal the early damage from sexual abuse. Perhaps her wounds will not heal completely, until the day she finds herself in a warm and genuine relationship.

Discussion

It is not always possible to work on a certain event in life during therapy. Sometimes the event is thoroughly repressed, even though well-defined symptoms may have begged the patient to deal with it. Often, the reason for this is that the traumatic event is not a singular event, but occurred as follow-on from earlier traumas and life-denying decisions.

Indeed, in our culture it is common to have experienced a handful or more traumatic events that are related to our problematic themes in life, as mentioned previously. The reason why the individual trauma, which need not be particularly severe, may tip the balance is its contact with earlier, underlying traumas in the particular situation, reactivating their painful content. Most people believe that the anxiety, pain, shame and hopelessness, come from the most recent event. The most recent events have much deeper and more serious roots.

The patient has to reconsider his or her entire life philosophy and large parts of his or her personal history in order to regain balance. The patient needs to be relieved of what may appear, in retrospect, to be a considerable amount of naivety and shallowness. Not until the patient has developed and raised his personal level of responsibility can he integrate the underlying traumas. The patient is now facing two choices: To shut off emotionally and survive, perhaps sustained by symptom-relieving medication such as antidepressants, or to give life a thorough clean up.

With love for our patient comes trust, holding and processing and results in holistic healing. Instead of giving commands, giving a surplus of care and resources invites the patient to spontaneously return to the painful events of life. Spontaneous regression seems to be an almost pain free way of integrating even severe traumas, like the traumas that result from rape or incest (affecting at least 15% of the population) (1,4,5). Interestingly, most of the incest traumas remains hidden in the biomedical clinic, but are often revealed in the holistic clinic, where love or professional care and intimacy is an important part of the therapy.

When traumatized patients distance themselves from their soul, feelings, sexuality, and existential depth, they can easily lose their energy and enjoyment of life. But this does not mean that they are out of the game of life. Although it may seem paradoxical, a severe trauma may be a unique opportunity to gain new understanding and regain participation and full enjoyment of life. The patient will often be richly rewarded for the extensive work of clearing and sorting out and will often experience a new depth in his or her existence and emotional life with a new ability to understand life in general and other people in particular.

So what may look like a tragedy in the beginning of the therapy can be transformed into a unique gift. If the patient gets the sufficient support there is a possibility of healing and learning. Consciousness-based, holistic medicine and sexology seem to provide the severely traumatized patient with the quality of support and care needed for their soul and deepest existence to heal.

The most important prerequisite for the healing to happen is the physician's or sexologist's love or care for the patient and every physician with a loving heart can learn to use the holistic medical toolbox and thus help his patients to heal existentially. We recommend the holistic psychiatrist to also be thoroughly familiar with holistic sexology (56), as the formal distinction between psychiatry and sexology cannot be obtained for patients with sexual traumas causing their mental symptoms.

References

[1]   Russell D. The secret trauma: Incest in the lives of girls and women. New York: Basic Books, 1986.
[2]   Green AH. Child sexual abuse: Immediate and long-term effects and intervention. J Am Acad Child Adolesc Psychiatry 1993;32(5): 890-902.
[3]   Miller J, Moeller D, Kaufman A, Divasto P, Fitzsimmons P, Pother D, Christy J. Recidivism among sexual assult victims. Am J Psychiatry 1978;135:1103-4.
[4]   Wilson JP, Raphael B. International handbook of traumatic stress syndromes. New York: Plenum Press, 1993.
[5]   Backe L, Leick N, Merrick J, Michelsen N, eds. [Incest. A book on child sexual abuse]. Copenhagen: Hans Reitzel, 1983. [Danish].
[6]   Briere J. The long-term effects of childhood sexual abuse: Defining a post-sexual abuse syndrome. Washington, DC: Presentation Third Natl Conf Sex Victimization Children, 1984.
[7]   Armsworth MW. Therapy of incest survivors: abuse or support? Child Abuse Negl 1989;13(4):549-62.

[8] Ventegodt S, Merrick J. Clinical holistic medicine: Applied consciousness-based medicine. ScientificWorldJournal 2004;4: 96-9.

[9] Ventegodt S, Morad M, Merrick J. Clinical holistic medicine: Classic art of healing or the therapeutic touch. ScientificWorldJournal 2004;4:134-47.

[10] Ventegodt S, Morad M, Merrick J. Clinical holistic medicine: The "new medicine", the multi-paradigmatic physician and the medical record. ScientificWorldJournal 2004;4:273-85.

[11] Ventegodt S, Morad M, Merrick J. Clinical holistic medicine: Holistic pelvic examination and holistic treatment of infertility. ScientificWorldJournal 2004;4:148-58.

[12] Ventegodt S, Morad M, Hyam E, Merrick J. Clinical holistic medicine: Use and limitations of the biomedical paradigm ScientificWorldJournal 2004;4:295-306.

[13] Ventegodt S, Morad M, Kandel I, Merrick J. Clinical holistic medicine: Social problems disguised as illness. ScientificWorldJournal 2004;4:286-94.

[14] Ventegodt S, Morad M, Andersen NJ, Merrick J. Clinical holistic medicine Tools for a medical science based on consciousness. ScientificWorldJournal 2004;4:347-61.

[15] Ventegodt S, Morad M, Hyam E, Merrick J. Clinical holistic medicine: When biomedicine is inadequate. ScientificWorldJournal 2004;4:333-46.

[16] Ventegodt S, Morad M, Merrick J. Clinical holistic medicine: Holistic sexology, sexual healing, and treatment of vulvodynia through existential therapy and acceptance through touch. ScientificWorldJournal 2004;4:571-80.

[17] Nishith P, Duntley SP, Domitrovich PP, Uhles ML, Cook BJ, Stein PK. Effect of cognitive behavioral therapy on heart rate variability during REM sleep in female rape victims with PTSD. J Trauma Stress 2003;16(3):247-50.

[18] Nishith P, Resick PA, Griffin MG. Pattern of change in prolonged exposure and cognitive-processing therapy for female rape victims with posttraumatic stress disorder. J Consult Clin Psychol 2002; 70(4):880-6.

[19] Resick PA, Nishith P, Weaver TL, Astin MC, Feuer CA. A comparison of cognitive-processing therapy with prolonged exposure and a waiting condition for the treatment of chronic posttraumatic stress disorder in female rape victims. J Consult Clin Psychol 2002;70(4):867-79.

[20] Jaycox LH, Zoellner L, Foa EB. Cognitive-behavior therapy for PTSD in rape survivors. J Clin Psychol 2002;58(8):891-906. 1.

[21] Cryer L, Beutler L. Group therapy: an alternative treatment approach for rape victims. J Sex Marital Ther 1980;6(1):40-6.

[22] Glover NM. Play therapy and art therapy for substance abuse clients who have a history of incest victimization. J Subst Abuse Treat 1999;16(4):281-7.

[23] McMahon B. Positive use of a traumatic reawakening. Therapy with incest survivors. Prof Nurse 1992;8(1):21-2, 24-5.

[24] Winick C, Levine A, Stone WA. An incest survivors' therapy group. J Subst Abuse Treat 1992;9(4):311-8.

[25] Urbancic JC. Resolving incest experiences through inpatient group therapy. J Psychosoc Nurs Ment Health Serv 1989;27(9):4-10.

[26] Maltz W. Identifying and treating the sexual repercussions of incest: a couples therapy approach. J Sex Marital Ther 1988;14(2):142-70.

[27] Lutz SE, Medway JP. Contextual family therapy with the victims of incest. J Adolesc 1984;7(4):319-27.

[28] Hartman CR, Burgess AW. Treatment of rape trauma. In: Wilson JP, Raphael B. International handbook of traumatic stress syndromes. New York: Plenum Press, 1993:507-16.

[29] Ventegodt S, Kroman M, Andersen NJ, Merrick J. The life mission theory VI: A theory for the human character: Healing with holistic medicine through recovery of character and purpose of life. ScientificWorldJournal 2004;4:859-80.

[30] Huxley A. Island. New York: Harper Row, 1962.

[31] Ventegodt S, Andersen NJ, Merrick J. The life mission theory III: Theory of talent. ScientificWorldJournal 2003;3:1286-93.

[32] Ventegodt S, Andersen NJ, Merrick J. Editorial: Five theories of human existence. ScientificWorldJournal 2003;3:1272-6.

[33] Ventegodt S. The life mission theory: A theory for a consciousness-based medicine. Int J Adolesc Med Health 2003; 15(1):89-91.

[34] Ventegodt S, Andersen NJ, Merrick J. The life mission theory II: The structure of the life purpose and the ego. ScientificWorldJournal 2003;3:1277-85.

[35] Ventegodt S, Merrick J. The life mission theory IV. A theory of child development. ScientificWorldJournal 2003;3:1294-1301.

[36] Ventegodt S, Andersen NJ, Merrick J. The life mission theory V. A theory of the anti-self and explaining the evil side of man. ScientificWorldJournal 2003;3:1302-13.

[37] Ventegodt S, Andersen NJ, Merrick J. Holistic medicine: Scientific challenges. ScientificWorldJournal 2003;3:1108-16.

[38] Ventegodt S, Andersen NJ, Merrick J. Holistic Medicine II: The square-curve paradigm for research in alternative, complementary and holistic medicine: A cost-effective, easy and scientifically valid design for evidence based medicine. ScientificWorldJournal 2003;3: 1117-27.

[39] Ventegodt S, Andersen NJ, Merrick J. Holistic Medicine III: The holistic process theory of healing. ScientificWorldJournal 2003;3: 1138-46.

[40] Ventegodt S, Andersen NJ, Merrick J. Holistic Medicine IV: The principles of the holistic process of healing in a group setting. ScientificWorldJournal 2003;3:1294-1301.

[41] Ventegodt S, Merrick J, Andersen NJ. Quality of life theory I. The IQOL theory: An integrative theory of the global quality of life concept. ScientificWorldJournal 2003;3:1030-40.

[42] Ventegodt S, Merrick J, Andersen NJ. Quality of life theory II. Quality of life as the realization of life potential: A biological theory of human being. ScientificWorldJournal 2003;3:1041-9.

[43] Ventegodt S, Merrick J, Andersen NJ. Quality of life theory III. Maslow revisited. ScientificWorldJournal 2003;3:1050-7.

[44] Ventegodt S, Andersen NJ, Merrick J. Quality of life philosophy: when life sparkles or can we make wisdom a science? ScientificWorldJournal 2003;3:1160-3.

[45] Ventegodt S, Andersen NJ, Merrick J. QOL philosophy I: Quality of life, happiness, and meaning of life. ScientificWorldJournal 2003;3:1164-75.

[46] Ventegodt S, Andersen NJ, Kromann M, Merrick J. QOL philosophy II: What is a human being? ScientificWorldJournal 2003;3: 1176-85.

[47] Ventegodt S, Merrick J, Andersen NJ. QOL philosophy III: Towards a new biology. ScientificWorldJournal 2003;3:1186-98.

[48] Ventegodt S, Andersen NJ, Merrick J. QOL philosophy IV: The brain and consciousness. ScientificWorldJournal 2003;3:1199-1209.

[49] Ventegodt S, Andersen NJ, Merrick J. QOL philosophy V: Seizing the meaning of life and getting well again. ScientificWorldJournal 2003;3:1210-29.

[50] Ventegodt S, Andersen NJ, Merrick J. QOL philosophy VI: The concepts. ScientificWorldJournal 2003;3:1230-40.

[51] Merrick J, Ventegodt S. What is a good death? To use death as a mirror and find the quality in life. BMJ. Rapid Responses 2003 Oct 31.

[52] Ventegodt S, Merrick J, Andersen NJ. Quality of life as medicine. A pilot study of patients with chronic illness and pain. ScientificWorldJournal 2003;3:520-32.

[53] Ventegodt S, Merrick J, Andersen NJ. Quality of life as medicine II. A pilot study of a five day "Quality of life and health" cure for patients with alcoholism. ScientificWorld Journal 2003;3:842-52.

[54] Ventegodt S, Clausen B, Langhorn M, Kromann M, Andersen NJ, Merrick J. Quality of life as medicine III. A qualitative analysis of the effect of a five days intervention with existential holistic group therapy: a quality of life course as a modern rite of passage. ScientificWorld Journal 2004;4:124-33.

[55] Ventegodt S. Consciousness-based medicine [Bevidsthedsmedicin – set gennem lægejournalen.] Copenhagen: Forskningscenterets Forlag, 2003. [Danish].

[56] Ventegodt S, Merrick J. Sexology from a holistic point of view. A textbook of classic and modern sexology. New York: Nova Science, 2010.

The existential crisis – life crisis, stress and burnout

The triple and parallel loss of quality of life, health and ability without an organic reason is what we normally recognize as a life crisis, stress or a burnout. Not being in control is often a terrible and unexpected experience. Failure on the large existential scale is not a part of our expectations, but most people will experience it.

The key to getting well again is getting resources and help, which most people experience with shame and guild. Stress and burnout might seem temporary problems easily handled, but often the problems stay. It is very important for the physician to identify this pattern and help the patient realise the difficulties and seriousness of the situation, helping the patient to assume responsibility and prevent existential disaster, suicide or severe depression. As soon as the patient is an ally in fighting the dark side of life and works with him/herself the first step has been reached.

Existential pain is really a message to us indicating that we are about to grow and heal. In our view, existential problems are gifts, which are painful to receive, but wise to accept. Existential problems require skill on the part of the holistic physician or therapist in order to help people return to life – to their self-esteem, self-confidence and trust in others. In this paper we describe how we have met the patients soul to soul, and guided him or her through the old pains and losses in order to get back on the track to life.

Introduction

Events that overwhelm us emotionally and "shock" us may have very serious consequences for our lives. Typical examples are painful, violent and sexual assaults, incest, war traumas, accidents with near-death experiences and other serious events. Actually, seemingly harmless events, such as a stressful exam, scolding, rejection or neglect in childhood – even terrible things that we witness – can move us and overwhelm us enough to make the "shock" reside in us and make us think, feel and act in irrational and disturbed ways. Many small events, where we little by little let go of our sound and true self, for example in the workplace, have similar undermining effects on our life. The essence of what we usually give the scientifically vague terms "life crisis", "spiritual crisis", "stress" and "burnout" are basically the triple loss of quality of life, health and ability to function.

The holistic process theory (1) claims that the physical, emotional and mental aspects of the trauma can be handled in a simple way, by helping the patient to feel, understand and let go of negative beliefs and decisions. The acute trauma is the easiest to treat, as the patient will often heal spontaneously with a little support and holding. Old traumas, such as multiple rape in childhood are often so repressed that they will not resurface without massive "holding" and support of the patient with a particularly close and trusting relationship from a loving and caring physician or other therapist. Love, trust and holding are central concepts in our style of holistic medicine (2-24) and discussed in a number of our books and papers (25-44). Holistic medicine is basically about providing sufficient support in the therapeutic situation to enable the patient to confront the old painful traumas in his or her life. The holding take five forms: awareness to the mind, respect to the feelings, care to the body, acknowledgment to the wholeness of the person (the "soul") and acceptance of the physical aspect, the gender and the sexuality of the person.

The events of life seem to be controlled by a strange inner logic. Our consciousness seems to be tied up in certain patterns manifested as problematic themes of life with which we struggle. These themes appear as painful events with mysterious problems and these events seem to repeat themselves indefinitely, until the moment that we fully understand our own part in them. We all know the cases similar to those of women, who keep falling for boyfriends who eventually beat them. Not until she realises her part in the pattern can she escape from it. Fortunately, it is not that difficult to sort out such themes in life, although it is very painful to acknowledge one's own responsibility for them. When the inescapable feeling of guilt finally wears off, we often also get rid of a number of emotional disturbances the tendency towards depression, for example, may cease.

People react very differently to traumatic events. Some women recover from rape in a relatively short time, while others fall apart and only able to get themselves together again after several years of therapy. Some victims of violence return from a night out with a broken nose and laugh about it; apparently suffering no harm from the incident, while others become frightened of other people and public places and need long-term treatment to recover. Basically, you can say that everybody has an inner physician or healer, but not everybody knows how to use "him". When the self-healing process is stuck then the holistic physician comes into play.

Clinical holistic medicine

The life mission theory (25-30) states that everybody has a purpose of life, or huge talent. Happiness comes from living this purpose and succeeding in expressing the core talent in your life. To do this, it is important to develop as a person into what is known as the natural condition, a condition where the person knows himself and uses all his efforts to achieve what is most important for him. The holistic process theory of healing (1,45-47) and the related quality of life theories (39-41) state that the return to the natural state of being is possible, whenever the person gets the resources needed for the existential healing. The resources needed are holding in the dimensions: awareness, respect, care, acknowledgment, acceptance with support and processing in the dimensions: feeling, understanding and letting go of negative attitudes and beliefs. The preconditions for the holistic healing to take place are trust and the intention for the healing to take place. Existential healing is not a local healing of any tissue, but a healing of the wholeness of the person, making him much more resourceful, loving, and knowledgeable of his own needs and wishes. In letting go of negative attitudes and beliefs the person returns to a more responsible.

Existential problems are gifts

Generally, personal problems are difficulties in achieving what we want in life. Because deep inside us there is something that we desperately want – the purpose of life – we often seem to face great difficulties. Painful experiences can easily make us change course. We lie about what we want and in so doing fail our purpose in life.

When life is painful it is very tempting to disclaim responsibility and escape. We may run away from the pain, but cannot remove it and we carry it around deep inside us. Then, as we try during our lives to return to our original, true course, the same old difficulties show up again. The old pains and life lies resurface from the subconscious mind and distort our entire life. Indeed, the subconscious implies that we are not aware of what lies buried there, because of repression and denial. The only trace of what we once suffered is the pain, suffering, anxiety or however it is that the disturbance is manifested.

From this point of view, existential pain is a message to us indicating that we are about to be healed. We are about to pick up something precious, from which we once fled. We are about to rediscover something that we still need, now more than ever. In our view, existential problems are gifts. They are gifts which are painful to receive, but which it is wise to accept. It requires skill on the part of the holistic physician or therapist to help people return to life – to their self-esteem, self-confidence, and to trust in others. We need to meet the patient or client soul to soul, take him by the hand and guide him through the old pain or loss and back to life. That is the essence of holistic medicine.

Improving one's life perspective is connected with having to let go of old perceptions, to which one has become attached. It is connected with anxiety. As one lets go of one's fundamental perceptions – known as ego death – one is reborn as a true and more genuine person. The way out is the way through it. Mostly, meeting the pain face to face hurts much less than one would expect, having avoided it so long. Sometimes it does not hurt at all, rather it feels good to be relieved of the existential pain. And invariably it teaches us something important about life. Once the patient's pain has shifted into acknowledgement and once the negative decisions have been released, the patient has grown as a person. Sometimes a small and seemingly insignificant event may tip the balance, even though previous violent events apparently did not have any major effect.

> Male, aged 31 years with traumas
> Presents with palpitation and fear of death. Auscultation of the heart: normal. Slightly increased pulse, which soon decreases during the consultation. One month ago the patient nearly died together with his whole family in a car accident, in which the car overturned. None of the family members were injured, but the 7-year-old son is still very frightened. We talk about the fact that we are mortal and that life is

precious and fragile. Went through the incident a couple of times. The patient should write it down.

This patient moves back and forth on the time line, harmoniously and spontaneously, guided by inner logic and necessity, so stereotyped commands are not required. The patient's resources are so large that he may even finish the work at home. It takes great skill to know whether the patient needs to be held by the hand or whether he can manage on his own. It is not good for the patient, if the physician misjudges him and sends him home with a task that he cannot tackle alone.

The existential crises in the holistic clinic – life crises, stress and burnout

Existential pain is one of our basic conditions as human beings – life hurts. Many people are unaware of the pain residing in their inner layer. They lead superficial lives, which appear successful, although they are suffering deep inside their souls. The reason for this division of the individual into superficial layers and deep existential layers lies at the very root of our conscious nature. We can choose, and when we choose we define our own reality. We can choose to live in several worlds at the same time and we can choose to be aware of and attentive to one of these worlds and unaware of and inattentive to another world.

To a great extent, we get away with such divisions as mind and soul or feeling and reason. We function, live our lives, and things turn out the way we want them to, but not always. The existential crisis occurs if we do not reclaim resources and qualities that we have placed in the repressed layers. If we fail, we have to acknowledge that life does not provide us with what we need and deep down want. In the course of weeks, months or years, a person who experiences an existential crisis may change from being a jolly, extrovert person who functions well into being gloomy, introvert and socially isolated. It is as though a bomb has gone off in that person's life. Everything is turned upside down, the most fundamental things in life no longer function. This calls for a radical clearing-out, a new orientation in life. Frequently, the person has failed in his present version and needs to renew himself

> Male, aged 45 year with a life crisis
> Eats very little, has no appetite. Very tired, but is constantly active. Is no longer happy. On examination: Fast-paced, very tense in all major muscle groups – neck, back, arms, legs. I (SV) see a marathon runner, running away from his own feelings. EXERCISE: Take three days off and come to a complete stop. Just be, and feel all the emotions that emerge inside. That is the problem, in my opinion.

The picture is clear: a marathon runner, running away from himself. We frequently obtain very distinct and clear pictures, that for a brief moment, reveal something essential about the patient's current problem. When the patients confront and acknowledge the current problem, it often diminishes. Often the patient needs some time and peace to chew on the underlying gestalts. We do not hesitate to give patients a sick leave certificate for a few days to allow them to work it out. We do not care for long-term sick leave, however. In our opinion, being unoccupied for a long time does not provide any therapeutic benefit for the patient, unless the patient has a large, relevant project, like writing a complete autobiography. In that case, this may occupy the patient for three to six months.

> Female, aged 26 years with stress
> Presents with "stress" – manifesting as a "clamp" around her head – has been off work from her job as a middle manager in a large enterprise. Married to a man from the same place, talks and thinks a lot about her job in her spare time, cannot let go of it. Three EXERCISES: Let go of the job after working hours (let go physically of the uniform). Write down all your thoughts about the job on paper and leave them there until you return to work. Make an agreement with your husband not to talk about work in your spare time. Feels an extra heart beat. ECG examination normal. BP 120/85. Next appointment in one week.

Many patients claim to suffer from "stress", but we do not buy that. In our opinion, stress comprises two element (this is the excellent stress model from the Karolinska Hospital in Stockholm) namely discomfort and strain. People complain about the strain, but the discomfort is the problem. There is nothing wrong with being busy, being active, committed and strained. That is human nature. But the discomfort should not be there. It occurs when we act contrary to ourselves. In this case, working the same place, as her husband is not a good idea, it means that work is the sole content of both her life and her marital relationship. That is all wrong. The term "stress" covers something completely different. Stress cannot be treated, but should be perceived as a manifestation of some kind of acute crisis. The patient has to understand herself better and sort out her life.

Life crises

Apparently, external factors may trigger a life crisis. Sometimes the problems accumulate – in relation to work, the family with children and partner, friends and acquaintances or the financial situation. Suddenly immense problems may exist everywhere. Sometimes we may even experience misfortunes from which we cannot recover completely, like being left by our partner, the death of a child, our home being gutted by fire or a serious physical or mental illness, which makes us question our entire existence and the meaning of life. Often, the life crisis is not caused by external factors or illness, but rather inner, existential factors. The life crisis is manifested as strange and incomprehensible mental and physical symptoms: the feeling of having wasted one's life, of not being able to realise our great dreams in life. In short the feeling of being a failure.

Some patients suddenly feel terribly old, tired and wonder why life has suddenly turned so grey, dull and monotonous. Something is wrong, but they do not know what it is. Colours are no longer bright. The enjoyment of life has disappeared. Nevertheless, the patient is not just depressed. Something has gone completely wrong. Something worse than transient depression.. Something in life has to be changed completely. When the existential pain breaks through to the surface of the conscious mind, it is unhealthy to ignore it or suppress it from a holistic perspective. The rational approach is to take it seriously, to address it in an analytical and exploring manner and to do something about the situation. A patient experiencing a life crisis often needs help to move on. The patient needs support to summon the courage to face himself deep down in his soul.. Perhaps our patient needs the physician to be another human being, who can reflect him and make him see himself with greater clarity.

> Female, aged 51 years with problems in life
> Quality-of-life (QOL) conversation: She attended the course "Life Philosophy that Heals". Has major problems in life – she wants to change now. List of problems: Grinds her teeth at night – the dentist is willing to arrange an occlusal splint, but the treatment is expensive. Major marital problems with her husband for six years. No sexual relations for the past year. She does not want any closeness or intimacy with him. Physical/mental health: troubled by headache, depressed for many years, never treated medically, had her uterus removed when she was 36 years old. Low back pain occasionally. Impaired memory. Describes herself as: too nice, forbidding, prim, inhibited. "I cannot express myself," "I'm in charge." Social, in general: Problems with her daughter-in-law who is an incest victim. In my opinion, she lacks clarity – I get the impression of a 1,000 kg rope tied into a huge knot. EXERCISE: Write your autobiography – start from the present – what happened, how did you feel, what did you decide (write down your negative decisions on paper and bring them here – let go immediately, if possible). PLAN: Gestalt therapy – 20 hours. Can be supplemented with Rosen therapy. Session with me (SV) every month or every other month.

The fact that I get the impression of a 1,000 kg rope tied into a huge knot probably means years of work for the patient. Twenty hours of gestalt therapy is a good start. Unfortunately, after referring the patient for gestalt therapy we lost contact with her, so we do not know how the story ends.

The following case record describes a patient, who relived a trauma that made him leap half a metre out of his stomach, mentally speaking. This is very odd and difficult to understand, but apparently in the conscious mind we can adopt any vantage point. Incredible precision and intelligence in life means that distances, times – indeed any measurable qualities – are handled elegantly and smoothly, including when it comes to early traumas. Scientifically, this is disconcerting, because no developed nervous system so far can be behind this, so which part of life provides the intelligence? Conventional medical science would reject the reports as unreliable interpretations by the adult, but we sense that it is wise to believe that life does actually possess such embedded intelligence. We believe that it exists at the cellular level, but proving it is extremely difficult.

> Male, aged 33 years: I am nothing
> Patient has felt completely stuck and depressed for six weeks. "I run away," he says. We agree that a more accurate description is that he is paralysed with fear. He wants to go into process NOW. On the couch, we work with "rebirthing" [the patient breathes forcefully, heavily and regularly until the gestalt crystallises]. "There is nothing", "I am outside", "It's all black" he says. And later "I am blissful out there" ("I am nothing"). Re-experience himself as a 5-month-old foetus with umbilical cord, where he is half a metre outside the stomach – there is emptiness and freedom. He lets go of the statements by means of a roll and sense that he is back in the stomach. He breathes again, and this time he breathes heavily and naturally, with his entire body. He then experiences being a rejected little boy 2 or 3 years old. EXERCISE: Write down your life's story starting with the statements that you let go – how you were always rejected and excluded.

Life crises may sometimes refer directly back to a large, early gestalt, which can be released on the couch, for example by means of breathing techniques as in this case. In the same way that time line therapy is rarely necessary, breathing techniques are only necessary, when we seek to overcome mental resistance here and now. This patient had been making tentative efforts for a long time and really needed a breakthrough, which he achieved.

Spiritual crises

A special form of life crises is the spiritual crises. They are troublesome elements in the life of the conscious individual. But such crises make sense. We are not quite true to ourselves. We do not lead our lives in accordance with our personal project of life. Therefore, problems arise. The patient may be an academic or a businessman experiencing good personal growth. He may be professionally and personally successful and have many challenges at work and in life. Then, one day, everything comes to a halt. The patient has hit a wall and is unable to move on. We had for example a patient who was an artist, who had enjoyed rapid growth for a couple of years. Then, all of a sudden, a terrible pain caught up with her, which made her want to get away from it all. She never wanted to touch a paintbrush again. She needed a fundamental shift in perspective.

> Male, aged 45 years with spiritual crisis
> A man who had experimented with sexual tantra techniques [meditation with channelling of sexual energies] and experienced supreme ecstasy – he had made love to his goddess in the form of his partner – experienced the most devastating, unrequited love for her; total dependence, laying his emotional life in ruins. When his girlfriend, who has now left him, was having sex with another man, he is still so connected to her that he can feel everything that is going on and he suffers terribly. The crisis lasted for several years, during which he meditated on the problem until it finally wears off and he met another woman.

Religious people may experience a struggle within them between God and the Devil, eventually making them wonder whether they are going insane. Such patients usually experience peace following a night-time visit by the Holy Spirit. Patients with known mental disorders fall into what we would call a genuine spiritual crisis, when the evil inside them appears to have won the first round, and they refuse to surrender, because they know that basically they are not evil. This type of crisis is extremely unpleasant for patients, but can often have a positive outcome, when good ultimately triumphs. We believe that the patient should go through such crises with a maximum of personal support and care with a minimum of medication.

Spiritual crises may also be insidious: perhaps the patient shows no signs of a mental disorder or external problems. In spite of this, the patient describes a profound sense of meaninglessness or perhaps even a death wish, which has broken through from the subconscious mind and now demanding the patient's unremitting attention. The way we see it, this is about spiritual growth, about a side of the patient that has been hurt and has been hidden for an entire life and suddenly demands to be healed.

Creativity and imagination in therapy

It often requires a vivid imagination to help people in spiritual and existential crisis. There is no conventional treatment and the symptoms displayed by the patients are peculiar, to put it mildly. Such was the case with the following patient, who was so devoid of intelligence and so stagnant that it was totally unbearable for her and for the people around her.

A young, rather overweight and single woman with a young child came to the clinic in Copenhagen (which attracts people with all sorts of strange problems) to be cured of being a "stupid cow". She was very kind-hearted and her entire life concerned with being a good mother. For a mother that is commendable, of course, but her own life and personal development had come to a complete standstill and now she felt that all that was left of her was this stupid cow grazing in the field, while her child was sucking power and sustenance from her. In a few years, when the child would grown up, she would still be that stupid cow, but without the calf that put at least a minimum of meaning into her life here and now. That thought tormented her terribly. She wanted to move on with her life, but felt hopelessly stuck. First, we (SV) tried to talk to her about the great philosophical questions such as the meaning of life and gratification of needs. This is what was written after one session:

> ... evoked little response from her. Discussing Kierkegaard with cows simply cannot be done. I do not consider women to be stupid cows, on the contrary, a healthy woman is highly intelligent and alert. So, there was something completely wrong with her. In short, her brain was completely blocked. She had fallen into a deep slumber. In my view, she identified herself with the cow character and used up so much energy on playing the part that it took up all her mental capacity. The situation was desperate, and I struggled with it for some time. Then I had a bright idea. In principle, there are two ways of escaping from such a trap. Being caught in an existential crisis is more or less like being locked up in a cage or in prison. One has to break down the wall to become free. Sometimes, this can be done provided the person has masses of self-confidence, free energy and intellectual resources. But if it cannot be done, which was the case for this plump, young woman – who, in a way, resembled a patient with terminal cancer – an alternative solution must be sought: transcendence.

If we totally accept being what we are and the way we are, where we are, we achieve taking responsibility for it. Suddenly, we become who we are, of our own free will, by our own choice – and then we are also free to choose being something else. After all, the cage in which we are trapped is our own minds, rather than external circumstances, as we tend to believe. The woman felt enslaved by her situation in life, but actually she was enslaved only by her own previous choices and decisions. She had worked herself into a corner from which she could not escape on her own. She had fallen into a "cow trap".

My insight immediately led to the solution: She had to be a cow – in every sense! "Do you feel like trying an experiment, something I have not tried before, but which may help even if it seems crazy?" I asked her. Naturally, the obedient patient agreed with her doctor's advice, so I continued: "Get down on the floor with me, then we will crawl about on all fours and pretend to be cows!" Following the predictable protests and bursts of laughter, I convinced the patient to get down on the floor and for a full ten minutes we crawled about like cows, while I mooed and the patient did the same, cringing with embarrassment and laughing hysterically. "If you won't say 'moo', it will be your homework," I threatened her, and so managed to get a proper 'moo!' out of the patient. "Now, don't file a complaint about the treatment," I told her after having recovered my breath. "If you do, I'll spend two years in prison for professional misconduct as a doctor." I spoke to her two weeks later, when she was making good progress. She had crawled about on all fours, mooing, together with her child, who had had a marvellous time, until finally she realised that the reason why she was such a stupid cow was that she had once made the intellectually restrictive decision that she simply was stupid. Now, she was in the process of letting go of the decision and was already experiencing a great improvement. She laughed, when I asked her permission to publish this brief account of her miraculous recovery through "cow therapy" and she promptly gave her permission. This is the case record:

Female, aged 32 years with a life crisis
First quality-of-life (QOL) session: Men make her sick. Literally had to get out and throw up on the way over here. The Rosen practitioner found: Throbbing aorta deep in the abdomen above the sacral promontory; does not feel dilated, but tender. A scan should be considered if tenderness persists. Patient has major problems with her stomach, which is too fat, too tender and nauseous. During Rosen session with the practitioner she felt immense anger, as though she were about to explode. On the couch, we work on the feelings of anger, disgust and grief, where the patient says that her father did her wrong, when she was five years old. Misses someone to care for her; we talk about how such a relationship is formed. Continue Rosen treatments.

Second QOL session: The patient wants to break away from correctness, but that is difficult as she has a young child, who needs her. The child has been very ill and she has been the good mother, which has benefited the child. She feels an urge to scream, but cannot. We practise screaming, and the patient screams with great difficulty. The diminutive scream "h" gradually becomes "ah", and ultimately a fully developed scream. The patient screams herself hoarse across the fields. The patient is stuck in a "stupid cow" gestalt, as she is present in her stomach and heart, but not in her head. She does not want to do anything, she does nothing, has no ambition or drive. The image of her is a cow at pasture. Until acceptance transcends, we practise being cows, mooing on the floor. EXERCISE: Walk about on all fours for ten minutes and "act like the cow that you are", until you can handle being what you are. On examination: The previous abdominal complaints with intense tenderness around the aorta have decreased. On palpation today there are no problems. The patient continues to see the Rosen practitioner, which is beneficial for her. She is showing good progress. She had crawled about on all fours, mooing, together with her child, who had had a marvellous time, until finally she realised that the reason why she was such a stupid cow was that she had once made the intellectually restrictive decision that she simply was stupid. Now, she was in the process of letting go of the decision and already experiencing a great improvement.

Third QOL session: Has turned her back on correctness following cow exercises. Now she does all kinds of crazy things. Her child is very happy. Went outdoors to scream and shout. It was very good and powerful. She does not believe that she has any opinion, in fact she believes that she is stupid. We talk about this and find out that she has nothing but opinions, which she needs to let go in order to reach the point, where she sees the world as it is: perfect, her natural condition. Has a large hump, excessive flexion of the thoracic spine from T1 to T8, locked into a hunchback. The "hump" hurts, she sits and stands with stooped shoulders, looking very stupid. On the couch, the hump is manipulated and straightened out with five loud snaps, and the pain in the hump disappears. In front of a mirror we work on the patient's posture, sagging breasts being transformed into nice breasts, which the patient is told to be proud of and show off next summer. Posture with retroflexion of the pelvis is straightened. With these exercises, the patient is transformed from a deformed person into a handsome woman. EXERCISE: Be proud of yourself and show it. She had breast-lifting surgery for sagging breasts when she was 20 years old. The problems with which the patient presented have been resolved, but she will not stop. Must find new goals, can return.

Burnout

Why is it that a job or activity that used to be immensely interesting years ago, can end up being a completely uninteresting duty that torments you day after day? Where did the interest go? What happened to that tickling sensation, the sense that it was so exciting and so challenging? What became of the enthusiastic and committed young man or woman, reading, studying, writing and engaging in all kinds of discussions? What became of the power of concentration, the wide fingertip knowledge, creativity, good perspectives and visions? What became of the quiet satisfaction of a job well done that lasted a surprisingly long time?

Burnout is a problem that torments hundreds of thousands of people. It is a mysterious ailment, the greatest problem being that nobody is willing to acknowledge it. The burnt-out person lies to himself about how well he is doing, while knowing instinctively that that is not the case, but the fear of losing his job, status, identity and income makes it difficult to face. Burnout is basically a consequence of a loss of interest in what one is doing due to a lack of intellectual stimulation, growth and development. When we fail to renew ourselves, we gradually decline. Plenty of qualities and talents in a person can be developed. There is enough to learn and take an interest in, but personal development does not occur automatically. It is a laborious and often painful process. The burnt-out person has to understand himself better and learn how to apply himself and his talents in a more lively and creative way. The key is a new perspective; not just in respect of working life, but of life itself. An attentive physician can help his patient recognise the true nature of the problem and how to become committed again – perhaps to something entirely different.

The individual's fundamental life philosophy is crucial for the ability to create satisfaction and development in his job. The burnt-out person has to rescue his working life by incorporating the ideas of personal development in his perception of life. The patient holds great potential, regardless of the apparent degree of burnout. Contrary to what one might think, when looking into those dull eyes, it will often be possible for the patient once again to become lively and interested and have a good, long and active working life, if supported by a sympathetic person. Frequently, the burnt-out patient needs extensive rehabilitation. It is important that the physician does not underestimate the extent of the problem and give the patient false hope.

Female, aged 42 years with burnout
QQL session: Receptionist, aged 42 years, burnout.. Feels like a 90-year-old. Looks like a 55-year-old, listless and tired. Gives a very confusing and mixed-up account of her problems, which she cannot identify herself. Worried, afraid of hurting others.

Has not had sex for years, does not feel the need, she believes. Scared of contact. She looks delightful and lovely, but has made herself unnatural and messy – as though she is wearing 1,000 cactus prickles to avoid being eaten. Asks for help in becoming herself again. We talk about what it would take for her to become alive again – she has nearly made herself dead, like driving with one foot on the brake. EXERCISE: What is the meaning of life? EXERCISE: Feel your inner emotions without changing anything. Next appointment in three weeks.

This example clearly shows that the patient has to find a new meaning of life to become 20 years younger. The project is difficult, but not impossible.

Discussion

The triple and parallel loss of quality of life, health and ability is a terrible experience. The feeling that you are not in control or on top of you own life, but lying down under your own world hardly able to move is often felt as a surprising defeat. Failure on the large existential scale is not a part of our expectations for our life, but nevertheless most people will experience it before they die.

The key to getting well again is getting resources or help from outside and this is often connected with shame, guild and hard for most people. Taking care of the patient's difficult emotions in a vulnerable existence is the essence of the treatment in major crises in life. Stress and burnout might seem to be temporary problems easily handled, but all too often the problems will not go away. They remain and after a short period of recovery the problem returns in an even worse form. It is very important for the physician to identify this pattern and help the patient realise the difficulties and seriousness of the situations. Thus the patient is helped to assume responsibility for his or her own future and thus preventing an existential disaster, suicide or severe depression.

As soon as the patient is an ally in fighting the dark side of life (30) using the holistic approach to treatment the physician will be able to assist in recovery. Coaching is an important concept after an acute life crisis is over. When life is painful it is very tempting to disclaim responsibility and escape. The old pains and negative decisions lye in our subconscious mind and distort our entire lives and as we accumulate pain and life-lies throughout our lives we gradually loose our quality of life, health and ability (51). Existential pain is really a message to us indicating that we are about to grow and to be healed. In our view, existential problems are gifts. Gifts which are painful to receive, but which it is wise to accept. It requires skill on the part of holistic physicians and therapists to help people return to life – to their self-esteem, self-confidence, trust in others. We have to meet the patient or client soul to soul, take him by the hand and guide him through the old pain and loss in order for him to come back to life. That is the essence of holistic medicine.

Improving your life perspective is connected with having to let go of old perceptions, to which one has become attached. Once the pain has shifted into acknowledgement and the negative decisions released, the patient can grow as a person. Sometimes a small and seemingly insignificant event may tip the balance, even though previous violent events apparently did not have any major effect. Even the most severe life crisis can be turned into positive development, if the physician understands the situation of the patient on an existential level. Using this understanding he can support the patients in feeling, understanding and letting go of negative convictions and beliefs (1).

References

[1] Ventegodt S, Andersen NJ, Merrick J. Holistic Medicine III: The holistic process theory of healing. ScientificWorldJournal 2003;3: 1138-46.
[2] Ventegodt S, Merrick J. Clinical holistic medicine: Applied consciousness-based medicine. ScientificWorldJournal 2004;4:96-9.
[3] Ventegodt S, Morad M, Merrick J. Clinical holistic medicine: Classic art of healing or the therapeutic touch. ScientificWorldJournal 2004;4:134-47.
[4] Ventegodt S, Morad M, Merrick J. Clinical holistic medicine: The "new medicine", the multi-paradigmatic physician and the medical record. ScientificWorldJournal 2004;4:273-85.
[5] Ventegodt S, Morad M, Merrick J. Clinical holistic medicine: Holistic pelvic examination and holistic treatment of infertility. ScientificWorldJournal 2004;4:148-58.
[6] Ventegodt S, Morad M, Hyam E, Merrick J. Clinical holistic medicine: Use and limitations of the biomedical paradigm ScientificWorldJournal 2004;4:295-306.
[7] Ventegodt S, Morad M, Kandel I, Merrick J. Clinical holistic medicine: Social problems disguised as illness. ScientificWorldJournal 2004;4:286-94.
[8] Ventegodt S, Morad M, Andersen NJ, Merrick J. Clinical holistic medicine Tools for a medical science based on consciousness. ScientificWorldJournal 2004;4:347-61.
[9] Ventegodt S, Morad M, Hyam E, Merrick J. Clinical holistic medicine: When biomedicine is inadequate. ScientificWorldJournal 2004;4:333-46.
[10] Ventegodt S, Morad M, Merrick J. Clinical holistic medicine: Prevention through healthy lifestyle and good quality of life. Oral Health Prev Dent 2004;2(suppl 1):239-245.
[11] Ventegodt S, Morad M, Vardi G, Merrick J. Clinical holistic medicine: Holistic treatment of children. ScientificWorldJournal 2004;4:581-8.
[12] Ventegodt S, Morad M, Kandel I, Merrick J. Clinical holistic medicine: Problems in sex and living together. ScientificWorldJournal 2004;4:562-70.
[13] Ventegodt S, Morad M, Hyam E, Merrick J. Clinical holistic medicine: Holistic sexology and treatment of vulvodynia through existential therapy and acceptance through touch. ScientificWorldJournal 2004;4:571-80.
[14] Ventegodt S, Morad M, Kandel I, Merrick J. Clinical holistic medicine: A psychological theory of dependency to improve quality of life. ScientificWorldJournal 2004;4:638-48.
[15] Ventegodt S, Morad M, Kandel I, Merrick J. Clinical holistic medicine: Treatment of physical health problems without a known cause, exemplified by hypertension and tinnitus. ScientificWorldJournal 2004;4:716-24.
[16] Ventegodt S, Morad M, Merrick J. Clinical holistic medicine: Developing from asthma, allergy and eczema. ScientificWorldJournal 2004;4:936-42.
[17] Ventegodt S, Merrick J. Clinical holistic medicine: Chronic infections and autoimmune diseases. ScientificWorldJournal 2005;5:155-64.
[18] Ventegodt S, Flensborg-Madsen T, Andersen NJ, Morad M, Merrick J. Clinical holistic medicine: A Pilot on HIV and Quality of Life and a Suggested treatment of HIV and AIDS. ScientificWorldJournal 2004;4:264-72.
[19] Ventegodt S, Merrick J. Clinical holistic medicine Chronic pain in the locomotor system. ScientificWorldJournal 2005;5:165-72.
[20] Ventegodt S, Gringols M, Merrick J. Clinical holistic medicine: Whiplash, fibromyalgia and chronic fatigue. ScientificWorldJournal 2005;5:340-54.
[21] Ventegodt S, Merrick J. Clinical holistic medicine: Chronic pain in internal organs. ScientificWorldJournal 2005;5:205-10.
[22] Ventegodt S, Gringols M, Merrick J. Clinical holistic medicine: Holistic rehabilitation. ScientificWorldJournal 2005;5:280-7.

[23] Ventegodt S, Andersen NJ, Neikrug S, Kandel I, Merrick J. Clinical holistic medicine: Mental disorders in a holistic perspective. ScientificWorldJournal 2005:5:313-23.

[24] Ventegodt S, Meerick E, Merrick J. Clinical holistic medicine: the Dean Ornish program ("opening the heart") in cardiovascular disease. ScientificWorldJournal 2006;6:1977-84.

[25] Ventegodt S, Andersen NJ, Merrick J. Editorial: Five theories of human existence. ScientificWorldJournal 2003;3:1272-6.

[26] Ventegodt S. The life mission theory: A theory for a consciousness-based medicine. Int J Adolesc Med Health 2003;15(1):89-91.

[27] Ventegodt S, Andersen NJ, Merrick J. The life mission theory II: The structure of the life purpose and the ego. ScientificWorldJournal 2003;3:1277-85.

[28] Ventegodt S, Andersen NJ, Merrick J. The life mission theory III: Theory of talent. ScientificWorldJournal 2003;3:1286-93.

[29] Ventegodt S, Merrick J. The life mission theory IV. A theory of child development. ScientificWorldJournal 2003;3:1294-1301.

[30] Ventegodt S, Andersen NJ, Merrick J. The life mission theory V. A theory of the anti-self and explaining the evil side of man. ScientificWorldJournal 2003;3:1302-13.

[31] Ventegodt S, Andersen NJ, Merrick J. Quality of life philosophy: when life sparkles or can we make wisdom a science? ScientificWorldJournal 2003;3:1160-3.

[32] Ventegodt S, Andersen NJ, Merrick J. QOL philosophy I: Quality of life, happiness, and meaning of life. ScientificWorldJournal 2003;3: 1164-75.

[33] Ventegodt S, Andersen NJ, Kromann M, Merrick J. QOL philosophy II: What is a human being? ScientificWorldJournal 2003;3:1176-85.

[34] Ventegodt S, Merrick J, Andersen NJ. QOL philosophy III: Towards a new biology. ScientificWorldJournal 2003;3:1186-98.

[35] Ventegodt S, Andersen NJ, Merrick J. QOL philosophy IV: The brain and consciousness. ScientificWorldJournal 2003;3:1199-1209.

[36] Ventegodt S, Andersen NJ, Merrick J. QOL philosophy V: Seizing the meaning of life and getting well again. ScientificWorldJournal 2003;3:1210-29.

[37] Ventegodt S, Andersen NJ, Merrick J. QOL philosophy VI: The concepts. ScientificWorldJournal 2003;3:1230-40.

[38] Merrick J, Ventegodt S. What is a good death? To use death as a mirror and find the quality in life. BMJ. Rapid Response 2003 Oct 31.

[39] Ventegodt S, Merrick J, Andersen NJ. Quality of life theory I. The IQOL theory: An integrative theory of the global quality of life concept. ScientificWorldJournal 2003;3:1030-40.

[40] Ventegodt S, Merrick J, Andersen NJ. Quality of life theory II. Quality of life as the realization of life potential: A biological theory of human being. ScientificWorldJournal 2003;3:1041-9.

[41] Ventegodt S, Merrick J, Andersen NJ. Quality of life theory III. Maslow revisited. ScientificWorldJournal 2003;3:1050-7.

[42] Ventegodt S. Quality of life. To seize the meaning of life and become well again. [Livskvalitet – at erobre livets mening og blive rask igen.] Copenhagen: Forskningscentrets Forlag, 1995. [Danish].

[43] Ventegodt S. Philosophy of life that heals. [Livsfilosofi der helbreder.] Copenhagen: Forskningscenterets Forlag, 1999. [Danish].

[44] Ventegodt S. Consciousness-based medicine [Bevidsthedsmedicin – set gennem lægejournalen.] Copenhagen: Forskningscenterets Forlag, 2003. [Danish].

[45] Ventegodt S, Andersen NJ, Merrick J. Holistic medicine: Scientific challenges. ScientificWorldJournal 2003;3:1108-16.

[46] Ventegodt S, Andersen NJ, Merrick J. Holistic Medicine II: The square-curve paradigm for research in alternative, complementary and holistic medicine: A cost-effective, easy and scientifically valid design for evidence based medicine. ScientificWorldJournal 2003;3:1117-27.

[47] Ventegodt S, Andersen NJ, Merrick J. Holistic Medicine IV: The principles of the holistic process of healing in a group setting. ScientificWorldJournal 2003;3:1294-1301.

[48] Ventegodt S, Merrick J, Andersen NJ. Quality of life as medicine. A pilot study of patients with chronic illness and pain. ScientificWorld Journal 2003;3:520-32.

[49] Ventegodt S, Merrick J, Andersen NJ. Quality of life as medicine II. A pilot study of a five day "Quality of Life and Health" cure for patients with alcoholism. ScientificWorld Journal 2003;3:842-52.

[50] Ventegodt S, Clausen B, Langhorn M, Kromann M, Andersen NJ, Merrick J. Quality of Life as Medicine III. A qualitative analysis of the effect of a five days intervention with existential holistic group therapy: a quality of life course as a modern rite of passage. ScientificWorldJournal 2004;4:124-33.

[51] Ventegodt S, Flensborg-Madsen T, Andersen NJ, Nielsen M, Mohammed M, Merrick J. Global quality of life (QOL), health and ability are primarily determined by our consciousness. Research findings from Denmark 1991-2004. Soc Indicator Res 2005;71:87-122.

Chapter 39

Holistic rehabilitation

Quality of life, health and ability are often lost in the same time and most often in one decaying existential movement over five or ten years. The loss of life is mostly too slow to be felt as life threatening, but once awakening to reality it provokes the deepest of fears, the fear of death itself and destruction of our mere existence. The horrible experience of having lost life, often without even noticing how, can be turned into a strong motivation for improvement. Personal development is about finding the life deeply hidden within in order to induce revitalization and rehabilitation. Rehabilitation is about philosophy of life with the integration of the repressed painful feelings and emotions from the past and the letting go of the associated negative beliefs and decisions.

The holistic medical tool box builds on existential theories (the quality of life theories, the life mission theory, the theory of character, the theory of talent and the holistic process theory) and seems to have the power to rehabilitate the purpose of life, the character of the person and fundamental existential dimensions of man: 1) love, 2) strength of mind, feelings and body and 3) joy, gender and sexuality allowing the person once again to express and realize his talents and full potential.

The principles of rehabilitation is not very different from other healing, but the task is often more demanding for the holistic physician, as the motivation and resources often are very low and the treatment can take years.

Introduction

Holistic rehabilitation (1-3) is revitalisation, which actually means resuscitation and that is exactly what it is about. Rehabilitation is for patients, who need a new and radically improved life. A patient in need of rehabilitation may feel that he or she has reached the end of his or her old life or in other words the patient is emotionally or existentially dead. We believe that a patient with such an experience of life is in serious difficulty and at risk of dying in the near future, for instance from excessive drinking or suicide, if the rehabilitation project fail. On the other hand, the patient is often motivated to take a giant leap with appropriate guidance.

The existential healing project, in all its difficult simplicity, is about teaching the patient the following: life is your own responsibility, so you have to take fate into your own hands to return from the abyss that you are facing. You must find out what you want to do with your life - your purpose of life (4) and your personal character (5). Although life has gone completely off track and the future seems hopeless, it is our job as physicians and therapists to convince our patients that this is not the case and show them the road back to life. The road is bumpy, but often also fantastic and wonderful. Our firm conviction that life is not over, but merely lost, often inspire enough hope in patients to make them embark on their journey back to life. Clinical holistic medicine (4-28) can offer a solution to this scenario and help the patient reverse the sad negative development.

Creating a new and better life

Many people feel as though they are drifting aimlessly. It is as if they are not in control of their direction in life, but merely have to submit to the caprices of fortune. "I have met my fate," the patient says, when everything has fallen apart and there is some truth in that, because was this person not heading towards this very wasteland that he or she is currently in?

The concept of fate has been misused, but basically it is a sound concept. Fate is our direction through life and many people sense a sinister undertone in life indicating that they are moving towards an unfortunate place. This forewarning has not been taken seriously by the rational mind. Many people in the western world believe in chance. But scientific studies of the correlation between lifestyle and illness indicate that we are indeed on an existential course, which in time will lead us to a good or perhaps a bad place. Fate seems to be a fact of life. We shape our own personal future by the way we relate to life in the present – in a constructive or destructive manner. Let us look at a simple example and a more complex one.

> Male, aged 47 years and overweight
> BP check: 145/100, OK. Weight today: 138 kg. A brief discussion about weight loss strategies – taking hold – letting go – both roads can lead to the intended destination.

Overweight is related to eating patterns, which are in turn related to self-esteem and self-appraisal, more precisely to the quality of self-care and contact with body and soul. The existential problems, of which overweight is a symptom, are therefore fundamental and can only be resolved with a whole-hearted effort. There are two paths, however. One can solve the problem by force and control – the most obvious approach in the form of weight-loss plans – or one can let go of the fundamental disturbances, which are the cause of the problem. Naturally, the latter approach is better, as a causal solution is also a lasting solution. Symptomatic treatment almost invariably has a temporary effect. In the following example, the patient has met his fate, so to speak. Nevertheless he is not beyond therapeutic reach and his life can still be put right.

> Male, aged 65 years with overweight, diabetes, stroke
> Patient has been overweight for many years and diabetes since 1997, today's BMI: 30. Episode of TIA [transient ischaemic attack] 10 days ago. He was driving the car, his wife was in the passenger seat, he started swaying more and more and increased his speed, became angry when his wife took the wheel, was driving at more than 100

km/h, when his wife resolutely pulled the hand brake and forced the car over to the side. Then the patient became paralysed on the right side; now hardly any after-effects, except impaired sense of taste. /TIA focused around right motor cortex [cerebral cortex controlling movements of the left side of the body] or perhaps thalamus [central structure in the brain]/ Examination: BP 155/65, now well-controlled. Fasting blood glucose 6.2 in latest test, i.e. only marginally increased, we will wait and see. PLAN: Intervention according to Ornish: Has now stopped smoking. Dietary advice. Weight-loss advice – should lose some weight, ideally 1 kg a week for nine weeks. Advice on physical exercise, e.g. 1 hour of swimming daily. Conversation on values in life. EXERCISE: For next time, think about improvements in life to become healthier. N.B.: should not drive a car, for at least 3 months.

His overweight is severe and has led to Type 2 diabetes. This has not prompted the patient to lose weight despite the risk of degeneration of eyes, vascular system and nervous system. But once the patient suffered the minor stroke he became much more motivated to do something about it. And then it is a matter of seizing the opportunity. If the patient achieve substantial weight-loss the diabetes is very likely to disappear and that would improve the patient's prospects considerably. Why do we have to be close to falling over the edge before we take it seriously?

Life is created by you, not by coincidence

When people who believe in chance have got into trouble, they have been "unlucky". They do not explain their misfortune by systematically having lived life wrongly and thus having failed themselves. The notion that we control our own fate is not particularly attractive, when things go wrong, but as long as everything is fine, it is much easier to accept. On further reflection, however, this notion has a certain appeal: once we realise that we are responsible for what happens, it becomes possible to do things differently and then to fare much better in future. The awareness that we create our own fate through our attitudes to and actions in life – our life perspective – thus brings about the interesting possibility that we can save ourselves. It is possible for us to rescue our exhausted, lost, failed and tormented existence and start afresh in a new and rich territory.

Life fell apart because we were thinking, deciding and acting contrary to our own life and the life of others. We were not good to ourselves, but bad. We were not good and constructive in relation to other people, but bad and destructive. Negative attitudes and perceptions were followed by inappropriate behaviour, which in turn had unfortunate consequences. The patient has started on a downward path and will hit rock bottom unless he or she can stop it.

> Male, aged 31 years with dizziness caused by life crisis and stress
> Borreliosis excluded, IgG negative. Persistent dizziness for nine months, no major palpitations, patient is afraid that it will return. Excessive workload – last working week he worked three days from 8 a.m. to 11.30 p.m. – and two young children also require full attention. No time for leisure, sports, friends etc. /Dizziness of disorientation type /acute stress/. Prescribed support/relief, time off work, peace and quiet. EXERCISE: Make an outline of what takes away energy and what provides energy in life. Then new appointment.

If we dissipate our energy, we may end up lacking it. The symptoms described above are common. There are many different types of dizziness, but the disorientation type is a characteristic sign of a lack of energy. It should also be noted that the suspicion was that something was wrong with his brain; that is how poorly he felt. That does not appear to be the case. If he is able to balance his "energy accounts", the dizziness will pass.

> Female, aged 34 years and everything is going off the rails
> Comes in desperation – everything is going off the rails – her husband wants a divorce, they have a two-year-old child together and she herself has two children from a previous relationship, two girls aged 5 and 8 years. Is no longer able to remember things, cannot concentrate, cannot watch television, cannot find her way to places, is completely out of it. Has considered taking her own life, but no specific plans, thinks about the children. What is to happen next week when she is due to meet her husband for the first time in a long while to make arrangements for a divorce and so on? Her husband says she is always morose and negative and critical, and that is also correct. We talk about it probably being best to divorce if it is simply not working, but that it is important to find an arrangement that works for the children. She has friends to talk to. On examination: assessed as not seriously depressive, no reduction in speed of speech, no waking in the early hours, slight loss of appetite, very little lowering of mood. EXERCISE: Should compile a list of all her problems. We talk about being true to oneself and about emptying one's "internal waste bin" – but first looking at and accepting everything that is in it. Can return next week, when a plan will be made.

When the bin falls over, all the waste is plainly visible. The more unresolved and repressed problems we throw into our internal waste bin, the more full it becomes, draining our energy and resources. Our energy and emotional fullness go into the waste bin along with the repression. And eventually it becomes full to the brim. The patient above became increasingly childish and unreasonable and her husband became fed up and walked out on her. The children will become the losers, unless the two adults pull themselves together and turn sober in less than a split second. Now is the time to think straight. Not only do the daughters need both a mother and a father, they also need their external woman to remain friends with their internal man.

Discussion

Taking control of your fate is a major, difficult and important decision. It is not impossible, far from it. It is difficult because it is so painful to see and acknowledge all the misery that one has caused oneself and others, while blindly and stubbornly insisting on pursuing the wrong path. Native Americans say that it is never too late to turn around, if one is on the wrong path. But in the Western world many people seem to believe that the fact that one has already been following that path for so long as a good argument for continuing all the way to the bitter end.

The holistic therapist supports the patient in rediscovering himself, his constructive and affirmative soul perspective. The patient should practise good and sustainable attitudes and in that way establish the good relations, internally and externally, that is needed in life. When your entire life has to be rebuilt from scratch and your entire existence needs to be rehabilitated, this often requires a combination of long-term training in life philosophy, psychotherapy and body therapy. This is because the patient's dark side – the neurosis resulting from pain in life and life-limiting decisions – is tied into the body, feelings and mind. To recover, the patient has to find the answers to some essential questions: What is kindness and ethical behaviour? How can I become useful to myself and to others? What is my personal vocation in life, my life mission? What is the meaning of life, and where do enjoyment of life, vital energy and wisdom come from? To find these answers the patient has to become fully aware of what has happened to him and what caused him to lose his enjoyment of life, vital energy and direction in life. Usually, our advice to the patient is along the lines of: "You need to understand the principles according to how the life works inside you. You need to understand yourself. You need to get to know yourself all over again."

> Male, aged 37 years, depressive and dull
> First consultation: 1. His wife has decided that she wants a divorce. They are getting divorced after 12 years of marriage, and they share the 7-year-old boy so that he stays with his father for three weekends every month. The patient is satisfied with this arrangement and pleased that his wife took the initiative, as he once suggested it, which crushed her completely. 2. He is constantly tired. Probably a manifestation of depression. We go through some painful events with his own parents. He stayed with his father for one week, when he was 12 years old. Emotional pain, disappointment, hope and frustration. Angry with his father for deserting him. To return for conversation in two weeks.
>
> Second consultation: 1. Small varicose veins, which the patient has had for many years and now, as a single, wants to have removed. It is agreed that the patient can be referred for surgery when they become worse. 2. Has decided that their 7-year-old son should stay with his mother, who has found a new husband with a 10-year-old daughter. Sees him every other weekend. Feels "selfish" after having been self-effacing his entire life. We discuss that. 3. We talk about his tendency towards depression. He describes himself as "dry, bare and dull", albeit with a few bright spots. We discuss the fact that the patient exists in a better version, and he will make an effort to retrieve it for next appointment. EXERCISE: The patient has read the book "Conversations with God", which is about creating the best version of yourself; his task for the next consultation is to find the passages of the book that can help him do that.

A person seeing himself as dull can work on that. He does not have to be dull, because as a living individual he has the alternative of being vibrant. But it takes an effort to rediscover one's life. This patient will most likely attain a whole new life, far better than he had previously. But it requires a big effort.

Quality of life, health and ability are often lost at the same time, most often in one decaying existential movement over five or ten years. The loss of life is mostly too slow to be felt as life threatening, but when it is finally realized, the awakening to reality provokes the deepest of fears in us, the fear of death itself, of destruction of our mere existence. The horrible experience of having lost life, often without even noticing how, can be turned into a strong motivation for improvement and betterment of life. Personal development is about finding the life so deeply hidden within. It is still there and a full revitalization and rehabilitation is often possible, much to the patient's surprise. Interestingly, success in rehabilitating a patient's quality of life, health and ability in general normally follows the successful rehabilitation of the person's philosophy of life. This rehabilitation follows the integration of the repressed painful feelings and emotions from the past and the letting go of the associated negative beliefs and decisions.

The holistic medical tool box (29-54) seems to have the power to rehabilitate the purpose of life (4), the character of the person (5) and fundamental existential dimensions of man: 1) love, 2) strength of mind, feelings and body, and 3) joy, gender and sexuality (8) allowing the person once again to express and realize his talents and full potential.

The principles of rehabilitation is not very different from the healing of other diseases and syndromes, but the task is often more demanding for the holistic physician, as the motivation and resources is often very low, and the treatment can take years.

References

[1]   Webb CY, Anderson JM. The relevance of education training for therapists in promoting the delivery of holistic rehabilitation services for young school children with disabilities in Hong Kong. Disabil Rehabil 2003;25(13):742-9.

[2]   Fridlund B. A holistic framework for nursing care. Rehabilitation of the myocardial infarction patient. J Holist Nurs 1994;12(2):204-17.

[3]   Aronoff GM. A holistic approach to pain rehabilitation: the Boston Pain Unit. NIDA Res Monogr 1981;36:33-40.

[4]   Ventegodt S. The life mission theory: A theory for a consciousness-based medicine. Int J Adolesc Med Health 2003;15(1):89-91.

[5]   Ventegodt S, Kroman M, Andersen NJ, Merrick J. The life mission theory VI: A theory for the human character. ScientificWorldJournal 2004;4:859-80.

[6]   Ventegodt S, Andersen NJ, Merrick J. Editorial: Five theories of human existence. ScientificWorldJournal 2003;3:1272-6.

[7]   Ventegodt S, Andersen NJ, Merrick J. The life mission theory II: The structure of the life purpose and the ego. ScientificWorldJournal 2003;3:1277-85.

[8]   Ventegodt S, Andersen NJ, Merrick J. The life mission theory III: Theory of talent. ScientificWorldJournal 2003;3:1286-93.

[9]   Ventegodt S, Merrick J. The life mission theory IV. A theory of child development. ScientificWorldJournal 2003;3:1294-1301.

[10] Ventegodt S, Andersen NJ, Merrick J. The life mission theory V. A theory of the anti-self and explaining the evil side of man. ScientificWorldJournal 2003;3:1302-13.

[11] Ventegodt S, Andersen NJ, Merrick J. Holistic medicine: Scientific challenges. ScientificWorldJournal 2003;3:1108-16.

[12] Ventegodt S, Andersen NJ, Merrick J. Holistic Medicine II: The square-curve paradigm for research in alternative, complementary and holistic medicine: A cost-effective, easy and scientifically valid design for evidence based medicine. ScientificWorldJournal 2003;3:1117-27.

[13] Ventegodt S, Andersen NJ, Merrick J. Holistic Medicine III: The holistic process theory of healing. ScientificWorldJournal 2003;3: 1138-46.

[14] Ventegodt S, Andersen NJ, Merrick J. Holistic Medicine IV: The principles of the holistic process of healing in a group setting. ScientificWorldJournal 2003;3:1294-1301.

[15] Ventegodt S, Merrick J, Andersen NJ. Quality of life theory I. The IQOL theory: An integrative theory of the global quality of life concept. ScientificWorldJournal 2003;3:1030-40.

[16] Ventegodt S, Merrick J, Andersen NJ. Quality of life theory II. Quality of life as the realization of life potential: A biological theory of human being. ScientificWorldJournal 2003;3:1041-9.

[17] Ventegodt S, Merrick J, Andersen NJ. Quality of life theory III. Maslow revisited. ScientificWorldJournal 2003;3:1050-7.

[18] Ventegodt S, Andersen NJ, Merrick J. Quality of life philosophy: when life sparkles or can we make wisdom a science? ScientificWorldJournal 2003;3:1160-3.

[19] Ventegodt S, Andersen NJ, Merrick J. QOL philosophy I: Quality of life, happiness, and meaning of life. ScientificWorldJournal 2003;3: 1164-75.

[20] Ventegodt S, Andersen NJ, Kromann M, Merrick J. QOL philosophy II: What is a human being? ScientificWorldJournal 2003;3:1176-85.

[21] Ventegodt S, Merrick J, Andersen NJ. QOL philosophy III: Towards a new biology. ScientificWorldJournal 2003;3:1186-98.

[22] Ventegodt S, Andersen NJ, Merrick J. QOL philosophy IV: The brain and consciousness. ScientificWorldJournal 2003;3:1199-1209.

[23] Ventegodt S, Andersen NJ, Merrick J. QOL philosophy V: Seizing the meaning of life and getting well again. ScientificWorldJournal 2003;3:1210-29.

[24] Ventegodt S, Andersen NJ, Merrick J. QOL philosophy VI: The concepts. ScientificWorldJournal 2003;3:1230-40.

[25] Merrick J, Ventegodt S. What is a good death? To use death as a mirror and find the quality in life. BMJ. Rapid Response 2003 Oct 31.

[26] Ventegodt S, Merrick J, Andersen NJ. Quality of life as medicine. A pilot study of patients with chronic illness and pain. ScientificWorld Journal 2003;3:520-32.

[27] Ventegodt S, Merrick J, Andersen NJ. Quality of life as medicine II. A pilot study of a five day "Quality of Life and Health" cure for patients with alcoholism. ScientificWorld Journal 2003;3:842-52.

[28] Ventegodt S, Clausen B, Langhorn M, Kromann M, Andersen NJ, Merrick J. Quality of life as medicine III. A qualitative analysis of the effect of a five days intervention with existential holistic group therapy: a quality of life course as a modern rite of passage. ScientificWorld Journal 2004;4:124-33.

[29] Ventegodt S, Merrick J. Clinical holistic medicine: Applied consciousness-based medicine. ScientificWorldJournal 2004;4:96-9.

[30] Ventegodt S, Morad M, Merrick J. Clinical holistic medicine: Classic art of healing or the therapeutic touch. ScientificWorldJournal 2004;4:134-47.

[31] Ventegodt S, Morad M, Merrick J. Clinical holistic medicine: The "new medicine", the multi-paradigmatic physician and the medical record. ScientificWorldJournal 2004;4:273-85.

[32] Ventegodt S, Morad M, Merrick J. Clinical holistic medicine: Holistic pelvic examination and holistic treatment of infertility. ScientificWorldJournal 2004;4:148-58.

[33] Ventegodt S, Morad M, Hyam E, Merrick J. Clinical holistic medicine: Use and limitations of the biomedical paradigm. ScientificWorldJournal 2004;4:295-306.

[34] Ventegodt S, Morad M, Kandel I, Merrick J. Clinical holistic medicine: Social problems disguised as illness. ScientificWorldJournal 2004;4:286-94.

[35] Ventegodt S, Morad M, Andersen NJ, Merrick J. Clinical holistic medicine Tools for a medical science based on consciousness. ScientificWorldJournal 2004;4:347-61.

[36] Ventegodt S, Morad M, Hyam E, Merrick J. Clinical holistic medicine: When biomedicine is inadequate. ScientificWorldJournal 2004;4:333-46.

[37] Ventegodt S, Morad M, Merrick J. Clinical holistic medicine: Prevention through healthy lifestyle and good quality of life. Oral Health Prev Dent 2004;2(suppl 1):239-45.

[38] Ventegodt S, Morad M, Merrick J. Clinical holistic medicine: Holistic treatment of children. ScientificWorldJournal 2004;4:581-8.

[39] Ventegodt S, Morad M, Merrick J. Clinical holistic medicine: Problems in sex and living together. ScientificWorldJournal 2004;4:562-70.

[40] Ventegodt S, Morad M, Hyam E, Merrick J. Clinical holistic medicine: Holistic sexology and treatment of vulvodynia through existential therapy and acceptance through touch. ScientificWorldJournal 2004;4:571-80.

[41] Ventegodt S, Morad M, Kandel I, Merrick J. Clinical holistic medicine: A psychological theory of dependency to improve quality of life. ScientificWorldJournal 2004;4:638-48.

[42] Ventegodt S, Morad M, Kandel I,.Merrick J. Clinical holistic medicine: Treatment of physical health problems without a known cause, exemplified by hypertension and tinnitus. ScientificWorldJournal 2004;4:716-24.

[43] Ventegodt S, Morad M, Merrick J. Clinical holistic medicine: Developing from asthma, allergy and eczema. ScientificWorldJournal 2004;4:936-42.

[44] Ventegodt S, Merrick J. Clinical holistic medicine: Chronic infections and autoimmune diseases. ScientificWorldJournal 2005;5: 155-64.

[45] Ventegodt S, Flensborg-Madsen T, Andersen NJ, Morad M, Merrick J. Clinical holistic medicine: A pilot on HIV and quality of life and a suggested treatment of HIV and AIDS. ScientificWorldJournal 2004;4:264-72.

[46] Ventegodt S, Merrick J. Clinical holistic medicine Chronic pain in the locomotor system. ScientificWorldJournal 2005;5:165-72.

[47] Ventegodt S, Gringols M, Merrick J. Clinical holistic medicine: Whiplash, fibromyalgia and chronic fatigue. ScientificWorldJournal 2005;5:340-54.

[48] Ventegodt S, Merrick J. Clinical holistic medicine: Chronic pain in internal organs. ScientificWorldJournal 2005;5:205-10.

[49] Ventegodt S, Kandel I, Neikrug S, Merrick J. Clinical holistic medicine: Holistic treatment of rape and incest trauma. ScientificWorldJournal 2005;5:288-97.

[50] Ventegodt S, Morad M, Merrick J. Clinical holistic medicine: The existential crisis – life crises, stress and burnout. Submitted ScientificWorldJournal 2005;5:300-12.

[51] Ventegodt S, Clausen B, Nielsen ML, Merrick J. Clinical holistic medicine: Advanced tools for holistic medicine. ScientificWorldJournal 2006;6:2048-65.

[52] Ventegodt S, Morad M, Press J, Merrick J, Shek DTL. Clinical holistic medicine: Holistic adolescent medicine. ScientificWorldJournal 2004;4:551-61.

[53] Ventegodt S, Morad M, Hyam E, Merrick J. Clinical holistic medicine: Induction of spontaneous remission of cancer by recovery of the human character and the purpose of life (the life mission). ScientificWorldJournal 2004;4:362-77.

[54] Ventegodt S, Solheim E, Saunte ME, Morad M, Kandel I, Merrick J. Clinical holistic medicine: Matastatic cancer. ScientificWorldJournal 2004;4:913-35.

A psychological theory of dependency to improve quality of life

In this chapter we suggest a psychological theory of dependency, as an escape from feeling the existential suffering and poor quality of life. The ways the human being escape hidden existential pains are multiple. The wide range of dependency states seems to be the most commonly escape strategy used. If the patient can be guided into the hidden existential pain to feel, understand and integrate it, we believe that dependency can be cured.

The problem is that the patient must be highly motivated, sufficiently resourceful and supported to want such a treatment that is inherently painful. Often the family and surrounding world is suffering more that the dependent person himself, because the pattern of behaviour the patient is dependent on, makes him or her rather insensitive and unable to feel. If the patient is motivated, resourceful and trusts his physician, recovery from even a severe state of dependency is not out of reach, if the holistic medical tools are applied wisely.

The patient must find hidden resources to take action, then in therapy confront and feel his old emotional pains, understand the source and inner logic of it and finally learn to let go of negative attitudes and beliefs. This way the person can be healed and released of the emotional suffering and no longer a slave to the dependency-pattern.

Introduction

In his book "Women who love too much", the author Robin Norwood (1) has the outstanding insight that dependency is generally due to an urge to escape from oneself into something else. A dependent person has leaped out of himself or herself, from his or her existence and abdomen, into whatever it is that he or she is dependent on. The purpose of leaping out of oneself is quite simple: to avoid feeling the pain in life. To avoid feeling everything in life that is far removed from the way it ought to be.

The interesting aspect is that many different things can be used to escape to, resulting in dependency: sex, television, work, alcohol, drugs, the lottery, the internet, other people and more. It is always a habit that provides freedom from pain by diverting attention from your own emotions, body and existence. The pain the patient is escaping from is always immense suffering in the patient's present-day existence, which is located in his or her repressed side, in the internal waste bin, the "sack" (2). Because of the discomfort involved, the patient cannot be blamed for trying to avoid this apparently meaningless pain.

When the patient, supported by a holistic therapist, takes on the emotional pain and accommodates it, explores it and gets to know it, he or she discovers that there is actual meaning to it. The pain conceals something that we need to learn, if we are to become whole people. The dependency is according to this understanding not a product of genetic predispositions, although there could be a genetic component also, but a product of a personal history with intensive and repressed existential suffering. Dependency can be cured if this existential pain is integrated and the existence healed. This is the general purpose of holistic medicine (3-26).

The many faces of dependency

Hardly anybody can say that they are not dependent on something or somebody. The existential ideal of health with total presence in life with no escape and repression is not of this world. The problem with dependency is not that you spent too much time working or being with your friends or partner or behind the computer, but that you miss your opportunity to live. Many people do not have a life. They are deeply in pain and only because they manage to escape, can they avoid feeling how bad and miserable their life really is. An even more serious problem is the tendency of dependent people to be abusive and violent, because they cannot manage the emotional pain, when it surfaces, in the moments where their "heroin-like habits" are disturbed. Fortunately, the holistic medicine provides us with tools to help the dependent patient integrate his or her life-pains and grow from the dependency. But these tools must be used wisely.

> Female, aged 22 years with dependency
> First session: The patient presents with a dependency problem – she left her boyfriend a year ago after living with him for three and a half years. She is unable to move on, would like to go back but that is not possible either. Works 60 hours a week – workaholic – she cannot be alone with herself and her emotions, which appear to be denied. Third eye - appears as though the brain is running on half power – "Am I stupid?" Hara: is not really at home in her stomach, pelvis and uterus. We work on this on the couch. Heart – appears to be quite closed. Purpose of life: something about being healthy and lovely – right now she is like a flat, lukewarm soda water. EXERCISE 1: One day a week you must do nothing other than being there and living in your emotions. Do not do anything, just be there and feel what you feel. These will be uncomfortable days. EXERCISE 2: Make a complete list of all your problems, describe them on half a sheet of A4 each. About 10 problems. Diagnosis: existential pain, repressed and leaps out of herself and into her boyfriend /dependency/. PLAN: she should come back in 2 to 4 weeks.
>
> Second session Has been very miserable, but that is a sign that there is progress and the patient now in contact with her emotions. EXERCISE 1: When you feel something, stop and note what it is that happens. Catch your shadow with your attention. See the little, neglected and lonely girl in you - study her. Do not change. "I am alone" – is let go of with a roll [the kitchen roll which the hand slowly releases

as the statement is released]. EXERCISE 2: When you are together with other people, note what you feel - is there pain in closeness? EXERCISE 3: Describe the good in you, all your talents. Another appointment in 2 to 3 weeks. Next time – talk about good books.

Here the physician (SV) unfortunately makes the mistake of overburdening the patient with more exercises than she has the resources to cope with. She consequently failed to turn up for the next conversation. It must be acknowledged that the physician in this case was too ambitious on behalf of the patient and consequently deprived her of the chance to receive help.

The "co-dependent" person is a key part of the problem

There is often a "co-dependent" person close to the dependent person, who in turn is dependent on the dependent person. The co-dependent person leaps over to the dependent person in the same way that the dependent person leaps out of himself or herself into food, sex, alcohol, work etc. The co-dependent person is someone who "loves too much" – an angel whom the severe alcoholic, the workaholic etc. is so fortunate to have by their side and who makes a sacrifice for the other person. But in reality this person is not a victim, but a "criminal". The co-dependent person is not just dependent on being able to help and support the dependent person, but often holds the dependent person fastened in his dependency.

The co-dependent person is an active participant in the person's dependency, but often plays the role so well that the dependent person does not see through the game, but weighed down by the feeling of guilt, reproaches himself for his weak character. A co-dependent person for an alcoholic will ensure, for example, that there is always plenty of alcohol within reach. It is difficult for the dependent person to escape from his dependency, when someone close is dependent on the person being dependent! Such complicated correlations may be difficult to see through for the person suffering from dependency, who fails time after time when he tries to give up drinking, to the great dismay of friends and family. There is a need for an outsider with a better overview and understanding of the dynamics of dependency.

> Male, aged 55 years, female aged 43years – alcoholic, co-alcoholic
> Quality-of-life conversation – Couple session: They come on her initiative. "We have to change from I to we," she says, but I do not agree. She wishes to devour him. She has a long history of being a "co-alcoholic" in a previous relationship, where the man was weak, with alcoholic tendencies. She and her present partner came together last autumn, and now he feels enveloped and half-smothered. We talk about this and discover that she plays the role of the "criminal", while he is the "victim". EXERCISE for her: Stop saying we. There are only two selves here. Stop dominating and "nudging" - that is to say forcing through your will. Let him take most of the initiatives and let him be in charge when you are together. Let him come onto the stage. Forget yourself. Wait for him. EXERCISE for him: Say no if you feel uncomfortable. Say "it's private" if there is something you do not want to share. PLAN: Five Rosen sessions for her, so that she can perceive the cause of her need to dominate, session as a couple again with SV in six to eight weeks.

The path out of dependency is the path through pain

To become free of abuse, it is necessary at the same time to look at the historical life pain within and the present-day life situation. Becoming free will also mean becoming free in relationships with other people and that is sometimes the scariest aspect. Because we do not really need to be dependent on anyone, if we can fully and completely count on ourselves. Then we can live, as we want, with those we want to. It is only in freedom that love and spirit can flourish.

We have conducted projects with people in severe social distress and with severe dependency, for instance on alcohol (25). We have also used students to conduct in-depth interviews with substance abusers and prostitutes with drug addictions at the street level. On the face of it, the picture looks bleak for many of them. However, we have been surprised how relatively easy it has been in practice to do something for those of them, who wanted to help themselves. Nine out of sixteen alcoholics we have been working with on an intensive 5-day residential course with a view to improving their life philosophy and life practice drank less and apparently leading a much better life, when we examined them six months after the course – and three of them had only sporadic episodes of drunkenness and had returned to work (25,26).

The medical consultation for a patient of this type typically comes about as a result of the patient having suffered an acute crisis, which has caused him to reach a decision that now is the time to stop! Our treatment does not, however, always prove successful. The next patient came full of eagerness and enthusiasm and promised firmly that she would improve, but she was never seen again.

> Female, aged 50 years, alcoholic and heavy smoker, who would like to stop this abuse
> The patient is an alcoholic, who drinks 7-14 units of alcohol daily and smokes 50 cigarettes, but has not been involved in prostitution or drug addiction. Three weeks ago her boyfriend, whom she had known for 17 years, died from drinking. This has stirred things up. There are family problems, as her brother wants her to renounce her inheritance. The patient has been "nice" throughout her life and done what other people expected of her, but now wishes to become free and alive. INTERPRETATION: It is precisely this attempt to break out that has brought her to the hell - the tormented and death-like state – she now finds herself in and is trying to drink her way out of. When a woman tries to get away from being nice, she goes through the pain it cost to become a nice and disciplined girl to begin with. PLAN: To go from nice to free, the patient has to go through a period of pain and suffering, with all the old failures and decisions to die coming to the surface. As an alcoholic, she can join our programme for holistic rehabilitation and would like to have the quality-of-life package [the clinic's six-month treatment offer]. She goes to see our clinic's gestalt therapist for a treatment and development plan. We expected three phases with this patient: An orientation phase, in which she understands her personal recovery project, a process phase, in which she goes through her old sufferings in therapy and rediscovers her enjoyment of life and hidden resources. A rehabilitation phase, where she acknowledges her personal purpose of life and has her new life arranged accordingly. The patient is informed of these expectations and that it will be hard work, possibly taking three years, but initially six months. The patient is a

candidate for the growth group [a network group in which patients and people taking the course meet every fortnight to support one another], which will take place in our lecture hall every second Tuesday. AGREEMENT: The patient has four weeks to overcome her excessive alcohol and tobacco consumption. It should preferably also be down after four weeks. EXERCISE: She has been given quality of life and life philosophy to read. She scales down her alcohol consumption over the next four weeks, after which she comes to see the gestalt therapist again.

This patient came a long way in learning about her problems. The next step was to go through old sufferings, which often is the problematic part. Because whatever for? Why should I suffer the hurt? What am I to live for, when life just causes pain? This is the reason that alcohol and pills makes it easy to escape. That is why many people in the Western world have excess consumption and dependency problems. Although the outlook appears bleak, we always choose to believe the best about patients, who wish to improve their lives. Occasionally we are positively surprised.

> Male, aged 63 years and co-alcoholism
> 1. His sciatica is coming along fine.
> 2. Swollen left leg. On examination there is nothing other than the swelling. No tenderness in the calf, no discoloration or heat. Discontinue Centyl Mite [bendroflumethiazide + potassium chloride] as the patient does not tolerate Centyl. Prescribe Furix [furosemide] 40 mg + KCl.
> 3. Problems with drinking. His partner is at a loss what to do, it is affecting him greatly. We talk about dependency and about co-alcoholism/co-dependency. EXERCISE: Read "Women who love too much" (on the topic of dependency)(1).

In the same way that the husband is dependent on alcohol, she is dependent on being the good, great and strong person who protects and takes care of him (it is typical for the man to cling to the bottle and the wife to cling to her identity as helper/mother/martyr). A single well-chosen book that illustrates the problem is very often all it takes to create awareness and set the wheels in motion.

Dependency as the key problem in a relationship

One of the places where dependency is most common and troublesome is in our close and intimate relationships. Some case reports will illustrate this relationship.

> Female, aged 40 years with dependency on boyfriend
> There have been problems with her boyfriend, whom she has moved in with. She makes sexual demands on him, and he backs off. We talk about her making demands, because she feels that she "has a need" and about the dependency being a manifestation of her escaping from herself instead of being at ease in her own centre. Confronted with this, she cries. We talk about being at ease and being in balance. EXERCISE: Sit and be where you are. Stop making demands, stop criticising and controlling. Focus in terms of your thoughts, in terms of your emotions.

Dependency often takes the form of an urge to demand, control, and criticise. When the dependency becomes extreme, as in the next case, it may be reflected in disease caused by the life pain behind the dependency. A patient of this kind is treated holistically in such a way that the physical pain is taken back to the dependency, which is taken back to the original pain of existence.

This history is also concerned with a major existential problem on how to relate to being the daughter of a prostitute. The person concerned was in the situation of being unwanted and sullied with shame from the start. How can you find self-esteem and worth against such a background? The patient had a hidden history, which was gradually confronted and put into place. At first it was highly embellished and idealised, then she realised the awful truth, and later an even deeper truth revealed itself, life's own truth, which resulted in resuming her course. The case illustrates how complex the situation often can be, since many things happen during life that it can be difficult to keep up with. The case history showed how disease is due to dependency, which in turn is due to an underlying existential emptiness. On the way through the course of the person's life, internal chaos is manifested as disease and external chaos as a miserable relationship, which ultimately in the case history was resolved in a necessary divorce.

Female, aged 38 years, where dependency is the actual problem underlying arthritis
First conversation: The patient has a history of rheumatoid arthritis. She is on medication for this. She has three children, boys aged 8 and 12 years and a girl aged 6 years. Trained as auxiliary nurse, at present off work due to arthritis. She has previously had several operations on her knee for excrescences. Since the time she was very young, where she grew up with a hippie mother and does not know her father. Her mother was living in a lesbian relationship, when she was small. She had to take responsibility for both her mother and her sister at an early age. She therefore had to be strong. "I'm disappointed," says the patient, and she looks very disappointed. She is disappointed with her husband, children, parents, family, friends and everything. We work on this and talk about her use of power over those around her, who hurts her and others and about her general malice towards herself and others. She finds it difficult to see this. EXERCISE for next time: Make a complete list of your power games. Another appointment in two weeks.

Second conversation: Many thoughts about power games and about being domineering. Her father had ended up in institutional care and her best friend falling into alcohol abuse and she is also carrying her husband. She is a mother to them all, but is tired of fulfilling this role, and everyone around her is dropping like rotting tree trunks. On the couch I (SV) work on her stomach, in which "she is not present" [I place one hand on the skin of her stomach and ask her to meet me there, while we talk together about topics relevant to the stomach]. She talks about her two childbirths, the first was terribly difficult, the second went fairly well. She finds it difficult to let go, to abandon herself, to be a woman. She has always been very masculine. It appears as though she allows herself to be a woman more on the couch. She is taking NSAID [drugs such as Ibuprofen] for her arthritis. She has started school. Next appointment in a week with the topic: letting go.

Third conversation: "I am a woman," says the patient, and that does a lot for her, and she feels like kissing. She is living with a man she does not love, she is considering an affair, but I recommend that she should divorce straightaway so that the children come out of it unscathed. She is very anxious, and sits clutching her stomach. She radiates "like a beautiful goddess" and talks about being sexually assaulted as a six-year-old, how she was always afraid of men and was very attractive as a teenager, before she became tough, masculine and a driving force. We talk about her having to go back and feel the anxiety, but she is afraid of becoming fragile and being completely squashed, if that happens. Sometimes her legs turn to jelly. She will probably soon have to go for Rosen sessions[27]. Another appointment in one week. She must accept her anxiety, be fragile and emotional as a woman. She has the power in the relationship with her husband and therefore responsibility for it. She now has to live up to it. Her dependency on him must be broken and it is likely to be tough for her.

Fourth conversation: She has been through a lot since last session. Has suffered, been ill and vomiting. "It's dangerous to think about what I want from life," says the patient. She reveals her deep and shameful secret, which she has been battling with, alone for seven years: that she is the result of rape. The story her mother has told her is as follows: Her mother was an escort and one day she had a very good-looking man as a client. It was in the sixties and at that time many girls earned money that way and they did not take it very seriously. The mother was very attracted to this man, who had apparently become hooked on her and eventually forced himself on her. She apparently gave in to him, let go, enjoyed it and allowed herself to become pregnant; she did not have any regrets about it later, even though it did not fit in well with the social order. But the mother had lived in a lesbian relationship beforehand. The father left his visiting card and greatly regretted that he had not been able to control himself. On the couch, "I take her back to the time of conception", where we both look together at what actually happened. Very strong divine energy was present, from which sprang her purpose of life, she feels. She could not express this purpose in words today, but we will continue working on this. Another appointment in 1-2 weeks. Her arthritis is dormant. Today we worked on the content of the incident, which was extremely charged emotionally. It is not up to me to question the story; the patient's reality is what is concerned and that is what has to be handled if she is to be redeemed. The two main aspects focused on are the enormous sexual attraction that lie behind a case of rape - perhaps even mutual - and the subsequent moral condemnation. Gradually, as we work our way deeper into it, the polarisation of the sexual pleasure and the shame is strengthened. In the patient's consciousness it emerges as an almost divine joining of the two sexual poles during the rape, which leads to her own creation and afterwards unbearable shame and guilt, which she shares with her mother. It is an extremely redeeming experience for the patient to have this dark side of her life confronted and integrated.

Fifth conversation: She phoned on Friday, having had too much to drink and said that she was deeply in love with me. Today we have talked about it and she is ashamed that she is unable to control herself. Much has opened up since the last session and she is full of feelings of all kinds. Her arthritis has disappeared completely, she has been able to do ballet on her toes again, which she had not been able to do for many years, and her pain has completely vanished. She herself thinks that her arthritis has been cured. We (SV and the patient) talk about how she fell in love, about it being "fine safe" to fall in love with a physician, who will not and cannot use it against her. She must accommodate her emotions for better or worse, until they calm down and fit into her new life. It is important not to shut herself off from her emotions again, because if she does her arthritis will return. The emotions must be accommodated and developed, so that her emotionality and femininity are rehabilitated.

Sixth conversation: She has been to the rheumatology department and reports that the physician there told her, that she had miraculously recovered - joints and cartilage have healed completely, no scarring can be seen on the X-ray and the radiologist has never seen that before, the patient reports. Her symptoms started, when she had salmonella poisoning, was in such a poor state that she was unable to run, bicycle and barely walk, after the physicians had saved her life. She felt terribly let down by her husband, who did not help her when it mattered. She now wants a divorce. Time line therapy on this incident results in contact with a new incident, when the patient was ten years old and bought trainers for her step-father, who two days later falls off a ladder and only comes home after a year in intensive care, he died six years later from cancer. He was a good father of whom the patient was very fond. Scared of the ladder. Must never cry for her mother. Chain of anxiety? The patient promises to provide a copy of the hospital case record. EXERCISE 1: Write about the two incidents. EXERCISE 2: Tell your husband that you want a divorce, ask how long it will take him to find somewhere else to live, if appropriate find a place yourself. Suggestion for sharing daughter: every other weekend from Friday to Monday plus every Wednesday afternoon to Thursday afternoon plus first half of each holiday. If necessary, put this in writing for him.

Seventh conversation: The patient says: "I am stupid, I am stupid, I am stupid," and works on her duplicity, as she does not admit to her husband that she does not love him, that she does not like kissing him, that she does not like making love with him, that she does not fancy him, that she does not find him sexually attractive at all. There is no doubt about the need for them to separate, but it is very difficult for the patient to free herself of her dependency; she hides behind examinations, the children's needs and so on. During the session the patient became very disappointed and very angry with me and had an urge to strike me with flowers she had brought along to give me. We agreed, however, that she should come again. "You're so false the falseness runs down your teeth!" she says.

Eighth conversation: She has lost her appetite and is not eating. On examination, she is very sore below the navel, "dependency relationship stomach". She is about to separate, but her partner ignores her requests for him to move out, her 8-year-old son is in crisis. We talk about the patient having to review her superficial life and become genuine, deep, alive and true. She is a facade person, and it is very difficult for her to admit that she is in crisis; she is unable to accept the help that is offered. We talk about this. "I don't know whether I would resist if someone held my head under water." I suggest that we find a bucket at once, and that makes her laugh. She is not considered to be suicidal.

Ninth conversation: The patient is doing fine, she has found a new job, has developed really well and feels sure that she will return to full health. /Finished/.

She was contacted by telephone one year later and she said: "I felt terribly cheated and helpless, which I think was the cause of the arthritis." She said that the X-rays of her joints and lungs have again shown her to be completely healthy and the arthritic nodules have not returned. Her knee, which she was once told would never be repaired, now works perfectly. She says that she has changed many things in her life; she has divorced, she has changed her diet so that she eats less meat and animal fat, and taken a part-time job 25 hours a week, which is what she is able to cope with now.

Discussion

The problem with dependency is that we are empty. Feeling this emptiness is almost unbearable. It is as though we would rather die than be empty. We have leaped out of ourselves and into the person we are dependent on. In psychodynamic terms, the dependency is a consequence of very severe neglect, which we repeat in relation to ourselves by completely omitting to feel what we need, where we are and where we are to go. We are "in the other person" – when it is a person we are dependent on, as in this case above– and barely sense ourselves or our own needs any longer. When we come "back home" to ourselves, we find a smoking ruin instead of our own good and orderly existence. There is a lot of clearing-up to be done. The focus in the described case study was on the stomach and uterus (in the oriental tradition called the hara center), as it so often is with dependency.

The reward was reaped. The arthritis disappeared half-way through the course of the treatment. This happened, when she became willing to live with her emotional pains. The moment she did that, the problems moved out of her body, back into the emotions they come from and the body was healed. She is still insecure and could still carry out manoeuvres, where her defences cleverly will take over. She can still get her arthritis back and she might perhaps simply find a new partner to be dependent on. She was over the worst after the last consultation and at the follow-up conversation one year afterwards she was in good form with a new job and a good life, which appeared to be a stable improvement.

Conclusion

The ways we escape hidden existential pains are multiple. The wide range of dependency states seems to be one of the most commonly used. If the patient can be guided into the hidden existential pain to integrate it, in accordance with holistic process theory (9-12), dependency can be cured. The problem is that the patient must be highly motivated, sufficiently resourceful and supported to want such a treatment, which is inherently painful. Often the family and surrounding world are suffering more that the dependent person himself, since the pattern of behaviour the patient is dependent of, makes him or her rather insensitive and unable to feel. If the patient is motivated, resourceful with a trusts in his physician, recovery from even a severe state of dependency is not out of reach, if the holistic medical tools are applied wisely. The patient must feel his old emotional pains, understand the source and inner logic of it and finally "take to learning" and let go of negative attitudes and beliefs. This way fundamental existence can be healed and without the emotional suffering, the patient is no longer a slave of the dependency-pattern moving the attention away from the core of existence and life.

References

[1]   Norwood R. Woman who love too much. Los Angeles, CA: JP Tarcher, 1985.
[2]   Bly R. A little book on the human shadow. San Francisco: Harper, 1988.
[3]   Ventegodt S, Andersen NJ, Merrick J. Five theories of human existence. ScientificWorldJournal 2003;3:1272-6.

[4]   Ventegodt S. The life mission theory: A theory for a consciousness-based medicine. Int J Adolesc Med Health 2003;15(1):89-91.

[5]   Ventegodt S, Andersen NJ, Merrick J. The life mission theory II: The structure of the life purpose and the ego. ScientificWorldJournal 2003;3:1277-85.

[6]   Ventegodt S, Andersen NJ, Merrick J. The life mission theory III: Theory of talent. ScientificWorldJournal 2003;3:1286-93.

[7]   Ventegodt S, Merrick J. The life mission theory IV. A theory of child development. ScientificWorldJournal 2003;3:1294-1301.

[8]   Ventegodt S, Andersen NJ, Merrick J. The life mission theory V. A theory of the anti-self and explaining the evil side of man. ScientificWorldJournal 2003;3:1302-13.

[9]   Ventegodt S, Andersen NJ, Merrick J. Holistic medicine: Scientific challenges. ScientificWorldJournal 2003;3:1108-16.

[10] Ventegodt S, Andersen NJ, Merrick J. Holistic Medicine II: The square-curve paradigm for research in alternative, complementary and holistic medicine: A cost-effective, easy and scientifically valid design for evidence based medicine. ScientificWorldJournal 2003;3:1117-27.

[11] Ventegodt S, Andersen NJ, Merrick J. Holistic Medicine III: The holistic process theory of healing. ScientificWorldJournal 2003;3:1138-46.

[12] Ventegodt S, Andersen NJ, Merrick J. Holistic Medicine IV: The principles of the holistic process of healing in a group setting. ScientificWorldJournal 2003;3:1294-1301.

[13] Ventegodt S, Merrick J, Andersen NJ. Quality of life theory I. The IQOL theory: An integrative theory of the global quality of life concept. ScientificWorldJournal 2003;3:1030-40.

[14] Ventegodt S, Merrick J, Andersen NJ. Quality of life theory II. Quality of life as the realization of life potential: A biological theory of human being. ScientificWorldJournal 2003;3:1041-9.

[15] Ventegodt S, Merrick J, Andersen NJ. Quality of life theory III. Maslow revisited. ScientificWorldJournal 2003;3:1050-7.

[16] Ventegodt S, Andersen NJ, Merrick J. Quality of life philosophy: when life sparkles or can we make wisdom a science? ScientificWorldJournal 2003;3:1160-3.

[17] Ventegodt S, Andersen NJ, Merrick J. QOL philosophy I: Quality of life, happiness, and meaning of life. ScientificWorldJournal 2003;3: 1164-75.

[18] Ventegodt, S., Andersen, N.J, Kromann, M., and Merrick, J. (2003) QOL philosophy II: What is a human being? ScientificWorldJournal 2003;3:1176-85.

[19] Ventegodt S, Merrick J, Andersen NJ. QOL philosophy III: Towards a new biology. ScientificWorldJournal 2003;3:1186-98.

[20] Ventegodt S, Andersen NJ, Merrick J. QOL philosophy IV: The brain and consciousness. ScientificWorldJournal 2003;3:1199-1209.

[21] Ventegodt S, Andersen NJ, Merrick J. QOL philosophy V: Seizing the meaning of life and getting well again. ScientificWorldJournal 2003;3:1210-29.

[22] Ventegodt S, Andersen NJ, Merrick J. QOL philosophy VI: The concepts. ScientificWorldJournal 2003;3:1230-40.

[23] Merrick J, Ventegodt S. What is a good death? To use death as a mirror and find the quality in life. BMJ Rapid Response 2003 Oct 31.

[24] Ventegodt S, Merrick J, Andersen NJ. Quality of life as medicine. A pilot study of patients with chronic illness and pain. ScientificWorld Journal 2003;3:520-32.

[25] Ventegodt S, Merrick J, Andersen NJ. Quality of life as medicine II. A pilot study of a five day "Quality of Life and Health" cure for patients with alcoholism. ScientificWorld Journal 2003;3:842-52.

[26] Ventegodt S, Clausen B, Langhorn M, Kromann M, Andersen NJ, Merrick J.Quality of Life as Medicine III. A qualitative analysis of the effect of a five days intervention with existential holistic group therapy: a quality of life course as a modern rite of passage. ScientificWorld Journal 2004;4:124-33.

[27] Rosen M, Brenner S. Rosen method bodywork. Accessing the unconscious through touch. Berkeley, CA: North Atlantic Books, 2003.

Section 10. Children and adolescence

Children and teenagers are more and more often treated by psychiatrists as their poor thriving and inadequate behaviour is becoming more and more the center of attention. But children and teenagers cannot be seen as isolated individuals. When a child is dysfunctional, this signifies serious problem in the family to which it belongs. When a teenager has mental problems these problems are often just simple symptoms of emotional problems only too natural to have in this difficult period.

The holistic perspective is therefore more relevant here than anywhere else. The trend in society is to see the young person as an individual with individual problems of growth and development. This perspective is anti-holistic and the holistic psychiatrist is standing before a challenging task when a family is bringing its child or teenager for psychiatric treatment.

Children and young people somatisize and physical pain is very common during childhood and adolescence. Often psychosomatic pains are untreatable by the biomedical physician so patients with treatment-resistant physical pain often end up in psychiatric treatment as well. When the pain is connected to genitals and is of unbearable intensity, as is sometimes the case with vulvodyni, the young patient also often is referred to psychiatric treatment. To help here the holistic psychiatrist must also be sexologist and often also gynecologist. This is more specialties than can be expected from a physician, and the sad result is that the patient that could be cured from an integrated treatment stays chronically ill and untreated. In this case the physician must do his or her best in spite of not having all the formal competencies necessary for the treatment.

A strict ethics is necessary in holistic medicine. When the ethical code is known and well respected the holistic physician that come from good intent cannot do any harm (1). Fortunately holistic medicine is so safe that even formal errors are not harming the patient but just making the treatment taking longer time.

References

[1]   de Vibe, M., Bell, E., Merrick, J., Omar, H.A., Ventegodt, S. Ethics and holistic healthcare practice. Int J Child Health Human Dev 2008;1(1):23-8.

Chapter 41

Holistic treatment of children

We believe a holistic approach to mental and behavioral problems in childhood and adolescence will benefit the child, adolescent and the whole family. As nearly a rule, children have far less to say in the family than their parents. It is therefore the parents who set the agenda and decide how things are done at home and in relation to the child. It is therefore most often also the parents, who have a problem when the child is not thriving. The child thus acts as the thermometer of the family. When children are not feeling well or sick, the parents are not doing so well either.

Most problems arising from dysfunctional patterns are almost impossible for the parents to solve on their own, but with help and support from the holistically oriented physician, we believe that many problems can be discovered and solved. Not only can health problems, but also problems of poor thriving in the family in general, be addressed, but with the physician in the role of a coach the family can be provided with relevant exercises, that will change the patterns of dysfunction. Consciousness-based medicine seems to be efficient also with children and adolescents, which are much more sensitive to the psycho-social dimensions than adults.

Five needs seem to be essential for the thriving and health of the child: the need for attention, for respect, for love, for touch and for acknowledgment. The physician should be able to see if the child lacks the fulfilment of one or more of these needs, and he can then demonstrate to the parents how these needs should be handled. This should be followed by simple instructions and exercises to the parents in the spirit of coaching. This approach is especially relevant, when the child is chronically ill or presenting a hyperactive behavioural pattern often diagnosed as Attention Deficit Hyperactivity Disorder (ADHD).

Introduction

Sometimes you will hear the following sentence: "If your child is impossible for you, you are also impossible for your child." A number of recent studies have shown that around one in four children in Denmark have social, psychological or health problems (1-3). Some of these studies have been conducted by professor Per Schultz Jørgensen from the Royal Danish School of Educational Studies, who also chaired the Danish National Council for Children

(Children Ombudsman) during 1998 – 2001 and these studies (1-3) make sad and dismal reading. We find it even more upsetting that the numbers of children and families in distress does not appear to be changing, despite the fact that increasing attention has been given to the problem.

When children are not feeling well psycho-socially it can be manifested by a range of symptoms, such as frequent bedwetting, stomach ache, sleep problems, disruption at school, bullying, problems with learning or concentration. The parents may also find their children to be completely impossible, non-receptive to common sense or any reasonable attempt at upbringing. The physician will often find it impossible to treat these symptoms with biomedicine. We generally do not like giving children drugs that suppress symptoms, because of the consequences long term. Our holistic approach to children are not in principal different from our holistic approach to the adult patient, except that psychosocial factors seems to be of even more importance with children. Let us therefore first take a short review of our work relevant for holistic medicine in general.

The foundation of clinical holistic medicine

The life mission theory (4-9) state that everybody has a purpose of life or a huge talent. Happiness come from living this purpose and succeeding in expressing the core talent in your life. To do this, it is important to develop as a person into what is know as the natural condition, a condition where the you know yourself and use all your efforts to achieve what is most important for you. The holistic process theory of healing (10-13) and the related quality of life theories (14-16) state that the return to the natural state of being is possible, whenever the person gets the resources needed for the existential healing. The resources needed are "holding" in the dimensions: awareness, respect, care, acknowledgment and acceptance with support and processing in the dimensions: feeling, understanding and letting go of negative attitudes and beliefs. The preconditions for the holistic healing to take place is trust and the intention of the healing taking place. Existential healing is not a local healing of any tissue, but a healing of the wholeness of the person, making him much more resourceful, loving, and knowledgeable of himself, his own needs and wishes. In letting go of negative attitudes and beliefs the person returns to a more responsible existential position and an improved quality of life. The philosophical change in the person healing is often a change towards preferring difficult problems and challenges, instead of avoiding difficulties in life (17-24). The person who becomes happier and more resourceful is often also becoming more healthy, more talented and able of functioning (25-27).

The child as the thermometer of the family

It is of great advantage to be able to adopt a holistic perspective in relation to the child. If it is possible to assess and observe the whole family and not just the child, it is often possible to understand the interaction and where the problem arises. As a rule, children have far less say in the family than their parents with the parents setting the agenda and deciding how things are done at home and in relation to the child. It is therefore most often also the parents, who have a problem when the children are impossible. You can say that the children function as the thermometer of the family. When children are ill or not doing well, this is often due to the parents not doing well either or unable to cope with themselves, with each other and with the children. This is especially relevant, when the child is not developing normally or presenting a hyperactive behavioural pattern often diagniosed as Attention Deficit Hyperactivity Disorder (ADHD).

Children cooperate

It is a natural reaction to blame impossible children for their impossibility. But, as the family therapist Jesper Juul, the founder of the Scandinavian Kempler Institute in Denmark, has so outstandingly explained in his book "Your competent child" (28), children like to cooperate and they will do whatever they can to be loved by their parents. But children have their needs, which they are compelled to fight for in order to have fulfilled, even if this cuts across their parents. The following things in particular are concerned:

- The need for attention: being seen and understood
- The need for respect: being met and acknowledged as an independent living being
- The need for love: care, loving touch and loving words.
- The need for touch and acceptance
- The need for acknowledgment: the parents must see and fully acknowledge the character of body, mind, and spirit

Instead, children are often given the brush-off, met with emotional coldness or perhaps even punished with studied indifference or in some other way by their frustrated parents. When parents and children get on well together, the child is the source of the greatest joy in the world. Many modern parents appreciate their children, they are very attentive to their children and very aware of the relationship, but they nevertheless often overlook a number of serious imbalances. The child may be suffocated by too much care and protection, or may become domineering, even a complete prima donna, from receiving too much attention or attention of a neurotic and idolising nature. The child might even become domineering and taking up to much space from too much misunderstood respect of boundaries and independence. It is more usual, however, for the children to be neglected, ignored, insulted, scolded, and condemned.

It is not easy to be a child, but it is just as true to say that it is not easy to be a parent. A good holistic cure for the child is therefore support for the parents in being good parents with an understanding of the needs of their children.

The project is not concerned with the child, but with the parents and how they deal with the child. As they are the adults, they must also take responsibility and stop being impossible for the child, because when they do the child will start to do well and if he or she is sick, to get better. And soon the child will flourish and be a joy to the parents, which they had never thought to be possible.

Male, age 1 year and neglect
12-month well-baby examination in the family practice with vaccination. Seems a
little neglected. The mother also has another young child in her care, who is a late
developer and to whom she often gives priority. There is clear jealousy and demand
for attention, which triggers scolding. Ears: nothing abnormal discovered. Talk about
it. Recommended reading: Jesper Juul: "Your competent child" (28).

It is upsetting that so many small children 'maltreated" in Denmark. Physical violence is
prohibited, but neglect and other forms of abuse are "permitted". At the well-baby visits it
also seems that quite a number of mothers do not even know what they are doing, when they
scold a one-year-old child. Criticism is experienced by the child as if the "King" himself told
him and can be experienced as blows, just as bad as if they had been physical blows - indeed,
perhaps worse. In our clinical life we try to use any opportunity to teach parents about the
need for care, attention and respect of children. But with parents, who themselves have "been
failed" in their childhood, must face up to their failures and old wounds in order to be able to
act better towards their own children. This is very painful. We therefore proceed very slowly
with them. A good book, which they can take at their own pace to read is a good idea.

Male, aged 3 years and agitated
3-year development examination in the family practice. Good development, he has
very good motor skills, but his language skills are less well developed, he is unable
or unwilling to repeat syllables. Not so cooperative in the vision test, which will have
to be carried out in a later examination. Some problems in day care, where the
teacher finds him too agitated. Here he tears up the paper on the couch. Perhaps he
needs to be met at his boundary [i.e. in balanced contact with his mother, when she
crosses the boundary her son has dominated] more than the mother is doing at
present. We talk briefly about this.

A 3-year-old boy, who acts in protest would seem to have been browbeaten rather than met.
He "fights for his life", everywhere including when he is brought to see the family physician.
There is no reason to be angry with him. On the contrary – it is fine that he fights. As a
holistic physician one has "a bone to pick" with the mother, to whom the problem and its
possible causes must be discreetly turned over. If she makes changes and meets him at his
boundary, their life together will be completely transformed, into fun and games instead of
war and argument, from pain to joy for them both in the years to come. Think what a
difference such a small change from battling with the boy to showing him respect will make!
If not handeld correctly the child might be diagniosed with ADHD in a few years from now.

Female, aged 5 years with problems concerning respect
5-year examination – development good, but there are probably some problems with
being respected. Has a great need to take care of herself. Does not want to be
vaccinated, and I do not wish to enforce it. Is to come back in 3 months for
diphtheria-tetanus vaccination. Social: Today appears shy and inhibited. It appears as
though the father violates the patient's boundaries. Says in as many words that he has
to put her in her place the whole time. He regards her as impossible and has some
problems in bringing her up. He gets on better with his son. Discussion on children's
needs: care, attention and respect. I am not sure that he understood. They are to come
back in 3 months for a further attempt at vaccination. This is a good opportunity to
return to the subject.

In this case the needs of the girl was discussed with the father, who seemed to have difficulties to provide care and respect, because of lack of knowledge. Our function as physician is not to become emotional and condemnatory, but to remain neutral and helpful. The lack of self-respect in the father, which deep down is what it is about, is a widespread condition and the father needs our respect, not our disrespect. If we are to break the social heritage, we need to make him understand what is going on. If he does understand, a long and difficult process will be started in him, where he gradually takes responsibility for all the pain there is in him from long ago in his own childhood, which having a young child constantly reminds him of. The alternative is for him to continue to take out his frustration on his child, become angry with her and irritated by her instead of taking responsibility for the pain in himself. The child is blamed for the discomfort he feels (that is, the discomfort he felt when he himself was a child).

> Female, aged 3 years and afraid of animals (arachnophobia)
> Increasingly afraid of small animals over the course of a year – she now screams and becomes completely hysterical as soon as she sees a small animal – she says herself that she is most afraid of spiders. Father and mother immediately kill all the small animals they can find and equipped the girl with a fly-swat so that she can defend herself. The father, who comes with his daughter, also says that he really cannot stand seeing the patient become so frightened. I ask the father whether it is OK for his daughter to become afraid - and we are in agreement that it is. She is allowed to have the feelings she has. So he must just hold onto her and support her as well as he can in the meantime. I capture a small animal outside and show it to the patient, while the father holds onto her, and she is not afraid. It appears as though the pattern has been broken. They are to come back if the problem persists.

To us, it is great medical art, although it is extremely simple: The girl did not receive support from her father when she was afraid. On the contrary, he reacted inappropriately – in a neurotic manner – and in so doing reinforced the girl's anxiety. From our point of view, not only did he reinforce her anxiety – it is actually the disturbance in him that has made the girl afraid of animals in the first place. So in reality it is the father we are treating here under the disguise of attending to the girl. A more difficult, but in the longer term more effective strategy would be to make the father understand that he is himself disturbed and over-protective.

> Male, aged 10 years with pain in the foot due to a "I hide myself" posture
> Walks on the inside of the foot and is in pain after sport – judo and badminton. As a result of a stooping, "I hide myself" posture the pelvis is tilted, and the knees are turned inward, producing functional flat-footedness. On examination: when the knees are bent out over the foot, the flat-footedness is straightened out and the arch is lifted off the floor. The metatarsal arch is flattened. Conclusion: There is no major anatomical defect, the problem is functional. The patient is instructed to lift his knee up over the side of the mid-foot and to "walk like a cowboy". Social: Patient appears to be affected by having moved, at his own request, from his mother to his father and stepmother, with whom he has a very good relationship (she comes along with him). However, he still sees his mother every other weekend. He is to come back in a

month, when we will see whether there has been any improvement following the exercises.

Social and family-related problems hit children and adolescents hard. The defence mechanism is often some negative attitudes in life, which are directly reflected in the way the body is used. Often incorrect use of the body in turn leads to problems with the locomotor system, as in the case described above. A problem of this kind is difficult to solve with insoles in the shoes. But when the problem is seen in context and thoroughly understood, it is not difficult to do something about it.

> Female, 39 years, setting boundaries for oneself, not for one's child
> 1. Inflammation particularly in left Achilles tendon. On examination: slight reddening around the skin, resembles streptococcal infection. Prescribe Fucidin cream tid, washing occasionally with soapy water.
> 2. The problem with regard to setting boundaries in relation to her domineering daughter has improved greatly now that the mother sets boundaries for herself.

The patient presents with a minor physical complaint and we talk about how she can become a better mother for her daughter by setting boundaries for herself - staying in her own area - instead of setting boundaries for her daughter - stamping on her and trying to solve the problems by subjugating her.

Either the daughter can be supported in applying her intelligence and her desire to cooperate - or an attempt can be made to condition her; in the same way that Pavlov trained his dogs. The former leads to lively, happy and healthy children, while the latter results in neurotic children and later in neurotic adults.

Discussion

Many parents do not understand the ill health of their child as they often have difficulties seeing the child's unfulfilled needs and the dysfunctional patterns in the family. The idea that psychosocial dynamics is a co-factor in the etiology is often strongly provoking, so the perspective must be presented wisely and cautiously to avoid psychological resistance with a poor outcome of holistic therapy.

Many parents hope that the disease of their child will be cured by a simple pharmacological treatment. When the child remain sick, parents will eventually, if guided by physician proficient in using the holistic tools (29) gradually open up to a psycho-social perspective, where the physician can support the development of the quality of life of the child and the quality of life in the whole family. Another problem more and more often seen in the clinic is the holistically oriented parent, who do not want to give the children the prescribed drugs. In this case holistic medicine is an obvious choice if appropriate in the situation.

Sometimes a biomedical treatment is needed also, like in the case, where antibiotics is the right choice to cure the child and here the role of the physician will be to teach the parents the use and limitations of the different medical paradigms (30) – a job that in the end might save even the life of the child. Developmental problems i.e. ADHD almost always take a holistic approach.

Conclusion

Many problems with children that can be noticed in the clinic are almost impossible for the parents to solve on their own. The holistically oriented physician, who understand that the child is the thermometer of the family functioning, and that the observed problems regarding thriving or behaviour are only a question of arrested psychosexual development, can easily alleviate the problem by accelerate the arrested development. In this way many future problems can be prevented or solved in an early phase.

Not only health problems, but also problems of poor thriving and behaviour i.e. ADHD in school or home can be addressed. When the physician takes on a role as coach and provide the family with small relevant exercises, even larger patterns of dysfunction can be turned. Consciousness-based medicine seems to be extremely efficient with children and adolescents, which are much more sensitive to the psychosocial dimensions than adults. Five needs seems to be essential for the thriving and health of the child: the need for attention, for respect, for love, for touch and for acknowledgment (28).

The physician should be able to see if the child lacks the fulfilment of one or more of these needs, and he can then demonstrate to the parents how these needs should be taken care of. This should be followed by simple instructions and exercises to the parents in the spirit of coaching. This approach is especially relevant, when the child is chronically ill.

References

[1] Polakow V, Halskov T, Jørgensen PS. Diminished rights. Vulnerable lone mothers and their children in Denmark. Bristol: Policy Press, 2001.

[2] Jørgensen PS. Familieliv i børnefamilien. In: Dencik L, Jørgensen, PS, eds. Børn og familie i det postmoderne samfund. Copenhagen: Hans Reitzel, 1999:108-131. [Danish].

[3] Jørgensen PS, Holstein BE, Due P. Sundhed på vippen. En undersøgelse af de store skolebørns sundhed, trivsel og velfærd. Copenhagen: Hans Reitzel, 2001. [Danish].

[4] Ventegodt S, Andersen NJ, Merrick J. Editorial: Five theories of human existence. ScientificWorldJournal 2003;3:1272-6.

[5] Ventegodt S. The life mission theory: A theory for a consciousness-based medicine. Int J Adolesc Med Health 2003;15(1):89-91.

[6] Ventegodt S, Andersen NJ, Merrick J. The life mission theory II: The structure of the life purpose and the ego. ScientificWorldJournal 2003;3:1277-85.

[7] Ventegodt S, Andersen NJ, Merrick J. The life mission theory III: Theory of talent. ScientificWorldJournal 2003;3:1286-93.

[8] Ventegodt S, Merrick J. The life mission theory IV. A theory of child development. ScientificWorldJournal 2003;3:1294-1301.

[9] Ventegodt S, Andersen NJ, Merrick J. The life mission theory V. A theory of the anti-self and explaining the evil side of man. ScientificWorldJournal 2003;3:1302-13.

[10] Ventegodt S, Andersen NJ, Merrick J. Holistic medicine: Scientific challenges. ScientificWorldJournal 2003;3:1108-16.

[11] Ventegodt S, Andersen NJ, Merrick J. Holistic Medicine II: The square-curve paradigm for research in alternative, complementary and holistic medicine: A cost-effective, easy and scientifically valid design for evidence based medicine. ScientificWorldJournal 2003;3:1117-27.

[12] Ventegodt S, Andersen NJ, Merrick J. Holistic Medicine III: The holistic process theory of healing. ScientificWorldJournal 2003;3:1138-46.

[13] Ventegodt S, Andersen NJ, Merrick J. Holistic Medicine IV: The principles of the holistic process of healing in a group setting. ScientificWorldJournal 2003;3:1294-1301.

[14] Ventegodt S, Andersen NJ, Merrick J. Quality of life theory I. The IQOL theory: An integrative theory of the global quality of life concept. ScientificWorldJournal 2003;3:1030-40.

[15] Ventegodt S, Merrick J, Andersen NJ. Quality of life theory II. Quality of life as the realization of life potential: A biological theory of human being. ScientificWorldJournal 2003;3:1041-9.

[16] Ventegodt S, Merrick J, Andersen NJ. Quality of life theory III. Maslow revisited. ScientificWorldJournal 2003;3:1050-7.

[17] Ventegodt S, Andersen NJ, Merrick J. Quality of life philosophy: when life sparkles or can we make wisdom a science? ScientificWorldJournal 2003;3:1160-3.

[18] Ventegodt S, Andersen NJ, Merrick J. QOL philosophy I: Quality of life, happiness, and meaning of life. ScientificWorldJournal 2003;3: 1164-75.

[19] Ventegodt S, Andersen NJ, Kromann M, Merrick J. QOL philosophy II: What is a human being? ScientificWorldJournal 2003;3:1176-85.

[20] Ventegodt S, Merrick J, Andersen NJ. QOL philosophy III: Towards a new biology. ScientificWorldJournal 2003;3:1186-98.

[21] Ventegodt S, Andersen NJ, Merrick J. QOL philosophy IV: The brain and consciousness. ScientificWorldJournal 2003;3:1199-1209.

[22] Ventegodt S, Andersen NJ, Merrick J. QOL philosophy V: Seizing the meaning of life and getting well again. ScientificWorldJournal 2003;3:1210-29.

[23] Ventegodt S, Andersen NJ, Merrick J. QOL philosophy VI: The concepts. ScientificWorldJournal 2003;3:1230-40.

[24] Merrick J, Ventegodt S. What is a good death? To use death as a mirror and find the quality in life. BMJ. Rapid Response 2003 Oct 31.

[25] Ventegodt S, Merrick J, Andersen NJ. Quality of life as medicine. A pilot study of patients with chronic illness and pain. ScientificWorld Journal 2003;3:520-32.

[26] Ventegodt S, Merrick J, Andersen NJ. Quality of life as medicine II. A pilot study of a five day "Quality of Life and Health" cure for patients with alcoholism. ScientificWorld Journal 2003;3:842-52.

[27] Ventegodt S, Clausen B, Langhorn M, Kromann M, Andersen NJ, Merrick J. Quality of Life as Medicine III. A qualitative analysis of the effect of a five days. intervention with existential holistic group therapy: a quality of life course as a modern rite of passage. ScientificWorld Journal 2004;4:124-33.

[28] Juul J. Your competent child: Toward new basic values for the family. New York: Farrar Straus Giroux, 2001.

[29] Ventegodt S, Morad M, Merrick J. Clinical holistic medicine: Prevention through healthy lifestyle and quality of life. Oral Health Prev Dent 2004;2(Suppl 1):239-45.

[30] Ventegodt S, Merrick J. Clinical holistic medicine: The "new medicine", the multi-paradigmatic physician and the medical record. ScientificWorldJournal 2004;4:273-85.

Chapter 42

Adolescent holistic medicine

Effective caring for adolescents hinges on trust. Establishment of trusting relationships with health care providers opens the door for discussion of sensitive issues such as, sexuality and risk-taking behavior. Methods to gain trust on the part of the provider include: being relaxed, genuine, friendly, open, making eye contact. Additionally, being an authority not authoritarian, and understanding that development of full trust may take time. Adolescents view health care providers as an important source for information and education especially regarding healthy sexual development.

Mental problems are a normal part of puberty and even more severe mental symptoms should be seen as problems regarding psychosexual development with the problematic development supported. Rehabilitation of self-esteem might be the key to normalization.

Introduction

Understanding adolescent development and the psychosocial developmental stages of adolescence is helpful and necessary for anyone working with adolescents. Adolescents undergo three stages of development: early adolescence (ages 12-14 years), middle adolescence (15-17 years), and late adolescence (18-20 years) (1). Early adolescence is characterized by concrete thinking necessitating the importance of keeping explanations short and to the point. In contrast, middle adolescence is defined by the development of abstract thinking. Risk-taking behavior is mostly likely to occur within this age group and peer influence is significant (1). Older adolescence is the transition to adulthood. Adolescents in this age group have a clear understanding that their actions will result in consequences. Yet they still need support and encouragement to understand that they should make their own health care decisions.

Effective caring for adolescents hinges on trust. Establishment of trusting relationships with health care providers opens the door for discussion of sensitive issues such as, sexuality and risk-taking behavior (1). Methods to gain trust on the part of the provider include: being relaxed, genuine, friendly, open, making eye contact. Additionally, being an authority not authoritarian, and understanding that development of full trust may take time (1). Adolescents view health care providers as an important source for information and education especially regarding healthy sexual development (2).

Leading causes of mortality and morbidity in adolescents continue to be mainly preventable, such as: accidents, homicide, suicide, sexually transmitted infections, teen pregnancy, eating disorders and drug abuse related consequences (3). All these factors in morbidity and mortality are directly related to risk-taking behaviors (3). The above factors were part of the development of adolescent medicine as a new subspecialty (4-6), while continuing to be an integral part of general practice. With the teenagers preventive medicine is extraordinarily important as so many problems are preventable in this age: pregnancy and contraception (7), HIV (8,9), substance use and abuse (10-12), ethics, law, sports (13), violence (14), prostitution and victimization (15). In adolescent medicine, knowledge of psychosomatics is very important as they are related to the 20-30% of the teenagers suffering from either chronic pains (16), psychiatric disturbances (17-19), eating disturbances (20-22), vulvodynia and other gynaecological problems (23-25). Many of the problems can be seen as disturbances in the teenagers psycho-social and sexual development, often with patterns going back to their childhood (26).

As an example, fifty percent of both anorectic and bulimic patients reported a history of sexual abuse, while only 28% of a non-anorexic, non-bulimic control population reported similar problems (27) leading the authors to recommend that sexual issues be addressed early in the treatment of patients with eating disorders. In this article we will attempt to illustrate the need for more comprehensive and preventive approach to the adolescent in the clinical setting for a better outcome.

Case story 1

14 year old girl referred to our clinic for evaluation of recurrent pelvic pain. She was seen in the emergency department seven days ago, where she was diagnosed with pelvic inflammatory disease. Review of the emergency department physician records showed "Sexually active teen with multiple partners, diagnosis: pelvic inflammatory disease, standard treatment regimen prescribed".. During interview in our clinic, the patient appeared depressed, shy, not making eye contact and complained of recurrent abdominal and pelvic pain for the last six years. Once a rapport was established, the patient disclosed that she had been sexually abused by her biological father since age five, until she became pregnant at age 11 years.

At that time the father was sent to prison, the patient underwent elective abortion and her parents divorced. A year later the mother remarried and the stepfather also started abusing the patient sexually. At that point both her mother and stepfather were imprisoned and the patient was taken into state custody, where she has been placed in 13 different foster homes over a two-year period.

During that time, she has been occasionally seen by a psychologist and given antidepressant medication. Her main question in our clinic was "I am worthless, nobody likes or wants me, why would you be any different and can you change my life?"

Case story 2

14 year-old girl referred to our clinic for evaluation of "conduct problems".. According to her mother, during a church sponsored trip, the patient was caught having sex with a male of the same age in the back of the bus, she also had multiple school absences and possible drug use. She has been seen by a psychiatrist and placed on antidepressant medication. In our clinic, the patient stated that "I am a worthless person, why should I go to school".. Ultimately we found out that the father was from eastern Indian origin and the mother a religious fanatic. When the patient was born after unplanned pregnancy, the father refused to marry or to recognize the child until three years later, when he finally married the mother and had two further children. During the patient's life however the father never treated her as his child and always put her down, while loving his other children and treating them well. The mother was always after her, because she is "Godless". The patient said "I do not like or enjoy sex, I do it hoping to get someone to like me". The patient is very intelligent and beautiful with very low self-esteem. She feels hopeless, ugly and unloved, but is not planning suicide, because "that is what everybody wants, to get rid of me". She said: "At least boys care for me, if I have sex with them, but my parents do not no matter what I do". In response to the question about taking her antidepressant, she says: "Yes, I am taking my medicine daily, but do you really believe that it will make my life better?"

Discussion

Adolescents are basically healthy in the physical sense and most of their morbidity and mortality are due to preventable causes that are the product of risk taking behavior. This is the result of either poor quality of life, problems in development or combination of multiple factors. Attempting to help these adolescents with a dogmatic, narrow-minded approach may frequently fail as illustrated by the cases above. Often adolescents present at the clinic with a host of complaints that have nothing to do with their actual problem with the hope of finding help from the physician, who may be able to figure out the real agenda behind their complaints. Over the past three years, a total of 132 adolescents were referred to one of our clinics for evaluation of long lasting recurrent abdominal pain and only three (2.34%) had an actual physical pathology.

The patients in the cases above cannot be helped with a simple approach: you are depressed, here is a prescription for antidepressant and you will attend weekly counseling. Their quality of life is very poor and until that changes, they will continue to have problems. The holistic approach to adolescents, helps define their quality of life, find out the underlying causes of their problem and if there is a good social system, that will help alleviate their suffering and provide them with a better quality of life. In a survey of adolescents in Europe, 10% reported having chronic illness and only 10-15% thought they were healthy (28).

Adolescent medicine specialists tend to be more active in screening adolescents for quality of life issues and risk taking behaviors. The initial visit by an adolescent to any clinic, especially to a reproductive health care provider may illicit fear and anxiety among adolescents, however simple guidelines outlined by Burgis and Bacon (1) can help set the ground work for a positive experience for patient and provider. Tips for an initial visit include, a) an interview that should be conducted with the teen fully clothed, b) an interview with limited interruptions, c) inquiry about and assessment of the home situation, d) learning about the adolescents relationship with parents, peers and school environment. Establishment and maintenance of confidentiality, as well as trust, cannot be over emphasized. A successful visit also encompasses the encouragement of forthright conversations with a parent or trusted adult regarding sexuality. Adolescents living in a perceived supportive environment report more communication with sexual partners about sexual risks, close relationships with supportive parents seem to be related to later onset of sexual activity and improved contraceptive use. In contrast less frequent parent/adolescent communication is associated with less contraceptive use, lower self-efficacy to negotiate safe sex and less communication between adolescents and their sexual partners (1).

Conclusions

Adolescents are a vulnerable population, undergoing a complicated development. This development occurs in the context of external factors: peers, family, school and society as a whole. Interruption of the normal development process or changes in perceived quality of life may lead to risk taking behaviors above and beyond the usual experimentation by the adolescent and may lead to chronic morbidity or early mortality. A holistic approach to the adolescent that includes investigating quality of life issues and provides proper rapport and caring may help prevent significant mortality and morbidity in this population. The rehabilitation of self-esteem is often followed by spontaneos recovery from mental symptoms.

References

[1]   Burgis JT, Bacon JL. Communicating with the adolescent gynecology patient. Obstet Gynecol Clin 2003;30(2):1-9.
[2]   Blythe M J, Rosenthal SL. Female adolescent sexuality. Obstet Gynecol Clin North Am 2000;27(1), 125-141.
[3]   Centers for Disease Control and Prevention. Surveillance Summaries. MMWR 2004:53.
[4]   Alderman EM, Rieder J, Cohen MI. The history of adolescent medicine. Pediatr Res 2003;54(1):137-47.
[5]   Joffe A. Why adolescent medicine? Med Clin North Am 2000;84(4):769-85.
[6]   Mackenzie RG. Adolescent medicine: a model for the millennium. Adolesc Med 2000;11(1):13-8.
[7]   Bradford BJ, Lyons CW. Adolescent medicine practice in urban Pittsburgh--1990. Clin Pediatr (Phila) 1992;31(8):471-7.
[8]   Murphy DA, Moscicki AB, Vermund SH, Muenz LR. Psychological distress among HIV(+) adolescents in the REACH study: effects of life stress, social support, and coping. The Adolescent Medicine HIV/AIDS Research Network. J Adolesc Health 2000;27(6):391-8.
[9]   Holland CA, Ma Y, Moscicki B, Durako SJ, Levin L, Wilson CM. Seroprevalence and risk factors of hepatitis B, hepatitis C, and human cytomegalovirus among HIV-infected and high-risk uninfected adolescents: findings of the REACH Study. Adolescent Medicine HIV/AIDS Research Network. Sex Transm Dis 2000;27(5):296-303.
[10] 10, Ungemack JA, Hartwell SW, Babor TF. Alcohol and drug abuse among Connecticut youth: implications for adolescent medicine and public health. Conn Med 1997;61(9):577-85.
[11] Hicks RD, Bemis Batzer G, Bemis Batzer W, Imai WK. Psychiatric, Developmental, and Adolescent Medicine Issues in Adolescent Substance Use and Abuse. Adolesc Med 1993;4(2):453-68.

[12] Adger H Jr, DeAngelis CD. Adolescent medicine. JAMA 1994;271(21):1651-3.

[13] Saperstein AL, Nicholas SJ. Pediatric and adolescent sports medicine. Pediatr Clin North Am 1996;43(5):1013-33.

[14] Wilson MD, Joffe A. Adolescent medicine. JAMA 1995;273(21):1657-9.

[15] Johnson RL, Shrier DK. Sexual victimization of boys. Experience at an adolescent medicine clinic. J Adolesc Health Care 1985;6(5):372-6.

[16] Strasburger VC, Reeve A. The adolescent with chronic pains: Basic principles of psychosomatic medicine. Adolesc Med 1991;2(3):677-96.

[17] Fisman S, Sangster J, Steele MM, Stewart MA, Rae-Grant N. Teaching child and adolescent psychiatry to family medicine trainees: a pilot experience. Can J Psychiatry 1996;41(10):623-8.

[18] DuPont RL, Saylor KE. Depressant substances in adolescent medicine. Pediatr Rev 1992;13(10):381-6.

[19] Bartlett JA, Schleifer SJ, Johnson RL, Keller SE. Depression in inner city adolescents attending an adolescent medicine clinic. J Adolesc Health 1991;12(4):316-8.

[20] Fisher M, Burns J, Symons H, Schneider M. Treatment of eating disorders in a division of adolescent medicine. Int J Adolesc Med Health 2002;14(4):283-95.

[21] Luiselli JK, Medeiros J, Jasinowski C, Smith A, Cameron MJ. Behavioral medicine treatment of ruminative vomiting and associated weight loss in an adolescent with autism. J Autism Dev Disord 1994;24(5):619-29.

[22] Silber TJ, Delaney D, Samuels J. Anorexia nervosa. Hospitalization on adolescent medicine units and third-party payments. J Adolesc Health Care 1989;10(2):122-5.

[23] Rabinovitz S, Neinstein LS, Shapiro J. Effect of an adolescent medicine rotation on pelvic examination skills of paediatric residents. Med Educ 1987; 21(3):219-26.

[24] Reed BD, Haefner HK, Cantor L. Vulvar dysesthesia (vulvodynia). A follow-up study. J Reprod Med 2003;48(6):409-16.

[25] Newman DK. Pelvic disorders in women: chronic pelvic pain and vulvodynia. Ostomy Wound Manage 2000;46(12):48-54.

[26] Ventegodt S, Merrick J. The life mission theory IV. A theory of child development. ScientificWorldJournal 2003;3:1294-1301.

[27] Tice L, Hall RC, Beresford TP, Quinones J, Hall AK. Sexual abuse in patients with eating disorders. Psychiatr Med 1989;7(4):257-67.

[28] Suris J, Blum RW. Adolescent health in Europe: An overview. Int J Adolesc Med Health 2001;13(2):91-9.

Chapter 43

Chronic pain in the locomotor system

In children and teenagers the distance between mind and body observed in adults rarely exists. This means that mental and emotional problems – psychosexual developmental disturbances – often somatise and present as physical pain. To help these patients the psychosomatic pain must be taken well care of.

Most pains from the locomotor system arise due to involuntary, chronic tensions in the muscles or other tissues. When the patient is motivated, the pain is easily cured in most of the cases by using the tools of consciousness-based medicine, primarily therapeutic touch, conversation, and coaching the patient in a positive philosophy of life. The pains are often caused by "blockages" that may cause problems other than just pain. Often it turns out that the blocked areas develop actual physical damage over time: a slipped disk in the back, articular degeneration, or osteoarthritis when the cartilage is affected, can often be explained in this way. Apparently, the exact areas where the blockage is situated cause cellular problems, disrupting cellular order.

The holistic process theory of healing and the related quality of life theories state that return to the natural state of being is possible, whenever the person gets the resources needed for existential healing. The resources needed are "holding" in the dimensions of awareness, respect, care, acknowledgment, and acceptance with support and processing in the dimensions of feeling, understanding, and letting go of negative attitudes and beliefs. The preconditions for holistic healing are trust and the intention for the healing to take place.

Case stories of holistic treatment of patients with chronic back pain, low back pain, muscle problems, knee pain, and symptoms of rheumatoid arthritis are discussed with exercises relevant for patients with these conditions in the holistic clinic.

Introduction

Pain is the most common reason for consultation with a physician (1). Many of these pains are not cured by standard biomedical treatment (2), but become chronic with staggering negative health and economic consequences (3). Pain is an extremely complex and difficult subject as it involves a whole range of aspects of the human being from the most bodily-physical to the most mental and spiritual (2-5). Pain in children and teenagers can be caused by physical disease, but are more likely somatisations of emotional and psychosexual problems.

Emotions seems to play an important role and pain is statistically connected to depression and anxiety (6). The problem is that the pain will not go away, no matter what, and experiments with alternative methods like psychotherapy (7), relaxation techniques (8), and "spiritual healing" (9,10) seem only to have very limited effect.

When in severe or constant pain in the locomotor system, most patients go to see a physician and, in our experience, many patients can obtain partial or complete freedom from pain with consciousness-based holistic medicine. This is not the case when we are talking about terminal cancer or other terminal diseases, but even many of these patients can benefit from a holistic approach, as most patients have large hidden resources they can use. However, to obtain pain relief, the patient must be dedicated to develop into a more positive and happy individual who is less tense about him/herself and life. In our natural state, which holistic medicine helps us to recover, life is good and does not make the body hurt.

About 20% of the Danish population suffers from chronic pain and both children and adults are affected (11). Often the pain of the locomotor system is in the neck, upper or lower back, shoulders, elbows, knees, hands, or feet. Closer analysis shows that pain is often located in particularly sensitive areas in muscles, tendons, connective tissues, joints, and bones. These areas are often called trigger points and are located in the parts of the body where we find most local tensions or blockages.

There are many theories about why we have those tensions. The most common explanation is that tension is due to tenseness, meaning a tendency to develop a "tense" personality. Instead of relaxing and being our own good self, we strain ourselves in many ways, consciously or unconsciously. We become tense while trying to fit, cope, and adapt in a different way than we actually are deep down in our nature. The tensions go all the way down to the deepest level of our existence. As we find this level (our soul or whole being) causal to the pain, this is the level we primarily address in our holistic medicine.

Clinical holistic medicine

The life mission theory (12-17) states that everybody has a purpose of life or huge talent. Happiness comes from living this purpose and succeeding in expressing the core talent in life. To do this, it is important to develop as a person into what is known as the natural condition, a condition where the person knows himself and uses all efforts to achieve what is most important for him. The holistic process theory of healing (18-21) and the related quality of life theories (22,23,24) state that the return to the natural state of being is possible whenever the person gets the resources needed for existential healing.

The resources needed are "holding" in the dimensions of awareness, respect, care, acknowledgment, and acceptance with support and processing in the dimensions of feeling, understanding, and letting go of negative attitudes and beliefs. The preconditions for holistic healing are trust and the intention for the healing to take place. Existential healing is not a local healing of any tissue, but a healing of the wholeness of the person, making him much more resourceful, loving, and knowledgeable of himself, his needs, and his wishes. In letting go of negative attitudes and beliefs, the person returns to a more responsible existential position and an improved quality of life.

The philosophical change of the person healing is often a change towards preferring difficult problems and challenges, instead of avoiding difficulties in life (25-32). The person who becomes happier and more resourceful often also becomes more healthy, more talented, and more able to function (33-35).

Case stories from the holistic clinic

Blockages encompass old feelings and can be dissolved once the feelings are liberated. It is difficult to explain the pain from "tensions", because we cannot just feel joint capsules or bones where blockages are sometimes located. Since it is often possible to provoke pain by pressing swollen or tense body areas without any muscle function (for instance, connective tissue above the sternum or fatty tissue above the low back), there must be some other explanation. Blockages are not tensions in the traditional sense, although they may be the cause of chronic muscle tensions.

> Female, aged 30 years, with pain in fingers
> A 30-year-old woman presents with large swollen and tender finger joints. Signs of inflammation – sterile inflammation – and blood test results consistent with arthritis. The question is how the patient can strain her finger joints. By touch and massage ("manipulation") of the joints in her fingers, hands, arms, legs, feet and spinal column in holistic body therapy, an emotional tension was "released", as the patient becomes cross, angry and grumpy during the intense body therapy. Subsequently in gestalt therapy, the patient verbalised her feelings and finally understood who she is cross with and why. The arthritic symptoms – swelling and pain – vanished during the weeks that followed.

Clinical experience indicates that physical pain can be released when the patient can accommodate emotional pain. In holistic medicine, the theory concerning chronic pain in the locomotor system is supported by clinical experience. When patients are touched on tense and tender areas of the body, they often come into contact with old, unresolved problems and painful feelings from their personal lives.

> Male, aged 39 years, with low back pain
> A 39-year-old man suffering from recurrent low back pain. Examination: his back is very tense and the facet joints in the low back have almost come apart in some places. Conversation revealed that he was suffering from anxiety. During gestalt therapy his anxiety was released, when he looked at his relationship with his authoritarian mother. Afterwards the back pain was resolved and did not return.

When the patients remembered and fully understood what went wrong, the blockage and the pain disappeared. This experience forms the basis of the Rosen method (36) and holistic body therapy.

Blockages that are not released can cause tissue damage

Blockages may cause problems other than just pain. Often it turns out that the blocked areas develop actual physical damage over time such as a slipped disk in the back, articular degeneration, or osteoarthritis when the cartilage is affected. Apparently, the exact areas where the blockage is situated cause cellular problems, disrupting cellular order. This disruption is reversible. The renowned international medical textbook, Harrison's Internal Medicine, states that even degenerated cartilage, as it occurs in osteoarthritis, is sometimes seen on X-rays to have regenerated. That is the sort of healing effect that may occur once blockages around the joint are released. We have performed pilot studies in groups of pain patients with a regime combining life philosophy, psychotherapy, and body therapy. Some of the participants had severe physical disabilities and damage. The preliminary results of treating patients with different diagnoses indicate that, in general, working on the release of blockages in the body can be an effective way of abolishing chronic pain.

> Female, aged 38 years, with chronic back pain
> Conversation: She has had chronic back pain for over 12 years. On examination: Very tense in back muscles between iliac crest and column. She believes that the pain has a psychological explanation. She wants to work on herself to get rid of pain and arrive highly motivated. Subjective: She explains that her younger brother is mentally ill – anxiety, depression and attempted suicide – and starts crying. There have also been problems with the parents. "I am the one who has to cope with it all," she says when we talk about self-esteem, "but I'm not there." She can see that she is suppressing her feelings to make herself strong, and that this is how she avoids being present in life. She can feel that she does so by tensing the low back, exactly where it hurts. EXERCISE for next time: "Find out where you are – where did you go?"

PLAN: When she is ready, she should have physiotherapy with massaging of back. Once one has seen how people suppress their lives to adjust to people around them, this pattern becomes easily recognizable in the patient. This woman has completely opted out of her own existence to be as sensible as she felt she needed to be in order to survive at the social level. The problem is that in the middle of all her control and sense, she is not at all present as a human being with feelings and presence.

She is hiding; she has fled life. Unfortunately, the feelings of anxiety and discomfort are parked in her upper and lower back as tension, and that gives her great problems. Once she learns to apply herself better, her chronic back pain will go away. This typically takes six sessions over 3 months of exercise and assignments.

> Male, aged 51 years, with chronic back pain
> His back snapped following construction work. Pain and some throbbing down into the legs. Saw a chiropractor twice with no effect. On examination: no significant back pathology (in spite of X-rays), swollen and tender at sacroiliac joints and piriformis, which are massaged with some effect. The patient believes that this is old damage that cannot be helped. Very tense between shoulder blades, where the back has not yet "snapped". Manipulation not possible, because of muscle tension. He will come back for treatment of this region and further assessment in 14 days. EXERCISE: Pelvic exercises and examine at home why he is so tense.

The idea that the body is a machine that may break down irretrievably is widespread. If you understand the body the way we do, as a dynamic colony of cells controlled by the information flow, you would have to smile wryly at remarks of the type made by this patient: "Old damage that cannot be helped." When people "break their back", they believe that the back is almost torn apart, never to be put together again, like a trunk that has broken. In general, it is quite astonishing how little patients know about the anatomy of the back. Fortunately back problems can usually be resolved when the patient finds out why he or she is tense and tackles the underlying emotional issue. Once the patient has assumed responsibility for this, it is usually possible to manipulate the vertebrae back into place. Actually, vertebrae and joints, which can be quite distorted and shifted in relation to each other, will usually fall spontaneously into place once the muscles relax. Often a 10-minute talk on the couch before the manipulation will do the trick. It is peculiar how you tear and press and nothing happens, then you talk for a while and snap!.... it yields to the smallest pressure and the pain goes away.

> Male, aged 61 years, with chronic back pain for 20 years
> Immigrant presenting with back pain dating back 20 years. He has taken analgesics over the years. Now distinct tenderness (doorbell) corresponding to about L2. No other symptoms. Says chiropractor could not help. Remarkably rigid gait. Needs to exercise his back. Instructed in back exercises. Advised to swim once or twice a day. The effect will take a while to appear, perhaps months or years. But that is the only way out of the problem.

Cultural differences and language barriers mean that we cannot apply a psychosomatic approach, but must try a combination of exercise and remarks to strengthen the patient's physical confidence. This is harder work, painful and sad.

> Female, aged 24 years, with low back pain
> Presents with low back pain corresponding to right sacroiliac joint (between os sacrum and pelvis). On examination: Articular tenderness consistent with /sprained left sacroiliac joint/. Very tense in scalenus muscles, neck, shoulders and particularly the center of the back, where large groups of muscle are organised as tethered and tense muscular masses causing /enlarged kyphotic curve/ that is compensated by /enlarged low-back lordosis/, which is presumably the cause of the low back pain. So the problem lies in the tensions. We talk about where they come from and the patient mentions her parents' divorce. EXERCISE: Tilting and rotating the pelvis ("pelvic rotations" (good exercise in which the patient swings the abdomen around in a horizontal circle in a diameter of about one metre)). Can return if the problem persists.

Young people almost never process their parent's divorce. It is quite surprising how little it takes to start relevant processing. When the patient has some exercises that gently release the blockages from the body, combined with one that supports processing of the emotional trauma, a clear and motivated individual can rid himself of a chronic, low back condition fairly rapidly. Other times it may bother him for years.

Male, aged 61 years, with severe pain in thigh following intercourse

Left thigh very sore, daily attacks corresponding to posterior side of thigh, a piercing, throbbing, hammering pain, sometimes the whole day, sometimes up to a whole week after intercourse. Pain brought on by flexing of hips. Rectal exploration: no tumours, no tenderness, nothing abnormal. Free hernial orifices. Muscle tension corresponding to quadriceps femoris and psoas major muscles. The familiar pain is induced by pressing on these muscles. /Muscle pain/ – does not want analgesics. He is instructed to try to breathe instead of tensing up and shutting off at attacks. Can come back if pain persists; then we shall have another talk about medication.

When the familiar pain is induced by pressing on certain muscles, the patient knows that we are aware of his pain and why he is in pain. This means that the patient should be given a confrontational exercise where he can use his breathing (breathe in deeply and into the abdomen and then exhale) to be present when he is cramped and sore. That can often deal with the problem. The focused consciousness, where you become more familiar with yourself and your body, is a brilliant tool for the patient to use.

Male, aged 30 years, with knee pain

Presents with problems in left knee: hurts after he
has been sitting for 10 min. On examination: oedema in legs and around the knee. Talk about job, using the body, etc. We talk about him getting away from cyberspace (spending hours on the Internet) and finding a girlfriend – getting out into the world where his body is. His body would benefit from that. Guidance. Get a life! The body does not much like sitting in front of a computer screen day in, day out, completely denied by its owner.

Female, aged 55 years, with muscle problems

QOL conversation: Problems with muscles, tendons and joints for 12 years. Pain and reduced strength, particularly in the arms, the left being worse. Reduced mobility of shoulder. On examination: very small muscles that are chronically tense and resemble "steel strings" in shoulder girdle. Seems to be as frozen as an ice-lolly in the upper part of the chest. We talk about feelings, which in my opinion do not come alive in the patient. It is as if she is very warm, but has decided to be cold. PLAN: The patient is adept at avoiding emotional pain, so we prescribe Rosen method 6 times every 14 days, which supports the patient in registering all those old, painful feelings that she has denied. EXERCISE: Welcome all negative feelings. Be with them, inside them, allow them space. Come back in three months.

Some patients are really hard to get through to. It is good for them to lie on a couch and feel, feel, feel, until one day they finally realize what it is all about. Then they can come back to our clinic and unable us to move on.

Discussion

Pain in children and teenagers can be somatizations of emotional and psychosexual developmental problems. The understanding of this fact empowers the holistic physician to intervene and cure the pain by accelerating the arrested development.

The case stories show, in many different ways, how the physician assuming the holistic medical perspective addresses the physical pain. Not all patients welcome this perspective, as it inevitably ends with the patient going through often severe emotional difficulties, confronting negative attitudes and shadowy aspects of their own existence. A lot of trust in the physician is necessary before the holistic toolbox (37) can be used freely. To win the trust, the physician needs to care for his patient and express this care, which is difficult for many physicians with traditional biomedical training. When the trust is won, the patient must accept the holding and support and in this privileged state, the patient can heal.

Therapeutic touch (38) is often helpful when trust is obtained. Often the problems are more of a social type than of a somatic type (39). What might look easily treatable turns out to be very difficult, unless the social circumstance is handled successfully through coaching of the patient to help him create value and mobilize resources and talent in the social relationships. Sometimes, the physician must face severe problems connected with interpersonal chemistry; this is the case when he has something to learn from his patient because he is not sufficiently developed in the existential aspects relevant for the holistic treatment of this special patient (18).

Most pain from the locomotor system arises because of involuntary, chronic tensions in the muscles or other tissues. When the patient is motivated, the pain is easily cured in most of the cases by using the tools of consciousness-based medicine, primarily therapeutic touch, conversation, and coaching the patient in a philosophy of life that supports life and a constructive behavior. As previously discussed, the holistic process theory of healing (18-21) and the related quality of life theories (22-24) state that the return to the natural state of being is possible whenever the person gets the resources needed for existential healing.

The resources needed are holding in the dimensions of awareness, respect, care, acknowledgment, and acceptance with support and processing in the dimensions of feeling, understanding, and letting go of negative attitudes and beliefs. The precondition for the holistic healing is deep trust and the intention of the healing to take place.

The holistic cure for chronic pains and discomfort can be used on almost all patients independent of the site and affected tissue, but the efficiency of the cure has yet to be documented clinically in larger series of patients.

The treatment of children and teenagers must always involve an analysis of the whole family and its function as pain in children can be an indication of dysfunctional family patterns.

References

[1]   McGuire D, Luther RR, DuBois M. The management of severe chronic pain with a focus on new treatment modalities. Drugs Today (Barc) 1998;34(5):481–86.

[2]   Rosenow JM, Henderson JM. Anatomy and physiology of chronic pain. Neurosurg Clin North Am 2003;14(3):445–62.

[3]   Holden JE, Pizzi JA. The challenge of chronic pain. Adv Drug Deliv Rev 2003;55(8):935–48.

[4]   McCaffrey R, Frock TL, Garguilo H. Understanding chronic pain and the mind-body connection. Holist Nurs Pract 2003;17(6):281–7.

[5]   Rashbaum IG, Sarno JE. Psychosomatic concepts in chronic pain. Arch Phys Med Rehabil 2003;84(3 Suppl 1):S76–80.

[6]   McWilliams LA, Cox BJ, Enns MW. Mood and anxiety disorders associated with chronic pain: an examination in a nationally representative sample. Pain 2003;106(1–2):127–33.

[7]   Tumlin TR, Kvaal S. Psychotherapeutic issues encountered in the psychotherapy of chronic pain patients. Curr Pain Headache Rep 2004;8(2):125–9.

[8]   Lecky C. Are relaxation techniques effective in relief of chronic pain? Work 1999;13(3):249–56.

[9]   Abbot NC, Harkness EF, Stevinson C, Marshall FP, Conn DA, Ernst E. Spiritual healing as a therapy for chronic pain: a randomized, clinical trial. Pain 2001;91(1–2):79–89.

[10] Sundblom DM, Haikonen S, Niemi-Pynttari J, Tigerstedt I. Effect of spiritual healing on chronic idiopathic pain: a medical and psychological study. Clin J Pain 1994;10(4):296–302.

[11] Ventegodt S. [Livskvalitet I Danmark.] Quality of Life in Denmark. Results from a Population Survey. Copenhagen: Forskningscentrets Forlag, 1995. [Partly in Danish].

[12] Ventegodt S, Andersen NJ, Merrick J. Five theories of the human existence. ScientificWorldJournal 2003;3:1272–6.

[13] Ventegodt S. The life mission theory: a theory for a consciousness-based medicine. Int J Adolesc Med Health 2003;;15(1):89–91.

[14] Ventegodt S, Andersen NJ, Merrick J. The life mission theory II. The structure of the life purpose and the ego. ScientificWorldJournal 2003;3:1277–85.

[15] Ventegodt S, Andersen NJ, Merrick J. The life mission theory III. Theory of talent. ScientificWorldJournal 2003;3:1286–93.

[16] Ventegodt S, Merrick J. The life mission theory IV. A theory of child development. ScientificWorldJournal 2003;3:1294–1301.

[17] Ventegodt S, Andersen NJ, Merrick J. The life mission theory V. Theory of the anti-self (the shadow) or the evil side of man. ScientificWorldJournal 2003;3:1302–13.

[18] Ventegodt S, Andersen NJ, Merrick J. Holistic medicine: scientific challenges. ScientificWorldJournal 2003;3:1108–16.

[19] Ventegodt S, Andersen NJ, Merrick J. The square curve paradigm for research in alternative, complementary, and holistic medicine: a cost-effective, easy, and scientifically valid design for evidence-based medicine and quality improvement. ScientificWorldJournal 2003;3:1117–27.

[20] Ventegodt S, Andersen NJ, Merrick J. Holistic medicine III: the holistic process theory of healing. ScientificWorldJournal 2003;3:1138–46.

[21] Ventegodt S, Merrick J. The life mission theory IV. A theory of child development. ScientificWorldJournal 2003;3:1294–1301.

[22] Ventegodt S, Merrick J, Andersen NJ. Quality of life theory I. The IQOL theory: an integrative theory of the global quality of life concept. ScientificWorldJournal 2003;3:1030–40.

[23] Ventegodt S, Merrick J, Andersen NJ. Quality of life theory II. Quality of life as the realization of life potential: a biological theory of human being. ScientificWorldJournal 203;3:1041–9.

[24] Ventegodt S, Merrick J, Andersen NJ. Quality of life theory III. Maslow revisited. ScientificWorldJournal 2003;3:1050–7.

[25] Ventegodt S, Andersen NJ, Merrick J. Quality of life philosophy: when life sparkles or can we make wisdom a science? ScientificWorldJournal 2003;3:1160–3.

[26] Ventegodt S, Andersen NJ, Merrick J. Quality of life philosophy I. Quality of life, happiness, and meaning of life. ScientificWorldJournal 2003;3:1164–75.

[27] Ventegodt S, Andersen NJ, Kromann M, Merrick J. Quality of life philosophy II. What is a human being? ScientificWorldJournal 2003;3:1176–85.

[28] Ventegodt S, Merrick J, Andersen NJ. Quality of life philosophy III. Towards a new biology. ScientificWorldJournal 2003;3:1186–98.

[29] Ventegodt S, Andersen NJ, Merrick J. Quality of life philosophy IV. The brain and consciousness. ScientificWorldJournal 2003;3:1199–1209.

[30] Ventegodt S, Andersen NJ, Merrick J. Quality of life philosophy V. Seizing the meaning of life and becoming well again. ScientificWorldJournal 2003;3:1210–29.

[31] Ventegodt S, Andersen NJ, Merrick J. Quality of life philosophy VI. The concepts. ScientificWorldJournal 2003;3:1230–40.

[32] Merrick J, Ventegodt S. What is a good death? To use death as a mirror and find the quality in life. BMJ Rapid Response, 2003 Oct 31 October.

[33] Ventegodt S, Merrick J, Andersen NJ. Quality of life as medicine: a pilot study of patients with chronic illness and pain. ScientificWorldJournal 2003;3:520–32.

[34] Ventegodt S, Merrick J, Andersen NJ. Quality of life as medicine II. A pilot study of a five-day "quality of life and health" cure for patients with alcoholism. ScientificWorldJournal 2003;3:842–52.

[35] Ventegodt S, Clausen B, Langhorn M, Kromann M, Andersen, NJ and Merrick J. Quality of life as medicine III. A qualitative analysis of the effect of a five-day intervention with existential holistic group therapy: a quality of life course as a modern rite of passage. ScientificWorldJournal 2004;4:124–33.

[36] Rosen M, Brenner S. Rosen method bodywork. Accessing the unconscious through touch. Berkeley, CA: North Atlantic Books, 2004.

[37] Ventegodt S, Morad M, Andersen NJ, Merrick J. Clinical holistic medicine: tools for a medical science based on consciousness. ScientificWorldJournal 2004;4:347–61.

[38] Ventegodt S, Morad M, Merrick J. Clinical holistic medicine: classic art of healing or the therapeutic touch. ScientificWorldJournal 2004;4:134–47.

[39] Ventegodt S, Morad M, Kandel I, Merrick J. Clinical holistic medicine: social problems disguised as illness. ScientificWorldJournal 2004;4:286–94.

Chapter 44

Chronic pain in internal organs and genitals

Holistic medicine seems able to work in the treatment of chronic pain in the internal organs, including the genitals, especially when the pain has no known cause. It is quite surprising that while chronic pains can be one of the toughest challenges in the biomedical clinic, it is often possible to alleviate in the holistic clinic.

These pains are regarded as caused by repressed emotions and explained as a psychosomatic reaction. Using holistic medicine, the patient can often be cured of the sufferings, when he or she assumes responsibility for the repressed feelings. The holistic process theory of healing states that the return to the natural (pain free) state of being is possible, whenever the person obtains the resources needed for the existential healing. This shift is explained by the related quality of life and life mission theories.

The resources needed are "holding" or genuine care in the dimensions: awareness, respect, care, acknowledgment and acceptance with support and processing in the dimensions: feeling, understanding and letting go of negative attitudes and beliefs.

The preconditions for the holistic healing to take place are "love" and trust by obtaining full confidence of the patient, which seems to be the biggest challenge of holistic medicine, especially when dealing with a patient in pain.

For the holistic physicians or psychiatrist as well as the sexologst the patients chronic sexual or genital pain (dyspareuni, vulvodyni etc) is often a challenge, and often patients have their genital pains almost unchanged for many years in spite of visiting physicians, gynechologists and sexologists. But genital pain follows the same basic pattern of establishment (patogenesis) and healing (salutogenesis) as all other chronic pain syndroms caused by psychosocial, "non-organic" ("non-anatomic") causes. Understanding the elementary dynamics regarding pain and healing empowers the holistic psychiatrist to help the majority of patients with sexual and genital pain. As many of these patients end up in psychiatric treatment as the biomedical physicians give up on them, this is an important observation.

Introduction

About one in twenty Danes suffer from recurrent or chronic pain in their internal organs (1). If we use the example of chronic pelvic pain (2), it can result from a variety of abdominal and pelvic causes, including endometriosis, pelvic inflammatory disease, adhesions, urogenital causes and from bladder complaints, including overactive bladder, urinary tract infection and interstitial cystitis (IC). Often, there seems to be no medical explanation for the pain – apparently there is no ill health that can be detected within the internal organs (i.e. the stomach, intestines, gall bladder, pancreas, liver, bladder, kidneys or reproductive organs). In spite of numerous in-depth medical examinations nothing is revealed. Nevertheless, the pain such as for example primary vulvodynia (3) continues even for years resulting in severe disability for the patient.

To our knowledge and experience, even analgesics such as morphine, have little effect on chronic pain. Many patients have surgery on the suspicion that the problems may have a hidden, structural cause, which sometimes turns out to be the case, especially in acute pain. However, the operation may also result in adhesions and other sequelae, which might even aggravates the patient's pain. Sometimes the patients are repeatedly operated upon. This may even take place at the patient's instigation in the hope of sudden freedom from pain.

If pain is of a chronic nature it is our impression that exploratory surgery rarely produces significant findings and that it has little effect on the pain. Often, no physical reason can be detected for chronic pain in internal organs, leading us to assume that the pain is psychosomatic. Psychosomatic pain is often randomly distributed in the body and cannot be located within specific physical structures, tissues or organs. You believe that you have located it when pressing on a certain point, but the next moment it is gone again. It is as if the obstruction behind the pain is living its own life in the body. The pain is a warning sign of something that has been repressed and something in the life of the patient is not as it ought to be. This type of pain does not go away until the patient understands what he or she needs to "learn from the pain". The problems will persist until the patient takes up the challenge, begins investigating what is going on (or in popular terms the body is trying to tell you something), learns the lesson and take proper steps to amend it.

Part of the underlying, emotional pain that the patient is unwittingly trying to avoid by somatising the pain lies in the acknowledgement that he or she has a personality imbalance, due to personal flaws and weaknesses. Once patients reach this acknowledgement of their health status, they may soon achieve pain relief. When the patients understand the problem, they can also find a way to solve it. Then it is mostly just a question of time, before they can move on. As simple as it might seem when expressed in this way, the process of supporting the patient and helping him or her go through the emotional pain and "take learning", is quite multidimensional. Let us again take a brief look at some of the dimensions in the field of "quality of life as medicine".

Clinical holistic medicine

The life mission theory (4-9) states that anyone has a purpose in life, or a huge talent. Happiness comes from living this purpose and success in expressing the core talent in your life. To do this, it is important to develop as a person into what is known as: "the natural condition". The "natural condition" accrues when the person knows himself and uses all his efforts to achieve his most important personal goals. The holistic process theory of healing (10-13) and the related quality of life theories (14-16) states that the return to the natural state of being is possible, whenever the person gets the resources needed for the existential healing. The resources needed are "holding" in the dimensions such as: awareness, respect, care, acknowledgment and acceptance with support and processing in dimensions such as: emotion, understanding and letting go of negative attitudes and beliefs. The precondition for the holistic healing to take place is trust and the intention for the healing to take place. Existential healing is not a local healing of any tissue, but a healing of the wholeness of the person, making him much more resourceful, loving, and knowledgeable of himself and of his own needs and wishes. In letting go of negative attitudes and beliefs the person returns to a more responsible existential position and thus achieves improved quality of life. The philosophical change of the person healing is often a change towards facing and struggling difficult problems and challenges, instead of avoiding difficulties in life (17-24). The person, who becomes happier and more resourceful often becomes healthier, more talented and capable of better functioning (25-27).

Case stories

The treatment of pain in the internal organs begins with a comprehensive physical examination with the necessary tests to exclude somatic illness. According to the holistic process theory, the treatment involves a combination of body therapy, psychotherapy and life philosophy exercises, where the patients are first supported in achieving better understanding of their inner self by formulating a more positive attitude towards life and finally by living accordingly.

> Female, aged 28 years with psychosomatic abdominal complaints
> First visit: Diarrhoea for ten days with nausea; vomits every morning, complete loss of appetite, but drinks plenty. She was admitted to hospital by an emergency physician and referred for colonoscopy, numerous faecal cultures all turned out negative [faeces are stools; they are tested for amoebic abscesses, and parasites such as worms]. Current medication: Losec [omeprazole], Alopam [oxazepam], nausea-relieving suppositories of unknown brand. Something is wrong. I (SV) cannot immediately diagnose the source of the patient complaints. A second appointment for in-depth assessment is scheduled.
>
> Second visit: Abdominal problems persist. I (SV) detect that the patient is anxious due to the death of her aunt at the age of 31 years by stomach cancer. In the aunts case her disease was wrongly diagnosed as gall-bladder stones. So far the patient has been to the emergency medical services, where she was given large numbers of pills, including Losec – which did not help. She is determined to be admitted to hospital immediately and regrets the fact that she did not accept the offer to remain in the hospital until her assessment was complete. My decision is to readmit the patient, since the thought of waiting for a distant appointment is greatly distressing the patient.

Third visit: when arriving at our third meeting she feels much better, now that the physical examinations in the hospital have shown her to be in good health. I postulate that her basic problem might be fear of dying, which leads to muscle tension, which causes abdominal and chest pain. We discuss her reasons for fear of dying, but the patient cannot concur. Further discussion into the matter unveils the amount of anxiety that disturbs the patient and she is advised to confront her fears instead of constantly avoiding it. At the end of the meeting the patient is diagnosed with anxiety neurosis. EXERCISE: She is than given an exercise to support her in confronting her anxiety and accommodating her feelings, when they overwhelm her.

The symptoms expressed by the patient looked like serious abdominal illness, but in fact diagnosed eventually as a simple somatisation of anxiety. As the patient will gather better control, she will understand the essence of her suffering and might be prepared to confront and process her anxiety. After such a process will take place the abdominal problems will disappear and replaced by the underlying problem of which they were symptomatic. Once the anxiety is integrated, she will have learnt something existential about life. This insight will strengthen her and will enable her to achieve a fuller life.

Female, aged 31 years with abdominal pain and pain during intercourse
The patient complains of continuous abdominal pain, which at times becomes severe. Pain is usually present during intercourse, especially during orgasm. The patient reveals that she suffered during previous relationship and suspects that the pain may be connected with her previous negative experience. Pelvic examination: normal. Smear taken. EXERCISE: The patient was instructed to write about her negative experiences during her previous relationships in as much detail as possible. When completing this task she was asked to read it aloud to a female friend or come for a second appointment to discuss her former experiences.

The patient showed many internal resources and needed little external help in order for her to solve her problems. The issue in this case was about getting the patient to change to a responsible and constructive perspective. Once the perspective is in place, the task is straightforward.

Female, aged 39 years with lower abdominal pain despite hysterectomy
Medical history: She had lower abdominal surgery with removal of uterus and ovaries. After surgery pain was reduced, but problems persisted. There are accompanying sleeping problems. She often stays at home sick and not attending work. Her family physician has prescribed Pantoloc [pantoprazole] for chronic gastritis. She is also taking antidepressants. "I have many skeletons in the cupboard that I can't or don't want to remember," she says, sadly, thinking of her childhood. Physical examination: Presents with chronic pain in the flanks that can be provoked by pressing on psoas muscles. Quality-of-life conversation: I (SV) explain the correlation between pain and a full "internal waste bin" and we agree to try gestalt therapy to go over the patient's difficult past. We can prepare a development plan, if the patient benefits from gestalt therapy. EXERCISE: Read books about topics resembling what you have experienced. PLAN: Trial gestalt session.

Patient history revealed that the patient had her uterus removed, which helped a little, but did not resolve the problem. At this stage it is more difficult to process the patient, due to the fact that the medical profession has burdened her with yet another trauma to process. Final developments of the patient will hopefully be gained during the gestalt therapy. Although the patient was found to have very little inner strengths and courage to clear up and thus eliminating the pain, we must not give up on her beforehand.

Discussion

According to the holistic medical theory (5,12) physical pains are often existential pains that the patient will not assume responsibility for. This perspective can be sometimes difficult to understand for a person, who has been educated within the biomedical paradigm, not acknowledging the depth of existence, the nature of the human wholeness and the causal nature of consciousness (17-24,28).

It is very important to rule out any serious and life-threatening diseases, when a patient presents with complains such as stomach pain, but when all medical enquiries and examinations have been exhausted without any results, treating the pain is often a simple procedure, using the holistic medical toolbox (3,29). In some cases, when the pain is in the region of the pelvis and a pelvic examination is to be carried out, we find it of value to use the holistic approach to the pelvic examination (30). This is extremely crucial in a case, where the patient is scared and sensitive. If the complaints of the patient are related to social problems (31) these must be resolved. If the patient is a child, the parents might be involved in the process of healing (32).

It is quite surprising, that what can be considered one of the toughest challenges in the biomedical clinic can sometimes be one of the simplest problems to deal with in the holistic clinic.

In our experience pains in the internal organs of an unknown origin are almost always caused by repressed emotions, giving the psychosomatic reaction. Using holistic medical toolbox, the patient is motivated towards personal development and can often be cured of the pains, when he or she assumes responsibility for the repressed feelings. The holistic process theory of healing (10-13) and the related quality of life theories (14-16) states that the return to the natural and pain free state of being is possible, whenever the person gets the resources needed for the existential healing.

We believe and our clinical experience has constantly verified that the resources needed are "holding" or genuine care in the dimensions: awareness, respect, care, acknowledgment and acceptance with emotional support and processing in the dimensions: emotion, understanding and abandoning negative attitudes and beliefs.

The precondition for the holistic healing to take place is trust between the physician and the patient, which seems to be the biggest challenge of holistic medicine, especially when dealing with the patient in pain.

Patients with genital pain often ends up in psychiatric treatment as the biomedical physician give up on them. Luckily the holistic psychiatrist that understands the process of holistic healing can easily help a large fraction of these patients. We recommend that the holistic psychiatrist that intents to treat chronic genital pain, also become familiar with holistic sexology (33).

References

[1] Ventegodt S. Quality of life in Denmark. Results from a population survey. Copenhagen: Forskningscentrets Forlag, 1995. [Partly in Danish].

[2] Sand PK. Chronic pain syndromes of gynecologic origin. J Reprod Med 2004;49(3 Suppl):230-4.

[3] Ventegodt S, Merrick J. Clinical holistic medicine: Holistic sexology, sexual healing, and treatment of vulvodynia through existential therapy and acceptance through touch. ScientificWorldJournal 2004; 4:571-80.

[4] Ventegodt S, Andersen NJ, Merrick J. Editorial: Five theories of human existence. ScientificWorldJournal 2003;3:1272-6.

[5] Ventegodt S. The life mission theory: A theory for a consciousness-based medicine. Int J Adolesc Med Health 2003;15(1):89-91.

[6] Ventegodt S, Andersen NJ, Merrick, J. The life mission theory II: The structure of the life purpose and the ego. ScientificWorldJournal 2003;3:1277-85.

[7] Ventegodt S, Andersen NJ, Merrick J. The life mission theory III: Theory of talent. ScientificWorldJournal 2003;3:1286-93.

[8] Ventegodt S, Merrick J. The life mission theory IV. A theory of child development. ScientificWorldJournal 2003;3:1294-1301.

[9] Ventegodt S, Andersen NJ, Merrick J. The life mission theory V. A theory of the anti-self and explaining the evil side of man. ScientificWorldJournal 2003;3:1302-13.

[10] Ventegodt S, Andersen NJ, Merrick J. Holistic medicine: Scientific challenges. ScientificWorldJournal 2003;3:1108-16.

[11] Ventegodt S, Andersen NJ, Merrick J. Holistic Medicine II: The square-curve paradigm for research in alternative, complementary and holistic medicine: A cost-effective, easy and scientifically valid design for evidence based medicine. ScientificWorldJournal 2003;3:1117-27.

[12] Ventegodt S, Andersen NJ, Merrick J. Holistic Medicine III: The holistic process theory of healing. ScientificWorldJournal 2003;3:1138-46.

[13] Ventegodt S, Andersen NJ, Merrick J. Holistic Medicine IV: The principles of the holistic process of healing in a group setting. ScientificWorldJournal 2003;3:1294-1301.

[14] Ventegodt S, Merrick J, Andersen NJ. Quality of life theory I. The IQOL theory: An integrative theory of the global quality of life concept. ScientificWorldJournal 2003;3:1030-40.

[15] Ventegodt S, Merrick J, Andersen NJ. Quality of life theory II. Quality of life as the realization of life potential: A biological theory of human being. ScientificWorldJournal 2003;3:1041-9.

[16] Ventegodt S, Merrick J, Andersen NJ. Quality of life theory III. Maslow revisited. ScientificWorldJournal 2003;3:1050-7.

[17] Ventegodt S, Andersen NJ, Merrick J. Quality of life philosophy: when life sparkles or can we make wisdom a science? ScientificWorldJournal 2003;3:1160-3.

[18] Ventegodt S, Andersen NJ, Merrick J. QOL philosophy I: Quality of life, happiness, and meaning of life. ScientificWorldJournal 2003;3: 1164-75.

[19] Ventegodt S, Andersen NJ, Kromann M, Merrick J. QOL philosophy II: What is a human being? ScientificWorldJournal 2003;3: 1176-85.

[20] Ventegodt S, Merrick J, Andersen NJ. QOL philosophy III: Towards a new biology. ScientificWorldJournal 2003;3:1186-98.

[21] Ventegodt S, Andersen NJ, Merrick J. QOL philosophy IV: The brain and consciousness. ScientificWorldJournal 2003;3:1199-1209.

[22] Ventegodt S, Andersen NJ, Merrick J. QOL philosophy V: Seizing the meaning of life and getting well again. ScientificWorldJournal 2003;3:1210-29.

[23] Ventegodt S, Andersen NJ, Merrick J. QOL philosophy VI: The concepts. ScientificWorldJournal 2003;3:1230-40.

[24] Merrick J, Ventegodt S. What is a good death? To use death as a mirror and find the quality in life. BMJ. Rapid Responses 2003 Oct 31.

[25] Ventegodt S, Merrick J, Andersen NJ. Quality of life as medicine. A pilot study of patients with chronic illness and pain. ScientificWorld Journal 2003;3:520-32.

[26] Ventegodt S, Merrick J, Andersen NJ. Quality of life as medicine II. A pilot study of a five day "Quality of Life and Health" cure for patients with alcoholism. ScientificWorld Journal 2003;3:842-52.

[27] Ventegodt S, Clausen B, Langhorn M, Kroman M, Andersen NJ, Merrick J. Quality of Life as Medicine III. A qualitative analysis of the effect of a five days intervention with existential holistic group therapy or a quality of life course as a modern rite of passage. ScientificWorld Journal 2004;4:124-33.

[28] Ventegodt S, Flensborg-Madsen T, Andersen NJ, Nielsen M, Morad M, Merrick J. Global quality of life (QOL), health and ability are primarily determined by our consciousness. Research findings from Denmark 1991-2004. Soc Indicator Res 2005;71:87-122.

[29] Ventegodt S, Morad M, Andersen NJ, Merrick J. Clinical holistic medicine Tools for a medical science based on consciousness. ScientificWorldJournal 2004;4:347-61.

[30] Merrick J, Ventegodt S. Medicine and the past. Lesson to learn about the pelvic examination and its sexually suppressive procedure. BMJ Rapid Responses 2004 Feb 20.

[31] Ventegodt S, Morad M, Kandel I, Merrick J. Clinical holistic medicine: Social problems disguised as illness. ScientificWorldJournal 2004;4:286-94.

[32] Ventegodt S, Morad M, Merrick J. Clinical holistic medicine: Holistic treatment of children. ScientificWorldJournal 2004;4:581-8.

[33] Ventegodt S, Merrick J. Sexology from a holistic point of view. A textbook of classic and modern sexology. New York: Nova Science, 2010.

Section 11. Tools for Holistic medicine

In this section we describe the tools of holistic medicin. This is not so simple, for in a way everything can be a tool, and in another there is only one tool: the physician or holistic therapist him or herself. From an abstract point of view healing comes from love. On a concrete level healing comes from thousand small things that together make a whole; thousand words said, small actions, holding the patients hand when the time is exactly right etc. We have already presented the five principles of holistic healing; they are very important but we will not repeat them; instead we encourage the reader who forgot them to read the introduction to section one again. We have also mentioned the five derived formal errors of holistic therapy in the same section.

In this section we will look at holistic healing from a lot more concrete perspective: as something the holistic physician or holistic psychiatrist does. In chapter 46 we look at the fundamental job of talking, touching and setting philosophical perspective. This is the well-known job of the practitioner of mind-body medicine. Then in chapter 47 we look at the same but from the angle of "Primum non nocere" – using the tools in a strategic way as to minimize the damage and inconvenience caused by the therapeutic interventions.

In a way this is highly practical, as it always will allow the holistic medical practitioner to pick a tool that is useful and not too big. In spite of the elegance of this approach it is not too helpful. Holistic medicine is not a science; healing and helping is not really a question of methods and skills as we would like it to be. In chapter 28 we talked about "crazy wisdom" and without a huge measure of intuition and emotional intelligence the process of holistic healing cannot be done. So beware not to take the methods described in these chapters 45-47 to literally. If you do you will fail miserably to help you patient.

Chapter 45

Applied consciousness-based medicine

Consciousness-based medicine is our term for a form of medical treatment that works by direct appeal to the consciousness of the patient, in contrast to modern biomedical treatment where drugs are used to affect body chemistry. With this concept, maybe we are (in a sense) turning back to the "old medicine", where the family physician was the all-concerned "old country doctor" who knew the child, the siblings, the parents, the family, and the village.

Consciousness-based medicine is the classic art of healing, where the physician works mostly with his hands, whereas the modern biomedical physician performs with biochemistry. Some of our questions are: If you improve your quality of life, will you also improve your health? Will learning more about yourself bring more purpose in your life? Will finding someone to live with in a loving and mutually respectful relationship improve your health? Scientists and thinkers like Antonovsky, Frankl, Maslow, and Jung have pointed to love as a unique way to coherence in life, and thus to biological order and a better health. Several scientific studies have also suggested that patients who focus on improving their quality of life usually will not follow the general statistics for survival, since somehow other factors are at play, which sometimes you will find referred to as "exceptional".

Introduction

Consciousness-based medicine is our term for a form of medical treatment that works by direct appeal to the consciousness of the patient. This is in contrast to modern biomedical treatment, where drugs are usually used to affect body chemistry. In a sense, maybe we are turning back to the "old medicine", where the family physician was the all-concerned "old country doctor" who came to your home to see your sick child, who you could talk to when social or economic problems became to hard to handle, or who came to be with you when your loved one(s) were dying or had an accident. He knew you and your family and could bring strength, comfort, and support to all.

It is our belief that we all have unlimited hidden resources for healing and curing, which we can call forth when we receive the necessary attention, respect, and care. In the long run, touch, love, and being there for somebody may prove more effective than even the best pills. Perhaps the conscious or unconscious choices that we make every day are decisive for whether we feel well or poorly, healthy or ill. What we experience, decide, anticipate, and feel may affect illness and health far more than we have traditionally assumed. That is what consciousness-based medicine or holistic medicine is about.

Will improving your quality of life also improve your health? Will learning more about yourself bring more purpose in your life? Will finding someone to live with in a loving and mutually respectful relationship improve your health? The case stories presented in this book are mainly patients who remain chronically ill despite conventional medical treatment and often also despite alternative treatment. We wish to show readers how consciousness-based medicine, by supporting personal development, can help patients to tackle conditions hitherto out of therapeutic reach: chronic pain, rheumatoid arthritis, cancer, heart conditions, psychoses, or dementia.

In our perspective, physical and mental disorders and complaints are often symptoms of a mistaken basic attitude to life. Obviously disorders and complaints may also have different causes, such as purely genetic disorders like muscular atrophy and purely traumatic illnesses like physical injuries caused by accidents, but general practitioners rarely see those in surgery or clinic. They affect a few percent of the population, represent a large cost to the health system, and are usually managed by specialist units at major hospitals or medical centers (1,2).

The more common complaints that we have seen and studied in patients may have hidden genetic or traumatic aspects. First of all, people seem to suffer mostly from complaints caused by their inability to understand themselves, life, or how to relate to others. It is almost as if sick people do not fulfill their destiny in life. Instead, they suppress and fail themselves. Deep down in our existence, we have great hidden resources that are best described in words like wisdom, joy, and energy of life. Once we uncover these resources in ourselves and rely on them more, we slowly change from being dissatisfied, sad, and ill to being far more alive, healthy, and happy.

Consciousness-based medicine and quality of life

Consciousness-based medicine is about improving the quality of life through personal development. A few studies in particular seem to indicate that survival in cancer and cardiovascular disorders can be drastically improved or prolonged by a targeted improvement of life (3,4). Other diseases, like management of autoimmune diseases such as juvenile diabetes (type 1) could probably also be promoted by tackling the patient's inner conflicts, when the first symptoms appear. It is important to underline that hundreds of scientific studies have shown a statistical correlation between health and dimensions like love, intimacy, good relationships, positive philosophy of life, and constructive life strategy (5). What we need now are suggestions for cures that provide efficient results, which can be scientifically documented with standard protocols or with a method appropriate for consciousness-based medicine (6). We aim to suggest twenty new holistic cures to be scientifically tested in the near future and with our series of papers on clinical holistic medicine, to accelerate the important development of an evidence-based, consciousness-based medicine, a development that in the end can give the physician another toolbox, more effective and cheaper for the patient, than the pharmaceutical toolbox he has today.

It is evident that we have full confidence in consciousness-based medicine, and we hope that the case histories in this series, which come from our clinical experiences and with qualitative documentation, will confer that confidence on our readers. Our basic perspective in life is that once we humans understand what a mystery we present and what energies we command, and once we take in how we connect to the universe surrounding us, we can also acknowledge our freedom to recreate ourselves as good or evil, healthy or sick, strong or weak.

This does not render our lives free of problems; quite the contrary. We are created with a will to do things, and this is likely to entail problems. The good life is intense and vibrant for better or for worse. The intense emotional pain of the will of doing should be balanced by the intense joy and pleasure of existing, being alive and conscious. That is the great art of living, which the holistic physician should share with his patients.

Love and tender care

We have in the Copenhagen Clinic seen some unusual cases stories, who suffered from serious injuries to their soul and through treatment and intervention were helped back on track again with an intervention that consisted of love and care. Scientists and thinkers like Antonovsky (7), Frankl (8), Maslow (9) and Jung (10,11) have pointed to love as a unique way to coherence in life, and thus to biological order and a better health; these case histories seem to support that idea.

On the other hand, we want to caution our readers to the fact that we believe all disorders should be investigated and diagnosed. Although the authors believe that improving the quality of life will often be the best and most effective way of preventing and treating illness, efforts to improve the quality of life should be seen as a supplement to conventional medical treatment and not as a replacement for it. We would encourage anyone suffering from or suspecting illness to seek complete medical assessment and subsequently decide what treatment would be desirable for the disease in question based on current experience with different treatment options. Several scientific studies suggest though that patients focused on improving their quality of life usually do not follow the general statistics for survival, since somehow other factors are at play, which sometimes you will find referred to as "exceptional".

References

[1]   Lewis R, Dixon J. Rethinking management of chronic diseases. BMJ 2004;328:220–2.

[2]   Wagner EH. Chronic disease care. BMJ 2004;328:177–8.

[3]   Spiegel D, Bloom JR, Kraemer HC, Gottheil E. Effect of psychosocial treatment on survival of patients with metastatic breast cancer. Lancet 1989;2(8668):888–91.

[4]   Ornish D, Brown SE, Scherwitz LW, Billings JH, Armstrong WT, Ports TA, et al. Can lifestyle changes reverse coronary heart disease? Lancet 1990;336(8708):129–33.

[5]   Ornish D. Love and survival. The scientific basis for the healing power of intimacy. Perennial, NY: HarperCollins 1999.

[6]   Ventegodt S, Andersen NJ, Merrick J. The square-curve paradigm for research in alternative, complementary and holistic medicine: a cost-effective, easy, and scientifically valid design for evidence based medicine. ScientificWorldJournal 2003;3:1117–27.

[7]   Antonovsky A. Unravelling the mystery of health. How People manage stress and stay well. San Francisco: Jossey-Bass, 1987.

[8]   Frankl V. Man´s search for meaning. New York: Pocket Books, 1985.

[9]   Maslow AH. Toward a psychology of being. New York: Van Nostrand, 1962.

[10] Jung CG. Psychology and alchemy. Collected works of CG Jung, Vol. 12. Princeton, NJ: Princeton Univ Press, 1968.

[11] Jung CG. Man and his symbols. New York: Anchor Press, 1964.

Tools for a medical science based on consciousness

Biomedicine focus on the biochemistry of the body, while consciousness-based medicine – holistic medicine – focus on the individual's experiences and conscious whole (Greek: holos, whole). Biomedicine perceive diseases as mechanical errors at the micro level, while consciousness-based medicine perceive diseases as disturbances in attitudes, perceptions and experiences at the macro level – in the organism as a whole. Thus, consciousness-based medicine is based on the whole individual, while biomedicine is based on its smallest parts, the molecules. These two completely different points of departure make the two forms of medicine very different; they represent two different mind-sets, two different frames of reference or medical paradigms. This chapter explains the basic tools of clinical holistic medicine based on the life mission theory and holistic process theory with examples of holistic healing from the holistic medical clinic.

Introduction

This chapter is the practical pendent to a series of theoretical papers on quality of life as medicine and holistic medicine to be reviewed below. After the short review, we explain the three basic tools of consciousness-based medicine, where feelings are at the core of holistic medicine. Holistic medicine is dealing with man as a whole, and this wholeness, global level of existence or "soul" is integrating all the being, having and doing of the individual. We believe this top level of the biological organism to be the seat of consciousness, which is the reason why we focus on consciousness in our holistic medicine. The first step for the patient is therefore to reach inside the body to reveal the feelings and impressions hidden there. They are often rooted in the personal history (unfinished issues or the so-called gestalts). The next step is to verbalise the feelings, to understand and finally let go of the life-limiting perspective in order to find a new perspective, which is more nourishing and supporting for life. We will see how this is done in a case story. Based on this example we will analyse the main differences between biomedicine and consciousness-based medicine.

As will be demonstrated in other articles in our series on clinical holistic medicine, there are still a number of important aspects of being a person and working on one's health, which are difficult to fit into the holistic theories, so the job of developing the new medicine is far from finished. We hope for the medical community to engage in the exiting challenge of making consciousness-based medicine work in the medical clinic, hopefully to the benefit of thousands of chronic patients, not sufficiently helped neither by bio-medicine nor alternative treatment as we know it today.

It is important to stress that the word holistic has been used in many different meanings, so there are many different kinds of "holistic medicine". Often spirituality has been stressed in holistic medicine, but the meaning of this word has not always been clear. In our version of holistic medicine spirituality is the abstract. The life mission theory (1-6) states that essence of man is his life purpose, and this is the abstract core of the being. The ideal contact between two persons is the contact we call "love", so important in our clinical work, where our wholeness ("soul") openly and in full acknowledgment meets the other persons wholeness ("soul"). This is a meeting "soul to soul", where we connect as deeply as humanly possible. In a way we merge our consciousness with the consciousness of the other, in the intention to serve this other person, while realizing our own purpose of life, which is always about creating value for the other (2). All this and more sum up the scientific holistic medicine (1-24).

Two simple clinical examples

Female, aged 35 years – Feel!
The patient presents with neck pain and tensions in the thoracic and intercostal muscles [the muscles between the ribs]. We talk about the presence of a feeling, which the patient does not want to acknowledge.
EXERCISE: Sit down for 10 minutes every day with your eyes closed and sense your feelings. Make room for all negative and positive feelings.

Another physician might refer this woman to a physiotherapist and prescribe analgesics, if the neck pain is severe. Contrary to this, we recommend that she take the time to listen to her emotional life. Unprocessed feelings – anger, anxiety or frustration – often manifest themselves as tensions in the body. If that is the case for this woman, we may be able together to solve her troubling and probably recurring problems without any physical or chemical intervention.

That is how consciousness-oriented medicine differs from biomedicine. The biomedical physician typically resorts to medication and physical manipulation, while consciousness-based medicine will often begin by turning the patient's attention to the underlying emotional problems. Our feelings are a great source of knowledge of the unique causes of our diseases and health.

In modern society we often fail to recognise the importance of feelings. We rely on reason and suppress many of the painful reactions to our less than perfect reality, which are basically natural and require some space. But suppressed feelings tie into knots, and frequently we will not get rid of a symptom, until we open ourselves to the repressed emotional pain.

Female, aged 20 years – abortion trauma
Quality-of-life conversation. The patient presents with fatigue and persistent low spirits. "I feel bad about my body and myself" – low self-esteem – e.g. the statement "I am worthless". Had an abortion six months ago, which still troubles her. Cries on the couch, I hold her hand and she talks about the abortion. Conclusion: She has no close, intimate friends whom she trusts. A consequence of low self-esteem , which makes her certain that once she is seen, she will be rejected. Early problem when the patient felt rejected.
EXERCISE: List of problems – describe your social, psychological, physical, educational and sexual problems
EXERCISE: Write a description of the course of the abortion from beginning to end, and bring it back for follow-up conversation.
PLAN: Feel, acknowledge, let go – for the next six months. Another appointment in two weeks.

It is estimated that there is at least 26 million legally terminated pregnancies each year throughout the world, at least 20 million illegally terminated with the result of at least 78,000 maternal deaths (25). Every abortion is an emotional trauma that often is not processed and will torment the woman for years. This is a great shame, since the problem can be solved by relatively simple means. In this specific case the problem was low self-esteem, a feeling with which so many young people struggle today. When we take a look together behind the facade and view her self-esteem as the essential problem, she also will be able to see that her entire existence reflects her low self-esteem. The abortion is like an emotional plug in her, and once it is removed, it releases a number of emotional problems that concerns her relationship with the significant individuals in her life.

As homework, the physician asks her to describe the abortion and make a list of all the problems in her life. These two exercises deal with the past and the present and, if successful, she will feel as if she has been relieved of a great burden. Once she has confronted the painful feelings, she will get a much clearer view of her position in life, and she will be able to let go of many negative attitudes towards herself and others.

In our view, these three steps are required to sort things out and heal: First, one has to feel the old emotional pain again, then clearly acknowledge the nature of the problem and where life took the wrong track, and finally let go of the negative attitudes to life that accumulate in all of us, when life is hard on us or we fail at something we want.

Holistic process theory

We formulated these three steps – feel, acknowledge and let go – following studies of therapeutic approaches of alternative therapists. What do alternative therapists do for their patients and clients? Well, either they touch the patients and help them feel the emotions and "energies" that are restrained in their bodies, for example by means of massage, zone therapy, Rosen sessions, kinesiology, acupuncture, craniosacral therapy, bioenergy, primal therapy or holotropic breathwork. Or they help their patients verbalise their feelings and sensations and support them in acknowledging the structure of their lives, for example through Gestalt therapy and other psychotherapy, cognitive therapy, transaction analysis or existential group therapy sessions. They can also work with the patients' thinking and consciousness and help them towards new perspectives and life philosophies, for example through Body Mirror System Healing, psychosynthesis, NLP, philosophical counselling, existential therapy, thought field therapy and on life philosophy courses such as our own summer courses "Life philosophy that heals" in Denmark. With these measures and techniques, alternative therapists can help the patients let go of physical tension, emotional tension or tension in their minds.

We call the combination of these three essential steps: "feel, acknowledge, let go" holistic process theory. "Holistic", because it draws on the whole formed by the body, emotional life and mind. And "process" because it describes the process, where the pain load that a person has repressed earlier in life (from the spiritual to the physical level through life), once more becomes conscious and integrated. Thus, through the holistic healing process one becomes aware of the causes of one's diseases and disorders, and at the same time as the misfortunes of the past are sorted out, one's quality of life, health and functional capacity improve.

Let us provide an example from the clinic: A woman suffers from urinary tract infections that keep recurring, and she is treated over and over again – we see that in the clinic occasionally. What could be the cause, seen from a holistic angle, and how should it be treated holistically?

As children we need love; without love we become anxious and insecure. If the anxiety becomes unbearable, we can escape from it by a "decision" that we are not worth loving. The pain may, in this perspective, be wrapped up and placed, for instance in the skeletal muscles between the ribs or in the smooth muscles in the pelvis. Indeed, therapy often reveals that as adults we carry the anxiety from our childhood hidden in the organs of the pelvis – in the intestine, bladder, sexual organs or skeletal muscles.

If the anxiety is hidden away in the pelvis, it may weaken our bladder region and cause repeated or chronic infection of the urinary tract. To get rid of such chronic infection the patient has to "become present in the pelvis" and feel the anxiety again. The gestalt – "the frozen now" with the original emotional pain – must be caught, verbalised and made conscious. Finally, the patient must let go of his or her old perception of being unlovable. Not only will the cystitis go away as a result of this process; the patient will also attain higher self-esteem and thereby become easier to love. The patient has learned from his or her disease, the disease has been cured and the patient has re-emerged in an improved version.

The holistic process theory thus implies that the patient must work with body, feeling and mind at the same time. A practical solution is to let the patient draw on a team of therapists, some specialised in work on the body, others in words and feelings, and yet others in the mind and life philosophy. At the Quality of Life Research Center and Clinic in Copenhagen, the patient will typically see a body therapist, a psychotherapist and a physician trained in the holistic-oriented approach, who also is in charge of referrals and the overall therapy. In our experience with this kind of work, a course of treatment to improve quality of life typically lasts about six months – consisting of 10 to 15 individual sessions at two-week intervals. The treatment should be supplemented by reading relevant literature, perhaps a course in life philosophy and possibly participation in a "growth and development group" directed by a psychotherapist. In this group, patients join and support each other in the development process.

Regardless of their practical focus, the holistic treatment regime share the approach of working with the patient rather than with the disease. The focus is on improving the quality of life. That is the reason, why we often say "quality of life as medicine", when we explain the concept of consciousness-based medicine.

Theory of cognitive dissonance

Let us take a closer look at what will happen, when a person establish the traumas, which the holistic process theory seek to eliminate. Let us draw on the classic socio-psychological theory of cognitive dissonance[26]. According to this theory, a person has a number of cognitions at any time, i.e. beliefs, attitudes and perceptions. These cognitions may be more or less inconsistent. When there is a conflict between them, which Leon Festinger (1919-1990) from Stanford University calls cognitive dissonance, this is perceived as discomfort. Festinger viewed people as thinking individuals, who need to have balance in their thoughts as well as their actions. This idea of balance is key to his theory of cognitive dissonance. Much research is still being conducted today in social psychology to answer some of the questions that cognitive dissonance has raised.

Let us look at an example. A small child begins by having the attitude "I am worth loving". But if the child feels constantly punished by its father, the child will acquire the experience "I see that I am not loved". Such dissonance is unpleasant and, according to Festinger, the child will attempt to change it to create consonance (harmony) between the cognitions. If the child cannot make the father stop the punishment so that the child achieves the cognition "I experience being loved", it is forced to change the cognition that it controls, i.e. the attitude "I am lovable". Consequently, the child will gradually change it into "I am unlovable". Now there is cognitive consonance between the child's two cognitions: "I experience being punished" and "That is because I am unlovable".

Festinger used his theory to explain why and how we change our own and others' attitudes and values (cognitions). It provides an excellent framework for our observations at the clinic of both traumatised children and adult patients reliving a traumatic childhood. However, we will demonstrate further below that patients often harbour numerous, mutually conflicting perspectives. Not until the traumatic material becomes conscious can the patient heal and become himself again. This healing can only take place once the gestalt – the painful "frozen now" – has moved from the body, where it is apparently stored and kept, and into the emotional dimension, where the old painful feelings should be contained and confronted, and further into the mind as a clear acknowledgement that can make us re-assess our old choices of existential survival.

If we come to grief so early in life and make such self-destructive decisions as is often the case – I am unlovable, I am no good, I am hopeless, there is something wrong with me – we take vast amounts of vital energy from our living and bind this life force in unfinished gestalts. If we are to get well again and regain our vital energy, we have to melt the ice cubes of the past and in this way restore the exchange of information in the body. We must make the separate "parts" of ourselves, our denied sides, merge into our whole again. That is how we heal and regain our health and life force.

"The frozen now" is the essential element that binds our vital energy, and that is conventionally called a "gestalt" (we sometimes use the phrase holo-gestalt, when body, feeling and mind are involved at the same time). The gestalt begins as a pain that is unbearable, the next step is a life lie that relieves us from responsibility for the pain, and the third step is the parking of the entire gestalt in the part of the body that is able to contain it (typically a group of muscles or another organ structure).

Tools

"Please – tame me!" he said.
"I want to, very much," the little prince replied. "What must I do, to tame you?" asked the little prince.
"You must be very patient," replied the fox. "First you will sit down at a little distance from me – like that – in the grass. I shall look at you out of the corner of my eye, and you will say nothing. But you will sit a little closer to me, every day..." (Saint-Exupéry: The Little Prince)(27)

According to Irvin D Yalom, Emeritus Professor of Psychiatry at Stanford University School of Medicine (28), the good therapist must invent a unique treatment for each patient, and the only thing that can really make a difference is attention, as Jiddu Krishnamurti (1895-1986)(29) pointed out throughout his life. Nevertheless, there appear to be some more concrete tools, which the therapist can acquire and learn to master, in the interest of the patient.

When we meet a patient, the first thing we notice is typically how much closeness the patient allows between us. Some patients are good at closeness and intimacy; they have come far in their personal development and are very open and honest, both to themselves and to us. They trust in us and our good intentions as physicians and immediately accept our attention, respect, care, acknowledgement and acceptance, which we consider the five fundamental therapeutic tools that any holistic doctor has to master to provide optimal holding, and on which every treatment should be based. The trusting patient often makes rapid progress, if the therapist succeeds in combining these fundamental qualities in a smooth and unbiased manner, in the exact proportions needed by the patient, guided by the therapist's kindness towards – or perhaps even love of – the patient.

Other patients show little trust, they are emotionally distant and characterised by being equally unable to give and take. Attention hurts them, so we need to be very careful, when we show them our attention and treat them. We experience these patients as severely damaged. In such cases, the first therapeutic goal is to restore their trust by supporting them to feel, acknowledge and let go of the trust-damaging traumas. The most important tools to achieve this goal are touch, conversation and sharing of life perspective.

Touch comes at all levels of intensity, from the handshake to the embrace. Conversation comes in all degrees of intimacy, from the entirely impersonal to the most intimate conversation. Sharing of life perspective ranges from sharing of trivial, shallow views to generous sharing of our greatest moments and most significant experiences. People, who cannot show trust can be very difficult to like and very difficult to help. The most damaged patients will not establish eye contact, when they first visit the clinic, they are unable to see the world from any other viewpoint than the one in which they are stuck. We are not allowed to respect them, because they cannot meet us at the line between us, but are either below or above that line. Nor are we allowed to touch them, for they cannot bear close contact with others. These patients may be normal in the psychiatric sense, but from an emotional view they are terrible, and from an existential view they are very ill. They have withdrawn from life completely and are stuck in a negative, mental position of defence.

One patient is an example, a 50-year-old man, whom I (SV) perceived as totally impossible. All that I was allowed to do was to share his perspective, namely that he wanted to die. I could not talk him out of it in any way. I ended up giving him the only thing that I could, namely my meeting him concerning his death. Intuitively I felt that meeting him there was the only right thing to do, so we discussed suicide methods to find the exact method that would best suit him. Then, gradually I felt how his basic attitude changed: since I no longer tried to pull him from the grave, but accepted his independence and will to die and cooperated with him on his departure, part of him awoke. Ever so slowly he started struggling to live, rather than struggling to die. At the end of the session he declared that he no longer wanted to die.

We had but a single tool, one single straw to which the physician could cling as therapist, namely to join him unreservedly and without resistance where he was, in his mental perspective. The attitude and in a way generosity of the physician at this point apparently set him free. Half an hour later he was laughing at himself and his futile suicidal thoughts and the crisis had passed. The physician used his last and perhaps most important tool, namely to look at the situation from the patient's point of view, supported by the intention to help him.

Ideally, the holistic therapist is able to support the patient in all the processes concerned with feeling, acknowledging and letting go. The goal of the therapy is to help the patient return to his or her natural state, where the patient surrenders to life and find peace in life. The care of the physician helps the patient to be present in order to feel what is hidden away in the body. The respect of the physician enables the patient to establish his own well-defined space, which in turn enables the patient to understand himself and his life. The attention of the physician enables the patient to see himself and his life from many perspectives and to choose the very best and most affirmative views. Care, respect and attention will not help the patient until he can accept them, and that is a question of trust. Trust enables the patient to accept the most nourishing support (called "holding""), which makes the deep and spiritual processes take their course.

Holding requires that the patient lets himself "be held", i.e. surrenders and lets the therapist take full control of the situation. That is the control held naturally by the parents, before the fundamental breach of trust occurred. Usually the patient would not let the parents or anyone else take control ever again. Healing takes place through surrender, where the patient once more let go of all the ways he or she holds back: physical tension, emotional dissociation and all the mental reservations. When the patient lets go, life returns. Healing will only be possible, when the patient can accept being held, almost like a trusting infant. These resources – being met with respect and love, being seen, touched – are the very resources that were missing in the original traumatic situation in life. In the successful cases, the ability to be close is recreated slowly, but steadily.

It is quite remarkable that one is able to provide parenthood with a delay of 30, 50 or 70 years, and in that way make up for a terrible, traumatic loss of love and closeness in the past of the patient that has damaged the patient right up to the present. In therapy, the road to sufficient trust and profound healing is often long. Some of our patients have already been in therapy for many years, before seeing us without having found help in relation to their fundamental problems. The first three months are sometimes spent unlearning bad habits and misapprehensions, which the patient has picked up during therapy or in other contexts.

Just how long that road is, seems to be a question of the therapist's professional skill, emotional generosity and intention. The therapist may be infinitely wise, but to no avail if he is unable to give. The ability to give must be sincere and loving. To be a good holistic therapist, one must make sure that one's own feelings are available for the encounter with the patient and that one is aware of one's own intentions. One must be able to withstand being reflected by the patient. One must master the classic concepts, such as transference and projection. As a person the therapist should be attentive, respectful and caring. Then we can begin practising the three tools mentioned above that create trust and closeness. Let us take a closer look at them.

1. Touch

A caressing touch is the essence of care and as such one of the most natural and vital things for us as children. Most of us do not receive the care we need as children and are still deeply hurt. Therefore, when the therapist touches his patient, there is a risk that he may open some of the most painful wounds and expose the patient to more than he or she can handle. If we are not attentive and respectful, and attain the patient's complete acceptance, it may easily seem like an assault. On the other hand, there is no other way of healing the old wounds than to go back and relive the pain. Therefore, there is no alternative to touching the patient. The simplest and most natural thing is thus the hardest for us as therapists in the clinic. It is in the touching of our patient that we prove our worth as holistic physicians.

When supporting the patient to feel what lies hidden in the body – as being taught by Marion Rosen who developed the Rosen method (30) – the holistic therapist should place his hands on the patient and support the tense, blocked and perhaps diseased area of the body. The purpose of the touch is to meet the patient soul to soul through the two bodies. In order for the touch to establish contact with repressed matter, the therapist's genuine intention with the touch should be to encounter the patient's self, not just the patient's body. Therefore, the therapist has to recognise qualities in himself such as curiosity towards the other person, pleasure in the contact or wanting to touch, all qualities which are considered unwanted and unwelcome in general medical practice. Marion Rosen (30): "When you touch the client, the client also touches you". That is true, which for a while can cause some difficulties, because it means that a therapeutic touch performed correctly in the holistic context leads to uncompromising and quite provocative closeness. When the patient, slowly and step by step, becomes present in a sick and blocked area, the repressed feelings and problems, which are often placed there in early childhood, will slowly rise to the surface of consciousness. The patient becomes present and meets the therapist and the gestalt that was hidden in the tissue resurfaces with all its negative feelings. Mostly, this process is gradual and quiet, but sometimes it is explosive. And then the trick is not to comfort the patient.

We begin the physical touch of the patient in a fairly neutral place, on the hands or knees; on the couch we proceed to touch the head, chest and abdomen, corresponding to the third eye, the heart/solar plexus and the Hara centre. When we touch a patient on the forehead and a handbreadth below the navel, this double touch can lead to deep contact, which triggers the holistic healing process. Two dormant intelligences, intuition in the body and the analytical intelligence in the mind, can be activated in this way, and applying these talents may really speed up the patient's process.

Touch combined with conversation can change the patient's well being radically over a short time. It is always surprising for the patient, when an opening appears and feelings return. Not always pleasant, of course, as the patient finds the feelings exactly the way they were left: often in unbearable pain. The patient may suddenly begin to laugh and then to cry bitterly on the couch – in a way that the patient has not cried for half his life. The 'feel therapy' is the port of entry. Without it, there is no hope of therapeutic progress in the context of consciousness-based medicine.

2. Conversation

The holistic conversation has the same purpose as holistic touch: soul-to-soul contact, this time through our two minds. Conversation has it all: body, feelings and thought. A voice contains so much body, so much feeling with so much to tell about the person it belongs to. And the choice of words tells its own story, the tone of voice and finally the sentences and the intention behind them that carry them forth. It is tempting to believe that conversation embraces all of it. What else is needed when we meet, but to speak together sincerely, openly, honestly and intimately?

In the same way that touch becomes extremely difficult due to old neglect, the conversation which is supposed to be so natural, becomes so difficult because of all the abuse, verbal assaults and mental defeats that we have suffered in our lives. Conversation is therefore also a door to awareness, but many feelings and events are so painful or so well repressed that they are actually unreachable through conversation and memory. As with touch, important questions relate to conversation. What happens when two people are good at talking to each other, and what is it about conversation that really redeems and develops the patient? How to help a person towards consciousness and clarification?

In our experience, the conversation does not take on real value until the patient begins to express himself. It seems that every person contains a very large, inner truth, and only when it is verbalised can the person live and apply that truth. The conversation should support the patient to find his own unique and original expression, which is verbal, emotional and spiritual all at once.

We really mean something; we are not vacillating or indifferent. Deep down, we represent something. Finding this content in life, verbalising what we feel and think so that our mind become clear – that is where conversation supports the patient. In a way, each fruitful conversation is like a vortex, pulling the meaning and content towards its centre and down towards the depth of the soul. And not until the basin is emptied and the vortex has become completely still and is completely centred in it own centre, is the process over. The person has become aware, emotionally focused and conscious. The patient has "opened up his heart" as the feelings returned, and mind and body reach each other once again. The opening of the heart and the recuperation of feelings reopen the door to the depth of existence, the wholeness of man – or the soul.

3. Setting perspectives

Generally, we may not notice that our attention changes its nature in relation to what we do and the place within us from which we work, but this is a very important point in the holistic clinic. Touch, for instance, works best when the physician is centred in the abdomen and pelvis, in the Hara centre, which is our centre of being and physical desire. Conversation is most constructive and natural with the centre in the heart and solar plexus, since the heart creates connection and the solar plexus creates clarity and definition.

When we become centred in the centre of the mind, traditionally called the third eye, we gain access to the quality we call acuity. It is a frightening quality that relates to making conscious choices. What we can choose in a state of acuity is our philosophical position, our perspective. It appears that over time most people move away from a perspective close to life, often towards a very strange perspective distant from life.

When we, as holistic physicians, are to help our patients, perhaps our strongest tool is the awareness of life perspective and the invitation to a shift in perspective. Once we have gained the patient's trust, we can make a journey together, exploring a number of alternative life perspectives and their consequences for our lives. It often comes as a shock to discover the decisive influence of our personal life perspective on our quality of life and well-being. If we succeed in helping the patient return to his or her natural life perspective, which is in full harmony with the inner life, this patient will often get well. As the patient lets go of all mental difficulties and firm views, he or she will return to the natural life perspective that expressed the patient's inner truth. At last the patient can experience the correlation between the inner and outer life, which was disturbed temporarily by the old traumas. The inner conflicts and contrasts dissolve, and the patient can experience happiness, perhaps for the first time. When we succeed in helping the patient become focused in his or her own mind, we say that the patient has become conscious. From that moment on, the patient is in control of his or her own destiny. Choosing a life perspective that is in harmony with one's inner life means taking responsibility for life.

Let us look at an example of this. The patient in the following case presented with a terribly disfiguring scar in the lower part of the face. She wanted to die, because she looked so ugly that nobody could love her, not even her own parents. The physician (SV) first made her choose to live by setting a dramatic perspective, where she is made aware of the choice between life and death, and she chooses life. Subsequently, he applied touch, with her permission, first resting his hands on her old disfiguring scar, and then massaging the scarred tissue. She starts crying hysterically, as she spontaneously goes back to the time, when she suffered burns. The re-experience is so intense that her lips turn blue again, and she gasps desperately for air as if the flames prevent her from breathing here and now.

> Female, aged 20 years – healing scars on face after severe burns
> First session. She had a large scar on her face after suffering burns at the age of three. On the couch, therapy centres on spontaneous regression to the episode with massaging of the scar, which healed nicely in terms of energy. She cried and relived a lot of suffering, which was processed. Before this we talked about choosing a life of suffering or a peaceful death. She disclaimed responsibility based on karma theory [it is not her fault that things are the way they are, it is because of her bad karma, i.e. the consequences of harmful actions in previous lives that pursue her], which we discussed. Another appointment in two weeks.

EXERCISE: Write a complete list of all your problems in life. Write half a page on each problem.

The physician touched her, and she felt. The healing process was underway. The patient must then be supported in acknowledging, and she has to verbalise the difficult feelings that emerged. The physician then joined her in her feelings. It was important that the physician accommodate the patient with all her feelings, allowed her to express herself and her feelings in the situation, even if she was very childish, very aggrieved and very hurt. All these feelings have nothing to do with the physician, they are things of the past, which the patient really needed to talk about and express. This took place during the second session with the patient.

> Second session. She has done her homework – about 10 pages about her problems – she will type it out and improve it for next appointment. Her father abused her sexually, when she was 16 years old. "Perhaps before that, too?" the patient asked. Has a boyfriend, but right now neither of them knows whether they should keep seeing each other. She is very dependent on the security and closeness that she gets with him. She feels very sorry for herself. Her wicked mother has ruined her life.
> EXERCISE: Write an essay on your self-pity. Also write a little about your conceitedness.
> Next time: We continue to work on the scar. Have a portrait taken that clearly shows your scars.

In helping the patient to acquire a more down-to-earth and constructive life philosophy, we have to join her in her perception of reality. Again, we can meet soul to soul, this time through the mind, and together examine whether the patient's present life perspective is the view of life that she basically has and wants to have. Massive self-expression concerning life perception, perhaps in the form of a written biography, promotes this process considerably. The therapist must be able to accommodate even the most sinister view of life and existence to help the patient acquire a more down-to-earth life perspective. In this session preparations are made for the major shift in perspective, which the patient needs in order to regain her enjoyment of life.

> Third session. She has done her homework – about ten A4 pages, partly about self-pity.
> The patient's name used to be P, but she went to a numerologist and then changed her name to the present one. That way she felt that she got away from her old life. It felt good. "Have barely seen my parent for a couple of years – they sort of destroyed me," she says. She cries and refuses to take responsibility for her past.
> EXERCISE: Write from the present and go back through all the major events that have evoked feelings in you: what happened, what did you feel, what happened, what did you feel, etc. – and what did you decide in each situation. May take up to 100 pages. One hour a day. Another appointment in two weeks.

To help the patient experience a real breakthrough to herself, she now has to begin sorting out everything that keeps her from being herself. It is a vast job, but it can be done. Now our job is to motivate her to make a persistent and substantial effort, perhaps for a year or so, until she finally and inevitably breaks through to her real self. A patient who chooses the soul's perspective often experiences a more profound meaning of life, joy in being alive and fundamental peace and being. It feels like coming home, like knowing oneself again, like being back in control. Like this statement from one of our patients: "I haven't felt like this before. I have always been insecure. People have always led me by the nose. Now it is completely different, and now I am back in charge. And I am happy."

This experience of things falling into place in life triggers an inner revolution, which frees the self-healing powers of the body and mind. Personal development is a life-long process, but the road to health need not be as long. And in the long term, we also develop good quality of life and good functional capacity – at work, socially or sexually. Therefore we believe, holistic medicine is a key to the good life in a broad sense, and also a key to help people become useful to and coherent with those around them and society. Holistic medicine is thus also a sustainable project of public utility, which optimises the value of the individual in relation to its fellow human beings, society and the ecosystem.

It should be emphasised that the starting point of consciousness-based medicine also includes the individual's physical and mental appearance, first and foremost the body, which can be regarded as a direct manifestation of the patient's consciousness. In our view, the body and feelings contain just as much consciousness as the head and mind. That is because our consciousness cannot be narrowed down to the mind and therefore does not reside in the head, but indeed in the whole that embraces all our parts.

It is an interesting fact that what patients need to heal spontaneously is the combination of attention, respect and care. And it is an interesting fact that this very combination cannot be given without profound and genuine love of the other person. What may appear to be technique and scientific knowledge in the eyes of the young therapist, gradually – as experience and wisdom grow – increasingly resemble genuine love and kindness towards one another. Consciousness-based medicine thus moves towards what we call social utopia. We consider the holistic process the first step towards consciousness-based medicine.

Discussion

Biomedicine focus on the biochemistry of the body, while consciousness-based medicine (holistic medicine) focus on the individual's experience and conscious whole (Greek: holos, whole). Biomedicine perceive diseases as mechanical errors at the micro level, while consciousness-based medicine perceives diseases as disturbances in attitudes, perceptions and experiences at the macro level – in the organism as a whole. Thus, consciousness-based medicine is based on the whole individual, while biomedicine is based on its smallest parts, the molecules.

These two completely different points of departure make the two forms of medicine very different, they represent two different mind sets, two different frames of reference or medical paradigms. Some of the differences may be listed as follows:

The greatest and most conspicuous difference between biomedicine and consciousness-based medicine concerns the perception of resources. According to biomedicine, you need support in the form of chemical substances, when you are ill or weak, while according to consciousness-based medicine you need to mobilise your hidden resources. This does not imply that a holistic physician will not prescribe penicillin to treat pneumonia, or that the biomedical oriented physician will not talk to his patient. But it does imply a totally different perception of the resources required to help the patient get better and function better.

Biomedicine	Consciousness-based medicine (holistic medicine)
The physician helps you	The physician supports you in helping yourself
The physician is responsible for how you are doing	You are responsible for how you are doing
The physician treats you with medicine and surgery	You develop by feeling, understanding and letting go of negative perceptions
Based on body and compliance	Based on consciousness and learning
Biomedicine	Consciousness-based medicine (holistic medicine)
Disease controls the individual	Health and quality of life are created through personal development
Peace and quiet to recover	Inspiration to rediscover hidden resources
Focus on lifestyle and physical factors	Focus on life philosophy, wholeness or " soul", responsibility, love, respect and care
Your genes determine how beautiful, good and true you are	Your degree of inner consonance determines how beautiful, good and true you are

Another highly striking difference between biomedicine and consciousness-based medicine is the relationship with quality of life. To biomedicine, good quality of life is a result of health, meaning that the patient's quality of life will improve when the doctor treats the body or mind with medicine. To the holistic doctor, improvement of the quality of life is the very key to mobilising the hidden resources. To the biomedical doctor, increased quality of life is a result of improved health, while to the consciousness-oriented doctor improved health is a result of increased quality of life. According to consciousness-based medicine the patient acquires quality of life, when he or she takes responsibility for his or her life. According to biomedicine the patient acquires quality of life, when the doctor takes responsibility for the patient. Hence, the perception of the patient's responsibility for his or her own life and illness is another important difference between biomedicine and consciousness-based medicine.

Therefore biomedicine may be defined simply as medicine based on a biochemical perception of man: we are chemical machines. Similarly, consciousness-based medicine is founded on the consciousness of man: we are conscious beings, who choose our own lives and thereby to a great extent create our own lives. The biomedical perception of reality is that everything consists of atoms, and that experiences and consciousness are kind of by-products of the chemical processes in the brain. The brain chemistry makes all decisions, consciousness actually lags far behind, but merely imagines that it matters. Consciousness-based medicine considers consciousness to be just as real as – but not more real than – substance. Consciousness is a real phenomenon, an element, if you will, in the same way as atoms. And our consciousness has great influence. Through all our minor and major, conscious choices, consciousness is the primary cause of our present lives.

In this chapter we have compared biomedicine and consciousness-based holistic medicine. It is very important to stress that we imagine the excellent physician to use both toolboxes and more (31) in his treatment of his patients, we actually want the physician to be multi-paradigmatic (32). Often both biomedicine and holistic medicine must be taken into use to cure a patient; mostly the acute problems can be solve using biomedicine, while chronic health problems needs a holistic approach (33-37).

Using holistic medicine and therapeutic touch, being very intimate with and very close to the soul of the patient, emotions and body, is only possible with an ethical consciousness on the part of the physician (31,37). We strongly believe that the results of a holistic physician never will be better than his ethical standard.

There are many great theories and philosophies in favour of a holistic approach to human health, like the works of Maslow[38], Antonovsky (39,40), Frankl (41) and Jung (42), but what is a thousand times more important for medicine than the opinions and perspectives of wise old men is your own understanding in the daily clinical practice of what it takes for you as the physician to cure your patient and make him or her well again.

Conclusions

One of the great advantages of consciousness-based medicine is that, in an abstract sense, the physician should always do the same thing, regardless of what is wrong with the patient, namely support the patient in becoming more conscious, more whole and more himself. Biomedicine often requires advanced technological assessment programmes and completely accurate diagnoses prior to implementing a successful treatment. In the field of consciousness-based medicine, it is far more important – as Hippocrates (460-400 BCE) already taught us – which person has a disease, than which disease a person suffers from. The holistic medicine is basically, as it was in the days of Hippocrates, about the recovery of the human character, serving the realization of our purpose of life.

References

[1]   Ventegodt S, Andersen NJ, Merrick J. Editorial: Five theories of human existence. ScientificWorldJournal 2003;3:1272-6.
[2]   Ventegodt S. The life mission theory: A theory for a consciousness-based medicine. Int J Adolesc Med Health 2003;15(1):89-91.
[3]   Ventegodt S, Andersen NJ, Merrick J. The life mission theory II: The structure of the life purpose and the ego. ScientificWorldJournal 2003;3:1277-85.
[4]   Ventegodt S, Andersen NJ, Merrick J. The life mission theory III: Theory of talent. ScientificWorldJournal 2003;3:1286-93.
[5]   Ventegodt S, Merrick J. The life mission theory IV. A theory of child development. ScientificWorldJournal 2003;3:1294-1301.
[6]   Ventegodt S, Andersen NJ, Merrick J. The life mission theory V. A theory of the anti-self and explaining the evil side of man. ScientificWorldJournal 2003;3:1302-13.
[7]   Ventegodt S, Andersen NJ, Merrick J. Holistic medicine: Scientific challenges. ScientificWorldJournal 2003;3:1108-16.
[8]   Ventegodt S, Andersen NJ, Merrick J. Holistic Medicine II: The square-curve paradigm for research in alternative, complementary and holistic medicine: A cost-effective, easy and scientifically valid design for evidence based medicine. ScientificWorldJournal 2003;3:1117-27.
[9]   Ventegodt S, Andersen NJ, Merrick J. Holistic Medicine III: The holistic process theory of healing. ScientificWorldJournal 2003;3:1138-46.
[10] Ventegodt S, Andersen NJ, Merrick J. Holistic Medicine IV: The principles of the holistic process of healing in a group setting. ScientificWorldJournal 2003;3:1294-1301.
[11] Ventegodt S, Merrick J, Andersen NJ. Quality of life theory I. The IQOL theory: An integrative theory of the global quality of life concept. ScientificWorldJournal 2003;3:1030-40.

[12] Ventegodt S, Merrick J, Andersen NJ. Quality of life theory II. Quality of life as the realization of life potential: A biological theory of human being. ScientificWorldJournal 2003;3:1041-9.

[13] Ventegodt S, Merrick J, Andersen NJ. Quality of life theory III. Maslow revisited. ScientificWorldJournal 2003;3:1050-7.

[14] Ventegodt S, Andersen NJ, Merrick J. Quality of life philosophy: when life sparkles or can we make wisdom a science? ScientificWorldJournal 2003;3:1160-3.

[15] Ventegodt S, Andersen NJ, Merrick J. QOL philosophy I: Quality of life, happiness, and meaning of life. ScientificWorldJournal 2003;3:1164-75.

[16] Ventegodt S, Andersen NJ, Merrick J. QOL philosophy II: What is a human being? ScientificWorldJournal 2003;3:1176-85.

[17] Ventegodt S, Merrick J, Andersen NJ. QOL philosophy III: Towards a new biology. ScientificWorldJournal 2003;3:1186-98.

[18] Ventegodt S, Andersen NJ, Merrick J. QOL philosophy IV: The brain and consciousness. ScientificWorldJournal 2003;3:1199-1209.

[19] Ventegodt S, Andersen NJ, Merrick J. QOL philosophy V: Seizing the meaning of life and getting well again. ScientificWorldJournal 2003;3:1210-29.

[20] Ventegodt S, Andersen NJ, Merrick J. QOL philosophy VI: The concepts. ScientificWorldJournal 2003;3:1230-40.

[21] Merrick J, Ventegodt S. What is a good death? To use death as a mirror and find the quality in life. BMJ. Rapid Response 2003 Oct 31.

[22] Ventegodt S, Merrick J, Andersen NJ. Quality of life as medicine. A pilot study of patients with chronic illness and pain. ScientificWorld Journal 2003;3:520-32.

[23] Ventegodt S, Merrick J, Andersen NJ. Quality of life as medicine II. A pilot study of a five-day "Quality of Life and Health" cure for patients with alcoholism. ScientificWorld Journal 2003;3:842-52.

[24] Ventegodt S, Clausen B, Langhorn M, Kromann M, Andersen NJ, Merrick J. Quality of Life as Medicine III. A qualitative analysis of the effect of a five days intervention with existential holistic group therapy: a quality of life course as a modern rite of passage. ScientificWorld Journal 2004;4:124-33.

[25] Kandel I, Merrick J. Late termination of pregnancy. Professional dilemmas. ScientificWorldJournal 2003;3:903-12.

[26] Festinger L. A theory of cognitive dissonance. Stanford, CA: Stanford Univ Press, 1957.

[27] Saint-Exupéry AMR. The little prince. New York: Harcourt Brace, 1943.

[28] Yalom ID. The gift of therapy. New York: Harper Collins, 2002.

[29] Krishnamurti J. On relationships. San Francisco: Harper, 1992.

[30] Rosen M, Brenner S. The Rosen method of movement. Berkeley, CA: North Atlantic Books, 1992.

[31] Ventegodt S, Morad M, Merrick J. Clinical holistic medicine: Classic art of healing or the therapeutic touch. ScientificWorldJournal 2004;4:134-47.

[32] Ventegodt S, Morad M, Merrick J. Clinical holistic medicine: The "new medicine", the multi-paradigmatic physician and the medical record. ScientificWorldJournal 2004;4, 00-00.

[33] Ventegodt S, Morad M, Hyam, E, Merrick, J. Clinical holistic medicine: Use and limitations of the biomedical paradigm ScientificWorldJournal 2004;4:295-306.

[34] Ventegodt S, Morad M, Kandel I, Merrick J. Clinical holistic medicine: Social problems disguised as illness. ScientificWorldJournal 2004;4:286-94..

[35] Ventegodt S, Morad M, Haym E, Merrick J. Clinical holistic medicine: Induction of spontaneous remission of cancer by recovery of the human character and the purpose of life (the life mission). ScientificWorldJournal 2004;4:362-77.

[36] Ventegodt S, Morad M, Hyam E, Merrick J. Clinical holistic medicine: When biomedicine is inadequate. ScientificWorldJournal 2004;4:333-46.

[37] Ventegodt S, Morad M, Merrick J. Clinical holistic medicine: Holistic pelvic examination and holistic treatment of infertility. ScientificWorldJournal 2004;4:148-58.

[38] Maslow AH. Toward a psychology of being, New York: Van Nostrand Nostrand, 1962.

[39] Antonovsky A. Health, stress and coping. London: Jossey-Bass, 1985.

[40] Antonovsky A. Unravelling the mystery of health. How people manage stress and stay well. San Francisco: Jossey-Bass, 1987.

[41] Frankl V. Man´s search for meaning. New York: Pocket Books, 1985

[42] Jung CG. Man and his symbols. New York: Anchor Press, 1964.

Chapter 47

Advanced tools for holistic medicine

According to holistic medical theory the patient will heal, when old painful moments, the traumatic events of life often called "gestalts", are integrated in the present now. The advanced holistic physician's and sexologist's expanded toolbox has many different tools to induce this healing, some which are more dangerous and potentially traumatic than others.

The more intense the therapeutic technique, the more emotional energy will be released and contained in the session, but the higher is also the risk for the therapist to loose control of the session and loose the patient to his or her own dark side. To avoid harming the patient must be the highest priority in holistic existential therapy making sufficient education and training an issue of highest importance.

The concept of "stepping up" the therapy using more and more "dramatic" methods to get access to repressed emotions and events, has lead us to a "therapeutic staircase" with ten steps: 1) establishing the relation, 2) establishing intimacy, trust and confidentiality, 3) giving support and holding, 4) taking the patient into the process of physical, emotional and mental healing, 5) social healing of being in the family, 6) spiritual healing – returning to the abstract wholeness of the soul, 7) healing the informational layer of the body, 8) healing the three fundamental dimensions of existence: love, power and sexuality in a direct way, using among other classical techniques "controlled violence" and "acupressure through the vagina", 9) mind-expanding and consciousness-transformative techniques like psychotropic drugs used by most medicine men and shamans of the pre-modern cultures, but only rarely by contemporary therapists and 10) techniques transgressing the patients borders, and therefore often traumatising, like the use of force against the will of the patient.

We believe that the systematic use of the staircase will greatly improve the power and efficiency of the holistic medicine and sexology for the patient and we invite a broad cooperation in scientifically testing the efficiency of the advanced holistic medical and sexological toolbox on the many chronic patients in need for cure.

Introduction

In principle, holistic healing of a person is a simple thing: an old and frozen "now" or "gestalt" containing repressed and painful emotions from past life events need to merge with the present and when this process of integration of denied parts of existence is successfully done, the healing is completed (1-4). In practice the merging is often everything, but simple.

One of the strongest reasons is that the patient really does not want to suffer again (because he has to deal with old "hidden" pain). So the most fundamental principle in clinical holistic medicine is working with the patient's resistance towards feeling, remembering and confronting the content of the sub-conscious (5). In principle the holistic physician or therapist can do this work in two opposite directions and either go with the resistance or go against it.

In therapeutic practice this is always "a dance", one step in the one direction and one step in the other (compare with chapter 17 on the often problematic decision making in the holistic medical and sexologic clinic). When you go with the resistance you comfort your patient and win sympathy, when you go against it you raise the patient's consciousness, awareness and presence. When you go with your patient's true self, you go against the resistance and when you go with the resistance you go against the patient's true self.

Unfortunately, because of the patient's repression of the true self, going with the deepest emotional layer of the patient is often going against the more superficial layer of the patient's existence and paradoxically this is often experienced by the patient as going against him or her – hence the dance.

As the therapy progress successfully, earlier experiences for the patient's personal history– the still old repressed painful gestalt – are appearing in the therapeutic sessions. As therapy goes back to earlier in life, more and more abstract existential problems are confronted and the philosophy of life of the patients are gradually turning more positive and responsible (4), while the negative attitudes serve the purpose of justification of displacement of responsibility from self to the outer world.

As the patient often spontaneously moves back in time during the therapy, integrating more and more of the repressed material, the "energy" of the gestalts are normally raising. The reason for this paradoxical situation is that the patient will confront still stronger emotional pains as the therapy goes deeper due to the level of arousal and the intensity of emotions, which is generally higher if the traumas were from childhood.

When the patient is back in early childhood, the emotional intensity is normally quite extreme (compare to Janov's "Primal Scream") compared to the emotional intensity of adults and as the regression progresses further into the re-experience of the life in the womb (6). These well-repressed traumas are often so intense, that is takes several persons to support the patient to give enough holding for him or her to fully confront the extremely intense both pleasant and unpleasant subconscious material (7).

The dark side of therapy

To get a patient, who is in need of care and attention, to work in therapy is often quite easy. Physicians often work as therapists after only a few weeks of training, as we know it from young physicians entering psychiatry. Working with biography and personal history, perception of self and reality, and similar issues are also often quite easy with a motivated patient.

As the therapy goes deeper the patient will reveal a higher and higher degree of resistance and the competence of the physician or therapist must rise accordingly to match the needs. When the therapy takes the patient into the deepest layers of the consciousness the experiences often get quite disturbing for the patient.

The emotional pain will often be overwhelming and the therapist will then meet the dark side, the shadow, of the patient and in this meeting the therapist will often also meet his own shadow. In some cases this shadow can materialise as directly evil towards the physician and others (8).

This can be shocking for the therapist, when the patient suddenly turns with evil intentions towards the therapist, who is only trying to help the patient from the best of intentions. When the therapist uses strong therapeutic techniques to confront the shadow side of the patient, the patient cannot escape and all the negative aspects can then arrange itself around an abstract centre of evil, which in many ways are similar to the good essence of the person, which is his purpose of life, or life mission (9).

Confronting the patient in his negative, evil intended side can take form as the classical ritual of "exorcism" (8), where the patient is completely obsessed with "the devil" or the patient can enter into a psychotic state of mind lasting for minutes, hours or days (10,11). If the therapist is not experienced or confident with the holistic treatment of insanity, the therapist can be overwhelmed as the resistance of the patient "wins the game" and then the holistic therapy can be turned into traditional psychiatry with the danger of creating further trauma and without healing of the patient's existence, which was the purpose of the therapy.

If the therapist is caught unprepared in the process of meeting the shadow side, which we call negative transference (often happening after a period of positive transference, where the patient has been into strong admiration or even secretly in love with the therapist) and working into the dangerous trap of counter-transference and suddenly being the weaker part, instead of staying strong, balanced and in control of the session, the therapist can also be deeply hurt emotionally.

If the therapist goes completely out of control and into emotionally driven, highly irrational behaviour (it can happen when the therapist is strongly hit by what is happening), very unfortunate things can happen. Sometimes the patient will fight to leave the room, while the physician will physically hold him or her back. Afterwards the patient might complain that the therapeutic contract was violated, or even accuse the physician of violent or sexual abuse. Such an experience can be so embarrassing, that it can tempt even a trained therapist to drop his whole carrier as a therapist.

So "the dance" of therapy, as it grows in intensity can turn into a fight and a true nightmare, where the therapist loose all control and the patient's dark side take over the session. What normally happens in this situation is from a depth-psychological perspective, that powerful gestalts of the therapist himself – his own inner conflicts - materialise during the therapy. The better the therapist knows himself, the farther the therapist has come in his own therapy, the farther into the depth of the ocean of consciousness the therapist himself has penetrated, the farther he/she can also take the patient.

But everybody has their repressed emotions and every therapist must learn in order for severe errors, mistakes and failures not to happen. Constant supervision and personal therapy is a must and lifelong supervision strongly recommended. Over time the therapist will normally step by step be more confidant and competent and able to use still stronger tools from the advanced holistic medical toolbox.

The holistic therapist or sexologists should therefore not expect to be able to use the most difficult tools for the first several years, since it takes a lot of time and experience to learn to lead the session at that speed and intensity; the maturity of the therapist must also be taken into consideration here.

When regular therapy is not enough

The holistic physician and sexologist normally work with love, trust, holding (awareness, respect, care, acceptance and acknowledgment), therapeutic touch, conversational therapy and exercises intended to upgrade the philosophy of life of the patient, combined with the standard medical or sexological assessment and examination (12,13) (see also chapter 27).

Except for a modest risk of verbal abuse and physical intimidation, these techniques must be considered safe for the patient, if they are done correctly and according to a previous therapeutic contract. But these rather risk-free techniques are not always enough to make the patient heal. And failure is not really an option, as failure normally means the patient's gradual or sudden loss of health, ability, and quality of life.

In the many cases where a mental or physical disease is not disappearing in spite of more superficial therapy it is sometimes necessary to use techniques, which helps the patient to match the high levels of neural arousal and emotional intensity of the early traumas. Some patients with a more reflectory nature will need a deeper process and some diseases like cancer often needs a deeper process, than a less severe disease like arthritis.

To fully rehabilitate the three most fundamental dimensions of existence, which according to our thinking is: love, power and sexuality (14-16), the therapist will need to guide the patient into the deepest corners of the soul, mind and spirit or life itself. This journey goes into the famous underworld and inferno of Dante (Dante Alighieri,1265-1321) (17), which will take the patient through the most intense emotional and spiritual pains.

Life is suffering, as Gautama Buddha (563-483 BCE) taught, and deep existential therapy often reveals this fundamental truth. Only when we let go of what we cling to, Buddha also said, the suffering will disappear. Letting go of what we cling to in our mind and life is essentially what existential holistic therapy is about.

In the situation where the patient is not healing because deeper existential layers need to be integrated, the physician is obliged to take the art of healing a step further. A "radical new cure" must now be invented for the patient and the means must be judged against the risks. The physician must deeply consider the old Hippocratic saying: "First do no harm".

It is true that no physician can be expected to cure all patients, but still it is the duty of the physician – as long as the patient himself insists on fighting for his life - to do his best and continue to do so, until the day the battle is either definitely won or definitely lost. The physician must judge in every case, if it is possible at all to cure the patient, and if this is really within his reach as physician.

As the outcome of any treatment is really unknown beforehand, because it is strongly dependent on the patient himself, the physician must also estimate a likelihood that the intended cure will help in order not to waste time and resources on a hopeless case.

									10 Border transgressing techniques
								9 Mind expansion	
							8 Existential work		
						7 Energy work			
					6 Spiritual healing				
				5 Social healing					
			4 Emotional healing						
		3 Support							
	2 Intimacy								
1 Relation									

Figure 1. The staircase of advanced tools for holistic medicine.

Table 1. The staircase of increasingly intense and potentially traumatic and dangerous holistic medical therapeutic tools: 1) love, 2) trust, 3) holding, 4) healing, 5) group therapy, 6) life purpose-character-coherence, 7) "energy" work, 8) cathartic work, 9) mind-expanding/ego-transformative techniques, 10) extreme (often traumatising) techniques (see text)

1 Relation	2 Intimacy	3 Support	4 Emotional healing	5 Social healing
Love and acknowledgment Talking about Pt's biography	Winning the patients trust, music and art therapy Dance and movements Massage	Giving holding: Awareness, respect, care acceptance and acknowledgement. Coaching Time line therapy	Taking the pt. into the process of healing by touching, talking and setting perspective. Intentional work (Sweat lodge ritual)	Active work with projections. Mirroring good and evil in the pt. Working visibly with and against the pt's resistance Group therapy, psychodrama, body dynamics Sharing circle (native social rituals)

6 Spiritual healing	7 Energy work	8 Existential work	9 Mind expansion	10 Border transgressing
Rehabilitation of life purpose, character and coherence Acceptance through touch Soul-body-body-soul Deep coherence between patient and therapist	Rising energy circles Holistic breath work Painful provocative body work Sexual polarity work	"Controlled violence" Acupressure through the vagina and anus. Direct sexual stimulation "Controlled sexual abuse" "Exorcism" "Controlled fail of the patient"	Psychotropic drugs Substitute partners Death-rebirth rituals Mitote ritual Ritual life burial Killing and revival Sundance ritual Shamanism (i.e. materialization)	Sedating drugs, antipsychotic drugs. NCE. Use of force against patient's will. Institutionalisation Surgery in general Mutilating rituals like hanging in the chest muscles (native American procedures). [Direct sexual involvement]

When everything else has been tried, but the healing has occurred and the physician still sense that there is more to be done, the holistic physician can – if he has the necessary qualifications, such as training in medical ethics and in the different treatment techniques, combined with a sufficient level of personal development and sufficient courage - use the advanced tools of holistic medicine.

The advanced holistic physician's expanded toolbox contains powerful tools, which can be organised into a staircase of the intensity of the therapeutic experience that they provoke and the level of expertise they take to master (see figure 1 and table 1).

The more intense a therapeutic technique, the more emotional energy will normally be contained in the session and the higher the risk for the therapist to loose control or loose the patient to the dark side, which can make the therapeutic session very traumatic and damaging.

These induced problems can almost always be healed, if the patients stays in the therapy, so the real risk is loosing the patient, because he or she completely drops out of the therapy.

As demonstrated throughout our many papers on clinical holistic medicine (10-13,18-49), almost everything can be used as a tool, since only the imagination sets the limit. To induce the state of consciousness we call "being in the process of healing" (4) the physician according to Yalom (50,51) needs to invent a new cure for every patient.

This ability to be imaginative, creative and use whatever is necessary to induce the healing is the hallmark of the excellent therapist. Good intent, balanced action, and good results are definitely needed in holistic medicine. Giving up on your patient and not doing anything at all might in many cases be a bigger sin, than doing your best as a holistic physician and still loose your patient.

Still you need to use any tool only after careful consideration, respecting the golden rule never to use a tool more powerful and dangerous than necessary (compare that both in surgery and with chemotherapy the patient is risking death as a result of the treatment).

Almost everything in the world can be used as a tool, but as the physicians line up his tools, some tools are naturally to use before others and some might be painfully out of reach, because of lack of expertise or due to the laws of your country. The ranking of tools after intensity, danger, and needed expertise of the physician gives a "staircase" of advanced tools of holistic medicine; its function is to help the holistic physician to "step up" in the use of the techniques one level at a time.

Let us admit that holistic medical and sexological therapy often is a little "messy" with the combination of a number of classical and modern tools and techniques (see chapter 17). To think of therapy as the clear-cut process of "walking the staircase" is too simple. Often many of the steps are used in subtle and symbolic ways of the skilful therapist, i.e. hidden in jokes and ironic remarks. So this staircase is meant for education, training and treatment strategy, not to limit the flexibility and spontaneity of the therapy.

The concept of "stepping up" in the therapy using more and more "dramatic" methods to get access to repressed emotions and events, has lead to the common notion of a "therapeutic staircase" with still stronger, more efficient and more dangerous potentially traumatic methods of therapy (see figure 1).

We have identified 10 steps of this staircase: 1) is about establishing the relation, 2) is about establishing intimacy, trust and confidentiality, 3) is about giving support, 4) is about taking the patient into the process of physical, emotional and mental healing, 5) is about social healing of being in the family, 6) is about spiritual healing – returning to the abstract wholeness of the soul, 7) is about healing the informational layer of the body (from old times called the ethereal layer), 8) is about healing the three fundamental dimensions of existence: love, power and sexuality in a direct way; 9) is mind-expanding and consciousness-transformative techniques, and 10) are techniques transgressing the borders of the patient and therefore often traumatising, like using force and going against the will of the patient.

When the holistic physician, sexologist or therapist masters one step, he can go on to training and using the techniques of the next step of the staircase. As step 10 is often traumatising for the patient even with the best of physicians, it is generally advised that the holistic physician or therapist do not go there.

When well mastered by the physician step 5-8 (9) can be used, when step 1-4 does not help the patient sufficiently. The tools must be used one level at the time and each step imply an increasing risk for traumatising the patient. Level 8 and 9 often takes many years of practice to master.

Level 1: relationship/love

Loving (caring for) your patient is the first step of helping, since only with love can you be at service in an unselfish, ego-less way and love is the strongest resource in the art of helping another fellow human being. If love is not there it cannot be forced or willed; maybe there is kindness and care, maybe an interest in the other person, which can be turned into a relationship. Just establishing a relationship is a powerful thing to do and in the acknowledgment of the other person's personal history will you be able to help many wounds to be healed. It is important to say that love in our understanding originates from the urge to use your personal talents and give what you need to give to the world. Love is about living your personal mission.

Level 2: Intimacy/trust

When there is love, the patient's trust can be won, often little by little during time. With thrust comes intimacy – physical, emotional and mental closeness. Then many things are possible, like massage, dance, art therapy etc. Just learning how to trust and be intimate is a giant step forward for most patients, and their quality of life and self-esteem can be radically improved by the techniques of this level.

Level 3: Support and holding

When the patient trusts you, you can get permission to give holding; the five dimension of this crucial existential support is 1) awareness to the mind, 2) respect for the patient's emotional space, 3) care for the body, 4) acceptance of gender and sexuality, and 5) acknowledgement of the soul and personal character. In giving these five qualities in a rich blend you can help almost everybody to feel good and right.

Level 4: Physical, emotional and mental healing

When the holding is there, the patient can get the support in the actual moment, which empowers him/her to go back to the old, emotionally painful and confront the repressed content of the traumas. Getting help now to process the old trauma is the secret of healing. To take the patient into the state of mind, which we call "being in the process of healing" is what holistic medicine basically is about[4]. To get the patient into this state is really a question of intention; both the physician and the patient must intent the healing and "the bobble" the patient is isolated in must be open from inside and from outside at the same time, as the shamanistic tradition claims[52].

Level 5: Social healing – healing the being in the family

This level is about healing the relation with the group and the family, where using a group for this kind of healing is a must. The native Americans had their sharing circle and the talking stick, today we have the holistic existential group therapeutic process (7). In the group everybody can watch everybody, and one great advantage of this kind of work compared to individual therapy is that the process of working with or against the resistance becomes obvious to every member of the group.

This makes it possible to help the member to watch his own projective mechanism of the consciousness, helping him or her to assume responsibility for the unconscious attitudes, the "colour of the glasses of the spectacles" so to speak. This makes it possible for the therapist to effectively mirror the patients in the group, effectively helping the patients to realize their own idiosyncrasies, blind spots and neurotic survival patterns.

Level 6: Spiritual healing - healing the abstract wholeness of the patient

On this level the therapist must use his ability to sense the purpose of life (6,9) and the physical, mental and spiritual character of the patient (7). The purpose of life, or the life mission, is the core talent of this person, and happiness is about using this talent to be of value to the world. Other supporting talents surround the core talent and when claiming them yet another series of tertiary talents comes into use.

Being gifted and contributing to the persons dear to him or her and to society at large rehabilitate the existential coherence, the deep feeling of connectedness and belonging, which we long for deepest in our hearts. Rehabilitating the spiritual side of the patient is really allowing the patient to dig deeply into the hidden resources for healing him or her.

Unfortunately, the ability to use the abstract sense necessary to master this level takes a lot of practice and time, often years. It develops as you obtain coherence with the outer world yourself, as a product of your own successful personal development. As you find this coherence you will notice that you can connect soul to soul with you patient through your body and the body of the patient. When you take this skill into the sexual area and give acceptance to the body, the organs, the gender and the sexuality of the patient, you master the technique called "acceptance through touch" (13); the touching may simply just be placing your hand on the patient's body.

Level 7: Healing the informational system of the body (ethereal healing)

Consciousness meet the body in a peculiar way, creating what is often experienced as "circles of energy", the different qualities of the body and mind being sensed as circulating sexual, emotional, mental and spiritual energy [see (16) for an overview of the qualities]. Raising these subjective circles of "energy" is called "working with the energy" and it really is difficult to describe what is going on in this work, as it is about supporting the patient in exploring all the hidden qualities of body, mind and spirit.

Often breathing is involved in this work with holotropic breath work (53) as a fine example of this kind of energy work. It often helps the patient to integrate very early gestalts and spontaneous regression into the womb is normal in this kind of work. Some patients recall earlier incarnations, especially if the physician is open for this.

Working with the energies of the body often leads to recollection of extremely painful memories from early life. Also intense sexual energies are often awakened and training the patient to be a male/female pole in the universe is a part of the successful balancing of the patient's energy.

This level of biological information is poorly understood by contemporary science and for the last two centuries occult research has been carried out referring to this layer of the human being as the "ethereal body" (54).

Level 8: Direct existential healing of love, power, and sexuality

According to the theory of talent, there are tree fundamental dimensions of existence: love, power and sexuality. These dimensions can be confronted en bloc, which gives overwhelming and extremely intense experiences in the therapy. When all the evil sums up to the essence of the shadow, the person manifests his evil alter-ego and it really looks like he is obsessed by Satan; hence the name "exorcism" for this tool (see chapter 4).

When a person has been violently violated throughout his childhood, anger can be so repressed that only hitting him again can release it. This can be used as the therapeutic technique originally developed by the famous founder of gestalt therapy, Perls (3) and we call this method for "controlled violence".

Actually every time the therapist goes against the resistance, there is an element of controlled violence toward the patient's emotions, who often reacts hurt and offended. Every time the therapist goes against the patient's true self, there is an element of controlled violence against the patient's soul. But violation of emotions and the soul is often not seen and is widely accepted. Violating the body physically be beating it (with open hand not to cause any harm though) is seen as many people as unacceptably violent. From a theoretical analysis there is really no difference, it is all controlled violence.

Another set of very strong and efficient techniques at this level is the technique's relation to sexuality. The therapist can work against the resistance and with the patient by directly stimulating the patient sexually, which is a seldom-used technique. More often the therapist will use a formalised technique like the classical Hippocratic method of acupressure though the vagina, to rise the energies in the pelvic area (55) or to confront repressed material connected to sexual abuse or neglect by the stimulating the relevant tender-points in the genitals and deep pelvis reached through the anus and the vagina.

The last technique has an aspect related to controlled violence, and this kind of work is called "controlled sexual abuse", as the patient in this kind of healing often will find the old painful emotions from the trauma in the present moment, not in the past (see chapter 21). This seems to be a general rule of all high-energy traumas: the higher the energy and the more intense the emotional pain, the higher the likelihood for the trauma to manifest itself in present time during life or in therapy.

This means that you as a therapist should not always expect a child rape trauma to be presented to the patient as a child-rape trauma, but sometimes as an – initial - experience of the patient of being abused in present time in the clinic by the physician, because of the transferences.

The only way that the therapist can survive this legally is to address the problem directly and to make a therapeutic contract of "controlled sexual abuse", for the trauma to re-appear in the session under controlled conditions and not allowing the patient to get away with the transference of the old, extremely painful material (47-49).

This kind of work takes a high level of expertise and years of practice to master. It must always be done with supervision, to be completely sure that the physician or sexologist is not involving his own shadow in this kind of work. If the physician subconsciously is engaging in counter-transference here, is can be very traumatic for the patient.

The most painful and difficult of the tools on this level is the controlled fail of the patient. There is hardly a patient, who has not extremely severe wounds on their soul from early childhood, as it really is impossible to be a perfect parent, since just 30 minutes of mental distraction or physical absence in some cases can be experienced as a complete loss of both parents, by a sensitive and vulnerable child.

Some patients are worse of, as they as children had experienced systematic fail from their parents. Often they had the role as parents for their own parents from early childhood and to compensate for this, they developed a tendency to cling and adhere to finally obtain the love and contact they needed. In theory this failure should be easy to alleviate, but as love is what is most important for us as human being, systematically not getting the love we need and fight for throughout out childhood is giving such a traumatic series of emotionally painful wounds, that the moment the therapist intent to give his love, the resistance of the patient will be so intense that no love can be received.

So going with the resistance is the only way to proceed and this means ignoring and abandoning the patient, while he or she is in the therapeutic session. This really is a paradox: the patient is paying for therapy and nothing is happening, no, less that nothing! Only the philosophically highly developed patient will understand what is going on and even this mental understanding will not help. This is as terrible as it gets, since this is sheer hell raised once again, but it is not really happening in present time in the therapy, as a normal sound person will not enter into deep process of holistic healing feeling emotionally completely destroyed, just from being ignored by an other person. But these patients will. As the therapist can easily feel the transference he must now avoid getting into counter-transference and starting to feel evil himself.

The technologies on this level are highly efficient, yet they are just drills derived from the inner logic of the therapeutic process of holistic healing. In the hand of an untrained and poorly developed therapist, these are the cruel tools of torture and abuse that finally gives him the dark power over another person that his own evil shadow side has longed for a whole life. It is really easy to be tricked into the dark side using the tools of level 8, so never start using level 8 tools without intense supervision and coaching by an experienced holistic physician mastering this level himself.

Level 9: Mind-expanding and consciousness-transformative techniques

If level 8 was difficult, then level 9 is an art that really cannot be mastered without perfect mastery of the tools of level 8. One of the techniques of this level is being a substitute partner. To give yourself to this process of pairing up with a sexually dysfunctional person with the only purpose of healing their sexuality takes a rare kind of devotion. When it is done professionally and according to a contract – which normally implying only seeing each other for 14 days or so - it really works wonders for the patients (56,57).

Some of the techniques in this group are so difficult that in the pre-modern societies it took a shaman or high priest, one of the highest developed persons in the tribe, who had devoted their whole life to this kind of practise and service. This is very much still the case. You can only develop the mastery of the skills of level 9 by being completely devoted to this kind of work for decades - unless you have a very special gift for it, as a few students have.

Gifted or not, you need to be a trained by a master in these techniques for years, before you can do them on your own.

Some of the tools that demand this kind of mastery are the healing rituals, mostly carried out by Native Americans and other pre-modern cultures as extremely intense rituals, taking you all the way down to the core of your existence. One ritual takes you through a subjective experience of death and rebirth, while others makes your worst nightmare come through in the form of a life burial, to (almost) die from suffocation alone in darkness (used for integrating some of the most terrible foetal experiences, compare Stanislav Grof's BPM2) (6) and thereafter miraculously coming back to life as your true self that you felt you had lost forever.

To master such rituals takes the most loving and empathic of therapist, who minutely can read the state of mind and observe all changes of the patient's consciousness accurately enough throughout every moments of the whole ritual to meet the needs for the healing of the patient. It takes a therapist, who is completely familiar with the whole range of experiences of ego-death and personal transformation. This competence is only slowly developed though supervised training and personal experience throughout years.

Other tools of the ninth level that take similar mastery are the use of psychotropic drugs in therapy. In many ways this is a lost art, but it has been extremely widely used, as most pre-modern cultures has used them for millenniums. The word for medicine is the same as the word for the peyote cactus in many native North American tribes (58-60).

Other tribes have used the fungi of the species Psilopsybe (containing psilosybine) and the cactus called San Pedro (Trichocereus pachanoi), which like peyote contains mescaline as its major active substance. The liana called ayahuasca (Banisteriopsis caapi) has been used in the South America, while other cultures like the old Egyptians used an LSD like alkaloid derived from the Ergot of Rye, a plant disease caused by the fungus Claviceps purpurea (61).

All these drugs contains psychotropic (mind-expanding, active placebo) drugs or the hallucinogens, but with a different profile from the recreational drugs in popular use among young people all over the world today (62), like ecstasy, cocaine, and amphetamine, which has a strong CNS-stimulating effect in addition to a more modest, mind-expanding quality.

The purpose of the use of the mescaline-cacti among native Americans is to bring the patient to a state of consciousness, where he can realise how he makes himself ill by not living in accordance with the deep self (58) or in our interpretation with the true human character and the purpose of life (63). This makes the fairly mysterious native medicine, often completely incomprehensible due to the use of massive symbolism, very difficult to understand.

We are proud to say that the consciousness-based medicine we have developed these years normally do not use any kinds of drugs, as this has not been necessary, because of highly efficient therapeutic techniques and strategies, many inherited from the classical Hippocratic tradition that does not use pharmaceutical drugs at all.

Level 10: Techniques that transgresses the patient's personal borders (often traumatising)

It is obvious from figure 1, that many of the level 10 tools are in frequent use in modern day medicine. When the use of moderate power does not work, more powerful tools are frequently used; this is techniques like brute force against the patients will, sedating drugs, institutionalisation, and in some countries even imprisonment and severe invalidations of basic human rights, even though most researchers agree that they are often severely traumatising the patient. The reasons why they are in use are of cause the failure to help the patients with less radical means, or the failure of confidence in the lover steps, making the physician skip the try, jumping directly to level 10. Most of the steps of the staircase are not taken into use by many modern physician in the western world; sadly in many highly developed countries often only level 1 techniques are tried before going to level 10.

It seems that the art of holistic healing using the first nine steps are sadly lost in many countries and instead of practicing love and healing the patient, brute force is in use. We hope that re-introducing the therapeutic staircase will inspire many physicians and therapists to use less powerful and less traumatising means of the lower steps to heal their patients in the future.

One other potent tool, which is often used by modern day therapists, sometimes motivated by love, sometimes motivated by abusive intentions is direct sexual involvement with the patient. While such endeavour has been talked strongly against ever since Hippocrates, it seems that there has been a constant decay of some therapist's ethics throughout the last century. One female patient around 25-years old with a personality disturbance could tell us about at least four different therapists, who had abused her sexually.

The reason for not having sex with a patient is that this behaviour completely disturbs the relation, turning it upside down, giving the power to the patient and making therapy impossible. As the patient often love and admire the therapist this can also be seen as abuse of the power of the therapist and all too often the girl is left behind as the therapist moves on to abusing yet another patient and thereby failing the patient and their profession.

Direct sexual involvement with the patient are rarely the right thing to do from a therapeutic perspective, except in one special occasion: when the patient and the therapist has fallen mutually in love; when the therapy has gone definitely stock; and when none of them has obligations towards others, which forces them to fail each other at a later occasion. As the laws of almost all countries forbid the physician to have sex with a patient, the therapy must then be formally ended, there must be an appropriate gab in time from ending it to engaging sexually, and the relationship must also be successfully re-defined, before direct sexual involvement is possible.

Because of the negative view of such a relationship from the society, it is still recommended to keep such an engagement within the frames of the tool of substitute partner. Direct sexual engagement with a patient is a good example of a level 10 tool often having a traumatizing effect. The level 10 tools are in general so traumatising in spite of all good intentions that they cannot be recommended in the holistic medical clinic; although the use of them cannot always be completely avoided.

Using the staircase for training the holistic physician or sexologist

The training of the holistic therapist is difficult, since the only way to learn is to practice and doing it. Learning by doing means that the student in the beginning will make every possible mistake and error and the coach must be very involved and close to correct the errors and mistakes, before they lead to any serious consequence. In practice it is often very easy for a skilled therapist to correct the errors, if the student looses control of the session the senior therapist will take over and reinsert the student very much the way a new driver learns to drive a car.

Interestingly, in therapy the situation with the patient is as a rule better after a failure and a recovery that before the failure. This happy situation is a result of the mutual learning of the patient and the physician or student. Not being willing to learn from mistakes, and therefore hiding them for oneself or others is the most dangerous behaviour a trainee or physician can have.

Unfortunately many university hospitals have little mercy with physicians and students making mistakes, which create an environment of fear and of hiding. The most important thing in good training is the rule that all mistakes are allowed, but only once. In biomedicine, when a mistake with drugs and surgery is often fatal, this kind of freedom is more difficult to give students, while in the holistic clinic the most difficult of tools are hardly ever fatal.

Complete familiarity and mastery of one level of techniques leads naturally to the next and after many years of training and practice all the levels can be used. Using the level 10 tools is something even the most skilled holistic therapist only will do hesitatingly. It is of utmost importance to know how to use these tools to use them wisely and avoid traumatisation.

If force is necessary or if the use of strong sedatives and antipsychotic drugs are necessary (i.e. because the patient is trying to kill somebody or trying to commit suicide), the physician must know exactly how to react concerning force or drugs used.

If the physician or sexologist has fallen in love with a patient bringing therapy to an end, he or she must know how to deal with this extremely difficult situation, by finding a supervisor for support, avoiding sexual contact before the roles are sufficiently re-defined and the relationship balanced, so that this can be considered safe for the patient.

Not knowing how to use these tools can be very dangerous for both the patient and the physician. Lets underline that we most strongly do recommend that a sexual relationship between a physician and his patient are to be avoided at al times, also after the treatment is formally terminated.

Discussion

One of the most important principles in medicine since Hippocrates has been "first do no harm". The medical ethics is therefore every holistic physician's primary concern, when using advanced and emotionally intense tools of holistic medicine with the potential to afflict further traumas instead of helping.

Often in the clinical practice even a severe mistake can fortunately be corrected, as traumas induced by therapy can be healed in the same way as every other trauma. On the other hand it will take a therapeutic session of similar intensity as the damaging session to heal the wound and sometimes this is not possible as the patient is not willing to give it another try. if the first session was very painful and scary.

In daily practice this means that every procedure must be justified in two ways: 1) No procedure should be carried out, when one with less risk and less intensity of the impact/emotionally, physically and otherwise - can do the job. 2) What is likely to be won for the patient by using this procedure should be much more that will likely be lost. The patient must always be informed of the risk involved in the treatment and must give his or her consent after this information.

The basic principle for holistic healing (4) is to reverse the pathogenetic process, by taking the patient into a holistic process of healing, which has been called salutogenesis by the great Jewish thinker Aaron Antonovsky (1923-1994) (1,2). In the holistic clinic this is done by giving the patient the love, support and holding (awareness, care, respect, acceptance and acknowledgement), which was so intensely lacking in the original traumatic events, which caused the loss of inner balance, the disturbances and the inner conflicts and being the cause of the disease for which the patient now needs healing. The trauma was caused by the repression of unbearable negative emotions and the healing must be the reverse process of the pathogenetic process according to Antonovsky. This can only happen when the patient confront and integrate these painful emotions.

The characteristics of the state of consciousness in which patients heal (which we normally call "being in the process of healing"), is the same emotions and neural arousal as the original trauma. Because of the extreme intensity of emotions connection to certain traumas, especially from violent and sexual abuse, and especially if this happens in early childhood, is often difficult to get these patents into the state of healing.

Often lengthy therapy is needed, and patience is a must with these patients, but sometimes the therapy comes to a seemingly dead end and only more drastic and intense methods will yield the result of taking the patient into the old traumas again.

In general, what gives the holistic physician the ability of use a tool of a certain level is the complete mastery of the tools of the former steps of the staircase. Many fine books have been written on most of the techniques and level 7 and level 9 have been intensively researched, while research done with the tools at level 8 have been modest. The reason for that seems obvious: both sex and violence is taboo in our culture, while being among the best selling commercial products (i.e. in movies and pornography), medical science in its attempt to be clean and pure has avoided working seriously with these issues.

The problem by excluding level 8 tools is that without mastering this level, the next level 9 becomes very difficult to handle for the therapist. Only a few contemporary therapist have used psychotropic drugs successfully, like the LSD therapy pioneer Stanislav Groff, while most often drugs has been seen as a fast route to enlightenment, the most prominent example being the drug guru Timothy Leary.

More reflective people like the brilliant philosopher Aldous Huxley and Hoffmann understood perfectly well the potential of the drugs, but could not really tell how to use the drugs in therapy. The native Americans have undoubtedly done this for years using many different drugs derived from plants and mushrooms.

The rationale for the techniques found on the therapeutic staircase [originally introduced to us by Gormsen (68)] is the most simple of all: healing happens when the present moment or now of the patient, and the old repressed and emotionally painful now are taken together and integrated. Healing is thus the opposite of cutting your existence into parts as you do when you repress a trauma.

You heal when you in present time get what you could not get and needed in the past traumatic old now. So the art of holistic existential healing is really keeping the patient in the present moment giving him or her everything needed, and at the same time taking him or her back in time into the old painful now, confronting what happened when the fundamental needs was not met. If the trauma was less intense, just talking about personal history might do the job (biography work).

With more intense feelings, trust and physical contact is often needed; massage is a fine example of this level 2. With more severe trauma, as neglect in early childhood, re-parenting is necessary, giving the patient the care needed but not received in childhood (level 3).

Level 4 takes care of deeps wounds in the existence, so this is the first level of holistic existential healing. It involves a mysterious dimension of intent, and all higher level of healing work is dependent of this. Often the trauma happened in a group setting, taking us to the logic of level 5: working with the patient in a group, re-creating the sound family, healing trauma from dysfunctional families.

Level 6 is rehabilitating the character and purpose of life (the soul); these deeper layers of existence are often wounded already in the womb and without the art of deep coherence between physician and patient, allowing for an energetic imitating the connection of the foetus and his/her mother these wounds cannot be healed.

Level 7 takes care of the body and of deep and early wounds in sexuality and gender. Level 8 integrates trauma with severe sexual and violent abuse. Direct sexual stimulation can be necessary to awaken a deeply repressed sexuality, although we strongly recommend that a patient is not stimulated into orgasm, to avoid the risk of the relationship turning into a sexual relationship.

Level 9 awakens the deepest layers of consciousness; the psychotropic drugs destabilises the old patters of perception making a breakthrough possible, where the patient leaves a mental survival perspective (being in the head) to experience life fully. This project has been described as "no mind" by the Zen Buddhists.

The holistic physician only uses level 10 in exceptional cases: when nothing else has worked, or when time or other serious conditions does not allow for trying many different things, i.e. with terminal and suicidal patients. Direct sexual involvement with the patient will often harm the patient and cannot be recommended.

The concept of controlled violence is somewhat disturbing, and it is very important that the beating is done only with open hand and extremely carefully, symbolically. The ethical problems using the holistic medical tools in general and especially the level 8, 9 and 10 techniques has been researched intensively by our team the last several years.

The tool of controlled violence is highly efficient to provoke anger in patients, who are so damaged by violent abuse that they no longer are able to feel and express anger, but it is difficult to avoid strong transferences of the therapist being the violator in stead of the original violator from the patients past, making controlled violence a very dangerous tool to use for the therapist, if the patients chooses to complain.

Most often the patients in need for this tool will be severely repressed and they often live in chronic fear, or complete emotionally numbness, socially isolated from the world. The danger of this treatment is obviously not to get them sufficiently into healing to be whole and well functioning, but sufficiently into their old material to be projecting the anger towards the therapist, in worst case complaining or even suing you for malpractice.

Another unwanted side effect are in rare cases temporary psychotic episodes normally followed by recovery within hours; happily such episodes do not seem correlated to any negative effects of the treatment. Having a legal system in most countries not accustomed to the level 8,9 and 10 techniques make the use of these tools some what difficult; we must recommend that you always comply rigidly to the laws of your country to avoid compromising yourself or holistic medicine and sexology in general.

In spite of the dramatic qualities of the therapeutic tools we know from large reviews of the litterature that side effects of holistic medicine and sexology are very rare (NNH=64,000) (69).

Conclusions

The patient will be able to heal, when old painful moments, the gestalts or trauma, are taken into the present and integrated. The holistic physician has many different tools to induce this kind of healing, some of which are more dangerous and potentially traumatic than others. Using the less powerful tool is of utmost importance to live up to Hippocrates principle of "first do not harm".

The more intense the therapeutic technique, the more emotional energy will normally be contained in the session and the higher the risk for the therapist to loose control or loose the patient to his or her own dark side, which can make the therapeutic session very traumatic and damaging to the patient.

The concept of "stepping up" in the therapy using more and more "dramatic" methods to get access to repressed emotions and events, has lead to the common notion of a "therapeutic staircase" with still stronger, more efficient and more dangerous potentially traumatic methods of therapy (see figure 1). This advanced expanded toolbox contains powerful tools, which can be organised into a staircase of intensity of therapeutic experience, both according to the effect they provoke and the level of expertise they take to master.

We believe that the systematic use of the staircase will greatly improve the power and efficiency of the holistic physician and sexologist and encourage governments and medical communities to work to make the whole toolbox legal for the holistic physicians and sexologists of their country, as many therapists are not free to use it today, which is sad for the many chronically ill patients desperately needing more efficient holistic therapy.

References

[1] Antonovsky A. Health, stress and coping. London: Jossey-Bass, 1985.
[2] Antonovsky A. Unravelling the mystery of health. How people manage stress and stay well. San Francisco: Jossey-Bass, 1987.
[3] Perls F, Hefferline R, Goodman P. Gestalt therapy. New York: Julian Press, 1951.
[4] Ventegodt S, Andersen NJ, Merrick J. Holistic medicine III: The holistic process theory of healing. ScientificWorldJournal 2003;3:1138-46.
[5] Jones E. The life and works of Sigmund Freud. New York: Basic Books, 1961.
[6] Grof S. The cosmic game: Explorations of the frontiers of human consciousness. New York: State Univ New York Press, 1998.
[7] Ventegodt S, Andersen NJ, Merrick J. Holistic medicine IV: Principles of the holistic process of healing in a group setting. ScientificWorldJournal 2003;3:1294-1301.
[8] Ventegodt S, Andersen NJ, Merrick J. The life mission theory V. A theory of the anti-self and explaining the evil side of man. ScientificWorldJournal 2003;3:1302-13.

[9] Ventegodt S. The life mission theory: A theory for a consciousness-based medicine. Int J Adolesc Med Health 2003;15(1): 89-91.

[10] Ventegodt S, Andersen NJ, Neikrug S, Kandel I, Merrick J. Clinical holistic medicine: Mental disorders in a holistic perspective. ScientificWorldJournal 2005;5:313-23.

[11] Ventegodt S, Merrick J. Clinical holistic medicine: The patients with multiple diseases. ScientificWorldJournal 2005;5:324-39.

[12] Ventegodt S, Morad M, Andersen NJ, Merrick J. Clinical holistic medicine: Tools for a medical science based on consciousness. ScientificWorldJournal 2004;4:347-61.

[13] Ventegodt S, Morad M, Hyam E, Merrick J. Clinical holistic medicine: Holistic sexology and treatment of vulvodynia through existential therapy and acceptance through touch. ScientificWorldJournal 2004;4:571-80.

[14] Jung CG. Psychology and alchemy. Collected works of CG Jung, vol 12. Princeton, NJ: Princeton Univ Press, 1968.

[15] Jung CG. Man and his symbols. New York: Anchor Press, 1964.

[16] Ventegodt S, Andersen NJ, Merrick J. The life mission theory III: Theory of talent. ScientificWorldJournal 2003;3:1286-93.

[17] La Divina Commedia (The Divine Comedy), written during Dante's exile (after 1302) and finished shortly before his death in 1321; a trilogy: Inferno, Purgatorio, Paradiso; spiritual journey through the spiritual realms of the afterlife and toward Beatrice and salvation.

[18] Ventegodt S, Merrick J. Clinical holistic medicine: Applied consciousness-based medicine. ScientificWorldJournal 2004;4:96-9.

[19] Ventegodt S, Morad M, Merrick J. Clinical holistic medicine: Classic art of healing or the therapeutic touch. ScientificWorldJournal 2004;4:134-47.

[20] Ventegodt S, Morad M, Merrick J. Clinical holistic medicine: The "new medicine", the multi-paradigmatic physician and the medical record. ScientificWorldJournal 2004;4:273-85.

[21] Ventegodt S, Morad M, Merrick J. Clinical holistic medicine: Holistic pelvic examination and holistic treatment of infertility. ScientificWorldJournal 2004;4:148-58.

[22] Ventegodt S, Morad M, Hyam E, Merrick J. Clinical holistic medicine: Use and limitations of the biomedical paradigm ScientificWorldJournal 2004;4:295-306.

[23] Ventegodt S, Morad M, Kandel I, Merrick J. Clinical holistic medicine: Social problems disguised as illness. ScientificWorldJournal 2004;4:286-94.

[24] Ventegodt S, Morad M, Hyam E, Merrick J. Clinical holistic medicine: When biomedicine is inadequate. ScientificWorldJournal 2004;4:333-46.

[25] Ventegodt S, Morad M, Merrick J. Clinical holistic medicine: Prevention through healthy lifestyle and quality of life. Oral Health Prev Dent 2004;2(Suppl 1):239-45.

[26] Ventegodt S, Morad M, Merrick J. Clinical holistic medicine: Holistic treatment of children. ScientificWorldJournal 2004;4:581-8.

[27] Ventegodt S, Morad M, Merrick J. Clinical holistic medicine: Problems in sex and living together. ScientificWorldJournal 2004;4: 562-70.

[28] Ventegodt S, Flensborg-Madsen T, Andersen NJ, Morad M, Merrick J. Clinical holistic medicine: A pilot on HIV and quality of life and a suggested treatment of HIV and AIDS. ScientificWorldJournal 2004;4:264-72.

[29] Ventegodt S, Morad M, Merrick J. Clinical holistic medicine: Induction of spontaneous remission of cancer by recovery of the human character and the purpose of life (the life mission). ScientificWorldJournal 2004;4:362-77.

[30] Ventegodt S, Morad M, Kandel I, Merrick J. Clinical holistic medicine: Treatment of physical health problems without a known cause, exemplified by hypertension and tinnitus. ScientificWorldJournal 2004;4:716-24.

[31] Ventegodt S, Morad M, Merrick J. Clinical holistic medicine: Developing from asthma, allergy and eczema. ScientificWorldJournal 2004;4:936-42.

[32] Ventegodt S, Morad M, Press J, Merrick J, Shek, DTL. Clinical holistic medicine: Holistic adolescent medicine. ScientificWorldJournal 2004;4:551-61.

[33] Ventegodt S, Solheim E, Saunte ME, Morad M, Kandel I, Merrick J. Clinical holistic medicine: Metastatic cancer. ScientificWorldJournal 2004;4:913-35.

[34] Ventegodt S, Morad M, Kandel I, Merrick J. Clinical holistic medicine: A psychological theory of dependency to improve quality of life. ScientificWorldJournal 2004;4:638-48.

[35] Ventegodt S, Merrick J. Clinical holistic medicine: Chronic infections and autoimmune diseases. ScientificWorldJournal 2005;5:155-64.

[36] Ventegodt S, Merrick J. Clinical holistic medicine: Chronic pain in the locomotor system. ScientificWorldJournal 2005;5:165-72.

[37] Ventegodt S, Gringols M, Merrick J. Clinical holistic medicine: Whiplash, fibromyalgia and chronic fatigue. ScientificWorldJournal 2005;5:340-54.

[38] Ventegodt S, Merrick J. Clinical holistic medicine: Chronic pain in internal organs. ScientificWorldJournal 2005;5:205-10.

[39] Ventegodt S, Kandel I, Neikrug S, Merrick J. Clinical holistic medicine: Holistic trauma treatment, for example following rape or incest – spontaneous regression and time line therapy. ScientificWorldJournal 2005;5:288-97.

[40] Ventegodt S, Kandel I, Neikrug S, Merrick J. Clinical holistic medicine: The existential crisis – life crises, stress and burnout. ScientificWorldJournal 2005;5:300-12.

[41] Ventegodt S, Gringols M, Merrick J. Clinical holistic medicine: Holistic rehabilitation. ScientificWorldJournal 2005;5:280-7.

[42] Ventegodt S, Morad M, Merrick J. Clinical holistic medicine: Holistic adolescent medicine. ScientificWorldJournal 2004;4:551-61.

[43] Ventegodt S, Andersen NJ, Neikrug S, Kandel I, Merrick J. Clinical holistic medicine: Mental disorders in a holistic perspective. ScientificWorldJournal 2005;5:313-23.

[44] Ventegodt S, Andersen NJ, Neikrug S, Kandel I, Merrick J. Clinical holistic medicine: Holistic treatment of mental disorders. ScientificWorldJournal 2005;5:427-45.

[45] Ventegodt S, Merrick J. Clinical holistic medicine: The patients with multiple diseases. ScientificWorldJournal 2005;5:324-39.

[46] Ventegodt S, Solheim E, Saunte M, Morad M, Kandel I, Merrick J. Clinical holistic medicine: Metastatic cancer. ScientificWorldJournal 2004;4:913-35.

[47] Ventegodt S, Clausen B, Merrick J. Clinical holistic medicine: The case story of Anna I. Long-term effect of childhood sexual abuse and incest with a treatment approach. ScientificWorldJournal 2006;6:1965-76.

[48] Ventegodt S, Clausen B, Merrick J. Clinical holistic medicine: The case story of Anna II: Patient diary as a tool in treatment. ScientificWorldJournal 2006;6:2006-34.

[49] Ventegodt S, Clausen B, Merrick J. Clinical holistic medicine: The case story of Anna III: Rehabilitation of philosophy of life during holistic existential therapy for childhood sexual abuse. ScientificWorldJournal 2006;6:2080-91.

[50] Yalom ID. Existential psychotherapy. New York: Basic Books, 1980.

[51] Yalom ID. The gift of therapy. New York: Harper Collins, 2002.

[52] Castaneda C. The art of dreaming. New York: Harper-Collins, 1993.

[53] Ventegodt S, Andersen NJ, Merrick J. Holistic medicine: Scientific challenges. ScientificWorldJournal 2003;3:1108-16.

[54] Baker D. Esoteric healing (I). London: Essendon, 1975.

[55] Kjems C. Vaginal acupressure. Personal communication.

[56] Masters WH, Johnson VE. Human sexual inadequacy. Philadelphia, PA: Lippincott Williams Wilkins, 1970.

[57] Masters WH, Johnson VE. Human sexual response. Boston: Little Brown, 1966.

[58] Anderson EF. Peyote. The divine cactus. Tucson, AZ: Univ Arizona Press, 1996.

[59] Bruhn JG, De Smet PA, El-Seedi HR, Beck O. Mescaline use for 5700 years. Lancet 2002;359(9320):1866.

[60] Mumey N. The peyote ceremony among the American Indians. Bull Med Libr Assoc 1951;39(3):182-8.

[61] Stafford P. Psychedelics encyclopedia. Berkeley, CA: Ronin Publ, 1992.

[62] Ventegodt S, Merrick, J. Psychoactive drugs and quality of life. ScientificWorldJournal 2003;3:694-706.

[63] Ventegodt S, Kromann M, Andersen NJ, Merrick J. The life mission theory VI: A theory for the human character. ScientificWorldJournal 2004;4:859-80.

[64] Castaneda C. The teachings of Don Juan: A yaqui way of knowledge. New York: Harper-Collins, 1968.

[65] Grof S. LSD psychotherapy: Exploring the frontiers of the hidden mind. Alameda, CA: Hunter House, 1980.

[66] Luna LE, White S. Ayahuaasca reader. Santa Fe, NM: Synergetic Press, 2000.

[67] Strassman RJ. Adverse reactions to psychedelic drugs. A review of the literature. Nerv Ment Dis 1984;172(10):577-95.

[68] Gormsen C. [Gensidig terapi]. Copenhagen: Lindeløvs Forlag, 1984.

[69] Ventegodt S, Merrick J. A review of side effects and adverse events of non-drug medicine (non-pharmaceutical CAM): Psychotherapy, mind-body medicine and clinical holistic medicine. J Compl Integr Medicine 2009, In press.

Section 12. Suicide and suicide prevention

Suicide is one of the most problematic issues in psychiatry; fortunately holistic medicine has recently been found to prevent suicide (1). A metaanalysis found that about 100 patients that entered therapy after taking the decision of committing suicide all survived. In the therapy the patient found resources to let go of the decision of killing themselves. In general holistic therapy therefore seems to be the preferred treatment for patients in danger of committing suicide.

But things are not that simple. Many countries have special laws installed to protect the life of patients wanting to commit suicide. Often force is used to save the patients, in spite of the use of force obviously violating the sacred principle of patient autonomy. The holistic physician or therapist must obey the laws in spite of these not being rational according to the latest scientific knowledge (1).

Death can be good or bad. In this section we also discuss what a good and a bad death is. Understanding this has by existential thinkers been seen as crucial for the whole understanding of life itself. We have included chapter 49 which is of little practical value, to give the reader an example of contemporary holistic philosophy of life.

References

[1] Ventegodt S, Andersen NJ, Kandel I, Merrick J. Effect, side effects and adverse events of non-pharmaceutical medicine. A review. Int J Disabil Hum Dev 2009;8(3):227-35.

Chapter 48

Suicide from a holistic approach

Suicide has been honoured and respected in the eastern culture, especially in Japan with the famous tradition of Hara-kiri or seppuku, while in most western societies suicide has been seen negatively and many contemporary physicians tend to consider suicide the most self-destructive and evil thing a human being can do and something that should be avoided at all cost. Religions also have different viewpoints on suicide, but from a philosophical point of view we believe that considering the choice of life and dead to be extremely relevant for a good living. The choice of life and dead is real, since responsibility for life is necessary in order to live life and even the best physician cannot keep a patient alive, who deep inside wants to die. In this chapter we present parts of a story of a young girl who had experienced child sexual abuse. In holistic existential therapy it is our experience, when the patient is well supported in the confrontation of the fundamental questions related to assuming responsibility for the coherence, that this confrontation will almost always lead to a big YES to life. Without confronting the fundamental question of "to be or not to be" life can never be chosen 100% and thus never be lived fully.

Introduction

Suicide (from latin sui caedere, self killing) is the act of ending your own life, which has been considered a sin and crime in many religions and societies, but some cultures have viewed it as an honorable way to exit certain shameful or hopeless situations. Parasuicide is the term for "attempted suicide".

Suicide has been honoured and respected in the eastern cultures with the famous tradition of Hara-kiri (called seppuku) as a well-known example. Hara-kiri is a ritual and honorable suicide with Japanese origins. Traditionally, it is done in a spiritually clean temple by cutting open your abdomen with a wakizashi (traditional Japanese sword with a shoto blade between 30 and 60 cm, with an average of 50 cm), thereby releasing the soul. The traditional form is one deep cut down and one across, while a slightly less honorable version (and much less painful) is that at the same time, a friend severs the head for an instant death. Hara-kiri was traditionally used as the ultimate protest, when your own morals stood in the way of executing an order from the master. It was also permissible as a form of repentance when one had committed an unforgivable sin, either by accident or on purpose.

History and religion

Many famous people through history have committed suicide, such as Cleopatra VII of Egypt, Hannibal, Nero, Adolf Hitler, Ernest Hemingway or Vincent van Gogh.

In Buddhism, the past influence our present and what an individual does in the present influence his or her future, in this life or the next. This is cause and effect, as taught by Gautama Buddha. Known as karma, intentional action by mind, body or speech has a reaction and its repercussion is the reason behind the conditions and differences we come across in the world. Suffering primarily originates from past negative deeds or just from being in samsara (the cycle of birth and death). Another reason for the prelvalent suffering we experience is due to impermanence. Since everything is in a constant state of flux, we experience unsatisfactoriness with the fleeting events of life. To break out of samsara, one simply must realize their true nature, by Enlightenment in the present moment; this is Nirvana. For Buddhists, since the first precept is to refrain from the destruction of life (including oneself), suicide is clearly considered a negative form of action. But despite this view, an ancient Asian ideology similar to Hara-kiri persists to influence Buddhists by, when under oppression, commiting the act of "honorable" suicide.

Christianity is traditionally opposed to suicide, and assisted suicide and especially in Catholicism, suicide has been considered a grave and sometimes mortal sin. The chief Catholic argument is that your life is the property of God and to destroy your own life is to assert dominion over what belongs to God. Many Christians believe in the sanctity of human life, a principle which, broadly speaking, says that all human life is sacred - a wonderful, even miraculous creation of the divine God - and every effort must be made to save and preserve it whenever possible.

In Islam, God is creator, he is the giver of life, and he alone has the right to end it. Suicide is forbidden in Islam and listed as a sin among the "enormities" in Reliance of the Traveller, a manual of Sharia in the tradition of Imam Shafi'i. Those who commit suicide should be *roasted in a fire* (do not kill yourselves, for Allah is compassionate towards you. Whoever does so, in transgression and wrongfully, We shall roast in a fire, and that is an easy matter for Allah. (an-Nisaa 4:29-30)), *forbidden Paradise* (the Prophet said, "Whoever intentionally swears falsely by a religion other than Islam, then he is what he has said, (e.g. if he says, 'If such thing is not true then I am a Jew,' he is really a Jew). And whoever commits suicide with piece of iron will be punished with the same piece of iron in the Hell Fire." Narrated Jundab the Prophet said, "A man was inflicted with wounds and he committed suicide, and so Allah said: My slave has caused death on himself hurriedly, so I forbid Paradise for him." (Sahih Bukhari 2.445) *and will be punished in hell by whatever used for suicide* (the Prophet said, "He who commits suicide by throttling shall keep on throttling himself in the Hell Fire (forever) and he who commits suicide by stabbing himself shall keep on stabbing himself in the Hell-Fire." (Sahih Bukhari 2.446, 2.445)).

Judaism views suicide as one of the most serious of sins. Suicide has always been forbidden by Jewish law, except for three specific cases: if one is being forced by someone to commit murder, forced to commit an act of idolatry, or forced to commit adultery or incest. However, outside those cases, suicide is forbidden, and this includes taking part in assisted suicide. One may not ask someone to assist in killing themselves for two separate reasons: (a) killing oneself is forbidden, and (b) one is then making someone else accomplice to a sin.

Western society

In most western societies suicide has mostly been seen negatively, and many contemporary physicians tend to consider suicide the most self-destructive and evil thing a human being can do and something that should be avoided at all cost. Even the patient's contemplation of suicide is often considers harmful and treated as a disease in itself.

From a philosophical point of view considering the choice of life and dead is extremely relevant to good living and very sound considerations. The choice of life and dead is real, since responsibility for life is necessary in order to live life and even the best physician cannot keep a patient alive, who deep inside wants to die.

The reason for the western suicide is normally bad thriving as the tendency to have suicidal thoughts are closely connected to poor quality of life or a feeling of having no value or even harmful to the surrounding world. One in 20 of the Danish population is at a given point in time considering suicide (1).

Holistic medicine

In the process of holistic medical treatment the physician or therapist must some times use a deep existential rehabilitation process (2), which can include a crisis where the patient will consider committing suicide (3) and this danger must be considered as real. On the other hand, the deep contemplation of suicide and the following unconditional choice of life seem to be extremely beneficial for the patient deeply involved with personal development. This turns our view of suicide upside down and forces us to analyse the phenomenon of urge for suicide (or urge for dead as described by Freud (4)) in the existential perspective of healing the "soul" or core of existence.

Freud stated that the subconscious of man contains two fundamental forces: a life force (or sexual force) and a death force. The life mission theory states that to annulate a painful life purpose, one must intent destruction of self and other (5). The logic is that we deepest down in existence wants to do good, but when this is to difficult it turns so emotionally painful that we want to get out of this purpose and the only way to do so is to repress is by intending the opposite of the original purpose. This dynamic seems to be highly active in early childhood.

To understand the process of healing, the concept of "peeling the onion" is relevant (6). In therapy the patient digs deeper and deeper down the historical layers of traumas, and deeper and deeper into the heart of being. Three layers of existence can be identified, as they reveal themselves during holistic existential therapy (see figure 1):

1) the layer of global quality of life (QOL), mental/physical health and ability
2) the layer of love, power/consciousness and sexuality
3) the layer of existential coherence, where life inside the human being cohere with the outside world

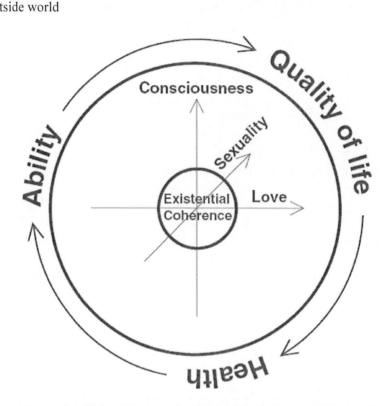

Figure 1. The human existence consist of three layers: 1) the layer of global quality of life (QOL), mental/physical health and ability, 2) the layer of love, power/consciousness and sexuality, and 3) the layer of existential coherence, where life inside the human being cohere with the outside world. When the patient or spiritually seeking person go still deeper towards the innermost core of existence (s)he will one day confront the most fundamental question in life: To be or not to be. This is the birth of the suicidal crises, which can only be definitely terminated by the patient deciding unconditionally to live. This decision must be taken autonomously, that is without any kind of pressure of external motivation.

Normally what brings the patient to the clinic is a problem with one of the major issues of the first layer: quality of life – the patient is unhappy, stressed or in a crisis; health – the patient is sick, in pain or mentally disturbed or depressed or ability – the patient is poor functioning and of little value to self or others. Searching for the causes of the problems in this layer normally will bring the patient to the second, inner layer of existence, where often the disturbances in the dimensions of love, understanding and gender/character can be seen as the diseases causing the problems of health, QOL and ability. The problems of love, consciousness and sexuality are often emotionally overwhelmingly painful, and only with great support and intense "holding" will the roots of the existential imbalances be healed in the holistic medical clinic.

As the therapy goes still deeper, one day a third layer of existence is revealed. This layer seems to contain the core of existential responsibility. We call this innermost layer "coherence", or existential coherence (7) or Antonovsky coherence after the researcher naming it first (Aaron Antonovsky, 1923-1994) (8,9). The problem of this layer is that it cannot really be processed in therapy as the question is: Do I want to be connected to the world? Do I want to be a part of this world? Do I want to live or do I want to die? So we are back at the famous core question of existence, so beautifully worded by William Sheakspeare (1564-1616)(10): "To be or not to be".

The value of our autonomy is our free will, the prize of it is our loneliness. Only I can say if I want to live. So in the course of personal development, people who seek all the way to the basis of existence will face this question: when it comes down to it, do you want to live of do you want to die? The urge to die is very logical at this level: to be connected is to painful, to reach for the meaning of life is too much for me, to be is connected with to unbearable feelings and emotions for me to be acceptable. The urge to live is as logical: I am here as a gifted person, and the meaning of my life is to share my gift with other people and to the world in order to create value, as I was meant to.

The internal struggle on life and death that follows from these contradictory and opposing forces in the root of every individual human soul is from this perspective what causes the suicidal crises of man. Interestingly, therefore, the suicidal crisis becomes extremely important in the process of healing with the understanding and wise handling of the suicidal patient guiding the patient towards confronting the fundamental existential question "To be or not to be". This question is what brings growth, learning and personal progress to the troubled patient.

A case history

Anna was a student aged 22 years, who had completely repressed over 100 episodes of sexual abuse, incest and rape throughout her early childhood. She now seems to have recovered completely, including regaining her full emotional range, though holistic existential therapy, individually and in a group. The therapy took 18 month and more than one hundred hours of intensive therapy. In the beginning of the therapy, the issues were her physical and mental health, in the middle of the therapy the central issue was about her purpose of life and her love life. In the end of the therapy the issue was gender and sexuality. The strategy was building up her strength for several months, mobilising all her hidden resources and motivation for living, before the painful old traumas were confronted and integrated.

The following is from her own case diary, just before she ends her therapy, the suicidal crisis came and choosing life in the end of this crisis was what gave her the final breakthrough to life (3).

> Saturday
> After a nice bath I dressed and got ready to go out enjoying the nature. To begin with I must say that the sun had been shining on me the whole day; so beautiful and fine it was that I couldn't help saying hallo, while warming me on the outside and on the inside. This grew into many greetings. I was down near the Marienlyst Castle and was sitting at the end of the avenue, of course with the sun on my chins. The place was really beautiful and minimalistic. I proceeded a bit towards Helsingoer, but it wasn't the right way; too many cars, houses and first and foremost, too much noise. Therefore I went back to Hellebaek and followed the beach with my recently purchased goods in the bag: chips and white bread, uhmmm. How great an outing it

had been! I could sense how I got calmed and at the same time boosted from listening to the roar of the waves. I sat down on a big stone, on the cushion I had brought along, enjoyed the sound of the water and shuddered slightly at the warm sunbeams. While sitting there I thought of it once again: that I am an unwritten leaf and that right now I am exceptionally lucky, because I have got the chance of shaping my life and myself like I want it most. Now I can cultivate the capacities, skills and qualities I greatly prefer to possess, and this without the usual, rotten wreckage in tow, which could prevent me from doing it. There is a huge opportunity right now! I was also thinking this means that now I will actually be capable of getting/achieving ANYTHING I want. I just have to set about getting/achieving it. I walked to Hellebaek, about 6 km, along the beach and walked back via the woods. I thought of the song "The woods around the country are turning yellow now" and changed the title into "The woods around the country are glowing now" because I found that was what they actually did. The woods were unbelievably beautiful right now, in fact got my eyes filled with tears. It's indeed a huge gift for me to be up here in the beautiful nature. It was, no doubt, the completely right impulse to follow! As I returned here I began to paint/colour a bit in the colouring book. However, it didn't really mean anything to me though, so I didn't finish the drawing. It was so boring … Then I laid down to rest. I dreamed a little, but as I didn't manage to maintain the dream, I forgot it again. Now I have been taking a bath thus, and I want to read a little before going to sleep again. Tomorrow I shall check out at 9:30 a.m. I am curious to know whether I'll wake up, having got no watch. What I have been experiencing has been right: To stay in the pleasure: going for a walk today, giving myself fully into the pleasure; not holding back at all and being able to stay in it. To give myself for: the anger. The same principle as for the pleasure: not holding back, being one hundred percent in it. - This is to be alive!

Saturday night
I twist about miserably in my bed, sweat as if I had got a very high temperature. The anger is huge and while lying here I am full of it. I beat the mattress, swear, snub them, and then begin projecting anger onto Søren (the therapist/physician). I get angry with him at the way he treated me this week; the rough way mixed with an apparent indifference as to the way he had been reflecting me. Then the suicide thoughts appeared:

- pistol: too much mess and too traumatic for those who find me
- cut my throat: same thing as with the pistol
- cut the wrists: then I shall suffer too long
- liquidation: I could pay someone to do it; this one is the best I immediately find until I am thinking of:
- overdose: which would be much better. A second later I think that I would probably not hit the correct dose, but would brain-damage myself and end as a vegetable, dribbling and not even being able to communicate to people that they must kill me. Then Søren would call on me, hold me close, and this would be the ultimate hell; me not being able to communicate, only dribble.

Now I cry and am totally miserable. I still sweat fever. I think then: Stop – just be quiet. One day at the time. I say aloud: "I bring life and joy. I bring life. I bring life" quite a lot of times and this calms me; this slowly makes me to relax. [Anna is here assuming responsibility for her own existence at the most deep level; she is facing the need of choosing to live or to die, accepting life on its own conditions or not accepting it. This is really the deepest level of existential choice for any human being: do you want to live or do you want to die? And it is a strictly personal question; nobody can really help you out here, you need to solve this for yourself, as Anna instinctively did.]

Monday

At long last I had a decent conversation with Søren. I had hurt his feelings, made him sad. He said I did it to create a distance between us. I told him that I was fond of him. He thanked and finished the conversation saying he was fond of me too. Subjects: detachment, independence. I slept very bad tonight, Søren and our understanding dialogue about "what did happen" the last few days being constantly in my thoughts. I even wrote a poem while shifting about restlessly.

Tuesday

I was at my gestalt therapist today. Further I am thinking that if I play my cards well I can end as something big. With my story, my intuitive intelligence and my courage I think I can become an entirely tough therapist. Watch me! Later I talked with Søren; he was making fun and said I would soon be able to take my gestalt therapist in therapy. It was funny said, and I must admit that later I will be forgetting her face while telling her how I had been experiencing my therapy. Not only was she gaping, she also realized that she was facing a very intelligent girl who had just discovered how intelligent she was. An educational experience, indeed! Let me finish here by mentioning that my personal development will no doubt carry on. I have been releasing so amazingly much insecurity. Never before have I been feeling so confident that everything will turn out all right. I find I keep on getting ever more gorgeous, and I am sure I shall get the best boyfriend in the whole world. I am in the process of being quite happy; I am not miserable any more. I am convinced I shall become entirely happy.

Discussion

Fear of letting the patient confront the deep existential pain of loneliness and low coherence often makes the physician use force to save the patient's life. Often the physician use strong antipsychotic drugs and conversational therapy of a cognitive type to turn the patient's attention outwards against the outer world and away from the existential problems, thus avoiding the patient's confrontation of the emotional pain and the temptation of the suicidal perspective.

From a holistic perspective this approach is only dealing with the symptoms of the real disease, which is lack of existential coherence, and can thus not be recommended as the problem stays with the patient and can surface anytime again leaving the patient in tremendous danger of actually committing the suicide, the physician so eagerly tries to prevent.

There is always a risk that the patient during the process of confronting the original painful causes of the existential disconnection can waste his or her own life, if not sufficiently supported.

In holistic existential therapy it is our experience, when the patient is well supported in the confrontation of the fundamental questions related to assuming responsibility for the coherence, that this confrontation will almost always lead to a big YES to life. Without confronting the fundamental question of "to be or not to be" life can never be chosen 100% and thus never be lived fully.

Conclusions

The dynamics of suicide, wanting to die so much that self-destruction of the body becomes an issue, is the most painful a human being can go through. On the other hand it seems that solving the existential problems at the deepest level is the most beneficial achievement of all and the most important thing a person can be supported in doing. The taboo of dead in most western cultures has turned an existentially sound quest for meaning and search for healing of the soul and reconnection to the world into something shameful and bad, something that are often condemned. With a more profound, honest and brave understanding of life and personal growth, the reflection on suicide can be changed from being something we in our society and medical facilities try to avoid at all cost, to something natural and beautiful, we as holistic physicians and health professionals must support and guide our patients through.

The intense suffering connected to the dynamics of suicide is something we cannot spare the patient, but we can give him the benefit of his hard work, which only becomes obvious when the choice of life and dead is real, and life is finally chosen unconditionally. With a lot of "holding" and caring support even the most painful feelings of being completely worthless and unwanted on this planet is easier to deal with, contain and finally integrate for the patient.

References

[1]   Ventegodt S. Quality of life in Denmark. Results from a population survey. Copenhagen: Forskningscentrets Forlag, 1995. [Danish].
[2]   Ventegodt S, Gringols M, Merrick J. Clinical holistic medicine: Holistic rehabilitation ScientificWorldJournal 2005;5:280-7.
[3]   Ventegodt S, Clausen B, Merrick J. Clinical holistic medicine: The case story of Anna. II Patient diary with the holistic process of healing seen from within the patient. Submitted to ScientificWorldJournal.
[4]   Freud S, Brill AA, ed. The basic writings of Sigmund Freud. New York: Modern Library, 1938.
[5]   Ventegodt S. The life mission theory: A theory for a consciousness-based medicine. Int J Adolesc Med Health 2003;15(1):89-91.
[6]   Perls F, Hefferline R, Goodman P. Gestalt therapy. New York: Julian Press, 1951.
[7]   Ventegodt S, Flensborg-Madsen T, Andersen NJ, Merrick J. Life Mission Theory VII: Theory of existential (Antonovsky) coherence: a theory of quality of life, health and ability for use in holistic medicine. ScientificWorldJournal 2005;5:377-89.
[8]   Antonovsky A. Health, stress and coping. London: Jossey-Bass, 1985.
[9]   Antonovsky A. Unravelling the mystery of health. How people manage stress and stay well. San Franscisco: Jossey-Bass, 1987.
      Alexander P. William Sheakspeare: The complete works. London: Collins. 1991.

Chapter 49

Death: What is a good death?

To live with the awareness of death – death is around somewhere, waiting for our final slip in order to sweep us away – is a sinister but also wonderful situation. When we are aware of death and know that we have too little time left and that time is the only thing we do not have, then we really do our best. When we acknowledge the unique opportunity we have to become aware, straighten our lives to get a better life while there is still a chance, then we can live the way that makes each day better than the previous and the next year better than this. We can live in such a way that we are on our way up. A force stronger than reason is needed, when the course of your life is to be altered. Let us call it the will to a better life. If this will is present people will possess real humility, making them open and willing to learn and change. The strange thing about this will is that it is an irrational, nonverbal force that pulls up your existence. To rediscover the meaning of life means finding yourself and the values that you can always, and without faltering, use as foundation for your own life. To regain the meaning of life means that you acknowledge that you are a human being, subject to the conditions and laws applicable to humans.

Introduction

Death can be seen as the real enemy (1). Death puts life in perspective as we finally see it as the very fragile, easily lost and infinitely valuable thing that it is. When you do not sense that death is after you, you relax and think yourself out of danger. But you have no guarantee that you are alive in five minutes. It is already later than you think. In a little while we are gone. In a moment we have all turned to dust.

To live with the awareness of death – death is around somewhere, waiting for our final slip in order to sweep us away – is a sinister but also wonderful situation. When we are aware of death and know that we have too little time left and that time is the only thing we do not have, then we really do our best. When we acknowledge the unique opportunity we have to become aware, straighten our lives to get a better life while there is still a chance, then we can live the way that makes each day better than the previous and the next year better than this. We can live in such a way that we are on our way up.

Ask yourself: "Am I on my way up or on my way down?" Do you have to admit that you are on your way down, even though of course it is a slow descent? The only thing that can make most of us change our course, so that we live in a manner that leads us upwards is the distinct awareness of death. When we see death threatening us all the time and coming at us in many various forms like loneliness, illness or hopelessness and when we realize that we constantly feed death with great chunks of our own flesh, because we do not make the right choices and thus unconsciously take one step further towards the grave, then we are motivated to correct these systematic faults.

Only death has the power to really make us want to change our course in life. All lesser problems and crises throughout life may be unpleasant, but not really unpleasant enough to make us want to succeed in changing ourselves. The reason for this extreme conservatism is that we already have dedicated most of our decisions to survive, i.e. to avoid dying. Therefore, the death that threatens us now is computed in our minds as more important than the death threatening us in the past. But awareness of death does not come to us easily when we are only slowly decaying. We can see people die in front of us without understanding that we, too, consist of fragile flesh and that we have to depart soon. No force in life can change this: In a little while we are gone. We have to live here and now. This moment is all we have got (2).

When you have only 700 days left

When "terminal" cancer patients (the quotation marks are because maybe the patients are not as terminal as we usually think) visit their physician some time after they have received the diagnosis and the verdict, that according to the statistics they only have about two years left to live, they often say strange things like: "I am grateful that I got cancer." The physician thinks that this is strange and asks why. "I have never felt so well," the patient says. Most physicians tend to think that is peculiar, because here we have Mrs Larsen, who lost 35 kilogram, lost all her hair because of chemotherapy and her cancer has metastasized throughout the body. Also she looks like something the cat dragged in and then she insists that…". "But it is true, doctor," she insists. "My life has never had so much meaning, my life is more intense than it has ever been now that I know that I have only 700 days left. Now I have let go on all my worries and idiosyncrasies. I have turned simple. I see the sun rise, I feel the wind on my skin, I talk honestly with my friends and I have stopped arguing with my husband. And best of all I have started to say no in order to only do the things I really like".

However absurd it may seem, people with their back against the wall and knowing their days are numbered often live much more intensely than the rest of us, who imagine that we will live forever. Face to face with death we suddenly appear to remember that this is what life is all about, to feel good within ourselves and with each other and to do something we really like. "What a fool I have been" people often say and think. Time possesses the strange capacity to expand enormously, when we live intensely. A moment can feel like eternity or a year can appear to pass within a minute (have you ever experienced a New Year's Eve, where you feel that the past year has been uneventful, so totally empty of anything essential ?). If you know that you only have a short while left before death, then even such a moment may be enough to change the course, that fate had in store for you.

We may call this very strange power that steps in when you are facing death "the will to live." We really do possess enormous potentials for growth and change, but only rarely do these potentials come into use. Our reason and our total naiveté towards the tough and wonderful conditions that apply to us prevent us from changing. You can reclaim the meaning of life. You can break through to the experience of being totally and fully alive, to your life having meaning and your existence making a real difference to the world you live in and yourself. Patients who become well again, drug addicts who become clean, prostitutes who succeed in love, all the miracles people talk about, but do not believe in. All this happens during this process. But, of course, up to this day it has been rare. If our culture held more insight into these things they would probably be much more common, the way they appear to have been in other cultures at other times. A holistic physician often has the great fortune to live in a world, where these miracles are almost normal. In our "quality of life as medicine" projects they occur surprisingly often (3,4).

To pull yourself up

A force stronger than reason is needed, when the course of your life is to be altered. Let us call it the will to a better life. If this will is present people will possess real humility, making them open and willing to learn and change. The strange thing about this will is that it is an irrational, nonverbal force that pulls up your existence.

When the will influences your view of the world it becomes altered in a strange way. This happens because the will to live supplies a fixed point, namely what you have to believe in when you really love life, beyond all reason, beyond everything you have learnt and experienced in life. This fixed point can serve as a new foundation for your personal philosophy of life. From this moment on you will feel that deep down life is good and valuable, the world is full of opportunities, people are trustworthy, you are able to solve the problems in life on your own and through this battle you can make everything cohere.

The experience of pulling yourself up by the roots of your hair literally means that you raise or lift your own existence. You correct your faults and close up all the holes that drain your vital energy. You remove all the good reasons for not having any self-respect and start a new life on a totally new foundation. You take responsibility for your own life.

The essential part of the will is that it is able to cut through all the confusion and doubt that normally characterize human life. In reality, there is no rational way of determining the truth value of statements or philosophies of life. You cannot guess the truth about life and the world. Reason cannot distinguish very well between personal philosophies of life, because they all basically rest on principles that are irrational, ethical or even emotional. However, the will to live a good life cuts cleanly through doubt and mental fog and points out clearly and directly what is right and wrong in relation to our love of life.

Some decisions and choices are in harmony with life, others bring ruin and destruction. Some decisions lead towards the top, others towards the bottom. Some views of the world can sustain life, others weigh it down. Only the will to live a good life can make a person rise above the immaterial, the meaningless, doubt and nonsense. You rarely discover that the will is the real resource for improving life, until you are facing death. When that happens, the will to live is often the only reason why you survive.

The experience of pulling yourself up by the roots of your hair is quite amusing. But really, if we are to live fully and completely for just a moment this is what is needed, the ability to lift ourselves and take wings, despite the thousands of weights that are dragging us down. Taking responsibility for our own lives is really a process during which we elevate our own existence, in spite of all barriers and difficulties. The will to live a good life is the only thing that can create this effect.

To find quality of life

We are free to choose our values, the things we think are important and good. Some people's lives are centered on collecting stamps, while others collect good friends. Some chose expensive clothes or fast cars as values, while others grow ecological vegetables and wear only clothes made of recycled material. Some people collect dirty videos, while others are into bible studies. In our minds we are free to chose our own personal values, just as we have an enormous freedom to describe the world whatever way we want.

One thing is values, another thing is how we feel or what state we are in. Something makes one person happy, something else makes another person happy. But what about the happiness we feel: is it the same kind of happiness or are there different kinds of happiness? And what about satisfaction with life? Do we all possess the same sense of satisfaction or do we experience satisfaction in different ways? What about the meaning of life itself? When we feel deep within ourselves, in our very souls and hearts (if we are able to find it), do we then feel the same meaningfulness in life, when it is meaningful and the same senselessness, when it is not? Do two people experience the same kind of love, the same feeling of hate or sexual desire?

It is obvious that each experience carries its own qualities and intensity. But is the actual quality of the experience connected to the individual, to our egos and learned descriptions of the world? Or is the actual quality of happiness, satisfaction or the meaning of life something that is given by human nature? As it appears from this paper, we believe very strongly in nature and that life within us never has let go of its habitat in nature, because we possess our common description of the world not just as a possibility, but as a necessity. This is a given, because we are constructed the way we are and have to live together.

The decisive factor for being able to change yourself is that you are able to regain your belief, that fundamentally life is good. When we here use the word 'belief' it is because from a rational point of view, such an attitude will always be a question of belief. Subjectively, of course, it can also be experienced as certain knowledge. And it is this inner certain conviction that makes the difference.

You can believe nature as being the essential thing. Not, as is often suggested, in a primitive way, with coarse instincts and pre-programmed behavior parallel to animal behavior, but more refined. The idea is that deep down in our biological matter we possess a nature as humans. This nature is in the shape of an abstract recipe for being a human, and life is about expressing this recipe to the full, unfolding and manifesting its potential for a good life.

In this light, our nature holds the potential for all the dimensions of our lives. It is in our nature to feel good or bad, to be satisfied or dissatisfied, to have sexual feelings, to be happy and feel there is a meaning in life or to work for our innermost visions and longings. Our nature is such, that we have a heart that we need to discern and obey so that we may lead the good life.

To seize the meaning of life

When we finally acknowledge that the world extends beyond our reason or that there are forces at large that matter more than our impulses then we can proceed. When we realize that there are values on Earth that far surpass the value of our small life, then we will be humble enough to accept the gift (and task) that is life. Then we can put our faith in authority and our loyal, but out-of-date and limited description of the world behind us.

To rediscover the meaning of life means finding yourself and the values that you can always, and without faltering, use as foundation for your own life. To regain the meaning of life means that you acknowledge that you are a human being, subject to the conditions and laws applicable to humans. We am not talking about the highway code, but more profound laws that apply to all living beings. To take responsibility, to see yourself as active and not as a victim, to work at correcting your personal faults and repair the bumps in your inner map of the world.

To regain the meaning of life does not mean to be forever happy. It means that you find your fundamental challenge as a human being and take up the challenge. You become a person with a mission. There are things to be corrected both on the inside and the outside, things within yourself and things in the world around you. If you are really clever you will see that in reality there is often little difference between the two. The flaws in the world are evident to you, because you also sense and work on similar weaknesses and flaws within yourself. The great struggle for a better world, that all people become involved in, when they acknowledge that the meaning of life is about coherence. They cannot escape this world, however much they want to, because of all its superficiality, materialism, abuse of power and false values, then their realize that this struggle is very much about improving that part of the world that is you. To clean the place you occupy, to cultivate your own spirit.

Everything starts with yourself. Because all the barriers you see are actually within you, in your own personal view of the world. Becoming free means first and foremost becoming free of the constraints imposed by your own rational description of reality. It does not actually mean that you must get rid of this description or the framework it puts around your self-expression, but you can loosen the constraints so much that they no longer limits life, but support life. You need to get rid of the negativity in the description and the old pains that hold your limiting decisions in their place.

What is the purpose of life?

Imagine that you really wish to know the meaning of your life. You rent a small cabin in the mountains, where nobody can disturb you for the next three or four weeks. You buy provisions for the whole stay. You go alone and you spend your time on only one thing, namely answering the question: 'What is the meaning of my life'? Of course you have to find a wording that is all your own, which exactly fits you and your life. But it must be deep enough to penetrate all the way into your soul.

What is the purpose of life for you? Why are you on the surface of the Earth for a short while? In what way do you make a difference in the world? What are your dreams in life, love, real friendship, a good job or harmony with nature ?

When you compare the life you lead with your dreams, how do you measure up ? Is your personal relationship the love of your life or is it boring routine in bed and arguments at breakfast and before the evening news? Do you actually have one single friend with whom you can and do talk about everything and who does not begrudge you real progress ? A friend who can meet you right where you are and just wish you all the best and therefore ask you all the questions you should already have asked yourself, but did not dare to out of fear of meeting yourself ? Questions like what is it you want, what are your opportunities and what is needed for you to obtain what you want with the opportunities you have ?

What about your work? Do you really exert yourself and improve anything? Do you gain the expertise necessary to express yourself creatively and spontaneously? Do you solve your tasks to your own personal satisfaction? Do you have enough influence on your own work? Do you actually accept what your company produces or should you be doing something quite different in order to be of use in the world?

What about your time off? Do your holidays fulfill your dreams or do you just end up in some bar in Mallorca wasting your time on casual pursuits, before returning home to your boring routine? Do you burn for your life, your work and your love? Does you or your life contain any nerve at all? In the final analysis, how do you feel, if you are really and totally honest? Are you OK? Do you get out of life, what it can give you? Do you exploit all your opportunities? Have you accepted the challenge that is yours and is your life in balance? Are you at peace with yourself, because you have acknowledged your own personal mission in life?

We suspect that after a couple of days you are having no more fun at the cabin. After all, to study the meaning of life is rather unpleasant. The really sad truth is that we have no wish to know the truth about ourselves or the deeper meaning of life, because it is painful to learn something decidedly new and we only do this if it is absolutely necessary.

Actually, what began as a straightaway philosophical experiment now appears to be a dramatic process, where you have to confront and process the pains of a lifetime! All the bad things you have done since early childhood will come to you and ask you for a clean-up! This is not our favorite perspective, but the only perspective that will make us change into better, more innocent and more loving persons.

The pain of knowing the meaning of your life

Our problem is that deep down we do not really want to know the meaning of our lives, because if we do we have to acknowledge that the life we actually live is a pale shadow of the opportunities we hold, no matter how good life is, when compared to that of other people.

We are not at all interested in realizing that we almost live in an existential gutter, when we compare our life with what we were actually created for. Our life is not first-class and maybe it is not even second-class, which we thought, but actually third-class, because our life is more or less without love to life, to other people or even to ourselves.

We are also not the decent folks we thought we were, but rather harbor fairly violent and destructive tendencies. Not a fun perspective at all. Let us assure you that one of us was surprised when, one sunny day some years ago, he finally came to the realization that his basic intentions toward other people were basically mean, while he himself thought he was such a well-meaning fellow. A close examination showed otherwise. There is a reason why we do not want to know ourselves: It hurts. This realization that our life does not have the meaning it could have or that our life is far poorer than it needs to be does not give us a nice feeling. That we are actually at fault for wasting our life and perhaps about to lose something precious, our actual existence, this realization is actually very unpleasant.

The unpleasantness lies in the realization of the magnitude of the problem, because it obliges us to do something about it for our own sake. We must take responsibility and see ourselves as the cause of our own personal mess. We must learn to associate with others and change our attitudes towards all kinds of things. We need to let go of all out-dated points of view for which we have fought and battled forever, ever since we learned them from our parents.

It is important that you can face yourself in the mirror every morning. One reason this may be difficult is the painful feeling that you are not faithful to yourself. When you know deep down what life is about and what your real purpose and meaning of life are, it hurts inside if you just continue living as always and not true to your own intuitions.

When you are conscious of your big dream, but shy away from working to make it come true, you suppress yourself. This works fine only as long as you are not too aware of it, but with the growing awareness the suppression of your own life becomes still harder to bear. The more you understand the game of life, the more you are obliged to engage in it. Knowing what you like, makes it much more difficult not to be good to yourself. When you face yourself in the mirror, you will know how much work you have to do to bring your life in better accord with the innermost wishes of your soul.

Everybody, who engages totally in the challenge of improving his or her relationship with the self will find that this game can be won. It takes a real effort, though. For most of us it is hard work every day for many years. Frankly, because our state of being is so lousy, when we start out. We are rather far from being happy, cheerful and easygoing.

One of us with the experience of this process felt a strong and almost unbearable sensation of unworthiness. When you develop an excellent inner standard of existence, you are likely to feel less proud of yourself. When you realize the brilliant standard that all mankind inhabits deep down in his soul (5) – all that we are meant to be, our real potential – then our present existence often seems pretty pale, insignificant, sometimes close to a total failure. As long as you compare yourself with your next-door neighbor you can always claim success. But when your start comparing your present state of being with that of a person at his full peek – like Moses, Buddha, Jesus, Leonardo da Vinci or and maybe spiritual masters like the Dalai Lama, Sai Baba or Baal Shem Tov– it is difficult not to feel gray.

Now, humility and humor will always be helpful. It is quite funny to be an action hero, when you compare yourself to your friends and be an existential midget, when you compare yourself to your own potentials. You might find that what nature or God intended you to be is amazingly different from whatever you thought at first. The gift of knowing the meaning of life is energy. When we see our true potential it is tempting to reach for the power and glory, the creativity and the divinity that lie within. When we do this we will immediately get all kinds of problems with the outer world and we will get an immense amount of energy. An unsurpassed energy kick.

People who know their hidden potentials and dig into them without hesitation or second thoughts will always blossom. They will soon be transformed into original beings, colorful, intelligent, troublesome, creative, lovely and often annoying like hell. These people will normally get everything they want. If they are sick they will get healed, if they are artists they will get fame, if they are scientists they will get a unique understanding of their field of research. Eventually, as their personal growth continues they might be recognized as the geniuses of this world.

The secret of these success stories is lots and lots of energy drawn from the source of existence combined with other amazing qualities like intuitive competence and emotional intelligence. These qualities pour from one single source: life. More precisely, the abundant source of energy and motivation is "the joy of life". Joyfulness seems to be the most basic and most mysterious quality of all living beings. The nature of joy is by the way still completely unexplained by science.

The no man"s land between your old and new life

Knowing what life is about does not necessarily mean that life becomes any easier. It is often quite the opposite: life turns even more difficult, when you wake up. But a conscious life has a peculiar quality. A person who experiences the deepest meaning in his or her life discovers that life now has touch of bliss and fragrance (6). No matter how chaotic, no matter how painful, deep down the new life is sweet.

This fine sweetness makes it possible for a human being to endure almost incredible pain and sorrow. When you strive to realize yourself and your utopian dreams many people will react as if you have the plaque. You will often turn into an incomprehensible and disturbing element of other people's worlds. To be sure, after some years of hard work you will come back as a beautiful, peaceful and happy person, but often the first thing that happens is that you turn annoying, selfish, difficult or even angry.

The fine, inner sweetness gives these people an unstoppable quality. They turn into fighters. They have seen the light and they follow it. New jobs, divorces, new friends, new habits and values, new sexual and professional interests... we are talking about major transformations here. People are not the same and will never be the same again. They are forever lost for you, if you do not follow them by developing yourself.

If you get a metastasized cancer and you heal yourself by letting go of the negative beliefs and self-suppressing decisions of a lifetime, you will be changed. You now have dramatically improved your quality of life and inner coherence. But you might also be in the situation, where you find yourself as reborn to the degree that not even your old clothing fits you any more. The price to be paid for personal growth is, unfortunately, chaos. As most people are very conservative they will try to oppose your growth the best they can. So, people who supported you, when you were down suddenly do their best to suppress you. It is sometimes difficult to believe that your relatives can jump on your back trying to hold you back. It is sometimes grotesque that you will have to escape from your whole family.

Between your new blossoming life and the old normal, boring life of habits and routines is a no man's land of very difficult nature. You discover that nothing is as your thought is was – it might be that your beloved does not really love you or that what you thought was the essence of your life is simply a substitution for a sound and healthy interest. Often people going through this transformation will at some point in time feel that they are going crazy. But relax: your are not going crazy. You have been crazy for half a lifetime living with values that did not make you happy. And now your are waking up. You are in the middle of a speedy, but unpleasant recovery. Loneliness of the most painful kind is normal at this stage. You are alone with your thoughts, and you are confused, unhappy, not seen, not loved and not understood. You cannot continue to live your old life, but you have not yet found your new ways. The fine order of your life has been broken and now chaos prevails both on the surface and in the debts of our soul.

We are healing, but first we must acknowledge that we really are sick. The pain of a whole lifetime is often overwhelming us and survival becomes dependent on our ability to be good to ourselves. Nobody but yourself is there now to show you love and concern. The miracle is that it is enough: when we love ourselves we do not really depend on other people's concern for us. But before we can enjoy the luxury of relying fully on ourselves, living in perfect inner balance, we must heal a lot of old painful wounds. This is why loneliness bites us at this stage.

Most people live lives that are not truly a life. They sense this intuitively, but they do not want to look at it at all. There are plenty of symptoms telling you that everything is not as it is supposed to be. The terrible headache or low back pain that returns still more often, problems sleeping at night, the growing sexual problems that are taking the fun out of this part of life, problems with your skin, the slips of memory, maybe the arthritis making every step you take even more painful. Enough is enough. Some day you realize that this is not how you want to life. Enough of lies and politeness and pretension. Air! You need fresh air, renewal, new inspiration. The way you live brings you slow death and this is not how life was meant to be. It takes a lot of courage to break the well-known order of daily life.

Sometimes we are lucky enough to be forced to make the move and wake up: the physician gives you the malignant diagnosis, the boss says he is sorry he has to let you go, because of your still poorer performance. This is the end. You have reached the end of the road. You only have one chance now: renewal from within. Your whole life needs repair. It is time to clean up the mess. Now a hard time usually follows. It is difficult not to feel that a lot of time is wasted living your old life. Realizing the distance to the existence you have been living, you are often overwhelmed with sorrow and bitter regrets. But eventually you will find mercy and realize that life is never wasted, you have learned your lesson, you suffered for as long as you had to. As time goes by you will appreciate a still deeper pattern of order and inherent logic in the universe.

Conclusions

We have a nature as human beings. It is this nature that makes it possible for us to be happy, cheerful, wise and lovely. When we turn natural and innocent, the extraordinary freedom that characterizes life at its fullest will return to us. All the life we hold as living organisms will now blossom and grow. Our love and passion will come back, a burning interest for our work will unexpectedly catch us, deep friendships will form and this divine creativity and humor will mark our new personality. All of us have the possibility do make a difference. The quality of our own life can be drastically improved and so can our use to people around us. We can be of real value to ourselves and to the world around us. Instead of being one more of these human beings tearing down the global ecosystem you will understand the web of life in all its forms and shadows and do what is needed to make mankind and our beautiful culture survive. As we see it, mankind is a highly endangered species, and only by transforming our old materialistic culture into a new spiritual culture with honesty, truthfulness and contributing people can humanity survive. The right place for all of us to begin is by saving ourselves. All it takes is that we decide to seize the meaning of life. But this must be one whole-hearted move: you must give it everything you have got if you want to succeed. You can change a poor life to an excellent life (5,6-11), but you must risk your life to win. One day you will find the courage. Maybe the day is today. The wise Jewish Rabbis have a few good sayings: "Live todays as if tomorrow is your last day" or "in order to perfect yourself, one must renew oneself day by day".

Let us conclude by telling the story of Sol Gordon (1923-2008), who was professor of Child and Family Studies at Syracuse University and a good friend: "Growing up as an idealistic youth, I was determined to save the world and even the more I tried, the world became worse and worse. Then I decided I had taken on too much. I thought I would just try to save the United States. The more I tried -- conditions in the US got worse and worse. So again I thought I had taken on too much. So I decided I would just try to save my neighborhood. My neighbors told me to mind my own business. But just as I was about to give up in despair, I read in the Talmud (Jewish teachings) that if you can save one life, it is as though you have saved the world. That is now my mission -- one person at a time (12). When you start there, then you will have a good death.

References

[1]   What is a good death? Join in our online discussions. BMJ 2003;327: 66.
[2]   Ventegodt S, Andersen NJ, Merrick J. Quality of life philosophy V: Seizing the meaning of life and becoming well again. Accepted by ScientificWorldJournal 2003;3:1210-29.
[3]   Ventegodt S, Merrick J, Andersen NJ. Quality of life as medicine: A pilot study of patients with chronic illness and pain. ScientificWorldJournal 2003;3:520-32.
[4]   Ventegodt S, Merrick J, Andersen NJ. Quality of life as medicine II: A pilot study of a five day "Quality of Life and Health" cure for patients with alcoholism. ScientificWorldJournal 2003;3:842-52.
[5]   Ventegodt S. The life mission theory: A theory for a conciousness based medicine. Int J Adolesc Med Health 2003;15(1):89-91.
[6]   Huxley A. The perennial philosophy. New York, NY: Harper Collins, 1972.
[7]   Antonovsky A. Unravelling the mystery of health. How people manage stress and stay well. San Francisco, CA: Jossey-Bass, 1987.
[8]   Maslow A. Toward a psychology of being. New York: Van Nostrand, 1968.
[9]   Ventegodt S. Quality of life: Seizing the meaning of life and becoming well again. Copenhagen: Forskningcentrets Forlag, 1995. [Danish]
[10]   Saint-Exupéry AMR. The little prince. New York: Harcourt Brace, 1943.
[11]   Castaneda C. The art of dreaming. New York: HarperCollins, 1993.
[12]   Gordon S. When living hurts. New York: UAHC Press, 1994.

Section 13. Clinical results in holistic psychiatry

Evidence-based holistic medicine means that the treatment efficacy and safety are thoroughly documented by clinical research. Research in holistic medicine needs to have the same quality as biomedical research protocols. The lack of research expertise and national organs to regulate this kind of research and assure its quality has lead us to develop the concept "Open Source Research Protocol", where all important procedures, treatment techniques, ethical considerations, documentation standards, systems for quality assurance, including instruments for measurement of effect like questionnaires that have been published in peer-reviewed scientific journals (see table 1) (1).

Table 1. The peer-reviewed journals that have published the research protocols and scientific papers on quality of life research and clinical holistic medicine

- Arch Sex Behaviour (sexology) (Medline/PubMed)
- BMJ (medicine) (Medline/PubMed)
- Child Care Health Dev (pediatrics) (Medline/PubMed)
- Eur J Surg (surgery) (Medline/PubMed)
- Int J Adolesc. Med Health (adolescent medicine, pediatrics) (Medline/PubMed)
- Int J Child Health Human Dev (pediatrics, human development) (PsycINFO, PubMedCentral)
- Int J Disabil Hum Dev (disability, human development) (PsycINFO)
- Ital J Pediatr (pediatrics, adolescent medicine)
- J Altern Med Res (alternative medicine)
- J Coll Physicians Surg Pak (Medicine) (Medline/PubMed)
- J Compl Integr Medicine (alternative medicine) (Medline/PubMed)
- J Pediatric Adolesc Gynecol (gynecology, pediatrics) (Medline/PubMed)
- J Pain Management (medicine) (PsycINFO, PubMedCentral)
- Med Sci Monit (medicine) (MedLine/PubMed)
- Oral Health Prev Dent (dentistry) (Medline/PubMed)
- South Med J (medicine) (Medline/PubMed)
- Social Indicators Research (sociology) (PsycINFO)
- ScientificWorldJournal (medicine) (Medline/PubMed)
- Ugeskrift for Læger (medicine) (Medline/PubMed)

The publication of all aspects of the protocol and the research that resulted has made it possible to have an excellent standard of research. We also believe that by publishing all part of the protocol and receiving critique from internationally recognized scientific journals have avoided much of the bias that all research obviously contain.

The research papers have been arranged according to several systematic categories according to the headlines and topics listed in table 2. The general title of the papers is mentioned in the title of the paper to make it easy to identify all papers of a series.

Table 2. The most important series of papers that constitute the research protocol in clinical holistic medicine

- QOL methodology describes the method used to measure quality of life used with the Quality of Life Survey Study at the Copenhagen University Hospital (Rigshospitalet), Denmark.
- QOL philosophy describes the philosophy behind our work with quality of life presented in the books "Quality of life. To seize the meaning of life and get well again" (1995), "Life philosophy that heals. Quality of life as medicine" (1999), "Consciousness-based medicine" (2003) and "Principles of Holistic Medicine. Philosophy behind quality of life" (2005). These are publications describing the philosophy on which the entire project is based.
- QOL theory covers the related life and human points of view described theoretically.
- QOL questionnaires are the questionnaires used in the Quality of Life Survey Study and later studies.
- QOL results are results from the Quality of Life Survey Study.
- Theories of existence are new theories on quality of life and the human nature described coherently and concisely.
- Holistic medicine describes our research program for the holistic-medical project ? a new research paradigm for researching alternative and holistic medicine and a theory for process of holistic healing.
- QOL as medicine describes results from the treatment of patients suffering from various chronic diseases, like chronic pains, alcoholism and Whiplash Associated Disorders.
- Clinical holistic medicine describes how to deal with the variety of problems presented by the patients in the medical clinic using holistic medicine.
- Human development is a series of papers to address a number of unsolved problems in biology today. First of all, the unsolved enigma concerning how the differentiation from a single zygote to an adult individual happens has been object for severe research through decades. By uncovering a new holistic biological paradigm that introduces an energetic-informational interpretation of reality as a new way to experience biology, these papers try to solve the problems connected with the events of biological ontogenesis from a single cell involvement in the fractal hierarchy, to the function of the human brain and "adult human metamorphosis".
- Quality of working life research is a series of paper that addresses the fundamental needs for happiness and efficiency the working situation. This applies to physicians and therapists as well as other occupations. The series of paper analyses how we can develop in our job, and continue to learn and grow, and avoid the routine and boredom that in the end forces us to compromise with quality and patience.

Research in clinical holistic medicine

Millennia ago, around the year 300 BCE, at the island of Cos in old Greece, the students of the famous physician Hippocrates (460-377 BCE) worked to help their patients to step into character, get direction in life, and use their human talents for the benefit of their surrounding world. For all we know this approach was efficient medicine that helped the patients to recover health, quality of life, and ability for which Hippocrates gained great fame. For more than 2,000 years this was what medicine was about in most of Europe.

On other continents similar medical systems were developed. The medicine wheel of the native Americans, the African Sangoma culture, the Samic Shamans of northern Europe, the healers of the Australian Aboriginals, the ayurvedic doctors of India, the acupuncturists of China, and the herbal doctors of Tibet all seems to be fundamentally character medicine (2-8). All the theories and the medical understanding from these pre-modern cultures are now being integrated into what has been called integrative or transcultural medicine. Many of the old medical systems are reappearing in modern time as alternative, complementary and psychosocial medicine. This huge body of theory is now being offered as a European Union Master of Science degree (2-8).

Interestingly, two huge movements of the last century have put this old knowledge into use: psychoanalysis (9) and psychodynamic therapy (10,11) (most importantly STPP or short term psychodynamic psychotherapy) (12,13) going though the mind on the one hand and through the body on the other. Bodywork developed through most importantly Reich (14), Lowen (15) and Rosen (16) with sexual therapy along the tantric tradition (17). A third road, but much less common path has been directly though the spiritual reconnection with the world (18,19).

Our international research collaboration became interested in existential healing from the data that originated from the epidemiological research at the Copenhagen University Hospital (Rigshospitalet) starting in 1958-61 at the Research Unit for Prospective Pediatrics and the Copenhagen Perinatal Birth Cohort 1959-61. Almost 20 years ago we were conducting epidemiological research on quality of life, closely examining the connection between global quality of life and health for more than 11.000 people in a series of huge surveys (see 20 for a review of these studies) using large and extensive questionnaires, some of them with over 3,000 questions. We found (quite surprisingly) from this huge data base that quality of life, mental and physical health, and ability of social, sexual and working ability seemed to be caused primarily by the consciousness and philosophy of life of the person in question. Objective data were only to a small extent involved, like being adopted, coming from a family with only one breadwinner, mother being mentally ill, or the person in question financially poor or poorly educated (which are obviously very much socially inherited) (20). Clinical holistic medicine is holistic mind-body medicine, which is also clinical medicine, i.e. medicine based on patient self-exploration and self-insight for obtaining existential healing. It is also called holistic body psychotherapy, mindful mind-body medicine, and similar names.

In Denmark where we have conducted the research, almost all patients that seek complementary medical treatment of the holistic, existential type, has tried biomedical treatment first, and after this often several complementary and alternative types of treatment, before they came to the Copenhagen Research Clinic for Holistic Medicine and Sexology and entered our research protocol. In one study, the patients had their problems and suffering for

8.9 years (mean) (1). As nothing had helped these patients before they came to our clinic, we find it justified to use them as their own controls. Quite remarkably we have been able to help every second of the patients independent of the type of problem they have presented, and independent of the seriousness of the problem (table 3) (21-28). In our recent protocols we have only included patients, who experienced their problem as "bad" or "very bad" on a five point Likert scale (1).

We have used a new research paradigm called the "square curve paradigm" that documents the lasting effect of an immediate significant improvement that comes simultaneously with the process of existential healing of the patient – the process that we call Antonovsky-salutogenesis (1). One of the great concerns in our project has been to cover also the philosophical, methodological, and interdisciplinary aspects of the research, which has lead to many series of papers. We have also found it extremely important to find the dimensions we need to intervene on to help the patients in many different research designs to avoid the bias from one specific research strategy. Therefore the prospective cohort design has been extremely important in our research.

The international collaboration has constantly been expanded and today about 30 different researchers have participated in the scientific work that constitutes the Open Source Research Protocol. Most importantly we have developed a unique concept of recording the case, including measuring before and after the treatment with validated quality of life and health questionnaire, which has allowed us to monitor every side effect and unexpected event during the treatment (see table 4).

We are happy to notice that clinical holistic medicine seems to be an extremely efficient type of treatment that causes no harm without side effects (1). We also know that this kind of therapy can prevent suicide, and even side effects from biomedical, pharmaceutical treatments (1).

Table 3. Treatment success rate when all treatment failures (non-responders), drop-outs of the survey, and dropouts of treatment are taken as non-responders. Patient's own experience as measured self-rated with the questionnaire QOL10, and the patient is taken as cured if the state of the measured factor was bad or very bad before treatment and not bad after treatment (and one year after treatment, statistically, using the square curve paradigm). The data comes from clinical studies covering the holistic treatment of 600 patients. (CHM: Clinical holistic medicine. (21-26) (HMS: Holistic manual sexology (27). HMS-D: Holistic manual sexology – Dodson's method for treating chronic anorgasmia) (28)

Physical illness (CHM)	39%(p=0.05) (21)
Mental illness (CHM)	57% (p=0.05) (22)
Low quality of life (CHM)	56% (p=0.05) (23)
Low self-esteem (CHM)	61% (p=0.05) (24)
Low working ability (CHM)	52% (p=0.05) (25)
Sexual dysfunction(CHM)	42% (p=0.05) (26)
Sexual dysfunction (HMS)	56% (p=0.05) (27)
Sexual dysfunction (HMS-D)	93% (p=0.05) (28)

Table 4. Yearly itemized account of side effects and serious complications or events for the treatment with clinical holistic medicine

Itemized account 31/12 1991: No side effects or serious complications or events

Itemized account 31/12 1992: No side effects or serious complications or events

Itemized account 31/12 1993: No side effects or serious complications or events

Itemized account 31/12 1994: No side effects or serious complications or events

Itemized account 31/12 1995: No side effects or serious complications or events

Itemized account 31/12 1996: No side effects or serious complications or events

Itemized account 31/12 1997: No side effects or serious complications or events

Itemized account 31/12 1998: No side effects or serious complications or events

Itemized account 31/12 1999: No side effects or serious complications or events

Itemized account 31/12 2000: No side effects or serious complications or events

Itemized account 31/12 2001: No side effects or serious complications or events

Itemized account 31/12 2002: No side effects or serious complications or events

Itemized account 31/12 2003: No side effects or serious complications or events

Itemized account 31/12 2004: No side effects or serious complications or events

Itemized account 31/12 2005: No side effects or serious complications or events

Itemized account 31/12 2006: No side effects or serious complications or events

Itemized account 31/12 2007: No side effects or serious complications or events

Itemized account 31/12 2008: No side effects or serious complications or events

Quality assurance

The strategy for data collection and quality assurance in the clinic for CAM (complementary and alternative medicine) and holistic medicine has been developed in the Research Clinic for Holistic Medicine and Sexology, where it has been used since 2004 (1). We are using a questionnaire (QOL10) measuring global quality of life (QOL1, QOL5), self-rated mental and physical health, self-rated social, sexual and working ability, self-rated I-strength, self-rated self esteem (relation to self) and relation to partner and friends. We measure before treatment, after treatment (three month) and again one year after the treatment has been completed.

The complete lack of side or adverse effects from ethical and professionally conducted consciousness-based medicine has been documented through a systematic review of the literature (1,29).

This is an extremely lucky situation, meaning that the physician, who is working with holistic medicine does not need a clinical assurance.

In Denmark the Scientific Ethical Committee (Helsinki) accepted from the very beginning that our research in "quality of life as medicine" (holistic medicine) was not covered by their domain (Copenhagen Scientific Ethical Committee under the numbers (KF)V. 100.1762-90, (KF)V. 100.2123/91, (KF)V. 01-502/93, (KF)V. 01-026/97, (KF)V. 01-162/97, (KF)V. 01-198/97).

Ethical aspects

The rationale for treating with clinical holistic medicine is naturally its high efficacy (see table 4) (see 1 for a review) compared with the complete lack of adverse/side effects. Hippocrates' ethics "primum non nocera", "first do no harm", is fully respected in clinical holistic medicine, but not always adapted or possible in biomedicine. Scientific holistic medicine has had its highly developed ethics already from its first days, when it was created as a science by Hippocrates and his students. We have carefully considered all ethical aspects relevant for today's practice of holistic medicine and holistic sexology and have participated in the development of the ethical rules of the International Society of Holistic Health that organise holistic medical practitioners worldwide (1) (see also the society's homepage on www.internationalsocietyforholistichealth.com). A more thorough ethical discussions is found in the protocol (1).

Informed consent

The most important aspect of ethical conduct is full information to the patient and the openness of the protocol with public and scientific publications that will give every patient the possibility to see exactly what the principles, procedures, results, and side effects of the treatment are. An important aspect of communication and decision making by the patients is the selection of material for reading by the patient and also verbally explained to the patient, before initiating the treatment and making the therapeutic contract. The patient filling in the questionnaire and the other papers related to the treatment is legally taken as a written consent. As not every patient is able to read scientific papers, we have also published easy-to-read books on quality of life philosophy, clinical holistic medicine and the results from the research, which have been included as a part of the research protocol. In the Research Clinic for Holistic Medicine in Copenhagen, we also have one page of written patient information giving just the core information and we have put a summary of the research on our homepage (www.livskvalitet.org). For researchers we have collected the most important papers in a series of books on principles of holistic medicine (30-33).

Before treatment in holistic medicine the patient should be informed about the course of the treatment in general terms and it is recommended to also receive a written contract for the treatment signed by the patient.

Political and financial aspects

Fortunately national authorities as well as international experts have recently started to recognize the clinical, holistic medicine as scientific and efficient. Recently the Interuniversity College, Graz, has graduated a number of therapists with the master degree on the basis of their research work in clinical holistic medicine (1), making Austria the first country to officially acknowledge clinical holistic medicine as a scientific complementary-medical treatment system. In USA the conflicts between biomedicine and complementary medicine (CAM including holistic medicine) has often reached the court system and the supreme court of California has in the last decade realised this and systematically judged in support of the practitioners of CAM and holistic medicine in these conflicts.

Conclusions

Evidence-based holistic medicine takes thorough clinical research that documents the efficacy and safety of the treatment. For almost two decades we have been conducting research in "quality of life as medicine". The Open Source Research Protocol gives all interested parties – patients, physicians, therapists, researchers and politicians direct admission to all important parts of the protocol, allowing for peer review and critique of all part of it. The publication allows other researchers to be inspired and use part for their own research and practice. This is important, because the trend of chronic illness/disability in our societies has been on the increase.

We encourage all public and private, national and international research organs, foundations and institutions to support the development of scientific, holistic medicine and its institutions financially and politically.

References

[1]   Ventegodt S, Andersen NJ, Kandel I, Merrick J. The open source protocol of clinical holistic medicine. J Altern Med Res 2009;1(2), 129-44.

[2]   Antonella R. Introduction of regulatory methods. Graz, Austria: Interuniversity College, 2004.

[3]   Blättner B. Fundamentals of salutogenesis. Graz, Austria: Interuniversity College, 2004.

[4]   Endler PC. Master program for complementary, psychosocial and integrated health sciences Graz, Austria: Interuniversity College, 2004.

[5]   Endler PC. Working and writing scientifically in complementary medicine and integrated health sciences. Graz, Austria: Interuniversity College, 2004.

[6]   Kratky KW. Complementary medicine systems. Comparison and integration. New York, Nova Sci, 2008.

[7]   Pass PF. Fundamentals of depth psychology. Therapeutic relationship formation between self-awareness and casework Graz, Austria: Interuniversity College, 2004.

[8]   Spranger HH. Fundamentals of regulatory biology. Paradigms and scientific backgrounds of regulatory methods Graz, Austria: Interuniversity College, 2004.

[9]   Jones E. The life and works of Sigmund Freud. New York: Basic Books, 1961.

[10]   Jung CG. Man and his symbols. New York: Anchor Press, 1964.

[11]   Jung CG. Psychology and alchemy. Collected works of CG Jung, Vol 12. Princeton, NJ: Princeton Univ Press, 1968.

[12]   Leichsenring F, Rabung S, Leibing E. The efficacy of short-term psychodynamic psychotherapy in specific psychiatric disorders: a meta-analysis. Arch Gen Psychiatry 2004;61(12):1208-16.

[13]   Leichsenring F. (2005) Are psychodynamic and psychoanalytic therapies effective? A review of empirical data. Int J Psychoanal 2005;86(Pt 3):841-68.

[14]   Reich W. [Die Function des Orgasmus]. Köln: Kiepenheuer Witsch 1969. [German].

[15]   Lowen A. Honoring the body. Alachua, FL: Bioenergetics Press, 2004.

[16]   Rosen M, Brenner S. Rosen method bodywork. Accessing the unconscious through touch. Berkeley, CA: North Atlantic Books, 2003.

[17]   Anand M. The art of sexual ecstasy. The path of sacred sexuality for western lovers. New York: Jeremy P Tarcher/Putnam, 1989.

[18] Antonovsky A. Health, stress and coping. London: Jossey-Bass, 1985.

[19] Antonovsky A. Unravelling the mystery of health. How people manage stress and stay well. San Francisco: Jossey-Bass, 1987.

[20] Ventegodt S, Flensborg-Madsen T, Andersen NJ, Nielsen M, Mohammed M, Merrick J. Global quality of life (QOL), health and ability are primarily determined by our consciousness. Research findings from Denmark 1991-2004. Soc Indicator Res 2005;71:87-122.

[21] Ventegodt S, Thegler S, Andreasen T, Struve F, Enevoldsen L, Bassaine L, Torp M, Merrick J. Clinical holistic medicine (mindful, short-term psychodynamic psychotherapy complemented with bodywork) in the treatment of experienced physical illness and chronic pain. ScientificWorldJournal 2007;7:310-6.

[22] Ventegodt S, Thegler S, Andreasen T, Struve F, Enevoldsen L, Bassaine L, Torp M, Merrick J. Clinical holistic medicine (mindful, short-term psychodynamic psychotherapy complemented with bodywork) in the treatment of experienced mental illness. ScientificWorldJournal 2007;7:306-9.

[23] Ventegodt S, Thegler S, Andreasen T, Struve F, Enevoldsen L, Bassaine L, Torp M, Merrick J. Clinical holistic medicine (mindful, short-term psychodynamic psychotherapy complemented with bodywork) improves quality of life, health, and ability by induction of Antonovsky-salutogenesis. ScientificWorldJournal 2007;7:317-23.

[24] Ventegodt S, Thegler S, Andreasen T, Struve F, Enevoldsen L, Bassaine L, Torp M, Merrick J. Self-reported low self-esteem. Intervention and follow-up in a clinical setting. ScientificWorldJournal 2007;7:299-305.

[25] Ventegodt S, Andersen NJ, Merrick J. Clinical holistic medicine in the recovery of working ability. A study using Antonovsky salutogenesis. Int J Disabil Hum Dev 2008;7(2):219-22.

[26] Ventegodt S, Thegler S, Andreasen T, Struve F, Enevoldsen L, Bassaine L, Torp M, Merrick J. Clinical holistic medicine (mindful, short-term psychodynamic psychotherapy complemented with bodywork) in the treatment of experienced impaired sexual functioning. ScientificWorldJournal 2007;7:324-9.

[27] Ventegodt S, Clausen B, Merrick J. Clinical holistic medicine: Pilot study on the effect of vaginal acupressure (Hippocratic pelvic massage). ScientificWorldJournal 2006;6:2100-16.

[28] Struck P, Ventegodt S. Clinical holistic medicine: Teaching orgasm for females with chronic anorgasmia using the Betty Dodson method. ScientificWorldJournal 2008;8:883-95.

[29] Ventegodt S, Merrick J. A review of side effects and adverse events of non-drug medicine (non-pharmaceutical CAM): Psychotherapy, mind-body medicine and clinical holistic medicine. J Compl Integr Medicine 2009, In press.

[30] Ventegodt S, Kandel I, Merrick J. Principles of holistic medicine. Philosophy behind quality of life. Victoria, BC: Trafford, 2005.

[31] Ventegodt S, Kandel I, Merrick J. Principles of holistic medicine. Quality of life and health. New York: Hippocrates Sci Publ, 2005.

[32] Ventegodt S, Kandel I, Merrick J. Principles of holistic medicine. Global quality of life.Theory, research and methodology. New York: Hippocrates Sci Publ, 2005.

[33] Ventegodt S, Merrick J. Sexology from a holistic point of view. A textbook of classic and modern sexology. New York: Nova Science, 2010.

Chapter 50

Mental health intervention and follow-up

Holistic medicine intervention can be especially useful with chronic patients that present the triad of low quality of life, poor health (physical and/or mental) and poor ability of functioning, which are very difficult to help – not to say cure - by traditional psychiatric treatment. We found in 54 patients with experienced mental illness (half had already had the traditional psychiatric treatment that did not work), that 31 patients were cured. This is 57,4% of the patients and with a confidence interval calculated after p=0.05 we found that: 95% CI: 43.21% - 70.77% of the patients had been cured. Calculated in this simplistic way we found the Number Needed to Treat (NNT) of clinical holistic medicine with mentally ill patients to be 1.41-2.31 (1.41<NNT<2.31). None of over 500 patients treated complained of any serious side effects and none harmed by the treatment; estimated from this we find the Number needed to harm to be NNH>500. The rate of cure is comparable to the most successful interventions with psychiatric treatment, and as clinical holistic treatment seems to have almost no side effects. On average the patients received less than 20 treatments over 14 month at a cost of 1,600 EURO per patient. The efficiency, low cost, lack of negative side effects, lasting results and preventive dimension of clinical holistic medicine makes it the treatment of choice for the patient that is able to manage to develop as a person.

Introduction

A meta study of 2,000 papers on the general effect of psychopharmacological treatment showed that 1 in 3 could not be helped, 1 in 3 improved a little, and 1 in 3 was helped; unfortunately half of the last group became ill again after two years (1), giving the sad result that 1/6 was helped for a two year period; nobody seems to know the treatment effect long term.

A problem with psychopharmacological treatment seems to be an increased tendency of the patients to commit suicide (2,3). After introduction of psychopharmacological treatment in Norway, Sweden and Finland the number of suicide was dramatically increased, in Norway the suicide rate 8-doubled in 1970-1974 compared to before the introduction of these drugs in

1950-54 (4) amd from 1955 the rate of suicide in mental institutions increased markedly and continuously (5). A new Danish study found that about 1/7 of all suicides in Denmark was related to psychiatric hospitalisation (6).

Psychodynamic short time therapy has in several meta-studies been found successful with many different kinds of mental illnesses (7-10), even when the patients were suffering from the most extreme conditions like schizophrenia (10,11). In avoiding drugs if possible at all the suicide risk and other side effects seems to be reduced. This has motivated us to start developing clinical holistic medicine to help the mentally ill patient (12,13). After testing this cure on 54 patients who entered our Research Clinic for Holistic Medicine in 2004 and 2005 and rated their own mental health as "bad" or "very bad" (4 or 5 on the five point Likert scale in the questionnaire QOL5 (14) measuring self-assessed mental health) we are now able to present the results.

We believe that these patients all would have had a psychiatric diagnosis and psychiatric treatment, if they had chosen psychiatric treatment instead of our holistic treatment using no drugs. The reason for believing this is that we know that the 34 patients who already before coming to us had been to a GP, psychologist or psychiatrist for treatment had a self-evaluated mental health on this scale of in average 3.7 (standard deviation 0.76) (15). 54.4% of 109 patients entering the clinic had mental problems, and this group received on average 11.7 session of a prize of 938.40 EURO. The actual group of 54 severely ill patients received about 20 sessions on average of a prize of 1,600 EURO. Please see (16) for more details on the study.

Our study

The patients came in from the street after having read about holistic medicine in our books (17-20), or after our clinic had being recommended by former patients. The patients wanted a different approach than psychiatry to their problems, either because of their personal philosophy of life believing in insight and personal development, or they came because they had experienced that the traditional treatment did not help them. The later group, about half the patients [21 patients, see figure 26 in (16)], had already been diagnosed with depression, anxiety/GAD, bulimia/anorexia, borderline, skizotypia or schizophrenia. This group rated 3.7 on average so we decided to include all patients rating <=40 in this study, excluding more than half of these patients as not ill enough to enter the study.

When we only included patients scoring <=4 – that is the group that felt mentally ill or very ill - we felt pretty sure that these patients would all have been diagnosed and treated if they had gone to psychiatrist.

As many patients had lost faith in the psychiatric approach that did not help them, it was important for the patients that they did not get a psychiatric diagnosis, but that we worked on their self-evaluated health. Using this diagnosis was also a strong message to the patients on a different health-philosophy stressing healing of the patient's whole life, not only of the mental disease.

Our findings

We found the following (see table 1):

- Mentally ill before treatment (self-assessed physical health: bad or very bad): 54 Patients
- Mentally well after treatment: (self-assessed physical health: very good, good, or neither good nor bad): 31 Patients
- Mentally ill after treatment (self-assessed physical health: bad or very bad): 6 Patients
- Response rate of follow up study: 58.1%
- Non-responders or dropouts: 17 patients
- Total of mentally ill after treatment, non-responders and dropouts: 23 patients

Success rate of treatment: 31/54 = 57.4% (95% CI: 43.2% - 70.8%) (15). Calculated in this simplistic way we found the Number Needed to Treat (NNT) of clinical holistic medicine with mentally ill patients to be 1.41-2.31 (1.41<NNT<2.31). None of these patients complained of any side effects, and none harmed. Estimated from this we found the Number Needed to Harm to be NNH>50. This is comparable to or better that the results from interventions with psychopharmacological treatment. If we look at the whole group of more than 500 patients who has been treated with clinical holistic medicine at our clinic 2000-2006 by eight different therapists, none of these 500 patients had severe or lasting side effects or committed suicide, or harmed in other ways, giving an estimated NNH>500.

In an earlier paper (16) we have documented that the treatment of mental problems with clinical holistic medicine is lasting, using the square curve paradigm (21) as the survey instrument and the results did not deteriorate one year after therapy.

After the treatment we found that 57.47% of the mentally ill patients (see table 1) did not feel ill any more; here we have calculated our success rate conservatively, taking dropouts and non-responders of the follow up questionnaire as negative responders to the treatment. Of the 31 therapeutic responders 21 patient (67.7%) felt completely cured (good or very good self-assessed mental health) and 10 patients (32.3%) was improving (felt neither bad nor good).

Table 1. After treatment with clinical holistic medicine 31 of 54 mentally ill patients were cured. These 31 patients were 57,4% of the group (p=0.05: 95% CI: 43.2% - 70.8%, CI being the binominal confidence interval) (15)

	Before treatment	After treatment
Mentally ill	54	6
Mentally well (not ill)	0	31 = 57.41 (95% CI: 43.2% - 70.8% [15]).
Non-responders or dropouts	-	17
Mentally ill, non-responder or dropout	23	23

Table 2. T-Test. Study of 31 patients which therapy changed their ratings of self-evaluated mental health from ill to not ill (from 4=bad or 5=very bad, to 1=very good, 2=good, or 3=neither good nor bad)

Paired Samples Statistics

		Mean	N	Std. Deviation	Std. Error Mean
Pair 1	T1Q1	2,9333	30	,94443	,17243
	T3Q1	2,3333	30	,88409	,16141
Pair 2	Tid 1, Q2	4,1613	31	,37388	,06715
	T3Q2	2,1935	31	,65418	,11749
Pair 3	T1Q3	3,5161	31	,76902	,13812
	T3Q3	2,2903	31	,73908	,13274
Pair 4	T1Q4	2,5161	31	,92632	,16637
	T3Q4	2,0000	31	,85635	,15380
Pair 5	T1Q5	4,7419	31	1,71207	,30750
	T3Q5	2,9355	31	1,94826	,34992
Pair 6	T1Q6	3,7742	31	1,05545	,18956
	T3Q6	2,4194	31	1,14816	,20622
Pair 7	T1Q7	3,4516	31	1,05952	,19030
	T3Q7	2,4194	31	1,02548	,18418
Pair 8	T1Q8	3,2258	31	,95602	,17171
	T3Q8	2,0645	31	,67997	,12213
Pair 9	T1Q9	3,3333	30	,99424	,18152
	T3Q9	2,4333	30	,97143	,17736
Pair 10	T1Q10	3,9677	31	,60464	,10860
	T3Q10	2,2581	31	,85509	,15358

Table 3. Paired samples test. 31 patients that heal mentally also significantly improved their self-evaluated physical health, relationship with self, friends, and partner, ability to love, sexual ability of functioning, social ability, working ability, and self-assessed quality of life

Paired Samples Test

| | | Paired Differences | | | | | | | |
| | | | | | 95% Confidence Interval of the Difference | | | | |
		Mean	Std. Deviation	Std. Error Mean	Lower	Upper	t	df	Sig. (2-tailed)
Pair 1	T1Q1 - T3Q1	,6000	,89443	,16330	,2660	,9340	3,674	29	,001
Pair 2	Tid 1, Q2 - T3Q	1,9677	,79515	,14281	1,6761	2,2594	13,778	30	,000
Pair 3	T1Q3 - T3Q3	1,2258	1,11683	,20059	,8161	1,6355	6,111	30	,000
Pair 4	T1Q4 - T3Q4	,5161	,92632	,16637	,1764	,8559	3,102	30	,004
Pair 5	T1Q5 - T3Q5	1,8065	2,27185	,40804	,9731	2,6398	4,427	30	,000
Pair 6	T1Q6 - T3Q6	1,3548	1,60309	,28792	,7668	1,9429	4,706	30	,000
Pair 7	T1Q7 - T3Q7	1,0323	1,35361	,24312	,5358	1,5288	4,246	30	,000
Pair 8	T1Q8 - T3Q8	1,1613	1,12833	,20265	,7474	1,5752	5,730	30	,000
Pair 9	T1Q9 - T3Q9	,9000	1,06188	,19387	,5035	1,2965	4,642	29	,000
Pair 10	T1Q10 - T3Q10	1,7097	1,03902	,18661	1,3286	2,0908	9,162	30	,000

For the 31 therapeutic responders, the self-assessed mental health, relationship with self, friends, partner, ability to love, have sex, have social activities, and to work, and the self-assessed quality of life (QOL1)(14) were radically improved (see tables 2 and 3). Their relationships in general, measured QOL (with the validated questionnaire QOL5)(14) and life's total state (mean of health, QOL and ability) was also statistically and clinically significantly improved (see tables 4 and 5).

Tables 2 and 3 show that the 31 patients that heal mentally also improved their self-evaluated physical health, relationship with self, friends, and partner, ability to love, sexual ability of functioning, social ability, working ability, and self-assessed quality of life (QOL1[14]). Please notice that the results are both statistically and clinically highly significant.

Table 4. Paired samples statistics. The 31 patients who healed mentally improved their relationships with self, partner, and friends, their self-evaluated ability of functioning socially, sexually and work-related, and their selfassess global quality of life

Paired Samples Statistics

		Mean	N	Std. Deviation	Std. Error Mean
Pair 1	RELAT1	3,5914	31	,76357	,13714
	RELAT3	2,4086	31	,79214	,14227
Pair 2	FUNK1	3,4333	30	,62950	,11493
	FUNK3	2,3250	30	,59867	,10930
Pair 3	QOL5_1	3,5611	30	,44092	,08050
	QOL5_3	2,3278	30	,60566	,11058
Pair 4	QOL10_1	3,5220	29	,41264	,07662
	QOL10_3	2,2998	29	,55174	,10246

Table 5. Paired samples test. The 31 patients who healed mentally improved their relationships with self, partner, and friends, their self-evaluated ability of functioning socially, sexually and work-related, and their selfassess global quality of life

Paired Samples Test

	Paired Differences							
	Mean	Std. Deviation	Std. Error Mean	95% Confidence Interval of the Difference		t	df	Sig. (2-tailed)
				Lower	Upper			
Pair 1 RELAT1 - RELAT3	1,1828	,98822	,17749	,8203	1,5453	6,664	30	,000
Pair 2 FUNK1 - FUNK3	1,1083	,94158	,17191	,7567	1,4599	6,447	29	,000
Pair 3 QOL5_1 - QOL5_3	1,2333	,71999	,13145	,9645	1,5022	9,382	29	,000
Pair 4 QOL10_1 - QOL10	1,2222	,68260	,12676	,9626	1,4819	9,642	28	,000

Tables 4 and 5 show that the 31 patients, who healed mentally, also improved their relationships (with self, partner, and friends), their self-evaluated ability of functioning, and their quality of life as measured with the validated questionnaire QOL5 (14). When health, quality of life, and ability is combined, it is clear that these patients have healed their whole life (as measured by QOL10) (16). This healing of all aspects of life is often seen with clinical holistic medicine and is called (Antonovsky-) salutogenesis after the researcher who discovered this kind of global healing of the patient's existence.

Discussion

These results are comparable to the best results from established treatments. Most importantly, all aspects of life are improved simultaneously because of induction of Antonovsky-salutogenesis (22,23), which we understand as existential healing (24) according to the life mission theory (25). The treatment of mental patients with clinical holistic medicine had no observed side effects except for a few days of feeling bad when old painful, repressed material from old trauma re-appeared in patients consciousness. During the most intense phase of therapy many patients felt very bad for a few days, but no patients experienced severe or lasting side effects. Two patients needed support 24 hours for a few days. No patients committed suicide or attempted to do so, in spite of the provoked existential crises; we thus believe the treatment with clinical holistic medicine to be safer that psychiatric treatment.

The condition for this treatment is that you as patient is willing to assume responsibility for your own life, and develop as a person, even when this is emotionally difficult. We believe that the recent development in this kind of therapy (17-20) has made clinical holistic medicine more "mindful" and much less emotionally painful and much more enjoyable, focusing much more on the patients meaning of life, talents and positive abilities and on the patient's inner potentials and resources for healing.

Clinical holistic medicine – mindful psychodynamic short time therapy complemented with bodywork - can cure many of the severely ill mental patients. This is done fast, efficient, cheap, without side effects, and the effect seem to be lasting and preventive. Most interesting, by the successful inducing of existential healing – called Antonovsky salutogenesis, or just salutogenesis – all aspects of life is improved at the same time – physical and mental health, quality of life, ability of function in a number of important areas: with partner and friends, sexually, and work-related.

The self-assessed physical health, relationship with partner, ability to work, self-assessed quality of life, relationships in general, measured QOL (with the validated questionnaire QOL5), and life's total state (mean of health, QOL and ability) was also statistically and clinically significantly improved. Most importantly, all aspects of life are improved simultaneously because of induction of Antonovsky-salutogenesis.

The medicine is especially useful with chronic patients that present the triad of low quality of life, poor health (physical and/or mental) and poor ability of functioning, which are very difficult to help – not to say cure - by traditional psychiatric treatment. The efficiency, low cost, lack of negative side effects, lasting results, lack of use of psychopharmacological drugs with side effects like increased tendency to suicide, and preventive dimension of clinical holistic medicine makes it the treatment of choice for the patient that is able to manage to develop as a person.

References

[1]   SBU-rapport nr. 133/1 og 133/2. [Behandling med neuroleptika.] Stockholm: Statens beredning för
        utvärdering av medicinsk metodik, 1997. [Swedish].

[2]   More TJ. Hidden dangers of antidepressants. Washingtonian Dec 1997:68-71,140-5.

[3]   Jick S, Dean A, Jich H. Antiderssants and suicide. BMJ 1995;310:215-8.

[4]   Retterstøl NA. Increasing suicidal rate in Scandinavian psychiatric hospitals. In: Moller HJ, Schmidtke
        A, Welz R, eds. Current issues of suicidology. Berlin: Springer, 1988:75-82.

[5]   Retterstøl NA. [Selvmord, død og sorg.] Oslo: Universitetsforlaget, 1978:85. [Norwegian].

[6]   Qin P, Nordentoft M. Suicide risk in relation to psychiatric hospitalization: evidence based on
        longitudinal registers. Arch Gen Psychiatry 2005;62(4):427-32.

[7]   Anderson EM, Lambert MJ. Short term dynamically oriented psychotherapy: A review and meta-
        analysis. Clin Psychol Rev 1995;15:503-14.

[8]   Crits-Cristoph P. The efficacy of brief dynamic psychotherapy: A meta-analysis. Am J Psychiatry
        1992;149: 151-8.

[9]   Svartberg M, Stiles TC. Comparative effects of short-term psychodynamic psychotherapy: A meta-
        analysis. J Consult Clin Psychol 1991;59:704-14.

[10]   Bechgaard B. [The relationship between psychological and medical treatment of schizophrenia. In:
        Bechgaard B, Jensen HH, Nielsen T, eds. Forholdet mellem psykologisk og medicinsk behandling af
        psykiske lidelser.] Copenhagen: Reitzel, 2001:34-93.

[11]   Karon BP, VendenBos G. Psychotherapy of schizophrenia. The treatment of choice. New York: Jason
        Aronson, 1981.

[12]   Ventegodt S, Andersen NJ, Neikrug S, Kandel I, Merrick J. Clinical holistic medicine: Mental
        disorders in a holistic perspective. ScientificWorldJournal 2005;5:313-23.

[13]   Ventegodt S, Andersen NJ, Neikrug S, Kandel I, Merrick J. Clinical holistic medicine: Holistic
        treatment of mental disorders. ScientificWorldJournal 2005;5:427-45.

[14]   Lindholt JS, Ventegodt S, Henneberg EW. Development and validation of QoL5 clinical databases. A
        short, global and generic questionnaire based on an integrated theory of the quality of life. Eur J Surg
        2002;168:103-7.

[15]   Diem K, ed. Documenta Geigy. Scientific tables. Basel: Geigy, 1962.

[16]   Ventegodt S, Thegler S, Andreasen T, Struve F, Enevoldsen L, Bassaine L, et al. Clinical holistic
        medicine: Psychodynamic short-time therapy complemented with bodywork. A clinical follow-up
        study of 109 patients. ScientificWorldJournal 2006;6:2220-38.

[17]   Ventegodt S, Kandel I, Merrick J. Principles of holistic medicine. Philosophy behind quality of life.
        Victoria, BC: Trafford, 2005.

[18]   Ventegodt S, Kandel I, Merrick J. Principles of holistic medicine. Quality of life and health. New
        York: Hippocrates Sci Publ, 2005.

[19]   Ventegodt S, Kandel I, Merrick J. Principles of holistic medicine. Global quality of life.Theory,
        research and methodology. New York: Hippocrates Sci Publ, 2006.

[20]   Ventegodt S. Consciousness-based medicine [Bevidsthedsmedicin – set gennem lægejournalen.]
        Copenhagen: Forskningscenterets Forlag, 2003. [Danish].

[21]   Ventegodt S, Andersen NJ, Merrick J. Holistic Medicine II: The square-curve paradigm for research in
        alternative, complementary and holistic medicine: A cost-effective, easy and scientifically valid design
        for evidence based medicine. ScientificWorldJournal 2003;3: 1117-27.

[22]   Antonovsky A. Health, stress and coping. London: Jossey-Bass, 1985.

[23]   Antonovsky A. Unravelling the mystery of health. How people manage stress and stay well. San
        Francisco: Jossey-Bass, 1987.

[24]   Ventegodt S, Andersen NJ, Merrick J. Holistic Medicine III: The holistic process theory of healing.
        ScientificWorldJournal 2003;3:1138-46.

[25]   Ventegodt S. The life mission theory: A theory for a consciousness-based medicine. Int J Adolesc
        Med Health 2003;15(1):89-91.

Chapter 51

Self reported low self-esteem

43 patients, who presented with low or very low self-esteem at the Research Clinic for Holistic Medicine in Copenhagen were treated with psychodynamic short-term therapy complemented with bodywork. They received in average of 20 sessions at a cost of 1,600 EURO. The bodywork helped the patients to confront old emotional pain from childhood trauma repressed to the body-mind. Results showed that 60.5% recovered from low self-esteem (95% CI: 44.41% - 75.02%). Calculated from this we have NNT=1.33-2.25. Almost all aspects of life improved at the same time (p<0.01): physical health, mental health, quality of life and ability to function in a number of important areas (partner, friends, sexually and socially). This indicated that we had successfully induced existential healing (Antonovsky salutogenesis). The strategy of improving self-esteem can be the key to a new life for patients presenting with low quality of life, poor health (physical and/or mental) and poor ability of functioning. The patients were strongly motivated and willing to endure strong emotional pain provoked by the therapy. The rate of recovery is comparable to the most successful interventions with psychological and psychiatric treatment. Clinical holistic treatment has many advantages: efficiency, low cost, lack of negative side effects, lasting results, lack of use of psychopharmacological drugs often with side effects and an important preventive dimension.

Introduction

The most fundamental problem of human existence seems to be how to love oneself (1,2). The reason for this is our triple nature (3,4): having body, mind and soul, each carrying its own representations of self: the Id, the Ego and – Me! So who am I? When a patient start to become a wholeness, he subjectively recovers his sense of coherence (5,6). Looked upon from the outside, he becomes more alive, more real and solid. But much more than that is happening: the patient is gaining health, quality of life, and ability on all areas of life. Sexual and social ability are often radically improved with the ability to love and work also rehabilitated. This process of gaining existential health was called salutogenesis by Aaron Antonovsky (1923-1994)(5,6). Taking the patient into such a process of existential healing might be the medical strategy for the new millennium (7,8).

Our experience

Psychodynamic short term therapy (9-11) combined with "spiritual" mindfulness (12,13) and bodywork (14-16) was used in this study in order to work with all aspects of body, mind and spirit at the same time, as conversational therapy is often mainly mind-work. From 1990 to 2004 we analysed how more than 2,000 life-factors affected quality of life and health in order to conclude that philosophy of life was the single most important causal factor (17), which we afterwards have used in therapy. From 1997 to 2005 we have treated more than 500 patients using this new combined method, which we have called clinical holistic medicine (18-20). We have recently been able to demonstrate that this intervention is safe and efficient with patients suffering from physical, mental and sexual problems with the effect of therapy lasting for more than a year (21). The clinic has an open door policy and the patients are all coming "from the street" having read our books (18-23) or – most commonly - by recommendation from other patients (word by mouth). They entered this study if they rated 4 or 5 on the five point Likert Scale for quality of life (QOL5)(24): How do you feel about yourself at the moment? 1: "Very good", 2: "Good", 3: "Neither good nor bad", 4: "Bad", 5: "Very bad". Eight therapists performed the therapy under supervision (by SV). There were four major common themes in the therapy: sex and the body; consciousness and mind; love and spirit; and using your own talents and true self to be of real value to others (18-20).

The patients were measured with a five item quality of life and health questionnaire QOL5 (a five questions on self-assessed physical health, mental health, relation to self, relation to partner, and relation to friends)(24), a one-item questionnaire of self-assessed quality of life (QOL1)[24] and four questions on self-rated ability to love, self rated ability of sexual functioning, self rated social ability and self-rated working ability (ability to sustain a full time job) (together QOL10 questionnaire). These questionnaires were administered before entering the study, after the treatment and after one year (20,21).

Our findings

A: How many recovered their self-esteem?
Out of 43 patients, who entered the study (see table 1), only three continued to feel bad about themselves after an average of 20 sessions. 14 patients did not complete therapy, or failed to fill in the follow-up questionnaire. The therapy confronted the patients with their many repressed and often painful emotions from childhood of anger, guild, shame, hopelessness, despair and anxiety. Two patients had severe existential crisis lasting for a few days, but soon recovered and no patient was harmed from the intervention or had severe side effects. Not all patients were sufficiently motivated to confront the painful emotions from the past, which made them drop out. Success rate of treatment: 26/43 = 60.47% (95% CI: 44.41% - 75.02% [25].) Number Needed to Treat (NNT) of clinical holistic medicine with patients with low self esteem is therefore NNT = 1.33-2.25. As we have treated more than 500 patients with no patient harmed we estimate the Number Needed to Harm (NNH) to be >500.

Table 1. Clinical holistic medicine cure 60.47% (95% CI: 44.41%-75.02%, CI being the binomial confidence interval) of patients from self-assessed self-esteem

	Before treatment	After treatment
Low or very low self-esteem	43	3
Very high, high or intermediate self-esteem	0	26 (17 high or very high, 9 intermediate); 26/43 = 60.47% (95% CI: 44.41% - 75.02%) %%)[25].
Non-responders or dropouts	-	14
Low or very low self-esteem, non-responder or dropout	43	17

B: What happened to the responders?

Most interestingly, the patients who responded to the holistic existential therapy and improved their self-esteem (relationship with self), also improved all other areas of life: quality of life (both self-assessed with QOL1 (20,24) and measured by the validated questionnaire QOL5)(20,24), self-evaluated physical and mental health, and self-evaluated ability of functioning. All these improvement were about one step up the 5-point Likert scale, making them both statistically and clinically highly significant (see tables 2,3,4 and 5).

We found (tables 4 and 5) that the 26 patients, who recovered their self-esteem in the therapy, also improved their relationships in general (with self, partner, and friends), their self-evaluated ability of functioning in general (love-, sex-, and social ability), and their quality of life as measured with QOL5. When health, quality of life, and ability were combined (in the measure called QOL10 that take the average of these three domains), it was clear that the patients had healed their whole life (as measured by QOL10)(21), not only their self-esteem.

Tables 2 and 3 show that the 26 patients that recovered their self-esteem also improved their self-evaluated physical and mental health, relationship with friends and partner, ability to love, sexual ability of functioning, social ability, and self-assessed quality of life (QOL1)(24).

Please notice that the results are both statistically and clinically highly significant (self-assessed physical health p<0.05, working ability is not improved significantly, all other results p<0.01).

Tables 4 and 5 shows that the 26 patients, who recovered their self-esteem in the therapy, also improved their relationships (with self, partner, and friends), their self-evaluated ability of functioning (love-, sex-, work- and social ability), and their quality of life as measured with the validated questionnaire QOL5 (20,24). When health, quality of life and ability is combined, it is clear that these patients have healed their whole life (as measured by QOL10)(23).

Table 2. Study of 26 patients which therapy changed their ratings of self-esteem (feeling about them self) from bad to not bad (from 4=bad or 5=very bad, to 1=very good, 2=good, or 3=neither good nor bad). Paired samples statistics

		Mean	N	Std. deviation	Std. error mean
Physical Health	Before	2.5769	26	.80861	.15858
	After	2.1538	26	.78446	.15385
Mental health	Before	3.8000	26	.81650	.16330
	After	2.3600	26	.99499	.19900
Self esteem	Before	4.0769	26	.27175	.05329
	After	2.2692	26	.60383	.11842
Relation to friends	Before	2.6923	26	1.04954	.20583
	After	2.0385	26	.82369	.16154
Relation to partner	Before	4.6154	26	1.65111	.32381
	After	3.0385	26	1.94896	.38222
Ability to love	Before	3.8846	26	.99305	.19475
	After	2.3846	26	1.06120	.20812
Sexual ability	Before	3.5000	26	1.02956	.20191
	After	2.6154	26	1.09825	.21538
Social ability	Before	.3.3077	26	1.01071	.19822
	After	2.2308	26	.90808	.17809
Work ability	Before	3.1538	26	1.00766	.19762
	After	2.8462	26	1.22286	.23982
Quality of life	Before	3.8462	26	.73170	.14350
	After	2.2308	26	.86291	.16923

Table 3. Study of 26 patients which therapy changed their ratings of self-esteem (feeling about them self) from bad to not bad (from 4=bad or 5=very bad, to 1=very good, 2=good, or 3=neither good nor bad). Paired samples test

	Paired Differences					t	df	Significance (2 – tailed)
	Mean	Std. Deviation	Std. Error mean	95% confidence interval of difference				
				Lower	Upper			
Physical health	.4231	.98684	.19353	.0245	.8217	2.186	25	.038
Mental health	1.4400	1.15758	.23152	.9622	1.9178	6.220	24	.000
Self esteem	1.8077	.63367	.12427	1.5517	2.0636	14.546	25	.000
Relation to friends	.6538	1.12933	.22148	.1977	1.1100	2.952	25	.007
Relation to partner	1.5769	2.17574	.42670	.6981	2.4557	3.696	25	.001
Ability to love	1.5000	1.20830	.23697	1.0120	1.9880	6.330	25	.000
Sexual ability	.8846	.95192	.18669	.5001	1.2691	4.738	25	.000
Social ability	1.0769	1.09263	.21428	.6356	1.5182	5.026	25	.000
Work ability	.3077	1.43581	.28158	-.2722	.8876	1.093	25	.285
Quality of life	1.6154	1.20256	.23584	1.1297	2.1011	6.849	25	.000

Table 4. Paired samples statistics

		Mean	N	Std. deviation	Std. error mean
Relations	Before	3.7949	26	.70602	.13846
	After	2.4487	26	.76561	.15015
Ability	Before	3.4615	26	.59453	.11660
	After	2.5192	26	.74473	.14605
QOL (QOL 5)	Before	3.6200	25	.45775	.09155
	After	2.3400	25	.63915	.12783
Health-QOL-Ability (QOL 10)	Before	3.4800	25	.44866	.08973
	After	2.3878	25	.64132	.12826

Table 5. Paired samples test

	Paired differences					t	df	Significance (2) – tailed
	Mean	Std. deviation	Std. Error mean	95% confidence interval of difference				
				Lower	Upper			
Relations	1.3462	.80267	.15742	1.0219	1.6704	8.552	25	.000
Ability	.9423	.82252	.16131	.6101	1.2745	5.842	25	.000
QOL (QOL 5)	1.2800	.67309	.13462	1.0022	1.5578	9.508	24	.000
Health-QOL-Ability (QOL 10)	1.0922	.65752	.13150	.8208	1.3636	8.306	24	.000

Discussion

Although research has stressed the connection between health and self-esteem with development of self-esteem often suggested as one of the most important ways to prevent illness, improve health and fortune, it has been difficult to understand, conceptualise, measure or improve self-esteem (26-31). Even though self-esteem is strongly related to quality of life, health and ability, the connection between them still remain quite obscure (26-32).

It seems that in order to change a person's self-esteem, the most fundamental dimensions of existence much be analysed and developed, and such a development of the person's innermost layer seems to be a true transformation of personality. We have induced this transformation with the patients in the clinic through the development of sense of coherence by development of character and purpose of life, which actually seems to be a very old strategy.

This healing of almost all aspects of life is often seen with clinical holistic medicine and is called (Antonovsky-) salutogenesis after the researcher who discovered this type of immediate, lasting, and all-inclusive healing of the patient's existence. The most remarkable thing is that this seems to be the kind of healing that was induced by Hippocrates and his students 2,300 years ago at the island of Cos (33), where recovering of the human character was the primary tool for this. Physicians have been laughing for centuries of Hippocrates theory of "black and white bile" (the humeral medicine using the four elements), but it can still today work wonders to recover the human soul and character. It is possible, because this is the door to the purpose of life, where we use our primary talents (often called our life-purpose or "mission of life") in order to be of value to others (34) and give from our own gift to others.

Clinical holistic medicine – mindful psychodynamic short term therapy complemented with bodywork – seems from this study to be the perfect tool for helping the patients to recover their self-esteem. This can be done fast, efficient, cheap, and without side effects. Most interesting, by the successful inducing of existential healing (salutogenesis), almost all aspects of life were improved at the same time – physical and mental health, quality of life, ability of function in a number of important areas: with partner and friends, sexually, and socially. Most importantly from a philosophical point of view the patient's ability to love was recovered, when the patient started to love him- or herself again. The strategy of improving self-esteem can be the key to a new life for chronic patients, who present the triad of low quality of life, poor health (physical and/or mental) and poor ability of functioning. This combination is very difficult to help – not to say cure - by traditional biomedical or psychiatric treatment.

Conclusions

43 patients entered the study with low or very low self-esteem, but after an average of 20 sessions 26 persons (60.5%) were cured (95% CI: 44.41% - 75.02%). Number Needed to Treat (NNT) in clinical holistic medicine with patients with low self esteem was thus calculated to NNT = 1.33-2.25. As we have treated more than 500 patients with no patient harmed we estimate the Number Needed to Harm (NNH) as >500.

The rate of recovery was comparable to the most successful interventions with psychological and psychiatric treatment, and as clinical holistic treatment seems to have almost no side effects it seems as the choice of treatment for the patients, who are able to endure the emotional pain it provokes. In average the patients received 20 treatments over 14 month at a cost of 1,600 EURO.

References

[1]   Fromm E. The art of loving. New York: HarperCollins, 2000.
[2]   Buber M. I and thou. New York: Charles Scribner's Sons, 1970.
[3]   Jones E. The life and works of Sigmund Freud. New York: Basic Books, 1961.
[4]   Jung CG. Man and his symbols. New York: Anchor Press, 1964.
[5]   Antonovsky A. Health, stress and coping. London: Jossey-Bass, 1985.
[6]   Antonovsky A. Unravelling the mystery of health. How people manage stress and stay well. San Francisco: Jossey-Bass, 1987.
[7]   Ornish D. Love and survival. The scientific basis for the healing power of intimacy. Perennial, NY: HarperCollins, 1999.
[8]   Chopra D. Quantum healing. Exploring the frontiers of mind body medicine. New York: Bantam Books, 1990.

[9]   Anderson EM, Lambert MJ. Short term dynamically oriented psychotherapy: A review and meta-analysis. Clin Psychol Rev 1995;15:503-14.

[10]   Crits-Cristoph P. The efficacy of brief dynamic psychotherapy: A meta-analysis. Am J Psychiatry 1992;149:151-8.

[11]   Svartberg M, Stiles TC. Comparative effects of short-term psychodynamic psychotherapy: A meta-analysis. J Consult Clin Psychol 1991;59:704-14.

[12]   de Vibe M, Moum T. [Training in mindfulness for patients with stress and chronic illness.] Tidsskr Nor Laegeforen 2006;126(15):1898-902. [Norwegian].

[13]   de Vibe M. [Mindfullness training--a method for self-regulation of health.] Tidsskr Nor Laegeforen 2003;123(21):3062-3. [Norwegian].

[14]   Rosen M, Brenner S. Rosen method bodywork. Accessing the unconscious through touch. Berkeley, CA: North Atlantic Books, 2003.

[15]   Rothshild B. The body remembers. New York: WW Norton, 2000.

[16]   van der Kolk BA. The body keeps the score: memory and the evolving psychobiology of post traumatic stress. Harv Rev Psychiatry 1994;1(5):253–65.

[17]   Ventegodt S, Flensborg-Madsen T, Andersen NJ, Nielsen M, Morad M, Merrick J. Global quality of life (QOL), health and ability are primarily determined by our consciousness. Research findings from Denmark 1991-2004. Soc Indicator Res 2005;71:87-122.

[18]   Ventegodt S, Kandel I, Merrick J. Principles of holistic medicine. Philosophy behind quality of life. Victoria, BC: Trafford, 2005.

[19]   Ventegodt S, Kandel I, Merrick J. Principles of holistic medicine. Quality of life and health. New York: Hippocrates Sci Publ, 2005.

[20]   Ventegodt S, Kandel I, Merrick J. Principles of holistic medicine. Global quality of life.Theory, research and methodology. New York: Hippocrates Sci Publ, 2006.

[21]   Ventegodt S, Thegler S, Andreasen T, Struve F, Enevoldsen L, Bassaine L, et al. Clinical holistic medicine: Psychodynamic short-time therapy complemented with bodywork. A clinical follow-up study of 109 patients. ScientificWorldJournal 2006;6:2220-38.

[22]   Ventegodt S. Quality of life. To seize the meaning of life and become well again. [Livskvalitet – at erobre livets mening og blive rask igen.] Copenhagen: Forskningscentrets Forlag, 1995. [Danish].

[23]   Ventegodt S. Consciousness-based medicine [Bevidsthedsmedicin – set gennem lægejournalen.] Copenhagen: Forskningscenterets Forlag, 2003. [Danish].

[24]   Lindholt JS, Ventegodt S, Henneberg EW. Development and validation of QoL5 clinical databases. A short, global and generic questionnaire based on an integrated theory of the quality of life. Eur J Surg 2002;168:103-7.

[25]   Diem K, ed. Documenta Geigy. Scientific tables. Basel: Geigy, 1962.

[26]   Goodson P, Buhi ER, Dunsmore SC. Self-esteem and adolescent sexual behaviors, attitudes, and intentions: a systematic review. J Adolesc Health 2006;38(3):310-9.

[27]   Kermode S, MacLean D. A study of the relationship between quality of life, health and self-esteem. Aust J Adv Nurs 2001;19(2):33-40.

[28]   Shimizu M, Pelham BW. The unconscious cost of good fortune: implicit and explicit self-esteem, positive life events, and health. Health Psychol 2004;23(1):101-5.

[29]   Willoughby C, Polatajko H, Currado C, Harris K, King G. Measuring the self-esteem of adolescents with mental health problems: theory meets practice. Can J Occup Ther 2000;67(4):230-8.

[30]   Mann M, Hosman CM, Schaalma HP, de Vries NK. Self-esteem in a broad-spectrum approach for mental health promotion. Health Educ Res 2004;19(4):357-72.

[31]   MacInnes DL. Self-esteem and self-acceptance: an examination into their relationship and their effect on psychological health. J Psychiatr Ment Health Nurs 2006;13(5):483-9.

[32]   Berge M, Ranney M. Self-esteem and stigma among persons with schizophrenia: implications for mental health. Care Manag J 2005;6(3):139-44.

[33]   Jones WHS. Hippocrates. Vol. I–IV. London: William Heinemann, 1923-1931.

[34]   Ventegodt S. The life mission theory: A theory for a consciousness-based medicine. Int J Adolesc Med Health 2003;15(1): 89-91.

Chapter 52

Improvement of QOL, health and ability

We had a success rate of treating low self-assessed global quality of life (measured by QOL1: How would you assess the quality of your life now?) with clinical holistic medicine of 56.4% (95% CI: 42.3% - 69.7%); calculated from this the Number Needed to Treat (NNT) is 1.43 - 2.36. We found the Number Needed to Harm (NNH) >500, estimated from more that 500 patients being treated with no patients harmed.

We found that the patients during treatment entered a state of Antonovsky's salutogenesis (holistic, existential healing) and that they also improved their self-assessed health and general ability about one whole step up the 5-point Likert Scale. The treatment-responders radically improved their self-assessed physical health (0.6 step), self-assessed mental health (1.6 step), their relation to self (1.2 step), friends (0.3 step), and partner (2.1 step on a 6-step scale), and their ability to love (1.2 step) and work (0.8 step), and to function socially (1.0 step) and sexually (0.8 step).

Treatment with clinical holistic medicine is the cure of choice when the patients; 1) present the triad of low quality of life, pour self-assessed physical and/ or mental health, and pour ability of functioning, and 2) are willing to suffer during the therapy from confronting and integrating old emotional problems and traumas from early childhood. For these patients the treatment provides lasting benefits, with out the negative side effects of drugs. A lasting positive effect seems to prevent many different types of problems in the future. The patients had in average about 20 sessions at a total cost of 1,600 EURO.

Introduction

The last 20 years, the concept of quality of life (QOL) has been the subject for intensive research, and the medical society have been using this concept more and more often as the primary goal for care and prevention, even more important than health itself. There are many different measures of QOL, from highly complex and compound measures, to the most simple one, QOL1: Asking the person to rate his own quality of life today (1). The last two decades have made the medical society expert in measuring QOL, so now we can easily say if a treatment improved a patent's global (total) QOL or not. Still, we miss the simple answer to the question on how to improve a patient's QOL. Sometimes a very substantial intervention does not improve a patient's QOL, and sometimes a very subtle intervention changes the patient's whole life. We know that QOL can change dramatically, and when this happens, even the most severe of somatic diseases seems to respond positively (2-4).

After studying 2,000 factors related to eight different dimensions of QOL we found that a positive philosophy of life seems to be the most important causal factor of global QOL (5-9); or more precisely: the patients consciousness seems to be the primary determinant of both QOL, health and ability (10). As a more positive philosophy of life in principle can be developed in any patient, wee started in 1997 to improve the QOL and health with interventions on philosophy of life. Unfortunately we did not succeed in this endeavour before we finally understood that negative philosophy of life was rooted in emotional traumas; when we started working with psychodynamic short time therapy patients started to improve (by a few percent)(11,12) and when we added bodywork giving much more support to the patients process of healing, we suddenly had a dramatic improvement of our results (13). From year 2000 we added bodywork and training in philosophy of life when needed, and since them more than 500 patients have been treated, with increasing success.

Our experience

The literature of psychodynamic short time therapy demonstrates that many sufferings can be cures when old emotional and existential problems are solved in the therapy (14-16). Bodywork ads efficiency and speed to this method (17-19). Philosophy of life gives direction and allows the patient to reach their goal with less deviation from the planed route of therapy. We call the combination of philosophy of life, psychodynamic short time therapy, and bodywork for clinical holistic medicine, as this combination seems to be very much the same therapy – often called character medicine or humeral medicine - as was used in old Greece by Hippocrates and his disciples on the island of Cos (20).

55 patients with low or very low self-assessed quality of life (measure with the validated questionnaire QOL1 (1) were treated with clinical holistic medicine (mindful psychodynamic therapy with bodywork) inducing holistic healing (Antonovsky-salutogenesis)(21,22) from 2004 to 2005. All eight therapist had had training in clinical holistic medicine from the Nordic School of Holistic Medicine, and the students also attended a EU-master program to improve their consciousness as therapists (23-29).

The purpose was to see if patients with a low global QOL could improve this, if they healed their whole life, increasing their sense of coherence by use of Antonovsky salutogenesis as proposed by Aaron Antonovsky in the 1980s (21,22). We expected all aspects of life to improve if the patients were able to heal their whole existence, so we measured their QOL, health and ability before and after the treatment. 55 motivated patients entered the study and received clinical holistic medicine our Research Clinic for Holistic Medicine in Copenhagen. For more details, please see (13,30-32).

Our findings

We found self-assessed quality of life low before treatment (bad or very bad) in 55 patients, self-assessed quality of life high after treatment: (very good, good, or neither good nor bad) in 31 patients, self-assessed quality of life low after treatment (bad or very bad) in 10 patients with a response rate of follow up study: Non-responders or dropouts: 14 patients and self-assessed quality of life low after treatment, non-responders and dropouts: 24 patients (see table 1).

We had a success rate of treating low quality of life of 31/55 = 56.4% (95% CI: 42.3% - 69.7%) (33); calculated in this simplistic way we found the number needed to treat (NNT) of clinical holistic medicine with patients with low self-assessed QOL to be NNT = 1.43 - 2.36. We found the number needed to harm to be NNH>500 (estimated from more that 500 patients treated with no patients harmed).

Interestingly, we found that the patients had actually not only improved their self-assessed QOL (QOL1)(1) and their QOL measured with a more complex questionnaire (QOL5)(1], see table 4 and 5, they had also dramatically improved their physical health, mental health, relation to self, friends, and partner, and their ability to love and work, and to function socially and sexually (see tables 2 and 3). Most importantly, we found (using the square curve paradigm)(34) that these positive effects for the patients were lasting; after one year the effect of treatment had not significantly deteriorated (13). So salutogenesis seems to provide lasting benefits from the patients, without the side effects of drugs.

Tables 2 and 3 show that the 31 patients that healed existentially through salutogenesis and improved self-assessed quality of life (QOL1)(1) also improved their self-evaluated physical and mental health as measured with QOL5 (1), relationship with self, friends, and partner, ability to love, sexual ability of functioning, social ability, working ability, and. Please notice that the results are both statistically and clinically highly significant.

If we look at their relations to self and other people (average of relation to self, partner and friends), and their overall ability of functioning (average of love- work – sex- and social ability) these measures had also improved. When we combined health, quality of life, and ability in the combined measure QOL10, we also found that life as a whole had dramatically improved. This is the characteristic of salutogenesis. So we found that what happened for our patients were the healing of their existence and whole life.

Table 1. Characteristics of sample

	Before treatment	After treatment
Self-assessed quality of life low	55	10
Self-assessed quality of life high	0	31
Non-responders or dropouts		14
Self-assessed quality of life low,		
non-responder or dropout	31	24

Table 2. Study of 31 patients where therapy changed their ratings of self-evaluated quality of life from low to not low (from 4=bad or 5=very bad, to 1=very good, 2=good, or 3=neither good nor bad) (T-test)

		Mean	N	Std. Deviation	Std. Error Mean
Physical health	Before	2.900	30	0.9595	0.1751
	After	2.300	30	0.8366	0.1527
Mental health	Before	3.806	31	0.7491	0.1345
	After	2.193	31	0.7032	0.1263
Self-esteem	Before	3.451	31	0.8098	0.1454
	After	2.258	31	0.6815	0.1224
Relation to friends	Before	2.387	31	0.8032	0.1442
	After	2.064	31	0.7718	0.1386
Relation to partner	Before	4.548	31	1.8044	0.3240
	After	2.483	31	1.6905	0.3036
Ability to love	Before	3.580	31	1.0574	0.1899
	After	2.419	31	1.1187	0.2009
Sexual ability	Before	3.290	31	1.0390	0.1866
	After	2.483	31	1.0286	0.1847
Social ability	Before	3.096	31	0.9075	0.1630
	After	2.096	31	0.7463	0.1340
Work ability	Before	3.096	31	0.8700	0.1562
	After	2.322	31	0.7910	0.1420
QOL	Before	4.129	31	0.3407	0.0612
	After	2.193	31	0.7032	0.1263

*   From 4 = bad or 5 = very bad, to 1 = very good, 2 = good, or 3 = neither good nor bad.

Table 3. Paired sample test

	Paired Differences					t	df	Significance (Two–Tailed)
	Mean	Std. Deviation	Std. Error Mean	95% CI of Difference				
				Lower	Upper			
Physical health	0.6000	0.8550	0.1561	0.2807	0.9193	3.844	29	0.001
Mental health	1.612	1.0855	0.1949	1.214	2.011	8.272	30	0.000
Self-esteem	1.193	1.0776	0.1935	0.7983	1.588	6.167	30	0.000
Relation to friends	0.3226	0.8321	0.1494	0.0173	0.6278	2.158	30	0.039
Relation to partner	2.064	2.1899	0.3933	1.261	2.867	5.249	30	0.000
Ability to love	1.161	1.5512	0.2786	0.5923	1.730	4.168	30	0.000
Sexual ability	0.8065	1.3017	0.2338	0.3290	1.283	3.449	30	0.002
Social ability	1.000	1.0954	0.1967	0.5982	1.401	5.083	30	0.000
Work ability	0.7742	1.0865	0.1951	0.3756	1.172	3.967	30	0.000
QOL	1.935	0.8538	0.1533	1.622	2.248	12.62	30	0.000

Tables 4 and 5 show that the 31 patients, who healed existentially, also improved their relationships (with self, partner, and friends), their self-evaluated ability of functioning, and their quality of life as measured with the validated questionnaire QOL5 (1). When health, quality of life, and ability is combined, it is clear that these patients have healed their whole life (as measured by QOL10)(13). This healing of all aspects of life is often seen with clinical holistic medicine and is called (Antonovsky-) salutogenesis after the researcher who discovered this kind of global healing of the patient's existence. The patients had in average about 20 sessions at a total cost of 1,600 EURO.

Table 4. Study of 31 patients where therapy changed their ratings of self-evaluated quality of life from low to not low (from 4=bad or 5=very bad, to 1=very good, 2=good, or 3=neither good nor bad) (T-test)

		Mean	N	Std.	Std. Mean
Relations	Before	3.462	31	0.7634	0.1371
	After	2.268	31	0.7119	0.1278
Ability	Before	3.266	31	0.6121	0.1099
	After	2.330	31	0.5715	0.1026
QOL (QOL 5)	Before	3.416	30	0.5061	0.0924
	After	2.244	30	0.5685	0.1038
Health-QOL-Ability (QOL 10)	Before	3.353	30	0.4536	0.0828
	After	2.265	30	0.5262	0.0960

Table 5. Paired sample test

	Paired Differences					t	df	Significance (Two–Tailed)
	Mean	Std. Deviation	Std. Error Mean	95% CI of Difference				
				Lower	Upper			
Relations	1.193	0.8596	0.1544	0.8782	1.508	7.730	30	0.000
Ability	0.9355	0.8802	0.1581	0.6126	1.258	5.917	30	0.000
QOL (QOL 5)	1.172	0.6829	0.1246	0.9172	1.427	9.401	29	0.000
Health-QOL-Ability (QOL 10)	1.088	0.6590	0.1203	0.8419	1.334	9.042	29	0.000

Discussion

Holistic healing improving all aspects of life at the same time was predicted to be a possibility by Antonovsky; it seems that it can be done by rehabilitating a persons character, mission of life and sense of coherence, which is the aim for clinical holistic medicine (35-37). We found the process to be possible for the patients who were prepared to assume responsibility for own life, also when this meant confronting old emotional problems. Of 55 patients starting 14 patients dropped out of the study and 10 did not improve. 31 patients were helped to a QOL that was no longer bad or very bad. 20 of these had a good or very QOL after treatment, and 11 rated their QOL as neither good nor bad.

According to the square curve paradigm is has no meaning to use a placebo-control when we use shifts in consciousness to induce Antonovsky's salutogenesis. What we need to do is to demonstrate that the process of healing is actually taking place in a very short time, to exclude any likelihood of the patients being helped any other way than by our treatment; the patients must also be chronically ill or in a similar chronically poor condition, so that they do not shift by themselves. We believe that both these conditions has been fulfilled (13); all the patients had been to their own general practitioner without getting the help their needed from him. About one in three of the patients had been to psychiatrist, psychologist or had had psychopharmacological treatment before entering the study.

The most severe problem with this study is that our patients my be highly motivated for personal development, because they were attracted to the clinic by books and other material presenting the idea of personal growth as key to life's problems (35-38). This makes it a relevant question whether a random sample of the Danish population with pour QOL would have done similarly well. Further research is needed to answer the import question of who can be helped this way.

Conclusions

We had a success rate of treating low self-assessed global quality of life (as measured with QOL1: How would you assess the quality of your life now?[1]) of 31/55 = 56.4% (95%CI: 42.3% - 69.7%); calculated in the most simplistic way we found the Number Needed to Treat (NNT) of clinical holistic medicine with patients with low self-assessed QOL to be NNT = 1.43 - 2.36. We found the number needed to harm to be NNH>500 (estimated from more that 500 patients being treated with no patients harmed).

We found that the patients had entered a state of salutogenesis (existential healing) and that they besides their global QOL also improved their self-assessed health and ability about one step up the 5-point Likert Scale. They treatment responders dramatically improved their self-assessed physical health and mental health, their relation to self, friends, and partner, and their ability to love and work, and to function socially and sexually. In spite of having treated more than 500 patients no patient has yet been harmed, indicating that the induction of Antonovsky's salutogenesis is the most efficient and least dangerous method of healing we have to day. Unfortunately this cure is not yet for everybody but only for the motivated patients who are willing to suffer during the therapy from confronting and integrating old emotional problems and traumas all the way back from early childhood. For the patients that are able to endure the therapy, the treatment seems to provide lasting benefits for the patients, with out the side effects of drugs. The lasting positive effects also seem to prevent many problems in the future.

References

[1]   Lindholt JS, Ventegodt S, Henneberg EW. Development and validation of QoL5 clinical databases. A short, global and generic questionnaire based on an integrated theory of the quality of life. Eur J Surg 2002;168:103-7.

[2]   Spiegel D, Bloom JR, Kraemer HC, Gottheil E. Effect of psychosocial treatment on survival of patients with metastatic breast cancer. Lancet 1989;2(8668):888-91.

[3]   Ornish D. Love and survival. The scientific basis for the healing power of intimacy. New York: HarperCollins, 1999.

[4]   Ornish D, Brown SE, Scherwitz LW, Billings JH, Armstrong WT, Ports TA, et al. Can lifestyle changes reverse coronary heart disease? Lancet 1990;336(8708):129-33.

[5]   Ventegodt S. Measuring the quality of life. From theory to practice. Copenhagen: Forskningscentrets Forlag, 1996.

[6]   Ventegodt S. [Livskvalitet I Danmark.] Quality of life in Denmark. Results from a population survey. Copenhagen: Forskningscentrets Forlag, 1995. [Danish].

[7]   Ventegodt S. [Livskvalitet hos 4500 31-33 årige.] The Quality of Life of 4500 31-33 year-olds. Result from a study of the Prospective Pediatric Cohort of persons born at the University Hospital in Copenhagen. Copenhagen: Forskningscentrets Forlag, 1996. [Danish].

[8]   Ventegodt S. [Livskvalitet og omstændigheder tidligt i livet.] The quality of life and factors in pregnancy, birth and infancy. Results from a follow-up study of the Prospective Pediatric Cohort of persons born at the University Hospital in Copenhagen 1959-61. [partly in Danish] Copenhagen: Forskningscentrets Forlag, 1995. [Danish].

[9]   Ventegodt S. [Livskvalitet og livets store begivenheder.] The quality of life and major events in life. Copenhagen: Forskningscentrets Forlag, 2000.

[10]   Ventegodt S, Flensborg-Madsen T, Andersen NJ, Nielsen M, Morad M, Merrick J. Global quality of life (QOL), health and ability are primarily determined by our consciousness. Research findings from Denmark 1991-2004. Soc Indicator Res 2005;71:87-122.

[11]   Ventegodt S, Merrick J, Andersen NJ. Quality of life as medicine. A pilot study of patients with chronic illness and pain. ScientificWorld Journal 2003;3:520-32.

[12]   Ventegodt S, Merrick J, Andersen NJ. Quality of life as medicine II. A pilot study of a five day "Quality of Life and Health" cure for patients with alcoholism. ScientificWorldJournal 2003;3:842-52.

[13]   Ventegodt S, Thegler S, Andreasen T, Struve F, Enevoldsen L, Bassaine L, et al. Clinical holistic medicine: Psychodynamic short-time therapy complemented with bodywork. A clinical follow-up study of 109 patients. ScientificWorldJournal 2006;6:2220-38.

[14]   Anderson EM, Lambert MJ. Short term dynamically oriented psychotherapy: A review and meta-analysis. Clin Psychol Rev 1995;15:503-14.

[15]   Crits-Cristoph P. The efficacy of brief dynamic psychotherapy: A meta-analysis. Am J Psychiatry 1992;149:151-8.

[16]   Svartberg M, Stiles TC. Comparative effects of short-term psychodynamic psychotherapy: A meta-analysis. J Consult Clin Psychol 1991;59:704-14.

[17]   Rothshild B. The body remembers. New York: WW Norton, 2000.

[18]   Rosen M, Brenner S. Rosen method bodywork. Accessing the unconscious through touch. Berkeley, CA: North Atlantic Books, 2003.

[19]   van der Kolk BA. The neurobiology of childhood trauma and abuse. Child Adolesc Psychiatr Clin North Am 2003;12(2):293–317.

[20]   van der Kolk BA. The body keeps the score: memory and the evolving psychobiology of post traumatic stress. Harv Rev Psychiatry 1994;1:253–65.

[21]   Lowen A. Honoring the body. Alachua, FL: Bioenergetics Press, 2004.

[22]   Jones WHS. Hippocrates. Vol. I–IV. London: William Heinemann, 1923-1931.

[23]   Antonovsky A. Health, stress and coping. London: Jossey-Bass, 1985.

[24]   Antonovsky A. Unravelling the mystery of health. How people manage stress and stay well. San Franscisco: Jossey-Bass, 1987.

[25]   Endler PC. Master program for complementary, psychosocial and integrated health sciences Graz, Austria: Interuniversity College, 2004.

[26]   Blättner B. Fundamentals of salutogenesis. Health promotion and individual promotion of health: Guided by resources. Graz: Interuniversity College, 2004.

[27]   Pass PF. Fundamentals of depth psychology. Therapeutic relationship formation between self-awareness and casework Graz, Austria: Interuniversity College, 2004.

[28]   Endler PC. Working and writing scientifically in complementary medicine and integrated health sciences. Graz, Austria: Interuniversity College, 2004.

[29]   Spranger HH. Fundamentals of regulatory biology. Paradigms and scientific backgrounds of regulatory methods Graz, Austria: Interuniversity College, 2004.

[30]   Rodari A. Introduction of regulatory methods and systematics. Description and current research. Graz: Interuniversity College, 2004.

[31]   Kratky KW. Complementary medicine systems: Comparison and integration. New York: Nova Sci, 2008.

[32]   Ventegodt S, Kandel I, Merrick J. Principles of holistic medicine. Philosophy behind quality of life. Victoria, BC: Trafford, 2005.

[33]   Ventegodt S, Kandel I, Merrick J. Principles of holistic medicine. Quality of life and health. New York: Hippocrates Sci Publ, 2005.

[34]   Ventegodt S, Kandel I, Merrick J. Principles of holistic medicine. Global quality of life.Theory, research and methodology. New York: Hippocrates Sci Publ, 2006.

[35]   Diem K, ed. Documenta Geigy. Scientific tables. Basel : Geigy, 1962.

[36]   Ventegodt S, Merrick J, Andersen NJ. Holistic Medicine II: The square-curve paradigm for research in alternative, complementary and holistic medicine: A cost-effective, easy and scientifically valid design for evidence based medicine. ScientificWorldJournal 2003;3: 1117-27.

[37]   Ventegodt S. The life mission theory: A theory for a consciousness-based medicine. Int J Adolesc Med Health 2003;15(1):89-91.

[38]   Ventegodt S, Merrick J, Andersen NJ. The life mission theory VI: A theory for the human character. ScientificWorldJournal 2004;4:859-80.

[39]   Ventegodt S, Flensborg-Madsen T, Andersen NJ, Merrick J. Life mission theory VII: Theory of existential (Antonovsky) coherence: a theory of quality of life, health and ability for use in holistic medicine. ScientificWorldJournal 2005;5:377-89.

[40]   Ventegodt S, Merrick J, Andersen NJ. Holistic Medicine III: The holistic process theory of healing. ScientificWorldJournal 2003;3:1138-46.

[41]   Ventegodt S. Consciousness-based medicine [Bevidsthedsmedicin – set gennem lægejournalen.] Copenhagen: Forskningscenterets Forlag, 2003. [Danish].

Chapter 53

Impaired self-rated ability of sexual functioning improved

We have conducted a clinical follow-up study, where we examined the effect of clinical holistic medicine (psychodynamic short-term therapy complemented with bodywork) on patients with poor self-assessed sexual ability of functioning and found that this problem could be solved in 41.67% of the patients ((95% CI: 27.61% - 56.7%; $1.75 < NNT < 3.62$, $p=0.05$). The bodywork was inspired by the Marion Rosen method and helped the patients to confront painful emotions from childhood trauma(s) and thus accelerated and deepened the therapy. The goal of therapy was the healing of the whole life of the patient through Antonovsky salutogenesis. In this process, rehabilitation of the character and purpose of life of the patient was essential, and assisted the patient to recover his sense of coherence (existential coherence). We conclude that clinical holistic medicine is the treatment of choice if the patient is ready to explore and assume responsibility for his existence (true self) and willing to struggle emotionally in the therapy to reach this important goal. When the patient heals existentially, both quality of life, health and ability of functioning in general was improved at the same time.

Introduction

About 25-50% of the western population complain about sexual issues (1) and with more specific questions asked, the larger the group of patients that have such problems. In our clinical work we measured sexual ability in 109 patients who entered the Research Clinic for Holistic Medicine during the 2004-2005 period and found that 48 of these patients complained about significant sexual issues regarding their self-assessed ability of sexual functioning. These patients entered a treatment process, where their sexual ability could be addressed though rehabilitation of their natural being and knowledge of self. The intention was healing their whole life through induction of Antonovsky salutogenesis (2,3). In this chapter we analyze the effect that our treatment had on the patients, who presented with self-assesed sexual problems.

Our study

The patients were included in this study if they assessed their own sexual ability of functioning (each patient received a questionnaire before start of treatment) as impaired or very impaired before treatment start. They received treatment according to clinical holistic medicine (4-6), a kind of psychodynamic short-term therapy earlier found effective on a long list of health problems (7,8). The patients were also evaluated for sexual issues that existed along three axis: desire, orgasmic dysfunction, and sexually related pain (mostly pain during intercourse, primary vulvodynia, or pelvic tension pain) (9). The body work was inspired by Marion Rosen and helped the patients to confront old emotional pain from childhood trauma repressed to the body-mind (10).

Forty-eight patients entered the study having self-assessed impaired ability of sexual function before treatment (self-assessed as being 'impaired' or 'very impaired'. Twenty patients rated their sexual functioning as adequate after treatment: (self-assessed sexual ability of functioning: very good, good, or neither good nor bad). Of those 20 patients, eight of these completely resolved their problem (rating good or very good) and twelve were improving (rating: neither good nor bad). Eleven of the patients continued to self-assess their sexual functioning as impaired after the treatment (self-assessed sexual ability of functioning: bad or very bad). The response rate of follow-up survey one year after was 64.6%. Seventeen patients were classified as non-responders upon follow-up. After the treatment, 28 patients were either still poorly functioning sexually, or classified as non-responders upon follow-up, or withdrew from the study early.

The "rate of cure" of the treatment was 20/48 = 41.7% (95%CI: 27.6% - 57.0%) (see table 1) (11). Number needed to treat (NNT) of clinical holistic medicine with sexually poorly functioning patients = 1.75-3.62. Number needed to harm (NNH) was estimated from treating more than 500 patients in our clinic since year 2000 with this therapy none of which had severe side effects or harmed themselves or other people during the therapy; NNH estimated >500. The patients healed not only their sexuality, but also their whole being, because of the induction of Antonovsky salutogenesis. Both physical and mental health, relations to self, friends, and partner, and ability of function socially and to work was improved, as was the self-assessed quality of life. Quality of life, health and relations were measured with QOL1 and QOL5 (6,12).

Tabel 1. 48 patients with severe sexual problems of functioning entered the study; 20 = 41.67% (95% CI: 27.61% - 56.7%) of these was helped with clinical holistic medicine

	Before treatment	After treatment
Low self-assessed sexual ability of functioning	48	11
High ability of sexual functioning	0	20
Non-responders or dropouts	-	17
Low sexual ability of functioning, non-responder or dropout	-	28

Table 2. Summary of patient identified sexual issues

Self evaluated Physical health

		Before	After	Δ	p
Desire	Val	2.7	2.33	0.37	.019
	N	43	33	10	
Pain	Val	3	2.4	0.6	NS
	N	16	10	6	
Orgasmic dysfunction	Val	2.75	2.35	0.4	.016
	N	24	17	7	
Other problems	Val	2.76	2.21	0.55	NS
	N	33	24	9	

Self evaluated Mental health

		Before	After	Δ	p
Desire	Val	3.65	2.42	1.23	.000
	N	43	33	10	
Pain	Val	3.25	2.4	0.85	NS
	N	16	10	6	
Orgasmic dysfunction	Val	3.17	2.29	0.88	.000
	N	24	17	7	
Other problems	Val	3.55	2.63	0.92	.002
	N	33	24	9	

Relation to myself

		Before	After	Δ	p
Desire	Val	3.28	2.41	0.87	.000
	N	43	34	9	
Pain	Val	3.19	2.2	0.99	.032
	N	16	10	6	
Orgasmic dysfunction	Val	3.04	2.39	0.65	.006
	N	24	18	6	
Other problems	Val	3.24	2.36	0.88	.001
	N	33	24	9	

Relation to friends

		Before	After	Δ	p
Desire	Val	2.61	2.18	0.43	.011
	N	43	34	9	
Pain	Val	2	1.5	0.5	NS
	N	16	10	6	
Orgasmic dysfunction	Val	2	1.89	0.11	NS
	N	24	18	6	
Other problems	Val	2.61	2.04	NS	.012
	N	33	24	9	

Relation to your partner

		Before	After	Δ	p
Desire	Val	5	3.88	1.12	.016
	N	43	34	9	
Pain	Val	4.3	2.9	1.4	NS
	N	16	10	6	
Orgasmic dysfunction	Val	4	3.11	0.89	NS
	N	24	18	6	
Other problems	Val	4.72	3.46	1.26	NS
	N	32	24	8	

Self evaluated Ability to love

		Before	After	Δ	p
Desire	Val		2.5	0.86	.001
	N	42	34	8	
Pain	Val	3.31	1.9	1.41	.011
	N	16	10	6	
Orgasmic dysfunction	Val	3	2.44	0.56	NS
	N	24	18	6	
Other problems	Val	3.39	2.29	1.1	.002
	N	33	24	9	

Self evaluated Sexual function

		Before	After	Δ	p
Desire	Val	3.35	2.71	0.64	.014
	N	43	34	9	
Pain	Val	3.94	3	0.94	.004
	N	16	10	6	
Orgasmic dysfunction	Val	3.21	2.78	0.43	NS
	N	24	18	6	
Other problems	Val	3.46	2.67	0.79	.029
	N	33	24	9	

Self evaluated Social function

		Before	After	Δ	p
Desire	Val	2.79	2.18	0.61	.002
	N	43	34	9	
Pain	Val	2.63	1.8	0.83	.025
	N	16	10	6	
Orgasmic dysfunction	Val	2.42	2.17	0.25	NS
	N	24	18	6	
Other problems	Val	3.06	2.29	0.77	.001
	N	33	24	9	

Self evaluated Working capacity

		Before	After	Δ	p
Desire	Val	3.09	2.53	0.56	.025
	N	43	34	9	
Pain	Val	3.38	2.4	0.98	.037
	N	16	10	6	
Orgasmic dysfunction	Val	3	2.67	0.33	NS
	N	24	18	6	
Other problems	Val	3.06	2.46	0.6	NS
	N	33	24	9	

Self evaluated Quality of life (QOL1)

		Before	After	Δ	p
Desire	Val	3.44	2.32	1.12	.000
	N	43	34	9	
Pain	Val	3.31	2.3	1.01	.029
	N	16	10	6	
Orgasmic dysfunction	Val	3.46	2.61	0.85	.000
	N	24	18	6	
Other problems	Val	3.36	2.33	1.03	.001
	N	33	24	9	

Table 3. T-test (20 patients with sexual problems who succeeded in experiencing Antonovsky salutogenesis) Paired samples statistics

		Mean	N	Std.	Std. mean
Physical Health	Before	2.7368	19	.87191	-20003
	After	2.2105	19	.85498	.19615
Mental health	Before	3,7000	20	.86450	.19331
	After	2.1000	20	-85224	-19057
Self esteem	Before	3.5000	20	.76089	.17014
	After	2.3500	20	-98809	.22094
Relation to friends	Before	2.5500	20	.99868	.22331
	After	1.9500	20	..88704	.19835
Relation to partner	Before	4.2000	20	2.01573	.45073
	After	2.6500	20	2.05900	.46041
Ability to love	Before	3-6500	20	1.18210	.26433
	After	2.1500	20	1.26803	.28354
Sexual ability	Before	4.4000	20	.50262	.11239
	After	2-5000	20	.68825	.15390
Social ability	Before	3-0500	20	1.14593	.25624.
	After	2.0000	20	.79472	.17770
Work ability	Before	3.1053	19	.93659	.21487
	After	2.1579	19	1.06787	.24499
Quality of life	Before	3.6000	20	.99472	.22243
	After	2.2500	20	1.01955	.22798

Table 4. Paired samples test

	Paired Differences					t	df	Significance (2 – tailed)
	Mean	Std. Deviation	Std. Error mean	95% confidence interval of difference				
				Lower	Upper			
Physical health	.5263	.84119	.19298	.1209	.9318	2.727	18	.014
Mental health	1.6000	1.18766	.26557	1.0442	2.1558	6.025	19	.000
Self esteem	1.1500	1.18210	.26433	.5968	1.7032	4.351	19	.000
Relation to friends	.6000	1.18766	.26557	.0442	1.1558	2.259	19	.036
Relation to partner	1.5500	2.06410	.46155	.5840	2.5160	3.358	19	.003
Ability to love	1,5000	1.50438	.33639	7959	2.2041	4.459	19	.000
Sexual ability	1.9000	.85224	.19057	1.5011	2.2989	9.970	19	.000
Social ability	1.0500	1.31689	.29447	.4337	1.6663	3.566	19	.002
Work ability	.9474	1.22355	.28070	.3576	1.5371	3.375	18	.003
Quality of life	1.3500	1.34849	.30153	.7189	1.9811	4.477	19	.000

Table 2 shows that 43 patients had sexual issues related to desire, 16 patients had problems related to sexually related pain; 24 patients suffered from orgasmic dysfunction, and 33 patients had other sexual problems. One patient could have more that one problem. Interestingly, physical health, mental health, relation to self, friends and partner, ability to love, function socially, working ability [meaning ability to sustain a full time work], and self-evaluated quality of life by QOL1 (12) did also improve for many of the patients during the therapy. The general beneficial effect of the therapy is due to the induction of Antonovsky-salutogenesis (2,3).

Fifty-six percent of the clinics patients reported sexual problems and received on average 14.8 sessions at the cost of 1,188 EURO. Tables 3-6 shows that when the patient with the experience of sexual inadequacy healed her/his life (enters the state of salutogenesis) the sexual issues were resolved and all other dimensions of existence were improved as well.

Table 5. Paired samples statistics

		Mean	N	Std. deviation	Std. error mean
Relations	Before	3.4167	20	.93580	.20925
	After	2.3167	20	.86839	.19418
Ability	Before	3.5395	19	.65226	.14964
	After	2.1842	19	.75389	.17295
QOL (QOL 5)	Before	3.3509	19	.64763	.14858
	After	2.2456	19	.68351	.15681
Health-QOL-Ability (QOL 10)	Before	3.3735	18	.59609	.14050
	After	2.1574	18	.58049	.13682

Table 6. Paired samples test

	Paired differences					t	df	Significance (2) – tailed
	Mean	Std.	Std. Error mean	95% confidence interval of difference				
				Lower	Upper			
Relations	1.1000	.99766	.22308	.6331	1.5669	4.931	19	.000
Ability	1.3553	.89488	.20530	.9239	1.7866	6.601	18	.000
QOL (QOL 5)	1.1053	.76419	.17532	.7369	1.4736	6.304	18	.000
Health-QOL-Ability (QOL 10)	1.2160	.65814	.15512	..8888	1.5433	7.839	17	.000

Discussion

Sexual issues are very common and often related to existential and mental problems. In spite of good medical advice and sexological training programs most patients with a compromised sexual ability of functioning continue to have sexual problems, which can continue even for years. We have learned from working with many patients during the last six years, that even severe sexual inadequacy, both male and female, is often due to existential factors, like not knowing one self sufficiently. Sexual problems are not only connected to physical or mental factors and this is why psychotherapy alone often is not able to solve sexual problems, while holistic existential therapy combined with bodywork often is.

A successful strategy to solving sexual problems of general sexual inadequacy seems to be personal development of the sense of coherence, healing the whole being, not only of sexual life. The combination of psychodynamic therapy and bodywork are helping the patient to confront the painful sexually related emotion in an efficient way and creates fast, affordable, and lasting results with no side effects.

The patient must in the course of the treatment be willing to face deep existential problems and often very unpleasant feelings like shame, guilt and hopelessness, when the often very early traumas are confronted, and the old emotional charge is re-integrated. The goal of the psychodynamic therapy is for the patients to learn to know their true self. Not all patients are ready for that, so we believe that clinical holistic therapy is the therapy of choice, when the patient is motivated for a deep inner exploration.

Conclusions

Clinical holistic medicine is our name for psychodynamic short-term therapy complemented with bodywork. The rehabilitation of character and purpose of life is essential, and assisting the patient recover his existential coherence is the primary intent of the therapy. In this paper, we found that 41.67% (95% CI: 27.61% - 56.7%) were helped. The number needed to treat (NNT) of clinical holistic medicine with sexually poorly functioning patients = 1.75-3.62. The number needed to harm (NNH) was estimated as >500.

References

[1]   Ventegodt S. Sex and the quality of life in Denmark. Arch Sex Behav 1998;27(3):295-307.
[2]   Antonovsky A. Health, stress and coping. London: Jossey-Bass, 1985.
[3]   Antonovsky A. Unravelling the mystery of health. How people manage stress and stay well. San Franscisco: Jossey-Bass, 1987.
[4]   Ventegodt S, Kandel I, Merrick J. Principles of holistic medicine. Philosophy behind quality of life. Victoria, BC: Trafford, 2005.
[5]   Ventegodt S, Kandel I, Merrick J. Principles of holistic medicine. Quality of life and health. New York: Hippocrates Sci Publ, 2005.
[6]   Ventegodt S, Kandel I, Merrick J. Principles of holistic medicine. Global quality of life. Theory, research and methodology. New York: Hippocrates Sci Publ, 2006.
[7]   Abbass AA, Hancock JT, Henderson J, Kisely S. Short-term psychodynamic psychotherapies for common mental disorders. Cochrane Database Syst Rev 2006;18;(4):CD004687.
[8]   Leichsenring F. Are psychodynamic and psychoanalytic therapies effective? A review of empirical data. Int J Psychoanal 2005;86(Pt 3):841-68.
[9]   Ventegodt S, Vardi G, Merrick J. Holistic adolescent sexology: How to counsel and treat young people to alleviate and prevent sexual problems. BMJ Rapid Response 2005 Jan 15.
[10]   Rosen M, Brenner S. Rosen method bodywork. Accessing the unconscious through touch. Berkeley, CA: North Atlantic Books, 2003.

[11]   Diem K, ed. Documenta Geigy. Scientific tables. Basel: Geigy, 1962.
[12]   Lindholt JS, Ventegodt S, Henneberg EW. Development and validation of QOL5 clinical databases. A short, global and generic questionnaire based on an integrated theory of the quality of life. Eur J Surg 2002;168:103-7.

Chapter 54

Recovery of working ability using Antonovsky salutogenesis

40 patients with low or very low self-assessed working ability were treated with psychodynamic short time therapy complemented with body-work. They received in average 20 sessions at a prize of 1,600 EURO. The Body Work was inspired by Marion Rosen and helped the patients to confront old emotional pain from childhood trauma repressed to the body-mind. Results: 52.5% (95% CI: 36.1% - 68.5%) of patients recovered their self-assessed working ability (from 4.2 to 2.4 up the five point Likert scale (p<0.01)). From this we have NNT = 1.46-2.77. We estimate the Number Needed to Harm to be NNH>500. The responders improved their self-assessed physical health (from 3.3 to 2.6; 0.6 step up the five point Likert Scale, p=0.01), self-assessed mental health (from 3.8 to 2.5, p<0.01), self-esteem (from 3.4 to 2.5, p<0.01), self-assessed quality of life (QOL1) (from 3.7 to 2.4p<0.01), QOL measured by QOL5 (from 3.3 to 2.6p<0.01), the quality of relations (from 3.2 to 2.6p<0.01), general ability of functioning (from 3.5 to 2.5; p<0.01). Combining quality of life, health, and ability showed large improvements of the patient's whole life (p<0.01). The simultaneous improvement in all aspects of life can be explained as caused by existential healing (Antonovsky salutogenesis). The patients of this study have been strongly motivated, and willing to endure the strong emotional pain provoked by the therapy.

Introduction

The experience of having lost the ability to work is to many people a destiny worse than death; quite surprisingly we have found that this condition is often easily curable with psychodynamic short time therapy (1-6) complemented with bodywork. The key to recovery of working ability seems to be rehabilitation of the patients character (7) and purpose of life (8), as already Hippocrates knew (9). The basic idea of the therapy is that what limits our performance is not knowing our own talents and not understanding the joy of using these gifts to create value for others.

Modern psychodynamic theory states that the lack of personal power primarily is caused by a lack of insight in self, which originally was caused by the patient's childhood traumas ("gestalts") (10-12). These traumas carry both painful emotions and negative life-denying, decisions, which materialize a negative philosophy of life, which again limits the patient's self-confidents, self-esteem, sense of coherence, and willingness to accept life's challenges. This becomes a major hindrance to the personal development, and shuts the patient's life down.

Our study

In this study we included the 40 patients that entered our Research Clinic for Holistic Medicine 2004 and 2005, and before starting therapy rated their own ability to work as bad or very bad. In average these patients (from 20 to 60 years, both gender) had about 20 sessions of clinical holistic therapy (10-12) for 1600 EURO. Most patient paid for their own treatment, indicating a strong motivation to receive the treatment. The clinic was build with financial support from the "IMK Almene" Foundation, which is a non-for profit organisation supporting research in complementary medicine. The patients approached the clinic themselves, mostly because of recommendation from former patients. The mission of the clinic is to improve psychodynamic short term therapy to make it more efficient and useful for patients with physical, mental, existential, sexual, and working-ability issues. The Body Work was inspired by Marion Rosen and helped the patients to confront old emotional pain from childhood trauma repressed to the body-mind[13], thus accelerating therapy, and making it less painful (11). See Ventegodt et al 2006 (14) for more details on the study.

Our findings

After the treatment we found that 21 patients (52.5%, 95%CI: 36.1% - 68.5% [15]) rated their working ability as "very good" (1 patients), "good"(11 patients), or "neither good nor bad" (9 patients); 7 completed the treatment but did not improve, and 12 patients dropped out of the study. Table 1 shows the results.

Table 1. Charateristics of sample

	Before treatment	After treatment
"Low" or "very low" self-assessed working ability	40	7
Self-assessed working ability	0	21; 21/40 = 52.5% (95%CI: 36.1% - 68.5%) [15] Fully recovered ("good" or "very good"): 12 Improved ("neither good nor bad"): 9
Non-responders or dropouts	-	12
"Low" or "very low" self-assessed working ability, non-responder or dropout	40	19

We found that the 21 patients who improved their working ability (from 4.2 to 2.4; a radical improvement 1.8 step up the five point Likert scale (p<0.01)) also statistically and clinically significantly improved their self-assessed physical health (from 3.3 to 2.6; 0.6 step up the five point Likert Scale (p=0.01)), self-assessed mental health (from 3.8 to 2.5; 1.3 step up the five point Likert Scale (p<0.01)), self-esteem (from 3.4 to 2.5; 0.9 step up the five point Likert scale (p<0.01)), and their self-assessed quality of life (measured by QOL1[16]) (from 3.7 to 2.4; 1.3 step on the five point Likert Scale p<0.01)). We also found large improvements of QOL (measured by QOL5[16]) (from 3.3 to 2.6; 0.8 step on the five point Likert Scale (p<0.01)), the quality of relations (mean of relation to self, friends, and partner) (from 3.2 to 2.6; 0.7 step on the five point Likert Scale (p<0.01)), general ability of functioning (mean of ability to love, sexual ability, social ability and working ability) (from 3.5 to 2.5; 0.9 step on the five point Likert Scale p<0.01)). Combining quality of life, health, and ability in a measure called QOL10 showed large improvements of the patients whole life (from 3.4 to 2.6; 0.9 step on the five point Likert Scale p<0.01)) (see table 2). This over-all improvement is the indication of the phenomena of holistic healing that Antonovsky predicted and called "salutogenesis" – the inverse process of pathogenesis. A one-year follow up indicated the therapeutic benefits to be lasting [14].

Table 2. The 21 patient who improved working ability also improved QOL, relations, and ability in general (p<0.01). They also improved the whole life (QOL10, which is an average of QOL, self-assessed health, and self-assessed ability)
Paired T-Test

| | Paired | | | | | t | df | Significance (2 – tailed) |
| | Mean | Std. | Std. mean | 95% interval of difference | | | | |
				Lower	Upper			
Relations before/after	.634	.8938	.1950	.228	1.041	3.25	20	.00
Ability beore/after	.940	.8547	.1865	.551	1.329	5.04	20	.00
QOL5 before/after	.783	.7236	.1618	.444	1.122	4.84	19	.00
QOL10 before/after	.850	.6680	.1493	.537	1.162	5.69	19	.00

Discussion

We have seen 21 patients of 40 recover self-assessed working ability though clinical holistic medicine. Quality of life, health and ability were regained at the same time. We suggest that this happened because the therapy healed the patient's existence as a whole. Antonovsky predicted that this dramatic event of total recovery could happen, when sense of coherense was recovered, which is what we are noticing happening; he called this process of healing the patients total life for "salutogenesis" (17,18). We find that the present study strongly indicates that Antonovsky's concept of salutogenesis might be a key to solve one of the most important problems of our time: how to help people recover their working ability when this is lost to pour health, low self-confidence and self-esteem, and pour quality of life. The secret seems to be to find the patients inner resources and help him set these free.

We were told that several of the patients actually got full-time work after the treatment, but unfortunately this "objective" side of the improvement was not well documented in the study, which primarily had an existential focus. Further research is needed to document that improved self-assessed working ability is also actually making the patient regain his job.

Conclusions

Antonovsky predicted that man could heal his whole existence and called this salutogenesis. Clinical holistic medicine seems to be efficient in inducing salutogenesis, and lost working ability seems to be regained in 52.5% (36.1% - 68.5% of the patients, p=0.05). The patients are motivated for human development and engage in existential therapy in spite of this being highly emotionally painful at times where old trauma are confronted and integrated. The study was a non-controlled, non-blinded prospective intervention study.

We found that the 21 patients who improved their working ability (from 4.2 to 2.4; a radical improvement 1.8 step up the five point Likert scale (p<0.01)) also statistically and clinically significantly improved their self-assessed physical health (from 3.3 to 2.6; 0.6 step up the five point Likert Scale (p=0.01)), self-assessed mental health (from 3.8 to 2.5; 1.3 step up the five point Likert Scale (p<0.01)), self-esteem (from 3.4 to 2.5; 0.9 step up the five point Likert scale (p<0.01)), and their self-assessed quality of life (measured by QOL1) (from 3.7 to 2.4; 1.3 step on the five point Likert Scale p<0.01)). We also found large improvements of QOL (measured by QOL5) (from 3.3 to 2.6; 0.8 step on the five point Likert Scale (p<0.01)), the quality of relations (mean of relation to self, friends, and partner) (from 3.2 to 2.6; 0.7 step on the five point Likert Scale (p<0.01)), general ability of functioning (mean of ability to love, sexual ability, social ability and working ability) (from 3.5 to 2.5; 0.9 step on the five point Likert Scale p<0.01)).

Combining quality of life, health, and ability in a measure called QOL10 showed large improvements of the patient's whole life (from 3.4 to 2.6; 0.9 step on the five point Likert Scale p<0.01).

This over-all improvement is the indication of the phenomena of holistic healing that Antonovsky predicted and called "salutogenesis" (17,18) – the inverse process of pathogenesis.

References

[1]   Anderson EM, Lambert MJ. Short term dynamically oriented psychotherapy: A review and meta-analysis. Clin Psychol Rev 1995;15:503-14.
[2]   Crits-Cristoph P. The efficacy of brief dynamic psychotherapy: A meta-analysis. Am J Psychiatry 1992;149:151-8.
[3]   Svartberg M, Stiles TC. Comparative effects of short-term psychodynamic psychotherapy: A meta-analysis. J Consult Clin Psychol 1991;59:704-14.
[4]   Leichsenring F, Rabung S, Leibing E. The efficacy of short-term psychodynamic psychotherapy in specific psychiatric disorders: a meta-analysis. Arch Gen Psychiatry 2004;61(12):1208-16.

[5]   Leichsenring F. Are psychodynamic and psychoanalytic therapies effective?: A review of empirical data. Int J Psychoanal. 2005;86(Pt 3):841-68.

[6]   Abbass AA, Hancock JT, Henderson J, Kisely S. Short-term psychodynamic psychotherapies for common mental disorders. Cochrane Database Syst Rev 2006;(4):CD004687.

[7]   Ventegodt S, Andersen NJ, Merrick J. The life mission theory VI: A theory for the human character. ScientificWorldJournal 2004;4:859-80.

[8]   Ventegodt S. The life mission theory: A theory for a consciousness-based medicine. Int J Adolesc Med Health 2003;15(1): 89-91.

[9]   Jones WHS. Hippocrates. Vol. I–IV. London: William Heinemann, 1923-1931.

[10]   Ventegodt S, Kandel I, Merrick J. Principles of holistic medicine. Philosophy behind quality of life. Victoria, BC: Trafford, 2005.

[11]   Ventegodt S, Kandel I, Merrick J. Principles of holistic medicine. Quality of life and health. New York: Hippocrates Sci Publ, 2005.

[12]   Ventegodt S, Kandel I, Merrick J. Principles of holistic medicine. Global quality of life.Theory, research and methodology. New York: Hippocrates Sci Publ, 2005.

[13]   Rosen M, Brenner S. Rosen method bodywork. Accessing the unconscious through touch. Berkeley: North Atlantic Books, 2003.

[14]   Ventegodt S, Thegler S, Andreasen T, Struve F, Enevoldsen L, Bassaine L, Torp M, Merrick J. Clinical holistic medicine: Psychodynamic short-time therapy complemented with bodywork. A clinical follow-up study of 109 Patients. ScientificWorld Holistic 2006;6:2220-38.

[15]   Diem K, ed. Documenta Geigy. Scientific tables. Basel: Geigy, 1962.

[16]   Lindholt JS, Ventegodt S, Henneberg EW. Development and validation of QoL5 clinical databases. A short, global and generic questionnaire based on an integrated theory of the quality of life. Eur J Surg 2002;168:103-7.

[17]   Antonovsky A. Health, stress and coping. London: Jossey-Bass, London, 1985.

[18]   Antonovsky A. Unravelling the mystery of health. How people manage stress and stay well. San Franscisco: Jossey-Bass, 1987.

Section 14. Tools for research and quality assurance

Clinical research in holistic medicine needs the endpoints shown to be the best predictors of future health and survival. We know that such endpoints are self-evaluated health and self-evaluated quality of life. Fortunately these endpoints are extremely easy to collect with small questionnaires that only take a few minutes to fill out for the patient (like QOL1, QOL5 and QOL10)(see chapters 55 and 56) (1-4), meaning that every physician or therapist can easily conduct clinical research and also use the measurements by such questionnaire for quality assurance of his clinic and the therapists working there.

To be sure that such research will be up to standard we have made the Open Source Protocol that can be used by everybody (5).

An important research question is if the clinical results are temporary or permanent and in order to answer this question we have developed a special research design called the "square curve paradigm" (6). This is also easy to use; it simply says that you need to measure your patients before and after intervention, and then again sufficiently long time after to be sure that the results of therapy is lasting. We recommend at least one year before follow up. When we did such a study in our clinic (7) we noticed that the clinical results were not only lasting, but also improved over time. It seems like the holistic treatment is able to heal the patient and also teach the patient how to continue growing and learning. This is a very encouraging finding, which has also been found by other researchers.

So, when you start treating your patients with holistic medicine, give them the QOL10 questionnaire before and after treatment and calculate the QOL1, QOL5 and QOL10 scores before and after to learn how much your patients has improved (see appendix A in chapter 56) – it can be used free of charge for all non-commercial clinical research. Notice also the specific areas, where your patients have improved and the areas where improvement has been less positive. If the patients end up at a lower stage that the beginning point and no serious progressive illness like cancer can explain that, you might have ended therapy prematurely, which is also important to notice. It is normal that the patient will have a healing crisis with lower marks in the middle of the therapy. This is also where some patients have a tendency to drop out of treatment. If you suspect that your patient is in a crisis you can have him or her answering the questionnaire at that point in time, and the ratings will show this right away. So there are many practical applications of scientific measuring.

We always measure the patient with QOL10 before therapeutic intervention to set goals for the treatment. It is easy to remember such goals and very easy to see, if they are accomplished. Naturally all measurements and goals are noted in the case record.

We have also noticed that when people are related in time and space and grounded existentially your rating of the patient and the patients' own rating will often be very similar. If there is a large discrepancy this is a good subject for a talk in order to help the patient to be more down to earth and centered.

References

[1]   Lindholt JS, Ventegodt S, Henneberg EW. Development and validation of QOL5 for clinical databases. A short, global and generic questionnaire based on an integrated theory of the quality of life. Eur J Surg 2002;168(2):107-13.

[2]   Ventegodt S, Merrick J, Andersen NJ. Measurement of quality of life IV: Use of the SEQOL, QOL5, QOL1 and other global and generic questionnaires. ScientificWorldJournal 2003;3:992-1001.

[3]   Ventegodt S, Merrick J, Andersen NJ. Measurement of quality of life V: How to use the SEQOL, QOL5, QOL1 and other and generic questionnaires for research. ScientificWorldJournal 2003;3:1002-14.

[4]   Ventegodt S, Andersen NJ, Merrick J. QOL10 for clinical quality-assurance and research in treatment-efficacy: Ten key questions for measuring the global quality of life, self-rated physical and mental health, and self-rated social-, sexual and working abulity. J Altern Med Res 2009;1(2):113-22.

[5]   Ventegodt S, Andersen NJ, Kandel I, Merrick J. The open source protocol of clinical holistic medicine. J Altern Med Res 2009;1(2): 129-44.

[6]   Ventegodt S, Andersen NJ, Merrick J. The square-curve paradigm for research in alternative, complementary and holistic medicine: a cost-effective, easy and scientifically valid design for evidence based medicine. ScientificWorldJournal 2003;3:1117-27.

[7]   Ventegodt S, Thegler S, Andreasen T, Struve F, Enevoldsen L, Bassaine L, Torp M, Merrick J. Clinical holistic medicine: Psychodynamic short-time therapy complemented with bodywork. A clinical follow-up study of 109 patients. ScientificWorldJournal 2006;6:2220-38.

Chapter 55

Square curve paradigm used in integrative medicine

In this chapter we present a research paradigm for integrative, alternative, complementary and holistic medicine. A low cost, effective and scientifically valid design for evidence based medicine. Our aim was to find the simplest, cheapest and most practical way to collect data of sufficient quality and validity to determine: 1) which kinds of treatment give a clinically relevant improvement to quality of life (QOL), health and/or functionality, 2) which groups of patients can be aided by alternative, complementary, or holistic medicine, and 3) which therapists have the competence to achieve the clinically relevant improvements. Our solution to the problem is that a positive change in QOL must be immediate to be taken as caused by an intervention. We define "immediate" as within one month of the intervention. If we can demonstrate a positive result, with a group of chronic patients (20 or more patients who had their disease or state of suffering for one year or more), who can be significantly helped within one month and the situation still improved one year after, we find it scientifically evidenced that this cure or intervention has helped the patients. We call this characteristic curve for a "square curve".

If a global, generic QOL questionnare like QOL5, or even better a QOL-Health-Ability questionnaire (a QOL questionnaire combined with a self-evaluated health and ability of functioning quationnaire), is administered to the patients before and after the intervention, it is possible to document the effect of an intervention to a cost of only a few thousand Euros/USD. A general acceptance of this research design will solve the problem of not enough money in alternative, complementary and holistic medicine to pay the normal cost of a biomedical Cochrane study. As financial problems must not hinder the vital research in non-biomedical medicine, we ask the scientific community to accept this new research standard.

Introduction

Today every second person in Scandinavia is chronically ill, if you include minor diseases like allergies, eczema, low back pain or migraine and 94% of the population in Denmark has one or another symptom of ill health (1). The National Health Service, supplied free or almost free of charge in Scandinavia, is to an increasing degree being supplemented by alternative, complementary and holistic medical services paid by the individual user. There are numerous anecdotes of patients with cancer, arteriosclerosis, tinnitus, schizophrenia and other serious or incapasitating diseases being helped or even cured by these treatments (2), but at the same time there is no evidence that explains the spontaneous remissions from schizophrenia (ten international studies with 25-35 year follow-up showed 46-64 % complete og near complete recovery) or cancer and not much connects these remissions to any kind of treatement.

One reason for the scarcity of scientific evidence could be that the extensive use of alternative and holistic therapy – 800.000 persons using it now in Denmark or about 15% of the population (3)- is actually not linked to the improvement of health of the patients. Another and much more likely reason for the scarcity of documented success could be that the economic interest in alternative and holistic medicine, so far has been much too small to finance the necessary research. It is, however, of utmost importance that the non-biomedical medicine is carefully examined for possible positive effects on a variety of different diseases and human states of sufferings, since one must suspect that some of the alternative and holistic medicine provided by the most competent of the therapists do actually help at least some patient groups.

Let us therefore think about ways to solve that problem. If the problem is getting the money for research, one way is raising more money, but that is obviously the hard road. Another way is making the research cheaper. It seems that this is possible, if we can agree on some rules. As we definitely do not want to accept a method with less evidence, less plausibility, certainty and validity, we have to design a new method giving all these fine qualities of science, but at a cost of about 1% of the normal budget for research.

The theoretical advantage of alternative and holistic medicine

Alternative treatment (complementary and alternative medicine, CAM) is normally defined as treatment that is not provided by the established health service. Since many physicians have started to use alternative methods in their practice, most commonly a simple form of acupuncture, it is necessary to define alternative treatment as a treatment, which in contrast to biomedicine, builds openly on the self-healing resources and potentials of the patient him/herself. This is, of course, true for any treatment from the time of Hippocrates until today, but much modern medicine has forgotten this. In alternative and holistic medicine these hidden resources are considered a vital part of the human whole. In most kinds of alternative medicine these self-healing resources are triggered into use, i.e. by helping the patients to change attitudes, resulting in general improvement of the human global quality of life, health and ability of functioning. That is why we use the expression consciousness-oriented medicine about the "alternative and holistic medicine" and also why we imagine that, in spite of the obvious lack of evidence, the best of the alternative and holistic medicine might actually have the power to help.

The empowerment of the patient though personal development mobilise these hidden resources, so this "medicine" has many advantages. It is affordable for all patients, it is cheap for the society, a benefit to the workplace due to satisfied and healthy workers, it does not deprive the patient of the responsibility for his og her own existence, it is "organic", takes care of the ecosystem, it does not pollute, it has almost no side effects, and finally it might give the patient a permanent benefit if successful. If the person who takes his hidden resources into use does this so well as to improve the global quality of life, this person might even get less sick in the future, which is of great value to his or her surrounding world. So we can say that this consciousness-oriented medicine might also be preventive and societally constructive.

Can we have good medical science?

Research can be a value enhancing activity. This happens when research produce data of necessary certainty and quality. It happens when the data is produced in relation to the relevant endpoints and the basic intention of the research. If, on a scientific basis, one wishes to improve the subjective experience of health, one must measure psychometrically in order to retrieve the data necessary to evaluate own health and verify improvement. Therefore, in research we must keep track of both intention and endpoints in order to secure that these are always alligned with eachother.

One serious difficulty with research in consciousness-based medicine is that alternative and holistic treatments seldom live up to the general demands of scientific theory and method. Therefore the research must, if at all possible, be arranged so it can be used on all forms of treatment, regardless of the theory and method underlying this treatment.

When research shows that an alternative or holistic treatment give the patients a significant improvement, there is apparently something to gain from that treatment. This documentation is in itself of great value. Of cause this is not the end of the research, but only the beginning. There must now be established new research projects to clarify the theory and method. Only when the method of treatment is understood, described rationally and linked to sound scientific theory, can we make a valid scientific contribution to the treasure of medical knowledge. A scientifically trained physician will never use meaningless rituals or substances to the patient, no matter how well it works for an alternative therapist. Without scientific understanding, an alternative or holistic cure will never be used by the medical community. But without examining the effects of the new or alternative cures and interventions, medicine will never be able to develop in a positive direction.

Below, we suggest a simple and scientifically trustworthy research design, which can be accomplished within the economical limits of a small public or private research centre or corresponding organisations. It has been developed to study the effects of alternative and holistic therapies at the "Frisklivssenteret" (the "Healthy Life Centre") in Porsgrunn, Norway, in co-laboration with the independent non-profit organisation "The Scandinavian Foundation for Holistic Medicine".

Scientific demands for evidence based alternative and holistic medicine

We make the following demands on the quality and validity of the collected results:
1. The results are qualitatively meaningful and the applied endpoints correspond closely to the intention behind all sound, alternative and holistic treatment, namely the

general improvement of quality of life, health and functionality. It is these dimensions, which must be measured in the study (see tables 1 and 2).

Table 1. The points to be included in surveys with adults

Quality of life
Self-evaluated, global quality of life

Health
Self-evaluated physical health
Self-evaluated psychic health

Ability of functioning
Self – evaluated, global ability of functioning, assessed in three sub-dimensions, corresponding to life's three dimensions of leisure time, work and family:
Self-evaluated social functionality
Self-evaluated working ability
Self-evaluated functionality concerning love
Self-evaluated functionality concerning sexuality

2. The quantitative results are valid (4) and statistically significant at a $p = < 0.05$ level (95 % probability that the proven effect is true).
3. That the results are visibly and directly observed as an immediate consequence of a treatment. By immediate, we mean within one month from the start of the intervention. A survey before and after the intervention must show a significant and clinically relevant improvement of the patient's condition regarding self-evaluated quality of life, health and or functionality. Is this case, a control group is not needed..

Table 2. The points to be included in surveys with children

Quality of life
Self-evaluated, global quality of life
Parent-evaluated, global quality of life

Health
Parent-evaluated physical health
Parent-evaluated mental health

Ability of functioning
Parent-evaluated global ability of functioning, evaluated by the following sub dimensions:
Parent-evaluated functionality in the family
Parent-evaluated functionality at school / institution
Parent-evaluated social functionality with the same and opposite sex

4. The questionnaire(s) must be appropriate and validated. They must have the correct amount of questions necessary to document a clinically and statistically significant

improvement of the relevant dimensions. We accept an average improvement of ½ point on a 5-point "Likert"-scale as adequate to call a treatment good, but an improvement of ¼ of a point is of clinical relevance.

5. There must be at least 20 patients in the group receiving the treatment, and the patients must be sufficiently well characterised to allow falsification of the formulated hypothesis: Therapist (x) can, with method (y), help patients with diagnosis (z), in the age interval (p), the degree of motivation (q), the resources (r), etc. improve their QOL/physical health/psychological health/ability of functioning.

A simple way to ensure valid results is to demand that the results are significant and produced immediately (within one month). This intervention can naturally be repeated a desired number of times, to increase or secure a result of treatment. In case of repeated treatments, ratings of endpoints must show a postive trend on a run-chart (5). The rating is repeated again after an appropriate length of time to see the long-term effect of the treatment, at least one year after the initial treatment.

Effect of Intervention

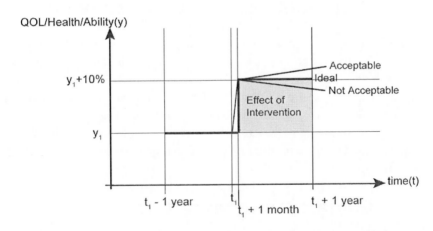

Figure 1. The "square" curve. The ideal curve that documents scientifically valid and clinically relevant effect of holistic medicine is squared, since the group, on average, is on one level before and a higher level after the treatment. The treatment intervention must be of limited duration. Endpoints are QOL, health and/or ability of functioning. The area under the square curve (grey) is the documented gain of the patients. For the square curve to appear time must be measured at T1 minus one year (sufficiently long time before the intervention), at T1 (immediately before the intervention), at T1 plus one month (immediately after the intervention), and at T1 plus one year (sufficiently long time after the intervention). If the patients are chronically ill and the situation is stabile, the measurement T1 minus one year is not necessary. Please note that if the effect is lost through time, which is when the difference between Y(T1 plus one year) and Y(T1 plus one month) is negative and larger that the insecurity of the measurement, the effect is not documented (the curve marked "not acceptable"). T0: a long time before the intervention (T1 minus one year); T1: immediately before the intervention ;T2: immediately after the intervention (one month after T1); T3: a long time after the intervention (T1 plus one year).

The ideal form of the curve, that can document significant effects from alternative and holistic medicine, is in fact a "square" (see figure 1). An even better curve is an opward slope as QOL, health and ability continues to improve after the intervention (6). The patient baseline level regarding quality of life and/or health and/or functionality is lifted, within one month after initiation of the intervention, to a new, significantly higher and stabile level of quality of life and/or health and/or functionality. Since these three factors are closely related statistically (1,7), it is expected that the patients will receive a similar increase in both quality of life, health and functionality, but an improvement in one of these three dimensions alone is acceptable for a treatment to be of value.

In figure 1 the x-axis represents time and the y-axis represents condition of quality of life/health/functionality. The leap up has to be clinically significant, and must be as well defined as possible. It must come as a consequence of our intervention so there can be no doubt that it is caused by it. Whether the intervention is made one patient at a time and summed up to the collective curve, or all patients are treated at once, has no significance for the scientific validity of the documentation. The state of QOL, health and/or Ability must have been at the baseline level for at least one year. The improvement must be found unchanged one year after the intervention. If this is the case, there is no need for a control group.

Comments to point one above

Endpoints must always correspond to the intention of the treatment. In the case of alternative and holistic medicine the intention is a general improvement of quality of life, health and functionality. It is these dimensions that are to be measured, in a way that will make comparison possible. Since we are facing a common intention, we can measure all enterprises with the same endpoints, which make the research very rational and thereby economically reasonable. This is how it must be, when hundreds of kinds of treatment, hundred different groups of patients, and hundreds of different therapists are to be submitted to evidence-based medical research.

Comments to point two above

Results can be documented quantitatively or qualitatively. Qualitative documentations, that are often based on the patient's own statements, are difficult and demand large resources to compare and are not very reliable. A patient may feel that he/she has received good help even though quality of life, health and functionality have not been improved, i.e. that a patient is aided in resignation, or that symptoms are suppressed without the existing suffering being treated. It is not possible to statistically analyse qualitative data. Therefore, to be certain of documenting an improvement, we have to demand numbers that in a simple way can show the improvement, and fulfil the demands of medical science for statistical analysis, namely a generally accepted probability of 95%. This kind of data can easily be provided by using psychometric tools; namely appropriate and validated questionnaires.

Comments to point three above

One big difficulty with alternative treatment is that one seldom, in a sensible way, can create a blinded control group. One can create a group that does not receive the treatment that is offered, but since many alternative therapies are accessible on the market in one form or another, one cannot in any way prevent those who are not included in the test group from buying a corresponding service outside the normal program. Since a substantial part of the healing on a long term basis comes as a consequence of the initiatives and programs people do on their own, one cannot exclude, if an intervention takes place over a certain period of time, that a corresponding healing in a motivated control group is caused by a corresponding treatment. Thereby the control group loses its fundamental idea and validity. One can argue that if the intervention is no better than the control group finds out and fixes themselves, then the treatment given is unnecessary, but this is not a valid statement, as people pay for these services and they are often willing to pay surprisingly much money for them – often thousands of EURO/USD. To know if they actually help people is therefore an important question.

It is difficult to document progress with alternative treatment where the intervention takes place over a long time. Many alternative systems of treatment lets patients go for years waiting for progress that maybe will never come. That is not what we want to offer our patients in modern medical science, and that is why that kind of treatment is not in correspondence with the intention of effective improvement of life quality, health and functionality. Thus it is important the the treatments given can show rapid and visual results.

The reason why we say that one month is "immediate", is that within one month it is very unlikely that something happens that changes the quality of a patient's life. On the other hand, it is sufficient time to give at least eight sessions of most therapies. If eight sessions do not create a vissible result in at least some of the patients, giving a significant rise in the measured QOL, health and ability of functioning, we must conclude that the cure is not effective.

Comments to point four above

At the moment there are economical limitations restricting the research of alternative and holistic medicine. Therefore documentation must be necessary and adequate, but not more. Since what troubles the patients are always their own experience of life quality, health and functionality, it is sufficient to examine this to document the effect we wish to give our patients by alternative and holistic medicine.

Objective examinations are desirable, but very expensive and not necessary at this stage. Psychometric tools; questionnaires concerning quality of life, health and functionality, that measure exactly what they should and that have the correct amount of questions that are necessary to prove a clinically essential improvement of the relevant dimensions are therefore the right choice for this research. This can work with a five point (Likert) - scale with a neutral centre as in the extremely short, validated QOL1 questionnaire (8):

How do you assess the quality of your life now?

1. very high
2. high
3. neither high nor low
4. low
5. very low

The difference in quality of life, health and functionality required to call a treatment clinically relevant (clinically significant) must be one-fourth of the difference between two points of the scale, and a good intervention must raise the intervention group in average at least one-half step on the scale. The rationale for this is that people with a global QOL rating below 3.5 on a five point symmetrical Likert scale (between "high" and "neither high nor low", calculated as 60%) often are unable to work while people above 4.0 ("high" calculated as 70%) often are able to work. Being able to work seems to be an important indicator of ressources and health, and we want a valid treatment to be able to bring people back to work.

If the patients are on a level of i.e. "low" at the beginning, the therapist must lift the group to a level between "low" and "neither high nor low". This will not make the patient able to work, but the improvement is thought to be of value to the individual. It is obvious that an optimal treatment would lift the group four or even six times as much, namely to the level "high" or "very high". But for a single intervention taking less that one month, we are willing to acknowledge the increase of one-half step on a five-point (Likert) - scale as fine and remarkable. An improvement of one step (20%) is acknowledged as excellent.

Comments to point five above

The desired difference of one-half a step (calculated as 10%) (9) can be statistically significantly documented (with the given one-half steps on the scale as above) with 19 patients, as shown for the question of quality of life (questionnaire with one question called QOL1) (8). If five questions are used (QOL5) (8), a difference of a one-fourth step can easily be detected with 20 patients. Therefore the number of 20 people is adequate for a statistically significant measuring of the difference, before compared to after the intervention.

Global QOL and self-assessed health (physical and mental) can be measured with the QOL1 and QOL5 questionnaires (8).

Discussion

The proposed research design is not without difficulties, as psychometrics is a complex issue, and consciousness in general poorly understood. A consciousness-based medicine is basically using changes in consciousness, well exemplified by the placebo-effect, that is such an annoyance in biomedical research. Working directly on the consciousness is infinitely more powerful that just tricking it with a pill.

The presented square curve paradigm aims to eliminate the highly esteemed control group of the traditional clinical testing. Before judging the scientific value of this paradigm, please consider the fact that the standard procedure in biomedical research using the control group is not without difficulties either. When a company select drugs that give the patients an internal sensation of receiving a drug, they boost the placebo-effect ("active placebo") and so the "blinded" test is not at all blind, since all patients should have a similar experience of getting an active drug. So the control group in a fair trial should also be "boosted" with an internal clue of receiving a drug. The placebo effect is well known to be enhanced dramatically by this internal clue, as experienced when physicians for centuries have administrated strychnine and other poisonous substances with absolutely no specific therapeutic effect to their patients. So please do not be naive about the validity of even the finest scientific designs.

The best proof for an clinically significant effect of an intervention is that our patients actually improve their health, feel better today, and that they stay this way. Is it the case when our patients with problem X gets intervention Y? This is exactly what the square curve paradigm tells us to test for in a reliable way.

A problem with the square curve paradigm is of course that it is insensitive to slow improvements made over a longer time, but this can be made visible using statistical process control methods like run-charts.

Conclusions

If the scientific community can acknowledge an effect on quality of life (QOL), health and ability of functioning to be caused by an intervention, if the patients have been in a stable state for a year, if they are raised to a better state within a month, and if they stay in this better state for another year, the effect of alternative and holistic medicine can be evaluated effectively and scientifically with very simple and affordable means. A simple, easily administered, quickly answered, validated and adequate questionnaire, containing less than 100 questions on quality of life, health and functionality can give the necessary data, of sufficient quality, for evidence based alternative and holistic medicine. Ideally the questionnaire(s) contain(s) no more than 20 core questions, supplied by the necessary background information on name, age, sex, diagnosis etc. Any therapists, who wish to be a part of the study, can easily administrate the questionnaire to his or her patients. Studies are easy to do, and can include any kind of alternative and holistic treatment, any groups of patients, recruited from hospitals, clinics, practising physicians, homes for the mentally ill, or any other organizations of treatment and care.

Thus, with this new suggested "square curve" research paradigm for consciousness-based medicine, it will be possible, with a minimum of resources, to collect the necessary evidence to answer the three fundamental questions in alternative, complementary and holistic medicine, namely:

- Who can be helped? – Which group of patients can benefit from alternative or holistic treatment? We know that an important factor in healing is the patient's own degree of competence, resources, and motivation. Must patients be subdevided into groups according to motivation, to understand the process of healing?
- What helps? – Which kinds of alternative and holistic treatment give, with certainty, a clinically relevant improvement of the patient's quality of life, health and/or functionality?
- Who can help? – Over all in the Nordic countries there is an explosive increase of alternative and holistic therapists, available forms of treatment and alternative institutes training new therapists, giving diplomas to everybody who pays the fee often more or less regardles of the obtained skills. It is therefore decisively important to find out which therapists are competent, and what one must demand from an alternative or holistic therapists` competence.

Every year thousands of new alternative and holistic therapists and several new kinds of treatment enter the market, but the population surveys show no improvement of the public health. The most likely explanation is that the methods often are not very efficient, or that the competence of the alternative therapists often is too modest to give the patients clinically relevant improvement.

When the therapist works primary with the consciousness of the patients, it is very difficult to identify faults and errors in the alternative and holistic treatments. The nessesary research in alternative and holistic medicine will show which methods (together with the associated theories) are good tools to support the patient's personal development of quality of life, health and functionality. It is of great value if the research also can document the level of competence of a therapist giving alternative and holistic treatments.

The suggested research design, where several therapists, treatment systems and patient groups are included in a time-limited study, with the improvement of quality of life, health and functionality as endpoints, is believed to be scientifically reasonable, financially sound, practical and without compromising the patients ethically or otherwise, naturally providing one upholds standard research customs, i.e. regarding confidentiality regarding collected data, written patient documentation and the like.

The square curve paradigm is also a general method for quality improvement of any treatment, which takes place in the timespan of one month or less, which is supposed to give a lasting improvement, and which has the purpose of improving QOL, health and ability of functioning.

References

[1]   Ventegodt S. *Quality of Life in Denmark: Results from a population survey.* Copenhagen: Forskningscentrets Forlag, 1995. [Danish].

[2]   Ventegodt S, Andersen NJ, Merrick J. Holistic medicine: Scientific challenges. ScientificWorldJournal 2003;3:1108-16.

[3]   Rapport from the Technology Council on alternative treatment to the Danish Parliement. Christiansborg, Copenhagen, 19 Mar 2002. [Danish].

[4]   Ventegodt S, Hilden J, Merrick J. Measurement of quality of life I: A methodological framework. ScientificWorldJournal 2003; 3:950-61.

[5]   5 .   Carey RG, Lloyd RC. Measuring quality improvement in healthcare. Milwaukee, WI: Quality Press, 2000.

[6]   Ventegodt S, Merrick J, Andersen NJ. Quality of life as medicine II. A pilot study of alcoholics. ScientificWorldJournal 2003;3:842-52.

[7]   Ventegodt S. *Quality of life of 4500 31-33 year olds. Copenhagen: Forskningscentrets Forlag,* 1996. [Danish].

[8]   Lindholt JS, Ventegodt S, Henneberg EW. Development and validation of QOL5 for clinical databases. A short global and generic questionnaire based on an integrated theory of the quality of life. Eur J Surg 2002;168:107-13.

[9]   Ventegodt S, Merrick J, Andersen NJ. Measurement of Quality of life II. From the philosophy of life to science. ScientificWorldJournal 2003;3:962-71.

Chapter 56

Quality assurance and research in treatment efficacy

Quality of life and self-rated health are important health measures. They are simple to use and highly efficient for accurate documentation of treatment effects and thus for securing the quality of a clinical practice. We have developed the 10-item QOL10 questionnaire measuring self-assessed quality of life, health and ability. We need to measure both self-rated physical health and self-rated mental health, to be certain that we know how the patients are in both these dimensions. The QOL10 combined with the Square Curve Paradigm data-collecting-procedure seem to be an extremely efficient, fast, in-expensive and valid method of documenting total treatment effect and securing high quality of a treatment facility. In this paper we demonstrate how easy data are collected and analyzed. The time consumption of administering, collecting and analyzing the QOL10 was only 10 minutes per patient. The QOL10 is free for all to use. People even without statistical training can make the statistics in a few hours. The use of QOL10 and its 10 key questions makes it possible to group the patients into treatment groups according to their health/QOL/functional problems, and follow the development of each group to see how well they are helped in the clinic. We found the following dimensions to be of primary interest in quality assurance and documentation of treatment effect: 1) Health: Self-assessed physical health, self-assessed mental health, 2) Quality of life: Self-assessed QOL (QOL1), QOL measured with a small questionnaire (i.e. QOL5) 3) Ability: Self-assessed sexual ability, self-esteem social ability and working ability.

Introduction

During the last two decades a large number of papers have documented that the most important factor and most significant endpoint in studies of effects of medical treatments is the self-rated health (1-11).

> "Self-rated health (SRH) is considered a valid measure of health status as it has been shown to predict mortality in several studies" (4)

"Self-assessed health status has been shown to be a powerful predictor of mortality, service use, and total cost of medical care treatment" (5)

"Self-rated health contributes unique information to epidemiologic studies that is not captured by standard clinical assessments or self-reported histories" (7)

"Self-evaluations of health status have been shown to predict mortality, above and beyond the contribution to prediction made by indices based on the presence of health problems, physical disability, and biological or life-style risk factors" (8)

"The results suggest that poor self rated health is a strong predictor of subsequent mortality in all subgroups studied, and that self rated health therefore may be a useful outcome measure" (11)

Self-rated health has been documented to predict survival time and future health better than any other known health parameter. This means that self-rated health has been found to be a valid and possibly the most valid health measure. To document improvement of health we need to measure self-rated health; and to measure health we need to measure self-rated health. Most unfortunately the research has worked with a single item questionnaire of self-assessed health, making it very difficult to understand what is measured by the questionnaire. We have as a part of the validated QOL5 questionnaire included two items on self-assessed physical health and self-assessed mental health (see appendix 1). We have found that these two items function extremely well in quality assurance and in documentation of treatment effect (12,13). We therefore recommend that these two measures, together with measures of self-assessed global quality of life (like the single item QOL1 (14) or QOL5 (14)) and self-assessed measures of ability are used for quality assurance and documentation of research effect. We have combined ten key questions into the QOL10-battery measuring self-assessed health, quality of life, and ability in general, and found this to be of immense value.

The use of QOL10 and its ten key questions makes it possible to group the patients into treatment groups according to their health/QOL/functional problems, and follow the development of each group to see how well they are helped in the clinic setting (12,13,15-18).

The QOL10

The idea behind QOL10 is the *sense of coherence (SOC)*, a very important dimension in life developed by Aaron Antonovsky (1923-1994). The subjective experience of sense of coherence stem from a line going from life inside us to reality outside us (19). Sense of coherence is thus closely related to the concept of meaning of life and global QOL, as we find it for example in the IQOL theory (20). You can say that sense of coherence is the experience of being an integrative part of the world. The world is your home, you have come home in the world. Psychologically the secure base that your mother was, when you were a child has become the whole world. In religious terms, you live in God, or in Sunya (the great emptiness), and no longer in Maya, the illusionary world.

QOL is determined by the global state of the person, while self-assessed health is determined by the inner state of this person. Self-assessed ability in the relevant dimensions (work, social, sex, love) is determined by the social state of the person. In our experience health, QOL and ability are improved simultaneously, when the person is healing his existence though the process of salutogenesis.

Due to our experience with the symmetric 5-point Likert scales for psychometric research (21), we selected this scale for all items. The QOL5 and QOL1 questionnaire was validated earlier (14) and we also plan to validate the QOL10 questionnaire.

Analysing the data

For research in treatment effects and quality assurance you need about 20 patients in each group for a valid test. You need according to our experiences to measure the patients before and after treatment with a one year follow-up questionnaire. If the treatment is taking place over a long period of time you need to measure before treatment, then three months later and then again a year after treatment. If you do it this way, you can measure a change in health that is highly likely to be the effect of your treatment, meaning that you can use the patients as their own control (we call this the Square Curve Paradigm) (22).

The simplest way to analyze data is by dichotomizing the scale in a "bad" and "well" part. We normally use the bottom values [4 and 5] on the Likert scale as an indication of "bad" and the top part of it [1,2 and 3] as "well". You include all starting participants in the study. Only patients who comply with the treatment and answer the questionnaire in the end of the study, and report that they are well now, are included in the "cured" group; all the dropouts, non-responders of questionnaires, and not-cured are treated as not cured. We finally used a statistical table (23) to establish the confidence interval.

The time consumption of administering, collecting and analyzing the QOL10 were only ten minutes per patient. The QOL10 is free for all to use. The statistics can be made in e few hours and by people with no statistical education. We found in our study of the treatment effects of clinical holistic medicine (CHM) (24-58) that the six following dimensions measured by the QOL10 questionnaire were of primary interest:

1. Self-assessed physical health (12)
2. Self-assessed mental health (13)
3. Self-assessed QOL (measure with QOL1) (17)
4. Self-assessed sexual ability (16)
5. Self-assessed self-esteem (relation with self) (15)
6. Self-assessed working ability (18)

1) and 2) are the self-assessed physical and mental health, and the average of this corresponds well to the single item questionnaire of self-assessed health (statistical validation of this statement is planed).

An example

Data is taken from one of our studies (13). 54 patients felt mentally ill before treatment (rating 4 or 5 on the 5-point Likert scale of self-assessed mental health of QOL5). 31 Patients did not feel mentally ill any more after treatment (rating 1, 2 or 3 on the Likert scale). Six patients still felt mentally ill after treatment (rating 4 or 5). 17 patients were non-responders upon follow-up of withdrew during the study.

We thus treated 54 patients, who rated themselves mentally ill before treatment, 31 patients did not do so after treatment. From this we calculate a curing rate of 57,4%. The table (23) gives us 95% CI: 43.21% - 70.77%). From this we estimated: $1.41 < NNT < 2.31$. We then analysed the changes in all QOL10 measures for the treatment responders using paired samples T-test, and found that all measured aspects of life improved significantly, simultaneously, and radically (see table 1): somatic health (from 2.9 to 2.3), self-esteem/relationship to self (from 3.5 to 2.3), relationship to partner (from 4.7 to 2.9 [no partner was rated as "6"]), relationship to friends (from 2.5 to 2.0), ability to love (from 3.8 to 2.4), and self-assessed sexual ability (from 3.5 to 2.4), self-assessed social ability (from 3.2 to 2.1), self-assessed working ability (from 3.3 to 2.4), and self-assessed quality of life (from 4.0 to 2.3) (see table 1). Quality of life as measured with QOL5 improved (from 3.6 to 2.3 on a scale from 1-5 ($p < 0.001$)).

Most radically the self-rated mental health improved by 1.97 steps on the Likert scale, from a bad mental health to a good mental health. This documents that the patients were not just "flipped" over the artificially defined border between the two dichotomised groups, but their mental health were actually radically improved.

All this data documents a general improvement that strongly indicates that the patient had healed existentially and experienced what Antonovsky called "salutogenesis" (59,60), defined as the process exactly the opposite of pathogenesis.

As reference value we have "2" (good) on the 5-point Likert scale, which corresponds to being well and normal (this is in accordance with what have been found empirically in large population surveys in Denmark) (61). We therefore see that the 31 mentally ill patients, that where helped with holistic therapy, actually almost normalised all their scores, signifying that they were indeed cured, not only improved.

It is very important to have a system to collect side effects and we therefore observed for brief reactive psychosis, suicide attempts, suicide, and signs of re-traumatisation (62), but did not observe these side effects in over 500 patients. The therapy was found to be safe, (estimated from this: NNH>500). We then could present the NNtH/NNtB as $500/(1.41 < NNT < 2.31)$. As we for medical-ethical reasons need to use the most pessimistic number for the calculation we find NNtH/NNtB/NNtH=500/2.31= 216.5.

We can compare this with the treatment of mentally ill schizophrenic patients with Clorpromazine (63): Number Needed to Treat: Prevents relapse, longer term data: NNT 4 CI 3 to 5. Improves symptoms and functioning NNT 6 CI 5 to 8. Number Needed to Harm: Sedation: NNH 5 CI 4 to 8.

Acute movement disorder NNH 32 CI 11 to 154. Need for antiparkinson drugs NNH 14 CI 9 to 28. Lowering of blood pressure with accompanying dizziness NNH 11 CI 7 to 21. Considerable weight gain NNH 2 CI 2 to 3. Thus we find NNtH/NNtB=2/5=0.4. If we treated schizophrenics only, our treatment would have been 543.5 times more valuable than the treatment with chlorpromazine, but we did not as our group was an undiagnosed, mixed group of patients feeling mentally very ill.

Table 1. 31 patients who changed from feeling mentally ill to mentally well (defined as "not ill"), healed all measured aspects of life due to Antonovsky salutogenesis: Somatic health, relationship to self, relationship to partner, relationship to friends, ability to love, and self-assessed sexual ability, self-assessed social ability, self-assessed working ability, and self-assessed quality of life. Paired samples T-test

	Paired Differences					t	df	Significance (2 – tailed)
	Mean	Std. Deviation	Std. Error mean	95% confidence interval of difference				
				Lower	Upper			
Physical health	.6000	.89443	.16330	.2660	.9340	3.674	29	.001
Mental health	1.9677	.79515	.79515	1.6761	2.2594	13.778	30	.000
Self esteem	1.2258	1.11683	1.11683	.8161	1.6355	6.111	30	.000
Relation to friends	.5161	.92632	.92632	.1764	.8559	3.102	30	.004
Relation to partner	1.8065	2.27185	2.27185	.9731	2.6398	4.427	30	.000
Ability to love	1.3548	1.60309	1.60309	.7668	1.9429	4.706	30	.000
Sexual ability	1.0323	1.35361	1.35361	.5358	1.5288	4.246	30	.000
Social ability	1.1613	1.12833	1.12833	.7474	1.5752	5.730	30	.000
Work ability	.9000	1.06188	1.06188	.5035	1.2965	4.642	29	.000
Quality of life	1.7097	1.03902	1.03902	1.3286	2.0908	9.162	30	.000

Conclusions

The QOL10 combined with the Square Curve Paradigm data collecting procedure seems to be an extremely efficient, fast, in-expensive and valid method of documenting treatment effect and securing quality of a treatment facility. Self-rated health seems to be the most important health measure we have. It is simple to use and eminent for documenting treatment effects and securing quality of a clinical practice.

The use of QOL10 and its 10 key questions makes it possible to group the patients into treatment groups according to their health/QOL/functional problems, and follow the development of each group to see how well they are helped in the clinic. We found the following dimensions to be of primary interest in quality assurance and documentation of treatment effect:

- Health: Self-assessed physical health, self-assessed mental health,
- QOL: Self-assessed QOL, QOL measured with a small questionnaire like QOL5
- Ability: Self-assessed sexual ability, self-assessed self-esteem (relation to self), self-assessed social ability, and self-assessed working ability.

Also important are the self-rated quality of relation to partner, self-rated quality of relation to friends, and self-assessed I-strength (ability to love). We thus recommend the QOL10 (see appendix 1) measuring the global quality of life, self-rated physical and mental health, and self-rated ability for inexpensive, fast and reliable clinical quality-assurance and for research in treatment-efficacy in biomedicine, complementary and holistic medicine.

Appendix 1. The QOL10 – a 10 item questionnaire on health, QOL and ability including the validated QOL5 and QOL1

Q 1 How do you consider your physical health at the moment?

[1] very good
[2] good
[3] neither good nor bad
[4] bad
[5] very bad

Q 2 How do you consider your mental health at the moment?

1   very good
2   good
3   neither good nor bad
4   bad
5   very bad

Q 3 How do you feel about yourself at the moment?

1   very good
2   good
3   neither good nor bad
4   bad
5   very bad

Q 4 How are your relationships with your friends at the moment?

1   very good
2   good
3   neither good nor bad

4   bad
5   very bad

Q 5 How is your relationship with your partner at the moment?

1   very good
2   good
3   neither good nor bad
4   bad
5   very bad
6   I do not have one (This is scored like "5" very bad)

Q 6 How do you consider your ability to love at the moment?

1   very good
2   good
3   neither good nor bad
4   bad
5   very bad

Q 7 How do you consider your sexual functioning at the moment?

1   very good
2   good
3   neither good nor bad
4   bad
5   very bad

Q 8 How do you consider your social functioning at the moment?

1   very good
2   good
3   neither good nor bad
4   bad
5   very bad

Q 9 How is your working ability at the moment?

1   very good
2   good
3   neither good nor bad
4   bad
5   very bad

Q 10 How would you assess your quality of your life now?

1   very high

2   high
3   neither low nor high
4   low
5   very low

The Endpoints you collect are:

QOL1: Self assessed (global) quality of life[]
QOL5: Measured global quality of life[]
QOL10: QOL+Health+Ability/3

To calculate QOL1: Q10

To calculate QOL 5: ((Q1+Q2):2+Q3 + (Q4+Q5):2):3

To calculate QOL 10 "Health-QOL-Ability":

([Health] ((Q1 + Q2):2) + [QOL] ((Q10)+(Q3+Q4+Q5):3):2)+ [ability] ((Q6+Q7+Q8+Q9):4)):3

The result is comparable to a five point Likert scale of global QOL but more informative. QOL10 is a "global life status", we like to think of this measure as a "subjective sense of coherence(SOC)" measure. We just call the measure "Health-QOL-Ability".

The normal values for Danes for QOL1, QOL5 and QOL10 are around "2" [Ventegodt, S. (1995) *Livskvalitet I Danmark. Quality of life in Denmark. Results from a population survey.* [partly in Danish] Copenhagen: Forskningscentrets Forlag.] (you will see that "2" equals "70%" in the Table if you transform the result to "percent of maximum" as described in [Ventegodt, S. (1996) Measuring the quality of life. From theory to practice. Copenhagen: Forskningscentrets Forlag.].

To keep it simple we recommend the use of this scale for comparison:

Q 10 Measured quality of your life:

1   very high
2   high
3   neither low nor high
4   low
5   very low

Interpretation: 1 is great, 2 is normal, 3 is bad for QOL1 and very bad for QOL5 and QOL10; 4 is very bad for QOL1 and deadly for QOL5 and QOL10; 5 is dying for QOL1, QOL5 and QOL10 - you cannot survive for very long with this low rating.

I would say; if your patients in average are doing worse than QOL1=3 and QOL5= 2.7.5 and QOL10 =2.5 then a significant number of your patients might have severe existential problems and significant suffering.

References

[1] Fylkesnes K, Førde OH. Determinants and dimensions involved in self-assessment of health. Soc Sci Med 1992;35(3):271-9.

[2] Jylhä M. Self-rated health revisited: Exploring survey interview episodes with elderly respondents. Soc Sci Med 1994;39(7):983-90.

[3] Jylhä M, Leskinen E, Alanen E, Leskinen A-L, Heikkinen E. Self-rated health and associated factors among men of different ages. J Gerontology 1986;41(6):710-7.

[4] Singh-Manoux A, Dugravot A, Shipley MJ, Ferrie, JE, Martikainen, P, Goldberg, M, Zins M. The association between self-rated health and mortality in different socioeconomic groups in the GAZEL cohort study. Int J Epidemiol 2007;36(6):1222-8.

[5] Long MJ, McQueen DA, Bangalore VG, Schurman JR, 2nd. Using self-assessed health to predict patient outcomes after total knee replacement. Clin Orthop Relat Res 2005;434: 189-92.

[6] Long MJ, McQueen DA, Lescoe-Long M, Schurman JR, 2nd. Capturing the full measure of patient outcome improvement using a self-assessed health adjustment. J Eval Clin Pract 2005;11(5):484-8.

[7] Idler EL, Russell LB, Davis D. Survival, functional limitations, and self-rated health in the NHANES I Epidemiologic Follow-up Study, 1992. First National Health and Nutrition Examination Survey. Am J Epidemiol 2000;152(9):874-83.

[8] Idler EL, Kasl S. Health perceptions and survival: do global evaluations of health status really predict mortality? J Gerontol 1991;46(2):S55-65.

[9] Idler EL. Age differences in self-assessments of health: Age changes, cohort differences, or survivorship? J Gerontol Soc Sci 1993;48(6):289-300.

[10] Idler EL. Self-assessed health and morality: A review of studies. Int Rev Health Psychol 1992;1:33-54.

[11] Burström B, Fredlund P. Self rated health: Is it as good a predictor of subsequent mortality among adults in lower as well as in higher social classes. J Epidemiol Community Health 2001;55(11):836-40.

[12] Ventegodt S, Thegler S, Andreasen T, Struve F, Enevoldsen L, et al. Clinical holistic medicine (mindful, short-term psychodynamic psychotherapy complemented with bodywork) in the treatment of experienced physical illness and chronic pain. ScientificWorldJournal 2007;7:310-6.

[13] Ventegodt S, Thegler S, Andreasen T, Struve F, Enevoldsen L, et al. Clinical holistic medicine (mindful, short-term psychodynamic psychotherapy complemented with bodywork) in the treatment of experienced mental illness. ScientificWorldJournal 2007;7: 306-9.

[14] Lindholt JS, Ventegodt S, Henneberg EW. Development and validation of QoL5 clinical databases. A short, global and generic questionnaire based on an integrated theory of the quality of life. Eur J Surg 2002;168:103-7.

[15] Ventegodt S, Thegler S, Andreasen T, Struve F, Enevoldsen L, et al. Self-reported low self-esteem. Intervention and follow-up in a clinical setting. ScientificWorldJournal 2007;7:299-305.

[16] Ventegodt S, Thegler S, Andreasen T, Struve F, Enevoldsen L, et al. Clinical holistic medicine (mindful, short-term psychodynamic psychotherapy complemented with bodywork) in the treatment of experienced impaired sexual functioning. ScientificWorldJournal 2007;7:324-9.

[17] Ventegodt S, Thegler S, Andreasen T, Struve F, Enevoldsen L, et al. Clinical holistic medicine (mindful, short-term psychodynamic psychotherapy complemented with bodywork) improves quality of life, health, and ability by induction of Antonovsky-salutogenesis. ScientificWorldJournal 2007;7:317-23.

[18]   Ventegodt S, Kandel I, Merrick J. Clinical Holistic Medicine in the recovery of working ability. A
       study using Antonovsky salutogenesis. Int J Disability and Human Development 2008;7(2):219-22.

[19]   Ventegodt S, Flensborg-Madsen T, Andersen NJ, Merrick J. Life Mission Theory VII: Theory of
       existential (Antonovsky) coherence. ScientificWorldJournal 2005;5:377-89.

[20]   Ventegodt S, Merrick J, Andersen NJ. Quality of life theory I. The IQOL theory: An integrative theory
       of the global quality of life concept. ScientificWorldJournal 2003;3:1030-40.

[21]   Ventegodt S. Measuring the quality of life. From theory to practice. Copenhagen: Forskningscentrets
       Forlag, 1996.

[22]   Ventegodt S, Andersen NJ, Merrick J. Holistic Medicine II: The square-curve paradigm for research in
       alternative, complementary and holistic medicine: A cost-effective, easy and scientifically valid design
       for evidence based medicine. ScientificWorldJournal 2003;3: 1117-27.

[23]   Diem K, ed. Documenta Geigy. Scientific Tables (several editions, 1962 and later). Basel: Geigy,
       1962.

[24]   Ventegodt S, Merrick J. Clinical holistic medicine: Applied consciousness-based medicine.
       ScientificWorldJournal 2004;4:96-9.

[25]   Ventegodt S, Morad M, Merrick J. Clinical holistic medicine: Classic art of healing or the therapeutic
       touch. ScientificWorldJournal 2004;4:134-47.

[26]   Ventegodt S, Morad M, Merrick J. Clinical holistic medicine: The "new medicine", the
       multiparadigmatic physician and the medical record. ScientificWorldJournal 2004;4:273-85.

[27]   Ventegodt S, Morad M, Merrick J. Clinical holistic medicine: Holistic pelvic examination and holistic
       treatment of infertility. ScientificWorldJournal 2004;4:148-58.

[28]   Ventegodt S, Morad M, Hyam E, Merrick J. Clinical holistic medicine: Use and limitations of the
       biomedical paradigm. ScientificWorldJournal 2004;4:295-306.

[29]   Ventegodt S, Morad M, Kandel I, Merrick J. Clinical holistic medicine: Social problems disguised as
       illness. ScientificWorldJournal 2004;4:286-94.

[30]   Ventegodt S, Morad M, Andersen NJ, Merrick J. Clinical holistic medicine Tools for a medical
       science based on consciousness. ScientificWorldJournal 2004;4:347-61.

[31]   Ventegodt S, Morad M, Merrick J. Clinical holistic medicine: Prevention through healthy lifestyle and
       Quality of life. Oral Health Prev Dent 2004;1:239-45.

[32]   Ventegodt S, Morad M, Hyam E, Merrick J. Clinical holistic medicine: When biomedicine is
       inadequate. ScientificWorldJournal 2004;4:333-46.

[33]   Ventegodt S, Morad M, Merrick J. Clinical holistic medicine: Holistic treatment of children.
       ScientificWorldJournal 2004;4:581-8.

[34]   Ventegodt S, Morad M, Merrick J. Clinical holistic medicine: Problems in sex and living together.
       ScientificWorldJournal 2004;4:562-70.

[35]   Ventegodt S, Morad M, Hyam E, Merrick J. Clinical holistic medicine: Holistic sexology and
       treatment of vulvodynia through existential therapy and acceptance through touch.
       ScientificWorldJournal 2004;4:571-80.

[36]   Ventegodt S, Flensborg-Madsen T, Andersen NJ, Morad M, Merrick J. Clinical holistic medicine: A
       Pilot on HIV and Quality of Life and a Suggested treatment of HIV and AIDS. ScientificWorldJournal
       2004;4:264-72.

[37]   Ventegodt S, Morad M, Merrick J. Clinical holistic medicine: Induction of spontaneous remission of
       cancer by recovery of the human character and the purpose of life (the life mission).
       ScientificWorldJournal 2004;4:362-77.

[38]   Ventegodt S, Morad M, Kandel I, Merrick J. Clinical holistic medicine: Treatment of physical health
       problems without a known cause, exemplified by hypertension and tinnitus. ScientificWorldJournal
       2004;4:716-24.

[39]   Ventegodt S, Morad M, Merrick J. Clinical holistic medicine: Developing from asthma, allergy and
       eczema. ScientificWorldJournal 2004;4:936-42.

[40] Ventegodt S, Morad M, Press J, Merrick J, Shek D. Clinical holistic medicine: Holistic adolescent medicine. ScientificWorldJournal 2004;4:551-61.

[41] Ventegodt S, Solheim E, Saunte ME, Morad M, Kandel I, Merrick J. Clinical holistic medicine: Metastatic cancer. ScientificWorldJournal 2004;4:913-35.

[42] Ventegodt S, Morad M, Kandel I, Merrick J. Clinical holistic medicine: a psychological theory of dependency to improve quality of life. ScientificWorldJournal 2004;4:638-48.

[43] Ventegodt S, Merrick J. Clinical holistic medicine: Chronic infections and autoimmune diseases. ScientificWorldJournal 2005;5:155-64.

[44] Ventegodt S, Kandel I, Neikrug S, Merrick J. Clinical holistic medicine: Holistic treatment of rape and incest traumas. ScientificWorldJournal 2005;5:288-97.

[45] Ventegodt S, Morad M, Merrick J. Clinical holistic medicine: Chronic pain in the locomotor system. ScientificWorldJournal 2005;5:165-72.

[46] Ventegodt S, Merrick J. Clinical holistic medicine: Chronic pain in internal organs. ScientificWorldJournal 2005;5:205-10.

[47] Ventegodt S, Kandel I, Neikrug S, Merrick J. Clinical holistic medicine: The existential crisis – life crisis, stress and burnout. ScientificWorldJournal 2005;5:300-12.

[48] Ventegodt S, Gringols G, Merrick J. Clinical holistic medicine: Holistic rehabilitation. ScientificWorldJournal 2005;5:280-7.

[49] Ventegodt S, Andersen NJ, Neikrug S, Kandel I, Merrick J. Clinical holistic medicine: Mental disorders in a holistic perspective. ScientificWorldJournal 2005;5:313-23.

[50] Ventegodt S, Andersen NJ, Neikrug S, Kandel I, Merrick J. Clinical Holistic Medicine: Holistic Treatment of Mental Disorders. ScientificWorldJournal 2005;5:427-45.

[51] Ventegodt S, Merrick J. Clinical holistic medicine: The patient with multiple diseases. ScientificWorldJournal 2005;5:324-39.

[52] Ventegodt S, Clausen B, Nielsen ML, Merrick J. Advanced tools for holistic medicine. ScientificWorldJournal 2006;6:2048-65.

[53] Ventegodt S, Clausen B, Merrick J. Clinical holistic medicine: The case story of Anna: I. Long term effect of child sexual abuse and incest with a treatment approach. ScientificWorldJournal 2006;6:1965-76.

[54] Ventegodt S, Clausen B, Merrick J. Clinical holistic medicine: the case story of Anna. II. Patient diary as a tool in treatment. ScientificWorldJournal 2006;6:2006-34.

[55] Ventegodt S, Morad M, Merrick J. Clinical holistic medicine: The case story of Anna. III. Rehabilitation of philosophy of life during holistic existential therapy for childhood sexual abuse. ScientificWorldJournal 2006;6:2080-91.

[56] Ventegodt S, Merrick J. Suicide from a holistic point of view. ScientificWorldJournal 2005;5:759-66.

[57] Ventegodt S, Clausen B, Omar HA, Merrick J. Clinical holistic medicine: Holistic sexology and acupressure through the vagina (Hippocratic pelvic massage). ScientificWorldJournal 2006;6:2066-79.

[58] Ventegodt S, Clausen B, Merrick J. Clinical holistic medicine: Pilot study on the effect of vaginal acupressure (Hippocratic pelvic massage). ScientificWorldJournal 2006;6:2100-16.

[59] Antonovsky A. Health, stress and coping. London: Jossey-Bass, 1985.

[60] Antonovsky A. Unravelling the mystery of health. How people manage stress and stay well. San Franscisco: Jossey-Bass, 1987.

[61] Ventegodt S. [Livskvalitet i Danmark]. Quality of life in Denmark. Results from a population survey. Copenhagen: Forskningscentrets Forlag, 1995. [Danish].

[62] Ventegodt S, Merrick J. A review of side effects and adverse events of non-drug medicine (nonpharmaceutical complementary and alternative medicine): Psychotherapy, mind-body medicine and clinical holistic medicine. J Complement Integr Med 2009;6(1):16.

[63] Adams CE, Awad G, Rathbone J, Thornley B.Chlorpromazine versus placebo for schizophrenia. Cochrane Database Syst Rev 2007;18(2):CD000284.

Chapter 57

Consensus paradigm for qualitative research in holistic medicine

In every treatment it should be important what the patient feel, experience and if there has been gained an improvement or cure to the problem the patient originally gave to you with. . If both the physician and his patient, after careful investigation before and after the treatment, find that the treatment has helped, this is most likely the case. The more precise the target group and the treatment are defined the more valuable the documentation. We recommend for securing the validity that the presented method is used with five highly comparable patients receiving five highly comparable treatments. The patient needs to express the gain as a "significant improvement". When both patient and observer find improvement of quality of life (QOL), health and functional ability significant, then we can call the treatment "good".

Introduction

What is it that people want from primary care and what are the priorities for primary care and the views of the patient on quality of care? (1). There are basically two ways of documenting an effect of a holistic medical intervention, the quantitative and the qualitative approach. Much effort has been given to developing valid methodology and measuring tools, but the art of documentation has become a complex and expensive task.

Due to lack of resources we have been forced to seek simple, but still valid ways of documenting effect (2). In this small chapter we will focus on the qualitative research method.

What do we investigate in holistic medicine?

Fortunately the holistic approach makes it much simpler, because there are always three domains to investigate: health, quality of life (QOL) and ability. These three domains can be subdivided in as many detailed domains as one wishes, but often three are sufficient for most purposes.

There are two qualitative aspects of documenting effect in medicine, often called subjective (that is from the perspective and experience of the patient) - and objective (that is from the perspective of the therapist or researcher). To document effect of an intervention using both perspectives, the patient must be interviewed before and after the intervention. Semi structured interviews with interviewer rating of the state immediately before and after the intervention can be used to give the objective perspective on the effect of the intervention. Interviewing the patient after the intervention can give the patient's subjective experience of the effect.

Most importantly these perspectives often leads to two different results, but confronting the patient with the observed improvement, after the patient has given his own experience of the effect, can be very enlightening.

The consensus paradigm states that only to the degree that there is consensus between patient and therapist/observer, the treatment has an effect. If the patient experience an effect that cannot be observed, something else is likely to have happened, i.e. an upgrade of other dimensions than the three defined as outcome. Instead of QOL, health and ability the patient has gained self-esteem, confidence, admiration from others etc. As holistic medicine aims to improve life in these three domains a pleasant experience with the therapy is not the same as en effect of a treatment.

If the patient does not experience an observed effect, this effect is most likely to be happening only in the observer's mind. Very often a therapist is convinced that a cure or intervention gave a positive result, but the fact that the patient did not experience that is then often neglected. In holistic medicine the dimensions we want to improve are highly experiential, so if the patient did not experience any improvement, such an improvement is most likely not to have happened.

Interestingly one single patient is enough to document effect with the consensus paradigm. If both the physician and his patient, after careful investigation before and after the treatment, find that the treatment has helped, this is most likely the case. The more precise the target group and the treatment are defined the more valuable the documentation. We recommend for securing the validity that the presented method is used with five highly comparable patients receiving five highly comparable treatments.

As always we recommend for the observer rating a five point symmetrical Likert scale with neutral middle point and equidistance (3). A clinically significant improvement must be half a step on this scale or more. The patient needs to express the gain as a "significant improvement". When both patient and observer find improvement of QOL, health, and ability significant (according to the above), we call the treatment "good".

References

[1]   Counter A. What do patients and the public want from primary care? BMJ 2005;331:1199-1201.
[2]   Ventegodt S, Andersen NJ, Merrick J. Holistic Medicine II: The square-curve paradigm for research in alternative, complementary and holistic medicine: A cost-effective, easy and scientifically valid design for evidence based medicine. ScientificWorldJournal 2003;3:1117-27.
[3]   Ventegodt, S. Measuring the quality of life. From theory to practice. Copenhagen: Forskningscentrets Forlag, 1996.

Section 15. Ethical aspects

Each patient carries with him his own doctor... They come to us without knowing this.
We do our best when we give the doctor within each patient a chance to do its work.
Albert Schweitzer (1875-1965)

The aim is to support, nourish and remove obstacles for nature's inherent health-
promoting and healing forces.Illness can be looked upon as a reaction to conditions we
have placed ourselves in conditions inappropriate for maintaining health and well-being.
Florence Nightingale (1820-1910)

This section contains in chapter 58 a comparison of the risk aspects of holistic medicine and biomedical psychiatry. In chapter 59 we present a theory of integrative ethics we have found useful in our practical clinical work, when we want to make ethical decisions regarding the treatment before, during and after the intervention is done.

The development of patient healthcare has brought with it new discussions about the ethical obligations of practitioners delivering holistic healthcare (1,2). Holistic, complementary and alternative medicine (CAM) treatments are being used in many western countries by up to half the population, but there has not been enough dialogue between mainstream health practitioners and CAM practitioners, about many issues of care delivery, including ethics (3,4). Ethical issues for physicians and allied health providers, who practice CAM are a related but quite distinct area, because these practitioners have been medically trained and operate in the legal and regulatory frameworks of mainstream medicine and health. Ethical issues for this group have not been well explored in the published literature.

However, we know that holistic healthcare involves a different conceptualisation of healing that through its engagement with the whole patient (mind-body-spirit) creates quite different physician-patient relationships. These in turn raise new ethical considerations to do with vulnerabilities, ethical self awareness and trust (5). We also know that new treatments, such as touch therapy, whether integrated with mainstream approaches or not, also present new ethical considerations (6).

Such ethical issues have been of interest to the International Society of Holistic Health (ISHH) and addressed in a recent paper (1). This paper, developed by a collaboration between holistic practitioners and researchers, offers information, content and implications of the ISHH guidelines. It aims to be useful to those wanting to reflect further on ethical practices in holistic healthcare. In a context where health practice is about integrative multidisciplinary approaches and inter-professional teams (7) with medical, nursing and allied health professionals increasingly engage with notions of ethical virtues (8), such matters are of interest to both healthcare practitioners and educators in general. Ethics for health professionals has increasingly been conceptualised as being about an integrated set of knowledge, skills and attributes such that the literature speaks of ethics as being about personhood and the evolution of the whole practitioner (9).

Definitions and importance of ethics

Ethics are reflections and guidelines on how to act, while morals describe how we act. Ethics can be based on duty, on rights, on virtues, on consequence, on usefulness or on relations (10). The fundamental premise for all ethics is that every human being is equally valuable and demands the same respect and consideration. The main role of ethical guidelines is to protect those, who cannot fully defend themselves and who cannot voice their demands or stand up for their rights.

Ethical principles and guidelines are important, because they help encourage reflections on how to act. Unless human behaviour is audited against well-theorised and developed ethical statements, it is difficult for practice to be consistently ethical. Holistic healthcare practice involves a proactive approach to multidisciplinary treatments, often involving diverse teams of professionals. This can create new pressures and ethical decision-making situations for practitioners. Accordingly, the 'whole-of-patient' focus of holistic practice requires careful development of authentic and useful guidelines for practices that are not narrowly bio-medical.

Vision and aims

The International Society of Holistic Health (ISHH) is comprised of physicians, allied health professionals, and researchers, who have a commitment to developing high quality, whole-of-patient, integrative healthcare. The association has members across the world, in the Middle East, Europe, America, Asia, Australia and elsewhere. This international group have been interested in and published on contemporary developments in healthcare that reflect our emphasis on multidisciplinary, holistic, innovative—and above all effective and ethical—care for patients. It undertakes collaborative international research on healthcare practices that integrate bio-psycho-social and other medical approaches to achieve quality, patient-centred care. ISHH also organize conferences that are an international meeting place of all those interested in advancing practices in holistic healthcare. The aims of the ISHH are:

- To promote holistic health awareness among health care providers, organizations and the general public
- To foster and stimulate the highest quality of health care provision in all communities.

Holistic health care is defined as the art and science of healing the whole person—body, mind and spirit, by prevention and treatment—to promote optimal health. The ISHH believes that health is a holistic concept, because it is impossible to be healthy without taking into account the physical, mental, social, environmental, and spiritual aspects of life. The fields of knowledge and experience that can inform this area are therefore vast. Accordingly, the ethical decision-making situations that can arise in holistic practice are many and varied. Yet we believe they can be guided by simple universal principles that can be agreed-upon by those in many cultures and countries.

The ethical principles and guidelines endorsed by ISHH aim to help us fulfil another aspect of our vision: to build bridges between the various factions of medicine and healthcare providers that shares a goal in creating high quality holistic healthcare services. This emphasis upon building bridges across different areas of practice, services, cultures, and countries is why our emphasis is on simplicity and clarity of ethical statements.

Key ethical principles for holistic practice

Two key principles underline high quality holistic healthcare practices:

1. Do to others as you want to be done by them
2. Ask if it would be okay if everybody acted the way you plan to act.

The first principle is common to many world religions. It requires the practitioner to imagine being the patient and to ask yourself if the behaviour would be desirable if you were on its receiving end. The second principle comes from Kant's writings. Kant suggests that the basis for immorality is to make an exemption for oneself (11). This principle invites you as practitioner to ask yourself if your behaviour would be good for society if it were universally adopted.

Aims of holistic practice

The aims of holistic practice are fourfold:

1. Heal, help and comfort the patient
2. Support and strengthen the internal healing forces of each person
3. Treat the person as a whole (bio-psycho-social-spiritual being)
4. Focus on prevention when possible.

The first aim positions the health practitioner as a holistic helper of those experiencing illness and related hardships. The second aim focuses the attention of holistic healthcare on developing the capacities of healing of the patient, rather than acting upon the patient. The third aim emphasises the importance of whole-of-patient care and the interrelatedness of the different dimensions of being in any consideration of how best to meet the patient's needs.

The fourth aim emphasises the value of prevention, positioning holistic healthcare as being about proactive approaches to health: education for health, healthy behaviours, and so on.

Together these aims suggest quite different relationships between the patient and practitioner than are suggested by either traditional bio-medical models or more modern corporate models of healthcare. In the holistic model the practitioner focuses on empowering the patient and delivers services that cannot be so easily commoditised—it is difficult to see how empathy as a basis for giving comfort, or an engagement with the spiritual dimensions of the patient as part of whole-of-patient approaches, could ever be authentically priced on the healthcare marketplace.

If the holistic practitioner takes on different roles and responsibilities from those found in bio-medical traditions of care, or new corporate models of care, it follows that there will be ethical considerations in holistic care that are related, but not exactly the same, as those found in these two other models of healthcare. In developing ethical practices the holistic practitioner will want to be aware that holistic practice may involve applying universal ethical principles to new practice contexts. Recognising how a universal ethical principle—such as that treatment be evidence-based—is relevant to new practice contexts is an important part of developing deeper ethical awareness. This is a truism of learning generally: a generic knowledge or skill can only be internalised and reproduced in daily practice when it has been applied to enough diverse contexts to make it deeply understood.

The ethical guidelines of ishh

1. The values and laws on which the practitioner should build holistic practices are:

    a.   compassion
    b.   mutual trust
    c.   respect for the patient's integrity
    d.   human rights
    e.   truth and justice to the patient and society
    f.   national laws
    g.   informed consent
    h.   confidentiality.

2. In delivering healthcare, the practitioner should:

    a.   give information regarding the purpose, content, duration, cost of treatment and complaint rules
    b.   build the practice on evidence
    c.   use methods that are validated
    d.   use methods one can master
    e.   use methods that do not harm
    f.   place concern for the patient as paramount when trying out methods
    g.   keep records (10 years) that patients can read

h. conduct research, develop and test new methods of diagnosis and treatment to high standards of quality research practice

i. monitor and evaluate results

j. develop and improve one's practice

k. use one's resources fairly

l. where possible, develop the tool (oneself).

3. The practitioner's relationship to colleagues should:

a. be respectful

b. involve raising misconduct by other practitioners directly with them in a caring way; secondly with authorities

c. not express criticism of colleagues in front of patients

d. be transparent, sharing, and open, assuming informed consent in patient matters

e. not involve inappropriate interference in, or prevention of, treatment given by others.

5. In relations with patients, the practitioner must not:

a. disrespect the patient's right to choose (treatment, life or death)

b. assist actively in ending life

c. exploit or manipulate the patient economically, philosophically, religiously,

d. sexually or in any other way (the consent of the patient does not free the practitioner from this duty)

e. engage in a sexual relationship with the patient

f. promise to cure the patient, or hinder the patient receiving help from others.

The first part of the guidelines focuses on broad values and laws that should govern holistic practice. The emphasis upon compassion suggests the way in which holistic care involves practitioner empathy for the patient, which is critical to an engagement with the whole patient. The second part of the guidelines emphasises that holistic practice is accountable, evidence based, and rigorously developed. The third part of the guidelines emphasises high standards in collegial interactions in ways that serve the interests of rigorous and accountable healthcare services. The last and fourth part of the guidelines emphasise what the practitioner should not do in interactions with patients, consistent with other parts of the guidelines.

Considered as a whole, these guidelines suggest that if holistic practice involves the integration of mainstream approaches and CAM to deliver whole-of-patient healthcare, such healthcare is not exempt from the high standards of rigour, accountability, transparency, and duty of care expected of practitioners everywhere.

For example, when tailoring treatments from different disciplines to meet complex healthcare needs, the practitioner must be able to point at the evidence that informs decision-making about the appropriate treatments.

Ethics and quality of care

Ethical healthcare practices and quality healthcare practices are related but different aspects of healthcare delivery. The personal ethics of the practitioner set the pre-conditions for quality healthcare at the micro-level of provider and patient; the quality of the care systems sets the macro pre-conditions for provider-patient interactions. Provider practices that are ethical are also practices that aim for high quality. Holistic healthcare should aim to deliver services with the same quality aims as those set by the World Health Organisation (WHO), which have also been adopted by many countries in the world (12).

Conclusions

In contrast to some representations of alternative therapeutic approaches as not involving, for example, a reliance on evidence-based approaches (13), the foregoing suggests that many of the principles and guidelines that apply to mainstream medicine apply to holistic healthcare. Expectations of quality and safety also apply.

ISHH does not give a simple 'yes' or 'no' answer to the question of whether ethical frameworks that apply to narrow bio-medical healthcare approaches apply to holistic healthcare. The health ethics literature suggests that one error to avoid in developing ethical statements is the assumption that frameworks developed for one health context can be simply applied to another (14). ISHH take the view that holistic healthcare involves many common ethical principles and guidelines that can find new challenges of application in the multidisciplinary contexts of whole-of-patient care.

Of course, most people from vastly different contexts of care can agree upon a set of common principles and guidelines if they are broad enough. The real challenges of obtaining real, in-practice agreement on ethics comes when practitioners need to make sound decisions about a familiar principle in an unfamiliar context. The meaning of ethics in holistic practice requires an effort of understanding precisely because holistic care opens up new contexts for the application of familiar ethical principles and guidelines. Thus, the restatement of familiar ethical principles and guidelines in ways that are nuanced to the contexts of holistic healthcare is important to developing understandings of how the former applies to the new contexts. This is the task that ISHH is engaged in as it develops these working principles and guidelines. ISHH challenges healthcare educators to design undergraduate and continuing professional development courses that provide learners with opportunities to understand how familiar ethics principles and guidelines apply across diverse healthcare contexts.

References

[1] de Vibe M, Bell E, Merrick J, Omar HA, Ventegodt S. Ethics and holistic healthcare practice. Int J Child Health Human Dev 2008;1(1):23-8.
[2] Slater L. Person-centredness: a concept analysis. Contemp Nurs 2006;23(1):135-44.
[3] Robotin MC, Penman AG. Integrating complementary therapies into mainstream cancer care: which way forward? Med J Aust 2006;185(7):377-9.

[4]   Ernst E, Cohen MH, Stone J. Ethical problems arising in evidence based complementary and alternative medicine. J Med Ethics 2004;30(2):156-9.

[5]   Geller G. A "holistic" model of the healing relationship: what would that require of physicians? Am J Bioethics 2006;6(2):82-5.

[6]   Wardell DW, Engebretson J. Ethical principles applied to complementary healing. J Holistic Nurs 2001;19(4):318-34.

[7]   Artnak KE. A comparison of principle-based and case-based approaches to ethical analysis. HEC Forum 1995;7(6):339-52.

[8]   Sprengel A, Kelley J. The ethics of caring: a basis for holistic care. J Holistic Nurs 1992;10(3):231-9.

[9]   Keegan L, Keegan GT. A concept of holistic ethics for the health professional. J Holistic Nurs 1992;10(3):205-17.

[10]   Buber M. Ich und du [I and thou]. New York: Touchstone, 1966.

[11]   Syse H. Veier til et godt liv Filosofiske tanker om hverdagslivets etikk. [Ways to a good life] Oslo: Aschehoug, 2006. [Norwegian].

[12]   Norwegian National Strategy for Quality Improvement of Health and Social Services 2005 - 2015. http://www.ogbedreskaldetbli.no/237/IS-1162_E_5484a.pdf.

[13]   Kottow MH. Classical medicine versus alternative medical practices. J Med Ethics 1992;18(1):18-22.

[14]   McCarthy J. A pluralist view of nursing ethics. Nurs Philosophy 2006;7(3):157-64.

Chapter 58

First do no harm. Risk aspects and side effects of clinical holistic medicine

Clinical holistic medicine (CHM) is short-term psychodynamic pshychotherapy (STPP) complemented with bodywork and philosophical exercises, to be more efficient in treating patients with severe mental and physical illness. STPP has already been found superior to psychiatric treatment as usual (TAU) and thus able to compete with psychiatric standard treatment as the treatment of choice for all non-organic mental illnesses; we have found the addition of bodywork and philosophy of life to STPP to accellerate the process of existential healing and recovery (salutogenesis). In this paper we compare the side effects, suicidal risk, problems from implanted memory and implanted philosophy of CHM with psychopharmacological treatment. Method: Qualitative and quantitative comparative review. Results: In all aspects of risks, harmfulness, and side effects, we have been considering, CHM was superior to the standard psychiatric treatment. The old principle of "first do no harm" is well respected by CHM, but not always by standard psychiatry. CHM seems to be able to heal the patient, while psychopharmacological drugs can turn the patient into a chronic, mentally ill patient for life. Based on the available data CHM seems another alternative to patients with mental illness. There seem to be no documentation at all for CHM being dangerous, harmful, having side effects of putting patients at risk for suicide. As CHM uses spontaneous regression there is no danger for the patient developing psychosis as, according to some experts, has been seen with earlier intensive psychodynamic methods. Conclusion: CHM is an efficient, safe and affordable cure for a broad range of mental illnesses.

Introduction

Integrated science and integrative medicine has become increasingly popular, both with scientists and with patients. The research in issues like scientific holistic medicine and quality of life has exploded the last decades, as a search on www.pubmed.gov will show. Out of the boiling pot of contemporary, integrative, medical science has several, quite different, new treatment systems crystallized. One of the most interesting new systems is clinical holistic medicine (CHM) (1-40) developed in an international network of medical and psychological researchers and tested at the Research Clinic for Holistic Medicine at the Quality of Life Research Center (NGO) in Denmark. CHM aims to integrate epidemiological research on quality of life and health (41), Hippocratic character Medicine (42-44), psychosocial medicine focusing on Antonovsky and sense of coherence (45,46), psychoanalysis and psychodynamic therapy (primarily short-term psychodynamic psychotherapy, STPP) (47,48,49), and finally transcultural medicine and CAM, both in theory, methodology and clinical practice (primarily bodywork addressing the patients unconsciousness and emotional layers, like the Marion Rosen Method)(50).

The most resent development has been an attempt to treat mentally ill patients with CHM, often psychiatric patients not responding to biomedicine and quite surprisingly it seems that this system is able to help most of the patients, without the suicidal risk and the other severe side effects of the traditional psychiatric biomedical treatment (35,39). Unfortunately the documentation is still based on a limited number of mentally ill patients. Because of its offspring in quality of life research it is focusing on the subjective experience of being mentally ill, not on objective symptoms and diagnoses of specific psychiatric disorders. Most fortunately CHM is build on the strong traditions of clinical practice and research of psychodynamic psychotherapy (STPP) that is known to be almost completely free of side effects/adverse-effects as documented by a a search on Medline (www.pubmed.gov). The search for "psychodynamic psychotherapy AND adverse effects" gave only 16 hits with none of them reporting adverse effects and some reporting no adverse-affects. A similar search for "psychodynamic psychotherapy AND side effects" gave 19 hits none reporting side effecs and some reporting no side effects. A similar search for "drugs AND side effects" gave 138,726 hits, and "drugs AND adverse-effects" gave 128,059 hits, a large fraction of these with postive findings. Side effects and adverse-effects are obviously a problem connected to the use of drugs, and not to psychodynamic psychotherapy.

As the experience of being mentally ill is what basically torments the patients the most, the subjective improvement of this aspect might very well be the most important dimension of any psychiatric quality assessment and treatment-effect evaluation. More research should definitely be done to also document the objective aspects of the process of healing the mentally ill with CHM.

This chapter is going to examine the most important differences between CHM and standard psychiatry regarding the risk aspects and side effects of the treatment.

Standard psychiatry

In biomedical psychiatry the theory is that mental illness is product of disturbed or dysregulated brain chemistry. The cure is therefore drugs that regulate the brain activity in different neurotransmitter pathways. The reality is complex with many antipsychotic and antidepressive drugs acting on many different transmitter systems. Effective drugs are available for stimulating depressed patients, tranquilizing anxiety patients, and down regulating overactive, psychotic patients.

Unfortunately these drugs all have quite severe side effects, with a number needed to treat to harm (NNTH) around two and a number needed to treat to cure (NNTC) around four.

Major side effects are excessive overweight, sedation, involuntary movements (dyskinesia), Parkinson's disease, suicide, and sudden, unexpected death.

The drugs are in most cases not curative. When the patients stop taking the psychopharmacological drugs the original disease and the disturbed mental state of the patients is seldom bettered but quite often worsened. These facts make the standard psychiatric treatment a less than perfect treatment.

As many of the drugs are affordable and easy to use for the patient, in contrast to most relevant psychotherapy, and as mental illness are very common, these drugs have become extremely popular in most western countries. The strategy of treating symptoms with drugs and not curing the patients is creating a huge number of chronically ill patients, and the society at large is thus paying a huge prize in so many of its citizens not being able to function and work properly, and most mentally ill patients continue to suffering though their life, just at a diminished scale.

Clinical holistic medicine

In scientific holistic medicine the theory is that mental illness is a product of disturbed or dysregulated consciousness, causing disturbed brain neurophysiology, which again gives the behavior we observe as mental illness. The subjective experience of a dysfunctional or disturbed consciousness is the feeling of being mentally ill.

The disturbance is due to compromised psychosocial and psychosexual development because of traumatic events and adaptation to a less-than-perfect childhood environment. These events has lead to negative learning about the world, "destructive decisions" in the language of CHM, an only by de-learning this, the normal mental functionality can be restored.

The de-learning is happening though a process of healing that is facilitated by the combination of giving resources to the patient, and taking the patient back to the old wounds. The purpose of the treatment is to cure somatoform and psychoform dissociation (51,52), to enable the patient to once again be in full contact with the surrounding world though mind and body. This is also called the rehabilitation of the "sense of coherence"(53-57), or existential healing (58). The sign of the healing taking place is first that the patient re-enters a number of historic life-crises with destructive learning, and then the sudden and dramatic improvement of self-assessed mental health, followed by rehabilitation of the patient's ability of functioning.

In the end the cure the patient knows himself and his major talents, and assumes responsibility to be an integrated and valuable part of the world. Thus CHM is curative, and helps the patient to get back to a normal function in society. The use of CHM takes a certain understanding of life and a certain level of willingness to suffer the old pains once again, and it can take years before a substantial betterment has occurred. About half of the mentally ill patients have been helped in one year and with 20 sessions of CHM, making CHM affordable for most patients[39]. The curative aspect means that all expenses to medicine come in the first years of treatment.

Negative and positive effects

Physical – the body

Standard psychiatric pharmacological treatment: The psychopharmacological drugs are known to be very hard to the body, with overweight, sedation, and involuntary movements and the most common, but hundreds of quite severe side effects are known, and sudden, unexpected death is happening 150% as often for patients using antipsychotic drugs (59).

CHM treatment: As this system avoid the use of drugs, all the negative side effects of the drugs are not present in this system. The treatment is taking the patient back to old life crises, which is often very unpleasant, but as this is a part of treatment, and only lasting for hours or a few days, this is not considered a side effect. The most advanced tools of CHM like intensive bodywork on a floor with many holdings, taking the patient into re-experiencing birth (re-birth exercises)(60) has been seen to give the patients bruises and scratches but nothing that could not heal within a week. CHM has thus no known physical side effects.

Physical – future health

Standard psychiatric pharmacological treatment: The future health of most mentally ill patients is pour, with a substantial loss of number of life years. The physical side effects tend to accumulate though the years, increasing the probability for the drugs being harmful.

CHM: As the treatment addresses existence as a whole, subjective physical health is normally also improved, when subjective mental health is improved. CHM is effective as preventive medicine, and both physical, mental, sexual, and existential health problems seem to be prevented.

Mental – the mind

Standard psychiatric pharmacological treatment: The psychopharmacological treatment with psychopharmacological drugs are known to be very hard to the state of mind, with loss of motivation, interest, libido, sedation, lack of self-confidence and self-esteem, and suicidal thoughts and attempts (61). Advanced studying is often not possible on these drugs (62), as they are known to give a restriction of the patient's learning capacity, which also may represent an obstacle to the application of other treatment modalities, e.g. behaviour modification, or to the patient's social re-adaptation. Thus the patients and the experiential life is often dramatically reduced (62). The consequence of this is that the development of insight in self, others, and society often is arrested, and the patient remains though life at an infantile level of mental development.

CHM: As this treatment is accelerated personal development, it develop self-insight and responsibility for own life, and increases dramatically the experiential life and the reflections upon the experiences. The use of talents is often dramatically improved, and training the patient in being of value to the surrounding world is a standard part of CHM treatment. The ability to go though advances studies, like university studies, are often dramatically increased.

As CHM uses spontaneous regression, where the patient returns to the trauma in surplus of resources, the therapeutic process cannot get stuck, and there is therefore no danger for the patient developing psychosis, as has been seen with earlier, intensive psychodynamic regression methods.

Mental – the mental future of the patient

Standard psychiatric pharmacological treatment: The most important negative statistically documented consequence of using psychopharmacological drugs is chronicity – becoming a chronic patient. The reason for this is arresting personal development and the drugs directly and indirectly hindering existential healing and recovery.

Another serous problem is the psychopharmachological drugs psychodynamic interference with psychotherapy, e.g. by diminishing the patient's motivation to pursue this type of treatment or by disturbing the structure of his defences[62].

An important problem arising from the implanted philosphy of psychiatric treatment is what could be called "the trap problem": If a patient chooses to enter psychiatric treatment, and gets the diagnosis of schizophrenia, and is having the antipsychotic drug treatment, the philosophical impact of this treatment is often so dramatic that the patient is trapped in his own understanding of himself as a chronic mentally ill patient with no future socially or work-wise, and in this resignation all motivation for helping himself to healing and recovery is lost. The trap-problem is mirrored in the finding that there exist almost no successful studies of hospitalized patients being cured by psychodynamic psychotherapy (63), while there are many such reports independently of the psychiatric treatment institution (64). Because of the faith-determining step of psychiatric hospitalization the conclusion that schizophrenia cannot be cured with psychodynamic psychotherapy is not likely to be correct, and we have seen schizophrene patients seemingly being cured with CHM.

CHM: With the development of sense of coherence and increased responsibility and self-insight, the mental future for the CHM patients healing successfully in therapy is bright. They will most often be an integrated an active part of society though their life, and they will fight for what they believe, because of the level of self-consciousness and self-esteem they develop in the therapy.

Sexual

Standard psychiatric pharmacological treatment: The drugs are known to be very hard on the libido as well as on the general motivation (62) and mood (65). Lack of desire and sexual interest is normal with the mentally ill treated with antipsychotic and antidepressant drugs. In the male, a common problem seems to be diminished potency; as this has not been thoroughly investigated more research is needed on the side effects on sexuality.

CHM: rehabilitation of sexuality of a standard element of the CHM treatment, as psychosexual health is seen as closely connected to mental health. Therefore the sexual life of CHM patients is most often radically improved (36,37,39).

Behavioral

Standard psychiatric pharmacological treatment: The behavior of the patients is often quite bizarre, with many involuntary movements, and a most peculiar movement pattern easy to detect for a normal person, which often leads to severer marginalisation of the mentally ill patients on psychopharmacological drugs. As years goes by, the arrested psychosocial and psychosexual development from the reduced experiential life, will also lead to a behavior that is very characteristic and often seen as infantile. The sedation, overweight and other side effects often also impacts the behavior negatively, giving the patient on psychopharmacological drugs a severe disadvantage compared to the normal population.

   CHM: The accelerated personal development and increased self-insight from cultivated reflection is often making the behavior of the patient more elegant and attractive. In general the CHM patients are doing very well socially, work wise, sexually etc (35-39). The negative side effects seen with drugs are not present here.

Financial

Standard psychiatric pharmacological treatment: As most mentally ill patients using psychopharmacological drugs are not able to compete with normal individuals, their ability to get and function in a job is often compromised. This leads to a severely reduced personal income; often the patients will end up with a social pension.

   CHM: As the mentally ill patients not only is cured but also taking into accelerated personal development, witch often will continue after therapy, the ability to work will often increase radically, giving the patient not only a normal ability to work, but often allowing the cured patient to study at university and rehabilitate the use of core talents, to the benefit of themselves and their surrounding world.

   The cost of treating a patient with STPP or CHM is between 1-4,000 Euros; the standard psychiatric treatment that reduces the patients to chronic mentally ill patients for life with frequent hospitalization is often over 1 mill. Euros (64).

Social

Standard psychiatric pharmacological treatment: All the above-mentioned aspects sums up to a severe social handicap for mentally ill patents using the psychopharmacological drugs.

   CHM: All the above mentioned aspects sums up to a severe social empowerment for the mentally ill patients choosing accelerated personal development as way out of the mental illness.

Quality of life

Standard psychiatric pharmacological treatment: In Denmark this is the standard treatment for mental illness, and the mentally ill is known to have a very low QOL in Denmark. We found found the happiness of these patients to be 21.4% under average, and the IQOL to be 21.8% under. The use of drugs to the central nervous system is also directly associated with a very poor QOL; the happiness for the patients using this was 19.7% below average of the Danish population (62,63).

CHM: CHM is known to improve QOL, as it was originally designed exactly to do this. Ventegodt et all. found a very strong association between self-asses mental health and QOL in nine different dimensions, signifying the importance for QOL of improving subjective mental health (63).

Spiritual

Standard psychiatric pharmacological treatment: The spiritual well-being is in science most often connected with the experience to be an integrated and happy part of the world; the concept of "sense of coherence" developed by Antonovsky and further by Lindström et al (64), Flensborg-Madsen et al (52-57),and Ventegodt et al (44), is strongly connected to subjective mental health, and quality of life. As neither global quality of life nor subjective mental health seems to be normalized with psychopharmacological drugs in general, we must assume that SOC is not reestablished either by this treatment.

CHM: Improvement of SOC is the core ambition in CHM; this happens in the process of existential healing described in (58). The common patent's experience of this treatment is that spiritual well-being is radically improved; the meaning of life is appearing, the libido and reason to be is enhanced, and the being in general is consolidated. CHM makes the patient a happy and uncomplicated part of the world. .

Implanted philosophy, implanted memory, and suicide

Standard psychiatric pharmacological treatment: In this system the patients is thought the psychiatrists belief about their mental illness. Most often they learn that their disease is inborn, presumably a consequence of some dysfunctional or mutated genes (DNA) causing disturbances in the brains chemistry, and therefore giving the patient her symptoms; The patient will learn that the illness is incurable but that the drugs are likely to alleviate many of the symptoms of the disease. The side effects of the drugs are a reasonable prize, and most be tolerated.

This learned view of self as chronically ill is often putting the patient into deep existential trouble: why am I here, if I am no good? What is the meaning of my life, if I am to be a burden to the world for life? Why am I so unlucky that I got the bad genes so I cannot improve? The understanding that the patient is chronically ill and must lean all his hope for cure and comfort onto the doctor, is severely disempowering him, and often leading to severely diminished self-esteem and self-confidence. The suicidal thoughts are a logical consequence of this implanted philosophy. When the patient re-interpret his whole personal history, he will be more likely to blame the "genes" for all the things that went wrong for him, putting his own responsibility aside, hindering him learning from his past. This is "implanting memories", in the most general and destructive meaning of the concept.

The tremendous raise of suicidal attempts and suicides after the patients enter the standard psychiatric treatment is showing that the problems of psychological side effects of the psychopharmachological drugs and of implanted philosophy by the treatment has not been solved by the psychiatrists[61]. It has been suggested that the many suicides and suicide attempts is a direct consequence of the well-known dysphoria often induced by the psychopharmacological drugs (65).

CHM: The CHM treatment is often extremely intense emotionally, and it is implanting the CHM philosophy of personal development of life, existence and consciousness, into the patient: "Everything that happens is in the end your responsibility, as you are free to perceive the world as you please. The gab you see is your responsibility, so please go and make your life good as your want it. Every defeat and failure is an occasion to take learning, and the fundamental reason to be here is to be so intimately connected to the world that you can use your talents to create value for your self, your loved ones, and your surrounding world".

Very often symbolic traumas of sexual nature is encountered in CHM therapy, rehabilitation also the libido of the patient, and quite often these traumas are taken for real in a phase of the therapy, but in the end they will be correctly perceived as the CHM therapy is ingeniously designed to help the patient to de-learn the implanted philosophy an to conquer true independence of other people, also the therapist himself, in the end of the therapy. Therefore the CHM is not implanting philosophy of memory in the patient, unless the CHM treatment for some reason is disrupted, which is most unfortunate; no severe harm to the patient has seemingly be done to any patient, even in this case. Suicide or suicide attempts provoked by CHM has not been observed in spite of many hundred patients now treated with this new method.

Ethics – to heal the patient, alleviate human suffering, and do no harm

Standard psychiatric pharmacological treatment: what has been characterizing psychiatry through the last century is extensive use of force. The problem is that use of force almost always is harmful an giving trauma. And in a way a sedating drug is also a forceful intervention in itself. The behavior of the psychiatric patient has often been severely impacted by the collection of trauma from the forceful psychiatric treatment itself. The classical "madman" almost exploding with rage just from a minute provocation is the typical consequences of massive use of force in psychiatry. The sad fact that QOL and subjective mental health is not alleviated in most cases by the use of psychopharmacological drugs, while the negative side effect and negative consequences of implanted memories are massive, like suicide and suicide attempt, is making the standard psychiatric treatment a less than optimal treatment. The fine Hippocratic principle of "First do no harm"[42] seems therefore not well respected by standard psychiatry.

A more complicated, ethical aspect of psychiatric standard treatment is the objectification and alienation of the patient that is a consequence of the objective analysis made of the patient in this system.

Another problem is the reduction of the physicians' therapeutic efficacy if he relies exclusively on psychotropic agents (62).

CHM: "First do no harm" is a principle well respected by CHM. The use of force is normally very moderate or absent. The patient is seen and met as a living, autonomous, responsible, and consciousness subject. The existential healing is improving all aspects of patient's life, and is giving the patient a huge empowerment, by accelerating his personal development and self-insight. The patient is likely to be cured and thereafter lead a life of high quality, being happy and of value to himself, his family and friends, working place, and surrounding world at large. As conscious being he is likely to take good care of his world, from his son and loved one to the global ecosystem.

Conclusions

In all aspects of risks, harmfulness, and side effects, we have been considering, CHM is superior to the standard psychiatric treatment. The old principle of "first do no harm" is well respected by CHM and seems to be able to heal the patient, while psychopharmacological drugs can turn the patient into a chronic, mentally ill patient for life. Based on the available data CHM seems to be an alternative choice regarding patients with mental illness. There seem to be no documentation at all for CHM being dangerous, harmful, having side effects of putting patients at risk for suicide. As CHM use spontaneous regression there is no danger for the patient developing psychosis as, according to some expert's opinions, in single cases has been provoked by earlier intensive psychodynamic methods; we find it more likely that these episodes were what we today call "developmental crisis" [32] and not real psychotic episodes. As the documentation still only includes a very limited number of patients treated with CHM, more research is needed to allow for stronger conclusions related to the specific psychiatric diseases, especially schizophrenia where the treatment with drugs like Chlorpromazine has shown itself to be particularly problematic (69).

Clinical holistic medicine (CHM) is based on short-term psychodynamic psychotherapy (STPP) that has a well-documented effect on the specific psychiatric disorders (47-49); CHM seems to intensify and accelerate therapy so we have no reason to believe that CHM is less effective than STPP. CHM is an efficient, safe and affordable cure for a broad range of mental illnesses.

References

[1]   Ventegodt S, Merrick J. Clinical holistic medicine: Applied consciousness-based medicine. ScientificWorldJournal 2004;4:96-9.
[2]   Ventegodt S, Morad M, Merrick J. Clinical holistic medicine: Classic art of healing or the therapeutic touch. ScientificWorldJournal 2004;4:134-47.
[3]   Ventegodt S, Morad M, Merrick J. Clinical holistic medicine: The "new medicine", the multi-paradigmatic physician and the medical record. ScientificWorldJournal 2004;4:273-85.
[4]   Ventegodt S, Morad M, Merrick J. Clinical holistic medicine: Holistic pelvic examination and holistic treatment of infertility. ScientificWorldJournal 2004;4;148-58.
[5]   Ventegodt S, Morad M, Hyam E, Merrick J. Clinical holistic medicine: Use and limitations of the biomedical paradigm ScientificWorldJournal 2004;4:295-306.
[6]   Ventegodt S, Morad M, Kandel I, Merrick J. Clinical holistic medicine: Social problems disguised as illness. ScientificWorldJournal 2004;4:286-94.
[7]   Ventegodt S, Morad M, Andersen NJ, Merrick J. Clinical holistic medicine Tools for a medical science based on consciousness. ScientificWorldJournal 2004;4:347-61.
[8]   Ventegodt S, Morad M, Merrick J. Clinical holistic medicine: Prevention through healthy lifestyle and quality of life. Oral Health Prev Dent 2004;1:239-45.
[9]   Ventegodt S, Morad M, Hyam E, Merrick J. Clinical holistic medicine: When biomedicine is inadequate. ScientificWorldJournal 2004;4:333-46.

[1]   Ventegodt S, Morad M, Merrick J. Clinical holistic medicine: Holistic treatment of children. ScientificWorldJournal 2004;4:581-8.

[2]   Ventegodt S, Morad M, Merrick J. Clinical holistic medicine: Problems in sex and living together. ScientificWorldJournal 2004;4:562-70.

[3]   Ventegodt S, Morad M, Hyam E, Merrick J. Clinical holistic medicine: Holistic sexology and treatment of vulvodynia through existential therapy and acceptance through touch. ScientificWorldJournal 2004;4:571-80.

[4]   Ventegodt S, Flensborg-Madsen T, Andersen NJ, Morad M, Merrick J. Clinical holistic medicine: A pilot on HIV and quality of life and a suggested treatment of HIV and AIDS. ScientificWorldJournal 2004;4: 264-72.

[5]   Ventegodt S, Morad M, Merrick J. Clinical holistic medicine: Induction of spontaneous remission of cancer by recovery of the human character and the purpose of life (the life mission). ScientificWorldJournal 2004;4:362-77.

[6]   Ventegodt S, Morad M, Kandel I, Merrick J. Clinical holistic medicine: Treatment of physical health problems without a known cause, exemplified by hypertension and tinnitus. ScientificWorldJournal 2004;4:716-24.

[7]   Ventegodt S, Morad M, Merrick J. Clinical holistic medicine: Developing from asthma, allergy and eczema. ScientificWorldJournal 2004;4:936-42.

[8]   Ventegodt S, Morad M, Press J, Merrick J, Shek DTL. Clinical holistic medicine: Holistic adolescent medicine. ScientificWorldJournal 2004;4:551-61.

[9]   Ventegodt S, Solheim E, Saunte ME, Morad M, Kandel I, Merrick J. Clinical holistic medicine: Metastatic cancer. ScientificWorldJournal 2004;4:913-35.

[10]   Ventegodt S, Morad M, Kandel I, Merrick J. Clinical holistic medicine: a psychological theory of dependency to improve quality of life. ScientificWorldJournal 2004;4:638-48.

[11]   Ventegodt S, Merrick J. Clinical holistic medicine: Chronic infections and autoimmune diseases. ScientificWorldJournal 2005;5:155-64.

[12]   Ventegodt S, Kandel I, Neikrug S, Merrick J. Clinical holistic medicine: Holistic treatment of rape and incest traumas. ScientificWorldJournal 2005;5:288-97.

[13]   Ventegodt S, Morad M, Merrick J. Clinical holistic medicine: Chronic pain in the locomotor system. ScientificWorldJournal 2005;5:165-72.

[14]   Ventegodt S, Merrick J. Clinical holistic medicine: Chronic pain in internal organs. ScientificWorldJournal 2005;5:205-10.

[15]   Ventegodt S, Kandel I, Neikrug S, Merrick J. Clinical holistic medicine: The existential crisis – life crisis, stress and burnout. ScientificWorldJournal 2005;5:300-12.

[16]   Ventegodt S, Gringols M, Merrick J. Clinical holistic medicine: Holistic rehabilitation. ScientificWorldJournal 2005;5:280-7.

[17]   Ventegodt S, Andersen NJ, Neikrug S, Kandel I, Merrick J. Clinical holistic medicine: Mental disorders in a holistic perspective. ScientificWorldJournal 2005;5:313-23.

[18]   Ventegodt S, Andersen NJ, Neikrug S, Kandel I, Merrick J. Clinical holistic medicine: Holistic treatment of mental disorders. ScientificWorldJournal 2005;5:427-45.

[19]   Ventegodt S, Merrick J. Clinical holistic medicine: The patient with multiple diseases. ScientificWorldJournal 2005;5:324-39.

[20]   Ventegodt S, Clausen B, Nielsen ML, Merrick J. Clinical holistic health: Advanced tools for holistic medicine. ScientificWorldJournal 2006;6:2048-65.

[21]   Ventegodt S, Clausen B, Merrick J. Clinical holistic medicine: The case story of Anna: I. Long term effect of child sexual abuse and incest with a treatment approach. ScientificWorldJournal 2006;6:1965-76.

[22]   Ventegodt S, Clausen B, Merrick J. Clinical holistic medicine: the case story of Anna. II. Patient diary as a tool in treatment. ScientificWorldJournal 2006;6:2006-34.

[23]   Ventegodt S, Clausen B, Merrick J. Clinical holistic medicine: The case story of Anna. III. Rehabilitation of philosophy of life during holistic existential therapy for childhood sexual abuse. ScientificWorldJournal 2006;6:2080-91.

[24] Ventegodt S, Clausen B, Omar HA, Merrick J. Clinical holistic medicine: Holistic sexology and acupressure through the vagina (Hippocratic pelvic massage). ScientificWorldJournal 2006;6:2066-79.

[25] Ventegodt S, Clausen B, Merrick J. Clinical holistic medicine: Pilot study on the effect of vaginal acupressure (Hippocratic pelvic massage). ScientificWorldJournal 2006;6:2100-16.

[26] Ventegodt S, Thegler S, Andreasen T, Struve F, Enevoldsen L, Bassaine L, et al. Clinical holistic medicine: Psychodynamic short-time therapy complemented with bodywork. A clinical follow-up study of 109 patients. ScientificWorldJournal 6, 2220-2238.

[27] Ventegodt S, Thegler S, Andreasen T, Struve F, Enevoldsen L, Bassaine L, et al. Clinical holistic medicine (mindful, short-term psychodynamic psychotherapy complemented with bodywork) in the treatment of experienced impaired sexual functioning. ScientificWorldJournal 2007;7: 324-9.

[28] Ventegodt S, Thegler S, Andreasen T, Struve F, Enevoldsen L, Bassaine L, et al. Clinical holistic medicine (mindful, short-term psychodynamic psychotherapy complemented with bodywork) improves quality of life, health, and ability by induction of Antonovsky-salutogenesis. ScientificWorldJournal 2007;7:317-23.

[29] Ventegodt S, Thegler S, Andreasen T, Struve F, Enevoldsen L, Bassaine L, et al. Clinical holistic medicine (mindful, short-term psychodynamic psychotherapy complemented with bodywork) in the treatment of experienced physical illness and chronic pain. ScientificWorldJournal 2007;7:310-6.

[30] Ventegodt S, Thegler S, Andreasen T, Struve F, Enevoldsen L, Bassaine L, et al. Clinical holistic medicine (mindful, short-term psychodynamic psychotherapy complemented with bodywork) in the treatment of experienced mental illness. ScientificWorldJournal 2007;7:306-9.

[31] Ventegodt S, Thegler S, Andreasen T, Struve F, Enevoldsen L, Bassaine L, et al. Self-reported low self-esteem. Intervention and follow-up in a clinical setting. ScientificWorldJournal 2007;7:299-305.

[32] Ventegodt S, Flensborg-Madsen T, Andersen NJ, Nielsen M, Morad M, Merrick J. Global quality of life (QOL), health and ability are primarily determined by our consciousness. Research findings from Denmark 1991-2004. Soc Indicator Res 2005;71:87-122.

[33] Jones WHS. Hippocrates. Vol. I–IV. London: William Heinemann, 1923-1931.

[34] Ventegodt S, Kromann M, Andersen NJ, Merrick J. The life mission theory VI: A theory for the human character. ScientificWorldJournal 2004;4;859-80.

[35] Ventegodt S, Flensborg-Madsen T, Andersen NJ, Merrick J. Life Mission Theory VII: Theory of existential (Antonovsky) coherence: a theory of quality of life, health and ability for use in holistic medicine. ScientificWorldJournal 2005;5:377-89.

[36] Antonovsky A. Health, stress and coping. London: Jossey-Bass, 1985.

[37] Antonovsky A. Unravelling the mystery of health. How people manage stress and stay well. San Francisco: Jossey-Bass, 1987.

[38] Leichsenring F, Rabung S, Leibing E. The efficacy of short-term psychodynamic psychotherapy in specific psychiatric disorders: a meta-analysis. Arch Gen Psychiatry 2004;61(12):1208-16.

[39] Leichsenring F. Are psychodynamic and psychoanalytic therapies effective?: A review of empirical data. Int J Psychoanal 2005;86(Pt 3):841-68.

[40] Rosen M, Brenner S. Rosen method bodywork. Accessing the unconscious through touch. Berkeley, CA: North Atlantic Books, 2003.

[41] Punamäki L, Komproe I, Quota S, El Masri M, De Jong JTVM. The role of peritraumatic dissociation and gender in the association between trauma and mental health in a Palestinian community sample. Am J Psychiatry 2005;162:545–51.

[42] De Jong JTVM, Komproe I, Van Ommeren M. Common mental disorders in post-conflict settings. Lancet 2003;361(9375):2128-30.

[43] Flensborg-Madsen T, Ventegodt S, Merrick J. Sense of coherence and physical health. A Review of previous findings. ScientificWorldJournal 2005;5:665-73.

[44] Flensborg-Madsen T, Ventegodt S, Merrick J. Why is Antonovsky's sense of coherence not correlated to physical health? Analysing Antonovsky's 29-item sense of coherence scale (SOCS). ScientificWorldJournal 2005;5:767-76.

[45] Flensborg-Madsen T, Ventegodt S, Merrick J. Sense of coherence and health. The construction of an amendment to Antonovsky's sense of coherence scale (SOC II). ScientificWorldJournal 2006;6:2133-9.

[46] Flensborg-Madsen T, Ventegodt S, Merrick J. Sense of coherence and physical health. A cross-sectional study using a new SOC scale (SOC II). ScientificWorldJournal 2006;6:2200-11.

[47] Flensborg-Madsen T, Ventegodt S, Merrick J. Sense of coherence and physical health. Testing Antonovsky's theory. ScientificWorldJournal 2006;6:2212-9.

[48] Flensborg-Madsen T, Ventegodt S, Merrick J. Sense of coherence and health. The emotional sense of coherence (SOC-E) was found to be the best-known predictor of physical health. ScientificWorldJournal 2006;6: 2147-57.

[49] Ventegodt S, Andersen NJ, Merrick J. Holistic Medicine III: The holistic process theory of healing. ScientificWorldJournal 2003;3:1138-46.

[50] Lindhardt A, et al. [Forbruget af antipsykotika blandt 18-64 årige patienter med skizofreni, mani eller bipolar affektiv sindslidelse]. Copenhagen: Sundhedsstyrelsen, 2006. [Danish].

[51] Stern B. [Att må dåligt är en bra början : En bok om den obegränsade människan.] Stockholm: Förlaget Mullingstorp, 2000. [Swedish].

[52] Qin P, Nordentoft M. Suicide risk in relation to psychiatric hospitalization: evidence based on longitudinal registers. Arch Gen Psychiatry 2005;62(4): 427-32.

[53] Lehmann HE. Negative aspects of psychotherapeutic drug treatment. Prog Neuropsychopharmacol 1979;3(1-3):223-9.

[54] Malmberg L, Fenton M. Individual psychodynamic psychotherapy and psychoanalysis for schizophrenia and severe mental illness. Cochrane Database Syst Rev 2001;3:CD001360.

[55] Karon BP, VandenBos G.R. Psychotherapy and schizophrenia: The treatment of choise. New York: Aronsen, 1981.

[56] The Swedich Council of Technology Assessment in Health care. SBU-repport 133/1 and 133/2. Treatment with antipsychotic drugs [Behandling med neuroleptika.] Stockholm: SBU, 1997 [Swedish]

[57] Ventegodt S. [Livskvalitet I Danmark.] Quality of life in Denmark. Results from a population survey. Copenhagen: Forskningscentrets Forlag, 1995. [Danish].

[58] Ventegodt S. [Livskvalitet hos 4500 31-33 årige.] The Quality of Life of 4500 31-33 year-olds. Result from a study of the Prospective Pediatric Cohort of persons born at the University Hospital in Copenhagen. Copenhagen: Forskningscentrets Forlag, 1996. [Danish].

[59] Lindstrom B, Eriksson M. Contextualizing salutogenesis and Antonovsky in public health development. Health Promot Int 2006;21(3):238-44.

[60] Adams CE, Awad G, Rathbone J, Thornley B. Chlorpromazine versus placebo for schizophrenia. Cochrane Database Syst Rev 2007;18(2): CD000284.

Chapter 59

Integrative ethical theory

We have constructed an integral ethical theory with three dimensions: 1) intent, 2) outcome and 3) the quality of the act, well known from a) the duty ethics, b) the utilitarian ethics and c) the feministic ethics. This theory makes it possible to give a complex evaluation of the ethics of a complex holistic medical or sexological treatment. We have introduced a new "rule of integrative ethics" that allows us to evaluate the medical ethics of complex therapeutic behaviour. This ethical model is useful for clinical holistic medicine, especially to evaluate the ethics of concrete therapeutic actions in advanced holistic medical and sexological treatment. An integrative medical ethic is useful for teaching ethics to holistic therapists and physicians and for training students in holistic medicine.

Introduction

Ethics is the philosophy and science about doing good. It must be discriminated from the moral of society, which is the set of moral rules that a specific society requests its members to respect and follow. Medical ethics can sometimes be in conflict with the morals of society; it can be immoral to kill but ethical to perform euthanasia or it can be immoral for 13-year old teenagers to have sex but ethical to give them birth control. In a society physicians often receive permission to violate moral rules of society, if the actions are well based in medical ethics. Therefore it is urgent that the principles of medical ethics are clear, logical, fair and practical.

The medical ethics has its roots with Hippocrates (460-377 BCE), who worked with non-drug therapy. His aim was to help people cure their diseases by stepping into character, knowing themselves, and using all their talents to create value in the world. One thing that could seriously harm a physician's ability to help was if his reputation was destroyed, if he was mistrusted, or if he destroyed his therapeutic relationships by having sex with his patients. All this meant special demands and conduct for the behaviour of a physician, hence the famous medical ethics (1).

With the establishment of the Research Clinic for Holistic Medicine in 1997, expanding to the Research Clinic for Holistic Medicine and Sexology in 2003, and into the Nordic School of Holistic Medicine in 2004, all under the auspices of the Quality of Life Research

Center in Copenhagen, we have gone back to clinical medicine, i.e. a medicine that is examination and cure in the same process (2-4). For almost two decades we have been doing research in non-drug medicine - clinical holistic medicine - which is basically the combination of conversation and touch therapy (5-9). Of talking and touching, touching is far the most emotional, and the most difficult to master. In spite of this, it is well known that bodywork and touch therapy has no adverse effects, if it is done gently and without use of perfumed, aromatic oils (10). Even the most vulnerable and fragile of patients, the mentally ill children and teenagers has been shown to benefit from therapeutic touch (11), but even if you avoid extremely vigorous touch, the patient can still be violated sexually, hence the classical Hippocratic rule of the physician avoiding abusing his patients sexually. We know of no therapist that does not agree in this simple and basic rule of professional behaviour. So this is simple.

What is not so simple is to create value for the patient just by talking and touching. When the therapist's words and behaviour is used as medicine – when the doctor is himself the tool (12) - the need for a clear and practical medical ethics becomes obvious. Most unfortunately medical ethics has not developed much since Hippocrates, while the ethics as a philosophical subject had undergone a tremendous development. Most unfortunately, philosophical ethics had divided into three major schools, none of them completely efficient in guiding the practice of medicine and therapy. We therefore in our research project on clinical holistic medicine started to develop an integrated medical ethics that could fill the gab (13).

As teachers of the therapy and the training of therapists we have assumed responsibility for our patients and for our student's behaviour. The practical training of the student to behave optimally together with the patient was what most urgently forced us to work on formulating a new more comprehensive medical ethic.

Holistic medicine and ethics

The Nordic style of holistic medicine and therapy is somewhat different from many other countries, especially America. In the Nordic countries sexology is often an integrated part of the medical clinic, while in other parts of the world the sexological clinics are separated from the medical facilities. In the US, a doctor is rarely a sexologist and a sexologist is rarely a doctor. In Europe, strongly inspired by Freud (14), Jung (15,16) Reich (17) and many other therapists, researchers and sexologists (18-20) including many physicians has included work with the patient's sexuality in their clinical work.

As most other holistic therapists we believe that the process of healing one's existence comes about when sufficient resources are available for the patient. Our concept for giving this support is the four steps of 1) love, 2) trust, 3) holding and 4) processing the patient (3-9). This often leads to close intimacy between the therapist and the patient, often leading further into re-parenting and spontaneous regression into the most emotionally painful childhood and adolescent life events. The extreme closeness and intimacy needed for the patient's healing and the material of the patient's case story is not always as neutral to the therapist as wished for. The experienced therapist knows how to deal with all kinds of reactions, from intense emotional suffering, resentment and aggression, to transference, projections of love, strength and desire, all the way up to sexual excitement.

In the beginning the student and the inexperienced therapist often feels it both awkward and somewhat flattering, when the patient falls in love with them. The reaction to the patient turning on sexually, are often either disgust and condemnation or excitement and desire. The student is before anything a human being with his/her own repressed material, own vulnerable borders, and own sexuality. The repressed material can be activated, the borders violated, the sexual desire awakened, and from this arises many problems for most students.

It takes about 10 minutes to read the standard medical ethical rules for a student and unfortunately the sexual desire is often not well controlled by such rules. The inexperienced student is often in a very difficult situation regarding ethics, because of the rules being very tempting and very easy to go about. The only solid thing granting an ethical behaviour is the therapist being deeply founded in his/her own inner ethics, or "natural ethics" known from philosophy. The fundamental idea is that every man has an ethical nature, which often must be discovered in serious self-contemplation; what is almost always discovered is that in the essence of our soul, we are loving beings who wants to contribute with something of value to our fellow men.

Sexual issues in clinical practice

A rule will often seem ridiculous, when reality comes marching in and a young man and a young woman fall in love and want each other. Such a relationship will often appear more important than anything else, including the whole education and medical carrier. In this situation ethical rules are much more likely to make the involved persons keep the relationship secret than to make them abstain from having the relationship.

When it comes to personal development, secrecy about a relationship between a patient and a therapist or student with elements of love and sexuality is almost certain to disturb or even arrest it. Applying standard ethical rules, which often cannot be respected even by experienced therapists to the students, are therefore not only meaningless, but even damaging to the learning and development of the student. As we definitely need our students to be ethical and well behaved therapists, the problem is now what kind of ethics we need to impose on them as their teachers, or more precisely: how we can make them solve their own ethical problems by doing a thorough analyses of their personal ethics and the consequent medical ethics.

If possible to formulate at all, we need an ethical theory to guide this important endeavour; we need a general and fundamental understanding of human ethics to enlighten all students and therapists about our deeply ethical nature and the extreme value of ethics. In addition to such a theory we need a strategy for couching the students into the development of a perfectly ethical practice.

The use of ethics

First we need to understand that ethics is meant to guide our actions in order to do good for others in this life. Judging and punishing is generally not good. It leads to conditioned learning (Pavlovian, unconscious learning), with reflex inhibitions and accumulations of life-pain, thus crippling of the soul and existence, instead of facilitating conscious learning, awareness and enlightenment. If we want to create a community of conscious and responsible people, we need everybody to develop a high degree of self-esteem, a full permission to acting on any urge, and a flexible system of feedback to notice impact of any action and efficient learning. The environment must be open and friendly, and everybody must assume that the other person come with a good intent.

Ethics can be used to judge the actions of other people, but being judgemental is often not of any value, unless the offender is completely expelled from the society. If one can choose between being a good example and being judgemental, the impact on a family or on the community will normally be a hundred times more constructive if you elect to be the good example. Rules are often carried in our minds and not in our hearts, making them easy to neglect, when a person can gain a personal advantage or can avoid confronting a neurotic pattern of behaviour dictated by un-integrated life-pain.

Depending on the understanding of human nature, ethics is something natural that must be looked for and found at the bottom of your soul, or something un-natural that must be imposed on man from the outside world. The life-mission theory (21-28) states that everybody the essentially in his soul carry a wish to do good in the world, using specific talents and gifts. According to this theory ethics is not only something that we can find and discover within ourselves, but something that is a direct expression of our innermost nature. Doing good for other people is what life is about. Doing good and making a difference in the world is the meaning of life, the fundamental reason why we are here. The more ethical rules, the easier it is to go into the mind, to go to a place of judging another person, and to loose connection to the heart and deep nature of self; ideally therefore we all carry a non-rule based ethics, customized to completely fit our own understanding of life and self.

A timeline strategy for integrating ethics

There have been three major directions in ethical thinking: the duty ethics, the utilitarian ethics and the feministic ethics. With duty ethics the intention is what is important. If you kill a person with no intention whatsoever to do so, your action can still be ethical. The utilitarian ethics looks at the result of the action: if the person died, the action was wrong, even if you desperately tried to help him as a physician. The feministic thinkers have been looking very much into the balance between the male and the female components in ethical situations.

To integrate these three seemingly contradictory ethical philosophies has been a very difficult task, but obviously this is what must be done for us to have the best ethics, as most people will choose the combination of a good intention, good result and balanced actions. Only a fanatic will say that we just need to look into our heart, the result of our action is not important. Only an opportunistic person deprived of any scruple will say that we can be as evil as we want, as long as it maximizes the profit for me or for the world at large. And only a person with no roots into reality would state that now is all that counts, intention and result are not important at all.

So how can the three different ethical perspectives become integrated into a common ethical theory for use in holistic medical practice? A simple way is to use the timeline: Before an action we must look at our intention (or the intention of another person, directly if possible, or through his/her statement of the intent), we must look at the probable outcome of our different choices of action, and for each of them we must visualise the events that will come in order to see which line of events born from these different possible actions will be the most harmonious.

In the middle of an action, after choosing the fundamental direction, we must keep an eye on our intent to be sure not to depart from an ethical route. Due to the emotional aspects involved, we must be keenly aware to interact in our best way, reflect and at all time notice our impact in order to evaluate if there is anything in our behaviour, understanding, or perspective that we need to correct. Finally we must be certain that every present situation is balanced between female and male energies, not being too much coloured by the element of "water" or of to much "fire".

After the action we must contemplate on what we did, how we did it, and what we accomplished. Did I come from a good intent or did I catch myself coming from my shadow (25)? Did I act in fine balance, respecting both the male and the female aspects of the universe? Did I do the good I intended? What did I learn? What is the urge in myself and in the space and universe that I now feel? What will be my next step? Is there something or some relationship I involuntarily damaged, which I now need to repair before I can move forward?

An ethical theory based on the theory of existence

To create a formal theory of ethics we need to map the dimensions of existence relevant for human ethics and to be sure to encompass the totality. The extended version of the life mission theory called the theory of talent (23) gives fundamental dimensions of human existence: love/intent, power/consciousness and gender/sexuality. Interestingly, these three dimensions correspond to the three ethical perspectives of duty ethics (love/intention), utilitarian ethics (power/consciousness), and feministic ethics (gender/balance between the male and the female). That makes the life mission theory an excellent framework for an ethical theory with the axes: 1) Intent, 2) impact, and 3) balance between male and female.

In a way, the ethical debate is done with, if one can use such a simple theoretical framework for ethical guidance in all our actions. The strength of such a model is that it invites anybody who knows it to look for these dimensions in themselves, and thus it helps developing natural ethics. This is especially important where a flawless ethics is a must, as in the training of students in holistic medicine.

A strategy for coaching

It only takes about ten minutes to read and explain the ethical rules of physicians or other therapists to a class of students. The issue most intensely stressed is the ethical rules regarding sexuality. Sexual abuse cannot be tolerated and just one student or physician caught in severe misconduct can bring shame over a whole hospital or university, actually over the whole medical society. In spite of this obvious fact, sexual misconduct has continuously been a problem, ever since the ethical rules handed down by Hippocrates.

In the modern medical clinic, sexual abuse during the therapy is extremely rare, as people not being able to control their sexual behaviour are likely to be regarded as compulsive sexual offenders and sent away for psychiatric care. The problem is when a physician or student and a patient fall in love. In this situation everything including the education or whole medical career looses its significance, compared to this relationship now commencing. In practice it is almost impossible to keep the two parties from each other and even awareness of the strict ethical rules forbidding a sexual relationship will most likely make the two persons engage in a hidden relationship instead and anyway.

Case study one

A 50-year old, married psychotherapist and his 27-year old patient fell in love. She was in his therapy group. They started a sexual relationship, which they kept secret for about 6 month, until the day when she finally broke down and told another person that he drank and had sexually abused her. He was drinking, because he had severe emotional problems from this double life: a sexually highly dissatisfying life in his marriage and in the darkest secrecy, a promiscuous life with prostitutes and now also the sexual abuse of a patient. She had not been able to get help from another therapist, neither could she tell her girlfriends about the relationship, because she was afraid that the new therapist or some of the girlfriends would denounce him and thus ruin his career. After this incident the patient was supported and refused to see him again, which he insisted. Only after she had threatened him with the possibility of reporting to the ethical committee of the psychotherapist association did he stop bothering her. The psychotherapist is still working as a therapist. The patient is now in therapy healing her wounded heart and body, but the new therapy is facing severe difficulties, because of her serious distrust and intentions of her new therapist. She has seemingly been severely damaged existentially by the abusive relationship.

This situation is unfortunately not unusual and in one study 23% of the incest victims reported a new sexual violation from their therapist (29). Seemingly we are facing a paradox: all the ethical rules are working fine, except with the people, who really need them. Instead of helping, the ethical rules seems to be a destructive barrier making it impossible to talk about what is really going on, making the patients and therapist who fall in love and engage in a relationship so wrong that they must keep it a secret forever. Not being able so share this with anybody, the relationship turns out to but much more harmful, than it would have been in an open and accepting society. The conclusion is that a sexual relationship between a therapist and a patient is damaging; but what seems to be most damaging is the consequences of the wrong and the deep secrecy making it impossible for both the patient and the therapist to talk about it with anybody and to seek supervision and help.

If the therapist in the above mentioned case had been open about his sexual problems in the first place, if not with anybody else then just with his wife, the situation could not have persisted for years and developed as it did. If he just could admit it to his own supervisor and therapist, the situation would not have gone completely out of control and he could have been helped to confront his own feelings and personal problems creating the emotional pull in order to take his projections back (30). If it was not a "deathly sin" leading to expulsion from the society of psychotherapists, the patient could have gone to another therapist for help, or she could have talked with her friends about it.

Case study two

A 30-year old student in holistic medicine fell in love with a mentally ill participant of the same age in a quality of life course and shared her experience and different thoughts with her supervisor. As a sexual relationship seemingly could not be avoided, she asked permission to sleep with him. The supervisor gave the permission, under the condition that she takes full responsibility for the impact of her actions. She slept with him and a month afterwards he entered an almost suicidal crisis. In the middle of the night she took her car and drove 300 km to assist him and help him through his crisis. She felt an extreme degree of empathy and responsibility and knew that she was in it with everything she has got. She stayed intimate and closely emotionally connected to him for about 100 intensive hours in a row during which she connected with her supervisor by phone. Finally she managed to get him to trust her and to receive the holding he needed for healing existentially. He now succeeded to integrate the strong life-pains that made him want to die. After this dramatic culmination of his old tendency to attempt suicide and his spontaneous regression to early childhood and poor mothering, it seemed that his mental and existential problems were to a large extent solved.

Box 1. CAM often use one or more of the five central, holistic principles of healing the whole person (from 31)

a) The principle of salutogenesis: the whole person must be healed (existential healing), not only a part of the person. This is done by recovering the sense of coherence, character and purpose of life of the person

b) The similarity principle: only by reminding the patient (or his body, mind or soul) of what made him ill, can the patient be cured. The reason for this is that the earlier wound/trauma(s) live in the subconscious (or body-mind)

c) The Hering's law of cure (Constantine Hering, 1800-1880): that you will get well in the opposite order of the way you got ill

d) The principle of resources: only when you are getting the holding/care and support you did not get when you became ill, can you be healed from the old wound (2-4)

e) The principle of using as little force as possible (primum non nocere or first do no harm), because since Hippocrates (460-377 BCE) statement "Declare the past, diagnose the present, foretell the future; practice these acts. As to diseases, make a habit of two things - to help, or at least to do no harm" (1), it has been paramount not to harm the patient or running a risk with the patient's life or health.

She on her part took her projections back from him too, so her sexual desire was gone. In her next supervision session it looked more to her like an intense wish to help the young man, than it looked like a sexual intention in its own right. Giving her body will not be a part of her treatments, but here for some idiopathic reason this was inevitable. So they were in the end both set free by the episode, which from normal moral and medical-ethical standards would have been unacceptable. She also learned about the dramatic impact of a sexual relationship with a patient, and why she needs to be extremely careful with this kind of involvement in the future. Without wise guidance this relationship could have ended tragically.

Therapeutic behaviour in clinical holistic medicine

According to the holistic process theory of healing, holistic and existential healing happens when the patient encounters the repressed content of his or her unconscious. There are three steps in holistic healing: 1) feel, 2) understand and 3) let go (31). To facilitate healing, the therapist must support the patient, which is called "holding" (known as the "principle of resources") (32, Box 1). At the same time the therapist must take the patient into painful emotions and gestalts - the traumas from early life - by exposing the patient to small doses of that originally made him ill (this is known as the "principle of similarity") (32-39). The latter therapeutic re-exposure to the evil is called "processing". As most of what gave us our traumas originally was evil, the key to healing is really treating the patient "bad" with the good intention of healing them. This is what happens in the therapeutic processing.

So the skilful therapist treats the patient good and bad at the same time; holding takes love, devotion, acceptance, patience, acknowledgement, respect and so forth (23), while processing takes small doses of controlled violence, abuse, neglect etc. as is well known from the advanced toolbox of clinical holistic medicine (8) and intensive holistic therapy (40-43). The necessity of "evil" actions in holistic therapy calls urgently for an ethical tool that allows us to evaluate each therapeutic action regarding its ethical standing. Below we present three examples in need of ethical evaluation.

Example one: A patient physically abused as a child

A patient was severely beaten as a child. According to the principle of similarity, the therapist must beat him again, or do something similar to provoke and process him. The therapist must take the patient back to his childhood traumatic violence and (after getting consent) once again beat him. This is what has been called "encounter" (44). During such a session, the therapist through role-play, invite the patient to go back in time, into re-experiencing being children beaten by his father (now the therapist) and to once again feel all the anger and fear that the beating made him feel, and little by little understand what the violent abuse and repression did to him as child. What it did do his personality - to allow him to let go of all his repressed hate and anger and in the end to embrace, understand his father, and forgive him. This is a most difficult therapeutic process, as any therapist will know.

Is this an ethical action? To answer this question, we can look at 1) the intent, 2) the way the exercise was done and 3) the outcome. We need to compare it to the three steps of healing: feel, understand and let go. Regarding the first: If it was done with a good intent – to heal – then we believe it was ethical. Concerning the second: If it was done in an empathic and balanced way, helpful to the patient, facilitating the recall of old feelings and emotions, facilitating reflection and understanding, and facilitating forgiveness and letting go of negative beliefs and learning from the childhood violent abuse, then it was ethical in our opinion. Regarding the last: If it helped the patient to heal and forgive, it was ethical as we understand it– if it healed or supported healing, because it provoked emotion, understanding and letting go, it was ethical. If the patient learned from it and gained understanding and self-insight it was ethical in our opinion.

The "rule of integrative ethics"

It is always difficult to balance these three factors: Intent, outcome and quality of action. The "rule of integrative ethics" is that if two or three out of these three ethical dimensions were fine, then the action was all together ethical in our opinion. Imagine that the exercise was well performed, and everything in principle went well, but the patent was not helped. We would not blame the therapist in that situation. Imagine that the therapist failed to do the therapy empathically, but that it was done in the best of intentions, and that it really helped the patient. Again, we would not blame the therapist. Imagine that the intent was not good, but selfish, as the therapist himself had been beaten as a child, and needed to do this exercise for his own sake; if it was done emphatically and skilfully, and if it really helped the patient, we would not accuse him for being a bad therapist – but of course we would still give him critique and encourage him to take the therapy he needs himself.

But, if this was done with a selfish intent, and it did not help the patient, we would reject it as unethically therapy. If it was done in the best of intentions, but performed badly, so it did not help the patient, we would say, that it was not good therapy. If the intention was evil, and the act cruel and it really did help the patient, we would still blame the therapist for not giving good and ethical therapy.

Example 2: A cancer patient in existential trouble

Now let's take a little more difficult example. A cancer patient wants to life, but feels that she is loosing herself – her hair, her body tissues, her dignity, wearing a ridiculous wig. The therapist wants to encourage her to be what she is, and love just that, and in this intent he makes a role play with her where he puts her wig in the office's paper-bin (it does not destroy the wig, as the bin is clean and empty). After this she feels courageous enough to be bald and she does not wear the wig anymore. Was that ethical?

It was done in a good intent. It was – at least according to the moral of society - a violation of her integrity and the outcome was good. As two out of three of these ethical dimensions were positive, the action was all in all ethically acceptable and good in our opinion.

Example 3: Holistic sexology: Healing a sexually abused woman using "acceptance through touch"

Sexual dysfunctions often come from lack of self-acceptance. A traditional cure for this is therapeutic touch especially if the therapist is able to signify acceptance by the touch, a technique known as "acceptance through touch" (1,8,45). Around the year 1900 therapeutic touch was often practiced as a swift kiss, but due to moral reflections this practice has now become rare. Let us use such a controversial practice as the next example.

A holistic therapist works on a severely sexually abused 21-year old woman. The therapist feels that just touching the patient by hand is not enough to heal her, and chooses therefore, after getting her consent for this action, to gently kiss her mons pubis (over the pubic hair and the pubic bone, at one of the acupressure points related to sexuality known as "Conception Vessel 4" in Chinese medicine (46)). The intention is to let her know that her body and genitals are completely lovely, acceptable and fine for him or indeed taking her father's place psychodynamically.

The rationale for this action is clear: a kiss is maybe the most powerful bodily sign of acceptance, and the genital kiss is a well-known sexological procedure developed by van der Velde around 1900 as an exercise for couples (47). The genital kiss was a non-sexual interaction indented for lovers; it allowed a man to heal his women for sexual frigidity. Brecher wrote in 1969: "The genital kiss, van der Velde adds, "is particularly calculated to overcome frigidity and fear in hitherto inexperienced women who have had no erotic practice, and are as yet scarcely capable of specific sexual desire". In the example the procedure of the genital kiss seemingly did the job and helped the woman to acceptance of own body and sexuality. After the therapy she is able to enter a happy sexual relationship for the first time in her life.

Was this action ethical? Let's analyse according to the "rule of integrative ethics":

- It was done in the best of intentions.
- It was not sex and therefore not in conflict with the ethics of Hippocrates (but as it was close to the vulva it was still in conflict with the moral of society).
- The woman was helped but it is difficult to say if it was this kiss that healed her.

The score are as follows: a) It was done with a good intention, b) the action was not sex so it was ethical according to medical ethics but at the same time not morally acceptable by society, c) the outcome was good. All in all this is therefore still an ethical act.

Discussion

This kind of "doubtful" actions as shown in example three has been quite normal in the classical holistic therapy of Asia, guided by the principle often called "holy madness" or "crazy wisdom" (48,49). Holy madness is today often used in advanced holistic therapy and at advanced courses in self-knowledge and personal development.

With a traditional duty-ethic many actions performed in the state of "holy madness" must be rejected as unethical, but in the light of a complex, integrated ethics, many of the actions become also ethically acceptable. They are actually very helpful for learning and personal development, because they turn reality up-side-down and force the students to think and reflect.

It must be admitted, that according to the integrative ethics, sex with a patient, if done with a good intent, and with a good outcome, is in principle ethical, in spite of validating the famous ethical rule of Hippocrates of not having sex with your patient. In spite of this, modern holistic therapists agrees, that this rule is so important, that even the best of intentions and the best of outcomes cannot allow for a dispensation from it. Therefore, we strongly advise that the "rule of integrative ethics" is not used to justify sex with the patient. The suspicion, that the therapist did it for himself, and not for his patient, will always be there, making the action unethical.

Conclusions

An integral ethical theory can integrate the three ethical core dimensions: 1) intent, 2) outcome and 3) the quality of the act, well known from a) the duty ethics, b) the utilitarian ethics and c) the feministic ethics. This theory makes it possible to give a complex evaluation of the ethics of a complex holistic medical or sexological treatment. We have introduced a new "rule of integrative ethics" that allows us to evaluate the medical ethics of complex therapeutic behaviour, even if such a behaviour be judged as immoral by society in general. This ethics is useful for clinical holistic medicine, especially to ethically evaluate the concrete therapeutic actions in advanced holistic medical and sexological treatment. An integrative medical ethic is useful for teaching ethics to holistic therapists and physicians and for training students in holistic medicine.

References

[1]   Jones WHS. Hippocrates. Vol. I–IV. London: William Heinemann, 1923-1931.
[2]   Ventegodt S, Kandel I, Merrick J. A short history of clinical holistic medicine. ScientificWorldJournal 2007;7:1622-30.
[3]   Ventegodt S, Kandel I, Merrick J. Principles of holistic medicine. Philosophy behind quality of life. Victoria, BC: Trafford, 2005.
[4]   Ventegodt S, Kandel I, Merrick J. Principles of holistic medicine. Quality of life and health. New York: Hippocrates Sci Publ, 2005.
[5]   Ventegodt S, Kandel I, Merrick J. Principles of holistic medicine. Global quality of life.Theory, research and methodology. New York: Hippocrates Sci Publ, 2005.
[6]   Nielsen ML. Advanced tools for holistic medicine. Dissertation. Graz: Interuniversity College, 2008.
[7]   Ventegodt S, Morad M, Andersen NJ, Merrick J. Clinical holistic medicine. Tools for a medical science based on consciousness. ScientificWorldJournal 2004;4:347-61.
[8]   Ventegodt S, Clausen B, Nielsen ML, Merrick J. Advanced tools for holistic medicine. ScientificWorldJournal 2006;6:2048-65.
[9]   Ventegodt S, Andersen NJ, Kandel I, Merrick J. Five tools for manual sexological examination and treatment. J Altern Med Res, in press.
[10]   Vickers A, Zollman C. ABC of complementary medicine. Massage therapies. BMJ 1999;319(7219):1254-7.

[11] Field T, Morrow C, Valdeon C, Larson S, Kuhn C, Schanberg S. Massage reduces anxiety in child and
      adolescent psychiatric patients. J Am Acad Child Adolesc Psychiatry 1992;31:125-31.
[12] de Vibe M, Bell E, Merrick J, Omar HA, Ventegodt S. Ethics and holistic healthcare practice. Int J
      Child Health Human Dev 2008;1(1):23-8.
[13] Ventegodt S, Andersen, NJ, Kandel, I, and Merrick, J. The open source protocol of clinical holistic
      medicine J Altern Med Res 2009;1(2):129-44.
[14] Jones E. The life and works of Sigmund Freud. New York: Basic Books, 1961.
[15] Jung CG. Man and his symbols. New York: Anchor Press, 1964.
[16] Jung CG. Psychology and alchemy. Collected works of CG Jung, Vol 12. Princeton, NJ: Princeton
      Univ Press, 1968.
[17] Reich W. [Die Function des Orgasmus]. Köln: Kiepenheuer Witsch 1969. [German].
[18] Lowen A. Honoring the body. Alachua, FL: Bioenergetics Press, 2004.
[19] Rosen M, Brenner S. Rosen method bodywork. Accessing the unconscious through touch. Berkeley,
      CA: North Atlantic Books, 2003.
[20] Anand M. The art of sexual ecstasy. The path of sacred sexuality for western lovers. New York:
      Jeremy P Tarcher/Putnam, 1989.
[21] Ventegodt S. The life mission theory: A theory for a consciousness-based medicine. Int J Adolesc
      Med Health 2003;15(1):89-91.
[22] Ventegodt S, Andersen NJ, Merrick J. The life mission theory II: The structure of the life purpose and
      the ego. ScientificWorldJournal 2003;3:1277-85.
[23] Ventegodt S, Andersen NJ, Merrick J. The life mission theory III: Theory of talent.
      ScientificWorldJournal 2003;3:1286-93.
[24] Ventegodt S, Merrick J. The life mission theory IV. A theory of child development.
      ScientificWorldJournal 2003;3:1294-1301.
[25] Ventegodt S, Andersen NJ, Merrick J. The life mission theory V. A theory of the anti-self and
      explaining the evil side of man. ScientificWorldJournal 2003;3:1302-13.
[26] Ventegodt S, Andersen NJ, Merrick J. The life mission theory VI: A theory for the human character.
      ScientificWorldJournal 2004;4:859-80.
[27] Ventegodt S, Flensborg-Madsen T, Andersen NJ, Merrick J. Life Mission Theory VII: Theory of
      existential (Antonovsky) coherence: a theory of quality of life, health and ability for use in holistic
      medicine. ScientificWorldJournal 2005;5:377-89.
[28] Ventegodt S, Merrick J. Life mission theory VIII: A theory for pain. J Pain Manage 2008;1(1):5-10.
[29] Ventegodt S, Kandel I, Neikrug S, Merrick J. Clinical holistic medicine: Holistic treatment of rape and
      incest traumas. ScientificWorldJournal 2005;5:288-97.
[30] Ventegodt S, Kandel I, Merrick J. Clinical holistic medicine: avoiding the Freudian trap of sexual
      transference and countertransference in psychodynamic therapy. ScientificWorldJournal
      2008;14(8):371-83.
[31] Ventegodt S, Andersen NJ, Merrick J. Holistic Medicine III: The holistic process theory of healing.
      ScientificWorldJournal 2003;3:1138-46.
[32] Ventegodt S, Merrick J. Complimentary and alternative medicine. In: Lopex SJ, ed. The encyclopedia
      of positive psychology. Oxford, UK: Wiley-Blackwell, 2009;1:216-7.
[33] Antonella R. Introduction of regulatory methods. Graz, Austria: Interuniversity College, 2004.
[34] Blättner B. Fundamentals of salutogenesis. Graz, Austria: Interuniversity College, 2004.
[35] Endler PC. Master program for complementary, psychosocial and integrated health sciences Graz,
      Austria: Interuniversity College, 2004.
[36] Endler PC. Working and writing scientifically in complementary medicine and integrated health
      sciences. Graz, Austria: Interuniversity College, 2004.
[37] Kratky KW. Complementary medicine systems. Comparison and integration. New York, Nova Sci,
      2008.
[38] Pass PF. Fundamentals of depth psychology. Therapeutic relationship formation between self-
      awareness and casework Graz, Austria: Interuniversity College, 2004.
[39] Spranger HH. Fundamentals of regulatory biology. Paradigms and scientific backgrounds of
      regulatory methods Graz, Austria: Interuniversity College, 2004.

[40] Stern, B. Feeling bad is a good start. San Diego: ProMotion Publ, 1996.

[41] Fernros L, Furhoff AK, Wändell PE. Quality of life of participants in a mind-body-based self-development course: a descriptive study. Qual Life Res 2005;14(2):521-8

[42] Fernros L, Furhoff AK, Wändell PE. Improving quality of life using compound mind-body therapies: evaluation of a course intervention with body movement and breath therapy, guided imagery, chakra experiencing and mindfulness meditation. Qual Life Res 2008;17(3): 367-76.

[43] Ventegodt S, Kandel I, Merrick J. Positive effects, side effects and negative events of intensive, clinical holistic therapy. A review of the program "meet yourself" characterized by intensive body-psychotherapy combined with mindfulness meditation at Mullingstorp in Sweden J Altern Med Res 2009;1(3):275-86.

[44] Perls F, Hefferline R, Goodman P. Gestalt Therapy. New York: Julian Press, 1951.

[45] Ventegodt S, Morad M, Hyam E, Merrick J. Clinical holistic medicine: Holistic sexology and treatment of vulvodynia through existential therapy and acceptance through touch. ScientificWorldJournal 2004;4:571-80.

[46] Young J. Acupressure: Simple steps to health. Discover your bodies powerpoints for health and relaxation. London: Thorsons HarperCollins, 1994.

[47] Brecher EM. The sex researchers. Boston, MA: Little Brown, 1969:93.

[48] Feuerstein G. Holy madness. Spirituality, crazy-wise teachers and enlightenment. Arkana, London, 1992.

[49] Ventegodt S, Kandel I, Merrick J. Clinical holistic medicine: Factors influencing the therapeutic decision-making. From academic knowledge to emotional intelligence and spiritual "crazy" wisdom. ScientificWorldJournal 2007;7:1932-49.

Chapter 60

Acknowledgments

The Danish Quality of Life Survey and the Quality of Life Research Center was 1991-2004 supported by grants from the 1991 Pharmacy Foundation, the Goodwill-fonden, the JL-Foundation, E Danielsen and Wife's Foundation, Emmerick Meyer's Trust, the Frimodt-Heineken Foundation, the Hede Nielsen Family Foundation, Petrus Andersens Fond, Wholesaler C.P. Frederiksens Study Trust, Else and Mogens Wedell-Wedellsborg's Foundation and IMK Almene Fond.

The research in quality of life and scientific complementary and holistic medicine was approved by the Copenhagen Scientific Ethical Committee under the numbers (KF)V. 100.1762-90, (KF)V. 100.2123/91, (KF)V. 01-502/93, (KF)V. 01-026/97, (KF)V. 01-162/97, (KF)V. 01-198/97 and further correspondence.

Staff from the National Institute of Child Health and Human Development, Office of the Medical Director, Jerusalem in Israel was supported by the Israel Foundation for Human Development in New York.

We also thank Frank Columbus of Nova Science and his staff in New York for their support and guidance.

Chapter 61

About the authors

Søren Ventegodt, MD, MMedSci, EU-MSc is the director of the Nordic School of Holistic Health and Quality of Life Research Center in Copenhagen, Denmark. Director and lecturer, Inter-University College, International Campus, Denmark in collaboration with Inter-University Consortium for Integrative Health Promotion, Inter-University College Graz, Austria and the Austrian Ministry of Education, Science and Culture. He is also responsible for a Clinical Research Clinic for Holistic Medicine in Copenhagen and used as a popular speaker throughout Scandinavia. He has published numerous scientific or popular articles and a number of books on holistic medicine, quality of life and quality of working life. His most important scientific contributions are the comprehensive SEQOL questionnaire, the very short QOL1, QOL5, and QOL10 questionnaires, the integrated QOL theory, the holistic process theory, the life mission theory, and the ongoing Danish Quality of Life Research Survey, 1991-94 in connection with follow-up studies of the Copenhagen Perinatal Birth Cohort 1959-61 initiated at the University Hospital of Copenhagen by the late professor of pediatrics, Bengt Zachau-Christiansen, MD, PhD. E-mail: ventegodt@livskvalitet.org. Website: www. livskvalitet.org.

Joav Merrick, MD, MMedSci, DMSc, is professor of pediatrics, child health and human development affiliated with Kentucky Children's Hospital, University of Kentucky, Lexington, United States and the Zusman Child Development Center, Division of Pediatrics, Soroka University Medical Center, Ben Gurion University, Beer-Sheva, Israel, the medical director of the Health Services, Division for Mental Retardation, Ministry of Social Affairs and Socail Services, Jerusalem, the founder and director of the National Institute of Child Health and Human Development. Numerous publications in the field of pediatrics, child health and human development, rehabilitation, intellectual disability, disability, health, welfare, abuse, advocacy, quality of life and prevention. Received the Peter Sabroe Child Award for outstanding work on behalf of Danish Children in 1985 and the International LEGO-Prize ("The Children's Nobel Prize") for an extraordinary contribution towards improvement in child welfare and well-being in 1987. E-mail: jmerrick@zahav.net.il; Homepage: http://jmerrick50.googlepages.com/home.

Chapter 62

About the Quality of Life Research Center in Copenhagen, Denmark

The Quality of Life Research Center in Copenhagen was established in 1989, when the physician Søren Ventegodt succeeded in getting a collaboration started with the Department of Social Medicine at the University of Copenhagen in response to the project "Quality of life and causes of disease". An interdisciplinary "Working group for the quality of life in Copenhagen" was established and when funds were raised in 1991 the University Hospital of Copenhagen (Rigshospitalet) opened its doors for the project.

The main task was a comprehensive follow-up of 9,006 pregnancies and the children delivered during 1959-61. This Copenhagen Perinatal Birth Cohort was established by the a gynecologist and a pediatrician, the late Aage Villumsen, MD, PhD and the late Bengt Zachau-Christiansen, MD, PhD, who had made intensive studies during pregnancy, early childhood and young adulthood. The cohort was during 1980-1989 directed by the pediatrician Joav Merrick, MD, DMSc, who established the Prospective Pediatric Research Unit at the University Hospital of Copenhagen and managed to update the cohort for further follow-up register research, until he moved to Israel. The focus was to study quality of life related to socio-economic status and health in order to compare with the data collected during pregnancy, deliverty and early childhood.

The project continued to grow and later in 1993, the work was organized into a statistics group, a software group that developed the computer programs for use in the data entry and a group responsible for analysis of the data.

Quality of life research center at the university medical center

The Quality of Life Center at the University Hospital generated grants, publicity with research and discussions among the professionals leading to the claim that quality of life was significant for health and disease. It is obvious that a single person cannot do much about his/her own disease, if it is caused by chemical defects in the body or outside chemical-physical influences. However, if a substantial part of diseases are caused by a low quality of life, we can all prevent a lot of disease and operate as our own physicians, if we make a personal effort and work to improve our quality of life. A series of investigations showed that this was indeed possible. This view of the role of personal responsibility for illness and health would naturally lead to a radical re-consideration of the role of the physician and also influence our society.

Independent quality of life research center

In 1994, The Quality of Life Research Center became an independent institution located in the center of the old Copenhagen. Today, the number of full-time employees have grown. The Research Center is still expanding and several companies and numerous institutions make use of the resources, such as lectures, courses, consulting or contract research. The companies, which have used the competence of the reseach center and its tools on quality of life and quality of working life, include IBM, Lego, several banks, a number of counties, municipalities, several ministries, The National Defense Center for Leadership and many other management training institutions, along with more than 300 public and private companies. It started in Denmark, but has expanded to involve the whole Scandinavian area.

The center's research on the quality of life have been through several phases from measurement of quality of life, from theory to practice over several projects on the quality of life in Denmark, which have been published and received extended public coverage and public impact in Denmark and Scandinavia. The data is now also an important part of Veenhoven's Database on Happiness at Rotterdam University in the Netherlands.

New research

Since The Quality-of-Life Research Center became independent a number of new research projects were launched. One was a project that aimed to prevent illness and social problems among the elderly in one of the municipalities by inspiring the elderly to improve their quality of life themselves. Another a project about quality of life after apoplectic attacks at one of the major hospitals in Copenhagen and the Danish Agency for Industry granted funds for a project about the quality of work life.

Quality of life of 10,000 danes

There is a general consensus that many of the diseases that plague the Western world (which are not the result of external factors such as starvation, micro-organisms, infection or genetic defects) are lifestyle related and as such, preventable through lifestyle changes. Thus increasing time and effort is spent on developing public health strategies to promote "healthy" lifestyles. However, it is not a simple task to identify and dispel the negative and unhealthy parts of our modern lifestyle even with numerous behavioural factors that can be readily highlighted harmful, like the use of alcohol, use of tobacco, the lack of regular exercise and a high fat, low fibre diet.

However there is more to Western culture and lifestyle than these factors and if we only focus on them we can risk overlooking others. We refer to other large parts of our life, for instance the way we think about and perceive life (our life attitudes, our perception of reality and our quality of life) and the degree of happiness we experience through the different dimensions of our existence. These factors or dimensions can now, to some degree, be isolated and examined. The medical sociologist Aaron Antonovsky (1923-1994) from the Faculty of Health Sciences at Ben Gurion University in Beer-Sheva, who developed the salutogenic model of health and illness, discussed the dimension, "sense of coherence", that is closely related to the dimension of "life meaning", as perhaps the deepest and most important dimension of quality of life. Typically, the clinician or researcher, when attempting to reveal a connection between health and a certain factor, sides with only one of the possible dimensions stated above. A simple, one-dimensional hypothesis is then postulated, like for instance that cholesterol is harmful to circulation. Cholesterol levels are then measured, manipulated and ensuing changes to circulatory function monitored. The subsequent result may show a significant, though small connection, which supports the initial hypothesis and in turn becomes the basis for implementing preventive measures, like a change of diet. The multi-factorial dimension is therefore often overlooked.

In order to investigate this multifactorial dimension a cross-sectional survey examining close to 10,000 Danes was undertaken in order to investigate the connection between lifestyle, quality of life and health status by way of a questionnaire based survey. The questionnaire was mailed in February 1993 to 2,460 persons aged between 18-88, randomly selected from the CPR (Danish Central Register) and 7,222 persons from the Copenhagen Perinatal Birth Cohort 1959-61.

A total of 1,501 persons between the ages 18-88 years and 4,626 persons between the ages 31-33 years returned the questionnaire (response rates 61.0% and 64,1% respectively). The results showed that health had a stronger correlation to quality of life ($r= 0.5$, $p<0.0001$), than it had to lifestyle ($r=0.2$, $p< 0.0001$).

It was concluded that preventable diseases could be more effectively handled through a concentrated effort to improve quality of life rather than through n approach that focus solely on the factors that are traditionally seen to reflect an unhealthy life style.

Collaborations across borders

The project has been developed during several phases. The first phase, 1980-1990, was about mapping the medical systems of the pre-modern cultures of the world, understanding their philosophies and practices and merging this knowledge with western biomedicine. A huge task seemingly successfully accomplished in the Quality of Life (QOL) theories, and the QOL philosophy, and the most recent theories of existence, explaining the human nature, and especially the hidden resources of man, their nature, their location in human existence and the way to approach them through human consciousness.

Søren Ventegodt visited several countries around the globe in the late 1980s and analysed about 10 pre-modern medical systems and a dozen of shamans, shangomas and spiritual leaders noticing most surprisingly similarities, allowing him together with about 20 colleagues at the QOL Study Group at the University of Copenhagen, to model the connection between QOL and health. This model was later further developed and represented in the integrative QOL theories and a number of publications. Based on this philosophical breakthrough the Quality of Life Research Center was established at the University hospital. Here a brood cooperation took place with many interested physicians and nurses from the hospital.

A QOL conference in 1993 with more than 100 scientific participants discussed the connection between QOL and the development of disease and its prevention. Four physicians collaborated on the QOL population survey 1993. For the next 10 years the difficult task of integrating bio-medicine and the traditional medicine went on and Søren Ventegodt again visited several centers and scientists at the Universities of New York, Berkeley, Stanford and other institutions. He also met people like David Spiegel, Dean Ornish, Louise Hay, Dalai Lama and many other leading persons in the field of holistic medicine and spirituality.

Around the year 2000 an international scientific network started to take form with an intense collaboration with the National Institute of Child Health and Human Development (NICHD) in Israel, which has now developed the concept of "Holistic Medicine". We believe that the trained physician today has three medical toolboxes: the manual medicine (traditional), the bio-medicine (with drugs and pharmacology) and the consciousness-based medicine (scientific, holistic medicine). What is extremely interesting is that most diseases can be alleviated with all three sets of medical tools, but only the bio-medical toolset is highly expensive. The physician, using his hands and his consciousness to improve the health of the patient by mobilising hidden resources in the patient can use his skills in any cultural setting, rich or poor.

Contact person

Director Søren Ventegodt, MD, MMedSci, MSc
Quality of Life Research Center
Frederiksberg Alle 13A, 2tv
DK-1661 Copenhagen V
Denmark
E-mail: ventegodt@livskvalitet.org
Website: www.livskvalitet.org

Chapter 63

About the National Institute of Child Health and Human Development in Israel

The National Institute of Child Health and Human Development (NICHD) in Israel was established in 1998 as a virtual institute under the auspicies of the Medical Director, Ministry of Social Affairs and Social Services in order to function as the research arm for the Office of the Medical Director. In 1998 the National Council for Child Health and Pediatrics, Ministry of Health and in 1999 the Director General and Deputy Director General of the Ministry of Health endorsed the establishment of the NICHD.

Mission

The mission of a National Institute for Child Health and Human Development in Israel is to provide an academic focal point for the scholarly interdisciplinary study of child life, health, public health, welfare, disability, rehabilitation, intellectual disability and related aspects of human development. This mission includes research, teaching, clinical work, information and public service activities in the field of child health and human development.

Service and academic activities

Over the years many activities became focused in the south of Israel due to collaboration with various professionals at the Faculty of Health Sciences (FOHS) at the Ben Gurion University of the Negev (BGU). Since 2000 an affiliation with the Zusman Child Development Center at the Pediatric Division of Soroka University Medical Center has resulted in collaboration around the establishment of the Down Syndrome Clinic at that center. In 2002 a full course on "Disability" was established at the Recanati School for Allied Professions in the Community, FOHS, BGU and in 2005 collaboration was started with the Primary Care Unit of the faculty and disability became part of the master of public health course on "Children and society". In the academic year 2005-2006 a one semester course on "Aging with disability" was started as part of the master of science program in gerontology in our collaboration with the Center for Multidisciplinary Research in Aging.

Research activities

The affiliated staff have over the years published work from projects and research activities in this national and international collaboration. In the year 2000 the International Journal of Adolescent Medicine and Health and in 2005 the International Journal on Disability and Human development of Freund Publishing House (London and Tel Aviv), in the year 2003 the TSW-Child Health and Human Development and in 2006 the TSW-Holistic Health and Medicine of the Scientific World Journal (New York and Kirkkonummi, Finland), all peer-reviewed international journals were affiliated with the National Institute of Child Health and Human Development. From 2008 also the International Journal of Child Health and Human Development (Nova Science, New York), the International Journal of Child and Adolescent Health (Nova Science) and the Journal of Pain Management (Nova Science) affiliated and from 2009 the International Public Health Journal (Nova Science) and Journal of Alternative Medicine Research (Nova Science).

National collaborations

Nationally the NICHD works in collaboration with the Faculty of Health Sciences, Ben Gurion University of the Negev; Department of Physical Therapy, Sackler School of Medicine, Tel Aviv University; Autism Center, Assaf HaRofeh Medical Center; National Rett and PKU Centers at Chaim Sheba Medical Center, Tel HaShomer; Department of Physiotherapy, Haifa University; Department of Education, Bar Ilan University, Ramat Gan, Faculty of Social Sciences and Health Sciences; College of Judea and Samaria in Ariel and recently also collaborations has been established with the Division of Pediatrics at Hadassah, Center for Pediatric Chronic Illness, Har HaZofim in Jerusalem.

International collaborations

Internationally with the Department of Disability and Human Development, College of Applied Health Sciences, University of Illinois at Chicago; Strong Center for Developmental Disabilities, Golisano Children's Hospital at Strong, University of Rochester School of Medicine and Dentistry, New York; Centre on Intellectual Disabilities, University of Albany, New York; Centre for Chronic Disease Prevention and Control, Health Canada, Ottawa; Chandler Medical Center and Children's Hospital, Kentucky Children's Hospital, Section of Adolescent Medicine, University of Kentucky, Lexington; Chronic Disease Prevention and Control Research Center, Baylor College of Medicine, Houston, Texas; Division of Neuroscience, Department of Psychiatry, Columbia University, New York; Institute for the Study of Disadvantage and Disability, Atlanta; Center for Autism and Related Disorders,

Department Psychiatry, Children's Hospital Boston, Boston; Department of Paediatrics, Child Health and Adolescent Medicine, Children's Hospital at Westmead, Westmead, Australia; International Centre for the Study of Occupational and Mental Health, Düsseldorf, Germany; Centre for Advanced Studies in Nursing, Department of General Practice and Primary Care, University of Aberdeen, Aberdeen, United Kingdom; Quality of Life Research Center, Copenhagen, Denmark; Nordic School of Public Health, Gottenburg, Sweden, Scandinavian Institute of Quality of Working Life, Oslo, Norway; Centre for Quality of Life of the Hong Kong Institute of Asia-Pacific Studies and School of Social Work, Chinese University, Hong Kong.

Targets

Our focus is on research, international collaborations, clinical work, teaching and policy in health, disability and human development and to establish the NICHD as a permanent institute at one of the residential care centers for persons with intellectual disability in Israel in order to conduct model research and together with the four university schools of public health/medicine in Israel establish a national master and doctoral program in disability and human development at the institute to secure the next generation of professionals working in this often non-prestigious/low-status field of work.

Contact

Joav Merrick, MD, MMedSci, DMSc
Professor of Pediatrics, Child Health and Human Development
Medical Director, Health Services, Division for Mental Retardation, Ministry of Social Affairs and Social Services, POB 1260, IL-91012 Jerusalem, Israel.
E-mail: jmerrick@inter.net.il

Chapter 64

About the book series "health and human development"

Health and human development is a book series with publications from a multidisciplinary group of researchers, practitioners and clinicians for an international professional forum interested in the broad spectrum of health and human development.

- Merrick J, Omar HA, eds. Adolescent behavior research. International perspectives. New York: Nova Science, 2007.
- Kratky KW. Complementary medicine systems: Comparison and integration. New York: Nova Science, 2008.
- Schofield P, Merrick J, eds. Pain in children and youth. New York: Nova Science, 2009.
- Greydanus DE, Patel DR, Pratt HD, Calles Jr JL, eds. Behavioral pediatrics, 3 ed. New York: Nova Science, 2009.
- Ventegodt S, Merrick J, eds. Meaningful work: Research in quality of working life. New York: Nova Science, 2009.
- Omar HA, Greydanus DE, Patel DR, Merrick J, eds. Obesity and adolescence. A public health concern. New York: Nova Science, 2009.
- Lieberman A, Merrick J, eds. Poverty and children. A public health concern. New York: Nova Science, 2009.
- Goodbread J. Living on the edge. The mythical, spiritual and philosophical roots of social marginality. New York: Nova Science, 2009.
- Bennett DL, Towns S, Elliot E, Merrick J, eds. Challenges in adolescent health: An Australian perspective. New York: Nova Science, 2009.
- Schofield P, Merrick J, eds. Children and pain. New York: Nova Science, 2009.
- Sher L, Kandel I, Merrick J. Alcohol-related cognitive disorders: Research and clinical perspectives. New York: Nova Science, 2009.
- Anyanwu EC. Advances in environmental health effects of toxigenic mold and mycotoxins. New York: Nova Science, 2009.
- Bell E, Merrick J, eds. Rural child health. International aspects. New York: Nova Science, 2009.

- Dubowitz H, Merrick J, eds. International aspects of child abuse and neglect. New York: Nova Science, 2010.
- Shahtahmasebi S, Berridge D. Conceptualizing behavior: A practical guide to data analysis. New York: Nova Science, 2010.
- Wernik U. Chance action and therapy. The playful way of changing. New York: Nova Science, 2010.
- Omar HA, Greydanus DE, Patel DR, Merrick J, eds. Adolescence and chronic illness. A public health concern. New York: Nova Science, 2010.
- Patel DR, Greydanus DE, Omar HA, Merrick J, eds. Adolescence and sports. New York: Nova Science, 2010.
- Shek DTL, Ma HK, Merrick J, eds. Positive youth development: Evaluation and future directions in a Chinese context. New York: Nova Science, 2010.
- Shek DTL, Ma HK, Merrick J, eds. Positive youth development: Implementation of a youth program in a Chinese context. New York: Nova Science, 2010.
- Omar HA, Greydanus DE, Tsitsika AK, Patel DR, Merrick J, eds. Pediatric and adolescent sexuality and gynecology: Principles for the primary care clinician. New York: Nova Science, 2010.
- Chow E, Merrick J, eds. Advanced cancer. Pain and quality of life. New York: Nova Science, 2010.
- Latzer Y, Merrick, J, Stein D, eds. Understanding eating disorders. Integrating culture, psychology and biology. New York: Nova Science, 2010.
- Sahgal A, Chow E, Merrick J, eds. Bone and brain metastases: Advances in research and treatment. New York: Nova Science, 2010.
- Postolache TT, Merrick J, eds. Environment, mood disorders and suicide. New York: Nova Science, 2010.
- Maharajh HD, Merrick J, eds. Social and cultural psychiatry experience from the Caribbean Region. New York: Nova Science, 2010.
- Mirsky J. Narratives and meanings of migration. New York: Nova Science, 2010.
- Harvey PW. Self-management and the health care consumer. New York: Nova Science, 2011.
- Ventegodt S, Merrick J. Sexology from a holistic point of view. New York: Nova Science, 2011.
- Ventegodt S, Merrick J. Principles of holistic psychiatry: A textbook on holistic medicine for mental disorders. New York: Nova Science, 2011.

Contact

Professor Joav Merrick, MD, MMedSci, DMSc
Medical Director, Medical Services
Division for Mental Retardation
Ministry of Social Affairs
POBox 1260
IL-91012 Jerusalem, Israel
E-mail: jmerrick@zahav.net.il
Home-page: http://jmerrick50.googlepages.com/home

Index

C

D

E

F

N

Q

R

S

T

U

V

W

X

Y

Z